A Companion to American Foreign Relations

BLACKWELL COMPANIONS TO AMERICAN HISTORY

This series provides essential and authoritative overviews of the scholarship that has shaped our present understanding of the American past. Edited by eminent historians, each volume tackles one of the major periods or themes of American history, with individual topics authored by key scholars who have spent considerable time in research on the questions and controversies that have sparked debate in their field of interest. The volumes are accessible for the non-specialist, while also engaging scholars seeking a reference to the historiography or future concerns.

Published:

A Companion to the American Revolution
Edited by Jack P. Greene and J. R. Pole
A Companion to 19th-Century America
Edited by William L. Barney
A Companion to the American South
Edited by John B. Boles
A Companion to American Indian History
Edited by Philip J. Deloria and Neal Salisbury
A Companion to American Women's History
Edited by Nancy A. Hewitt
A Companion to Post-1945 America
Edited by Jean-Christophe Agnew and Roy Rosenzweig
A Companion to the Vietnam War
Edited by Marilyn B. Young and Robert Buzzanco
A Companion to Colonial America
Edited by Daniel Vickers

A Companion to 20th-Century America
Edited by Stephen J. Whitfield
A Companion to the American West
Edited by William Deverell
A Companion to American Foreign Relations
Edited by Robert D. Schulzinger
A Companion to the Civil War and Reconstruction
Edited by Lacy K. Ford
A Companion to American Technology
Edited by Carroll Pursell
A Companion to African-American History
Edited by Alton Hornsby
A Companion to American Immigration
Edited by Reed Ueda

In preparation:
A Companion to American Cultural History
Edited by Karen Haltunnen

BLACKWELL COMPANIONS TO HISTORY

Published

A Companion to Western Historical Thought
Edited by Lloyd Kramer and Sarah Maza

A Companion to Gender History
Edited by Teresa A. Meade and Merry E. Wiesner-Hanks

BLACKWELL COMPANIONS TO BRITISH HISTORY

Published

A Companion to Roman Britain
Edited by Malcolm Todd
A Companion to Britain in the Later Middle Ages
Edited by S. H. Rigby
A Companion to Tudor Britain
Edited by Robert Tittler and Norman Jones
A Companion to Stuart Britain
Edited by Barry Coward
A Companion to Eighteenth-Century Britain
Edited by H. T. Dickinson

A Companion to Nineteenth-Century Britain
Edited by Chris Williams
A Companion to Early Twentieth-Century Britain
Edited by Chris Wrigley
A Companion to Contemporary Britain
Edited by Paul Addison and Harriet Jones

In preparation
A Companion to the Early Middle Ages: Britain and Ireland
Edited by Pauline Stafford

BLACKWELL COMPANIONS TO EUROPEAN HISTORY

Published

A Companion to Europe 1900-1945
Edited by Gordon Martel
A Companion to Nineteenth-Century Europe
Edited by Stefan Berger
A Companion to the Worlds of the Renaissance
Edited by Guido Ruggiero

A Companion to the Reformation World
Edited by R. Po-chia Hsia

In preparation
A Companion to Europe Since 1945
Edited by Klaus Larres
A Companion to Eighteenth-Century Europe
Edited by Peter H. Wilson
A Companion to the Medieval World
Edited by Carol Lansing and Edward D. English

BLACKWELL COMPANIONS TO WORLD HISTORY

Published

A Companion to the History of the Middle East
Edited by Youssef M. Choueiri

In preparation

A Companion to Japanese History

Edited by William M. Tsutsui
A Companion to Latin American History
Thomas H. Holloway
A Companion to Russian History
Edited by Abbott Gleason

A Companion to American Foreign Relations

Edited by

Robert D. Schulzinger

Blackwell
Publishing

© 2003, 2006 by Blackwell Publishing Ltd
except for editorial material and organization © 2003, 2006 by Robert D. Schulzinger

BLACKWELL PUBLISHING
350 Main Street, Malden, MA 02148-5020, USA
9600 Garsington Road, Oxford OX4 2DQ, UK
550 Swanston Street, Carlton, Victoria 3053, Australia

The right of Robert D. Schulzinger to be identified as the Author of the Editorial Material in this Work
has been asserted in accordance with the UK Copyright, Designs, and Patents Act 1988.

First published 2003 by Blackwell Publishing Ltd
First published in paperback 2006

1   2006

Library of Congress Cataloging-in-Publication Data

A companion to American foreign relations / edited by Robert D. Schulzinger.
     p. cm. – (Blackwell companions to American history)
   ISBN 0-631-22315-0 (alk. paper)
   1. United States – Foreign relations.   2. United States – Foreign relations – Historiography.
I. Schulzinger, Robert D., 1945–   II. Series.

E183.7 .C658 2003
327.73–dc21

                                                                    2002153754

ISBN-13: 978-0-631-22315-3 (alk. paper)
ISBN-13: 978-1-4051-4986-0 (paperback)
ISBN-10: 1-4051-4986-8 (paperback)

A catalogue record for this title is available from the British Library.

Set in 10 on 12.5 pt Galliard
by SetSystems Ltd, Saffron Walden, Essex
Printed and bound in the United Kingdom
by TJ International Ltd, Padstow, Cornwall

The publisher's policy is to use permanent paper from mills that operate a sustainable forestry policy, and
which has been manufactured from pulp processed using acid-free and elementary chlorine-free practices.
Furthermore, the publisher ensures that the text paper and cover board used have met acceptable
environmental accreditation standards.

For further information on
Blackwell Publishing, visit our website:
www.blackwellpublishing.com

Contents

Notes on Contributors

Lloyd E. Ambrosius is Professor of History at the University of Nebraska-Lincoln. His publications include *Woodrow Wilson and the American Diplomatic Tradition: The Treaty Flight in Perspective* (1987), *Wilsonian Statecraft: Theory and Practice of Liberal Internationalism During World War I* (1991), and *Wilsonianism: Woodrow Wilson and His Legacy in American Foreign Relations* (2002). He was a Fulbright Professor at the University of Heidelberg (1996) and the University of Cologne (1972–3), and the Mary Ball Washington Professor of American History at University College, Dublin (1977–8).

David L. Anderson is Dean of the College of University Studies and Programs at California State University, Monterey Bay. He is the author or editor of numerous books and articles on the Vietnam War. His book *Trapped by Success: The Eisenhower Administration and Vietnam, 1953–1961* (1991) was a co-winner of the Robert H. Ferrell Book Prize from the Society for Historians of American Foreign Relations. His most recent books are *The Human Tradition in the Vietnam Era* (2000) and *The Columbia Guide to the Vietnam War* (2002).

Michael A. Barnhart is Distinguished Teaching Professor of History at State University of New York at Stony Brook. He is the author of *Japan Prepares for Total War* (1988) and *Japan and the World Since 1968* (1995). He is currently co-editor of a series of books about World War II.

H. W. Brands is Dickson Centennial Professor of History at the University of Texas, Austin.

He is the author of *TR: The Last Romance* (1997), *What America Owes the World* (1998), *The First American: The Life and Times of Benjamin Franklin* (2000), and other books. His brief biography of Woodrow Wilson was published in 2003.

Susan Brewer is Professor of History at the University of Wisconsin-Stevens Point. She is the author of *To Win the Peace: British Propaganda in the United States during World War II* (1997). She continues her examination of culture and foreign relations in her current project on American wartime propaganda in the twentieth century.

Andrew DeRoche received his PhD in diplomatic history from the University of Colorado. He teaches at Front Range Community College. His first book, *Black, White, and Chrome: The US and Zimbabwe, 1953–1998* (2001), was published by Africa World Press. He is currently writing a biography of Andrew Young that will be published by Scholarly Resources Press.

Justus D. Doenecke is Professor of History at New College of Florida in Sarasota. His book *In Danger Undaunted: The Anti-Interventionist Movement of 1940–1941 as Revealed in the Papers of the America First Committee* (1990) was awarded the Arthur S. Link Prize for Documentary Editing by the Society for Historians of American Foreign Relations. His book *Storm on the Horizon: The Challenge to American Intervention, 1939–1941* (2000) received the annual Herbert Hoover Book Award from the Hoover Presidential Library, West Branch, Iowa, as the best book on any topic of American history spanning the years 1914–64.

Kurk Dorsey is an Associate Professor of History at the University of New Hampshire. In 1999, his book, *The Dawn of Conservation Diplomacy: US–Canadian Wildlife Protection Treaties in the Progressive Era*, was co-winner of the Stuart Bernath Prize for the best first book in US foreign relations. Continuing his interest in environmental diplomacy, he is now working on a book on international efforts to regulate whaling in the twentieth century.

Rosemary Foot is Professor of International Relations and John Swire Senior Research Fellow in the International Relations of East Asia, St. Antony's College, Oxford. Her latest book is entitled *Rights Beyond Borders: The Global Community and the Struggle over Human Rights in China* (2000).

Mark T. Gilderhus is Lyndon B. Johnson Chair in US History at Texas Christian University. His specialties center on American diplomatic history, especially US relations with Latin America, and historiography. His recent publications include *The Second Century: US–Latin American Relations since 1889* (2000) and *History and Historians: A Historiographical Introduction* (5th edn., 2003). He is a former president of SHAFR (Society for Historians of American Foreign Relations).

Evelyn Goh is Assistant Professor at the Institute of Defence and Strategic Studies, Nanyang Technological University, Singapore. She completed a D.Phil. in International Relations at Nuffield College, Oxford, in 2001, and is revising her doctoral thesis, *From Red Menace to Tacit Ally: Constructing the US Rapprochement with China, 1961–1974*, for publication. Her main research interests lie in the areas of US foreign policy, US–China relations, and the international relations of East Asia.

Peter L. Hahn is Associate Professor of History at Ohio State University and Executive Secretary-Treasurer of the Society for Histo-

rians of American Foreign Relations. He is the author of *The United States, Great Britain, and Egypt, 1945–1956: Strategy and Diplomacy in the Early Cold War* (1991) and co-editor of *Empire and Revolution: The United States and the Third World since 1945* (2001). He is completing a major monograph on US policy toward the Arab–Israeli conflict, 1945–61.

Peter P. Hill is Professor Emeritus of History at George Washington University. In addition to publishing numerous scholarly articles on the diplomacy of the early national period, he is the author of *William Vans Murray, Federalist Diplomat: The Shaping of Peace with France* (1971) and *French Perceptions of the Early American Republic* (1988). Hill formerly chaired the GWU history department and once served as acting dean of what is today its Elliott School of International Affairs. Since 1996 he has been the university's historian.

Richard H. Immerman is Professor and Chair of History and Director of the Center for the Study of Force and Diplomacy at Temple University. His books include *The CIA in Guatemala: The Foreign Policy of Intervention* (1981); *Milton S. Eisenhower: Portrait of an Educational Statesman* (1983), co-authored with Stephen E. Ambrose; *John Foster Dulles and the Diplomacy of the Cold War* (1990); *Waging Peace: How Eisenhower Shaped an Enduring Cold War Strategy for National Security* (1998), co-authored with Robert R. Bowie; and *John Foster Dulles: Piety, Pragmatism, and Power in US Foreign Policy*. Immerman is a recipient of Temple's Paul W. Eberman Faculty Research Award, the Regents' Faculty Award for Excellence in Scholarship from the University of Hawaii, and the Society for Historians of American Foreign Relations' Stuart Bernath Book and Lecture Prizes.

Robert J. McMahon is Professor of History at Ohio State University. A past president of the Society for Historians of American Foreign Relations, he is the author of several books, including *The Cold War on the Periph-*

ery: The United States, India, and Pakistan (1994), *The Limits of Empire: The United States and Southeast Asia since World War II* (1999), and *The Cold War: A Very Short Introduction* (2003).

James I. Matray is Professor of History and Department Chair at California State University, Chico. He has published many articles on US–Korean relations during and after World War II. Author of *The Reluctant Crusade: American Foreign Policy in Korea* (1985) and *Japan's Emergence as a Global Power* (2000), his most recent publication is *East Asia and the United States: An Encyclopedia of Relations since 1784* (2002).

Keith L. Nelson is a Professor of History at the University of California, Irvine, where he has taught since the campus was founded in 1965. A graduate of Stanford University, he did graduate work at the Free University of Berlin and took his doctorate in history at the University of California, Berkeley. His books include *Victors Divided: America and the Allies in Germany* (1975), *Why War? Ideology, Theory, and History* (with Spencer C. Olin, 1985), and *The Making of Détente: Soviet–American Relations in the Shadow of Vietnam* (1995).

Frank Ninkovich is Professor of History at St. John's University. He is the author of several books on United States foreign policy, including *Germany and the United States: The Transformation of the German Question since 1945* (updated edition, 1994), *Modernity and Power: A History of the Domino Theory in the Twentieth Century* (1994), *US Information Policy and Cultural Diplomacy* (1996), *The Wilsonian Century: US Foreign Policy since 1900* (1999), and *The United States and Imperialism* (Blackwell, 2000).

Stephen G. Rabe is a Professor of History at the University of Texas at Dallas. He is the author of *The Road to OPEC: United States Relations with Venezuela* (1982), *Eisenhower and Latin America* (1988), and *The Most Dangerous Area in the World: John F. Kennedy Confronts Communist Revolution in*

Latin America (1999). He is currently working on a study of US intervention in British Guiana, 1953–66.

Darlene Rivas is Associate Professor of History at Pepperdine University. She is the author of *Missionary Capitalist: Nelson Rockefeller in Venezuela* (2002).

Robert D. Schulzinger is Professor of History and Director of the International Affairs Program at the University of Colorado at Boulder. A former president of the Society for Historians of American Foreign Relations, he is the editor-in-chief of the society's journal, *Diplomatic History.* Among his many books are *A Time for War: The United States and Vietnam* (1997) and *US Diplomacy since 1900* (5th edn., 2002).

Melvin Small is a Professor of History at Wayne State University. A former president of the Peace History Society, he has authored or edited several books on American foreign relations, the Vietnam War, and the peace movement, including *Democracy and Diplomacy: The Influence of Domestic Politics on US Foreign Relations* (1994) and *The Presidency of Richard Nixon* (1999).

Mark A. Stoler is a Professor of History at the University of Vermont. He is the author of *The Politics of the Second Front: American Military Planning and Diplomacy in Coalition Warfare, 1941–1943* (1977), *The Origins of the Cold War* (1981), *George C. Marshall: Soldier-Statesman of the American Century* (1989), and *Allies and Adversaries: The Joint Chiefs of Staff, the Grand Alliance, and US Strategy in World War II* (2000), which received the 2002 Distinguished Book Award of the Society for Military History. He has been the recipient of the Univesity of Vermont's George V. Kidder Award, University Scholar Award, and Dean's Lecture Award for his scholarship and teaching.

Jeremi Suri is an Assistant Professor of History at the University of Wisconsin-Madison. He is the author of *Power and Protest: Global Revolution and the Rise of Détente* (2003).

Professor Suri has also published articles in *Diplomatic History, Reviews in American History, Cold War History,* and the *Journal of Cold War Studies.* He teaches courses in international history, American foreign relations, and the history of the Cold War.

William E. Weeks is an independent scholar living in Garrett County, MD. He is the author of *John Quincy Adams and American Global Empire* (1992), *Building the Continental Empire* (1996), and most recently, co-author of the entry "Freedom of the Seas" in *The Encyclopedia of American Foreign Policy* (2nd edn., 2002).

Randall B. Woods is Cooper Distinguished Professor of History at the University of Arkansas. Among his publications are *A Changing of the Guard* (1990), *The Dawning of the Cold War* (1991), and *Fulbright: A Biography* (1995). He is currently writing a life-and-times biography of Lyndon B. Johnson.

Introduction

ROBERT D. SCHULZINGER

The history of American foreign relations is the story of power – power in its many forms. Historians have written thousands of books describing, explaining, analyzing, puzzling over, praising, and criticizing the application of American power. In its broadest sense, power consists of the ability to affect the behavior of others. It can involve the use of physical force, but there is also soft power. The modes of influence and compulsion are as much cultural and intellectual as they are political and military.

The essays in this *Companion* explore the ways in which Americans have understood and applied power and influence from the beginning of the Republic to the beginning of the twenty-first century. They explain how this understanding has grown and changed over the centuries. They analyze the ways in which advocates of the use of power have praised the men and women who have wielded it. They also show how critics of the misuse of power have presented their arguments and sometimes prevailed in the struggle for intellectual primacy.

The contributors to this *Companion*, all prominent scholars of the history of US foreign relations, have explained the ways in which the study of US diplomatic history has changed in the last generation. These changes occurred alongside a major transformation of the study of American history more generally. Both occurred as part of the major upheavals in American society during the 1960s. Foreign affairs, especially the agony of the Vietnam War, played a prominent role in this transformation.

As many Americans questioned the assumptions, activities, and integrity of leaders of public and private institutions, the study of history itself became more critical of these institutions. Historians looked at the inarticulate, those without a voice, people left out. History of government, public institutions, leaders, politics at one time or another in the last thirty years seemed to some historians increasingly irrelevant to understanding how American society developed.

In some forums, the study of diplomatic history became emblematic of the limitations of traditional history. Some advocates of new ways of looking at the past decried what they perceived to be the narrowness of vision of traditionally trained diplomatic historians. The cruel jibe, heard often twenty-five years ago, that diplomatic history was the story of what one clerk said to another encapsulated much of the criticism aimed at the field. Diplomatic historians themselves sometimes were among the loudest critics of their own work.

And yet, even as some scholars of the history of US foreign relations felt embattled, the books and articles kept coming. They had a ready audience. Consult any bestseller list, see what people are buying at Amazon.com, or stroll through any bookstore (be it an independent, a college bookstore, or one of the mega chains) and it is obvious that no subject is more written about than America in the world. Classes in foreign relations, America abroad, or the wars of the nineteenth and twentieth centuries are packed.

As much as historians of American foreign relations have felt embattled by the criticism directed at them, they have also taken it to heart and learned from it. The essays in this *Companion* show that the recent scholarship on the history of US foreign relations has been deeply informed by many of the same theoretical consider- ations historians of American culture and society have used to transform their parts of the study of American history. Recent scholarship on American foreign relations explores the views and actions of those previously ignored. It is anything but the story of what one clerk says to another. The works analyzed in this collection deal with the use of state power. In the first seventy-five years of the twentieth century, international historians worked within a framework of the state as the principal, usually sole actor, on the world stage. The state is still vitally important, and these essays show how the understanding of state power has been enriched by the insights of political scientists and cultural analysts.

One major and often overlooked project of the modern state is the keeping and preservation of records. The United States excels in opening archival material. Government archives are open to all. Other depositories maintain different rules of access. Taken together, the hundreds of public and private archives throughout the United States set the standard for access to scholars. A major product of this archival abundance appears in the books and articles discussed in this *Companion*. Many of these essays show how contemporary scholarship has been able to get inside the highest levels of the US government to show how real men and women applied their ideas and their assumptions, sifted evidence, explored alternatives and made decisions. This abundance of archival material has made it possible to explore the actual workings of the state.

The idea of narrative has undergone serious scrutiny in the last twenty-five years. The multiplicity of sub-fields within the larger discipline of history has forced teachers to scramble to incorporate the new material into a master narrative. Teachers of the history of US foreign relations face the same problem. In the old days, before 1970, most courses followed a straightforward narrative of the rise of America to world power. Courses followed the contours of presidential administrations, alternat- ing between and among the major political parties. Wars and other diplomatic crises provided the points of punctuation. The ways in which public officials and members of the general public behaved in crisis and war became the major subject matter of the history of foreign relations. The United States had relations in many parts of the world, but clearly some areas took precedence over others. Americans paid more attention to Europe and Asia than other regions.

That master narrative has broken down. The essays in this *Companion* demon- strate the rich variety of ways in which the narrative of US foreign relations has changed. The first three essays cover ideas, culture, and the environment throughout the course of American history. Essays that follow explore a mixture of chronology, regional relations, and the major wars and crises from the late nineteenth to the early twenty-first century. No single college course could hope to cover this variety of subject. Indeed, most of these essays could be considered guides to the literature of individual courses of interest to specialists in the field.

This *Companion* is a snapshot of the state of diplomatic history at the beginning of the twenty-first century. It shows a vibrant discipline, one that absorbs the attention of scholars, students, and, more than most aspects of American history, the reading public. For a brief period after the end of the Cold War, many people interested in foreign affairs observed a distressing insularity among Americans. Newspapers, news magazines, and television networks devoted less and less attention to news from beyond American shores.

When people spoke, either hopefully or in dismay, in the early 1990s of the end of history, they meant both that the great ideological struggles of the twentieth century were over and that people no longer cared about the past. Neither concern seemed to be very salient after the attacks on New York and Washington, DC on September 11, 2001. Even at the supposed height of American indifference to foreign affairs, students filled courses on the history of US foreign relations. Books on the wars and great crises of US foreign relations filled readers' shelves.

It is likely that the next twenty-five years will see as many changes in the shape and subject matter of US foreign relations as did the last decade of the twentieth century. Archives around the world will continue to release new documentary evidence showing the way people in power made real decisions. Diplomatic historians will continue the dialogue with other historians and other scholars in disciplines now considered to be unimaginably remote. As long as the United States continues to play a predominant role in world affairs, the origins, development, consequences, and alternatives of that role are bound to attract serious attention.

CHAPTER ONE

Ideas and Foreign Affairs

H. W. Brands

Ideas are nebulous things, and often trade at a discount in the material world of international affairs. "How many divisions has the pope?" Stalin sneeringly asked, exemplifying what that generation's high priest of historical materialism thought of the power of ideas detached from the tools of force. Yet the fact that the question came up illustrates a deeper truth: if force is the final arbiter of international affairs, ideas are the trigger of force, the governor of force, the measure of whether force has accomplished what its authors desire. Force may be *how* international affairs are waged; ideas are *why*.

Consequently, any study of international affairs must start with a study of ideas. *Whose* ideas need to be studied depends on the regimes, polities, and societies examined. A student of Soviet foreign affairs during Stalin's long reign might credibly concentrate on what Stalin and perhaps a few of his closest henchmen thought about the world and Russia's place therein. Dictatorships have advantages – for those who study them if not necessarily those who live under them. By contrast, in a pluralist democracy such as the United States, the larger number of actors influencing foreign affairs necessitates a broader field of inquiry. Historians have entered this field from various directions. Some have taken important individuals – presidents, secretaries of state, influential legislators, the occasional executive of a multinational corporation – and probed their minds. Other historians have assessed the *Zeitgeist* of generations – Manifest Destiny, the Munich syndrome, the shadow of Vietnam – to establish the boundaries within which policymakers have been constrained to operate.

On account of the diversity of approaches to the ideas that drive US foreign relations, it is impossible to identify a literature of the subject in a way that includes all and only what deals with ideas and foreign affairs. Every study of Thomas Jefferson or Woodrow Wilson treats their ideas and motivations; no serious account of the 1840s or 1960s ignores popular attitudes toward the world beyond American borders. This said, though, certain historians have placed the ideas of foreign relations front and center.

Any student of the subject ought to start with Norman Graebner's *Ideas and Diplomacy* (1964). The book combines essential documents from the history of American foreign relations with Graebner's insightful commentary on those documents and the way they reveal American thinking about the world. For readers at the start of the twenty-first century, the principal drawback of the book is that it was published too soon, leaving out lots that happened since. Even so, it serves as a model for sensible analysis of the intellectual wellsprings of foreign policy; an aspiring young scholar could do far worse than essay an update. Brands (1998) covers some of the same ground, although from a different angle. Identifying key thinkers during two centuries of American foreign relations (but concentrating on the twentieth century), Brands hangs what might be called an intellectual history of American foreign policy on the question of the title.

The stepsister of ideas is ideology – a term that once meant the innocent study of ideas but has long since shifted to denote a system of ideas, especially a rigid system into which reality is forced. The ideology of American decision-makers is discussed in nearly every study of American foreign relations; the best book devoted to ideology on its own terms is Hunt (1987). Dallek (1983) employs a different lexicon but investigates many of the same phenomena.

The ideas of American foreign relations have typically arisen from questions regarding the national interest: to wit, what is the national interest, and how might it be promoted? During the late eighteenth and early nineteenth centuries, the national interest was competitively defined as supporting the republican ideals of the French Revolution, opposing the terror and eventual Bonapartism of the same revolution, or steering clear of the whole mess. The Jeffersonians and Republicans leaned in the first direction, the Hamiltonians and Federalists in the second, and President Washington in the third (to the extent that neutrality could be considered leaning). Jeffersonian thinking is traced authoritatively in Kaplan (1967) and more recently and impressionistically in O'Brien (1996). Because Hamilton was less literary than Jefferson, more commercially minded, and died relatively young (in the infamous duel with Aaron Burr), he has never, as an intellectual, attracted the kind of attention Jefferson has. But his thoughts are vigorously presented in Brookhiser (1999). They also appear in treatments of Washington's thinking on foreign affairs, which though it gave rise to an official neutrality between Britain and France, drew more heavily from Hamilton than from Jefferson; the best of these treatments is Gilbert (1961). With no disrespect to Gilbert, it is fair to say that subsequent scholarship in the period of the early republic, including the publication of new editions of the papers of the founders, as well as a wonderful documentary collection entitled *The Emerging Nation* (Giunta 1996), makes this field a promising one for students of the intellectual origins of American foreign policy.

After 1815 problems with Britain and France diminished, largely because Britain's principal problem with France, Bonaparte, disappeared (to St. Helena and beyond). Americans turned to the issue that would preoccupy them for the rest of the nineteenth century: Western expansion. Most Americans assumed expansion to be in the national interest, but the nature and extent of expansion occasioned considerable debate. The Mexican War, for example, was the most controversial conflict in American history until the Vietnam War (excluding, for obvious reasons, the Civil War). Many Whigs and northerners decried it as a conspiracy of slaveholders, while Democrats, southerners, and assorted others defended it as nothing less than God's will afoot. The arguments on both sides are thoroughly aired in Weinberg (1935), and Merk (1963). As one might guess, Merk was reinterpreting Weinberg; considering the time that has passed since Merk, a reinterpretation of him is in order. Stephanson (1995) briefly addresses the subject, but a more comprehensive account is needed. To some extent the spirit of Manifest Destiny is present in every generation of Americans, and studies of the subject reveal at least as much about the generations doing the writing as about the subject itself. (This is true of most histories, but particularly of those dealing with continuing issues.) At the beginning of the twenty-first century, Americans are feeling rather full of themselves, making the topic of Manifest Destiny all the more natural for a new study.

The Spanish–American War – or, more precisely, the Philippine war that followed the war against Spain – pricked the bubble of American territorial expansionism. The anti-guerrilla action in the Philippines killed far more Americans than the conflict against Spain, and it disabused Americans of the idea that their hegemony would be readily embraced by foreigners. American expansionism would subsequently take more subtle forms, but not again the ambitious territorial kind that had marked American history since the nation's birth.

This change of thinking came just in time for Americans to revert to their preoccupation of the early national period. In 1914 the century of European peace (or almost peace) ended, and Americans once more had to pay close attention to transatlantic affairs. The historically minded among them might have concluded that America's long isolation from Europe had more to do with Europe than with America, and some did. But others disputed the issue, provoking an aspect of the debate over the national interest that has persisted to the present – namely, how closely is America's fate tied to Europe's? At the time, Europe seemed the world to many Americans, and the debate soon ratcheted slightly upward to become one about how closely America's fate was tied to that of the world. This question has been the hinge of all discussions of American foreign policy ever since.

Woodrow Wilson had one answer, at least after the 1916 election. Although the Democratic president avowed neutrality at the outset of World War I, by early 1917 he became convinced of two things: that the United States couldn't thrive in a world that included a triumphant Germany, and that the world couldn't survive without an engaged United States. Wilson's ideas are analyzed with subtlety and sympathy – but not uncritical sympathy – in Knock (1992). The ethos of Wilsonianism is described in Kennedy (1980). Wilsonians – especially Wilsonian intellectuals – are portrayed in Forcey (1961). The star of that trio, and an ardent Wilsonian before becoming disillusioned at the Paris peace conference, was Walter Lippmann, the subject of Ronald Steel's outstanding life-and-times (Steel 1980).

Many besides Lippmann grew disillusioned with Wilsonianism, which came to mean a belief that both American interest and world welfare required a continuing American commitment to international institutions, preeminently the League of Nations. The term "idealism" was attached to this belief, by critics as often as by supporters; the implication of the critics was that Wilson's acolytes were wooly-minded theorists out of touch with the world's hard realities. Yet the Wilsonians were not necessarily less in touch with reality than self-proclaimed "realists"; the two schools simply interpreted reality differently. The "idealists" – often but not always liberals in domestic politics – believed humanity could learn from its mistakes and do progressively better. The "realists" – often domestic conservatives – had little faith in human betterment. Human nature was essentially flawed, they said; prudence consisted in expecting the worst, and preparing to deal with it. Typically this meant building warships and other weapons and girding to use them. Wilson may have lost the argument in his day (when the Senate rejected the Treaty of Versailles and

American membership in the League of Nations), but he framed the debate for decades to come. Two of the best treatments of the debate are Smith (1994), by a latter-day Wilsonian, and Kissinger (1994), by the high priest of realism among American policymakers. (Readers who desire more of Kissinger can get their fill in his three-volume memoir (Kissinger 1979, 1982, 1999). Whatever one thinks of Kissinger's policies, these massive tomes are a *tour de force* of a keen mind in action – both in real time and in retrospect.)

For all their differences, the idealists and the realists concurred on one fundamental premise: that the United States must continually engage the world diplomatically, politically, or militarily. During the 1920s and 1930s, however, there were many Americans who rejected this idea. Watching Europe and Asia slide toward fascism, they contended that the appropriate American response was disengagement. Dubbed (pejoratively) "isolationists," this group held that every people must save itself; the best America could do was keep the democratic beacon burning till the rest of the world was able to appreciate its light. Charles A. Beard was the most penetrating thinker among the disengagers; his political works from the period, especially *The Idea of the National Interest* (with G. H. E. Smith, 1934), still bear reading. (H. W. Brands (1999) stole Beard's title for an essay evaluating varying interpretations of the national interest during the twentieth century: "The Idea of the National Interest.") During his prime one of America's most respected intellectuals, Beard fell into dark disfavor after Pearl Harbor made his skepticism of foreign engagement seem unpatriotic, if not downright seditious. His reputation never recovered; at least partly for this reason he has never received satisfactory biographical treatment.

Pearl Harbor changed everything about American thinking about the world, and Hiroshima changed everything again, but in the same direction. By the end of World War II it was almost impossible to advocate the kind of standoffishness that had been both conventional wisdom and American policy during the 1920s and 1930s. In an egregious example of post-hoc-ergo-propter-hoc thinking, American leaders and the American people assumed that their country's complacence regarding the rise of Hitler and the Japanese militarists had been responsible for World War II, and that similar complacence toward communism in Eastern Europe and China would bring on World War III. As it applied to Hitler and the Japanese, this conclusion was not implausible, although it was hardly conclusive; its application to Stalin and Mao was little more than a leap of frightened faith. Yet it was a leap Americans made because they *could* make it. Emerging from World War II as the world's sole superpower, Americans were uniquely situated to attempt a kind of security vouchsafed to no great power since imperial Rome. Americans could afford to arm themselves against nearly every conceivable threat, to cajole or purchase the cooperation of allies around the world, and to encircle the one country – imperial Russia – that seriously threatened American security, and then solely by Russia's possession of nuclear weapons.

Curiously, perhaps, America was led into the era of postwar realism by intellectuals, whose native country lies closer to the realm of theory than to practice. On the other hand, George Kennan, the most visible of the Cold War intellectuals, was a foreign-policy practitioner before making a name as an intellectual. Kennan cut his diplomatic teeth at the American embassy in Moscow during Stalin's 1930s reign of terror – an experience that would have knocked the Wilsonianism out of anyone.

Long before Kennan returned to Moscow after the war, he concluded that the US–Soviet alliance was one of convenience only: anti-Hitler convenience. Kennan allowed the Kremlin a brief period of grace – in which to condemn itself by its own actions – then wrote home a long telegram declaring that the only appropriate attitude for Americans to adopt toward the Russians was one of trenchant opposition. After this hard line appealed to his superiors in the Truman administration, Kennan went public, in a briefly anonymous article in the establishment organ *Foreign Affairs*. Soon the Kennanesque lexicon, including the catchword "containment," was the lingua franca of American policy.

Kennan's emergence as intellectual icon of the Cold War is traced in his *Memoirs* (Kennan 1967–72). Kibbitzers include Mayers (1988), Stephanson (1989), and Miscamble (1992). Kennan has been a darling of historians and other students of the early Cold War, partly because he was peculiarly literate and partly because he subsequently disavowed his early hard line. (By the time Kennan became fair game for historians, most of them had grown squishy on the Cold War. One who hadn't, and whose biography of Kennan was still in the works in 2000, was John Lewis Gaddis; for this reason, in addition to Gaddis's preeminence in the field of Cold War studies, his Kennan was eagerly awaited.)

Another reason for the great interest in the early Cold War is its easy accessibility, especially via the State Department's ongoing collection, *The Foreign Relations of the United States*. This venerable series shifted into high gear for the period after 1945; in many respects the volumes for the years from 1945 to the early 1950s are the best in the entire series. (By the early 1950s much of the record of American diplomacy was being generated by agencies beyond the State Department; some such agencies – notoriously the Central Intelligence Agency – resisted seeing themselves in print. Too often for scholarly preferences, and for democratic accountability, their resistance succeeded.)

Much of Kennan's cachet came from having been inside the policy apparatus (he left the government in 1953); by contrast, the influence of Hans J. Morgenthau derived from his sheer intellectual power. Morgenthau's *Politics Among Nations* (1948) became the manifesto of an entire generation of Cold War realists, and the phrase he offered as an all-encompassing explanation, prescription, and justification of international behavior – the "balance of power" – became their mantra. The book, which went through numerous editions, bears reading today both for its theoretical power and as a window on that generation of realists. Morgenthau sketched a few notes toward an autobiography but got sidetracked; oddly, no biographer has taken up the thread of a life that was fascinating (flight from German anti-Semitism in the 1930s, etc.) even apart from the unfolding of a first-class mind.

Realism sometimes sat uncomfortably with Americans who had long considered their country exceptional, for Morgenthau's balance of power was nothing more or less than what Europe had been practicing during all those years Americans had disdained Europe for its anachronistic – even atavistic – ways. Reinhold Niebuhr solved the problem by bringing God explicitly into the equation of international affairs. The foremost American theologian of his day, Niebuhr crafted a kind of Christian realism (identified as such in *Christian Realism and Political Problems*, 1953) that allowed an end run around the moral equivalency (or perhaps amoral equivalency) between democracy and communism implicit in the Morgenthavian version of realism, which treated all polities as black boxes, the moral and other contents of which had almost no bearing on the practice of diplomacy. Niebuhr was a deep and subtle thinker who reveled in irony (for example in *The Irony of American History*, 1952); his depth and subtlety were what made him appealing to a couple of generations of American intellectuals ("The father of us all," Kennan called him). But it was his reassuring conclusion – that whatever the systemic sins of the democrats, they were merely venial next to the mortal transgressions of the communists – that won him the imprimatur of the Cold War establishment.

The realists reigned through the 1950s and into the 1960s, although certain cracks in their intellectual hegemony developed. Part of the problem was that realism (like idealism) operated better at the level of strategy than at the level of tactics. It was one thing to say, as the realists did, that the Soviet Union must be contained; it was another thing to determine whether, for example, containment required a nuclear policy of "massive retaliation," or whether it dictated an open-ended commitment to defend Indochina against communist guerrillas.

Questions of nuclear strategy gave birth to an entire intellectual industry during the Cold War. In certain respects, the nuclear theologians (as they were often called, derisively) were the purest intellectuals, the dealers in ideas least sullied by application, of the whole postwar period. Like the schoolmen of medieval Europe, they argued endlessly about questions that couldn't be answered short of Armageddon – which in their case had a very real meaning. Would it take ten hydrogen bombs to deter a Soviet attack on Washington, or a hundred? If the United States suffered 50 million dead in a nuclear war, and the Soviet Union 100 million, who would be the winner?

At the time, the theorizing seemed worthwhile, although some of it – particularly by the irrepressibly outrageous Herman Kahn – struck many readers as distastefully ghoulish. "Thermonuclear pornography," one reviewer called Kahn's *On Thermonuclear War* (1960), a book that provided the plot-pivot (the "doomsday machine") of Stanley Kubrick's 1964 black comedy, *Dr. Strangelove: or, How I Learned to Stop Worrying and Love the Bomb.* Yet whether all the analysis accomplished anything is hard to say, even decades later. The nuclear war theorized about never befell humanity; whether it would have occurred had such capable intellects as Bernard Brodie (1946, 1959), Henry Kissinger (1957), Thomas Schelling (1960), and many others devoted an equal number of mind-years to more peaceable pursuits must rest in the realm of all historical imponderables. On the other hand, a student unfazed by imponderables might interestingly try to calculate the intellectual cost of the Cold War, in terms of individuals and institutions drawn into defense work at the expense of other endeavors. Needless to say, the accounting isn't all on one side of the ledger; numerous technologies, from jet aircraft to the Internet, have spun off the Cold War scientific–defense complex – which means the student who takes on this assignment must be open-minded and ecumenically educated, in addition to being bold.

In the end, of course, it was more mundane matters, most conspicuously the American intervention in Indochina, that forced a change in American Cold War thinking. Since the onset of the Cold War, a dissenting school had challenged the communists-are-coming view that undergirded containment. The skeptics included, at one time or another, Walter Lippmann, by now the dean of American pundits;

Robert Taft, the Ohio senator who warned, accurately, that a North Atlantic alliance would lead to the garrisoning of Europe by American troops; and the later George Kennan, who complained that he had been misunderstood and his subtle concepts hijacked by the military–industrialists.

The skeptics also included such neo-Beardians as William Appleman Williams, the author of *The Tragedy of American Diplomacy* (1959, 1962), who contended, as Beard had a generation earlier, that the United States was using foreign affairs – in particular, the alleged communist threat – as a way of avoiding its problems at home. The habit hadn't started with communism. Since the late nineteenth century American leaders had insisted on establishing an "open door" for American products, investment, and values overseas; by opposing this open door, the communists had simply situated themselves in a long line of groups defined as enemies of the American way of life. Again like Beard, Williams wrote more in sorrow than in anger. He thought the open-door obsessives were wrong; American civilization would not collapse if certain portions of the planet were cut off from the American sphere. He called on Americans to come home, to allow other countries to find their own way to their own fates.

For Williams and others on what might have been called the soft left of criticism of the Cold War realist school, the link between ideas and policy was direct; by simply swapping wrongheaded ideas about America's purpose for sound ones, American leaders and the American people could put American policy on the path of righteousness. For Gabriel Kolko and those on the hard left of Cold War criticism, however, the connection between ideas and policy was indirect. Kolko was a Marxist, and with other Marxists he perceived policy as reflecting a certain set of property relations – in the case of the United States, reflecting the capitalism that constituted the American political economy. The capitalists who controlled American foreign policy acted as they did not because they had bad ideas, but because they were capitalists. (Actually, they did have bad ideas, but those too followed from the fact that they were capitalists.) As the dominant capitalist power, Kolko explained in such works as *The Politics of War* (1968) and *The Roots of American Foreign Policy* (1969), the United States sought economic stability above all. Stability had been challenged by Hitler in the 1930s and 1940s; hence the war against Germany. Stability had been threatened by Stalin and Mao in the 1940s and 1950s; hence the Cold War. Stability was being challenged by Ho Chi Minh in the 1960s; hence the war in Vietnam. Where Williams and the Beardians believed struggle might end once American leaders got their heads straight, Kolko and the Marxists judged struggle inevitable and endless – at least until the great revolution that got property relations straight once and for all.

If the Vietnam War prompted a challenge to American thinking about the Cold War and about the world generally, that challenge – in a dialectic Marx would have appreciated, despite his dismissal of ideas as secondary to property relations – in turn prompted a counter-challenge. Many of those who became prominent as neoconservatives during the 1970s had been Marxists during the 1930s. For many of them, the intellectual migration commenced with the Nazi–Soviet nonaggression pact of 1939, which demonstrated how cynical Stalin, until then the only reliable antifascist, could be. By temperament true believers, the zealots of the Old Left became zealots of the New Right, requiring only a suitable issue to rally around. They got their issue in détente, the Nixon administration's effort to end the Vietnam War and rationalize American relations with the Soviet Union and China. Détente was widely popular: after Vietnam seemed to have revealed the bankruptcy of containment, most Americans were willing to try something new. But the neoconservative personality thrived on adversity, and the initial unpopularity of their message – that détente was a snare and a delusion, making the communists more dangerous than ever – merely intensified their convictions. Norman Podhoretz, the archetypal neoconservative, regularly assaulted détente in the pages of *Commentary* magazine (which he edited), and although he spared no epithets regarding Nixon, he reserved his special vitriol for Henry Kissinger, who, as an intellectual, should have known better.

The neocons cultivated the ground for Ronald Reagan, who rode into office on their present-dangerist message. (*The Present Danger: Do We Have the Will to Reverse the Decline of American Power?* (1980), was Podhoretz's contribution to the Reagan campaign.) One neocon who did yeoman – in this case, yeowoman – service was Jeane Kirkpatrick, author of *Commentary*'s most noticed article, and perhaps the piece most influential for foreign affairs since Kennan's "X" article in *Foreign Affairs* in 1947. Entitled "Dictatorships and Double Standards" (Kirkpatrick 1979), the essay argued that there were dictators, and dictators. Neither were folks you'd want to bring home to dinner, but where dictators of the right ("authoritarians") allowed private life to continue largely undisturbed, dictators of the left ("totalitarians") claimed control over every aspect of existence. The former – such as the Shah of Iran and Anastasio Somoza of Nicaragua – deserved American support in this less-than-ideal world; the latter – the rulers of communist countries and fellow-travelers across the Third World – deserved America's undying opposition. Kirkpatrick's reasoning so impressed Reagan that he picked her to be ambassador to the United Nations, where she had a chance to parse repression on a daily basis.

Much has been written about both the New Left and the New Right, but for the student of ideas and foreign relations, most of it is unsatisfactory, focusing on the politics and personalities of the movements, and in any event being written by people too close to the movements to do them justice. A single intellectual thread runs through the story of the breakdown and attempted resuscitation of the American Cold War consensus; the story itself has yet to be written. John Ehrman (1995) tried, but much more remains to be done.

The resuscitation was mightily attempted by Reagan and the neoconservatives who staffed his foreign-policy team. In terms of rhetoric and defense spending, the effort succeeded: while Reagan railed at the "evil empire" of the Soviets, production lines at America's arms-makers hummed as they hadn't since the heyday of Vietnam. But Cold War II never really caught on among the American people, who had been hearing that the communists were coming for forty years and wondered where they were. In one memorable speech Reagan contended that the Marxist Sandinistas of Nicaragua were only a two-days' drive from Texas – an estimate that brought laughs to Brownsville and other border towns where people had actually *driven* the roads of Central America and Mexico. Americans generally yawned at Reagan's threat-mongering; Congress went further, banning American aid to the anti-Sandinista *contras*. (Which ban the Reaganistas ignored, undertaking the efforts that produced the Iran–contra scandal.)

But what really killed the new Cold War (and flummoxed Kirkpatrick and other neoconservatives, who had said that such could never happen) was the emergence of fundamental reform in the Soviet Union. For months and then years, American analysts inside government and out debated whether Mikhail Gorbachev was the genuine article, a Peter-the-Great wannabe, or a shill for closet reactionaries. It was a glorious time to be a pundit, since no one knew any more than anyone else, and events regularly raced ahead of everyone's expectations. All jockeyed to be first to spy the end of the Cold War – or to reveal that the end wasn't even close.

George Kennan called it over in the summer of 1988. "The Marxist–Leninist ideology is a stale and sterile ritual to which lip service must be given because it is the only ostensible source of legitimacy for the Communist Party in Russia," Kennan wrote in *New Perspectives Quarterly*. "Beyond that, nobody takes it seriously." To Kennan, ideology was the defining characteristic of the Cold War; having lost its ideological way, the Soviet Union had lost the Cold War.

Zbigniew Brzezinski, the Democrats' answer to Henry Kissinger, agreed with Kennan that ideology was the key to understanding what was happening in the Soviet Union. Describing what he called *The Grand Failure* (1979), Brzezinski saw the layers of communist rule falling away one by one. First went Brezhnevism: the pretense that the Soviet Union might ever match the West in the production of consumer goods and other elements of a decent life for the Soviet masses. Next went Stalinism: the apparatus of state security that rendered everyone in the country insecure. Leninism – the claim of the communist to exclusive wisdom and right to rule – would be the last to go. But given the rate of change in Russia under Gorbachev, it couldn't hold on much longer.

An innocent observer might have supposed the neoconservatives would have been quick to claim victory in the Cold War, but in fact they were remarkably slow. In part their hesitance reflected career considerations: having ridden into office on opposition to Moscow and all its works, they were reluctant to retire that hobby-horse. In part it reflected the curious circumstance that, for a bunch of intellectuals, they were skeptical of the power of ideas – at least ideas within a communist regime. Even if Gorbachev were sincere in his desire for reform at home and relaxation abroad – and the neoconservatives had grave doubts on this point – a turn of the political wheel in Moscow might oust Gorbachev and replace him with some old Bolshevik. If Americans put down their guard, they might never get it back up. Jeane Kirkpatrick, answering Kennan in *New Perspectives* (winter 1988–9), said she was watching events in Russia with "rapt attention" but meanwhile was keeping her powder dry.

When the Berlin Wall fell in late 1989, not even the neoconservatives could deny that the changes in Eastern Europe were genuine; when Germany was reunified the following year, the changes were admitted to be far-reaching; when the Soviet Union dissolved the year after that, the changes were reckoned to be irreversible. Ideas are always both lagging and leading indicators of reality. They lag events in that people require time to figure out what is happening and what it means. This is why, for all the punditry surrounding Gorbachev's *glasnost* and *perestroika*, almost none of it counted for anything six months after seeing print. No one has chronicled the response of American intellectuals to the revolutionary events in Eastern Europe in the late 1980s, and – not to put too fine a point on it – no one should bother. It was forgettable at the time, and hasn't improved with age.

Ideas are leading indicators of foreign policy in that they condition people to interpret events in particular ways, and thereby tend to shape those events. (It is when the ideas become so rigid as to straitjacket interpretations that they are called ideologies.) Ideas led the collapse of communism in Europe – but those ideas were European rather than American. Almost no one in America, and certainly no substantial school of American thinkers, foresaw the rapid demise of the Russian empire. On the contrary, political scientists for years had been fabricating models to explain the stability of the bipolar system of international affairs. When that system proved spectacularly *un*stable, the model-makers were forced back to their workbenches.

The foreign-affairs intelligentsia spent most of the late 1980s and 1990s trying to make sense of the new reality. Paul Kennedy (1987) suggested that large empires are vulnerable to "imperial overstretch" – when commitments outstrip resources – but all his evidence pointed to the problem afflicting the United States before the Soviet Union. "Decision-makers in Washington must face the awkward and enduring fact that the sum total of the United States' global interests and obligations is now far larger than the country's power to defend them all simultaneously," Kennedy wrote. The model seemed compelling until the Soviet empire collapsed, enormously lightening the American burden.

Francis Fukuyama, as deputy director of the State Department's policy planning staff (Kennan's old shop), would have won career points for correctly calling events in Eastern Europe; having failed at that (along with everyone else), Fukuyama proceeded to predict something far more sweeping. In "The End of History?" (1989; later expanded into *The End of History and the Last Man*, 1992), Fukuyama suggested that the demise of European communism signaled the end of history itself. Fukuyama had a rather idiosyncratic definition of history; he meant the struggle between competing systems of ideas, lately represented, on one hand, by liberal individualism and, on the other, by various brands of collectivism. The collectivists – chiefly fascists and communists – had lost World War II and now the Cold War; there was nothing left for them but the ash heap of history. For someone on the winning side, Fukuyama was surprisingly subdued. Societies thrived on challenge, and the great challenge to American society was disappearing. "The end of history will be a very sad time," he predicted.

Samuel Huntington didn't think history had ended at all. But then Huntington didn't buy Fukuyama's premise that the only history that really counted was the history of ideas. Huntington didn't dismiss ideas, but he wrapped them in the cultures that produced – or, as frequently, borrowed – them. In "The Clash of Civilizations?" (1993) and *The Clash of Civilizations and the Remaking of World Order* (1996), Huntington contended that the world's struggles were only beginning. (Like Fukuyama, Huntington dropped the question mark from his title in moving from journal to book. Book publishers prefer certitude, if not certainty.) Moreover, though the liberal West had apparently won Fukuyama's struggle of ideas, there was no guarantee it would win the clash of civilizations. Hindu India, the Muslim Middle East, and Confucian China were at least as good bets.

The arguments of Kennedy, Fukuyama, and Huntington had policy implications for the United States, but on the whole they described rather than prescribed. Other authors devoted more attention to how Americans should deal with a world in which their country was the sole superpower. (Some now accepted the argument that the United States had been the only superpower since 1945 – the Soviet Union simply having grafted an elephantine military arsenal on a third-world economy. To the extent this argument was accurate, it raised the question – still unanswered, and a suitable subject for investigation – as to how Americans fooled themselves so long.) Joseph S. Nye (1990) took umbrage at Kennedy's contention that American power was on the wane. Maybe America overspread the globe less dramatically than in 1945, Nye conceded, but the American sun remained high in the sky, and of all the nations on earth, only the United States possessed the power to shape the future to its designs. Americans must not lose confidence, and must employ their power to the world's and their own benefit.

American power *was* employed in various regions during the 1990s, most notably in the Persian Gulf and, less confidently and decisively, in the Balkans. The Gulf War against Saddam Hussein promised – or, more precisely, the Bush administration during the Gulf crisis promised – to establish a precedent for American intervention on behalf of small countries mugged by their bigger neighbors. But what might have been a Bush doctrine of the early post-Cold War, perhaps comparable to the Truman doctrine of the early Cold War, never materialized, and the "new world order" of which George Bush spoke so confidently fizzled in the face of an alarmingly ubiquitous new world disorder. The principal question for American policymakers – and the principal point of debate for policy analyzers – was how to establish a framework for American intervention. None doubted that the United States would defend its own interests overseas, as it did in the Gulf, where Saddam Hussein threatened the oil supplies on which Western economies depended. The crux of the issue was whether the United States would defend the interests of other people overseas. Of course, there remained many who held that American interests couldn't be so easily divorced from the interests of others – that mayhem and anarchy anywhere would eventually reach American shores. Even so, almost no one contended that genocide in Rwanda (where the United States did not intervene) posed a serious threat to American security. The argument from security for intervention in the Balkans was stronger, although this argument was as often backward looking ("Here's where World War I started") as forward looking.

The debate over American intervention unfolded in the pages of such specialized journals as *Foreign Affairs* and *Foreign Policy*, and on the opinion pages of the *New York Times*, the *Wall Street Journal*, and the *Washington Post*. Numerous conferences took place, some giving rise to compilations, on the order of *The Use of Force after the Cold War* (Brands 2000). But the muddiness of world affairs precluded much clarity in the intellectual accompaniment to policy-making, and readily discernible schools of thought were slow to develop. Robert D. Kaplan (2000) suggested that the mud wouldn't clear for some time.

At the dawn of the new millennium, the buzz word was "globalization." The concept was slippery, but its economic emphasis – the growing interconnectedness of the world economy, resulting from trade liberalization and advances in telecommunications – underscored the degree to which traditional notions of security continued to diminish. Proponents of globalization claimed the largest share of space in the published media; none spoke more cogently than Thomas L. Friedman of the *New York Times*, who gathered his thoughts into book form in *The Lexus and the Olive Tree* (2000). Skeptics followed themes set out earlier by Benjamin R. Barber in *Jihad vs. McWorld* (1995), but many of their complaints were registered on the Internet – which, ironically, was a principal agent of the globalization they decried.

By some measures, ideas mattered more than ever in foreign affairs. The end of the Cold War diminished the likelihood of armed conflict between great powers; the answer to Stalin's question about how many divisions the pope had was now, Who cares? The idea of trade liberalization was powerful – otherwise the anti-globalist protesters wouldn't have bothered disrupting meetings of the World Trade Organization and other global bodies. And ideas of another sort – the technical ideas behind the Internet and other forms of telecommunications – were rendering borders more permeable, in some respects, than invading armies ever had. The pope didn't need divisions as long as he had a broadband connection to the Internet.

Under the circumstances, the role of ideas in foreign affairs appeared a promising field of study. The present always influences perceptions of the past, and as ideas emerged more clearly as arbiters of here-and-now, it became easier to appreciate the influence of ideas in the there-and-then. The old questions – of ideology, of American exceptionalism or banality, of realism versus idealism, of American imperialism, of the exportability of democracy – remained as valid as ever. New questions – of technology and the dissolving of borders – offered fresh ways of examining the past.

REFERENCES

Barber, Benjamin R.: *Jihad vs. McWorld* (New York: Times Books, 1995).

Beard, Charles A. (with G. H. E. Smith): *The Idea of the National Interest: An Analytical Study of American Foreign Policy* (New York: Macmillan, 1934).

Brands, H. W.: *What America Owes the World: The Struggle for the Soul of Foreign Policy* (New York: Cambridge University Press, 1998).

Brands, H. W.: "The Idea of the National Interest." In Michael J. Hogan (ed.), *The Ambiguous Legacy: US Foreign Relations in the "American Century"* (New York: Cambridge University Press, 1999).

Brands, H. W. (ed.): *The Use of Force after the Cold War* (College Station, TX: Texas A&M University Press, 2000).

Brodie, Bernard: *The Absolute Weapon: Atomic Power and World Order* (New York: Harcourt Brace, 1946).

Brodie, Bernard: *Strategy in the Missile Age* (Princeton, NJ: Princeton University Press, 1959).

Brookhiser, Richard: *Alexander Hamilton, American* (New York: Free Press, 1999).

Brzezinski, Zbigniew: *The Grand Failure* (New York: Scribner, 1979).

Dallek, Robert: *The American Style of Foreign Policy: Cultural Politics and Foreign Affairs* (New York: Oxford University Press, 1983).

Ehrman, John: *The Rise of Neoconservatism: Intellectuals and Foreign Affairs, 1945–1994* (New Haven, CT: Yale University Press, 1995).

Forcey, Charles: *The Crossroads of Liberalism: Croly, Weyl, Lippmann, and the Progressive Era, 1900–1925* (New York: Oxford University Press, 1961).

Friedman, Thomas L.: *The Lexus and the Olive Tree* (New York: Farrar Straus Giroux, 2000).

Fukuyama, Francis: "The End of History?" *National Interest* (summer 1989).

Fukuyama, Francis: *The End of History and the Last Man* (New York: Free Press, 1992).

Gilbert, Felix: *To the Farewell Address: Ideas of Early American Foreign Policy* (Princeton, NJ: Princeton University Press, 1961).

Giunta, Mary A. (ed.): *The Emerging Nation: A Documentary History of the Foreign Relations of the United States under the Articles of Confederation, 1780–1789*, 3 vols. (Washington, DC: Scholarly Resources, 1996).

Graebner, Norman: *Ideas and Diplomacy: Readings in the Intellectual Tradition of American Foreign Policy* (New York: Oxford University Press, 1964).

Hunt, Michael H.: *Ideology and US Foreign Policy* (New Haven, CT: Yale University Press, 1987).

Huntington, Samuel: "The Clash of Civilizations?" *Foreign Affairs* (summer 1993).

Huntington, Samuel: *The Clash of Civilizations and the Remaking of World Order* (New York: Simon and Schuster, 1996).

Kahn, Herman: *On Thermonuclear War* (Princeton, NJ: Princeton University Press, 1960).

Kaplan, Lawrence: *Jefferson and France* (New Haven, CT: Yale University Press, 1967).

Kaplan, Robert D.: *The Coming Anarchy: Shattering the Dreams of the Post Cold War* (New York: Yale University Press, 2000).

Kennan, George: *Memoirs* (Boston, MA: Houghton Mifflin, 1967–72).

Kennedy, David M.: *Over Here: The First World War and American Society* (New York: Oxford University Press, 1980).

Kennedy, Paul: *The Rise and Fall of the Great Powers: Economic Change and Military Conflict from 1500 to 2000* (New York: Random House, 1987).

Kirkpatrick, Jeane: "Dictatorships and Double Standards." *Commentary* (November 1979).

Kissinger, Henry: *Nuclear Weapons and Foreign Policy* (New York: Council on Foreign Relations/Harper, 1957).

Kissinger, Henry: *White House Years* (Boston, MA: Houghton Mifflin, 1979).

Kissinger, Henry: *Years of Upheaval* (Boston, MA: Houghton Mifflin, 1982).

Kissinger, Henry: *Diplomacy* (New York: Simon and Schuster, 1994).

Kissinger, Henry: *Years of Renewal* (New York: Simon and Schuster, 1999).

Knock, Thomas: *To End All Wars: Woodrow Wilson and the Quest for a New World Order* (New York: Oxford University Press, 1992).

Kolko, Gabriel: *The Politics of War* (New York: Random House, 1968).

Kolko, Gabriel: *The Roots of American Foreign Policy* (Boston, MA: Beacon Press, 1969).

Mayers, David Allan: *George Kennan and the Dilemmas of US Foreign Policy* (New York: Oxford University Press, 1988).

Merk, Frederick: *Manifest Destiny and Mission in American History: A Reinterpretation* (New York: Knopf, 1963).

Miscamble, Wilson D.: *George Kennan and the Making of American Foreign Policy, 1947–1950* (Princeton, NJ: Princeton University Press, 1992).

Morgenthau, Hans J.: *Politics Among Nations: The Struggle for Power and Peace* (New York: Knopf, 1948).

Niebuhr, Reinhold: *The Irony of American History* (New York: Scribner, 1952).

Niebuhr, Reinhold: *Christian Realism and Political Problems* (New York: Scribner, 1953).

Nye, Joseph S.: *Bound to Lead: The Changing Nature of American Power* (New York: Basic Books, 1990).

O'Brien, Conor Cruise: *The Long Affair: Thomas Jefferson and the French Revolution, 1785–1800* (Chicago, IL: University of Chicago Press, 1996).

Podhoretz, Norman: *The Present Danger: Do We Have the Will to Reverse the Decline of American Power?* (New York: Simon and Schuster, 1980).

Schelling, Thomas: *The Strategy of Conflict* (Cambridge, MA: Harvard University Press, 1960).

Smith, Tony: *America's Mission: The United States and the Worldwide Struggle for Democracy in the Twentieth Century* (Princeton, NJ: Princeton University Press, 1994).

Steel, Ronald: *Walter Lippmann and the American Century* (Boston, MA: Houghton Mifflin, 1980).

Stephanson, Anders: *Kennan and the Art of Foreign Policy* (Cambridge, MA: Harvard University Press, 1989).

Stephanson, Anders: *Manifest Destiny: American Expansionism and the Empire of Right* (New York: Hill and Wang, 1995).

Weinberg, Albert K.: *Manifest Destiny: A Study of Nationalist Expansion in American History* (Baltimore, MD: Johns Hopkins University Press, 1935).

Williams, William Appleman: *The Tragedy of American Diplomacy* (1959; expanded edn., New York: Dell, 1962).

Chapter Two

"As Far As We Can": Culture and US Foreign Relations

Susan Brewer

"If we seek to understand a people, we have to try to put ourselves, as far as we can, in that particular historical and cultural background," said Indian Prime Minister Jawaharlal Nehru to a New York audience in 1949. In *Visit to America*, Nehru observes that understanding the way of life of a people or a country is not easy. The effort, he admits, can cause "great irritation." Nor does he promise success as he insists that the attempt must be made (Nehru 1950: 58). Historians who analyze culture and American foreign relations know these motivations, challenges, limitations, and rewards. In the last decade, they have produced an impressive number of books and articles contributing fresh perspectives to the analysis of US foreign relations. As this survey of the recent literature demonstrates, studies of culture and American foreign relations are a diverse lot, embracing a variety of traditional and non-traditional approaches, new methodologies, and a multitude of sources, written by historians who are convinced that the ways in which people understood their world affected their international interactions.

The new questions raised have been in part inspired by the changing times. After decades of defining its global role in terms of the confrontation with the Soviet Union, how would the United States determine its international identity? Some historians wish to test what Robert J. McMahon describes as the popular perception that the United States "won" the Cold War because of the superiority of its "values and institutions" (McMahon 1995: 530). Others see the United States, no longer contained, embarked upon, as the Clinton administration put it, the enlargement of market democracy. Along with economic power and technological advances, Americans spread their popular and consumer culture, exciting a global dialogue about such issues as Americanization, globalization, and Westernization. In addition, historians, who found that the hard evidence of troop deployments, military strength, foreign trade, and investment failed to adequately explain the use and misuse of power that distinguished US policy during the Cold War era, looked for answers elsewhere. Finally, the so-called culture wars in the United States engaged historians in clashes over popular and scholarly interpretations of the past. Feuds over the plans for the Smithsonian's exhibit on the *Enola Gay* and the end of World

I wish to thank Sally Kent, David Langbart, Linda Nemec, Emily Rosenberg, and Marjorie Thompson for their contributions to this essay.

War II at the National Air and Space Museum in 1995 and the development of National History Standards exposed the gap between patriotic memory and the more ambiguous conclusions of historical scholarship. In these national and international debates over America's image in the world, history and culture mattered.

In their investigations of culture and American foreign relations, historians have been influenced by scholarship from within and without the discipline. Some have found inspiration in William Appleman Williams' use of the concept of *Weltanschauung* to consider how Americans defined and explained their world, given that their "immediate and remembered" reality was shaped by "personal motives, group interests, and class ideologies." Williams quotes a revealing statement by Secretary of State Dean Acheson: "We are willing to help people who believe the way we do to continue to live the way they want to live" (Williams 1966: 17, 20). Two influential studies that emphasized culture in the Williams tradition of exploring the expansion of the American way of life are Emily Rosenberg's *Spreading the American Dream* (1982) and Frank Costigliola's *Awkward Dominion* (1984). Michael Hunt examined the role of culture in shaping "visions of national greatness" and beliefs in racial hierarchies in his often cited *Ideology and US Foreign Policy* (1997). Over the years, Akira Iriye has written trailblazing studies on culture. In *Cultural Internationalism and World Order* (Iriye 1997), he investigates the efforts of individuals and groups to influence world affairs through cross-national cultural cooperation with the goal of promoting internationalism in place of parochialism or nationalism.

As in the past, historians tapped into political science, security studies, and economics for new ideas, historians of culture and foreign relations have turned to cultural and social history, literary theory, mass communication and media studies, postcolonial studies, anthropology, and sociology, among others. They examine the ways in which the cultural constructions of national identity, gender, race, and class have affected power relationships, exposing long-standing assumptions and beliefs. They analyze culture as an instrument of power, discussing how those in authority employed language and symbols appealing to emotions, religious beliefs, and attitudes in an attempt to build consensus. They consider the complicated cultural context in which all involved in foreign relations must make sense of their world. They combine traditional multi-archival research in government documents with such non-traditional sources as mass media, art, advertisements, world fairs, fast food, fashion, guidebooks, and landscapes.

All of these influences have stimulated a lively exchange among scholars from the United States, Latin America, Europe, Asia, Africa, and the Middle East who study US foreign relations. Defenders and critics of cultural approaches have articulated their views in *Diplomatic History*'s roundtables and symposiums on "Culture, Religion, and International Relations" (Fall 2000), "Cultural Transfer or Cultural Imperialism?" (Summer 2000), "The American Century – Part II" (Summer 1999), "Imperial Discourses: Power and Perception" (Fall 1998), and "Culture, Gender, and Foreign Policy" (Winter 1994). During the discussion following a 1995 Society for Historians of American Foreign Relations conference roundtable with the state-of-the-art title "Culture and Diplomacy, or What are You Trying to Do?" a number of historians argued that diplomatic history should focus primarily on the nation-state and its exercise of power through economic and strategic policies. After a time, a member of the audience remarked that hearing American music broadcast in China when he was growing up had meant everything to him. What scholars are trying to do, while not at all dismissing the importance of strategic and economic policies, is examine how culturally constructed meanings influence international relations. In addition, historians using cultural approaches take seriously the points of view of those considered to be outsiders as well as insiders in US foreign relations. Much less likely, to quote Anders Stephanson, to write as "ersatz policymakers," they consider diverse perspectives (Stephanson 1993: 287).

With humility and conviction, historians grapple with how and why culture affects American foreign relations. As Michael Sherry observed, it's "what we all know but still have trouble explaining – that foreign policies rest on and arise from the mainsprings of culture" (Sherry 1995b: 718). Everyone admits that culture is notoriously difficult to define. Noting that the term applies to "everything from anorexia to zydeco," K. Anthony Appiah (1997) suggests that we might give it a rest. Without an alternative, however, we are left to cope as best we may. Historians of culture and foreign relations, well aware of the many uses of the term, take pains to explain their definitions. Most begin with a basic definition of culture as the beliefs, customs, arts, language, memory, and symbols of a society. Beyond that, there are numerous approaches investigating cultural diplomacy, cultural expansion, cultural interactions, cultural internationalism, cultural transmission, and cultural imperialism. As a starting point, Akira Iriye suggests three useful levels of analysis: national, cross-national, and global (Iriye 1991: 216). As he admits, even as we attempt to create categories of analysis for purposes of presenting a range of scholarship, it is immediately clear that these studies defy strict boundaries. Emily Rosenberg, a leading advocate of cultural approaches, encourages us to walk the borders (Rosenberg 1991: 27).

National Terrains

Historians combine an interest in the domestic influences on foreign policy with a cultural approach to examine beliefs about national identity, ideology, race and ethnicity, gender, and class in order to understand why Americans acted as they did. Their studies show how US policy-makers saw themselves and their counterparts. They investigate how policymakers presented their policies to the nation and the world. Often, they analyze how cultural attitudes shaped the exercise of economic, political, or military power. For example, in *In the Shadow of War* (1995), Michael Sherry argues that the militarization of American life since the late 1930s has tied culture, politics, and the economy to the images and reality of war. Emily Rosenberg (1999) examines how American dollar diplomacy from 1900 to 1930 was understood in terms of a civilizing mission shaped by gendered and racialized perceptions of power relationships.

Many new studies unite foreign and domestic policy with a specific focus on race, gender, class or national identity. For example, Thomas (Tim) Borstalmann has never been comfortable with what he considers the artificial separation of the internal and external history of the United States. He opens *The Cold War and the Color Line* (2001) with an account of how in 1961 the ambassador to the United States from the new African state of Chad was refused service in a Maryland restaurant, introducing his analysis of the intersection of Cold War ideological competition, decolonization in Africa, and the American civil rights movement. Race has influenced Americans' perceptions of themselves, their relations with other nations, and the conduct of their day-to-day diplomacy. Mary L. Dudziak (2000) shows how the case of Jimmy Wilson, an African-American handyman who in 1958 was sentenced to death in Alabama for stealing $1.95, prompted international condemnation and challenged America's vaunted image as leader of the free world. Policymakers, embarrassed by the contradictions to their story of American progress raised by the Little Rock Nine, the Freedom Riders, and the marchers on Selma, pushed for formal civil rights reforms such as the Voting Rights Act, if not for fundamental social change.

Recent studies explore the meanings of race in US foreign relations from the perspective and experience of African-American officials and activists. Michael L. Krenn (1999) notes that international awareness of American racism created an unexpected snag for the State Department's feeble attempt to use African-American diplomats as representatives of the United States. Newly independent African countries, knowing that black Americans were second-class citizens in their own country, resented what they saw as the patronizing posting of African Americans to their capitals. Marc Gallicchio (1998) investigates the wartime efforts of the National Association for the Advancement of Colored People (NAACP) to secure Nationalist China's participation in a global coalition against racism. He concludes that although these efforts failed, as demonstrated by Chiang Kai-shek's request that the black GIs who had helped to build the Burma Road be banned from China, because "they might excite undue sensation," the disappointed NAACP became more determined to pursue equal rights at home (p. 571). These studies begin with W. E. B. DuBois' assertion that "the problem of the twentieth century is the problem of the color line" and pursue its implications.

A growing number of historians have explored the ways in which gendered images illustrated, symbolized, and influenced perceptions of power relationships. Kristin Hoganson (1998) argues that anxieties over changing male and female roles at the end of the nineteenth century helped push the United States into war. Theodore Roosevelt called to the "lusty youth" of his generation to demonstrate a "virile manhood unequalled in the world." With their eye on the economic advantage of US territory in the Pacific, American imperialists claimed that white middle-class and upper-class American men could avoid degeneracy and prove their manhood by wielding authority over the Filipinos, considered to be childlike, feminine, and savage. Robert D. Dean (1998) explains that Kennedy and his administration were concerned that America had "gone soft." Sensitive to Cold-War era Republican attacks on the internationalist and upper-class foreign policy establishment as "effete homosexual Communist sympathizers subverting America from within," they responded with tough talk and policies asserting manliness from counterinsurgency to the Peace Corps as the embodiments of pioneer virtue and virility (p. 33). These studies take rhetoric seriously, analyzing what policymakers and political leaders said and the meanings behind those statements. Both tie together notions of manliness and American justifications of the acquisition and exercise of power. By examining what was said and what was meant, they help to explain what was done and why.

Historians have examined how the domestic cultures of nations have shaped their relations with each other. John Dower's (1986) pathbreaking study analyzed the role of racism in US policies toward Japan and Japanese policies toward the United States. Andrew J. Rotter (2000) explores how ideas about their nation's social systems shaped American and Indian worldviews. During a famine in 1950, Indian Prime Minister Nehru asked the United States for 2 million tons of wheat. A food loan bill was finally passed, only after a hard Congressional debate during which the Indian people were portrayed as a mass of starving beggars, and some members of Congress questioned the failure of India to support the UN action in Korea and demanded that, in return for wheat, India supply the United States with such strategic materials as manganese. Instead of advancing Indo-US relations, or in other words, making India more supportive of US foreign policy, as the Truman administration expected, Indian leaders were offended, humiliated, and suspicious of "political strings." Rotter explains that, in the Indian tradition of "dana" or "royal giving," a wealthy and powerful superior is expected to be generous to those less so and, when asked to give, should do so without hesitation and without expecting acknowledgment. Americans, expecting gratitude, were angry and annoyed when Nehru failed to demonstrate it, making the loan of wheat a low point in US–India relations.

Such brief summaries do not do justice to tightly woven analyses on the national level, or any other for that matter. They do call attention to a paradox in many of these works, however. Borstalmann, Hoganson, and Rotter, for example, have written studies that closely and carefully intertwine issues of race and ethnicity, gender, class, economic interests, and political power. Yet their titles and arguments isolate the single theme of race or gender or class. This focus allows the writers to highlight a significant aspect of culture, muster their evidence, and make their case, but denies the quite complex context they provide. Their arguments, however, have a clarity that studies which present a highly descriptive synthesis of the ways race, class, and gender influence US foreign relations seem to lack. The question of where to draw the line regarding inclusion and presentation is one of the dilemmas for historians of culture and foreign relations.

Cross-national Contacts

At the cross-national level, historians examine the ways in which the United States transmits and exchanges culture with other nations. Just as important, they analyze the ways in which governments and peoples have responded to those interactions, finding a range from acceptance to rejection. Here we consider another, related definition of culture, familiar to diplomats past and present, as literature, the arts, education, religion, sports, and entertainment. This version of culture has been subjected to division into categories of highbrow, defined as refined and enlightening (ballet, opera, symphony orchestra) and lowbrow, described as popular, vulgar, and common (ragtime and blues, vaudeville, dime novels). These divisions frequently call up Old and New World identities, prompting both derision and celebration of American popular culture. Cultural exchange includes such traditional foreign relations actors as policymakers, diplomats, and political leaders, along with the nontraditional – scholars, missionaries, tourists, artists, athletes, and activists. Cultural interactions may have been sponsored by governments and run by the Department of State's Cultural Relations Division, for example. They might be a product of public and private collaboration, as when the Departments of State and Commerce assisted Hollywood studios in obtaining access to foreign markets. Or they may be entirely private.

Traditionally, governments and diplomatic historians relegated cultural diplomacy to the bottom of the hierarchy below political and economic relations. Reflecting this ranking, the National Archives, wrestling with the problem of the volume of State Department records and limited space, decided to discard the Foreign Service Post files on "Informational, Cultural, and Scientific Affairs" for the period beginning in 1949 and designated other headquarters files on culture and information as temporary; only bits and pieces of the records of the Bureau of International Cultural Relations, for instance, survive. For some consolation, perhaps, we can turn to Frank Ninkovich's claim that the consignment of American cultural programs "to the diplomatic basement, so to speak, gave them access to the foundations of US foreign policy" (Ninkovich 1981: 3). For policymakers, the promotion of culture raised essential questions. What were US foreign policy goals and how might cultural exchange advance them? How would the United States project its way of life? Historians examine the intent behind the programs, the assumptions of policymakers, the sometimes quite different agendas of the Americans involved, and the diverse reactions of elite and popular audiences.

Cultural exchange has been used as a weapon of war and diplomacy. Walter L. Hixson states that the US–Soviet Cultural Agreement of 1958 "may well have proven to be one of the most successful initiatives in the history of US cold war diplomacy" (Hixson 1997: 153). The resulting American National Exhibition in Moscow, where Soviet Premier Nikita Khrushchev and US Vice President Richard Nixon discussed kitchen appliances, Hixson claims, introduced the Russians to an interest in and desire for American consumer culture that eventually would help undermine the Soviet system. Seth Fein (1998) describes the cooperation between American and Mexican officials over the distribution of US films about public health, agricultural methods, and American lifestyles. While officials collaborated in using film "as a shared instrument of modernization and sociopolitical control," their agendas diverged. The Mexicans sought to promote national modernization and political popularity; the Americans aimed for "transnational social engineering and ideological persuasion." Fein argues that the impact of films should not be overestimated or underestimated. Even though the official aims went unrealized, the films "shaped discourse, introduced new symbols, and spread the practice of movie going" (ibid: 401, 437). Hixson and Fein, while able to define US purposes, acknowledge the difficulty of measuring the effects of propaganda and are careful to suggest their conclusions.

Historians have followed the trail of jazz, seen as a distinctly American popular alternative to the highbrow music, art, and dance of the Old World. The State Department, as Penny Von Eschen (2000) has shown, exported jazz to represent the freedom and vitality of the United States in contrast to the repression of the Soviet Union. The State Department deployed musicians to the Cold War front lines, sending them on tours of Eastern Europe, the Middle East, Africa, and Asia, often to places of strategic economic interest. In the experience of the Dave Brubeck quartet, Secretary of State John Foster Dulles turned out to be a tyrannical booking agent, canceling the group's US engagements to extend their tour in Iraq and Iran, where they were sponsored jointly by the Iranian Oil Refining Company and the United States Information Agency. To the chagrin of the State Department, jazz musicians frequently asserted their own versions of freedom and democracy. They insisted on playing for ordinary people, rather than only for elite audiences. Dizzy Gillespie, who enjoyed representing America, but didn't want to downplay its racist history, avoided his State Department briefing, saying, "I've got three hundred years briefing." At home, the State Department felt pressure from conservatives who opposed the promotion of integrated bands abroad. The examination of jazz as a cultural export, used to project an image of racial progress, egalitarianism, and democratic values, shows how this agenda contrasted with the effects of US policy as it displayed its military dominance, sought access to strategic materials, and exerted its political and economic power.

Governments have attempted to manipulate or suppress culture to advance their power, while people have used it to assert their own interests and desires. From the other side of the "Iron Curtain," the Czechoslovakian government viewed jazz as an offensive danger. There, Josef Jařab explains in his study of the conflict between the government and the enthusiasts and musicians known as the Jazz Section it deemed as dissenters, "culture had functioned in the dark times also as alternative politics." During the Velvet Revolution in 1989, student protesters expressed their dissent by singing the American civil rights anthem "We Shall Overcome" with the lyrics "Truth Shall Prevail," inspired by Thomas Masaryk (Jařab 1993: 215). Reinhold Wagnleitner (1994) explores how even as US officials attempted to present the United States of Aaron Copland and Samuel Barber as superior to European "high culture," Austrian youth embraced cokes, jeans, and rock and roll in the spirit of rebellion, freedom, and modernity.

State-sponsored cultural exchange offers a compelling subject for analyzing foreign policy and culture. Officials must identify their aims, determine their messages, select mediums such as exhibits, films, or music, and evaluate their intended audiences. It is also worthwhile for historians to consider what is deemed ineligible for cultural exchange. When an American, on behalf of a Croatian teenager, requested a copy of the Declaration of Independence at the US Consulate in Zagreb in the early 1990s, the American official declined, indicating that the State Department considered the document to be too inflammatory for certain regions where it might be "misunderstood." The Constitution, by the way, was good to go. In addition, as historians emphasize that cultural exchange is a two-way street, it is important to consider programs and propaganda directed at the United States, evaluating another nation's reading of American culture and foreign policy goals. For instance, in my *To Win the Peace* (Brewer 1997), a study of British propaganda in the United States during World War II, I examine how, finding inspiration in Hollywood westerns, British propagandists hit upon the theme of "white men in tough places" to promote the empire by portraying American settlers and English colonizers as allies in a worldwide civilizing mission.

Recent studies of the cross-cultural interactions of such non-government actors as missionaries, artists, and tourists throw considerable light on perceptions of national identity, modernity, and power. Jon Thares Davidann (1998) examined two national histories to write what he calls an intercultural history. The conservative and evangelical American YMCA missionaries, who "linked Protestantism and nationalism by identifying Americans as the 'chosen people,'" wanted their converts to choose "Jesus over Japan." Japanese Christians wanted a liberal, modern faith, but one connected to the ancient *bushido* tradition of warrior ethics that satisfied their nationalism (ibid: 13, 62). Helen Delpar (1992) describes how Americans, turning their backs on Europe following World War I, sought an authentically American culture, celebrated what they saw as the primitive and romantic, and embraced Mexican arts as their own, in effect colonizing their southern neighbor's preconquest heritage. Traveling north, muralist Diego Rivera found beauty in American factories and technology even as he pointed out how workers suffered dehumanizing conditions.

Dennis Merrill reminds us that mass tourism is theater, "a dramatic and comedic play in which hosts and guests alike display their self-importance and choreograph their responses to cultural modernity"(Merrill 2001: 212). Appealing to middle- and upper-class American visitors who they saw as potential investors, Puerto Rican officials carefully created an image of an island that preserved the gracious traditions of the past with the amenities of modern life. Ambivalent Puerto Ricans, regretting the erosion of their way of life, welcomed the advantages of jobs, investment capital, and a forum for displaying their multicultural heritage. US visitors could find in the glamorous beachfront hotels validation of the superiority of their model of consumer capitalism over Soviet communism. Or, in the case of a few "nonconformist" Americans, who with their Puerto Rican counterparts were uneasy with the pace of technology and commercialism, the tourist centers were rejected in the search for what they hoped would be more authentic interactions with the people and the place.

Although the purpose of their studies is to illuminate private cultural interaction, Davidann, Delpar, and Merrill recognize and consider briefly its connection to government policy. Merrill points out that the Puerto Ricans had constructed a stage set for their visitors featuring a charming past and an enterprising future, while they heatedly debated without resolution their status as independent, a state, or common-wealth. Davidann observes with some irony that after resisting the American YMCA's attempt to impose its standards on them, Japanese Christians went off to Korea to do the same, only to set up YMCA organizations that became dominated by anti-Japanese Korean nationalists. He notes that the competition for influence on the Asian mainland between Japanese and American Christians paralleled the competition between the Japanese and US governments. Delpar explains that US ambassadors to Mexico held two typical, but contrasting attitudes about the role of culture in diplomatic relations. James Rockwell Sheffield (1924–7) viewed cultural relations as a tool that could be implemented to further one country's agenda to the detriment of the other's. Dwight Morrow, Sheffield's successor, promoted cultural exchange in the hope that mutual understanding would lead to better economic and diplomatic relations. As we have seen, these studies and others discussed earlier complicate these typical views by showing that culture as a tool does not always work as policymakers assume it will, that cultural exchange does not always lead to better understanding, and that better understanding if achieved might or might not lead to improved economic and diplomatic relations.

Global Grounds

In 2000 in the alpine resort town of Davos, Switzerland, the heads of state, CEOs, media moguls, and academics who attended the private World Economic Forum saw an inflatable, illuminated, 30-foot tall Ronald McDonald, seated in the lotus position, floating above the Golden Arches of the town's only McDonald's. Dubbed the Anti-Buddha by Danish journalist Mads Brügger (2000), Ronald was removed by the time 1,300 Italian, Spanish, German, and Swiss activists, protesting against globalization and multinational corporations, destroyed the fast food restaurant, injuring the locals who were trying to defend it. During the riot, protesters set fire to a huge plastic yellow McDonald's banner that read, "Think global, Eat local." As the activists moved on the square in front of the luxury hotel where Palestinian leader Yassir Arafat was supposedly staying, Kurdish activists burned a Turkish flag and others burned an American flag. Brügger compared the scene to a colorized version of the old movie *Frankenstein*, where outraged townspeople, brandishing torches, clubs, and pitchforks, made their way to the castle to punish the monster, although he is vague about who or what might be considered the monster. As this incident at Davos illustrates, global grounds include the local, national, regional, and multinational. To make sense of this event and others like it, some historian will have to examine the beliefs, assumptions, symbols, images, and rhetoric that made up the cultural context of this clash over globalization.

Worldwide movements promoting religion, the abolition of slavery, women's rights, the preservation of art, health, the environment, peace, and security engage historians of culture and US foreign relations. Increasingly taught on college campuses, world history covers movements of people, plants, diseases, information, technology, capital, and culture. International organizations such as the League of Nations' Committee on Intellectual Cooperation and the United Nations Educational, Scientific, and Cultural Organization (UNESCO) sponsored cultural programs to promote better understanding among nations. Many national groups have international agendas. They may pursue worldwide recognition to mobilize forces to advance their cause on a global scale or to transcend marginalization at the national level.

Some private organizations have closer relations with official American foreign policy than others. Volker Berghahn explores the close ideological collaboration between such large philanthropic foundations as the Carnegie Endowment for International Peace, the Ford Foundation, and the Rockefeller Foundation and the US government, while noting that collaboration went beyond ideological for the Congress of Cultural Freedom which received its funding publicly from the Ford Foundation and covertly from the CIA (Berghahn 1999: 416). Citing De Tocqueville's observation that Americans were keen on "private associations," Akira Iriye (1999) calls for international historians to explore the over 1 million non-government organizations (NGOs) as a link between world and US history. NGOs and the international non-government organizations (INGOs) are non-profit, non-political, private, and voluntary organizations such as the American Friends Service Committee, Social Science Research Council, Save the Children Foundation, Women's International League for Peace and Freedom, Amnesty International, and the Red Cross. An investigation of the activities of private organizations reveals that ordinary Americans have been quite persistent about participating in foreign relations.

A number of historians of American foreign relations have explored the link between culture and power on a global level by investigating the issue of Americanization. In the United States of the late 1800s, the term applied to the assimilation of its immigrant population. Celebrated as progress, Americanization was the subject of dispute over its Old World or New World origins. Frederick Jackson Turner argued that Americanization, "English in neither nationality or character," took place on the frontier. His British contemporary, liberal journalist W. T. Stead, saw it differently. In his 1902 book, *The Americanization of the World*, Stead claimed that, as the Americans carried out "the refashioning of the world in their image," they were in fact anglicizing it. As for the "American invasion" of "the typewriter, the sewing-machine, the Linotype, the automobile, the phonograph, the telephone, the elevator, and the incandescent electric light," Stead declared, "We want these things. We want them now" (Stead 1972: 135–7). The expanding American system of mass production, mass marketing, and mass consumption sold itself with the advertised promise of individual freedom, success, and happiness. To the bemusement of satirical artist George Grosz (1998), recalling the 1920s, the home of standardization and commercialization produced the newest fads in Germany – teddy bears, cocktails, and cowboy movies. Americanization was embraced as liberating and intoxicating, condemned as repressive and conforming.

Historians have analyzed the responses of resistance, adaptation, and acceptance to Americanization ranging from love to hate. Masako Notoji contrasts the immense popularity of everything Disney in Japan with the dismay of new parents whose baby's first word was "Mickey" (Notoji 2000: 223). In *Americanization and Australia*, Philip Bell and Roger Bell see a shift in the 1980s from focusing on the mighty American dollar to global capital, thereby leaving fears of Americanization to rest on the influence of American culture, in particular, sports, language, and fashion. They conclude that Australians, in a process they call "creolization" or "hybridization," often took what they wanted from American culture, blended it with their own traditions, and considered the result as part of their own national identity (Bell and Bell 1998: 7).

In their exploration of the Americanization of Australian sport, Richard Cashman and Anthony Hughes (1998) challenge popular myths of cultural dominance, while acknowledging that in the 1990s, American basketball superstar Michael Jordan was more famous than any Australian athlete. For instance, they show that instead of being a recent presence carried by television, American sport had a long-time role in Australia, from harness racing in the 1860s, to lacrosse in the 1870s, to rodeo in the 1890s. At the same time, they conclude that American sport has limited influence in Australia in part because US baseball and football competition culminating in the "World Series" and the Superbowl are open only to American and Canadian teams and because the Australians play sports such as cricket, netball, and forms of football that Americans do not. A quite different approach to the worldwide reach of American sports is Walter LaFeber's *Michael Jordan and the New Global Capitalism*. LaFeber uses Jordan's phenomenal career as well as his role as the "greatest endorser" to examine ways in which the combination of professional sports, multinational corporations, and media technology dominate the global marketplace, often overwhelming, displacing, or destabilizing traditional, local cultures. LaFeber concludes that in the contest between capital and culture, capital will win (LaFeber 1999: 162).

Certainly, historians investigating culture and foreign relations on a global level must reckon with defining the boundaries of their analysis. Distinguishing between Americanization and globalization is one challenge. Richard Kuisel (2000) suggests that, as one rather large chapter in the history of globalization, Americanization contributed to its spread by promoting and exporting mass consumer culture. It is also difficult to reconcile the detailed exploration of many perspectives with a global vision. One alternative are collections of studies on local or national levels linked by region or theme, such as *Close Encounters of Empire: Writing the Cultural History of US–Latin American Relations* (Joseph, LeGrand, and Salvatore 1998), *Cultural Transmissions and Receptions: American Mass Culture in Europe* (Kroes, Rydell, and Bosscher 1993), *Drugs in the Western Hemisphere: An Odyssey of Cultures in Conflict* (Walker 1996), and *"Here, There and Everywhere": The Foreign Politics of American Popular Culture* (Wagnleitner and May 2000). The editors and some of the contributors draw the larger conclusions about the hemispheric or global reach of culture and US foreign relations, as may the readers.

Whether they use analytical frameworks based on the nation-state, cross-cultural exchange, global interactions, or some combination of these, foreign relations scholars have explored the power of culture to shape people's perceptions of the world. They have investigated the ways in which beliefs about race, gender, class, and national identity have affected the creation and conduct of US foreign policy. Their championship of culture counters its traditionally low placement in the diplomatic hierarchy where the need to understand another culture was seen sometimes as a sign of weakness, only necessary if a nation did not have the military or economic power to get its way. At face value this view is illustrated by the difference between Nehru, who needed American aid and called for understanding history and culture, and Acheson, who had it to give and expected recipients to share American beliefs. As numerous historians have pointed out over the years, this disregard or ignorance of the cultures of the nations with which Americans have conducted relations has been one of the major flaws in US foreign policy. And to figure out why this has been so, historians, walking through the door opened by William Appleman Williams and others, investigate the cultural roots of American foreign relations.

In addition, they have recognized the importance of non-governmental actors in constructing the diverse identities of the United States in the world. Consider John F. Sears' (1993) discussion of the many effects of the tremendously popular "Buffalo Bill's Wild West Show" in late nineteenth- and early twentieth-century Europe. As it traveled, the show, featuring gunfights, bucking broncos, trick riding, and dramatic rescues of white settlers from savages, demonstrated the triumph of industrial civilization's revolver and repeating rifle, the effectiveness of sensational mass adver-tising, and such efficient transportation and setup that Prussian army officers took detailed notes. With Buffalo Bill, Sears concludes, the audience "could have it both ways." They could cheer the "freedom, mobility, wildness, and violence" of Buffalo Bill and the Indians, while celebrating the "triumph of European civilization over savagery." In many ways, with and without state sponsorship, the expansion of American mass culture and its message of "having it all," have served US interests.

In answer to Thomas Paterson's call that historians "have a responsibility to combat the American public's ignorance about US foreign relations," studies of culture and foreign relations can make a real contribution (Paterson 1991: 53). People often look upon the subject of foreign relations as boring, serious, and important and therefore having nothing to do with them. As historians have pointed out, this response has been encouraged. For example, here is columnist Walter Lippmann on British economist John Maynard Keynes' plan regarding negotiations in Washington over Anglo-American wartime economic policies: "Keynes told me last night that he wanted to keep the whole subject dull and important, so that the general public will accept the views of the experts on their authority, rather than try to understand them and form an independent judgment" (Brewer 1997: 219). Although the "trust me" approach to policymaking obviously may vary in quality depending upon the policy and the expert, it always, it must be noted, requires a passive public. As we've seen, studies of culture and foreign relations do not view publics as puppets; instead they show people in the United States and elsewhere acting in a variety of ways, initiating, protesting, adapting, rejecting, and participating. Foreign relations, while serious and important, are shown to be far from dull and having everything to do with people's way of life.

Histories of culture and foreign relations also contribute by exploring understanding and misunderstanding among peoples and nations. Sometimes a small detail can have a big impact. In *Backfire*, a study of the Vietnam War and American culture, Loren Baritz describes how the common custom in Vietnam for friends, including South Vietnamese soldiers, to hold hands when walking down the street was viewed with shock and disgust by American marines, thereby adding more fear and mistrust to an already strained alliance (Baritz 1985: 6). Many times, students have commented on how this account of cultural misperception opened their eyes, making them rethink customs that they take for granted as universal. From there, they questioned the roles of race, gender, class, and national identity in shaping hearts and minds. This investigation of how peoples understand each other seems especially relevant after the September 11, 2001 terrorist attacks when a common question was "why do they hate us?" Therefore, it is important for historians to write in an accessible, engaging way on the complications of a world growing at once closer and more fragmented. To make sense of US foreign relations the cultural complexities past and present must be addressed, so that we may understand as far as we can.

REFERENCES

Appiah, K. Anthony: "The Multiculturalist Misunderstanding." *The New York Review of Books* (October 9, 1997), 30–6.

Baritz, Loren: *Backfire: A History of How American Culture Led Us into Vietnam and Made Us Fight the Way We Did* (New York: Ballantine Books, 1985).

Bell, Philip and Roger Bell (eds.): *Americanization and Australia* (Sydney: University of New South Wales Press, 1998).

Berghahn, Volker: "Philanthropy and Diplomacy in the 'American Century'." *Diplomatic History* 23 (summer, 1999), 393–419.

Borstalmann, Thomas: *The Cold War and the Color Line: American Race Relations in the Global Arena* (Cambridge, MA: Harvard University Press, 2001).

Brewer, Susan: *To Win the Peace: British Propaganda in the United States during World War II* (Ithaca, NY: Cornell University Press, 1997).

Brügger, Mads: "Six Days that Shocked the World." *Virus* 5 (May 2000).

Cashman, Richard and Anthony Hughes: "Sport." In Philip Bell and Roger Bell (eds.) *Americanization and Australia* (Sydney: University of New South Wales Press, 1998).

Costigliola, Frank: *Awkward Dominion: American Political, Economic, and Cultural Expansion, 1919–1933* (Ithaca, NY: Cornell University Press, 1984).

Davidann, Jon Thares: *A World of Crisis and Progress: The American YMCA in Japan, 1890–1930* (Bethlehem: Lehigh University Press, 1998).

Dean, Robert D.: "Masculinity as Ideology: John F. Kennedy and the Domestic Politics of Foreign Policy." *Diplomatic History* 22 (winter 1998), 29–62.

Delpar, Helen: *The Enormous Vogue of Things Mexican: Cultural Relations between the United States and Mexico, 1920–1935* (Tuscaloosa: University of Alabama Press, 1992).

Dower, John W.: *War Without Mercy: Race and Power in the Pacific War* (New York: Pantheon Books, 1986).

Dudziak, Mary L.: *Cold War Civil Rights: Race and the Image of American Democracy* (Princeton, NJ: Princeton University Press, 2000).

Fein, Seth: "Everyday Forms of Transnational Collaboration: US Film Propaganda in Cold War Mexico." In Gilbert M. Joseph, Catherine C. LeGrand, and Ricardo D. Salvatore (eds.) *Close Encounters of Empire: Writing the Cultural History of US–Latin American Relations* (Durham, NC: Duke University Press, 1998).

Gallicchio, Marc: "Coloring the Nationalists: The African-American Construction of China in the Second World War." *International History Review* 20 (September 1998), 571–96.

Grosz, George: *Ein kleines Ja und ein grosses Nein* [1946], trans. Nora Hodges, *George Grosz: An Autobiography* (Berkeley: University of California Press, 1998).

Hixson, Walter L.: *Parting the Curtain: Propaganda, Culture, and the Cold War, 1945–1961* (New York: St. Martin's Press, 1997).

Hoganson, Kristin L.: *Fighting for American Manhood: How Gender Politics Provoked the Spanish–American and Philippine–American Wars* (New Haven, CT: Yale University Press, 1998).

Hunt, Michael H.: *Ideology and US Foreign Policy* (New Haven, CT: Yale University Press, 1997).

Iriye, Akira: "Culture and International History." In Michael J. Hogan and Thomas G. Paterson (eds.) *Explaining the History of American Foreign Relations* (New York: Cambridge University Press, 1991).

Iriye, Akira: *Cultural Internationalism and World Order* (Baltimore, MD: Johns Hopkins University Press, 1997).

Iriye, Akira: "A Century of NGOs." *Diplomatic History* 23 (summer 1999), 421–35.

Jařab, Josef: "The Story of the Jazz Section in Czechoslovakia." In Rob Kroes, Robert W. Rydell, and Doeko F. J. Bosscher (eds.) *Cultural Transmissions and Receptions: American Mass Culture in Europe* (Amsterdam: Vu University Press, 1993).

Joseph, Gilbert M., Catherine C. LeGrand, and Ricardo D. Salvatore (eds.): *Close Encounters of Empire: Writing the Cultural History of US–Latin American Relations* (Durham, NC: Duke University Press, 1998).

Krenn, Michael L.: *Black Diplomacy: African Americans and the State Department 1945–1969* (Armonk, NY: M. E. Sharpe, 1999).

Kroes, Rob, Robert W. Rydell, and Doeko F. J. Bosscher (eds.): *Cultural Transmissions and Receptions: American Mass Culture in Europe* (Amsterdam: Vu University Press, 1993).

Kuisel, Richard: "Americanization for Historians." *Diplomatic History* 24 (summer 2000), 509–15.

LaFeber, Walter: *Michael Jordan and the New Global Capitalism* (New York: W.W. Norton, 1999).

McMahon, Robert J.: "The Cold War in Asia: The Elusive Synthesis." In Michael J. Hogan (ed.) *America in the World: The Historiography of American Foreign Relations since 1941* (New York: Cambridge University Press, 1995).

Merrill, Dennis: "Negotiating Cold War Paradise: US Tourism, Economic Planning, and Cultural Modernity in Twentieth-Century Puerto Rico." *Diplomatic History* 25 (spring 2001), 179–214.

Nehru, Jawaharlal: *Visit to America* (New York: John Day, 1950).

Ninkovich, Frank A.: *The Diplomacy of Ideas: US Foreign Policy and Cultural Relations, 1938–1950* (New York: Cambridge University Press, 1981).

Notoji, Masako: "Cultural Transformation of John Philip Sousa and Disneyland in Japan." In Reinhold Wagnleitner and Elaine Tyler May (eds.) *"Here, There, and Everywhere": The Foreign Politics of American Popular Culture* (Hanover, NH: University Press of New England, 2000).

Paterson, Thomas G.: "Defining and Doing the History of American Foreign Relations: A Primer." In Michael J. Hogan and Thomas G. Paterson (eds.) *Explaining the History of American Foreign Relations* (New York: Cambridge University Press, 1991).

Rosenberg, Emily S.: *Spreading the American Dream: American Economic and Cultural Expansion, 1890–1945* (New York: Hill and Wang, 1982).

Rosenberg, Emily S.: "Walking the Borders." In Michael J. Hogan and Thomas G. Paterson (eds.) *Explaining the History of American Foreign Relations* (New York: Cambridge University Press, 1991).

Rosenberg, Emily S.: *Financial Missionaries to the World: The Politics and Culture of Dollar Diplomacy, 1900–1930* (Cambridge, MA: Harvard University Press, 1999).

Rotter, Andrew J.: "Feeding Beggars: Class, Caste, and Status in Indo–US Relations, 1947–1964." In Christian G. Appy (ed.) *Cold War Constructions: The Political Culture of United States Imperialism, 1945–1966* (Amherst: University of Massachusetts Press, 2000).

Sears, John F.: "Bierstadt, Buffalo Bill, and the Wild West in Europe." In Rob Kroes, Robert W. Rydell, and Doeko F. J. Bosscher (eds.) *Cultural Transmissions and Receptions: American Mass Culture in Europe* (Amsterdam: Vu University Press, 1993).

Sherry, Michael S.: *In the Shadow of War: The United States since the 1930s* (New Haven, CT: Yale University Press, 1995a).

Sherry, Michael S.: "Projections of Hegemony and Consent in Film." *Diplomatic History* 19 (fall 1995b), 713–18.

Stead, William.T.: *The Americanization of the World or the Trend of the Twentieth Century* [1902] (New York: Garland Publishing, 1972).

Stephanson, Anders: "Commentary: Ideology and Neorealist Mirrors." *Diplomatic History* 17 (spring 1993), 285–95.

Von Eschen, Penny M.: " 'Satchmo Blows Up the World': Jazz, Race and Empire during the Cold War." In Reinhold Wagnleitner and Elaine Tyler May (eds.) *"Here, There and Everywhere": The Foreign Politics of American Popular Culture* (Hanover, NH: University Press of New England, 2000).

Wagnleitner, Reinhold: *Coca-Colonization and the Cold War: The Cultural Mission of the United States in Austria after the Second World War* (Chapel Hill: University of North Carolina Press, 1994).

Wagnleitner, Reinhold and Elaine Tyler May (eds.): *"Here, There and Everywhere": The Foreign Politics of American Popular Culture* (Hanover, NH: University Press of New England, 2000).

Walker, William O., III (ed.): *Drugs in the Western Hemisphere: An Odyssey of Cultures in Conflict* (Wilmington, DE: Scholarly Resources, 1996).

Williams, William Appleman: *The Contours of American History* (Chicago, IL: Quadrangle Books, 1966).

FURTHER READING

Bennett, Todd: "Culture, Power, and *Mission to Moscow*: Film and Soviet–American Relations during World War II." *Journal of American History* 88 (September 2001), 489–518.

Costigliola, Frank: "'Unceasing Pressure for Penetration': Gender, Pathology, and Emotion in George Kennan's Formation of the Cold War." *Journal of American History* 83 (March 1997), 1309–39.

DeConde, Alexander: *Ethnicity, Race, and American Foreign Policy: A History* (Boston, MA: Northeastern University Press, 1992).

Foglesong, David S.: "'Roots of Liberation': American Images of the Future of Russia in the Early Cold War, 1948–1953." *International History Review* 21 (March 1999), 57–79.

Haddow, Robert H.: *Pavilions of Plenty: Exhibiting American Culture Abroad in the 1950s* (Washington, DC: Smithsonian Institution Press, 1997).

Hogan, Michael J. (ed.): *Hiroshima in History and Memory* (New York: Cambridge University Press, 1996).

Hoganson, Kristin: "Cosmopolitan Domesticity: Importing the American Dream, 1865–1920." *American Historical Review* 107 (February 2002), 55–83.

Iriye, Akira: "Cultural Diplomacy." In Bruce W. Jentleson and Thomas G. Paterson (eds.) *Encyclopedia of US Foreign Relations* (New York: Oxford University Press, 1997).

Jarvie, Ian: *Hollywood's Overseas Campaign: The North Atlantic Movie Trade, 1920–1950* (New York: Cambridge University Press, 1992).

Kroes, Rob: *If You've Seen One, You've Seen the Mall: Europeans and American Mass Culture* (Urbana: University of Illinois Press, 1996).

Kuisel, Richard: *Seducing the French: The Dilemma of Americanization* (Berkeley: University of California Press, 1993).

LaFeber, Walter: "The World and the United States." *American Historical Review* 100 (October 1995), 1015–33.

Linenthal, Edward T. and Tom Engelhardt (eds.): *History Wars: The Enola Gay and Other Battles for the American Past* (New York: Henry Holt, 1996).

Lytle, Mark: "NGOs and the New Transnational Politics." *Diplomatic History* 25 (winter 2001), 121–8.

Mart, Michelle: "Tough Guys and American Cold War Policy: Images of Israel, 1948–1960." *Diplomatic History* 20 (summer 1996), 357–80.

May, Elaine Tyler: *Homeward Bound: American Families in the Cold War Era* (New York: Basic Books, 1988).

Pells, Richard: *Not Like Us: How Europeans Have Loved, Hated, and Transformed American Culture Since World War II* (New York: Basic Books, 1997).

Plummer, Brenda Gayle: *Rising Wind: Black Americans and US Foreign Affairs, 1935–1960* (Chapel Hill: University of North Carolina Press, 1996).

Prevots, Naima: *Dance for Export: Cultural Diplomacy and the Cold War* (Hanover, NH: University Press of New England, 1998).

Robin, Ron: *The Making of the Cold War Enemy: Culture and Politics in the Military–Industrial Complex* (Princeton, NJ: Princeton University Press, 2001).

Rosenberg, Emily S.: "Cultural Interactions." In Stanley Kutler (ed.) *Encyclopedia of the United States in the Twentieth Century* (New York: Scribners, 1996).

Rosenberg, Emily S.: "Turning to Culture." In Gilbert M. Joseph, Catherine C. LeGrand, and Ricardo Salvatore (eds.) *Close Encounters of Empire: Writing the Cultural History of US–Latin American Relations* (Durham, NC: Duke University Press, 1998).

Rotter, Andrew: "Gender Relations, Foreign Relations: The United States and South Asia, 1947–1964." *Journal of American History* 81 (September 1994), 518–42.

Rotter, Andrew J.: "Saidism without Said: *Orientalism* and US Diplomatic History." *American Historical Review* 105 (October 2000), 1205–17.

Rydell, Robert W.: *All the World's a Fair: Visions of Empire at American International Expositions, 1876–1916* (Chicago, IL: University of Chicago Press, 1984).

Shulman, Holly Cowan: *The Voice of America: Propaganda and Democracy* (Madison: University of Wisconsin Press, 1990).

Smith, Geoffrey S.: "National Security and Personal Isolation: Sex, Gender, and Disease in the Cold-War United States." *International History Review* 14 (May 1992), 307–37.

Smith, Shannon: "From Relief to Revolution: American Women and the Russian–American Relationship, 1890–1917." *Diplomatic History* 19 (fall 1995), 601–16.

Von Eschen, Penny M.: *Race Against Empire: Black Americans and Anticolonialism, 1937–1957* (Ithaca, NY: Cornell University Press, 1997).

CHAPTER THREE

International Environmental Issues

KURK DORSEY

The great untapped vein of American diplomatic history is the environment. Several prominent diplomatic historians have called for more work on the place of the environment in US foreign policy, but few have taken up the challenge. Instead, most of the history of international environmental issues has been written by environmental historians, policymakers, and political scientists. Of the three groups, the environmental historians probably have the most to say to diplomatic historians. The political scientists and analysts tend to be grounded either in theory or their own personal experiences – not to mention being quite present-minded. In fact, Patricia Limerick (2001), one of the leaders of Western and environmental history, noted that many of her ideas closely mirror those of William Appleman Williams. Williams and his descendants in the Wisconsin school of diplomatic history would seem well-suited to begin the development of an environmental analysis of US foreign policy. Their emphasis on economics often raises, at least implicitly, questions about American consumption of natural resources, and their emphasis on informal empire has contributed to an understanding of the limitations of political borders. The potential for innovative and important research on environmental diplomacy rivals that provided by the opening of Eastern European archives.

Those who would like a primer on the complexities of the subject would do well to consult Lawrence Susskind's book *Environmental Diplomacy* (1994). Susskind laid out a framework for negotiators to use in crafting environmental treaties, so in that sense his scholarship is primarily policy oriented. Still, he based his conclusions on studying fifteen recent treaties, which gave him historical perspective. In particular, he concluded that environmental diplomacy had unique features, such as a need to consider scientific findings, the uncertainty of ecological change, and the input of non-governmental organizations. National delegations to negotiation sessions not only have to account for all of the above factors, but they also have to sort out all of their own differences and competing claims, while hammering out differences with delegations from scores of other countries. Susskind made another important point, that traditional allies will often butt heads when it comes to environmental issues. The United States has frequently disagreed with its closest European allies on environmental issues, from whaling to global warming; likewise, the rivals on the Indian subcontinent often find themselves united against the industrialized nations on environmental issues.

Susskind's book suggests some of the reasons that diplomatic historians have not known what to do with the environment. First, few diplomatic historians have much background in the sciences, especially ecology, that are so important to environmental diplomacy and environmental history. Attempts to employ an environmental analysis, much as some have employed gender analysis, to revitalize well-studied topics require a specific, non-traditional approach, to which few diplomatic historians have been exposed. Second, such diplomacy, because it often cuts across those traditional alliances and rivalries, does not really fit into the broad frameworks that we construct. Specifically environmental issues, such as wildlife protection treaties, often do have a clear relationship with, and in fact appear to be less crucial than, the various crises of the Cold War, which account for about half of the research of diplomatic historians. Thus historians are more likely to study Nixon's summit diplomacy than the US position at the UN Conference on the Human Environment held at Stockholm in 1972, and they are completely unlikely to see any link between the two.

The end of the Cold War in 1989, and subsequent premature claims about the end of history, paved the way for diplomats and diplomatic historians to re-evaluate their work and the field, and four prominent scholars noted the opportunity to include the environment. In 1990, *Diplomatic History* published a symposium on the writing of the history of US foreign relations, prompted largely by Christopher Thorne's accusation that US diplomatic historians were a parochial, narrow-minded lot. In his piece, Thomas Paterson wrote that both communications and the environment needed more attention. As he noted, activists had identified a long list of international environmental crises, enough that the State Department was trumpeting its own – belated – acknowledgment of environmental issues. These crises, though seemingly new, were "rich in history," stretching back decades. They also fit the interests of diplomatic historians because so often they were about power, such as control of food in a time of famine.

Paterson's essay made an important first step, but it was only that. He devoted just two pages to this point, because his larger goal was to analyze the field in general, including what had been done well and what should be done. In addition, he acknowledged that to get to the core of environmental issues diplomatic historians might well have to acquire a great deal of basic knowledge in history of science and similar fields. In other words, scholars would have to be interdisciplinary. Like calls for historians to learn Russian and mine the Kremlin's archives, Paterson's suggestion realistically could be taken up only by graduate students.

Four years later, in *America, Russia and the Cold War, 1945–92*, Walter LaFeber (1993) suggested that the end of the Cold War would force the United States to reconsider the place of the environment in diplomacy. As LaFeber noted, the number and magnitude of international environmental problems were growing, but US leaders were slow to grapple with those problems. Implicit in his comment was a call for diplomatic historians to study them and explain their significance. In 1995, Gaddis Smith added his voice to the chorus. In reviewing Henry Kissinger's gargantuan *Diplomacy* for the *Boston Globe*, Smith commented that Kissinger somehow managed to overlook the state of the chessboard in his obsession with the chess game. Kissinger apparently missed the point, as his most recent book, *Does America Need a Foreign Policy?*, mentions neither the environment nor natural resources.

But not until 1996 did anyone try to develop a coherent vision for what an environmental approach to diplomatic history might look like. In that year, *Diplo-*

matic History carried an article by Mark Lytle that expanded on Paterson. Arguing that diplomatic historians risked increasing irrelevancy if they did not adopt an environmental perspective, Lytle urged his colleagues to take up "the rich agenda and fresh perspectives" promised by an environmental approach. Two possible avenues stood out. First, diplomatic historians could tackle questions that were "self-evidently environmental," such as the 1973 Convention on International Trade in Endangered Species. Second, they could attempt the admittedly "somewhat more elusive" task of re-analyzing traditional diplomatic topics, such as the Vietnam War. In either case, they had a long way to go.

In searching for an explanation for the lack of cross-pollination between diplomatic and environmental historians, Lytle focused on two important differences. First, environmental history grew largely out of the field of Western history, while diplomatic history has largely been concerned with power elites in Washington, DC and New York. This sectional difference certainly does not explain the whole gap, but it certainly fits with Edmund Morgan's conclusion that the great split in the United States is not north–south but east–west. Second, and far more important, Lytle pointed to the different sources for theories and ideas. Ecology has played a huge role in shaping environmental historians' thinking about their field, but very few diplomatic historians think like ecologists do. As an example, diplomatic historians are nearly obsessed with political borders, but ecologists largely view them as arbitrary means of dividing ecosystems. Lytle noted that many diplomatic historians sympathized with environmentalist views, but they had largely failed to see the connection to historical events.

This comment suggests one more reason that diplomatic historians have not done much with the environment – they imagine that environmental diplomacy is a very new phenomenon, too young perhaps to be history. This notion is reinforced by environmental activists, who often act as if they recently invented environmental diplomacy. In 1995, an official of the environmental group Worldwatch, Hilary French, claimed that environmental diplomacy "began to gather serious momentum" only in 1972, although she did note that there had been occasional treaties as long ago as the 1870s. Most environmentalists and activists treat these pre-1972 treaties as oddities with no direct relevance to the vastly more complex problems of today. In a similar way, diplomatic historians may see all of these treaties largely as an extension of domestic politics, as the treaties of the last thirty years seem to fit better into a domestic framework than into the diplomatic one.

In fact, the environment has played a key role in US foreign policy, especially expansion, from independence. The United States found itself wrestling with Great Britain over fisheries issues at the peace conference that resulted in the Treaty of Paris of 1783, and the issue remained a contentious one for more than a century. Treaties in 1815, 1818, 1854, 1871, and 1888 all addressed access to the cod fisheries of the Grand Banks and other areas of the Northwest Atlantic. The two nations did not resolve their dispute until 1910, when an arbitration tribunal finally set permanent rules for the fishery. Historians such as Harold Innis (1940) paid a great deal of attention to the cod wars, but most of the analysis came down to fisheries as a piece of the Anglo-American friction and *rapprochement* of the nineteenth century. Historians like to tell the tale of Robert Benchley, who was faced with an essay question at Harvard on the fisheries dispute. Allegedly, he noted that while everyone had analyzed the British and American positions, few had considered the viewpoint of the fish. He proceeded to analyze the dispute from their wall-eyed perspective. While diplomatic historians chuckle at the idea, it is not far removed from what Lytle would ask of them, that they consider the life-cycles of fish, climatological influences that might bring scarcity or abundance, and the role of other species and human influences. At the same time, Benchley might have received a better grade if he had instead placed the fisheries dispute into a broader context of an American quest for resources and other environmental amenities.

Meanwhile, on the other side of North America, the United States and the British Empire spent the years 1886–1911 embroiled in another dispute over marine resources, in this case fur seals. The seals are born on two small Alaskan islands, but they spend roughly 75 percent of their lives on the high seas. Canadians hunted the seals on the open ocean; Americans hunted them on the islands under a lease from the government; both sold the pelts to furriers in London. Beginning in 1886, the fur seal dispute held the attention of officials in London, Washington, and Ottawa, as the United States used force to confiscate Canadian sealing vessels. Seven years later, in a famous case, arbitrators created rules restricting access to the seals by Canadian sealers, while preserving their right to hunt seals. Instead of solving the problem, the ruling opened the way for Japanese sealers to fill the void, thus complicating an already murky dispute. Finally, in 1911, with the seal on the verge of extinction, the interested parties cut a deal that allowed harvesting of seals on land in exchange for splitting the proceeds among them.

Diplomatic historians did not ignore these conflicts. After all, it was Samuel Flagg Bemis who so eloquently summed up the biological knowledge of fur seals: "Amphibious is the fur seal, ubiquitous and carnivorous, uniparous, gregarious, and withal polygamous." Rather they examined them through a traditional diplomatic lens within the context of the Anglo-American *rapprochement*. Thomas Bailey (1935) described the 1911 North Pacific Fur Seal Convention as a victory for conservation, but his article in *Pacific Historical Review* had as much to do with the old-fashioned triumph of diplomacy and cooperation. Charles Campbell, Jr., in a pair of articles in the 1960s, defined fur seal diplomacy as a story about arbitration and power rivalries. Neither man attributed any agency to the seals or their behavior, nor expressed any appreciation of the seals' place in a complex ecosystem, even though the seals' biology had placed them in the center of a diplomatic conflict.

It was possible, though, to see the North Pacific Fur Seal Convention as part of a trend of environmental diplomacy in the early twentieth century, and it was possible to see the seal's behavior as an important factor in shaping that diplomacy. First in a 1995 article and then in a 1998 book, *The Dawn of Conservation Diplomacy: US–Canadian Wildlife Protection Treaties in the Progressive Era*, Kurk Dorsey made an attempt to place the fur seal dispute into a different context. While acknowledging the importance of Anglo-American relations and successful resolution of disputes, he linked the fur seal convention with two treaties meant to protect fish and birds, the 1908 Inland Fisheries Treaty and the 1916 Migratory Bird Treaty (MBT). The former was an attempt by the United States and United Kingdom to resolve long-standing questions about fisheries along the US–Canadian border, from Passama-quoddy Bay to Puget Sound. Although the treaty received formal approval, the United States Congress failed to pass enabling legislation, and the treaty's provisions did not become law. The MBT stands as one of the few environmental treaties to be a clear success. It regulated hunting of migratory birds north of Mexico and provided the basis for further bird-protection treaties with Mexico, the USSR, and Japan; but also the MBT lives on today, as its enabling legislation, in amended form, stands as the core of bird-hunting regulations in Canada and the United States.

Dorsey (1998) argued that these three treaties fit together. Their success or failure depended on a combination of science, sentiment, and economics. The fisheries treaty went belly-up because the science in favor of it was thin, the fishermen argued persuasively that their economic interests would be harmed for little societal gain, and there was no groundswell of sentimentalism for a treaty to regulate fish. In the case of the fur seal convention, diplomats were able to snatch the seal from the brink of extinction in part because the scientific evidence proved that pelagic sealing was driving it toward extinction, in part because some clever public relations work created the notion that seals are what might now be called charismatic megafauna, and in part because the diplomats devised a fair means of sharing the costs. The Migratory Bird Treaty emerged as the most successful of the three because conservationists harnessed a natural human sympathy for birds, while scientists generated evidence that birds had economic value as insectivores.

In the end, these treaties were a product of both the unique relationship between Canada and the United States and the behavior of the species themselves. While many people have rhapsodized about the longest undefended border in the world, another way of thinking about that border is that it cuts across the ranges of many species of migratory animals. Valuable migrants, whether birds, fish, or seals, were bound to become the subject of dispute and therefore of diplomacy. For all of the occasional sniping across the border, private citizens and public officials in both countries by the turn of the century saw that they had to cooperate to save migratory species. They shared a concern about the inefficient use of resources or short-sighted destruction of species such as the bison and passenger pigeon. It is worth noting that US officials had first looked to Mexico as a partner for a migratory bird treaty, but, with the revolution there well under way and a small conservationist community, Mexico did not seem ready for a migratory bird treaty. Canada and the United States, because of their cultural similarity and huge border, went on to produce an admirable record of bilateral environmental cooperation.

One lesson was that environmental diplomacy interested a collection of groups, which often worked at cross-purposes. The decision to work with Canada, not Mexico, reflected the origins of the MBT, which had been conjured up by conservationists as a means to solidify the constitutionality of federal bird protection laws. The State Department looked at the treaty as something of a nuisance, and in fact diplomats have almost never been crucial advocates of an environmental treaty. Likewise, the tireless advocates of fisheries and sealing conservation were more often scientists or activists, while the diplomats tended to see the treaties as means of disposing of impediments to smoother Anglo-American relations. Sometimes the scientists and the activists clashed, as in the discussions about sealing, when most scientists thought that some sealing could continue, while the activists thought that it all had to stop. Then there were the treaties' opponents. Driven by a desire to protect their own livelihoods or by their interpretations of constitutionality, they fought hard to derail conservation treaties. As many diplomatic historians have recognized, diplomacy is often a product of domestic politics, and environmental diplomacy even more so.

Although Dorsey's book is the only monograph by a diplomatic historian to deal with environmental issues, environmental diplomacy between the two countries certainly did not end in 1916. The United States and Canada continued their fruitful conservation relationship by signing treaties to regulate fishing for halibut in 1922 and salmon in 1937, and the International Joint Commission (IJC), established in 1909, continued to deal with boundary issues between the two nations. From the 1952 agreement to build the St. Lawrence Seaway, to the 1970s agreements to restore the Great Lakes, to a 1987 treaty to protect caribou, the two nations have had the most negotiated environmental relationship in the diplomatic world. Most of these agreements have undergone frequent up-dating and revision to reflect both changing scientific understanding and increased public acceptance of restrictions on pollution and fishing.

The most thorough single book on a number of these recent US–Canadian issues comes from John Carroll (1983). Approaching the topic from the Natural Resources discipline, Carroll covered a wide range of topics, from acid rain, to flood control, to oil pollution. While acknowledging the great similarity between the two nations and the importance of their shared "ecosphere," Carroll emphasized how the differences between the two nations led to unique problems. Most notably, he described Canada as still something of a frontier society, hungering for industrialization. In contrast, more Americans had developed an ecological sensitivity as a result of witnessing the impact of full industrialization. His chapter on wilderness and development described the Cabin Creek conundrum, as Canadians had discovered a huge coal deposit in British Columbia just across the border from Glacier National Park. Carroll asked: do citizens have a right to influence economic decisions on the other side of the border in the interest of protecting a national treasure? Montana and US officials certainly answered "yes," as they pressured Canadian and British Columbia authorities to prevent mining at Cabin Creek. Carroll's work suggested that no matter how similar they might appear on the surface, any two countries would have substantial differences that would hinder environmental relations.

Carroll concluded that the long list of bilateral agreements and the fundamental differences necessitated a formalized approach to environmental diplomacy between Canada and the United States. The current scheme, which he described as "ad hoc with a light patina of order and governance," left too much to chance and shifting political winds. In its place, Carroll proposed a treaty to cover the complete range of transborder environmental problems. The two nations would have to agree not to surprise one another with an issue, not to score too many rhetorical points at the other's expense, to arbitrate points of fact and legality, and to anticipate national and bilateral problems before they arise. No progress has been made on such an approach, and none seems likely anytime soon, although the Commission on Control, set up by the North American Free Trade Agreement, at least nods in that direction.

While Carroll surveyed a broad spectrum of issues, one transborder pollution issue has drawn sustained attention, the Trail Smelter. The smelter began operation in 1927 in Trail, British Columbia, just across the border from Stevens County, Washington. Toxic fumes from lead and zinc smelting harmed the farms on both sides of the border, despite construction of a 400-foot smokestack. The parent company, Canadian Pacific Railroad, agreed in principle to pay damages to area farmers, but the farmers rejected the offer as inadequate. Transborder smelter pollution was nothing new, but it had not drawn diplomatic attention until US farmers appealed to the State Department for assistance. After years of disagreement and acrimony, the two nations resolved their differences in 1941 through the International Joint Commission.

Much of the analysis of this dispute has celebrated the legal precedents of arbitration and the "polluter pays" ruling, but environmental historian John Wirth (2000) has offered a new interpretation. Instead of seeing the Trail Smelter case as a victory for international cooperation, Wirth argued that the case damaged efforts to regulate pollution for nearly thirty years. Faced with an enormous amount of scientific evidence, much of it incompatible; conflicting economic interests; and recognition that the Trail case could have a major impact on factories on both of North America's borders, the IJC issued a narrow ruling on the pollution problem rather than a broad one. Instead of investigating pollution thoroughly and in a way that would have set a powerful precedent, the arbitrators did little more than was necessary to make the problem go away.

Wirth's book made two major contributions. First, he elaborated on the notion of borderlands, regions bisected by a political boundary but united by cultural and natural features. Certainly the 49th parallel made the Trail Smelter case different from previous smelter cases that had been wholly domestic, and yet, as Wirth noted, farmers on both sides of the border had a common interest, as did the smelting companies. The mining and smelting industries, he argued, had been thinking continentally since the late nineteenth century. On the other hand, the scientific community fractured for a variety of reasons, only some of them having to do with nationality. Scholars such as Samuel Truett (1997) have shown how the US–Mexican border was similarly no impediment to the creation of interlocking communities based on mineral extraction more than a century ago. The environmental impact of the North American Free Trade Agreement, then, should be seen largely as an extension of an old trend, not something new. Diplomatic historians would do well to consider borderlands theory, because of its emphasis on environmental and cultural similarities, while they also continue with traditional notions of political differences.

Second, Wirth drew an explicit connection from Trail – which might have been left as an isolated incident – to modern disputes about acid rain. In the second half of his book, Wirth discussed the Gray Triangle, a collection of three smelters along the US–Mexican border, which became the center of controversy in the 1970s. As early as the 1930s, some US officials understood that the smelter in Douglas, Arizona presented as much of a transborder problem as did the one in Trail. But not until the 1970s, when Mexican companies began to construct two new smelters near their northern border, did both governments move to tackle the pollution problem. The smelters promised to deliver acid rain throughout the mountain southwest, prompting a diplomatic exchange between Mexico and the United States. The 1983

La Paz agreement set rules for curbing pollution from these three sites, eight years before the US and Canada resolved their long-standing dispute over acid rain in the northeastern part of the continent.

Wirth's book implicitly answered Donald Worster's (1985) call to environmental historians to think beyond their own national borders. Worster, one of the most accomplished environmental historians, argued that traditional historians had been reasonably well-served by their use of the nation-state as a vital historical actor, but new immigrants to the field, such as environmental historians, could provide a needed spark by challenging such standard notions. As long as environmental historians put a national label in front of themselves – whether French, British, or American – they would fail to attain their greatest chances for success, which come from moving across boundaries. In a sense, he urged historians to conceptualize the intersection of ecosystems rather than the clash of nations. Worster gave several examples of what historians might study: the Yale graduates who came to teach forestry and the Rockefeller scientists who promoted the Green Revolution in the Philippines, all of whom had a profound impact on that society; the transition in some places from "ecosystem cultures" to those tied in to the world market; and the way in which ideas of conservation and environmentalism transcend borders. Worster was not arguing that boundaries were irrelevant, just that environmental historians would do well to avoid a fixation on them. In similar ways, diplomatic historians were urging their colleagues to get out and expand their horizons and to conduct more research in foreign archives. Two environmental historians have recently provided examples of what might be done. Richard Tucker's *Insatiable Appetite* (2000) and John McNeill's *Something New Under the Sun* (2000) demonstrate the connections that can be made between environmental and international history, not to mention their authors' ability to synthesize an enormous amount of information.

Tucker's book is a broad survey of the impact of the US economy on tropical ecosystems from the 1890s to the 1960s. He argued that the United States created an "ecological empire," similar to the informal empire that diplomatic historians discuss, in such places as Liberia, Cuba, Central America, and the Philippines. The soldiers in this empire were rarely in the military but instead came from the ranks of businessmen, government officials, and scientists – such as the aforementioned Yale foresters. Much as the miners and smelters whom Wirth discussed had a continental vision, these men had something of a global vision. US citizens desired a higher standard of living, and that meant bananas and coffee with breakfast, sugar constantly, rubber for tires, and tropical hardwoods for a variety of purposes. None of those things would come from temperate North America, but all could be found in places where US economic power might dominate, even if formal empire would be a rarity.

To diplomatic historians, the broad outline of Tucker's book is well known. US power in Cuba displayed itself not just through military conquest but also through economic hegemony. Sanford Dole and other sugar and fruit growers brought Hawaii under the US umbrella against the wishes of native Hawaiians. Liberia's chaos allowed Harvey Firestone to make extremely favorable deals in an attempt to break the British stranglehold on rubber. American markets and capital encouraged landowners around the world to produce huge monocultures of sugar or coffee, leading to calls for land reform from poor peasants, who in their frustration often turned to violence directed at the United States and its political allies. Those who believe in the primacy of markets as a motivating force in US foreign policy will find little to disagree with here.

But Tucker's book comes closer to achieving what Lytle called for, an environmental analysis of foreign policy, than any diplomatic history. He explains US expansionism in this period as a product – primarily, but not exclusively – of a shortage of resources. Whether the empire was to be formal or informal is really not relevant to Tucker's story; what is relevant is that Americans wanted goods from ecosystems that did not exist in the United States. Had he pushed his argument a little harder, to encompass Williams and the Wisconsin School, Tucker might have analyzed how US citizens could have been complicit in the ecological and societal degradation of tropical societies. Few Americans understood the true costs of their bananas – monocultures susceptible to disease and insects, displaced peasants, increased use of marginal land for peasant subsistence, disparity of wealth in tropical society, and, on occasion, open rebellion. Chiquita was not about to tell them. And yet, even as they were nibbling away at the tropical ecosystem and unintentionally undermining tropical societies, most US citizens would have gladly agreed with President John Kennedy's rhetoric calling for an Alliance for Progress.

The displacement of peasants is central to Tucker's story, because it suggests the full impact of US economic power abroad, even when that impact was unintended. When local landowners or foreign investors decided that the market was ready for more sugar or coffee or bananas, they usually held the power simply to expropriate the best agricultural land. The poor had little choice but to move aside, although certainly some found work on the plantations. Those who moved on settled on marginal land, often using swidden agriculture, with all of the long-term problems associated with that practice. If plantation agriculture wore out the land, then investors might well be able to pick up and move to some other site, but the people left behind would have even less than they had had years before. The source of instability in the tropics, then, was not just inequitable distribution of land, but also the way that the land was used. Tucker is careful not to blame the United States exclusively, both in noting that the United States was acting within a 500-year pattern of Western exploitation and that local citizens in the tropics were hardly innocent dupes, but he left no doubt that so much of the trouble that the United States encountered in the tropics during the Cold War was a product of its appetite.

As ambitious as Tucker's book is, it pales besides John McNeill's environmental history of the twentieth century. McNeill, who appears to have read everything written about the century in question, acknowledged the importance of political boundaries, but he emphasized the patterns that emerged over the face of the earth. People around the world understood that they were changing their ecosystems, and by the end of the century, McNeill argued, they had wrought unprecedented changes, from extinction of species to deforestation to climate change. By and large, these changes were again unintended consequences of a range of decisions, mostly related to rapid economic growth. Humans, then, have been adapting to their planet even as they have dramatically changed it.

Certainly, international politics mattered. Not only did nations sign a plethora of treaties and conventions in the twentieth century to regulate or protect the environment, but they also engaged in any number of wars and standoffs that had profound environmental effects. Chewing up northern France from 1914–18, flattening Tokyo in 1945, and dumping oil into the Persian Gulf in 1991 – all were examples of the massive, although usually temporary, environmental change brought about by modern warfare. More damaging, McNeill argued, was the preparation for war. Throughout the century, nations built up their military–industrial complexes, in part to sustain quick mobilization. At the extreme, during the Cold War, that meant that at least seven nations invested in the most dangerous technology of all, nuclear weaponry. Both the United States and, to a far greater extent, the USSR tended to ignore the long-term consequences of radioactive wastes while focusing on the immediate priority of surviving their rivalry.

But perhaps most important, the rise of the United States led to a shift in human perceptions of the place of nature. US ideas about economics, in particular, dominated any number of countries outside of the Iron Curtain. The economists who had gotten the assignment to reshape the global economy at Bretton Woods, New Hampshire in 1944 established, according to McNeill, a new orthodoxy. In it, nature did not exist. Rather, human ingenuity could tackle any problem, because nature was a largely inert pool of resources waiting to be used. The World Bank and the International Monetary Fund, as many environmentalists have argued, approved projects without any serious concern for their environmental impact.

The shift was not one way, however. Out of the United States also came the environmental movement, which McNeill saw as partially a response to the new economic orthodoxy. Certainly, there were home-grown environmentalists in countries around the world, and other nations developed powerful Green parties while the United States was backing down from many environmental commitments. But there can be no doubt that as environmentalist ideas entered US popular culture and academia they began to reach audiences around the world, occasionally even in the Soviet bloc. One crucial shift came from ecology, which had for many years mirrored economics by pretending that people did not exist. With authors such as Rachel Carson taking on political activism, American ecologists began to influence world opinion.

This global environmental movement accounts in part for the many treaties in the postwar world. With the United Nations serving sometimes as a framework, sometimes as a model, complex multilateral treaties became the solution of choice for troubling environmental problems. These conventions have revealed some of the difficulties of environmental diplomacy that had not been especially obvious in the US–Canadian schemes. First, the governments involved have been generally very reluctant to yield their sovereignty without a compelling crisis and clear benefits. Second, the vast disparities in how nations use resources have made it very difficult for them to equalize the costs and benefits of a treaty meant to encourage conservation. Third, the sheer number of nations involved has made diplomacy remarkably complex.

The longest-standing and perhaps least understood of these postwar deals was the 1946 International Convention for the Regulation of Whaling (ICRW). The ICRW created the International Whaling Commission (IWC) in 1949 as a regulatory body to conserve whale populations and develop the industry. Those two goals certainly seemed contradictory in later years, but in 1946 they reflected both a postwar demand for whale products – mainly oil to be converted to margarine – and a faith that science could answer any problems. The sixteen original members of the IWC ranged from long-time whaling states, such as Norway, to consumer states, such as the Netherlands, to those with a political stake in the outcome of a conservation treaty, such as the United States. They included the main protagonists in the Cold War as well as nations leaning toward neutrality. They included states that had huge pelagic whaling fleets, nations whose whaling industry was based on shore stations, and nations whose whaling operations existed only in the distant past or fertile imaginations. The IWC, for a time, was paralyzed by a feud between the conservationist nations, led by the United States, and the strange whaling bedfellows, Norway, Japan, the United Kingdom, the Netherlands, and the Soviet Union. It was, in short, an international body that required delicate diplomacy and a willingness to set aside preconceived notions.

Judged by the two goals it set for itself, the IWC failed completely. The stocks of whales were not conserved but largely destroyed. Blue whales, which had been the prize target of whalers, are nearly extinct; other species suffered precipitous declines that have left them on endangered species lists. The industry was not developed but rather left to a boom–bust cycle. Whaling companies in the UK, Australia, the Netherlands and other countries collapsed; in Japan and Norway they survive only because of subsidies and controversial practices that skirt the recent ban on commercial whaling. Whalers and environmentalists agree on one thing: the IWC has been a disaster.

A more nuanced view would not only be more fair, but it would also suggest ways in which historians could examine many of the environmental treaties of the last fifty years. The great diversity in members' interests manifested itself in the clause that allowed any member to opt out of an amendment to the original IWC schedule. Likewise, the convention contained no enforcement mechanism, so a country that chose to violate the rules it had agreed to would face no more than a potentially embarrassing lecture. In fact, nations were reluctant to confront one another for fear that the embarrassed party would simply leave the commission and be completely free from rules. Few nations were willing to risk their sovereignty over a national industry, and that very natural concern tied up the commission. The IWC's founders had hoped that scientific evidence would be impartial, so nations would study the data and agree on a logical course of action. If they could not agree, then no one would be compelled to accept any new rules. What they learned was that scientists were prone to nationalism, too, and were occasionally even for sale. With the stakes so high, whaling companies and their governments could find scientists who supported more whaling, even when the data clearly called for less. These were hard lessons to learn.

The lessons were not all negative. Governments learned how to promote conservation even when the rules were against it, scientists learned how to use their expertise, and non-governmental organizations learned how to bring pressure to bear. Through the Packwood–Magnusson Amendment of 1979, the United States reinforced the power of the IWC's conservationist wing by threatening sanctions against those countries which ignored the scientific consensus on whaling regulations. That action did not just occur in a vacuum; rather, it was the product of the kind of ecological awareness that McNeill discussed, as well as political calculations that any diplomatic historian would understand. Diplomats also appreciated the symbolic value of their institutions. When the IWC was under attack around 1960 and looked to be on the verge of extinction itself, US diplomats fought hard to save it. Their interest in whales was less of a factor than their interest in sustaining the ideal of international cooperation on the high seas. The IWC as a living, struggling institution could stir people to make better institutions. The IWC as a disbanded body would only reinforce those who said that cooperation and conservation were impossible and not worth the effort.

The many perils of the IWC were hardly unique, and diplomats and environmentalists worked to avoid them in later treaties, especially after the 1972 Stockholm meeting raised the profile of environmental diplomacy. The 1973 Convention on International Trade in Endangered Species (CITES) is a prime example. The goal of CITES is to protect species that have commercial value if their numbers decline, and it includes enforcement clauses that make it possible to levy sanctions on member states who refuse to accept rulings. As such, it has reduced trade in many important endangered species. At the same time, it respects sovereignty, both by allowing nations a great deal of power over which species get listed as endangered and by turning a blind eye to minor infractions. About 150 nations have signed CITES, but fewer than a quarter of those really enforce the rules. This disparity suggests both that nations join largely for the public relations value of doing so, and that they also realize that they will surrender very little sovereignty.

The balancing act between protecting sovereignty and protecting the biosphere is the subject of several books by policymakers who have been directly involved in diplomacy with an environmental twist. Ralph and Miriam Levering (1999) reinforced the notion that private citizens could have influence in grand global diplomacy. Miriam and Sam Levering, Ralph's parents, helped organize the Neptune Group, which altered the course of the UN Conference on the Law of the Sea (UNCLOS). There were actually three UNCLOS rounds, beginning in 1958, as the nations of the world tried to regularize the use of the high seas and their resources. The last one attracted the Leverings' attention, as it ran from 1972 to 1982, with the most serious disagreements about the proposal to make deep-seabed minerals global property, even though only Western nations had the technology and resources to recover them.

Over time, the Neptune Group emerged from obscurity to a position of influence as an honest broker of information among competing blocs of nations. The Group of 77 developing nations had the ability to out-vote nearly any other group, but the wealthy nations, such as the United States, had the power to walk away from the negotiations. That the UNCLOS negotiations took so long could be attributed then in part to the enormous complexity of the topic – from access to marine life to freedom of navigation – and in part to the great gap between various nations' interests. In these circumstances, the Neptune Group found that it could provide moderate solutions that bridged the gaps and allowed nations to back down from extreme positions.

In many ways, the Leverings' book demonstrates that environmental diplomacy is surprisingly accessible to private citizens and NGOs. Sam and Miriam Levering had no special knowledge, nor were they wealthy and powerful. Instead, they offered hard work and a determination to search for a just convention, plus they studied the issues thoroughly from many different angles. People on almost every side of the various debates were able to set aside any preconceived notions about the Leverings and others in the Neptune Group and work with them. Private citizens can make a difference in regulating natural resources.

In contrast, Richard Benedick's *Ozone Diplomacy* (1991) revealed a diplomat's perspective on the inner workings of the various meetings surrounding the 1987 Montreal Protocol on Substances That Deplete the Ozone Layer, which banned chlorofluorocarbons (CFCs), the chemicals responsible for thinning the ozone layer. As the leader of the US delegation to the negotiation sessions in Geneva, Vienna, and Montreal and a career foreign service official, Benedick had a rare view of this protocol, which he described as unique. Never before, he argued, had nations taken a preventative step based on extremely complex, theoretical science rather than hard evidence. And more remarkable, they did so in the face of determined opposition from powerful industrial concerns, although they received some support from environmental and other industrial groups.

The problem that diplomats faced came from previously heralded chemicals, CFCs, which turned out to be quite insidious. Invented in the 1930s, CFCs had been used primarily as refrigerants and propellants for aerosol sprays. They had been thoroughly tested and seemed harmless. But in 1974 scientists developed a theory that when CFCs floated to the upper atmosphere they reacted with – and destroyed – ozone, which protected life on the planet by intercepting ultraviolet radiation from the sun. For forty years, people had been producing CFCs and unwittingly chipping away at the barrier between the earth and cancer-causing solar radiation. Even worse, with a desire for higher standards of living around the world, the demand for CFCs was rising faster than the ozone was disappearing. Not surprisingly, it took time for people to accept this theory, especially because there was no actual evidence that the ozone was in decline until 1987. Even then, scientists were not sure of the cause of the decline, and powerful political and economic actors in the United States were still fighting hard against the very notion that international regulation was a better response than big hats and lots of sunscreen.

Still, the Reagan administration threw off its anti-regulatory cloak and led the fight to set a timetable to ban CFC production and use. Opposition came from Japan and Western Europe, where industry was not as prepared to replace CFCs as in the United States. Developing world nations also objected because there was no procedure for transferring new technology to them, which was both very expensive and necessary if the convention was to have any strength. At later meetings in Helsinki and London, diplomats ironed out these details. The diplomatic effort to save the ozone layer, so far, has been a grand success. Of course, we may well be doing something now that is, unknown to us, destroying the ozone layer, but as Benedick articulated, US diplomats can be proud that they mobilized to accomplish an amazing feat of preventative diplomacy.

One of the key players in the CFC drama was Mostafa Tolba, the executive director of the UN Environment Programme from 1976 to 1992. In that position and others, Tolba was one of the most active figures in environmental diplomacy, from the 1972 UN Conference on the Human Environment in Stockholm, to the 1992 UN Conference on Environment and Development in Rio de Janeiro. In his book, Tolba (1998) focused on the notion of sustainable development, a new idea that came to dominate environmental diplomacy after Stockholm. Such development does not imply a static economy or society, but it does mean that countries need to re-evaluate their most basic economic activities. Industrializing nations face the reality that their activities will contribute to global pollution, but they need to provide for their citizens. Industrialized nations may well have to give up some of their cherished goods, such as the private automobile. At the same time, the developing nations could well benefit from the transfer of technology from the wealthier nations, which could cut down on the environmental damage of their economic progress. But technology is not a magic weapon, as it too often blurred the reality that, for instance, plants grow more because of natural processes than anything people do.

Tolba represents a new facet of environmental diplomacy in the UN era: the man without a nation. Although he was born an Egyptian and served his country with distinction, in environmental affairs Tolba represented the United Nations. In other words, his job was to represent humanity. Such a position does not fit easily into the frameworks used by diplomats or diplomatic historians, both of whom are prone to see such a man as still a national actor. It seems unlikely that anyone can separate himself totally from his nation, but men like Tolba and Maurice Strong had to seek impartiality and balance, and when they did that well they enhanced the chances of successful diplomacy.

Like the Neptune Group, Tolba often found himself bridging the gaps between nations, especially the North–South splits that plague so many attempts to solve global problems. The developmental differences that form the basis of the North–South chasm do more to derail environmental diplomacy than anything else, as poorer nations demand assistance from wealthier nations to pay for any costs associated with these treaties. In turn, the wealthier nations argue that the developing nations cannot follow the same resource-depleting paths to development that the wealthy pursued before. Compromise has been difficult; Kipling might well have written that "north is north and south is south and never the two shall meet."

But Oran Young, the dean of political scientists who study the environment in foreign policy, has done his best to bring them together. In *Global Environmental Change and International Governance* (1996), Young noted that one of the basic problems was that North and South had very different concerns, with northerners often worrying about things like ozone depletion and biodiversity while southerners had to start with the basics, like clean water and sufficient food. Young assembled a series of authors to address the differing North–South perspectives on the use of such resources as the oceans, freshwater, biodiversity, forests, and the atmosphere – in short, everything on earth. Their goal was to present ideas for improving global governance based both on past attempts at environmental regulation and an under-standing of these different regional agendas. They concluded that one of the most basic tasks had to be a global educational campaign covering both the environmental problems and the options for international governance to address them. Beyond that, they drafted a long list of goals, such as calculating true social costs of using the environment, encouraging local communities to participate in research, and defining problems more effectively. As a work of political science, Young's book is naturally aimed at suggesting models for effective action, but because it is grounded in the study of the past it should also appeal to historians looking for broad coverage of older environmental treaties.

While Tolba did not say so directly, one of the central stories of the time since the Montreal Protocol has been the decline of US leadership. At the Earth Summit in 1992, the United States found itself more often fighting rearguard actions. The Biodiversity Convention drew wide support, but the United States refused to sign until it had negotiated exceptions to protect its industries. President George H. W. Bush publicly wrestled with the decision to attend the conference, concerned that he might be trapped politically by environmentalists if he attended. In the end, he made an appearance but undermined his own credibility by proposing a new forest protection convention, even though delegates had been working for years to iron out details on other conventions that were, at the moment, hanging in the balance.

An even more striking abdication of leadership came with negotiations about global climate change. Many scientists believed that industrial emission of gasses such as carbon dioxide was causing the atmosphere to trap more of the sun's radiation. With industrial production and pollution steadily growing in the West and exploding in the developing world, many feared that temperatures might rise more rapidly than they had at any time in the past, leading to melting ice caps, drought, floods, and a range of unpredictable effects. Most frightened were those living in low-lying nations, which faced literal inundation by rising oceans. Following the model of the ozone convention, the solution seemed to be more preventative diplomacy to reduce greenhouse gas emissions. Even then, many scientists believed that it could take decades to rectify the problems.

In the negotiations on this complex subject, the United States has often found itself in the role of vocal minority. At Rio, the Western European nations joined with some in the developing world to push for a detailed treaty setting targets for pollution control. The Bush administration was adamant that it would not sign anything more than a broad statement of goals, with specifics coming later. The United States won that round, and preparations began for the Kyoto meeting in 1997, which produced a detailed protocol. The Clinton administration chose not to push for ratification and in fact took the unpopular stance in further negotiation sessions that having forests should count toward pollution reduction. In 2001, George W. Bush furthered the pattern of US independence by announcing a unilateral withdrawal from the Kyoto protocol, a move roundly criticized around the world. Whether these positions will be permanent or even detrimental is not clear yet, but there is no doubt that the United States no longer strives to lead nations toward more stringent environmental protection.

This uncertainty seems an appropriate place to end, because it reflects a general uncertainty about the course of past environmental diplomacy. To return to Thomas Paterson's and Mark Lytle's essays, diplomatic historians need to begin taking the environment seriously. They could, first, begin to explore those environmental conventions and conferences that have drawn little attention, whether the CITES, the range of US–Canadian fisheries deals, or the Stockholm meeting. In studying these issues, they could ask not only the standard questions about motivations, results, and the relationship of these acts to the larger trends of US foreign policy, but more importantly they could understand the science behind these treaties and the ecology that made them possible. So for CITES, a historian might well ask how it related to the larger diplomatic goal of the Nixon administration as well as whether it succeeded in protecting endangered species. They might also ask which species were endangered and why, which species got listed and why, which nations relied on scientists and why, and finally whether the convention reflected scientific reality. Diplomatic historians would do well to begin studying ecology and history of science to be more conversant with these kinds of topics.

While it would be more difficult, it is also time for diplomatic historians to heed Lytle's call for a reinterpretation of wars and other events through an environmental prism. The model here could be Kristin Hoganson's (1998) use of gender to explain the Spanish–American War. Given the Wisconsin School's emphasis on markets and resources as the goal of US expansionism, this would not seem to be a large step. Some diplomatic historians might cringe at the thought, but perhaps it is time for a book entitled *An Environmental Interpretation of the Cold War*.

REFERENCES

Bailey, Thomas: "The North Pacific Sealing Convention of 1911." *Pacific Historical Review* 4 (1935), 1–14.

Benedick, Richard: *Ozone Diplomacy: New Directions in Safeguarding the Planet* (Cambridge, MA: Harvard University Press, 1991).

Campbell, Charles, Jr.: "The Anglo-American Crisis in the Bering Sea, 1890–1891." *Mississippi Valley Historical Review* 66 (1961), 395–410.

Campbell, Charles, Jr.: "The Bering Sea Settlements of 1892." *Pacific Historical Review* 32 (1963), 347–68.

Carroll, John: *Environmental Diplomacy: An Examination and Prospective of Canadian–US Transboundary Environmental Relations* (Ann Arbor: University of Michigan Press, 1983).

Dorsey, Kurk: "Scientists, Citizens, and Statesmen: US–Canadian Wildlife Protection Treaties in the Progressive Era." *Diplomatic History* 19 (1995), 407–30.

Dorsey, Kurk: *The Dawn of Conservation Diplomacy: US–Canadian Wildlife Protection Treaties in the Progressive Era* (Seattle: University of Washington Press, 1998).

French, Hilary: *Partnership for the Planet: An Environmental Agenda for the United Nations* (Washington, DC: Worldwatch, 1995).

Hoganson, Kristin: *Fighting for American Manhood: How Gender Politics Provoked the Spanish–American and Philippines–American Wars* (New Haven, CT: Yale University Press, 1998).

Innis, Harold: *The Cod Fisheries: The History of an International Economy* (New Haven, CT: Yale University Press, 1940).

LaFeber, Walter: *America, Russia, and the Cold War, 1945–92*, 7th edn. (New York: McGraw-Hill, 1993).

Levering, Ralph and Miriam Levering: *Citizen Action for Global Change: The Neptune Group and Law of the Sea* (Syracuse, NY: Syracuse University Press, 1999).

Limerick, Patricia: "Dilemmas in Forgiveness: William Appleman Williams and Western American History." *Diplomatic History* 25 (2001), 293–300.

Lytle, Mark: "An Environmental Approach to American Diplomatic History." *Diplomatic History* 20 (1996), 279–300.

McNeill, John: *Something New Under the Sun: An Environmental History of the Twentieth-Century World* (New York: W. W. Norton, 2000).

Paterson, Thomas: "Defining and Doing the History of American Foreign Relations: A Primer." *Diplomatic History* 14 (1990), 584–601.

Susskind, Lawrence: *Environmental Diplomacy: Negotiating More Effective Global Agreements* (New York: Oxford University Press, 1994).

Tolba, Mostafa: *Global Environmental Diplomacy: Negotiating Environmental Agreements for the World, 1973–1992* (Cambridge, MA: MIT Press, 1998).

Truett, Samuel: "Neighbors by Nature: Rethinking Region, Nation, and Environmental History in the US–Mexican Borderlands." *Environmental History* 2 (1997), 160–78.

Tucker, Richard: *Insatiable Appetite: The United States and the Degradation of the Tropical World* (Berkeley: University of California Press, 2000).

Wirth, John: *Smelter Smoke in North America: The Politics of Transborder Pollution* (Lawrence: University Press of Kansas, 2000).

Worster, Donald: "World Without Borders: The Internationalizing of Environmental History." In Kendall Bailes (ed.) *Environmental History: Critical Issues in Comparative Perspective* (Lanham, MD: University Press of America, 1985).

Young, Oran, George Demko, and Kilaparti Ramakrishna (eds.): *Global Environmental Change and International Governance* (Hanover, NH: University Press of New England, 1996).

CHAPTER FOUR

The Early National Period, 1775–1815

PETER P. HILL

Research in the foreign relations of the early national era might be likened to a well-worked strip-mine, the first-comers having published such nearly definitive works from its documentary mother lode as to discourage any further digging by would-be prospectors. Whether it be a Samuel F. Bemis or a Richard B. Morris sorting out the multi-archival dimensions of diplomacy in Paris in the early 1780s, or a Dexter Perkins analyzing the circumstances that gave rise to the Monroe Doctrine forty years later, historians who came early to the scene appear to have left the late-comers panning for nuggets. Nor can the latter take heart from realizing that the careers of the major diplomatic players have already been chronicled by outstanding biographers. For all its apparent barrenness, however, the field is not without its opportunities; first, because the traditional lines of inquiry are still being nourished by the ongoing publication of the papers of the founding policymakers, but also because a new generation of historians has succeeded in coming up with new approaches and new analytical frameworks which, if they take hold, bid fair to broaden the very definition of foreign relations. For a look at such developments, the reader might begin with William Weeks' (1994) article in the scholarly journal *Diplomatic History*; and for specific areas still in need of research, Bradford Perkins' (1998) article in the same journal. The following overview, for its part, will attempt to explain why the era still attracts scholars of diplomatic history, point to some of the recent scholarship in the field, and (like the Perkins article) suggest avenues for further inquiry.

The early period retains its allure in large part because it abounds in foreign relations issues. Indeed, one can make a strong case that foreign relations so dominated the public discourse during the first forty years of our national existence that no domestic issue of consequence, except Hamilton's financial program, seems worth considering. As is well known, much of that discourse centered on the fledgling republic's uncertain ability to cope with European powers believed to be inherently hostile to its existence. Despite outpourings of gratitude to France, for example, many Americans in the postwar era felt uneasy about owing that country their nation's independence and suspected that Britain was already plotting to steal it away. They fretted, too, over the likely hostility of Spain's presence to the south and west. And perhaps most uncertain of all was the future of their vital commerce with Europe, visibly in need of central regulation if it were to prosper. Not surprisingly and perhaps overdue, the historian Frederick W. Marks (1986) singled out this widespread awareness of dangers from abroad as one of the most compelling factors in the movement to supersede the Articles of Confederation. Marks made a convincing case that the Constitutional Convention sprang in large part from the public's perception that without a stronger central government, its life-giving commerce would remain the victim of European exploitation and the nation itself at risk from foreign enemies who, some believed, would partition it if they could. Marks' thesis has not gone unchallenged, of course. Historians are a disputatious lot. Norman Graebner (1987), for example, points to the equally widespread belief among contemporary Anti-federalists that the proposed Constitution seriously threatened states rights and that its proponents exaggerated the dangers to national security. That Jefferson then in Paris concurred on both counts is the theme of Lawrence Kaplan's (1987b) article. Still, there is no denying the centrality of foreign relations in the consciousness of a people whose commercial ties with Europe were its life-blood and whose fears for its future were bound up with European events.

Such fears became more explicit in the 1790s when in response to the revolution in France, the Republican faction in this country rallied to the French cause with a fervor that threatened to override Washington's chosen course of neutrality. Before the decade ended, partisans on both sides, already divided over domestic issues, were to charge each other with being in thrall to a foreign enemy. For a time, the impassioned rhetoric heard in coffee houses and the halls of Congress seemed to presage either war, disunion, or perhaps both. Of a piece with this "phrenzy," it is worth remarking that the most controversial domestic legislation of the late Federalist era – the Alien and Sedition laws – were themselves a response to fears of foreign subversion. The ensuing Napoleonic wars, though somewhat less heatedly divisive on foreign issues, nonetheless continued to stoke the fires of political controversy over whether Presidents Jefferson and Madison had it in them to stop the belligerents from seizing American ships, cargoes, and crewmen. In sum, the early national era saw a sustained tension in international relations that challenged American leaders to secure for the United States a safe and respected place within the community of nations. Hence the need to devise a foreign policy.

Although the terms foreign policy and diplomacy are often used interchangeably, it may be useful to make a distinction. Foreign policy by and large speaks to a nation's aims in dealing with other powers; diplomacy is the means of attaining those aims. American statesmen of the early national era had no difficulty identifying their foreign policy objectives. Besides peace and prosperity, they intended to guard the nation's independence, security, and neutrality, and to foster its expansion, both commercial and territorial; and historians have gone to great lengths to explain why individual leaders and their followers acted vigorously to ward off what they perceived as foreign threats to the fulfillment of these objectives. Overlapping the study of goal-oriented policy is the study of American diplomacy, a closely related enterprise in which historians describe and assess how well the actors played their part in achieving these ends. In the early period, the distinction between the major shapers and actors was often blurred because many were both. Thus, while George Washington laid down lines of national policy with his neutrality proclamation and his farewell, he also acted the diplomat in signing Jay's treaty. President Jefferson, while reinforcing the policy dictum of "entangling alliances with none," spent much of his second term testing the diplomatic potential of economic sanctions. Between

Washington and Jefferson, John Adams might be said to have practiced the policy of war-avoidance and acted "diplomatically" when he sent a second peace mission to Paris in the wake of the XYZ affair. The wholeness of foreign relations, then, comes from joining the analysis of aims, including motives, to a description of means.

Ideology

Ideology, too, has left its imprint on early foreign policy, most lastingly perhaps in Thomas Paine's published prediction that the United States by dint of its republican institutions would set a liberating example to the world. How lastingly is apparent today in the readiness of Americans who, having progressed from exemplars to leaders in fulfilling this prediction, accept the notion that under most circumstances, they will support democratic regimes wherever they spring up. Michael Hunt in his *Ideology and US Foreign Policy* (1987) asserts flatly that "ideology is central, not incidental, to policymaking" (p. 3), and urges fellow historians to bring more clearly to public view "the remarkable continuity of our thinking on basic foreign policy issues." Arguing that this continuity "is not sufficiently recognized" (p. xii), Hunt proceeds to find it in such ideological elements as Americans' vision of their own national greatness, their attitudes toward various races, and their disappointment with other people's revolutions. Hunt's work, it should be noted, has met with some criticism, most notably in a 1989 review article by James Field who questions whether Hunt's chosen elements of ideology are borne out by his illustrations of their operation.

If ideology has come to figure more prominently in the study of foreign relations, cultural factors have remained relatively unexplored. As recently as 1998, Bradford Perkins notes that only three of the chapters in Heald and Kaplan's *Culture and Diplomacy*, published some twenty-five years ago, address this component for the early period. These chapters, he writes, "are very acute, but they also are suggestive rather than comprehensive and necessarily do not incorporate conceptual approaches developed since that time" (Perkins 1998: 117). He cites racism as one of the still-scanted cultural components in US foreign relations and calls for a greater awareness of other "often distorting prisms through which [national] interests are seen." He finds a similar deficiency in foreign policy studies which, though based on multi-archival research, are still too one-sided. Such studies broaden our understanding of the American side of various relationships, he writes, but "the same has not often been true of investigations of those nations with which the United States interacted" (p. 116). He takes as an example histories of early US relations with Latin America, faulting them for their too narrow focus on the US end of the relationship. While John J. Johnson's *A Hemisphere Apart* (1990) makes a "very suggestive beginning" toward illuminating Latin American views about the United States, he finds that it starts too late (1815) and covers too much else (Perkins 1998: 116). For the early period, then, there is still work to be done in broadening "the view from the other side."

The Jeffersonian Controversy

Of the five presidential practitioners of foreign relations in this era, Jefferson and to a lesser extent Madison have attracted the most critical notice from historians, early and late, if for no other reason than that despite their commitment to all of the foreign policy goals listed above, their diplomacy failed to prevent the War of 1812. An avoidable war in their estimate, they tend to ascribe this failure to what they regard as the third president's wrong-headed idealism, his instinctive pacifism and, not least of all, his Francophilia. Thus, they find him wanting because he allowed his visionary ideology to blind him to the power realities of his times while permitting his aversion to war and his attachment to France to sap the strength of his diplomacy. Historians writing in this fault-finding vein range from Henry Adams, whose multi–volume critique was published more than a century ago, to that of Robert W. Tucker and David C. Hendrickson (1990), who find astonishing gaps between Jefferson's avowed ideology and his actions as president. Other historians have entered qualified demurrers.

In considering the first of these Jeffersonian "flaws," one might note that idealism in the conduct of foreign policy has acquired a bad name in recent times. The "realist" school, that is to say, the latter-day pundits of power politics, blame much of the mistaken and self-damaging directions taken by past policymakers on their too nebulous view of America's aims and capabilities in world affairs. As a counter-vailing reminder, however, William Weeks (1994) observes that "Much of the nation's history can be understood as a triumph of the visionary over the practical, beginning with the American Revolution. Realist calculations about power," he notes, "would have prevented the War of Independence" (p. 82). As for Jefferson's alleged failing in this respect, James R. Sofka's (1997) article finds him capable of practicing his statecraft with a classic eighteenth-century awareness of the uses of power nowhere more evident than in his readiness to quash the piratical activities of the Barbary powers. As early as 1786, Sofka's Jefferson is less concerned with propagating republican principles – a presumed purpose of the "new diplomacy" – than with protecting and expanding American commerce. Thus, when Jefferson despatched naval forces against Tripoli in 1801, Sofka sees him acting from a realistic assessment of the US navy's capability, embracing limited war rather than continue to pay tribute to the North African regimes. He concludes that "Like most diplomats of the mid-eighteenth century, Jefferson quoted liberal maxims but practiced the diplomacy of power, especially commercial power" (p. 544).

As for the broader scholarly debate over whether early American statesmen practiced a "new diplomacy," which is to say one idealistically dismissive of the Old World's balance of power, or whether they operated pretty much in eighteenth-century European traditions, the reader is referred to Felix Gilbert's (1961) case for the former and James H. Hutson's (1977) counter-argument. The "traditional" school – Hutson's – appears to have triumphed, although David M. Fitzsimons (1995) makes a strong case for what he also sees as an early strain of "idealistic internationalism" originating in the highly influential writings of Thomas Paine. And Peter Onuf (1998) believes that diplomatic historians have been too quick to dismiss Gilbert's "classic essay on the intellectual origins of American foreign policy" (p. 75). Whatever the merits of this debate, most historians today would agree that early

American statesmen were fully aware of their new nation's place in Europe's shifting balance of power and sought ceaselessly to exploit its opportunities. At the same time, any depiction of early American foreign policy must take into account the driving force of the "idealistic" opinion, proclaimed mostly by the followers of Thomas Jefferson, that America's republican experiment had a message for the rest of the world. If the Old World resisted the appeal of republican principles, Americans at least would carry them westward to create an expanding and beneficent "empire of liberty." Whether in turn this early zest for expansion should be labeled imperialism (a sometimes contrived pejorative), Americans moving westward (as Albert Weinberg (1935) ably documents) never lacked for an accompaniment of justificatory rationales.

Finally, Jefferson's presumably debilitating Francophilia has met with Lawrence Kaplan's recurrent observation that his diplomacy was driven more by his fear of Britain than by his fondness for France. Kaplan (1980) asks and answers the critical question: "Did Jefferson's widely advertised Francophilia compromise his position as a public man? In my judgment [Kaplan replies] the direct effect was slight, but he provided enough material in his writings nevertheless to keep the question alive for future generations of historians and politicians to debate" (p. 50). In sum, the last word on Jefferson as Francophile may never be written.

In a related controversy, Doron Ben-Atar in his *Origins of Jeffersonian Commercial Policy and Diplomacy* (1993) sees his subject avidly pursuing overseas markets for the agricultural surpluses needed to support an agrarian way of life. To Ben-Atar, Jefferson's diplomacy ran aground because he "vacillated between viewing commerce as a threat to republican virtue, and as a necessary vehicle for promoting the maintenance of prosperity in the new nation" (p. 170). Like Kaplan (1987a: ch. 8), Ben-Atar directs his sternest reproach at Jefferson's inability or unwillingness to recognize America's larger stake in defeating Napoleonic France. "Jeffersonian commercial policy and diplomacy, in effect, assisted the French aggressor," he argues, whereas "America's best interest would also have been served had it reached an accommodation with the country that protected it." He adds significantly that "Great Britain was also America's most important trade partner" (p. 172). This judgment raises a still-debated question: could the Jeffersonians have reached an accommodation with Britain as the Federalists had with Jay's treaty? Some would say maybe, pointing out that except for the failure of James Monroe and William Pinkney to settle the impressment issue, the treaty they drafted with London in 1806 gave genuine promise of resolving some serious commercial problems. Tucker and Hendrickson (1990), for example, call Jefferson's refusal to submit this treaty to the Senate "a fateful step," adding that "had it been accepted at this moment, much danger and difficulty might have been avoided" (p. 202). These authors, however, seem to share Burton Spivak's (1979) analysis of the potentially direful consequences of the treaty's commercial clauses in the long run (pp. 61–7) and are not far from echoing Dumas Malone's still earlier judgment of the treaty that "there were entirely too many things wrong with it" (Malone 1974: 411). Finally, perhaps, Bradford Perkins speculates that even if Jefferson had accepted the Monroe–Pinkney treaty, Britain's subsequent conduct would have rendered an accommodation short-lived (Perkins 1961: 130). Doubtless, historians will continue to debate whether 1806 was a year of lost opportunity.

For purposes of further speculation, one might also pick up on Ben-Atar's (1993) disparagement of Jefferson's efforts to make France "a viable commercial alternative" to Britain (ch. 4). During his years as US minister to Paris, Jefferson obviously made little headway in his efforts to break through the stifling mercantilist restrictions France placed on her external trade. The revolutionary regimes that followed were no less restrictive. But his failure might also be seen in the light of the curious indifference or resistance on the part of French manufacturers to seek out and adapt to American markets. This non-response to opportunity is all the more remarkable in view of the urgings of French consuls here in the 1780s and 1790s that even a modicum of market research would have enabled France to compete successfully in producing goods of the same size, shape, and color that Americans were accustomed to buying from Britain. Although Peter Hill (1988: ch. 3) adduces a number of explanations for this phenomenon, certain structural and cultural factors remain to be examined more systematically.

Jefferson's most triumphant foreign policy coup, although its final accomplishment took more politicking than diplomacy, was his acquisition of Louisiana. George Dangerfield's (1960) magisterial biography of Robert Livingston, taken in conjunction with Alexander DeConde's (1976) study of the Louisiana Purchase, would seem to foreclose any further major research on this topic. Still open to debate, however, is the tantalizing question of how much weight ought to be given to the several factors that appear to have counted in Napoleon's decision to part with this piece of real estate. Seminar students will surely continue to debate this question, warned, however, that even if they could resurrect Bonaparte and Talleyrand for polygraph tests, two such practiced deceivers would not likely provide conclusive answers. Further efforts to come to an accurately weighted conclusion may serve simply to underscore the wisdom of accepting the likelihood of multi-causality.

The Military Factor

Until military history gained its present-day respectability, diplomatic historians took it as their own, logically assuming that war (reckoned as a failure of diplomacy) fell naturally within their purview. Not surprisingly, the causes, conduct, and consequences of the War of 1812 have come under close, one might say incessant, scrutiny. Major conclusions as to its significance appear to have been reached. Writing as recently as 1989, for example, Donald Hickey strikes the already familiar note that failed military objectives paled in significance alongside the popular perception of victory which in turn boosted national self-confidence and set the stage for exuberant westward expansion (Hickey 1989: 3). Hickey's work, like that of J. C. A. Stagg (1983), is more fully rounded than most in that it adds political and economic context to military operations. In this respect, Hickey's and Stagg's coverage of the war years is not unlike, although better informed than, Henry Adams' treatment published a century ago. To the much-debated explanations of why Congress voted for war in 1812, however, neither author adds much. Hickey, for example, settles ultimately on the primacy of maritime causes, which is to say, the issues of impressment and Britain's refusal to revoke her orders-in-council (ch. 1). He takes little notice of historians whose efforts to find alternative or at least supplementary explanations stretch from Adams through Julius Pratt to Bradford Perkins and Roger Brown.

When Marshall Smelser wrote in 1968 that "perhaps as many as fifty historians have offered original explanations of the war in the past seventy-five years" (p. 219), he was acknowledging historiographical perplexity on a grand scale. To make sense of this array, historians have tried periodically to sort out and categorize these findings of causes. By the end of the 1960s they seemed to have settled on what was called the "Republican Synthesis," whose foreign policy component (as described by Hatzenbueler and Ivie 1983: 1–2), "rests on the conviction that the War of 1812 was fought to preserve the republic's existence, threatened internally by a faction bent on destroying virtue and by a country determined to destroy the young nation." While summarizing this and other explanations, Hatzenbueler and Ivie add still others. They purport to go "Beyond the Republican Synthesis" (ch. 1) to explore the ostensibly neglected factors of rhetoric, leadership, and partisanship. For those tempted to conduct their own explorations, their opening chapter offers a useful roadmap into the historiographical past. For a more detailed picture of where the profession has traveled along the way, quoted passages from the major explicators can be found in Bradford Perkins' (1983) edited collection.

Parenthetically, it might be noted that the Republican Synthesis has been attacked most recently by Peter Onuf and Doron Ben-Atar. Onuf's (1998) article, "A Declaration of Independence for Diplomatic Historians," hails its demise as clearing the way for a return to a more cosmopolitan approach to thinking about the roots of US foreign policy; whereas Ben-Atar (1998) enjoins historians to reject as a frayed paradigm the supposedly unifying nature of republican rhetoric/ideology and accept instead the centrality of Americans' early "ideological commitment to liberate the world from mercantilist trade barriers while at the same time promising to open markets for American agricultural surpluses" (p. 103). Apparently, the debate over what to put in place of the "Synthesis" will prolong historians' search for a unified field theory of early foreign relations for some time to come.

Meanwhile, in a review article of Hickey's work, Reginald Horsman (1991) suggests that the seemingly endless parade of "causes" of the War of 1812 has some distance to go. He believes, for example, that Pratt's expansionist thesis, so vigorously contested by historians in the 1960s, may need to be reopened. Admitting that he once accepted the view that the campaigns against Canada were merely a means to an end, Horsman writes: "I now believe that there were many politicians in the United States who saw the invasion and retention of Canada as a useful side benefit of a war that had become necessary largely because of British maritime policies" (p. 118). Besides urging scholars to continue to re-examine the war from the perspective of such national issues, Horsman welcomes the wider inquiry recently launched into "the economic and social impact of the war at the regional or state level" (p. 121). In this more narrowly focused field, he points approvingly to such groundbreaking works as those of Victor Sapio, Allan S. Everest, Sarah M. Lemmon, and James W. Hammack.

Among the myriad "causes," the impressment issue, arguably the most inflammatory, might also be re-examined. The British navy's forced conscription of American seamen, though intermittent, unquestionably sparked anger on this side of the Atlantic from the days of the Nootka Sound crisis of 1790 until it became one of the announced reasons for war in 1812. By that time, however, recent historians typically take a somewhat dismissive view of its importance. They point out that Britain's smashing victory at Trafalgar in 1805 had led to a downsizing of her navy which meant that fewer American seamen were needed to man her fleet. They also note that the nearer we drew to war the less often impressment was mentioned in Congress or in diplomatic correspondence between Washington and London. Finally, they find it hard to explain why, after London agreed to suspend its obnoxious orders-in-council, impressment remained a hot enough issue to justify continuing the war. The apparent insignificance of this grievance by the year 1812 has doubtless been a major factor in the profession's unremitting quest for more satisfying explanations. For the sake of argument, however, one might posit that repeated failures to resolve this issue may have engendered a sullen resentment among a populace which having despaired of a solution merely fell silent. As Bradford Perkins writes, "Although officially the American government made very little of impressment from 1808 onward, the people could not forget it" (Perkins 1961: 429). Reviving its status as a major motivation for war, however, poses a major research problem. How does one prove the potency or even the existence of unspoken anger?

Schools of Interpretation?

In the writings on our early foreign relations, overarching schools of historical interpretation have been around since at least 1926, when Samuel Flagg Bemis' thematic treatment of Pinckney's treaty first sent graduate students looking for other instances of Europe's distress working to America's advantage. More recently, the economic determinist school of William Appleman Williams, despite its claim to universality, has not taken hold in the early period, indeed has been dismissed as a paradigm for any era by economic historian William H. Becker and his co-editor, the diplomatic historian Samuel F. Wells, Jr., who find no support, early or late, for an interpretation of American diplomacy "which emphasizes an ideologically based consensus in the United States on the need for foreign economic expansion to solve domestic economic and social problems" (Becker and Wells 1984: 460). James A. Field's essay in the Becker and Wells collection argues that the nation's continental expansion sprang not from a need to solve domestic problems but from the "imperative to put Europe at a distance." Sweeping aside as unlikely the operation of any socioeconomic principle in the early period, Field writes:

> The purchase of Louisiana, unintended and unexpected, stemmed from a European threat, and the acquisition of an empire from the attempt to gain a riverbank. The conquest of Canada was attempted as means rather than end, a way to free the seas and control the Indians rather than a method of gaining real estate. In the negotiation of the Florida treaty, the central aims were economic and strategic: the acquisition of river openings to the Gulf and the removal of Europe from the southern border. The reassertion of title to the Columbia River and Adams' restriction of Spanish and Russian claims reflected the same desire to push back European political and commercial influence. (Ibid: 52)

Cautionary Notes

Partisan passions, past and present, obviously need to be approached with caution. Just as historians today must be wary of imposing on the past the questionable lessons of their own time, Jerald Combs (1983) would also have them aware of the doubtful "lessons" learned by those they write about. He notes, for example, that on the eve of war in 1812 Federalists and Republicans were prone to hark back some thirty years to explain each other's reprehensible "foreign attachments." Federalists, he finds, were wont to see the beginnings of their rivals' shameless Francophilia in Franklin's submissiveness to Vergennes during the Paris peace negotiations. Republicans, for their part, believed they detected the first stirrings of Federalist hostility toward France in the unseemly end-runs Adams and Jay made around the French foreign minister's larger policy objectives (ibid: 4–5). Combs' broader purpose, however, is to illustrate the role played by historical memory in shaping political debates in times of foreign policy crisis. Unlike the Munich paradigm that haunted the Vietnam era, however, he concludes that nineteenth-century historians writing of the Federalist–Republican era "probably had little effect on the diplomatic thinking of their time" (p. 19).

Relatedly, fear of anachronistic lapses has not deterred historians (nor should it) from exposing hypocrisy whenever it sticks out in the conduct of foreign relations. A recent excursion in this direction is the extended and ironic commentary of the French historian Marie-Jeanne Rossignol (1994) in addressing the spectacle of American leaders irrespective of party proudly championing the cause of liberty for themselves but not black Haitians (ch. 6). "Relations" with this first black republic, with all its subtexts of racism and fear of slave uprisings, seem to call for more systematic exploration. A warning note should be sounded, however. If some values are time-related, others would seem to be timeless and universally accepted. Thus, for example, historians sometimes find it tricky to make clear their distinction between "understanding" a slave-holding Jefferson who hated slavery and their own abhorrence of the South's peculiar institution.

As recently as the terrorist attacks in New York and Washington and as far back as the 1790s, Americans have puzzled over how far the nation can resort to the use of military and legal force in the name of national security without impairing civil rights. Among the examples of dubious domestic law spawned by foreign crisis, few can match for virulence the Alien and Sedition acts of 1798. Curiously, however, historians having vented their wrath on the Federalist perpetrators of this legislation seem to have lost interest. While memories of the McCarthy era were still fresh, however, John C. Miller (1951) and James Morton Smith (1956) voiced much the same damning judgments. From Miller came the ringing declaration that "where men cannot freely convey their thoughts to one another, no liberty is secure" (p. 232). And from Smith, "Without free speech and a free press, representative government is not truly representative" (p. 433). A few years later in his biography of John Adams, Page Smith (1962) observed wryly and perhaps terminally: "We can leave the Alien and Sedition Acts to the periodic indignation of righteous historians who will be happy if their own nation and their own times show no grosser offenses against human freedom" (p. 978). Case closed?

Of John Adams' part in these "gross offenses," virtually all historians give him a pass, excusing him on grounds that the laws were largely the work of Federalist warhawks in Congress. Indeed, some might have us believe the president signed them in his sleep. Perhaps worthy of further inquiry, however, is why Congress having prepared to cope with subversion on the home front pulled back from making a formal declaration of war on France that spring.

The Gender Factor

A contemporary question nearly as interesting, though of lesser consequence: was Abigail Adams more of a warhawk than her husband during those exciting weeks? Her letters to her "dearest friend" suggest she was. Whether she had a hand in John Adams' contrary decision to seek peace is as yet unclear, although few would deny her ability to influence him in other matters.

Of other women on the fringes of foreign relations, a recent gender study by Catherine Allgor (1997) suggests that the Adams' daughter-in-law, Louisa Catherine, like many diplomats' wives, played a vitally supportive role during John Quincy's mission to St. Petersburg a decade later. Allgor points out that while historians often ascribe the male Adams' success to his informal encounters with an all-powerful tsar, Louisa's regular attendance at court meant that she spoke with the emperor "almost daily" (p. 40). Having made the case that court gossip and whispered secrets constituted significant elements in discerning the directions of Russian foreign policy, Allgor seems justified in characterizing Louisa as an indispensable asset to her husband's diplomacy. She writes that "if historians conclude that this mission was a significant one in American history, and they do, and that John Quincy Adams was a significant player, and they do, then we must insist on as meaningful a place for Louisa Catherine" (p. 43). For those uninitiated in scholarly approaches to the role of women in foreign relations, either of Emily Rosenberg's essays, both entitled "Walking the Borders" (1990, 1991), is a good place to begin.

Addressing another highlight of the elder Adams' presidency, Richard Rohrs (1998) takes a closer look at the Federalist Party's disarray during the Senate's ratification of the Franco-American Convention of 1800. Too often, it seems, historians in their haste to raise the curtain on the Jeffersonians have brushed past this political end game of the Adams years. Rohrs, while conceding that Alexander DeConde's (1966) coverage of the Senate debates (pp. 288–93) is "the most complete," focuses on the shifting factional divisions within the Federalist ranks throughout the series of votes that first defeated the treaty, then revived it, and finally ratified it with amendment. Central to this article is the emerging picture of a political party already showing signs of terminal disintegration, its major figures (Hamilton and Adams) unlistened to at any stage of the debate; and the outcome influenced more by economic than sectional considerations. Future historians who believe they can find signs of life in the Federalist Party after the spring of 1801 will have to deal with Rohrs' assessment that the party's "handling of the Treaty of Mortefontaine challenges descriptions of its viability" (p. 260).

The Public Sphere of Diplomacy

Ransacking newspapers of the era (many now on microfilm) often turns up insights into the social, economic, and political forces at work in the staging of foreign policy dramas. Historians who once regarded newspapers merely as useful sources for "public opinion" studies now look to their columns for evidence of a "public sphere" of diplomacy operating outside official channels to sustain or oppose certain directions in foreign policy. While they still draw on the formal opinion pieces appearing in the press over Roman pseudonyms, they now give weight to such sources as the letters from merchants, sea captains, and foreign travelers which when they attracted public notice the political leadership clearly had to reckon with. Those leaders themselves, as Harry Ammon pointed out some years ago, were not above mobilizing the public in support of their own foreign policy causes. Writing of the Genet affair in 1971, Ammon notes ironically that it was not the people-pleasing Republicans who first took to the field. Rather, "It was the Hamiltonians who invaded the public arena, summoning citizens . . . to public meetings at which resolutions were adopted endorsing the administration policy of neutrality and condemning Genet for threatening an appeal to the people" (Ammon 1971: 132). In this instance the impetus for engaging the public came from the top. Likewise, the Democratic Republican societies, of the same era and similarly engaged, had identifiable leaders. Other issues touching on foreign relations, however, seem to bubble below the printed surface waiting for the historian to give them meaning. A case in point comes from a scholarly paper given by Lawrence Peskin in the fall of 2001. Peskin details how effectively the published accounts of individuals, often victims of Algerian piracy, kept public attention focused on this perennial trouble spot between 1785 and 1797. Four newspapers in this period, he notes, published no fewer than 285 items on the "Algerian crisis," thereby demonstrating "the important connection between foreign affairs and the domestic public sphere," the former, he concludes, "no longer the exclusive province of elites" (p. 49). Scholars entering the public sphere may, of course, find it risky to draw a straight line of cause and effect between popular clamors and official responses. As Peskin says of his own inquiry, it would be "too simplistic" to infer, for example, that "the Algerian crisis caused the creation of the United States Navy." Nevertheless, further forays into the public sphere, especially if they add convincingly to explanations of outcomes already seen as multi-causal, will surely be undertaken.

Likewise, we can expect to hear more of the policy pressures exerted by prominent individuals like John Jacob Astor. Inevitably, Astor's fur trading enterprise at the mouth of the Columbia intersected with the efforts of American diplomats to keep a territorial foothold on the Pacific. For this conjuncture of private and public objectives, James Rhonda's *Astoria and Empire* (1990) helps to flesh out the narrative of the "Oregon Question" where Frederick Merk left off in 1967.

The Genet Affair and the Law of Nations

Because the Constitution made no mention of how the law of nations might fit into the conduct of American foreign relations, early leaders adopted its precepts gradually and only when pressed. Americans first became aware of this constitutional hiatus when in 1793 Citizen Genet set out to make the United States a base for hostile land and sea operations against both Britain and Spain. The possibility that Genet's activities might sweep Americans into an unwanted war fixed attention on what the law of nations had to say about neutrality. Basically, it implied that if a nation defended its neutral rights and observed its neutral duties, it would offer no pretext for getting involved. Accordingly, Washington's so-called neutrality proclamation threatened to punish "under the law of nations" any American citizen caught "committing, aiding, or abetting hostilities against any of the said powers." Genet's subsequent fitting out of privateers in American ports and allowing French consuls to dispose of the prize vessels they brought in led the administration to add to the list of actions it believed prohibited by the law of nations as well as by the existing treaties with France. That Congress in 1794 gave legislative support to Washington's extra-constitutional rule-making did much to confirm the place of international law in American jurisprudence. The most recent analysis of this process appears in Stephen Rosen's (1981) article, "Alexander Hamilton and the Domestic Uses of International Law." In Hamilton's intellectual wrestling with international realities, presidential power, and national self-interest, Rosen finds a key to understanding not only the administration's response to the Genet crisis but also its defense of Jay's treaty. Moreover, he concludes, Washington and Hamilton "used the unique occasion of Washington's Farewell Address to associate the prestige of Washington not with the idea of permanent neutrality but with the principle of popular deference to . . . the law of nations" (p. 201).

Adding measurably to Ammon's account of Genet's recall, Eugene Sheridan (1994) probes more deeply the political factors attending this event on both sides of the Atlantic. He argues that the divisions within Washington's cabinet as to how to go about this delicate matter were "far more complex than the usually emphasized polarity between pro-French Republicanism and anti-French Federalism" (p. 464). Sheridan proceeds to analyze the divergent but sometimes overlapping motives of the principal players as they set about to end the French minister's mission. He also goes beyond Ammon's depiction of Genet's recall having been made easy by the Jacobin takeover in Paris to elaborate on such other "key variables" as "Genet's failure to adjust to a radical change in French foreign policy . . . and the Jacobin belief that his challenge to American neutrality was part of a wide-ranging counter-revolutionary plot." Sheridan's article demonstrates that even one of the most studied and written-about events of the era is susceptible to further inquiry.

Including Indian Treaties?

The discomfort Americans feel today about their forebears' treatment of Native Americans has its lesser counterpart in the uneasiness diplomatic historians feel about counting as "foreign relations" the 200-odd treaties US commissioners negotiated with Indian tribes prior to 1840. Jay Gitlin (1998) argues that whatever the anomalies, both parties benefited from this mode of arranging their relations. The government, for its part, used the treaties to prevent public lands from slipping into the hands of private speculators; while "many, if not most tribal peoples recognized the importance of dealing with outsiders in a controlled and unified manner" (pp. 86–7). Such dealings, he contends, not only strengthened the tribes' sense of nationality (with all the ramifications implied by nationhood), but the sheer number of treaties revealed their adeptness in using market forces to their advantage. By negotiating away tribal lands piecemeal and at intervals, they profited from the gradual rise in land values. As Gitlin puts it, "treatymaking in a sense became marketmaking – not only for whites, but for some tribesmen" (p. 91). Moreover, prior to the "removal" era, Gitlin cites enough instances of tribal affluence resulting from such marketing success as to suggest that not all Indians were "passive victims of the [treaty] process." Bradford Perkins (1998), seconding the need to know more about the place as well as the fate of Native Americans in the history of American diplomacy, notes that "even the most comprehensive textbooks seldom insert more than a disconnected paragraph or two on tribal–white relations" (p. 119). Besides the historiographical shortfall on such face-to-face encounters, there remain largely unwritten chapters about how the tribes figured in our relations with neighboring Canada and Mexico. A notable opening is this direction is Richard White's publication in 1991 of *The Middle Ground: Indians, Empires, and Republics in the Great Lakes Region, 1650–1815.*

Diplomatic Biographies

Although biographers appear to have thoroughly illuminated the careers of the principal foreign policy figures of the era, more "diplomatic biographies" continue to appear. Even Samuel F. Bemis' exhaustive treatment of John Quincy Adams' long and distinguished diplomatic career has left enough room for William Weeks to elaborate on JQA's tortuous role in negotiating the Transcontinental Treaty of 1819. Similarly, Greg Russell (1995) examines the self-conscious ethical and moral factors in Adams' conduct; and James Lewis (2001) develops the theme that Adams was most skilled at settling what problems he could within "the constraints imposed by the nation's federal and republican system" while postponing those problems that might have led to war (p. 141). The careers of lesser diplomats, too, may be found fit subjects for expanded treatment. Thus far, American statesmen who undertook diplomatic missions often as a reward for their achievements on the domestic scene have rated only a chapter or two in their biographers' accounts of these episodes. Some may be found worthy of full-length accounts of their overseas accomplishments. But even the major figures call for re-examination. As Bradford Perkins (1998) points out, if four authors publishing over the past twenty year can reshape how we think about Thomas Jefferson's foreign policy, "surely there are many opportunities for innovative biographical treatments of other important figures" (pp. 118–19). But whether it is in biography or by following up on some of the new approaches and new expectations suggested by this essay, an active future for research in the foreign policy of the early era seems assured.

REFERENCES

Adams, Henry: *History of the United States under the Administrations of Jefferson and Madison,* 9 vols. (New York: Scribner and Sons, 1889–91).
Allgor, Catherine: "'A Republican in a Monarchy': Louisa Catherine Adams in Russia." *Diplomatic History* 21 (winter 1997), 15–43.

Ammon, Harry: *The Genet Mission* (New York: W. W. Norton, 1971).

Becker, William H. and Samuel F. Wells, Jr.: *Economics and World Power: An Assessment of American Diplomacy Since 1789* (New York: Columbia University Press, 1984).

Bemis, Samuel Flagg: *Pinckney's Treaty: A Study of America's Advantage from Europe's Distress, 1783–1800* (Baltimore, MD: Johns Hopkins University Press, 1926).

Bemis, Samuel Flagg: *John Quincy Adams and the Foundations of American Foreign Policy* (New York: A. A. Knopf, 1949).

Ben-Atar, Doron S.: *The Origins of Jeffersonian Commercial Policy and Diplomacy* (London: Macmillan, 1993).

Ben-Atar, Doron S.: "Nationalism, Neo-Mercantilism, and Diplomacy: Rethinking the Franklin Mission." *Diplomatic History* 22 (winter 1998), 103–14.

Brown, Roger H.: *The Republic in Peril: 1812* (New York: Columbia University Press, 1964).

Combs, Jerald A.: *American Diplomatic History: Two Centuries of Changing Interpretations* (Berkeley: University of California Press, 1983).

Dangerfield, George: *Chancellor Robert R. Livingston of New York* (New York: Harcourt Press, 1960).

DeConde, Alexander: *The Quasi War: The Politics and Diplomacy of the Undeclared War with France, 1797–1801* (New York: Scribner, 1966).

DeConde, Alexander: *This Affair of Louisiana* (New York: Scribner, 1976).

Everest, Allan S.: *The War of 1812 in the Champlain Valley* (Syracuse, NY: Syracuse University Press, 1981).

Field, James A., Jr.: "Novus Ordo Seclorum" [Feature review on Michael Hunt's *Ideology and US Foreign Policy*]. *Diplomatic History* 13 (winter 1989), 113–22.

Fitzsimons, David M.: "Idealistic Internationalism in the Ideology of Early American Foreign Relations." *Diplomatic History* 19 (fall 1995), 569–82.

Gilbert, Felix: *To the Farewell Address: Ideas of Early American Foreign Policy* (Princeton, NJ: Princeton University Press, 1961).

Gitlin, Jay: "Private Diplomacy to Private Property: States, Tribes and Nations in the Early National Period." *Diplomatic History* 22 (winter 1998), 85–99.

Graebner, Norman: "Isolationism and Antifederalism: The Ratification Debates." *Diplomatic History* 11 (fall 1987), 337–70.

Hammack, James W., Jr.: *Kentucky and the Second American Revolution* (Lexington: University of Kentucky Press, 1976).

Hatzenbueler, Ronald L. and Robert L. Ivie: *Congress Declares War: Rhetoric, Leadership, and Partisanship in the Early Republic* (Kent, OH: Kent State University Press, 1983).

Heald, Morrell and Lawrence S. Kaplan: *Culture and Diplomacy: The American Experience* (Westport, CT: Greenwood Press, 1977).

Hickey, Donald R.: *The War of 1812: A Forgotten Conflict* (Urbana: University of Illinois Press, 1989).

Hill, Peter P.: *French Perceptions of the Early American Republic, 1783–1793* (Philadelphia, PA: American Philosophical Society, 1988).

Hogan, Michael J. and Thomas G. Peterson (eds.): *Explaining the History of American Foreign Relations* (Cambridge: Cambridge University Press, 1991).

Horsman, Reginald: "Feature Review; The War of 1812 Revisited." *Diplomatic History* 15 (winter 1991), 115–24.

Hunt, Michael H.: *Ideology and US Foreign Policy* (New Haven, CT: Yale University Press, 1987).

Hutson, James H.: "Intellectual Foundations of Early American Diplomacy." *Diplomatic History* 1 (winter 1977), 1–19.

Johnson, John J.: *A Hemisphere Apart: The Foundations of US Policy toward Latin America* (Baltimore, MD: Johns Hopkins University Press, 1990).

Kaplan, Lawrence S.: "Reflections on Jefferson as a Francophile." *South Atlantic Quarterly* 79 (winter 1980), 38–50.

Kaplan, Lawrence S.: *Entangling Alliances with None: American Foreign Policy in the Age of Jefferson* (Kent, OH: Kent State University Press, 1987a).

Kaplan, Lawrence S.: "Jefferson and the Constitution: The View from Paris, 1786–89." *Diplomatic History* 11 (fall 1987b), 321–35.

Lemmon, Sarah M.: *Frustrated Patriots: North Carolina and the War of 1812* (Chapel Hill: University of North Carolina Press, 1973).

Lewis, James E., Jr.: *John Quincy Adams: Policymaker for the Union* (Wilmington, DE: Scholarly Resources, 2001).

Malone, Dumas: *Jefferson the President: Second Term, 1805–1809*, vol. 5 in *Jefferson and His Time* (Boston, MA: Little, Brown, 1974).

Marks, Frederick W., III: *Independence on Trial* (Wilmington, DE: Scholarly Resources, 1986).

Merk, Frederick: *The Oregon Question: Essays in Anglo-American Diplomacy and Politics* (Cambridge, MA: Harvard University Press, 1967).

Miller, John C.: *Crisis in Freedom: The Alien and Sedition Acts* (Boston, MA: Little, Brown, 1951).

Onuf, Peter S.: "A Declaration of Independence for Diplomatic Historians." *Diplomatic History* 22 (winter 1998), 71–83.

Perkins, Bradford: *Prologue to War: England and the United States, 1805–1812* (Berkeley: University of California Press, 1961).

Perkins, Bradford: *The Causes of the War of 1812: National Honor or National Interest?* (Malabar, FL: Krieger Publishing, 1983).

Perkins, Bradford: "Early American Foreign Relations: Opportunities and Challenges." *Diplomatic History* 22 (winter 1998), 115–20.

Peskin, Lawrence A.: "Caught in the Web: Algerian Pirates and the Early National Public Sphere." Paper presented at the Washington Area Early American Seminar, College Park, MD, September 20, 2001.

Rhonda, James P.: *Astoria and Empire* (Lincoln: University of Nebraska Press, 1990).

Rohrs, Richard C.: "The Federalist Party and the Convention of 1800." *Diplomatic History* 12 (summer 1998), 237–60.

Rosen, Stephen Peter: "Alexander Hamilton and the Domestic Uses of International Law." *Diplomatic History* 5 (summer 1981), 183–202.

Rosenberg, Emily S.: "Walking the Borders." *Diplomatic History* 14 (fall 1990), 565–73. Also ch. 3 in Michael J. Hogan and Thomas G. Paterson (eds.) *Explaining the History of American Foreign Relations* (Cambridge: Cambridge University Press, 1991).

Rosenberg, Emily S.: "A Call to Revolution: A Roundtable on Early US Foreign Relations." *Diplomatic History* 22 (winter 1998), 63–70.

Rossignol, Marie-Jeanne: *Le Ferment nationale: aux origines de la politique extérieures des Etats-Unis, 1789–1812* (Paris: Editions Belin, 1994).

Russell, Greg: *John Quincy Adams and the Public Virtues of Diplomacy* (Columbia: University of Missouri Press, 1995).

Sapio, Victor A.: *Pennsylvania and the War of 1812* (Lexington: University of Kentucky Press, 1970).

Sheridan, Eugene R.: "The Recall of Edmond Charles Genet: A Study in Transatlantic Politics and Diplomacy." *Diplomatic History* 18 (fall 1994), 463–88.

Smelser, Marshall: *The Democratic Republic, 1801–1815* (New York: Harper and Row, 1968).

Smith, James Morton: *Freedom's Fetters: The Alien Sedition Laws and American Civil Liberties* (Ithaca, NY: Cornell University Press, 1956).

Smith, Page: *John Adams* (Garden City, NY: Doubleday, 1962).

Sofka, James R.: "The Jeffersonian Idea of Security: Commerce, the Atlantic Balance of Power, and the Barbary War, 1786–1805." *Diplomatic History* 21 (fall 1997), 519–44.

Spivak, Burton: *Jefferson's English Crisis* (Charlottesville: University Press of Virginia, 1979).

Stagg, J. C. A.: *Mr. Madison's War: Politics, Diplomacy and Warfare in the Early American Republic, 1783–1830* (Princeton, NJ: Princeton University Press, 1983).

Stevens, Kenneth R.: "Thomas Jefferson, John Quincy Adams, and Foreign Policy in the Early Republic" [feature review]. *Diplomatic History* 19 (fall 1995), 705–11.

Stuart, Reginald C.: "Confederation Diplomacy" [feature review]. *Diplomatic History* 22 (spring 1999), 371–8.

Tucker, Robert W. and David C. Hendrickson: *Empire of Liberty: The Statecraft of Thomas Jefferson* (New York: Oxford University Press, 1990).

Weeks, William Earl: *John Quincy Adams and the American Global Empire* (Lexington: University of Kentucky Press, 1992).

Weeks, William Earl: "New Directions in the Study of Early American Foreign Relations." *Diplomatic History* 17 (winter 1994), 73–96.

Weeks, William Earl: *Building the Continental Empire: American Expansion from the Revolution to the Civil War* (Chicago, IL: American Way Series, 1996).

Weinberg, Albert K.: *Manifest Destiny: A Study of National Expansion in American History* (Baltimore, MD: Johns Hopkins University Press, 1935).

White, Richard: *The Middle Ground: Indians, Empires, and Republics in the Great Lakes Region, 1650–1815* (New York: Cambridge University Press, 1991).

CHAPTER FIVE

American Expansion, 1815–1860

WILLIAM E. WEEKS

Bracketed by the end of one war and the beginning of another, the period 1815–61 is possibly the least examined era in the history of American foreign relations, perhaps overshadowed by the momentous events occurring both before and after that time. Nonetheless, since 1983 it has been rediscovered as a critical era in US history by a new generation of scholars, most of whom would not characterize themselves as historians of American foreign relations. Yet the redefinition of the field to include not just a narrow focus on diplomacy but rather to address the range of interactions between Americans of all sorts – diplomats, missionaries, merchants, entrepreneurs, filibusters, sailors, whalemen, pioneers, and the like – and the world beyond the nation's borders has radically altered our conception of the era. The last twenty years has seen a flowering of work on the foreign relations of the era from a diversity of approaches, perspectives, and backgrounds. This essay will examine some of the more significant books and historiographical trends in the literature of the period 1815–61 to have appeared since 1983.

Expansion Into the Americas

Significant reconceptualization has occurred on what already had been one of the most worked topics of the era: continental expansionism. Whether dealing with new approaches to the foreign policy of the Monroe administration, fleshing out an evolving understanding of the Texas question in American foreign policy, or redefining the causes and legacy of the Mexican–American War, knowledge of the period has increased substantially since 1983 over what was even then an impressive body of work. Perhaps the most profound redefinition of the topic has been done by the emerging group of scholars known as the "new" Western historians, including, among others, Patricia Nelson Limerick, Richard White, and Clyde Milner. Over roughly the past fifteen years, this group collectively has altered the terms of the debate over the historical meaning(s) of the "American West."

Basic to this transformation has been situating the history of the American West in world history as a critical meeting ground in the transmigration of the peoples of the world. The emphasis is on the West as a geographic region where Native

Portions of this essay were first delivered as a paper entitled "The Economic Sources of American Foreign Policy in the Early Republic: Another Look," delivered at the SHAFR annual convention in Waltham, MA, June 22–25, 1994.

Americans, Hispanics, and Asians interacted both with each other and with the advancing Anglo-American and African-American civilizations in ways that affirm each group's distinctiveness and importance even after the formal transfer of sovereignty to the United States. Patricia Nelson Limerick, one of the most notable of the "new" Western historians, writes in *Something in the Soil* (2000): "In earlier versions of western history, the doings of white people, especially white men, controlled center stage . . . White Americans were the leading men (and much more rarely, women) of Western history." The new perspective assumes that the doings of Native Americans, Asians, Hispanics, and African Americans deserve as much attention as that bestowed on Euro-Americans in order for the history of the region to be truly told. Also new is a supposed neutrality and embrace of complexity in the telling of the story, in place of what she represents as "The desire for a telling of Western history in which good guys are easily distinguished from bad guys" (ibid: 19, 21).

Yet it would be inaccurate to argue that Limerick's work lacks good guys and bad guys. It is easy to tell who the bad guys are – they are almost invariably white, male, and middle class or better, while the good guys are almost invariably non-white, non-male, or non-middle class. Limerick, typical of many "new" Western historians, responds to the triumphalist myths of Manifest Destiny with the creation of an anti-myth in which subjugated peoples are surprisingly successful in resisting, directly or indirectly, the domination of Anglo-American civilization. That civilization is represented as patriarchal, racist, genocidal, and destructive of the environment, in addition to hypocritically betraying the ideals on which it supposedly is built. In place of a Turnerian model of progress along successive frontiers Limerick substitutes a "legacy of conquest" for both the history of the West and as "the historical bedrock of the whole [American] nation" (Limerick 1987: 27).

It is Turner who is the prime historiographical antagonist of Limerick and other "new" Western historians. His "frontier thesis" of American growth and development stands accused of erasing the stories of the victims of progress. What, Limerick asked in *The Legacy of Conquest* (1987), had happened to Western history? "Paradoxically, the problem stemmed from the excess of respect given to the ideas of the field's founder, Frederick Jackson Turner" (p. 27). These lines were a prelude to what became a category-5 tempest in an academic teapot over the meaning and continued significance of Turner and his thesis.

On the one hand it is almost impossible to resist the tendency to contradict Turner. My particular complaint is that his notion of "the frontier," defined as successive lines of contact between Anglo-American and Native-American civilizations in North America radically understates the level of engagement of the US and its citizens in the Pacific, Asia, and Central and South America in the nineteenth century. Yet Turner's ideas have shown a Rasputin-like ability to survive in the face of assault from many scholars and by a variety of rhetorical and conceptual weapons. Limerick's work evidences this phenomenon. Her observation that "conquest forms the historical bedrock of the whole nation" seems little different from Turner's notion that successive struggles at the "meeting place between savagery and civilization" (i.e., the frontier) continually reinvigorated the nation. Limerick's analysis views this struggle from the barrel-end of the American expansionist gun and offers condemnation of it rather than praise, but the historical model is essentially the same.

Limerick's intense desire to nail Turner's scalp to the wall leads her to stub her toe in other ways as well, such as her conclusion that "under the Turner thesis, Western history stood alone" (Limerick 1987: 26). Of course, Turner's "frontier" was a series of contact/conflict zones beginning in eastern North America. It is Limerick, not Turner, who makes the notion of "the West" synonymous with "the frontier."

Although the "new" Western historians' notions of the West as a critical convergence zone in world history have reinvigorated the field by situating it in the context of global history, the tendency to overemphasize race and gender as categories of analysis preempts understanding of the complex interrelationship of peoples, ideologies, and cultures that gave the frontier regions their fluid nature. The key question in the nineteenth-century history of the geographic region known as western North America is not how much text space is given over to white males versus that given to non-white males, but rather, as Turner argues, how the reality of "Americanization" (a complex multi-racial, multi-class, multi-gender and multicultural phenomenon) achieved such dominance. At the same time it is the story of how the process of "Americanization" changed and was changed by the peoples and cultures it encountered, as Turner also suggests.

The "spread-eagle" expansionism of the 1815–61 era and its unembarrassed rhetoric of triumphalist nationalism has made it an attractive target of study by a number of the innovative approaches to the writing of history to emerge in the past twenty years or so, including feminist, cultural, and postcolonial studies. Westward expansion, dripping as it is with images of a feminized landscape ready to be taken by a hyper-masculine expansionist male "subject," is particularly ripe for such a "critical" approach. A prominent example of this is Annette Kolodney's *The Land Before Her* (1984). In Kolodney's scheme, American white female pioneers play Eve to their husbands' Adam, venturing into a western frontier that was imagined as a New World Garden of Eden. Although this pilgrimage often occurred against their will, Kolodney represents females as resisting their husbands' visions of exploitation and domination of the landscape, preferring instead to see the frontier as "potential sanctuary for an idealized domesticity" (p. xiii) in which the garden was tended, not raped. She positions herself unambiguously when she comments: "given the choice, I would have had women's fantasies take the nation west rather than the psychosexual dramas of men intent on possessing a virgin continent" (p. xiii). Kolodney frankly admits her disappointment that, in spite of their differing responses to the landscape, the written record substantially implicates American females in the conquest of the West.

A similar approach is found in Brigitte Georgi-Findlay's *The Frontiers of Women's Writing* (1996). Georgi-Findlay subjects the private and public writings of selected American frontier white females to feminist theory and poststructuralist analysis. The author candidly admits that she began her study expecting to find female voices offering a dissenting view, or at least a more critical response to American continental expansionism than their male counterparts. To her apparent dismay, the record suggests that females were substantially implicated in the conquest of the continent and the "Americanization" of the Indians. The author acknowledges that American white females "adopted many representational practices that can be identified as part of the colonialist discourses, using them in the service of their own empowerment"

(p. 291). In the end, Georgi-Findlay argues that women writers "authorized" themselves not chiefly as women but rather as individuals. Whatever grievances they may have felt regarding their subordination within American civilization, they did not lead to radical or even liberal critiques of the system they inhabited.

Reading Kolodney and Findlay, one is left with the impression that virtually all US history is an expression of a despicable patriarchy, unredeemable in any aspect. As Findlay terms it, "The feminist revision of the frontier myth has exposed the androcentric bias underlying the pastoralization of America – a bias that either neutralizes women completely or colonizes them as captives within the story of the male innocent" (Georgi-Findlay 1996: 8). As with the "new" Western historians, American history generally and American expansionism in particular are cast as a series of fiendishly oppressive ideologies and practices inflicted on a range of racial, ethnic, and gender groups.

What the work of Kolodney and Georgi-Findlay establishes, notwithstanding their *a priori* theoretical convictions, is the centrality of a nationalist ideology in the identities of both male and female Americans. The controlling variable in the behavior of the individuals studied is nationality, not racial, class, or gender identities. The latter three categories, while significant, are subordinated to some notion of a still imperfectly understood American nationality that, while comprised of race, class, and gender dimensions, is far more than the sum of those particular parts. American nationalism remains oddly underexamined given its role, particularly during the first half of the nineteenth century, as one of the great revolutionary forces in the modern world. Some scholars appear to believe that American nationalism does not exist, insofar as it bears little in common with other forms of nationalism. Benedict Anderson's *Imagined Communities: Reflections on the Origins and Prospects of Nationalism*, widely lauded as the best text on the topic in the past twenty years, locates the origins of modern nationalism in Latin America, virtually ignoring US nationalism.

In spite of the uneven analyses of various insurgent scholarly tendencies, there can be no doubt that language was critical to the creation of American nationalism and expansionism. The nationalist project and the expansionist project, both rhetorically and actually, proceeded hand in hand in the ideology of Manifest Destiny. Analyses that aim to foreground gender or race are missing the most important part of the vocabulary, in that the nationalist/expansionist project was built on a series of hierarchies – of race, gender, culture, religion, economics, technology, and politics – that assumed the superiority of all things American over all things not-American. The racial and cultural affinity felt by many Americans for Great Britain existed side-by-side with an intense suspicion of British motives and the assumption of the inferiority of its society and politics. The conquest of the West and Southwest would have occurred whatever the racial and cultural makeup of the peoples of the area. The alleged inferiority of the diverse civilizations of North America was a rationalization for conquest, not a cause.

The historiography of westward expansionism has been radically altered since 1983 both by the incorporation of federal Indian policy as a foreign relations topic and by the inclusion of tribal histories of the era. The full dynamic of American expansionism cannot be understood unless it is viewed from the perspective of those at whose expense expansionism occurred. One of the most perceptive of authors on federal Indian policy is George Harwood Phillips. His *Indians and Intruders in Central California, 1769–1849* (1993) and *Indians and Indian Agents* (1997) combine solid archival research with a detailed narrative in which historical judgments are rooted in historical evidence. Phillips rightly characterizes federal Indian policy as a critical part of the larger expansionist policy.

A landmark study is William G. McLoughlin's three volumes of *Cherokees and Missionaries* (1984), *Cherokee Renascence in the New Republic* (1986), and *After the Trail of Tears* (1993). In the middle volume, McLoughlin eloquently illustrates the dilemmas faced by the Cherokees as they attempted to adapt (some more than others) to the revolution in modernity brought by the Americans. McLoughlin suggests a split in Cherokee opinion between those who wished to cleave to more traditional communal/matrilineal ways of living and those who more fully embraced the individualist/patrilineal practices of the Americans. In the end, white racism rendered the question moot for the Cherokees. McLoughlin concludes: "The more successfully an Indian nation acculturated itself, the more dangerous it became to American expansionism" (McLoughlin 1986: 423).

Also valuable is Dianna Everett's *The Texas Cherokees* (1990). Everett chronicles the Texas Cherokees' efforts to exercise tribal self-determination in the face of Anglo-Americans advancing from the east and other Indian tribes pressing from the west before final removal to the north in 1840. Her work provides further evidence that Indian tribes were autonomous entities in the diplomacy of expansionism, combining strategies of cooperation and resistance in forestalling their eventual subjugation. Similarly, James Taylor Carson's *Searching for the Bright Path* (1999) chronicles the tribes' struggle to adapt to the revolution wrought by the arrival of Europeans in general and by Americans in particular. Carson emphasizes the role of contingency in the historical outcome: "The history of the Choctaws involved a complex interaction between received culture and personal choice" (p. 132).

The "winning of the West" has lost much of its luster by viewing the process from the perspective of the vanquished. The frontier heroes of old increasingly are viewed as bloodthirsty and genocidal, the memory of whom should be roundly criticized if not merely forgotten. In recent years something of a backlash to this trend has occurred, as scholars have attempted either to deny or at least put into a palatable context the alleged transgressions. Robert V. Remini's *Andrew Jackson and his Indian Wars* (2001) portrays Old Hickory, depending on the circumstances, as both a friend and foe of Indians. Drawing on decades of experience with his Jackson and the era, Remini asserts that "although no one in the modern world wishes to accept it or believe it" Jackson's removal policy saved the tribes "from inevitable annihilation" at the hands of white frontiersmen (p. 281). Similarly, Thomas Dunlay's *Kit Carson and the Indians* (2000) attempts to rehabilitate the frontier trapper, guide, and military commander from the harsh criticism bestowed upon him in recent decades by Clifford Trafzer and others. Dunlay portrays Carson for most of his life occupying a "middle ground" between Indian and white civilizations, and claims that Carson's alleged responsibility for the savage subjugation of the Navajos has been exaggerated.

Less persuasive is Francis Paul Prucha's *American Indian Treaties* (1994), which argues that US treaties with Native-American tribes were not treaties at all, but political anomalies in need of being viewed in a different light as history and voided as contemporary law. Prucha suggests that it would be better to understand them as part of the civilizing mission of the US in teaching the cultivation of the soil, the importance of private property, and the principles of democracy.

Prucha's bold thesis that Indian affairs ultimately were a "domestic issue" is contradicted by authorities ranging from John Marshall to the large body of recent scholarship on Native-American affairs which affirm the existence of tribal autonomy. Prucha not only denies that the "trail of broken treaties" were in fact treaties, he even denies that the agreements were broken, whatever their nature, seeing arguments to the contrary as a historically fabricated guilt trip conjured up by Native-American scholars and acquiesced in by scholarly liberals. The underlying motive appears to be undermining the status of present-day tribal treaty claims in the federal courts. Prucha candidly calls for the treaties to be nullified. Such a course, in light of the history of Native-American subjugation and removal, would be the final expression of imperial conquest.

The inescapable consequence of the evolution of the historiography of expansionism since 1983 is the realization that one can no more examine US continental expansionism without examining the Indian side of affairs than one can study Anglo-American relations without consulting the British archival record. Indians were neither depraved savages of traditional historiography nor the innocent victims of revisionist interpretation, but autonomous entities that more or less skillfully resisted American encroachment by accommodation, assimilation, and resistance.

Mexican–American War

The period since 1983 has seen an abundance of work on Mexican–American relations both prior to and after the war between the two nations. The sesquicentennial of the conflict in particular elicited a flood of work, especially from scholars or American scholars writing from a Mexican, Chicano, or Mexican-American perspective. Richard Griswold del Castillo's *The Treaty of Guadelupe-Hidalgo* (1990) is part of the new wave of critical studies on the making and long-term implications of the treaty ending the Mexican–American War. It is the first book in English to consider the treaty as a key determinant in the long-term trajectory of US–Mexican relations. Griswold del Castillo provides a lucid discussion on the negotiation and ratification of the treaty and additional chapters detailing how its terms have structured bilateral relations since then between the two countries. The seemingly ironclad nature of the treaty's guarantees to Mexican-Americans has led to a political and legal strategy that, much like Native Americans and their treaties with the US, aims to use a relic from the Age of Manifest Destiny to compel contemporary policy changes. The treaty remains a rallying point for groups who continue to see the Southwest portrayed as "occupied America."

The cultural and psychological roots of American relations with Latin America more generally are examined in Frederick B. Pike's *The United States and Latin America* (1992), which analyzes a wide range of literary, documentary, and personal sources to probe the assumptions that structured US relations with Hispanic America. In Pike's view, Latin America was another frontier of renewal on which Americans could revitalize both their civilization and their manhood. Pike documents the conflicting North American responses to race mixing and concludes that

US perceptions of Latin America across the political spectrum were more a projection of their hopes and fears than a result of direct engagement with the region.

Vivien Green Fryd's *Art and Empire* (1992) provides a vivid reading of the intertwining rhetorics of American nationalism and American expansionism known as "Manifest Destiny." Fryd combines a social and political history with the interpretative techniques of art history to argue that the form and content of much of the art of the Capitol "forms a remarkably coherent program of the early course of North American empire, from the discovery and settlement to the national development and westward expansion," a theme visible only in retrospect (p. 1). She claims that those responsible both for the planning and making of the artworks aimed to create a national "semblance of consensus" in the face of intractable political and sectional divisions, thus enabling expansion and the removal of Native Americans (p. 4). The artwork of the Capitol is portrayed as analogous to the popular dime novel scenarios of the regeneration of American civilization through violence against a racial or cultural "other." In this scheme the domination of Indians is on a continuum with the domination of Hispanics, African Americans, and females.

Fryd suggests that most people who visit the Capitol in the present day (that is, when security concerns allow for visits) still fail to notice the artworks' expansionist ideology of progress and narrative of exclusion, which are literally hidden in plain sight. This interpretation can be taken a step further. The architecture of the Capitol itself is so unambiguously a past-as-prelude evocation of the Roman republic that one wonders how any scholar can deny the world-redeeming imperial aspirations at the center of the "American experiment." The building itself is perhaps the single most significant document from the Age of Manifest Destiny.

More analysis of the complex nature of the ideology of Manifest Destiny is found in Peter Antelyes' *Tales of Adventurous Enterprise* (1990). In the tradition of Sacvan Bercovitch, Antelyes details how Washington Irving's fictions celebrate market expansion while acknowledging its personal and ethical pitfalls. The West – open, rugged, and full of opportunity – is the playing field for the "spirit of enterprise," and the (ad)venture capitalist is engaged in both a sacred and secular enterprise. Once again, a myth of eternal return is seen as central to the American story, which Antelyes characterizes as "a repeated exercise in regression and mastery, a drama presented as dynamic and progressive but founded on ideological principles that remained static and repetitive" (p. 15). In Antelyes' view, the entire American West was "a threshold, the boundary line of the American mission" (p. 16). Equally important, the author argues that the expansion of the marketplace was a *de facto* expansion of the nation's boundaries.

The role of American Christian missionaries must be an important part of the consideration of the foreign policy of the era 1815–61. It is sometimes said that all Americans (particularly those of the early nineteenth century) are missionaries of one sort or another. If that is true, it is equally true that Christian missionaries were, as a group, the most zealous American emissaries not just of their religion but also of their nationality, which was bound inextricably to their faith.

This last point is demonstrated in William R. Hutchison's *Errand to the World* (1987), a major contribution to the growing awareness that missionaries were central to American cultural and ideological expansionism. As Hutchison observes, missionaries were "too admirable to be treated as villains and too obtrusive and self-righteous to be heroes" (p. 2). Missionaries combined a powerful mix of American nationalism and evangelical religiosity with fervent determination to accomplish their spiritual mission. Hutchison sees the American desire to reform and rehabilitate the secular world given a powerful stimulus by Christian evangelical zeal. The comparison is apt – American antebellum nationalism, like evangelical Christianity, was a faith that would not keep on the shelf. Both had to expand in order to survive, part of a process of continual rebirth and reinvigoration. The missionary frontier was a critical facet of the expansionist thrust of the era, whether that frontier was located in Hawaii, China, or Georgia.

Patricia Grimshaw's *Paths of Duty: American Missionary Wives in Nineteenth Century Hawaii* (1989) examines the lives and sentiments of the wives of American missionaries during the early years of US engagement with the islands. Similarly to Kolodney and Georgi-Findlay, Grimshaw finds that the women, while possessed of a distinct social and cultural perspective as women, nonetheless were themselves enthusiastic proponents of the American missionary endeavor, contributing "substantially to the religious conversion and reorientation of Hawaiian culture in the first half of the nineteenth century" (p. 195). Once again, it was the national and religious identities of Americans that, more than gender, defined their beings.

Expansion Into the Pacific

The US's expansionist successes of the era remain astounding. In 1815, the nation's claim to the Louisiana Territory continued uncertain and ill defined. The region west of the Mississippi River was generally so unknown that it had not yet acquired the mistaken appellation of the "Great American Desert" given to it as a result of the Long–Atkinson Expedition of 1819. Yet by 1861 all of the region eventually known as the "lower forty-eight" had been acquired, and Americans had made major inroads into most of the rest of the world of the sort that had not existed prior to 1815. By 1861, California had become the new pivot point of the nation, functioning not just as the westernmost edge of a North American empire but also as the easternmost edge of an emerging Pacific empire. The importance of California's ports in the expansionist process has been recognized since at least 1956 with the publication of Norman Graebner's *Empire on the Pacific*. Recent scholarship has now recognized California as an important intercultural zone of the time – a meeting ground of many different nationalities and ways of living brought together by the promise of wealth, especially gold. The gold rush accelerated an already rapidly expanding Pacific basin trading zone; by the 1850s, California was part of a network that looked north to Oregon and Alaska, south to the isthmus of Panama, and Chile and Peru, west to the Hawaiian Islands, and beyond that to the emerging markets of Asia.

The functioning of this regional trading network is deftly chronicled by a scholar who is not a historian at all, much less a diplomatic historian. Thomas N. Layton's *The Voyage of the Frolic* (1997) is the work of an anthropologist by training whose interest in the wreck of the clipper ship *Frolic* off the California coast led him down a trail of discovery that ended in the present. Layton tracked the ship from Baltimore, where the *Frolic* was built in 1844 (in the same shipyard where a young Frederick

Douglass had been employed), to Bombay, where it procured its supply of opium, to Canton, where it traded that opium for Chinese silver, and finally to California, where the *Frolic*'s owners met with American consul and trader Thomas O. Larkin, hoping to profit from a new trade between California and China fueled by the prosperity of the gold rush. Finally, in July 1850, the *Frolic* collided with offshore rocks 100 miles north of San Francisco and sank, to be forgotten until rediscovered by recreational salvage divers in the 1960s. Layton's investigation of the historical record of the voyage of the *Frolic* and of the controversy surrounding the "owner-ship" of its broken chinaware and other treasures in the late twentieth century is a model foreign policy study. The book provides further proof that the record of the American empire, far from being confined to the archives, is in evidence all around us, even under the sea.

Given the importance of the Hawaiian Islands as a crucial spot in the Pacific Ocean, and given the fact that it was the US that by 1842 had issued to the world what was in essence a Monroe Doctrine of Hawaii, warning other states not to attempt to control the islands, it is surprising that the topic is so often overlooked in discussions of American foreign relations of the time. Again, some of the best new work on the islands' conquest is by a non-diplomatic historian. Sally Engle Merry's *Colonizing Hawaii* (2000) probes the paternalistic, capitalistic, and moralistic moti-vations of New England missionaries and lawyers in their efforts to colonize Hawaii via the implementation of a Western legal system. "During the brief period from 1825–1850 the Kingdom of Hawaii was transformed from a system of governance based on sacred laws, hereditary rank, and religious authority to one based on Anglo-American common law, a written constitution, and an elected legislature" (p. 35). Based on records from the Hilo District Court, *Colonizing Hawaii* provides new insight into the very distinct methods by which Americans exerted imperial control over a new land.

The presentation weakens considerably when the author makes glib comparisons to contemporary events, as when she equates missionary efforts to control the sexual behavior of Hawaiian women to modern discussions over "the loss of 'family values,' with its depiction of frightening rates of teen pregnancy and divorce" (p. 261). An open-minded scholar might acknowledge that the politics of such matters can cut in more than one direction. "Protecting women from degrading status" may have been a "frequent justification for colonialism in Hawaii," but it is also a frequent justification for much of what now constitutes sexual harassment law (p. 261). Merry's evident political orientation does not allow for these sorts of decentering observations and her rhetorical strategies throughout the book tend to exclude those who might think differently from her or be different from her. This lessens the effectiveness of her work.

Discussions of the origins of an American Pacific empire must include the whaling frontier, a critical if often overlooked industry in antebellum America. Whalers, along with missionaries, spread the American idea (if their own distinct version of that idea) to the farthest reaches of the Pacific during that time. Notable recent books include Briton C. Busch's *"Whaling Will Never Do For Me"* (1994), which provides a social history of the sailors who signed on with American vessels. Busch is especially good at demonstrating the key role of American consular agents in the Pacific region in administering some semblance of the rule of law to what was often an unruly and lawless enterprise. The book again illustrates how the federal government of the era, though minuscule by today's standards, provided essential support to American economic enterprise in the far reaches of the world. Also valuable is Margaret S. Creighton's *Rites and Passages* (1995).

Perhaps the most impressive recent piece of work on whaling is *In Pursuit of Leviathan* (1997) by Davis, Gallman, and Gleiter. Massively researched and tightly argued, the book shows how, during the period 1815–42, the US overtook Great Britain as the world's leading producer of a critical commodity. Essential to that shift in global economic power was the expansion of the American whale fleet, first into the central Pacific and then to the seas around Japan. The whalers, much like the fur traders before them, operated as the front edge of American expansionism, pushing out the boundaries of US influence and directing the attention of elite opinion and the federal government to new areas of the globe. Whaling, basically overlooked in the 1983 edition of the SHAFR Guide, now stands as a key intercultural conflict/contact zone between American sailors and the world and, increasingly after 1830, in the multi-ethnic makeup of whaling crews.

Expansion Into Asia

No examination of the expansionist impulse of the era 1815–61 would be complete without looking at American commercial penetration of Asia generally and China in particular. As the second largest participant in the China trade during this era, the American role in opening the Canton trade should not be underestimated. A major contribution to an enlarged understanding of this key role is Jacques M. Downs' *The Golden Ghetto* (1997). Downs, acknowledged as the unrivaled authority on the American trading community at Canton, has written what stands as the definitive history on that community and its influence over US policy. Downs amplifies Layton's point about the importance of the opium trade, describing it as the economic foundation of American interest in China and the source of many a great fortune. Downs details the social history of the American mercantile elite, from their palatial homes in Canton to their only slightly less palatial residences in the US. He argues that it was the extreme isolation of the Treaty Port culture (an isolation founded and enforced by the Chinese) that prevented the development of "enlightened social attitudes" towards the Chinese (p. 340). Part economic history, part diplomatic history, part social and cultural history, *The Golden Ghetto* occupies a key spot in the emerging historiography of US expansionism.

Matthew C. Perry's "opening" of Japan is another event of epochal importance that is often overlooked or underappreciated when assessing the key events of the era. As is the case with Hawaii, any number of European nations could have forced open Japan to the world, but in the end it was the US that did the deed, further testimony to the nation's high profile in world affairs even then. Peter Booth Wiley's *Yankees in the Land of the Gods* (1991) takes a fresh look at a topic at once well worked and yet surprisingly obscure. Wiley situates the Perry expedition in the context of the US's new Pacific orientation resulting from the conquest of California. The expedition's most basic motive – to establish protections for shipwrecked American sailors from abuse at the hand of the Hermit Kingdom – speaks loudly of the awesome reach of the federal government even in the years prior to the Civil

War. The federal government, via the use of the navy and the diplomatic corps, took it upon itself to secure justice for its citizens throughout the world. At the same time, American policymakers pushed for an international maritime regime that would facilitate commerce on the world's oceans.

Along the same lines, the editorial decision to "mainstream" American military history into the relevant chapters in the new edition of the SHAFR Guide rather than provide a separate chapter casts a new perspective on the expansionism of the era. The nation's participation in the emerging global trade network would have occurred much more slowly (and maybe not have occurred at all) had the federal government, through the agency of the army and navy, not defended the rights of Americans outside the nation's boundaries. Almost as important as the direct military support was the military's role in mapping and exploring both the land and the high seas. J. Valerie Fifer's *United States Perceptions of Latin America* (1991) observes that "In the early 1850s, the United States Government carried out the most ambitious, far-reaching series of land surveys of the New World since the days of the conquistadores" (p. 6). The army explored the Trans-Mississippi West while the navy explored South America, having previously explored and mapped much of the entire Pacific basin. Who can deny the long-term significance of the Wilkes expedition of 1838–42, which, besides making the first confirmed sighting of Antarctica, drew the Pacific Ocean navigation charts used by the navy in World War II?

The success of the expansionist project depended on the conquest of the immense spaces encompassed by the American territorial, commercial, and ideological empires. Without the revolutionary advances in transportation, communication, and military technologies during this time, expansionism could not have occurred as it did, and perhaps could not have occurred at all. The role of the telegraph in that process is suggested in Menahem Blondheim's *News Over the Wires* (1994). Blondheim demonstrates how the telegraph nationalized the news of the day and facilitated timely access on the periphery to the critical developments. Astoundingly, the nascent Associated Press's ability to disseminate news actually outpaced the rapidly growing territorial extent of the republic. The technology allowed the new acquisitions of the nation to quickly be bound to the national community by a common news source and, more significantly, by a common set of cultural reference points. The railroad, the steamship, and the telegraph effectively made manageable a domain that many feared would be too large to hold together.

The Economic Dimension

Finally, one of the most significant trends in the literature since 1983 has been a renewed emphasis on the role of economic motives in the making of American foreign policy. Foreign policy scholars of the era of diverse backgrounds and approaches have confirmed the primacy of economic considerations. A prominent example of this trend is Becker and Wells' *Economics and World Power* (1984). This edited collection is intended to assess the importance of economic motives in American foreign policy and more generally to consider the influence of economic factors in America's rise to world power. Kinley J. Brauer's "Economics and the Diplomacy of American Expansionism" persuasively argues for the central importance of economic motives in the making of antebellum American foreign policy. Brauer views the period 1821–60 as a time "when economic considerations played a particularly important role in American diplomacy." American leaders, Brauer writes, "were well aware of the vital relationship between American prosperity and American diplomacy" (Becker and Wells 1984: 55). He sees the primary focus of policymakers as "widening old markets and opening new ones, expanding production, and promoting industry." He concludes that "since a crucial part of American prosperity and growth stemmed from international trade, since nature and history had dictated that America's primary relations with other nations would be economic, economic considerations provided the fundamental framework for American foreign relations during this period" (pp. 55, 59, 113). In this scheme, national security became synonymous with the protection of American economic interests.

Along similar lines, Mary W. M Hargreaves' *The Presidency of John Quincy Adams* (1985) argues that Adams "regarded foreign affairs as the focus of his administration and, under that category, the interests of the United States' commerce as paramount" (p. 67). Adams perceived that the nation's economic well-being hinged on the expansion of foreign trade, and that the development of the home market was inextricably linked to expanding foreign markets. Adams also vigorously pursued claims against foreign states for depredations against American commerce either on land or at sea, putting the world on notice that violating the property rights of American citizens would have certain and long-term consequences. Yet Hargreaves emphasizes that Adams viewed the creation of a liberal international trade regime as the chief means by which the United States would spread its gospel of republicanism, individual liberty, and free enterprise.

Likewise, John Belohlavek's *"Let the Eagle Soar!" The Foreign Policy of Andrew Jackson* (1985) portrays Old Hickory as both a vigorous nationalist and a zealous expansionist. Revising the traditional notion of the Jacksonian era as a quiescent time in the history of American foreign relations, Jackson is described as having "formulated the most expansive and aggressive foreign policy between the presidencies of Thomas Jefferson and James K. Polk." At the center of this activist foreign policy lay commercial expansionism. Jackson, Belohlavek writes, crafted an "aggressive, bold, and imaginative" policy aimed at solidifying existing trade ties and developing new markets in Latin America, the Middle East, and the Far East. Via the negotiation of reciprocity treaties, the expanded use of the consular services, special agents, appointed ministers, and a revitalized navy that was able to defend American interests anywhere in the world, Jackson by 1836 had fostered a 75 percent increase in exports and a 250 percent increase in imports over his first year in office. The net result was increased respect worldwide for the American flag and increased security for the American carrying trade, which by the 1830s was second in the world only to that of the British. *"Let the Eagle Soar!"* reveals how commercial questions became questions of national honor and national interest in the early republic. Belohlavek concludes that "the advance of commerce . . . was virtually inseparable from the promotion of and defense of American nationalism" (pp. 257, 252, 10).

The work of Brauer, Hargreaves, and Belohlavek makes a strong case that global commercial expansionism was of primary importance in the making of antebellum American foreign policy. This body of work challenges the traditional notion that the foreign policy of the era lacked a global dimension. On the contrary, the picture that has emerged is of a federal government that linked the nation's security to its economic well-being and with considerable long-term consistency pursued policies designed to support both American global commercial expansionism and American principles of international law and commerce.

Seen as a whole, the literature that has appeared in the last twenty years on the period 1815–61 requires scholars of American foreign relations to redraw their mental maps of the era. No longer can the "Age of Manifest Destiny" be seen exclusively or even primarily in continentalist terms. Continental expansion was but one aspect of an integrated expansionist thrust that by 1861 had spread throughout the Western hemisphere and had laid the foundations of a US Pacific empire. Americans, self-conscious bearers of the future, in the end racked up a list of accomplishments during this time that somehow exceeded their inflated rhetoric. The speed and scope of that imperial thrust continues to astound and outrage in our own time. The task that remains is to continue to elaborate the distinctive elements – private, public, and ideological – that gave that empire its unique aspect.

REFERENCES

Antelyes, Peter: *Tales of Adventurous Enterprise: Washington Irving and the Poetics of Western Expansion* (New York: Columbia University Press, 1990).

Becker, William H. and Samuel F. Wells, Jr. (eds.): *Economics and World Power: An Assessment of American Diplomacy since 1789* (New York: Columbia University Press, 1984).

Belohlavek, John: *"Let The Eagle Soar!" The Foreign Policy of Andrew Jackson* (Lincoln: University of Nebraska Press, 1985).

Blondheim, Menahem: *News Over the Wires: The Telegraph and the Flow of Information in America, 1844–1897* (Cambridge, MA: Harvard University Press, 1994).

Busch, Briton Cooper: *"Whaling Will Never Do For Me": The American Whalemen in the Nineteenth Century* (Lexington: University of Kentucky Press, 1994).

Calloway, Colin G.: *Our Hearts Fell to the Ground: Plains Indians Views of How The West Was Lost* (Boston, MA: Bedford Books, 1996).

Carson, James Taylor: *Searching for the Bright Path: The Mississippi Choctaws from Prehistory to Removal* (Lincoln: University of Nebraska Press, 1999).

Chavezmontes, J.: *Heridas Que No Cierran* [Wound That Will Not Heal] (Mexico City: Grijalbo, 1988).

Creighton, Margaret S.: *Rites and Passages: The Experience of American Whaling, 1830–1870* (Cambridge: Cambridge University Press, 1995).

Davis, Lance E., Robert E. Gallman, and Karen Gleiter: *In Pursuit of Leviathan: Technology, Institutions, Productivity, and Profits in American Whaling, 1816–1906* (Chicago, IL: University of Chicago Press, 1997).

Downs, Jacques M.: *The Golden Ghetto: The American Commercial Community at Canton and the Shaping of American China Policy, 1784–1844* (Bethlehem: Lehigh University Press, 1997).

Dunlay, Tom: *Kit Carson and the Indians* (Lincoln: University of Nebraska Press, 2000).

Engstrand, Iris W.: Poniatowska, Elena: *Culture y Cultura: Consequences of the US–Mexican War, 1846–1848* (Los Angeles: Autry Museum of Western Heritage, 1998).

Everett, Dianna: *The Texas Cherokees: A People Between Two Fires, 1819–1840* (Norman: University of Oklahoma Press, 1990).

Faragher, John Mack (ed.): *Rereading Frederick Jackson Turner: The Significance of the Frontier and Other Essays* (New York: Henry Holt, 1994).

Fifer, J. Valerie: *United States Perceptions of Latin America, 1850–1930: A "New West" South of Capricorn?* (Manchester: Manchester University Press, 1991).

Figueroa, E. R.: *La Guerra De Corso De Mexico Durante La Invasion Norteamericana, 1845–1848* [The War In Mexico During the North American Invasion, 1845–1848] (Mexico City: Instituto Tecnologico Autonomo De Mexico, 1996).

Flynt, Wayne and Gerald W. Berkley: *Taking Christianity to China: Alabama Missionaries in the Middle Kingdom, 1850–1950* (Tuscaloosa: University of Alabama Press, 1997).

Fryd, Vivien Green: *Art and Empire: The Politics of Ethnicity in the United States Capitol, 1815–1860* (New Haven, CT: Yale University Press, 1992).

Georgi-Findlay, Brigitte: *The Frontiers of Women's Writing: Women's Narratives and the Rhetoric of Westward Expansionism* (Tucson: University of Arizona Press, 1996).

Goetzmann, William H.: *New Lands, New Men: America and the Second Great Age Of Discovery* (New York: Viking, 1986).

Grimshaw, Patricia: *Paths Of Duty: American Missionary Wives in Nineteenth Century Hawaii* (Honolulu: University of Hawaii Press, 1989).

Griswold del Castillo, Richard: *The Treaty of Guadelupe-Hidalgo: A Legacy of Conflict* (Norman: University of Oklahoma Press, 1990).

Hagan, Kenneth J.: *This People's Navy: The Making of American Sea Power* (New York: Free Press, 1991).

Hague, Harlan: *Thomas O. Larkin: A Life Of Patriotism and Profit in Old California* (Norman: University of Oklahoma Press, 1990).

Hargreaves, Mary W. M.: *The Presidency of John Quincy Adams* (Lawrence: University of Kansas Press, 1985).

Harlow, Neal: *California Conquered: War and Peace on the Pacific, 1846–1850* (Berkeley: University of California Press, 1982).

Hutchison, William R.: *Errand to the World: American Protestant Thought and Foreign Missions* (Chicago, IL: University of Chicago Press, 1987).

Kidwell, Clara Sue: *Choctaws and Missionaries in Mississippi, 1818–1918* (Norman: University of Oklahoma Press, 1995).

Kolodney, Annette: *The Land Before Her: Fantasy and Experience of the American Frontiers, 1630–1860* (Chapel Hill: University of North Carolina Press, 1984).

Layton, Thomas N.: *The Voyage of the Frolic: New England Merchants and the Opium Trade* (Palo Alto, CA: Stanford University Press, 1997).

Limerick, Patricia N.: *The Legacy of Conquest: The Unbroken Past of the American West* (New York: W. W. Norton, 1987).

Limerick, Patricia N.: *Something in the Soil: Legacies and Reckonings in the New West* (New York: W. W. Norton, 2000).

Limerick, Patricia N. and Clyde A. Milner: *Trails: Toward a New Western History* (Lawrence: University of Kansas Press, 1991).

Long, David F.: *Gold Braid and Foreign Relations: Diplomatic Activities of US Naval Officers, 1798–1883* (Annapolis, MD: Naval Institute Press, 1988).

MacDougall, Walter A.: *Let the Sea Make a Noise: A History of the North Pacific from Magellan to MacArthur* (New York: Basic Books, 1993).

McLoughlin, William G.: *Cherokees and Missionaries: 1789–1839* (New Haven, CT: Yale University Press, 1984).

McLoughlin, William G.: *Cherokee Renascence in the New Republic* (Princeton, NJ: Princeton University Press, 1986).

McLoughlin, William G.: *After the Trail of Tears: The Cherokees Struggle For Survival, 1839–1880* (Chapel Hill: University of North Carolina Press, 1993).

Meinig, D. W.: *The Shaping of America: A Geographical Perspective on 500 Years of History, Volume 2: Continental America, 1800–1867* (New Haven, CT: Yale University Press, 1993).

Meinig, D. W.: *The Shaping Of America: A Geographical Perspective on 500 Years of History, Volume 3: Transcontinental America, 1850–1915* (New Haven, CT: Yale University Press, 1998).

Merry, Sally Engle: *Colonizing Hawaii: The Cultural Power of Law* (Princeton, NJ: Princeton University Press, 2000).

Miller, Angela: *The Empire of the Eye: Landscape Representation and American Cultural Politics, 1825–1875* (Ithaca, NY: Cornell University Press, 1993).

Perry, John Curtis: *Facing West: Americans and the Opening of the Pacific* (Westport, CT: Praeger, 1994).

Phillips, George Harwood: *Indians and Intruders in Central California, 1769–1849* (Norman: University of Oklahoma Press, 1993).

Phillips, George Harwood: *Indians and Indian Agents: The Origins of the Reservation System in California, 1849–1852* (Norman: University of Oklahoma Press, 1997).

Pike, Frederick B.: *The United States and Latin America: Myths and Stereotypes of Civilization and Nature* (Austin: University of Texas Press, 1992).

Prucha, Francis Paul: *American Indian Treaties: The History of a Political Anomaly* (Berkeley: University of California Press, 1994).

Remini, Robert V.: *Andrew Jackson and his Indian Wars* (New York: Viking Press, 2001).

Schroeder, John H.: *Shaping a Maritime Empire: The Commercial and Diplomatic Role of the American Navy, 1829–1861* (Westport, CT: Greenwood Press, 1985).

Turner, Frederick J. and Martin Ridge: *History, Frontier, and Section: Three Essays* (Albuquerque: University of New Mexico Press, 1993).

Unrau, William E.: *The White Man's Wicked Water: The Alcohol Trade and Prohibition in Indian Country, 1802–1892* (Lawrence: University of Kansas Press, 1996).

Weeks, William E.: *John Quincy Adams and American Global Empire* (Lexington: University of Kentucky Press, 1992).

Wiley, Peter Booth: *Yankees in the Land of the Gods: Commodore Perry and the Opening of Japan* (New York: Viking Penguin, 1991).

CHAPTER SIX

The United States and Imperialism

FRANK NINKOVICH

An understanding of imperialism needs to be built upon a solid foundation of reading in theory and in broad works of historical interpretation. While it is true that the debates about imperialism, like most scholarly discussions of large themes, are inconclusive, a critical familiarity with the arguments at least makes it possible to choose intelligently the conceptual ground upon which one stands. A good place to begin is Williams (1976: 132–3). Koebner and Schmidt (1965) trace the story from the time when the word was first applied to the policies of Napoleon III of France to the middle of the twentieth century. Mommsen (1980) provides concise summaries of the most important interpretive approaches. Osterhammel (1996) wrestles productively with some of the complexities that arise from attempts at conceptualization. The essays in Osterhammel and Mommsen (1986) are quite helpful. Thornton (1965) repays reading for its wealth of interesting ideas.

Many of the classic works also deserve to be consulted. Hobson (1902) remains important for its lucidly put, if factually suspect, argument that the causes of imperialism are traceable to the workings of special interests that are not necessarily essential to capitalism. V. I. Lenin's *Imperialism: The Last Stage of Capitalism* relies significantly upon Hobson to make the entirely different point, quickly adopted as the keystone of Marxist theory in the twentieth century, that imperialism was a consequence of capitalism's built-in need to find outlets for surplus capital. Economist Joseph Schumpeter's widely reprinted essay, "The Sociology of Imperialism," portrays imperialism as an "atavism," i.e., as the product of vestigial premodern military institutions. Schumpeter's argument that capitalism is a peaceful social order is usefully read as a liberal rebuttal to the Leninist thesis.

In addition, it is helpful to be able to put American imperialism into comparative perspective. The European experience was far grander in scale, but how exactly it differed in administration, economic features, geopolitical implications, and cultural impact remains to be addressed. Carr and Hopkins (1993) is a magisterial work. Comparisons with Great Britain can be found in Darby (1987) and Smith (1981). Two broad and insightful studies are Fieldhouse (1965: 138–47) and Doyle (1986). Semmel (1960), a classic study of how British imperialism was linked to leftist ideologies, stimulates thinking about the relationship between progressive thought and empire in the United States. There are also a host of good studies of French, German, Russian, and Japanese imperialism.

For many scholars, imperialism is not restricted solely to the exercise of formal colonial control. An extraordinarily influential concept holds that "informal empire" can be cemented largely by means of economic contacts. The classic source of this argument is Robinson and Gallagher, with Denny (1961). A more succinct statement of their views, along with critiques, can be found in Louis (1976), but see also Landes (1972: 134–8). Semmel (1970) gives an excellent account of anti-colonial liberal ideology in Great Britain.

The idea that imperialism is essentially economic in nature has had many radical offshoots, most of which sprouted up after World War II following the rapid decolonization of the world. The failure of many newly independent nations to achieve political stability or economic prosperity led to a school of thought – most often categorized under the heading of neocolonialism or dependency theory – which argued that imperialism had reverted to informal or non-political modes of control. Circa 1950, the Argentine economist Raul Prebisch, associated with the UN's Economic Commission on Latin America, put forth the case for what came to be known as "dependency theory," which argued that international trade was the principal cause of underdevelopment. The works of Fernando Cardoso and Johan Galtung provide important statements of this thesis, but the most influential arguments for dependency theory have come in the numerous writings of Andre Gunder Frank. Insisting that "third world" poverty was no accident, but instead the consequence of the systematic "development of underdevelopment," he argued that non-industrial societies would remain hewers of wood and drawers of water as long as they were attached to the capitalist center. Perhaps the most seminal of his many works is *Capitalism and Underdevelopment in Latin America* (1967).

By the 1970s these perspectives were modified and incorporated into a more ambitious interpretation known as world-system theory, which was inspired by the writings of the sociologist Immanuel Wallerstein, first in his *The Modern World System I* (1974) and subsequently in many elaborations and refinements. According to this interpretation, continuing backwardness was the consequence of the structural requirement of the capitalist "world system" for an underdeveloped periphery. An excellent place to begin exploring the arguments for and against this approach is Shannon (1989).

The concept of informal empire lies squarely at the center of historical debate about American imperialism. It is undeniable that the United States was an imperial power, but historians have not been able to agree on important questions. Was imperialism an accidental minor episode or did it flow ineluctably from an earlier history of expansion? Did the US continue on an imperialist course even after it had abandoned its colonial possessions? The different answers given to these kinds of questions are attributable, to a significant degree, to the way that imperialism is defined. The historian most influential in articulating the continuity thesis is William Appleman Williams, founder of the Open Door school of interpretation which enjoyed great popularity in the 1960s and 1970s, largely as a result of widespread dissatisfaction with the Vietnam War. In a series of works, which include *The Tragedy of American Diplomacy and the Roots of the American Empire* (1969), Williams outlined his thesis that a constant preoccupation with economic expansion, under the ideological banner of the Open Door, was intended to meet the needs of a capitalist system. Domestic crises of overproduction, which were structurally rooted in an unequal distribution of income, could be resolved only by opening up new markets overseas. Americans were confident about the ability of the nation's economic power to control and shape other societies as dependencies in an "Open World." Inevitably, however, Washington's support of American economic expansion abroad had adverse political consequences. It led to frictions with other powers, generated revolutionary unrest, and in the end produced war. For an intellectual biography of Williams, see Buhle and Rice-Maxim (1995). A good introduction to his work is provided by Berger (1992).

According to Williams, the felt need for economic expansion was not a product of economic determinism. Instead, he argued that a *Weltanschauung*, the ideology or worldview shared by the elites that made US foreign policy, was the proximate cause of expansion, though in so doing he failed to show why it was that economic preoccupations necessarily dominated their thinking. However, this emphasis on a rationally changeable worldview, which suggested that policymaking was a voluntarist process, clearly positioned his critique within the progressive tradition of historiography. Williams' best-known student, who has surpassed the master in the quantity and quality of his historical output while continuing to promote the basic line of interpretation laid down by Williams, is Walter LaFeber. His *The New Empire* (1963) remains the most closely argued statement of the Wisconsin School on behalf of the continuity thesis, though the argument of continuity is more subtle than this simple statement makes it appear. LaFeber's *The American Search for Opportunity, 1865–1913* (1993) provides a more mature statement of his views on this critical era. Kiernan (1978) is a work by a European historian who attempts to put the American experience into a more deterministic Marxist framework.

A rather different historiographical tradition sees American imperialism as a short-lived phenomenon that resulted from the convergence of some unique historical circumstances. The long-dominant account is May (1973), which argues that President William McKinley was on the fence until he became convinced that public opinion favored empire. May (1968) takes the next step by trying to explain why the American public thirsted for empire in the 1890s. This pioneering application of social scientific public opinion theory argues that Americans were influenced by the thinking of a cosmopolitan opinion elite that followed changing political and intellectual fashions in Europe in the 1880s, when imperialism came into vogue. Surprisingly, to date no one has tested this thesis, all the more so as it prefigures the new wave of scholarly interest in globalization. In a far more critical manner, Kennan (1950) makes the "realist" case that an irrational public opinion was at work in the war with Spain.

More recently, interpretations centering on gender, a term that connotes cultural definitions of manhood and womanhood, have begun to make their presence felt. An important new work that provides insights into jingoism – an aspect of public opinion often mentioned but rarely analyzed – is Hoganson (1998). Why were Americans so enthusiastic for war and empire? One must look to American definitions of manhood, says Hoganson. For a general discussion of the connection between gender and imperialism, see "Empires and Intimacies" (2001). However, once again we stand to benefit by consulting the work dealing with the British experience. Ronald Hyam's *Empire and Sexuality* (1992) has no American counterpart, a shortcoming that, one hopes, will soon be remedied. McClintock (1994) looks at Victorian Britain from a feminist perspective in which imperialism becomes a vehicle for patriarchy.

Gender is but one way of applying cultural analysis to the study of imperialism. Another new approach emphasizes the study of language and rhetoric, or, more trendily, "discourse." Some notable examples are Kaplan and Pease (1993), Spurr (1993), Rowe (2000), and, for Great Britain, MacDonald (1994).

More exciting for its potential to explore hitherto closed regions of the imperial experience is a new emphasis on intercultural contacts. Many of the essays in Joseph, Legrand, and Salvatore (1998) are excellent examples of this new approach. Not only does the emphasis on culture as opposed to high politics offer a broader perspective on imperial contacts, but these kinds of studies also have the virtue of providing two-sided looks at events and thus have the potential to broaden enormously our understanding of what went on at a people-to-people level. Yet, for all its virtues, this kind of approach is micro-historical in emphasis. It remains to be seen how well it can illuminate larger themes or draw convincing connections between culture, the policymaking process, and global events.

Finally, there is another theoretical style that goes under the name of "postcolonial studies" or "subaltern studies." Following in the footsteps of Edward Said's influential *Orientalism* (1978), which argued that Western scholarship never really took pains to understand the oriental "other," a diverse group of scholars has attempted to correct the imbalance. The theory used by many of the writers, which mixes postmodernism, feminism, Marxism, and racial theory in varying degrees, can be frustratingly opaque and off-putting when presented in an intentionally obscure form. But there is no quarreling with their insistence that the colonized "other" has an identity that is deserving of serious historical exploration. The same holds true for the need to explore the ways in which colonial subjects accepted, rejected, and modified foreign institutions and values, not to mention the impact that colonialism had upon the self-definition of the colonizers. One might do well to start with Ashcroft et al. (1989) and Ashcroft, Griffiths, and Tiffin (1995). Appadurai (1996) is quite stimulating and written in an accessible style. Bhabha (1990) and his *Location of Culture* are far more dense yet quite influential. For a sampling of the influential work of Gayatri Chakravorty Spivak, see Landry and MacLean (1996).

Quick background on American imperialism can be found by consulting the essays and entries in the following reference works: DeConde (1978), Jentleson and Peterson (1997), Findling (1989), and Flanders (1993). As one might expect of such a controversial topic, these essays are more useful as guides to the literature than for stating definitive points of view. Crapol (2000) provides a fine critical survey of the literature. De Santis (1981) is still valuable for its critique.

Surprisingly, there are few scholarly overviews of American imperialism. For a classic indictment of many of the traditional arguments, see Field (1978: 665). Pratt (1950) remains useful for its down-to earth explication of the details of colonial administration. A more recent general interpretation is Ninkovich (2000). Imperialism is here defined very broadly as occupying a continuum between outright colonialism and informal empire. This work also tries to situate imperialism within a broader context of US foreign relations by viewing it as but one facet of America's response to globalization.

A key issue in the historical debate over American imperialism is whether the imperialist surge of the 1890s was a natural outgrowth of a century of overland expansion. Were the 1890s an aberration or a product of historical continuity? The issue is important because it colors one's view of the history of US foreign relations as a whole. If one perceives continuity, then one is more likely to sympathize with the view that imperialism is a central theme of US foreign relations. If not, one is likely to see imperialism as only one element, albeit an important one, of broader national and international processes. One's position on imperialism is also a marker of where one is likely to stand on a host of interpretive and methodological issues: e.g., on the relative importance of internal and external causes, structures and ideas, opinions and interests, economic and political factors, culture and ideology, individuals and social forces, necessity, contingency, irony, voluntarism, the role of historian as critic, and so on. Unfortunately, there is no study that convincingly treats the similarities and differences between republican and industrial expansion and the relationship of imperialism thereto.

The works of Williams and LaFeber cited above are canonical texts of the continuity argument. Albert Weinberg's *Manifest Destiny* is somewhat dated but remains an important work that is still well worth reading for its discussion of American exceptionalism. Williams (1980) argues – rather too simplistically, in my opinion – that there is a direct causal connection between US policy toward Native Americans and colonial expansion. Stephanson (1995) also sees continuity at work, although he places greater emphasis on the role of religion and the American belief that the nation's global spread was God-given.

Frederick Merk, in his classic *Manifest Destiny and Mission in American History* (1963), argues that the two periods of expansion were fundamentally different because overland expansion was the product of republican land hunger in which new territories were being added to the national domain with the expectation that they would eventually become equal states in the federal Union. Perkins (1993) calls this a period of "republican expansion." Johannsen (1985) highlights the degree to which republican ideology was at work in this war. Merk stressed land hunger as a primal drive among American settlers, but Graebner (1955) cautions against single-factor explanation by arguing convincingly that the desire to expand the nation's maritime commerce across the Pacific was also at work in the expansionist outburst of the 1840s. Thomas A. Hietala's *Manifest Design* looks at racial fears, Anglophobia, and fear of economic constriction as reasons for expansion. Graebner (1968) contains some useful introductory materials. Other notable works on overland expansion are Billington and Ridge (1982) and Goetzmann (1966).

Many historians believe that racism was a driving force in both periods of expansion, though some have argued that racism worked more against expansion than for it. For the early development of the sense of global Anglo-Saxon mission, see Horsman (1981: 272–97). It seems clear, however, that the imperialist position on race was moderate when compared to other racialist points of view. Most imperialists seemed to favor Lamarckism, which was the reigning scientific outlook in the 1890s. Lamarckism was a hybrid concept that combined race and culture – concepts that today are rigidly separated – in such a way that learned characteristics were thought to be hereditarily transmissible. Consequently, the "civilizing mission" found support in the scientific understanding of the day. On the emergence of Lamarckian thought, see Stocking (1968) and Bowler (1983).

Not surprisingly, the perceptions of African Americans on the relationship between race and empire have differed significantly from those of white Americans.

Gatewood (1975) looks at the conflicted images of American blacks. For the mid-century years, see Von Eschen (1997). An important new work that draws connections between perceptions of race, imperialism, and geopolitics is Gallicchio (2000). Borstelmann (2001) provides an excellent overview of more recent developments, though he concentrates primarily upon Africa.

Social Darwinism is another frequently mentioned cause of imperialism. For example, Karsten (1972) argues that US naval officers looked at the world from a perspective that fused Darwinian notions of competition with sentiments of Anglo-Saxon solidarity. However, this ritualistic formulation is past due for reassessment. In domestic policy, where it is used as a synonym for a laissez-faire approach to society and politics, Social Darwinism fits very well. But when applied to American images of international relations, it is quite misleading. The problems are evident in the classic study by Hofstadter, *Social Darwinism in American Thought* (1955), whose last chapter, in particular, runs together a number of concepts that fit together uneasily, if at all. Bannister (1979) makes it quite clear that applications of European conceptions of Social Darwinism to the American context find little support in the thinking of American imperialists. Indeed, a sizable body of work demonstrates that Social Darwinism had little connection to *European* imperialism. Unfortunately, the reception of Bannister's attempt to rethink the historical meaning of Social Darwinism in the American context has been less enthusiastic than the pathbreaking quality of the work deserves.

A good deal of the confusion results from the tendency to equate Social Darwinism with the evolutionary thinking of Herbert Spencer. Spencer's ideas on the internal workings of society were indeed quite Darwinian, but in foreign affairs they translated into a liberal advocacy of free trade, anti-militarism, and anti-imperialism. For the confusion between Darwinism and Spencerianism, see Bowler (1988: 156–65). Darwinism was part of a wider current of evolutionist thought in the late nineteenth century, much of which was progressive in character. This current could drift in an imperialist direction, but it could just as well take an anti-imperialist turn depending on the circumstances. In support of this view, see Crook (1994). For other important discussions of evolutionism, see Stocking (1987) and Burrow (1966). That being said, Spencerian liberalism, like liberalism today, could be quite harsh when applied to the analysis of relations between cultures at different levels of material development. The idea of "creative destruction," often applied to the description of change within free market societies, appeared to be the governing outlook in intercultural affairs as well.

Works on the 1890s are more closely attuned to particular circumstances and the unpredictable play of events. General works on the 1890s are Brands (1995), a lively account. Healy (1970) is in the Open Door school of interpretation. Offner (1992) is the standard work detailing the diplomatic events that led to the war. Other useful accounts are Leech (1959), Morgan (1965), and Gould (1980). Unfortunately, our understanding of McKinley remains spotty and is not likely to improve much over time given the scarcity of archival sources.

Pratt (1936) is a multi-causal account that is especially notable for its yet-to-be-refuted demonstration that American business interests were not in favor of imperial expansion until the summer of 1898. Those who believe that imperialism was economically motivated have always had to contend with Pratt's work. For the older view that "yellow journalism," and in particular the circulation war in New York City between the Pulitzer and Hearst newspapers, caused the war, see Wisan (1934) and Brown (1967). In a classic essay on "Cuba, the Philippines, and Manifest Destiny" (1997), Richard Hofstadter located the source of American imperialism in what he called the "psychic crisis" of the 1890s. The US was in such disarray, he argued, that the resulting "status anxieties" found an aggressive outlet in foreign policy. A recent Columbia University dissertation by Michelle Morgan, "Imperialists of 1898: Transatlantic Conceptions of American Expansion," reveals the hitherto unacknowledged role played by imperialist English naval figures.

Pérez (1998) takes dead aim at those historians who continue to believe that a jingoist public opinion was the cause of the war. It provides a scathing critique of the existing historiography of the war and it makes a compelling case for seeing it as a three-sided Cuban–Spanish–American conflict in which the Cuban rebels were major actors in their own right. His argument that the United States was guided by traditional interests is less novel but cannot be ignored. An interesting compendium of recent research is provided in Bouvier (2001). By underscoring the importance of the war in defining American identities, Bouvier shies away from interest-based interpretations. Rystad (1975) is a detailed examination of how imperialism played out in domestic politics.

The best account of the military side of the war is Trask (1981), but see also Musicant (1998), Tebbel (1996), and Traxel (1998). Some useful essays can still be found in Miller (1970).

No study of American imperialism would be complete without a consideration of Theodore Roosevelt and other proponents of a "Large Policy" who saw a connection between imperialism and world power. Some important biographical treatments of TR are Brands (1997) and Morris, *Mornings on Horseback*. A major new work on Roosevelt is Dalton (2001), which provides a badly needed sense of proportion in our views of Roosevelt. She argues, among other things, that the War of 1898 would have occurred without his presence on the scene and that our views of TR as an avid imperialist need to be counterbalanced by an understanding of his internationalism.

Still chock-full of information and perhaps the leading treatment of TR as a realist is Beale (1956). A hagiographic account of TR as realist is provided by Marks (1979). Easy to caricature, TR was in fact a quite complicated figure. For Roosevelt as an internationalist who was guided by a belief in civilization, see Ninkovich (1986). In differing ways, Roosevelt's cultural side is emphasized in Burton (1968) and Collin (1985). Dyer (1980) drives home the point that, for his time, TR held progressive views on race.

Important studies of Roosevelt's response to the diplomacy of imperialism in Asia are Neu (1967) and Esthus (1970). On Henry Cabot Lodge, who was a more important political figure than TR in 1898 and 1899, see Widenor (1980). Braeman (1971) is the standard account of this important pro-imperialist progressive.

The ease with which the empire fell into the nation's hands was balanced by the difficulty in coming to terms with it. For the debate on empire, Beisner (1968) is unlikely soon to be surpassed as the dominant account. For the domestic response to the conflict in the Philippines, Welch (1965) is standard, but see also Tompkins, Osborne (1981), Graff (1969), Schirmer (1972), and Zwick.

The Philippines were America's most prominent colonial possession. For an excellent critical survey of the scholarship on the relationship, see May (1996: 286). Brands (1992) is an excellent overview, though like most works it is far stronger on the pre-World War II years. Karnow (1989) is also useful, though not as methodical and well organized as Brands. Schirmer and Shalom (1987) provides some interesting documents. Stanley (1984) has some important essays.

On the Filipino-American war, see Miller (1982), Wolff (1991), Linn (1902), and May (1983). Glenn A. May's *Battle for Batangas* (1991) is an account notable for its two-sided look at the war. De Bevoise (1995) is useful in sorting out the issue of how and why so many Filipinos died during the war. Some hot-button issues are addressed in Welch (1974).

For the early years, Peter Stanley's *A Nation in the Making* (1974) still provides the best account of American thinking. Minger (1975) provides a solid account of the outlook of William Howard Taft, who was the first US Governor-General of the islands. May (1980) is the best recounting of attempts to put into practice the civilizing mission. Salamanca (1968) looks at developments from the other side. Clymer (1986) explores the half-hearted and only marginally successful attempt to Christianize the predominantly Catholic Filipinos. Friend (1965) covers the years leading to independence.

Given the many pie-in-the-sky predictions in 1898 about the economic advantages of annexing the Philippines, it is important to get a sense of how much of an economic stake the US developed in the islands. On this issue, see Pringle (1980), Jenkins (1954), and Irvine (1959). Pomeroy (1970) is interesting not only for its Marxist perspective but also for its frank acknowledgment of the difficulty of explaining the US–Philippine relationship in terms of the profit-motive.

The literature on the relationship during the independence period is rather thin. Cullather (1994) is easily the best work on the post-World War II relationship. As the title suggests, the author believes that neocolonialism is not the best way of conceptualizing a relationship that was driven, from the American side, by geopolitical motives, and, on the Philippine side, by the remarkable ability of a small elite to manipulate the Americans to suit their interests. Overall, despite its frequently high level of quality, one is impressed by the one-sidedness of the literature. No doubt the future will bring studies that provide us with deeper insights into the Filipino dimension.

In contrast to the manageable body of scholarship on US–Philippine relations, the literature on Latin America is immense. Among the many overviews that, for different reasons, cannot be ignored are Gilderhus (2000), Langley (1992), Schoultz (1998), Smith (1996), Coatsworth (1994), LaFeber (1983), Blasier (1985), Schmitz (1999), and Lowenthal (1991). Pérez (1982) is also well worth consulting.

American images of Latin America were at least as important as "interests" in shaping US policy toward the region. A good account is Berger (1995). Johnson (1980) offers abundant evidence from the cartoon literature of the many ways in which Latin Americans were stereotyped. But the study of images takes one only so far. An excellent work that goes beyond images to take a hard look at American-promoted social and economic development in the region is O'Brien (1996). For better or worse, American imperialism has been associated with the protection of corporate interests like those of the United Fruit Company. For some surprising twists and turns in the US government's relationship with United Fruit, see Dosal (1993).

For the early years of the twentieth century, see Healy (1988), Langley (1983), and Perkins (1981: 160). Munro (1964, 1974) offer accounts sympathetic to the official US position. For the 1920s, Johnson (1994) offers some new insights. Wood (1961) remains an important work, but should be read in conjunction with Gellman (1979).

The literature on the post-World War II period is too large to summarize conveniently in this essay. Some useful and suggestive works are Rabe (1999), Latham (1998), Domínguez, Pastor, and Worrell (1993), and May (1998). There is, in addition, a large monographic literature on relations with specific countries.

The United States became an imperial power in the Caribbean with its occupation of Cuba (1899–1902) and the imposition of the Platt Amendment. Incorporated into the Cuban Constitution until its abrogation in 1934, the Platt Amendment made Cuba a formal protectorate by giving the United States the right to intervene in Cuba and to control Cuba's foreign policy. Healy (1963) chronicles the occupation period. For an account sympathetic to the technocratic reformism of the US army, see Millett (1968). Lane, *Armed Progressive: General Leonard Wood* and Hagedorn (1969) are valuable for their treatment of Wood, the military governor of Cuba, who believed, unlike many of his countrymen, that Cuba could be groomed for statehood. Lockmiller (1938) continues the story of US attempts to transform Cuba.

For the relationship as it developed subsequently, see Benjamin (1977). The work of Luis A. Pérez, Jr. has been particularly valuable for telling the story of the war from the standpoint of Cubans, who all too often have been treated as marginal figures: see Pérez (1986, 1990). Other useful works are Hernández's *Cuba and the United States* and Gellman (1973).

Central to the image of Yanquí imperialism in Latin America was the virtual annexation of the Canal Zone in Panama. Marks (1979: 96–105) makes a spirited (perhaps recklessly so) defense of TR's seizure of Panama. LaFeber (1989) is the best survey. The early story is told compellingly by McCullough (1977). Major (1993) is the best account of the canal's construction; see also Hogan (1986) and also Ealy (1971).

The United States also conducted lengthy occupations of the Dominican Republic (1916–24) and the adjoining republic of Haiti (1915–34); see Calder (1984) and Schmidt (1971). Renda (2001) takes another look from the standpoint of race and gender.

The acquisition of Puerto Rico was not much debated in the decision for empire, and historians have since done little to end the silence. Although it seems reasonable to infer that Puerto Rico's strategic value as a base astride a vital approach to a new isthmian canal had something to do with it, there can be no certainty until historians delve into the archives and unearth the evidence. For the ways in which the US assumed control and governed the island, see Wells (1969), Carr (1984), the relevant sections of Johnson (1988), Fernandez (1992), and, for a gendered view, Findlay (1999).

The literature on US relations with China is a scholarly world unto itself. Despite the huge body of work, with the exception of the Open Door historians there has

been surprisingly little effort to situate US–Chinese relations within a larger history
of imperialism. Much of the earlier work had an idealistic tinge that focused on
American opposition to the diplomacy of imperialism in China to the neglect of the
widespread belief in the civilizing righteousness of the treaty-port imperialism in
which the US was a full participant. The essays in Cohen (1996) provide indispensable historiographical overviews for specific periods of the relationship, especially
Michael Hunt's essay, "New Insights But No New Vistas." Somewhat earlier but by
no means outdated is the review by Akira Iriye, "Americanization of East Asia:
Writings on Cultural Affairs Since 1900."

One could do worse than begin with the classic survey by John King Fairbank,
The United States and China (1983). Cohen (1990) continues to hold its place as
the standard survey. The dominant overview of US–Chinese relations to 1914 is
Hunt (1983), notable for its pioneering reliance on Chinese-language sources.
Thomson, Stanley, and Perry (1982) remains popular, but is flawed because of its
outmoded emphasis on sentimentality to the neglect of more serious themes. An
element central to the imperial relationship was the extraterritoriality regime that
shielded Americans from Chinese law, which is ably studied by Scully (2001).
Schaller (1979a) remains useful as a quick survey.

For a discussion of some of the tensions and contradictions that plagued the
simultaneous pursuit of treaty port imperialism and developmentalism, see Anderson
(1985). Varg's *Missionaries, Chinese, and Diplomats* still provides a good introduction to the nineteenth-century relationship. Reed (1983) focuses on an important
interest group at a critical point in time. Women, particularly the wives of missionaries, played a significant role in people-to-people relations. An especially sensitive
account is Hunter (1984), while Scully (2001) shows that other kinds of women,
including prostitutes, also played a significant role.

An influential statement of the thesis that American relations with China were
economically driven is McCormick (1967). A more balanced view of economic
factors is provided by Campbell (1951). On the gap between the desires of Open
Door ideologues and the limited willingness of the government to pursue them, see
Young (1968).

For the immediate post-1900 period, Israel (1971) chronicles the emergence of a
more serious interest in China's modernization. McKee (1977) covers a tumultuous
period. Hunt (1973) is a seminal work that gives equal weight to the Chinese side.
Hunt's important essay (1972) shatters forever the view that the Boxer remission
was an act of pure idealism.

Historians of US–Chinese relations have long been interested in the cultural
dimension of the relationship, a pioneering approach that is now being widely
applied to other aspects of US foreign relations. For some early examples, see
Fairbank (1975) and Chi-Pao Cheng (1965). While avoiding cultural analysis per se,
Iriye (1967) studies mutual images based on readings of source materials in China,
Japan, and the United States to throw significant light on complex interactions. The
relevance of images to an understanding of international relations was given its
seminal statement in Isaacs (1980). For some more recent applications, see Jesperson
(1996) and also the essays in Goldstein, Israel, and Conroy (1991).

The desire to modernize China by generating a cultural revolution has been a
constant feature of the American side of US–Chinese relations. Bullock (1980) is an

excellent account of a prominent attempt to promote modernization through education in scientific medicine. Ninkovich (1984) looks at some modernizing initiatives in the 1920s and 1930s. Ninkovich (1980) is an attempt to draw some explicit connections between cultural and political relations for the World War II years. Cohen (1992) shows how the trans-Pacific cultural relationship developed at the institutional and artistic levels. Spence (1969) and Thomson (1969) are notable descriptions of attempts to modernize China from the outside.

With the coming of World War I, the US–Chinese relationship merges into the study of diplomatic history on a global scale. The years following World War I brought tumultuous changes in the US–China relationship. Iriye (1990) is a now-classic account of how the optimistic quest for great power cooperation broke down in the course of the 1920s. Dorothy Borg's works (1947, 1964) remain indispensable.

The US relationship with China reached new heights of intimacy during World War II by virtue of the alliance against Japan. Nevertheless, serious tensions emerged between the partners as a result of Chiang Kai-shek's perceived refusal to adopt a modernizing approach to governance that, many Americans believed, would pay dividends in a more robust war effort. For some accounts of this turbulent relationship, see Tuchman (1971), Schaller (1979b), and Tang Tsou's *America's Failure in China*. In the post-World War II years, one could argue that imperialism disappeared as the newly created People's Republic of China flaunted its sovereignty and cultural autonomy. However, Taiwan remained a military and, to some extent, cultural protectorate of the United States. For this story, consult Tucker (1994)

John King Fairbank's memoirs, *Chinabound* (1982), provide an enthralling account from the scholar who pioneered the modern academic study of China and was personally involved in the tumultuous domestic politics surrounding China's postwar turn to communism. The biographies of many of the China specialists in the Department of State who were caught up in the political firestorm also make for instructive reading, not least for their recollections of their experiences in China.

Despite the almost complete severance of contact between the PRC and the US, many American institutions with deep historical ties to China refused to abandon the dream of cultural transformation. That story is told in outline form by Warren Cohen in "While China Faced East: Chinese-American Cultural relations, 1949–71." The rocky geopolitical relationship is well-analyzed by Chang (1990).

Imperialism involves a relationship between the imperial power and its dependency, but it also brings with it relations with other imperial powers, a diplomacy of imperialism. There are two contrasting points of view on this topic. The first, connected to the economic school of interpretation, sees world politics as a function of imperial drives and imperialist competition. An understanding of imperialism therefore has the bonus of explaining world politics. The second, and contrasting, perspective sees imperialism and anti-imperialism as only one hue in the broader palette of world politics. The problem, if one adopts this second perspective, is to figure out where and how imperialism "fits" into the larger picture as a complicating causal factor.

Still very useful in providing the diplomatic context of international history at the *fin de siècle* is Langer (1972). It is clear from Langer's detailed account that at this time the United States was still a bit player in a global drama. The United States first became involved in the diplomacy of imperialism as a treaty power in China, but with its acquisition of the Philippines it became more active in promoting the Open Door policy, which was intended to maintain the imperialist status quo in China. Most of the works cited above in the section on China touch upon this topic.

Anti-imperialism is a topic that has received insufficient attention from historians. It has been neglected by realists and radicals alike; by the first, as a result of the belief that it was an unimportant symptom of a more general susceptibility to idealism; by the second, because, in their minds, American imperialism overshadowed all other outlooks. Although a solid beginning has been made in the works of Beisner, Tompkins, and Zwick cited above, our understanding of this phenomenon quickly turns hazy after the first decade of the twentieth century. Leuchtenberg (1952) makes the point, still commonly accepted, that progressives were originally in favor of empire. But sometime around World War I progressivism and liberalism began to take on an anti-imperialist cast as intellectuals like Walter Lippmann and Walter Weyl began to argue that imperialism had been the chief cause of World War I.

Anti-imperialism first emerges as a strain of geopolitical thinking in the US during the presidency of Woodrow Wilson, formerly an enthusiast for empire. By the time of the Great War, Wilson had come to believe that imperialism was partly, but not exclusively, responsible for the war. His chief objection to empire was thus geopolitical in character. The ideological bifurcation between geopolitical and progressive interpretations of the war as an imperialist event is made clear in Lasch (1972), in Levin's still influential *Woodrow Wilson and World Politics* (1968), and to a lesser extent in Herman (1969). However, new studies of the expectations and disappointments generated by Wilsonian rhetoric are sorely needed. The role of anti-imperialism in Wilsonian foreign policy still awaits its historian.

For the postwar period, Johnson (1995) is a pioneering attempt to describe the connection between progressivism and anti-imperialism in the 1920s. Interestingly, he makes the point that many of them lapsed into isolationism in the 1930s. Johnson takes a closer look at a single anti-imperialist in his *Ernest Gruening and the American Dissenting Tradition* (1998). For a critical view from the left, see Nearing and Freeman (1969).

Anti-imperialism emerges more robustly as a mainstream element of US policy during World War II. The works of Christopher Thorne are indispensable guides to the diplomacy of imperialism in the 1930s and after. See in particular his *Allies of a Kind* (1978). Louis (1978) remains the major work on this theme. For insights into Franklin D. Roosevelt's anti-imperialism, see portions of Warren Kimball's *The Juggler* (1991). Jeffreys-Jones (1983) contains some interesting essays. Gary Hess' *America Encounters India, 1941–1947* (1971) tells the story of America's position towards Great Britain's most important colony.

The often conflicting American attitudes toward imperialism from the time of World War II and after are the subject of a growing literature. Robert J. McMahon's books, *The Limits of Empire* (1999) and *Colonialism and Cold War* (1981), are must reading. Despite a declared policy of opposition to imperialism, to its embarrassment the United States often found itself on the wrong side of the issue after World War II as a result of overriding Cold War imperatives. For this aspect of the story, see Bills (1990), Brands (1989), Borstelmann (1993), and Hahn (1991).

On Vietnam, a notable new work by Mark Bradley, *Imagining Vietnam and*

America (2000), argues that American relations with Vietnam need to be understood from within a larger historical perspective of racial condescension and Western imperialism. Another work that explores cultural themes is Christian G. Appy's *Cold War Constructions* (2000). The idea of imperialism is placed in a first-world context by Geir Lundestad, whose *United States and the World, 1945–1989* (1989) posits an "empire by invitation" that arose when the United States was seduced by Europe into playing an imperial role on the continent after World War II.

The postwar triumph of decolonization and the end of the Cold War's diplomacy of imperialism did not bring an end to critiques of imperialism in American foreign policy. With the spotlight of attention now focused on globalization as the key international phenomenon of the age, dependency theory and world-systems theory have metamorphosed into a general critique of globalization. For some preliminary readings, see Hopkins (2002), Appadurai (2001), and Held and McGrew (2000).

Many analyses of globalization are quite critical. While the works in this genre are too numerous to list here, Greider (1997) and Gray (1998) provide good starting points. An influential postmodern attempt to update Marxism by pushing beyond the boundaries of Leninist analysis is Hardt and Negri's *Empire* (2000). The title is somewhat misleading, as the authors argue that the natural result of globalization is neither imperialism nor war.

But globalization also has many defenders, who see in its continued development the best hope for human freedom and prosperity. Thus it is not uncommon to see calls for a return to imperialism, under the cover of international organization, as a way of dealing with "failed states" that have been unable to cope with the new global order. This would seem to suggest that globalization is a direct consequence of American imperialism, but it is not clear that this is in fact the case. It is not simply a matter of imperialism being replaced or succeeded by globalization. It is also possible to rewrite the history of imperialism as but one episode in a long process of globalization in which the United States has played an important, and perhaps even decisive, role.

In any event, globalization has pushed debates about American imperialism in new directions. In the past, imperialism has been associated with the existence of polyglot empires in which cultural pluralism was generally accepted; if not, however, it was then usually dealt with by forceful attempts at conversionism. In the modern era, however, the civilizing mission is ruthlessly anti-cultural and anti-particularist, but it is at the same time more dependent on voluntary acceptance than coercion for its success. Partly because of this tendency, the perceived importance of the cultural dimension has increased. As traditional colonialism has waned, the tendency in historical scholarship has been away from structural and economic forms of explanation in favor of cultural modes of analysis. Many of the theoretical approaches dealt with in the opening section of this essay focus on such cultural themes. John Tomlinson's *Globalization and Culture* (1999) centers on this controversial aspect of globalization, while his *Cultural Imperialism* (1991) connects previous debates about imperialism to contemporary global developments. The new concerns are evident in many of the essays found in Hogan (2000). LaFeber (1999), in defining the contemporary world in terms of a conflict between capitalism and culture, is a notable attempt at pouring old Open Door wine into the new bottle of globalization.

Where will the study of American imperialism go in future? The record of past debates on empire offers only limited help in answering that question. As the foregoing discussion makes clear, the scholarly literature on imperialism encompasses a broad array of research strategies and interpretive outlooks. It ranges from a focus on the simplest human encounters to events of world-historical proportions. It takes in relations between developed and underdeveloped peoples as well as relations among great powers; it encompasses the actions of domestic and transnational interest groups; it deals with issues of race, culture, gender, class, religion, political economy, and other social phenomena; it includes the study of ideas at a number of levels. When it comes to the future, nothing is certain except that our understanding of imperialism will continue to evolve. Yet, whatever paths imperialism takes in the future, its complex history suggests that the study of imperialism will continue to open fascinating conceptual windows to every conceivable dimension of international relations and world history.

REFERENCES

Anderson, David L.: *Imperialism and Idealism: American Diplomats in China, 1861–1898* (Bloomington: Indiana University Press, 1985).

Appadurai, Arjun: *Modernity at Large: Cultural Dimensions of Globalization* (Minneapolis: University of Minnesota Press, 1996).

Appadurai, Arjun (ed.): *Globalization* (Durham, NC: Duke University Press, 2001).

Appy, Christian G. (ed.): *Cold War Constructions: The Political Culture of United States Imperialism, 1945–1966* (Amherst: University of Massachusetts Press, 2000).

Ashcroft, Bill, Gareth Griffiths, and Helen Tiffin (eds.) *The Post-colonial Studies Reader* (New York: Routledge, 1995).

Ashcroft, Bill et al.: *The Empire Writes Back* (London: Routledge, 1989).

Bannister, Robert C.: *Social Darwinism: Science and Myth in Anglo-American Social Thought* (Philadelphia, PA: Temple University Press, 1979).

Beale, Howard K.: *Theodore Roosevelt and the Rise of the United States to World Power* (Baltimore, MD: Johns Hopkins University Press, 1956).

Beisner, Robert: *Twelve Against Empire: The Anti-Imperialists, 1898–1900* (New York: McGraw-Hill, 1968).

Benjamin, Jules: *The United States and Cuba: Hegemony and Dependent Development, 1880–1934* (Pittsburgh, PA: University of Pittsburgh Press, 1977).

Berger, Henry W.: *A William Appleman Williams Reader: Selections from his Major Historical Writings* (Chicago, IL: Ivan R. Dee, 1992).

Berger, Mark T.: *Under Northern Eyes: Latin American Studies and US Hegemony in the Americas 1898–1990* (Bloomington: Indiana University Press, 1995).

Bhabha, Homi (ed.): *Nation and Narration* (London: Routledge, 1990).

Bhabha, Homi: *The Location of Culture.*

Billington, Ray Allen and Martin Ridge: *Westward Expansion*, 5th edn. (New York, 1982).

Bills, Scott: *Empire and Cold War: The Roots of US–Third World Antagonism, 1945–1947* (New York: St. Martin's Press, 1990).

Blasier, Cole: *The Hovering Giant: US Responses to Revolutionary Change in Latin America, 1910–1985*, revd. edn. (Pittsburgh, PA: University of Pittsburgh Press, 1985).

Borg, Dorothy: *American Policy and the Chinese Revolution, 1925–1928* (New York: Macmillan, 1947).

Borg, Dorothy: *The United States and the Far Eastern Crisis of 1933–1938* (Cambridge, MA: Harvard University Press, 1964).

Borstelmann, Thomas: *Apartheid's Reluctant Uncle: The United States and South Africa in the Early Cold War* (New York: Oxford University Press, 1993).

Borstelmann, Thomas: *The Cold War and the Color Line: American Race Relations in the Global Arena* (Cambridge, 2001).

Bouvier, Virginia (ed.): *Whose America? The War of 1898 and the Battles to Define the Nation* (Baltimore, MD: Johns Hopkins University Press, 2001).

Bowler, Peter J.: *The Eclipse of Darwinism: Anti-Darwinian Evolution Theories in the Decade Around 1900* (Baltimore, MD, 1983).

Bowler, Peter J.: *The Non-Darwinian Revolution: Reinterpreting a Historical Myth* (Baltimore, MD: Johns Hopkins University Press, 1988).

Bradley, Mark: *Imagining Vietnam and America: The Making of Postcolonial Vietnam, 1919–1950* (Chapel Hill: University of North Carolina Press, 2000).

Braeman, John: *Albert Beveridge: American Nationalist* (Chicago, IL: University of Chicago Press, 1971).

Brands, H. W.: *The Specter of Neutralism:The United States and the Emergence of the Third World, 1947–1960* (New York: Columbia University Press, 1989).

Brands, H. W.: *Bound to Empire: The United States and the Philippines* (New York: Oxford University Press, 1992).

Brands, H. W.: *The Reckless Decade* (New York: St. Martin's Press, 1995).

Brands, H. W.: *TR: The Last Romantic* (New York: Basic Books, 1997).

Brown, Charles H.: *The Correspondents' War: Journalists in the Spanish–American War* (New York: Scribner, 1967).

Buhle, Paul M. and Edward Rice-Maxim: *William Appleman Williams and the Tragedy of Empire* (New York: Routledge, 1995).

Bullock, Mary Brown: *An American Transplant: The Rockefeller Foundation and Peking Union Medical College* (Berkeley: University of California Press, 1980).

Burrow, J. W.: *Evolution and Society: A Study in Victorian Social Theory* (Cambridge: Cambridge University Press, 1966).

Burton, David H.: *Theodore Roosevelt: Confident Imperialist* (Philadelphia, PA, 1968).

Calder, Bruce J.: *The Impact of Intervention: The Dominican Republic During the US Occupation of 1916–1924* (Austin: University of Texas Press, 1984).

Campbell, Charles S., Jr.: *Special Business Interests and the Open Door Policy* (New Haven, CT: Yale University Press, 1951).

Carr, P. J. and A. G. Hopkins: *British Imperialism*, 2 vols. (London, 1993).

Carr, Raymond: *Puerto Rico: A Colonial Experiment* (New York: Vintage Books, 1984).

Chang, Gordon: *Friends and Enemies: The United States, China, and the Soviet Union, 1948–1972* (Stanford, CA: Stanford University Press, 1990).

Chi-Pao Cheng (ed.): *Chinese American Cultural Relations* (New York: China Institute in America, 1965).

Clymer, Kenton J.: *Protestant Missionaries in the Philippines 1898–1916* (Urbana, IL, 1986).

Coatsworth, John H.: *Central America and the United States: The Clients and the Colossus* (New York: Twayne, 1994).

Cohen, Warren: *The United States and China* (New York: Columbia University Press, 1990).

Cohen, Warren: *East Asian Art and American Culture* (New York: Columbia University Press, 1992).

Cohen, Warren (ed.): *Pacific Passages: The Study of American–East Asian Relations on the Eve of the Twenty-First Century* (New York: Columbia University Press, 1996).

Cohen, Warren: "While China Faced East: Chinese–American Cultural Relations, 1949–71." In Joyce Kallgren and Simon, *Educational Exchanges*.

Collin, Richard: *Theodore Roosevelt, Culture, Diplomacy, and Expansion: A New View of American Imperialism* (Baton Rouge: Louisiana State University Press, 1985).

Crapol, Edward D.: "Coming to Terms With Empire: The Historiography of Late Nineteenth Century American Foreign Relations." In Michael J. Hogan (ed.) *Paths to Power: The Historiography of American Foreign Relations to 1941* (New York, 2000).

Crook, Paul: *Darwinism, War and History: The Debate Over the Biology of War from the 'Origin of Species' to the First World War* (Cambridge: Cambridge University Press, 1994).

Cullather, Nick: *Illusions of Influence: The Political Economy of United States–Philippine Relations, 1942–1960* (Stanford, CA: Stanford University Press, 1994).

Dalton, Kathleen: *Theodore Roosevelt: A Strenuous Life* (New York: Knopf, 2001).

Darby, Philip: *The Faces of Imperialism: British and American Approaches to Asia and Africa, 1870–1970* (New Haven, CT: Yale University Press, 1987).

De Bevoise, Ken: *Agents of Apocalypse: Epidemic Disease in the Philippines* (Princeton, NJ, 1995).

De Santis, Hugh: "The Imperialist Impulse and American Innocence, 1865–1900." In Gerald K. Haines and Samuel K. Walker (eds.) *American Foreign Relations: A Historiographical Review* (Westport, CT, 1981).

DeConde, Alexander (ed.) *Encyclopedia of American Foreign Policy: Studies of the Principal Movements and Ideas* (New York: Scribner, 1978).

Domínguez, Jorge I., Robert A. Pastor, and R. DeLisle Worrell (eds.) *Democracy in the Caribbean: Political, Economic, and Social Perspectives* (Baltimore, MD: Johns Hopkins University Press, 1993).

Dosal, Paul J.: *Doing Business With the Dictators: A Political History of United Fruit in Guatemala, 1899–1944* (Wilmington, DE: Scholarly Resources, 1993).

Doyle, Michael: *Empires* (Ithaca, NY: Cornell University Press, 1986).

Dyer, Thomas G.: *Theodore Roosevelt and the Idea of Race* (Baton Rouge: Louisiana State University Press, 1980).

Ealy, L. O.: *Yanqui Politics and the Isthmian Canal* (University Park: Pennsylvania State University Press, 1971).

"Empires and Intimacies: Lessons From (Post) Colonial Studies: A Round Table." *Journal of American History* 88 (December 2001), 829–93.

Esthus, Raymond: *Theodore Roosevelt and the International Rivalries* (Claremont, CA: Regina Books, 1970).

Fairbank, John King: *Chinese–American Interactions: A Historical Summary* (Rahway, NJ: Rutgers University Press, 1975).

Fairbank, John King: *Chinabound: A Fifty Year Memoir* (New York: Harper and Row, 1982).

Fairbank, John King: *The United States and China*, 4th edn., enlarged (Cambridge, MA: Harvard University Press, 1983).

Fernandez, Ronald: *The Disenchanted Island: Puerto Rico and the United States in the Twentieth Century* (Westport, CT: Praeger, 1992).

Field, James A., Jr.: "American Imperialism: The Worst Chapter in Almost Any Book." *American Historical Review* 83 (1978), 665.

Fieldhouse, D. K.: *The Colonial Empires: A Comparative Survey From the Eighteenth Century* (New York: Delacorte Press, 1965).

Findlay, Eileen Suarez: *Imposing Decency: The Politics of Sexuality and Race in Puerto Rico 1870–1920* (Durham, NC, 1999).

Findling, John E.: *Dictionary of American Diplomatic History*, 2nd edn. (New York: Greenwood Press, 1989).

Flanders, Stephen E.: *Dictionary of American Foreign Affairs* (New York: Macmillan, 1993).

Frank, Andre Gunder: *Capitalism and Underdevelopment in Latin America: Historical Studies of Chile and Brazil* (New York: Monthly Review Press, 1967).

Friend, Theodore: *Between Two Empires: The Ordeal of the Philippines, 1929–1946* (New Haven, CT: Yale University Press, 1965).

Gallicchio, Marc: *The African American Encounter with Japan and China: Black Internationalism in Asia, 1895–1945* (Chapel Hill: University of North Carolina Press, 2000).

Gatewood, William B., Jr.: *Black Americans and the White Man's Burden 1898–1903* (Urbana: University of Illinois Press, 1975).

Gellman, Irwin F.: *Roosevelt and Batista: Good Neighbor Diplomacy in Cuba* (Albuquerque: University of New Mexico Press, 1973).

Gellman, Irwin F.: *Good Neighbor Diplomacy: United States Policies in Latin America, 1933–1945* (Baltimore, MD: Johns Hopkins University Press, 1979).

Gilderhus, Mark T.: *The Second Century: US–Latin American Relations Since 1889* (Wilmington, DE: Scholarly Resources, 2000).

Goetzmann, William: *Exploration and Empire: The Explorer and the Scientist in the Winning of the American West* (New York: Knopf, 1966).

Goldstein, Jonathan, Jerry Israel, and Hilary Conroy (eds.) *America Views China: American Images of China Then and Now* (Bethlehem, PA: Lehigh University Press, 1991).

Gould, Lewis L.: *The Presidency of William McKinley* (Lawrence: University of Kansas Press, 1980).

Graebner, Norman: *Empire on the Pacific: A Study in American Continental Expansion* (New York, 1955).

Graebner, Norman (ed.): *Manifest Destiny* (Indianapolis, IN, 1968).

Graff, Henry F.: (ed.): *American Imperialism and the Philippine Insurrection* (Boston, MA: Little, Brown, 1969).

Gray, John: *False Dawn: The Delusions of Global Capitalism* (New York: New Press, 1998).

Greider, William: *One World Ready or Not: The Manic Logic of Global Capitalism* (New York: Simon and Schuster, 1997).

Hagedorn, Hermann: *Leonard Wood: A Biography* (New York: Kraus, 1969).

Hahn, Peter L.: *The United States, Great Britain, and Egypt, 1945 1916: Strategy and Diplomacy in the Early Cold War* (Chapel Hill: University of North Carolina Press, 1991).

Hardt, Michael and Antonio Negri: *Empire* (Cambridge, MA: Harvard University Press, 2000).

Healy, David: *The United States in Cuba, 1898–1902* (Madison: University of Wisconsin Press, 1963).

Healy, David: *US Expansionism: The Imperialist Urge in the 1890s* (Madison, 1970).

Healy, David: *Drive to Hegemony: The United States in the Caribbean 1898–1917* (Madison: University of Wisconsin Press, 1988).

Held, David and Anthony McGrew (eds.): *The Global Transformations Reader: An Introduction to the Globalization Debate* (Cambridge, MA: Blackwell, 2000).

Herman, Sondra: *Eleven against War: Studies in American Internationalist Thought, 1898–1921* (Stanford, CA: Stanford University Press, 1969).

Hernández, José M.: *Cuba and the United States: Intervention and Militarism, 1868–1933.*

Hess, Gary: *America Encounters India, 1941–1947* (Baltimore, MD: Johns Hopkins University Press, 1971).

Hietala, Thomas A.: *Manifest Design.*

Hobson, John: *Imperialism* (London, 1902).

Hofstadter, Richard: *Social Darwinism in American Thought* (Boston, MA: Beacon Press, 1955).

Hofstadter, Richard: "Cuba, the Philippines, and Manifest Destiny." In *The Paranoid Style in American Politics and Other Essays* (New York: Vintage Books, 1997).

Hogan, J. Michael: *The Panama Canal in American Politics: Domestic Advocacy and the Evolution of Policy* (Carbondale: Southern Illinois University Press, 1986).

Hogan, J. Michael (ed.): *The Ambiguous Legacy: US Foreign Relations in the "American Century"* (New York: Cambridge University Press, 2000).

Hoganson, Kristin L.: *Fighting for American Manhood: How Gender Politics Provoked the Spanish–American and Philippine–American War* (New Haven, CT: Yale University Press, 1998).

Hopkins, A. G. (ed.): *Globalization in World History* (London: Pimlico, 2002).

Horsman, Reginald: *Race and Manifest Destiny: The Origins of American Racial Anglo-Saxonism* (Cambridge, MA: Harvard University Press, 1981).

Hunt, Michael H.: "The American Remission of the Boxer Indemnity: A Reappraisal." *Journal of Asian Studies* 31 (May 1972).

Hunt, Michael H.: *Frontier Defense and the Open Door: Manchuria in Chinese–American Relations, 1885–1911* (New Haven, CT: Yale University Press, 1973).

Hunt, Michael H.: *The Making of a Special Relationship: The United States and China to 1914* (New York: Columbia University Press, 1983).

Hunter, Jane: *The Gospel of Gentility: American Women Missionaries in Turn-of-the-Century China* (New Haven, CT: Yale University Press, 1984).

Hyam Ronald: *Empire and Sexuality: The British Experience* (New York: St. Martin's Press, 1992).

Iriye, Akira: "Americanization of East Asia: Writings on Cultural Affairs Since 1900." In Warren Cohen (ed.) *New Frontiers in American–East Asian Relations.*

Iriye, Akira: *Across the Pacific: An Inner History of American–East Asian Relations* (New York: Harcourt, Brace, 1967).

Iriye, Akira: *After Imperialism: The Search for a New Order in the Far East, 1921–1931* (Chicago, IL: Imprint Publications, 1990).

Irvine, Reed J.: "American Trade with the Philippines." In Robert J. Barr (ed.) *American Trade With Asia and the Far East* (Milwaukee, WI: Marquette University Press, 1959).

Isaacs, Harold: *Scratches on Our Minds: American Views of China and India* (Armonk, NY: M. E. Sharpe, 1980).

Israel, Jerry: *Progressivism and the Open Door: America and China, 1905–1921* (Pittsburgh, PA: University of Pittsburgh Press, 1971).

Jeffreys-Jones, Rhodri: *Eagle Against Empire: American Opposition to European Imperialism* (Aix-en-Provence: Université de Provence, 1983).

Jenkins, Shirley: *American Economic Policy Toward the Philippines* (Stanford, CA: Stanford University Press, 1954).

Jentleson, Bruce W. and Thomas G. Peterson (eds.): *Encyclopedia of US Foreign Relations* (New York: Oxford University Press, 1997).

Jesperson, T. Christopher: *American Images of China 1931–1949* (Stanford, CA: Stanford University Press, 1996).

Johannsen, Robert H.: *To the Halls of the Montezumas: The Mexican War in the American Imagination* (New York: Oxford University Press, 1985).

Johnson, John H.: *Latin America in Caricature* (Austin: University of Texas Press, 1980).

Johnson, Robert David: *Ernest Gruening and the American Dissenting Tradition* (Cambridge, MA: Harvard University Press, 1988).

Johnson, Robert David: "The Transformation of Pan-Americanism." In Robert David Johnson (ed.) *On Cultural Ground: Essays in International History* (Chicago, IL: Imprint Publications, 1994).

Johnson, Robert David: *The Peace Progressives and American Foreign Relations* (Cambridge, MA: Harvard University Press, 1995).

Johnson, Robert David: *Ernest Gruening and the American Dissenting Tradition* (Cambridge, MA: Harvard University Press, 1998).

Joseph, Gilbert M., Catherine C. Legrand, and Ricardo D. Salvatore (eds.) *Close Encounters of Empire: Writing the Cultural History of US–Latin American Relations* (Durham, NC: Duke University Press, 1998).

Kaplan, Amy and Donald Pease (eds.) *Cultures of Imperialism* (Durham, NC: Duke University Press, 1993).

Karnow, Stanley: *In Our Image: America's Empire in the Philippines* (New York: Random House, 1989).

Karsten, Peter: *The Naval Aristocracy: The Golden Age of Annapolis and the Emergence of Modern American Navalism* (New York, 1972).

Kennan, George F.: *American Diplomacy 1900–1950* (Chicago, IL: University of Chicago Press, 1950).

Kiernan, V. G.: *America: The New Imperialism* (London: Zed Books, 1978).

Kimball, Warren: *The Juggler: Franklin D. Roosevelt as Wartime Statesman* (Princeton, NJ: Princeton University Press, 1991).

Koebner, Richard and Helmut Dan Schmidt: *Imperialism: The Story and Significance of a Political Word, 1840–1960* (Cambridge: Cambridge University Press, 1965).

LaFeber, Walter: *The New Empire: An Interpretation of American Expansion 1860–1898* (Ithaca, NY: Cornell University Press, 1963).

LaFeber, Walter: *Inevitable Revolutions: The United States in Central America* (New York: W. W. Norton, 1983).

LaFeber, Walter: *The Panama Canal: The Crisis in Historical Perspective* (New York: Oxford University Press, 1989).

LaFeber, Walter: *The American Search for Opportunity, 1865–1913*. Vol. 2 in *The Cambridge History of American Foreign Relations* (New York: Cambridge University Press, 1993).

LaFeber, Walter: *Michael Jordan and the New Global Capitalism* (New York, 1999).

Landes, David S.: "The Nature of Economic Imperialism." In Kenneth E. Boulding and Tapan Muskerjee (eds.) *Economic Imperialism: A Book of Readings* (Ann Arbor: University of Michigan Press, 1972).

Landry, Donna and Gerald MacLean (eds.) *The Spivak Reader* (New York: Routledge, 1996).

Lane, Jack C.: *Armed Progressive: General Leonard Wood.*

Langer, William L.: *The Diplomacy of Imperialism*, 2nd edn. (New York: Knopf, 1972).

Langley, Lester D.: *The Banana Wars: An Inner History of American Empire, 1900–1934* (Lexington: University of Kentucky Press, 1983).

Langley, Lester D.: *The United States and the Caribbean in the Twentieth Century* (Athens: University of Georgia Press, 1992).

Lasch, Christopher: *The American Liberals and the Russian Revolution* (New York: McGraw-Hill, 1972).

Latham, Michael E.: "Ideology, Social Science, and Destiny: Modernization and the Kennedy-Era Alliance for Progress." *Diplomatic History* 22 (spring 1998).

Leech, Margaret: *In the Days of McKinley* (New York: Harper, 1959).

Leuchtenberg, William E.: "Progressivism and Imperialism: The Progressive Movement and American Foreign Policy, 1898–1916." *Mississippi Valley Historical Review* 39 (June 1952).

Levin, N. Gordon, Jr.: *Woodrow Wilson and World Politics: America's Response to War and Revolution* (New York: Oxford University Press, 1968).

Linn, Brian McAllister: *The Philippine War 1899–1902* (Lawrence, KS, 1902).

Lockmiller, David: *Magoon in Cuba: A History of the Second Intervention, 1906–1909* (Chapel Hill: University of North Carolina Press, 1938).

Louis, W. Roger (ed.): *Imperialism: The Robinson and Gallagher Controversy* (New York: New Viewpoints, 1976).

Louis, W. Roger: *Imperialism at Bay: The United States and the Decolonization of the British Empire, 1941–1945* (New York: Oxford University Press, 1978).

Lowenthal, Abraham (ed.): *Exporting Democracy: The United States and Latin America* (Baltimore, MD: Johns Hopkins University Press, 1991).

Lundestad, Geir: *The United States and the World, 1945–1989* (Washington, DC, 1989).

McClintock, Anne: *Imperial Leather: Race, Gender, and Sexuality in the Colonial Conquest* (New York: Routledge, 1994).

McCormick, Thomas: *The China Market: America's Quest for Informal Empire, 1893–1901* (Chicago, IL, 1967).

McCullough, David: *The Path Between the Seas: The Creation of the Panama Canal 1870–1914* (New York: Simon and Schuster, 1977).

MacDonald, Robert H.: *The Language of Empire: Myths and Metaphors of Popular Imperialism, 1880–1918* (Manchester: Manchester University Press, 1994).

McKee, Delber L.: *Chinese Exclusion Versus the Open Door Policy 1900–1906* (Detroit, MI: Wayne State University Press, 1977).

McMahon, Robert J.: *Colonialism and Cold War: The United States and the Struggle for Indonesian Independence, 1945–1949* (Ithaca, NY: Cornell University Press, 1981).

McMahon, Robert J.: *The Limits of Empire: The United States and Southeast Asia Since World War II* (New York: Columbia University Press, 1999).

Major, John: *Prize Possession: The United States and the Panama Canal 1903–1979* (New York: Cambridge University Press, 1993).

Marks, Frederick W., Jr.: *Velvet on Iron: The Diplomacy of Theodore Roosevelt* (Lincoln: University of Nebraska Press, 1979).

May, Ernest: *American Imperialism: A Speculative Essay* (New York: Atheneum, 1968).

May, Ernest: *Imperial Democracy: The Emergence of the United States as Great Power* (New York: Harper Torchbooks, 1973).

May, Ernest: "The Alliance for Progress in Historical Perspective." In Akira Iriye (ed.) *Rethinking International Relations: Ernest R. May and the Study of Foreign Affairs* (Chicago, IL: Imprint Publications, 1998).

May, Glenn Anthony: *Social Engineering in the Philippines: The Aims, Execution, and Impact of American Colonial Policy, 1900–1913* (Westport, CT: Greenwood Press, 1980).

May, Glenn Anthony: "Why the United States Won the Philippine–American War, 1899–1902." *Pacific Historical Review* 52 (1983), 353–77.

May, Glenn Anthony: *Battle for Batangas: A Philippine Province at War* (New Haven, CT: Yale University Press, 1991).

May, Glenn Anthony: "The Unfathomable Other: Historical Studies of US–Philippine Relations." In Warren I. Cohen (ed.) *Pacific Passages: The Study of American–East Asian Relations on the Eve of the Twenty-First Century* (New York: Columbia University Press, 1996).

Merk, Frederick: *Manifest Destiny and Mission in American History: A Reinterpretation* (New York: Vintage Books, 1963).

Miller, Richard H. (ed.): *American Imperialism in 1898: The Quest for National Fulfillment* (New York: John Wiley and Sons, 1970).

Miller, Stuart Creighton: *"Benevolent Assimilation": The American Conquest of the Philippines, 1899–1903* (New Haven, CT: Yale University Press, 1982).

Millett, Allan Reed: *The Politics of Intervention: The Military Occupation of Cuba 1906–1909* (Columbus: Ohio State University Press, 1968).

Minger, Ralph Eldin: *William Howard Taft and United States Foreign Policy: The Apprenticeship Years, 1900–1908* (Urbana: University of Illinois Press, 1975).

Mommsen, Wolfgang J.: *Theories of Imperialism*, trans. P. S. Falla (New York: Random House, 1980).

Morgan, H. Wayne: *America's Road to Empire: The War with Spain and Overseas Expansion* (New York: Wiley, 1965).

Morris, Edward: *Mornings on Horseback*.

Morris, Edward: *Theodore Rex* (New York: Random House, 2001).

Munro, Dana: *Intervention and Dollar Diplomacy in the Caribbean, 1900–1921* (Princeton, NJ: Princeton University Press, 1964).

Munro, Dana: *The United States and the Caribbean Republics, 1921–1933* (Princeton, NJ: Princeton University Press, 1974).

Musicant, Ivan: *Empire By Default* (New York: Henry Holt, 1998).

Nearing, Scott and Joseph Freeman: *Dollar Diplomacy: A Study in American Imperialism* (New York: Modern Reader Paperbacks, 1969).

Neu, Charles: *An Uncertain Friendship: Theodore Roosevelt and Japan, 1906–1909* (Cambridge, MA: Harvard University Press, 1967).

Ninkovich, Frank: "Cultural Relations and American China Policy, 1942–1945." *Pacific Historical Review* 49 (August 1980), 471–98.

Ninkovich, Frank: "The Rockefeller Foundation, China, and Cultural Change." *Journal of American History* 70 (March 1984), 799–820.

Ninkovich, Frank: "Theodore Roosevelt: Civilization as Ideology." *Diplomatic History* 10 (summer 1986), 221–45.

Ninkovich, Frank: *The United States and Imperialism* (Oxford, 2000).

O'Brien, Thomas F.: *The Revolutionary Mission: American Enterprise in Latin America, 1900–1945* (New York: Cambridge University Press, 1996).

Offner, John L.: *An Unwanted War:The Diplomacy of the United States and Spain over Cuba, 1895–1898* (Chapel Hill: University of North Carolina Press, 1992).

Osborne, Thomas J.: *"Empire Can Wait": American Opposition to Hawaiian Annexation, 1893–1898* (Kent, OH, 1981).

Osterhammel, Jürgen: *Colonialism: A Theoretical Overview*, trans. Shelley L. Frisch (Princeton, NJ: M. Wiener, 1996).

Osterhammel, Jürgen and Wolfgang J. Mommsen (eds.) *Imperialism and After: Continuities and Discontinuities* (London: Allen and Unwin, 1986).

Pérez, Louis A., Jr.: "Intervention, Hegemony, and Dependency: The United States in the Circum-Caribbean, 1898–1980." *Journal of American History* 51 (May 1982), 165–94.

Pérez, Luis A., Jr.: *Cuba Under the Platt Amendment, 1902–1934* (Pittsburgh, PA: University of Pittsburgh Press, 1986).

Pérez, Luis A., Jr.: *Cuba and the United States: Ties of Singular Intimacy* (Athens: University of Georgia Press, 1990).

Pérez, Louis A., Jr.: *The War of 1898: The United States and Cuba in History and Historiography* (Chapel Hill: University of North Carolina Press, 1998).

Perkins, Bradford: *The Creation of a Republican Empire, 1776–1865, vol. 1: The Cambridge History of American Foreign Relations*, ed. Warren I. Cohen (New York: Cambridge University Press, 1993).

Perkins, Whitney T.: *Constraint of Empire: The United States and Caribbean Interventions* (Westport, CT: Greenwood Press, 1981).

Pomeroy, William J.: *American Neo-Colonialism: Its Emergence in the Philippines and Asia* (New York: International Publishers, 1970).

Pratt, Julius: *Expansionists of 1898: The Acquisition of Hawaii and the Spanish Islands* (New York: Quadrangle Books, 1936).

Pratt, Julius: *America's Colonial Experiment: How the United States Gained, Governed, and in Part Gave Away Its Colonial Empire* (New York: Prentice-Hall, 1950).

Pringle, Robert: *Indonesia and the Philippines: American Interests in Island Southeast Asia* (New York: Columbia University Press, 1980).

Rabe, Stephen G.: *The Most Dangerous Area in the World: John F. Kennedy Confronts Communist Revolution in Latin America* (Chapel Hill: University of North Carolina Press, 1999).

Reed, James: *The Missionary Mind and American East Asia Policy 1911–1915* (Cambridge, MA: Harvard University Press, 1983).

Renda, Mary: *Taking Haiti: Military Occupation and the Culture of US Imperialism, 1915–1940* (Chapel Hill, NC, 2001).

Robinson, Ronald and John Gallagher, with Alice Denny: *Africa and the Victorians: The Official Mind of Imperialism* (London: Macmillan, 1961).

Rowe, John Carlos: *Literary Culture and US Imperialism: From the Revolution to World War II* (New York: Oxford University Press, 2000).

Rystad, Goran: *Ambiguous Imperialism: American Foreign Policy and Domestic Politics at the Turn-of-the-Century* (Lund, Sweden, 1975).

Said, Edward: *Orientalism* (New York: Pantheon, 1978).

Salamanca, Bonifacio S.: *The Filipino Reaction to American Rule, 1901–1913* (Shoe String Press, 1968).

Schaller, Michael: *The United States and China in the Twentieth Century* (New York: Oxford University Press, 1979a).

Schaller, Michael: *The US Crusade in China, 1937–1945* (New York: Columbia University Press, 1979b).

Schirmer, Daniel B.: *Republic or Empire: American Resistance to the Philippine War* (Morristown, NJ: Schenkman Books, 1972).

Schirmer, Daniel B. and Stephen Rosskamm Shalom (eds.) *The Philippines Reader: A History of Colonialism, Neocolonialism, Dictatorship, and Resistance* (Boston, MA: South End Press, 1987).

Schmidt, Hans: *The United States Occupation of Haiti, 1915–1934* (New Brunswick, NJ: Rutgers University Press, 1971).

Schmitz, David F.: *Thank God They're on Our Side: The United States and Right-Wing Dictatorships, 1921–1965* (Chapel Hill: University of North Carolina Press, 1999).

Schoultz, Lars: *Beneath the United States: A History of United States Policy Toward Latin America* (Cambridge, MA: Harvard University Press, 1998).

Scully, Eileen: *Bargaining with the State from Afar: American Citizenship in Treaty Port China, 1844–1942* (New York: Columbia University Press, 2001).

Semmel, Bernard: *Imperialism and Social Reform: English Social-imperial Thought, 1895–1914* (Cambridge, MA: Harvard University Press, 1960).

Semmel, Bernard: *The Rise of Free Trade Imperialism: Classical Political Economy, the Empire of Free Trade and Imperialism 1750–1850* (Cambridge: Cambridge University Press, 1970).

Shannon, Thomas: *An Introduction to the World-System Perspective* (Boulder, CO: Westview Press, 1989).

Smith, Peter H.: *Talons of the Eagle: Dynamics of US–Latin American Relations* (New York: Oxford University Press, 1996).

Smith, Tony: *The Pattern of Imperialism: The United States, Great Britain, and the Late-industrializing World since 1815* (New York: Cambridge University Press, 1981).

Spence, Jonathan: *To Change China: Western Advisers in China 1620–1960* (Boston, MA: Little, Brown, 1969).

Spurr, David: *The Rhetoric of Empire: Colonial Discourse in Journalism, Travel Writing, and Imperial Administration* (Durham, NC: Duke University Press, 1993).

Stanley, Peter W.: *A Nation in the Making: The Philippines and the United States, 1899–1921* (Cambridge, MA: Harvard University Press, 1974).

Stanley, Peter W. (ed.): *Reappraising an Empire: New Perspectives on Philippine–American History* (Cambridge, MA: Harvard University Press, 1984).

Stephanson, Anders: *Manifest Destiny: American Expansion and the Empire of Right* (New York: Hill and Wang, 1995).

Stocking, George W., Jr.: *Race, Culture, and Evolution: Essays in the History of Anthropology* (New York, 1968).

Stocking, George W., Jr.: *Race, Culture, and Victorian Anthropology* (New York: Free Press, 1987).

Tang Tsou, *America's Failure in China*.

Tebbel, John: *America's Great Patriotic War With Spain* (Manchester, VT: Marshall Jones, 1996).

Thomson, James C., Jr.: *While China Faced West: American Reformers in Nationalist China, 1928–1937* (Cambridge, MA: Harvard University Press 1969).

Thomson, James C., Jr., Peter W. Stanley, and John Curtis Perry: *Sentimental Imperialists: The American Experience in East Asia* (New York: Harper and Row, 1982).

Thorne, Christopher: *Allies of a Kind:The United States, Britain, and the War against Japan, 1941–1945* (New York: Oxford University Press, 1978).

Thornton, A. P.: *Doctrines of Imperialism* (New York, 1965).

Tomlinson, John: *Cultural Imperialism: A Critical Introduction* (Baltimore, MD: Johns Hopkins University Press, 1991).

Tomlinson, John: *Globalization and Culture* (Chicago, IL: University of Chicago Press, 1999).

Tompkins, E. Berkely: *Anti-Imperialism in the United States: The Great Debate 1890–1920* (Philadelphia, PA).

Trask, David: *The War With Spain in 1898* (New York: Macmillan, 1981).

Traxel, David: *1898: The Birth of the American Century* (New York: Knopf, 1998).

Tuchman, Barbara: *Stilwell and the American Experience in China* (New York: Macmillan, 1971).

Tucker, Nancy Bernkopf: *Taiwan, Hong Kong, and the United States, 1945–1992: Uncertain Friendships* (New York: Twayne, 1994).

Varg, Paul: *Missionaries, Chinese, and Diplomats*.

Von Eschen, Penny M.: *Race Against Empire: Black Americans and Anticolonialism, 1937–1957* (Ithaca, NY: Cornell University Press, 1997).

Wallerstein, Immanuel: *The Modern World System I: Capitalist Agriculture and the Origins of the European World Economy in the Sixteenth Century* (New York: Academic Press, 1974).

Weinberg, Albert: *Manifest Destiny*.

Welch, Richard E., Jr.: *Response to Imperialism: The United States and the Philippine War, 1899–1902* (Chapel Hill: University of North Carolina Press, 1965).

Welch, Richard E., Jr.: "American Atrocities in the Philippines: The Indictment and the Response." *Pacific Historical Review* 43 (1974), 233–53.

Wells, Henry: *The Modernization of Puerto Rico: A Political Study of Changing Values and Institutions* (Cambridge, MA: Harvard University Press, 1969).

Widenor, William C.: *Henry Cabot Lodge and the Search for an American Foreign Policy* (Berkeley: University of California Press, 1980).

Williams, Raymond: *Keywords: A Vocabulary of Culture and Society* (London: Croom Helm, 1976).

Williams, Walter: "The United States Indian Policy and the Debate Over Philippine Annexation: The Implications for the Origins of American Imperialism." *Journal of American History* 66 (March 1980), 810–31.

Williams, William Appleman: *The Tragedy of American Diplomacy and the Roots of the American Empire: A Study of the Growth and Shaping of Social Consciousness in a Mass-Market Society* (New York, 1969).

Wisan, Joseph E.: *The Cuban Crisis as Reflected in the New York Press (1895–1898)* (New York: Columbia University Press, 1934).

Wolff, Leon: *Little Brown Brother: How the United States Purchased and Pacified the Philippines* (New York: Oxford University Press, 1991).

Wood, Bryce: *The Making of the Good Neighbor Policy* (New York: Columbia University Press, 1961).

Young, Marilyn B.: *The Rhetoric of Empire: American China Policy 1895–1901* (Cambridge, MA, 1968).

Zwick, Jim (ed.): *Mark Twain's Weapons of Satire: Anti-Imperialist Writings on the Philippine–American War.*

CHAPTER SEVEN

Relations with Africa since 1900

ANDREW DEROCHE

The history of United States relations with Africa in the twentieth century is a rich field, with many exciting new publications and a lot of active scholars with projects underway. The important themes in US relations with Africa represent the entire spectrum of critical issues in the field of international relations: culture, economics, national security, domestic influence, Cold War rivalry, decolonization, and race relations, among others. One sign of the maturity and richness of a historical sub-field is the existence of master narratives, which encapsulate the major themes in a dramatic style that never strays too far from the individual people who drive history. For example, beginning students of the US Civil War should read James McPherson's *Battle Cry of Freedom*. Thanks to Robert Massie, the field of US relations with Africa now has a similar starting point. Massie's *Loosing the Bonds: The United States and South Africa in the Apartheid Years* (1997) is the type of historical writing that brings a topic to life even for people with no prior knowledge of the subject.

Massie provided a thorough examination of the key events in South Africa from 1960 to 1990, from the massacre at Sharpeville to the release of Nelson Mandela. He discussed the policies of the Kennedy and Reagan administrations in depth. He examined the influence of several non-government organizations such as the African National Congress and the American Committee on Africa. He featured famous individuals such as Mandela, but also detailed the crucial contributions of Jennifer Davis and Randall Robinson. He traced the origins and implementation of American sanctions against South Africa, then insightfully analyzed their impact. In short, Massie crafted the definitive study of American relations with South Africa; however, he did much more than that. He provided a snapshot of the field of US relations with Africa, elucidating the importance of factors such as the Cold War, race relations, domestic politics, economics, national security, and individual initiative. For many reasons, therefore, Massie's *Loosing the Bonds* is the place to begin studying US relations with Africa.

Liberia

From 1900 until 1935, American relations with Africa focused primarily on Liberia. The United States first had contact with the area that would become Liberia in the 1820s, when the US government provided funds to support settlement by African Americans. A small group of Americo-Liberians, who never constituted more than 5 percent of the population, exercised an inordinate amount of control over the nation's politics. Great Britain dominated the economy, however, with major loans in 1870 and 1906 making Liberia practically a British protectorate. A major change in that situation began in 1909, when the United States sent an investigatory commission to Liberia.

Booker T. Washington played a central role in determining the makeup of the commission, submitting a list to the State Department of acceptable candidates for the two white slots. Washington himself was the leading choice for the one black slot, but when William Taft requested that Washington stay in the United States to help with his transition, Washington chose his close friend and secretary Emmett Scott as his replacement. The commission visited Liberia in May 1909, and returned to the United States with the recommendation that the American government provide substantial assistance to help Liberia establish true independence. President Taft supported the proposed treaty as it made its way through Congress, but in May 1910 the Senate rejected the treaty.

Taft wanted to help Liberia, so he advised the State Department to arrange for a private loan from a combination of American, British, French, and German banks. State officials were successful, and Liberia received the funds early in 1912. This ended British dominance of Liberia's economy, which would be overseen by Americans for decades to come. The collection of customs in Liberia would be controlled by an American adviser, Reed Clark, who was approved by Washington. The training of the Liberian military was also placed into American hands, with three black officers and a black military attaché taking over for British advisers. Again Washington made his mark on US relations with Liberia, selecting Major Charles Young as the military attaché. Young proved a wise choice, training a Liberian force that put down a rebellion in 1915.

Liberia joined the allied cause during World War I, further improving its relations with the United States. Despite continuing American supervision of customs, however, Liberia struggled financially. After the war ended the Liberian government sought a $5 million loan from the United States. A delegation of Liberians led by President Charles King arrived in Washington in March 1921, and soon met with Secretary of State Charles Evans Hughes. A month later President Warren Harding hosted them at the White House. King thanked Harding for past American support, and expressed his hope that it would continue. Harding explained that he knew of the key role Americans had played in Liberia's history, and that the United States "stands always ready to support" Liberia (Skinner 1992: 445).

Harding may well have been sympathetic to the Liberian cause, but there were limits on how far the United States government could go in 1921. The postwar climate was hostile to foreign aid, and the Senate had made known its intention to cut off aid to several nations. In November 1921 the Liberians returned to Africa still uncertain about their loan request. In May 1922 the House approved the loan, but the Senate hesitated. Harding was aware that support for Liberia was a key issue among leading African Americans, and he urged the Senate to approve the loan. He appealed to Senator Henry Cabot Lodge, but to no avail. In November the Senate voted to send the loan bill back to committee, effectively killing it. Upon hearing of the verdict, DuBois informed Secretary of State Hughes that he was "very alarmed by the failure of the American Congress to confirm the Liberian loan" (Skinner 1992: 480).

Throughout the 1920s DuBois stayed very involved with US relations with Liberia, and in December 1923 he journeyed to Liberia as President Calvin Coolidge's special envoy. DuBois himself realized that his appointment was primarily symbolic, but his opinion did matter to Liberians. One important issue he may have discussed with the Liberian government was the effort by Marcus Garvey to organize a mass exodus of African Americans to West Africa. Garvey, through his Universal Negro Improvement Association, had a massive following in the United States. He never got the ear of leaders in Washington or Monrovia as DuBois did, nor did he ever establish a settlement in Liberia. Arrested for tax evasion in 1924, he was jailed and then deported. Nevertheless, there is no doubt that he made a huge impact on US relations with Africa. The rivalry between Garvey and DuBois, particularly regarding Liberia, is discussed in great depth in the final chapter of Skinner (1992).

American relations with Liberia were a key focus of Skinner's work, and he traced the story up to the mid-1920s. There were a number of significant occurrences between 1926 and 1935, however, which he did not cover in any depth. First, the Firestone Rubber Company secured a 99-year lease on a million acres in Liberia on which to produce rubber. In exchange for the lease, Firestone arranged a $5 million loan to Liberia. Second, an international commission reported slavery-like conditions in Liberia in 1930, prompting President King to resign. The United States refused to recognize the government of his successor Edwin Barclay and called for League of Nations supervision of Liberia. Barclay refused to be controlled by external powers, and in 1935 the United States helped draft some reforms and renewed official recognition.

For these events, the authoritative source is Emily Rosenberg's "The Invisible Protectorate" (1985). Rosenberg went far beyond detailing the events of US relations with Liberia. She provided the most insightful analysis of Liberia's overall significance in the history of American foreign policy. She rejected the notion that Firestone completely dominated US policy, and instead contended that "there were a number of political, racial, strategic, and economic considerations" (p. 210). She characterized Liberia as an American protectorate, but an "invisible" one. This invisibility was due to the fact that policy was not overseen by Congress, but rather through private contracts. The State Department played a key role in encouraging these contracts, and thus emerged a relationship Rosenberg referred to as "colonialism by contract" (p. 212).

Ethiopia, 1935–1936

In October 1935, the Italian forces of Benito Mussolini attacked Ethiopia. This prompted debate in the United States over the best policy regarding Europe, with Congress and President Franklin Roosevelt disagreeing over the nature of neutrality. Because Italy's target was Ethiopia, the only independent black nation in Africa, the war aroused African Americans who had developed many ties to Ethiopia. Black leaders ranging from DuBois to Garvey agreed on the importance of it maintaining independence. African Americans joined in the defense of Ethiopia before the war even began, with the most notable contributor being Hubert Julian. A pilot known as the "Black Eagle of Harlem," Julian served as Emperor Haile Selassie's personal pilot and helped to train the Ethiopian air force.

Julian was replaced as commander of Selassie's air force in 1935 by a black Tuskegee graduate named John Robinson, called the "Brown Condor." The exploits of Robinson and the fate of Ethiopia in general dominated discussions across Harlem in the fall of 1935. During the winter of 1935–6 the attention of black leaders focused on the debate over neutrality legislation in Washington. Walter White, leader of the National Association for the Advancement of Colored People (NAACP), and Congressman Arthur Mitchell from Illinois opposed an amendment that would exempt both Italy and Ethiopia from neutrality legislation, because that would effectively favor Italy. The amendment did not pass, but the policy enacted favored Italy nonetheless. American companies contributed significantly to Mussolini's war machine, while isolated Ethiopia had no access to American goods. In late May, the Ethiopian forces surrendered.

The news from Africa cheered Italian Americans, who had supported Mussolini's invasion from the start. The Italian communities in New York, Philadelphia, and Chicago had raised hundreds of thousands of dollars and sent the donations to Italy. Italian Americans had swarmed into the Italian embassy in Washington in hopes of joining Mussolini's military, but the Italian ambassador turned them away. Despite warnings about fines and imprisonment, nearly 200 Italian Americans sailed from New York in late 1935 for Rome and a chance to fight for their fatherland. Voters of Italian heritage lobbied their representatives to maintain a neutrality that would continue to favor Mussolini, and ultimately their side prevailed. Blacks and Italians expressed comparable levels of interest in the Ethiopian conflict, but Italian Americans had more influence in the United States. In his fine study, *African-American Reactions to War in Ethiopia, 1936–1941* (1994), Joseph Harris included a chapter on Italian Americans, and provided a rare look at the influence on US relations with Africa by a minority other than blacks.

The Italian Americans' success in influencing US relations with Africa during the Ethiopian war, as detailed by Harris, illuminated the obstacles preventing similar success by African Americans. Harris himself devoted most of his study to discussing the often-futile efforts of African Americans. However, blacks' ineffectiveness was perhaps most clearly analyzed in another major work on Ethiopia, William Scott's *The Sons of Sheba's Race* (1993). Scott identified several powerful factors that undermined the ability of African Americans to influence the outcome of the war. First was the poverty that debilitated the vast majority of blacks during the Depression. Another key factor was that most blacks lacked experience in international relations. Finally, African Americans in the 1930s possessed very little political power.

World War II

World War II made a major impact on US relations with Africa in several ways. It established in the minds of leading policymakers the strategic importance of Africa, mainly as a location for bases and a source for raw materials. Wartime events prompted the State Department to increase its attention to Africa. Some high-level diplomacy was conducted regarding Ethiopia. While most American diplomats paid little attention to Africa and had no respect for black Africans, ideas about the need to end colonialism began to take hold among some Americans, especially blacks.

Many African Americans included African independence in their vision for a "Double Victory" after the war.

One obvious reason that World War II sparked an increase in African-American interest in Africa was that black units of the US army were stationed there. Nearly 5,000 African-American soldiers served in Liberia. The United States constructed an airport in Liberia, and also rebuilt much of the country's infrastructure. The two nations signed a mutual defense agreement, and the United States provided Liberia with Lend Lease funds. Although there had been a very long history of contact between the United States and Liberia, only the wartime realization of Liberia's strategic value resulted in major concrete activities there by the American government. The same could be said for the Horn of Africa. The United States set up a radio communications center near Asmara, Eritrea, in 1943. Eritrea was then under British occupation, but its status was at the heart of negotiations between Ethiopia, Britain, and the United States during the latter stages of the war.

During World War II the United States supported Ethiopia in its quest to reassert its independence after the Italian occupation. In July 1942 Emperor Haile Selassie asked President Roosevelt for American acknowledgment of Ethiopia's sovereignty. Roosevelt responded in August that "It is a source of much satisfaction to me and to the people of the United States that your country . . . has regained its independence" (Marcus 1995: 14). State Department officials realized that recognizing Ethiopia would lead to Lend Lease assistance. This could eventually benefit the United States in the form of trade with Ethiopia and commercial flight routes through the region. In the summer of 1943 American diplomats advocated Ethiopian control of Eritrea, and pledged Lend Lease to Selassie in a Mutual Aid Agreement. In February 1945 Roosevelt and Selassie discussed Ethiopia's future in Egypt, and Roosevelt was supportive if non-committal. In 1945 Selassie requested nearly $6 million in loans from the Import–Export bank, and was granted $3 million for the purchase of trucks and spare parts.

As demonstrated by the examples of Liberia and Ethiopia, the US government established unprecedented concrete ties with Africa during World War II, due mainly to strategic concerns. That did not necessarily mean the United States would be working on the behalf of black Africans. Key American officials did not believe Africans were ready for independence, including influential Undersecretary of State Sumner Welles. He considered Africans to be "in the lowest rank of human beings." President Roosevelt visited Gambia early in 1943 and characterized the conditions in Gambia as "the most horrible thing I have ever seen in my life" (Plummer 1996: 110).

African Americans saw Africa very differently. According to Brenda Plummer, a key aspect of US relations with Africa during World War II was the contrast between white and black Americans' opinions of the continent. During the war African Americans talked of "Double V," a victory against fascism abroad and racism at home, and many blacks included independence for the African colonies in this equation. Just as the war gave a boost to the civil rights movement in the United States, it sparked the struggle for liberation in Africa. The interaction between the two movements became a crucial element of US relations with Africa in the 1960s and 1970s. World War II did much to catalyze that dynamic reaction.

The Truman Administration

During the presidency of Harry Truman, relations with Africa became more extensive, but also more challenging for US policymakers. The key example was South Africa, where the Nationalist Party gained control of parliament in 1948. Led by extremist Afrikaners, the Nationalists constructed their system of institutionalized racism known as apartheid. They passed the legal foundations of apartheid in 1950: the Population Registration Act, the Group Areas Act, and the Suppression of Communism Act. These allowed the government to classify all South Africans by race, segregate them in residential areas, and crush any criticism of their policies. The emergence of apartheid presented the US government with a dilemma. Maintaining friendly relations with South Africa would open the United States to criticism from black Africans, especially at the United Nations. The Soviet Union would jump on the propaganda bandwagon, too. On the other hand, the international anti-communism of the Afrikaner regime was helpful during crises such as the Korean War.

Despite reservations about associating with a racist state, the Truman administration fostered close ties with Pretoria. The State Department upgraded its presence in South Africa to an embassy, and abstained on anti-apartheid measures at the United Nations. The Pentagon negotiated a Mutual Defense Assistance Pact, and in 1952 agreed to sell over $100 million in weapons to South Africa. Furthermore, the Central Intelligence Agency initiated a close relationship with their counterparts in Pretoria, helping to build a surveillance and covert operations unit in South Africa. In an agreement in 1950, in exchange for scientific, technical, and financial support, the United States received a supply of uranium. Over the next fifteen years South Africa shipped over $1 billion worth of uranium to the US nuclear industry (Schraeder 1994: 193–6).

While scholars basically agree on the main factors influencing Truman's policy towards South Africa, there is some difference in emphasis. In his groundbreaking book *Cold War and Black Liberation* (1985), Thomas Noer argued that Pretoria's support for the US intervention in Korea was the key. American officials such as Dean Acheson contended that the United States should judge other nations by their foreign policy, not domestic politics, and his view won the day. Pretoria sent an air squadron and ground troops to Korea. Concrete assistance in the Asian conflict trumped any concerns about apartheid and "effectively determined US policy toward South Africa" (Noer 1985: 27–9).

In his major study of Truman's policy towards South Africa, *Apartheid's Reluctant Uncle* (1993), Thomas Borstelmann offered a slightly different interpretation. He stated that among the reasons why American officials built bonds with Pretoria, the key was uranium. Although there were historic, geostrategic, and economic motives, uranium stood out as the "most important single interest of the United States" (Borstelmann 1993: 198). In addition to taking a firm stand in the debate over what influenced the Truman administration the most, Borstelmann raised some very compelling questions about the long-term significance of US cooperation with the apartheid regime. He pointed to the insidious link between racism and anti-communism, both in the United States and South Africa. Furthermore, he concluded that American support for Pretoria in the early 1950s foreshadowed future US policy throughout the Third World, where American officials repeatedly opposed liberation movements in the name of anti-communism.

In the most recent work to consider the Truman administration's policy towards Africa, Ebere Nwaubani (2001) extended several of the points made by Noer and Borstelmann regarding South Africa to other nations. Just as American officials supported apartheid, so they also sided with European colonial regimes in the Congo, Nigeria, and Ghana. For US diplomats, Africa was seen as a source of raw materials for the defense industry, which cranked up in response to the war in Korea. Nigeria, the Congo, and Ghana provided high percentages of the necessary columbium, cobalt, and manganese to the US military machine. According to Nwaubani, the Truman administration had a "dual mandate" in Africa: one, the United States sought minerals; and two, the United States wanted to help Europe continue its postwar recovery. Helping to maintain the strong center–periphery relations between Europe and its African colonies would both strengthen the economies of US allies and eventually integrate Africa into the worldwide economic web being weaved by the United States (Nwaubani 2001: 84–5).

The Eisenhower Administration

According to Noer, the Eisenhower administration's policy toward southern Africa essentially continued the Truman policy of seeking a moderate, "middle road" position. American officials condemned apartheid at the United Nations, but simultaneously maintained close ties with the Pretoria regime. In dealing with colonial areas, US policy continued to take a "Europe first" approach (Noer 1985: 60). The Eisenhower administration hoped that a middle course in African relations would allow them to have it both ways: on the one hand they could support European allies and receive strategic metals, and on the other hand they would please critics of apartheid. Nwaubani further refined this "middle road" interpretation. He acknowledged that the rhetoric of the Eisenhower administration criticized apartheid and supported black Africa. However, he insisted that "a distinction must be made between rhetoric and actual policy" (Nwaubani 2001: 93). He pointed out that during the Eisenhower years, less than 2 percent of American foreign aid went to Africa, and most of that went to North Africa or to white regimes. The emerging black African states in West Africa got virtually no concrete support from the United States. American diplomats perceived no Soviet threat and relatively little strategic value in West Africa, so they deferred to European preferences and preferred little aid to states such as Ghana.

Nwaubani's argument that the Eisenhower administration did almost nothing to assist black Africans is certainly accurate. However, important distinctions can be made between US relations with Africa during Eisenhower's first and second terms. Policy towards Africa became a higher priority during the second term. In March 1957 Vice President Richard Nixon visited several African countries, and attended the independence ceremony in Ghana on March 6. Upon returning to Washington, Nixon submitted a report that stressed the importance of Africa in the Cold War struggle against the Soviets. In August 1958 the State Department formed a separate Bureau of African Affairs.

In "Crossing the Color Line in Little Rock" (2000) Cary Fraser detailed another way that 1957 represented a turning point in Eisenhower's policy towards Africa. According to Fraser, the showdown over school integration in Little Rock in September 1957 necessitated changes in American relations with Africa, particularly with South Africa. Before Little Rock, American officials constructed strong bonds with their counterparts in Pretoria that rested firmly on "segregation, investment, and security" (Fraser 2000: 241). After the crisis the United States shifted its stance at the United Nations regarding South Africa, and in 1958 voted in favor of a resolution condemning apartheid. American policy towards Africa had entered a "state of flux," but ambivalence on apartheid and colonialism remained strong among US officials, including Eisenhower himself. The events at Little Rock manifested the link between domestic race relations and African policy, but the Eisenhower administration was "unable to mount the necessary effort to devise a legitimate solution" (ibid: 257–64).

Fraser's work exemplifies a growing body of scholarship on the relationship between the African-American civil rights movement and United States foreign relations. Another important sub-field in the study of international affairs considers the importance of culture, and Penny Von Eschen made a major contribution with her *Race Against Empire* (1997). Von Eschen described the efforts of the US State Department to use culture in the Cold War competition with the Soviet Union. During the Eisenhower era the State Department funded trips to Africa by "Goodwill Ambassadors," notable black athletes and musicians, to underline the great achievements of African Americans. On an unofficial trip to Ghana in 1956 Louis Armstrong played before lively crowds of 100,000, which prompted the State Department to hire him as one of their "jambassadors" in 1957. Before he actually represented the United States overseas, however, events in Little Rock convinced Armstrong to change his tune. Disappointed by Eisenhower's slow response to the crisis in Arkansas, Armstrong exclaimed: "The way they are treating my people in the South, the government can go to hell" (Von Eschen 1997: 179–80). As Von Eschen clearly demonstrated, the escalating civil rights movement made it increasingly complicated for the United States to use culture in its Cold War competition.

A crisis in the Congo brought that competition to the boiling point during the last six months of the Eisenhower administration, starting with the rapid Belgian evacuation of their former colony in July 1960. Patrice Lumumba emerged as the most promising leader in the Congo, but his efforts to lead an orderly transition to independence were immediately frustrated by a rebellion in the mineral-rich province of Katanga. After the United Nations refused to provide sufficient support to his attempts to crush the Katanga uprising, Lumumba requested assistance from the Soviet Union. The Soviets sent advisers and planes, which sparked a stern reaction in Washington. Eisenhower believed it was necessary to thwart Soviet influence in any Third World country but wanted to avoid direct confrontation, so he opted for covert action. With Eisenhower's approval the National Security Council authorized the CIA to remove Lumumba. The CIA set in motion a plan to kill Lumumba, and simultaneously began supporting Colonel Joseph Mobutu. It was actually Mobutu's forces that killed Lumumba on January 17, 1961, but American officials deserve their fair share of blame. In its eleventh hour the Eisenhower administration took notice of Africa, and in an attempt to prevent Soviet influence facilitated the rise of one of the twentieth century's most notorious dictators (Schraeder 1994: 53–9).

According to Peter Schraeder, the Eisenhower administration's policy towards the Congo crisis represented an effort to prevent Soviet influence in Africa. In *The Political Economy of Third World Intervention* (1991), David Gibbs offered a very different analysis. Gibbs contended that economic motives drove Eisenhower's policy. He identified several Eisenhower officials with ties to mining in the Katanga province, including Allan Dulles and Secretary of State Christian Herter. For these men, ongoing Belgian control of the mines was beneficial, whereas Lumumba posed a threat. Gibbs concluded: "The economic perspective explains the Eisenhower policy quite well" (Gibbs 1991: 101).

The New Frontier

Crisis in the Congo continued throughout the presidency of Eisenhower's successor, John Kennedy. Kennedy adopted a very different policy towards the Congo, most importantly by deciding in November 1962 to support a United Nations operation that crushed the Katanga rebellion. Gibbs argued that Kennedy was able to pursue this policy because high-level officials in his administration had virtually no economic interests at stake in Katanga, thus they could seek Cold War strategic objectives. In Gibbs' view, the lack of economic interests in the Congo allowed the Kennedy administration to focus on fighting the Cold War.

Many scholars have emphasized the unique and progressive nature of Kennedy's relations with Africa. Thomas Noer challenged this notion in his "New Frontier and African Neutralism" (1984), which examined the Kennedy administration's decision to fund the Volta River Project in Ghana. Kennedy's support for the dam has often been cited as proof that he would gladly overlook Cold War neutrality to back important African nationalists like Kwame Nkrumah. Noer convincingly demonstrated that Kennedy granted the assistance to Nkrumah reluctantly, after Nkrumah pledged to assert his belief in American economic and political principles. Forcing Nkrumah to advocate American ideals allowed the Kennedy administration to justify the Volta River dam as a strategic maneuver. According to Noer, when concrete issues were at stake relations with Africa under Kennedy adhered to the Cold War pattern.

Thomas Borstelmann reinforced Noer's argument in his article, "Hedging Our Bets and Buying Time" (2000), which compared Kennedy's policies towards the African-American civil rights movement and southern Africa. While Kennedy became more supportive of civil rights at home in the second half of his presidency, he simultaneously became less critical of the white regime in Pretoria. At the same time Borstelmann acknowledged that Kennedy desired to help black Africans attain independence and equality. He praised Kennedy for appointing liberal officials such as G. Mennen Williams, Assistant Secretary of State for Africa, and for establishing the Peace Corps.

In the long run the formation of the Peace Corps was probably Kennedy's most significant contribution to US relations with Africa, and Elizabeth Cobbs Hoffman demonstrated this in *All You Need Is Love* (1998). From the beginning the Kennedy administration conceived of the Peace Corps as a tool to show people in less-developed areas, such as Africa, that Americans were not all racist monsters. With this in mind, Kennedy officials chose Ghana as the first destination for Peace Corps volunteers. The concrete impact on the lives of Africans was tremendous, particularly in education. About 675,000 Ghanaians learned from Peace Corps teachers between 1961 and 1991. In addition to being inspiring teachers, many of the volunteers contributed outside the classroom. They worked in remote areas where most Ghanaians would not go, and made an incredible difference. This was also true in other parts of Africa, particularly Nigeria. Cobbs Hoffman concluded: "In both Ghana and Nigeria between 1960 and 1977, the Peace Corps was the only part of overall US policy toward the continent that Africans viewed favorably" (Cobbs Hoffman 1998: 181).

The Johnson Administration

Lyndon Johnson attempted to continue the positive relations with Africa that Kennedy initiated. He supported the Peace Corps, met with many African leaders, gave a speech in honor of the Organization of African Unity, and sent Vice President Hubert Humphrey on a major tour of Africa. But in terms of high-level policymaking, Johnson and his top advisers spent nearly all of their time discussing Vietnam and paid very little attention to Africa, and that was mostly in response to crises. The two most revealing case studies occurred in the Congo and Southern Rhodesia.

Whereas Kennedy's Congo policy was progressive in that he strongly supported a United Nations peacekeeping operation, Johnson's Congo policy promoted neocolonialism and racism. Piero Gleijeses detailed the events in his article, "Flee! The White Giants Are Coming!" (1994). Early in 1964 a revolt led by former followers of Lumumba started, and it expanded in June. At that point Moise Tshombe, who had instigated the Katanga rebellion, returned from exile and joined his former foes in the central government. In August they named him prime minister, and fighting escalated further. The Johnson administration decided it could not afford to let the rebels defeat Tshombe, because they viewed the rebels as anti-American. Takeover of the Congo by an unfriendly regime would be a political loss for Johnson in the fall of 1964, and it would constitute a strategic blow as well.

Assistant Secretary Williams suggested helping Tshombe hire mercenaries, and the United States pursued a dual policy of providing military assistance to Tshombe in public and facilitating his use of mercenaries in private. The mercenaries were white, and in spite of efforts to recruit in Europe, most of them were from South Africa and Southern Rhodesia. Four American C-130 planes with American crews transported the soldiers, and the operation was overseen by the CIA. The attacks on the rebels received heavy air support from American B-26s. Most support the rebels got from outside came from Tanzania, but the CIA stopped that by establishing a naval patrol on Lake Tanganyika. The mercenaries ruthlessly suppressed the rebellion, justifying their vicious tactics as necessary to preserve white status in Africa, and by August 1965 they eliminated virtually all resistance. As fighting died down, political bickering renewed, with Tshombe and other leaders in the central government refusing to work together. In late November General Mobutu terminated the turmoil, seizing power and beginning in earnest his long reign of terror and greed.

The CIA, who had been working with Mobutu since 1960, considered his takeover of the Congo as "the best thing that could possibly have happened" (Gleijeses 1994: 235). Future events proved otherwise. In his top-notch article,

Gleijeses depicted Johnson's morally bankrupt policy in the Congo and its tragic results. Moreover, his article stands as a model of the finest scholarship available on US relations with Africa. His writing is clear and compelling, and his research is even more impressive. He combed the archival sources in the United States, interviewed key players, and consulted sources in at least three other languages (French, Italian, and German). Gleijeses revisited the story in his book *Conflicting Missions* (2002), and by utilizing archival research in Cuba succeeded in painting an even more thorough picture of events in the Congo.

The second major African crisis to receive high-level attention from the Johnson administration occurred in Southern Rhodesia, where a white minority ruled the black majority with institutionalized racism that resembled South Africa's apartheid. Since the Kennedy years the US State Department had advocated reform in Southern Rhodesia to allow for political and economic opportunity for blacks; however, with the election of Ian Smith as prime minister in 1964 the chance of such reform vanished. While the British granted independence to colonies throughout Africa in the early 1960s, they refused to grant independence to Southern Rhodesia unless race relations improved. Smith intended to maintain white domination, and in November 1965 declared independence from Great Britain. The Johnson administration's response to Smith's unilateral declaration of independence (UDI) is thoroughly discussed in my own recent work, *Black, White, and Chrome* (DeRoche 2001).

With Secretary of State Dean Rusk involved so extensively with Vietnam, oversight of Southern Rhodesia policy fell to Undersecretary George Ball. In the days following UDI, it was clear from Ball's conversations that the most critical issue in his mind was the copper industry of Zambia. Any strong measures against Smith would result in retaliatory measures against neighboring Zambia, which depended on Southern Rhodesia for fuel and transportation. Ball generally viewed events through an economic lens. Had policy been entirely up to him, harsh sanctions against Smith would probably have been avoided. He felt that in the long run the health of the copper industry was in the best interests of all the residents of southern Africa. Closing Zambia's copper mines, in addition, could limit supply and raise prices to the point where American jobs could be threatened.

Yet Ball was a brilliant advocate who could see both sides of any issue. As the weeks passed after UDI, it became clear to Ball that the gravest immediate threat was a backlash against the British by black African nations at the UN. Furthermore, he sensed the growing dissatisfaction with US policy among civil rights leaders – particularly Whitney Young. For these reasons, then, Ball championed US participation in an oil embargo against the Smith regime. American officials were responsive to the attitudes of black leaders in Africa and the United States. Moreover, once the decision to embargo oil was reached, Ball did his best to see that the embargo succeeded. Ultimately, South Africa foiled the effectiveness of the oil embargo, but it was not from a lack of effort by George Ball and other US diplomats (DeRoche 2001: 128–30).

The Nigerian Civil War, 1967–1970

The next major crisis in Africa, a civil war in Nigeria, began during Johnson's presidency and lasted one year into the tenure of Richard Nixon. Both administrations basically refrained from any major involvement in the conflict, as Robert Shepard demonstrated in his *Nigeria, Africa, and the United States* (1991). When the Biafra region of Nigeria seceded in May 1967 and fighting began in July, the Johnson administration decided to embargo arms from both sides. Although the United States had provided $150 million to Nigeria since its 1960 independence, Johnson had his hands full with Vietnam in 1967. Furthermore, there was considerable public support for the Biafran cause, most notably from Senator Edward Kennedy. In June 1968, press reports of widespread starvation in Biafra forced Johnson to authorize official US support for the relief efforts by agencies such as the Red Cross. The United States provided funds and planes to the Red Cross, but did not intervene directly.

Nixon criticized Johnson's policy on Nigeria during the 1968 campaign, and as he took office he intended to play a significant role in the conflict. He envisioned himself mediating a settlement, and possibly recognizing an independent Biafra. Nixon's hopes proved unrealistic, as the Nigerian federal forces steadily encircled the Biafran forces. On January 12, 1970 the Biafran commander surrendered. Although Nixon had increased the relief effort to Biafra somewhat, he had essentially continued the Johnson policy of staying out, in deference to the military realities. The Nixon administration's top priority was maintaining US influence in Nigeria and retaining access to its tremendous oil reserves. Shepard concluded: "The whole affair left Nixon with a distinct distaste for African issues" (Shepard 1991: 49).

The Byrd Amendment

Section 503 of the 1971 Defense Procurement Bill, commonly referred to as the Byrd Amendment, allowed for the importation into the United States of any strategic mineral being imported from a communist country. As an upshot of the amendment, which Nixon signed into law on November 17, American firms renewed shipments of Southern Rhodesian chrome. The United States, therefore, joined South Africa and Portugal as the major culprits violating sanctions against the Smith regime. The United States continued to participate in the sanctions, but no longer applied them to the one product it had historically imported from Southern Rhodesia in the greatest quantity: chrome. How and why did this happen? Congress initiated the amendment, corporate lobbyists advocated it, and Nixon and National Security Adviser Henry Kissinger ignored the debate in the months before its passage. These are all components of the complete explanation, but none were new elements in 1971. The catalyst, in fact, was the skill of Senator Harry Byrd, Jr. (D. – Va.) and his supporters in Congress.

Why did Byrd do it? There is no doubt that he was influenced by the stainless steel industry's lobbyists. However, a more fundamental reason lay beneath Byrd's efforts. Byrd's father, a former senator from Virginia, had been one of the most outspoken adversaries of the civil rights movement. Harry Byrd, Jr., descended from one of the arch segregationists of US history. Several of his allies in the fight had similar pedigrees, particularly Strom Thurmond. These men, who had battled integration in the American South, identified with Ian Smith and his struggle for white supremacy in southern Africa.

The United States imported Southern Rhodesian chrome, in violation of the sanctions, until 1977. The economic effect on Southern Rhodesia of the amendment is difficult to measure. Ironically, American stainless steel manufacturers would be hurt by the amendment, because it allowed for importation of stainless steel as well as chrome. The impact on security was dubious, furthermore, as the United States continued to import Soviet chrome. But there was no doubt about the psychological boost for Smith, whose Minister of Foreign Affairs personally thanked Byrd. Reaction from the other side of the struggle was equally strong. Ndabaningi Sithole, a leader of the liberation movement in Zimbabwe, blasted the Byrd Amendment. The developments that made Sithole's words ring true had occurred because in 1971 Nixon and Kissinger simply did not care about events in southern Africa (DeRoche 2001: 170–7).

Kissinger Notices Africa

Henry Kissinger finally noticed Africa in 1975, when Angola's independence from Portugal resulted in a complicated civil war. Angolan guerrillas had been fighting against the Portuguese since 1962. Despite considerable aid from the United States, the Portuguese forces could not crush the rebellion. A coup in Lisbon in 1974 ousted Antonio Salazar, and his leftist successors withdrew the troops from Angola and negotiated independence in 1975. Three main groups had waged the war against Portugal: Agostinho Neto's Popular Movement for the Liberation of Angola (MPLA), Holden Roberto's Front for the Liberation of Angola (FNLA), and Jonas Savimbi's National Union for the Total Independence of Angola (UNITA). In the wake of Portuguese withdrawal these three groups began a bitter struggle for power that would last for over fifteen years.

In June 1974 the Central Intelligence Agency (CIA) started secretly supporting Roberto's FNLA in the escalating struggle. In January 1975 Kissinger approved an increase in support to the FNLA. In March 1975 Neto's MPLA began receiving Soviet military supplies, and in September the first Cuban advisers arrived to further assist the MPLA. Kissinger responded with $14 million for the FNLA, approved by President Gerald Ford. Kissinger also backed Savimbi's UNITA, and ultimately spent $32 million in his effort to overthrow the MPLA. In October 1975 South African troops joined the fray against the MPLA, making the United States and South Africa allies in the Angolan civil war. With more Soviet support and additional Cuban troops, however, the MPLA retained the upper hand through the end of 1975.

The CIA operation in Angola drew fire from many quarters, including Congress. Senator Dick Clark (D. – Iowa) proposed an amendment blocking future covert funds for Angola, and the Senate approved it in December. The House did likewise in January 1976. Rebuffed by Congress, Kissinger tried a different angle and attempted to rally black African support for Savimbi's UNITA. Furious because the United States had sided with South Africa, the Nigerian government attacked Kissinger and Ford in the newspapers. Headlines screamed "To Hell with America" and Nigeria banned Kissinger from future visits. By treating the Angolan civil war as a Cold War battleground, Kissinger had alienated much of black Africa, including oil-rich Nigeria. As Piero Gleijeses demonstrated in his groundbreaking book *Conflicting Missions* (2002), the American policy towards Angola not only was immoral and racist, but also was a complete failure.

With his hands tied by Congress regarding Angola, Kissinger sought a new strategy for southern Africa. Unable to fight the Soviets and the Cubans militarily, he tried removing future battlefields. Thus his attention turned in the spring of 1976 to Southern Rhodesia, where the intensifying conflict offered ripe ground for Soviet influence. By negotiating an end to the war and a transition to majority rule, Kissinger could head off the Soviets. From spring to fall 1976, Kissinger paid considerable attention to the Southern Rhodesian situation. He made two trips to Africa, gave an impressive speech, and practiced his famous shuttle diplomacy. He met personally with nearly all the principal actors, and most importantly convinced Ian Smith to accept majority rule. What can we conclude about Kissinger's foray into African affairs in 1976? On one level, his efforts were a failure which reinforce scholarly opinions about his personal flaws. The war raged for three more years, during which Smith retained control of the power structure. Kissinger's tactical mistakes, especially ignoring the views of Joshua Nkomo and Robert Mugabe, foiled any hope of a settlement in 1976.

On the other hand, in some ways Kissinger succeeded. A consensus exists regarding the importance of Kissinger coercing Smith to accept majority rule. Success or failure aside, personal mediation in the dispute by an American official at as high a level as Secretary of State set a precedent. Kissinger deserves some credit, then, for initiating the high-level US mediation that would eventually contribute to the formation of Zimbabwe. There is scholarly debate about other results of Kissinger's diplomacy, however. In *Kissinger* (1992) Walter Isaacson credited the Secretary with building trust among black Africans. As my own research demonstrated, Kissinger's dishonest methods actually alienated key black Africans like Joshua Nkomo and Julius Nyerere. If anything, Kissinger raised the barrier between black African leaders and the US government (DeRoche 2001: 209–28).

The Carter Administration

After defeating Gerald Ford in the 1976 election, Jimmy Carter intended to change the nature of US relations with Africa, shifting away from Kissinger's Cold War lens to a more regional lens. Carter himself desired this change, as did his Secretary of State Cyrus Vance. The most important American official in terms of overhauling US relations with Africa, however, was Andrew Young. An African-American minister, former assistant to Martin Luther King, and congressman from Georgia from 1973–7, Young played a key role in Carter's election to the White House. Carter asked Young to be his ambassador to the United Nations. Hoping to focus on Africa and take King's vision onto the world stage, Young accepted.

As Bartlett Jones detailed clearly in *Flawed Triumphs* (1996), Young succeeded in improving relations with Africa in many ways. Perhaps most importantly, he regained the trust of key black leaders such as Julius Nyerere. Arguably his greatest break-through with an African leader, though, was the bond he built with Nigerian president Olusegun Obasanjo. Whereas Kissinger had been banned from Nigeria,

Carter visited Nigeria in 1978 and was warmly welcomed. Dramatically improving relations with Nigeria, the most populous African nation and home to massive oil reserves, was a major accomplishment of the Carter administration.

Young and others also initiated a change in policy towards South Africa, especially regarding the issue of Namibian independence. Young, with help from his assistant Donald McHenry, spearheaded a move at the United Nations to negotiate Namibia's freedom from South African control. Although unsuccessful during Carter's tenure in the Oval Office, the peace process begun by Young and McHenry came to fruition in the early 1990s. In addition to pushing for Namibian independence the Carter administration confronted the Pretoria regime over their oppressive apartheid system, with Vice President Walter Mondale publicly condemning the South African government. In the wake of the police murder of Steve Biko in September 1977, Young advocated mandatory sanctions against South Africa. That was too radical a step for Carter, however, and only a limited arms embargo was applied in November. Although it was not as tough a response as Young desired, it was a concrete sign of a new American approach to Africa.

While for the most part the Carter administration retained its regional approach, battling institutionalized racism and seeking peace, there were instances of old-fashioned Cold War confrontation. The most significant case occurred in the Horn of Africa, starting with Somalia's invasion of Ethiopia in July 1977, by which Somalia hoped to gain the Ogaden region. The Soviets had traditionally backed Somalia, but had switched to supporting the new Marxist regime in Ethiopia. As fighting intensified, some Carter officials wanted to support Somalia in its fight against Soviet-backed Ethiopia. However, because Somalia was the clear aggressor, the United States remained neutral. In January 1978, with the crucial assistance of 20,000 Cuban troops, Ethiopia defeated Somalia. On the surface the American policy of neutrality seemed to be the right choice, as the conflict never escalated into a full-blown superpower showdown. The crisis is worthy of further analysis, however, and Nancy Mitchell is examining the Ogaden War in her research on Carter's foreign policy.

While Carter's policies towards Nigeria, South Africa, and the Ogaden War can all be interpreted as successes on some level, his greatest accomplishment regarding Africa was contributing to the transition from Southern Rhodesia to Zimbabwe. Carter, Vance, and Young sought peace and majority rule in Southern Rhodesia from day one. They quickly repealed the Byrd Amendment, returning the United States to compliance with the UN sanctions. Carter played a key role in maintaining the sanctions through 1978 and 1979, fighting off serious challenges from Byrd and Jesse Helms. Meanwhile, Young built positive relationships with Joshua Nkomo and Robert Mugabe on one side, and with Ian Smith on the other side, ultimately helping to keep negotiations alive. Finally, in December 1979, a settlement was reached, and in April 1980 the independent nation of Zimbabwe was born. The Carter administration's policy not only reflected a new approach to Africa, but also the rising influence of African Americans in US foreign relations (DeRoche 1999: 683–5). With the Zimbabwe case as a warm-up, African Americans were prepared to make their greatest contribution to US foreign relations in the battle against apartheid in the 1980s.

Ending Apartheid

The formation of Zimbabwe left only one minority-ruled nation in Africa, the notorious apartheid regime of South Africa. The central question for the United States was whether or not to apply sanctions. The administration of Ronald Reagan firmly opposed sanctions, instead initiating a policy of constructive engagement. Engineered by Assistant Secretary of State Chester Crocker, constructive engagement attempted to encourage reform by working with the South African white leadership. Simultaneously, Crocker convinced Congress to provide significant aid to Zimbabwe and Mozambique in order to maintain stability in southern Africa. Crocker was very knowledgeable about southern Africa and practiced nuanced diplomacy towards the area. Critics ignored all of this as the debate over sanctions heated up, however, and focused only on the Reagan administration's ties to Pretoria.

Randall Robinson emerged as Crocker's leading critic. Head of TransAfrica, which was formed in the late 1970s to lobby for more progressive policies towards Africa and the Caribbean, Robinson and his followers transformed the debate over South Africa into a question of civil rights. Indeed, the anti-apartheid movement practiced many of the tactics of Martin Luther King and included many former King supporters, such as Andrew Young and Walter Fauntroy. Like the civil rights struggle of the 1960s, the push for sanctions in the mid-1980s became a national grassroots movement. At the same time, Representative Ronald Dellums (D. – CA) led an increasingly powerful Congressional Black Caucus that strongly championed sanctions. In 1986 Randall Robinson and his allies in Congress triumphed, imposing tough sanctions against South Africa over Reagan's veto.

As discussed at the start of this essay, the best work on South Africa is Robert Massie's *Loosing the Bonds* (1997). The key point Massie clearly demonstrated is the impact that the Comprehensive Anti-Apartheid Act ultimately had. He argued that the sanctions applied by the United States helped convince the Pretoria regime to dismantle apartheid: freeing Nelson Mandela, recognizing the African National Congress (ANC), and holding elections in 1994. The triumph of the ANC and Mandela represented one of the great moments of the twentieth century, and a bright spot in US relations with Africa. The end of apartheid is the final example of US relations with Africa that has received scholarly treatment. Major events of the 1990s, such as the lack of a strong US response to the genocide in Rwanda or the unsuccessful American intervention in Somalia, will undoubtedly be explored by historians in future research. Those topics, along with works in progress identified in the above essay, guarantee that the study of American relations with Africa will remain alive and well for many years to come.

REFERENCES

Borstelmann, Thomas: *Apartheid's Reluctant Uncle: The United States and Southern Africa in the Early Cold War* (New York: Oxford University Press, 1993).
Borstelmann, Thomas: "'Hedging Our Bets and Buying Time': John Kennedy and Racial Revolutions in the American South and Southern Africa." *Diplomatic History* 24 (2000), 435–63.

Cobbs Hoffman, Elizabeth: *All You Need Is Love: The Peace Corps and the Spirit of the 1960s* (Cambridge, MA: Harvard University Press, 1998).

DeRoche, Andrew: "Standing Firm for Principles: Jimmy Carter and Zimbabwe." *Diplomatic History* 23 (1999), 657–85.

DeRoche, Andrew: *Black, White, and Chrome: The United States and Zimbabwe, 1953–1998* (Trenton, NJ: Africa World Press, 2001).

Fraser, Cary: "Crossing the Color Line in Little Rock: The Eisenhower Administration and the Dilemma of Race for US Foreign Policy." *Diplomatic History* 24 (2000), 233–64.

Gibbs, David: *The Political Economy of Third World Intervention: Mines, Money, and US Policy in the Congo Crisis* (Chicago, IL: University of Chicago Press, 1991).

Gleijeses, Piero: " 'Flee! The White Giants Are Coming!': The United States, the Mercenaries, and the Congo, 1964–65." *Diplomatic History* 18 (1994), 207–37.

Gleijeses, Piero: *Conflicting Missions: Havana, Washington, and Africa, 1959–1976* (Chapel Hill: University of North Carolina Press, 2002).

Harris, Joseph: *African-American Reactions to War in Ethiopia, 1936–1941* (Baton Rouge: Louisiana State University Press, 1994).

Isaacson, Walter: *Kissinger: A Biography* (New York: Simon and Schuster, 1992).

Jones, Bartlett: *Flawed Triumphs: Andy Young at the United Nations* (New York: University Press of America, 1996).

Marcus, Harold: *The Politics of Empire: Ethiopia, Great Britain and the United States, 1941–1974* (Trenton, NJ: Red Sea Press, 1995).

Massie, Robert: *Loosing the Bonds: The United States and South Africa in the Apartheid Years* (New York: Doubleday, 1997).

Noer, Thomas: "The New Frontier and African Neutralism: Kennedy, Nkrumah, and the Volta River Project." *Diplomatic History* 8 (1984), 61–79.

Noer, Thomas: *Cold War and Black Liberation: The United States and White Rule in Africa, 1948–1968* (Columbia: University of Missouri Press, 1985).

Nwaubani, Ebere: *The United States and Decolonization in West Africa, 1950–1960* (Rochester, NY: University of Rochester Press, 2001).

Plummer, Brenda: *Rising Wind: Black Americans and US Foreign Affairs, 1935–1960* (Chapel Hill: University of North Carolina Press, 1996).

Rosenberg, Emily: "The Invisible Protectorate: The United States, Liberia, and the Evolution of Neocolonialism, 1909–1940." *Diplomatic History* 9 (1985), 191–214.

Schraeder, Peter: *United States Foreign Policy Toward Africa: Incrementalism, Crisis and Change* (Cambridge: Cambridge University Press, 1994).

Scott, William: *The Sons of Sheba's Race: African Americans and the Italo–Ethiopian War, 1935–1941* (Bloomington: Indiana University Press, 1993).

Shepard, Robert: *Nigeria, Africa, and the United States: From Kennedy to Reagan* (Bloomington: Indiana University Press, 1991).

Skinner, Elliott: *African Americans and US Policy Toward Africa, 1850–1924* (Washington, DC: Howard University Press, 1992).

Von Eschen, Penny: *Race Against Empire: Black Americans and Anticolonialism, 1937–1957* (Ithaca, NY: Cornell University Press, 1997).

FURTHER READING

Anderson, Carol: "From Hope to Disillusion: African Americans, the United Nations, and the Struggle for Human Rights, 1944–1947." *Diplomatic History* 20 (1996), 531–63.

Crocker, Chester: *High Noon in Southern Africa: Making Peace in a Rough Neighborhood* (New York: Norton, 1992).

Fredrickson, George: *Black Liberation: A Comparative History of Black Ideologies in the United States and South Africa* (New York: Oxford University Press, 1995).

Gordon, David: *The United States and Africa: A Post-Cold War Perspective* (New York: Norton, 1998).

Krenn, Michael: *Black Diplomacy: African Americans and the State Department, 1945–1969* (Armonk, NY: M. E. Sharpe, 1999).

Lyon, Judson: "Informal Imperialism: The United States in Liberia, 1897–1912." *Diplomatic History* 5 (1981), 221–43.

Minter, William: *King Solomon's Mines Revisited: Western Interests and the Burdened History of Southern Africa* (New York: Basic Books, 1986).

Staniland, Martin: *American Intellectuals and African Nationalists, 1955–1970* (New Haven, CT: Yale University Press, 1991).

Wall, Irwin: "The United States, Algeria, and the Fall of the Fourth French Republic." *Diplomatic History* 18 (1994), 489–511.

Williams, G. Mennen: *Africa For The Africans* (Grand Rapids, MI: William Eerdmans, 1969).

CHAPTER EIGHT

History as Victim:
The Sorry State of the Study of
US–Japanese Relations, 1900–1945

MICHAEL A. BARNHART

It was perhaps inevitable that the study of US–Japanese relations from 1900 to 1945 would slip into the realm of myth-making. At the time of writing, the United States Congress passed legislation overriding the usual and customary procedures in order to ensure the rapid construction of a memorial to veterans of World War II in the middle of the Washington mall. A popular new Japanese prime minister vowed to pay a visit to the Yasukuni war shrine. The movie *Pearl Harbor* opened to near-record crowds despite its mangling of the past and three-hour length. Controversies still swirl over what the atomic bombing of Hiroshima and Nagasaki were really about, with renewed acrimony over the Nanjing massacre becoming a part of an increasingly heated exchange among caretakers of national pasts who present themselves, with varying degrees of insistence, as professional historians.

All this would be troubling enough, at least for those of us who insist very strongly on our professionalism, but it is compounded by a remarkable lack of interest among academic historians in this field and this period. The field is not entirely fallow. Strong work has appeared on new aspects of Japanese–US relations during World War I and the 1920s. But the grand conflagration and the critically important roads to it have been left, frankly, to the amateurs. While their output is prodigious, their methods, more often than not, are appalling. This output circles around three episodes, all much in the general public's eye and their leaders' political agendas: Hiroshima, Pearl Harbor, and Nanjing. In each case, the focus is not about events and motives of policymakers to explain what happened. Rather, it is about what should be remembered of the victims.

Leading the way is Iris Chang's impassioned *The Rape of Nanking: The Forgotten Holocaust of World War II* (1997).[1] Angry enough at the Japanese for the original atrocity, Chang reserves her full fury for their continued efforts to blind the world to that crime or deny its very existence. She is appalled that highly educated Americans have heard of Pearl Harbor and Hiroshima, but not Nanjing, and astounded that a "prominent government historian" admitted that Nanjing had never been studied even at the graduate level as a matter of course (pp. 199–200). Fortunately for American graduate instructors, Chang lays the blame for this ignorance squarely at the feet of Japanese politicians such as Ishihara Shintaro or

Hashimoto Ryutaro, who either deny the rape altogether or blame it on a war forced upon Japan by the West, and a Japanese academic establishment that knowingly conspires with such politicians to keep the Japanese people in ignorance. Those few Japanese who have sought the real story or, worse, to tell it have been victimized by an incessant campaign of official harassment and public hate, such as Motoshima Hitoshi, former mayor of Nagasaki, who was shot for questioning the Japanese emperor's responsibility for war crimes (pp. 213–14).

This is not to say that professional works by Western academics get off lightly. Rather, Chang ignores them. Her attention is reserved for the audience much more than the accuracy of the story. High school textbooks and pictorial histories of World War II give Nanjing too short shrift. Churchill's memoirs offer no mention at all. Gerhard Weinberg's *A World at Arms* (1995) has a mere two references (Chang 1997: 6–7). Chang, however, can claim barely more herself. While her research, oral and in records in China and the United States, is studious on the horrors of the rape itself, it is minuscule as to why it occurred.

Chang's aim is to get headlines for the Nanjing massacre. But, as history, *The Rape of Nanking* is caricature, so much so as to invite precisely the criticism it has received, especially in Japan. Chang's treatment of the origins of the massacre is at best a cardboard account of a Japanese culture thoroughly imbued with the warrior spirit of *bushidō*, led by officer-propagandists who dedicated their careers to provoking war with China. Finally achieving it by the summer of 1937, these officers were outraged by the audacity of the Chinese to actually resist. They determined to have their revenge through the systematic humiliation of Nanjing – then China's capital.[2] There is no mention, let alone appreciation, of the far more complex situation inside Japan's imperial army itself, much less that army's status within a far-from-monolithic Japanese government. Impressive studies on important dissenters, such as Peattie (1976) on Ishiwara Kanji, have no place in Chang's riveting but one-dimensional story.[3]

Chang's book was a bestseller in America. For that very reason, it attracted immediate condemnation by right-wing Japanese and, as importantly, Japanese war veterans. The most important of these latter was Tanaka Masaaki, who had been General Matsui Iwane's secretary at the time of the massacre and who wrote *What Really Happened in Nanking: The Refutation of a Common Myth* (2000). Originally published in 1987, the book appeared thirteen years later – in English – in direct mailings to American scholars in Japanese studies. Its introduction minces no words: it has been translated and distributed specifically to refute Chang's attempts to induce hatred of Japan among Americans.

It may be tempting to dismiss Tanaka's work out of hand, but his derives from the same motive as Chang's: the need to capture the "correct" past for the public. Moreover, like Chang, Tanaka offers his own castigation of the professional historians' methods and priorities. He was there or, at the least, he personally visited Nanjing only months after the massacre and had personally interviewed the General immediately after the war. There was no real massacre then, in his view, so subsequent attempts to depict one are constructs of fiction. Constructs, Tanaka asserts, that were deliberately manufactured by the Guomindong regime in November 1945 for use in the Tokyo war crimes trials and that have been inflated by the communist Chinese government whenever it has been useful to bash Japan in recent decades.[4]

Tanaka's denial of the massacre is ludicrous, but his charges against China are not entirely off the mark. In a splendid volume on the massacre (Fogel 2000), Mark Eykholt agrees that it was not well known until after the war's end, when indeed the Nationalist government presented its evidence at the Tokyo trials. This evidence, however, was hardly a fabrication. Indeed, the Nationalists were at pains to document the slaughter precisely because it seemed so unbelievable. After all, by even the most conservative estimates, the imperial army had murdered by bludgeon, bullet, and bayonet more people than either atomic bomb. It had done so in a clearly organized campaign – the international Safety Zone was left largely unmolested and Westerners were not injured.

The Chinese may have assembled an impressive case, but its results were hugely disappointing, for two reasons. First, the Tokyo trials (like most American histories since) treated China as a tertiary, backwater front of the war. The Bataan Death March and fall of Singapore received more attention than any episode in the far longer and far bloodier Sino-Japanese conflict. Second, the emerging Cold War and concomitant rehabilitation of Japan in American eyes made the events in Nanjing awkward for the Chinese Nationalists, who used Japanese troops in important supporting roles during the civil war against the communists. After those communists came to power themselves, emphasizing years of China's common cause with the Americans was distinctly out of style.

As Tanaka charges and as Eykholt confirms, the communist government turned public attention away from or toward the Nanjing massacre as its diplomacy required. Its quest for Japanese goods and especially capital muzzled coverage of Nanjing through the 1970s.[5] This state of affairs ought to have continued, but Japan's insistence on its own construction of the past – especially a construction that essentially endorsed Tanaka's extreme position – so infuriated China (and many other Asian nations) that they sought rebuttal. Restoring the Nanjing massacre to the public's eye was a vital beginning of this effort, which saw the establishment of a massacre memorial in China and mandatory visits to it for Chinese schoolchildren.[6] Another aspect was the Chinese government's newfound encouragement of exposés such as Iris Chang's.

But why would Japan embrace such a radical view of its past, a view that at best ignores the massacre and insists instead that Japan was a pan-Asianist crusader out to rid that part of the world of the scourge of the West?[7] A sophisticated answer would require an in-depth examination of postwar Japanese politics and society. As Charles Maier (2000) has observed, however, the key is the strong emergence of the Japanese Right at least since the 1960s,[8] and the Right's use of its own theme of victimization – Japan as victim.

The cult of Japan-as-victim enjoys a considerable advantage over its Chinese rival. Whereas the Nanjing massacre was little known for decades, and has required great efforts in China and America to bring it to the public's attention, Hiroshima and Nagasaki were instant attractions with excellent public relations staying power. Better yet, the Americans themselves were willing, even eager, to portray the Japanese as victims. The keystone occasion was the decision by the Smithsonian's

National Air and Space Museum to present an exhibit marking the fiftieth anniversary of the use of the atomic bomb. One of the planners, Edward Linenthal, put it best: this exhibit was to be a "forum," not a "temple." And it was going to show the victims of the bomb along with the bomber *Enola Gay*, just as the museum's 1990 exhibit of a German V-2 missile included photographs of its human casualties (Linenthal and Engelhardt 1996: 23).

To the surprise of some museum staff and academic historians, but virtually no one else, this plan aroused immediate and strong protests from American veteran organizations and right-wing politicians.[9] For the Smithsonian, the timing was unfortunate, as the November 1994 elections swept in new Republican leaders who were vengefully partisan and determined to shift federal policies radically. Its budget under threat, the museum beat a hasty retreat and agreed to substantial revisions in the *Enola Gay* exhibit. The result was the worst of all worlds. Veteran groups, whose representatives were able to suggest specific changes in the exhibit, continued to complain that the real victims of Hiroshima would have been their comrades who would have perished had the atomic bomb not been dropped and an invasion of Japan taken place. Even more than the disputes over the number of massacred at Nanjing, the exchanges concerning how many Americans (and Japanese) would have perished in an invasion of the home islands have acquired an air of unreality or, as John Dower (1996) has put it, a "sacred numerology."

But the changes adopted to propitiate the veterans dismayed professional historians, such as Akira Iriye. "Balance" in the exhibit might be politically prudent, but the revisions were not historically accurate. These complaints, in turn, permitted opportunistic political leaders with further opportunities to claim that history was being "hijacked" by soft-hearted eggheads.[10] By the start of 1995, the exhibit had been cancelled.

The general public might have its myths left unstirred, but the eggheads had their journals to forward discussion of the American decision to use atomic weapons. *Diplomatic History* published an unusually useful collection of articles in its spring 1995 issue.[11] To be sure, there is still no total consensus on that decision, but it seems increasingly clear that a number of factors made the bomb's use practically unavoidable. By the spring of 1945 the top American military leaders – Generals George Marshall and Douglas MacArthur of the army and Hap Arnold of the army air force[s] – had prevailed over Admiral Ernest King's preference for a siege of Japan. Instead, all means would be used to induce surrender. The siege, by submarine, mining, and most spectacularly aerial bombardment, would continue, but it would be supplemented, and in fact made more effective, by an invasion of Kyushu, Japan's southernmost main island. Truman, newly come to office, was in no position to single-handedly veto this strategy, nor is there any indication that he wished to. Likewise, he was hardly inclined to block use of the atomic bomb, pushed vigorously by Manhattan Project supervisor General Leslie Groves. The bomb, as Barton Bernstein persuasively argues, was simply one more complement to the siege-and-invade strategy. Truman reserved any decision about an invasion of Honshu (the largest of the main islands), which would have been an even more daunting affair than the assault on Kyushu.[12]

This argument has the signal advantage of avoiding hindsight and eschewing the construction of memory. For all the post-Hiroshima impact of the atomic bomb, its use at the time was only a piece of a strategy – and not even the most expensive piece. Much has been made of the $2 billion price tag of the Manhattan Project. But the cost of deploying the fleet of B-29 bombers that rained more conventional (if that is the right word) destruction on Japan was nearly twice as great, as Kenneth Werrell (1996) makes clear in his study of those aircraft and their uses.[13]

Werrell's study is illuminating in other respects. His discussion of the American bombing campaign illustrates how utterly "pitiful" Japanese air and civilian defense measures were (ibid: 230). From the first meager efforts against the home islands in June 1944 to the horrific fire raid over Tokyo in March 1945, Japan had nine months to prepare countermeasures. When General Curtis LeMay briefed his pilots on the Tokyo raid, most thought it would be a suicide mission. In fact only fourteen planes were lost. The initial fire bombing campaign was paused not from Japanese opposition, but because the United States could not produce the bombs quickly enough (ibid: ch. 6). There were victims aplenty well before Hiroshima (and the Japanese authorities did not even undertake such basic steps as dispersing civilians and strengthening firefighting capabilities). But victims of what? An American decision to use fire and then atomic weapons, or a Japanese decision to continue a hopeless war that guaranteed large noncombatant casualties and horrific damage?

Any answer must examine the situation within the Japanese government during the last year of the war. Unfortunately, very few American scholars have done so.[14] One is Herbert Bix, whose work on Hirohito and Japan's "delayed surrender" compels rethinking both subjects (Bix 1996, 2000). The emperor perfectly understood that the loss of the Marianas in June 1944 meant the start of a bombing campaign over the home islands, so he ordered it retaken – a complete exercise in fantasy. Instead, Japan would rely upon sacrificial kamikaze tactics against new American offensives, arm women and children with bamboo spears, and release thousands of "balloon bombs," devices meant to drift across the Pacific and then drop on the American west coast. After Okinawa was lost, a year later, Hirohito approved plans for a defense of the home islands that heavily emphasized suicide tactics (Bix 2000: chs. 12–13).[15]

Much of Bix's biography portrays the great success the Japanese Right enjoyed – often with American assistance – in constructing a version of the Japanese past that exonerated Hirohito and, perhaps even more impressively, permitted the rapid political resurgence of that Right. It is ironic in no small way that Hiroshima and Nagasaki, actions made possible by the Right's utter disregard for the innocents of Japan, were instrumental in fostering a cult of victimization that ensured the Right's continued hold on the government after the war. Irony is present too in the Japanese Rightists' applauding of the efforts of American veterans' groups to "correct" the planned Smithsonian exhibition (Yoshida 2000). You keep your myths; we keep ours.

The most cherished American myth, however, remains Pearl Harbor. Even sixty years after the Japanese attack, books continue to be published with that ominous term "truth" in their titles or subtitles. As with the controversies and politics surrounding the Nanjing massacre and the atomic bombings, the Pearl Harbor debates focus on victims and ignore the wider contexts and histories of US–Japanese relations.

The latest screed is from Robert Stinnett (2000), a former naval officer certain that the biggest victim of the Pearl Harbor attack was Admiral Husband Kimmel. According to Stinnett, practically everyone in the United States government except Kimmel knew of the coming attack. The chief villain was Rear Admiral Walter Anderson, who had been promoted to be battleship commander out of purely political considerations, Stinnett argues, in order to serve as Roosevelt's henchman in Hawaii. Anderson, who had been posted to the Office of Naval Intelligence, ensured that Kimmel never received decrypts of intercepted Japanese transmissions. Anderson played a key role in calling off FBI surveillance of Japanese spy Yoshikawa Takeo so that he could provide detailed maps of Pearl Harbor to the imperial navy. Anderson made certain that RCA's offer to share its receipt of Japanese radio messages did not include Kimmel. Anderson even had the foresight, not to mention the gall, to take up residence on the side of Diamond Head facing Maui so that no stray bombs from the Japanese attack would damage his home (ibid: chs. 2, 3, 6, 7).[16]

Stinnett's analysis provides reassurance to academic historians that they must be doing something right in training their graduate students, who would be embarrassed to make some of the elementary errors of analysis that are commonplace in his book.[17] On the other hand, it is at least mildly troubling that Stinnett does not bother to cite – and clearly did not bother to read – a single account on US–Japanese relations by a professional historian.[18] His understanding of the Japanese side of the attack is remarkable only in its absence, which leaves him openly wondering why Japanese task force commander Nagano Osami so frequently and blatantly broke radio silence to reveal his position en route to Hawaii. Perhaps Nagano was trying to reach Anderson to arrange some real estate transactions once the war was over?

Whatever his faults, however, Stinnett did engage in archival research, particularly in the navy's signals sections. Most of the other books appearing cannot even make this claim.[19] One that does repay reading is H. P. Willmott's *Pearl Harbor* (2001). In a trenchant analysis, Willmott establishes the contexts – Japanese and American – of the origins of the attack in a way that quietly but overwhelmingly gives lie to the essence of Stinnett's and the other revisionists' position. In essence:

> Yamamoto's insistence that war begin with an attack on the American fleet at Pearl Harbor represented a demand for an operation which at the time could not be executed simply because the First Carrier Striking Force could have reached the Hawaiian Islands but lacked the range to return to home waters. The First Carrier Striking Force came within two days of having to sail without its full torpedo complement. It also had no guarantee that its Kates and Vals would be able to carry their designated ordnance and, stretching a point, no guarantee that its bombers could do anything but miss the target en masse while recording only the occasional hit. This was, to say the least, an extraordinary state of affairs. (Ibid: 62)

Unlike Chang or Stinnett, Willmott reminds us to see history as it unfolded, not with hindsight, much less a hindsight burdened by agenda. The remarkable contingency of events comes alive in these pages, as opposed to the wooden inevitability of revisionist accounts such as Stinnett's. As well, Willmott is a great deal more careful with his evidence. Could the Americans have been better prepared? he asks. Possibly, but events that in retrospect seem part of a whole, at the time would have been difficult to piece together. Willmott does not let high officials off unscathed by any means, and George Marshall in particular comes under scrutiny.[20]

Willmott's approach naturally raises again the question of why Japan attacked at all. There was no doubt in either Tokyo or Washington that the United States would prevail in the ensuing conflict. Collective insanity in the former hardly seems an ideal explanation, although the same narrow attachments to institutional loyalties that prolonged the agony of 1944–5 were certainly present four years earlier. While the most direct approach to these considerations has been curiously neglected by scholars,[21] recent years have seen the publication of studies on the 1910s and 1920s that help establish the context of America's and Japan's road to war in 1941.

Izumi Hirobe (2001) makes no attempt to link the American anti-immigration law of 1924 directly to Pearl Harbor, but he does show how corrosive that law was to interpersonal ties of friendship that had been built painstakingly since the Meiji Restoration. The law silenced (indeed, it outraged) influential pro-American leaders such as Shibusawa Eiichi, Kaneko Kentarō and Nitobe Inazō. It dismayed advocates for cooperation with the United States in the Japanese Foreign Ministry, who were bitterly surprised by Charles Evans Hughes' inability to block the legislation.[22] It encouraged right-wing organizations such as the Amur River Society (Kokuryūkai) to brand Americans as racists and claim that only Asians could make Asia free.[23]

Hirobe's focus is not on the 1924 law itself but rather on efforts to have it overturned or amended. Foreign Minister Shidehara Kijurō declined to participate, convinced that any official Japanese involvement would prove counterproductive. Japanese residing in the United States likewise kept silent. The initiative fell to American religious groups, women's clubs, and academics, which succeeded only in keeping the anti-Japanese forces active and vocal. Those forces were led by Valentine Stuart McClatchy of the *Sacramento Bee*, with generous funding from farm and labor organizations as well as the American Legion (Hirobe 2001: 14–16). This unequal contest continued until 1929, when new Japanese restrictions on lumber imports and the onset of the Great Depression brought several business leaders into the repeal movement. The new effort proved short-lived, a victim of growing hostility toward Japan among the American public at large due to the Shanghai Incident of 1932[24] and newly elected President Franklin Roosevelt's reluctance to make repeal an item of any priority. With the outbreak of general hostilities in the summer of 1937, Chinese leaders both in China and America were increasingly able to portray the Japanese as savage barbarians and render impossible any hope for repeal.[25] Throughout his study, Hirobe is careful to draw no direct connection between the immigration law and Pearl Harbor. Yet it is jarring to read his translation of a Foreign Ministry memorandum penned in February 1941: "The only solution to the fundamental question of the racial superiority of the white Americans is by a demonstration of the actual power and ability of Japan as a nation, ultimately, of course in our present world condition, by force of arms" (Hirobe 2001: 219).

Ironically, one of the sources for that sense of racial superiority was the very religious – especially missionary – groups that later worked for the repeal of the 1924 law. Jon Thares Davidann (1998) begins his study in the 1880s, when the American missionary movement revived. To his credit, Davidann takes care to trace the context of this revival, which took place as a reaction against "liberal theology" that had downplayed Christianity's uniqueness and the vitality of individual salvation.

Such an aggressive, even arrogant strain of Protestantism would seem ill suited to thrive abroad. Indeed, it converted remarkably few, primarily individuals, such as Nitobe Inazō, who detested Japan's old order (especially the Buddhist establishment) and sought moral regeneration for themselves and their nation. Nitobe, typical of the converts, was a veritable human dynamo.[26] While their energy allowed these men to survive often extreme social stigma, it also drove them to try to seize control of the missionary organizations – such as the YMCA or universities – the Americans had built and funded. It also led to increasing Japanese resentment of American mission activities in Korea and Manchuria, where the converts argued they could succeed better than the whites.[27] These frictions, coupled with a general decline of interest in the United States for sponsoring missionary activities, ended most American initiatives by the 1920s.

Hirobe and Davidann explore the role of private groups and non-governmental organizations in shaping US–Japanese relations, but there is still much to be learned from more traditional studies of the governments themselves. Two books in particular merit attention, both on Japan and World War I.

Noriko Kawamura's *Turbulence in the Pacific* (2000) sits squarely in the international arena. The main threads of her story will be familiar to scholars in the field. They focus on Japan's Twenty-one Demands upon China and Woodrow Wilson's Fourteen Points. Kawamura reminds us that the two were not equivalent. Japan's foreign policy during these years was devoted overwhelmingly to strengthening its position on the Asian continent, whereas Wilson was only fleetingly concerned with East Asian affairs. Some of his subordinates, however, most notoriously Paul Reinsch, saw themselves as virtual paladins for China. They were able to rally vocal blocs of Americans to their cause, especially the religious groups most active in the missionary movement.[28] Kawamura persuasively argues that the driving force behind the Lansing–Ishii agreement was not America's entry into the world war, but different views in Tokyo and Washington concerning China's possible entry. One issue that surfaced in negotiations leading to this agreement, and in internal American discussions on the Twenty-one Demands, was American land tenure legislation.[29] On both occasions, Wilson's senior advisers such as Edward T. Williams and Robert Lansing were willing to grant Japan relatively wide leeway in exchange for taking land tenure off the table for good (Kawamura 2000: chs. 2, 4).[30] Kawamura criticizes Wilson for proposing even a qualified, limited intervention in Siberia. Had he continued his opposition, she is confident that Japanese opponents could have held firm. As it was, Wilson yielded to the expansionists, whose radical steps in Siberia alienated Wilson (and those presidents who came after him) and tilted power within Japan to the imperial army (ibid: ch. 5).

Concerns about power within Japan dominate Frederick Dickinson's splendid *War and National Reinvention* (1999). Indeed, in his account, foreign policy is simply one tool employed by competing elites in their quest for political dominance within a still-undefined polity. Shaken by the Chinese Revolution of 1911, which threatened the sanctity of Japan's own monarchy, and the internal Taishō Crisis of 1912–13, astute Japanese leaders saw the outbreak of world war as a heaven-sent opportunity to create a stable (and conservative) political order in Japan. One of the most astute was Baron Katō Takaaki, Foreign Minister in 1915 and author of the Twenty-one Demands. Katō, previously regarded as a reckless, even bumbling, diplomat, emerges here as a skilled and ambitious politician acutely sensitive to the shifting political constellations of early Taishō Japan. Dickinson depicts his chief adversaries, many of them in the imperial army, as the real radicals, ready to consider even crises with America over China if that ensured the army's power at home.

Dickinson's interpretation of the Twenty-one Demands affair is illuminating on several counts. Katō did not require China to accept them, only for his Foreign Office to preempt the army in making them. Even Katō's resignation, after the affair led to American protests, was hardly a setback for him, as his political party (the Dōshikai) did exceptionally well in the 1915 elections and Katō had high hopes of becoming prime minister.

The United States was a tool of rival elites in the Demands affair, but it was central to that rivalry after it entered the war, for two reasons. First, the Bolshevik Revolution had shaken those elites to the core. Far more than the Chinese Revolution, the emergence of the Soviet Union was a deadly threat to conservative Japan. The arch-conservatives, with many again located in the imperial army, wanted the Bolsheviks overthrown. But that required, at the least, an invasion of Siberia and any such invasion required the consent, at the least, of the United States.[31]

Second, an America dedicated to Wilsonian ideals was itself a direct threat to conservative Japan. Wilson had made clear, after all, that while he was not opposed to monarchy itself, he was opposed – strongly – to militarism, a reference that made any self-respecting officer in the imperial army uncomfortable. Dickinson overthrows another myth by portraying Hara Takashi[32] as the civilian champion of the conservatives. As prime minister in 1918, Hara increased the army's budget. He agreed to naval arms limitation talks with the Americans primarily to reduce spending on the imperial navy. He undertook electoral reform to limit the expansion of voting rights. And his foreign policy, especially in China, was geared to minimizing American influence (and Wilsonian ideas) there. Indeed, Dickinson (p. 220ff.) maintains that Hara and Yamagata, a fascinating pair of allies, feared Wilsonianism more than Bolshevism.

If Dickinson is right, there is all the more reason for a fundamental reassessment of US–Japanese relations from 1920 to 1945.[33] It is all the more tragic that the story of these years has been surrendered to the myth-makers. Their purposes and agendas may be praised or condemned, but it is vital to stress that rendering an objective analysis of what happened in the past, and why, is not their concern. This sorry state of affairs leaves the biggest victim of all in its wake: history itself.

Postscript

Any written piece becomes dated as soon as pen lifts from paper. It is particularly perilous for an author to identify developments contemporary to his writing, inasmuch as subsequent events, especially great ones, can render all he has written incorrect, irrelevant, or simply quaint.

Certainly the attacks of September 11, 2001 qualify as an event, and certainly a great one. But the analysis that followed, and that has persisted for at least a year after, only seems to confirm the basic thrust of what has been argued above. The instant analogy of "9/11" to the "day of infamy" of Japan's attack on Pearl Harbor is fundamentally poor. It is bad history, an unenlightening use of the past.

For all the dastardly timing of the Pearl Harbor attack, and for Japan's conduct of its war elsewhere, the facts remain that the Japanese government attempted to provide notice of the opening of hostilities according to established international procedures and that the attack itself was concentrated upon military targets. Indeed, its execution has been criticized for being concentrated too heavily on such targets and ignoring such opportunities as fuel storage tanks.

As importantly, the United States government, for all the immediate intelligence failings relating to the attack, was well aware that hostilities with Japan were imminent. Washington already had taken steps, however inadequate they turned out to be, to prepare for attacks upon American military facilities, including those in Hawaii.

The atrocities of "9/11" bear closer similarity to an attack with a different date: June 25, 1950: the opening of the Korean War. The attackers of June were outraged with American support, however inconsistent or even bumbling, for a regime in Seoul that they saw as oppressive, corrupt, and foreign. American policy was indeed inconsistent and American attention uncertain. Certainly the June attack was a monumental surprise in all regards, just as 9/11 was.

The American reaction to June 25 was swift but mixed. The outbreak of the Korean War dramatically accelerated fears of domestic subversion within the United States and eroded civil liberties at exactly the moment when America's best weapon in foreign policy might have been an emphasis on the superiority, despite the drawbacks, of its open system as compared to its enemies. On the international front, however, President Harry Truman swiftly moved to assemble an international consensus and coalition to prosecute an armed and diplomatic response. The jury is still out on Washington's response to 9/11, of course, but there is little reason to believe, at least at this moment, that history's hijackers are becoming any wiser.

NOTES

1 Chang uses "Nanking," employing the older Wade–Giles method of romanizing Chinese terms.

2 Chang (1997: ch. 1). Although Chang makes no reference to the infamous "Tanaka Memorial," a forged document "leaked" in the 1930s that purported to be the secret Japanese plan to conquer China, her account of the background of the massacre bears an uncanny resemblance to it.

3 Chang employs Bergamini's questionable *Japan's Imperial Conspiracy* (1971) as her chief source, though she does refer once to Herbert Bix's earlier work on Hirohito.

4 Masaaki (2000: ch. 8). See also another Japanese work translated and distributed to American scholars: Takemoto and Ohara (2000).

5 In fact, the Chinese government suppressed survivors' testimonies about Nanjing during these years. See Daqing Yang, "The Challenges of the Nanjing Massacre: Reflections on Historical Inquiry," in Fogel (2000).

6 A chronic irritation has been the treatment of the war, including the massacre, in Japanese history texts, which are sanctioned by the Ministry of Education. For decades, the massacre was passed over entirely. Only in 1996 was accurate coverage inserted, over strong vocal opposition from Japanese conservatives, including over one hundred members of the Japanese Diet. See Takashi Yoshida, "A Battle over History: The Nanjing Massacre in Japan," in Fogel (2000).

7   This interpretation is as popular in Japan as ever. In the spring of 2001 *Merdeka*, a film portraying the Japanese army as instrumental in Indonesia's fight for independence, was released. Some Japanese critics deplored the film's scenes of Japanese officers slapping Indonesian trainees, even though they admitted that the practice had been common. See *Japan Times*, March 27, 2001.

8   Some would put this rightist reemergence before the 1960s. Indeed, some would argue that the Right in Japan never had to reemerge at all. Some of the work reflected in the Fogel volume has been continued and expanded in an international project on the Sino-Japanese conflict. See http://www.fas.harvard.edu/'asiactr/sino-japanese/sino-japanese_summary2.htm.

9   The chief driving force behind the attack on the exhibit came from the Air Force Association which, as Richard Kohn (1996) trenchantly observes, has never been happy with the Smithsonian as the curator of its service history, unlike the army and navy, which have their own historical units.

10   See the Introduction and Linenthal's "Anatomy of a Controversy," in Linenthal and Engelhardt (1996).

11   These articles were subsequently published in book form (Hogan 1996).

12   It is at least possible that Truman's subsequent claims of Japan's atomic-induced surrender saving a half-million lives arose from his inclusion of a Honshu operation. In any event, a fine study of the invasion, including the "sacred numerology" of the casualty controversy, is Skates (1994). Excellent discussions of the bomb decision are Walker (1996) and Bernstein (1996).

13   The cost of developing, deploying, and maintaining the B-29s was $3.75 billion, to be precise (Werrell 1996: 238). There seems to have been no Air Force Association protests over this book's publication.

14   It is a disgrace that there is no study of the politics of Japan's high command during the war in English.

15   In yet another irony, the Japanese press seized on Robert Sherrod's *Time* magazine account of the last days of the battle of Saipan to create the myth of civilians sacrificing themselves by the thousand rather than accept capture by the Americans. It was the perfect martyr myth to prepare for the invasion of the home islands. See Cook (2001).

16   The charge that Anderson deliberately located his home away from the fleet is made on p. 111. Anderson is not the only target. Stinnett bluntly accuses Edwin Layton of lying to Kimmel about the coming attack and Joseph Rochefort of misleading Kimmel by deliberately omitting reports of intercepts of the onrushing Japanese attack force: see Stinnett (2000: ch. 13).

17   To recount one: Stinnett cites a memorandum by a Lieutenant Commander in ONI written in October 1940 that laid out an eight-step program for provoking Japan into war. Roosevelt slavishly followed this program, although there is no evidence that the president ever saw the memo. See Stinnett (2000: 6–8).

18   There are references to works by William Manchester and Jonathan Marshall.

19   For example, there is Bruckheimer et al. (2001).

20   One example of care with evidence is Willmott's handling of the famous controversy over a "third strike" against Pearl Harbor, which he shows to be an historical figment, devoid of fact, that deceived even Gordon Prange in his otherwise outstanding study (see Willmott 2001: 154–7). Willmott also has interesting speculation about the American intelligence failures. For Marshall's role in them, see p. 198.

21   It has been thirty-five years since the appearance of the last study in English of the imperial Japanese army's senior officers and their internal politics: Crowley (1966).

22   At the 2001 conference of the Society for Historians of American Foreign Relations,

Hirobe argued that Hughes himself was so disappointed that the law's passage was critical in his decision to resign.

23 Hirobe (2001: 115) notes a passage in the diary of General Ugaki Kazushige, a central figure in the imperial army in the interwar period, on the increased likelihood of war with the United States. Unfortunately, there is no sustained discussion of the immigration law's wider impact on army thinking or planning during these years.

24 Interestingly, the imperial army's conquest of Manchuria, begun a year earlier, did not greatly affect the public at large according to Hirobe (2001: ch. 6, esp. p. 160).

25 Anti-Chinese provisions were repealed in 1943 as a gesture to an ally, exactly the same considerations that would drive the cancellation of the anti-Japanese law in 1952 (Hirobe 2001: 237–41).

26 Nitobe wrote *Bushidō* (The Way of the Warrior) in 1900. It became a school textbook and was widely translated (Davidann 1998: 72).

27 The converts often won these struggles. The Korean YMCA was absorbed into the Japanese Y in 1913 (Davidann 1998: 147).

28 During the height of the Twenty-one Demands affair, American religious leaders in China sent a twenty-page telegram to Wilson (paid for by the Chinese government) (Kawamura 2000: 49–51).

29 Specifically, state laws that barred Japanese from owning real estate.

30 In Kawamura's study, land tenure appears to have been a more important issue than the so-called "racial equality clause" (so-called because it did not request equality, just non-discrimination – an obvious reference to matters such as land tenure) that Japan wanted included in the League of Nations Covenant. The Japanese were surprised that Wilson was willing to approve any version of the clause, though disappointed that in its vote the United States abstained (Kawamura 2000: 143).

31 Indeed, the army's real head, Yamagata Aritomo, initially opposed the Siberian Expedition not out of restraint. Quite the opposite. He feared that any joint intervention with Washington would constrain Japan's wider aims (Dickinson 1999: 189–98).

32 Also known as Hara Kei.

33 And of course for the years after 1945 which saw, at best, only a limited introduction of Wilsonian ideas into the Japanese polity.

REFERENCES

Bergamini, David: *Japan's Imperial Conspiracy* (New York: William Morrow, 1971).

Bernstein, Barton J.: "Understanding the Atomic Bomb and the Japanese Surrender: Missed Opportunities, Little-Known Near Disaster, and Modern Memory." In Michael J. Hogan (ed.) *Hiroshima in History and Memory* (Cambridge: Cambridge University Press, 1996).

Bix, Herbert P.: "Japan's Delayed Surrender: A Reinterpretation." In Michael J. Hogan (ed.) *Hiroshima in History and Memory* (Cambridge: Cambridge University Press, 1996).

Bix, Herbert P.: *Hirohito and the Making of Modern Japan* (New York: HarperCollins, 2000).

Bruckheimer, Jerry et al. (ed.): *Pearl Harbor: The Movie and the Moment* (New York: Hyperion, 2001).

Chang, Iris: *The Rape of Nanking: The Forgotten Holocaust of World War II* (New York: Basic Books, 1997).

Cook, Haruko Taya: "The Myth of the Saipan Suicides." In Robert Cowley (ed.) *No End Save Victory: Perspectives on World War II* (New York: G. P. Putnam's Sons, 2001).

Crowley, James: *Japan's Quest for Autonomy* (Princeton, NJ: Princeton University Press, 1966).

Davidann, Jon Thares: *A World of Crisis and Progress: The American YMCA in Japan, 1890–1930* (Bethlehem: Lehigh University Press. 1998).

Dickinson, Frederick R.: *War and National Reinvention: Japan in the Great War, 1914–1919* (Cambridge, MA: Harvard University Press, 1999).

Dower, John W.: "Three Narratives of Our Humanity." In Edward T. Linenthal and Tom Engelhardt (eds.) *History Wars: The Enola Gay and Other Battles for the American Past* (New York: Henry Holt, 1996).

Eykholt, Mark: "Aggression, Victimization, and Chinese Historiography of the Nanjing Massacre." In Joshua A. Fogel (ed.) *The Nanjing Massacre in History and Historiography* (Berkeley: University of California Press, 2000).

Fogel, Joshua A. (ed.): *The Nanjing Massacre in History and Historiography* (Berkeley: University of California Press, 2000).

Hirobe, Izumi: *Japanese Pride, American Prejudice: Modifying the Exclusion Clause of the 1924 Immigration Act* (Stanford, CA: Stanford University Press, 2001).

Hogan, Michael J. (ed.): *Hiroshima in History and Memory* (Cambridge: Cambridge University Press, 1996).

Kawamura, Noriko: *Turbulence in the Pacific: Japanese–US Relations during World War I* (New York: Praeger, 2000).

Kohn, Richard H.: "History at Risk: The Case of the *Enola Gay*." In Edward T. Linenthal and Tom Engelhardt (eds.) *History Wars: The Enola Gay and Other Battles for the American Past* (New York: Henry Holt, 1996).

Linenthal, Edward T. and Tom Engelhardt (eds.): *History Wars: The Enola Gay and Other Battles for the American Past* (New York: Henry Holt, 1996).

Maier, Charles: "Foreword." In Joshua A. Fogel (ed.) *The Nanjing Massacre in History and Historiography* (Berkeley: University of California Press, 2000).

Masaaki, Tanaka: *What Really Happened in Nanking: The Refutation of a Common Myth* (Tokyo: Sekai Shuppan, 2000).

Peattie, Mark: *Ishiwara Kanji and Japan's Confrontation with the West* (Princeton, NJ: Princeton University Press, 1976).

Skates, John Ray: *The Invasion of Japan: Alternative to the Bomb* (Columbia: University of South Carolina Press, 1994).

Stinnett, Robert B.: *Day of Deceit: The Truth About FDR and Pearl Harbor* (New York: Touchstone, 2000).

Takemoto, Tadao and Yasuo Ohara: *The Alleged "Nanking Massacre": Japan's Rebuttal to China's Forged Claims* (Tokyo: Meisei-sha, 2000).

Walker, J. Samuel: "The Decision to Use the Bomb: A Historiographical Update." In Michael J. Hogan (ed.) *Hiroshima in History and Memory* (Cambridge: Cambridge University Press, 1996).

Weinberg, Gerhard L.: *A World at Arms: A Global History of World War II* (Cambridge: Cambridge University Press, 1995).

Werrell, Kenneth P.: *Blankets of Fire: US Bombers over Japan during World War II* (Washington, DC: Smithsonian Institution Press, 1996).

Willmott, H. P. with Tohmatsu Haruo and W. Spencer Johnson: *Pearl Harbor* (London: Cassell, 2001).

Yang, Daqing: "The Challenges of the Nanjing Massacre: Reflections on Historical Inquiry." In Joshua A. Fogel (ed.) *The Nanjing Massacre in History and Historiography* (Berkeley: University of California Press, 2000).

Yoshida, Takashi: "A Battle over History: The Nanjing Massacre in Japan." In Joshua A. Fogel (ed.) *The Nanjing Massacre in History and Historiography* (Berkeley: University of California Press, 2000).

CHAPTER NINE

US–Latin American Relations, 1898–1941: A Historiographical Review

MARK T. GILDERHUS

The centenary of the Spanish–American–Cuban–Filipino War in 1998 passed without much public notice from the masses or the media in the United States. For historians, in contrast, as if to compensate for such neglect, the event significantly marked the anniversary of a brief but portentous encounter between a declining empire of the Old World and the emerging colossus of the New. School children can enumerate the principal effects. The victory consolidated for the United States its hegemonic grip on the Caribbean region, resulting in the creation of, if not an empire, then something very much like one. It also extended United States influence across the Pacific through the annexation of the Philippines. These results had long-term impacts, notably upon the conduct of United States relations with the countries of Latin America. This essay reviews recent literature in English for the period from 1898 through 1941.

As readers know, fashions in history come and go. What scholars at one time have judged as enduring truths later may appear as ephemera. For that reason, historical discourse often assumes the form of an ongoing debate over evidence and points of view. Such is the case in the study of US diplomatic history. Historiographically, Samuel Flagg Bemis' classic work, *The Latin American Policy of the United States* (1967), is a place to begin. Bemis, a "founding father" of diplomatic history and a "nationalist" in his approach, presents his case for the most part in a positive fashion. According to him, the United States in modern times has behaved creditably by conforming with the requirements of the Monroe Doctrine and safeguarding the Western hemisphere against European intrusions, no matter whether Latin Americans displayed much appreciation or not. His emphasis on the defense of security interests qualifies Bemis as a traditionalist. Yet he reacts against the excesses of public enthusiasm for expansion at the turn of the century and castigates the McKinley administration for unwisely indulging in imperialism. Happily for him, the experiment lasted only for a short while. He calls it a "great aberration" (Gilderhus 1997: 1–3).

Traditional versions of the War with Spain emphasize distinctive themes. They depict a hapless President McKinley as a weak-kneed, easily intimidated bungler who collapsed before the demands of an outraged public opinion and accepted an unnecessary conflict when sound diplomacy could have avoided it. Such renditions highlight the importance of humanitarian goals. The people of the United States, genuinely distressed by the barbarism of Spanish pacification techniques in Cuba, set for themselves the task of restoring peace to the island. They meant well and sent in an army to prove it. Similarly, after the war, they acted with the best interests of the Cubans in mind by conforming to the self-denying requirements of the Teller Amendment. They refrained from annexing the island outright and, instead, beneficently placed it under US supervision as authorized by the Platt Amendment.

The recent literature no longer sustains such understanding. As Louis A. Pérez (1998: 36) shows, traditional accounts typically attribute too much benevolence to the United States. Also they distort or, worse, leave out the role of the Cubans, making them somehow peripheral to the story. In Pérez's view, the McKinley administration intervened in Cuba in 1898 not for the sake of Cuban independence but in opposition to it, thereby fulfilling the long-standing goal of transforming Cuba from a Spanish colony into a United States dependency. Moreover, as Pérez (1999) demonstrates, an array of official and unofficial connections with the United States contributed to the Cuban conception of self.

The modern debate over the causes of the war entered a new phase when Walter LaFeber published *The New Empire* (1963). Rejecting Bemis, this controversial book set forth a nuanced economic analysis, sometimes described as neo-Marxist. For LaFeber, the Industrial Revolution and the ensuing quest for markets and resources functioned as determinants of policy in conjunction with strategic and ideological considerations. Following in this tradition and elaborating upon it, Thomas Schoonover (1991) develops a conception of "social imperialism," underscoring the importance of overseas expansion as a means of relieving domestic tensions and problems with overproduction and underconsumption. LaFeber (1993) arrives even more emphatically at similar conclusions. McKinley preferred to achieve his goals through peaceful measures but, when other options closed down, he accepted war as a necessary means by which to expel Spain from the Western hemisphere and to extend United States influence into Asia.

LaFeber's work emphasizes continuities of purpose among US policymakers. By the end of the nineteenth century, the country entered the ranks of the Great Powers economically. At the same time, cyclical boom-and-bust tendencies brought about unpredictable fluctuations. Beginning with the Panic of 1873, the United States embarked upon twenty-five years of recurrent depression, occasioned in the popular understanding by too much supply and not enough demand. Ironically, rising productivity drove down prices by turning out more goods than consumers could buy. When market gluts resulted, the ensuing hard times meant reduced output and mounting unemployment. Meanwhile, strikes, riots, and other manifestations of class conflict suggested incipient revolution. In response, the leaders tried to dissipate adverse effects by increasing sales in the markets of Europe, Asia, and Latin America. For secretaries of state such as William Henry Seward in the 1860s, James G. Blaine in the 1880s, and their successors, visions of commercial empire and expanding trade formed the core of national aspiration.

Historians with other views sometimes concede an important point, acknowledging that foreign markets counted for something. Yet they warn of the dangers of oversimplification. For example, Robert Beisner (1986: 21) advises against exaggerating the effects of continuity. In his view, diplomats lacked the knowledge and ability consciously and systematically to execute "a farsighted economic diplomacy." During these "awkward years," as David M. Pletcher (1962) calls them, improvisational responses, based on habits, unplanned and uncoordinated, typified US behavior.

The transition from the Old Diplomacy to the New eliminated some of the liabilities. More assertively inclined to seize the initiative, as Beisner (1986: ch. 3) explains, the advocates of the New Diplomacy produced a paradigm shift, seeking to develop more effective responses in unsettled times. US policymakers preferred peace and trade without European entanglements but sometimes accepted such risks as unavoidable. The onset of the War with Spain marks a case in point, indicating a growing determination to take control of the Caribbean region as a sphere of influence.

The extent to which the United States' intentions actually dictated outcomes remains an object of debate. Some historians discern direct and constant connections between overseas expansion and economic drives for markets and resources. Others perceive the process as more disconnected, a herky-jerky affair reflecting also the multifarious effects of politics, strategy, and psychological states. Nonetheless, they all recognize the magnitude of change produced by the War with Spain. Whether these developments occurred because of contingency or design poses a significant question.

Theodore Roosevelt once claimed that William McKinley possessed "no more backbone than a chocolate éclair." Similarly, a contemporary cartoon showed "Willie" McKinley as a female, attired in a dress, holding a broom, seeking ineffectually to drive back huge waves called "Congress" and "The People." The caption read, "Another Old Woman Tries to Sweep Back the Sea" (Bailey 1974: 460–1). According to this view, the president, once submerged by a floodtide of public opinion, lacked the will to avoid an unnecessary war. As Joseph A. Fry (1979: 77–97) explains, this interpretation dominated historical writing until the 1960s, when revisionist accounts in contrast depicted McKinley as more courageous and capable than previously thought. Also, they described his decision in favor of war not so much as a capitulation to public and congressional pressure but, instead, a logical continuation of his own policy. In part a redemption of McKinley's historical reputation, this body of writing portrays the president as a shrewd practitioner of the diplomatic arts. Actually a strong leader, he understood relationships between means and ends, identified with the standards of the New Diplomacy, and accepted the use of force only as a last resort.

For the most part, recent studies of the War with Spain incorporate revisionist thinking. In *The Presidency of William McKinley*, Lewis L. Gould (1980: 79) argues the case for acknowledging the president's capabilities by demonstrating "the complexity of the diplomatic problems" and the extent of his efforts "to discover a way out of the impasse." In *An Unwanted War: The Diplomacy of the United States and Spain over Cuba, 1895–1898*, John L. Offner (1992: 225) characterizes the onset of the war as "inevitable" because of "the irreconcilable political positions dividing the Cuban, Spanish, and American people." According to this view, no grounds existed for a compromise as long as the Spanish government refused to relinquish royal authority, the Cuban rebels insisted upon independence, and the United States lacked the means for breaking the deadlock.

Recent works employ diverse approaches. Offner (1992) arrives at his conclusions by scrutinizing politics and diplomacy in traditional ways. In *The Diplomacy of Trade and Investment: American Expansion in the Hemisphere, 1865–1900*, a comprehensive account, David M. Pletcher (1998: 4, 325) examines the interplay among the various strategic, economic, political, and ideological incentives. His discussion highlights the discontinuities, calling the policymaking "tentative" and "experimental." Nevertheless, he acknowledges that the result, "a war of conquest," forever "changed the world outlook of the United States." Less conventional, Kristin Hoganson's *Fighting for American Manhood: How Gender Politics Provoked the Spanish-American and Philippine-American Wars* (1998) applies the techniques of cultural analysis. Hoganson posits the existence of a masculinity crisis among male elites. For reasons described by the author, men feared the effects of feminization and consequently experienced a need to accept stern tests, much as their fathers in the Civil War. As already suggested, the cartoon showing McKinley in drag typified such apprehension. Finally, in *The War of 1898* Louis A. Pérez (1998: ch. 4) exhorts historians to rectify previous errors and omissions, especially their disregard of the Cuban experience. For him, the usual designation for the conflict as "the Spanish–American War" exemplifies the problem. He identifies also another theme, a pervasive racism underlying the attitudes of US policymakers toward Cubans, resulting in patronizing condescension. This lamentable tendency to look upon Latin Americans as unruly children in need of supervision comes under extensive discussion in Schoultz (1998).

The conduct and consequences of the War with Spain also generate controversy. On the military phases, David F. Trask's *The War with Spain* (1981) is standard. Forcefully presented, it rejects some revisionist claims, regards the impact of public opinion as a prime impetus, and places the fighting in appropriate political and diplomatic contexts. Operational accounts of sea and land warfare typically applaud the Navy Department for high levels of performance and castigate the War Department for confusion and disorganization. Logistical difficulties impeded the tasks of arming and outfitting the army and transporting it to Cuba. Because of assorted confusions, the war in some renditions takes on a kind of comic-opera aspect, featuring traffic jams on the railroad leading into Tampa, the main port of embarkation, a 300-pound general who rode a mule because of his great girth, sweltering soldiers decked out in woolen uniforms for a summer campaign in the tropics because of the unavailability of light khaki cloth, and so forth. In narratives by US historians, as Pérez (1998: 94–5, 115–16) shows, the activities of Cuban rebels receive scant attention, except when white observers from the US characterized them as dirty, contemptible, and unreliable.

For Bemis (1967: 140, 151, 158, 165–6), the consequences of the War with Spain ushered the United States into "an era of protective imperialism focused on the defense of an Isthmian Canal." In his view, interventionist practices under authority of the Roosevelt Corollary and in conjunction with dollar diplomacy developed accordingly as methods for upholding order and stability. Of course, excesses occurred. Roosevelt's methods in Panama constituted a "black mark" on the record. Also, his corollary to the Monroe Doctrine had bad effects by transforming a prohibition on European intervention into a justification for action by the United States. Similarly, under Taft, the techniques of dollar diplomacy, especially in Nicaragua, appeared "high-handed," but Bemis assures us, the portly president "in his own inept way" had good intentions, seeking to "uphold continental security" and not "selfish private interests." The situation would not change until the 1920s. As Bemis explains, "Not until the menace of European intervention had temporarily disappeared as a result of the First World War could a President of the United States safely think of liquidating the protective imperialism that had been established in the vital Caribbean area."

In a classic work published twenty-one years later, *Intervention and Dollar Diplomacy in the Caribbean, 1900–1921* (1964), Dana G. Munro argues a similar case, holding that conditions of economic backwardness and political instability in the Caribbean basin compelled US intervention for security reasons in opposition to European threats. In the ensuing years, historians have elaborated upon the theme, debating the importance of security concerns in conjunction with other goals, assumptions, and perceptions. Lester D. Langley (1982) contends that the United States created an empire in the Caribbean but without colonies. His balanced and insightful account shows a complicated mix of selfish and unselfish motives in support of political order, economic tutelage, and civic morality. His book, *The Banana Wars* (1983), downplays the utility of economic explanations for US actions and attributes importance to political incentives calling for order among supposedly lesser peoples defined as uncivilized. Nonetheless, his work in collaboration with Thomas Schoonover, *The Banana Men* (1995), takes up other issues by exploring the economic implications within the context of "world-systems analysis." Finally, other illuminating books by David F. Healy (1988), Frederick S. Calhoun (1986, 1993), and Ivan Musicant (1990) show the complex impact and interplay of diverse purposes.

Scholars who admire Theodore Roosevelt's conduct of diplomacy usually pay tribute to his strengths, that is, his realism, his understanding of the uses of power, his moralistic convictions, and his fear of German intrusions. Such themes appear prominently in Marks (1979). Similarly, Gould (1991) portrays Roosevelt as a strong, vigorous, and determined leader who insisted upon keeping the Great European Powers out of the Western hemisphere. Richard H. Collin (1990) reacts vehemently against what he regards as deviant New Left depictions of Roosevelt as a grubby economic expansionist. To the contrary, Collin holds, Roosevelt acted out of concern for European incursions and not for reason of suppressing Latin Americans. Kaiser Wilhelm II's ambitions especially concerned him. Whether such fears had validity is not certain. Herwig (1986) gives them some credence. Focused on the German, British, and Italian blockade of Venezuela in 1902–3, this work rejects theories of economic motivation and attributes German actions to emotional and irrational incentives, such as pride, prestige, and national honor. In contrast, Nancy Mitchell (1999) concludes differently. Based on research in German archives, she finds no evidence of German designs on the Western hemisphere and suggests that such misapprehension, a kind of disinformation, well served US leaders as a subterfuge for their own aggressive intentions.

The practice of intervention resulted in the creation of five protectorates in Cuba,

Panama, Haiti, the Dominican Republic, and Nicaragua. The term "protectorate," a kind of euphemism, refers to sets of arrangements by which US leaders provided guarantees in defense of independence and self-determination against European violations but not against their own activities, typically regarded and defended by them as altruistic instruments of uplift, progress, and civilization. The Platt Amendment, later written into the Cuban constitution under pressure from the United States, established the means for creating an empire without colonies by bestowing upon the United States "the right of intervention for the preservation of Cuban independence and the maintenance of a stable Government adequately protecting life, property and individual liberty." According to Pérez (1991; 1998: 3–13), a leading critic, it served up "an adequate if imperfect substitute for annexation" by diluting Cuban sovereignty through incorporation into the "US national system." In his many writings on US–Cuban relations, oftentimes drawing on dependency theory, Pérez reveals the techniques for subjecting the island to an outside authority and the negative consequences for Cubans. In a devastating assessment, he describes what emerged as a "stunted Cuban republic fashioned by US proconsuls," the organization and institutions of which had "little relevance to Cuban social reality." Other works by David F. Healy (1963), Jules R. Benjamin (1977), and José M. Hernández (1993) develop related themes, for example, the role of complex motives among US policymakers, a readiness to employ flexibility in pursuit of hegemony, and the tight interrelationships between Cuban elites and the occupying military forces.

Similar arrangements based on the Cuban model emerged in dealings with the other protectorates. The recent literature incorporates impressive methodological feats by scrutinizing not only the aims and methods of US policymakers, but also the effects upon and responses by other peoples, sometimes showing how they employed "the weapons of the weak" to blunt the hegemonic presence of the United States. In *Prize Possession* (1993), John Major, a British historian, considers the importance of security considerations for the United States and also the limitations and disadvantages imposed on Panamanians, oftentimes for reasons of race. In *Haiti and the Great Powers, 1902–1915* (1988), Brenda Gayle Plummer analyzes the interplay among France, Germany, Great Britain, and the United States, the indigenous elites, and the foreign merchant community. Going beyond diplomacy, she incorporates a range of less official exchanges, highlighting the experiences of the relatively powerless. In a methodologically related work, Mary A. Renda in *Taking Haiti* (2001) focuses on issues of class, gender, and race while examining the cultural context. She sees paternalism with violent proclivities as a main characteristic of attitudes in the US Marine Corps. In *The Impact of Intervention: The Dominican Republic During the US Occupation of 1916–1924* (1984), Bruce J. Calder explains US policy as a mixture of economic and strategic motives and also explores the consequences for the country, notably Dominican responses taking the form of guerrilla war.

The Nicaraguan intervention receives attention in works already mentioned by Munro (1964), Langley (1983), and Musicant (1990), and also in *The Foreign Policies of the Taft Administration* (1970) by Walter and Marie Scholes. Though somewhat dated, this latter volume shows that Taft and his secretary of state, Philander C. Knox, hoped to benefit both the United States and the countries of Latin America by promoting stability and economic growth. Through the techniques of dollar diplomacy, they used US loans in conjunction with financial experts and typically failed to achieve their purposes. As they discovered, contrary to expectations, capitalist infusions in traditional societies all over the world had destabilizing effects tending toward revolution. Moreover, displays of paternalistic condescension aroused nationalist responses against them.

Similar themes appear in Emily S. Rosenberg's thoroughly up-to-date *Financial Missionaries to the World* (1999). This stimulating work takes a new look at an old subject and does so in revealing ways by connecting it with cultural history. As Rosenberg explains, the conduct of dollar diplomacy was "intertwined with cultural contexts that fostered the growth of professionalism, of scientific theories that accentuated racial and gender differences, and of the mass media's emphasis on the attractions and repulsions of primitivism." In other words, discourses about masculinity, money, whiteness, and professional expertise came together in close proximity, while affirming reasons why other peoples should take financial advice from the United States seriously. Nevertheless, the effects, often unanticipated by the experts, elicited resistance among foreign peoples, the supposed beneficiaries, and stimulated opposition among anti-imperialists everywhere. Connoisseurs of irony will appreciate these findings.

Peace and stability collapsed precipitously during the second decade of the twentieth century with the advent of World War I in Europe and the onset of revolutions in China, Mexico, and Russia. Faced with mounting disorder, President Woodrow Wilson reacted in distinctive ways. Bemis (1967: 168–9, 175–6) emphasizes a moralistic component, derived from "the Bible, Burke, and Bagehot," supposedly an inducement for respecting popular sovereignty and self-government. Sometimes Wilson spoke as a prophet, assuring Latin Americans of his friendship for them and his respect for constitutionalism. He also made promises holding that the United States "never again" would "seek one additional foot of territory by conquest." His subsequent interventions in Mexico and elsewhere left scholars wondering how to reconcile his words with his deeds. For Bemis, ostensibly not much bothered by the disparity, Wilson's diplomatic practices, though unexpressed, incorporated "the traditional Latin American policy of the United States: security of the Continental Republic in an independent republican New World." In recent times, historians have expanded upon Bemis' analysis by enlarging the context. Some portray Wilson's policies as responses to war and revolution, culminating in the Fourteen Points, a liberal–capitalist internationalist formulation, and the basis of his peace plan at the Paris Peace Conference.

The Mexican Revolution has generated an immense literature, most of which resides outside the bounds of this essay. Wilson's crusade against General Victoriano Huerta, his failed attempt to reconcile the factions headed by Francisco Villa and Venustiano Carranza, the ensuing Punitive Expedition into Mexico, and the hostile reactions to the Mexican Constitution of 1917 all form important parts of the story. Gilderhus (1977) argues that the president's policies sought to steer Mexicans away from revolutionary excesses and toward the principles of liberal capitalism. Similarly, Smith (1972) shows how successive administrations employed various diplomatic strategies to limit the adverse effects of the Mexican Constitution of 1917 on foreign-owned property, significantly without resorting to force after Pershing's withdrawal.

The works of Friedrich Katz, a foremost authority, hold special importance. In *The Secret War in Mexico* (1981), an exceptional book based on primary sources in many countries, Katz explores the economic competition over Mexican resources, especially oil, and an ongoing tendency among the Great Powers to support Mexican conservatives against radicals. International issues also receive attention in Katz's massive biography, *The Life and Times of Pancho Villa* (1998), notably his dealings with the United States, Great Britain, and Germany. It argues that Villa attacked Columbus, New Mexico, because of his belief that Carranza had sold out Mexican independence to the United States.

Other publications elucidate related issues. Two books by Linda B. Hall and Don M. Coerver, *Texas and the Mexican Revolution* (1984) and *Revolution on the Border* (1988), examine regional implications and show how state and national interests sometimes diverged. Linda B. Hall (1995) explains how politicians, financiers, and oil men responded to the nationalistic provisions of the Mexican Constitution. The activities of Mexican exiles come under consideration in Raat (1981) and Sandos (1992). A view of the Punitive Expedition from the Mexican side appears in Stout (1999).

The economic dimensions have received high levels of scholarly attention. In *Revolution from Without: Yucatán, Mexico, and the United States, 1880–1924* (1982), Gilbert M. Joseph examines a dependency relationship based on henequen production and the activities of the International Harvester Company. In *Capitalists, Caciques, and Revolution* (1984), Mark Wasserman shows how foreign investment linked northern Mexico with world economic cycles and contributed to the onset of revolution. In *Mexico and the United States in the Oil Controversy, 1917–1942* (1972), Lorenzo Meyer, a Mexican scholar, follows the dispute through the expropriation of foreign-owned oil properties by President Lázaro Cárdenas, using dependency as an interpretive device. Taking a broader approach in *Oil and Revolution in Mexico* (1992), Jonathan C. Brown argues that the exercise of governmental control over foreign-owned oil companies was part of a complex process of revolutionary state making. Finally, John A. Britton's intellectual history, *Revolution and Ideology: The Image of the Mexican Revolution in the United States, 1910–1960* (1995), analyses responses by a wide range of political commentators, academics, journalists, creative writers, politicians, businessmen, ministers, and diplomats.

Another aspect, examined in Gilderhus (1986), concerns the promotion of economic and political integration within the region. Taking advantage of opportunities created by World War I, the United States moved into Latin America with loans and goods but could not overcome resistance to Wilson's proposed Pan American treaty, an ambitious undertaking calling for a system of collective security in defense of self-determination. Bill Albert's *South America and the First World War* (1988) underscores the growing economic dominance of the United States. Focusing on bilateral relations, David Sheinin's book, *Searching for Authority: Pan Americanism, Diplomacy and Politics in United States–Argentine Relations, 1910–1930* (1998), examines the competition over leadership roles, while Joseph Smith's *Unequal Giants* (1991) shows why and how Brazilian leaders cultivated close relations with the United States as a counterweight against Argentina and Chile. Finally, in *The Revolutionary Mission* (1996), Thomas F. O'Brien examines the long-term impact of US corporate activity on Latin America and explains how the effects shaped social development and relationships with the United States.

The Republican Restoration in the 1920s produced significant shifts. Overall, historians have accepted Joan Hoff Wilson's (1971) characterization of Republican policy as "independent internationalism" and not "isolationism" (p. xvi). Unlike President Wilson, Republican leaders rejected collective security under auspices of the Treaty and the League but accepted other forms of international engagement on their own terms. Cohen (1998) provides an overview incorporating that insight. In the Western hemisphere, Republicans initiated a move away from military intervention, in part as Bemis suggests, because no threat of European incursions aroused anxiety. Consequently, as noted by Leffler (1984: 225–6, 242), "economic considerations" became primary, and the Monroe Doctrine, traditionally "the cornerstone" of policy, became less useful as "a viable guide to action."

In the postwar period, US trade and investment expanded impressively. Growing demand for US exports in Latin America meant high market shares and also opportunities for lenders. The process of infusing dollars became known as "the dance of the millions." In *The Money Doctor in the Andes* (1989), Paul Drake recounts the activities of Edwin W. Kemmerer, an economist from Princeton University, who functioned as a financial adviser in Columbia, Chile, Ecuador, Bolivia, and Peru, seeking to promote modernization through the creation of central banking facilities. Other works illuminate important aspects of US dealings with Latin America in the 1920s. In *Doing Business with the Dictators: A Political History of the United Fruit Company in Guatemala, 1899–1944* (1993), Paul Dosal examines the process by which a foreign-owned enterprise became the most important economic presence in the country. Thorp (1986) places such phenomena in a global context. Addressing another dimension, Krenn (1990) explores the negative response of US leaders to manifestations of Latin American radicalism and attributes it to economic self-interest, anti-communism, and racism. US elites didn't much care for Latin American nationalists and their economic schemes. In contrast, Delpar (1992) reveals how, especially in intellectual circles, presumed Mexican authenticities, particularly in art, became objects of admiration and special interest for gringos. Complex rivalries among the United States, Mexico, and regional factions, especially in Nicaragua, come under consideration in Salisbury (1989). Finally, a discussion of the "Clark Memorandum," a State Department document which disconnected the right of intervention from the Monroe Doctrine in 1930, appears in Fox (1980: ch. 26).

Under Franklin Roosevelt, the retreat from intervention turned into the "Good Neighbor Policy." This term, a kind of commonplace in diplomatic language, took on real meaning during the era of the Great Depression. For Latin Americans, it terminated for a time direct intervention by the United States in their affairs. For the Roosevelt administration, it initially functioned as an international counterpart of the New Deal by attacking economic problems through the expansion of trade and investment and later served as a means for mobilizing resistance within the Western hemisphere against the Axis powers. For Bemis (1967: 372–3), the wartime display of "hemispheric solidarity" with Latin Americans represented a great achievement. In his view, the United States had met "the supreme test" of Latin America policy by building upon "the basis of continental security, independence, and republican solidarity" in order to advance "the defense and well-being of the whole New World."

Frederick B. Pike's *FDR's Good Neighbor Policy* (1995) is the most significant and revealing work on the subject in recent times. An ambitious undertaking, this book effectively employs the techniques of cultural analysis to show how the people of the United States perceived their southern neighbors. Intriguingly, Pike suggests that during the Great Depression they could empathize more readily with Latin Americans because they became more like them. Economic hardship was a "great equalizer." Pike credits Roosevelt for making the policy distinctive. Presented as a "trickster" or political magician who obtained successes through the reconciliation of opposites, Roosevelt brought together the defense of vital US interests with some kind of regard for the requirements of Latin American sovereignty. Seldom preachy or racist, he earned respect and admiration from Latin Americans as "a gringo in the Latin mold, a man they could understand . . . as a projection of their own political and social style" (pp. 138–62, 350–3).

Pike's book, overall a sympathetic account, begins with a fundamental question: Have we been good neighbors? His brutally realistic reply says yes, some of the time, but really "no better . . . than we had to be." For Pike, "that seems the most one could expect. We might, after all, have been a good deal worse." This sage point establishes a main theme, emphasizing that, whatever the shortcomings, the Good Neighbor policy also obtained some successes. Seeking to situate his work historiographically, Pike notes a tradition of clashing interpretations. The one emphasizes the importance of trade and investment, and the other, strategic necessity. Pike (p. xii) remarks that, for him, "security and economic pursuits are so intimately intertwined as to be inseparable." As he sees it, the foreign policy of the United States "should attend principally to maintaining the military *and* the economic strength needed to defend its vital interests – meaning ultimately . . . the fundamental underlying values of its national culture." This compelling and insightful book presents Pike's case with reason and wit.

The interpretive clash to which Pike alludes intrudes upon most discussions of the Good Neighbor policy in one way or another. Smith (1976: 66–7) favors a synthesis incorporating diverse points of view. As he explains, taken together, the various components of the Good Neighbor policy formed "a massive, although ill-defined governmental effort" under US direction to create "an integrated hemisphere system" characterized by high levels of "political, economic and military cooperation." Similarly, Gellman (1979: 1–2) perceives "Good Neighbor diplomacy" as consisting of interlocking parts, some pursuing economic interests, and others, strategic concerns. He refers to such multifaceted policies as "sophisticated" because of their attentiveness to a variety of matters. Taking a more ideological approach drawn from New Left historiography, Grow (1981: 113–15) rejects depictions of the Good Neighbor policy as a manifestation of "liberal internationalism," characterized in his words as "an altruistic and pragmatic campaign to construct a prosperous, stable new hemispheric order mutually beneficial to the United States *and* the nations of Latin America." Instead, he presents it as an example of "liberal imperialism," described by him as "a concerted drive to achieve informal United States hegemony" primarily for reasons of "national economic self-interest." Such disputes, probably never resolvable, nonetheless allow historians to probe various aspects of the New Deal through the ongoing process of scholarly debate.

Recent monographic literature on the Good Neighbor policy reveals something of a shift in emphasis. Notably, it has given greater prominence to Latin American viewpoints and initiatives. Part of the change emanates from a reaction against the excesses of dependency theory. According to critics, *dependencia* too often depicted Latin Americans as helpless victims of *yanqui* imperialism without alternatives or recourse. As archival research has shown, such one-way representations deprive Latin Americans of "agency" and thereby distort complicated exchanges, official and unofficial, at many levels in which Latin Americans displayed some capacity to challenge and counter the effects of US hegemony. For example, important studies by Hilton (1975) and McCann (1973) demonstrate how Brazil under Getúlio Vargas played off Germany against the United States and obtained some space in which to maneuver in pursuit of national interests. In *Juan Vicente Gómez and the Oil Companies in Venezuela* (1983), B. S. McBeth shows how government authorities retained certain initiatives allowing for various advantages in dealing with foreign interests. In *The United States and Somoza, 1933–1956* (1992), Paul Coe Clark, Jr. argues against traditional views that presented the dictator as some kind of surrogate or puppet of the United States. To the contrary, Anastasio Somoza's survivability depended primarily on his political skills and ruthlessness and also on the Roosevelt administration's commitment to non-intervention. When taken seriously, the principle meant just that. In addition, Roorda (1998) applies similar arguments in reference to another unsavory regime, in the Dominican Republic. In a complex and revealing analysis, he explains how Rafael Trujillo retained leverage in dealings with the United States.

The possibility of achieving "hemispheric solidarity" during World War II depended heavily on resolving the differences with Mexico. Following the oil expropriation of 1938, negotiations headed off further trouble, paving the way for an eventual agreement with the petroleum companies on questions of compensation. Two recent books by Mexicanists bear upon such matters. Schuler (1998) elucidates the methods by which "the Mexican Government pursued its national interests" in a complicated and dangerous international environment and rejects the "simple clichés of dependency." Mexico was never merely "a Third World stage for great power conflict." Instead, Schuler argues, Mexican leaders demonstrated impressive skill in international negotiations, employed calculated realism in their evaluation of policy choices, and revealed a great deal of creativity in times of crisis, sometimes more so "than their European and US counterparts." When possible, Mexicans exploited weaknesses among the Great Powers and stayed focused on long-term objectives, using opportunities "to their own advantage" (1–2). Much less laudatory, Niblo (1995) explains how Mexican leaders devised a misguided program of industrial development that ultimately failed either to reduce poverty or underdevelopment.

The best source for the neutrality period and after is R. A. Humphreys' two-volume work, *Latin America and the Second World War* (1982). Noting the prevalence of atavistic competition among the Great Powers for markets and resources, Humphreys begins with an appropriate premise: "In 1939 Latin America was the richest raw material producing area in the world free from the control of any Great Power" (p. 1). At a time of global conflict, the region presented a prize well worth having. Humphreys discusses the various maneuvers by which the United States tried to cultivate Latin Americans, the sequence of Pan American conferences, and then, after Pearl Harbor, the reasons why Latin American nations declared war, severed diplomatic relations, or remained neutral. Among the latter, only two, Argentina and Chile, broke ranks, while the others, embracing "hemispheric solidarity" as a goal, rallied in opposition to the Axis powers and in support of the United States. From the standpoint of the Roosevelt administration, the adjustments undertaken in conjunction with the Good Neighbor policy really paid off.

In conclusion, this survey reveals intriguing historiographical tendencies. The methods and goals of US hegemony, whether exercised by direct or indirect means, remain issues of critical importance for historians and subjects of diverse interpretation. The asymmetries of power, wealth, and influence have shaped most aspects of US–Latin American relations, always bestowing inordinate advantages upon the United States but not complete domination. In the ensuing engagements, Latin Americans, though inhabitants of the periphery, possessed some means of acting upon and constraining the hegemonic capabilities of the United States. By shifting focus and scrutinizing also "the weapons of the weak," scholars can illuminate the process and show more clearly how the inhabitants of the Western hemisphere have conducted their international affairs.

REFERENCES

Albert, Bill: *South America and the First World War: The Impact of the War on Brazil, Argentina, Peru, and Chile* (New York: Cambridge University Press, 1988).

Bailey, Thomas A.: *A Diplomatic History of the American People*, 9th edn. (Englewood Cliffs, NJ: Prentice-Hall, 1974).

Beisner, Robert L.: *From the Old Diplomacy to the New, 1865–1900*, 2nd edn (Arlington Heights, IL: Harlan Davidson, 1986).

Bemis, Samuel Flagg: *The Latin American Policy of the United States: A Historical Interpretation* (New York: W. W. Norton, 1967 [1943]).

Benjamin, Jules R.: *The United States and Cuba: Hegemony and Dependent Development, 1880–1934* (Pittsburgh, PA: University of Pittsburgh Press, 1977).

Britton, John A.: *Revolution and Ideology: The Image of the Mexican Revolution in the United States, 1910–1960* (Lexington: University of Kentucky Press, 1995).

Brown, Jonathan C.: *Oil and Revolution in Mexico* (Berkeley: University of California Press, 1992).

Calder, Bruce J.: *The Impact of Intervention: The Dominican Republic During the US Occupation of 1916–1924* (Austin: University of Texas Press, 1984).

Calhoun, Frederick S.: *Power and Principle: Armed Intervention in Wilsonian Foreign Policy* (Kent, OH: Kent State University Press, 1986).

Calhoun, Frederick S.: *Uses of Force and Wilsonian Foreign Policy* (Kent, OH: Kent State University Press, 1993).

Clark, Paul Coe, Jr.: *The United States and Somoza, 1933–1956: A Revisionist Look* (Westport, CT: Praeger, 1992).

Cohen, Warren I.: *Empire Without Tears: American Foreign Relations, 1921–1933*, 2nd edn. (New York: McGraw-Hill, 1998).

Collin, Richard H.: *Theodore Roosevelt's Caribbean: The Panama Canal, the Monroe Doctrine, and the Latin American Context* (Baton Rouge: Louisiana State University Press, 1990).

Delpar, Helen: *The Enormous Vogue of Things Mexican: Cultural Relations between the United States and Mexico, 1920–1935* (Tuscaloosa: University of Alabama Press, 1992).

Dosal, Paul J.: *Doing Business with the Dictators: A Political History of the United Fruit Company in Guatemala, 1899–1944* (Wilmington, DE: Scholarly Resources, 1993).

Drake, Paul W.: *The Money Doctor in the Andes: The Kemmerer Missions, 1923–1933* (Durham, NC: Duke University Press, 1989).

Fox, Frank W.: *J. Reuben Clark: The Public Years* (Provo, UT: Brigham Young University Press, 1980).

Fry, Joseph A.: "William McKinley and the Coming of the Spanish–American War: A Study of the Besmirching and Redemption of an Historical Image." *Diplomatic History* 3 (winter 1979), 77–98.

Gellman, Irwin F.: *Good Neighbor Diplomacy: United States Policies in Latin America, 1933–1945* (Baltimore, MD: Johns Hopkins University Press, 1979).

Gilderhus, Mark T.: *Diplomacy and Revolution: US–Mexican Relations under Wilson and Carranza, 1913–1921* (Tucson: University of Arizona Press, 1977).

Gilderhus, Mark T.: *Pan American Visions: Woodrow Wilson in Latin America, 1913–1921* (Tucson: University of Arizona Press, 1986).

Gilderhus, Mark T.: "Founding Father: Samuel Flagg Bemis and the Study of US–Latin American Relations." *Diplomatic History* 21 (winter 1997), 1–13.

Gould, Lewis L.: *The Presidency of William McKinley* (Lawrence: Regents Press of Kansas, 1980).

Gould, Lewis L.: *The Presidency of Theodore Roosevelt* (Lawrence: University of Kansas Press, 1991).

Grow, Michael: *The Good Neighbor Policy and Authoritarianism in Paraguay: United States Economic Expansion and Great-Power Rivalry in Latin America during World War II* (Lawrence: University of Kansas Press, 1981).

Hall, Linda B.: *Oil, Banks, and Politics: The United States and Postrevolutionary Mexico, 1917–1924* (Austin: University of Texas Press, 1995).

Hall, Linda B. and Don M. Coerver: *Texas and the Mexican Revolution: A Study in State and National Border Policy, 1910–1920* (San Antonio, TX: Trinity University Press, 1984).

Hall, Linda B. and Don M. Coerver: *Revolution on the Border: The United States and Mexico, 1910–1920* (Albuquerque: University of New Mexico Press, 1988).

Healy, David F.: *The United States in Cuba, 1898–1902: Generals, Politicians, and the Search for Policy* (Madison: University of Wisconsin Press, 1963).

Healy, David F.: *Drive to Hegemony: The United States in the Caribbean, 1898–1917* (Madison: University of Wisconsin Press, 1988).

Hernández, José M.: *Cuba and the United States: Intervention and Militarism, 1868–1933* (Austin: University of Texas Press, 1993).

Herwig, Holger H.: *Germany's Vision of Empire in Venezuela: 1871–1914* (Princeton, NJ: Princeton University Press, 1986).

Hilton, Stanley E.: *Brazil and the Great Powers, 1930–1939: The Politics of Trade Rivalry* (Austin: University of Texas Press 1975).

Hoganson, Kristin: *Fighting for American Manhood: How Gender Politics Provoked the Spanish–American and Philippine–American Wars* (New Haven, CT: Yale University Press, 1998).

Humphreys, R. A.: *Latin America and the Second World War*, 2 vols. (London: University of London/Athlone Press, 1982).

Joseph, Gilbert M.: *Revolution from Without: Yucatán, Mexico, and the United States, 1880–1924* (New York: Cambridge University Press, 1982).

Katz, Friedrich: *The Secret War in Mexico: Europe, the United States, and the Mexican Revolution* (Chicago, IL: University of Chicago Press, 1981).

Katz, Friedrich: *The Life and Times of Pancho Villa* (Stanford, CA: Stanford University Press, 1998).

Krenn, Michael L.: *United States Policy toward Economic Nationalism in Latin America, 1917–1929* (Wilmington, DE: Scholarly Resources, 1990).

LaFeber, Walter: *The New Empire: An Interpretation of American Expansion, 1860–1898* (Ithaca, NY: Cornell University Press, 1963).

LaFeber, Walter: *The American Search for Opportunity, 1865–1913.* Vol. 2 in *The Cambridge History of American Foreign Relations* (New York: Cambridge University Press, 1993).

Langley, Lester D.: *The United States and the Caribbean in the Twentieth Century* (Athens, GA: University of Georgia Press, 1982).

Langley, Lester D.: *The Banana Wars: An Inner History of American Empire, 1900–1934* (Lexington: University of Kentucky Press, 1983).

Langley, Lester D. and Thomas Schoonover: *The Banana Men: American Mercenaries and Entrepreneurs in Central America, 1880–1930* (Lexington: University of Kentucky Press, 1995).

Leffler, Melvyn P.: "Expansionist Impulses and Domestic Constraints, 1921–32." In William H. Becker and Samuel F. Wells, Jr. (eds.) *Economics and World Power: An Assessment of American Diplomacy since 1789* (New York: Columbia University Press, 1984).

McBeth, B. S.: *Juan Vicente Gómez and the Oil Companies in Venezuela, 1908–1935* (New York: Cambridge University Press, 1983).

McCann, Frank D.: *The Brazilian–American Alliance, 1937–1941* (Princeton, NJ: Princeton University Press, 1973).

Major, John: *Prize Possession: The United States and the Panama Canal, 1903–1979* (New York: Cambridge University Press, 1993).

Marks, Frederick W., III: *Velvet on Iron: The Diplomacy of Theodore Roosevelt* (Lincoln: University of Nebraska Press, 1979).

Meyer, Lorenzo: *Mexico and the United States in the Oil Controversy, 1917–1942,* trans. Muriel Vasconcellos (Austin: University of Texas Press, 1972).

Mitchell, Nancy: *The Danger of Dreams: German and American Imperialism in Latin America* (Chapel Hill: University of North Carolina Press, 1999).

Munro, Dana G.: *Intervention and Dollar Diplomacy in the Caribbean, 1900–1921* (Princeton, NJ: Princeton University Press, 1964).

Musicant, Ivan: The Banana Wars: A History of United States Military Intervention in Latin America from the Spanish–American War to the Invasion of Grenada (New York: Macmillan, 1990).

Niblo, Stephen R.: *War, Diplomacy, and Development: The United States and Mexico, 1938–1945* (Wilmington, DE: Scholarly Resources, 1995).

O'Brien, Thomas F.: *The Revolutionary Mission: American Enterprise in Latin America, 1900–1945* (New York: Cambridge University Press, 1996).

Offner, John L.: *An Unwanted War: The Diplomacy of the United States and Spain over Cuba, 1895–1898* (Chapel Hill: University of North Carolina Press, 1992).

Pérez, Louis A., Jr.: *Cuba and the United States: Ties of Singular Intimacy* (Athens, GA: University of Georgia Press, 1990).

Pérez, Louis A., Jr.: "Dependency." In Michael J. Hogan and Thomas G. Paterson (eds.) *Explaining the History of American Foreign Relations* (New York: Cambridge University Press, 1991).

Pérez, Louis A., Jr.: *The War of 1898: The United States and Cuba in History and Historiography* (Chapel Hill: University of North Carolina Press, 1998).

Pérez, Louis A., Jr.: *On Becoming Cuban: Identity, Nationality, and Culture* (New York: Ecco Press, 1999).

Pike, Frederick B.: *FDR's Good Neighbor Policy: Sixty Years of Generally Gentle Chaos* (Austin: University of Texas Press, 1995).

Pletcher, David M.: *The Awkward Years: American Foreign Relations under Garfield and Arthur* (Columbia: University of Missouri Press, 1962).

Pletcher, David M.: *The Diplomacy of Trade and Investment: American Economic Expansion in the Hemisphere, 1865–1900* (Columbia: University of Missouri Press, 1998).

Plummer, Brenda Gayle: *Haiti and the Great Powers, 1902–1915* (Baton Rouge: Louisiana State University Press, 1988).

Raat, W. Dirk: *Revoltosos: Mexico's Rebels in the United States, 1903–1923* (College Station: Texas A&M University Press, 1981).

Renda, Mary A.: *Taking Haiti: Military Occupation and the Culture of US Imperialism, 1915–1940* (Chapel Hill: University of North Carolina Press, 2001).

Roorda, Eric Paul: *The Dictator Next Door: The Good Neighbor Policy and the Trumillo Regime in the Dominican Republic, 1930–1945* (Durham, NC: Duke University Press, 1998).

Rosenberg, Emily S.: *Financial Missionaries to the World: The Politics and Culture of Dollar Diplomacy, 1900–1930* (Cambridge, MA: Harvard University Press, 1999).

Salisbury, Richard V.: *Anti-Imperialism and International Competition in Central America, 1920–1929* (Wilmington, DE: Scholarly Resources, 1989).

Sandos, James A.: *Rebellion in the Borderlands: Anarchism and the Plan of San Diego, 1904–1923* (Norman: University of Oklahoma Press, 1992).

Scholes, Walter V. and Marie V. Scholes: *The Foreign Policies of the Taft Administration* (Columbia: University of Missouri Press, 1970).

Schoonover, Thomas: *The United States in Central America, 1860–1911: Episodes of Social Imperialism and Imperial Rivalry in the World System* (Durham, NC: Duke University Press, 1991).

Schoultz, Lars: *Beneath the United States: A History of US Policy Toward Latin America* (Cambridge, MA: Harvard University Press, 1998).

Schuler, Friedrich E.: *Mexico between Hitler and Roosevelt: Mexican Foreign Relations in the Age of Lázaro Cárdenas, 1934–1940* (Albuquerque: University of New Mexico Press, 1998).

Sheinen, David: *Searching for Authority: Pan Americanism, Diplomacy and Politics in United States–Argentine Relations, 1910–1930* (New Orleans, LA: University Press of the South, 1998).

Smith, Joseph: *Unequal Giants: Diplomatic Relations between the United States and Brazil, 1889–1930* (Pittsburgh, PA: University of Pittsburgh Press, 1991).

Smith, Robert Freeman: *The United States and Revolutionary Nationalism in Mexico, 1916–1932* (Chicago, IL: University of Chicago Press, 1972).

Smith, Robert Freeman: "The Good Neighbor Policy: The Liberal Paradox in United States Relations with Latin America." In Leonard P. Liggio and James Martin (eds.) *Watershed of Empire: Essays on New Deal Foreign Policy* (Colorado Springs, CO: Ralph Myles, 1976).

Stout, Joseph A., Jr.: *Border Conflict: Villistas, Carrancistas and the Punitive Expeditions, 1915–1920* (Fort Worth: Texas Christian University Press, 1999).

Thorp, Rosemary: "Latin America and the International Economy from the First World War to the World Depression." In Leslie Bethell (ed.) *The Cambridge History of Latin America, Vol. 4: c. 1870–1930* (New York: Cambridge University Press, 1986).

Trask, David F.: *The War with Spain in 1898* (New York: Macmillan, 1981).

Wasserman, Mark: *Capitalists, Caciques, and Revolution: The Native Elite and Foreign Enterprise in Chihuahua, Mexico, 1854–1911* (Chapel Hill: University of North Carolina Press, 1984).

Wilson, Joan Hoff: *American Business and Foreign Policy, 1920–1933* (Lexington: University of Kentucky Press, 1971).

Chapter Ten

Woodrow Wilson and World War I

Lloyd E. Ambrosius

Both Woodrow Wilson and World War I have received considerable attention in recent scholarship. His legacy and the war's impact on the twentieth century have been widely recognized. Although he failed to create the new world order he had promised, he did articulate ideas that Americans later embraced during World War II and used during the Cold War to fashion the global involvement of the United States. In different guises the Wilsonian legacy seemed relevant to successive generations. Subsequent presidents championed the rights of sovereign nations to self-determination, to global trade and investments, and to collective security against external aggression. Like Wilson during the Great War, they committed the United States to a progressive, democratic, capitalist, and peaceful world order. They believed history was progressing toward the worldwide attainment of these American ideals.

Wilsonianism, as Wilson defined it, offered four principles for a new world order. It proclaimed (1) national self-determination, affirming both national sovereignty and democratic self-government; (2) Open Door globalization, favoring a competitive marketplace for trade and financial investments across national borders; (3) collective security, finding expression in the League of Nations; and (4) progressive historicism, undergirding the promise of a better future. Wilson summarized this American ideology in his Fourteen Points address on January 8, 1918, as the foundation for peace and justice after the Great War.

Wilsonianism has continued to influence American thinking and policymaking throughout the twentieth century, emerging as the triumphant ideology after the Cold War. "For three generations," Henry Kissinger conceded in *Diplomacy* (1994), "critics have savaged Wilson's analysis and conclusions; and yet, in all this time, Wilson's principles have remained the bedrock of American foreign-policy thinking." Kissinger lamented that Americans have adopted Wilsonianism. He preferred Theodore Roosevelt's diplomacy, which had emphasized the balance of power and the national interest, to Wilson's promotion of democracy as the way to world peace. TR had epitomized geopolitical realism, in contrast to Wilson's crusading idealism. Unfortunately, in Kissinger's judgment, the United States had embraced Wilson's legacy of liberal internationalism. Despite his failure to win the US Senate's approval for the League of Nations after World War I, Kissinger concluded, "Wilson's intellectual victory proved more seminal than any political triumph could have been. For, whenever America has faced the task of constructing a new world order, it has returned in one way or another to Woodrow Wilson's precepts" (pp. 52, 54).

Other analysts of US foreign policy welcomed the triumph of Wilsonianism. Tony Smith applauded the liberal resurgence of democratic states after the Cold War. "Certainly the new global enthusiasm for democracy is the closest the United States had ever come to seeing its own traditional foreign policy agenda reflected on an international scale," he affirmed in *America's Mission* (1994). "Since Wilson's time," he added, "the most consistent tradition in American foreign policy with respect to this global change has been the belief that the nation's security is best protected by the expansion of democracy worldwide" (pp. 6, 9).

Amos Perlmutter agreed that Wilsonianism had significantly contributed to the defeat of totalitarianism in the twentieth century. In *Making the World Safe for Democracy* (1997), he noted that it provided the ideology for the United States to resist the two alternative world orders of communism and Nazism. During World War II, Franklin D. Roosevelt used Wilsonianism to defeat Adolf Hitler's Germany. Both Wilson and Roosevelt, Perlmutter explained, were "making the international system safe from rival hegemons – imperialist, revolutionary, or ideological." During the Cold War, US presidents from Harry Truman to Ronald Reagan utilized Wilsonianism against the Soviet Union, eventually defeating Leninism-Stalinism. Perlmutter emphasized that the United States deployed Wilsonian ideology in conjunction with other forms of power. Like Kissinger, he emphasized military force. He regarded US hegemony as a crucial contribution to world order, and thus gave a neoconservative spin to Wilson's liberal ideology. Throughout the century, Perlmutter concluded, "the Wilsonian legacy of democracy and self-determination cast a long shadow over US foreign policy concepts, and to some extent still does" (pp. 44, 134)

Perlmutter did not share Smith's optimistic version of Wilsonianism. "Under the banner of progressive internationalism and the ideal of democracy lies a nationalist concept," he affirmed. The United States should recognize that peace required enforcement by great powers. "A great misconception on the part of President Wilson was that the evolution of democratic regimes would lead to a peaceful international order. No such evidence has been seen in this century." Wilson had not realized his vision of peace after World War I, and Perlmutter doubted that it ever would be. "Peace is not guaranteed by democratic systems, nor is aggression uniquely the property of totalitarians" (pp. 35, 165–6). Thus, Perlmutter warned, the United States should not place false confidence in the liberal promise of Wilsonianism.

Frank Ninkovich concurred that Wilsonianism had guided US foreign policy throughout the twentieth century. He believed that this ideology had shaped the modern world. For him, this was the "Wilsonian Century." In fundamental ways, however, he rejected other schools of thought. He argued that realists, such as George F. Kennan, had missed the significance of Wilsonian idealism. So had revisionists, such as William Appleman Williams. They had offered "interest-based explanations" of US foreign relations, while neglecting ideology's vital contribution to the "real world." In *The Wilsonian Century* (1999), Ninkovich contended that: "For the United States, ideology worked. And, by that rather vulgar pragmatic standard, it was true – all of which helps to explain why Americans have been uninterested in learning from the alleged mistakes that realists and other critics continue to point out" (pp. 5–6). He attributed US victory against totalitarian enemies to Wilsonian ideology. Combining postmodernism with neoconservatism in his triumphalist history of US foreign policy, Ninkovich claimed that the United States derived its real power from ideology, whereas Perlmutter argued that this nation had used its multifaceted power to defeat Nazism and communism in the name of Wilsonianism. Oddly enough, the neoconservative Ninkovich and the liberal Smith both affirmed the efficacy of Wilsonian ideology.

So did Akira Iriye, who interpreted the "ideological offensive led by President Wilson" during World War I as the defining moment for the United States in the twentieth century. Iriye agreed that "'democracy' was a key guiding principle precisely in such a context, for it stood for a new political order at home and, therefore, abroad." Thus, he explained in *The Globalizing of America* (1993):

> Wilsonianism had provided the framework in which the United States redefined its external relations at a time when the age of European dominance was coming to an end. It combined America's military power, economic resources, and cultural initiatives in order to transcend traditional world affairs in which sovereign nations had pursued their interests with little regard for the welfare of the entire globe.

Although "realists" might criticize Wilsonian liberal internationalism, it prevailed. "Because the globalizing of America has been a major event of the century," Iriye concluded, "Wilsonianism should be seen not as a transient phenomenon, a reflection of some abstract idealism, but as a potent definer of contemporary history" (pp. 45, 71–2).

Euphoria over the apparent success of Wilsonian idealism at the end of the Cold War led other historians as well to conclude that Wilson's foreign policies and legacy were fundamentally sound. In a review for *Diplomatic History* of scholarship on Wilson's conduct of US foreign relations, David Steigerwald (1999) rejoiced over the "fading of realism" and the "obsolescence of revisionism," and jubilantly announced "the reclamation of Woodrow Wilson." In his view, realism was an outmoded school. He summarily dismissed my books on *Woodrow Wilson and the American Diplomatic Tradition* (1987) and *Wilsonian Statecraft* (1991). He likewise relegated revisionist interpretations to the past. He preferred historical studies, such as Thomas J. Knock's *To End All Wars* (1992), that praised Wilson's quest of a new order of "progressive internationalism." In *Wilsonian Idealism in America* (1994) as well as his article, Steigerwald embraced a liberal viewpoint, interpreting Wilson's legacy within his own ideological framework of progressive history rather than fundamentally questioning this tradition in US foreign relations.

Despite the resurgence of Wilsonianism as America's triumphal ideology in the 1990s, some observers continued to express skepticism. Realists voiced doubts about US foreign policy, questioning the wisdom of pursuing global hegemony. Ronald Steel observed in *Temptations of a Superpower* (1995) that both fragmentation and integration characterized the post-Cold War world. Both trends imposed limits on US power. As a consequence, he cautioned, the United States should not expect universal acceptance of American ideals, and therefore it might need to act on its own or with its allies to protect vital national interests and preserve a favorable balance of power. Reviewing Louis Auchincloss' *Woodrow Wilson*, Steel (2000) acknowledged that: "Today virtually every American concerned with international issues is, or at least claims to be, a Wilsonian . . . Dusted off after decades of neglect and ridicule, Wilson is now hailed as the prophet of the age." Steel, however, continued to identify with the realism of Wilson's critics and to question Wilsonian premises. "His schemes," Steel noted with reference to the Cold War years, "were mercilessly ridiculed by such analysts of power politics as George Kennan, Walter Lippmann, Hans Morgenthau, and, later, Henry Kissinger. To them, . . . Wilson's dream of a democratic world bound together by free trade and collective peacekeeping seemed simply irrelevant. And for the most part it was" (pp. 19–21).

Walter A. McDougall expressed a similarly realistic warning against Wilsonian ideology, which had characterized US involvement in Vietnam and reappeared after the Cold War. "Global Meliorism," he explained in *Promised Land, Crusader State* (1997), expressed "an American mission to make the world a better place. It is based on the assumption that the United States can, should, and must reach out to help other nations share in the American dream." If the United States were to pursue that kind of Wilsonian world order, he concluded, it might well repeat the Vietnam tragedy. "As a blueprint for world order," he warned, "Wilsonianism has always been a chimera, but as an ideological weapon against 'every arbitrary power anywhere,' it has proved mighty indeed. And that, in the end, is how Wilson did truly imitate Jesus. He brought not peace but a sword" (pp. 173, 146).

Historiographical controversies over Wilson's foreign policies have intertwined with concerns about contemporary US involvement in the world. This nexus between historiography and policymaking has characterized the ongoing debate since Wilson's time. Michael W. Doyle used the categories of realism, liberalism, and socialism for the three major schools of international relations theory, which he analyzed in *Ways of War and Peace* (1997). Steigerwald (1999) employed similar categories. Defining the schools as realism, liberal internationalism, and New Left revisionism, he rejoiced over the alleged demise of realism and revisionism, while proclaiming the triumph of Wilsonian liberal internationalism. He believed that history and historiography were progressing toward this end.

Historians from different schools of thought have adopted different approaches to study American foreign relations. Some have focused on diplomacy and statecraft, addressing questions of war and peace, or national security. Others have concentrated on international political economy, examining financial and economic linkages among countries. Still others have emphasized cultural or ideological dimensions. These various political, economic, and cultural approaches have coincided somewhat with the different schools. Thus, to some extent, realists have concentrated on diplomacy, statecraft, and national security, revisionists on international political economy, and liberal internationalists on ideology and culture. It is very important, however, to avoid assuming that historians from a particular school have all adopted the same approach or reached the same conclusions. It is essential to distinguish among different schools of thought, on the one hand, and different scholarly approaches on the other. The temptation to classify any interpretation by identifying it with one of the schools or with one of the approaches, and then to reject it categorically as irrelevant, must be avoided to appreciate the rich diversity of scholarship on Wilson and World War I.

Several historians have too quickly dismissed both realism and revisionism – or at least their caricatures of these schools – as outmoded. Iriye, Steigerwald, and

Ninkovich did so, while offering their versions of Wilsonian idealism. So did Michael H. Hunt in *Ideology and US Foreign Policy* (1987). They all emphasized ideology and culture, apparently assuming that other historians who focused on these dimensions would necessarily reject both realism and revisionism. They overlooked the possibility that realist and revisionist historians might also embrace a cultural approach. In my own studies of Wilsonian statecraft (Ambrosius 1987, 1991, 2002) I emphasized linkages between political culture and diplomacy, while identifying with the realist school of my mentor Norman A. Graebner. Critics of realism have seemingly overlooked that he focused in *Ideas and Diplomacy* (1964) on the intellectual tradition of American foreign policy. Critics of revisionism likewise ignored the importance of culture and ideology – not just material interests – in the best revisionist studies. Emily S. Rosenberg, in *Financial Missionaries to the World* (1999), emphasized both politics and culture in the dollar diplomacy of the 1900–30 era. She combined political, economic, and cultural approaches in her multifaceted study of dollar diplomacy in the international political economy. These books all illustrated the important point that historians may employ a cultural approach without embracing Wilsonianism or dismissing realism and revisionism.

Despite their common cultural approaches and similar critiques of realism and revisionism, it would not be fair to lump Hunt (1987), Iriye (1993), Ninkovich (1999), and Steigerwald (1994, 1999) together in a single school of thought without recognizing substantial distinctions among them. They offered different interpretations of Wilson's role and legacy in the history of US foreign relations. Hunt criticized Wilsonian ideology, noting, for example, its racism (as both Rosenberg and I did, too), while Iriye, Ninkovich, and Steigerwald embraced it. Hunt, Iriye, and Steigerwald did not espouse postmodernism, but Ninkovich did. They recognized the world's actual existence, whereas he regarded it as the projection of Wilson's perception. Viewing the world from the inside out, not as an external reality, Ninkovich reduced international history to his own understanding of Wilson's image of it. He eschewed any attempt to interpret international history from the comparative perspective of other peoples outside the United States, a hallmark of Iriye's and Hunt's scholarship. Iriye, Hunt, and Steigerwald avoided Ninkovich's postmodernism. Their interpretations, recognizing that the world actually existed beyond Wilson's mind, were thus closer to realism and revisionism than to Ninkovich's postmodern Wilsonianism.

From different schools and approaches, recent scholarship on World War I has shown the importance of Wilsonianism in modern world history. The four principles that Wilson combined in his vision of a new world order – national self-determination, Open Door globalization, collective security, and progressive historicism – have all received considerable attention. For my critique of Wilson's legacy in US foreign relations and of his continuing influence on recent scholarship, see *Wilsonianism* (Ambrosius 2002).

Wilson championed the right of national self-determination. In *Pandaemonium* (1993), Daniel Patrick Moynihan credited him with making it a key principle of modern international politics. He applauded Wilson's ideals, despite his pro-British bias, while criticizing Kissinger's "realist" perspective for overlooking ethnicity in world affairs. He identified the principle with ethnonationalism. Derek Heater likewise focused on this principle as Wilson's primary legacy. In *National Self-*

Determination (1994), Heater traced its origins and then concentrated on the president's advocacy of it. "National self-determination," he noted, "is a belief, which became a principle of international justice, that a people should have the right and opportunity to determine their own government." Combining national awareness and self-rule, this principle emphasized popular sovereignty within democratic nation-states. Heater claimed that language was "the best test of nationality" to decide which people were a particular nation entitled to self-government. He contrasted Wilson's advocacy of national self-determination at the 1919 Paris Peace Conference with the Allies' pursuit of secret diplomacy and treaties. The peacemakers faced difficulties, Heater acknowledged, "partly because the doctrine of national self-determination could not be readily made to fit the actual distribution of populations and partly because it came into collision with power politics." He thought Wilson too readily compromised his ideals to accommodate postwar realities (pp. 3, 26, 64).

Critical of the peace treaties with Germany, Austria, and Hungary for violating the principle of national self-determination, Heater overlooked that Wilson's Fourteen Points had never promised all Germans the right to live in postwar Germany or all other peoples of any ethnicity or language the right to inhabit their own nation-states. The problem at Paris in 1919 was that the principle gave no guidance for deciding whose claims should be recognized when more than one people occupied the same land. Democratic methods, such as plebiscites, were inadequate for solving this problem. In theory, Wilson failed to recognize this dilemma. In practice, his compromises appeared to sacrifice the principle. Heater appreciated the president's practicality in dealing with complicated choices, but nevertheless criticized his failure to fulfill his putative promise in the peace treaties.

Wilson's principles of national self-determination and collective security were at the heart of contemporary and historiographical controversy over his reaction to war and revolution. Lloyd C. Gardner, in his revisionist analysis of the Anglo-American response to revolution from 1913 to 1923, *Safe for Democracy* (1984), emphasized the tensions between these two principles. He also stressed the president's resolve to create an Open Door international economy. Focusing on British prime minister David Lloyd George and Wilson, Gardner argued that they both sought a middle way between traditional European imperialism and revolutionary chaos. This progressive alternative promised a new era of peace and order as the outcome of US intervention in World War I. "When Woodrow Wilson arrived at the Capitol on the evening of April 2, 1917," Gardner affirmed, "it was not to ask Congress to intervene in a European war. His quest was for a new world. Only that outcome of the Great War could ensure the conversion of the 'irrational' revolutionary impulses that surged up in the late imperial era from Mexico to China into steady forces supporting world equilibrium." Wilson began this pursuit in Mexico and China before concentrating on Germany and Russia. "What Mexico had to have, therefore," Gardner noted, "was an *American* revolution, if it was to break free from foreign economic dominion, avoid a violent lurching back and forth between reaction and anarchy, and, most important, not set the wrong precedent as the world moved out from under the shadow of the dying imperial order." Later pursuing this same global agenda in revolutionary Russia, the president explained: "My policy regarding Russia is very similar to my Mexican policy. I believe in letting them work out their own salvation, even though they wallow in anarchy for a while."

Wilson reconciled US dominance over foreign nations with self-determination and collective security, confident that history was progressing toward this end. Within his liberal ideology, as Gardner explicated it, the pursuit of a progressive, democratic, capitalist, and peaceful world order appeared internally consistent. It did as well for the new administration of Wilson's successor, Warren G. Harding. Gardner concluded that "in each instance, American policymakers thought they were devising a postimperialist blueprint flexible enough to permit nationalist shoots to grow safely, protected against the storms of revolution and war, espaliered along the wall of capitalist liberalism" (pp. vii, 62, 180, 313).

In contrast to revisionists such as Gardner, who noted the inherent tensions in Wilsonianism, defenders of the president's ideology and actions sought to reconcile the contradictions in his response to war and revolution. In *Power and Principle* (1986), Frederick S. Calhoun examined armed intervention in Wilsonian foreign policy. The president, he argued, frequently used military force to promote democracy in foreign lands. In Calhoun's view, "Wilson was a self-proclaimed idealist who understood, as well as any man can, the international problems and dangers of his time." Rather than naively expecting his ideals to win acceptance on their own merit, "Wilson used his idealism realistically to attack the problems confronting him." He resorted to armed intervention, using force as an important aspect of power in pursuit of principle. His statecraft was both idealistic and realistic. "However clumsy and high-handed," Calhoun claimed, "Wilson's efforts to assist the downtrodden achieve democracy were helped by the interventions." From Veracruz to Vladivostok, Wilson had adopted this model. "The intervention in Mexico, Haiti, Santo Domingo, World War I, and Russia illustrated the utility of armed power as a tool of foreign policy." Wilson had decided unilaterally to intervene with US troops in these cases, but Calhoun nevertheless interpreted these military actions as precursors of collective security, and thus he underscored the president's "cooperation with the Allies and the Czechs" in Russia. "By proving the utility of such collaborative action in Russia, he hoped to show how it could succeed in the postwar era." This future vision, Calhoun concluded, "was the main determinant for Wilson in approving American participation in the interventions" (pp. 5, 3, 220, 191, 212).

Focusing on Wilson's response to the 1917 Russian Revolution, Betty Miller Unterberger offered a similar justification for his military intervention. She argued in *The United States, Revolutionary Russia, and the Rise of Czechoslovakia* (1989) that he pursued "self-determination without dismemberment of nations." In other words, he placed a priority on self-rule within the traditional borders of existing states, and only reluctantly recognized new nations. Rather than dismember Russia, he wanted the Allies to respect its territorial integrity and its people's right to decide their own destiny. He advocated both national self-determination and collective security. "At the core of his thought," she maintained, "self-determination meant government by consent of the governed – a moral necessity. This logic did not conceive of the implementation of the concept in its broader sense apart from the parallel existence of a league of nations." This definition allowed Unterberger to interpret Wilson's decision to intervene in Russia as not really violating the principle of national self-determination. She underscored "his complete disapproval of military intervention." When he finally decided in July 1918 to send US troops into Siberia, she explained, "Wilson emphasized that his major objectives were to rescue the Czechs while adhering to the principle of noninterference in Russia's internal affairs" (pp. 90, 259, 263). US military assistance for the stranded Czech troops would presumably help them escape without jeopardizing the Russian people's right of self-determination. The Bolsheviks, however, viewed it from a different perspective. They understood that he regarded them as illegitimate, for he believed that the Russian people, if given a democratic choice, would never accept their revolutionary regime. But from Wilson's (and also Unterberger's) viewpoint, US intervention honored his pledge to self-determination by aiding the Czechs without meddling in Russia's internal affairs. He subsequently extended diplomatic recognition to Czechoslovakia after the breakup of the Habsburg empire, whose dismemberment he eventually accepted as unavoidable. The principle of national self-determination justified some new nations, but prohibited full-scale military intervention in Russia to shape its destiny.

From a critical perspective outside the Wilsonian ideology, David S. Fogelsong offered a new synthesis that combined realist and revisionist insights. According to George F. Kennan, World War I had shaped Wilson's decision to intervene in Russia. The realistic purpose for US intervention was to stop Imperial Germany from gaining strategic control over Russia. In contrast, revisionists from William Appleman Williams to Gardner had emphasized Wilson's antipathy toward Bolshevism. As a defender of Western capitalism, he had opposed the new Soviet regime. In *America's Secret War Against Bolshevism* (1995), Fogelsong combined these interpretations into his own synthesis. "Thus," he concluded, "while scholars have often portrayed the effort to support patriotic Russian elements as *either* a strategic move against Germany *or* an effort to extinguish the Soviet regime, it is more accurate to see the Wilson administration's policy as simultaneously anti-German and anti-Bolshevik" (p. 77). Avoiding a false dichotomy between strategy and ideology, Fogelsong recognized that US intervention served both purposes. He also rejected Calhoun's and Unterberger's rationalizations of Wilson's decision to intervene in Russia as the pursuit of democracy in accordance with the principles of national self-determination and collective security. Challenging their Wilsonianism, Fogelsong highlighted the covert aid that US officials, with the president's approval, channeled into Russia to assist anti-Bolshevik as well as anti-German factions. Perlmutter praised this interventionist feature of Wilsonian foreign policy, but Steigerwald dismissed it as unwarranted allegations. Their reactions to Fogelsong reflected their contrasting neoconservative and liberal views about covert aid and armed force as means of promoting democracy.

Unlike Fogelsong, who emphasized US–Bolshevik antagonism during the Russian civil war, David W. McFadden focused on early contacts between Americans and Soviets that potentially offered opportunities for cooperation. In *Alternative Paths* (1993), he examined these contacts. Downplaying Wilson's personal involvement, he observed that, when the president did involve himself, his liberal ideology shaped his statecraft. "Wilson struggled with the question of what to do with the Bolsheviks from the standpoint of his own ideals and values," McFadden noted. "He tried to apply his fundamental conviction that American democracy and American free enterprise were absolutely right, not just for America, but for Russia and the world. He believed himself to be a Christian statesman on a mission to bring the American way of life to the world." At the same time, he shunned a full-scale confrontation with the Bolsheviks. As both "the compromiser and the crusader," the president never took decisive action either to reconcile or overturn the Soviet government. As a result, McFadden concluded, he never developed a consistent American policy for dealing with the Bolsheviks until his secretary of state, Bainbridge Colby, announced non-recognition in 1920 (pp. 9, 50–1, 54).

Wilson's antagonism toward Bolshevism expressed his commitment to Open Door globalization. It emerged from his cultural understanding of the international political economy. N. Gordon Levin, Jr. examined this aspect of Wilsonianism in his influential analysis of America's response to war and revolution, *Woodrow Wilson and World Politics* (1968). This book, along with those of William Appleman Williams, helped shape the school of New Left revisionism. Revisionist studies examined the economic underpinnings for Wilson's foreign policy, and continue to influence historiography.

Contrary to Steigerwald's judgment about the obsolescence of revisionism, this school has endured. It has, however, become more complex and, in some instances, less critical of Wilson and his legacy. Leo J. Bacino acknowledged in *Reconstructing Russia* (1999) his indebtedness to Levin and Williams, and also to Linda Killen's innovative study of *The Russian Bureau* (1983). Recognizing the anti-Bolshevism of US policymakers, Bacino criticized McFadden for overstating the potential for Soviet–American *rapprochement* after 1917. Yet he downplayed anti-Bolshevik aspects of the American response to the Russian Revolution. Like Wilson, he regarded the Open Door principle as a progressive – and therefore non-intervention-ist – contribution to Russia's reconstruction. Bacino directed sharp criticism at Fogelsong: "By ignoring the significance and complexity of the interpower rivalry in Russia and the sophistication of the Wilson administration's assistance policy, Fogelsong mistakes the distinctly progressive character of Wilson's policy for a series of covert operations against the Bolsheviks" (p. 11). This Wilsonian perspective reduced Bacino's interpretation to a mild variant of the revisionist school.

Other historians have developed revisionism into a more sophisticated critique of Wilsonianism. In addition to Lloyd Gardner's (1984) and Emily Rosenberg's (1999) contributions, studies of US relations with Mexico have revealed both economic self-interest and aggressive impulses in US foreign policy during World War I. In *The Secret War in Mexico* (1981), Friedrich Katz examined the complex connections between international business and diplomacy during the Mexican Revolution. Showing that Americans as well as Europeans were pursuing their own economic and political advantages in Mexico by supporting or opposing different revolutionary factions, he challenged the Wilsonian belief in American exceptionalism. In Katz's multinational study, the United States did not appear as nearly so unique or virtuous as Wilson claimed. In *Oil, Banks, and Politics* (1995), Linda B. Hall likewise recognized that during and after World War I the United States sought to control postrevolutionary Mexico. More was involved than keeping European influences out of that neighboring country. Wilson's principles and diplomacy, she understood, safeguarded US economic interests. His appeal for an "open door" in Mexico justified the exploitation of its oil. "Mexican oil was a treasure at hand, and Americans intended to control it." Hall also observed that Wall Street bankers, in collaboration with the Wilson administration, intended to establish "US hegemony over Mexican financial affairs." The Mexicans, however, resisted these threats to their national sovereignty, and eventually won US diplomatic recognition as well as loans without abdicating control over their oil. Thus, Hall concluded, "the US stand – in both government and business – was ultimately counterproductive, leading to bad feelings and the further development of legal obstacles to US involvement in Mexican oil" (pp. 60, 85, 177). Rosenberg later developed the same crucial point, showing that dollar diplomacy generated a backlash in Latin America and the Caribbean, not international harmony as Wilson's liberal ideology had promised.

Some historians have employed the methodology of comparative history, which enabled them to comprehend how other peoples reacted to the United States. Their studies thereby escaped the ideological constraints of Wilsonianism. Besides Katz (1981), Gardner (1984), and Rosenberg (1999), Nancy Mitchell skillfully used this methodology. In *The Danger of Dreams* (1999), a comparative study of German and American imperialism in Latin America, she demonstrated that the United States was establishing its hegemony in the Western hemisphere before World War I. Imperial Germany as well as Great Britain, she argued, had recognized this reality and shown considerable deference toward the United States. Nevertheless, Americans needed an actual or potential enemy to justify their own imperial ambitions, given their sense of exceptionalism. Imperial Germany served this purpose for Wilson. The image of Europeans as a threat in the Americas allowed him to disguise US hegemony as a defensive response. He depicted American involvement in the Mexican revolution as protection against evil European intentions. This contrast between image and reality, Mitchell concluded, nurtured a negative view of Germany that would justify US intervention in 1917, thereby revealing "the utility of misperception" (pp. 216–28).

Image contradicted reality in the American pursuit of collective security as well as Open Door globalization in the Western hemisphere. In *Pan American Visions* (1986), Mark T. Gilderhus made this realistic point regarding Wilson's search for regional integration during World War I. While the president sought a new solidarity with the Latin American nations, they resisted his efforts to impose US hegemony. Argentina, Brazil, and Chile asserted their own leadership in the region, rejecting the president's combination of unilateral action and multilateral rhetoric. Like Mexico, they steadfastly refused to acquiesce in his hegemonial vision of Pan Americanism. As Gilderhus explained, Wilson believed that "the tenets of free trade, translated literally into practice, would open the doors of opportunity, roll back the European presence, and establish new connections between the United States and Latin America. Similarly, the cultivation of political ties would forge new bonds." But Latin Americans did not want these bonds, which would jeopardize their national sovereignty. They understood that Wilson's proposed Pan American Pact, while multilateral in form, would give legitimacy to unilateral US action. Consequently, they rejected this Wilsonian vision of collective security. "Wilson, to be sure," Gilderhus emphasized, "desired means of upholding national sovereignty and territorial integrity, but before recognizing any nation's unqualified right to self-determination, he insisted upon proper observance for the rules of civilized order" (pp. 156–7). He expected, moreover, to define those rules. This fundamental conflict between the Wilsonian vision and the Latin American reality doomed Wilson's Pan Americanism to failure.

In *Woodrow Wilson and the American Diplomatic Tradition* (1987), I featured the same inherent contradictions in the president's understanding of international relations, particularly in his conception of the new League of Nations. He emphasized global interdependence, but neglected to account for political, economic, and cultural diversity within and among nations. He expected his vision of a new world order to overcome the reality of pluralism. I emphasized that "global interdependence and pluralism combined to create a fundamental dilemma for the United States in the twentieth century." Wilson attempted to resolve this dilemma with the League of Nations, which would permit American control over foreign affairs. "By transforming international relations, the League would enable the United States to provide leadership overseas without entangling itself in the Old World's diplomacy and wars." Wilson's vision of collective security thus promised the United States the benefits of both unilateral control and multilateral action. "A redefinition of realism is required to provide a critical perspective on Wilson's particular combination of ideals and practicality," I argued (pp. ix–x, xii). Both universalism and unilateralism characterized his conception of the League. By joining this new regime of collective security, the United States would have involved itself in global obligations while reserving for itself the right to define them. I developed the themes of control, universalism, and unilateralism to explain Wilson's efforts to establish the League as the instrument of US hegemony. He failed to achieve this vision either at the Paris Peace Conference or in the US Senate. Wilson encountered limits to his power to create a new world order.

Other historians, besides Gilderhus and myself, have assessed Wilson's vision of collective security without embracing his liberal ideology. William C. Widenor, in *Henry Cabot Lodge and the Search for an American Foreign Policy* (1980), contrasted Lodge with Wilson. He contended that Lodge was both idealistic and practical, making the point about the senator that I made about the president. Both of us avoided the old, false debate between "realism" and "idealism," which had overlooked both Lodge's ideals and Wilson's practicality. Widenor and I agreed that Lodge offered a realistic alternative to Wilsonianism – a different combination of ideals and practicality. His alternative after World War I, including an Anglo-American guarantee of French security against future German aggression, recognized the limits of US power and thus avoided worldwide commitments. Lacking Wilson's belief in progress, Lodge doubted the liberal promise of universal peace through the League, whether the United States joined it or not, and thus sought to protect American national interests in the existing world of power politics.

In contrast to Widenor and myself, John Milton Cooper, Jr. sharply criticized Lodge and viewed Wilson more favorably in his interpretation of the treaty fight in 1919–20. In *Breaking the Heart of the World* (2001), he agreed, however, that the president was the primary obstacle to a compromise in the Senate that would have permitted the United States to join the League of Nations. He attributed this failure to Wilson's poor physical health, particularly his stroke in October 1919, and its consequent impact on his leadership. Although the president had adamantly and consistently rejected any compromise over his League before as well as after his major stroke, Cooper argued that he would surely have succeeded in winning the Senate's approval of the Versailles Treaty if his health had not broken. In other words, the problem was Wilson's health, not his rigid character or flawed ideology. Cooper also largely ignored the Republican senator's support for the French security treaty. Viewing the treaty fight within the framework of Wilsonian internationalism versus Republican isolationism, he agreed with Link and Knock, and also Thomas A. Bailey, that Wilson's peacemaking was essentially correct, despite his failure.

Recent studies of military strategy and operations during World War I have challenged the Wilsonian vision of collective security. These noted sharp differences between the United States and the Allies. With Wilson's firm support, General John J. Pershing refused to cooperate with either the British or the French on the Western front, risking a German victory in 1918 rather than allow the amalgamation of the American Expeditionary Forces into the Allied armies. David F. Trask in *The AEF and Coalition Warmaking* (1993) and David R. Woodward in *Trial by Friendship* (1993) stressed this point, as did Thomas H. Buckley and Edwin B. Strong, Jr. in *American Foreign and National Security Policies* (1987). Instead of providing a realistic model of collective security, wartime coalition relations evidenced Wilson's and Pershing's determination to retain unilateral US control over the warmaking and the future peacemaking.

Despite such critiques, champions of Wilsonianism have praised the president's concept of collective security. Thomas J. Knock (1992) contrasted "Wilsonian progressive internationalism" with "conservative internationalism." He traced the influences on Wilson's thinking, especially from left-wing liberals and socialists, and claimed that the president might have won the fight for the League in 1919–20 if he had maintained his contacts with these left-wing progressive internationalists. Knock failed to show, however, how the president might have gained a two-thirds majority in the Senate for the Versailles Treaty even if he had maintained close ties with them. Nor did Knock account for the negative domestic repercussions of Wilson's statecraft. His repressive actions at home alienated erstwhile supporters among progressive internationalists. Disregarding the hegemonial aspects of Wilson's evolving ideas, such as the Pan American Pact, Knock interpreted his quest for a new world order within the strictures of Wilson's own ideology, confident that it should have succeeded even if it did not. Progressive historicism undergirded their common affirmation of faith about a new world order, despite the predictable failure of Wilsonianism after World War I.

David M. Esposito, like Perlmutter (1997), stressed the geopolitical core of Wilson's liberal internationalism. Although the president had not given a strategic rationale for military intervention in 1917, Esposito argued in *The Legacy of Woodrow Wilson* (1996), his real purpose was to contain Imperial Germany. He did not articulate his geopolitical views prior to intervention because a direct threat to American national defense, beyond that of German submarines, became apparent only after the United States had entered the war. Pursuing both America's mission and its national interests in 1917–18, the president redefined modern American ideology as the foundation for a new foreign policy, and thus Wilsonianism anticipated the "domino theory" of the Cold War era. Esposito's thesis coincided with Frank Ninkovich's in *Modernity and Power* (1994) in attributing the domino theory to Wilsonian origins. "Today we are living through the consummate triumph of Wilsonianism," Esposito rejoiced, adding that "self-determination and collective security are no longer theories or slogans but pivots on which the modern world turns" (pp. 140–1). From this perspective, Wilsonian ideology appeared to coincide with geopolitical reality during World War I and throughout the twentieth century. It was not, as Nancy Mitchell (1999) would describe it, the creation of a dangerous dream.

Robert David Johnson highlighted another alternative for US involvement in world affairs in *The Peace Progressives and American Foreign Relations* (1995). In contrast to either Wilson's liberal internationalism or Republican corporatism (or to Knock's classifications of progressive and conservative internationalism), the peace progressives wanted to reform the international order in ways that were more sensitive to weaker nations in the financially and industrially underdeveloped world. Not really isolationist, despite their opposition to the League, they rejected both Wilsonian and corporatist visions of interdependence in favor of greater diversity among nations. As Johnson saw them, the peace progressives, mostly insurgent Republican senators and journalists, were anti-imperialist and anti-militarist dissenters against European power politics. Emerging as a movement against William Howard Taft's dollar diplomacy, they coalesced against Wilson's intervention in the Caribbean and Latin America and in World War I. They were committed to the principle of national self-determination, but not as Wilson understood it. They recognized that his League would threaten the right of revolution or genuine self-determination, and consequently worked to defeat it. In short, the peace progressives offered a left-wing alternative to both Wilsonianism and Republican corporatism. In contrast to Knock, who identified Wilson with left-wing progressive internationalism, Johnson grasped the profound differences between his ideology and that of peace progressives. They espoused quite divergent alternatives for US foreign relations during and after World War I.

William Jennings Bryan was the harbinger of the peace progressives. Johnson noted his contributions to this alternative to Wilson's liberal internationalism. Bryan did not share the president's hegemonial and interventionist tendencies, although their views of America's role in the world were similar in many respects. These underlying differences, not just their specific disagreements over US neutrality during the Great War, caused Wilson's first secretary of state to resign in 1915. In *The End of Neutrality* (1981), John W. Coogan examined the disagreements between Wilson and Bryan over maritime rights, noting that the president inclined toward a pro-British definition that would eventually take the United States into war against Germany. His new secretary of state, Robert Lansing, also espoused pro-British neutrality. Kendrick A. Clements, in *William Jennings Bryan* (1982), explicated the underlying ideological differences, observing that Bryan favored "a missionary isolationism that promised service to the world without involvement." World War I, Bryan believed, "presented to the United States, as the exemplar of Christian democracy, a unique opportunity to lead the exhausted belligerents to a permanent peace based on Christian principles" (pp. 22, 113). He hoped the United States could provide the democratic model for the world, but was less inclined than Wilson to use military force to achieve the goal they shared.

Outstanding biographies have shown the complexity of Wilson's personality and of the problems he faced during World War I. Clements examined his role as "world statesman" in *Woodrow Wilson* (1987) and further explained it in *The Presidency of Woodrow Wilson* (1992). He noted the fundamental dilemma that the United States confronted during the peacemaking after World War I. "Interdependence had made isolation impossible – and undesirable – in the future," he observed. Yet Americans wanted to preserve their national sovereignty in any new world order that Wilson might create. Clements emphasized Wilson's difficulty in trying to convince the

American people that the League of Nations could provide collective security without excessive sacrifice by the United States. "Wilson was asking Americans to accept a delicate structure, in which national independence was combined with a recognition of the reality of interdependence and with some limitations on sovereignty" (p. 196). Ultimately, the US Senate rejected the Wilsonian resolution of this fundamental dilemma.

John Milton Cooper, Jr., another outstanding biographer, recognized Wilson's practicality and downplayed his ideological zeal. In a comparative biography of him and Theodore Roosevelt, *The Warrior and the Priest* (1983), Cooper viewed Wilson as more of a practical statesman, and TR as more of a crusading ideologue. Contrary to Kissinger's (1994) stereotypical characterization of the two progressive presidents, Cooper regarded Wilson as more realistic than TR. He agreed with Arthur S. Link, who had emphasized in *Woodrow Wilson* (1979) that "Wilson . . . was no visionary idealist" (p. 11). That label was inadequate to describe the subtlety of Wilsonian statecraft. Wilson's brother-in-law, Stockton Axson, had earlier seen the same prudent qualities. Axson had observed that "he was an idealist with a strong realization of the practical." Wilson's thinking was "absolutely *non*-metaphysical." He was "the practical man" in comparison with Bryan, "the theoretical man" (pp. 4, 49, 184). Cooper made a similar comparison between the president and his wartime ambassador to the United Kingdom in *Walter Hines Page* (1977). The ambassador had crusaded for US intervention in the Great War after the 1915 sinking of the *Lusitania* by a German submarine. "Page had become an unwitting Rooseveltian in the Wilsonian camp," Cooper observed. "Behind these assertions lay a profound distaste for the president and his whole approach to world politics" (pp. 325, 372). In their crusades for or against US participation in the war, Page and TR, on one side, and Bryan, on the other, were all frustrated by the president's particular combination of idealism with practicality.

Foreign historians have contributed some keen insights into Wilson and World War I. Their non-US perspectives have sharpened their interpretations even when they did not explicitly adopt the methodology of comparative history. Dutch historian Jan Willem Schulte Nordholt focused in *Woodrow Wilson* (1991) on the president as "the first great advocate of world peace." Less encyclopedic than August Heckscher's *Woodrow Wilson* (1991), Nordholt's biography excelled as a realistic analysis. He noted that Wilson's belief in American exceptionalism undergirded his self-righteous attitude. As a reformer in international relations, he hoped to share the benefits of American capitalism, democracy, and Christianity with other nations. His response to revolutions in China, Mexico, and Russia expressed this hope. The president never comprehended that his foreign policy constituted American-style imperialism. Rather than being as benevolent as he claimed, the United States intervened in those revolutions to serve its own interests. Deceiving himself, he developed "the myth of the good people whose rulers are evil . . . It was a theory more democratic in appearance than in reality, however, for it was Wilson, not the people, who decided what the people should want" (pp. 5, 183). Nordholt did not accept the argument, which Link and Cooper had offered, that Wilson was realistic in seeking to preserve Europe's balance of power and create a new world order. Link (1971) had labeled this combination of strategy and ideology as "higher realism." Refuting that thesis, Nordholt perceived unrealistic features in Wilsonianism during

World War I. Although somewhat less critical, British historian John A. Thompson similarly recognized in *Woodrow Wilson* (2002) the president's distinctively American approach to world leadership. Thompson noted that "Wilson developed a rationale for the deployment of American power overseas that has remained central to subsequent debates in the United States over the role that the country should play in the world. Both abroad and at home, therefore, Wilson has been indissolubly associated with a particular, very American, version of internationalism that has continued to be the subject of lively debate" (p. 9).

German and Danish historians have contributed major studies of the US–German relationship and the Paris Peace Conference. Reinhard R. Doerries examined Count Bernstorff's unsuccessful service as Germany's ambassador to the United States until 1917 in *Imperial Challenge* (1989). Berlin's ineptitude, he concluded, contributed to the American perception of Germany as a danger, and thus to US intervention. Klaus Schwabe analyzed Wilson's missionary diplomacy and the realities of power in postwar Europe in *Woodrow Wilson, Revolutionary Germany, and Peacemaking* (1985). Like Link and Cooper, Schwabe generally applauded Wilsonian statecraft. He, too, embraced Wilsonianism. He commended the president for resisting excessive Allied claims against the new German republic at the peace conference, although ultimately Wilson failed to achieve what he had promised in the Fourteen Points. Inga Floto viewed Edward M. House, the president's intimate friend and adviser, from a more critical perspective. She perceptively examined his role at the peace conference and his eventual break with Wilson in *Colonel House in Paris* (1980).

British historian G. R. Conyne argued in *Woodrow Wilson* (1992) that the president was not a naive idealist, although that had become the stereotypical view of him in the United Kingdom after World War I, thanks to John Maynard Keynes and Harold Nicholson. Contrary to that stereotype, he was a more complex personality, combining shrewd practicality with moral principles. Reports from the British embassy in Washington had enabled Lloyd George to understand Wilson's political nature. Rather than arguing over the Fourteen Points, the prime minister affirmed these general principles and then interpreted them to protect British interests. Despite Anglo-American differences over war aims, this approach enabled British leaders to preserve relatively good relations with Wilson during the war and the peace conference.

In contrast, misperceptions plagued US–Japanese relations. Noriko Kawamura concluded that the president did not pursue a realistic policy toward East Asia during the war and at the peace conference. His ideology created problems. "Once Wilson assumed the universality of his ideals of liberal internationalism," she explained in *Turbulence in the Pacific* (2000), "nations that failed to adhere to the ideals were considered morally and legally wrong regardless of their reasons. He unilaterally applied his ideals to the East Asian situation without truly understanding the realities in that region" (p. 5). Wilsonianism blinded the president to East Asian realities.

Scholars who have embraced Wilsonianism have typically regarded it as a coherent, pragmatic ideology. They have praised Wilson's vision of a new world order based on national self-determination, collective security, and Open Door globalization. They have often assumed that world history was progressing toward the realization of these principles. That view, however, overlooked potential conflicts. It depended upon an often-unstated premise about the US role in world affairs. Wilsonianism provided a coherent ideology for Americans, given their assumption that this nation would become the dominant power in the new world order. Taking American hegemony for granted, Wilson's vision anticipated that the United States could control international relations and would determine how to reconcile his principles in practice. Questioning this underlying premise, whether in its liberal or neoconservative guises, scholars in the realist and revisionist schools have emphasized tensions between the Wilsonian vision of global interdependence and the reality of pluralism. They have emphasized the unresolved problems, noting, for example, that Open Door globalization and collective security would necessarily restrict national sovereignty and self-rule in other countries and even in the United States. It would not invariably promote democracy. Dollar diplomacy generated a backlash by pitting integration against fragmentation. Latin American nations rejected Wilson's Pan Americanism. Foreign revolutionaries pursued their own agendas, resisting American attempts to guide them toward a Wilsonian world order. Victorious allies as well as defeated enemies pursued their own interests during the peacemaking after World War I. Cultural, economic, and political diversity among peoples prevented the triumph of Wilsonianism. Despite Wilson's expectations, based on progressive historicism, the world did not achieve the liberal dream of peace and international harmony. A new progressive, democratic, and capitalist world order did not emerge from the ruins of World War I.

Even after the Cold War, that Wilsonian vision has not been realized. As long as pluralism remains among the world's peoples, despite the preferences of advocates of Wilsonianism for global interdependence and uniformity, the questions that realists and revisionists have raised will remain relevant. Viewing the history of US foreign relations through the eyes of faith in progress has obscured those questions for some, but scholars still need to address them. The insights of realism and revisionism should not be overlooked, despite the apparent triumph of Wilsonianism in recent years. In the ongoing debate over the US role in modern world history, Woodrow Wilson and World War I will most likely remain a focal point of controversy. That, too, is part of the Wilsonian legacy.

REFERENCES

Ambrosius, L. E.: *Woodrow Wilson and the American Diplomatic Tradition: The Treaty Fight in Perspective* (Cambridge: Cambridge University Press, 1987).

Ambrosius, L. E.: *Wilsonian Statecraft: Theory and Practice of Liberal Internationalism during World War I* (Wilmington, DE: Scholarly Resources, 1991).

Ambrosius, L. E.: *Wilsonianism: Woodrow Wilson and His Legacy in American Foreign Relations* (New York: Palgrave/Macmillan, 2002).

Axson, S.: *"Brother Woodrow": A Memoir of Woodrow Wilson* (Princeton, NJ: Princeton University Press, 1993).

Bacino, L. J.: *Reconstructing Russia: US Policy in Revolutionary Russia, 1917–1922* (Kent, OH: Kent State University Press, 1999).

Buckley, T. H. and E. B. Strong, Jr.: *American Foreign and National Security Policies, 1914–1945* (Knoxville: University of Tennessee Press, 1987).

Calhoun, F. S.: *Power and Principle: Armed Intervention in Wilsonian Foreign Policy* (Kent, OH: Kent State University Press, 1986).

Clements, K. A.: *William Jennings Bryan: Missionary Isolationist* (Knoxville: University of Tennessee Press, 1982).

Clements, K. A.: *Woodrow Wilson: World Statesman* (Boston, MA: Twayne Publishers, 1987).

Clements, K. A.: *The Presidency of Woodrow Wilson* (Lawrence: University of Kansas Press, 1992).

Conyne, G. R.: *Woodrow Wilson: British Perspectives, 1912–21* (London: Macmillan, 1992).

Coogan, J. W.: *The End of Neutrality: The United States, Britain, and Maritime Rights, 1899–1915* (Ithaca, NY: Cornell University Press, 1981).

Cooper, J. M., Jr.: *Walter Hines Page: The Southerner as American, 1855–1918* (Chapel Hill: University of North Carolina Press, 1977).

Cooper, J. M., Jr.: *The Warrior and the Priest: Theodore Roosevelt and Woodrow Wilson* (Cambridge, MA: Harvard University Press, 1983).

Cooper, J. M., Jr.: *Breaking the Heart of the World: Woodrow Wilson and the Fight for the League of Nations* (Cambridge: Cambridge University Press, 2001).

Doerries, R. R.: *Imperial Challenge: Ambassador Count Bernstorff and German–American Relations, 1908–1917* (Chapel Hill: University of North Carolina Press, 1989).

Doyle, M. W.: *Ways of War and Peace: Realism, Liberalism, and Socialism* (New York: W. W. Norton, 1997).

Esposito, D. M.: *The Legacy of Woodrow Wilson: American War Aims in World War I* (Westport, CT: Praeger, 1996).

Floto, I.: *Colonel House in Paris: A Study of American Policy at the Paris Peace Conference 1919* (Princeton, NJ: Princeton University Press, 1980).

Fogelsong, D. S.: *America's Secret War Against Bolshevism: US Intervention in the Russian Civil War, 1917–1920* (Chapel Hill: University of North Carolina Press, 1995).

Gardner, L. C.: *Safe for Democracy: The Anglo-American Response to Revolution, 1913–1923* (New York: Oxford University Press, 1984).

Gilderhus, M. T.: *Pan American Visions: Woodrow Wilson in the Western Hemisphere, 1913–1921* (Tucson: University of Arizona Press, 1986).

Graebner, N. A.: *Ideas and Diplomacy: Readings in the Intellectual Tradition of American Foreign Policy* (New York: Oxford University Press, 1964).

Hall, L. B.: *Oil, Banks, and Politics: The United States and Postrevolutionary Mexico, 1917–1924* (Austin: University of Texas Press, 1995).

Heater, D.: *National Self-Determination: Woodrow Wilson and His Legacy* (New York: St. Martin's Press, 1994).

Heckscher, A.: *Woodrow Wilson: A Biography* (New York: Charles Scribner's Sons, 1991).

Hunt, M. H.: *Ideology and US Foreign Policy* (New Haven, CT: Yale University Press, 1987).

Iriye, A.: *The Globalizing of America, 1913–1945* (Cambridge: Cambridge University Press, 1993).

Johnson, R. D.: *The Peace Progressives and American Foreign Relations* (Cambridge, MA: Harvard University Press, 1995).

Katz, F.: *The Secret War in Mexico: Europe, the United States, and the Mexican Revolution* (Chicago, IL: University of Chicago Press, 1981).

Kawamura, N.: *Turbulence in the Pacific: Japanese–US Relations during World War I* (Westport, CT: Praeger, 2000).

Killen, L.: *The Russian Bureau: A Case Study in Wilsonian Diplomacy* (Lexington: University of Kentucky Press, 1983).

Kissinger, H.: *Diplomacy* (New York: Simon and Schuster, 1994).

Knock, T. J.: *To End All Wars: Woodrow Wilson and the Quest for a New World Order* (New York: Oxford University Press, 1992).

Levin, N. G., Jr.: *Woodrow Wilson and World Politics: America's Response to War and Revolution* (New York: Oxford University Press, 1968).

Link, A. S.: *The Higher Realism of Woodrow Wilson and Other Essays* (Nashville, TN: Vanderbilt University Press, 1971).

Link, A. S.: *Woodrow Wilson: Revolution, War, and Peace* (Arlington Heights, IL: AHM Publishing, 1979).

McDougall, W. A.: *Promised Land, Crusader State: The American Encounter with the World Since 1776* (Boston, MA: Houghton Mifflin, 1997).

McFadden, D. W.: *Alternative Paths: Soviets and Americans, 1917–1920* (New York: Oxford University Press, 1993).

Mitchell, N.: *The Danger of Dreams: German and American Imperialism in Latin America* (Chapel Hill: University of North Carolina Press, 1999).

Moynihan, D. P.: *Pandaemonium: Ethnicity in International Politics* (New York: Oxford University Press, 1993).

Ninkovich, F.: *Modernity and Power: A History of the Domino Theory in the Twentieth Century* (Chicago, IL: University of Chicago Press, 1994).

Ninkovich, F.: *The Wilsonian Century: US Foreign Policy since 1900* (Chicago, IL: University of Chicago Press, 1999).

Nordholt, J. W. S.: *Woodrow Wilson: A Life for World Peace* (Berkeley: University of California Press, 1991).

Perlmutter, A.: *Making the World Safe for Democracy: A Century of Wilsonianism and Its Totalitarian Challengers* (Chapel Hill: University of North Carolina Press, 1997).

Rosenberg, E. S.: *Financial Missionaries to the World: The Politics and Culture of Dollar Diplomacy, 1900–1930* (Cambridge, MA: Harvard University Press, 1999).

Schwabe, K.: *Woodrow Wilson, Revolutionary Germany, and Peacemaking, 1918–1919: Missionary Diplomacy and the Realities of Power* (Chapel Hill: University of North Carolina Press, 1985).

Smith, T.: *America's Mission: The United States and the Worldwide Struggle for Democracy in the Twentieth Century* (Princeton, NJ: Princeton University Press, 1994).

Steel, R.: *Temptations of a Superpower* (Cambridge, MA: Harvard University Press, 1995).

Steel, R.: "Mr. Fix-It." *New York Review of Books* 47 (October 5, 2000), 19–21.

Steigerwald, D.: *Wilsonian Idealism in America* (Ithaca, NY: Cornell University Press, 1994).

Steigerwald, D.: "Reclamation of Woodrow Wilson." *Diplomatic History* 23 (1999), 79–99.

Thompson, J. A.: *Woodrow Wilson: Profiles in Power* (London: Longman, 2002).

Trask, D. F.: *The AEF and Coalition Warmaking, 1917–1918* (Lawrence: University of Kansas Press, 1993).

Unterberger, B. M.: *The United States, Revolutionary Russia, and the Rise of Czechoslovakia* (Chapel Hill: University of North Carolina Press, 1989).

Widenor, William C.: *Henry Cabot Lodge and the Search for an American Foreign Policy* (Berkeley: University of California Press, 1980).

Woodward, D. R.: *Trial by Friendship: Anglo-American Relations, 1917–1918* (Lexington: University of Kentucky Press, 1993).

FURTHER READING

Boemeke, M. F., G. D. Feldman, and E. Glaser, E. (eds.): *The Treaty of Versailles: A Reassessment after 75 Years* (Cambridge: Cambridge University Press, 1998).

Chickering, R. and S. Forster (eds.): *Great War, Total War: Combat and Mobilization on the Western Front* (Cambridge: Cambridge University Press, 2000).

Cooper, J. M., Jr. and C. E. Neu: *The Wilson Era: Essays in Honor of Arthur S. Link* (Arlington Heights, IL: Harlan Davidson, 1991).

Ferrell, R. H.: *Woodrow Wilson and World War I, 1917–1921* (New York: Harper and Row, 1985).

Winter, J., G. Parker, and M. R. Habeck (eds.): *The Great War and the Twentieth Century* (New Haven, CT: Yale University Press, 2000).

CHAPTER ELEVEN

Recent Explorations Concerning the Interwar Period

JUSTUS D. DOENECKE

In the 1990s and beyond, historians have pursued research on the interwar period, here defined as the two decades before the United States entered World War II. The emphasis is hardly surprising, for the period marks the end of one world war and the beginning of another. This chapter centers on fresh contributions to the study of diplomatic maneuvers and military policy beginning with the Washington Naval Conference of 1921–2 and going down to Japan's attack on Pearl Harbor. Many discoveries have been described in the bibliographical essays edited by Michael J. Hogan (2000), which were based on articles published in *Diplomatic History* throughout the 1990s. Nonetheless, thanks to the bibliography project of the Society for Historians of American Foreign Relations, one can even trace fresher material as well as attempt to find some long-range patterns on crucial aspects of the period 1920–41.

In retrospect one sees that the previous decade, the 1980s, produced some memorable and at times provocative scholarship. In *Threshold of War* (1988), dealing with Franklin D. Roosevelt during the months of March through December 1941, Waldo Heinrichs argues that the very centerpiece of the president's strategy lay in his concern with maintaining the Russian front. Indeed, FDR had little choice, for the United States lacked the ships and planes needed to check the Axis. In examining activities in the Pacific, Jonathan G. Utley denies that in the summer of 1941 FDR sought to confront Japan. His *Going to War with Japan, 1937–1941* (1985) stresses the role of bureaucratic underlings in the State Department, namely Assistant Secretary Dean Acheson, who in July 1941 ignorantly and arrogantly altered presidential freezing orders. Acheson on his own, says Utley, converted Roosevelt's order of a partial embargo into a total one and hence made war inevitable. In covering the major opposition to the president, Wayne S. Cole (1983) emphasizes how many of the so-called isolationists in Congress were Western Progressives, people who had often started to the left of the New Deal, though usually backing FDR's major reform measures. Only when World War II broke out in Europe did

Much of this material was presented in somewhat different form to a plenary session of the Siena College Annual Conference on World War II, May 31, 2001. The author is grateful to J. Garry Clifford, Wayne S. Cole, Warren F. Kimball, Leo P. Ribuffo, and Mark A. Stoler for suggestions. All views expressed are solely the author's.

relations become strained, with the president meeting legitimate political opposition with wiretaps and federal probes.

Three books of the 1980s triggered particular controversy. Marks (1988) argued that "FDR accumulated the largest overseas credibility gap of any president on record." Marks' chapter "From the Potomac to the Rhine" accused FDR of seeking to be the architect of Munich, then of encouraging outright war by prodding Britain and France to resist Germany. At the same time, Marks indicts Roosevelt for trimming American armaments below "a level commensurate with the nation's national defense" (pp. 167, 287). Far more friendly to FDR but creating equal debate is Robert Edwin Herzstein's *Roosevelt and Hitler: Prelude to War* (1989). To Herzstein, the crux of the president's foreign policy was based on his sympathy with Europe's persecuted Jews. FDR was so concerned about this matter that he became the virtual architect of Germany's defeat. Presenting a view very much to the contrary, Patrick J. Hearden (1987) sees US involvement rooted in market factors. "American leaders," Hearden writes, "were primarily concerned about the menace that a triumphant Germany presented to the free enterprise system of the United States" (p. x).

In the 1990s, scholars did relatively little with the 1920s. Seldom do we have the sweeping works on reconstruction, reparations, commerce, and arms control produced in previous decades. There is, however, one new work of synthesis concerning this period. Following in the footsteps of L. Ethan Ellis (1968) and Warren I. Cohen (1987), Margot Louria (2001) examines 1920s diplomacy as a whole. Focusing on the three secretaries of state holding office during this time, she presents a positive report, finding them acting most responsibly. Charles Evans Hughes fostered serious disarmament, Frank B. Kellogg created a legal framework for a world bound by law, and Henry L. Stimson sought to check Japanese expansion. Conversely, in examining much of the literature existing in 1992, Kathleen Burk (1992) indicts American diplomacy for attempting to build an entire world order on financial stability, thereby neglecting crucial balance-of-power considerations on the European continent.

Disarmament, however, continues to fascinate researchers. In covering the naval conferences of the 1920s and 1930s, political scientist Robert Gordon Kaufman (1990) finds the varied agreements resting on fallacious assumptions concerning new technologies, the dynamics of Japanese politics, and Japan's strategic intentions. The naval treaties, he claims, benefited Japan far more than it did the US and Britain. Similarly, Murfett (1992) sees the Washington Conference of 1921–2 making far more concessions to Japan than to Britain. In dealing with the aftermath of the conference, Buckley (1994) emphasizes a missed opportunity for a lasting peace. Likewise, Maurer (1994) notes that the arms control created by the Washington meeting could not endure in a political vacuum. Fanning (1995) explores the effect of public opinion on policymaking, tracing how the failure of the 1927 Geneva (or Coolidge) Conference led to the success of the one held in London in 1930. The Geneva meeting, Fanning claims, fell victim to bureaucratic infighting as well as strategic and technical differences. Epstein (1992) in fact calls upon scholars to take the Geneva meeting more seriously. Challenging the picture of "perilous equilibrium" advanced by O'Connor (1962), Kennedy (1992) denies that the London meeting embodied such a concept.

Several historians have stressed US–British rivalries during the 1920s. McKercher (1993) notes how Britain saw the United States as a potential naval rival; only in the 1930s did it envision cooperation with the US. Bell (1997) traces contingency plans for a British–American war, the US basing its strategy on an overland invasion of Canada and the British sending a battle fleet over the ocean.

There is practically nothing new on the Manchurian crisis of 1931–3, the first major onslaught on the international systems created at Paris in 1919 and at Washington three years later. Waldron (1992) has edited the famous 1935 memorandum of John Van Antwerp MacMurray, praised in Kennan (1950), in which the senior diplomat called for moderation in confronting Japan and restraint in backing China. Clavin (1996) has covered the economic interaction of the US and the major European powers from 1931 through 1936. She challenges the traditional interpretation, which centers on FDR's "bombshell" message of July 3, 1933 to the London Economic Conference. Instead, Calvin pins the blame on the British tariff and the imperial preference system. As far as US recognition of the Soviet Union is concerned, Morris (1994) indicts the State Department, seeing it so anxious to open diplomatic relations that it ignored all reports concerning a forced famine.

Turning to the Ethiopian crisis of 1935–6, Schmitz (1990) claims that the Italian invasion had little effect on FDR or the State Department. "Actions were limited," Schmitz argues, "so as not to antagonize Mussolini to the point that he would precipitate a war with Britain or break relations." He continues, "It was Mussolini's methods and not his objectives which led to Roosevelt's anger and the desire to try and isolate Italy" (pp. 11–12). Cole (1990), taking issue with Schmitz, finds that FDR always remained indifferent to any accord with Italy. Roosevelt, Cole asserts, "never really thought an accord with Fascist Italy was terribly important one way or the other" (pp. 87–8).

A similar debate concerns the Spanish Civil War. In 1985 Douglas Little published *Malevolent Neutrality*, covering the years 1931–6. In that work, Little posited that American and British policy could only be understood in terms of their fear of communism. In taking the story down through 1939, Little continues his argument, finding the reason for non-intervention lying "less from fear of a general European war than from suspicion that a Loyalist victory would open the door to bolshevism from the Aegean to the Atlantic" (Little 1990: 21). Again, Cole (1990) differs, stressing domestic pressures on FDR, in particular his desire to retain support from Roman Catholics.

In analyzing the Nye Committee, Coulter (1997) challenges the picture presented in Wiltz (1963), which – according to Coulter – is too hostile. Coulter claims that Senate investigators deserved credit for probing the nation's modern military establishment. Moreover, he goes on, the inquiry did not block a realistic American response to aggression, never labeled arms dealers "merchants of death," and found war profiteering far from being limited to the so-called "munitions makers." Scheer (1994), who covers the Ludlow war referendum amendment of 1938, denies that its proponents were diehard isolationists; rather, they were idealists seeking to initiate nothing less than a world revolution against war and dictatorship.

Various studies of British–American relations have been written, often spearheaded by Canadian scholar Brian McKercher and all challenging widely held assumptions concerning British decline and a corresponding American rise. Although

McKercher focuses more on the 1920s, he claims that until the summer of 1940 Britain was correctly perceived as the world's leading power, as it expressed its national strength far more vigorously. McKercher (1991) has the not-so-subtle subtitle "Great Britain Pre-eminent in the 1930s."

During the late 1930s, it could well have been the Americans who took the greater initiative in trying to check Germany and Japan. According to Harrison (1990), FDR continually sought to cooperate with the British. In August 1936 and again in January 1938, Roosevelt wanted to convene an American-led conference. In October 1937, he proposed peacefully blockading any aggressor nation. "Because of Roosevelt," claims Harrison, "there was an alternative available to appeasement" yet "thanks mostly to Chamberlain it was never fully explored" (p. 132).

The Munich conference still creates debate. As early as 1969, in his book *American Appeasement*, Arnold Offner argued that "by and large Roosevelt had convinced himself that Munich opened the way to a new and better world" (p. 268). Offner (1991) continues his indictment. During those crucial weeks of September 1939, he says, FDR never took into account such vital matters as the status of Czechoslovakia's army, Germany's weak western fortifications, France's preponderant military force, Britain's naval supremacy, and the possibility of Soviet intervention.

Only in 1997, however, did we get an entire book on FDR and the Munich crisis. Farnham (1997) denies that Roosevelt was either a tacit isolationist or a drifting opportunist; rather, he long sought to check aggressors. As early as 1935, Farnham claims, Roosevelt sought to blockade Germany, turning only to neutrality legislation after his proposals were ignored. Similarly, she finds his quarantine speech of October 1937 a "strategic probe" in which the president sought to warn the dictators, shape world opinion, and educate the American public. When the Western powers first began to negotiate with Hitler over the Sudetenland, FDR initially wanted to strengthen the will of the democracies. After the Munich conference ended, Roosevelt became committed, even eager, to check Germany. Because FDR believed that Hitler's aggressiveness would ultimately threaten American security, with Brazil serving as Germany's launching pad, he desired to aid Britain and France, particularly with planes. Yet one can ask, as does Kimball (1998), why then was Roosevelt so reluctant to be more overtly confrontational towards Hitler in 1940 and 1941?

In a highly readable study of the destroyer-bases deal, journalist Robert Shogan (1995) offers a thorough if polemical analysis of its topic. The title and subtitle reveals his thesis at the outset: *Hard Bargain: How FDR Twisted Churchill's Arm, Evaded the Law, and Changed the Role of the American Presidency.* Shogan claims that the deal, because of its secrecy, served as precedent for such surreptitious commitments as the Korean War, the Vietnam War, and the Iran–Contra scandal. "At each critical step along the convoluted path to consummation," he writes, "nearly everyone involved always held the end to justify whatever means came to hand. No one can accurately measure how much the trade contributed to Great Britain's ability to resist its foes and to the ultimate victory over the Axis. But whatever the benefit, a high price was paid in undermining the rule of law" (p. 259). Stephen Ambrose claims on the book jacket that the study shows "FDR at his best and worst." Ironically, according to Shogan, the destroyers far from measured up to expectations, while the American naval installations in the Caribbean and Newfoundland ended up serving little purpose. A related article by Whitham (1996) finds the British government by no means a willing partner in the negotiations, coming close in early 1941 to a serious diplomatic break over the terms of the leases.

The Roosevelt–Churchill summit held in August 1941 has been subject to fresh examination. In 1991 Theodore A. Wilson updated his definitive work, *The First Summit: Roosevelt and Churchill at Placentia Bay, 1941* (1969). Using materials recently available from the British Public Record Office, Wilson shatters what he calls "the Churchillian paradigm," that is the assertion that the prime minister and the president shared a unique friendship devoid of major differences. Furthermore, says Wilson, Roosevelt "was unwilling to face the risks that accompany aggressive leadership." Given the Axis threat, however, "allowing oneself to drift with the tide of events embodies irresponsible if not downright idiotic behavior" (pp. 230, 235).

At a special fiftieth anniversary conference held, most appropriately, at Memorial University in Newfoundland, Wilson (1994) stresses several matters that are often overlooked. The two world leaders were in each other's company less than 24 hours. The meeting is most remembered for the famous Atlantic Charter, but that document needed neither FDR nor Churchill on hand to help write it; it could just as well have been drafted in Washington by Ambassador Halifax and Secretary of State Cordell Hull. The conversations between the British and American military were useful but inconclusive, as were discussions over production priorities and meeting Axis threats in North Africa, Southeast Asia, and the islands of the eastern Atlantic.

Also at the Newfoundland meeting was David Reynolds, a British historian whose book on the creation of the Anglo-American alliance remains one of the great studies of this quarter-century (Reynolds 1982a). Reynolds notes Churchill's famous report to the cabinet once the conference ended, in which Churchill claimed that FDR had told him that he, that is Roosevelt, "would wage war but not declare it, and that he would become more and more provocative. If the Germans did not like it, they could attack American forces" (p. 214). Far from honoring such a commitment, FDR – according to Reynolds – was painfully slow in fulfilling any such promise. Nor did Roosevelt back Churchill in the Pacific, for FDR really made no commitment of American help, particularly concerning Singapore, Britain's main naval base in Southeast Asia.

Speculation remains as to why Hitler declared war on the US. Weinberg (1992a, 1992b) argues that once Japan took the plunge, Germany eagerly sought a fight. Weinberg, a specialist in Nazi foreign policy, concludes that the Führer believed he could draw upon the full-scale participation of the Japanese navy, therefore compensating for his own weakness at sea. Furthermore, a major war with the US would give his U-boats the chance to impose crippling strikes. One should realize, Weinberg asserts, that Hitler was always biding his time, awaiting the day when the Russian campaign had ended and he had built enough battleships to attack the United States. Asher (2000) stresses a psychological motive, rooted in Hitler's irrational urge for self-destruction. With the situation on the Russian front rapidly deteriorating, the German dictator deliberately sought to speed up the defeat he now saw as all but certain.

In asking what would have happened had the US not entered World War II, Cole (1995a) has proposed some counterfactual scenarios for 1941. He sees three possibilities: Hitler's army might have crushed the Soviet Union; Stalin's forces might have driven west across all of Europe, thereby reaching the English Channel; a bloody stalemate could have resulted, in which both powers would have exhausted themselves. Not only, says Cole, was the third alternative the most likely, but also the mutual losses would have left the US more secure.

In the 1990s, we lacked the major studies of US Asia policy that had made works by Jonathan Utley, Dorothy Borg, and Robert Butow so prominent (e.g., Utley 1985; Borg 1964; Butow 1974). Historians, however, have not remained dormant. In evaluating FDR's early China policy, Cohen (1990) claims that the chief executive was never really focused on China per se, where he saw no American vital interest; rather, the president increasingly found Germany and Japan destroying a world order in which American ideals and interests could prosper. No better evidence of his apathy to China's own plight could be offered than his indifference to the ruinous effect of the US silver purchase act of 1934, which created deflation and sharp recession for the Chinese. Another treatment of the silver policy, this one by Chinese historian Wang Xi (1990), sees the US forcing China to the brink of economic collapse, thereby critically weakening its ability to resist Japan.

Certainly in confronting American Far Eastern policy in 1940 and 1941, one finds controversy remaining strong. Particularly revealing is the anthology edited by Conroy and Wray, *Pearl Harbor Reexamined* (1990), to which seventeen historians contributed. Its Americans contributors include Gary Dean Best, Jonathan Utley, Norman Graebner, Akira Iriye, Alvin D. Coox, Waldo Heinrichs, Michael Barnhart, and John K. Emmerson. Among the Japanese contributors is Tsundoa Jun, the dean of Japanese historians and adviser to several prime ministers. Despite the use of Pearl Harbor in the title, the volume really centers on the diplomacy leading to the war, not on the attack itself. If the essays are often far too brief to develop an argument fully, they are still quite spirited. The authors sharply differ among themselves, revealing a surprising lack of consensus on such fundamental matters as the skill of specific diplomats, the wisdom of the bargaining positions, and just exactly what were the events that made war a certainty. Graebner and Barnhart, for example, are at odds on the role of Stanley K. Hornbeck, special adviser to Secretary Hull. Two Japanese historians, Tsunoda Jun and Fujiwara Ikira, differ radically over the feasibility of a summit between Roosevelt and Prime Minister Konoye. What the Conroy–Wray collection reveals is that one is often in the realm of weighting existing evidence, not necessarily digging up new material, and the editors acknowledge "no definite answer on the inevitability of the Pacific War." It seems most unlikely that there will be some hidden cache of documents that will put a stop to all the arguments.

Even the famous decoded Japanese messages are the subject of fresh research. In a work entitled *Origins of the Pacific War and the Importance of Magic* (1999), Keiichiro Komatsu stresses the mistranslations of American cryptologists. He argues that the efforts on both sides to avert the conflict, or at least to delay it, "might have been much closer to achieving success than is generally believed up to now." Jonathan Marshall offers one of the most provocative arguments of all. Again, the title reveals the argument: *To Have and Have Not: Southeast Asian Raw Materials and the Origins of the Pacific War* (1995). Marshall finds that this contested area was crucial to the thinking of American policymakers. In 1997, Walter LaFeber's sweeping account on Japanese–American relations, *The Clash*, was published. In this work, LaFeber claims that the war occurred because Japan sought to obtain economic self-sufficiency, only to be stymied by Hull and Hornbeck.

Of course, the matter of the Pearl Harbor attack itself never dies. In 1992 Henry C. Clausen and Bruce Lee published a work offering the traditional view that the two American commanders in Hawaii, Admiral Husband E. Kimmel and General Walter C. Short, were in dereliction of duty. As Clausen was a leading army prosecutor in the Pearl Harbor case, his interpretation is not unexpected. More writing, though, remains revisionist. In 1991 two intelligence specialists, one Australian and the other British, argued that Winston Churchill had foreknowledge of the Pearl Harbor attack. The prime minister, they claim, failed to warn FDR, doing so deliberately in order to drag the US into a war in order to defend his nation's Far Eastern interests. In 1995 retired naval captain Edward L. Beach came out with *Scapegoats: A Defense of Kimmel and Short at Pearl Harbor*. Beach was a submarine expert who had been President Eisenhower's naval aide. He denies that Roosevelt manipulated the Pearl Harbor attack, but maintains that the military commanders on Hawaii were not negligent. Another navy veteran, Robert Stinnett, claims in *Day of Deceit* (2000) that the US deliberately provoked war in accordance with a long-standing plan. None of these latter broadsides have found scholarly support.

Historians are still exploring FDR's fundamental goals and policies as war approached. One cannot really talk about this topic without being grounded in the extensive work of Warren F. Kimball, editor of one of the two major collections of the Roosevelt–Churchill correspondence (Kimball 1984). The 1990s were a vintage decade for Kimball, as he published a set of essays on FDR titled *The Juggler* (1991) and a general narrative, *Forged in War: Roosevelt, Churchill, and the Second World War* (1997). In his treatment of FDR's 1937 quarantine speech, Kimball – unlike Farnham – denies that the president had any real plan. He was thinking out loud and backed off in the face of vocal opposition. Turning to Munich, Kimball claims that Roosevelt's support for the agreements did not reflect any liking for appeasement; instead, it showed FDR's understanding that leadership for Europe had to come from within. Unlike many historians, Kimball takes the mission of Undersecretary Sumner Welles to Europe in February 1940 quite seriously; it was neither whimsical nor a device to delay a German offensive against France. FDR was anxious to convince the public he was doing everything possible to broker a peace settlement; moreover, he could well have hoped to avoid what seemed inevitable – all-out war on the Western front. At no time, however, does Kimball see chances for the Welles mission strong, as Hitler would certainly have found unacceptable any proposal by Roosevelt.

In dealing with the wider issue of the overall leadership of FDR, Kimball argues that by 1941, Roosevelt was a skillful leader, though at times "disingenuous, deceptive, and devious." In contrast to the picture of a masterful Roosevelt given by Waldo Heinrichs (1992), Kimball sees the president often muddling through, sweeping "obstacles under the rug in the hope that they would go away in time." Yet, says Kimball, by 1941 FDR had a genuine foreign policy, one centering on the containment of Hitler and the survival of Britain. At the same time, Roosevelt always sought to avoid large-scale American intervention. Until the Japanese attack on Pearl Harbor, FDR had hoped that the US would only have to use naval and air forces. In a sense, Kimball's Roosevelt was fighting a proxy war, hoping that the British (and after June 1941, the Russians) would do the real fighting for him. If the Russians pinned the Germans down, there might be no need for American ground forces on the European continent. In short, the president wanted both victory and influence without paying the price. Yet, unlike Theodore Wilson, Kimball defends Roosevelt's caution in this regard. Given the slim margin for extending the terms of draftees, FDR was simply exercising common sense.

Nor, according to Kimball, did FDR want to fight the Japanese. Even Roosevelt's remarks to Ambassador Halifax, made early in December 1941 and apparently indicating support in Southeast Asia, were indirect and possibly misleading. He calls FDR a master of indirection in this matter. Roosevelt never gave an outright commitment promising war if Japan invaded the British or Dutch colonies, but made it clear Congress would have the final say.

Moreover, Kimball challenges any assertion that FDR lied actively and consistently to the American people about his ultimate intentions. Admittedly, concedes Kimball, Roosevelt did not take the public into his confidence during the 1940 election campaign, lacked candor about convoys during the debate over Lend Lease, and evaded questions as to just how the US could be neutral and still provide warships to a belligerent. However, all elements concerned, from pollsters to administration figures to the public itself, sought "to be lied to," that is, they willingly went along with the president's subterfuges in order to avoid hard decisions. Kimball, like Cole and Offner, indicts FDR for treating his opposition most unfairly, that is, painting his opponents as extreme isolationists and dupes of Hitler.

Heinrichs (1992, 1995) concurs with the general claim that FDR sought to avoid direct American entry into the war as long as possible, for the president feared the US would be overextended. At the same time, says Heinrichs, Roosevelt grew increasingly hawkish towards Japan once the Soviets entered the war; FDR feared that any American compromise in the Pacific could free Japan to strike at the Soviet Union. Were the Russians forced to fight on two fronts, Britain and the US would themselves be imperiled.

Offering a wider focus, Harper (1994) portrays Roosevelt as a neo-Jeffersonian who found the US alone the sanctuary of civilized values. Conversely, Harper claims that FDR saw Europe as corrupt. Even his feelings towards Britain were, in Harper's words, "always a fluid mixture of resentment, rivalry, and regard." If, as Harper claims, Roosevelt saw American entry into the European war as inevitable by June 1941, he still adhered to his vision of a morally superior US, a belief that in his eyes made an American-made peace even more crucial.

Certainly, Roosevelt's attitude towards France could fit right into this mold. Rossi (1993) notes that FDR was disillusioned by French leadership in the 1930s and bitterly disappointed by its surrender in 1940. The president, writes Rossi, misread the degree of independence from Germany enjoyed by Marshal Pétain, unwisely recognizing the collaborationist Vichy regime as soon as it was formed.

Gellman (1995) asks pointedly if FDR's handling of his own diplomatic apparatus was counterproductive. Gellman's *Secret Affairs* covers the complex interaction between FDR, Secretary Hull, and Undersecretary Sumner Welles. The book goes into detail concerning Hull's abysmally bad health, Welles' hidden homosexuality, and FDR's deliberate fostering of bureaucratic rivalry between the two subordinates. Seeing the president engaged in petty and pointless manipulation, Gellman finds a "mean streak" in the man. Furthermore, so Gellman asserts, Roosevelt had no business allowing a man in Hull's condition (he was tuberculous) to handle sensitive Far Eastern negotiations. In the first three months of 1941, when the US was engaged in the most sensitive of negotiations with the Japanese, Hull was absent from his office for three months. FDR often turned to such personal assistants as Harry Hopkins for crucial diplomatic tasks, thereby undermining his own State Department, which embodied the very organizational structure he needed to sustain long-range objectives.

Harper (1994: 48–73) divides Roosevelt's foreign policy establishment into four major groups. First, there are the "Hullian" liberals, represented by Secretary Hull, Norman H. Davis, Leo Pasvolsky, and to some degree FDR himself. Their agenda centered on disarmament, massive exports, and an end to European imperialism. Second, one finds the advocates of "protocontainment," seeking above all the weakening of the Soviet Union, even at the risk of making common cause with Nazi Germany. Diplomats Joseph P. Kennedy, Breckinridge Long, John Cudahy, and Robert Kelley all articulated such sentiments, though usually without Roosevelt's backing. Third, one sees a school calling for what Harper terms "Europhobic-hemispherism" (which he finds more accurate than "appeasement"); this group stressed integration of the Western hemisphere and alleviation of "legitimate" German economic grievances. Represented by Adolf Berle, William C. Bullitt, and Sumner Welles, it dominated American policy through the spring of 1940. Fourth, the diplomatic establishment possessed a pro-British party that linked US security to the continental balance of power, friendly control of the Atlantic, and the defeat of Nazi Germany. Frank Knox, Henry L. Stimson, and Felix Frankfurter embodied such thinking. By the summer of 1940, this fourth school had gained the ascendancy.

Other studies of individual diplomats have recently been published. In tackling Hull's activity during FDR's first term, Butler (1998) seeks to recover the secretary's reputation. Given the fact that the US shrank from wider political and military involvement, Butler finds Hull's trade policy offering the most effective diplomacy with which to counter Hitler's Germany. Burke (1994) has contributed a biography of Frederic Sackett, Herbert Hoover's ambassador to Germany. Burke shows how such a conservative Republican saw the salvation of the German Republic lying in organized labor and the Social Democrats. Bailey (1992) deals with Sackett's successor, William E. Dodd, whom he portrays as a Wilsonian idealist. Dodd saw the leaders of the Third Reich as German counterparts to the planters of his native South that he treated so critically in the scholarly histories he wrote at the University of Chicago. Castle (1998) covers Hoover's undersecretary of state, William R. Castle, Jr., whose lively diary has long been a major source for historians. Briefly Hoover's ambassador to Japan in 1930, by the late 1930s Castle was outspoken in seeking accommodation with Japan.

Some demythologizing has been done in regard to Stanley K. Hornbeck. Shizhang Hu (1995) portrays the State Department hand as cautious concerning both a potential Asian market and China's national aspirations. During the 1920s and 1930s, according to Hu, Hornbeck's China policy remained passive, in fact negative.

Emissaries to the Soviet Union have received extensive treatment. Brands' (1991) biography of Loy Henderson shows how the American diplomat, secretary to the US Embassy in Moscow from 1934 to 1938, grew increasingly skeptical concerning

Soviet motives, Dunn's (1998) general work on Roosevelt's ambassadors praises the astuteness of William Bullitt and Laurence A. Steinhardt and condemns Joseph Davies. Dunn finds Roosevelt himself far from blameless, attacking FDR for not applying sufficient pressure during the Winter War with Finland or using sufficient leverage with Stalin once Hitler invaded Russia. MacLean (1992) offers a slightly more positive picture of Davies, conceding his abysmal *naïveté* concerning the show trials, in fact Stalin's rule in general, but seeing him perceptive on the strength of the Red Army, the power of Stalin's dictatorship, and the resiliency of the Soviet economy. Mayers (1992) goes even further, claiming that some of Davies' private correspondence suggests a person alert to the "grim realities" of Stalinism.

Far more, however, is needed on other major figures of the Roosevelt administration. Work is particularly vital on Treasury Secretary Henry Morgenthau, Jr., not to mention such diplomats as William Phillips, John Cudahy, Jay Pierrepont Moffat, John Winant, and Lawrence Steinhardt. There has been preliminary work on some of these figures. Hearden (1986) demolishes many stereotypes by showing that until 1941, Cudahy combined his belief in German access to world markets with calls for US military preparedness. Cudahy's anti-interventionism surfaced in June 1941 after his *Life* interview with Hitler. A general study of Winant is found in Howland (1983). For the role of the British Left in influences on Winant's appointment as US ambassador, see Reynolds (1982b).

The correspondence of Joseph P. Kennedy has been collected by his granddaughter, Amanda Smith, a graduate student at Harvard. In her introduction, Smith (2001: xxxii) writes of offering a representative sampling of the ambassador's papers, selecting documents that were "particularly characteristic of moments or figures in history." She also claims she possessed unlimited access and that no documents were restricted from publication. Much of the material is not surprising to anyone who works in the period, indeed anyone who has read the major biographies of Joe Kennedy or his dispatches from London published in *Foreign Relations*. One does find that the ambassador did fear Hitler's designs on Latin America and that one son, 23-year-old John F. Kennedy, suggested that his father refrain from making public comments that would lead Americans to minimize aid to Britain.

General military strategy and tactics have received extensive investigation. Coletta (1991) notes how both the US and Japan ignored the true potential of aircraft carriers, for they believed future engagements would resemble Jutland, with battleships remaining the crucial instrument. Kennedy (1995), seeking to meet accusations that President Hoover irresponsibly weakened the navy, sees him limited by technological change, budgetary constraints, and a lack of national will. In covering War Plan Orange, the strategy designed over decades to defeat Japan, Miller (1991) attempts to deflate the myth that American naval leadership was obsessed by defensive thinking and the construction of battleships. Naval planners, he claims, were quite far-sighted, devising an offensive strategy later used to defeat Japan.

Building on Michael S. Sherry's comprehensive *Rise of American Air Power* (1987), several scholars describe how American planners thought that aviation alone would achieve victory by destroying the enemy's will to resist (see Clodfelder 1994; Underwood 1991). Furthermore, by abandoning the confrontation tactics of Billy Mitchell, the army air corps convinced FDR and the general staff to support air power.

Several studies of war mobilization have appeared. Koistinen (1998) examines preparations by military and industrial elites, then covers congressional investigations that focused on the emerging military–business partnership. Gough (1991) describes an army unprepared to cooperate with business as war approached, as its officers distrusted the corporate ethic. In turn, industrialists felt the top brass was unaware of a competitive system. Kirkpatrick (1990) offers thorough coverage of the overseas victory program drafted in September 1941 by Major Albert C. Wedemeyer for the War Department. Contrary to legend, this massive blueprint – entailing 5 field armies, 215 divisions, and 6 million men – involved sheer contingency, being "a hypothesis without real influence."

Certain works deal with the American military presence in the Pacific. In his study of the American army there, Linn (1997) finds the US fully recognizing the Japanese danger to both Hawaii and the Philippines. It was, however, confronted with numerous obstacles, including inadequate manpower, insufficient resources, service competition, professional rivalries, and public and congressional indifference. Arguing somewhat to the contrary, McPoil (1991) sees wisdom in the navy's decision, made in 1934, to regard Wake Island as expendable. To sustain attack, Wake needed three to four times the defense force and aircraft it was allotted.

Some historians find Roosevelt himself negligent. Robert W. Love, Jr., a professor at the Naval Academy, goes so far as to indict FDR for failing to rearm during the 1930s and then for incorrectly blaming his failure upon Congress. Furthermore, according to Love (1995), Roosevelt kept subordinates in the dark about his views on key questions, postponed decisions until the last minute, and lacked candor as to his goals and policies. Christman (1992) finds the president overestimating Germany's military strength while underestimating that of Japan. Ambrose (1995) scores FDR in late 1941 for refusing to engage in an all-out effort against Germany. The president, Ambrose continues, was just plain lucky that Hitler declared war after Pearl Harbor, for otherwise FDR would have been forced of necessity to devote most of his attention to the less important Pacific theater.

Mark A. Stoler has contributed a major work on American planning: *Allies and Adversaries: The Joint Chiefs of Staff, the Grand Alliance, and US Strategy in World War II* (2000). Stoler clearly captures the sense of anarchy that existed among military planners in the late 1930s. The navy opposed withdrawal from East Asia and the Western Pacific, while the army focused far more on hemispheric defense. In late summer 1941 the War Department itself acted under an "extraordinary delusion," one that Stoler says "defies comprehension"; it suddenly thought that the sending of thirty-six B-17s to the Philippines would deter attack. Roosevelt himself, Stoler claims, appeared to lack direction. FDR, for example, sought a massive naval and air buildup but did not provide the backup personnel and ground forces needed. Similarly, he vetoed a major base in the Philippines while opposing any American withdrawal from the islands.

We have also benefited from various intelligence studies, so much so that we can appear downright obsessed by them. Brown and Troy (1996) stress the close liaison between British and American intelligence in 1940 and 1941. Here the focus is on William ("Wild Bill") Donovan, founder of the Office of Strategic Services, and Canadian super-sleuth William Stephenson, "the man called Intrepid." (Several historians have warned us how careful we should be in evaluating anything about

William Stephenson, including his own autobiography, for there is incredible exaggeration at work.) Mahl (1998) took the pursuit further, ably illuminating the complicated network of British intelligence groups, though incorrectly implying that leading backers of Roosevelt's policy were British puppets.

MacDonnell (1995) finds FDR manipulating the nation's fears to weaken the anti-interventionist movement. At the same time, MacDonnell sees Roosevelt's critics in this regard underestimating the barrage of warnings FDR receives from reporters, diplomats, and intelligence officers. He gives FDR credit for not establishing another Creel committee. Two studies have covered Roosevelt's use of the FBI against the anti-interventionists in general and Charles Lindbergh in particular (Croog 1992; Charles and Rossi 1997).

Nicholas John Cull of the University of Birmingham uses untapped British sources to show the strong effectiveness of British propaganda once it entered World War II. British propaganda in the US was subtle and indeed wisely so, for heavy-handed efforts would have been disastrous. Even World War II scholars might be surprised by some of Cull's findings. When, for instance, FDR met with George VI at Hyde Park several months before war broke out, he assured the king that any bombing of London was bound to bring the US into war (Cull 1995, 1993).

Certain prominent interventionists of the 1939–41 period have been given new attention, including theologian Reinhold Niebuhr and Henry R. Luce (Doenecke 1995; Herzstein 1993). Surprisingly, there has been proportionately more detailed work on FDR's critics, in reality a minority, than on his more outspoken backers or on those who found Roosevelt too slow in checking the Axis. Roberts (1995) shows how American labor, originally quite anti-interventionist, became a powerful backer of FDR's foreign policy. Comparative studies of business are still needed. Platt's (1991) full-scale study of the congressional representation of one southern state, Virginia, ascribes the state's militant interventionism to concerns over democracy, security, and trade, plus a shared British heritage. One would like to see similar state studies, particularly concerning the South. After all, certain leading southern senators had been on FDR's purge list as late as fall 1938.

Lynne Dunn has revised the rough manuscript of Warren Kuehl, our foremost scholar of classic American internationalism (centering on efforts to advance world order), whose untimely death occurred in 1987. What comes through most strongly in the volume *Keeping the Covenant* (Kuehl and Dunn 1997) are the divisions among the varied internationalists, a situation that even prevented them from forming a consensus behind the League. Moreover, the League of Nations Association itself was ambivalent about collective security.

In a pioneering work on certain Senate anti-interventionists, Robert David Johnson (1995) effectively finds the term "peace progressive" superior to that of "isolationist." Such figures as William E. Borah, George Norris, and Gerald P. Nye, so Johnson asserts, sought to achieve a more peaceful world order by directing American foreign policy along anti-imperialist lines. These figures sought worldwide disarmament, backed the Weimar Republic, and supported democratic revolutions in Mexico, Nicaragua, and China. One of Johnson's subjects, Senator Hiram Johnson, finally has an able biographer in Richard Coke Lower (1993), who shows why California's arch foe of intervention could no longer lead decisive battles.

There is fresh material on other FDR critics. Berg's massive 1998 biography of

Charles Lindbergh has little that is new on his political views, but does show that the published diaries of Charles and Anne Morrow Lindbergh had some embarrassing sections edited. A fresh study of William Randolph Hearst denies that the Lord of San Simeon was blindly insisting on a Fortress America. In standing for American sovereignty, freedom of action, and good relations with the rest of the world, Hearst – says Ian Mugridge (1995) – held a view of American conduct overseas that was "basically sensible and reasonable." John Moser's (1999) study of Anglophobia between the wars, however, finds such Americans acting irresponsibly, as they would not address themselves to the concrete problems faced by Britain.

The 1990s gave us some fresh studies of individual pacifist groups and leaders. In covering the interwar period as part of a more encompassing work, Cecelia Lynch (1999) challenges the dichotomy advanced by those who still see the era as dominated by the struggle between naive "appeasers" and a small but noble band of Churchillian (and "Rooseveltian") "realists." The debate, Lynch argues, was far more complicated, the impact of the peace movement far less destructive.

The role of women in foreign policy has received new impetus. Foster (1995) has written a study of the Women's International League for Peace and Freedom, and Bacon (1993) offers a life of the WIL's national organization secretary, Mildred Scott Olmsted. Both works show the splits within the peace lobby over such matters as mandatory neutrality and collective security, as well as the personal conflicts within the WIL, particularly between the more reserved Olmsted and Dorothy Detzer, its militant national secretary. Sittser's (1997) work on the American churches indicates the high degree to which pacifists permeated these bodies. Sittser does differ from the conventional interpretation in his ability to recognize that Reinhold Niebuhr misrepresented the views of his opponents, ascribing to them a utopianism many did not possess.

Doenecke continues his work on anti-interventionism, coming forth with studies on the *Weekly Foreign Letter*, edited by the self-styled American fascist Lawrence Dennis, and *Scribner's Commentator*, a digest-sized monthly that spoke for the militant right wing of FDR's critics. In 1990 Doenecke edited the papers of the America First Committee, the nation's leading anti-interventionist group in 1940 and 1941. His labors have culminated in *Storm on the Horizon* (2000). Here he focuses on the underlying military, economic, and geopolitical assumptions of his subjects, tracing how they perceived the ideology, armed potential, territorial aspirations, and commercial aims of Germany, Japan, the Soviet Union, and the British Empire.

All in all, as we look over the research conducted during the past decade, we can be glad there is still so much interest in what was obviously one of the most exciting spans in world history. It is to be hoped that the quite natural interest in the Cold War does not totally overshadow it.

REFERENCES

Ambrose, Stephen E.: " 'Just Dumb Luck': American Entry into World War II." In Robert W. Love, Jr. (ed.) *Pearl Harbor Revisited* (New York: St. Martin's Press, 1995).
Asher, Harvey: "Hitler's Decision to Declare War on the United States Revisited: A Synthesis

of the Secondary Literature." *Newsletter of the Society for Historians of American Foreign Relations* 31 (September 2000), 2–20.

Bacon, Margaret Hope: *One Woman's Passion for Peace and Freedom: The Life of Mildred Scott Olmsted* (Syracuse, NY: Syracuse University Press, 1993).

Bailey, Fred Arthur: "A Virginia Scholar in Chancellor Hitler's Court: The Tragic Ambassadorship of William Edward Dodd." *Virginia Magazine of History and Biography* 100 (July 1992), 323–42.

Barnhart, Michael A.: "Hornbeck Was Right: The Realist Approach to American Policy Toward Japan." In Hilary Conroy and Harry Wray (eds.) *Pearl Harbor Reexamined: Prologue to the Pacific War* (Honolulu: University of Hawaii Press, 1990).

Barnhart, Michael A. "The Origins of the Second World War in Asia and the Pacific: Synthesis Impossible?" In Michael J. Hogan (ed.) *Paths to Power: The Historiography of American Foreign Relations to 1941* (New York: Cambridge University Press, 2000).

Beach, Edward L.: *Scapegoats: A Defense of Kimmel and Short at Pearl Harbor* (Annapolis, MD: Naval Institute Press, 1995).

Bell, Christopher M.: "Thinking the Unthinkable: British and American Strategies for an Anglo-American War, 1918–1931." *International History Review* 19 (November 1997), 789–808.

Berg, A. Scott: *Lindbergh* (New York: G. P. Putnam, 1998).

Borg, Dorothy: *The United States and the Far Eastern Crisis of 1933–1938* (Cambridge, MA: Harvard University Press, 1964).

Brands, H. W.: *Inside the Cold War: Loy Henderson and the Rise of the American Empire, 1918–1961* (New York: Oxford University Press, 1991).

Brown, Anthony Cave and Thomas F. Troy: *Wild Bill and Intrepid: Bill Donovan, Bill Stephenson, and the Origins of the CIA* (New Haven, CT: Yale University Press, 1996).

Buckley, Thomas H.: "The Icarus Factor: The American Pursuit of Myth in Naval Arms Control, 1921–36." In Eric Goldstein and John H. Maurer (eds.) *The Washington Conference, 1921–22: Naval Rivalry, East Asian Stability and the Road to Pearl Harbor* (Portland, OR: Frank Cass, 1994).

Burk, Kathleen: "The Lineaments of Foreign Policy: The United States and a 'New World Order,' 1919–1939." *Journal of American Studies* 26 (1992), 377–91.

Burke, Bernard V.: *Ambassador Frederic Sackett and the Collapse of the Weimar Republic, 1930–1933: The United States and Hitler's Rise to Power* (New York: Cambridge University Press, 1994).

Butler, Michael A.: *Cautious Visionary: Cordell Hull and Trade Reform* (Kent, OH: Kent State University Press, 1998).

Butow, Robert J. C.: *The John Doe Associates: Backdoor Diplomacy for Peace, 1941* (Stanford, CA: Stanford University Press, 1974).

Castle, Alfred A.: *Diplomatic Realism: William R. Castle Jr. and American Foreign Policy, 1919–1953* (Honolulu: Samuel L. and Mary Castle Foundation, 1998).

Charles, Douglas M. and John P. Rossi: "FBI Political Surveillance and the Charles Lindbergh Investigation, 1939–1944." *Historian* 59 (summer 1997), 831–47.

Christman, Calvin L.: "Franklin D. Roosevelt and the Craft of Strategic Assessment." In Williamson Murray and Allan R. Millett (eds.) *Calculations: Net Assessment and the Coming of World War II* (New York: Free Press, 1992).

Clausen, Henry C. and Bruce Lee: *Pearl Harbor: Final Judgment* (New York: Crown, 1992).

Clavin, Patricia M.: *The Failure of Economic Diplomacy: Britain, Germany, France, and the USA, 1931–36* (New York: St. Martin's Press, 1996).

Clodfelder, Mark: "Pinpointing Devastation: American Air Campaign Planning before Pearl Harbor." *Journal of Military History* 58 (January 1994), 75–101.

Cohen, Warren I.: *Empire Without Tears: American Foreign Relations, 1921–1933* (New York: Knopf, 1987).

Cohen, Warren I.: "American Leaders and East Asia, 1931–1938." In Akira Iriye and Warren I. Cohen (eds.) *American, Chinese, and Japanese Perspectives on Wartime Asia, 1931–1949* (Wilmington, DE: Scholarly Resources, 1990).

Cole, Wayne S.: *Roosevelt and the Isolationists, 1932–45* (Lincoln: University of Nebraska Press, 1983).

Cole, Wayne S.: "American Appeasement." In David F. Schmitz and Richard D. Challener (eds.) *Appeasement in Europe: A Reassessment of US Policies* (Westport, CT: Greenwood Press, 1990).

Cole, Wayne S.: "Franklin D. Roosevelt: Great Man or Man for His Times?" In Wayne S. Cole, *Determinism and American Foreign Relations During the Franklin D. Roosevelt Era* (Lanham, MD: University Press of America, 1995a).

Cole, Wayne S.: "The America First Committee – A Half-Century Later." In Wayne S. Cole, *Determinism and American Foreign Relations During the Franklin D. Roosevelt Era* (Lanham, MD: University Press of America, 1995b).

Coletta, Paolo A.: "Prelude to War: Japan, the United States, and the Aircraft Carrier, 1919–1945." *Prologue* 23 (winter 1991), 342–59.

Coulter, Matthew W.: *The Senate Munitions Inquiry of the 1930s: Beyond the Merchants of Death* (Westport, CT: Greenwood Press, 1997).

Croog, Charles E.: "FBI Political Surveillance and the Isolationist–Interventionist Debate, 1931–1941." *Historian* 54 (spring 1992), 441–58.

Cull, Nicholas John: "Radio Propaganda and the Art of Understatement: British Broadcasting and American Neutrality, 1939–1941." *Historical Journal of Film, Radio and Television* 13 (1993), 403–31.

Cull, Nicholas John: *Selling War: The British Propaganda Campaign Against American "Neutrality" in World War II* (New York: Oxford University Press, 1995).

Doenecke, Justus D. (ed.): *In Danger Undaunted: The Anti-Interventionist Movement of 1940–1941 as Revealed in the Papers of the America First Committee* (Stanford, CA: Hoover Institution Press, 1990).

Doenecke, Justus D.: "Reinhold Niebuhr and His Critics: The Interventionist Controversy in World War II." *Anglican and Episcopal History* 64 (December 1995), 459–81.

Doenecke, Justus D.: "Scribner's Commentator, 1939–1942." In Ronald Lora and William Henry Longton (eds.) *The Conservative Press in Twentieth-Century America* (Westport, CT: Greenwood Press, 1999).

Doenecke, Justus D.: "Weekly Foreign Letter, 1938–1942." In Ronald Lora and William Henry Longton (eds.) *The Conservative Press in Twentieth-Century America* (Westport, CT: Greenwood Press, 1999).

Doenecke, Justus D.: *Storm on the Horizon: The Challenge to American Intervention, 1939–1941* (Lanham, MD: Rowman and Littlefield, 2000).

Doenecke, Justus D.: "The United States and the European War, 1939–1941: A Historiographical Review." In Michael J. Hogan (ed.) *Paths to Power: The Historiography of American Foreign Relations to 1941* (New York: Cambridge University Press, 2000).

Dunn, Dennis J.: *Caught Between Roosevelt and Stalin: America's Ambassadors to Moscow* (Lexington: University of Kentucky Press, 1998).

Ellis, L. Ethan: *Republican Foreign Policy, 1921–1933* (New Brunswick, NJ: Rutgers University Press, 1968).

Epstein, Mark: "The Coolidge Conference of 1927: Disarmament in Disarray." In Brian J. C. McKercher (ed.) *Arms Limitation and Disarmament: Restraints on War, 1899–1939* (Westport, CT: Praeger, 1992).

Fanning, Richard W.: *Peace and Disarmament: Naval Rivalry and Arms Control, 1922–1933* (Lexington: University of Kentucky Press, 1995).

Farnham, Barbara Rearden: *Roosevelt and the Munich Crisis: A Study of Political Decision-Making* (Princeton, NJ: Princeton University Press, 1997).

Foster, Carrie A.: *The Women and the Warriors: The US Section of the Women's International League for Peace and Freedom, 1915–1946* (Syracuse, NY: Syracuse University Press, 1995).

Fujiwara Ikira: "The Road to Pearl Harbor." In Hilary Conroy and Harry Wray (eds.) *Pearl Harbor Reexamined: Prologue to the Pacific War* (Honolulu: University of Hawaii Press, 1990).

Gellman, Irwin: *Secret Affairs: Franklin Roosevelt, Cordell Hull, and Sumner Welles* (Baltimore, MD: Johns Hopkins University Press, 1995).

Gough, Terrence J.: "Soldiers, Businessmen, and US Industrial Mobilization Planning Between the Two Wars." *War and Society* 9 (May 1991), 68–98.

Graebner, Norman A.: "Nomura in Washington: Conversations in Lieu of Diplomacy." In Hilary Conroy and Harry Wray (eds.) *Pearl Harbor Reexamined: Prologue to the Pacific War* (Honolulu: University of Hawaii Press, 1990).

Harper, John Lamberton: *American Visions: Franklin D. Roosevelt, George F. Kennan, and Dean G. Acheson* (New York: Cambridge University Press, 1994).

Harrison, Richard A.: "The United States and Great Britain: Presidential Diplomacy and Alternatives to Appeasement in the 1930s." In David F. Schmitz and Richard D. Challener (eds.) *Appeasement in Europe: A Reassessment of US Policies* (Westport, CT: Greenwood Press, 1990).

Hearden, Patrick J.: "John Cudahy and the Pursuit of Peace." *Mid-America* (April–June 1986), 99–114.

Hearden, Patrick J.: *Roosevelt Confronts Hitler: America's Entry into World War II* (DeKalb: Northern Illinois University Press, 1987).

Heinrichs, Waldo: *Threshold of War: Franklin D. Roosevelt and American Entry into World War II* (New York: Oxford University Press, 1988).

Heinrichs, Waldo: "Franklin D. Roosevelt and the Risks of War, 1939–1941." In Akira Iriye and Warren I. Cohen (eds.) *American, Chinese, and Japanese Perspectives on Wartime Asia, 1931–1949* (Wilmington, DE: Scholarly Resources, 1990).

Heinrichs, Waldo: "The United States Prepares for War." In George C. Chalou (ed.) *The Secrets War: The Office of Strategic Services in World War II* (Washington, DC: National Archives and Records Administration, 1992).

Heinrichs, Waldo: "Pearl Harbor in a Global Context." In Robert W. Love, Jr. (ed.) *Pearl Harbor Revisited* (New York: St. Martin's Press, 1995).

Herzstein, Robert E.: *Roosevelt and Hitler: Prelude to War* (New York: Scribner's, 1989).

Herzstein, Robert E.: *Henry R. Luce: A Political Portrait of the Man Who Created the American Century* (New York: Scribner's, 1993).

Howland, Nina Davis: "Ambassador John Gilbert Winant: Friend of an Embattled Britain, 1941–1946." PhD dissertation, University of Maryland, 1983).

Johnson, Robert David: *The Peace Progressives and American Foreign Relations* (Cambridge, MA: Harvard University Press, 1995).

Kaufman, Robert Gordon: *Arms Control in the Pre-Nuclear Era: The United States and Naval Limitation Between the World Wars* (New York: Columbia University Press, 1990).

Keiichiro Komatsu: *Origins of the Pacific War and the Importance of Magic* (New York: St. Martin's Press, 1999).

Kennan, George F.: *American Diplomacy 1900–1950* (Chicago, IL: University of Chicago Press, 1950).

Kennedy, George C.: "The 1930 London Naval Conference and Anglo-American Maritime

Strength, 1927–1930." In Brian J. C. McKercher (ed.) *Arms Limitation and Disarmament: Restraints on War, 1899–1939* (Westport, CT: Praeger, 1992).

Kennedy, Greg: "Depression and Security: Aspects Influencing the United States Navy During the Hoover Administration." *Diplomacy and Statecraft* 6 (July 1995), 342–72.

Kimball, Warren F. (ed.): *Churchill and Roosevelt: The Complete Correspondence*, 3 vols. (Princeton, NJ: Princeton University Press, 1984).

Kimball, Warren F.: *The Juggler: Franklin Roosevelt as Wartime Statesman* (Princeton, NJ: Princeton University Press, 1991).

Kimball, Warren F.: *Forged in War: Roosevelt, Churchill, and the Second World War* (New York: William Morrow, 1997).

Kimball, Warren F.: *Times Literary Supplement*, February 20, 1998, 24.

Kirkpatrick, Charles E.: *An Unknown Future and a Doubtful Present: Writing the Victory Plan in 1941* (Washington, DC: Center of Military History, United States Army, 1990).

Koistinen, Paul A. C.: *Planning War, Pursuing Peace: The Political Economy of American Warfare, 1920–1939* (Lawrence: University of Kansas Press, 1998).

Kuehl, Warren F. and Lynne K. Dunn: *Keeping the Covenant: American Internationalists and the League of Nations, 1920–1939* (Kent, OH: Kent State University Press, 1997).

LaFeber, Walter: *The Clash: US–Japanese Relations Throughout History* (New York: Norton, 1997).

Linn, Brian McAllister: *Guardian of Empire: The US Army and the Pacific, 1902–1940* (Chapel Hill: University of North Carolina Press, 1997).

Little, Douglas: "Antibolshevism and Appeasement: Great Britain, the United States, and the Spanish Civil War." In David F. Schmitz and Richard D. Challener (eds.) *Appeasement in Europe: A Reassessment of US Policies* (Westport, CT: Greenwood Press, 1990).

Little, Douglas: "Influence Without Responsibility: American Statecraft and the Munich Conference." In Melvin Small and O. Feinstein (eds.) *Appeasing Fascism: Articles from the Wayne State University Conference on Munich After Fifty Years* (Lanham, MD: University Press of America, 1991).

Loewenheim, Francis L., Harold L. Langley, and Manfred Jonas (eds.) *Roosevelt and Churchill: The Secret Wartime Correspondence* (New York: Saturday Review Press/Dutton, 1975).

Louria, Margot: *Triumph and Downfall: America's Pursuit of Peace and Prosperity, 1921–1933* (Westport, CT: Greenwood Press, 2001).

Love, Jr., Robert W.: "FDR as Commander in Chief." In Robert W. Love, Jr. (ed.) *Pearl Harbor Revisited* (New York: St. Martin's Press, 1995).

Lowenthal, Mark M.: "INTREPID and the History of World War II." *Military Affairs* 41 (April 1977), 88–90.

Lower, Richard Coke: *A Bloc of One: The Politics and Career of Hiram W. Johnson* (Stanford, CA: Stanford University Press, 1993).

Lynch, Cecelia: *Beyond Appeasement: Interpreting Interwar Peace Movements in World Politics* (Ithaca, NY: Cornell University Press, 1999).

MacDonnell, Francis: *Insidious Foes: The Axis Fifth Column and the American Home Front* (New York: Oxford University Press, 1995).

McKercher, Brian J. C.: " 'Our Most Dangerous Enemy': Great Britain Pre-eminent in the 1930s." *International History Review* (November 1991), 565–98.

McKercher, Brian J. C.: "No Eternal Friends or Enemies: British Defence and the Problem of the United States, 1919–1939." *Canadian Journal of History/Annales Canadiennes d'Histoire* 28 (April 1993), 258–93.

McKercher, Brian J. C.: *Transition of Power: Britain's Loss of Global Pre-eminence to the United States, 1930–1945* (New York: Columbia University Press, 1999).

McKercher, Brian: "Reaching for the Brass Ring: The Recent Historiography of Interwar

American Foreign Relations." In Michael J. Hogan (ed.) *Paths to Power: The Historiography of American Foreign Relations to 1941* (New York: Cambridge University Press, 2000).

MacLean, Elizabeth Kimball: *Joseph E. Davies: Envoy to the Soviets* (Westport, CT: Praeger, 1992).

McPoil, William D.: "The Development and Defense of Wake Island, 1934–1942." *Prologue* 23 (winter 1991), 360–6.

Mahl, Thomas E.: *Desperate Deception: British Covert Operations in the United States, 1939–44* (Washington, DC: Brassey's, 1998).

Marks, Frederick W., III: *Wind over Sand: The Diplomacy of Franklin Roosevelt* (Athens, GA: University of Georgia Press, 1988).

Marks, Frederick W., III: "Prelude to Pearl Harbor: The Diplomatic Dress Rehearsal." In Robert W. Love, Jr. (ed.) *Pearl Harbor Revisited* (New York: St. Martin's Press, 1995).

Marshall, Jonathan: *To Have and Have Not: Southeast Asian Raw Materials and the Origins of the Pacific War* (Berkeley: University of California Press, 1995).

Maurer, John H. Maurer: "Arms Control and the Washington Conference." In Eric Goldstein and John H. Maurer (eds.) *The Washington Conference, 1921–22: Naval Rivalry, East Asian Stability and the Road to Pearl Harbor* (Portland, OR: Frank Cass, 1994).

Mayers, David: "Ambassador Joseph Davies Reconsidered." *Society for Historians of American Foreign Relations Newsletter* 23 (September 1992), 1–16.

Mayers, David: *The Ambassadors and America's Soviet Policy* (New York: Oxford University Press, 1995).

Miller, Edward S.: *War Plan Orange: The US Strategy to Defeat Japan, 1897–1945* (Annapolis, MD: Naval Institute Press, 1991).

Morris, M. Wayne: *Stalin's Famine and Roosevelt's Recognition of Russia* (Lanham, MD: University Press of America, 1994).

Moser, John E.: *Twisting the Lion's Tail: American Anglophobia Between the World Wars* (New York: New York University Press, 1999).

Mugridge, Ian: *The View from Xanadu: William Randolph Hearst and United States Foreign Policy* (Montreal: McGill–Queen's University Press, 1995).

Murfett, Malcolm H.: "Look Back in Anger: The Western Powers and the Washington Conference of 1921–22." In Brian J. C. McKercher (ed.) *Arms Limitation and Disarmament: Restraints on War, 1899–1939* (Westport, CT: Praeger, 1992).

Naftali, Timothy J.: "Intrepid's Last Deception: Documenting the Career of William Stephenson." *Intelligence and National Security* 8 (July 1993), 72–92.

O'Connor, Raymond G.: *Perilous Equilibrium: The United States and the London Naval Conference of 1930* (New York: Greenwood Press, 1962).

Offner, Arnold A.: *American Appeasement: United States Foreign Policy and Germany, 1933–1938* (Cambridge, MA: Harvard University Press, 1969), 268.

Offner, Arnold A.: "Influence Without Responsibility: American Statecraft and the Munich Conference." In Melvin Small and O. Feinstein (eds.) *Appeasing Fascism: Articles from the Wayne State University Conference on Munich After Fifty Years* (Lanham, MD: University Press of America, 1991).

Orde, Anne: *The Eclipse of Great Britain: The United States and British Imperial Decline, 1895–1956* (New York: St. Martin's Press, 1996).

Platt, Rorin M.: *Virginia in Foreign Affairs, 1933–1941* (Lanham, MD: University Press of America, 1991).

Platt, Rorin M.: "The Triumph of Interventionism: Virginia's Political Elite and Aid to Britain, 1933–1941." *Virginia Magazine of History and Biography* 100 (July 1992), 343–64.

Reynolds, David: *The Creation of the Anglo-American Alliance 1937–41* (Chapel Hill: University of North Carolina Press, 1982a).

Reynolds, David: "Roosevelt, the British Left, and the Appointment of John G. Winant as

United States Ambassador to Britain in 1941." *International History Review* 4 (August 1982b), 393–413.

Reynolds, David: "The Atlantic 'Flop': British Foreign Policy and the Churchill–Roosevelt Meeting of August 1941." In Douglas Brinkley and David R. Facey-Crowther (eds.) *The Atlantic Charter* (New York: St. Martin's Press, 1994).

Roberts, John W.: *Putting Foreign Policy to Work: The Organized Labor in American Foreign Relations, 1932–1941* (New York: Garland, 1995).

Rossi, Mario: *Roosevelt and the French* (Westport, CT: Praeger, 1993).

Rusbridger, James and Eric Nave: *Betrayal at Pearl Harbor: How Churchill Lured Roosevelt into World War II* (New York: Summit, 1991).

Scheer, Arthur: "Louis Ludlow's War Referendum of 1938: A Reappraisal." *Mid-America* 76 (spring–summer 1994), 133–55.

Schmitz, David F.: " 'Speaking the Same Language': The US Response to the Italo-Ethiopian War and the Origins of American Appeasement." In David F. Schmitz and Richard D. Challener (eds.) *Appeasement in Europe: A Reassessment of US Policies* (Westport, CT: Greenwood Press, 1990).

Sherry, Michael S.: *The Rise of American Air Power: The Creation of Armageddon* (New Haven, CT: Yale University Press, 1987).

Shizhang Hu: *Stanley K. Hornbeck and the Open Door Policy, 1919–1937* (Westport, CT: Greenwood Press, 1995).

Shogan, Robert: *Hard Bargain: How FDR Twisted Churchill's Arm, Evaded the Law, and Changed the Role of the American Presidency* (New York: Scribner, 1995).

Sittser, Gerald L.: *A Cautious Patriotism: The American Churches and the Second World War* (Chapel Hill: University of North Carolina Press, 1997).

Smith, Amanda (ed.): *Hostage to Fortune: The Letters of Joseph P. Kennedy* (New York: Viking, 2001).

Stinnett, Robert B.: *Day of Deceit: The Truth About Pearl Harbor* (New York: Touchstone, 2000).

Stoler, Mark A.: *Allies and Adversaries: The Joint Chiefs of Staff, the Grand Alliance, and US Strategy in World War II* (Chapel Hill: University of North Carolina Press, 2000).

Tsunoda Jun: "On the So-called Hull–Nomura Negotiations." In Hilary Conroy and Harry Wray (eds.) *Pearl Harbor Reexamined: Prologue to the Pacific War* (Honolulu: University of Hawaii Press, 1990).

Underwood, Jeffrey S.: *The Wings of Democracy: The Influence of Air Power on the Roosevelt Administration, 1931–1941* (College Station: Texas A&M University Press, 1991).

Utley, Jonathan G.: *Going to War with Japan, 1937–1941* (Knoxville: University of Tennessee Press, 1985).

Waldron, Arthur: *How the Peace Was Lost: The 1935 Memorandum – Developments Affecting American Policy in the Far East* (Stanford, CA: Hoover Institution Press, 1992).

Wang Xi: "A Test of the Open Door Policy: America's Silver Policy and Its Effects on East Asia, 1934–1937." In Akira Iriye and Warren I. Cohen (eds.) *American, Chinese, and Japanese Perspectives on Wartime Asia, 1931–1949* (Wilmington, DE: Scholarly Resources, 1990).

Weinberg, Gerhard: "Pearl Harbor: The German Perspective." In Gerhard Weinberg (ed.) *Germany, Hitler, and World War II: Essays in Modern German and World History* (New York: Cambridge University Press, 1992a).

Weinberg, Gerhard: "Why Hitler Declared War on the United States." *MHQ: The Quarterly Journal of Military History* 4 (spring 1992b), 18–23.

Whitham, Charlie: "On Dealing with Gangsters: The Limits of British 'Generosity' in the Leasing of Bases to the United States, 1940–41." *Diplomacy and Statecraft* 7 (November 1996), 589–630.

Wilson, Theodore A.: *The First Summit: Roosevelt and Churchill at Placentia Bay, 1941* (Boston, MA: Houghton Mifflin, 1969; revd. edn. Lawrence: University of Kansas Press, 1991), 230, 235.

Wilson, Theodore A.: "The First Summit and the Riddle of Personal Diplomacy." In Douglas Brinkley and David R. Facey-Crowther (eds.) *The Atlantic Charter* (New York: St. Martin's Press, 1994).

Wiltz, John Edward: *In Search of Peace: The Senate Munitions Inquiry, 1934–36* (Baton Rouge: Louisiana State University Press, 1963).

CHAPTER TWELVE

World War II

MARK A. STOLER

The historiography of US foreign relations during World War II possesses both standard and unique characteristics.[1] Similar to other subjects of intense historical dispute discussed within this volume, it has been influenced by both contemporary concerns and new schools of thought within diplomatic history and the historical profession as a whole. It is unique, however, in two important respects. First, the combination of massive documentary evidence and enormous popular interest in the war has resulted in a literature so huge as to merit special mention. One scholar has recently found more than 165,000 titles under World War II in the subject index of the OCLC's *First Search*, over half of them in English (Lee 2001: 367). Second, one event – the Cold War – has exercised an overwhelming influence over interpretations of World War II diplomacy. Indeed, for more than four decades most interpreters viewed wartime diplomacy as the first round in the Cold War, so much so that numerous historiographical and bibliographical studies combined the two conflicts instead of giving World War II separate treatment. The end of the Cold War in 1989–91, combined with changes within the historical profession as a whole, led to a partial shift in focus over the last two decades. But furious debates continue to swirl around specific World War II issues as a result of the continuing impact of the lengthy Soviet–American conflict, as well as the new impact of more recent events.

The tendency to view US World War II diplomacy as the opening round in the Cold War began with the earliest postwar interpretations. As a result, these interpretations did not follow the standard historiographical pattern of official version, revisionism, response, and synthesis. Instead, works highly critical of US wartime policies surfaced first and virtually became the official version. A few defenses of US policies did appear, but most of the major works published in the first two decades after the war accepted revisionist criticism to an extraordinary extent.

The focal points of this criticism were the supposed blunders and *naïveté* of President Franklin D. Roosevelt and his advisers in their wartime relations with the Soviet Union, which had resulted in a massive and dangerous extension of Soviet power. Early proponents of this interpretation included Roosevelt's prewar opponents, former advisers who had disagreed with his cooperative wartime approach to the Soviets (Bullitt 1948; Deane 1947), and Anglo-American journalists who favored the alternative approaches that British Prime Minister Winston S. Churchill had proposed (Baldwin 1949; Wilmot 1952). Churchill himself (1948–53) consciously downplayed such differences with Roosevelt on this and other issues so as not to damage postwar Anglo-American relations, but his memoirs nevertheless provided substantial ammunition for these attacks and exercised an extraordinary influence over World War II histories because of their high quality and early publication, before the declassification of most wartime documents.[2]

Events in the immediate postwar years made this assault on US wartime diplomacy not only popular, but also a very powerful and emotional political issue within the United States. Indeed, the frustrations of perceived Cold War defeats in China and Korea, combined with the loss of the US nuclear monopoly and revelations of wartime Soviet espionage, led Republican politicians such as Senator Joseph McCarthy to enormous popularity and power by accusing Roosevelt and his advisers of sins far worse than mere *naïveté*. By the early 1950s the 1945 Yalta conference had become the great symbol of such sins, with, as British historian D. C. Watt has noted (1989: 79), "a connotation of shameful failure, if not outright treason, matching that attached to the Munich conference of September 1938."

Roosevelt's supporters and numerous diplomatic historians within the "realist" school did criticize such interpretations for inaccurately projecting the Cold War environment back into World War II. US policies during the years 1941–5, they argued, had actually and properly been based upon military necessity and the need to maintain the alliance with Moscow in order to defeat the Axis powers. That defeat and need, as well as battlefield realities created by the advancing Soviet armies, rather than blunders, *naïveté* or treason, a few historians argued, had inevitably led to an enormous increase in Soviet power reflected in the Yalta accords (Snell 1956). Yet many defenses of US wartime diplomacy published in the first two decades after the war simultaneously agreed with the critics who argued that Roosevelt and his advisers had been naive in dealing with the Soviets. According to the realists, *naïveté* was one of the basic characteristics of US diplomacy in general. It was also a key component of American self-perception. Moreover, most of Roosevelt's defenders were by this time Cold Warriors themselves and thus neither willing nor able to defend his cooperative wartime policy toward the Soviet Union. In the process of defending US World War II diplomacy against its extreme critics, these individuals thus wound up attacking it on some of the same grounds the critics had used.

This duality was clearly visible in the comprehensive and excellent "first generation" histories of the wartime alliance by William H. McNeill (1953) and Herbert Feis (1957), as well as the numerous assessments of specific US wartime policies written between 1945 and 1965. During these years most scholars modified their general support of US wartime diplomacy by criticizing Roosevelt for placing faith in Soviet leader Josef Stalin's goodwill and his own powers of persuasion, and all US policymakers for their separation of military from political issues, their single-minded devotion to military victory, and naive Wilsonianism in their postwar planning. All of these points had originally been enunciated by Roosevelt's critics, and by the early 1960s they constituted the prevailing and dominant consensus. Indeed, by that time numerous scholars appeared to be agreeing with some of Roosevelt's harshest critics in the process of supposedly attacking them.

This historical consensus was clearly related to the Cold War consensus that had come to dominate American politics. And just as the latter was shattered by the events of the 1960s, most notably the Vietnam War, so too was the historical consensus as two new schools of interpretation arose to challenge it.

The first, which included historians writing the US army's massive official history of the war as well as others who made use of these volumes and/or the enormous documentary record then becoming available, argued that US wartime policies and strategies had been highly realistic rather than naive.[3] Indeed, John Snell maintained that it was Axis leaders who had based their policies on illusions and thereby lost the war, whereas Roosevelt's highly realistic policies had resulted in total victory. Since cooperation with the Soviets was essential to that victory and expanded Soviet power an inevitable outcome of it, Roosevelt's cooperative approach was "virtually imposed by necessity." Furthermore, FDR's heavily criticized Unconditional Surrender policy and postponement of territorial settlements were highly realistic and pragmatic attempts to promote US interests while simultaneously reconciling Allied differences and maintaining domestic support. His extraordinary success in these efforts resulted not only in military victory and the establishment of prerequisites for postwar cooperation with the Soviets, but also limits on Soviet expansion should cooperation not occur – limits illustrated by the fact that Stalin's territorial gains did not exceed those Tsar Nicholas II would have obtained at the end of World War I had he remained in power (Snell 1963: 116, 137–43, 209–16).

This thesis received strong reinforcement in the late 1960s from new studies of Roosevelt by Robert Divine (1969) and James MacGregor Burns (1970), both of whom portrayed FDR as highly pragmatic and realistic. Rather than being duped by Stalin, Divine argued, historians and the public had been duped by his Wilsonian public statements, which had been delivered to protect his domestic flank but had been contradicted by his pragmatic private comments and actions. Such pragmatism, both historians agreed, had helped to maintain the Grand Alliance but ironically doomed FDR's hopes for postwar cooperation – because it led him to misunderstand Stalin, according to Divine; and/or because it increased the Soviet leader's suspicions, according to Burns. Simultaneous reassessments of the supposedly realistic alternative strategies and policies proposed by Churchill led other scholars to conclude that fear of postwar Soviet power had not been the major factor he had claimed it to be, and that irrational as well as narrowly nationalistic factors had motivated him.[4]

The second school of interpretation to challenge the prevailing consensus on US wartime diplomacy, the so-called "New Left," also made extensive use of the massive documentation then becoming available to attack the notion of American blunders and *naïveté* during the war. But it sharply condemned rather than defended US policies, arguing that they had been highly aggressive and a cause, if not the primary cause, of the ensuing Cold War.

This assault was far from monolithic, however, as it included two very different approaches: a broad economic one and another focusing on the 1945 change in presidential administrations. Basing their work on the "Open Door" thesis that William Appleman Williams (and before him Charles Beard) had used to critique all of US foreign policy, Lloyd C. Gardner and other historians published during the 1960s and early 1970s a series of broad and highly critical economic interpretations of the entire Roosevelt foreign policy (Williams 1962; Gardner 1964, 1970). Gabriel Kolko (1968) provided the most extensive and extreme such critique of that foreign policy during World War II, maintaining that Washington had throughout the war aggressively promoted its own postwar capitalist expansion at the expense of the

British Empire, the Soviet Union, and the indigenous Left throughout the world. But other scholars such as Gar Alperovitz and Diane Clemens harkened back to D. F. Fleming's earlier and more limited Cold War revisionism (1961), rather than Williams' broad economic approach, to defend Roosevelt's policy with the Soviets as cooperative and instead to blame his successor, Harry S. Truman, for reversing it. Alperovitz (1985) found such a reversal in the atomic bombing of Hiroshima, which he argued had been motivated primarily by a desire to blackmail the Soviets rather than to end the war quickly, as Herbert Feis (1961) had earlier claimed. Clemens (1970) concluded her detailed revisionist analysis and defense of Yalta by maintaining that Truman rather than Stalin had broken the accords, even though Stalin rather than Roosevelt had made most of the concessions at the conference.

Consensus historians sharply attacked these New Left assaults on their interpretations of World War II diplomacy and the origins of the Cold War, with the debate often as heated as the larger political one over the Vietnam War. By 1973 it included name-calling and accusations of evidence distortion and had spilled beyond the confines of the profession and onto the pages of the *New York Times*. Ironically, however, new works were by that time moving far beyond such polarized confrontations and into an era of detailed monographs, new syntheses, and entirely new approaches.

This shift resulted from numerous causes. The interpretive debate had clearly reached a stalemate by the mid-1970s, while many historians had begun to realize that the divergent schools actually shared some important conclusions – such as the universalistic nature of US policies as compared with those of its wartime allies. As the years passed such shared conclusions became more visible, partially as a result of the calmer political environment that followed Watergate and the end of the Vietnam War, and partially as a result of the emergence of a new generation of historians not personally linked to the older historiographical battles – or the war itself for that matter.

That generation also possessed extensive and important new primary sources. Works written in the 1960s had relied primarily on documentary information provided in the numerous volumes published during those years in the State Department's *Foreign Relations* series and the British and US official history series, as well as memoirs and recently opened manuscript collections.[5] Most of the World War II documentary record remained classified until the early and mid-1970s, however, when much of it was opened in both the United States and the United Kingdom. The result was quantitatively and qualitatively staggering. US army files alone weighed 17,120 tons, enough to fill 188 miles of filing cases end to end (Greenfield 1954: 6). Those files contained enormously detailed evidence not only to revise previous analyses, but also to open entirely new areas of inquiry. Most publicized was the so-called "Ultra Secret," the Anglo-American interception and deciphering of the highest German military codes and messages that had been radio-transmitted through the now-famous Enigma machine. This great Allied success had remained secret for nearly three decades after the war's end. Its revelation in 1974 precipitated an explosion of scholarship in the field of intelligence, which one British diplomat had labeled "the missing dimension of most diplomatic history," and the creation of what constituted virtually a new and enormous sub-field in World War II scholarship (Dilks 1972: 21; Andrew 1984).[6]

Two additional and related factors also affected the scholarship of the 1970s, although their full impact would not be felt until the following decade. Historical study in general was being altered by the use of social science models and the computer as well as by a new emphasis on social, cultural, and comparative history; while diplomatic historians came under sharp attack for not participating in these changes and for limiting both their research and their focus to the United States. Although this criticism was overstated and ignored pioneering efforts in the new areas and methods of inquiry, it clearly affected numerous scholars who attempted to incorporate such approaches into their work.[7]

The resultant scholarly outpouring during the 1970s focused on numerous, diverse topics and areas of inquiry. The new availability of military as well as diplomatic, and British as well as US, documents led to numerous re-examinations of Anglo-American as well as Soviet–American wartime relations in general, as well as studies of such highly controversial specific issues as aid to Russia, the "second front" controversy, the Darlan affair, decolonization, postwar international organization and economic planning, Middle East oil, the atomic bomb decision, and the treatment of postwar Germany. Contradicting the image Churchill had sought to project in his memoirs, many of these studies revealed and emphasized intense Anglo-American as well as Soviet–American differences and tensions throughout the war.[8] William Roger Louis (1978) took such analyses a step further by examining intragovernmental conflicts in Washington and London, as well as conflicts between the two nations over postwar decolonization and trusteeships. Simultaneously, other historians made use of the newly available documents to shift the focus away from Allied relations and onto US policies in regard to other nations as well as specific colonies. Many of the nations and colonies selected illustrated a continued search for World War II roots to contemporary problems. As publication during the 1960s of studies on wartime Franco-American relations had coincided with Charles de Gaulle's return to power and removal of his country from the unified NATO military command, so did the large number of studies a decade later on US wartime policies regarding China, Indochina, and the Middle East parallel three areas of intense concern for US foreign policy during the 1970s.[9] But the enormous volume of the new documentation, combined with the rise of polycentrism and Third World issues in general during the 1970s, led to a similar flood of studies on wartime relations with a host of other countries.[10]

On some issues the result was a new consensus. Most notable in this regard were works on the atomic bomb by Barton J. Bernstein (1975, 1976) and Martin J. Sherwin (1975). Making use of newly declassified material as well as the existing and conflicting interpretations, each concluded independently that the United States had indeed practiced "atomic diplomacy" against the Soviets as Alperovitz had argued, but that this had been a secondary motive to ending the war quickly as Feis had earlier maintained. Each further emphasized that Roosevelt had initiated atomic diplomacy vis-à-vis the Soviets and that Truman had thus not reversed his predecessor's policies. A consensus also began to emerge on wartime policy toward China, although as a reversal rather than a synthesis of previous interpretations. Written at the height of Sino-American Cold War conflict, those previous interpretations had criticized US policymakers for insufficient support of Jiang Jieshi's Nationalists and non-recognition of the menace posed by the communist Mao Zedong. Writing in the very different environment of Sino-Soviet conflict and Sino-American *rapproche-ment* that marked the 1970s, Barbara Tuchman (1970) and Michael Schaller (1979) criticized policymakers for not having dropped the corrupt and incompetent Jiang in favor of Mao during the war.

The 1970s ended with the publication of two major works that attempted to synthesize the numerous recent studies into a new consensus and to point the way for new lines of inquiry. In his detailed and exhaustive analysis of all Roosevelt's foreign policies from 1932 to 1945, Robert Dallek (1979) sided with a decade of FDR defenders by dismissing what previous critics had labeled his blunders and by emphasizing instead his realism as well as the severe domestic and international constraints under which he had been forced to operate. Dallek did find fault with FDR, but on the same grounds as more recent critics for such "unnecessary and destructive compromises of legal and moral principles" as his sanctioning of illegal wiretaps and mail openings, the internment of Japanese Americans, and his overly cautious, virtual non-response to the Nazi murder of Europe's Jews. Simultaneously, British historian Christopher Thorne broke new ground with his *Allies of a Kind* (1978), a massive diplomatic history of the Anglo-American war against Japan and a pathbreaking work of multi-archival research that emphasized as key themes racism, anticolonialism, Anglo-American friction, and relations with other Pacific nations.

Additional studies in the 1980s both supported and filled gaps within these two seminal works. Although he focused on the postwar years, John L. Gaddis began his *Strategies of Containment* (1982) by crediting Roosevelt with a highly realistic though flawed wartime strategy of "containment by integration" of the USSR into his proposed postwar order and by arguing, as had Dallek and others, that had he lived longer FDR would have shifted to a tougher strategy after the Axis had been defeated (pp. 3–16). Simultaneously, Martin Gilbert (1981), David S. Wyman (1984) and others expanded upon previous criticisms on US and Allied refugee policy during the Holocaust in comprehensive, multi-archival works,[11] while numerous historians explored Anglo-American conflicts within their multi-archival analyses of US–British relations during and immediately after the war. In doing so they completed the destruction of Churchill's early and one-sided interpretation, exposing a relationship that, although "remarkable," had been marked by serious disagreements and had become "special" only gradually, fitfully, and incompletely (Reynolds 1986: 17–41).[12]

In regard to the culturally focused issues that Thorne had raised in *Allies of a Kind*, Akira Iriye's *Power and Culture* (1981) offered an original and provocative comparative analysis of US and Japanese societies and values that emphasized their similarities even in war. In his *War without Mercy* (1986), John Dower made extensive use of evidence within popular culture to analyze in detail the racist views each nation held and their wartime consequences. Thorne himself produced a comparative and thematic follow-up study that attempted to remove the boundaries between Western and non-Western history and to fuse diplomatic with economic and intellectual history as well as sociology and social psychology into a new "international history" (Thorne 1985). And both Frank A. Ninkovich (1981) and Michael S. Sherry (1987) made extensive use of cultural and intellectual history in their respective studies of US foreign policy regarding cultural relations from 1938 to 1950 and the rise of American air power before and during the war.

Many of these themes and approaches were also emphasized within the continuing flood of studies on US wartime relations with other nations and parts of the world. As in the 1970s, such studies continued to focus (though far from exclusively) on areas of recent and contemporary concern, most notably Indochina and the Middle East. With the opening of Korean War documentation came an additional focus on the wartime origins of that conflict. Many of these studies extended into the late 1940s and early 1950s rather than stopping in 1945, thereby continuing the tendency to focus on World War II diplomacy as a prelude to Cold-War era policies and issues. Unlike the studies of Roosevelt and the Grand Alliance, however, these tended to be highly critical of FDR for what appeared in the context of the 1980s to have been his ignorance and paternalism regarding the colonial world and his willingness to temporize with the colonial powers.[13]

The 1980s also witnessed a major outpouring of biographical studies of key Roosevelt advisers, most notably Harry Hopkins and the much-maligned wartime Joint Chiefs of Staff. These both represented and fueled a growing interest in the interaction between diplomatic and military issues during the war, while providing substantial additional evidence of political astuteness by the president and his advisers.[14]

The enormous impact of all these studies, from the late 1960s through the mid-1980s, and the differences between the old historiographical consensus and the newly emerging one, were clearly illustrated in the revisions within the second (1985) edition of Gaddis Smith's *American Diplomacy During the Second World War*, one of the major syntheses and undergraduate texts in the field. When first published in 1965, that volume had provided a vivid illustration of the extent to which Roosevelt's supposed defenders had accepted the critics' assault on his diplomacy. While claiming to analyze the issues in the context of 1941–5 rather than the ensuing Cold War, Smith did the reverse by sharply attacking Roosevelt for placing military above political considerations as well as putting too much faith in Wilsonian collective security concepts, and for naive efforts to "charm" Stalin. In the preface to the second edition, however, Smith admitted that the early 1960s environment had led him to be "too harsh" and "insufficiently appreciative" of the limits FDR faced. He still concluded that Roosevelt's policies for the postwar world had been a failure, but he did so in a tone far less strident than in 1965 and with a new admission that the president had been less naive than he had originally thought. In this regard Smith now questioned whether US interests, which focused on the need to militarily defeat the Axis powers, would have been better served by the open arguments within the Grand Alliance that would have flowed from different policies; perhaps FDR's cooperative approach, he concluded, had been based on a "deeper realism" (Smith 1985: vii–viii, 12–13). Equally noteworthy was Smith's much greater emphasis in the second edition on decolonization as a major wartime issue and on US policies regarding Latin America, the Middle East, and Asia – especially Korea, China, and Indochina.

Smith's work and others' notwithstanding, the promising new synthesis on World War II diplomacy did not continue far into the 1980s. Instead, the second half of the decade witnessed both extensive fragmentation and another massive interpretive debate, one that in many ways duplicated, with equal intensity, those that had taken place in the early 1950s and late 1960s. The focus was, once again, Roosevelt's policies toward the Soviet Union. Dallek's (1979) synthesis was essentially the capstone of the Roosevelt-as-realist interpretation that had become more pronounced and accepted throughout the 1960s and 1970s. As such it was able to successfully subsume earlier interpretations within this school and, to an extent, those of New Left critics. The critics of the 1950s and 1960s remained only partially convinced at best, however, and in the mid-1980s they replied.[15]

As previously noted, Smith had modified but not totally rejected his former critique of Roosevelt's *naïveté* and failure *vis-à-vis* the Soviet Union. Similar attacks emerged in two 1985 studies of the previously neglected 1943 Cairo–Tehran summit conferences by Keith Eubank and Keith Sainsbury. Both historians viewed Tehran as the pivotal wartime summit that in many ways determined the agenda and results of the more famous Yalta meeting, and both in effect projected the old criticism of American *naïveté* at Yalta back to this earlier meeting – although for the British Sainsbury, as for Smith, with clear recognition and admission of the numerous limits within which FDR had to work and the dangers posed by an alternative policy of confrontation (Eubank 1985; Sainsbury 1985). Russell D. Buhite criticized Roosevelt on similar grounds in his *Decisions at Yalta* (1986), as well as for being too concerned with the domestic consequences of failure at Yalta and, indeed, for having desired the conference in the first place: summit conferences in general, he concluded, were counterproductive and invited the misunderstandings and defeats that had taken place in the Crimea.

Other studies published in 1988 were far more critical, and indeed reminiscent of the attacks of the 1950s. In his brief *Roosevelt and Stalin* (1988), Robert Nisbet essentially updated and reiterated those attacks on Roosevelt for extraordinary *naïveté* regarding Stalin, with Tehran replacing Yalta as the place where FDR "played essentially the role Chamberlain had at Munich" and where the Cold War had actually begun (p. 12). Frederick W. Marks (1988) went even further, arguing that all of Roosevelt's diplomacy from 1933 to 1945 had been marked by ambivalence, indecisiveness, narrow domestic motivation, parochialism, and failure. Marks focused on events before Pearl Harbor, but in one chapter on the war years he argued that FDR had not been the "absolute prisoner of events" his defenders maintained and that he "gave away much of his hand in a game whose rules he did not comprehend." Moreover, he had as president "accumulated the largest overseas credibility gap of any president on record," been contemptuously disliked by his overseas contemporaries, and stood as the "fitting symbol" for an American "age of delayed adolescence in international affairs" (pp. 172, 260, 287).

This renewed assault on Roosevelt was clearly linked to the domestic and international environments of the 1980s, which differed substantially from those of the 1970s. Most important in this regard were the rise of the neoconservative movement and the revival of the Cold War that accompanied Ronald Reagan's election to the presidency in 1980, and the ensuing revival of a Manichaean worldview that labeled the Soviet Union the "evil empire." Along with this came a revival of the complementary view that cooperation with Moscow was and always had been impossible, and that Roosevelt had thus been a fool to try it.

Such conclusions were by no means limited to Nisbet and Marks. In a 1985 issue of the neoconservative magazine *Commentary*, Sir John Colville, Churchill's personal secretary whose diaries had just been published (Colville 1985a), used virtually the same words as had Bullitt, Wilmot, Baldwin, and others more than three decades earlier to attack FDR and his advisers for winning the war but losing the peace – Roosevelt by his *naïveté* and "complete sellout to Stalin" at Yalta regarding Poland, his military chiefs by their narrowly military and apolitical perspective, and all US policymakers by their anti-British bias based upon their negative view of colonialism (Colville 1985b). In another issue of *Commentary* a few months later ("How Has" 1985), Irving Kristol, Jeane Kirkpatrick, Lionel Abel, and Nisbet directly or indirectly supported Colville – on Yalta in particular and Roosevelt's overall policy in general. Abel and Nisbet were particularly sharp, with the former holding FDR personally responsible for the "terrible" decisions Colville had described and the latter blasting Roosevelt for "credulity" regarding Stalin, "pathetic ignorance of political history and geopolitics," and "colossal *naïveté*." Both also attacked what they labeled the broader liberal foreign policy, of which Roosevelt's policy had been but a part, and whose "pro- or at least anti-anti-Soviet" views, Nisbet argued, had severely hampered US policymakers during the Cold War.

Roosevelt's defenders quickly responded. In an early 1986 issue of the *New York Review of Books* an aroused Theodore Draper launched a massive counterattack against this "neoconservative history," which he bluntly labeled, in a thinly veiled reference to McCarthyism, another effort to make history "serve current political extremism." Making extensive use of the previous decade's defenses of Roosevelt and attacks on Churchill, as well as Warren F. Kimball's recently published complete Churchill–Roosevelt correspondence (1984), Draper maintained that the Red Army rather than FDR had given Stalin control of Eastern Europe, that conservatives such as John Foster Dulles had supported the same "illusions and compromises" as FDR, and that "the Western allies had not given away anything at Yalta that they actually had." The "defamatory fury" of the neoconservative assault on Roosevelt, he concluded, an assault based on "ignorance and effrontery," had "less to do with the past than with the present" – i.e., neoconservative hatred of "liberal international-ism." The real enemy and target of the neoconservative ideology, a new and extreme fusion of isolationism and internationalism, was the group of domestic liberals to which these neoconservatives had once belonged and which they were now attacking via historical character assassination as a means of displacing their own guilt for their previous actions (Draper 1986).

The ensuing rejoinders made such language appear mild in comparison. Nisbet and Draper traded accusations of misuse of the evidence, while Abel wrote that Draper's defense of Roosevelt made him as much as Roosevelt "the accomplice of Stalin . . . in the enslavement of Eastern Europe" – a remark Draper labeled a McCarthyite "political obscenity" (Draper 1986). Nor were these the last words on the subject. Nisbet followed with a long article that he expanded into his previously mentioned book, and Draper with an extensive review of David Eisenhower's wartime biography of his grandfather that emphasized his politico-military realism and the centrality of the Soviet war effort to all US wartime strategy and diplomacy; in 1990 he republished all of these within a book of essays (Draper 1990). Interestingly, although many of the participants in this debate were scholars, not one was a US diplomatic historian. Clearly, World War II diplomacy remained a heated issue of concern to many beyond the profession and specialization, with this particular confrontation boldly revealing its continued link to both the state of the Cold War and domestic politics.

Draper was of course far from the only writer to defend Roosevelt during the 1980s. Melvyn Leffler did so indirectly by boldly asserting, in a detailed assessment influenced by recent Soviet–American tensions and charges, that Washington as well as Moscow had broken the Yalta accords and, indeed, had used supposed Soviet violations as a "convenient lever" to justify its own (Leffler 1986). Moreover, most of the previously cited works published during the 1980s provided at least partial defenses of US wartime diplomacy and tended to echo Dallek and Draper in emphasizing the domestic and international constraints that Roosevelt faced and thus his lack of viable alternatives *vis-à-vis* the Soviets. In 1991, however, Warren F. Kimball, editor of the complete Churchill–Roosevelt correspondence, altered this focus in a volume of essays that concentrated on FDR's assumptions and worldview as well as his specific actions. Such an analysis was more an exploration and explanation than a defense of Roosevelt's ideas and policies, but in the environment of the 1980s simply to argue that Roosevelt possessed an overall vision and made logical choices was to defend him from his severe critics. Similarly, Kimball's use of "liberal" as a key descriptive term for the president's vision rather than as an epithet, and his equation of liberalism with "Americanism," constituted a powerful if indirect defense of Roosevelt against the neoconservative assault (Kimball 1991).

Reinforcement for both sides in this renewed debate came from scholars working with the still thin but growing trickle of available Soviet sources. Many of them emphasized Stalin's caution, pragmatism, and lack of any overall "master plan" during the war years, as well as his desire to obtain limited gains within a framework of continued collaboration with his wartime allies. They disagreed over how extensive those aims actually were, however, and over whether a clear FDR–Churchill definition of acceptable limits would have made any difference. Vojtech Mastny (1979) and William Taubman (1982) saw those aims as quite extensive and were highly critical of Roosevelt's refusal to state acceptable limits, but concluded that postwar Soviet suspicion, hostility, and aggression would have resulted from any US policy.[16] Edward Bennett (1990) launched similar criticisms and reached similar conclusions in a study of Roosevelt's wartime Soviet policy, though he defended Roosevelt's overall approach despite its shortcomings because it did secure his primary objectives: Axis defeat and "far more than the twenty-five years of peace he once said he hoped to ensure" (pp. 183–8).

Debate during the 1980s was not limited to the issue of Soviet–American diplomacy. The decade also witnessed an outpouring of scholarship on major British wartime figures, and on Anglo-Soviet as well as Anglo-American wartime relations.[17] The biographies naturally tended to defend the British position in Anglo-American disputes, while the Anglo-Soviet studies provided evidence for both sides in the debate over US policy by revealing sharp disagreements within the British government over Soviet policy and by reaching conflicting conclusions regarding these disagreements. Whereas Gabriel Gorodetsky (1984), for example, sharply criticized Churchill and his advisers for selecting a virtual non-policy – if not an anti-Soviet one – over the more cooperative approach recommended by Ambassador Sir Stafford Cripps in 1941–2, Steven M. Miner (1988) criticized Churchill for trying to appease

Stalin and pointed to the hardline US opposition to territorial settlements in 1941–2 as the policy London should have followed. Ironically, the pro-cooperation Gorodetsky thereby indirectly provided Roosevelt's anti-cooperation critics with additional ammunition while the anti-cooperation Miner did the same for Roosevelt's defenders.

As this irony illustrates, by the late 1980s the earlier conflicting schools of interpretation had become quite confused as a result of this complex outpouring of scholarship and polemics. Indeed, by decade's end at least five separate positions on Roosevelt and US wartime diplomacy, distinct from yet related to the earlier positions of the 1950s and 1960s, were clearly visible. At one extreme stood Roosevelt-as-ultimate-realist, a position supported by both his defenders, who praised this realism while emphasizing the domestic and international constraints under which he had to work, and some New Left critics who attacked it as aggressive. At the other extreme was Roosevelt the naive blunderer who had never understood the Soviet Union or international relations, a reiteration by neoconservatives of the charges originally leveled during the late 1940s and 1950s. In between were at least three composites: Roosevelt the realist who actually had more maneuverability than he had thought and who therefore could have done better than he did in checking Soviet expansion; Roosevelt the skillful pragmatist who unfortunately worked under a series of mistaken conceptions regarding the USSR; and Roosevelt the "idealist/realist" who possessed a clear and defensible vision of a reformed international order and who chose to compromise that vision because of wartime exigencies and dilemmas.

Where one stood on this spectrum depended not only on one's politics in the 1980s and interpretation of the documents, but also on whether one believed the "Yalta" or the "Riga" axioms regarding the USSR that Daniel Yergin had posited in 1977. Although somewhat artificial and overstated, this dichotomy remains as useful for understanding World War II historiographical disputes as the origins of the Cold War – if not more so. For one's opinion of Roosevelt's policies *vis-à-vis* the Soviet Union does depend to a large extent upon whether one views the USSR as simply a traditional Great Power with whom compromise was possible or as an ideological monstrosity incapable of cooperation or normal diplomatic behavior.

Reinforcing the importance of one's politics and preconceived notions regarding the USSR in assessing US wartime diplomacy was Roosevelt's notorious secrecy and deviousness, which, despite the enormous volume of his papers, resulted in a paucity of clear statements regarding what he truly believed. During the war he revealingly told his military chiefs to alter memoranda he feared future historians would interpret as proposing the abandonment of England (Stoler 2000: 87). He also told his secretary of state that publication of notes taken at the 1919 Paris Peace Conference should be postponed and that those notes should never have been taken in the first place (Burns 1970: 427–8). When the secretary of the Joint Chiefs of Staff tried to take notes during a meeting the president exploded and ordered a halt (Bland 1991: 623).

Even when Roosevelt did break down and say something meaningful for the record, one was often unsure if it was what he really thought – or indeed what it meant. A notable example was his 1942 comment to Churchill that he knew how to "handle" Stalin in regard to the latter's demand for recognition of his 1939–40 territorial conquests in Eastern Europe (Kimball 1984, I: 421). Nisbet and Draper each claimed in their 1986 debate that this comment supported his conclusion, the former arguing that it illustrated FDR's *naïveté vis-à-vis* Stalin and the latter that it showed the president's hard-headed realism in opposing recognition and taking the initiative from Churchill, who no longer did. One could almost hear FDR's ghost laughing as scholars argued over what in the world he had meant by this and similar comments, as well as empathize with Secretary of War Henry L. Stimson's 1940 comment that speaking with Roosevelt was "like chasing a vagrant beam of sunshine around a vacant room" (Kimball 1969: 4). One Roosevelt biographer, relating a "recurrent and maddening dream" about Roosevelt cheating at cards, aptly concluded that "all of Franklin Roosevelt's cards were never on the table" (Ward 1991: 119).

While Roosevelt and Grand Alliance scholars continued to argue throughout the 1980s, other diplomatic historians explored the new areas and approaches being illuminated by social scientists and social/cultural historians. In doing so they helped to redefine the major issues, questions, and themes to be addressed, and thus the terms of the debate over wartime diplomacy. Previously noted in this regard were the pathbreaking works of Thorne, Iriye, Dower, and others in the realms of multi-archival research and the comparative cultural approach of the new international history.[18] Equally notable was an increasing emphasis on bureaucratic politics. While numerous historians focused on this mode of analysis to explain US policies prior to Pearl Harbor, others such as Louis (1978) used it as one of their major tools for analyzing such wartime issues as decolonization, global strategy, postwar planning, and relations with Latin America and the Middle East.[19]

In one sense this was not new; analysis of disagreements within Roosevelt's notoriously chaotic bureaucracy had always been part of World War II diplomatic histories, and the archival openings of the 1970s enabled historians to trace and analyze them in great detail. Some scholars now began to argue, however, that social science theories of bureaucratic behavior were central to understanding why, not simply how, certain policies had been initiated and implemented. This interpretation held profound consequences for the debate over US wartime diplomacy, in that it implicitly rejected FDR's centrality by denying his ability, or that of any other single individual, to dictate or implement policy. Rather, policy often emerged from a welter of bureaucratic desires and conflicts that bore little if any relationship to US interests, to what Roosevelt had desired, or even to what he had ordered.[20] Political scientist Leon Sigal's *Fighting to a Finish* (1988) boldly illustrated the revolutionary consequences of such an analysis. Making use of the bureaucratic and "non-rational actor" models that Graham Allison had previously developed to analyze the 1962 Cuban Missile Crisis, Sigal dismissed all previous interpretations of the atomic bomb/Japanese surrender controversy by arguing that neither the United States nor Japan had followed any rational plan for ending the war. Rather, different segments of the bureaucracy in each country had proposed policies geared to their own worldviews and self-aggrandizement, none of which independently or in their interaction constituted a logical plan for war termination.

Culture and bureaucratic politics were by no means the only new areas to be explored in the 1970s and 1980s. Major analyses emphasizing gender, ideology, psychology, corporatism, "mental maps," public opinion, world systems, national security, balance of power, and international organization as explanations of US foreign relations in general also appeared during these decades.[21] Although only a few of them focused exclusively on World War II, that conflict played a major role in many of them. Numerous gender studies, for example, emphasized both the complex impact of the war on women and the relationship between gender, ideology, and war in general. In a fascinating article, Alan Henrikson (1975) explored the dramatic shift that had occurred in the American mental map of the globe during World War II and its impact on the origins of the Cold War. Les K. Adler and Thomas G. Paterson (1970) and Edward Mark (1989) similarly analyzed the impact of World War II on American ideological perceptions of Stalin and the Soviet Union, while Ralph Levering (1976) and others focused on wartime public opinion of the USSR.[22] Scholars also examined numerous other aspects of public opinion, with more than one asking if this might not be the key motivating factor in FDR's postwar planning (Widenor 1982). Thomas Campbell (1973) and Robert Hilderbrand (1990) explored the triumph of purely national over truly international definitions of security in the wartime formulation of the postwar international security organization, and Melvyn Leffler (1992) carefully noted the importance of the World War II experience in the new, global definition of American national security, which he viewed as central to the origins and development of the Cold War. Of related interest and focus were numerous works that reassessed US wartime attitudes toward spheres of influence.[23]

That these new approaches became increasingly voluminous as the 1980s came to an end and the 1990s began was far from accidental. Indeed, their rise coincided with the dramatic changes taking place within Eastern Europe, capped in the years 1989–91 by the end not only of the Soviet empire but also of the Cold War and the Soviet Union itself. These extraordinary events, it appeared, were breaking the virtual stranglehold the Cold War had held over interpretations of World War II diplomacy for the preceding four decades.

To an extent this was correct, and throughout the 1990s much World War II scholarship continued to explore these new approaches, most notably (but far from exclusively) the bureaucratic and social/cultural approaches. Many if not most of these studies focused on domestic history rather than foreign relations, but the line between the two was often blurred. Particularly noteworthy in this regard were studies of such previously unexplored or under-explored issues as the foreign policy attitudes of African Americans and women, the interactions between US service personnel stationed overseas and other cultures, and the impact of cultural perceptions on intelligence assessments (Reynolds 2001: 457–63). Equally noteworthy were studies on collective memories of the war – memories that focused on, included, or had a strong impact on foreign relations.[24]

Most if not all of these new approaches had first appeared while the Cold War was still in progress, however, and in many ways their appearance reflected changes within the United States more than changes in its foreign relations. Moreover, numerous scholars used these new approaches to reassess and reargue the traditional questions about Roosevelt and Cold War origins rather than to explore different themes. And although the dramatic events in Eastern Europe may have indirectly added to the popularity of different themes, those events were simultaneously laying the groundwork for another generation of Soviet–American studies by accelerating both scholarly contact between the two countries and the long-desired opening of Soviet World War II archives. Without those archives all diplomatic histories of the Grand Alliance had been woefully incomplete; with them, scholars began to glimpse the possibility of definitive, tri-archival histories of the coalition. Consequently the late 1980s and 1990s witnessed a continued deluge of Grand Alliance scholarship that paralleled and often intersected with the deluge of new approaches to the World War II years.

The increased scholarly contact that began in the mid-1980s included multinational World War II conferences in Britain, the Soviet Union, and the United States. These resulted not only in fascinating scholarly exchanges, but also in publication of some of the conferees' papers within each other's countries and languages. The meetings also had an obvious impact on the later publications of those involved, and they eventually led to such multilateral publications as *Allies at War* (Reynolds, Kimball, and Chubarian 1994), a tripartite and comparative analysis of the strategic, economic, home front, and foreign policy histories of the three nations during the war.[25]

Unfortunately, however, the release of Soviet documents during the 1980s and 1990s was highly erratic, unpredictable, and so incomplete as to preclude any definitive conclusions about Stalin's relations with Roosevelt or Soviet policies in general, claims to the contrary notwithstanding. Furthermore, neither the documents that were released nor the post-Cold War environment resulted in any resolution of the existing historiographical disputes. Rather, as illustrated by the conflicting alliance histories published in the early 1990s by Remi Nadeau and Robin Edmonds, the newly released documents and collapse of the Soviet empire provided additional ammunition for both sides to continue the debate rather than resolve it. Nadeau (1990) repeated the charges of FDR losing the peace because of his innocence and misplaced idealism, charges that others, labeled the "new perfectionists" by their critics, echoed and amplified throughout the decade (Kimball 2001: 351–42 and n. 15).[26] Edmonds (1991), on the other hand, emphasized the numerous successes of FDR and the Grand Alliance – most notably the destruction of Nazism and the creation of a United Nations that could now finally function as originally envisaged. Warren F. Kimball (1997) also praised Roosevelt and Churchill in his study of the two leaders during the war, though not without admission of their numerous shortcomings. By that date Churchill needed the defense as much as Roosevelt, for John Charmley (1993, 1995) had earlier launched a British neoconservative attack on Churchill that paralleled the 1980s American neoconservative attack on Roosevelt – though ironically for the prime minister's pro-American policy that Charmley argued had hastened if not caused the postwar demise of the British Empire.

Similar disagreements erupted during the 1990s within the field of wartime intelligence. The opening of certain US and Soviet intelligence files, most notably VENONA, appears to have proven beyond reasonable doubt the guilt of certain wartime Soviet spies and illustrated more extensive espionage than previously accepted. Yet the impact of such espionage activities, and implicitly one's judgments about the wisdom of US wartime behavior toward the Soviets, remains a hotly debated topic (Parrish 2001; Reynolds 2001: 460–1).

Intelligence studies during the 1990s were by no means limited to Soviet espionage and its impact. Numerous historians in this massively expanding field began during the decade to offer detailed analyses of the relationship of wartime intelligence to Allied relations in general. Sometimes the results were surprising. Bradley F. Smith (1996) revealed unexpected levels of intelligence sharing with the Soviets that did not parallel the ups and downs of Allied wartime relations, for example, while Richard J. Aldrich (2000) and Jay Jakub (1999) revealed major Anglo-American suspicion and conflict in the intelligence field. This challenged the rosy view of unprecedented collaboration that had emerged in the popular and unreliable early intelligence studies of the 1980s, while fitting in with the continued emphasis on Anglo-American conflict that marked numerous 1990s studies in the fields of wartime strategy, economics, and postwar planning.[27]

New disagreement erupted during the 1990s within another massively expanding World War II field: Holocaust studies. Here numerous scholars began to challenge the studies of the 1970s and 1980s (most notably but far from exclusively those by David Wyman) that had sharply condemned American inaction. Such condemnations, they argued, were one-sided and anachronistic in that they ignored both Roosevelt's accomplishments in this area and the context, limits, and priorities within which he operated.[28]

These disagreements were mild, however, compared to those focusing on the most hotly and extensively debated World War II issue during the 1990s: the atomic bombing of Hiroshima. That heated controversy would reoccur over this issue was in one sense surprising, as the works of Bernstein and Sherwin in the 1970s had established what appeared at the time to be a synthesis and new consensus that atomic diplomacy had existed and been initiated by Roosevelt, but that it was a secondary motive to ending the war as quickly as possible. Alperovitz had continued to challenge this conclusion in the 1980s, however, and in 1995 he published a second major work arguing once again that dropping the bomb had not been necessary to obtain Japanese surrender before any invasion and that it had been done primarily for indefensible political reasons. Others had by this time labeled as myth Truman's estimate that half a million American lives would have been lost in any invasion (Miles 1985; Bernstein 1986). Throughout the 1990s scholars both within and outside the profession published similar condemnatory conclusions based upon recently declassified documents as well as their reinterpretation of previously available ones. Simultaneously, however, numerous diplomatic and military historians found in those new documents substantial evidence that an invasion would have been both necessary and incredibly bloody. D. M. Giangreco (1997) even revisited and defended Truman's casualty projections, while Robert P. Newman (1995) bluntly accused Alperovitz and other A-bomb critics of being part of an historical "Hiroshima Cult."[29]

This heated debate was in one sense a continuation of the previous one that Alperovitz had helped to launch in the 1960s as part of the New Left revisionist assault on traditional Cold War history. But it was in a broader sense part of the separate though clearly related "culture wars" of the 1980s and 1990s, a fact boldly illustrated by the incredible public controversy that erupted in 1994–5 over the Smithsonian Institution's plans for an exhibition to mark the fiftieth anniversary of Hiroshima. Conservative critics bitterly attacked the original Smithsonian script as a "Politically Correct" Leftist whitewash of the Japanese and grossly unfair condemnation of the United States. Defenders responded that the script represented the present state of historical scholarship and debate. That in turn led some of the critics to respond that the job of the Smithsonian was to commemorate, not present history or historical disputes – a position defenders of the script labeled "Patriotically Correct" censorship. In the end attempted compromise totally broke down over the question of projected US casualties, and the Smithsonian wound up showing only a section of the *Enola Gay* with no explanation or analysis whatsoever – a result that appalled many in the historical profession. The *Journal of American History* published six articles on the controversy as a special roundtable in its December 1995 issue, some of them scathing in their condemnation of what they labeled political censorship. On the front cover of that issue was an Auth cartoon showing someone painting "Have a Nice Day" and a "smiley face" on the smiling nose of the *Enola Gay* with the comment, "It's all they can handle" (Thelen et al. 1995).

As the continued emphasis on new approaches to World War II diplomacy reflected domestic more than foreign policy issues in the 1990s, so did this furious public debate over Hiroshima. What was at stake, as numerous commentators pointed out, was nothing less than the public memory of World War II – a public memory now the subject of intense disagreement and part of a larger debate dividing Americans by age as well as political and cultural ideologies (Linenthal and Engelhardt 1996; Stoler 2001).

Many would argue this larger debate had actually begun during the 1960s, and that the historiographical controversy in that decade over World War II diplomacy and the origins of the Cold War had been a part of it from the start. In that sense contemporary domestic controversies have always been a fundamental source of historical disagreement over US diplomacy during World War II. But for half a century those domestic controversies as an issue in World War II historiography had focused on a single if lengthy event: the Cold War. The historiographical result has been, in Warren Kimball's apt phrase, the "Cold War colonization" of World War II scholarship (Kimball 2001). Although that colonization no longer dominates the field to the extent that it previously did, it still continues via the related culture wars. Simultaneously, however, the end of the Cold War and the rise of social/cultural history within the profession as a whole have helped to open numerous new areas of inquiry, and indeed to broaden the very definition of foreign relations. The result has been a continued deluge of World War II scholarship that shows no signs of abating in the foreseeable future.

NOTES

1 This is a revised, abridged and updated version of my 1994 historiographical article (Stoler, 1994)

2 This impact was far from accidental. "History will bear me out," Churchill had boasted, "particularly as I shall write that history myself." He certainly did, albeit with the knowledge, as paraphrased by Sir William Deakin, that "this is not history; this is my case" (Kimball 1993: 294).

3 The official army history of the war eventually included 79 volumes, as well as a special collection of essays (Greenfield 1960). See also Emerson (1958–9), Greenfield (1963), and Matloff (1962).

4 See Ambrose (1967), Higgins (1968), Howard (1968), and O'Connor (1971).

5   As a result of the domestic political uproar in the early postwar years over Yalta, a special
    Foreign Relations volume on that conference was published in 1955. Not until the 1960s,
    however, did the regular chronological series reach the war years (more than thirty volumes
    covering 1941–5 would be published during the decade) and companion volumes begin
    to appear for the other wartime summit conferences. The key British official and multi-
    volume histories were by Butler (1956–76) and Woodward (1962, 1970–6). In addition
    to the official US army history previously cited, see the multivolume Navy history by
    Morison (1947–62) and Army Air Forces history by Craven and Cate (1948–58).
        Roosevelt died before he could write his memoirs, but selections from his wartime
    correspondence with Churchill and Stalin were reproduced in *Foreign Relations*. Churchill
    (1948–53) also contained extensive Big Three correspondence, and in 1957 the Soviets
    published Stalin's complete correspondence with Churchill and Roosevelt (Ministry
    1957). The Churchill–Roosevelt correspondence received separate, full-length treatment
    only in the 1970s and 1980s (Lowenheim, Langley, and Jonas 1975; Kimball 1984)
6   The first work to reveal Ultra was Winterbotham's 1974 memoir. A complete note on all
    the related material published since then would require an entire book. The interested
    reader is advised to consult the Sexton guide (1996), which contains over 800 citations.
7   See Hogan and Paterson (1991) for an excellent series of essays on these new approaches
    in diplomatic history.
8   See, for example, Beitzell (1972), Gaddis (1972), Steele (1973), Lukas (1970), Funk
    (1974), Stoler (1977), Villa (1976, 1977–8), Dunn (1980), Herring (1973), Paterson
    (1973), and Kimball (1976), as well as ensuing text.
9   See, for example, Drachman (1970), Hess (1972), LaFeber (1975), Thorne (1976),
    Baram (1978), and DeNovo (1977). For France, see Viorst (1965) and White (1964).
10 See, for example, Roberts (1973), Bell (1977), Hess (1971), Lukas (1978), Gellman
    (1979), and Woods (1979).
11 See also Laqueur (1980), Penkower (1983), Breitman and Kraut (1987), and Lipstadt
    (1985).
12 See also Anderson (1981), Dobson (1986), Harbutt (1986), Hathaway (1981), and
    Sbrega (1983).
13 The number of pages in each work devoted to World War II rather than the early Cold
    War years varied enormously, with the 1941–5 period providing merely an introduction
    to some and nearly all the content of others. See, for example, Gallicchio (1988), Hess
    (1987), Matray (1985), Painter (1986), and Stoff (1980).
14 Biographies of each of the four members of the wartime Joint Chiefs of Staff appeared
    during the 1980s, as well as collective and individual biographies of Roosevelt's key
    officers and new biographies of Harry Hopkins. See in particular Ambrose (1983–4),
    James (1970–85, 1987), Larrabee (1987), McJimsey (1987), and Pogue (1963–87).
15 So too did some of the New Left historians. See below, for more detail on this.
16 For different conclusions see McCagg (1978) and Resis (1978, 1981)
17 See Barker (1978), Callahan (1984), Danchev (1986), Fraser (1982), and Gilbert (1986)
    on specific individuals, and Douglas (1981), Kitchen (1986), Reynolds (1990), Rothwell
    (1982), and Watt (1989) on British relations with the Soviet Union and the United
    States.
18 See above, and Iriye's essay in Hogan and Paterson (1991: 214–25).
19 See also Baram (1978), Martel (1979), Stoler (1977, 2000), and Woods (1979, 1990).
    For a discussion of bureaucratic politics as a model and the relevant literature, see J. Garry
    Clifford's "Bureaucratic Politics" in Hogan and Paterson (1991: 141–50).
20 Kolko (1968) had been one of the first scholars to challenge Roosevelt's centrality,
    though hardly on the basis of bureaucratic politics or a split between US policies and US
    interests.

21 All of these approaches are summarized in Hogan and Paterson (1991). See also directly below.
22 On other aspects of wartime public opinion and propaganda see Leigh (1976), Shulman (1990), and Winkler (1978).
23 See Davis (1974), Lundestad (1975), Mark (1981), and Gardner (1993). On international organization see also Divine (1971). On military/security issues see also Brower (1991), Sherry (1977), and Stoler (1977).
24 See, for example, Adams (1994), Gallicchio (2000), Linenthal (1996), Litoff and Smith (2000), Plummer (1996), Reynolds (1995), Schrijvers (1998), Stoler (2001), and Von Eschen (1997).
25 See also Sevostionov and Kimball (1989) and Lane (1995).
26 See also Aga-Rossi (1993), Dunn (1998), and Perlmutter (1993). A different type of criticism can be found in Harper's award-winning study (1994: 7–131).
27 See, for example, Danchev (1998), Jones (1996), Stoler (2000), Weiss (1996), and Woods (1990).
28 See in particular Rubinstein (1997) and the essays in Newton (1996).
29 Full listing and discussion of all the literature on the atomic bomb published in the 1980s and 1990s would require another full essay. Walker (1990, 1997) provides admirable summaries and assessments. See also directly below, and the compilation edited by Hogan (1996).

REFERENCES

Adams, Michael C. C.: *The Best War Ever: America and World War II* (Baltimore, MD: Johns Hopkins University Press, 1994).
Adler, Les K. and Thomas G. Paterson: "Red Fascism: The Merger of Nazi Germany and Soviet Russia in the American Image of Totalitarianism, 1930s–1950s." *American Historical Review* 75 (April 1970), 1046–64.
Aga-Rossi, Elena: "Roosevelt's European Policy and the Origins of the Cold War: A Reevaluation." *Telos* 96 (summer 1993), 65–85.
Aldrich, Richard J.: *Intelligence and the War Against Japan: Britain, America, and the Politics of Secret Service* (New York: Columbia University Press, 2000).
Alperovitz, Gar: *Atomic Diplomacy, Hiroshima and Potsdam: The Use of the Atomic Bomb and the American Confrontation with Soviet Power* (New York: Vintage, 1965; revd. edn. London: Penguin Books, 1985).
Alperovitz, Gar: *The Decision to Use the Atomic Bomb and the Architecture of an American Myth* (New York: Alfred A. Knopf, 1995).
Ambrose, Stephen E.: *Eisenhower and Berlin: The Decision to Halt at the Elbe* (New York: W. W. Norton, 1967).
Ambrose, Stephen E.: *Eisenhower*, 2 vols. (New York: Simon and Schuster, 1983–4).
Anderson, Irvine H.: *Aramco, the United States, and Saudi Arabia: A Study in the Dynamics of Foreign Oil Policy, 1933–1950* (Princeton, NJ: Princeton University Press, 1981).
Anderson, Terry H.: *The United States, Great Britain, and the Cold War, 1944–1947* (Columbia: University of Missouri Press, 1981).
Andrew, Christopher: *The Missing Dimension: Governments and Intelligence Communities in the Twentieth Century* (Urbana: University of Illinois Press, 1984).
Bagby, Wesley M.: *The Eagle–Dragon Alliance: America's Relations with China in World War II* (Newark: University of Delaware Press, 1992).
Baldwin, Hanson W.: *Great Mistakes of the War* (New York: Harper and Brothers, 1949).
Baram, Philip J.: *The Department of State in the Middle East, 1919–1945* (Philadelphia: University of Pennsylvania Press, 1978).

Barker, Elisabeth: *Churchill and Eden at War* (London: St. Martin's Press, 1978).

Beitzell, Robert: *The Uneasy Alliance: America, Britain and Russia, 1941–1943* (New York: Knopf, 1972).

Bell, P. M. H.: *John Bull and the Bear: British Public Opinion, Foreign Policy and the Soviet Union, 1941–1945* (London: Edward Arnold, 1990).

Bell, Roger J.: *Unequal Allies: Australian–American Relations and the Pacific War* (Melbourne: Melbourne University Press, 1977).

Bennett, Edward M.: *Franklin D. Roosevelt and the Search for Victory: American–Soviet Relations, 1939–1945* (Wilmington, DE: Scholarly Resources, 1990).

Bernstein, Barton J.: "Roosevelt, Truman and the Atomic Bomb, 1941–1945: A Reinterpretation." *Political Science Quarterly* 90 (spring 1975), 23–69.

Bernstein, Barton J.: "The Uneasy Alliance: Roosevelt, Churchill, and the Atomic Bomb, 1940–1945." *Western Political Science Quarterly* 29 (June 1976), 202–30.

Bernstein, Barton J.: "A Postwar Myth: 500,000 Lives Saved." *Bulletin of the Atomic Scientists* 42 (June/July 1986), 38–40.

Bland, Larry I. (ed.) *George C. Marshall Interviews and Reminiscences for Forrest C. Pogue* (Lexington, VA: George C. Marshall Research Foundation, 1991).

Breitman, Richard: *Official Secrets: What the Nazis Planned, What the British and Americans Knew* (New York: Hill and Wang, 1998).

Breitman, Richard and Alan M. Kraut: *American Refugee Policy and European Jewry, 1933–1945* (Bloomington: Indiana University Press, 1987).

Brower, Charles F., IV: "Sophisticated Strategist: General George A. Lincoln and the Defeat of Japan, 1944–1945." *Diplomatic History* 15 (summer 1991), 317–37.

Buhite, Russell D.: *Decisions at Yalta: An Appraisal of Summit Diplomacy* (Wilmington, DE: Scholarly Resources, 1986).

Bullitt, William C.: "How We Won the War and Lost the Peace." *Life* 25 (August 30, 1948), 82–97.

Burns, James MacGregor: *Roosevelt: The Soldier of Freedom, 1940–1945* (New York: Harcourt, Brace, Jovanovich, 1970).

Butler, J. R. M. (ed.): *Grand Strategy*, 6 vols. (London: Her Majesty's Stationery Office, 1956–76).

Callahan, Raymond A.: *Churchill: Retreat from Empire* (Wilmington, DE: Scholarly Resources, 1984).

Campbell, Thomas M.: *Masquerade Peace: America's UN Policy, 1944–1945* (Tallahassee: Florida State University Press, 1973).

Charmley, John: *Churchill: The End of Glory; A Political Biography* (New York: Harcourt Brace, 1993).

Charmley, John: *Churchill's Grand Alliance: The Anglo-American Special Relationship, 1940–1957* (New York: Harcourt Brace, 1995).

Churchill, Winston S.: *The Second World War*, 6 vols. (Boston, MA: Houghton Mifflin, 1948–53).

Clemens, Diane S.: *Yalta* (New York: Oxford University Press, 1970).

Colville, John: *The Fringes of Power: 10 Downing Street Diaries, 1939–1955* (New York: W. W. Norton, 1985a).

Colville, John: "How the West Lost the Peace in 1945." *Commentary* 80 (September 1985b), 41–7.

Craven, Wesley F. and James L. Cate (eds.): *The Army Air Forces in World War II*, 7 vols. (Chicago, IL: University of Chicago Press, 1948–58).

Dallek, Robert: *Franklin D. Roosevelt and American Foreign Policy, 1932–1945* (New York: Oxford University Press, 1979).

Danchev, Alex: *Very Special Relationship: Field-Marshal Sir John Dill and the Anglo-American Alliance, 1941–1944* (London: Brassey's, 1986).

Danchev, Alex: *On Specialness: Essays in Anglo-American Relations* (New York: St. Martin's Press, 1998).

Davis, Lynn E.: *The Cold War Begins: Soviet–American Conflict Over Eastern Europe, 1943–1947* (Princeton, NJ: Princeton University Press, 1974).

Deane, John R.: *The Strange Alliance: The Story of Our Wartime Co-operation with Russia* (New York: Viking, 1947).

DeNovo, John: "The Culbertson Economic Mission and Anglo-American Tensions in the Middle East, 1944–1945." *Journal of American History* 63 (March 1977), 913–36.

Dilks, David (ed.): *The Diaries of Sir Alexander Cadogan, 1938–1945* (New York: G. P. Putnam's Sons, 1972).

Divine, Robert A.: *Roosevelt and World War II* (Baltimore, MD: Johns Hopkins University Press, 1969).

Divine, Robert: *Second Chance: The Triumph of Internationalism in America during World War II* (New York: Atheneum, 1971).

Dobson, Alan P.: *US Wartime Aid to Britain, 1940–1946* (London: Croom Helm, 1986).

Douglas, Roy: *From War to Cold War, 1942–1948* (New York: St. Martin's Press, 1981).

Dower, John W.: *War without Mercy: Race and Power in the Pacific War* (New York: Pantheon, 1986).

Drachman, Edward R.: *United States Policy toward Vietnam, 1940–1945* (Rutherford, NJ: Fairleigh Dickinson University Press, 1970).

Draper, Theodore: "Neoconservative History." *New York Review of Books* (January 16 and 24; and April 24, 1986).

Draper, Theodore: *A Present of Things Past: Selected Essays* (New York: Hill and Wang, 1990).

Dunn, Dennis: *Caught between Roosevelt and Stalin: America's Ambassadors to Moscow* (Lexington: University of Kentucky Press, 1998).

Dunn, Walter S.: *Second Front Now 1943* (University Park: University of Alabama Press, 1980).

Edmonds, Robin: *The Big Three: Churchill, Roosevelt, and Stalin in Peace and War* (New York: W. W. Norton, 1991).

Eisenhower, David: *Eisenhower: At War, 1943–1945* (New York: Random House, 1986).

Emerson, William: "Franklin Roosevelt as Commander-in-Chief in World War II." *Military Affairs* 22 (winter 1958–9), 181–207.

Eubank, Keith: *Summit at Teheran* (New York: William Morrow, 1985).

Feis, Herbert: *Churchill, Roosevelt and Stalin: The War They Waged and the Peace They Sought* (Princeton, NJ: Princeton University Press, 1957).

Feis, Herbert: *Japan Subdued: The Atomic Bomb and the End of the War in the Far East* (Princeton, NJ: Princeton University Press, 1961).

Fleming, D. F.: *The Cold War and Its Origins, 1917–1960*, 2 vols. (New York: Doubleday, 1961).

Fraser, David: *Alanbrooke* (New York: Atheneum, 1982).

Funk, Arthur L.: *The Politics of TORCH: The Allied Landings and the Algiers Putsch, 1942* (Lawrence: University of Kansas Press, 1974).

Gaddis, John L.: *The United States and the Origins of the Cold War, 1941–1947* (New York: Columbia University Press, 1972).

Gaddis, John L.: *Strategies of Containment: A Critical Appraisal of Postwar American National Security Policy* (New York: Oxford University Press, 1982).

Gallicchio, Marc S.: *The Cold War Begins in Asia: American East Asian Policy and the Fall of the Japanese Empire* (New York: Columbia University Press, 1988).

Gallicchio, Marc S.: *The African American Encounter with Japan and China: Black Internationalism in Asia, 1895–1945* (Chapel Hill: University of North Carolina Press, 2000).

Gardner, Lloyd C.: *Economic Aspects of New Deal Diplomacy* (Madison: University of Wisconsin Press, 1964).

Gardner, Lloyd C.: *Architects of Illusion: Men and Idea in American Foreign Policy, 1941–1949* (Chicago, IL: Quadrangle, 1970).

Gardner, Lloyd: *Spheres of Influence: The Great Powers Partition Europe, from Munich to Yalta* (Chicago, IL: Ivan R. Dee, 1993).

Gellman, Irwin F.: *Good Neighbor Diplomacy: United States Policies in Latin America, 1933–1945* (Baltimore, MD: Johns Hopkins University Press, 1979).

Gellman, Irwin F.: *Secret Affairs: Franklin Roosevelt, Cordell Hull, and Sumner Welles* (Baltimore, MD: Johns Hopkins University Press, 1995).

Giangreco, D. M.: "Casualty Projections for the US Invasion of Japan, 1945–1946: Planning and Policy Implications." *Journal of Military History* 61 (July 1997), 521–81.

Gilbert, Martin: *Auschwitz and the Allies* (New York: Holt, Rinehart and Winston, 1981).

Gilbert, Martin: *Winston S. Churchill, 7: Road to Victory, 1941–1945* (Boston, MA: Houghton Mifflin, 1986).

Gorodetsky, Gabriel: *Stafford Cripps' Mission to Moscow, 1940–1942* (Cambridge: Cambridge University Press, 1984).

Greenfield, Kent Roberts: *The Historian and the Army* (New Brunswick, NJ: Rutgers University Press, 1954).

Greenfield, Kent Roberts (ed.): *Command Decisions* (Washington, DC: US Government Printing Office, 1960).

Greenfield, Kent Roberts: *American Strategy in World War II: A Reconsideration* (Baltimore, MD: Johns Hopkins University Press, 1963).

Harbutt, Fraser J.: *The Iron Curtain: Churchill, America, and the Origins of the Cold War* (New York: Oxford University Press, 1986).

Harper, John L.: *American Visions of Europe: Franklin D. Roosevelt, George F. Kennan and Dean G. Acheson* (Cambridge: Cambridge University Press, 1994).

Hathaway, Robert M.: *Ambiguous Partnership: Britain and America, 1944–1947* (New York: Columbia University Press, 1981).

Henrikson, Alan: "The Map as an 'Idea': The Role of Cartographic Imagery During the Second World War." *The American Cartographer* 2 (April 1975), 19–53.

Herring, George C.: *Aid to Russia, 1941–1946: Strategy, Diplomacy, and the Origins of the Cold War* (New York: Columbia University Press, 1973).

Hess, Gary R.: *America Encounters India, 1941–1947* (Baltimore, MD: Johns Hopkins University Press, 1971).

Hess, Gary R.: "Franklin Roosevelt and Indochina." *Journal of American History* 59 (September 1972), 353–68.

Hess, Gary R.: *The United States' Emergence as a Southeast Asian Power, 1940–1950* (New York: Columbia University Press, 1987).

Higgins, Trumbull: *Soft Underbelly: The Anglo-American Controversy over the Italian Campaign* (New York: Macmillan, 1968).

Hilderbrand, Robert C.: *Dumbarton Oaks: The Origins of the United Nations and the Search for Postwar Security* (Chapel Hill: University of North Carolina Press, 1990).

Hogan, Michael J.: *Hiroshima in History and Memory* (New York: Cambridge University Press, 1996).

Hogan, Michael J. and Thomas G. Paterson (eds.): *Explaining the History of American Foreign Relations* (New York: Cambridge University Press, 1991).

"How has the United States Met its Major Challenges since 1945: A Symposium." *Commentary* 80 (November 1985), 25–8, 50–2, 56–60, 73–6.

Howard, Michael: *The Mediterranean Strategy in the Second World War* (New York: Praeger, 1968).

Hurstfield, Julian G.: *America and the French Nation, 1939–1945* (Chapel Hill: University of North Carolina Press, 1986).

Iriye, Akira: *Power and Culture: The Japanese–American War, 1941–1945* (Cambridge, MA: Harvard University Press, 1981).

Jakub, Jay: *Spies and Saboteurs: Anglo-American Collaboration and Rivalry in Human Intelligence Collection and Special Operations, 1940–45* (New York: St. Martin's Press, 1999).

James, D. Clayton: *The Years of MacArthur*, 3 vols. (Boston, MA: Houghton Mifflin, 1970–85).

James, D. Clayton: *A Time for Giants: The Politics of the American High Command in World War II* (New York: Franklin Watts, 1987).

Jones, Matthew: *Britain, the United States and the Mediterranean War, 1942–44* (New York: St. Martin's Press, 1996).

Kimball, Warren F.: *The Most Unsordid Act: Lend-Lease, 1939–1941* (Baltimore, MD: Johns Hopkins University Press, 1969).

Kimball, Warren F.: *Swords or Plowshares?: The Morgenthau Plan for Defeated Nazi Germany, 1943–1946* (Philadelphia, PA: Lippincott, 1976).

Kimball, Warren F. (ed.): *Churchill and Roosevelt: The Complete Correspondence* (Princeton, NJ: Princeton University Press, 1984).

Kimball, Warren F.: *The Juggler: Franklin Roosevelt as Wartime Statesman* (Princeton, NJ: Princeton University Press, 1991).

Kimball, Warren F. (ed.): *America Unbound: World War II and the Making of a Superpower* (New York: St. Martin's Press, 1992).

Kimball, Warren F.: "Wheel Within a Wheel: Churchill, Roosevelt and the Special Relationship." In Robert Blake and William Roger Louis (eds.) *Churchill* (New York: W. W. Norton, 1993).

Kimball, Warren F.: *Forged in War: Roosevelt, Churchill and the Second World War* (New York: William Morrow, 1997).

Kimball, Warren F.: "The Incredible Shrinking War: The Second World War, Not (just) the Origins of the Cold War." *Diplomatic History* 25 (summer 2001), 347–65.

Kitchen, Martin: *British Policy Towards the Soviet Union During the Second World War* (New York: St. Martin's Press, 1986).

Kochavi, Arieh J.: *Prelude to Nuremberg: Allied War Crimes Policy and the Question of Punishment* (Chapel Hill: University of North Carolina Press, 1998).

Kolko, Gabriel: *The Politics of War: The World and United States Foreign Policy, 1943–1945* (New York: Random House, 1968).

LaFeber, Walter: "Roosevelt, Churchill, and Indochina, 1942–1945." *American Historical Review* 80 (December 1975), 1277–95.

Lane, Ann and Howard Temperly (eds.): *The Rise and Fall of the Grand Alliance, 1941–1945* (New York: St. Martin's Press, 1995).

Laqueur, Walter: *The Terrible Secret: Suppression of the Truth About Hitler's "Final Solution"* (Boston, MA: Little, Brown, 1980).

Larrabee, Eric: *Commander in Chief: Franklin D. Roosevelt, His Lieutenants, and Their War* (New York: Harper and Row, 1987).

Lee, Loyd E.: "We Have Just Begun to Write." *Diplomatic History* 25 (summer 2001), 367–81.

Leffler, Melvyn P.: "Adherents to Agreements: Yalta and the Experiences of the Early Cold War." *International Security* 11 (summer 1986), 88–123.

Leffler, Melvyn P.: *A Preponderance of Power: National Security, the Truman Administration, and the Cold War* (Stanford, CA: Stanford University Press, 1992).

Leigh, Michael: *Mobilizing Consent: Public Opinion and American Foreign Policy, 1937–1947* (Westport, CT: Greenwood Press, 1976).

Levering, Ralph B.: *American Opinion and the Russian Alliance, 1939–1945* (Chapel Hill: University of North Carolina Press, 1976).

Linenthal, Edward T. and Tom Englehardt (eds.) *History Wars: The Enola Gay and Other Battles for the American Past* (New York: Henry Holt, 1996).

Lipstadt, Deborah: *Beyond Belief: The American Press and the Coming of the Holocaust, 1933–1945* (New York: Free Press, 1985).

Litoff, Judy B. and David C. Smith (eds.): *What Kind of World Do We Want? American Women Plan for Peace* (Wilmington, DE: Scholarly Resources, 2000).

Louis, William Roger: *Imperialism at Bay: The United States and the Decolonization of the British Empire, 1941–1945* (New York: Oxford University Press, 1978).

Lowenheim, Francis L., Harold Langley, and Manfred Jonas (eds.): *Roosevelt and Churchill: Their Secret Wartime Correspondence* (New York: Saturday Review Press/E. P. Dutton, 1975).

Lukas, Richard C.: *Eagles East: The Army Air Forces and the Soviet Union, 1941–1945* (Tallahassee: Florida State University Press, 1970).

Lukas, Richard C.: *The Strange Allies: The United States and Poland, 1941–1945* (Knoxville: University of Tennessee Press, 1978).

Lundestad, Geir: *The American Non-Policy towards Eastern Europe, 1943–1947: Universalism in an Area Not of Essential Interest to the United States* (New York: Humanities Press, 1975).

Lytle, Mark H.: *The Origins of the Iranian–American Alliance, 1941–1953* (New York: Holmes and Meier, 1987).

McCagg, William O.: *Stalin Embattled, 1943–1948* (Detroit, MI: Wayne State University Press, 1978).

McCann, Frank D.: *The Brazilian–American Alliance, 1937–1945* (Princeton, NJ: Princeton University Press, 1973).

McJimsey, George T.: *Harry Hopkins: Ally of the Poor and Defender of Democracy* (Cambridge, MA: Harvard University Press, 1987).

McNeill, William H.: *America, Britain and Russia: Their Cooperation and Conflict, 1941–1946* (New York: Oxford University Press, 1953).

Mark, Edward: "American Policy toward Eastern Europe and the Origins of the Cold War, 1941–1946: An Alternative Interpretation." *Journal of American History* 68 (September 1981), 313–36.

Mark, Edward: "October or Thermidor? Interpretations of Stalinism and the Perception of Soviet Foreign Policy in the United States, 1927–1947." *American Historical Review* 94 (October 1989), 937–62.

Marks, Frederick W., III: *Wind Over Sand: The Diplomacy of Franklin Roosevelt* (Athens, GA: University of Georgia Press, 1988).

Martel, Leon: *Lend-Lease, Loans, and the Coming of the Cold War: A Study of the Implementation of Foreign Policy* (Boulder, CO: Westview Press, 1979).

Mastny, Vojtech: *Russia's Road to the Cold War: Diplomacy, Wafare, and the Politics of Communism, 1941–1945* (New York: Columbia University Press, 1979).

Matloff, Maurice: "Franklin Delano Roosevelt as War Leader." In Harry L. Coles (ed.) *Total War and Cold War: Problems in Civilian Control of the Military* (Columbus: Ohio State University Press, 1962).

Matray, James I.: *The Reluctant Crusade: American Foreign Policy in Korea, 1941–1950* (Honolulu: University of Hawaii Press, 1985).

Miles, Rufus E., Jr.: "Hiroshima: The Strange Myth of Half a Million Lives Saved." *International Security* 10 (fall 1985), 121–40.

Miller, Aaron D.: *Search for Security: Saudi Arabian Oil and American Foreign Policy, 1939–1949* (Chapel Hill: University of North Carolina Press, 1980).

Miller, John Edward: *The United States and Italy, 1940–1950* (Chapel Hill: University of North Carolina Press, 1986).

Miner, Steven M.: *Between Churchill and Stalin: The Soviet Union, Great Britain, and the Origins of the Grand Alliance* (Chapel Hill: University of North Carolina Press, 1988).

Ministry of Foreign Affairs, USSR: *Russia: Correspondence between the Chairman of the Council of Ministers of the USSR and the Presidents of the USA and the Prime Ministers of Great Britain during the Great Patriotic War of 1941–1945*, 2 vols. (Moscow: Foreign Languages Publishing House, 1957).

Morison, Samuel Eliot: *History of United States Naval Operations in World War II*, 15 vols. (Boston, MA: Little, Brown, 1947–62).

Nadeau, Remi: *Stalin, Churchill, and Roosevelt Divide Europe* (New York: Praeger, 1990).

Newman, Robert P.: *Truman and the Hiroshima Cult* (East Lansing: Michigan State University Press, 1995).

Newton, Verne W. (ed.): *FDR and the Holocaust* (New York: St. Martin's Press, 1996).

Ninkovich, Frank A.: *The Diplomacy of Ideas: US Foreign Policy and Cultural Relations, 1938–1950* (New York: Cambridge University Press, 1981).

Nisbet, Robert: *Roosevelt and Stalin: The Failed Courtship* (Washington, DC: Regnery Gateway, 1988).

O'Connor, Raymond G.: *Diplomacy for Victory: FDR and Unconditional Surrender* (New York: W. W. Norton, 1971).

Painter, David S.: *Oil and the American Century: The Political Economy of US Foreign Oil Policy, 1941–1954* (Baltimore, MD: Johns Hopkins University Press, 1986).

Parrish, Michael E.: "Soviet Espionage and the Cold War." *Diplomatic History* 25 (winter 2001), 105–20.

Paterson, Thomas G.: *Soviet–American Confrontation: Postwar Reconstruction and the Origins of the Cold War* (Baltimore, MD: Johns Hopkins University Press, 1973).

Penkower, Monty N.: *The Jews Were Expendable: Free World Diplomacy and the Holocaust, 1933–1945* (Urbana: University of Illinois Press, 1983).

Perlmutter, Amos: *FDR and Stalin: A Not So Grand Alliance, 1943–1945* (Columbia: University of Missouri Press, 1993).

Plummer, Brenda G.: *Rising Wind: Black Americans and US Foreign Affairs, 1935–1960* (Chapel Hill: University of North Carolina Press, 1996).

Pogue, Forrest C.: *George C. Marshall*, 4 vols. (New York: Viking, 1963–87).

Resis, Albert: "The Churchill–Stalin 'Percentages' Agreement on the Balkans, Moscow, October 1944." *American Historical Review* 83 (April 1978), 368–87.

Resis, Albert: "Spheres of Influence in Soviet Wartime Diplomacy." *Journal of Modern History* 53 (September 1981), 417–39.

Reynolds, David: "Roosevelt, Churchill, and the Wartime Anglo-American Alliance: Towards a New Synthesis." In William Roger Louis and Hedley Bull (eds.) *The "Special Relationship": Anglo-American Relations since 1945* (Oxford: Oxford University Press, 1986).

Reynolds, David: "The 'Big Three' and the Division of Europe, 1945–1948: An Overview." *Diplomacy and Statecraft* 1 (July 1990), 111–36.

Reynolds, David: *Rich Relations: The American Occupation of Britain, 1942–1945* (New York: Random House, 1995).

Reynolds, David: "World War II and Modern Meanings." *Diplomatic History* 25 (summer 2001), 457–72.

Reynolds, David, Warren F. Kimball, and A. O. Chubarian (eds.) *Allies at War: The Soviet, American, and British Experience, 1939–1945* (New York: St. Martin's Press, 1994).

Roberts, Walter R.: *Tito, Mihailovic and the Allies, 1941–1945* (New Brunswick, NJ: Rutgers University Press, 1973).

Rothwell, Victor: *Britain and the Cold War, 1941–1947* (London: Jonathan Cape, 1982).

Rubin, Barry: *The Great Powers in the Middle East, 1941–1947: The Road to the Cold War* (New York: Oxford University Press, 1980).

Rubinstein, William: *The Myth of Rescue: Why the Democracies Could Not Have Saved More Jews from the Holocaust* (New York: Routledge, 1997).

Sainsbury, Keith: *The Turning Point: Roosevelt, Stalin, Churchill, and Chiang Kai-shek, 1943: The Moscow, Cairo and Teheran Conferences* (New York: Oxford University Press, 1985).

Sbrega, John J.: *Anglo-American Relations and Colonialism in East Asia* (New York: Garland, 1983).

Schaller, Michael: *The US Crusade in China, 1938–1945* (New York: Columbia University Press, 1979).

Schaller, Michael: *Douglas MacArthur. The Far Eastern General* (New York: Oxford University Press, 1989).

Schrijvers, Peter: *The Crash of Ruin: American Combat Soldiers in Europe during World War II* (Washington Square, NY: New York University Press, 1998).

Sevostionov, G. N. and W. F. Kimball (eds.): *Soviet–US Relations, 1933–1942* (Moscow: Progress Publishers, 1989).

Sexton, Donal J., Jr. (compiler): *Signals Intelligence in World War II: A Research Guide* (Westport, CT: Greenwood Press, 1996).

Sherry, Michael S.: *Preparing for the Next War: American Plans for Postwar Defense, 1941–1945* (New Haven, CT: Yale University Press, 1977).

Sherry, Michael S.: *The Rise of American Air Power: The Creation of Armageddon* (New Haven, CT: Yale University Press, 1987).

Sherwin, Martin J.: *A World Destroyed: The Atomic Bomb and the Grand Alliance* (New York: Vintage, 1975).

Shulman, Holly C.: *The Voice of America: Propaganda and Democracy, 1941–1945* (Madison: University of Wisconsin Press, 1990).

Sigal, Leon V.: *Fighting to a Finish: The Politics of War Termination in the United States and Japan, 1945* (Ithaca, NY: Cornell University Press, 1988).

Smith, Bradley F.: *The Ultra-Magic Deals and the Most Secret Special Relationship, 1940–1946* (Novato, CA: Presidio, 1993).

Smith, Bradley F.: *Sharing Secrets with Stalin: How the Allies Traded Intelligence, 1941–1945* (Lawrence: University of Kansas Press, 1996).

Smith, Gaddis: *American Diplomacy During the Second World War, 1941–1945*, 2nd edn. (New York: Alfred A. Knopf, 1985).

Snell, John L. (ed.): *The Meaning of Yalta: Big Three Diplomacy and the New World Balance of Power* (Baton Rouge: Louisiana State University Press, 1956).

Snell, John L.: *Illusion and Necessity: The Diplomacy of Global War, 1939–1945* (Boston, MA: Houghton Mifflin, 1963).

Steele, Richard W.: *The First Offensive, 1942: Roosevelt, Marshall and the Making of American Strategy* (Bloomington: Indiana University Press, 1973).

Stoff, Michael: *Oil, War and American Security: The Search for a National Policy on Foreign Oil, 1941–1947* (New Haven, CT: Yale University Press, 1980).

Stoler, Mark A.: *The Politics of the Second Front: American Military Planning and Diplomacy in Coalition Warfare, 1941–1943* (Westport, CT: Greenwood Press, 1977).

Stoler, Mark A.: *George C. Marshall: Soldier–Statesman of the American Century* (Boston, MA: Twayne, 1989).

Stoler, Mark A.: "A Half Century of Conflict: Interpretations of US World War II Diplomacy." *Diplomatic History* 18 (summer 1994), 375–403.

Stoler, Mark A.: *Allies and Adversaries: The Joint Chiefs of Staff, the Grand Alliance, and US Strategy in World War II* (Chapel Hill: University of North Carolina Press, 2000).

Stoler, Mark A.: "The Second World War in US History and Memory." *Diplomatic History* 25 (summer 2001), 383–92.

Taubman, William: *Stalin's American Policy: From Entente to Détente to Cold War* (New York: W. W. Norton, 1982).

Thelen, David et. al.: "History and the Public: What Can We Handle? A Round Table about History after the *Enola Gay* Controversy." *Journal of American History* 82 (December 1995), 1029–135.

Theoharis, Athan: *The Yalta Myths: An Issue in US Politics, 1945–1955* (Columbia: University of Missouri Press, 1970).

Thorne, Christopher: "Indochina and Anglo-American Relations, 1942–1945." *Pacific Historical Review* 45 (February 1976), 73–96.

Thorne, Christopher: *Allies of a Kind: The United States, Britain and the War against Japan, 1941–1945* (New York: Oxford University Press, 1978).

Thorne, Christopher: *The Issue of War: States, Societies, and the Far Eastern Conflict of 1941–1945* (New York: Oxford University Press, 1985).

Tuchman, Barbara W.: *Stilwell and the American Experience in China, 1911–1945* (New York: Macmillan, 1970).

Tuttle, Dwight W.: *Harry L. Hopkins and Anglo-American–Soviet Relations, 1941–1945* (New York: Garland, 1983).

United States Army, Center for Military History: *United States Army in World War II*, 79 vols. (Washington, DC: US Government Printing Office).

Villa, Brian J.: "The US Army, Unconditional Surrender, and the Potsdam Declaration." *Journal of American History* 63 (June 1976), 66–92.

Villa, Brian J.: "The Atomic Bomb and the Normandy Invasion." *Perspectives in American History* 11 (1977–8), 463–502.

Viorst, Milton: *Hostile Allies: FDR and Charles de Gaulle* (New York: Macmillan, 1965).

Von Eschen, Penny M.: *Race Against Empire: Black Americans and Anticolonialism, 1937–1957* (Ithaca, NY: Cornell University Press, 1997).

Walker, J. Samuel.: "The Decision to Use the Bomb: A Historiographical Update." *Diplomatic History* 14 (winter 1990), 97–114.

Walker, J. Samuel.: *Prompt and Utter Destruction: Truman and the Use of the Atomic Bombs Against Japan* (Chapel Hill: University of North Carolina Pres, 1997).

Ward, Geoffrey: "On Writing about FDR." *American Heritage* 23 (summer 1991).

Watt, Donald Cameron: "Britain and the Historiography of the Yalta Conference and the Cold War." *Diplomatic History* 13 (winter 1989), 67–98.

Weiss, Steve: *Allies in Conflict: Anglo-American Strategic Negotiations, 1938–1944* (New York: St. Martin's Press, 1996).

White, Dorothy S.: *Seeds of Discord: De Gaulle, Free France and the Allies* (Syracuse, NY: Syracuse University Press, 1964).

Widenor, William C.: "American Planning for the United Nations: Have We Been Asking the Right Question?" *Diplomatic History* 6 (summer 1982), 245–65.

Williams, William Appleman: *The Tragedy of American Diplomacy*, enlarged revd. edn. (New York: Dell, 1962).

Wilmot, Chester: *The Struggle for Europe* (New York: Harper and Brothers, 1952).

Winkler, Allan M.: *The Politics of Propaganda: The Office of War Information, 1942–1945* (New Haven, CT: Yale University Press, 1978).

Winterbotham, F. W.: *The Ultra Secret* (London: Weidenfeld, 1974).

Woods, Randall B.: *The Roosevelt Foreign Policy Establishment and the Good Neighbor: The United States and Argentina, 1941–1945* (Lawrence: University of Kansas Press, 1979).

Woods, Randall B.: *A Changing of the Guard: Anglo-American Relations, 1941–1946* (Chapel Hill: University of North Carolina Press, 1990).

Woodward, Sir Llewellyn: *British Foreign Policy in the Second World War*, 1 vol. abridged and 5 vols. (London: Her Majesty's Stationery Office, 1962, 1970–6).

Wyman, David S.: *The Abandonment of the Jews: America and the Holocaust, 1941–1945* (New York: Pantheon, 1984).

Yergin, Daniel: *Shattered Peace: The Origins of the Cold War and the National Security State* (Boston, MA: Houghton Mifflin, 1977; revd. edn., New York: 1990).

CHAPTER THIRTEEN

The Early Cold War

JEREMI SURI

A half-century after the French Revolution, Alexis de Tocqueville concluded that this cataclysmic event grew from a series of developments under the Old Regime. The mass upheaval of 1789 transformed the landscape of Europe, but it also shared important continuities with social and political activities during prior decades. Historical perspective did not diminish the importance of the French Revolution; it blurred the lines of rupture between one era and another (de Tocqueville 1998).

The scholarship on the early Cold War has reached a similar Tocquevillian moment. More than fifty years removed from the "origins" of the Soviet–American conflict, historians have shifted their gaze from some of the questions that animated scholars of a prior generation: Who was responsible for the Cold War? When did the Cold War begin? What were the alternatives to the Cold War? These questions remain interesting, but they no longer dominate research and debate. Recognizing that the Cold War grew from conditions and circumstances in prior decades, historians now focus on the inherited assumptions, memories, and institutions that made Soviet–American hostility difficult to avoid. The most influential recent works have explained the events of the early Cold War in light of pre-1945 legacies. Conflict in Europe and Asia between 1945 and 1949 reflected the "lessons" that leaders believed they had learned in the immediate past.

US National Security

The United States was never really "isolated" from Europe and Asia, but after World War II even the illusion of isolation became untenable. The Japanese strike on Pearl Harbor illustrated how the Atlantic and Pacific Oceans no longer insulated North America from sudden foreign attack. Nazi Germany's near conquest of the entire European continent pointed to the vulnerability of American trade interests and cultural connections in the "Old World." Seared by their failure to prevent the rise of Japanese and German threats in the 1930s, American leaders vowed to replace prior policies of "neutrality" and "appeasement" with a firmer emphasis on long-run "national security."

This term became common among the men who planned for American foreign policy after World War II. "National security" expanded upon previous conceptions of territorial defense and hemispheric hegemony. American leaders now recognized that the nation's peace and prosperity required action against threatening "totalitarian" forces in far away areas. Despite their geographic distance, enemies could cut-off access to markets, foment revolution, and mobilize modern technology to threaten the physical safety of the United States and its allies. The American sense of democratic mission merged with a profound sense of foreign threat to make national security a truly international undertaking.

The most influential US policymakers after World War II – Harry Truman, James Byrnes, George Marshall, Dean Acheson, Averell Harriman, John McCloy, and George Kennan – worked to reconstruct Europe and Asia in ways that would replicate American values and, therefore, protect American interests. Melvyn Leffler explains that these values and interests went hand-in-hand. Leaders in Washington were "driven less by a desire to help others than by an ideological conviction that their own political economy of freedom would be jeopardized if a totalitarian foe became too powerful" (Leffler 1992: 13). The nation's security became synonymous with the spread of liberty and free enterprise, or at least the defeat of those regimes most antithetical to these inherited ideals.

The postwar American conception of national security emphasized strength, preparedness, and extensive reach as it never had before. In its most hopeful moments, this perspective promised a world of peace and cooperation dominated by President Franklin Roosevelt's "Four Freedoms" – freedom from fear, freedom from want, freedom of speech, and freedom of worship. In a return to the program of Woodrow Wilson, many Americans hoped to create a new international body – the United Nations – designed to promote peace, prosperity, human rights, and collective security. This vision, however, had a dark side. Recognizing that some states would continue to pursue aggression instead of cooperation, Washington prepared to act as a world policeman. American national security planners presumed that the nation faced evil and irredeemable threats that the United States had to "contain" or "rollback" with force.

Despite its experience as a US ally against Germany and Japan, the Soviet Union became the focus of American apprehensions by the end of World War II. Moscow's huge land army dominated the Eastern half of Europe, the area around the Middle East, and parts of Northeastern Asia. The Soviet Union also sponsored communist parties in many West European societies, particularly France, Italy, and the Western sectors of occupied Germany. Perhaps most significant for popular American perceptions, Soviet dictator Josef Stalin had displayed a pattern of brutality toward his own people and neighboring populations that included the purges and forced collectivization of the 1930s, the Nazi–Soviet Pact that divided Poland in 1939, and the forced deportations of ethnic groups that accompanied the defeat of Germany.

The distrust that characterized Stalin's relations with British Prime Minister Winston Churchill and American President Franklin Roosevelt deepened in the immediate postwar years. This was the point of Churchill's famous speech in Fulton, Missouri on March 5, 1946: "From Stettin in the Baltic to Trieste in the Adriatic, an iron curtain has descended across the Continent . . . This is certainly not the Liberated Europe we fought to build up. Nor is it one which contains the essentials of permanent peace" (James 1980: 881–2).

A traditional balance of power between the two strongest powers – the United States and the Soviet Union – was not enough. Nor was another war necessary. Churchill counseled that "there is nothing [the Soviets] admire so much as strength, and there is nothing for which they have less respect than for weakness, especially military weakness . . . We cannot afford, if we can help it, to work on narrow margins, offering temptations to a trial of strength" (ibid: 883). Through close political and economic cooperation, extensive military preparation, and American leadership, the "western democracies" could, according to Churchill, prohibit threatening Soviet expansion.

This perspective came to dominate American policymaking. One month before Churchill's speech, George Kennan – then the American chargé d'affaires in Moscow – outlined a similar argument in an 8,000 word "Long Telegram" to Washington. Describing the "negative" and "destructive" nature of Soviet power, Kennan predicted that Stalin would limit his expansion "when strong resistance is encountered at any point" (FRUS 1946: 706–7). Churchill and Kennan contributed to the formulation of the Truman Doctrine in March 1947, and the subsequent association of global Soviet "containment" with America's national security.

Recent debates among historians center on this moment between 1946 and 1947. The Cold War emerged during this period from the tensions, difficulties, and fears that lingered after World War II. Few scholars argue that Soviet–American tensions were avoidable, and few devote much time to spinning alternative scenarios for a complex postwar world. Many historians, however, disagree about the implications of Washington's containment policy. Was containment the most prudent response to the Soviet threat? What were its consequences for American foreign policy and domestic society in later years? To what extent did containment distort American perceptions of national security?

Melvyn Leffler's detailed and balanced account sets the standard for many of these debates. As noted above, he describes how American ideals and interests merged in the pursuit of a stable international order. Fearful of the threats that Soviet armies and ideas could pose to this order, the Truman administration hedged its bets. It emphasized strength and resolve along the lines articulated by Churchill and Kennan. The president predicated his commitment to Soviet containment on the assumption that the US could retain unparalleled capabilities in all areas of endeavor – military, economic, technological, and cultural. He and his advisers would not countenance the rise of another "totalitarian" enemy in control of Europe or Asia. "Prudent men aware of the wealth and power of the United States could not allow such worst-case scenarios to unfold" (Leffler 1992: 503).

America constructed an extraordinary international "preponderance of power" designed to ensure national security with maximum possible leverage over the Soviet adversary (ibid: 15–19). Through a mix of policies that included massive quantities of American aid under the Marshall Plan, anti-communist covert activities under the direction of the newly created Central Intelligence Agency (CIA), and the development of sophisticated nuclear weapons, the Truman administration prepared to negotiate with Moscow from a position of dominance. Stalin and other potential adversaries would never acquire the military and economic advantages that had fueled the advances of Hitler and Japanese Emperor Hirohito. Instead of appeasement or total war, a preponderance of power called for preventive action, designed to coerce good behavior from a dangerous adversary. This curious emphasis on strength without war kept the Cold War cold, but it also deepened its costs.

This is where Leffler sees American prudence turning to foolishness. In seeking preponderant power, American leaders exaggerated the Soviet threat. US conceptions of national security focused too narrowly on support for anti-communism, even at the cost of democracy. American leaders failed to differentiate nationalists like Mao Zedong and Ho Chi Minh from the Soviet puppets in parts of Eastern Europe. As a consequence, US aid went to dictators like Chiang Kai-shek and Syngman Rhee who were little better than Stalin. American military commitments stretched far beyond vital economic and strategic areas, supporting these corrupt and anti-democratic leaders in the cause of anti-communism. The US also built a huge military arsenal, including atomic weapons and after 1952 thermonuclear bombs, that far exceeded the necessities of Soviet containment in key areas. American power grew so great after World War II, Leffler argues, that it "engendered legitimate security apprehensions in the Soviet Union" (ibid: 516–17). In a classic case of what political scientists call the "security dilemma," Moscow perceived an offensive threat in America's defensive buildup (Jervis 2001). The pursuit of US national security through preponderance produced unintended insecurities.

For Leffler, the wisdom of Churchill and Kennan was misapplied. The Truman administration failed to discriminate between prudent analyses of Soviet threats in Europe and hysterical fears of Moscow's meddling in far away areas. The Cold War expanded to the detriment of America's core economic and security interests. Excessive militarism distracted attention from the most important and enduring American endeavors: European economic reconstruction, Japanese democratization, and international cooperation through the United Nations and other postwar organizations.

The institutions born of the Cold War departed from traditional American images of democracy. Drawing on Leffler's analysis, this is what Michael Hogan means when he writes of the post-World War II "national security state." According to the terms of the National Security Act of 1947 – "the Magna Carta" for the national security state, according to Hogan – a series of government bureaucracies emerged to keep the US permanently prepared for war. The National Security Council (NSC) became a central body where the White House coordinated the nation's military forces and economic activities with only very limited Congressional oversight. The creation of a secretary of defense (in place of the secretary of war) and a Joint Chiefs of Staff (JCS) allowed the armed forces to become a larger and more permanent presence in society. During World War II the Manhattan Project had been unusual in its coordination of military facilities, scientific research, and industrial resources. With the emergence of the Cold War national security state, however, these military–industrial activities grew in size and frequency, to the point where they pervaded American society. In addition, Hogan explains, the CIA developed as a mechanism for covert government activities, allowing the president to allocate national resources for secret meddling in foreign societies. These institutions, and many others, created "a permanent blurring of the usual distinctions between war and peace, citizen and soldier, civil and military" (Hogan 1998: 66). A policy that emphasized preponderant power gave priority to centralized armed forces. In this sense, the Cold War was an extension of World War II conditions (Sherry 1995).

While Leffler argues that the national security state perpetuated the Cold War by provoking Soviet insecurities, Hogan points to the incentives for anti-communist conflict inscribed in the functioning of American institutions. Each of the three armed services – the army, navy, and air force – played on public fears of war with the Soviet Union to justify expanded budgets. This was particularly the case in 1948, following the communist coup in Czechoslovakia that February. The evidence of Soviet aggression produced a $4.1 billion supplemental increase in the proposed $9.8 billion defense budget for the year, despite the president's fiscally conservative inclinations (Hogan 1998: 113). Peace with Moscow would remove the apparent need for these fiscal infusions. Cold War conflict, however, allowed the national security state to demand ever-increasing resources. Exaggerated Soviet fears gave the military priority over social services and other domestic programs that originally held higher importance for the Truman administration.

Hogan is careful to show that the demands of the national security state did not completely eradicate traditional attachments to free enterprise, individualism, and sound fiscal management. Conservative Republicans and Democrats distrusted centralized power, they abhorred higher taxes, and they rejected creeping infringements on the autonomy of small communities. Anti-communists to be sure, men like Ohio Senator Robert Taft drew on inherited symbols of the "American way of life" to warn against national security producing a "garrison state" that resembled Nazi Germany or the Soviet Union (ibid: 18). These apprehensions led to the congressional defeat of a bill for universal military training in 1948. Motivated to contain the Soviet Union without the creation of large "Prussian" standing armies, the Truman administration gave particular attention to the expansion of air power – long-range aircraft, warheads (conventional and atomic), and eventually rockets. Both Truman and his successor, Dwight Eisenhower, pressed for balanced budgets to prohibit profligate spending and excessive growth in the federal government.

The national security state constituted a compromise between various interests. It promoted the mobilization of preponderant American power for conflict with a perceived Soviet threat. It placed the United States on a permanent war footing, but it did so in a way that generally preserved core conceptions of democracy. McCarthyism was a moment of excess that revealed the domestic dangers of anti-communism, but also the eventual limits on militarization built into this system. In this context, Hogan's book shares many similarities in substance, if not in tone, with Aaron Friedberg's (2000) analysis of how the US avoided becoming a "garrison state" during the Cold War.

Curiously, Hogan refrains from associating the national security state and America's Cold War policies with the model of "corporatism" that he famously applied to the Marshall Plan in an earlier book (Hogan 1987). One can, however, see corporatism at the root of the national security state. Various constituencies – the president, the military, the Congress, the business community, organized labor, and the media – worked to create a set of Cold War institutions that served their mutual interests. A stronger military meant more presidential power, patriotic positions for congressional representatives, money for business and labor, and popular stories for journalists. Working to build preponderant power in a framework that appealed to symbols of democracy, all of these groups could claim that they were fighting to preserve the "American way" against communism. This fight ultimately defeated the Soviet Union, but Hogan joins Leffler in judging the costs – domestic and international – unnecessarily high (Hogan 1998: 481–2).

If the Truman administration overreacted to legitimate Soviet threats, Cold War conflict and the national security state were direct consequences. Arnold Offner agrees with this assessment. Unlike Leffler and Hogan, his book places the blame directly on the president, rather than a series of misperceptions and institutional interests. Offner argues that Truman was a "parochial nationalist" who relied on simple historical analogies, a narrow view of the international system, and a penchant for emotional toughness rather than creative thought (Offner 2002: 5, 470). From the first months when he succeeded Franklin Roosevelt in 1945, through the time of the Korean War (1950–3), the president assumed the worst in Soviet intentions, failing to pursue possible options for compromise and peaceful coexistence. He was insecure and woefully unprepared to assume the leadership of the free world. The "give 'em hell Harry" that some historians have looked back upon with nostalgia (McCullough 1992; Hamby 1995), was really simple-minded, belligerent, and self-centered.

A "give 'em hell" attitude, Offner explains, transformed the Soviet Union from a "difficult ally" into a "potential enemy who threatened America's vital interests and world peace." Making critical decisions in Europe and Asia when the international system was particularly susceptible to change, Truman reformulated policy "from the top down" (Offner 2002: 127). This was particularly the case with atomic weapons. In recent years many scholars have concluded that the American decision to drop two atomic bombs on Japan in August 1945 was a lamentable, but largely unavoidable climax to World War II in Asia. Truman authorized the bombings to end the war before a bloody American invasion of the main Japanese islands. Few presidents could have resisted the pressure to use atomic power in these circumstances (Bernstein 1995; Bundy 1988; Walker 1997). Offner differs with this interpretation. Drawing on the work of Gar Alperovitz (1985, 1995), he argues that Truman and his secretary of state, James Byrnes, "were inclined or readily tempted to use atomic bombs not merely to end the Second World War expeditiously but to 'win' the peace on US terms" (Offner 2002: 99). Instead of seeking a diplomatic end to the conflict in Asia – one that would include the Soviet Union – the president moved to create a *fait accompli* with American dominance in Japan, the southern half of Korea, and parts of mainland China. The atomic bombings were also designed to intimidate Stalin, showing him that the US had an "ace in the hole" to temper Soviet behavior, if necessary (ibid: 97). This was particularly the case for the second atomic explosion in Nagasaki on August 9, 1945. Offner explains that this bombing was unnecessary from a military point of view. It served primarily as a symbolic assertion of American toughness.

Offner's account of American "atomic diplomacy" does not provide any new evidence on this controversial topic, but it does place nuclear weapons and the Cold War in a revised narrative context. Instead of emphasizing strategic calculations like Leffler, or domestic political economy like Hogan, Offner elucidates a simpler pattern of presidential hostility to compromise with a perceived Soviet adversary. This carried through to the negotiations over international control of atomic weapons in 1946, the announcement of the Truman Doctrine (1947), the Berlin Blockade (1948–9), and the Korean War (1950–3). Churchill, Kennan, and other figures exerted influence over American foreign policy during this period because they confirmed an insecure president's inclination to lash out at his enemies. Legitimate Soviet anxieties about territorial insecurity, economic weakness, and technological inferiority failed to penetrate Truman's narrow considerations of national security.

Leffler, Hogan, and Offner have greatly advanced our understanding of the inner-workings of American foreign policy during the early Cold War. Motivated by the "lessons" of the last war and the fears of Soviet aggression, the United States formulated an expansive concept of national security that exceeded all precedents. The nation defined its political and economic interests to include nearly every corner of Europe and Asia, it pursued a strategy of preponderant power that militarized domestic politics, and it rejected compromise for toughness in its negotiations with adversaries. None of the three authors argues that the Cold War was avoidable, but all three blame American leaders for overreacting to what they contend was a limited Soviet threat.

The Soviet Threat

The collapse of the Soviet Union in 1991 has had a paradoxical effect on historical assessments of Moscow's foreign policy. On the one hand, the quick and peaceful demise of this empire, in the wake of Mikhail Gorbachev's reforms, indicates that the main communist adversary was more paper tiger than all-consuming threat. This observation confirms the perspective embedded in the books by Leffler, Hogan, and Offner. On the other hand, the fact that millions of people acted to destroy the Soviet Union at their first opportunity reveals how brutal this regime really was. East German women, to take one example, who suffered mass rape at the hands of occupying Soviet soldiers, saw Moscow as an aggressive, tyrannical power (Naimark 1995). The same cannot be said for West German views of the US (Schwartz 1991; Schwarz 1981–3). Many of the people who lived under or proximate to Soviet rule shared Truman's characterization of the Soviet threat. This observation has led some historians to see America's early Cold War foreign policy in a more favorable light.

Vladislav Zubok and Constantine Pleshakov provide an excellent example of how views of the United States change from a closer Soviet vantage point. The authors came of age in Soviet society during the Cold War: "As we grew up we discovered how influenced our flamboyant youth was by international tensions. Unfazed, we would watch our first girlfriends assembling Kalashnikov machine guns . . . Compulsory military training brought us to the Military Department of Moscow State University once a week, after which we would go drinking with friends" (Zubok and Pleshakov 1996: x). Josef Stalin, in particular, was responsible for creating an atmosphere of distrust at home and abroad that made a Cold War almost unavoidable.

Zubok and Pleshakov are careful not to place sole blame for the Cold War on Stalin, or the Soviet Union for that matter, but they argue that the Soviet dictator's insecurities and obsessions led to a "total collapse of relations between the [Soviet Union] and the Western democracies" (ibid: 36). Stalin combined a traditional Russian fear of foreign encirclement with strong Marxist convictions about the dangers of cooperation with capitalist states. He pursued a "revolutionary–imperial paradigm" that inspired foreign expansion for defensive reasons and for the pursuit of a world revolution that promised to fulfill long-standing messianic aspirations (ibid: 4). After centuries of foreign attack and historical "backwardness," the expansion of Soviet influence in Europe and Asia promised to make Russia a truly "great power."

This assessment of Stalin is crucial for analyzing American foreign policy in the early Cold War. The Soviet dictator's insecurities and aggressive inclinations made conflict with the United States difficult to avoid. He refused to accept a unified Germany that was not "friendly" to Moscow, he rejected Marshall Plan aid for its interference with Soviet dominance in Eastern Europe, and he repressed groups – especially in East Germany, Poland, and Czechoslovakia – who sought a cooperative relationship with both the Soviet Union and the United States. Some prominent Soviet figures – including former foreign minister and ambassador to the US, Maksim Litvinov – advocated a system of collective security with the US and Great Britain after World War II. Stalin never took these plans seriously; he never gave cooperation a chance (Roberts 2002).

The intermittent and still limited opening of former communist archives since 1991 has provided many new materials confirming the depth of Stalin's animosity toward the United States and other major capitalist states. He was pragmatic in his belief that another world war had to be avoided in the near term, but he also anticipated eventual armed conflict – first among the capitalist states, as Marx predicted, then between the capitalist and communist states. As early as January 1945, before the final defeat of Nazi Germany, Stalin was thinking this far ahead. He told Georgi Dmitrov, a Bulgarian communist leader, that "The crisis of capitalism revealed itself in the division of capitalists into two factions – one fascist, the other democratic . . . Now we side with one faction against the other, and in the future [we will also turn] against this faction of capitalists" (Zubok and Pleshakov 1996: 37). While Stalin did not have anything like a "master plan" for Cold War conflict, he prepared for hostility rather than alliance with the United States. The Truman administration emerged from World War II committed to a future of preponderant American power. Stalin anticipated another war.

The Soviet dictator's war preparations are most evident in his determination to match and surpass Washington's atomic capabilities. More than anyone else, David Holloway has made use of newly available Russian sources to tell this story and penetrate the inner-workings of Stalin's Cold War policies. The Soviet leader was surely shocked by American atomic power, on display in Hiroshima and Nagasaki during August 1945. His commitment to build a Soviet bomb is not surprising. Holloway, however, shows how the suspicions, insecurities, and terror that dominated Stalin's regime distorted atomic developments. Lavrentii Beria, the head of the feared Soviet Committee of State Security (KGB), supervised the nuclear scientists, providing them with extensive resources but also explicit threats of punishment if they failed to complete their work quickly. Stalin and Beria insulated their nuclear project from foreign influences, and they saw their activities as an extension of war. They combined their obsessive domestic secrecy with an extensive overseas espionage network, designed to steal information from the US, Great Britain, and other states.

After the Soviet Union tested its first atomic weapon in 1949, the regime proceeded with work on more powerful thermonuclear hydrogen bombs. This step was hotly debated in the United States, but for Stalin it was a foregone conclusion.

The Truman administration might have given too little attention to arms control in the early Cold War – as Leffler and Offner argue – but Holloway indicates that Stalin would not have changed course. He "committed the Soviet Union to a path of militarized development" that made a Cold War nearly impossible to avoid. "All attempts to imagine alternative courses of postwar international relations run up against Stalin himself . . . His malevolent and suspicious personality pervades the history of these years" (Holloway 1994: 369–70).

Vojtech Mastny concurs with this judgment. Like Zubok and Pleshakov, he came of age in the shadow of Soviet authority. Like Holloway, he sees Stalin's personality at the core of the early Cold War. Mastny explains that after World War II Stalin had an "insatiable craving" for "absolute security" (Mastny 1996: 23). Ideology was not so much the dictator's motive, as a desire to ensure his power – at home and abroad – from all challengers. This created an incoherent path for Soviet policy, oscillating between a desire for popular approval in places like Germany and a commitment to pursue power through force in Czechoslovakia and elsewhere. Moscow revitalized the Communist International (now called the "Cominform") to attract adherents, and it closed off areas under its control to foreign influence.

Stalin's unwillingness to accept deviation from his domination, in any form, produced what Mastny calls a "harvest of blunders" for the Soviet Union between 1948 and 1949 (ibid: 62). As mentioned earlier, in February 1948 Stalin provided support for a coup in Czechoslovakia that replaced a coalition government with hardline communist dominance. In June, Moscow attempted to blockade access to West Berlin – located deep within the territory of Soviet-controlled Eastern Germany. In both cases Stalin used brute force on behalf of alleged "democratic forces." His actions, however, exposed his aggressiveness. They also contributed to a spiral of Soviet insecurity that drove Stalin, in the next years, to act with even more belligerence.

Following the Czechoslovak coup, national communists began to fear similar Soviet actions in their own countries. Yugoslav leader Josip Broz Tito took his country out of the Cominform a few months later. He soon became one of the largest recipients of US foreign aid. In response to the Berlin blockade, the US government airlifted supplies into West Berlin, increasing European and American resolve to stay in this divided city and contain Soviet expansion. Stalin ended the Berlin blockade in May 1949 to find that he had stiffened resistance to his power throughout Eastern Europe, and among the allied governments of Western Europe and the United States.

The Soviet dictator triggered a militarization of American policy. In addition to the budget increases that Hogan describes, Mastny points to new US war plans that, for the first time, seriously contemplated the use of atomic weapons in response to Soviet aggression. The Truman administration increased the number of American bombers and foreign bases around Soviet territory. The US also began to enhance its capability for covert activities at this time. American support for anti-Soviet dissidents in Eastern Europe added to Stalin's difficulties in countries where the majority of people clearly resented communist tyranny. Stalin's attempts to overcome his insecurities only contributed to more of the same. The creation of what Hogan calls the "national security state," was, according to Mastny, a reaction to Soviet aggression.

Drawing on both his personal and scholarly knowledge of Soviet oppression, Mastny closes his book by reflecting on the "sheer evil of Stalinism. The depth of that evil was, if anything, underestimated even by its foreign critics" (Mastny 1996: 194). While he does not justify all of the major foreign and domestic facets of American behavior, Mastny argues that the US did not overreact to the Soviet threat. He views American policy in the early Cold War as a reasonable response to a brutal and expansive danger. Looking from the outside-in he judges the Truman administration on more favorable terms than those historians – Leffler, Hogan, and Offner, in particular – who examine US policy largely from the inside-out. "If the empire Stalin created was in fact every bit as evil as suspected and much more," Mastny writes, "then those who waged the Cold War against it need not apologize for the effort" (ibid).

This moralistic conclusion is shared by the most controversial recent book on the Cold War. In *We Now Know* John Lewis Gaddis highlights the dramatic differences between "Soviet authoritarianism and American democracy" (Gaddis 1997: 287). While the United States worked with Europeans to construct what Gaddis calls a "democratic empire" – allowing bargaining, conciliation, and even dissent – Moscow relied heavily on coercion. "The slightest signs of autonomy, for Stalin, were heresy, to be rooted out with all the thoroughness of the Spanish Inquisition" (p. 289). Soviet brutality made citizens and leaders look to Washington for economic and military support. Stalin undermined his own authority, contributing to the power of American liberal capitalism as a magnet for those fearing communist rule.

Gaddis shows that American policymakers – Harry Truman, George Marshall, Dean Acheson, and George Kennan, among others – only reluctantly assented to a permanent American military presence in Europe and Asia. Kennan, in particular, opposed the creation of the North Atlantic Treaty Organization (NATO) and argued for a withdrawal of US troops from Western Germany. The strongest and most consistent advocates of an expanded American international presence were foreign figures – in Great Britain, West Germany, Japan, and South Korea. Washington's Cold War empire was not an outgrowth of internal American developments, as Leffler, Hogan, and Offner argue. Gaddis points to the crucial role of overseas leaders who pulled Americans out of their more provincial horizons. In the words of Geir Lundestad (1990), the United States created an "empire by invitation." European and Asian invitations came from suitors fearful of a Soviet embrace.

Allied entreaties for support produced many American "blunders," where policymakers found themselves defending positions "they would never have thought worthy of defense" under other circumstances (Gaddis 1997: 84). US activities on the Korean and Indochinese peninsulas are excellent examples. In the case of Korea, the Truman administration sought to curtail its commitments to the undemocratic regime of Syngman Rhee in the South. This became most evident in Secretary of State Dean Acheson's January 12, 1950 speech, where he indicated, in Gaddis' words, that Washington wished to "avoid military conflicts on the Asian mainland" and "stay out of the Chinese civil war" (p. 72). Syngman Rhee depended on American aid for his survival and his ambition to reunite the Korean people. To prevent the planned US disengagement from the peninsula (the last American soldiers departed in 1949), Rhee trumpeted the communist threat in the region.

Bruce Cumings (1981–90) describes the long-standing civil conflict between the two Koreas that Rhee exploited to justify US support. When North Korea – in cooperation with the Soviet Union and the People's Republic of China – attacked the South on June 25, 1950, the US felt obligated to defend Rhee and turn back communist aggression. Despite its clear desire to reduce American military commitments in East Asia, the Truman administration fought an extensive land war against North Korean and Chinese forces. It also greatly increased its military aid to imperiled anti-communist regimes in Taiwan and Indochina. American attachments to allies prevented a desired disengagement from the region.

In Indochina it was the French who pulled the US in, despite contrary American inclinations (Lawrence, forthcoming). Gaddis explains that, after World War II, policymakers in Washington were committed to both anticolonialism and anti-communism. Franklin Roosevelt advocated "trusteeships" in Indochina and other areas of European imperialism. According to this model, the US would support a gradual movement away from colonialism to national independence under stable regimes with a Western orientation. Mark Bradley (2000) has shown that American ideas of trusteeship were serious, but also colored by racial presumptions of "Oriental" inferiority and American interests in regional influence.

As evidence for Bradley's analysis, American ideas of trusteeship led the US to support a return to French colonialism in Indochina. Paris appeared to provide the necessary source of regional order and anti-communism, en route to eventual national independence. The French were less serious about trusteeship than the Americans, but they emphasized – somewhat disingenuously – their asserted role as "Oriental" tutors to elicit political and economic aid from Washington. The government in Paris also exaggerated the importance of its Indochinese empire in reconstructing postwar national morale after the ignominy of defeat at the hands of Germany in Europe and Japan in Southeast Asia. To defend trusteeship, contain communism, and boost a critical European ally, Washington became an unintended colonial surrogate. Communist support for Ho Chi Minh's Vietminh forces from the Soviet Union and China – especially after the outbreak of the Korean War (Duiker 2000; Zhai 2000) – motivated a rapid militarization of American activity in the region. Following the French withdrawal in 1954, the US took over.

Attempts to support the independent "development" of an anti-communist state in South Vietnam gradually gave way to escalating US military intervention. American leaders sought to contain communism and justify prior commitments. Cold War threats and alliances made the US a belligerent in a land Americans poorly understood; populated by people Americans cared little about (Schulzinger 1997). This descent from the early Cold War to the Vietnam War, Gaddis writes, reflected the ways that the US was not "in charge much of the time." Conditions after World War II left "peripheries" – the French, their Indochinese collaborators, and others – "in a position to manipulate Washington about as often as the other way around" (Gaddis 1997: 187).

Gaddis distinguishes America's somewhat "democratic" empire from its predecessors, but he also draws heavily on the history of previous imperial projects. Like the British in the nineteenth century, Americans found that their preponderance of power after World War II created new vulnerabilities. With interests and allies around the globe, the US faced enemy threats on an incredibly broad geographic canvas. American leaders surely exaggerated dangers on the periphery, but the

Korean War provided evidence that perceived threats were, nonetheless, quite real. Allowing allies in far away corners of Asia to fall before communist aggression would undermine the resolve of allies elsewhere. European leaders like Konrad Adenauer never tired of making this point. Marc Trachtenberg (1999) has shown that Bonn and Paris, in particular, advocated an extended American hard line.

The US faced strong external pressures to expand its political, economic, and military commitments. American resources were bountiful, but they became over-extended due to widening foreign demands. The national security state that Hogan describes emerged as part of a historical pattern of "imperial overstretch" (Kennedy 1987). During the early Cold War years Gaddis argues that this pattern was largely imposed on the United States.

Assessments

Many historians have criticized Gaddis for his "triumphalism." Melvyn Leffler argues that *We Now Know* exaggerates the Soviet threat to justify American excesses. He also contends that Gaddis falsely presumes US "victory" in the Cold War was a consequence of Washington's policies. The collapse of the Soviet Union might have occurred despite, not because of, American activities (Leffler 1995, 1999). Marilyn Young adds to this criticism, arguing that Gaddis' approach centers too heavily on the US and Europe. She highlights the ways in which Washington contributed to rural devastation, economic inequality, and social injustice in "peripheral" countries like Vietnam, Iran, and Chile (Young 2002). Carolyn Eisenberg looks to the hardships of Germany's Cold War division to highlight the costs of US "victory," even in the center of Europe (Eisenberg 1996). For Young and Eisenberg, the early Cold War spread local tragedy along with communist containment.

These are powerful arguments. They remind us of how the implementation of US policies often departed from stated claims about democracy and anticolonialism. Gaddis' central theme, however, remains undisputed. The Cold War was almost unavoidable because of the global divisions after World War II, and the insecurities of Josef Stalin. Events surely might have played out differently – and here Gaddis' critics have a strong case – but to imagine a world without Cold War requires imagining away the Soviet leadership.

The debate among historians therefore revolves around how the Cold War was fought, not why. Gaddis, Mastny, Holloway, Zubok, and Pleshakov have assembled an impressive array of sources to show that the Soviet threat was not imagined. Leffler, Hogan, and Offner have, however, explained that American threat percep-tions – even if based in reality – did not constitute a simple reaction to external stimuli. Men like Harry Truman, Dean Acheson, and George Kennan had prejudices and interests, born of World War II and other experiences, which distorted their Cold War policies. These were leaders who emphasized "toughness" over compro-mise, containment over collective security, and free enterprise over economic regu-lation. They had an expansive view of threats to America, but also a very narrow view of the acceptable forms of social and political organization.

Scholarship that emphasizes the Soviet threat is not incompatible with work on the excesses of US national security. Both literatures use the legacies of World War II as their points of departure. Both begin with the division of Europe between

American and Soviet forces, examining how this division extended to Asia, and soon most of the globe. The early Cold War years were, in this sense, characterized by a Soviet–American struggle to dominate the postwar world. This bipolar competition included economic reconstruction, political party formation, cultural influence, and, of course, military conflict.

Recent analyses of the Soviet–American struggle differ most in their assignment of historical agency. Newly available sources from former communist countries point to the primacy of Soviet aggression. A fuller US and West European record illustrates American over-reaction. One can therefore see multiple Cold Wars occurring at the same time. The Soviet Cold War, as Mastny shows most clearly, was about Stalinist attempts to attain absolute security through force against rivals at home and abroad. The American Cold War, as Leffler describes most persuasively, was about US efforts to assure the international dominance of core values and interests through a preponderance of power. Gaddis' account is the most extended attempt to depict these two Cold Wars, but he gives too little attention to the American side. Future work by historians will endeavor to provide a richer synthesis of the Soviet threat and America's exaggerated vision of national security.

Allies and "peripheral" states are also likely to receive more attention in future work. New sources are becoming available and historians from these societies are beginning to give their perspectives voice. More important, the writings of Gaddis, Leffler, and others indicate how small states exerted extensive influence at critical moments. West Germany, Japan, and South Korea are the most obvious examples. Scholarship grounded in these and other areas is likely to emphasize culture, racism, and the legacies of prior conflicts. In these countries – where the United States attained dominance but not omnipotence – complex relationships emerged, producing many contradictions that do not fit any standard narrative of the Cold War. Internal conflicts over national identity, for example, created shifting alignments that defied capitalist–communist divisions. John Dower (1999) is surely correct when he extols the value of local studies that reach beyond standard Cold War dichotomies.

Historians, however, must situate local events within a larger context of international struggle. If anything, the recent literature on the early Cold War has shown the remarkable reach of the Soviet–American conflict. Even if disputes over national identity defied simple capitalist–communist divisions, they were deeply affected by this struggle. Moscow and Washington placed a premium on identifying friends and foes. They aided groups they perceived as friendly, they worked to undermine enemy influences, and they integrated allies into large empires. Soviet and American authority differed in important ways, as Gaddis explains, but both superpowers created extended empires in the years after World War II.

This attention to empires brings us back to de Tocqueville. Like the French Revolution, the early years of the Cold War transformed the international landscape. US perceptions of national security greatly expanded American political, economic, and military activities overseas. A growing Soviet threat heightened capitalist–communist conflict. The early Cold War was revolutionary because accumulated threats and interests came to a head, producing new political and social alignments. World War II was the "Old Regime": it nurtured the institutions, ideologies, and fears that dominated the years after 1945. In all its horror, the war against fascism presaged the rise of a new terror: global communism.

REFERENCES

Alperovitz, Gar: *Atomic Diplomacy: Hiroshima and Potsdam and the Use of the Atomic Bomb and the American Confrontation with Soviet Power*, revd. edn. (New York: Penguin Books, 1985).

Alperovitz, Gar: *The Decision to Use the Atomic Bomb and the Architecture of an American Myth* (New York: Alfred A. Knopf, 1995).

Bernstein, Barton J.: "Understanding the Atomic Bomb and the Japanese Surrender: Missed Opportunities, Little-Known Near Disasters, and Modern Memory." *Diplomatic History* 19 (1995), 227–73.

Bradley, Mark Philip: *Imagining Vietnam and America: The Making of Postcolonial Vietnam, 1919–1950* (Chapel Hill: University of North Carolina Press, 2000).

Bundy, McGeorge: *Danger and Survival: Choices About the Bomb in the First Fifty Years* (New York: Random House, 1988).

Cumings, Bruce: *The Origins of the Korean War*, 2 vols. (Princeton, NJ: Princeton University Press, 1981–90).

de Tocqueville, Alexis: *L'Ancien régime et la révolution* (Paris: 1856); trans. Alan S. Kahan, *The Old Regime and the Revolution* (Chicago, IL: University of Chicago Press, 1998).

Dower, John W.: *Embracing Defeat: Japan in the Wake of World War II* (New York: W. W. Norton, 1999).

Duiker, William J.: *Ho Chi Minh* (New York: Hyperion, 2000).

Eisenberg, Carolyn Woods: *Drawing the Line: The American Decision to Divide Germany, 1944–1949* (New York: Cambridge University Press, 1996).

Foreign Relations of the United States [FRUS], 1946, Vol. 6 (Washington, DC: US Government Printing Office, 1969).

Friedberg, Aaron L.: *In the Shadow of the Garrison State: America's Anti-Statism and its Cold War Grand Strategy* (Princeton, NJ: Princeton University Press, 2000).

Gaddis, John Lewis: *We Now Know: Rethinking Cold War History* (New York: Oxford University Press, 1997).

Hamby, Alonzo L.: *Man of the People: A Life of Harry S. Truman* (New York: Oxford University Press, 1995).

Hogan, Michael J.: *The Marshall Plan: America, Britain, and the Reconstruction of Western Europe, 1947–1952* (New York: Cambridge University Press, 1987).

Hogan, Michael J.: *A Cross of Iron: Harry S. Truman and the Origins of the National Security State, 1945–1954* (New York: Cambridge University Press, 1998).

Holloway, David: *Stalin and the Bomb: The Soviet Union and Atomic Energy, 1939–1956* (New Haven, CT: Yale University Press, 1994).

James, Robert Rhodes (ed.): *Churchill Speaks: Winston S. Churchill in Peace and War, Collected Speeches, 1897–1963* (New York: Chelsea House, 1980).

Jervis, Robert: "Was the Cold War a Security Dilemma?" *Journal of Cold War Studies* 3 (2001), 36–60.

Kennedy, Paul: *The Rise and Fall of the Great Powers: Economic Change and Military Conflict from 1500 to 2000* (New York: Random House, 1987).

Lawrence, Mark Atwood: *Constructing Vietnam: The United States, European Colonialism, and the Making of the Cold War in Indochina* (Berkeley: University of California Press, forthcoming.)

Leffler, Melvyn P.: *A Preponderance of Power: National Security, the Truman Administration, and the Cold War* (Stanford, CA: Stanford University Press, 1992).

Leffler, Melvyn P.: "New Approaches, Old Interpretations, and Prospective Reconfigurations." *Diplomatic History* 19 (1995), 173–96.

Leffler, Melvyn P.: "The Cold War: What Do 'We Now Know.'" *American Historical Review* 104 (1999), 501–24.

Lundestad, Geir: *The American "Empire" and Other Studies of US Foreign Policy in Contemporary Perspective* (New York: Oxford University Press, 1990).

McCullough, David: *Truman* (New York: Simon and Schuster, 1992).

Mastny, Vojtech: *The Cold War and Soviet Insecurity: The Stalin Years* (New York: Oxford University Press, 1996).

Naimark, Norman M.: *The Russians in Germany: A History of the Soviet Zone of Occupation, 1945–1949* (Cambridge, MA: Harvard University Press, 1995).

Offner, Arnold A.: *Another Such Victory: President Truman and the Cold War, 1945–1953* (Stanford, CA: Stanford University Press, 2002).

Roberts, Geoffrey: "Litvinov's Lost Peace, 1941–1946." *Journal of Cold War Studies* 4 (2002), 23–54.

Schulzinger, Robert D.: *A Time of War: The United States and Vietnam, 1941–1975* (New York: Oxford University Press, 1997).

Schwartz, Thomas Alan: *America's Germany: John J. McCloy and the Federal Republic of Germany* (Cambridge, MA: Harvard University Press, 1991).

Schwarz, Hans-Peter: *Die Ära Adenauer* [The Adenauer Era] (Stuttgart: Deutsche Verlags-Anstalt, 1981–3).

Sherry, Michael S.: *In the Shadow of War: The United States Since the 1930s* (New Haven, CT: Yale University Press, 1995).

Trachtenberg, Marc: *A Constructed Peace: The Making of the European Settlement, 1945–1963* (Princeton, NJ: Princeton University Press, 1999).

Walker, J. Samuel: *Prompt and Utter Destruction: Truman and the Use of the Atomic Bombs against Japan* (Chapel Hill: University of North Carolina Press, 1997).

Young, Marilyn B.: "The Age of Global Power." In Thomas Bender (ed.) *Rethinking American History in a Global Age* (Berkeley: University of California Press, 2002).

Zhai, Qiang: *China and the Vietnam Wars, 1950–1975* (Chapel Hill: University of North Carolina Press, 2000).

Zubok, Vladislav and Constantine Pleshakov: *Inside the Kremlin's Cold War: From Stalin to Khrushchev* (Cambridge, MA: Harvard University Press, 1996).

CHAPTER FOURTEEN

United States–Latin American Relations, 1942–1960

DARLENE RIVAS

International relations during the period 1942–60 were convulsive, shaped by enduring consequences of the global economic depression and by World War II and the emerging Cold War. After wooing the region with conciliatory policies during the 1930s, the administration of Franklin Delano Roosevelt hoped to rally Latin American nations to cooperate in hemispheric defense. During and after World War II, the Latin American nations increasingly found their international relations, political, economic, and military, defined primarily by their relationship to the United States. One result of global war was that the US, already dominant in the region, was in the unusual position of having no significant extra-hemispheric rivals for economic and political influence. The US continued to assert its power, and cultural and economic relations remained significant. However, with few exceptions, the US focused greater attention on other regions as the Cold War emerged and as Latin America seemed relatively safe from communism. Latin American leaders, faced with restless populations divided by historic inequities, and in some cases, the uncertainty of rapid social and economic change, chose to respond either through repression, reform, or revolution. By the late 1950s and the opening of the 1960s, US dominance was challenged, most directly when Cuba established close relations with the Soviet Union, but also as Latin American governments demonstrated their resolve to reduce dependence on the United States and to broaden their relations with the world. As a result, by the end of the era, the United States had begun wooing once again, and Latin American governments, Cuba excepted, continued efforts to harness resources and attention from the United States to help them fulfill their aspirations for economic development.

Scholarly writing on US–Latin American relations during this era is rich and varied. Traditional diplomatic history – narratives and analyses of policy development in Washington and the role of presidents and diplomats – provide a starting point for students seeking understanding of these relations. Some traditional diplomatic histories also use multi-archival approaches, providing understanding of Latin American (and sometimes extra-regional) perspectives and policies. Some scholars pay close attention to political, economic, and social contexts of the United States, Latin American nations, or both in order to explore the sources of policies and the extent of their impact. Some such works emphasize the substantive role of Latin Americans in shaping inter-American relations. Increasingly, scholars explore non-government relations, the role of individuals, popular culture, migration, and non-governmental organizations – such as corporations, civic groups, political movements, labor unions, religious groups, and educational, scientific, and technical organizations. Such subjects still remain fertile ground for future historians. Some scholars use theoretical concepts such as dependency theory, psychological theories, or poststructural theories to understand US–Latin American relations or US perceptions of Latin America. While some political and other social scientists have written on this period, especially the Cold War years, the boom in academic attention to the region sparked by the Cuban Revolution focused largely on events after 1960, so work on the pre-1960 era is still largely the province of historians.

Subjects that dominated early work on US–Latin American relations from 1942 to 1960 were the development of inter-American institutions, the effectiveness (or ineffectiveness) of policies by presidential administrations, and the impact of World War II and the Cold War on US–Latin American relations. Scholars have highlighted important themes, such as conflict and cooperation over economic development strategies, US relations with authoritarian governments, US promotion of democracy and liberal capitalism, alliance politics, and the relative importance of such ideas as economic and political nationalism and anti-communism. Bilateral studies highlight relations between the United States and particular countries in the region. Events of significant import have warranted great attention, especially the ongoing confrontation between the United States and Argentina during World War II and the early postwar period, the US covert involvement in the Guatemalan coup of 1954, and US–Cuban relations, primarily the response to Fidel Castro's revolution. Comparative work helps explain US responses to nationalism and revolutions, focusing in this period on revolutionary change in Bolivia, Guatemala, and Cuba. In general, accounts somewhat sympathetic to the United States are concentrated on US policy during World War II and the Roosevelt administration, while interpretations of the postwar period and the 1950s are for the most part highly critical of US policy. Underlying much of the scholarship on the era is the assumption that US policy was not only flawed, but also highly determinative in causing or exacerbating Latin American political instability and economic and social inequality. Increasingly, greater attention to the local and regional context has tempered this view. Still, overall, most scholars share a sense that US policy, often characterized by condescension and racism, should and could have been different and that the impact of US influence and power in the region has had largely negative consequences for Latin America.

Scholarship on the war years continues discussion of the character and evolution of the Good Neighbor policy begun during the late 1920s and reaching its fullest expression under the administration of Franklin Delano Roosevelt (see chapter 9, this volume). Shaped to a large extent by responses to the world depression and growing international tension in Europe, the Good Neighbor policy was characterized by US acceptance of the principle of non-intervention, growing emphasis on multilateral cooperation and "consultation" on issues of inter-American concern, and increasing trade between the United States and Latin American nations through the negotiation of bilateral reciprocal treaties. The administration of Franklin Roosevelt sought to improve its reputation and influence in the face of increasing political and economic nationalism in Latin America. Latin American nations sought to prevent US unilateral intervention in their countries, yet they also hoped to ensure that the United States would remain committed to hemispheric security from outside threats, and from potential threats from each other. Inter-American conferences during the 1920s and 1930s advanced this agenda, reaching a high point when the United States pledged in 1936 not to intervene unilaterally in the hemisphere. Inter-American meetings also served as venues for the United States to implement a policy of Western hemispheric (not merely continental North American) defense. These included an assertion of continental solidarity against any extra-hemispheric intervention in the Western hemisphere and the creation of a 300-mile security perimeter around the Western hemisphere.

During the war the United States drew on the reserves of good feeling awakened in Latin Americans by the Good Neighbor policy, rallying the nations of the hemisphere by providing economic and military aid with promises of more, to establish what the Roosevelt administration referred to as "hemispheric solidarity" for the war effort. Several studies of the Good Neighbor policy continue into the war years. They include Dozer (1961), Green (1971), Gellman (1979), Woods (1979), Wood (1985), and Pike (1995). In general they agree that the coming of war strained the relationship among the nations of the hemisphere, or at the least, posed new challenges. (More will be said on these works.) Another important source on US–Latin American relations during World War II is R. A. Humphreys' two-volume work, *Latin America and the Second World War* (1981–2).

After Pearl Harbor, Central American and Caribbean nations, most of them directly in the US orbit and dependent upon the United States for their security, almost immediately declared war on the Axis nations. More cautious, Colombia, Venezuela, and Mexico broke diplomatic relations. After consultation in Rio, where Assistant Secretary of State Sumner Welles made promises of economic assistance and deftly sidestepped Secretary of State Cordell Hull's pressure to seek firm commitments for war, six other Latin American nations broke relations with the Axis powers. In the summer of 1942, both Mexico and Brazil declared war, and each later sent armed forces into combat, with the Mexican air force represented in the Pacific and Brazilian troops in Italy. Two other nations represented challenges to American efforts at "hemispheric solidarity." Chile maintained neutrality until early 1943, mainly to keep Japan at bay because of a potential Japanese threat to its long coastline. US pressure and greater control of the seas by the US after 1943 contributed to Chile's eventual decision to declare war. Argentina became the thorn in the Roosevelt administration's side. In keeping with its tradition of diplomatic independence, and sensitive to historic ties to Germany, Argentina maintained its neutrality almost to the very end of the war. Led by a faction of military men with pro-Axis leanings and aspirations for Argentine hemispheric leadership, the Argentine government pursued an independent (and from the US perspective, contrary) foreign policy. Balancing their economic need for continued flow of beef to Britain with these other goals, Argentina was frequently at odds with the United States throughout the war. Humphreys, a British scholar with extensive knowledge of British sources, pays particular attention to the British–US–Argentine relationship, highlighting the role of the British as an important third party, more amenable to Argentina's independent stance.

Much scholarship on US–Latin American relations during the war period has focused on United States relations with the nations of the Southern Cone. The prickly US–Argentine relationship offered Brazil opportunities for more cozy relations with the United States, since these nations were frequently at odds and each sought hegemony in South America. Gary Frank's (1979) multi-archival work details this rivalry. Frank D. McCann (1973) explains that World War II closed options for Brazil, because it could no longer play off Germany and the US. McCann also emphasizes Brazil's desire for a special relationship, while the United States increasingly sought to pursue a regional policy. McCann suggests that at the war's end, the Truman administration began to abandon the emphasis that FDR had placed on Brazil. Other studies that examine US relations with nations of the Southern Cone include Grow (1981) and Francis (1977).

Following soon after the publication of these studies came work on espionage during World War II. Intelligence studies include Hilton (1981a), Rout and Bratzel (1986), and, more recently, Niblo (1995) and Paz (1997). Using multinational sources, these studies indicate that while foreign rivalry for influence in Latin America was real, German and Japanese intelligence operations were rarely efficient. In fact, by the outbreak of war, Herbert Hoover's FBI, acting largely independently rather than in collaboration with Latin American governments, had rooted out most spy rings. Hilton (1981a) and Rout and Bratzel (1986) focus on German efforts in the larger countries, especially Brazil, while Paz (1997) details Japanese activities in Mexico. Both Paz and Niblo (1995) go beyond the examination of espionage to shed light on the Mexican political struggles over cooperation with the United States, as well as upon Japanese and German intelligence operations in Mexico, largely through the use of documents in US archives. Niblo's work focuses more specifically on how cooperation for war led to joint efforts at economic development.

These books, along with studies of the Roosevelt administration and the Good Neighbor policy, explain US efforts at hemisphere security. Concerned about Axis influence through military advisers to Latin American armed services, German-owned airlines and other businesses, as well as potential for subversive activities by German immigrants, some of whom lived in colonies with German language schools and newspapers, the Roosevelt administration took action. The United States and Latin American governments developed a proclaimed list of individuals with Axis ties, interning almost 9,000 Latin Americans. Latin American militaries broke ties to continental European advisers, opening the door to increased US influence, which would grow even greater with the advent of the Cold War. In keeping with the principle of consultation, the hemispheric nations established the Inter-American Defense Board in 1942. Except in a few cases like Argentina (more on this later), Latin American militaries welcomed closer ties with the United States in the form of Lend Lease equipment. The US established air bases in Brazil, the closest Latin American nation to Africa. German submarines in the Caribbean disrupted shipping and led to increased activity by the United States to protect the Panama Canal. US desire for bases and military cooperation enhanced friendly ties with Central American and Caribbean dictators. For example, Eric Roorda (1998) argues that Dominican dictator Rafael Trujillo y Molina along with other dictators used anti-fascism (and later anti-communism) to win US support that would extend their ability to suppress opposition.

Hemispheric security had an economic component. Latin American economies, already damaged by depression, suffered further due to the war. The Roosevelt administration responded to Latin American economic concerns in a variety of ways. Negotiations led to such measures as the Inter-American Coffee Agreement in April 1941, which stabilized the coffee market. The US purchased strategic materials beyond war needs, stockpiling such commodities as tin, manganese, copper, quartz crystals, and rubber in part to help the Latin American economies, in part to reduce availability to enemy nations (at least early on). Latin American nations increasingly sought economic development, which required investment. Large nations like Brazil, Argentina, Chile, and Mexico especially began to push for industrial development rather than export-led growth. The economic disruptions of the preceding years led them to develop industries to supply their own needs and to develop a sector of manufactured goods for export. Talk of collaboration with the United States for economic development led to joint US–Brazilian financing of the Volta Redonda steel mill in Brazil in 1940 and Mexican railway improvements during the war. An Inter-American Development Commission served as a venue for discussion of development projects and cooperation between the public and private sectors in both the United States and Latin America, but it accomplished little in the way of actual projects. The Export–Import Bank offered loans to promote commercial relations, but it also developed technical assistance programs in places like Haiti and Ecuador that were intended to promote economic development. Buoyed by pledges such as that of Sumner Welles in 1942 that the United States would reward Latin American cooperation in the war effort, Latin American nations hoped for similar collaborative projects after the war. The US continued to resist Latin American requests for large programs of development assistance such as Volta Redonda, however, and the Roosevelt administration axed a proposal for an inter-American bank to provide investment capital. Bilateral studies on Brazil and Mexico already mentioned explore these policies and Latin American goals.

Roosevelt's economic policy is a primary focus of David Green (1971). Green argues that the United States sought "a closed hemisphere in an open world" (p. 255). The growing integration of Latin American economies with the United States created conditions for heightened conflict between Latin American nationalists who preferred means for developing their economies that the United States discouraged. The war disrupted the potential of development projects because of defense needs, and Green implies that continued and increased development assistance might have achieved Roosevelt's objective of dispelling revolutionary potential. Roosevelt's policy was "a failure" because he could not convince Latin Americans of US benevolence and ultimately failed to counter revolutionary nationalism, which Green sees as Roosevelt's fundamental purpose.

To achieve "hemispheric solidarity" for the war effort, stepped-up cultural initiatives, like economic development efforts, built on prewar precedents. Begun in 1938, the Cultural Relations Division of the State Department encouraged educational and technical exchanges. In 1940, Roosevelt created what became known as the Office of the Coordinator of Inter-American Affairs (OCIAA). Under the energetic leadership of Nelson Rockefeller, this well-funded agency pursued a variety of initiatives. The cultural activities of the OCIAA, although cloaked in the guise of promoting mutual understanding, were a blitzkrieg of US print, radio, and film propaganda promoting the US and its way of life. Included in these initiatives were exchange programs for educators, journalists, athletes, musicians, dancers, and artists. The office sponsored showings of US newsreels and animated shorts. Walt Disney contributed two feature films that introduced Latinized Disney characters, a Brazilian parrot named José Carioca and a Mexican rooster, Panchito. In a bid to enhance Pan-American feeling, the OCIAA encouraged the making of films with Latin American themes for a US audience as well. The OCIAA also compiled blacklists of properties owned by German, Italian, and Japanese nationals, created to encourage Latin American governments to confiscate such property. Through the establishment of the Institute of Inter-American Affairs, the OCIAA built on the earlier practice of loaning technical experts to give advice to Latin American governments by pioneering the first program of technical assistance administered jointly by US and local personnel. Sold to Congress as an emergency measure to provide for US military personnel as well as Latin Americans in areas producing strategic materials, the Basic Economy Program of the IIAA set up health and sanitation and food supply programs designed to promote economic development. The activities of the OCIAA are detailed in Haines (1977) and Erb (1985). The role of the State Department in cultural relations is described in Espinoza's *Inter-American Beginnings of US Cultural Diplomacy* (1976), which, as its title suggests, highlights the origins of cultural diplomacy in Latin America. Other sources, which explore cultural diplomacy in other regions as well, include Ninkovich (1981) and the classic work by Curti (1963) and Rosenberg (1982). Unfortunately, while these studies explore the cultural and propaganda activities by the United States, research is lacking on the reception by Latin Americans of all this flurry of activity.

By 1944 it was clear that the Allies would win World War II, and postwar planning began to impact US–Latin American relations. Latin American nations aspired to participate on an equal juridical basis not only in inter-American relations in the spirit of the Good Neighbor, but also in global international relations. As a result, they sought roles in the development of new international organizations like the World Bank, the International Monetary Fund, and the United Nations (UN). Full membership in the UN was a high priority for the Latin Americans, and the Brazilians hoped to gain a seat in the Security Council. Concerned by the US antagonism toward Argentina, some Latin American governments sought reconciliation at the Inter-American Conference on War and Peace, which met to discuss postwar collaboration in the inter-American community and participation in the UN. Meeting in Mexico in February 1945, the Latin American nations and the United States agreed in the Act of Chapultepec that a regional security arrangement for the hemisphere should be preserved, in harmony with the United Nations. At Chapultepec, tensions between the United States and the Latin Americans emerged on economic matters, particularly the US insistence on reliance on private capital flows for economic development and free trade over protectionism. Latin American nations generally sought greater flexibility for statist solutions to meet their economic goals. On the question of Argentina, the US agreed that if Argentina met certain conditions, including declaring war on the Axis, the US would support its admission to the UN.

At the UN Conference in San Francisco in June 1945, Latin American nations boldly spoke out for the rights of small nations and for their region. They insisted on the seating of Argentina and sought to preserve the regional security arrangements agreed upon at Chapultepec. The US response demonstrated deep divisions among the makers of US foreign policy. In the end, the United States supported the seating of Argentina and the adoption of Article 51 of the UN charter. Article 51 permitted regional security arrangements under the principle of collective self-defense, opening the door not only for the Rio Pact of the inter-American system, but for NATO and other regional security arrangements created during the Cold War. Some scholars and contemporary observers argued that Latin American delegates were pawns of US officials already firing early salvos in the Cold War. Tillapaugh (1978) argues that while there were some anti-Soviet worries among the US delegation, the Latin American delegates had their own concerns, which were both anti-communist and at the same time assertive of their goals of containing the United States from unilateral action in the hemisphere and maintaining US commitment to the hemisphere for the purposes of economic development. Tillapaugh insists that US effort to meet Latin American concerns was not part of a "shift toward an anti-Russian policy. The solution, collective defense, eventually did become significant in a divided world, but this was more a result than cause of the Cold War" (p. 26). On the region/UN conflict, see also Rippy (1958), Inis (1973), Divine (1967), and Campbell (1973).

Scholars of the Good Neighbor policy are keenly interested in the divisions among the members of the Roosevelt administration. Members of the two sides are variously labeled Latin Americanists/regionalists versus globalists/internationalists/ Europeanists. Gellman (1979) sees the Good Neighbor policy as a departure in US foreign relations from older policies of intervention. According to Gellman, the Good Neighbor policy effectively ended with the departure of key Roosevelt personnel who had particular affinity for Latin America, like Sumner Welles, who left under pressure in 1943, and Rockefeller, who pushed the regional perspective at Chapultepec and San Francisco over the protests of globalists. Woods (1979) uses a bureaucratic politics approach, a method popular in the 1970s that borrowed from the social sciences. While noting the significance of conflicts among members of the Roosevelt administration, Green (1971) argues that their differences were insignificant, since both sides pursued the same goals. For example, Green contends that only tactical differences separated varying approaches by policymakers to Argentina. In 1945 Assistant Secretary of State Nelson Rockefeller sought *rapprochement* with Argentine leader Juan Perón (according to Green, in keeping with Rockefeller's Wall Street interests), while the ambassador to Argentina, Spruille Braden (later named Assistant Secretary of State, replacing Rockefeller), took an aggressive stance toward Perón in order to undermine his authority. Green argues that Braden and Rockefeller's fundamental purpose was to "undercut . . . political and economic nationalism" in order to maintain US influence (p. 252). Woods (1979) agrees with Green that the Good Neighbor policy was characterized by economic concerns, but he argues that the direction of US policy was decisively influenced by rivalries among foreign policymakers in the United States government, such as the legendary feud between Welles and Hull and the disagreements between Rockefeller and Braden. For Woods, as for Gellman, the coercive policies of Hull and Braden toward Argentina undermined what these historians view as the genuine trust and mutual respect won by the Good Neighbor policy. Written when non-interventionist sentiment spawned by the Vietnam conflict was high, Woods finds more appealing the non-interventionist positions of regionalists Rockefeller and Laurance Duggan (which he sees as respecting the principle of self-determination), rather than crusades to export democracy like those of the internationalists Hull and Braden (which he sees as resulting in interference).

The Good Neighbor policy poses questions for scholars attempting to place it in the context of a longer view of US–Latin American policy. Does the transition between Roosevelt and his successor, Harry Truman, mark the end of a policy (and thus a period or era)? Was the Good Neighbor policy a significant departure in American foreign policy or was it merely a superficial change? When did the Good Neighbor policy end – with Roosevelt's death, or during the war, or at what point later? In other words, did Truman continue the Good Neighbor policy? Did Eisenhower? Such questions arose at once from contemporary critics of Truman and then of Eisenhower, who had earlier charged Truman with "neglect" of the region. Perhaps because of this "neglect" thesis there are no monographs solely on Truman's Latin American policy, although studies of the Good Neighbor policy like those of Woods and Green and monographs with broader topics do analyze it. Arguments about whether the Roosevelt, Truman, and Eisenhower administrations were marked by continuity or change in US–Latin American policy reflect the presidential synthesis approach, and derive from the premise that US policy is marked by discontinuity (and is even cyclical) and highly influenced by the partisan politics and the individual priorities and styles of American presidents. The lack of a "Latin American Policy of Truman" monograph may mean that, for Truman, there is some sense that discontinuity in policy is not just a function of politics and style, but also a function of incredible changes in the international system. On the other hand, it could also mean that scholars, convinced by the "neglect" thesis, have pursued topics of higher drama. Or scholars may simply reject the presidential synthesis approach because they see continuity in US–Latin American relations.

In an early scholarly approach, Donald Dozer addressed the continuity question in his aptly named *Are We Good Neighbors?* (1961). Dozer sketches US policy from the Good Neighbor through World War II and the early Cold War, but his narrative focuses on the responses by Latin Americans to US policy, which he gleaned largely from Latin American newspapers and other published sources. His understanding of the Good Neighbor policy is broad, as he considers the impact of the Roosevelt administration's political, economic, and cultural initiatives. He suggests that Roosevelt's Good Neighbor policy and wartime cooperation did indeed improve Latin American perspectives on the United States. Still, that view was ambivalent. During the war, for example, Latin Americans saw North Americans as possessing "economic and political power, but not intellectual and cultural" (p. 184). After the war, the United States failed to live up to the promise of the Good Neighbor, with the Truman and Eisenhower administrations failing to appreciate the role of state-directed economic development and nationalism in Latin America. Moreover, anti-Yankee feeling arose from a variety of other sources, including the interventionist policy of Braden toward Argentina, the continued ambivalence toward American culture, and reports of racism in the United States. Dozer advised that the United States government and Americans should treat Latin Americans with respect despite real differences, behave nicely, and provide economic assistance for Latin American modernization through industrialization and economic diversification. Latin America needed US capital, which Dozer argued that Latin Americans both sought and viewed with apprehension. Dozer is representative of the history of the era, as well as a scholar of it.

Bryce Wood, a diplomatic historian taking a traditional approach, uses both US and British sources in his *Dismantling of the Good Neighbor Policy* (1985) to trace the fate of the Good Neighbor. Unlike Green and Dozer, Wood sees the main feature of the Good Neighbor as political, namely, US commitments on non-intervention and non-interference. Wood argues that this commitment to non-interference faced challenges during World War II in the US pressure on Argentina and Bolivia (in 1943) and was demolished with the 1954 Guatemalan intervention by the Eisenhower administration. Wood believes the Good Neighbor policy marked a significant departure (and improvement) in US–Latin American relations, while David Green (1971) sees fundamental continuity. They both agree that the main features of the Good Neighbor policy extended beyond the Roosevelt administration, although they disagree about the fundamental nature of the Good Neighbor – to Wood a genuine effort to move US policy away from interference; to Green, an adjustment designed to further the ongoing US goal of preserving US political, and especially economic, hegemony.

Although the United States sought to preserve its influence in the region, methods changed in order to adapt to growing nationalist resentment and more popular political participation in Latin American nations. The US did not act as an equal partner, and intervention did not end, although increasingly it took the form of covert action and pressure through the use of foreign aid, in addition to the traditional form of commercial expansion and in contrast to direct military intervention. At the same time, in Latin America itself, the perception that Roosevelt acted in the interests of social and economic advancement of the people, as he had in the United States through the New Deal, persisted. Truman and Eisenhower were not viewed as fondly, and as we shall see, perceptions matter a great deal. Dozer makes this point, as does Fredrick Pike (1995). For Pike, who wryly answers Dozer's question by suggesting that the United States was "only as good as it had to be," there was not so much change in fundamental policy as there was a change in its reception in Latin America. To Latin Americans, Franklin Roosevelt was a sympathetic figure, both an aristocratic patron and a personalistic leader of the common people. Harry Truman was just a preoccupied haberdasher.

At war's end, the Truman administration focused its attention on Europe and Asia and relations with the Soviet Union. Despite the developing Cold War, Latin America seemed safe from communism. The Truman administration avoided meeting with Latin American nations on economic questions, delaying a promised economic conference with the excuse that Perón's Argentina refused to address inter-American (largely US) concerns about the repressive character of his regime and the harboring of fascists. To add insult to injury, Secretary of State George Marshall himself informed Latin Americans that there would be no Marshall Plan for Latin America. The US would offer no relief despite the complaint that Latin American dollar reserves evaporated, and prices for manufactured goods increased dramatically without price controls. The Truman administration at first sought to promote democratic governments, whose number had increased after 1944, in part from popular pressures fueled by strong labor movements and expanded suffrage and idealism spurred by the war against fascism. By 1948, democratic leftist governments, as in Peru and Venezuela, were toppled in military coups instigated by members of traditionally privileged sectors and by military leaders who were unsettled by the threat of rapid social change and who feared "communist" inroads in their countries. As the Cold War continued, the Truman administration dropped its emphasis on support for democracy, adopting a policy of recognizing governments regardless of internal conditions. NSC 141 argued that US policy should focus on "orderly political and economic development which will make the Latin American nations resistant to the internal growth of communism and to Soviet political warfare."

Scholars have paid close attention to US support for dictators who provided "order." The US exercised a more heavy-handed hegemony in Central America and the Caribbean than in other areas. While US leaders periodically expressed disgust with dictators, they valued their support for US global concerns. Valuable studies on the subject include regional studies like LaFeber (1983), Thomas (1984), and Schmitz (1999). Bilateral studies are also helpful, and often their detail provides more evidence of the Latin American context. For Nicaragua and the US ties to the Somoza regime, see Gambone (1997) and Clark (1992). For the Dominican Republic and Trujillo, see Roorda (1998), Atkins and Wilson (1998), and Hall (2000). Several of these studies (for example, Roorda's, Clark's, and Hall's) highlight the changing nature of US policy, noting turning points away from pressure on dictators for reform after 1948 and renewed pressure and even coercion in the late 1950s and early 1960s. These studies note that savvy dictators manipulated the US for their own ends, just as they had during World War II.

Dictators may have managed to stay in power through their own wiles, but they were aided by US military assistance, which they used to repress opposition. Chester Pach (1991) argues that despite the emphasis on military aid and integration during the Cold War, the Truman administration generally resisted Latin American requests for aid through 1950. However, the Korean War contributed to the militarization of US foreign policy. Under the Mutual Security program, military assistance to Latin American nations increased. Such aid would continue in the Eisenhower administration – to the delight of the dictators and to many, yet not all, Latin American military leaders.

US support for democracy and popular governments is discussed by Kyle Longley (1997), who seeks to explain why the United States supported José "Pepe" Figueres, who came to power in 1948 by extra-constitutional means. Figueres supported the Caribbean Legion, a group of former and future political leaders and intellectuals on the Democratic Left, which instigated attempts to overthrow dictators, particularly their favorite target, Somoza. Their story and details of their links to influential Americans who formed the Americans for Democratic Action is told in Ameringer (1974, 1996). Longley also argues that scholars' attention to crises has distorted understanding of US–Latin American relations. He points to the US–Costa Rican relationship as an example of the ability of small nations to use strategies of resistance and accommodation in their relations with stronger powers. He also highlights the role of perceptions, demonstrating that US views of Costa Ricans as white and democratic along with Figueres' staunch anti-communism contributed to US acceptance of his nationalist reforms.

The postwar period was characterized by two seemingly contrary developments: a decline in official and popular interest in Latin America and the institutionalizing of Pan Americanism with the signing of the Rio Pact and the creation of the Organization of American States. An imminent US historian of Latin America, Arthur Whitaker, traced the development of idealism regarding the potential for inter-American cooperation based on common values in *The Western Hemisphere Idea* (1954). Whitaker explained the high tide of Pan Americanism in the 1930s and war years, and its subsequent decline. Whitaker saw the notion of common ideas and interests, for example in republican government and rule of law, as having genuine roots, but he argued that significant cultural differences remained. The long-held notion that the people of the Americas were distinctive from Europe masked those differences. The global concerns of the United States after the war partially explain why the intensity of Pan Americanism declined. While the Latin American craze died down in the US and anti-Yankee feeling rose in Latin America, the nations of the region established formal mechanisms of cooperation: the Rio Pact for military cooperation in 1947 and the Organization of American States (OAS) in 1948 that replaced the Pan American Union.

The inter-American system, meaning the development of procedures and institutions of cooperation, has been primarily the focus of political scientists. The Rio Pact and OAS were in many respects a product of the Cold War and US efforts to protect the hemisphere from "Soviet" communism, but their origins were in Latin American attempts to contain the United States and to provide means for collective (now multilateral) action against threats from outside or each other. Drawing on published documents, J. Lloyd Mecham (1961) offered an early narrative and analysis of these developments. Writing just after the Cuban Revolution and at the height of the Cold War, Mecham's argument was shaped by his concern that communism posed a dangerous threat to the hemisphere. To Mecham, the development of the OAS and the 1954 Declaration of Caracas against communism in the hemisphere represented positive achievements for hemispheric security. Later scholars would see the inter-American system as a tool for continuing US hegemony. A good example is British political scientist Gordon Connell-Smith (1966, 1974), who also focused on inter-American institutions. To Connell-Smith, the notion of common values based on Western hemispheric ideals is nonsense. US peace and security interests are incompatible with the exercising of Latin American sovereignty, and Latin American economic and social goals are impossible given their dependence on the United States. These works, although dated by their Cold War perspective, are still useful for understanding evolving interpretations of the US–Latin American relationship, as well as for basic narratives of the development of the inter-American system. Political scientists continue to discuss the inter-American system at greater length than do historians. Atkins (1989) provides a more recent perspective.

One of the key issues of the postwar period was economic development. This was a priority of Latin American governments, and their goals are best explained in bilateral studies. Scholars have recently focused on how perceptions of Latin Americans and the region have shaped US policy toward economic development. James William Park (1995) traces the influence of academic ideas and popular perceptions of Latin America. Park sees continuity in ethnocentric and racist assumptions about Latin Americans (centered around views of Latin American racial inferiority, the debilitating effects of tropical climates, and negative features of the Spanish cultural legacy), but also by the 1930s and especially by the 1950s a greater willingness to consider external causes for Latin American "underdevelopment." Mark Berger (1995) focuses on perceptions of Latin America by academics – economists, social scientists, and historians. Both Park and Berger trace the emergence of developmentalism or modernization theory – the idea taking shape in the 1950s that Latin America would develop in a similar fashion to North America and required American capital infusions and tutelage along the way. While each notes the influence upon these ideas of arguments by Latin American economists associated with the United Nations Economic Commission on Latin America (ECLA), their focus is on North Americans. While both are critical of the ethnocentrism of US academicians, Park sees greater sophistication and good intentions in approaches to Latin America after the 1930s. Park's wider net suggests that modernization theory had roots in widely held American perceptions of Latin America and in the nature of economic and social progress. Berger highlights the intercourse among leaders of the power structure in the United States, arguing that academics (including Whitaker and Dozer) have helped shape failed US policies by their role in interpreting "Latin America" as an object of study. Despite North American efforts to "understand" Latin America, unequal power relations between the United States and Latin America make this impossible. Berger uses theories of language from Michel Foucault and Edward Said, and the imperial state theory of James Petras and Morris Morley. For Berger, "Latin America" is not a real object of study but a product of hegemonic discourses over time. Berger's discussion of the 1950s is minimal, since academic interest in Latin America, which had declined after World War II, rose abruptly after the Cuban Revolution. In general, Berger and Park both rely largely on published writing on Latin America by North Americans, rather than explore the activities and perceptions of Americans engaged in activities in Latin America. Fredrick Pike (1992) also discusses the perceptions North Americans held of Latin Americans and the impact of those perceptions, arguing the case for mutual misunderstanding.

Study of economic relations (in contrast to economic policy) includes examination of non-government organizations, including corporations and individuals. Mira Wilkins (1974) provides a survey of American corporate activity abroad and explains the shift of corporations toward multinational operations. World War II and its outcome boosted US direct investment, although most American private investment went to Europe rather than Latin America. Corporations adjusted to local conditions and demands by establishing subsidiaries, which sometimes courted local investors and employed local managers. Wilkins describes the expansion and strategies of large firms, but offers less information on the relations between corporations and the nations in which they invested. Thomas F. O'Brien (1996) focuses more specifically on the relations between host nations and corporations by discussing the transmission of US "corporate culture," but his work barely moves into the 1940s. He shows how corporations responded to the pressure of populist politics in the 1930s and 1940s by expanding worker benefits, improving working conditions, and hiring local mid-level management. O'Brien points out that corporations with operations in Central America were slower to adopt welfare capitalism. Other works that move beyond, yet incorporate, the activity of the state are two studies of Nelson

Rockefeller's postwar activities to promote economic development: Cobbs (1992) and Rivas (2002). Cobbs' work is important for the light it sheds on US economic development policy during and after World War II and on the business activities in Brazil of Nelson Rockefeller (in agriculture and mutual funds) and Henry Kaiser (in the automobile industry). Cobbs uses corporatist theory to describe how these two men worked with the Brazilian government in public–private ventures at a time when Brazilians felt the US government had reneged on its promises. Rivas discusses Rockefeller's similar efforts in Venezuela, where he attempted to model reform capitalism to Venezuelan and US investors. Rockefeller's divergent experiences in Brazil and Venezuela, and the insight from O'Brien on corporate resistance to reform in Central America, highlight the importance of considering the particularities of Latin American nations as well as of corporations. Rockefeller and Kaiser were not exploitative, but as Rivas notes, Rockefeller's attempts at operating a business with "social objectives" created contradictions that failed to inspire emulation. The more insidious impact of US corporate investment is explored in Paul J. Dosal's *Doing Business with the Dictators: A Political History of United Fruit in Guatemala, 1899–1944* (1993). UFCO's story is also told in studies of Central America and of the Guatemalan Revolution. Other scholars take an approach that sees the US capitalist system as necessarily promoting dependency. A good example is Walter LaFeber, whose *Inevitable Revolutions* (1983) has been reprinted in several revised editions. LaFeber uses a variant of dependency theory, which he calls neo-dependency theory. LaFeber argues that the assertion of US political, military, and economic power perpetuates a system in which only a few, namely foreign investors and local elites, profit, and in which social and political turmoil inevitably result. Despite his emphasis on corporate influences on US–Latin American relations, however, LaFeber's primary focus is US government policy.

One economic development initiative of the Truman administration – expansion of technical assistance – has received little attention from scholars of US–Latin American relations. Although the administration refused to grant significant economic aid to Latin America, Truman initiated a new technical assistance initiative to the Third World, known as Point Four (it was announced as the fourth point in his inaugural speech in 1949). Truman and his successors were confident that the transmission of American technical skill or "know-how" would over time transform other societies. Technical assistance was administered in Latin America through the Institute for Inter-American Affairs during the war, then the Technical Cooperation Agency, the International Cooperation Agency, and its successor, the Agency for International Development. Early technical assistance focused in such areas as agriculture or vocational education, but later expanded into the controversial area of community development. Early technical assistance was welcomed by Latin American governments, but it offered far less than they expected, which was substantial grants and loans. Rivas (2002) discusses the origins of Point Four and the implementation of private technical assistance, which offers a window into American perceptions of Latin American development as well as into interactions between Venezuelan and American technicians and officials. Haines (1989) offers a chapter on technical assistance in Brazil, and Streeter (2000) notes the political uses of technical assistance in Guatemala after the US-supported coup of 1954. Significantly, spending on technical assistance to Guatemala dramatically exceeded that of other Latin American nations, yet the program was plagued by shortages of qualified technicians and by the arrogance and perplexity of administrators and technicians toward local culture.

A number of bilateral studies also deal with the early Cold War years, many of which use the approaches and share similar interpretations with broader studies. An example is Haines' (1989) study on Brazil. Haines argues that US–Brazilian relations were dominated by Cold War concerns. Haines follows Green, agreeing that the US sought a "closed hemisphere in an open world," with the ultimate purpose to secure the world capitalist system. Thus, the Truman and Eisenhower administrations acted purposefully to promote a particular model of economic development that relied on private investment for limited industrialization and provision of raw materials for the US. Haines also notes the importance of perception or "projected images," arguing that "each side wrongly perceived the situation by projecting its own norms and values on the other. Each side, American as well as Brazilian, had a tendency to oversimplify and stereotype the others' motivations and to ignore the completely different frames of reference and cultural backgrounds" (Haines 1989: 6). After typical discussions of opposition to communism, and cultivation of the military, Haines moves beyond the traditional concerns of diplomatic historians through close investigation of economic and cultural relations between Brazil and the United States. He devotes a chapter to technical assistance in agriculture, and he notes the influx of US publications and popular media (for example, 70 percent of films shown in Brazil in 1952 were made in the USA) (p. 173). Haines does not discuss the reception of North American ideas and material or popular culture, as his focus is on the efforts of US officials.

The notion of "Americanization" which Haines employs is provocative, but despite the fact that US relations with Latin America were largely defined by non-governmental activity, discussions of Americanization still focus largely on Europe (see, for example, the American Century Roundtable in the summer 1999 issue of *Diplomatic History*). W. Michael Weis (1993) details the weakening of US–Brazilian diplomatic ties throughout the 1950s. Weis uses Brazilian sources, explaining in particular the role of President Juscelino Kubitschek in the formulation of a neutralist foreign policy in the latter part of the decade.

Unlike the Truman administration, the Eisenhower administration has received comprehensive treatment. In the 1980s, Eisenhower revisionism, fueled by access to newly opened documents, challenged traditional interpretations. The main thrust of this revisionism was that Eisenhower did not leave policy to subordinates, but was engaged and decisive. In the case of US–Latin American relations, early works agreed that Eisenhower did not respond to Latin America appropriately, leaving the Kennedy administration to come up with creative solutions to hemisphere problems. Burton I. Kauffman (1982) argued that the Eisenhower administration decided that conditions in Latin America, in particular growing economic nationalism and continued poverty, required a new approach, therefore setting precedents for the Kennedy administration. Thus, the Eisenhower administration recognized the need for significant foreign aid to promote economic development, which led to the creation of the Inter-American Bank (first proposed prior to World War II) and the Social Progress Fund.

Eisenhower's foreign policy is more thoroughly explained by Stephen Rabe (1988). Eisenhower's policies differed little from the Truman administration in their support of private sources of development capital and the primacy of Cold War concerns in dealing with the hemisphere. The administration increased the use of covert assistance and was warm in its embrace of Latin American dictators who espoused anti-communism. Rabe offers explanations of key events, such as the Guatemalan intervention, the Nixon tour of Latin America in 1958, and the US response to Cuban revolution. He explains the shifts in Eisenhower's policy toward increased foreign assistance to combat poverty, noting several important turning points: the post-1956 Soviet emphasis on the Third World as the new theater in the Cold War, growing pressure by liberal Democrats in Congress critical of his economic and military policy, the tour of Vice President Nixon in 1958, and of course, Fidel Castro's increasingly radical turn. Rabe, like Kauffman, argues that the Eisenhower administration set precedents to promote economic development and social and political reform upon which the Kennedy administration built.

The most studied event of the era is the Eisenhower administration's covert intervention in the Guatemalan Revolution of 1954. The pivotal significance of the 1954 intervention was pressed home by subsequent events, such as the violence and repression that ensued during the decades-long Guatemalan counter-revolution, rising anti-Americanism throughout Latin America in response to US intervention, and the Eisenhower administration's misplaced confidence in covert operations that resulted in the ill-planned CIA debacle at the Bay of Pigs.

The Guatemalan Revolution began with the administration of José Arevalo in 1944. His "spiritual socialism" did not threaten the social structure, but his successor, Jacobo Arbenz, initiated substantive reforms, with land reform the most ominous in the eyes of Guatemalan elites and US interests like the United Fruit Company. Increasingly convinced that communist influence in Guatemala would destabilize the region and result in a Soviet beachhead in the Americas, the Eisenhower administration sought to contain the red menace. First using the inter-American system, Secretary of State John Foster Dulles attempted to rally the Latin American nations behind an anti-communist resolution at the tenth inter-American conference in Caracas. Although the resolution passed with only Guatemala in opposition, the Latin American nations, except for a few headed by corrupt dictators, refused to certify that Guatemala posed such a communist threat. Unable to win Latin American support for intervention in Guatemala, the Eisenhower administration planned a covert CIA operation that brought to power the despicable regime of Castillo Armas. Despite denials by the Eisenhower administration, Latin Americans understood immediately that the US had aided Castillo Armas' revolt against the reformist Jacobo Arbenz. Resistance to land reform by the United Fruit Company drew immediate suspicion that the company exerted undue influence on the Eisenhower administration, where officials had close ties with the company and the law firm that represented it. Historical interpretations also demonstrated such suspicions. Schlesinger and Kinzer (1982) suggested as much and highlighted the intense anti-communism and rude behavior of Ambassador John Peurifoy. The nearly simultaneous publication of Richard Immerman's *The CIA in Guatemala* (1982) offered a more complex portrait of the Eisenhower administration, and offered evidence that UFCO had less pull than the strategic and ideological fears of US officials. Immerman, like Schlesinger and Kinzer, still concluded that US officials had overdrawn the communist threat in Guatemala. Immerman placed his work in the context of Eisenhower revisionism, using recently declassified documents to explain the intervention. He argued that with the Eisenhower administration the Cold War truly came to Latin America, contending that "Eisenhower, Dulles, and the Republican policymakers ushered in a new era in inter-American relations, an era marked by a protracted struggle between the United States and an assumed international Communist conspiracy" (Immerman 1982: 19).

Whereas Immerman argues that revolutionary policies adapted to Guatemalan conditions were mistaken for communism, Piero Gleijeses took seriously the influence of communists and of Marxist ideology influencing Arbenz. Gleijeses (1991) used Guatemalan evidence, including interviews with Jacobo's wife, Maria Arbenz, and Fortuny, communist leader of the Guatemalan Labor Party, to demonstrate that Arbenz had greater affinity to communists than historians such as Immerman had allowed. Gleijeses, like Immerman, does not see the interests of United Fruit as determinative in US policy. Indeed, he opens and closes his book with Fortuny's statement: "they would have overthrown us even if we had grown no bananas." Gleijeses suggests that "three forces" contributed to the American response: "the search for economic gain, the search for security, and imperial hubris" (p. 361). Ultimately, however, Gleijeses agrees with Immerman, Schlesinger and Kinzer, and others, that the United States' intervention was tragic. Arbenz's analysis that the great social inequities in Guatemala necessitated a courageous and radical response was essentially correct and his program promised progress. By 1954, 1.4 million acres of idle land, including government property and expropriations from large holdings, had been distributed to between 80,000 and 138,000 families, representing probably half a million Guatemalans.

Gleijeses represented a move away from Washington-centered "policy" approaches to analyses that took into account Guatemalan sources. Streeter (2000) takes the story beyond the 1954 coup to analyze US policy in the support of Castillo Armas. While the US offered large amounts of economic and technical assistance to Guatemala, Streeter argues that officials feared the consequences of social restructuring in Guatemala so much that the efforts were largely wasted. Streeter's recent analysis of US policy in the aftermath of the coup reinforces the conviction that PBSUCCESS was a terrible mistake.

Recent analyses of US responses to nationalism and revolutions in Costa Rica and Bolivia have offered comparisons that shed light on US Cold War policies, demonstrating that US policy was more nuanced than early interpretations of the US intervention in Guatemala allowed. Nationalism and efforts to reorder the social structure took place in other places in Latin America, notably Costa Rica and Bolivia. In these cases, however, US officials prized their relationship with Costa Rica's irascible yet staunchly anti-communist Jose "Pepe" Figueres and, in the case of Bolivia, offered the revolutionaries the greatest economic assistance of the era. In Bolivia, the US "tamed" the MNR through economic assistance, in part because years of civil and economic unrest had left Bolivia with no other choice than to restructure at some level. Longley (1997) and Lehman (1999) have emphasized the ability of Latin Americans to resist US policies, in part because of their accommodation on issues of key concern to US officials, namely anti-communist rhetoric and policies.

Several books have taken a comparative approach to revolutions. Cole Blasier

(1976) compares revolutionary movements in Mexico, Bolivia, Cuba, and Guatemala, with much of his focus on the period of the1940s and 1950s. Over space and
time, Blasier saw a general pattern: revolutionary change threatened US private
interests, but also "threatened to diminish US political influence, in that new
governments tended to adopt more independent domestic and foreign policies and
were less likely to conform to US policies" (p. 211). For Blasier, while economic
considerations often sparked US concern and meddling in the revolutionary process,
outright intervention occurred only where the United States feared outside influences. Blasier did not believe communism was a real threat in Latin America, but he
did not question that the Soviet Union was a threat to the United States during the
Cold War. Martha Cottam (1994) uses psychological theories in her comparisons of
revolution. In one chapter she compares Guatemala, Cuba, and Bolivia, arguing that
US policymakers held "cognitive images" that shaped their policies toward events in
these nations. A US "dependent" image of Cuba and Guatemala resulted in decisions
to intervene in a pattern that escalated from diplomatic coercion, to economic
sanctions, to paramilitary action. Bolivia was spared a similar response because,
Cottam argues, the MNR "manipulated" the image held by the Eisenhower administration, and successfully "separated the United States image of themselves from the
image of its enemy" (p. 53). James F. Siekmeier also offers a comparative analysis of
US responses in *Aid, Nationalism, and Inter-American Relations* (1999).

The postwar period was marked not only by assertion of US political and
economic power, but also by the spread of US material goods, popular culture, and
social values. Latin Americans, not unlike people in other parts of the world, worried
that the flood of American products, advertising, films, music, and, increasingly,
television and business and pleasure travelers – all transmitters of American popular
culture – threatened their culture. In addition to fearing economic domination,
there were concerns about homogenization and loss of unique identities and cultural
values. At the same time, many sought similar economic prosperity and found aspects
of American popular culture appealing. Books in the series "United States and the
Americas," published by the University of Georgia Press under the editorship of
Lester Langley, are helpful in this regard. Authors of books in this series define inter-
American relations broadly, attempting to write on the impact of policy as well as its
development, and more uniquely, authors in this series explore cultural relations as
well as economic and political policies. These books are generally written by
specialists who have previously written more focused monographs and who expand
on this primary research. While a love–hate response to the United States existed in
some form throughout the region, it was particularly strong in places with close ties
to the United States, like Cuba. Louis A. Pérez, Jr., a historian of both Cuba and
US–Cuban relations, includes discussion of the 1942–60 era in his work in this
series (Pérez 1997; see the list of references, below, for more books in this series,
which are valuable sources for cultural relations in the 1940s and 1950s). Pérez
discusses economic and political relations, but also cultural relations at length,
explaining the influence of US culture through television, film, and advertising,
movie stars, and acquisitiveness. The proximity of Cuba to the United States
enhanced influence, contributing, for example, to a steady flow of Cuban upper- and
middle-class travelers on shopping trips to Miami. Pérez casts his net widely in
seeking to explain the relationship between Cuba and the United States, noting, for

example, the cultural impact of the relaxing of relations between boys and girls, something that certainly appealed to many Cuban teenagers, but caused resentment and fear among Cuban traditionalists. By the late 1950s, American cultural influence also took the form of vice (gambling, drugs, prostitution) fueled by US tourism and the activities of organized crime. Perhaps because US influence in Cuba was so pervasive, Pérez does not suggest alternative explanations for such cultural changes, which were also occurring elsewhere.

Cubans had high expectations in the 1950s, yet they continued to experience the boom–bust cycles that the Cuban economy had long suffered. Pérez argues that Cubans, tied "directly into the larger US economic system and its concomitant consumption patterns," could live better than most Latin Americans, but because of Cuban economic stagnation they feared they could "not keep up with North America." Combined with the belief that "their national identity was succumbing slowly to North American material culture and vice," this sense of "relative deprivation" meant a "loss of confidence in the future." Revolution was thus "widely anticipated" and "initially welcomed" (Pérez 1997: 232).

The Cuban Revolution was a pivotal event in the Cold War and in US–Latin American relations. At first, the Eisenhower administration and the US public, as did most Cubans, welcomed revolution. In fact, the US had placed an arms embargo on dictator Fulgencio Batista's government in order to prevent him from using US military aid against insurgents. However, concerns about the course of the revolution and its anti-US character led the Eisenhower administration to increasingly coercive and hostile actions, including the termination of the sugar quota and CIA organization of Cuban exiles to destabilize Castro's government. Cuba's orientation toward the Soviet Union and later attempts to export revolution in Latin America and elsewhere antagonized the United States. These events also contributed to a surge in interest and writing on Latin America generally, and Cuba specifically. Writing on the revolution at first tended to focus on whether or not the US had properly or improperly supported or failed to support Batista; whether Castro was a communist from the beginning or a nationalist who had turned communist; whether or not the United States policy contributed to his turn to communism; and a related question, whether or not the Eisenhower administration had pushed Castro into the Soviet orbit. The overwhelming evidence that Castro was initially a revolutionary nationalist who turned communist has led to general consensus on that issue. Increasingly, scholars attribute Cuban factors to the direction of the Cuban Revolution, although criticism of the Eisenhower administration continues as well. Given Cuba's history, which was deeply intertwined with US pressure and influence on the island, scholars increasingly agreed that a nationalist revolution had to confront the United States, and that confronting the United States inevitably required radicalization of the revolution.

Readers seeking understanding of the development of US policy in response to the revolution may depend on works like Rabe's (1988) study of the Eisenhower administration, or upon monographs that focus on the US response, such as Welch (1985) and Benjamin (1990). While Welch does not offer details on the Cuban context, he attributes the radicalization of the revolution to Castro, who he describes as a charismatic leader of radical temperament. The popular Castro identified his cause with Cuban nationalism and history, and gradually moved leftward, blending

Marxism-Leninism with his own ideas. Welch argues that Castro pursued relations with the Soviet Union (rather than vice versa) "as a means of sustaining his social revolution while counteracting real and anticipated injury from the United States" (Welch 1985: 20–1). Welch is attentive to chronology, showing that as the revolutionaries determined that their internal opposition was weak, they sought to quicken the pace of change. Knowing this would antagonize the United States, they decided to continue their course, since US hostility would help increase support for the revolution among Cubans. Welch then describes the sequence of tit-for-tat events in Cuba and Washington. To Welch, the most significant factor in turning Eisenhower firmly against Castro was the latter's embrace of relations with the USSR. US policy impacted the course of the Cuban Revolution, but it was determined by Cubans.

Benjamin (1990) takes a longer-term approach, examining US relations with Cuba from the early nineteenth century, but much of his book focuses on US relations with Batista and the Eisenhower administration's response to the Cuban Revolution. Benjamin sees the United States as fearful of radical nationalism, favoring dictatorship over change. While Welch mentions Cuban conditions, Benjamin discusses them more fully, describing the Batista regime's decline and fall in the context of Cuban politics and economy. Benjamin also shows that the US policy was contested, highlighting conflicts between conservatives and liberals (who often had Latin American allies). Liberals expected and accepted a measure of Cuban nationalism or anti-Yankee feeling. But liberals who sought to distance the United States from Batista would be the same group who would later support US efforts to topple Castro. Benjamin argues that liberals held the mistaken belief that Cuba was so oriented toward North American values, that when Castro radicalized the revolution, strong opposition would emerge from Cubans who would fight for US and their common interests. Attentive to Cuban history, Pérez and Benjamin agree that US influence pervaded Cuba, contributing to the intense anti-Americanism that fueled Castro's success and at the same time creating the dependence upon North America that led Castro's opposition to rely upon salvation from the United States. Welch, Benjamin, and Rabe also discuss the Eisenhower administration's efforts to use the CIA and Cuban exiles to destabilize or overthrow the Cuban government, a policy that Kennedy would inherit. Rabe's (1988) book on the Eisenhower administration offers an additional perspective by placing Eisenhower's Cuban policy in the context of his larger Latin American policy. In particular, he shows how the administration sought to destabilize both the rightist dictator Rafael Trujillo of the Dominican Republic and the leftist Cuban Revolution. This larger context gives poignancy to Benjamin's argument that US policymakers, misled by their sense of harmony of interests between the Americans and Cubans, never reconciled their "contradictory need both to stabilize and to change Cuban society" (Benjamin 1990: 212). The conviction that reform, not revolution, was in the interests of both the United States and Latin America was not new, but the success of the Cuban Revolution and its ties to the Soviet Union altered the sense of urgency with which US policymakers sought to encourage reform and forestall revolution. The impact of the Cuban Revolution would dominate the contours of US–Latin American relations in the years to come.

In the period between 1942 and 1960 the effects of US power and interests in

Latin American nations were great, despite a sense that much of the period was marked by "neglect." The impact of US influence was particularly great in the Caribbean and Central America. US economic and security policy sometimes made or broke Latin American governments. US investments had consequences for local and national economies, and impacted societies through the introduction of American popular and corporate culture. Most North American scholarship on US–Latin American relations for the period 1942–60 explains the development of US policy, the methods and motives for assertion of political and economic power, and the projection of US perceptions upon Latin America. Increasingly, scholars demonstrate that Latin Americans also shape inter-American relations. Such efforts are challenging because of the diversity of the region and the difficulties North American scholars face as they attempt to understand other cultural contexts, so deeply are they enmeshed in their own. The ways in which the people of Latin America and their leaders – democratic or not – respond to US policy, power, and culture, and the process of interaction, remain unclear.

REFERENCES

Ambrose, Stephen E. and Richard H. Immerman: *Ike's Spies: Eisenhower and the Espionage Establishment* (Garden City, NY: Doubleday, 1981).

Ameringer, Charles D.: *The Democratic Left in Exile: The Anti-Dictatorial Struggle in the Caribbean, 1945–1975* (Coral Gables, FL: University of Miami Press, 1974).

Ameringer, Charles D.: *The Caribbean Legion: Patriots, Politicians, Soldiers of Fortune, 1946–1950* (University Park: Pennsylvania State University Press, 1996).

Atkins, G. Pope.: *Latin America in the International Political System* (Boulder, CO: Westview Press, 1989).

Atkins, G. Pope and Larman C. Wilson: *The United States and the Trujillo Regime* (New Brunswick, NJ: Rutgers University Press, 1972).

Atkins, G. Pope and Larman C. Wilson: *The Dominican Republic and the United States: From Imperialism to Transnationalism* (Athens, GA: University of Georgia Press, 1998).

Baily, Samuel L.: *The United States and the Development of South America, 1945–1975* (New York: New Viewpoints, 1976).

Baldwin, David A.: *Economic Development and American Foreign Policy, 1943–1962* (Chicago, IL: University of Chicago Press, 1966).

Baptiste, Fitzroy Andre: *War, Cooperation, and Conflict: The European Possessions in the Caribbean, 1939–1945* (New York: Greenwood Press, 1988).

Bemis, Samuel Flagg: *The Latin American Policy of the United States: An Historical Interpretation by Samuel Flagg Bemis* (New York: Harcourt, Brace, and World, 1943).

Benjamin, Jules R.: *The United States and the Origins of the Cuban Revolution: An Empire of Liberty in an Age of National Liberation* (Princeton, NJ: Princeton University Press, 1990).

Berger, Mark T.: *Under Northern Eyes: Latin American Studies and United States Hegemony in the Americas, 1898–1990* (Bloomington: Indiana University Press, 1995).

Bethell, Leslie and Ian Roxborough (eds.): *Latin America Between the Second World War and the Cold War, 1944–1948* (Cambridge: Cambridge University Press, 1992).

Blasier, Cole: *The Hovering Giant: US Responses to Revolutionary Change in Latin America* (Pittsburgh, PA: University of Pittsburgh Press, 1976).

Blasier, Cole: *The Giant's Rival: The USSR and Latin America* (Pittsburgh, PA: University of Pittsburgh Press, 1983).

Brands, H. W.: "Milton Eisenhower and the Coming Revolution in Latin America." In *Cold Warriors: Eisenhower's Generation and American Foreign Policy* (New York: Columbia University Press, 1988).

Campbell, Thomas M.: *Masquerade Peace: America's UN Policy, 1944–1945* (Tallahassee: Florida State University Press, 1973).

Clark, Paul Coe, Jr.: *The United States and Somoza, 1933–1956: A Revisionist Look* (Westport, CT: Praeger, 1992).

Clayton, Lawerence A.: *Peru and the United States: The Condor and the Eagle* (Athens, GA: University of Georgia Press, 1999).

Cobbs, Elizabeth A.: *The Rich Neighbor Policy: Rockefeller and Kaiser in Brazil* (New Haven, CT: Yale University Press, 1992).

Connell-Smith, Gordon: *The Inter-American System* (Oxford: Oxford University Press, 1966).

Connell-Smith, Gordon: *The United States and Latin America: An Historical Analysis of Inter-American Relations* (New York: John Wiley and Sons, 1974).

Conniff, Michael L.: *Panama and the United States: The Forced Alliance* (Athens, GA: University of Georgia Press, 1992).

Cottam, Martha L.: *Images and Intervention: US Policies in Latin America* (Pittsburgh, PA: University of Pittsburgh Press, 1994).

Cueto, Marcos (ed.): *Missionaries of Science: The Rockefeller Foundation and Latin America* (Bloomington: Indiana University Press, 1994).

Curti, Merle: *American Philanthropy Abroad: A History* (New Brunswick, NJ: Rutgers University Press, 1963).

Divine, Robert A.: *Second Chance: The Triumph of Internationalism during World War II* (New York: Atheneum, 1967).

Dosal, Paul J.: *Doing Business with the Dictators: A Political History of United Fruit in Guatemala, 1899–1944* (Wilmington, DE: Scholarly Resources, 1993).

Dozer, Donald M.: *Are We Good Neighbors? Three Decades of Inter-American Relations, 1930–1960* (Pittsburgh, PA: University of Pittsburgh Press, 1961).

Erb, Claude C.: "Prelude to Point Four: The Institute of Inter-American Affairs." *Diplomatic History* 9 (summer 1985), 249–69.

Espinoza, J. Manuel: *Inter-American Beginnings of US Cultural Diplomacy, 1936–1948* (Washington, DC: Bureau of Educational and Cultural Affairs, US Department of State, 1976).

Ewell, Judith: *Venezuela and the United States: From Monroe's Hemisphere to Petroleum's Empire* (Athens, GA: University of Georgia Press, 1996).

Findling, John E.: *Close Neighbors, Distant Friends: United States–Central American Relations* (New York: Greenwood Press, 1987).

Francis, Michael L.: *The Limits of Hegemony: United States Relations with Argentina and Chile during World War II* (Notre Dame, IN: University of Notre Dame Press, 1977).

Frank, Gary: *Struggle for Hegemony in South America: Argentina, Brazil, and the United States during the Second World War* (Miami, FL: University of Miami, 1979).

Frank, Gary: *Juan Perón v. Spruille Braden: The Story Behind the Blue Book* (Lanham, MD: University Press of America, 1980).

Gambone, Michael: *Eisenhower, Somoza, and the Cold War in Nicaragua, 1953–1961* (Westport, CT: Praeger, 1997).

Gardner, Lloyd C.: *Economic Aspects of New Deal Diplomacy* (Madison: University of Wisconsin Press, 1964).

Gellman, Irwin F.: *Good Neighbor Diplomacy: United States Policies in Latin America, 1933–1945* (Baltimore, MD: Johns Hopkins University Press, 1979).

Gellman, Irwin F.: *Secret Affairs: Franklin Roosevelt, Cordell Hull, and Sumner Welles* (Baltimore, MD: Johns Hopkins University Press, 1995).

Gleijeses, Piero: *Shattered Hope: The Guatemalan Revolution and the United States, 1944–1954* (Princeton, NJ: Princeton University Press, 1991).

Green, David: *The Containment of Latin America: A History of the Myths and Realities of the Good Neighbor Policy* (Chicago, IL: Quadrangle Books, 1971).

Grow, Michael: *The Good Neighbor Policy and Authoritarianism in Paraguay: United States Economic Expansion and Great-Power Rivalry in Latin America during World War II* (Lawrence: Regents Press of Kansas, 1981).

Haines, Gerald K.: "Under the Eagle's Wing: The Franklin Roosevelt Administration Forges an American Hemisphere." *Diplomatic History* 1 (fall 1977), 373–88.

Haines, Gerald K.: *The Americanization of Brazil: A Study of US Cold War Diplomacy in the Third World, 1945–1954* (Wilmington, DE: Scholarly Resources, 1989).

Hall, Michael R.: *Sugar and Power in the Dominican Republic: Eisenhower, Kennedy, and the Trujillos* (Westport, CT: Greenwood Press, 2000).

Hilton, Stanley E.: *Hitler's Secret War in South America, 1939–1945: German Military Espionage and Allied Counterespionage in Brazil* (Baton Rouge: Louisiana State University Press, 1981a).

Hilton, Stanley E.: "The United States, Brazil, and the Cold War, 1945–1969: End of the Special Relationship." *Journal of American History* 68 (December 1981b), 599–624.

Humphreys, R. A.: *Latin America and the Second World War, 1938–1945*, 2 vols. (London: University of London, 1981–2).

Immerman, Richard H.: *The CIA in Guatemala: The Foreign Policy of Intervention* (Austin: University of Texas Press, 1982).

Inis, Claude L., Jr.: "The OAS, the UN, and the United States." In Richard A. Falk and Saul H. Mendlovitz (eds.) *Regional Politics and World Order* (San Francisco: W. H. Freeman, 1973).

Kauffman, Burton Ira: *Trade and Aid: Eisenhower's Foreign Policy, 1953–1961* (Baltimore, MD: Johns Hopkins University Press, 1982).

Kofas, Jon V.: *The Struggle for Legitimacy: Latin American Labor and the United States, 1930–1960* (Tempe: Arizona State University Press, 1992).

Kolko, Gabriel: *Confronting the Third World: United States Foreign Policy, 1945–1980* (New York: Pantheon Books, 1988).

Krenn, Michael: *The Chains of Interdependence: US Policy Toward Central America, 1945–1954* (Armonk, NY: Sharpe, 1996).

LaFeber, Walter: *Inevitable Revolutions: The United States and Central America* (New York: Norton, 1983).

Langley, Lester D.: *America and the Americas: The United States in the Western Hemisphere* (Athens, GA: University of Georgia Press, 1989).

Lehman, Kenneth D.: *Bolivia and the United States: A Limited Partnership* (Athens, GA: University of Georgia Press, 1999).

Leonard, Thomas M.: *The United States and Central America, 1944–1949: Perceptions of Political Dynamics* (University Park: University of Alabama Press, 1984).

Leonard, Thomas M.: *Central America and the United States: The Search for Stability* (Athens, GA: University of Georgia Press, 1991).

Liss, Sheldon B.: *The Canal: Aspects of United States Panamanian Relations* (Notre Dame, IN: University of Notre Dame Press, 1967).

Longley, Kyle: *The Sparrow and the Hawk: Costa Rica and the United States during the Rise of José Figueres* (Tuscaloosa: University of Alabama Press, 1997).

McCann, Frank D.: *The Brazilian–American Alliance, 1937–1945* (Princeton, NJ: Princeton University Press, 1973).

Marks, Frederick W., III: "The CIA and Castillo Armas in Guatemala, 1954: New Clues to an Old Puzzle." *Diplomatic History* 14 (winter 1990), 67–86.

May, Ernest R.: "'The Bureaucratic Politics' Approach: US–Argentine Relations, 1942–1947." In Julio Cotler and Richard R. Fagan (eds.) *Latin America and the United States: The Changing Political Realities* (Stanford, CA: Stanford University Press, 1974).

Mecham, J. Lloyd: *The United States and Inter-American Security, 1889–1960* (Austin: University of Texas Press, 1961).

Niblo, Stephen R.: *War, Diplomacy, and Development: The United States and Mexico, 1938–1954* (Wilmington, DE: Scholarly Resources, 1995).

Ninkovich, Frank A.: *The Diplomacy of Ideas: United States Foreign Policy and Cultural Relations, 1938–1950* (New York: Cambridge University Press, 1981).

O'Brien, Thomas F.: *Revolutionary Mission: American Enterprise in Latin America, 1900–1945* (Cambridge: Cambridge University Press, 1996).

Pach, Chester, Jr.: "The Containment of US Military Aid to Latin America, 1944–1949." *Diplomatic History* 6 (summer 1982), 225–44.

Pach, Chester J., Jr.: *Arming the Free World: The Origins of the United States Military Assistance Program, 1945–1950* (Chapel Hill: University of North Carolina Press, 1991).

Packenham, Robert A.: *Liberal America and the Third World: Political Development Ideas in Foreign Aid and Social Science* (Princeton, NJ: Princeton University Press, 1989).

Park, James William: *Latin American Underdevelopment: A History of Perspectives in the United States, 1870–1965* (Baton Rouge: Louisiana State University Press, 1995).

Parkinson, F.: *Latin America, the Cold War, and the World Powers, 1945–1973*. Sage Library of Social Research, no. 9 (Beverly Hills, CA: Sage Publishers, 1974).

Paterson, Thomas G.: "Foreign Aid Under Wraps: The Point Four Program." *Wisconsin Magazine of History* 56, 2 (winter 1972–3), 119–26.

Paz, María Emilia: *Strategy, Security, and Spies: Mexico and the US as Allies in World War II* (University Park: Pennsylvania State University Press, 1997).

Pérez, Louis A., Jr.: "International Dimensions of Inter-American Relations, 1944–1960." *Inter-American Economic Affairs* 27, 1 (summer 1973), 47–68.

Pérez, Louis A., Jr.: *Cuba and the United States: Ties of Singular Intimacy* (Athens, GA: University of Georgia Press, 1997).

Pike, Fredrick B.: *The United States and Latin America: Myths and Stereotypes of Civilization and Nature* (Austin: University of Texas Press, 1992).

Pike, Fredrick B.: *FDR's Good Neighbor Policy: Sixty Years of Generally Gentle Chaos* (Austin: University of Texas Press, 1995).

Plummer, Brenda Gayle: *Haiti and the United States: The Psychological Moment* (Athens, GA: University of Georgia Press, 1992).

Rabe, Stephen G.: "The Elusive Conference: United States Economic Relations with Latin America, 1945–1952." *Diplomatic History* 2 (summer 1978), 79–294.

Rabe, Stephen G.: *The Road to OPEC: United States Relations with Venezuela, 1919–1976* (Austin: University of Texas Press, 1982).

Rabe, Stephen G.: *Eisenhower and Latin America: The Foreign Policy of Anti-Communism* (Chapel Hill: University of North Carolina Press, 1988).

Randall, Stephen J.: *Colombia and the United States: Hegemony and Interdependence* (Athens, GA: University of Georgia Press, 1992).

Rippy, J. Fred: *Globe and Hemisphere: Latin America's Place in the Postwar Foreign Relations of the United States* (Chicago, IL: H. Regnery, 1958).

Rivas, Darlene: *Missionary Capitalist: Nelson Rockefeller in Venezuela* (Chapel Hill: University of North Carolina Press, 2002).

Roorda, Eric: *The Dictator Next Door: The Good Neighbor Policy and the Trujillo Regime in the Dominican Republic, 1930–1945* (Durham, NC: Duke University Press, 1998).

Rosenberg, Emily: *Spreading the American Dream: American Economic and Cultural Expansion, 1890–1945* (New York: Hill and Wang, 1982).

Rout, Leslie B., Jr., and John F. Bratzel: *The Shadow War: German Espionage and United States Counterespionage in Latin America during World War II* (Frederick, MD: University Publications of America, 1986).

Sater, William F.: *Chile and the United States: Empires in Conflict* (Athens, GA: University of Georgia Press, 1990).

Schlesinger, Stephen C. and Stephen Kinzer: *Bitter Fruit: The Untold Story of the American Coup in Guatemala* (Garden City, NY: Doubleday, 1982).

Schmitz, David F.: *Thank God They're On Our Side: The United States and Right Wing Dictatorships, 1921–1965* (Chapel Hill: University of North Carolina Press, 1999).

Schoultz, Lars: *National Security and United States Policy toward Latin America* (Princeton, NJ: Princeton University Press, 1987).

Schoultz, Lars: *Beneath the United States: A History of US Policy Toward Latin America* (Cambridge, MA: Harvard University Press, 1998).

Siekmeier, James F.: *Aid, Nationalism, and Inter-American Relations: Guatemala, Bolivia, and the United States, 1945–1961* (Lewiston, NY: Mellen Press, 1999).

Skidmore, Thomas E.: *Politics in Brazil, 1930–1964: An Experiment in Democracy* (New York: Oxford University Press, 1967).

Smith, Gaddis: *The Last Years of the Monroe Doctrine, 1945–1993* (New York: Hill and Wang, 1994).

Steward, Dick: *Trade and Hemisphere: The Good Neighbor Policy and Reciprocal Trade* (Columbia: University of Missouri Press, 1975).

Streeter, Stephen M.: *Managing the Counter-Revolution: The United States and Guatemala, 1954–1961* (Athens, GA: University of Ohio Press, 2000).

Taylor, Graham D.: "The Axis Replacement Program: Economic Warfare and the Chemical Industry in Latin America, 1942–1944." *Diplomatic History* 8 (spring 1984), 145–64.

Thomas, Leonard: *The United States and Central America, 1944–1949: Perceptions of Political Change* (1984).

Tillapaugh, J.: "Closed Hemisphere and Open World? The Dispute over Regional Security at the UN Conference, 1945." *Diplomatic History* 2 (winter 1978), 25–42.

Trask, Roger R.: "The Impact of the Cold War on United States–Latin American Relations, 1945–1949." *Diplomatic History* 1 (summer 1977), 271–84.

Trask, Roger R.: "George F. Kennan's Report on Latin America (1950)." *Diplomatic History* 2 (summer 1978), 307–11.

Trask, Roger R.: "Spruille Brade versus George Messersmith: World War II, the Cold War, and Argentine Policy, 1945–1947." *Journal of Inter-American Studies and World Affairs* 26 (February 1984), 69–95.

Weis, W. Michael: *Cold Warriors and Coups d'Etat: Brazilian–American Relations, 1945–1964* (Albuquerque: University of New Mexico Press, 1993).

Welch, Richard E., Jr.: *Response to Revolution: The United States and the Cuban Revolution, 1959–1961* (Chapel Hill: University of North Carolina Press, 1985).

Whitaker, Arthur Preston: *The Western Hemisphere Idea: Its Rise and Decline* (Ithaca, NY: Cornell University Press, 1954).

Wilkins, Mira: *Maturing of Multinational Enterprise, 1941–1970* (Cambridge, MA: Harvard University Press, 1974).

Wood, Bryce: *The Dismantling of the Good Neighbor Policy* (Austin: University of Texas Press, 1985).

Woods, Randall Bennet: *The Roosevelt Foreign Policy Establishment and the "Good Neighbor": The United States and Argentina, 1941–1945* (Lawrence: Regents Press of Kansas, 1979).

Zoumaras, Thomas: "Containing Castro: Promoting Homeownership in Peru, 1956–1961."
    Diplomatic History 10 (spring 1986), 161–81.
Zoumaras, Thomas: "Eisenhower's Economic Policy, The Case of Latin America." In Richard
    A. Melanson and David Mayers (eds.) *Reevaluating Eisenhower: American Foreign Policy
    in the 1950s* (Urbana: University of Illinois Press, 1987).

CHAPTER FIFTEEN

From Containment to Containment? Understanding US Relations with China since 1949

EVELYN GOH AND ROSEMARY FOOT

At the start of the twenty-first century, the state of the US–China relationship to some degree resembles the period when the Cold War was at its height. Levels of distrust between the two major states are sufficiently high that points of contention often evolve into crises in relations; those in charge of determining the respective defense strategies pay close attention to the capabilities and intentions of the other side; and the Taiwan issue remains a major source of discord. Chinese perceptions of US policy exhibit considerable stability: US policy was one of containment and disruption of Chinese communist rule in the 1950s, they aver, and retains those goals today, even though America may occasionally dress up its stance as one designed to engage an important regional and increasingly global power. There are some similarities in perception and policy on the US side too. The Bush administration in 2002 registers a concern about China's rise reminiscent of the Eisenhower administration's fear of the People's Republic of China (PRC) as the "wave of the future," and searches for a policy that both satisfies domestic constituencies of importance to it, as well as the Asia–Pacific governments that are strongly concerned to maintain regional stability.

Unlike in the 1950s there are now multiple points of interaction between the two societies, whether we focus our attention on economic relations, educational and cultural exchanges, or military and political contacts. Each of these areas has provided us with important new information to interpret and weigh, well beyond the material that was available to those who chose to study this relationship prior to the time of normalization in 1979. Those writing about earlier phases of Sino-American inter-actions were unable to reach a consensus on the interpretation of major issues and events, a result, it was said, of the lack of sources (McMahon 1995). This lack of consensus has been evident, too, in later writings. In a valuable historiographical article, Nancy B. Tucker (1996) argued persuasively that, despite the addition of a range of important new materials, "Discovery and controversy are the norm rather than any fresh, satisfying, and widely accepted paradigm" (p. 215). In this review of the field, we concur broadly with this finding. Despite two decades or more of greater interconnectedness between the two countries, the literature on this topic still does not allow us easily to generalize about the quality or meaning of those ties:

are they "fragile" as Harry Harding (1992) has argued, or "substantial" (if often conflictual) as Steven Levine (1994) contends? Should we interpret the normalization policy in 1979 as an important chapter in the revitalization of an American-defined liberal world order (Madsen 1995), or as being about the need for the US to balance against its primary strategic enemy, the former Soviet Union (Ross 1993)? Do interdependence and reasonable prospects for stability define the predominant trend in US–China relations, or does China's growing economic and military strength connected with this interdependence portend future serious tension, if not military conflict, between the two countries? Students of this relationship face a hard task in the absence of settled responses to these and many similar questions.

Such students, however, do not lack material that can form the basis of an assessment. Archival and other sources have grown markedly in the last twenty years or so. The Foreign Relations series on US–China now covers the years until 1968, and presidential library materials are steadily opening, only beginning to become patchier after the Nixon era. The privately financed National Security Archive in Washington, DC has a wealth of documentation across the five decades of the relationship, and interview and oral history materials in this and many other locations abound. Tucker's (2001) collation of American foreign service personnel's recollections of the China relationship has added significantly to the oral history base.

With China's decision in 1978 to open up and embark on radical economic reform has come an inevitable flood of new materials from China itself, some available from official sources, others via more clandestine routes. Western and Chinese scholars, together with journalists, have mined these writings for important insights into Chinese society, policymaking, and elite perceptions. The international history of the Cold War has been transformed by major revelations from the Chinese side, as well as from materials gathered from a range of former Soviet bloc countries, many of which have appeared in the invaluable *Cold War International History Project Bulletin*. In the contemporary period, analyses of Chinese perceptions have been particularly important in shaping 1990s policy advice to the US government from the academic community. The *rapprochement* and normalization of US–China relations also guaranteed that many US policymakers had direct experience of negotiating with their Chinese counterparts, leading to the production of memoirs and articles in policy-relevant journals designed to impart something of the quality of that experience. Since many of those US officials involved in the process disagreed about how the relationship with China should be approached, these memoirs, together with investigations undertaken by US journalists (Mann 1998; Tyler 1999), have provided insight into the often warlike tactics used by policymakers and middle-ranking officials to ensure the outcomes they desired. As a result, we have also added to our knowledge of the operational procedures inside America's complex bureaucratic and governmental structures.

These new, multiple strands in the US–China relationship have been responsible for two additional developments: a growing number of writings about particular issue areas – economics, domestic sources of policy, human rights, Taiwan, and the like (Foot 1995; Ross 1998) – and a realization that both US and Chinese interactions involve a range of actors going well beyond the political elites based in Washington or Beijing. These actors often have different interests in or perspectives on the relationship. As Richard Madsen (1995: 218) has aptly put it: "It now makes less sense to speak of 'US–China Relations' than to talk of how one part of the United States (for instance, Chinese-Americans, southern black textile workers, or directors of multinational corporations) relates to one part of China (for instance, Beijing intellectuals, Guangdong entrepreneurs, or central government officials)."

If the relationship can now be approached from a variety of vantage points, it is also vital for an understanding of those ties that historians regularly go beyond the writings of their own disciplinary colleagues, and the journals that they habitually use. Diplomatic historians – more often than in the past – now bring insights into their work from cultural and economic history (Tucker 1994). Important too is the work of international relations specialists, especially those working in the various sub-branches of the field such as security studies, political economy, institutional analysis, foreign policy, and decision-making. For historians, investigating these writings is not a daunting enterprise. In general, political scientists working on US–China relations tend to deploy their conceptual and theoretical apparatuses with a light touch. For example, the political scientist Harry Harding in *A Fragile Relationship* (1992) adopts an analytical and thematic approach, utilizing the idea of different levels of analysis from international to individual, together with treatment of various issue areas, as a way of organizing a twenty-year span in the relationship; but he does not engage in theory testing. Robert S. Ross (1995), also from political science, looks at the internal and external factors that shaped negotiating behavior, but makes little reference to the broader theoretical literature on bargaining and negotiating strategies. Although their sources of evidence may be somewhat different from those that diplomatic historians traditionally deploy, neither their methods nor their language are difficult to penetrate.

In the pages that follow, we hope to be able to give a flavor of some of the best of this literature, focusing on the major events and issues that help to illuminate this relationship and area of study. We draw on the work of historians, international relations specialists, journalists, and memoirists, particularly those studies published since the 1990s, in order to demonstrate the range of work available to those intending to embark on the study of this topic. We would also like to convince those who need convincing that cross-disciplinary investigations are both rewarding in themselves and advance the primary goal of improving the levels of understanding of this crucial relationship.

Relations During the Cold War

US relations with the PRC began inauspiciously: the dust had barely settled after the communist victory on the mainland in late 1949 when a war broke out on the Korean peninsular (June 1950), which eventually pitted Chinese communist soldiers against US-led UN forces. For the next thirty years, US relations with "China" were formally conducted with the nationalist regime of the Republic of China (ROC) on Taiwan. US policy towards communist China from the Eisenhower administration to the Johnson administration was one of simultaneous diplomatic isolation and military-strategic containment. In this period, US antagonism towards China was situated firmly within the framework of the Cold War. It was premised on opposition to the spread of communist ideology and strategic containment of the communist-inspired threat to the national security of vital US allies and newly emerging states.

The Sino-American relationship was fundamentally altered only in the early 1970s, when Nixon negotiated a *rapprochement* with the PRC (1971–2), laying the foundations for diplomatic recognition and the "normalization" of relations under the Carter administration in 1979.

The changing US relationship with the PRC over these first thirty years was the result of evaluations and re-evaluations of China's identity and intentions, and the threat Beijing posed to US interests. Domestic politics, bureaucratic struggles, and policy debate influenced key policy actors' responses to the crises that buffeted and enveloped the two states. So too did culture, ideology, beliefs, and perceptions. The available literature on this period has focused on the strategic aspects of US–China policy: the origins of the Cold War in Asia, the two key "hot wars" in Korea and Vietnam, the strategic US–PRC–Soviet triangle, and the move towards normalization. More recent studies of this early phase in relations emphasize the contested policymaking processes; the importance of perceptions, mid-level official debates, and "secret" channels; and the Chinese perspective.

1949–1960: Crises and Confrontation

Viewed from the vantage point of the 1972 *rapprochement*, it would appear that realist balance-of-power logic had been flouted in US Cold War policy towards China prior to that breakthrough. Why did Washington not pursue accommodation with Beijing to forge a countervailing force against the Soviet Union, and why was it necessary to oppose the PRC to the extent of fighting two major wars in East Asia? An analysis of these questions must begin with the decision that faced the Truman administration in 1949. For the last twenty years, scholars working on the early US–PRC relationship have grappled with the idea that Washington might have missed an opportunity to reach an accommodation with the Chinese communists in the late 1940s. Such a development in turn might have forestalled the Sino-Soviet treaty of 1950, avoided the war with China in Korea, and moderated the imperative to contain China that ultimately led to the Vietnam debacle. The original debate over this "lost chance" thesis was published in a volume edited by Dorothy Borg and Waldo Heinrichs (1980). As presented by its most persuasive proponents, Warren Cohen and Nancy Tucker (see also Tucker 1983), the basic argument is that, prior to the Korean War, the Truman administration, led by Secretary of State Dean Acheson, had hoped to promote a Sino-Soviet breach and contemplated accommodation with Beijing to a greater extent than was recognized at the time or afterwards. It was the outbreak of the Korean War that put paid to this opportunity.

This contention has been challenged by scholars who emphasize Acheson's "Cold Warrior" outlook (Leffler 1992; McLean 1986) and domestic political constraints in the form of the conservative backlash to the "loss" of China. Cohen himself (2000) sees the latter as the key reason for Acheson's bureaucratic defeat over China policy. Furthermore, Thomas J. Christensen (1996) has persuasively demonstrated that China policy was an instrument for domestic mobilization behind the Truman administration's developing Cold War campaign in Europe: to maintain consistency in its anti-communist cause, Washington could not, in fact, seek accommodation with communist China in 1949.

However, it is with recent works by China scholars using Chinese documentary evidence that the debate has taken its most interesting turn. The significance of Cohen's thesis turns on the assumption that Mao seriously considered a formal relationship with the US to gain economic aid and insurance against Soviet expansionism. But these new works firmly oppose the idea of a "lost chance" and argue that China was never America's to "lose" in the first place. In a symposium in the journal *Diplomatic History* (1997), Chen Jian, John Garver, Michael Sheng, and Odd Arne Westad each reject the possibility of an alliance, or even diplomatic and economic relations, between the US and the PRC in 1949–50. These scholars assert that, because of their anti-imperialist ideology and the imperatives of regime security and nation-building, the Chinese communist leaders were not in a position to contemplate accommodation with the US. The debate is by no means over, but this new scholarship highlights the importance of studying the Chinese record and perspective on US–China relations. As we await the more comprehensive opening of Chinese and Soviet-era archives, we may move towards consensus on a more moderate version of the opportunities in 1949–50: in spite of the apparent realpolitik logic, there were serious domestic and ideological constraints on both sides, even granting that the two protagonists had seriously considered limited accommodation. Thus, it was a nascent but ultimately unfulfilled (or unfulfillable) opportunity.

We might note similar trends in studies of the US–PRC confrontation during the Korean War. New evidence pertaining to the Soviet, Chinese, and North Korean roles in the conflict has supplemented earlier scholarship concerned with explaining the nature of the US intervention in the war and its consequences. These earlier studies emphasized that the US made two somewhat contradictory miscalculations. First, Washington assumed that the North Korean attack on the South represented the latest advance in a Sino-Soviet instigated extension of communist influence. In this regard, Rosemary Foot (1985, 1990) has shown that US Cold War attitudes undermined a diplomatic approach to the crisis and reinforced the Truman and later Eisenhower administrations' predilections for a military solution to the extent of considering possible nuclear action. Second, the US decision to advance beyond the 38th parallel, which triggered the disastrous Chinese intervention, occurred because Washington had ignored Chinese warnings, failed to understand the security threat the UN advance posed to China, and underestimated Beijing's ability to mount a serious war effort (Whiting 1960; Stueck 1981).

Yet miscalculations occurred on both the American and the Chinese sides, contributing to the failure of deterrence strategies (Zhang 1992). Within the communist camp itself, misperceptions and disputes also rendered it predisposed towards confrontation with the US. The North Korean leader, Kim Il Sung, actively played on the Sino-Soviet alliance and international communism to further his own nationalist cause, and inflated the chances of his victory over the South to gain Stalin's support (Stueck 1995; Weathersby 1993). While Moscow's support was undoubtedly crucial for Kim's invasion of the South, in line with most post-revisionist assessments of Stalin's foreign policy, his agreement to support Pyongyang is seen as opportunistic and cautious. Initially reluctant to risk war with the US, Stalin changed his mind in the spring of 1950. While the reasons for this are still unclear, it probably stemmed from Stalin's perception that the threat of a confrontation with the US had receded after the latter acquiesced to the "loss" of China. Soviet miscalculation could also have related to Acheson's infamous speech in

January 1950 excluding South Korea from the US strategic line of defense (Stueck 1995). At the same time, the signing of the Sino-Soviet treaty of alliance in February 1950 allowed Stalin to delegate to the Chinese communists the direct military role in helping North Korea. Indeed, the Korean War can be regarded as an arena for the testing of the new Sino-Soviet alliance, and recent works have emphasized the tension and distrust in the partnership, particularly the confusion and discord as Beijing came closer to its decision to intervene after the landing of UN forces at Inchon in September 1950 (Goncharov, Lewis, and Xue 1993; Mansourov 1995/6).

The Korean War was the turning point in the globalization of the Cold War, and a crisis during which the key antagonists were still testing each other's resolve and evaluating the extent to which their respective interests coincided or diverged. In terms of the US–PRC confrontation, US actions in interposing the 7th Fleet in the Taiwan Straits and crossing the 38th parallel were crucial catalysts for the Chinese intervention. However, while earlier works asserted that Mao had reacted defensively (Whiting 1960), more recently, China scholars have argued that US action provided the justification, rather than the trigger, for Chinese involvement. Chen (1994) suggests that Mao had been ready to participate in the war well before US troops approached the Chinese border, primarily to demonstrate Chinese affinity with international communism and loyalty to the Sino-Soviet alliance, but also for reasons of domestic mobilization.

This image of communist Chinese belligerence appears to have been borne out in the two crises in the Taiwan Straits, which swiftly followed the Korean War in 1954/5 and 1958, when Beijing bombarded offshore islands held by the Nationalists. Orthodox accounts of the crises suggested that these were further instances of Chinese expansionism that were curbed by the Eisenhower administration's brinkmanship. The recent literature, in contrast, is more circumspect, and again features the twin themes of domestic mobilization and strategic misperception.

On the Chinese side, there is general agreement that Beijing's aim was not to seize the offshore islands, but rather to assert its sovereign claims to Taiwan, and to try to thwart US moves towards a "two Chinas" policy and closer relations with the ROC (He and Chang 1993). However, Zhang Shuguang (1992) points out that Beijing misperceived US intentions in that it was convinced that Washington wanted to control Taiwan as part of a policy to encircle China. Mao thus pursued "coercive diplomacy" to preempt more dangerous developments, but this was a costly miscalculation. In 1954 it led to precisely that deepening of US–ROC relations in the form of the mutual defense treaty; and in the 1958 crisis, it exacerbated Sino-Soviet tensions when Moscow proved reluctant to come to Beijing's aid. Similarly, Zhang suggests, US actions were underpinned by a fundamental misperception that Beijing's actions in the Taiwan Straits were an instance of Soviet-backed communist expansion, and that the reinforcement of US military deterrence in the area was the only reasonable response.

Robert Accinelli (1996, 2001) provides a more nuanced account. He emphasizes the Eisenhower administration's appreciation of the symbolic importance of the offshore islands to Chiang Kai-shek's regime, which led it to support the government on Taiwan, while also restraining both communists and nationalists from escalating the conflicts. He portrays a cautious Eisenhower, constrained by domestic and allied concerns about the danger of a nuclear war; and agrees with Tucker (1996), who particularly stresses that Eisenhower and Dulles were rhetorically belligerent, but cautious in practice, during the two crises. This is in line generally with the revisionist interpretation of Eisenhower and Dulles' China policy as having been more flexible than previously thought. These two US leaders recognized that the communist bloc was not monolithic and developed a "wedge" strategy to try to exacerbate Sino-Soviet differences (Mayers 1986; Gaddis 1989). Additionally, Dulles exercised significant restraint on the nationalist ambition to return to the mainland, and pursued a realistic "two Chinas" policy (Tucker 1990). Garver (1997b) makes the connection between these two aims, emphasizing the political usefulness of the US–ROC alliance to America's Cold War campaign in that, by denying Taiwan to Beijing, Washington helped to foster the Sino-Soviet split.

However, Dulles' attempt to shape a "two Chinas" policy came to nothing, fundamentally because the one issue on which Beijing and Taipei agreed was the principle of "one China." In the 1960s the Kennedy and Johnson administrations would continue to restrain Chiang and work to keep the PRC out of the UN, but the idea of actively fostering a "two Chinas" solution received very little sustained policy study. Ironically, it was the Nixon administration that eventually came closest to promoting this. When it seemed that the PRC would be voted in to replace the ROC at the UN in 1971, the administration officially supported and worked hard to gain support for a dual representation solution (Foot 1995; Ross 1995). In the event, though, Nixon's policy of *rapprochement* and Kissinger's dramatic secret trip to Beijing ahead of the UN vote undermined any chance of success, and Nixon officially subscribed to the principle of "one China" in the Shanghai Communiqué in February 1972.

1961–1968: Isolation, Containment, and Reassessment

US relations with China in the 1960s may be seen as an extension of the 1950s pattern of a hostile stalemate punctuated by periodic crises. Kennedy and Johnson continued the policy of containment and isolation towards China, and embarked on a large-scale military commitment in Indochina to counter what was regarded as the expansion of Chinese communist influence and aggression.

Some Kennedy-era officials have suggested that, had he lived, he would have modified China policy and sought diplomatic relations with China (Schlesinger 1965; Hilsman 1967). However, other works based on archival material contend that Kennedy's stance on China was less flexible. Principally, Kennedy was constrained by domestic politics because of his slim election victory, the legacy of McCarthyism, and the charge of "softness" towards the Chinese communists attending a Democratic administration (Cohen 1980b). Tucker (1996) and Leonard Kusnitz (1984) have additionally observed that Kennedy probably tried to foster the image of an aggressive, irrational China to provide an object to satisfy "domestic xenophobia," so as to allow Washington to cultivate a post-Cuban missile crisis détente with Moscow.

Recent scholarship has more clearly emphasized Kennedy's personal reservations as the obstacle to changing China policy: along with his preoccupation with demonstrating US credibility and his belief in the domino theory, he was also ethnocentric and particularly suspicious of the Chinese communists. Noam Kochavi (1998) asserts that Kennedy viewed China as the more unpredictable and dangerous of the two communist powers, and had little understanding of Chinese security fears of superpower encirclement and nuclear blackmail. Certainly, new evidence would seem to substantiate Gordon Chang's (1988) controversial thesis that Kennedy's fear of a nuclear China led him to explore the possibility of joint action with the Soviets to launch a preemptive strike on Chinese nuclear facilities. Working from newly declassified Kennedy administration records, William Burr and Jeffrey Richelson (2000/1) contend that in addition to a "massive" intelligence effort to monitor the Chinese nuclear program, Kennedy and his National Security Adviser McGeorge Bundy tried to enlist Soviet support for air attacks on Chinese facilities, and gave instructions that planning begin for covert CIA operations and possible unilateral military action.

On the other hand, the question remains as to whether the Kennedy administration was merely exploring various planning options rather than seriously contemplating such a strike. Beyond the nuclear issue, Kennedy was generally cautious and did not want war with China. This was evident in his reluctance to intervene militarily in Indochina; and in the crisis management during the third Taiwan Straits crisis in 1962, when Washington hastened to reassure Beijing through the Warsaw Ambassadorial channel that it was not supporting any nationalist attack on the mainland at a time when the communist regime was particularly vulnerable (Foot 1995).

The literature on the Johnson administration's China policy per se is still sparse, largely because of its recognized preoccupation with the Vietnam War. However, it is becoming clear that Vietnam did not have a straightforward effect of dampening Johnson's China policy. On the one hand, Washington certainly portrayed itself as fighting in Vietnam in order to contain Chinese communist influence and aggression. As Chang (1990) argues, the Johnson administration was cognizant of the Sino-Soviet ideological dispute, and portrayed the campaign against North Vietnam as a means to demonstrate that Beijing's radical brand of communism would fail, in contrast to Moscow's more moderate style. On the other hand, while the decision to escalate the war in 1965 was probably the result of an overestimation of the danger China posed to US interests, the parallel effort employed by Johnson and his advisers to avoid provoking a direct Chinese intervention is striking. In his sophisticated study of the 1965 decision-making process, drawing from the psychological-reasoning literature, Yuen Foong Khong (1992) relates Johnson's decision for graduated air attacks rather than large-scale heavy bombing directly to the lesson of China's intervention in Korea. More recently, Zhai Qiang (2000) and Chen and Hershberg (2000) use US and Chinese sources to document the conscious and conscientious crisis management process by which Beijing and Washington conveyed warnings, defined provocative actions, and signaled non-threatening intents to each other in the course of the war.

If the conduct of the Vietnam War helped to establish a modus vivendi of sorts between Washington and Beijing, it also spurred arguments for the reconsideration of China policy itself amongst certain officials in the Johnson administration. These recommendations included a relaxation of the embargo policy, and a reduction of anti-Chinese rhetoric in order to play down China's role in the war and reduce its leverage. Significant too is the extent to which a reassessment of China policy was underway during the Johnson administration in spite of Vietnam. Public opinion had moderated towards recognizing the importance of communicating with the PRC and including it in international forums (Kusnitz 1984). In a series of well-publicized Senate Foreign Relations Committee hearings in 1966, eminent China specialists spoke in favor of improving US–China relations, echoing the sentiments of mid-level China officials who had been arguing the need for more realistic contact, trade, and even a two-Chinas policy, in line with the diminished Chinese threat to US security, and international opinion (Foot 1995, 2001; Thomson 1972).

Indeed, there were signs of change in China policy: Johnson adopted the public line of "containment without isolation" of China in 1966, and there was some relaxation of travel policy in 1967. In view of these developments and the lack of reconciliation in the latter 1960s, might we therefore postulate a nascent "second lost chance" debate? No. To begin with, the perceived changes in China policy were fundamentally limited because officials were fully aware of the constraints of Vietnam. These "revisionist" officials' suggestions were predicated on the assumption that the PRC was not likely to change its hostile attitude; and indeed the recommendations for limited changes in trade and travel policy were suggested in the spirit of "shifting the monkey onto Peking's back" – to make clear that the blame for the strict China policy lay firmly with the intransigent leadership in Beijing, while demonstrating Washington's willingness to be reasonable (memorably Komer, and Thomson, to Bundy, in *Foreign Relations of the United States* 1964–8). Most importantly, there was no chance from the Chinese point of view. As Garver (1998) points out, Mao was still engrossed in promoting and securing the revolutionary character and strength of his regime, most dramatically by means of the Cultural Revolution which began in 1966, and was not prepared to improve relations with the US.

1969–1979: *Rapprochement*, Normalization, and Tacit Alliance

Nixon's "breakthrough" to the PRC in 1972 was the single most significant turning point in US–China relations in this period, and has been the subject of some of the most interesting new studies in the field in recent years. The significant declassification of Nixon administration documents from 1996 onwards and the availability of some Chinese material has also allowed new insights into the process of *rapprochement*.

In particular, documentary material pertaining to China policymaking allows us to assess the memoir accounts that have held center-stage so far. In his realpolitik treatment of the *rapprochement*, Kissinger (1979) has emphasized that Washington sought the opening to China in order to obtain leverage over Moscow in the pursuit of détente. Using newly available documents, Burr (2001) shows the cautious and somewhat ambivalent way in which the Nixon administration contemplated opening relations with the PRC in 1968–9. He confirms that Nixon and Kissinger's perceptions of the China threat shifted only after the Sino-Soviet dispute had escalated into border hostilities in March 1969, and he demonstrates the White House's initial reliance on State Department China expertise in this period, even though the latter was later cut out of the China policymaking circuit.

Analyses of the signals and messages between Washington and Beijing from 1968 to 1971 indicate that, while it was clearly a two-way process, recent Chinese sources suggest the critical importance of Chinese initiative in moving the two countries towards a *rapprochement*. For instance, Mao began reconsidering US policy in the wake of the Soviet invasion of Czechoslovakia in 1968, and ordered a PLA study of the implications of the Soviet action. This so-called Four Marshals' report provided powerful strategic justification for Beijing to improve relations with Washington (Chen and Wilson 1998; Yang 2000/1). In this respect, it is worth considering whether Beijing indeed played the determinative role in the *rapprochement*. Its willingness to "put aside" final resolution of the Taiwan issue was vital to pursuing contact and relations with the US. Mao and Zhou accepted US acknowledgment of the principle of "one China" and an undertaking to begin troop withdrawals from the Taiwan area, but did not press for either the immediate abrogation of the US–ROC Defense Treaty or for reunification (Ross 1995). Because of its national security considerations *vis-à-vis* the Soviet Union, Beijing would probably have negotiated with whichever party or president was in power at the time. As Mao told Nixon in 1972, if the Democrats won the elections that year, "we cannot avoid contacting them"; and many leading Democrats were certainly ready to negotiate with Beijing.

The majority of the transcripts of the Nixon–Kissinger talks with Mao and Zhou Enlai are now available, and many have been usefully collated in Burr's 1998 volume. They demonstrate two key points about the substance of the new relationship after 1971. First, as Solomon's (1999) study on Chinese negotiating behavior based on his earlier access to these records demonstrates, the Chinese successfully manipulated their American interlocutors towards preferred policy positions. Additionally, the transcripts reveal how, even though the strategic antipathy towards the Soviet Union had brought the two sides together, Kissinger had to work hard to convince the Chinese that the parallel US–USSR détente was not an exercise in collusion or appeasement, but rather a means of restraining and containing the Soviet Union. In addition, the disagreement about the direction of the Soviet threat (East or West), and the best means to combat it (military confrontation or negotiating a détente), continued throughout the 1970s.

Second, the records of the conversations reveal the extent to which Kissinger and Nixon "tilted" towards China in the strategic triangle. The policy of intelligence cooperation and military sales to China has been associated with the Carter administration in the late 1970s, but it is now evident that Kissinger tried to create a "tacit alliance" with the Chinese against the Soviets earlier on. For instance, during a trip to Beijing in November 1973, he secretly offered Zhou intelligence information on Soviet troop deployments, a Washington–Beijing hotline to convey information from American early-warning detection systems, and other forms of material and technological military assistance (Burr 1998). The reasons for these offers remain to be established. Burr suggests that Kissinger was genuinely fearful of a Soviet attack on China, but he draws this inference from what Kissinger himself told the Chinese, and it is at least as likely that it was more a symbolic means to appease Chinese worries about the superpower détente, and to maintain the momentum of the *rapprochement*.

What is clearer to us now is the degree of control Kissinger exercised in developing the new relationship: he carried out secret negotiations with the Chinese single-handedly, and maintained tight control over access to China policy formulation. While Nixon's ideas about improving relations with China can be traced further back into his political career and he certainly took the initiative in the opening to China, Kissinger dominated the implementation and development of the new China policy, particularly as the Watergate crisis reached its denouement in 1973 and 1974.

Kissinger and Nixon had promised the Chinese leaders that they would normalize relations during Nixon's second term, but domestic events such as Watergate and Nixon's resignation stalled the process. Documentary sources from the Ford and Carter administrations are still sparse, but it is apparent that domestic and bureaucratic politics in the United States again significantly influenced policymaking towards China. The best available account of China policymaking in this period is Ross' (1995) analysis, which emphasizes the importance of threat and security perceptions, as well as the constraints of domestic politics. He suggests that Ford, Kissinger, and Secretary of Defense Schlesinger perceived the Soviet challenge to have increased because a post-Vietnam Congress, wary of foreign intervention, had diminished the US ability to counter the Soviet threat. Thus, they wanted to move towards China in order to warn Moscow against the consequences of its adventurism, but domestic politics – including Ford's campaign considerations – again intervened.

In contrast, during the first year of Carter's presidency, he and Secretary of State Cyrus Vance felt secure about the US ability to stand up to the Soviet threat and so did not see the need for playing the "China card," but concentrated instead on developing détente with the Soviet Union. From 1978 onwards, though, Carter perceived a heightening of the Soviet threat, and began to favor National Security Adviser Zbigniew Brzezinski's position on the need to cooperate with China to balance Soviet power (Vance 1983; Brzezinski 1983). Washington was eventually able to negotiate an acceptable normalization agreement with Beijing at the end of 1978, largely due to Deng's consolidation of power and China's deteriorating strategic position *vis-à-vis* the Soviet Union and North Vietnam (Ross 1995).

As opposed to the literature on the 1950s and 1960s that often emphasizes misperceptions, the story of the US–China *rapprochement* and normalization is characterized by the convergence of strategic views – were the two sides, as Garrett (1991) suggests, "learning" at last? Yet Harding (1992) cautions that the new relationship has been fragile precisely because it was founded on antipathy towards the Soviet Union, rather than shared values or broader common worldviews. In particular, Taiwan remained the central unresolved bilateral irritant: as Ross (1995) points out, the normalization discussions in 1978 were dogged by serious conflicts over future US ties with Taiwan, particularly the continuation of arms sales. Furthermore, the "triangular politics" motivation for normalizing relations suffered from considerable limitations. For instance, Sestanovich (1993) and Ross (1993) argue that improved US–PRC relations had relatively little effect on US–Soviet relations in the 1970s, and in fact failed to restrain Moscow's adventurism, which culminated in the invasion of Afghanistan in 1979. Generally, a much more complex picture of the operation of the logic of triangular politics in US–China relations is emerging, and it is clear that the most useful studies will be those which successfully situate strategic analysis within domestic, ideological, and bureaucratic contexts on both the US and Chinese sides.

The Post-Normalization Era in the 1980s

The first decade after normalization of US–China relations is often depicted as the most productive period in the relationship. Ross (1998: vii), rather wistfully and somewhat neglecting his 1995 analysis of the underlying conflicts, records that, during this time, America and China "conducted high-level strategic dialogues, engaged in bilateral arms transfers, and developed and expanded economic and cultural relations." Some 75,000 Chinese students and scholars received visas to enter the United States, the US became a major source of direct foreign investment in China, second only to Hong Kong's investment, and the importance of the US market for Chinese goods steadily grew. Washington and Beijing also managed, especially after 1982, to put the Taiwan question to one side and to ignore until the second half of the 1980s the conflict of values over issues such as human rights.

China's role as tacit ally of the United States in containment of the Soviet Union primarily accounts for this relative steadiness in relations. Nevertheless, even during the Reagan period, as with the Carter administration before it, there were those who disagreed markedly on China's long-term importance to the United States. Whereas Secretary of State Alexander Haig saw it as "the most important country in the world" (Haig 1984: 194), Haig's successor, George P. Shultz (1993), concluded that Japan and not China was at the core of America's relations in Asia for ideological and strategic reasons. It is a debate over priorities that continues at the start of the twenty-first century.

Tiananmen and its Aftermath

The first ten years of normalization were ones of dramatic change, especially for the Chinese, but also for the former Soviet Union, and for the geo-strategic triangle that since the Nixon era had provided an overarching framework for the Sino-American relationship. China's economic reform program, begun in earnest after December 1978, was producing signal results, shaking up the society, and providing space for alternative ideas to be heard about how the society could best be organized and managed. Shultz's reference to the incompatibility of values between China and the United States looked in the late 1980s to be outdated as Deng Xiaoping rushed to adopt market-oriented reforms, and student demonstrators in Tiananmen Square set up the "Goddess of Democracy." As Levine has written, "American public opinion eagerly anticipated the Second Coming of Chinese Democracy" (Levine 1994: 80). The rude awakening of June 4, 1989 dashed these naive hopes. "Perhaps nowhere else in the world did the massacre engender more popular outrage, anguish, soul searching, and just plain fascination than in the United States," as Americans watched the horrifying events unfold on their television sets (Madsen 1995: 2).

The repression of the demonstrators occurred on the watch of President George Bush, the one president who tried to run his own China policy, because he believed he understood and had the right contacts with the Chinese leadership as a result of his time in the US liaison office in Beijing in the 1970s, and the long hours he had spent in the company of Deng, Li Peng, and Zhao Ziyang at the start of his administration. In those strained hours and days after the PLA's onslaught on the protesters, Bush tried to salvage the relationship he had long tried to cultivate. As he said in a letter to Deng, which Patrick Tyler rightly describes as "strikingly reverential" (Tyler 1999: 363), "I write asking for your help in preserving this relationship that we both think is very important," a request that resulted in the domestically ill-starred decision to send the US officials Brent Scowcroft and Lawrence Eagleburger on a secret mission to Beijing in July 1989. The Chinese repaid Bush's courage or appeasement – depending on one's perspective – by informing the Beijing press corps of the secret visit that had taken place just days after the US ban on high-level contacts (ibid: 367). The US Congress was outraged at Bush's behavior.

The Tiananmen bloodshed inevitably spawned much writing devoted to re-evaluating US–China policy, with some calling for a policy designed to overthrow communist rule in the country, and others trying to recapture the focus on the common interests that had brought the two societies closer together from the 1970s onwards. To some degree, this division depended on a supposed distinction between, on the one hand, US policies that reflected American values and, on the other, those that allowed the US to continue to play its international leadership role, which meant working with all major states, including China, in order to sustain global and regional order.

The latter approach was particularly difficult to advocate in the early 1990s with the events of 1989 still so fresh in the mind. Neither was it aided by the ending of the Cold War, the dissolution of the former Soviet Union, and the termination of the Warsaw Pact, which dramatically undercut the strategic rationale for the US–China relationship. Many scholars note that, combined with Tiananmen, the advent of the post-Cold War era rendered US policy towards China a branch of domestic policy, and that it "domesticated" Chinese policy too. Thus, the literature on US–China relations came to put even more emphasis on domestic factors, including the role of Congress, the development of a human rights policy, and the linking of Most Favored Nation (MFN) trading status to the pace of Chinese domestic political reform. Trying to respond to this variety of domestic pressures has made it more difficult for the US government to formulate a coherent China policy. It has also rendered academic writing on the topic less synthetic.

The intense struggle between the Bush administration and Congress over China policy in the immediate post-Tiananmen period can best be followed in articles by Ross (1992) and David Zweig (1991). James Mann (1998) provides valuable detail and evidence of policy disarray attendant on the sheltering and subsequent release of the renowned Chinese scientist and political activist, Fang Lizhi, from the US embassy in Beijing. Insight into the politicking over the MFN trading issue, and the peculiar domestic alliances that it brought into effect (anti-MFN brought together the US labor unions, the conservative Right, and some liberals, for example), is available in Lampton (1994, 2001) and Teles (1998). These writings show the extent to which the executive branch in these years had had control of foreign policy towards China wrested from its grasp. That control has not been fully returned to this day, although the sense of turmoil associated with policy formulation has been reduced.

The primary influences on reducing that turmoil and restoring a degree of stability to the relationship have been identified as ranging from the economic to the strategic. First is China's own economic and political recovery after Tiananmen, including Deng's 1992 decision to move ahead with economic reform, which quickly led to the return in China of extremely high growth rates. Economic factors, including the lobbying of Clinton by US businesses, did play a large role in overthrowing the president's earlier decision to link China's MFN status with progress on human rights issues, despite previous campaign pledges that he would abjure normal relations with the "butchers of Beijing" (Lampton 1994, 2001). Important to the change too was the realization that China had a key regional role to play in stabilizing relations in East Asia (such as diffusing the North Korean nuclear crisis, and controlling the Taiwan issue) and more broadly that China's participation in global regimes – including those pertaining to the environment, weapons proliferation, trade, and human rights – could help to boost the legitimacy of those regulatory arrangements.

The "Engagement" versus "Containment" Debate

Such reasoning about China's global and regional role underpins the arguments of those analysts and policymakers who describe themselves as being in favor of "engagement" with China. They are pitted against a group of scholars and policy advocates known as the "containers." Both sides tend to combine policy analysis with policy prescription.

This debate, which has flowered markedly from the second half of the 1990s, primarily arises from concerns about how best the United States can accommodate China's rise to power. As the authors of one major text on this topic state, "dramatic increases in China's economic and political power were among the most important changes in international politics during the 1980s and 1990s." They point to China's quadrupling of its gross domestic product between 1978 and 1999, its vast increases in foreign trade and levels of foreign reserves, and its decision to modernize its armed forces and buy advanced weapons from overseas suppliers (Brown et al. 2000: xi; non-US perspectives can be found in Harris and Klintworth 1995; Goodman and Segal 1997). Apart from the attempt to determine how real is this economic and military rise, the heart of the debate involves trying to establish China's intentions and particularly how the US and others should respond to this tectonic shift in the distribution of regional power. How should the United States, supposedly enjoying its "unipolar moment" and with the goal of maintaining its position of hegemony in East Asia, deal with China's rise? More specifically, what are the implications of China's growing power for America's Taiwan policy and for the possibilities of peaceful reunification?

Such questions have been hotly argued, particularly in the journals *Foreign Affairs* and *International Security*. Helpfully for us, a series of the best articles from the latter have been brought together in one volume (Brown et al. 2000). Not surprisingly, there is no consensus, but the terms of the argument are laid out clearly in this text, as well as in one devoted solely to an examination of engagement policies (Johnston and Ross 1999). Those wanting the United States to engage China state that this can be done via three mechanisms: developing bilateral policies that protect America's strategic interests but also take China's own interests seriously; drawing China in to membership of global regimes, which would help to underpin the notion of common interests and give China a greater stake in the global system; and finally deepening Chinese and American societal and institutional linkages in order – in the event of a breach in relations – to impose costs on those Chinese domestic political actors committed to reform and opening. For those advocating containment, this policy represents appeasement and fails to recognize that China's strategic goal in Asia is to challenge US supremacy in the region, achieve its territorial ambitions – including reunification with Taiwan and control over disputed islands in the south and east China seas – and establish its own hegemony in America's stead. "Containers" believe that China would even countenance war with the United States in order to achieve its revisionist aims.

The United States enjoys enormous superiority across all the dimensions of power, but Christensen (2001), focusing on the prospects of war between China and America, cautions us against looking exclusively at their relative military power to the neglect of China's development of specific kinds of military capabilities, the political geography of East Asia, Chinese domestic politics, and the perceptions – or misperceptions – of Chinese decision-makers. Christensen argues that a weaker China might well challenge the United States if the leadership sees itself as incurring greater regime costs from not attacking than from attacking (Taiwan is an issue that could lead to this reasoning); if actual or potential US casualties seem sufficiently high to force an early US withdrawal from any conflict; if the United States is tied down militarily in other parts of the world; and finally if Chinese leaders believe that regional allies can be encouraged to adopt policies different from America's own. Christensen's article makes the prospect of conflict seem more real, but it needs to be compared with other pieces in Brown et al. (2000), which argue variously that China is not in a position to conquer Taiwan, that its capabilities remain modest and would deter Chinese elites from taking military action, and that China and America can reach a modus vivendi based on a recognition of non-overlapping spheres of interest in East Asia. What this debate demonstrates in a more general sense is that the best of the scholars working on contemporary aspects of Chinese foreign policy and on US–China relations are diametrically opposed, depending on whether they put emphasis on China's need for regime security and the need for domestic mobilization, or more rationalist strategic calculations.

During the second term of the Clinton presidency, the preferred policy option was engagement. In the first years of the Bush administration, the policy was more distant than Clinton's, despite China's support in the aftermath of the terrorist assaults on September 11, 2001 and attempts at cooperation in the struggle against terrorism. This is because, as Friedberg (2002), among others, has argued, various points of contention between China and America still exist, especially over Taiwan, which has again taken center stage. Beijing believes – with some justification – that the United States has moved some distance from its previous policy stance of "strategic ambiguity" – a policy designed to discourage the Taiwanese leaders from becoming so bold as to declare independence, and China from using force to achieve its reunification goals. China also asserts that the United States is using a variety of means to prevent its rise. Certainly, some in the Bush administration advocated such policy positions, and if they eventually prevail over more moderate officials then US policy will almost have come full circle – from containment to containment. At the very least, we have witnessed in the period since normalization continued gyration around those "love–hate cycles" that Harding identified in 1982. Elizabeth Economy and Michel Oksenberg (1999: 1) seem to agree: with "dizzying rapidity," they state, the recommended US policy towards China has shifted from "cooperate with the mid-1980s reformers; sanction the late 1980s oppressors; profit from the early 1990s economic juggernaut; prepare for the Armageddon with the mid-1990s rising power; engage the late 1990s responsible China." We wait to see whether a later edition of the book might be forced to add "contain the fire-belching dragon."

Future Research in the Field

These matters of containment or engagement – in the absence of major change – are likely to shape the scholarly and journalistic writing on contemporary US–China relations for many years to come. On the other hand, the steady opening of US archives will allow some respite from this hot-house atmosphere of contemporary policy, and allow us to have a greater understanding of such events and issues as the moves towards normalization, the Soviet factor in the Sino-American relationship, and the means by which the Taiwan issue was finessed. It is in this realm that the greatest advances in understanding of this bilateral relationship are likely to come, although policy-relevant publications will continue to flow at a rapid rate. Chinese scholars' major contribution to the understanding of US–China relations in the Cold War era has been recognized. Their important interpretations of the early period in US–PRC relations based on the partial opening of Chinese archives, and their use of much Chinese memoir material, have been vital in making the writing on US–China relations less parochial and more subtle. Whether such scholars will be able to continue this important work in the wake of the Beijing regime's apparent sense of political vulnerability, shown in their recent detentions of a number of scholars of Chinese origin, remains to be seen. We can only hope so, for like Lampton (2001) we believe that understanding this relationship is vital to the maintenance of world peace, and represents a major challenge for both scholars and officials alike.

REFERENCES

Accinelli, Robert: *Crisis and Commitment: United States Policy Toward Taiwan, 1950–1955* (Chapel Hill: University of North Carolina Press, 1996).
Accinelli, Robert: "A Thorn in the Side of Peace: The Eisenhower Administration and the 1958 Offshore Islands Crisis." In Robert S. Ross and Jiang Changbin (eds.) *Re-examining the Cold War: US–China Diplomacy, 1954–1973* (Cambridge, MA: Harvard University Press, 2001).
Borg, Dorothy and Waldo Heinrichs (eds.): *Uncertain Years: Chinese–American Relations, 1947–1950* (New York: Columbia University Press, 1980).
Brown, Michael E., Owen R. Cote, Jr., Sean M. Lynn-Jones, and Steven E. Miller (eds.) *The Rise of China* (Cambridge, MA: MIT Press, 2000)
Brzezinski, Zbigniew: *Power and Principle: Memoirs of the National Security Adviser, 1977–1981* (New York: Farrar, Straus, Giroux, 1983).
Burr, William (ed.): *The Kissinger Transcripts: The Top Secret Talks with Beijing and Moscow* (New York: New Press, 1998).
Burr, William: "Sino-American Relations, 1969: The Sino-Soviet Border War and Steps Towards Rapprochement." *Cold War History* 1, 3 (April 2001), 73–112.

Burr, William and Jeffrey T. Richelson: "Whether to 'Strangle the Baby in the Cradle': The United States and the Chinese Nuclear Program, 1960–64." *International Security* 25, 3 (winter 2000/1), 54–99.

Chang, Gordon H.: "JFK, China, and the Bomb." *Journal of American History* 74, 4 (March 1988), 1289–310.

Chang, Gordon H.: *Friends and Enemies: The United States, China, and the Soviet Union, 1948–1972* (Stanford, CA: Stanford University Press, 1990).

Chen, Jian: *China's Road to the Korean War: The Making of the Sino-American Confrontation* (New York: Columbia University Press, 1994).

Chen, Jian: "The Myth of America's 'Lost Chance' in China: A Chinese Perspective in Light of New Evidence." *Diplomatic History* 21, 1 (winter 1997), 77–86.

Chen, Jian and James Hershberg: "Informing the Enemy: Sino-American 'Signalling' and the Vietnam War, 1965." Paper presented at CWIHP workshop on "New Evidence on China, Southeast Asia, and the Vietnam War," January 2000, Hong Kong University, Hong Kong.

Chen, Jian and David L. Wilson: "'All Under Heaven is Great Chaos': Beijing, the Sino-Soviet Border Clashes, and the Turn Toward Sino-American Rapprochement, 1968–69." *Cold War International History Project Bulletin* 11 (winter 1998), 155–75.

Christensen, Thomas J.: *Useful Adversaries: Grand Strategy, Domestic Mobilization, and Sino-American Conflict, 1947–1958* (Princeton, NJ: Princeton University Press, 1996).

Christensen, Thomas J.: "Posing Problems without Catching Up: China's Rise and Challenges for US Security Policy." *International Security* 25, 4 (spring 2001), 5–40.

Cohen, Warren I.: "Acheson, His Advisers, and China, 1949–1950." In Dorothy Borg and Waldo Heinrichs (eds.) *Uncertain Years: Chinese–American Relations, 1947–1950* (New York: Columbia University Press, 1980a), 15–52.

Cohen, Warren I.: *Dean Rusk* (Totawa, NJ: Cooper Square, 1980b).

Cohen, Warren I.: *America's Response to China: A History of Sino-American Relations*, 4th edn. (New York: Columbia University Press, 2000).

Economy, Elizabeth and Michel Oksenberg: *China Joins the World: Progress and Prospects* (New York: Council on Foreign Relations, 1999).

Foot, Rosemary: *The Wrong War: American Policy and the Dimensions of the Korean Conflict, 1950–1953* (Ithaca, NY: Cornell University Press, 1985).

Foot, Rosemary: *A Substitute for Victory: The Politics of Peacemaking at the Korean Armistice Talks* (Ithaca, NY: Cornell University Press, 1990).

Foot, Rosemary: *The Practice of Power: US Relations with China since 1949* (Oxford: Oxford University Press, 1995).

Foot, Rosemary: "Redefinitions: The Domestic Context and America's China Policy in the 1960s." In Robert S. Ross and Jiang Changbin (eds.) *Re-examining the Cold War: US–China Diplomacy, 1954–1973* (Cambridge, MA: Harvard University Press, 2001).

Foreign Relations of the United States 1964–8, vol. 30 (Washington, DC: US Government Printing Office, 1998).

Friedberg, Aaron: "11 September and the Future of Sino-American Relations." *Survival* 44, 1 (spring 2002), 33–50.

Gaddis, John Lewis: "The American 'Wedge Strategy,' 1949–1958." In Harry Harding and Yuan Ming (eds.) *Sino-American Relations 1945–1955: A Joint Assessment of a Critical Decade* (Wilmington, DE: Scholarly Resources, 1989).

Garrett, Banning N.: "The Strategic Basis of Learning in US Policy Toward China, 1948–1988." In George W. Breslauer and Philip Tetlock (eds.) *Learning in US and Soviet Foreign Policy* (Boulder, CO: Westview Press, 1991).

Garver, John: "Little Chance." *Diplomatic History* 21, 1 (winter 1997a), 87–94.

Garver, John: *The Sino-American Alliance: Nationalist China and American Cold War Strategy in Asia* (New York: M. E. Sharpe, 1997b).

Garver, John: "Food for Thought: Reflections on Food Aid and the Idea of Another Lost Chance in Sino-American Relations." *Journal of American–East Asian Relations* 7, 1–2 (spring/summer 1998), 101–6.

Goncharov, Sergei N., John W. Lewis, and Litai Xue: *Uncertain Partners: Stalin, Mao and the Korean War* (Stanford, CA: Stanford University Press, 1993).

Goodman, David S. G. and Gerald Segal (eds.) *China Rising: Nationalism and Interdependence* (London: Routledge, 1997).

Haig, Alexander, Jr.: *Caveat: Realism, Reagan, and Foreign Policy* (New York: Macmillan, 1984).

Harding, Harry: "From China with Disdain: New Trends in the Study of China." *Asian Survey* 22, 10 (October 1982).

Harding, Harry: *A Fragile Relationship: The United States and China since 1972* (Washington, DC: Brookings Institution, 1992).

Harris, Stuart and Gary Klintworth (eds.): *China as a Great Power: Myths, Realities and Challenges in the Asia–Pacific Region* (Sydney: Longman, 1995).

He, Di and Gordon H. Chang: "The Absence of War in the US–China Confrontation over Quemoy-Matsu in 1954–1955: Contingency, Luck, Deterrence?" *American Historical Review* 98 (December 1993), 1500–24.

Hilsman, Roger: *To Move a Nation: The Politics of Foreign Policy in the Administration of John F. Kennedy* (New York: Doubleday, 1967).

Johnston, Alastair, and Robert S. Ross (eds.): *Engaging China: The Management of an Emerging Power* (London: Routledge, 1999).

Khong, Yuen Foong: *Analogies at War: Korea, Munich, Dien Bien Phu, and the Vietnam Decisions of 1965* (Princeton, NJ: Princeton University Press, 1992).

Kissinger, Henry A.: *White House Years* (Boston, MA: Little, Brown, 1979).

Kochavi, Noam: "Kennedy, China, and the Tragedy of No Chance." *Journal of American–East Asian Relations* 7, 1–2 (spring/summer 1998), 107–16.

Kusnitz, Leonard: *Public Opinion and Foreign Policy: America's China Policy, 1949–1979* (Westport, CT: Greenwood Press, 1984).

Lampton, David M.: "America's China Policy in the Age of the Finance Minister: Clinton ends Linkage." *China Quarterly* 139 (September 1994).

Lampton, David M.: *Same Bed, Different Dreams: Managing US–China Relations, 1989–2000* (Berkeley: University of California Press, 2001).

Leffler, Melvyn: *A Preponderance of Power: National Security, the Truman Administration, and the Cold War* (Stanford, CA: Stanford University Press, 1992).

Levine, Steven I.: "Sino-American Relations: Testing the Limits." In Samuel S. Kim (ed.) *China and the World: Chinese Foreign Relations in the Post-Cold War Era* (Boulder, CO: Westview Press, 1994).

McLean, David: "American Nationalism, the China Myth, and the Truman Doctrine: The Question of Accommodation with Peking, 1949–50." *Diplomatic History* 10 (winter 1986), 25–42.

McMahon, Robert J.: "The Cold War in Asia: Toward a New Synthesis?" In Michael J. Hogan (ed.) *America in the World: The Historiography of American Foreign Relations since 1941* (New York: Cambridge University Press, 1995).

Madsen, Richard: *China and the American Dream: A Moral Inquiry* (Berkeley: University of California Press, 1995).

Mann, James: *About Face: A History of America's Curious Relationship with China, From Nixon to Clinton* (New York: Knopf, 1998).

Mansourov, Alexandre Y.: "Stalin, Mao, Kim, and China's Decision to Enter the Korean War, Sept. 16–Oct. 15, 1950: New Evidence from the Russian Archives." *Cold War International History Project Bulletin* 6–7 (winter 1995/6), 94–119.

Mayers, David: *Cracking the Monolith: US Policy Against the Sino-Soviet Alliance, 1949–1955* (Baton Rouge: Louisiana State University Press, 1986).

Ross, Robert S.: "National Security, Human Rights, and Domestic Politics: The Bush Administration and China." In Kenneth Oye, Robert J. Lieber, and D. Rothchild (eds.) *Eagle in a New World: American Grand Strategy in the Post-Cold War Era* (New York: Harper Collins, 1992).

Ross, Robert S. (ed.): *China, the United States, and the Soviet Union: Tripolarity and Policy Making in the Cold War* (Armonk, NY: M. E. Sharpe, 1993).

Ross, Robert S.: *Negotiating Cooperation: The United States and China, 1969–1989* (Stanford, CA: Stanford University Press, 1995).

Ross, Robert S.: *After the Cold War: Domestic Factors and US–China Relations* (Armonk, NY: M. E. Sharpe, 1998).

Schlesinger, Arthur M.: *A Thousand Days: John F. Kennedy in the White House* (London: Andre Deutsch, 1965).

Sestanovich, Stephen: "US Policy Toward the Soviet Union, 1970–90: The Impact of China." In Robert S. Ross (ed.) *China, the United States, and the Soviet Union: Tripolarity and Policy Making in the Cold War* (Armonk, NY: M. E. Sharpe, 1993).

Sheng, Michael: "The Triumph of Internationalism: CCP–Moscow Relations before 1949." *Diplomatic History* 21, 1 (winter 1997), 95–104.

Shultz, George P.: *Turmoil and Triumph* (New York: Scribners, 1993).

Solomon, Richard H.: *Chinese Negotiating Behaviour: Pursuing Interests through "Old Friends"* (Washington, DC: USIP, 1999).

Stueck, William Whitney, Jr.: *Road to Confrontation: American Policy Toward China and Korea, 1947–1950* (Chapel Hill: University of North Carolina Press, 1981).

Stueck, William Whitney, Jr.: *The Korean War: An International History* (Princeton, NJ: Princeton University Press, 1995).

Teles, Steven M.: "Public Opinion and Interest Groups in the Making of US–China Policy." In Robert S. Ross (ed.) *After the Cold War: Domestic Factors and US–China Relations* (Armonk, NY: M. E. Sharpe, 1998).

Thomson, James C., Jr.: "On the Making of China Policy, 1961–9: A Study in Bureaucratic Politics." *China Quarterly* 50 (1972), 220–43.

Tucker, Nancy Bernkopf: "Nationalist China's Decline and Its Impact on Sino-American Relations, 1949–1950." In Dorothy Borg and Waldo Heinrichs (eds.) *Uncertain Years: Chinese–American Relations, 1947–1950* (New York: Columbia University Press, 1980).

Tucker, Nancy Bernkopf: *Patterns in the Dust: Chinese–American Relations and the Recognition Controversy, 1949–1950* (New York: Columbia University Press, 1983).

Tucker, Nancy Bernkopf: "John Foster Dulles and the Taiwan Roots of the 'two Chinas' Policy." In Richard H. Immerman (ed.) *John Foster Dulles and the Diplomacy of the Cold War* (Princeton, NJ: Princeton University Press, 1990).

Tucker, Nancy Bernkopf: *Taiwan, Hong Kong and the United States 1945–1992: Uncertain Friendships* (New York: Twayne, 1994).

Tucker, Nancy Bernkopf: "Continuing Controversies in the Literature on US–China Relations Since 1945." In Warren I. Cohen (ed.) *Pacific Passage: The Study of American–East Asian Relations on the Eve of the Twenty-first Century* (New York: Columbia University Press, 1996).

Tucker, Nancy Bernkopf: *China Confidential: American Diplomats and Sino-American Relations, 1945–1996* (New York: Columbia University Press, 2001).

Tyler, Patrick: *A Great Wall: Six Presidents and China, An Investigative History* (New York: Century Foundation, 1999).

Vance, Cyrus: *Hard Choices: Critical Years in America's Foreign Policy* (New York: Simon and Schuster, 1983).

Weathersby, Kathryn: "The Soviet Role in the Early Phase of the Korean War: New Documentary Evidence." *Journal of American–East Asian Relations* 2, 4 (winter 1993), 425–58.

Westad, Odd Arne: "Losses, Chances, and Myths: The United States and the Creation of the Sino-Soviet Alliance, 1945–1950." *Diplomatic History* 21, 1 (winter 1997), 105–15.

Whiting, Allen S.: *China Crosses the Yalu: The Decision to Enter the Korean War* (Stanford, CA: Stanford University Press, 1960).

Yang, Kuisong: "The Sino-Soviet Border Clash of 1969: From Zhenbao Island to Sino-American Rapprochement." *Cold War History* 1, 1 (winter 2000/1), 21–52.

Zhai, Qiang: *China and the Vietnam Wars, 1950–1975* (Chapel Hill: University of North Carolina Press, 2000).

Zhang, Shuguang: *Deterrence and Strategic Culture: Chinese–American Confrontations, 1949–1958* (Ithaca, NY: Cornell University Press, 1992).

Zweig, David: "Sino-American Relations and Human Rights: June 4 and the Changing Nature of a Bilateral Relationship." In William T. Tow (ed.) *Building Sino-American Relations: An Analysis for the 1990s* (New York: Paragon House, 1991).

FURTHER READING

Chen, Jian: *Mao's China and the Cold War* (Chapel Hill: University of North Carolina Press, 2001).

Foot, Rosemary: "Making Known the Unknown War: Policy Analysis of the Korean Conflict Since the 1980s." In Michael J. Hogan (ed.) *America in the World: The Historiography of American Foreign Relations since 1941* (New York: Cambridge University Press, 1995).

Kochavi, Noam: *A Conflict Perpetuated: China Policy During the Kennedy Years* (Westport, CT: Praeger, 2002).

Sutter, Robert G.: *US Policy Toward China: An Introduction to the Role of Interest Groups* (Lanham, MD: Rowman and Littlefield, 1998).

Vogel, Ezra F. (ed.): *Living With China: US–China Relations in the Twenty-First Century* (New York: Norton, 1997).

Westad, Odd Arne (ed.): *Brothers in Arms: The Rise and Fall of the Sino-Soviet Alliance 1945–1963* (Stanford, CA: Stanford University Press; Washington, DC: Woodrow Wilson Center Press, 1998).

Zhang, Shu Guang: *Economic Cold War: America's Embargo Against China and the Sino-Soviet Alliance, 1943–1963* (Washington, DC: Woodrow Wilson Center Press, 2000).

CHAPTER SIXTEEN

The Korean War

JAMES I. MATRAY

Scholars devoted only modest attention to examining the causes and consequences of the Korean War for more than two decades after a truce ended the fighting in July 1953. This combined with the absence of public interest led Clay Blair to name his detailed study of the conflict *The Forgotten War* (1987). Other authors have labeled Korea "The War Before Vietnam" and "The Unknown War." This neglect at first had a decisive and negative impact on the place that the Korean War occupied in the history of US foreign relations. On June 27, 1950, President Harry S. Truman set the pattern for initial historical analysis of the conflict just two days after North Korea's attack when he declared that "communism has passed beyond the use of subversion to conquer independent nations and will now use armed invasion and war." The studies of Poats (1954), Leckie (1962), and Fehrenbach (1963) that dominated the literature on the war before the 1980s therefore focused on events starting with the North Korean invasion of South Korea on June 25, 1950. These accounts reflected and reinforced the almost universally accepted belief that the Soviet Union had ordered its puppet to attack as part of its plan for global conquest.

A consensus now prevails that the origins of the Korean War date from at least World War II. Rather than characterizing the conflict as the product of external aggression, scholars acknowledge the centrality of domestic factors. In fact, it became fashionable in the 1980s to portray the Korean conflict as a civil war, rejecting the argument that it was an example of Soviet-inspired, external aggression and even denying the Kremlin's involvement. Bruce Cumings, the leading proponent of this interpretation, insisted in the first volume of his *Origins of the Korean War* (1981) that a conventional war started in Korea in June 1950 because the United States prevented a leftist revolution on the peninsula in 1945 and thereafter imposed a reactionary regime on southern Korea. While Cumings discussed internal developments in Korea before and after World War II, other scholars were reassessing US foreign policy toward that nation during the same period. As classified US government documents became available during the 1970s, historians wrote detailed studies of US involvement in Korea from the start of World War II to the outbreak of hostilities a decade later. Stueck (1981), Dobbs (1981), and Matray (1985) all challenged the traditional characterization of the Korean War as the product of external aggression.

During the 1980s, access to primary documents in private manuscript collections and government archives both allowed and encouraged historians to re-examine the origins and impact of the Korean War. Previously, Appleman (1961), Hermes

(1966), Schnabel (1972), and Sawyer and Hermes (1979) had written the official history of the US army during the Korean War that had value for diplomatic historians. Also, Schnabel and Watson (1988) prepared for the Historical Office of the Joint Chiefs of Staff (JCS) a volume describing the history of the JCS in wartime policy formulation. Later, Condit (1988) added additional details in a study of the role of the Office of the Secretary of Defense in the Korean War. More important, by 1984, the State Department had published volumes reprinting US government documents covering the war years in *Foreign Relations of the United States*. Still, historians could not provide a complete picture of the Korean War without access to communist archival materials. In the late 1980s, Chinese scholars made available documents and firsthand personal accounts partially exposing Beijing's involvement in postwar Korea. But Russia's release of Soviet documents after the fall of the Soviet Union in 1991 had a dramatic impact on how historians interpreted the Korean War. No longer forgotten, Korea as the new century began was still the subject of intense debate after two decades of re-examination.

Historical analysis of the Korean War experienced a fundamental shift after 1981, as scholars no longer ignored the years before 1945. Contrasting sharply with traditional accounts, histories thereafter described US policy toward Korea before and during World War II. Prior to December 1941, the United States had no vital interests in this remote East Asian nation and was largely indifferent to its fate, despite the fact that it had been the first Western nation to sign a treaty with Korea in 1882. But after Japan's attack on Pearl Harbor, President Franklin D. Roosevelt and his advisers recognized at once the importance of this strategic peninsula for the maintenance of postwar peace in East Asia. Park Hong-kyu (1989) and Liu Xiaoyuan (1992) criticized Washington for not supporting the claims to political legitimacy of Korean exiles in China, but Matray (1985) argued that the United States was realistic in advocating creation of a trusteeship to manage Korea's transition to independence. At the Cairo conference in 1943, Roosevelt, British Prime Minister Winston Churchill, and China's Jiang Jieshi announced that the Allies, "mindful of the enslavement of the people of Korea, are determined that in due course Korea shall become free and independent." Given past Sino-Russian competition for control over Korea, Roosevelt knew that it was imperative to obtain Soviet support for the Cairo Declaration, and at Yalta, Soviet Premier Josef Stalin endorsed a four-power trusteeship plan.

During the McCarthy era, Oliver (1955) argued that just as communists in the State Department had helped Mao Zedong seize power in China, so too had they conspired to ensure Soviet control in North Korea. Korea's partition at the 38th parallel, according to McCune and Grey (1950) and Meade (1951), was part of the price that Roosevelt paid at Yalta for Soviet entry in the Pacific war. Mark Paul in Cumings' *Child of Conflict* (1983) and Sandusky (1983) set the record straight. When Harry S. Truman became president after Roosevelt's death in April 1945, he expected Soviet actions in Korea to parallel Stalin's expansionist policies in Eastern Europe. Within a week after taking office, Truman began to search for an alternative to trusteeship that would remove any chance for a repetition of "sovietization." The atomic bomb seemed to provide the answer. Japan's prompt surrender following an atomic attack would preempt Soviet entry into the Pacific war and allow the United States to occupy Korea unilaterally. But Truman's gamble failed. When the Soviet

Union declared war on Japan and sent the Red Army into Korea prematurely on August 12, 1945, Truman proposed and Stalin accepted Korea's division into Soviet and American zones of military occupation at the 38th parallel.

Korea soon became a captive of the Cold War. Attempts at reunification began when the United States and the Soviet Union agreed to implement a new trusteeship plan after the Moscow conference in late 1945. Eighteen months of intermittent negotiations at a Joint Soviet–American Commission failed to produce agreement on a representative group of Koreans to form a provisional government. Meanwhile, political and economic conditions in southern Korea deteriorated, prompting US occupation officials to urge military withdrawal as soon as possible. As the United States demobilized, reductions in defense spending intensified pressure for disengagement and ultimately forced the administration to develop a new policy. In September 1947, the JCS submitted an assessment concluding that Korea was without strategic significance, adding weight to the argument for early withdrawal. But with communist power growing in China, the Truman administration was unwilling to abandon southern Korea, fearing political criticism at home and damage to US credibility abroad. According to Van Ree (1989), the Soviet Union was far more purposeful, dominating northern Korea from the outset and establishing there a Stalinist satellite state. Cumings (1981) offered a very different assessment, applauding the Soviet occupation for sponsoring self-government and sweeping social and economic reforms.

Seeking an answer to its dilemma, Washington referred the Korean issue to the United Nations, resulting in passage of a resolution in November 1947 calling for reunification after internationally supervised nationwide elections. The Truman administration, knowing that the Soviet Union would refuse to cooperate with this plan, had shifted its policy to the creation of a separate government in southern Korea ultimately capable of defending itself. While the United States provided military and economic aid, a stamp of legitimacy from the United Nations would further enhance South Korea's chances of survival. The United Nations, bowing to American pressure, supervised and certified as valid elections in the south alone during May 1948, resulting in the formation of the Republic of Korea (ROK) the following summer. The Soviet Union responded in kind, sponsoring the formation in September of the Democratic People's Republic of Korea (DPRK). And so there were two Koreas. While President Syngman Rhee created a repressive, dictatorial, and anti-communist regime in the south, Kim Il Sung followed the Soviet model for political, economic, and social development in the north. These events magnified the need for the United States to withdraw, since Stalin, acting on a North Korean request, announced that Soviet troops would pull out of the north by the end of 1948. Despite plans to leave the south before 1949, Truman delayed military withdrawal until June 29, 1949 in response to a major uprising against the Rhee government in October 1948.

Berger (1964), Cho Soon-sung (1967), and Dobbs (1981) praised the United States for saving half the nation from communism, but they criticized it for not building a stronger South Korea and inviting an attack from North Korea. Buhite (1978), Matray (1985), and Ronald L. McGlothen (1993) countered that Washington in fact implemented a policy of qualified containment in Korea. Before withdrawal, the Truman administration had undertaken a commitment to train, equip, and supply a security force in the south that was capable of maintaining internal order and deterring an attack from North Korea. It also submitted to Congress a three-year program of technical and economic aid for recovery and self-sufficient growth. To build political support for the Korean assistance package, Secretary of State Dean G. Acheson delivered a speech before the National Press Club on January 12, 1950 that offered an optimistic appraisal of the ROK's future. Six months later, critics charged that Acheson's exclusion of South Korea from the US "defensive perimeter" gave the communists a "green light" to launch an invasion. Matray (2002) has argued, however, that Acheson's words had almost no effect on communist planning for the invasion, not least because only one available Soviet document even mentions the Press Club speech.

By June 1950, Truman's policy of containment through economic means seemed to be experiencing marked success in Korea. The ROK had acted vigorously to control spiraling inflation, and elections during May had given Rhee's opponents control over the legislature. Finally, the South Korean army virtually had eliminated guerrilla activities threatening internal order, prompting the United States to consider a sizable increase in military aid. While Washington was willing to be patient, awaiting the collapse of what it saw as Moscow's artificial client state in the north, South Korea's President Rhee was obsessed with accomplishing early reunification through military means. The Truman administration's fear that Rhee would stage an invasion prompted it to limit South Korea's military capabilities, refusing to provide tanks, heavy artillery, and combat planes. Merrill (1985) has shown that this did not stop South Korea from initiating most of the border clashes with North Korean forces at the parallel, beginning in the summer of 1948 and reaching a high level of intensity and violence a year later. Historians now acknowledge that the two Koreas already were waging a civil conflict when North Korea's attack opened the conventional phase of the war. This had a significant impact on Stalin, who was extremely concerned about the military threat that South Korea posed to North Korea's survival.

Soviet documents demonstrate that throughout 1949, Stalin consistently refused Kim Il Sung's persistent requests to approve an invasion of South Korea. North Korea, the Soviet leader believed, had not achieved either military superiority north of the parallel or political strength south of that line. While Stalin was not prepared to risk war with the United States in 1949, the communist victory in China that fall placed pressure on him to show his support for the same outcome in Korea. This allowed Kim Il Sung to play Moscow and Beijing against one another. In January 1950, Stalin approved Kim's request to visit Moscow, but, despite Acheson's speech, he was not ready to approve an invasion. At that time, he also approved a major expansion of North Korea's military capabilities, but this had as much to do with building its defense as preparing for aggressive expansion. When they met during April, Kim Il Sung persuaded Stalin that a military victory would be quick and easy largely because of support from southern guerrillas and an expected popular uprising against Rhee. But Stalin still feared US military intervention, advising Kim that he could stage an offensive only if China's Mao Zedong approved. During May, Kim traveled to Beijing to gain Chinese consent for the invasion. Significantly, Mao also voiced concern about US military intervention. But after Kim disingenuously explained that Stalin had approved his plans, Mao gave his reluctant consent as well.

Before Soviet documents became available, the most intensely debated issue among Korean War scholars was how the conflict began. US officials never doubted for a moment that North Korea had attacked on orders from Stalin as part of his blueprint for world conquest. The accounts of Generals Mark W. Clark (1954), Matthew B. Ridgway (1967), and J. Lawton Collins (1969) proceeded on this assumption. George F. Kennan (1967), the father of the containment strategy, however, disagreed, arguing instead that the Soviets saw conquest of Korea as a way to weaken the US position in Japan. Surprisingly, some writers challenged the Truman administration's position during the war. For example, Hitchcock (1951) claimed that Kim Il Sung "jumped the gun" and attacked the ROK before the Soviet Union was ready for the invasion. For proof, he pointed to the Soviet boycott of the UN Security Council that prevented Moscow from vetoing resolutions calling for UN military action to defend the ROK. According to Stone (1952), Rhee had initiated the border clashes to provoke North Korea's retaliatory attack. He then portrayed the orderly retreat of his forces as a military debacle to persuade Truman to commit US troops and save his corrupt regime.

Neither the Hitchcock nor Stone interpretation had won many adherents as the fighting in Korea ended. Thereafter, Truman's assessment of the war as a Soviet-inspired act of external aggression prevailed for a decade, largely because Soviet–American relations remained acrimonious. Consensus on the reasons for the Korean War brought a predictable shift toward investigation of other issues. For example, if the United States had decided before June 1950 to abandon South Korea, it begged the question of why Truman would reverse the policy and order military intervention. Paige (1968) and May (1973) provided an answer to this riddle. The United States, they argued, had to act against Soviet-inspired aggression or sustain irreparable damage to American credibility and prestige. Osgood (1957) and Halperin (1963) merely elaborated on the orthodox interpretation when they extolled the virtues of Truman resisting pressure for military escalation and fighting limited war in a nuclear age.

Meanwhile, a revisionist interpretation had emerged to challenge the traditional view that assigned responsibility to the Soviet Union for starting the Cold War. These writers contended that the United States had used superior economic power and an atomic monopoly in an effort to establish global political dominance in the postwar era. Fleming (1961) advanced a Left revisionist assessment of Korea in his two-volume study of the Cold War. Ironically, Korea otherwise escaped reinterpretation at first. US involvement in Vietnam, however, transformed Left revisionism into a plausible and legitimate explanation for the Korean War. Kolko and Kolko (1972) and Gupta (1972) boldly charged that South Korea struck first and North Korea's invasion was an act of self-defense. The most important impact of these revisionist accounts was to spark interest in the civil origins of the Korean War. Nikita Khrushchev (1970) added impetus to this trend when he reported that Stalin approved North Korea's attack with great reluctance because he feared US intervention. Simmons (1975) alleged that Moscow and Pyongyang had agreed on August 15, 1950 as an invasion date, but the attack came two months earlier because of the political rivalry between Kim and Foreign Minister Pak Hon-yong.

During the 1980s, Left revisionism peaked in popularity, as Korean War scholars accepted the accuracy of the Cumings interpretation. Lowe (1986), Kaufman

(1986), and MacDonald (1986) all agreed that Korea was really a civil war. Halliday and Cumings (1988) claimed that Rhee had sent his forces across the parallel before dawn on June 25 to provoke a communist invasion and bring US military intervention, thereby setting the stage for the ROK's conquest of North Korea. Cumings provided a detailed explanation of this "trap theory" in the second volume of his *Origins of the Korean War* (1990). But the emerging consensus that Korea was a classic civil war ended abruptly during the 1990s. Weathersby (1993, 1994) and Bajanov (1995/1996) used Soviet documents to establish that Stalin played a central role, albeit reluctantly, in igniting the Korean War. This renewed emphasis on international factors resulted in Goncharov, Lewis, and Xue (1993), Kim Chull Baum and Matray (1993), and Stueck (1995) arguing that Korea could best be understood as an "international civil war."

Neither Truman (1956) nor Acheson (1969) gave any thought in their memoirs to the domestic origins of the Korean War. The president equated Stalin's behavior in Korea with Adolf Hitler's aggression during the 1930s, arguing that if the North Korean aggression went "unchallenged, the world was certain to be plunged into another world war." Contrary to the popular belief that Truman acted with swiftness and courage to halt the communist invasion, he in fact did not commit US ground troops in Korea for almost a week, referring the matter instead to the UN Security Council and banking on South Korea's ability with US help to defend itself. At a June 29 press conference, the president was still optimistic that a total commitment was avoidable, agreeing with a newsman's description of the war as a "police action" rather than coining the phrase himself. After the DPRK ignored a UN resolution calling on North Korean forces to cease fire and withdraw, the Security Council passed a second resolution urging members to help defend South Korea. This would allow the Truman administration to portray US intervention as an act of collective security, although the United States had taken steps to halt invasion prior to passage of both UN resolutions.

Truman ordered US ground troops to Korea on June 30 after General Douglas MacArthur advised that without them, communist conquest of South Korea was certain. There is an extensive literature covering the ground, air, and sea operations that followed during the Korean War, but this essay will not survey studies of military engagements. Alexander (1986), Hastings (1987), Stokesbury (1988), and Hickey (1999) have provided detailed coverage of events on the battlefield. Knox (1985, 1988) and Tomedi (1993) have described the personal side of the soldiers' story with oral histories of the Korean War. Kim Chum-gon (1973), Kim Chull Baum (1991), and Paik Sun Yup (1992) have written about the conflict from the perspective of South Korea. Studies of the Korean War also have covered the contributions of the fifteen nations who fought with the United States to defend South Korea. Of most value are the accounts of Stairs (1974) on Canada, O'Neill (1981) on Australia, Farrar-Hockley (1987) and MacDonald (1990) on Britain, and McGibbon (1992) on New Zealand. These nations played important roles in the Korean War, but the United States and South Korea contributed 90 percent of the manpower. Not only were higher percentages of planes and ships American, but it was the United States that provided the bulk of the weapons, equipment, and logistical support to save South Korea.

For years, David Rees' *Korea: The Limited War* (1964) was the standard account on the course and outcome of the conflict. Joseph Goulden (1982) later offered a more entertaining alternative, but like earlier studies he devoted extraordinary attention to the first year of the Korean War, with MacArthur occupying a central place in the narrative. On July 7 1950, the UN Security Council passed a resolution providing for the creation of a United Nations Command (UNC) and calling upon Truman to appoint the UNC commander. The administration had blocked formation of a UN committee that would have had direct access to the UNC, adopting instead a procedure whereby MacArthur, Truman's choice as commander, received instructions from and reported to the JCS. As the United States sent more troops and supplies to Korea during July 1950, MacArthur pressed Lieutenant General Walton H. Walker, the battlefield commander, to halt North Korea's advance, but UN forces retreated to the Pusan Perimeter, a rectangular area in the southeast corner of the Korean peninsula. Both Perret (1986) and Weintraub (2000) have sharply criticized MacArthur for running the war by "remote control" from Tokyo and refusing to relieve ineffective officers.

Despite what seemed to be a desperate situation, MacArthur had devised plans during July for a counteroffensive in coordination with an amphibious landing behind enemy lines that would permit him to "compose and unite" Korea. But the JCS had serious reservations about MacArthur's intention to land at the port of Inchon, 30 miles west of Seoul, because of its narrow access and high tides. On September 15, however, MacArthur's landing at Inchon was a brilliant success. After the liberation of Seoul two weeks later, UN forces were poised for an advance across the 38th parallel. US leaders realized that extending hostilities northward would risk Soviet or Chinese entry and possibly a global war. Therefore, Truman's plan for the conquest of North Korea, which he approved on September 1, included precautions. First, only Korean forces would advance into the most northern provinces. Second, the US would obtain explicit UN support for reunification. After the DPRK refused to surrender, the United Nations passed a resolution of October 7 instructing MacArthur to "ensure conditions of stability throughout Korea." Historians agree that the decision to cross the 38th parallel was an incredible blunder because it provoked Chinese intervention. A consensus does not exist, however, on the reason behind this escalation of the war.

Administration officials later tried to deflect blame to MacArthur for the disastrous consequences of invading North Korea. Rees (1964) and Ridgway (1967) attributed the crossing of the parallel to "military momentum" and "a surge of optimism" after Inchon. Higgins (1960) and Caridi (1968) pointed to political motivation, arguing that Truman wanted to boost the Democratic Party's prospects in the November elections. Stueck (1981) and Kaufman (1986) have stressed how maintaining US credibility required pursuing Korea's reunification. But Matray (1979) has argued that the decision to cross the parallel reflected Truman's belief that conquest of North Korea would allow a united Korea to choose freely to follow the US model of economic, social, and political development. Many of his advisers had begun in July to lobby for forcible reunification once communist forces had been thrown out of the south. State Department official John M. Allison successfully overcame Acheson's initial opposition, arguing that the United States should destroy North Korea's army and then sponsor free elections for a government to rule a united Korea. US military leaders were reluctant to endorse this drastic change in war aims.

But on July 31, after defensive lines stabilized, the JCS advised Truman that occupying North Korea would be desirable if the Soviets did not intervene. During early August, Truman authorized the development of plans to achieve forcible reunification.

Whiting (1970), Spurr (1988), and Hao Yufan and Zhai Zhihai (1990) have argued that China intervened in the Korean War because the UNC advance to the Yalu constituted a grave threat to its national security. The People's Republic of China (PRC) was furious when Truman ordered the deployment of the Seventh Fleet into the Taiwan Strait on June 27 because this prevented Beijing from removing the nationalist redoubt on Taiwan. In late July, MacArthur visited the island and announced plans to strengthen the military capabilities of Jiang Jieshi's regime. Then, much to Truman's chagrin, the militantly anti-communist general dispatched a message to the Veterans of Foreign Wars that seemed to threaten the PRC. Nevertheless, Chinese Foreign Minister Zhou Enlai tried to avoid war, telling the Indian ambassador on October 2 that China would intervene in Korea if American forces crossed the parallel. Administration officials thought the Chinese were bluffing. At a personal meeting with Truman at Wake Island on October 15, MacArthur predicted that the Chinese would not intervene. Even after the first clash between UN troops and Chinese "volunteers" later that month, the general was supremely confident. On November 24, MacArthur launched his "Home by Christmas Offensive," with American troops in the vanguard. Two days later, the Chinese counterattacked in force, sending UN troops into a rapid mass retreat. An atmosphere of supreme crisis quickly gripped Washington as Truman declared a state of national emergency and spoke of using atomic weapons at a press conference.

China's decision to intervene in the Korean War has received a thorough re-examination in recent years as a result of access to information from the communist side. Chen Jian (1994), Zhang Shu Guang (1995), and Sheng (1997) contend that safeguarding the Chinese–Korean border was not the primary reason for Beijing's entry into the Korean War. Mao Zedong, Chen writes, sought "to win a glorious victory" that would restore China's world status as the "Central Kingdom." He also wanted to repay a debt to North Korea, which had sent thousands of soldiers to fight in the Chinese Civil War. Furthermore, after the Inchon landing, Stalin had been pressing Beijing to intervene and pledged Soviet air support. Some top PRC leaders opposed military intervention, but Mao used his authority and persuasive skill to convince his comrades that US conquest of North Korea would shatter China's credibility and prestige in Asia. Goncharov, Lewis, and Xue (1993) and Mansourov (1995/1996) have claimed that China balked in early October when Stalin reneged on his promise of air support, but then intervened to avoid the prospect of Kim Il Sung creating an exile government in Manchuria. According to Chen, Zhang, and Sheng, however, Chinese entry into the Korean War was certain because the triumph of Mao's revolutionary nationalist program was so vital to the PRC's future success.

During December 1950, MacArthur publicly defended his advance to the Yalu as a "reconnaissance in force" that had exposed a communist trap and averted disaster. He already had ridiculed Britain's "buffer zone" proposal and criticized US Allies for blocking approval of "hot pursuit" and bombing of the Yalu bridges. MacArthur pressed for adoption of his "Plan for Victory" that proposed blockading China's coast, bombing of military installations in Manchuria, using Chinese nationalist forces in Korea, and staging an assault from Taiwan against the mainland. Foot (1985) has demonstrated that the JCS, despite later denials, seriously considered implementation of these actions prior to receiving favorable reports from the battlefront late in December. Dingman (1988/1989) has shown that the president was prepared to use atomic weapons, an option that he had under consideration since the outset of the war. But after Chinese intervention, Truman decided to fight a "limited war" in Korea to accomplish the original goal of restoring the prewar status quo. James (1985), in the third volume of his authoritative biography of MacArthur, describes how the general opposed this strategy, arguing that escalation or evacuation were the only options. By March 1951, however, General Matthew B. Ridgway, who replaced Walker in December 1950, had proven that the adminis-tration's limited war strategy was feasible, driving Chinese communist forces back into North Korea.

In March 1951, Truman's plans to propose a ceasefire set the stage for the recall of MacArthur. Rovere and Schlesinger (1951) and Spanier (1959) established the consensus that still commends Truman for preserving the constitutional principle of civilian control over the military. In the first of two acts of insubordination, MacArthur scuttled Truman's planned peace initiative, issuing a humiliating public ultimatum to the Chinese communists demanding immediate surrender. Then, on the floor of the US House of Representatives, Republican Congressman Joseph W. Martin read a letter from MacArthur essentially charging that the Truman adminis-tration was guilty of appeasement in Korea. This directly violated a JCS directive of December 6, 1950 that required all government officials to obtain clearance for public comments on the war. Truman finally relieved MacArthur on April 11, but he did so for reasons related to military strategy and alliance politics. Schaller (1989) has explained how the JCS worried about a Chinese and Soviet military buildup in East Asia and thought the UN commander should have standing authority to retaliate against any communist escalation, even recommending deployment of atomic weapons to forward Pacific bases. Along with US allies, they mistrusted MacArthur and guessed he might provoke an incident in order to widen the war.

MacArthur's recall ignited a firestorm of criticism against Truman and the war. The general returned home to ticker-tape parades and delivered a televised address to a joint session of Congress, declaring that there was "no substitute for victory." During Senate hearings on his firing in May and later in his memoirs (1964), MacArthur denied he was guilty of insubordination. General Omar N. Bradley, the JCS chairman, made the administration's case, arguing persuasively that implement-ing MacArthur's proposals would lead to "the wrong war, in the wrong place, at the wrong time, and with the wrong enemy." Meanwhile, during April and May, the UNC had repulsed two huge Chinese communist offensives, establishing a defensive position just north of the parallel. Stalemate on the battlefield persuaded the belligerents to seek an armistice. After Soviet UN Ambassador Jacob Malik publicly advocated a ceasefire late in June, truce talks opened on July 10 at Kaesong. Washington was determined to limit the discussions to military matters, thus preventing the PRC from exploiting the talks to gain admission to the United Nations or control over Taiwan. The communists created an acrimonious atmos-phere at the start with efforts to score propaganda points, but Washington's desire for a political victory was behind its proposal on the first substantive issue for a demilitarized zone deep in North Korea. The nasty initial exchange on this issue established an acrid tone ensuring protracted negotiations.

Admiral C. Turner Joy (1955), head of the UNC delegation, and William H. Vatcher (1958) attributed the absence of progress toward an armistice to the inflexibility and intransigence of the communist delegation. Foot (1990) and Bailey (1992) blame the UNC delegation for the same reasons. Both sides shared responsibility for suspension of the truce talks in August after the communists protested an alleged UN violation of the neutral zone. Two months later, discussions resumed after Ridgway had forced movement of the negotiating site to Panmunjom. Rapid agreement was reached that the demilitarized zone would follow the line of battle. The delegations then approved inspection procedures to enforce the truce, as well as a postwar political conference to discuss withdrawal of foreign troops and unification. A tradeoff settled disputes on airfield rehabilitation and membership on a neutral supervisory commission. Ten months after talks began, negotiators would have signed an armistice agreement had they not deadlocked over the disposition of prisoners of war (POWs). To enlist world support to force the UNC to compromise, the communists charged that the United States was practicing bacteriological warfare in Korea. Gittings (1975), Halliday and Cumings (1988), and Endicott and Hagerman (1997) have presented evidence and argumentation to support these charges, but there are Soviet documents that suggest germ warfare was a hoax.

Orthodox accounts of the Korean War stress the humanitarian motivation behind the inflexible refusal of the United States to return communist POWs to China and North Korea against their will, endorsing Truman's portrayal of his decision at the time. Foot (1990) and Barton J. Bernstein in Cumings (1983) contend, however, that Truman's main goal was to win a propaganda victory in the Cold War, which necessitated a misrepresentation of the facts. The US stand on the principle of non-forcible repatriation contradicted the Geneva Convention, which required, as the communist side demanded, the return of all POWs. Far worse was the Truman administration's purposeful decision to allow the perception that those POWs refusing repatriation were communists defecting to the "Free World." McCormack (1983) and Kaufman (1986) have noted that the vast majority of the North Korean POWs were actually South Koreans who either had joined voluntarily or had been impressed into the communist army. And thousands of Chinese POWs were nationalist soldiers trapped in China at the end of the civil war who now had the chance to escape to Taiwan. Moreover, Chinese nationalist guards at UN POW camps had used terrorist "reeducation" tactics to compel prisoners to refuse repatriation. Goodman (1978), MacDonald (1986), and Foot (1990) have documented how those who resisted risked beatings or death.

In May 1952 the UNC's brutal suppression of an uprising at the Koje-do POW compound provided substantiation for communist charges of inhumane treatment. That summer, massive UNC bombing raids devastated the north, but failed to force communist concessions at Panmunjom. Despite intense efforts at the United Nations, the truce talks adjourned in October 1952. In November 1952, angry Americans elected Dwight D. Eisenhower president largely because they expected him to end what had become a very unpopular war in Korea. Fulfilling a campaign pledge, the general visited the Korean battlefront during December, concluding that further ground assaults would be futile. But Keefer (1986) and Stueck (1995) have shown that the new president entered office thinking seriously about using expanded conventional bombing and the threat of nuclear attack to force concessions from the communists. Eisenhower (1963) insisted that China agreed to an armistice after Secretary of State John Foster Dulles informed India's prime minister in May 1953 that in the absence of progress toward an armistice, the United States would expand the war. Divine (1981), Ambrose (1984), and Calingaert (1988) have argued that Beijing agreed to a truce because of US nuclear threats. Most scholars, however, doubt China was reacting to Eisenhower's atomic diplomacy because as yet no documentary evidence has surfaced to support his assertion.

How Eisenhower ended the Korean War thus remains contested terrain. Edward Friedman (1975) and Foot (1988/1989) contend that the Chinese, facing major domestic economic problems and wanting peaceful coexistence with the West, already had decided to make peace once Truman left office. Stalin's death in March only added to China's sense of political vulnerability, persuading Chinese negotiators to break the logjam at Panmunjom later that month when they accepted the UNC's proposal for an exchange of sick and wounded prisoners and then recommended turning non-repatriates over to a neutral state. More than a month later, when the administration delivered its nuclear threats to Beijing, Keefer (1986) and Dingman (1988/1989) have stressed that they were not clearly or forcefully delivered. Moreover, they were not substantively different from those implied threats that the Truman administration made during the fall of 1951, when B-29 bombers carried out atomic bombing test runs over North Korea with large conventional bombs. Ryan (1989) has added that the PRC did not view nuclear threats of any kind as credible. Finally, during late May and early June 1953, Chinese forces launched powerful attacks against positions that South Korean units were defending along the front line. Far from being intimidated, Beijing thus showed its continuing resolve, relying on military means to persuade the United States to compromise on the final terms of the armistice.

By January 1953, Washington and Beijing in truth wanted an armistice. Both had grown tired of the economic burdens, military losses, political and military constraints, worries about an expanded war, and the pressure from allies and the world community to end the stalemated war. Food shortages in North Korea, combined with an understanding that forcible reunification was no longer possible, had persuaded Pyongyang to favor an armistice even earlier. Moscow's new leaders thought that a more conciliatory approach in the Cold War not only would reduce the risk of general war, but also might create tensions in the Western alliance if Washington refused to reciprocate. Indeed, Bailey (1992) and Stueck (1995) have emphasized how a constant succession of issues during the Korean War threatened permanent damage to US relations with not only its allies in Europe, but also non-aligned members of the United Nations. For example, in May 1953, US bombing of North Korea's dams and irrigation system brought a new outburst of international criticism. Then, in June, Rhee, who opposed any armistice that left Korea divided, almost torpedoed the pending ceasefire when he released 27,000 North Korean POWs. Eisenhower bought Rhee's acceptance of an armistice with promises of financial aid and a mutual security pact. Fortunately, the incident only delayed until

July 27, 1953 the signing of an agreement to end this brutal conflict. Both sides committed atrocities in a "limited" war that killed over 2 million Koreans, 33,000 Americans, and 152,000 Chinese.

Whelan (1990), Toland (1991), and Catchpole (2000) have written the latest popular histories of the Korean War, but none adds much to the historical debate. Flaws of fact and interpretation appear throughout the works of Sandler (1999) and Wainstock (1999). Historians continue to neglect the domestic impact of the Korean War, with the exception of Pierpaoli (1999). The future release of more Soviet documents no doubt will revive debate on selected issues in the Korean War, but few specialists in US foreign relations now disagree that the conflict was the critical turning point in the Cold War. Reacting to North Korea's attack, the United States vastly increased defense spending, strengthened the North Atlantic Treaty Organization militarily, and pressed for West German rearmament. US relations with China were poisoned for twenty years, especially after Washington persuaded the United Nations in February 1951 to condemn the PRC for aggression in Korea. Moreover, the Korean War left the United States closely wedded to the odious regimes of Jiang Jieshi and Syngman Rhee. Korea's main legacy, however, was that the United States thereafter pursued a foreign policy of global intervention and paid an enormous price in death, destruction, and damaged reputation.

REFERENCES

Acheson, Dean G.: *Present at the Creation: My Years in the State Department* (New York: Norton, 1969).

Alexander, Bevin: *Korea: The First War We Lost* (New York: Hippocrene, 1986).

Ambrose, Stephen E.: *Eisenhower, Vol. 2: The President* (New York: Simon and Schuster, 1984).

Appleman, Roy E.: *South to the Naktong, North to the Yalu* (Washington, DC: US Government Printing Office, 1961).

Bailey, Sydney D.: *The Korean Armistice* (New York: St. Martin's Press, 1992).

Bajanov, Evgueni: "Assessing the Politics of the Korean War, 1949–1951." *Cold War International History Project Bulletin*, Issues 6–7 (winter 1995/1996), 54, 87–91.

Berger, Carl: *The Korean Knot: A Military–Political History* (Philadelphia: University of Pennsylvania Press, 1964).

Blair, Clay: *The Forgotten War: America in Korea, 1950–1953* (New York: Times Books, 1987).

Buhite, Russell D.: "'Major Interests': American Policy Toward China, Taiwan, and Korea, 1945–1950." *Pacific Historical Review* 47, 3 (August 1978), 425–51.

Calingaert, Daniel: "Nuclear Weapons and the Korean War." *Journal of Strategic Studies* 11 (June 1988), 177–202.

Caridi, Ronald J.: *The Korean War and American Politics: The Republican Party as a Case Study* (Philadelphia: University of Pennsylvania Press, 1968).

Catchpole, Brian: *The Korean War 1950–53* (London: Constable and Robinson, 2000).

Chen Jian: *China's Road to the Korean War: The Making of the Sino-American Confrontation* (New York: Columbia University Press, 1994).

Cho Soon-sung: *Korea in World Politics, 1940–1950: An Evaluation of American Responsibility* (Berkeley: University of California Press, 1967).

Clark, Mark W.: *From the Danube to the Yalu* (New York: Harper, 1954).

Collins, J. Lawton: *War in Peacetime: The History and Lessons of Korea* (Boston, MA: Houghton Mifflin, 1969).

Condit, Doris M.: *History of the Office of the Secretary of Defense, Vol. 2: The Test of War, 1950–1953* (Washington, DC: US Government Printing Office, 1988).

Cumings, Bruce (ed.): *Child of Conflict: The Korean–American Relationship, 1945–1953* (Seattle: University of Washington Press, 1983).

Cumings, Bruce: *The Origins of the Korean War*, 2 vols (Princeton, NJ: Princeton University Press, 1981, 1990).

Dingman, Roger: "Atomic Diplomacy during the Korean War." *International Security* 13, 3 (winter 1988/1989), 61–89.

Divine, Robert A.: *Eisenhower and the Cold War* (New York: Oxford University Press, 1981).

Dobbs, Charles M.: *The Unwanted Symbol: American Foreign Policy, the Cold War, and Korea, 1945–1950* (Kent, OH: Kent State University Press, 1981).

Eisenhower, Dwight D.: *The White House Years, Vol. 2: Mandate for Change, 1953–1956* (Garden City, NY: Doubleday, 1963).

Endicott, Stephen L. and Edward Hagerman: *The United States and Biological Warfare: Secrets from the Early Cold War and Korea* (Bloomington: Indiana University Press, 1997).

Farrar-Hockley, Anthony: *The British Part in the Korean War, Vol. 1: A Distant Obligation* (London: Her Majesty's Stationery Office, 1987).

Fehrenbach, T. R.: *This Kind of War: A Study in Unpreparedness* (New York: Macmillan, 1963).

Fleming, Denna Frank: *The Cold War and Its Origins*, 2 vols. (Garden City, NY: Doubleday, 1961).

Foot, Rosemary: *The Wrong War: American Policy and the Dimensions of the Korean Conflict, 1950–1953* (Ithaca, NY: Cornell University Press, 1985).

Foot, Rosemary: "Nuclear Coercion and the Ending of the Korean Conflict." *International Security* 13, 3 (winter 1988/1989), 92–112.

Foot, Rosemary: *A Substitute for Victory: The Politics of Peacemaking at the Korean Armistice Talks* (Ithaca, NY: Cornell University Press, 1990).

Friedman, Edward: "Nuclear Blackmail and the End of the Korean War." *Modern China* 1, 1 (January 1975), 75–91.

Gittings, John: "Talks, Bombs and Germs – Another Look at the Korean War." *Journal of Contemporary Asia*, 5, 2 (1975), 205–17.

Goncharov, Sergei N., John W. Lewis, and Xue Litai: *Uncertain Partners: Stalin, Mao, and the Korean War* (Stanford, CA: Stanford University Press, 1993).

Goodman, Allan E. (ed.): *Negotiating While Fighting: The Diary of Admiral C. Turner Joy at the Korean Armistice Conference* (Stanford, CA: Hoover Institution Press, 1978).

Goulden, Joseph C.: *Korea: The Untold Story of the War* (New York: Times Books, 1982).

Gupta, Karunakar: "How Did the Korean War Begin?" *China Quarterly* 52 (October–December 1972), 699–716.

Halliday, Jon and Bruce Cumings: *Korea: The Unknown War* (New York: Pantheon, 1988).

Halperin, Morton H.: *Limited War in the Nuclear Age* (New York: Wiley, 1963).

Hao Yufan and Zhai Zhihai: "China's Decision to Enter the Korean War: History Revisited." *China Quarterly* 121 (March 1990), 94–115.

Hastings, Max: *The Korean War* (New York: Simon and Schuster, 1987).

Hermes, Walter G.: *Truce Tent and Fighting Front* (Washington, DC: US Government Printing Office, 1966).

Hickey, Michael: *The Korean War: The West Confronts Communism, 1950–1953* (London: John Murray, 1999).

Higgins, Trumbull: *Truman and the Fall of MacArthur: A Precis on Limited War* (New York: Oxford University Press, 1960).

Hitchcock, Wilbur W.: "North Korea Jumps the Gun." *Current History* 20, 115 (March 20, 1951), 136–44.

James, D. Clayton: *The Years of MacArthur, Vol. 3: Triumph and Disaster, 1945–1963* (Boston, MA: Houghton Mifflin, 1985).

Joy, C. Turner: *How Communists Negotiate* (New York: Macmillan, 1955).

Kaufman, Burton I.: *The Korean War: Challenges in Crises, Credibility, and Command* (Philadelphia, PA: Temple University Press, 1986).

Keefer, Edward C.: "President Dwight D. Eisenhower and the End of the Korean War." *Diplomatic History* 10, 3 (summer 1986), 267–89.

Kennan, George F.: *Memoirs 1925–1950* (Boston, MA: Little, Brown, 1967).

Khrushchev, Nikita: *Khrushchev Remembers* (Boston, MA: Little, Brown, 1970).

Kim Chull Baum: *The Truth About the Korean War: Testimony 40 Years Later* (Seoul: Eulyoo, 1991).

Kim Chull Baum and James I. Matray (eds.): *Korea and the Cold War: Division, Destruction, and Disarmament* (Claremont, CA: Regina, 1993).

Kim Chum-gon: *The Korean War* (Seoul: Kwongmyong, 1973).

Knox, Donald: *The Korean War: Pusan to Chosin* (New York: Harcourt, Brace, Jovanovich, 1985).

Knox, Donald: *The Korean War: Uncertain Victory* (New York: Harcourt, Brace, Jovanovich, 1988).

Kolko, Joyce and Gabriel Kolko: *The Limits of Power: The World and United States Foreign Policy, 1945–1954* (New York: Harper and Row, 1972).

Leckie, Robert: *Conflict: The History of the Korean War, 1950–1953* (New York: Putnam's, 1962).

Liu Xiaoyuan: "Sino-American Diplomacy over Korea during World War II." *Journal of American–East Asian Relations* 1, 2 (summer 1992), 223–64.

Lowe, Peter: *Origins of the Korean War* (New York: Longman, 1986).

MacArthur, Douglas: *Reminiscences* (New York: McGraw Hill, 1964).

McCormack, Gavan: *Cold War/Hot War* (Sydney: Hale and Iremonger, 1983).

McCune, George M. and Arthur L. Grey, Jr.: *Korea Today* (Cambridge, MA: Harvard University Press, 1950).

MacDonald, Callum A.: *Korea: The War Before Vietnam* (New York: Free Press, 1986).

MacDonald, Callum A.: *Britain and the Korean War* (Oxford: Blackwell, 1990).

McGibbon, Ian: *New Zealand and the Korean War* (New York: Oxford University Press, 1992).

McGlothen, Ronald L.: *Controlling the Waves: Dean Acheson and US Policy in East Asia* (New York: Norton, 1993).

Mansourov, Alexandre Y.: "Stalin, Mao, Kim, and China's Decision to Enter the Korean War, September 16–October 15, 1950: New Evidence from the Russian Archives." *Cold War International History Project Bulletin*, Issues 6–7 (winter 1995/1996), 100–5.

Matray, James I.: "Truman's Plan for Victory: National Self-Determination and the Thirty-Eighth Parallel Decision in Korea." *Journal of American History* 66, 2 (September 1979), 314–33.

Matray, James I.: *The Reluctant Crusade: American Foreign Policy in Korea, 1941–1950* (Honolulu: University of Hawaii Press, 1985).

Matray, James I.: "Dean Acheson's National Press Club Speech Reexamined." *Journal of Conflict Studies* 22, 1 (spring 2002).

May, Ernest R.: *"Lessons of the Past": The Use and Misuse of History in American Foreign Policy* (New York: Oxford University Press, 1973).

Meade, E. Grant: *American Military Government in Korea* (New York: King's Crown Press, 1951).

Merrill, John: *Korea: The Peninsular Origins of the War* (Newark: University of Delaware Press, 1985).

Oliver, Robert T.: *Syngman Rhee: The Man Behind the Myth* (Tokyo: Tuttle, 1955).

O'Neill, Robert: *Australia in the Korean War, 1950–1953, Vol. 1: Strategy and Diplomacy* (Canberra: Australian Government Publishing Service, 1981).

Osgood, Robert E.: *Limited War: The Challenge to American Strategy* (Chicago, IL: University of Chicago Press, 1957).

Paige, Glenn D.: *The Korean Decision: June 24–30, 1950* (New York: Free Press, 1968).

Paik Sun Yup: *From Pusan to Panmunjom* (New York: Brassey's, 1992).

Park Hong-kyu: "From Pearl Harbor to Cairo: America's Korean Diplomacy, 1941–1943." *Diplomatic History* 13, 3 (summer 1989), 343–58.

Perret, Geoffrey: *Old Soldiers Never Die: The Life of Douglas MacArthur* (New York: Random House, 1996).

Pierpaoli, Paul G., Jr.: *Truman and Korea: The Political Culture of the Early Cold War* (Columbia: University of Missouri Press, 1999).

Poats, Rutherford B.: *Decision in Korea* (New York: McBride, 1954).

Rees, David: *Korea: The Limited War* (New York: St. Martin's Press, 1964).

Ridgway, Matthew B.: *The Korean War* (Garden City, NY: Doubleday, 1967).

Rovere, Richard and Arthur M. Schlesinger, Jr.: *The General and the President and the Future of American Foreign Policy* (New York: Farrar, Straus, and Giroux, 1951).

Ryan, Mark A.: *Chinese Attitudes toward Nuclear Weapons: China and the United States During the Korean War* (Armonk, NY: M. E. Sharpe, 1989).

Sandler, Stanley: *The Korean War: No Victors, No Vanquished* (Lexington: University of Kentucky Press, 1999).

Sandusky, Michael C.: *America's Parallel* (Alexandria, VA: Old Dominion Press, 1983).

Sawyer, Robert K. and Walter G. Hermes: *Military Advisors in Korea: KMAG in Peace and War* (Washington, DC: US Government Printing Office, 1979).

Schaller, Michael: *Douglas MacArthur: The Far Eastern General* (New York: Oxford University Press, 1989).

Schnabel, James F.: *Policy and Direction: The First Year* (Washington, DC: US Government Printing Office, 1972).

Schnabel, James F. and Robert J. Watson: *History of the Joint Chiefs of Staff, Vol. 3: The Korean War* (Washington, DC: US Government Printing Office, 1988).

Sheng, Michael M.: *Battling Western Imperialism: Mao, Stalin, and the United States* (Princeton, NJ: Princeton University Press, 1997).

Simmons, Robert R.: *The Strained Alliance: Peking, Pyongyang, Moscow and the Politics of the Korean Civil War* (New York: Free Press, 1975).

Spanier, John W.: *The Truman–MacArthur Controversy and the Korean War* (New York: Norton, 1959).

Spurr, Russell: *Enter the Dragon: China's Undeclared War Against the US In Korea, 1950–1951* (New York: Newmarket Press, 1988).

Stairs, Denis: *The Diplomacy of Constraint: Canada, the Korean War, and the United Nations* (Toronto: University of Toronto Press, 1974).

Stokesbury, James L.: *A Short History of the Korean War* (New York: William Morrow, 1988).

Stone, I. F.: *The Hidden History of the Korean War* (New York: Monthly Review Press, 1952).

Stueck, William W.: *The Road to Confrontation: American Foreign Policy toward China and Korea, 1947–1950* (Chapel Hill: University of North Carolina Press, 1981).

Stueck, William W.: *The Korean War: An International History* (Princeton, NJ: Princeton University Press, 1995).

Toland, John: *In Mortal Combat: Korea, 1950–1953* (New York: William Morrow, 1991).

Tomedi, Rudy: *No Bugles, No Drums: An Oral History of the Korean War* (New York: Wiley, 1993).

Truman, Harry S.: *Memoirs, Vol. 2: Years of Trial and Hope* (Garden City, NY: Doubleday, 1956).

Van Ree, Erik: *Socialism in One Zone: Stalin's Policy in Korea, 1945–1947* (Oxford: Berg, 1989).

Vatcher, William H.: *Panmunjom: The Story of the Korean Military Armistice Negotiations* (New York: Praeger, 1958).

Wainstock, Dennis D.: *Truman, MacArthur, and the Korean War* (Westport, CT: Greenwood Press, 1999).

Weathersby, Kathryn: "New Findings on the Korean War." *Cold War International History Project Bulletin*, Issue 3 (fall 1993), 1, 14–18.

Weathersby, Kathryn: "The Soviet Role in the Early Phase of the Korean War: New Documentary Evidence." *Journal of American–East Asian Relations* 3, 4 (winter 1994), 446–7.

Weintraub, Stanley: *MacArthur's War: Korea and the Undoing of an American Hero* (New York: Free Press, 2000).

Whelan, Richard L.: *Drawing the Line: The Korean War, 1950–1953* (Boston, MA: Little, Brown, 1990).

Whiting, Allen S.: *China Crosses the Yalu: The Decision to Enter the Korean War* (Stanford, CA: Stanford University Press, 1970).

Zhang Shu Guang: *Mao's Military Romanticism: China and the Korean War, 1950–53* (Lawrence: University of Kansas Press, 1995).

FURTHER READING

Anders, Roger M.: "The Atomic Bomb and the Korean War: Gordon Dean and the Issue of Civilian Military Control." *Military Affairs* 52, no. 1 (January 1988), 1–6.

Baldwin, Frank (ed.): *Without Parallel: The American–Korean Relationship since 1945* (New York: Pantheon Books, 1975).

Cumings, Bruce: "Korean–American Relations: A Century of Contact and Thirty-Five Years of Intimacy." In Warren I. Cohen (ed.) *New Frontiers in American–East Asian Relations: Essays Presented to Dorothy Borg* (New York: Columbia University Press, 1983).

Foot, Rosemary: "Making Known the Unknown War: Policy Analysis of the Korean Conflict in the Last Decade." *Diplomatic History* 15, 3 (summer 1991), 411–31.

George, Alexander L.: *The Chinese Communist Army in Action: The Korean War and Its Aftermath* (New York: Columbia University Press, 1967).

Heller, Frances H. (ed.): *The Korean War: A 25-Year Perspective* (Lawrence: University of Kansas Press, 1977).

Hunt, Michael H.: "Beijing and the Korean Crisis, June 1950–June 1951." *Political Science Quarterly* 107, 3 (fall 1992), 453–78.

Iriye, Akira and Yonosuke Nagai (eds.): *The Origins of the Cold War in Asia* (New York: Columbia University Press, 1977).

Jervis, Robert: "The Impact of the Korean War on the Cold War." *Journal of Conflict Resolution* 24, 4 (December 1980), 563–92.

Keefer, Edward C.: "The Truman Administration and the South Korean Political Crisis of 1952: Democracy's Failure?" *Pacific Historical Review* 60, 2 (May 1991), 145–68.

Khong, Yen Foon: *Analogies at War: Korea, Munich, Dien Bien Phu, and the Vietnam Decision of 1965* (Princeton, NJ: Princeton University Press, 1992).

Khrushchev, Nikita: *Khrushchev Remembers: The Glasnost Tapes* (Boston, MA: Little, Brown, 1990).

Lee, Steven Hugh: *Outposts of Empire: Korea, Vietnam and the Origins of the Cold War, 1949–1954* (Montreal: McGill-Queen's University Press, 1995).

Lee, Steven Hugh: *The Korean War* (New York: Longman, 2001).

Middleton, Harry: *The Compact History of the Korean War* (New York: Hawthorne, 1965).

Neary, Ian and James Cotton (eds.): *The Korean War in History* (Atlantic Highlands, NJ: Humanities Press International, 1989).

Noble, Harold J.: *Embassy at War* (Seattle: University of Washington Press, 1975).

Wilz, John E.: "The MacArthur Hearings of 1951: The Secret Testimony." *Military Affairs* 39, 4 (December 1975), 167–73.

CHAPTER SEVENTEEN

Foreign Relations in the 1950s

RICHARD H. IMMERMAN

US foreign relations from the decade following the Korean War to the inauguration of John F. Kennedy befuddled contemporary observers. Evaluating those foreign relations continues to befuddle today's scholars. The North Korean invasion of South Korea, especially because it occurred so soon after the communist forces of Mao Zedong expelled Jian Jieshi's (Chiang Kai-shek's) nationalists from mainland China and the successful Soviet test of an atomic device, appeared to confirm the premises – and nightmares – of advocates of a more aggressive and expensive US security policy. A decade later a central theme of Kennedy's campaign was that the security interests of the United States and the "Free World" demanded a more aggressive and expensive security policy. The inescapable conclusion was that foreign policy during the intervening years remained passive and insufficiently funded; hence, dangerously ineffective. Unless the United States took immediate and dramatic remedial measures, Kennedy proclaimed when debating Richard M. Nixon, "historians 10 years from now" would write that the 1950s "were the years when the tide ran out for the United States" (Kennedy and Nixon 1960).

Kennedy was not far off. Although, or perhaps because, he and his successor, Lyndon B. Johnson, took what they defined as remedial measures – the acceleration of nuclear missile production, increase of US conventional forces, development of special forces, generous distribution of foreign aid, and more – historians over the next decade with few exceptions portrayed the foreign policies of Dwight D. Eisenhower as fatally flawed. These policies produced a paralysis that precipitated scenarios that came perilously close to crossing the nuclear threshold, yet still allowed for communist expansion. The United States lurched spasmodically among Cold War battlefields even as it ceded the technological initiative to the Soviets. Historians attributed this bifurcation to the unfortunate combining of the naive, docile, and miserly Eisenhower with the inflexible, legalistic, and moralistic John Foster Dulles, his secretary of state. This combination also produced a perspective that alienated the Third World while placing countless strains on US relations with vital allies. Most analysts identified Eisenhower's culpability as primarily his delegating to Dulles primary responsibility for both the formulation and implementation of foreign policy. Eisenhower became a "captive hero" (Childs 1958).

Kennedy had been dead for about a decade before historians began to chip away at this orthodoxy (Parmet 1972; Bernstein 1973; Lyon 1974). But it took a confluence of events in the mid-1970s to generate the historiographic revolution known as Eisenhower revisionism. In Abilene, Kansas, thousands of pages of remarkably instructive archives became available to scholars. In Washington, DC elected and appointed officials struggled to resolve the pathologies of the economy while seeking out opportunities to demonstrate respect for the Constitution. And in Saigon, Vietnam, a US helicopter fled from the rooftop of the embassy. For many historians, America's tragedy in Vietnam was the most salient variable in the equation of Eisenhower revisionism. "The essence of Eisenhower's strength and the basis for any claim to presidential greatness," wrote Robert Divine in the year Ronald Reagan moved into the White House, "lies in his admirable self-restraint . . . His moderation and prudence served as an enduring model of presidential restraint – one that his successors ignored to their eventual regret" (Divine 1981: 155).

By appearing intent on refighting Vietnam in Nicaragua, Reagan added more fuel to Eisenhower revisionism. Divine published his *Eisenhower and the Cold War* in 1981. He relied largely on secondary sources. But a year later came Fred I. Greenstein's *The Hidden-Hand Presidency* (1982), which immediately became the exemplar of Eisenhower revisionism. Systematically exploiting the Eisenhower Library's archives, especially Eisenhower's private diary, his voluminous public and private correspondence, and detailed memoranda of the vigorous discussions at meetings of the National Security Council, Greenstein revealed a president who actually did rule and not merely reign. He, not Dulles, made the decisions. In fact, a politically savvy Eisenhower cultivated the misperception that he was Dulles' puppet so that he could avoid the debilitating criticism produced by unpopular policies and programs that he judged vital to pursue. Dulles and other subordinates served as lightning rods to insulate the president; the personable Ike could remain a symbol of national unity. Yet in heated debates behind closed doors, Eisenhower manifested great skill, sophistication, and expertise.

As a political scientist, Greenstein's concerns were largely instrumental. They lay in the areas of Eisenhower's leadership style. As a historian, Stephen Ambrose (1984) addressed more directly the policies' substance. Eisenhower emerged from these pages – many pages read by many readers – warranting the superlatives that Ambrose liberally used. Eisenhower "ran the show," effused Ambrose. "Firm, fair, objective, dignified," the president was "brilliantly right in his management of numerous war scares" and "consistently right in his opposition to putting ever greater sums into national defense." Ambrose identifies Eisenhower's Atoms-for-Peace proposal, which most scholars had dismissed or ignored as disingenuous or insignificant, as "the best chance [of] mankind . . . to redirect the arms race." He stood up to swashbucklers like Joint Chief of Staff Chairman Admiral Arthur Radford, who sought opportunities to put American power on display. His management of the first Quemoy–Matsu crisis was a "*tour de force.*" A "great and good man," Eisenhower "made peace, and he kept the peace" (Ambrose 1984: 9–12, 150, 245, 626).

The writings of Greenstein and Ambrose came to define Eisenhower revisionism. After their publication in the early 1980s, studies of foreign policy in the 1950s would never resemble those that characterized that decade and the succeeding two. This is not to say, however, that a new consensus emerged. In terms of Eisenhower's management of foreign policy, Greenstein convinced – with the exception of such partisan critics as Arthur Schlesinger, Jr., and even he mellowed (Schlesinger 1983, 2000). Subsequent scholars accepted and built on Greenstein's insights. Ambrose proved to be less convincing. He left the impression that, even taking into account the president's deep-seated hostility toward the Soviets and insensitivity to the dynamics of developing nations, Eisenhower got almost everything right. Subsequent scholars did not so much reject Ambrose's interpretations as argue that his judgments required greater nuance.

Indeed, even as Greenstein and Ambrose's works were being read widely, the publication of studies by other historians on US foreign policy in the 1950s foreshadowed what some would soon begin to call Eisenhower post-revisionism. Illustrative were several examinations of the CIA's 1954 operation in Guatemala to oust the government of Jacobo Arbenz. This illustration is apt because Divine invited criticism by pointedly excluding discussion of covert projects. How could he stress Eisenhower's prudent restraint by describing Eisenhower's "foreign policy achievements" as almost universally "negative in nature" without at least the qualifier that Eisenhower did behave aggressively albeit clandestinely in Guatemala, Iran, Indonesia, the Congo, and elsewhere (Divine 1981: 154)? Divine's claim that the lack of archives precluded considering such operations fell flat because many of the archives had become available.

Between 1981 and 1982 three different monographs appeared that, relying heavily on just-declassified materials, examined in detail PBSUCCESS, the CIA operation in Guatemala. Their interpretations varied substantially. One argued that the project reflected the degree to which Eisenhower had been bamboozled by the Eastern Establishment and other US elites (Cook 1981). A second asserted that PBSUCCESS revealed the influence of special economic interests – the United Fruit Company in particular – on US foreign policy (Schlesinger and Kinzer 1982). The third stressed America's geopolitical concerns and the pervasive and pernicious effects of a "cold war ethos" (Immerman 1982). These works were revisionist, for in each of them Eisenhower emerged as the central player – a smart man completely in command. Yet not one evaluated the quality of Eisenhower's policies as superior to what "orthodox" scholars had thought were Dulles' policies (Hoopes 1973).

Within a half-decade of the publication of Greenstein's *Hidden-Hand Presidency* and the trio of books on Guatemala, but only two years after Ambrose's biography captured such an immense readership, Robert McMahon threw down the gauntlet. McMahon did not challenge the "Greenstein revisionists." But the "Ambrose revisionists" caused him to pause. He conceded that on such issues as the arms race and handling Soviet relations, Eisenhower deserved credit. Deep down the World War II commander did champion peace. Yet while the potential for Armageddon was crucial to defining foreign policy in the 1950s, so was the challenge to the globe's colonial system. And in this area there was not much for Eisenhower revisionists to brag about. McMahon pointed out that although often denied access to archives comparable to those available on Guatemala, most scholars remained highly critical of US behavior on such Third World battlefields as Indochina (Herring 1979), the Philippines (Shalom 1981), the Middle East (Rubin 1980; Meyer 1980; Neff 1981; Spiegel 1985), Venezuela (Rabe 1982), and Africa (Noer 1985: Kalb 1982). "Some revisionists have badly overstated their case," McMahon's survey of the literature on the Third World suggested. "To understand a global foreign policy requires a systematic examination of *all* the areas of the world in which the United States tried to exert influence or affect developments." By its geopolitical selectivity,

Eisenhower revisionism was a "castle built upon sand" (McMahon 1986: 471–2, 457).

Historians of US foreign relations accepted McMahon's challenge. He dismissed the "preoccupation" of political scientists like Greenstein with Eisenhower's leadership and policymaking process as "at best peripheral" to historians' interest in assessing the goals and consequences of those policies (ibid: 455). According to Nelson (1983), however, the distinction between process and product is artificial. Studies published over the past fifteen years support Nelson's conclusions.

Journalists dubbed Eisenhower's global strategy the "New Look" in the first year of his presidency. Yet historians had to wait three decades for a sophisticated assessment of it; even then it comprised just two chapters in John Lewis Gaddis' *Strategies of Containment* (1982: 127–97). During the next several years there appeared important articles that enhanced Gaddis' depiction of Eisenhower's nuclear strategy, adding such terminology as "overkill" and "wasting asset" to the lexicon of historians of foreign and national security policy (Rosenberg 1983; Trachtenberg 1988/1989; Brands 1989). At the same time, examinations of policy toward China reinforced Gaddis' argument that the administration's behavior was not only surprisingly pragmatic and restrained, but also it appreciated the tension between Beijing and Moscow and acted belligerently because it thought that the best strategy for tearing apart the Sino-Soviet alliance (Chang 1990). The primary caveat was that luck as much as wisdom prevented this strategy from producing a nuclear exchange across the Taiwan Strait in 1954 and 1955 (Brands 1988; Chang 1988).

Influenced by the end of the Cold War and the collapse of the Soviet Union, the mid-1990s witnessed the emergence of a new literature on the New Look. At issue, at a most fundamental level, was the extent to which policies in the 1950s contributed to the events that occurred decades later. The flip side of this question was whether, in light of the death of Josef Stalin in 1953 and his denunciation by Nikita Khrushchev three years later, the United States "missed opportunities" to bring closure to the Cold War much earlier. And was the risk of a nuclear holocaust unnecessarily high? No amount of documentation can answer such questions, but for the historian writing after the end of the Cold War, it is fruitful to engage with them.

Halfway through the last decade two overviews of Eisenhower's New Look appeared in rapid succession. Each followed in Gaddis' interpretive footsteps by stressing Eisenhower's reliance on nuclear weapons, his preference for covert and paramilitary operations as opposed to deploying conventional forces, and the extent to which the president's fiscal conservatism influenced his strategic choices. Both also agreed with Gaddis in positively appraising the results. In his brief biography, William Pickett (1995) was necessarily selective in his coverage. Still, he found space to include a more informed discussion than Ambrose of how Eisenhower decided on his policies and programs. Pickett was one of the first historians to use reports of the Project Solarium task forces. He does not shy away from identifying Eisenhower's shortcomings. Nevertheless, as the "first Cold War commander-in-chief," he writes, Eisenhower's policies were on the whole "realistic and statesmanlike," embodying a "sense of the national interest" and "an awareness of obtainable goals" (pp. 136–7). Pickett leaves no doubt that Eisenhower contributed valuably to the collapse of the Soviet Union.

British historian Saki Dockrill (1996) took the analysis to the next level by seeking to describe and assess the New Look comprehensively: "as strategy, as policy, as diplomacy." Her explicit intention was to build on "revisionist themes," and she succeeded. Early chapters on the formulation of the New Look meld into subsequent chapters on its implementation worldwide and a scorecard on the outcomes. She uses relatively few of the materials that had become available from behind the Iron and Bamboo Curtains. Her research in US and British archives, however, is impressive.

Dockrill is positive yet measured in her judgments. For example, she faults Eisenhower for engaging in high-risk brinkmanship during both Quemoy–Matsu crises, for encouraging indigenous resistance to communist rule in Hungary but developing no instruments to assist those who resisted, and for failing to prepare for limited war even as the US strategic deterrent deteriorated. She even criticizes aspects of the president's vaunted leadership style. "Eisenhower was a determined and accessible leader." But he "assumed that his subordinates would obey his instructions, even if they could not understand them." In terms of global policy and strategy, nonetheless, Dockrill ends with applause. "Ultimately," she concludes, "the selectivity and flexibility built into the New Look was based on the sound judgment of the head of state." In addition, "massive retaliation was a sensible solution to the complex problem bedeviling US nuclear strategy at that time" (pp. xiv, 272, 276–7).

Dockrill's book was tantamount to a "first-cut" systematic analysis of the New Look in its entirety in the aftermath of the outbreak of the revisionist revolution. But in less than 300 pages of text she could not treat any component of the New Look thoroughly. Predictably, other scholarship was already in the pipeline that supplemented, and in some instances challenged, Dockrill's. Robert Bowie and I co-wrote a book that dissected the production of the New Look. As did Dockrill's analysis, *Waging Peace* (1998) exposed the strategy's constituent parts. To an extent greater than Dockrill, it defined the constituencies who participated in this process, identifying the sources each drew on, isolating the key debates, and explaining the outcomes. It also distinguished Eisenhower's strategy and policy from those of Harry S. Truman. Not only was it different, it was better.

In part, argue Bowie and Immerman, Eisenhower's superior product can be attributed to a more rigorous policymaking process than Truman's. In part it can be attributed to improved intelligence and extraordinary studies such as those under-taken during the Solarium exercise. But the most salient explanation is the contribution of Eisenhower himself – and to a lesser but nevertheless important extent, his secretary of state, Dulles (Immerman 1999). It was not so much Eisenhower's fiscal conservatism that drove his decisions – a central argument of both early critics and such subsequent fans as Gaddis and Dockrill – as his rejection of the alarmist estimates of the Soviet leadership, his belief that no country could win a nuclear war, and his efforts, even if unsuccessful in the short run, to negotiate a decrease in Cold War tensions. Scholars should not exaggerate his failure to achieve a settlement with the Soviets, as does Ambrose, nor the resistance of his successors to the vital tenets of the New Look – Dockrill's perspective. More important, the Eisenhower administration "developed the first coherent and sustainable Cold War strategy suitable for the basic conditions that would prevail during the following decades." Moreover, the "central concepts" of the New Look "served as enduring guides for the later stages of the Cold War" (Bowie and Immerman 1998: 3, 247).

The first three of these central concepts *Waging Peace* identifies are "The Imperative of Preventing Nuclear Holocaust," "The Feasibility of Deterrence," and "The Necessity of a Secure Second Strike." Clearly, the role of nuclear weapons in 1950s foreign and security policies is not contested. Evaluations of nuclear strategy, however, have become progressively more contested. Political scientist Peter Roman (1995), for example, concurs with the revisionist consensus that Eisenhower was at the center of his administration's decisions. He likewise concurs with Bowie and Immerman that Kennedy and others drew heavily on Eisenhower's legacy. That legacy includes the precept of strategic nuclear redundancy, and no less important, the shift from counterforce to countervalue targeting doctrine. To Roman, Eisenhower deserves credit for these vital innovations.

Yet Roman identifies much to complain about. Eisenhower fared poorly in his efforts to convince Congress and the public that his strategies were sound, and for that matter, that continental America (let alone continental Europe) was in fact secure. Thus he could not contain either the anxiety or criticism – as manifested by claims of a missile gap – produced by the flight of the Sputnik(s). A crucial consequence was that Eisenhower's effort to deflect this criticism, particularly in the context of the 1960 election, contributed to a lamentable spiral of nuclear arms-racing. In Roman's view, then, just as Kennedy does not deserve all the credit for the strategic innovations of the 1960s, so he does not deserve all the blame for the nuclear arms race. Eisenhower did his part, too.

In his study of the Gaither Report, which in juxtaposition with Sputnik was pivotal to the intensification of US nuclear anxiety in the last years of the 1950s, David Snead (1999) reaches parallel conclusions. Although a historian, Snead addresses the policymaking apparatus more extensively than Roman. He especially emphasizes Eisenhower's use of civilian advisers, in this case a panel to examine the adequacy of the existing civil defense programs chaired by H. Rowan Gaither, Jr. Snead considers this additional advisory layer a very good idea. Still, what intelligence this apparatus used to estimate Soviet strength and the threat it posed is to Snead a more salient issue, and on this score he agrees with Roman. Essentially, the administration was more ambivalent about Soviet capabilities and intentions than Immerman and Bowie allow. Thus the president had too few weapons with which to counter the dire forecasts of such Gaither committee members as Paul Nitze and George Lincoln. Consequently, with the notable exception of a vast fall-out shelter construction program, Eisenhower reluctantly adopted the Gaither Report, thereby fueling the arms race about which Roman writes.

Yet the most detailed study of Eisenhower's nuclear strategy, and the one that correlates that strategy most rigorously to events of the 1950s, is the most positive. In *Destroying the Village*, Campbell Craig (1998) takes on Eisenhower's critics dating back to the 1950s. He concedes that Eisenhower's reliance on nuclear weapons forfeited America's capability to respond flexibly to low intensity conflicts and limited wars. To Craig, however, this is not a shortcoming. It is the truest index of Eisenhower's genius – and commitment to humankind.

Craig provides robust evidence to support his contention that avoiding a war with the Soviet Union, which the president never doubted would entail nuclear weapons, was Eisenhower's chief priority. It had to be. The alternative would leave in its wake nothing worth defending. But he could not say this out loud. To admit that the United States was afraid of a general war was antithetical to the premises of both deterrence and collective security. Over the objections of many of his most valued advisers, including Dulles, Eisenhower therefore pursued a strategy that presented both the United States and the Soviets with only the starkest of choices: survival or annihilation – in Craig's terminology, "all-or-nothing." He uses carefully constructed and well-documented studies of the 1958 Taiwan Strait and Berlin crises to demonstrate Eisenhower's implementation of the strategy. Craig is confident that had the option of fighting a war in either case been viable, to Eisenhower's advisers as much if not more than to the Kremlin's, they would have exploited it. Eisenhower "evaded" Armageddon (Craig 1998: esp. pp. 152–62).

US nuclear strategy in the 1950s was intertwined with relations with allies, especially NATO allies. The literature on this general subject is too voluminous to include in this short essay, even selectively. Moreover, there has not been a great deal of revisionism over the past decades. As discussed below, a few provocative examinations of America's cultural influence on the Europeans – or vice versa – have been written. Nevertheless, historians continue primarily to address such overarching concerns as the European allies' need for assurance that the umbrella of America's nuclear power would protect them from Soviet aggression even as that power scared them to death; the roles played by such personalities as Winston Churchill, Anthony Eden, Konrad Adenauer, Charles De Gaulle, and others in forging relations with Eisenhower, Dulles, and "their others"; the tensions that arose over economic and trade issues; and the US effort to resolve traditional European rivalries and antagonisms. Regarding this last issue, predictably there has been an increase in scholarly attention to the relationship between America and European integration (Giauque 2002).

Still, a historiographic survey of US foreign policy in the 1950s must explicitly include Marc Trachtenberg's *Constructed Peace* (1999), a prize-winning work that among its strengths provides ballast to the brilliant Eisenhower portrayed by Craig. To Trachtenberg, what defined the Soviet–American relationship and the Cold War was the nuclear balance and the German question, which were symbiotically dependent. There could not be a stable Europe until the issue of Germany's division was settled – one way or the other – and this settlement required Soviet–American agreement on West German nuclear capabilities. Trachtenberg argues that Eisenhower, in a classic case of unintended consequences, was more than a little responsible for the failure to achieve an East–West accord on Germany. Hence, by extension, he helped ignite the Berlin crisis. His advocacy of a withdrawal of US forces from Europe at the first opportunity because, put simply, he was cheap, led a nervous Adenauer to suspect Washington's commitment to stand up to Russian aggression – or even coercion. The antidote was a West Germany with independent nuclear capabilities, a scenario the United States appeared not to rule out. The Soviets abandoned schemes to neutralize Germany once the 1954 Paris Accords paved the way for West Germany joining NATO. To accept a nuclear-armed West Germany, however, was beyond the Kremlin's pale. According to Trachtenberg, it took Kennedy to rectify Eisenhower's missteps by adopting a policy against nuclear sharing.

The above literature suggests that, although Eisenhower has not for the most part lost the luster accorded him by early revisionists, and in fact in many ways he shines even brighter in terms of his putative strengths, he has not emerged unscathed from the last decade of scholarship. The fundamental gripe that those like McMahon had with the revisionists, however, concerned the neglect of studies of policy toward the Third World in the 1950s. Historians have addressed his concern.

The evolution of the literature on Eisenhower's contribution to the evolving American tragedy in Vietnam is illustrative. There can be no doubt that what Melanie Billings-Yun (1988) praises as the administration's "Decision Against War" was integral to the surge of Eisenhower revisionism in the early and mid-1980s. By escaping the grief that befell his successors, Eisenhower's image and reputation retroactively improved substantially. Billings-Yun went beyond both Divine and Ambrose by arguing that Eisenhower not only wisely exercised restraint, but also his continuous intervention in his advisers' deliberations was pivotal in outflanking advocates of committing US forces at Dienbienphu. Writing with John Burke shortly thereafter, Greenstein compared how Eisenhower acquired and consumed information and advice when making his decisions about Vietnam to Lyndon Johnson – how the two presidents "tested reality." Johnson suffers in this comparison. Burke and Greenstein (1989) did not need to argue that just as Eisenhower's decision-making process was better than Johnson's, so his decision was better.

Yet there were differences between Billings-Yun and Burke and Greenstein that presaged arguments that surfaced more boldly in the 1990s. Eisenhower emerges more conflicted in the latter book than the former – he is no more sensitive to Vietnamese nationalism and culture than was Johnson. Accordingly, when historians began to examine more rigorously US policy toward Vietnam in the *aftermath* of Dienbienphu, the president and his advisory system received poorer grades. Sundry articles and Lloyd Gardner's multi-archival *Approaching Vietnam* (1988) raised serious questions about the administration's behavior during the 1954 Geneva conference and its decision to wrest responsibility from France and champion an independent Republic of South Vietnam governed by Ngo Dinh Diem (Kaplan, Artaud, and Rubin 1989). But it was the publication of David Anderson's *Trapped by Success* (1991) that best reflected the more furrowed historiographic terrain. Anderson argued forcefully that from the perspective of the legacy he bequeathed, Eisenhower's decision not to intervene in Dienbienphu does not loom as large as the political commitments he subsequently made to the Diem regime. "Taken as a whole," Anderson wrote, "the Eisenhower years were a time of deepening American commitment to South Vietnam premised on superficial assumptions about the government in Saigon, its future prospects, and the importance of its survival to US global strategic interests" (p. 200). No one has successfully challenged this argument.

Other than in the many surveys of US policy toward Latin America, particularly Central America, which appeared following the overthrow of the Somoza regime in Nicaragua and intensification of unrest in El Salvador, inter-American relations in the 1950s have not been extensively examined over the past several decades. In 1991

Piero Gleijeses used Guatemalan sources and personal interviews to produce an important book on PBSUCCESS (Gleijeses 1991). Since then only Nick Cullather, who served in the CIA's historical office, had access to enough new material on Guatemala to warrant publication. Cullather's *Secret History* (1999) filled in missing pieces of history, although it did not resolve the interpretive debates. The one effort to reveal a novel antecedent to the US hostility to the Sandinistas by examining Eisenhower's relationship with the Somozas, justifiably received little scholarly attention (Gambone 1997). Elizabeth Cobbs Hoffman (1992) made a promising start toward addressing the synergy between the US government and private interests, both economic and philanthropic, in an effort to promote American-style development in Latin America, but other historians have not followed suit.

Rich Neighbor Policy is an asset to the literature on both the diplomatic history of the 1950s and inter American relations overall. So is Stephen Rabe's *Eisenhower and Latin America* (1988). Indeed, so lucid is Rabe's argument and so comprehensive is his research that he preempted other scholarship. Instructively, in terms of McMahon's assessment of Eisenhower revisionism, Rabe's stinging criticism of the administration's hemispheric policies as driven by myopic anti-communism did not startle readers, including Eisenhower revisionists. Previous studies of PBSUCCESS in Guatemala were equally critical, and Rabe, although not focusing extensively on the policymaking process, does characterize that process as well managed and Eisenhower-centered. Even Rabe's artful assessment of the indigenous anti-Americanism that put Richard Nixon at risk when he toured South America in 1958 and provided the catalyst for Eisenhower's dramatic shift away from a policy of "trade not aid" reinforces work by others. Concurrently *Diplomatic History* published an article on Nixon's mission, and Eisenhower's changing attitudes toward extending foreign aid is a highlight of Burton Kaufman's *Trade and Aid* (1982; Zahnheiser and Weiss 1989).

Many of the scholars who built on Rabe's foundation began their research before the publication of *Eisenhower and Latin America*. For example, Stephen Streeter's revised dissertation, *Managing the Counterrevolution* (2000), examines Eisenhower policy toward Guatemala *subsequent* to Arbenz's overthrow. Using untapped sources, most notably USAID files, Streeter persuasively presents a damning indictment of America's "success" in promoting governments that it defined as serving US economic and strategic interests. The result was greater corruption, poverty, and oppression in Guatemala. To provide another example, Thomas Paterson (1994), Streeter's (and Rabe's) mentor, reached a similar judgment with regard to policy toward Cuba. Paterson's emphasis is not so much on the lamented "victims" of US policy as on the counterproductive outcome of that policy from the perspective of Washington's objectives. He demonstrates that Eisenhower, misled by his advisers, remained passive while Cubans' disenchantment with Fulgencio Batista festered. The United States was no more responsible for Fidel Castro's successful revolution than was the Soviet Union. US policy did, however, aggravate Castro's hostility toward America and help him gain leverage over his opponents and consolidate his regime.

The Near and Middle East has attracted more attention from historians of US foreign relations than has Latin America. The quality and quantity of the literature on the TPAJAX, the 1953 CIA operation that ousted the government of Mohammed Mossadegh and restored the Shah, nevertheless, compares unfavorably to that on Guatemala. In large part the reason is lack of archives. In contrast to documents concerning Guatemala, the CIA destroyed most of its files on Iran. Scholars rely heavily on what they can cull from other sources, including memoirs of questionable reliability. No study has surpassed that by Gasiorowski (1987). Future studies will benefit from the availability of the CIA's own history of the operation, written in 1954 and made public by the *New York Times* in 2000 (CIA 1954). Yet suits initiated for the purpose of gaining release of other documents are still pending. Mary Anne Heiss's (1997) examination of Mossadegh's decision to nationalize the Anglo-Iranian Oil Company in 1951 and the discord it created between London and Washington is very illuminating, but for more illumination of TPAJAX, historians must wait.

A plethora of works examines the Suez Crisis in 1956, however, and they add up to a wealth of riches. Moving beyond earlier works by Meyer (1980) and Neff (1981), both conceptually and in his multi-archival research, Peter Hahn's (1991) study of US, British, and Egyptian relations underscores the tensions that inhered in America's efforts to produce an effective and coherent policy toward the Third World. Hahn argues that dating back to the origin of the Cold War, US policymakers sought to resolve the riddle of responding sympathetically to Egyptian nationalism without undermining the "special relationship" with the British. Hahn does not suggest what strategy the Eisenhower administration could have pursued effectively to square this circle. He does suggest that its initiatives, from promoting the Baghdad Pact, to promising to help finance the Aswan Dam and then reneging to pursuing a secret plan for an Egyptian–Israeli settlement (Project Alpha), did not come close. According to Hahn, therefore, while it was not inevitable, the Suez Crisis was predictable.

To a large extent the monographs that followed emphasize one of the horns of this dilemma. Most of them concentrate on strategic issues, particularly US relations with its key NATO allies Britain and France, its access to oil, and the geopolitics of the Middle East. The perspectives and roles of the key actors, above all Eisenhower and Dulles on the one hand and Eden and Macmillan on the other, predictably receive close scrutiny. There is consensus on an array of issues, but some of the most fundamental ones remain intensely contested. Freiberger (1992) argues, for instance, that Suez must be understood in terms of the Anglo-American disagreement over membership in the Baghdad Pact, and that at least one of America's goals was to replace the British as the guardian of the Middle East. His hostility toward Dulles, moreover, is reminiscent of the venom spewed by Herman Finer (1964), even though Freiberger embraces the central tenets of Eisenhower revisionism. In Diane Kunz's equally stimulating study, Anglo-American tensions likewise take center stage, but Kunz (1991) focuses on economic issues rather than Freiberger's more conventional ones of politics and security. Kunz stresses that London and Washington were headed for a commercial and financial collision prior to Suez, and the United States' effective use of economic coercion to bring Britain to its knees demonstrated the folly of Britain's resting its fate on the "special relationship."

Kunz's account of the manner in which the United States imposed its will on the British (and to a lesser degree the French and Israelis) is compelling. Yet she all but begs the question of US motives. It is on this score that Louis (1990) advances a bold and provocative argument. Without minimizing Cold War influences on the administration's thinking, Louis argues that in the final analysis it was American idealism – as manifest in its anti-colonialism – that explains America's uncompromising opposition to the collusion among Britain, France, and Israel. Louis does not extend his framework to the US attitude toward Nasser. Still, his examination illustrates starkly the dilemma Hahn identified.

US relations with the Middle East during the 1950s enveloped more than the Suez Crisis. Yet the crisis influenced – or was influenced by – everything else. For example, to no one's surprise, works by several historians have examined America's relationship with Israel and highlight the 1950s. Suez figures prominently in each and in some cases appears to have most challenged the author. For example, Isaac Alteras' *Eisenhower and Israel* (1993) convincingly rebuts the conventional criticism that the administration normally supported the interests of Arab states at the expense of Israel. Yet in the context of Suez, Alteras portrays Washington as betraying Israel in much the same terms as do orthodox detractors (pp. 246–86). Abraham Ben-Zvi (1998) is more critical of the American posture, at least through the Suez Crisis. Only after Suez, Ben-Zvi argues, did the Eisenhower administration embrace "the preservation of Israel" and lay the foundations for the improved relationship mistakenly attributed to John F. Kennedy's initiative (p. 67).

America's difficult relations with Syria during Eisenhower's second term and the 1958 Marine landing in Lebanon, which more than the Suez Crisis signaled America's replacement of Britain as the lynchpin for Western influence in the Middle East, have finally begun to attract the attention they warrant (Ashton 1997). And the studies already in print augur well for the future. They do not augur well for the administration's reputation in the Middle East. Monographs written by David Lesch (1993), Erika Alin (1994), and Irene Gendzier (1996) effectively criticize the administration's ignorance of and insensitivity to indigenous dynamics. Gendzier is particularly scathing in indicting Washington for both Cold War tunnel vision and oil envy. Douglas Little's much-anticipated book will doubtless become the standard source on the tortuous efforts to implement the Eisenhower Doctrine in the wake of the Suez Crisis. Already his articles on policies and programs toward Syria, Jordan, and Lebanon are masterpieces of research and insight. They persuasively demonstrate the costs of the administration's meddling in the region, costs that the United States would have to pay for decades (Little 1990, 1995, 1996).

McMahon's research for a book on US policy toward India and Pakistan influenced his critique of the Eisenhower revisionists. His superb *Cold War on the Periphery* was published in 1994. Its evidence and logic leave little doubt that the Eisenhower administration's allergic response to Jawaharlal Nehru's insistence on non-alignment resulted in the misguided Mutual Defense Assistance Agreement with Pakistan in 1954 and drove New Delhi toward Moscow. McMahon compliments Eisenhower only for conceding that he made a "terrible error" and trying, with mixed success, to make amends (p. 207). Whereas McMahon stresses America's geopolitical anxiety, Andrew Rotter's concerns are primarily cultural: issues of religion, race, class, and gender. Rotter agrees with McMahon's argument. But, he maintains, McMahon "put the cart before the horse." US strategy in South Asia during the 1950s was predicated on culture, he concludes, not the other way around (Rotter 2000: 65).

Rotter is unusual but not unique in exploring the cultural dimensions of US foreign policy in the 1950s. While it concludes in 1955, Jessica Gienow-Hecht's *Transmission Impossible* (1999) examines the newspaper *Neue Zeitung*, run by the US army during the occupation, to determine how successfully Americans exported US culture to the Germans. Her evidence strongly suggests that Washington's influence was less than some have maintained, although local editors and journalists often accomplished what their superiors could not. More influential still, according to Uta Poiger (2000), were the stars of American movies, jazz, and rock 'n' roll.

Walter Hixson is more traditional, in that his gaze remains fixed on bipolarism. In his *Parting the Curtain* (1998), propaganda and cultural exports replace nuclear weapons, paramilitary and conventional forces, and trade embargoes as the means by which the United States projected its power against the Soviet Union. Although Hixson suggests that Eisenhower could have done even more to promote the infiltration of US culture behind the Iron Curtain, he points to the Soviet–American agreement that established a cultural and educational exchange program in 1958 and the notorious "kitchen debate" at the next year's American National Exhibition in Moscow as critical way stations on the road to the disintegration of the Kremlin's authority. In the Cold War battle for hearts and minds, concludes Hixson, "the outcome could only be decided on cultural ground" (p. 233).

Race is integral to culture. However, despite the impressive literature on the Civil Rights movement in the 1950s, historians have only recently begun to examine the international manifestations of African Americans' domestic struggles during the decade, especially but not exclusively in the context of policy toward Africa. Brenda Plummer's pioneering *Rising Wind* (1996) provides robust evidence that blacks in America, at least elite blacks in America, considered the "liberation" of colonial peoples of color inseparable from the struggle for racial justice in 1950s America. Plummer argues that the enthusiastic reception African Americans accorded Fidel Castro in 1959 signaled a break from the tactic of toeing Washington's Cold War line in order to garner support from White America for civil rights (pp. 285–97). Penny Von Eschen's equally pathbreaking *Race Against Empire* (1997) supports Plummer's argument, but it ends in 1957. Hence, Von Eschen stresses the priority African Americans placed on demonstrating that blacks were the equals of whites in vigorously crusading against communism. Later works have concentrated on the flip side by demonstrating that the Eisenhower administration promoted domestic civil rights largely for the purpose of coopting Soviet propaganda and winning converts in the global battle for hearts and minds. A healthy debate has thus ensued as to whether the Cold War accelerated or impeded US progress toward racial equality (Dudziak 2000; Fraser 2000; White 2000; Borstelmann 2001). This is a subject that promises exciting scholarship.

The fact of the matter is that the agenda for examinations of US foreign policy in the 1950s should be as fertile for the next several decades as it has been for the previous several. Surely scholars should seek to view America's international history through the lens of culture, race, gender, and other dimensions of the "new cultural history." Yet it is no less important that others continue to address the fundamental questions that remain. These questions include the relationship between the Greenstein and Ambrose revisionists – between the students of the policymaking process and students of that process's product. They also include the disconnection between grand strategy in the 1950s and policies toward the Third World. The literature produced over the past ten to fifteen years appears to confirm McMahon's argument that in the 1950s America did a better job of managing competition with the Soviets than promoting cooperation with peoples on the global periphery – or for that matter with allies. Was that indeed the case? And if so, why?

Part of the answer will arise from more studies of the objectives of policy in the 1950s – and the extent to which it represented change or continuity from the perspective of what preceded and succeeded it. To use the era's terminology, did the United States pursue containment or liberation? Mitrovich (2000) used more declassified documents to write about covert and paramilitary operations in the late 1940s and into the 1950s. His book won a prize, but it still left ambiguous the question of the aims of US policy, and more than that, the premises underlying those aims. This question is complicated further by recent definitional distinctions that have been drawn between liberation as a peaceful evolution and liberation as a coerced retraction of the Soviet orbit (Krebs 2001). As scholars continue to seek to understand what brought about the end of the Cold War, it is this last set of questions that will frame the next generation of literature on the 1950s.

REFERENCES

Alin, Erika: *The United States and the 1958 Lebanon Crisis* (Lanham, MD: University Press of America, 1994).

Alteras, Isaac: *Eisenhower and Israel: US–Israeli Relations, 1953–1960* (Gainesville: University of Florida Press, 1993).

Ambrose, Stephen E.: *Eisenhower: The President and Elder Statesman* (New York: Simon and Schuster, 1984).

Anderson, David L.: *Trapped by Success: The Eisenhower Administration and Vietnam* (New York: Columbia University Press, 1991).

Ashton, John Nigel: *Eisenhower, Macmillan and the Problem of Nasser: Anglo-American Relations and Arab Nationalism, 1955–1959* (New York: St. Martin's Press, 1997).

Ben-Zvi, Abraham: *Decade of Transition: Eisenhower, Kennedy, and the Origins of the American–Israeli Alliance* (New York: Columbia University Press, 1998).

Bernstein, Barton J.: "Foreign Policy in the Eisenhower Administration." *Foreign Service Journal* 50 (1973), 17–20, 29–30, 38.

Billings-Yun, Melanie: *Decision Against War: Eisenhower and Dien Bien Phu, 1954* (New York: Columbia University Press, 1988).

Bischof, Gunter and Saki Dockrill (eds.) *Cold War Respite: The Geneva Summit of 1955* (Baton Rouge: Louisiana State University Press, 2000).

Borstelmann, Thomas: *The Cold War and the Color Line: Race Relations and American Foreign Policy* (Cambridge, MA: Harvard University Press, 2001).

Bowie, Robert R. and Richard H. Immerman: *Waging Peace: How Eisenhower Shaped an Enduring Cold War Strategy* (New York: Oxford University Press, 1998).

Brands, H. W., Jr.: "Testing Massive Retaliation: Credibility and Crisis Management in the Taiwan Strait." *International Security* 12 (1988), 124–51.

Brands, H. W., Jr.: "The Age of Vulnerability: Eisenhower and the National Insecurity State." *American Historical Review* 94 (1989), 963–89.

Burke, John P. and Fred I. Greenstein: *How Presidents Test Reality: Decisions on Vietnam, 1954 and 1965* (New York: Russell Sage, 1989).

Chang, Gordon H.: "To the Nuclear Brink: Eisenhower, Dulles, and the Quemoy–Matsu Crisis." *International Security* 12 (1988), 96–123.

Chang, Gordon H.: *Friends and Enemies: The United States, China, and the Soviet Union, 1948–1972* (Stanford, CA Stanford University Press, 1990).

Childs, Marquis: *Eisenhower: Captive Hero: A Critical Study of the General and the President* (New York: Harcourt, Brace, 1958).

CIA Clandestine Service History: "Overthrow of Premier Mossadeq of Iran, November 1952–August 1953," March 1954, by Dr. Donald Wilber, available on the National Security Archive web page at: http://www.gwu.edu/'nsarchiv/NSAEBB/NSAEBB28/index.html#documents

Cobbs Hoffman, Elizabeth: *The Rich Neighbor Policy: Rockefeller and Kaiser in Brazil* (New Haven, CT: Yale University Press, 1992).

Cook, Blanche W.: *The Declassified Eisenhower* (Garden City, NY: Doubleday, 1981).

Craig, Campbell: *Destroying the Village: Eisenhower and Thermonuclear War* (New York: Columbia University Press, 1998).

Cullather, Nick: *Secret History: The CIA's Classified Account of its Operations in Guatemala, 1952–1954* (Stanford, CA: Stanford University Press, 1999).

Divine, Robert: *Eisenhower and the Cold War* (New York: Oxford University Press, 1981).

Dockrill, Saki: *Eisenhower's New-Look National Security Policy, 1953–61* (New York: St. Martin's Press, 1996).

Dudziak, Mary: *Cold War Civil Rights: Race and the Image of American Democracy* (Princeton, NJ: Princeton University Press, 2000).

Finer, Herman: *Dulles Over Suez: The Theory and Practice of His Diplomacy* (Chicago, IL: Quadrangle, 1964).

Fraser, Cary: "Crossing the Color Line in Little Rock: The Eisenhower Administration and the Dilemma of Race in US Foreign Policy." *Diplomatic History* 24 (2000), 233–64.

Freiberger, Steven Z.: *Dawn Over Suez: The Rise of American Power in the Middle East, 1953–1957* (Chicago, IL: University of Chicago Press, 1992).

Gaddis, John Lewis: *Strategies of Containment: A Critical Appraisal of Postwar American National Security Policy* (New York: Oxford University Press, 1982).

Gambone, Michael: *Eisenhower, Somoza and the Cold War in Nicaragua, 1953–1961* (Westport, CT: Praeger, 1997).

Gardner, Lloyd C.: *Approaching Vietnam: From World War II Through Dienbienphu, 1941–1954* (New York: Norton, 1988).

Gasiorowski, Marc J.: "The 1953 Coup D'État." *International Journal of Middle East Studies* 19 (1987), 261–86.

Gendzier, Irene E.: *Notes from the Minefield: United States Intervention, Lebanon and the Middle East, 1945–1958* (New York: Columbia University Press, 1996).

Giauque, Jeffrey Glen: *Grand Designs and Visions of Unity: The Atlanatic Powers and the Reorganization of Western Europe, 1955–1963* (Chapel Hill: University of North Carolina Press, 2002).

Gienow-Hecht, Jessica: *Transmission Impossible: American Journalism as Cultural Diplomacy in Postwar Germany 1945–1955* (Baton Rouge: Louisiana State University Press, 1999).

Gleijeses, Piero: *Shattered Hope: The Guatemalan Revolution and the United States, 1944–1954* (Princeton, NJ: Princeton University Press, 1991).

Greenstein, Fred I.: *The Hidden-Hand Presidency: Eisenhower as Leader* (New York: Basic Books, 1982).

Hahn, Peter L.: *The United States, Great Britain, and Egypt, 1945–1956: Strategy and Diplomacy in the Early Cold War* (Chapel Hill: University of North Carolina Press, 1991).

Heiss, Mary Anne: *Empire and Nationhood: The United States, Great Britain, and Iranian Oil, 1950–1954* (New York: Columbia University Press, 1997).

Herring, George C.: *America's Longest War: The United States and Vietnam, 1950–1975* (New York: McGraw Hill, 1979, 1986, 1996).

Hixson, Walter L.: *Parting the Curtain: Propaganda, Culture, and the Cold War, 1945–1961* (New York: St. Martin's Griffin, 1998).

Hoopes, Townsend: *The Devil and John Foster Dulles* (Boston, MA: Little Brown, 1973).

Immerman, Richard H.: *The CIA in Guatemala: The Foreign Policy of Intervention* (Austin: University of Texas Press, 1982).

Immerman, Richard H.: *John Foster Dulles: Piety, Pragmatism, and Power in US Foreign Policy* (Wilmington, DE: Scholarly Resources, 1999).

Kalb, Madeleine G.: *The Congo Cables: The Cold War in Africa – From Eisenhower to Kennedy* (New York: Macmillan, 1982).

Kaplan, Lawrence S., Denise Artaud, and Mark R. Rubin (eds.): *Dien Bien Phu and the Crisis of Franco-American Relations, 1954–1955* (Wilmington, DE: Scholarly Resources, 1989).

Kaufman, Burton I.: *Trade and Aid: Eisenhower's Foreign Economic Policy, 1953–1961* (Baltimore, MD: Johns Hopkins University Press, 1982).

Kennedy, John F. and Richard M. Nixon: Transcript of First Joint Radio–Television Broadcast, September 26, 1960, available on John F. Kennedy Library web page at: http://www.jfklibrary.org/60-1st.htm

Krebs, Ronald R.: *Dueling Visions: US Strategy Toward Eastern Europe under Eisenhower* (College Station: Texas A&M University Press, 2001).

Kunz, Diane: *The Economic Diplomacy of the Suez Crisis* (Chapel Hill: University of North Carolina Press, 1991).

Lesch, David: *Syria and the United States: Eisenhower's Cold War in the Middle East* (Boulder, CO: Westview Press, 1993).

Little, Douglas: "Cold War and Covert Action: The United States and Syria, 1945–1958." *Middle East Journal* 44 (1990), 51–75.

Little, Douglas: "A Puppet in Search of a Puppeteer? The United States, King Hussein, and Jordan, 1951–1970." *International History Review* 17 (1995), 512–44.

Little, Douglas: "His Finest Hour? Eisenhower, Lebanon, and the 1958 Middle East Crisis." *Diplomatic History* 20 (1996), 27–54.

Louis, William Roger: "Dulles, Suez, and the British." In Richard H. Immerman (ed.) *John Foster Dulles and the Diplomacy of the Cold War* (Princeton, NJ: Princeton University Press, 1990).

Lyon, Peter: *Eisenhower: Portrait of a Hero* (Boston, MA: Little, Brown, 1974).

McMahon, Robert J.: *The Cold War on the Periphery: The United States, India, and Pakistan* (New York: Columbia University Press, 1994).

McMahon, Robert J.: "Eisenhower and Third World Nationalism: A Critique of the Revisionists." *Political Science Quarterly* 101 (Centennial Year 1886–1986), 453–73.

Meyer, Gail E.: *Egypt and the United States: The Formative Years* (Rutherford, NJ: Fairleigh Dickinson University Press, 1980).

Mitrovich, Gregory: *Undermining the Kremlin: America's Strategy to Subvert the Soviet Bloc, 1947–1956* (Ithaca, NY: Cornell University Press, 2000).

Neff, Donald: *Warriors at Suez: Eisenhower Takes America into the Middle East* (New York: Linden Press/Simon and Schuster, 1981).

Nelson, Anna Kasten: "The 'Top of Policy Hill': President Eisenhower and the National Security Council." *Diplomatic History* 7 (1983), 307–26.

Noer, Thomas J.: *Cold War and Black Liberation: The United States and White Rule in Africa, 1948–1968* (Colombia: University of Missouri Press, 1985).

Parmet, Herbert S.: *Eisenhower and the American Crusades* (New York: Macmillan, 1972).

Paterson, Thomas G.: *Contesting Castro: The United States and the Triumph of the Cuban Revolution* (New York: Oxford University Press, 1994).

Pickett, William: *Dwight D. Eisenhower and American Power* (Wheeling, IL: Harlan Davidson, 1995).

Plummer, Brenda Gale: *Rising Wind: Black Americans and US Foreign Affairs, 1935–1960* (Chapel Hill: University of North Carolina Press, 1996).

Poiger, Uta G.: *Jazz, Rock, and Rebels: Cold War Politics and American Culture in a Divided Germany* (Berkeley: University of California Press, 2000).

Rabe, Stephen G.: *The Road to OPEC: United States Relations with Venezuela, 1919–1976* (Austin: University of Texas Press, 1982).

Rabe, Stephen: *Eisenhower and Latin America: The Foreign Policy of Anticommunism* (Chapel Hill: University of North Carolina Press, 1988).

Roman, Peter: *Eisenhower and the Missile Gap* (Ithaca, NY: Cornell University Press, 1995).

Rosenberg, David A.: "The Origins of Overkill: Nuclear Weapons and American Strategy, 1945–1960." *International Security* 7 (1983), 3–71.

Rotter, Andrew: *Comrades at Odds: The United States and India, 1947–1964* (Ithaca, NY: Cornell University Press, 2000).

Rubin, Barry: *Paved with Good Intentions: The American Experience and Iran* (New York: Oxford University Press, 1980).

Schlesinger, Arthur M., Jr.: *Reviews in American History* 11 (1983), 1–11.

Schlesinger, Arthur M., Jr.: "Effective National Security Advising: A Most Dubious Precedent." *Political Science Quarterly* 115 (2000), 347–51.

Schlesinger, Stephen and Stephen Kinzer: *Bitter Fruit: The Untold Story of the American Coup in Guatemala* (Garden City, NY: Doubleday, 1982).

Shalom, Stephen R.: *The United States and the Philippines: A Study of Neocolonialism* (Philadelphia, PA: Institute for the Study of Human Issues, 1981).

Snead, David: *The Gaither Committee, Eisenhower, and the Cold War* (Columbus: Ohio State University Press, 1999).

Spiegel, Steven L.: *The Other Arab–Israeli Conflict: Making America's Middle East Policy, from Truman to Reagan* (Chicago, IL: University of Chicago Press, 1985).

Streeter, Stephen M.: *Managing the Counterrevolution: The United States and Guatemala, 1954–1961* (Athens, GA: University of Ohio Press, 2000).

Trachtenberg, Marc: "A 'Wasting Asset': American Strategy and the Shifting Nuclear Balance." *International Security* 13 (1988/1989), 5–49.

Trachtenberg, Marc: *A Constructed Peace: The Making of the European Settlement, 1945–1964* (Princeton, NJ: Princeton University Press, 1999).

Von Eschen, Penny M.: *Race Against Empire: Black Americans and Anticolonialism, 1937–1957* (Ithaca, NY: Cornell University Press, 1997).

White, George: "Holding the Line: Race, Racism, and American Foreign Policy, 1953–1961." PhD dissertation, Temple University, 2000.

Zahnheiser, Marvin R. and W. Michael Weiss: "A Diplomatic Pearl Harbor: Richard Nixon's Goodwill Mission to Latin America in 1958." *Diplomatic History* 13 (1989), 163–90.

FURTHER READING

Bischof, Guenter and Saki Dockrill (eds.): *Cold War Respite: The Geneva Summit of 1955* (Baton Rouge: Louisiana State University Press, 2000).

Bose, Meena: *Shaping and Signaling Presidential Policy: The National Security Decision Making of Eisenhower and Kennedy* (College Station: Texas A&M University Press, 1998).

Brands, H. W., Jr.: *Cold Warriors: Eisenhower's Generation and American Foreign Policy* (New York: Columbia University Press, 1988).

Brands, H. W., Jr.: *The Specter of Neutralism: The United States and the Emergence of the Third World, 1947–1960* (New York: Columbia University Press, 1989).

Cullather, Nick: *Illusions of Influence: The Political Economy of United States–Philippines Relations, 1942–60* (Stanford, CA: Stanford University Press, 1994).

Divine, Robert: *The Sputnik Challenge: Eisenhower's Response to the Soviet Satellite* (New York: Oxford University Press, 1993).

Kingseed, Cole C.: *Eisenhower and the Suez Crisis of 1956* (Baton Rouge: Louisiana State University Press, 1995).

Lucas, W. Scott: *Divided We Stand: Britain, the US and the Suez Crisis* (London: Hodder and Stoughton, 1991).

McDougall, Walter: *The Heavens Can Wait: A Political History of the Space Age* (New York: Basic Books, 1985).

Merrill, Dennis: *Bread and the Ballot: The United States and India's Economic Development, 1947–1963* (Chapel Hill: University of North Carolina Press, 1990).

Pach, Chester J., Jr. and Elmo Richardson: *The Presidency of Dwight D. Eisenhower* (Lawrence: University of Kansas Press, 1991).

Wenger, Andreas: *Living with Peril: Eisenhower, Kennedy, and Nuclear Weapons* (Lanham, MD: Rowman and Littlefield, 1997).

Winand, Pascaline: *Eisenhower, Kennedy, and the United States of Europe* (New York: St. Martin's Press, 1993).

CHAPTER EIGHTEEN

The Vietnam War

DAVID L. ANDERSON

The Vietnam War may already be the most written about war in US history. All of this writing and rewriting – and refighting – of the war flows in large measure from the daunting reality that the United States lost the war. Victory has many fathers, but defeat is an orphan. World War II was the "good war" because Americans celebrated its outcome as evidence of their nation's power and moral virtue. The Korean War has been the "forgotten war" because its stalemated conclusion prompted neither congratulations nor recrimination. The Vietnam War is the "endless war," a subject locked into a protracted debate over the responsibility for and the significance of the outcome.

The absence of consensus on key questions about the origins, conduct, and results of the American war in Vietnam does not arise from an absence of information. On some aspects of US involvement there are vast amounts of documentation in presidential libraries, other government archives, media accounts, memoirs, and oral histories. Although secrecy of government records has plagued the work of historians of the Cold War era, many of the once-classified papers have been released in the years since the war ended in 1975. There are some significant exceptions to this pattern, such as Central Intelligence Agency materials and other records of covert operations, but thousands of pages of military, diplomatic, political, and personal papers are now accessible. Another source of information that is only partially open is the files of America's Cold War enemies. With the collapse of the Soviet Union, some of Moscow's documents relevant to Indochina opened, and in China since the late 1980s memoirs and official military histories have shed light on Beijing's role in the conflict. The government in Hanoi, too, has published some detailed but officially sanctioned accounts of the war. Some American and other non-Vietnamese researchers have been able to gain access to archives in Vietnam, but these records remain far from open (Bradley and Brigham 1993).

Gaps in the historical record produce some differences among historians, but what primarily fuels debate are divergent assumptions about US history, culture, and foreign policy. It is the seminal nature of many of the questions about the war that makes resolution so difficult and that, at times, even makes the evidence available seem incidental to ideological and moral considerations. Other major US international engagements, such as World War I and World War II, were perceived as contests in defense of civilization or at least national preservation, but in these cases the United States was victorious. Might may not have made right, but victory muted searching reflection on the rectitude of American foreign policy. The success of

American arms in World War II over the twin evils of European fascism and Japanese militarism produced self-congratulations among Americans and their leaders. With the onset of the Cold War, the presumed moral menace and national security threat posed by the Soviet Union further obscured critical examination of the goals of US foreign policy and careful definition of American interests and the means to secure those interests. Against this background, the United States entered the conflict in Vietnam, and when that American intervention ultimately failed to produce the desired outcome despite tremendous costs and effort, the soul searching and recrimination began in earnest.

The interpretive controversies created by the Vietnam War are not idle academic ruminations. The United States failed to preserve an independent South Vietnam allied to the West, but America did not exit from Vietnam as a defeated nation. Its military and economic power remained strong, and the likelihood of other interventions in other circumstances remained high. Consequently, historians, strategic analysts, policymakers, politicians, and pundits have offered numerous works to attempt to fathom the mysteries of the American experience with Vietnam in an effort to learn lessons to guide future actions. Some of this literature is polemical or exploitational, but much of it represents some of the finest and most careful studies in the field of American history. Basically, these studies divide into three areas (with subcategories): origins of the American involvement, the way the US chose to conduct the war, and how the American war finally ended. Permeating each area of inquiry is a search for lessons to be drawn from the experience for Americans individually and for the American nation.

If these categories appear to be America-centered, they are. Not only has much of the literature sought to answer questions about American conduct using American sources, this pattern reflects the history of the American war itself. The United States did not have a long experience of direct relations with Vietnam and the rest of Indochina, and hence for the history of US foreign relations, the war was and remains more of an event than a study of bilateral relations. American decision-makers often lacked understanding of Vietnamese history and made their policy choices from an assessment of global not local circumstances. For historians, delving into the Vietnamese historical and cultural context of the war reveals many flaws in US policy, but much of the available archival record of the American war is, indeed, American, and the available literature has been written that way.

Origins of the War

Since Vietnam and the adjoining areas of Southeast Asia were not of strategic value to the United States before World War II, the question of why the region grew to such importance to produce a major American war has attracted much scholarly attention. The search for the origins of the Vietnam War begins with World War II. In the late nineteenth and early twentieth centuries, as the United States emerged as a global power, Washington paid little heed to the French colonies in Indochina because the region was an already established European sphere of influence. Mark Bradley has noted that a cultural gap existed between the Vietnamese and Americans that explains more about their eventual conflict than does ideology or strategy. As Gary R. Hess observes in *The United States' Emergence as a Southeast Asian Power*

(1987), Japan's designs on the resources of Southeast Asia attracted US attention at the outset of World War II. After the Japanese occupation of bases in Indochina undermined France's control of its colonies, President Franklin D. Roosevelt spoke of replacing French colonialism after the war with a trusteeship system. Walter LaFeber and Lloyd Gardner have argued that Roosevelt saw an opportunity to advance American notions of liberal capitalism at the expense of European colonialism, but Roosevelt himself never moved to implement the trusteeship concept.

At the end of the world war in 1945, the new Truman administration faced a host of international problems, and the fate of French Indochina was not a high priority for Washington. The United States initially adopted a neutral stance as France moved to restore its former colonial position in Indochina against a nationalist resistance movement headed by Ho Chi Minh and his Vietminh movement. Like Roosevelt, Truman considered colonialism outmoded and illiberal, but the president and his aides could not overlook that Ho and other Vietminh leaders were communists.

Although President Harry S. Truman never faced the type of immediate-intervention decisions that later confronted his White House successors, it was during his administration that the fundamental questions about Vietnam emerged for policymakers and for historians. Most accounts of the American war in Vietnam connect its origins in a significant way to Truman's containment policy and the strategic goal of limiting the expansion of communist political and military power throughout the world. The Cold War with the Soviet Union spawned this global thinking. As Robert Schulzinger has asserted: "Had American leaders not thought that all international events were connected to the Cold War there would have been no American war in Vietnam" (Schulzinger 1997: 329). Many other historians support this basic contention, but much debate exists over why this particular local conflict in this particular place eventually rose to the level of becoming the largest US war and one of the most costly in American lives and resources.

How historians have answered the question of the importance of Vietnam to the United States parallels broader interpretive debates over US foreign policy that emphasize either geopolitical calculations or economic and ideological arguments. The geopolitical explanation tends to be multicausal and includes several elements in the definition of US national interests. The economic analysis tends to be monocausal and traces American intervention in Vietnam to the behavior of the United States as a capitalist nation pursuing its interests in a global economy. In practice, the first approach is often inductive and draws on extensive archival research, and the second is more deductive and theoretically based.

Near the end of 1946, an armed conflict erupted in Vietnam pitting French forces seeking to reimpose colonial control in Indochina against communist-led Vietminh resistance fighters. In March 1947 the American president announced the Truman Doctrine, which declared that the United States would aid governments threatened by communist insurrection. The French–Vietminh war lasted eight years and over that time the Truman and Eisenhower administrations gradually extended financial and material support to the French war effort in the name of containment. Thus, along with Schulzinger, authors such as Hess, Herring, Spector, Duiker, McMahon, and Immerman have noted that US involvement in the military conflict in Vietnam began as an application to Asia of the containment strategy, originally designed for

Europe. American leaders reasoned that any military, political, psychological, geographical, or economic advantage gained by an ally of the Soviet Union was a strategic loss for the United States. Such "zero sum" logic became a rationale for extending containment beyond Europe. As Robert Blum has written, this image of a global contest created domestic political pressures on the White House to be tough on communism in Southeast Asia in the same manner that it was declaring American resolve against communist expansion in the West.

The majority of the work on origins of the American war in Vietnam emphasizes the containment strategy, but a dissenting minority argues that Vietnam was not a militarily or politically vital spot for the United States. These alternative works maintain that Washington deemed the markets and raw materials of Southeast Asia as essential to the welfare of the US capitalist economy. Few historians argue that the United States had a direct economic stake in Indochina, but some develop a complex scenario in which France, Britain, and Japan – nations that were important trading partners of the United States – were helped by access to the region. William Borden, Michael Schaller, and Andrew Rotter have developed the thesis that a perceived need to keep open the markets of Indochina was the reason that a Vietminh victory over France was unacceptable to the United States. The concern was less that Vietnam might become communist than it was that the resources of the area would be closed to the United States and its commercial partners.

This difference in emphasis over why the United States had an interest in French Indochina in the late 1940s is part of a larger debate among historians of US foreign relations. Melvin Leffler and John Gaddis, for example, find that Soviet conduct after World War II and traditional definitions of national security in terms of geographical and political threats and opportunities explain much of the record of US strategic decisions throughout the world. Scholars such as William Appleman Williams, Thomas McCormick, and Bruce Cumings, on the other hand, maintain that the enormous material interest that the United States had in the world economy by the mid-twentieth century drove America inexorably into Eastern Europe, Southeast Asia, and other peripheral or developing economic areas. Such arguments have been labeled revisionist, New Left, or radical because they reflect the influence of Marxist historical theory, are critical of US behavior as acquisitive and aggressive, and challenge orthodox accounts that depict US actions as normal self-defense and as consistent with noble American traditions of defending freedom and peaceful resolution of conflicts against tyrants and aggressors.

As Robert Divine (1988) perceptively observed in a historiographical essay in *Diplomatic History*, however, there is an ironic twist to the orthodox and revisionist labels when applied to historical treatments of the Vietnam War. In the writing on other wars, Divine notes, the initial orthodox interpretations defended official US policies, for example, to enter into World War II against the threat of European and Asian aggressors or to respond to the danger of the Cold War with such containment steps as the Marshall Plan and NATO. During and after the Vietnam War, the standard or orthodox view of most scholars was that the decision of American leaders to support first France and later South Vietnam against an internal movement for independence and national unification was a mistake. Hence, the orthodox school was critical of US policy, and in the 1980s, Divine observes, a conservative revisionist school appeared. It was influenced by the prevailing political culture of the Ronald Reagan era and defended the decisions to enter the Vietnam conflict in the cause of anti-communism and opposition to tyranny. As useful as Divine's orthodox and revisionist labels are, however, they convey only part of the debate. He notes that the orthodox side itself divides into three arguments identified as quagmire, stalemate, and "flawed" containment. The revisionist side is also multifaceted, as Gary Hess (1994) describes in another essay in *Diplomatic History*. The disagreements among those revisionists who believe that the United States had reason to intervene in Vietnam are primarily over how rather than why the war was fought.

Among the initial orthodox criticisms of how and why the United States entered the war was one that became known as the quagmire theory, taking its name in part from David Halberstam's book, *The Making of a Quagmire* (1964). This interpretation held that, through ignorance of local conditions in Indochina and an overweening faith in American power and ideals, US leaders allowed the United States gradually to become trapped in a costly commitment in an area of limited strategic value with no clear way to proceed or withdraw without incurring further costs in men and materiel or in credibility. Robert Shaplen, Arthur Schlesinger, Jr., and Chester Cooper produced books characterizing the US intervention as a tragic mistake. George M. Kahin and John W. Lewis argued that America had placed itself on the wrong side of the Vietnamese nationalist revolution largely through a failure to heed the recent history of the country. In the early 1970s, two bestselling works by journalists – David Halberstam's *The Best and the Brightest* and Frances Fitzgerald's *Fire in the Lake* – presented the case that American arrogance about its own ability and ignorance of the revolutionary appeal of the Vietnamese communists had produced an avoidable American war.

With the leak and publication of the Pentagon Papers, a secret Department of Defense history of decision-making from 1945 to 1967, some analysts pointed out from this evidence that political leaders were not as ignorant as the quagmire view assumed and that, indeed, they knew there were few good options for the United States in Southeast Asia. Labeled the stalemate theory, this argument contended that for a variety of strategic, bureaucratic, and political reasons officials persisted in a costly holding action in Vietnam rather than incur the domestic political damage of acknowledging a mistake. Leaders kept escalating the US commitment in an effort not to win but simply to avoid losing. This cynical twist to the quagmire interpretation was not widely adopted by historians, but it is clearly articulated in *Papers on the War* (1972), a book by Daniel Ellsberg, the Department of Defense official who helped write the Pentagon Papers and then in an act of protest gave photocopies to the *New York Times*. Another author of the papers, Leslie Gelb, teamed with Richard K. Betts to write *The Irony of Vietnam* (1979), which also argues for the stalemate thesis. Gelb and Betts also summarize nine different interpretations of origins of the American war, and thus their book remains valuable as an introduction to historical debate on the war.

As more archival information and time for reflection became available to historians in the late 1970s and early 1980s, the most prevalent interpretation of origins came to be a combination of the quagmire and global containment perspectives. Divine and Hess have termed it the "flawed containment" school, and Robert McMahon labels it the "liberal–realist critique" (Divine 1988: 83; Hess 1994: 246; McMahon

1996: 316). Both of these phrases capture the theme in much of the Vietnam War literature that the United States was trying to apply to a social and political revolution in Asia a strategic concept first developed in response to a Soviet military and political presence in Eastern Europe. The liberal portion of this critique points out that the American fixation on the Marxism-Leninism of the Vietnamese Revolution (which linked it ideologically with the Soviet and Chinese revolutions) obscured the Vietnamese drive for self-determination, a principle also cherished by Americans. The realist aspect of these works notes that, regardless of political philosophies, the US national interest in Vietnam was small and the costs of intervention were great. From both theoretical and practical calculations of policy, this line of argument, which became the orthodox explanation of origins, generally produced the conclusion that US intervention was an error from the beginning or at least was wrong to have achieved a level of cost to the United States far exceeding the threat a communist success in Vietnam posed to America. As McMahon (1996) summarizes it, this body of scholarship finds the American war in Vietnam to have been an "avoidable tragedy" (p. 316).

One of the first books to synthesize the flawed containment thesis and what has become the standard liberal–realist work is *America's Longest War* by George Herring. The first edition appeared in 1979 and drew heavily but carefully on the Pentagon Papers. Subsequent editions have been enhanced by the steady release of previously classified documents and the outpouring of specialized monographs, but Herring's thesis has remained basically the same. The first edition concluded "Vietnam made clear the inherent unworkability of a policy of global containment." The problem, he found, was that "by wrongly attributing the Vietnamese conflict to external sources, the United States drastically misjudged its internal dynamics" (Herring 1979: 270). This same sentence continued to appear in subsequent editions. Even after the demise of the Soviet Union and end of the Cold War in the early 1990s, Herring still concluded: "That containment was misapplied in Vietnam . . . seems beyond debate" (Herring 1996: 314).

A number of other excellent overviews of the American war have appeared since Herring's original edition and have adhered to basically the same thesis, which Hess denotes as "neo-orthodox" to distinguish from the earlier quagmire arguments (Hess 1994: 246). Many of these works expand their coverage into areas only briefly mentioned by Herring, whose analysis is primarily diplomatic and strategic. Stanley Karnow's *Vietnam: A History* (1992) and A. J. Langguth's *Our Vietnam* (2000), with their colorful vignettes of people and events, are valuable narrative accounts from the liberal–realist perspective. Other overviews by Paul Kattenburg, Hugh Higgins, William S. Turley, and Gary Hess also fall into the neo-orthodox school, as do textbooks by George Donaldson Moss, James S. Olson and Randy Roberts, and Gerard J. DeGroot. Surveys by Marilyn Blatt Young and Robert Buzzanco add more of the American domestic turmoil caused by the war, and James Pinckney Harrison introduces more of the Vietnamese side of the conflict. Schulzinger's *A Time for War* incorporates diplomatic, military, and political analysis. David L. Anderson's *Shadow on the White House* (1993) concentrates on presidential leadership. Robert Mann's *A Grand Delusion* (2001) is an overview that devotes considerable attention to Congress, as does William Conrad Gibbons' *The US Government and the Vietnam*

War (1986–95). The analysis in all of these works remains, however, the liberal–realist model.

A radical critique of American policy is found in some other overviews written from a New Left or radical revisionist historical analysis. The most thoroughly developed of these is Gabriel Kolko's *Anatomy of a War* (1985). He argues that both the origins of US involvement in the Vietnamese Revolution and the dogged American persistence to defeat the Vietnamese communists derived from America's material interest in the world capitalist system. Proceeding from the assumptions of an economic determinist philosophy of history, Kolko arrives at the sweeping conclusion that the Vietnam War had "a significance greater than that of either of the two world wars" on America's "political structure and aspirations." Those wars "had only encouraged Washington's ambition to guide and integrate the world's political and economic system," he declares, "a goal which was surely the most important cause of its intervention in the Vietnam conflict after 1950" (pp. 547–8). Monographic studies such as those of Borden and Rotter on the Truman administration have marshaled evidence of economic calculations in American policy in Southeast Asia, and Thomas McCormick, Patrick Hearden, and Howard Schonberger have, like Kolko, placed the American intervention in Vietnam in the context of an American drive for hegemony in the world economic system. Many historians agree that economic interests are one factor in the calculations of US interest in Vietnam, but most do not make global markets the center of their explanation of American policy. The radical revisionists, like the stalemate theorists, however, prompt the more numerous liberal–realist scholars to consider that American intervention in Vietnam was not simply accidental or misguided, but, indeed, could have roots ingrained in American economic, social, and political culture.

In the various discussions of origins of America's Vietnam War, three chronological points attract most attention. The first is the time around the end of the French–Vietminh War and the emergence of the South Vietnamese government under Ngo Dinh Diem in 1954–5. The second is the period from the creation of the National Liberation Front in the South in December 1960 to the assassination of Diem in 1963. The third is the 1964–5 period when, after a series of post-Diem regimes, the government in Saigon neared collapse and presented the possibility of a failure after ten years of US support of South Vietnam. The Eisenhower administration faced the first situation, the Kennedy administration the second, and the Johnson administration the third.

When Eisenhower became president in January 1953, the French war in Indochina was reaching a critical phase. The Truman administration had gradually increased aid to the French against the Vietminh as the Korean War and the continuing Cold War in Europe had seemed to verify Paris' claims to be fighting for containment not colonialism in Indochina. Eisenhower further expanded US assistance, but he faced a major decision in 1954 as Vietminh forces besieged the French garrison at Dienbienphu and the French government, weary of the war, contemplated how to end the eight-year conflict. Invoking what became known as the domino theory, Eisenhower declared that if Vietnam fell to communist control, all of Southeast Asia would be vulnerable to being toppled. The president declined, however, to authorize US air strikes to break the siege at Dienbienphu. The French garrison surrendered, and shortly afterward, at an international conference in the Swiss city of Geneva, France agreed to a ceasefire and temporary north–south partition of Vietnam. So-called Eisenhower revisionists, such as Stephen Ambrose, John Burke, and Fred I. Greenstein, cite the former general's cautious response to Dienbienphu as evidence of Eisenhower's statesmanship, and Melanie Billings-Yun argues in a well-researched monograph that Eisenhower's strategic and political handling of the Dienbienphu decision was masterful. These historians basically absolve Eisenhower of responsibility for the American war in Vietnam.

Other scholars argue, however, that Eisenhower's actions significantly increased US involvement in the internal affairs of Vietnam. Lloyd Gardner finds that Eisenhower's secretary of state John Foster Dulles welcomed the end of France's neocolonial aspirations, which had been an obstacle to America's liberal capitalist goals in Asia. In a careful study of the Geneva conference, Anthony Short interprets the American opposition to permanent partition of Vietnam as contributing to continued hostility in the country. George M. Kahin's *Intervention* (1986) details the political anarchy that existed in South Vietnam after the Geneva conference and argues that the Eisenhower administration's decision to back Ngo Dinh Diem as a political alternative to Ho Chi Minh was foolish from the start. In *Trapped by Success*, David L. Anderson (1991) traces Eisenhower's policies beyond Dienbienphu and Geneva to the end of the administration. He argues that Washington artificially sustained a politically weak Diem regime while touting an image of South Vietnam as a miracle in nation building. In contrast to the Eisenhower revisionists, Anderson concludes that "the Eisenhower administration trapped itself and its successors into a commitment to the survival of its own counterfeit creation" (p. 197). By the end of the 1950s an American war in Vietnam could have still been avoided, but a decade of opposing Ho Chi Minh and the communists and supporting alternative leadership, first the French and then Diem, had made the option of abandoning support of the Saigon government very difficult.

When John Kennedy entered the White House in January 1961, an armed insurrection led by the National Liberation Front (NLF) of South Vietnam and a civil war in Laos were threatening to destabilize all of Indochina. In response to the threat that these worsening conditions posed for the Diem regime, Kennedy significantly increased the level of aid and the number of American military advisers to South Vietnam. Explanations differ on why he felt compelled to act to prevent the fall of the Saigon government. McCormick, Hearden, and other radical revisionists believe that the assumed need to shore up the outposts of American empire was at work, but R. B. Smith has argued that it was Soviet and Chinese support of Hanoi that gave Kennedy little choice. Consistent with the liberal–realist interpretation, Duiker maintains that Kennedy exaggerated the strategic importance of Vietnam, and Larry Berman notes how domestic American political calculations led Kennedy to take a tough anti-communist stand in Vietnam. Because Kennedy's assassination in 1963 cut short his administration, a large amount of counterfactual speculation has developed over what he might have done differently in Indochina than did his successor Lyndon Johnson. Kennedy expressed doubts about US involvement in Vietnam, and thus some writers, such as historians William Rust and John Newman and Kennedy aide Robert McNamara (1995: 96), have maintained that Kennedy would have withdrawn American military advisers after being reelected in 1964.

Other analysts, such as Lawrence Bassett and Stephen Pelz, argue that Kennedy's commitment to containment in Indochina was anything but cautious, and Hess, Berman, and other scholars have explicitly challenged the notion that Kennedy intended to withdraw.

President Johnson believed that the decisions of Truman, Eisenhower, and Kennedy had committed the United States to the defense of South Vietnam against North Vietnam. Still, it was Johnson who faced the ultimate choice of the United States taking over the military conduct of the war or accepting the military and political collapse of the Saigon government. Consequently, much of the historical debate over the origins of the American war centers on Johnson's actions. Survey works on the war tend to place his decisions in the context of their liberal–realist or radical revisionist theses, but there are many monographic or biographical works on Johnson himself or on the 1964–5 period that comprise a particularized Johnson historiography. There is no dispute that it was Johnson's orders that steadily raised US troop levels in South Vietnam to a half million, and this escalation led antiwar protesters to label the Americanization of the war Johnson's War. Scholars disagree, however, over the degree of control he had over this process, why he committed as much US force as he did, and why he did not do more.

Johnson was an energetic and demanding chief executive who scored enormous legislative victories in creating his domestic Great Society program, and writers such as Halberstam, Burke, and Greenstein have contended that he dominated Vietnam policymaking in a similar fashion. Herring acknowledges that Johnson was an impatient man whose temperament was ill-suited for the complex counterinsurgency warfare of Vietnam, but he warns against overdrawing the influence of the president's personality. Herring does describe Johnson, however, as having an almost pathologi cal inability to make a decision. Brian VanDeMark and David Barrett view Johnson as open to advice from others, and, like Herring, portray him as cautious, even reluctant, in deciding upon escalation. Whether or not Johnson gave consideration to different policy options, he and his advisers, in the opinion of most of these scholars, were not willing to accept the fall of South Vietnam to control by North Vietnam without some US effort to stop it. As Larry Berman has detailed in two books and as sympathetic Johnson biographer Doris Kearns notes, Johnson's domestic political instincts also compelled him to advocate a tough American stand in Vietnam in order not to appear to be a weak leader. He feared that conservatives who opposed his Great Society reforms would use any sign of retreat on his part in confronting world communism as a way to undermine his political position and defeat his domestic plans. Johnson biographer Robert Dallek portrays Johnson, despite his great leadership potential, as perceiving few options other than to stay the course in Vietnam. Lloyd Gardner also depicts him as an astute but surprisingly insecure domestic politician who felt trapped by limited policy choices in Indochina.

Since most of these studies see Johnson as a compromiser who wanted to do enough to help South Vietnam survive but not too much to risk a wider war with China or the USSR that would derail his ambitious domestic program, there are many shades of interpretation ranging from sympathetic to Johnson's leadership dilemma to highly critical of his choices. Several authors maintain that the president was poorly served by his advisers. H. R. McMaster faults the joint chiefs of staff for their lack of candor, Douglas Kinnard makes a similar indictment of Kennedy and

Johnson aide Maxwell Taylor, and David DiLeo argues that even the dovish undersecretary of state George Ball was too personally ambitious to risk his access to Johnson with an effective challenge to presidential decisions. Yuen Foong Khong finds that the thinking of Johnson and his aides was limited by the way they used historical analogies, such as the Munich conference and the Korean War, that did not fit the circumstances in Vietnam. In his much discussed memoir, *In Retrospect* (1995), Secretary of Defense Robert McNamara admits that he and others made monumental mistakes in Southeast Asia, a failing that he attributes in large part to their only superficial knowledge of the region.

A good example of how historical research has altered the image of Lyndon Johnson is the work on the Gulf of Tonkin incident of August 1964. Early studies, such as that by Eugene C. Windchy (1971), based upon congressional hearings and similar public sources, concluded that the president deliberately deceived Congress and the people about the details of North Vietnamese naval attacks on US vessels in the Gulf of Tonkin. Edwin E. Moïse's (1996) monograph based upon careful analysis of declassified documents finds, however, that Johnson and his aides actually believed there had been two attacks on US destroyers at the time Washington ordered a retaliatory bombing of North Vietnam. Moïse's findings do not dispute other evidence that the United States was on a collision course with North Vietnam regardless of the details of this one incident or that Johnson dissembled about his Vietnam policies. They do, however, give credence to the idea that Johnson often believed that he was simply doing what he had to do with little other choice.

Although the mounting volume of scholarship on Johnson's 1964–5 decisions has given greater understanding to the challenges and limitations that he faced, many obvious flaws in his actions remain visible. As Kahin (1986) has argued, for example, Johnson took the final step in a process begun by Eisenhower and Kennedy that made a compromise or "third force" – that is, neither communist nor neocolonialist – political outcome in Vietnam possible. The dogged American insistence on sustaining a Saigon government acceptable to Washington produced a major war. As Gelb and Betts (1979) and other stalemate proponents observe, Johnson and his team knew the chances of success were poor, but plunged ahead out of a political inability to risk an appearance of weakness. One of the most pointed revivals of the indictments of Johnson is Fredrik Logevall's *Choosing War* (1999), which maintains that Johnson knowingly rejected a negotiated settlement to the Vietnam War that was available in 1964 and 1965. Elements of Logevall's thesis are counterfactual. Since meaningful diplomacy was not attempted, the course it would have taken in terms of actual concessions by both sides is impossible to know. He also speculates that Kennedy, if he had lived past 1963, would have chosen negotiation. This provocative and thoroughly researched argument is ultimately unprovable, but it serves to place a glaring spotlight on Johnson as the most likely suspect in the search for origins of the American war in Vietnam.

Both the liberal–realist and radical revisionist explanations of the origins of the war conclude that it was not winnable in any meaningful sense for the United States and hence should never have been undertaken. To paraphrase General Matthew Ridgway's perception of possible US military involvement in Indochina during the French war, they contend that it was the wrong war, in the wrong place, and against the wrong enemy. They argue that American intervention was a misapplication of containment, a failure to understand local conditions in Southeast Asia, and a product of arrogance or ideological obsession. These factors prevented a clear definition of objectives and of the means available to attain those objectives. In other words, there was no successful American strategy that is apparent to these authors.

Course of the War

A number of military historians, many of whom are former military officers, have challenged this negative assessment and contend that the war was indeed winnable by the United States. These conservative revisionists tend to accept at face value the official US rationale that intervention in Vietnam was an important strategic move to contain international communist aggression. They focus their analyses on the way the war was fought and not on why it was fought. The victory scenarios that they advance come in basically two forms. As labeled by Hess (1994), they are the "Clausewitzian" revisionists and the "hearts-and-minds" revisionists (p. 241). Colonel Harry Summers of the US Army War College inspired the name of the first group after he based his analysis of the Vietnam War, *On Strategy* (1982), on Karl von Clausewitz's classic military treatise, *On War*. Summers contended that US forces in Vietnam never used Clausewitz's proven conventional principles, such as isolating the battlefield. Instead, an unconventional strategy largely shaped by civilian officials in the Pentagon dispersed American power in a futile search for guerrillas. Bruce Palmer, Philip B. Davidson, Shelby L. Stanton, and Dave Richard Palmer are other writers joining with Summers in maintaining that a conventional strategy with use of more American force could have compelled Hanoi to agree to a negotiated settlement that would have preserved South Vietnam. In their memoirs, some of America's principal commanders, such as General William C. Westmoreland and Admiral Ulysses S. Grant Sharp, support the view that fewer restrictions from Washington and higher levels of US ground forces and air power would have overwhelmed Hanoi.

These win arguments have prompted a host of rebuttals. Herring, Hess, Jeffrey Kimball, and other liberal–realist historians have penned reviews noting that the conservative revisionists' lack of attention to the political and social origins of the war make their prescriptions for military solutions to what were political problems unpersuasive. No amount of American power could make corrupt and repressive South Vietnamese officials popular. Indeed, some scholars maintain that excessive American use of its conventional military power was the source of US failure in Vietnam. James C. Thompson and Mark Clodfelter find fundamental flaws in the use of air power. Loren Baritz and James William Gibson believe that modern American society created an overconfidence in high technology warfare and in the effectiveness of managerial techniques borrowed from the corporate business world. This American way of war caused civilian and military strategists to inflict enormous damage on South Vietnam that destroyed not only people and homes but also any hope of village-level allegiance to the Saigon government. This response to the Clausewitzians drawn from an analysis of American culture suggests, like that of the liberal–realists, that the United States may have been incapable of winning the war.

The alternative school of military historians, the hearts-and-minds revisionists, argues that the United States could have responded more effectively to the communists' political threat to America's Saigon allies. These writers seek to demonstrate that Westmoreland and his generals would have had greater success with more attention to pacification, that is, efforts to provide security and government services to the people of South Vietnam rather than simply attempting to kill enemy soldiers in what was known as a war of attrition. Andrew Krepinevich, Larry Cable, Richard Hunt, Robert Komer, William Colby, and David Hackworth provide evidence that counterinsurgency tactics and pacification programs would have been no worse and likely better than the air bombardments and large unit ground operations that were actually used. One of the ardent believers in pacification was Colonel John Paul Vann, whose role as first a military and later civilian adviser in South Vietnam has been detailed by journalist Neil Sheehan (1988). A scholar who has taken exception to the notion that pacification was a key to American success, however, is Eric Bergerud. In two studies of the 25th Infantry Division in Hau Nghia Province (Bergerud 1990, 1993), he reports that American troops worked closely with Vietnamese villagers on local development and security, but these efforts did not translate into lasting political gains for Saigon.

As Bergerud's work reveals, any assessments of American military success and failure have to take into account the historical, political, and social realities of Vietnam itself. American historians have to be prepared to consider that the outcome of the Vietnam War was not an American failure but a Vietnamese success. As Spencer Tucker (1999) observes, the Vietnamese people have a long military tradition of effectively resisting outside foes. There are some Vietnamese histories of the American war in English translation, and several Western scholars have used Vietnamese-language sources and done research in Vietnam to study the Vietnamese side of the war. Frances Fitzgerald's *Fire in the Lake* (1972) is an older work that romanticizes the NLF, but her perception of the strength of the Vietnamese Revolution among the rural population has been verified by other studies. As Jeffrey Race, James W. Trullinger, Douglas Pike, and James P. Harrison have observed, the Vietnamese communists combined patriotic appeals with ruthless, disciplined political organization to mount and sustain an insurgency against the Saigon government, despite the South's significant level of US aid. The works of William Duiker, including his authoritative biography of Ho Chi Minh (Duiker 2000), reveal that the leaders in Hanoi were not supermen, that they argued among themselves and made mistakes, but also that they were formidable adversaries with a well-considered strategy for defeating the powerful Americans.

A third variation of the conservative revisionist school is a group of works that Hess (1994: 243–6) denotes as "legitimatists." These books do not necessarily assert that America could have won the war, but they forthrightly take the position that the effort and costs were morally and strategically justified. Guenter Lewy (1978) provided one of the first scholarly rejoinders to the orthodox view that the United States was wrong to wage such a destructive war in Vietnam. He rejects the notion that Americans should feel any guilt for the war, but he is critical of actual US tactics and regrets that a vigorous pacification strategy was not adopted. Reflecting on the repressive nature of the socialist government in Vietnam after the war, Norman Podhoretz believes the US intervention was morally justified, but he accepts much of the orthodox argument that the military and political chances for American success were never very good. Timothy Lomperis makes a related argument that Hanoi's military and political success did not mean that their claims of liberating the people were legitimate. Michael Lind's *Vietnam: The Necessary War* (1999) follows in the mode of Podhoretz and Lomperis. In contrast to the flawed containment school, these books and the multi–volume history by R. B. Smith (1984–90) maintain that US national security interests justified the United States fight in Vietnam, even at the levels ordered by Johnson. Another variant on the legitimist thesis is defense of the performance of the South Vietnamese government. Works by Ellen Hammer and Patrick Hatcher claim that the Diem government had more strengths than Americans recognized. Not surprisingly, memoirs by former South Vietnamese officials, such as Ambassador Bui Diem, also dispute the orthodox image of the Saigon regime as hopelessly corrupt.

The large outpouring of works dealing with questions of origins and conduct of the war continues because there is no consensus on the standards for judging the American policies. Both the liberal–realist contention that, from the outset, the war was unwinnable within the limits of prudent policy (for example, excluding the use of nuclear weapons on North Vietnam) and the conservative belief that a winning strategy existed but was not tried are basically unprovable. Thus analysts posit competing logical or ideological premises upon which to build their cases. In addition to origins and conduct, a third area of debate is over how the United States terminated its longest foreign war. The specialized literature in this area extends the debate and the basic interpretive positions in the other areas.

End of the War

On the subject of war-ending, much of the scholarship concentrates on the press, the antiwar movement, and diplomacy. Most historians agree that the communists' Tet Offensive of early 1968 marked the beginning of a deescalation process leading to an eventual end of the US military intervention in Vietnam. Why Tet can be considered a turning point, however, has led to debate among scholars over what actually occurred in the offensive and over the significance of how the American press, general public, and national leadership responded to Tet. Don Oberdorfer's *Tet!* (1971) and Marc Jason Gilbert and William Head's anthology, *The Tet Offensive* (1996), examine the diverse dimensions of the event. That enemy forces could mount a nationwide offensive after almost three years of American air and ground attacks was a psychological blow to American public opinion. In striking the blow, however, the NLF suffered heavy losses in men from which it never really recovered and which required North Vietnamese troops to assume the burden of fighting in the South. From these facts, Davidson (1988) and Sharp (1978) argue that Tet was a military victory for the United States upon which weak-willed politicians failed to capitalize. Buzzanco (1996: 324) observes, however, that the US army chief of staff declared after Tet that "we suffered a loss" that was a warning about the limits of American military power. Kolko, Harrison, and Young assert that a psychological victory was exactly what Hanoi sought. Conversely, Duiker and Bergerud detect a communist miscalculation because the popular uprising against the Saigon regime that Hanoi tried to spark did not occur. Although pleased by the American domestic turmoil Tet created, North Vietnam's leaders knew they had squandered men and materiel they could not afford to lose.

One of the lightning rods in the debate over the end of the American war and over Tet has been the press. Presidents Kennedy, Johnson, and Nixon often criticized reporters for lack of support of the war effort. Himself a journalist, Peter Braestrup argued in his book *Big Story* (1977) that media coverage of the Tet fighting helped convince the American public and politicians that what was a US military success in withstanding the Tet attacks was actually a disastrous American defeat. Westmoreland and other commanders agreed with this complaint. Careful studies of press coverage by Daniel Hallin (1986), William Hammond (1998), and others refute these claims. They find that most reporters, dependent on official sources of information, dutifully supported US policy in Vietnam until members of the public and people inside government were themselves raising doubts. These scholars conclude that the press was a mirror of changing American opinions on the war rather than a shaper of those opinions.

Related to press coverage but a broader issue is the question of what role the antiwar movement played in pressuring national leaders to seek a way to withdraw from the war. There are some good general surveys of the peace movement, such as DeBenedetti and Chatfield (1990), Wells (1994), and Zaroulis and Sullivan (1984). These works do not argue that antiwar activism itself ended the war, but they contend that what was largely a grassroots protest movement did have a restraining influence on policymakers. Books by David Levy and Rhodri Jeffreys-Jones focus on how different elements of American society responded to the war, and they detect a slowly evolving antiwar sentiment and an increasing war weariness in the public. Mel Small in *Johnson, Nixon, and the Doves* (1988) finds that the presidents were more influenced by the protests than they admitted. Adam Garfinkle (1995) takes a different approach and argues that the radicalism of some protestors alienated the public and may have thereby prolonged the war by discrediting the antiwar position. Research by Jeffrey Kimball indicates that, when the Nixon administration negotiated a final withdrawal of US forces from Vietnam, the action was primarily a traditional strategic calculation based upon national interest and not directly forced by the antiwar movement.

Although Hanoi and Washington both resisted a diplomatic solution throughout much of the conflict, the American war ended with a negotiated agreement signed in Paris on January 27, 1973. There are far fewer diplomatic than military studies of the war, but books by Allan Goodman (1978) and Gareth Porter (1975) on the Paris negotiations provide a narrative of what they see as missed compromise opportunities throughout the war. As noted, Logevall (1999) is especially critical of Johnson's rejection of diplomacy, and Wallace J. Thies (1980) explains how Johnson's attempt to use starts and stops in the air war was an unworkable way to coerce Hanoi into negotiations. Nixon entered the White House believing that he could force North Vietnam to agree to terms acceptable to the United States, but he quickly encountered the same stubborn refusal from Hanoi to make concessions that had frustrated Johnson. In their memoirs, Nixon and his chief foreign policy aide Henry Kissinger claim that their administration eventually wore down the North Vietnamese. Jeffrey Kimball's *Nixon's Vietnam War* (1998) details, however, how it was the American side that gradually modified its terms in order to obtain a settlement. In a purposeful public image campaign, Nixon declared that he had achieved "peace with honor," but historical accounts of the end of the American war, such as those by Larry Berman (2001) and Arnold Isaacs (1983), dispute the notion of honor.

At the end, the United States failed in Vietnam because its ally South Vietnam, which Washington had proclaimed to be an outpost of global containment, ceased to exist and the Democratic Republic of Vietnam united the country under communist rule. The effort to understand and give a context to this failure has generated an outpouring of broadly interpretive and narrowly detailed studies, all searching for answers. There is an additional library of memoirs, novels, short stories, poems, and cultural studies that explore the individual and collective impact of this war on American identity. As the debate over origins, conduct, and termination of the American war reveals, consensus remains elusive on the meaning of the experience for the United States. Life goes on, however, and Vietnam looms large for policymakers, just as Munich, Pearl Harbor, and Korea stood as examples for Vietnam-era leaders.

Although it may appear that historical analogies served as poor policy guides during the Vietnam War and that the interminable wrangling among historians over the war diminishes the value of historical perspective, lessons from the Vietnam experience remain for historians and for policymakers who use history. Differing philosophical understandings of the past will always generate debate, as the various orthodox and revisionist interpretations reveal, but all of this work demonstrates the formative process that perceptions of the past play. The liberal–realist authors argue that the documented record of past mistakes matters both in policymaking and in the writing of policy history. Many revisionists, whether radical or conservative, maintain that present thinking and theories about the past matter in the same way. What all of these historians are saying is that the conflict in Vietnam and the costly American intervention in that war are part of a continuous stream that connects the past, present, and future. Consequently, historians will and should continue to offer forthright lessons from the Vietnam War about tension between local and international forces in world affairs; about where, how, and when to use America's economic and military power; and about how Americans are viewed by other people and how Americans should perceive themselves.

REFERENCES

Anderson, D. L.: *Trapped by Success: The Eisenhower Administration and Vietnam, 1953–1961* (New York: Columbia University Press, 1991).

Anderson, D. L. (ed.): *Shadow on the White House: Presidents and the Vietnam War, 1945–1975* (Lawrence: University of Kansas Press, 1993).

Bergerud, E. M.: *The Dynamics of Defeat: The Vietnam War in Hau Nghia Province* (Boulder, CO: Westview Press, 1990).

Bergerud, E. M.: *Red Thunder, Tropic Lightning: The World of a Combat Division in Vietnam* (Boulder, CO: Westview Press, 1993).

Berman, L.: *No Peace, No Honor: Nixon, Kissinger, and Betrayal in Vietnam* (New York: Free Press, 2001).

Bradley, M. and R. K. Brigham: "Vietnamese Archives and Scholarship of the Cold War Period: Two Reports." Cold War International History Project, Working Paper No. 7 (1993).

Braestrup, P.: *Big Story: How the American Press and Television Reported and Interpreted the Crisis of Tet 1968 in Vietnam and Washington* (Boulder, CO: Westview Press, 1977).

Buzzanco, R.: *Masters of War: Military Dissent and Politics in the Vietnam Era* (Cambridge: Cambridge University Press, 1996).

Davidson, P. B.: *Vietnam at War: The History, 1946–1975* (Novato, CA: Presidio, 1988).

DeBenedetti, C. and C. Chatfield: *An American Ordeal: The Antiwar Movement of the Vietnam Era* (Syracuse, NY: Syracuse University Press, 1990).

Divine, R. A.: "Vietnam Reconsidered." *Diplomatic History* 12 (1988), 79–93.

Duiker, W. J.: *Ho Chi Minh* (New York: Hyperion, 2000).

Ellsberg, D.: *Papers on the War* (New York: Simon and Schuster, 1972).

Fitzgerald, F.: *Fire in the Lake: The Vietnamese and the Americans in Vietnam* (Boston, MA: Little, Brown, 1972).

Garfinkle, A. M.: *Telltale Hearts: The Origins and Impact of the Vietnam Antiwar Movement* (New York: St. Martin's Press, 1995).

Gelb, L. and R. K. Betts: *The Irony of Vietnam: The System Worked* (Washington, DC: Brookings Institution Press, 1979).

Gibbons, W. C.: *The US Government and the Vietnam War: Executive and Legislative Roles and Relationships*, 4 vols. (Princeton, NJ: Princeton University Press, 1986–95).

Gilbert, M. J. and W. Head (eds.): *The Tet Offensive* (Westport, CT: Praeger, 1996).

Goodman, A. E.: *The Lost Peace: America's Search for a Negotiated Settlement of the Vietnam War* (Stanford, CA: Hoover Institution Press, 1978).

Halberstam, D.: *The Making of a Quagmire* (New York: Random House, 1964).

Halberstam, D.: *The Best and the Brightest* (New York: Random House, 1972).

Hallin, D. C: *The "Uncensored War": The Media and Vietnam* (New York: Oxford University Press, 1986).

Hammond, W. M.: *Reporting Vietnam: Media and Military at War* (Lawrence: University of Kansas Press, 1998).

Herring, G. C.: *America's Longest War: The United States and Vietnam, 1950–1975* (New York: John Wiley and Sons, 1979).

Herring, G. C.: *America's Longest War: The United States and Vietnam, 1950–1975*, 3rd edn. (New York: McGraw-Hill, 1996).

Hess, G. R.: *The United States' Emergence as a Southeast Asian Power, 1940–1950* (New York: Columbia University Press, 1987).

Hess, G. R.: "Historians and the Vietnam War." *Diplomatic History* 18 (1994), 239–64.

Isaacs, A. R.: *Without Honor: Defeat in Vietnam and Cambodia* (Baltimore, MD: Johns Hopkins University Press, 1983).

Kahin, G. M.: *Intervention: How America Became Involved in Vietnam* (New York: Knopf, 1986).

Karnow, S.: *Vietnam: A History* (New York: Viking Press, 1992).

Kimball, J. P.: *Nixon's Vietnam War* (Lawrence: University of Kansas Press, 1998).

Kolko, G.: *Anatomy of a War* (New York: Pantheon Books, 1985).

Langguth, A. J.: *Our Vietnam: The War, 1954–1975* (New York: Simon and Schuster, 2000).

Lewy, G.: *America in Vietnam* (New York: Oxford University Press, 1978).

Lind, M.: *Vietnam: The Necessary War* (New York: Free Press, 1999).

Logevall, F.: *Choosing War: The Lost Chance for Peace and the Escalation of War in Vietnam* (Berkeley: University of California Press, 1999).

McMahon, R. J.: "US–Vietnamese Relations: A Historigraphical Survey." In W. I. Cohen (ed.) *Pacific Passage: The Study of American–East Asian Relations on the Eve of the Twenty-First Century* (New York: Columbia University Press, 1996).

McNamara, R. S.: *In Retrospect: The Tragedy and Lessons of Vietnam* (New York: Times Books, 1995).

Mann, R.: *A Grand Delusion: America's Descent into Vietnam* (New York: Basic Books, 2001).

Moïse, E. E.: *Tonkin Gulf and the Escalation of the Vietnam War* (Chapel Hill: University of North Carolina Press, 1996).

Oberdorfer, D.: *Tet!* (Garden City, NY: Doubleday, 1971).

Porter, G.: *A Peace Denied: The United States, Vietnam and the Paris Agreement* (Bloomington: Indiana University Press, 1975).

Schulzinger, R. D.: *A Time for War: The United States and Vietnam, 1941–1975* (New York: Oxford University Press, 1997).

Sharp, U. S. G.: *Strategy for Defeat* (San Rafael, CA: Presidio, 1978).

Sheehan, N.: *A Bright Shining Lie: John Paul Vann and America in Vietnam* (New York: Random House, 1988).

Small, M.: *Johnson, Nixon, and the Doves* (New Brunswick, NJ: Rutgers University Press, 1988).

Smith, R. B.: *An International History of the Vietnam War*, 3 vols. (New York: St. Martin's Press, 1984–90).

Summers, H. G., Jr.: *On Strategy: A Critical Analysis of the Vietnam War* (Novato, CA: Presidio, 1982).

Thies, W. J.: *When Governments Collide: Coercion and Diplomacy in the Vietnam Conflict, 1964–1968* (Berkeley: University of California Press, 1980).

Tucker, S. C.: *Vietnam* (Lexington: University of Kentucky Press, 1999).

Wells, T.: *The War Within: America's Battle over Vietnam* (Berkeley: University of California Press, 1994).

Windchy, E. C.: *Tonkin Gulf* (Garden City, NY: Doubleday, 1971).

Zaroulis, N. and G. Sullivan: *Who Spoke Up? American Protest against the War in Vietnam, 1963–1975* (New York: Doubleday, 1984).

FURTHER READING

Ambrose, S. E.: *Eisenhower: The President* (New York: Simon and Schuster, 1984).

Anderson, D. L.: *The Columbia Guide to the Vietnam War* (New York: Columbia University Press, 2002).

Baritz, L.: *Backfire: A History of How American Culture Led Us into Vietnam and Made Us Fight the Way We Did* (New York: Morrow, 1985).

Barrett, D. M.: *Uncertain Warriors: Lyndon Johnson and his Vietnam Advisers* (Lawrence: University of Kansas Press, 1993).

Bassett, L. J. and S. E. Pelz: "The Failed Search for Victory: Vietnam and the Politics of War." In T. G. Paterson (ed.) *Kennedy's Quest for Victory: American Foreign Policy, 1961–1963* (New York: Oxford University Press, 1989).

Berman, L.: *Planning a Tragedy: The Americanization of the War in Vietnam* (New York: Norton, 1982).

Berman, L.: *Lyndon Johnson's War* (New York: Norton, 1989).

Berman, L.: "NSAM 263 and NSAM 273: Manipulating History." In L. C. Gardner and T. Gittinger (eds.) *Vietnam: The Early Decisions* (Austin: University of Texas Press, 1997).

Billings-Yun, M.: *Decision Against War: Eisenhower and Dien Bien Phu, 1954* (New York: Columbia University Press, 1988).

Blum, R. M.: *Drawing the Line: The Origins of the American Containment Policy in East Asia* (New York: Norton, 1982).

Borden, W. S.: *The Pacific Alliance: United States Foreign Economic Policy and Japanese Trade Recovery, 1947–1955* (Madison: University of Wisconsin Press, 1984).

Bradley, M. P.: *Imagining Vietnam and America: The Making of Postcolonial Vietnam, 1919–1950* (Chapel Hill: University of North Carolina Press, 2000).

Brigham, R. K.: *Guerrilla Diplomacy: The NLF's Foreign Relations and the Viet Nam War* (Ithaca, NY: Cornell University Press, 1999).

Bui, D. and D. Chanoff: *In the Jaws of History* (Boston, MA: Houghton Mifflin, 1987).

Burke, J. P. and F. I. Greenstein: *How Presidents Test Reality: Decisions on Vietnam, 1954 and 1965* (New York: Russell Sage Foundation, 1989).

Buzzanco, R.: *Vietnam and the Transformation of American Life* (Cambridge, MA: Blackwell, 1999).

Cable, L.: *Unholy Grail: The US and the Wars in Vietnam, 1965–8* (New York: Routledge, 1991).

Clodfelter, M.: *The Limits of Air Power: The American Bombing of North Vietnam* (New York: Free Press, 1989).

Colby, W. and J. McCargar: *Lost Victory: A Firsthand Account of America's Sixteen-Year Involvement in Vietnam* (Chicago, IL: Contemporary Books, 1989).

Cooper, C. L.: *The Lost Crusade: America in Vietnam* (New York: Dodd, Mead, 1970).

Cumings, B.: "The Wicked Witch of the West is Dead. Long Live the Wicked Witch of the East." In M. J. Hogan (ed.) *The End of the Cold War: Its Meanings and Implications* (Cambridge: Cambridge University Press, 1992).

Dallek, R.: *Flawed Giant: Lyndon Johnson and His Times, 1961–1973* (New York: Oxford University Press, 1998).

DeGroot, G. J.: *A Noble Cause? America and the Vietnam War* (Harlow: Longman, 2000).

DiLeo, D. L.: *George Ball, Vietnam, and the Rethinking of Containment* (Chapel Hill: University of North Carolina Press, 1991).

Dommen, A. J.: *The Indochinese Experience of the French and the Americans: Nationalism and Communism in Cambodia, Laos, and Vietnam* (Bloomington: Indiana University Press, 2001).

Duiker, W. J.: *US Containment Policy and the Conflict in Indochina* (Stanford, CA: Stanford University Press, 1994).

Duiker, W. J.: *Sacred War: Nationalism and Revolution in a Divided Vietnam* (New York: McGraw-Hill, 1995).

Duiker, W. J.: *The Communist Road to Power in Vietnam*, 2nd edn. (Boulder, CO: Westview Press, 1996).

Gaddis, J. L.: *Strategies of Containment: A Critical Appraisal of Postwar American National Security Policy* (Oxford: Oxford University Press, 1982).

Gardner, L. C.: *Approaching Vietnam: From World War II through Dienbienphu, 1941–1954* (New York: Norton, 1988).

Gardner, L. C.: *Pay Any Price: Lyndon Johnson and the Wars for Vietnam* (Chicago, IL: Ivan R. Dee, 1995).

Gibson, J. W.: *The Perfect War: The War We Couldn't Lose and How We Did* (New York: Vintage, 1986).

Hackworth, D. H. and J. Sherman: *About Face: The Odyssey of an American Soldier* (New York: Simon and Schuster, 1989).

Hammer, E. J.: *A Death in November: America in Vietnam, 1963* (New York: Dutton, 1987).

Harrison, J. P.: *The Endless War: Vietnam's Struggle for Independence* (New York: Columbia University Press, 1989).

Hatcher, P. L.: *The Suicide of an Elite: American Internationalists and Vietnam* (Stanford, CA: Stanford University Press, 1990).

Hearden, P. J.: *The Tragedy of Vietnam* (New York: Harper Collins, 1991).

Herring, G. C.: "America and Vietnam: The Debate Continues." *American Historical Review* 92 (1987), 350–62.

Herring, G. C.: *LBJ and Vietnam: A Different Kind of War* (Austin: University of Texas Press, 1994).

Hess, G. R.: "The Military Perspective on Strategy in Vietnam: Harry G. Summers's *On Strategy* and Bruce Palmer's *The 25 Year War.*" *Diplomatic History* 10 (1986), 91–106.

Hess, G. R.: *Vietnam and the United States: Origins and Legacy of War*, revd. edn. (New York: Macmillan Library Reference, 1998).

Higgins, H.: *Vietnam*, 2nd revd. edn. (London: Heineman, 1982).

Hunt, R. A.: *Pacification: The American Struggle for Vietnam's Hearts and Minds* (Boulder, CO: Westview Press, 1995).

Immerman, R. H.: "Prologue: Perceptions by the United States of its Interests in Indochina." In L. S. Kaplan, D. Artaud, and M. R. Rubin (eds.) *Dien Bien Phu and the Crisis of Franco-American Relations, 1945–1955* (Wilmington, DE: Scholarly Resources, 1990).

Isaacs, A. R.: *Vietnam Shadows: The War, Its Ghosts, and Its Legacy* (Baltimore, MD: Johns Hopkins University Press, 1997).

Jacobs, S.: " 'Our System Demands the Supreme Being': The US Religious Revival and the 'Diem Experiment,' 1954–55." *Diplomatic History* 25 (2001), 589–624.

Jeffreys-Jones, R.: *Peace Now! American Society and the Ending of the Vietnam War* (New Haven, CT: Yale University Press, 1999).

Kahin, G. M. and J. W. Lewis: *The United States in Vietnam* (New York: Delta, 1969).

Kattenburg, P. M.: *The Vietnam Trauma in American Foreign Policy, 1945–75* (New Brunswick, NJ: Rutgers University Press, 1980).

Kearns, D.: *Lyndon Johnson and the American Dream* (New York: Harper and Row, 1976).

Khong, Y. F.: *Analogies at War: Korea, Munich, Dien Bien Phu, and the Vietnam Decisions of 1965* (Princeton, NJ: Princeton University Press, 1992).

Kimball, J. P.: "The Stab-in-the-back Legend and the Vietnam War." *Armed Forces and Society* 14 (1988), 433–58.

Kimball, J. P.: "How Wars End: The Vietnam War." *Peace and Change* 20 (1995), 183–202.

Kinnard, D.: *The War Managers* (Hanover, NH: University Press of New England, 1976).

Kinnard, D.: *The Certain Trumpet: Maxwell Taylor and the American Experience in Vietnam* (Washington, DC: Government Printing Office, 1991).

Kissinger, H. A.: *White House Years* (Boston, MA: Little, Brown, 1979).

Kissinger, H. A.: *Years of Upheaval* (Boston, MA: Little, Brown, 1982).

Kissinger, H. A.: *Years of Renewal* (New York: Simon and Schuster, 1999).

Kolko, G.: *Anatomy of a War* (New York: Pantheon Books, 1985).

Komer, R. W.: *Bureaucracy at War: US Performance in the Vietnam Conflict* (Boulder, CO: Westview Press, 1986).

Krepinevich, A. F., Jr.: *The Army and Vietnam* (Baltimore, MD: Johns Hopkins University Press, 1986).

LaFeber, W.: "Roosevelt, Churchill and Indochina, 1942–1945." *American Historical Review* 80 (1981), 1277–95.

Leffler, M. P.: *A Preponderance of Power: National Security, the Truman Administration and the Cold War* (Stanford, CA: Stanford University Press, 1992).

Levy, D. W.: *The Debate over Vietnam* (Baltimore, MD: Johns Hopkins University Press, 1995).

Lomperis, T. J.: *From People's War to People's Rule: Insurgency, Intervention, and the Lessons of Vietnam* (Chapel Hill: University of North Carolina Press, 1996).

McCormick, T. J.: *America's Half-Century: United States Foreign Policy in the Cold War* (Baltimore, MD: Johns Hopkins University Press, 1989).

McMahon, R. J.: *The Limits of Empire: The United States and Southeast Asia since World War II* (New York: Columbia University Press, 1999).

McMahon, R. J.: "Contested Memory: The Vietnam War and American Society, 1975–2001." *Diplomatic History* 26 (2002), 159–84.

McMaster, H. R.: *Dereliction of Duty: Johnson, McNamara, the Joint Chiefs of Staff, and the Lies that Led to Vietnam* (New York: Harper Collins, 1997).

McNamara, R. S., Blight, J. G., and Brigham, R. K.: *Argument without End: In Search of Answers to the Vietnam Tragedy* (New York: Public Affairs, 1999).

Military History Institute of Vietnam: *Victory in Vietnam: The Official History of the People's Army of Vietnam, 1954–1975*, trans. M. L. Pribbenow, foreword by W. J. Duiker (Lawrence: University of Kansas Press, 2002).

Moss, G. D.: *Vietnam: An American Ordeal*, 4th edn. (Upper Saddle River, NJ: Prentice-Hall, 2002).

Newman, J. M.: *JFK and Vietnam: Deception, Intrigue, and the Struggle for Power* (New York: Warner Books, 1992).

Nixon, R. M.: *RN: The Memoirs of Richard Nixon* (New York: Grosset and Dunlap, 1978).

Nixon, R. M.: *No More Vietnams* (New York: Arbor House, 1985).

Olson, J. S. and R. Roberts: *Where the Domino Fell: America and Vietnam, 1945 to 1995* (St. James, NY: Brandywine Press, 1999).

Palmer, B., Jr.: *The 25-Year War: America's Military Role in Vietnam* (Lexington: University of Kentucky Press, 1984).

Palmer, D. R.: *Summons of the Trumpet: US–Vietnam in Perspective* (San Rafael, CA: Novato, 1978).

Pike, D.: *Viet Cong: The Organization and Techniques of the National Liberation Front of South Vietnam* (Cambridge, MA: MIT Press, 1966).

Pike, D.: *History of Vietnamese Communism* (Stanford, CA: Stanford University Press, 1978).

Pike, D.: *PAVN: People's Army of Vietnam* (Novato, CA: Presidio, 1986).

Podhoretz, N.: *Why We Were in Vietnam* (New York: Simon and Schuster, 1983).

Race, J.: *War Comes to Long An: Revolutionary Conflict in a Vietnamese Province* (Berkeley: University of California Press, 1972).

Rotter, A. J.: *The Path to Vietnam: Origins of the American Commitment to Southeast Asia* (Ithaca, NY: Cornell University Press, 1987).

Rust, W. J.: *Kennedy in Vietnam* (New York: Scribners, 1985).

Schaller, M.: *The American Occupation of Japan: The Origins of the Cold War in Asia* (New York: Oxford University Press, 1985).

Schlesinger, A. M., Jr.: *The Bitter Heritage: Vietnam and American Democracy, 1941–1966* (Boston, MA: Houghton Mifflin, 1966).

Schonberger, H. B.: "The Cold War and the American Empire in Asia." *Radical History Review* 33 (1985), 140–8.

Shaplen, R.: *The Lost Revolution: The US in Vietnam, 1946–1966* (New York: Harper and Row, 1966).

Short, A.: *The Origins of the Vietnam War* (London: Longman, 1989).

Spector, R. H.: *The United States Army in Vietnam: Advice and Support: The Early Years, 1941–1960* (Washington, DC: Government Printing Office, 1983).

Stanton, S. L.: *The Rise and Fall of an American Army: US Ground Forces in Vietnam, 1965–1973* (San Rafael, CA: Presidio, 1985).

Thompson, J. C.: *Rolling Thunder: Understanding Policy and Program Failure* (Chapel Hill: University of North Carolina Press, 1980).

Trullinger, J. W.: *Village at War: An Account of Revolution in Vietnam* (New York: Longman, 1980).

Turley, W. S.: *The Second Indochina War: A Short Political and Military History, 1954–1975* (Boulder, CO: Westview Press, 1986).

VanDeMark, B.: *Into the Quagmire: Lyndon Johnson and the Escalation of the Vietnam War* (New York: Oxford University Press, 1991).

Wells, T.: *Wild Man: The Life and Times of Daniel Ellsberg* (New York: Palgrave, 2001).

Westmoreland, W. C.: *A Soldier Reports* (Garden City, NY: Doubleday, 1976).

Williams, W. A., C. McCormick, L. Gardner, and W. LaFeber (eds.) *America in Vietnam: A Documentary History* (New York: Norton, 1989).

Young, M. B.: *The Vietnam Wars, 1945–1990* (New York: Harper Collins, 1991).

CHAPTER NINETEEN

Beyond Vietnam: The Foreign Policies of the Kennedy–Johnson Administrations

RANDALL B. WOODS

John F. Kennedy's overriding interest had always been foreign policy. Most of his inaugural address was devoted to it, and he frequently justified his domestic policies in terms of America's ongoing competition with the Soviet Union. Kennedy's foreign policy suffered from a basic contradiction, however. He and his advisers insisted that they were out to make the world safe for diversity and that under their leadership the United States would abandon the status quo policies of the past and support change, especially in the developing world. At the same time, the administration was staunchly anti-communist. Like his two Cold War predecessors in the White House, Kennedy frequently found himself propping up, in the name of freedom and democracy, regimes that ranged from authoritarian to dictatorial, and combating political movements committed to social justice because they were in league, or alleged to be, with the forces of international communism.

Unlike the foreign policy of Dwight D. Eisenhower, which was determined in part by a fear that global activism and higher defense spending would bankrupt the nation, Kennedy's policy operated under no such constraints. The Kennedy administration was guided by economist John Kenneth Galbraith, who viewed the economy as one in the midst of indefinite expansion. Judicious government spending would only enhance the process. As far as defense was concerned, domestic and foreign interests were assumed to be complementary; the economy could withstand and even benefit from spending for national defense.

Insofar as process was concerned, Kennedy attempted to be less tied to what he conceived as the over-bureaucratized National Security Council. The new president utilized the private counsel of McGeorge Bundy, a former dean of the faculty at Harvard, whom he appointed as a national security adviser, but without ties to NSC proper. Kennedy continued to listen to Secretary of Defense Robert McNamara and Secretary of State Dean Rusk, but the president relied primarily on Bundy.

Kennedy's presidency was cut short by an assassin's bullet in Dallas on November 22, 1963. This event gave rise to the Kennedy legend, which in turn has had a major impact on the historiography of his presidency and policies. Biographers of Kennedy fall into three distinct camps. The first group may be called the Camelot historians, who heap praise on and deflect criticism of the mythic man. Schlesinger (1965) and

Sorensen (1965) are two of the most influential books in this genre. Both unabashedly praise Kennedy's accomplishments and generally ignore his faults and failings. Both men served with Kennedy, were his friends, and admit that their observations are biased.

In the 1980s, Kennedy historiography veered sharply away from mythology and toward a critical reappraisal. The public had become disenchanted with government because of Vietnam and Watergate, a disenchantment exacerbated by revelations in the Pentagon Papers and the report of the Church committee concerning the secret machinations of the national security state. A new group of counter-Camelot historians including Garry Wills and Thomas C. Reeves focused on Kennedy's sexual exploits and his arrogance. Wills (1985) blames Kennedy's disdain for bureaucracy for the failure of the Bay of Pigs invasion and argues that he did not learn from his mistakes, but continued to act without restraint. Reeves (1991) delves more into Kennedy's personal life. He argues that Kennedy had no moral compass and this lack of character affected his decision-making in both domestic and foreign policy.

Thomas G. Paterson's (1989) compilation of essays also fits into the counter-Camelot camp. Paterson contends that Kennedy's policies came up significantly short of their goals and most of his contributors agree. Included in the anthology are Frank Costigliola's look at Kennedy's policy toward Western Europe, Stephen Rabe's essay on Latin America in general, Paterson on Cuba, and Douglas Little on the Middle East. Written during the heyday of the Clinton scandals, Seymour Hersh's *Dark Side of Camelot* (1997) is an attempt to compile as much controversial material on Kennedy as possible. This most scathing critique of Kennedy yet details Kennedy's sexual life which, Hersh points out, continually opened him up to potential blackmail. According to Hersh, Kennedy's performance during the missile crisis was less than heroic; he brought the world dangerously close to nuclear annihilation and then swapped missiles with the Soviets. Unfortunately, Hersh's frequent reliance on hearsay and his indiscriminate use of sources undermines his work's credibility.

Over the past two decades a more balanced approach to the Kennedy historiography has emerged. Post-revisionist writings portray the president as a complex personality who both succeeded and failed during a pivotal time in Cold War history. Herbert S. Parmet (1983) renders a typically balanced look. Parmet's Kennedy was initially aggressive in the international arena, even risking nuclear war, while he appeased the Right and neglected his domestic agenda. But he learned on the job and matured in office. Parmet applauds Kennedy's diplomacy in the Middle East and Central Africa and criticizes his efforts in Cuba and Vietnam. Giglio (1991) provides a similar analysis. Despite a multitude of potential disasters lurking in a world that was trying to cope with decolonization, modernization, and a host of other problems in the midst of the Cold War, Cuba was the only major foreign policy crisis to emerge during Kennedy's presidency, and Vietnam was the only place that remained a hot spot after Kennedy's death. To Giglio, Kennedy was a good, though not great president; he concludes that the United States was better off after than before his tenure. Timothy P. Maga's (1994) contribution is a brief (159-page) look at the administration and some of its policies, including the Alliance for Progress, the Peace Corps, the Bay of Pigs fiasco, the Cuban missile crisis, and the isolation of China. Maga depicts Kennedy as a visionary, who was able to articulate lofty goals, but unable to carry through in policy implementation. Burner (1988) praises Kennedy's liberal rhetoric and his style and purpose, but lays bare his many shortcomings. Part of the Library of American Biography, Burner's brief synthesis was taken from a 1984 biography of Kennedy written with Thomas R. West. Nigel Hamilton's *Reckless Youth* (1992) focuses on the maturation of Kennedy. Hamilton discusses Kennedy's promiscuity, but praises Kennedy for refusing to assume some of his other traits, namely his anti-Semitism and his isolationism.

The most recent works regarding Kennedy's policies and his impact include *Kennedy: The New Frontier Revisited*, edited by Mark J. White (1998). Objective essays highlight the space program, the Cuban missile crisis, and Kennedy's dealings with Gaullist France, while Fredrik Logevall's essay concludes that Kennedy would have terminated US involvement in Vietnam after his reelection in 1964. In the same volume, Georg Schild praises Kennedy's handling of the Berlin crisis in 1961, but criticizes the president for an approach to US–German relations that was emotionally detached, thus prompting needless feelings of insecurity in the Federal Republic. Henggeler (1995) discusses the impact that the Kennedy mystique has had on successive presidents. Latham (2000) looks at Kennedy's policies of counter-insurgency, the Peace Corps, and the Alliance for Progress. He links the administration's national security strategies with the modernization theories posited by the social science community in the 1950s and 1960s. Latham compares the language used in classified meetings among the Kennedy elite with the rhetoric used for domestic and international consumption and finds that they were identical. Therefore, he concludes, the Kennedy team believed their own rhetoric, when it came to lifting up the masses of the Third World. (See also Kern, Levering, and Levering (1983) for the Kennedy administration's relationship with the press.)

Determined to deal with the Kremlin from a position of strength, Kennedy and McNamara announced soon after their accession to power that America's nuclear arsenal would increase until it contained 1,000 intercontinental ballistic missiles. Kennedy did not want to tempt the Soviets with weakness, he confided to reporters. The nuclear buildup frightened Nikita Khrushchev, the Soviet premier; as he well knew, his country already lagged far behind the United States in delivery vehicles. The "missile gap" was a fiction. Instead of stability, the Kennedy–McNamara buildup touched off an arms race that brought the world to the brink of nuclear war in 1962, and saddled the United States with a massive $50 billion annual military budget by 1963. A number of works have delved into Soviet–American relations and the strategic arms race during the Kennedy era.

Horelick and Rush (1966) look at the ways post-Stalinist Soviet leaders have attempted to take advantage of the changes in modern weapons technology and in the global distribution of strategic power. They found a systematic pattern of deception in the Kremlin's relations with the West. After the missile gap was proved to be a myth, Khrushchev turned to strategic placement to intimidate and contain the United States and its allies. The Cuban missile crisis called Khrushchev's bluff, however, and after 1962 the Soviet leader became increasingly willing to settle for strategic inferiority and a policy of détente with the Americans. According to the authors, following the confrontation with the United States, the Kremlin looked more to military and economic aid as a tool to acquire international power.

Zubok and Pleshakov (1996) use recently declassified Soviet documents to discuss

Soviet policies from 1945 to 1962, with particular emphasis on Josef Stalin and Nikita Khrushchev. The authors characterize Soviet policy as one that joined "imperial expansionism and ideological proselytism" (p. 3). Zubok and Pleshakov view Stalin as a flexible practitioner in pursuit of rigidly fixed goals and portray Khrushchev as a complex man whose policies were at times erratic as he attempted to maneuver outside of the Stalinist-molded box.

Beschloss (1986) discusses the evolution and purpose of the U-2 program and the events surrounding pilot Francis Gary Power's downing in Soviet territory. Beschloss concludes that the downing ended any possibility of détente with the Soviet Union in 1960. He stresses the importance of domestic and bureaucratic politics on foreign policymaking in both the United States and the Soviet Union.

Craig (1998) argues that Eisenhower's all-or-nothing approach to nuclear policy was an intelligent and purposeful approach in Cold War and nuclear policy formation. According to Craig, Eisenhower made no allowances for gradations or subtleties; it was either peace or nuclear annihilation. In so doing Eisenhower gave the Soviets and hardliners in the United States no choice but peace. When Kennedy took over the reigns of leadership his intellectual cadre thought up a whole host of military options. The result was conflict in Southeast Asia and a tortured debate within the NATO countries about the possibilities and potentials of limited nuclear war. Ultimately, according to Craig, Robert McNamara concluded after the Cuban missile crisis what Eisenhower had known all along: nuclear war could not be won and therefore should not be waged. Ball (1981) argues that despite the fact that the missile gap theory had been debunked, Kennedy supported a strategic missile program that provided for the production of a thousand Minuteman missiles, a figure the author believes was excessive. Ball also says that Kennedy made the decision more in a response to domestic politics than in regard to military needs.

McGeorge Bundy's *Danger and Survival* (1988) is a history of American strategic policy by an insider and first-hand witness to nuclear crises both actual and potential. In his discussion of the Cuban missile crisis, Bundy implies that nuclear attack was never really a viable option for either side and praises both nations' leaders for showing restraint during the crisis. Not surprisingly, he declares his support for nuclear deterrence and denies that nuclear superiority lends itself to political leverage because, he argues, there are no winners in a nuclear war.

Freedman (1977) blends political science theory with history in an examination of the US intelligence community and how intelligence estimates are made. Freedman analyzes the debates and estimates surrounding the perceived missile and ABM gaps in the 1940s and 1950s, and the Minuteman vulnerability issue of the 1960s and 1970s. Freedman emphasizes how estimates are determined as much by domestic politics, the prevailing strategic doctrine, and the defense budget, as much as based on the perceived Soviet force structure. An even more important work on this topic is John Prados' *The Soviet Estimate* (1982), a sweeping look at the history and evolution of the national intelligence estimates. He emphasizes the dangers in partisan interpretation of intelligence data, which he argues was largely responsible for the failure of SALT II.

Herken (1985) discusses the strategic planning activities of civilian and government defense intellectuals over the course of four decades. He discusses the origins and evolution of the strategic policy of deterrence and its counterpoint, flexible response. He explores the controversies and debates that took place within this tight-knit group of strategists that included academics from MIT and Harvard and think-tanks such as the RAND Corporation. This is an excellent book, despite that, except for the Vietnam time frame, Herken examines the strategic process without providing much political, economic, and social context.

A number of contemporary chroniclers of foreign affairs argue that in the modern nation-state substance and form are inseparable. Historian Meena Bose (1998) examines the way Eisenhower and Kennedy developed and communicated their national security strategies and stresses the difference in their policymaking styles. Kennedy discarded Eisenhower's formal advisory network in favor of a less structured consultative process. Bose concludes that both styles have pros and cons. Eisenhower's style was ordered, but seems to have squelched creativity, while Kennedy's fluid and accessible approach inundated the president with too much raw data. Bose argues that Kennedy pushed for an increase in defense spending in spite of hard data that cast serious doubt on the validity of the "missile gap." According to Bose, Kennedy's flexible response doctrine intensified apprehension in the Soviet Union and served to undo what Eisenhower had done to reduce Cold War tensions. Prados (1991) is rich in insights into the personalities and administrative structures of the national security state. Prados documents the relationship between the NSC and the various Cold War presidents. He emphasizes that the national security adviser had much more influence over both Kennedy and Johnson and easily overshadowed the NSC, pointing again to the influence of McGeorge Bundy. (For a look at other top advisers to the Kennedy and Johnson administrations, see Isaacson and Thomas 1986; Rusk 1990; Cohen 1980; Schoenbaum 1988; Brinkley 1992.)

In addition to promising to build bridges to the Third World by encouraging peaceful change, Kennedy outlined a "grand design" for Europe, a strengthened partnership based on closer ties between the United States and a politically and economically integrated Europe. By all accounts, Kennedy's vision was never realized. The decision by the president and his advisers to use the alleged missile gap as a lever to gain the presidency and the nuclear buildup that followed had profound consequences for Soviet–American relations and created major strains within NATO. Moreover, many Europeans, especially Charles de Gaulle, believed that what the American president wanted was a faithful and subservient helpmate rather than a full and equal partner. Part of the Kennedy and adviser George Ball's grand design was a foreign economic policy based on trade expansion and a resolution of the United States' balance of payments problems. However, like so many other modern American presidents, Kennedy proved unable to reconcile or defeat protectionists at home and abroad.

Brinkley and Griffiths (1999) is a compilation of seventeen essays on the relationship between the United States and Europe that grew out of a 1992 conference in Florence, Italy. Most of the essays focus on NATO's maneuverings to keep West Germany within the fold, and the Kennedy administration's efforts to preserve the alliance in the face of Charles de Gaulle's nationalism and his veto of British entry into the European Common Market. Somewhat surprisingly, there is no chapter devoted to the Berlin crisis. German scholar Oliver Bange (2000) argues that it was the irreconcilable goals of the four leaders in question that prevented an integrated Europe; especially vexing for de Gaulle was the Anglo-American Nassau agreement of December 1962. The author discusses Kennedy and Macmillan's plans to enlarge the EEC, the American campaign in behalf of a multilateral nuclear force, the events surrounding de Gaulle's veto of British membership in the EEC, and Adenauer's pursuit of a Franco-German treaty. He shows how each nation's leader blamed the others for Britain's exclusion, thus creating a xenophobia that would make the realization of true European integration just that much harder. Andrew Moravcsik plays moderate revisionist in "De Gaulle Between Grain and Grandeur" (2000) by arguing that economic considerations and not exclusively geopolitical interests determined events leading to the crisis of the European Economic Community (EEC). De Gaulle repeatedly compromised his geopolitical aims to placate powerful commercial interests, namely French farmers, Moravcsik argues.

Donette Murray (2000) analyzes the Anglo-American debate over nuclear weapons from 1960 to 1963. Murray credits the Kennedy administration's lack of understanding of the British political situation for generating the Skybolt crisis in late 1962. According to Murry, Skybolt had become the centerpiece of Prime Minister Macmillan's defense strategy and when the Kennedy administration backed out of the project, a crisis ensued not seen since the conflict over the Suez Canal. The crisis abated only after the Defense Department agreed to substitute Polaris for Skybolt. (See also Neustadt (1999) on the "report" ordered by Kennedy to determine why the Skybolt crisis had occurred; its contents were recently declassified.)

Winand (1993) depicts the Eisenhower administration as concerned primarily with strategic interests and how European integration would further those interests. Under the Kennedy administration emphasis shifted from military to economic interests. Like his predecessor, Kennedy wanted a partnership, but was determined that the Europeans should pull their own economic weight. Kennedy's grand design failed because the Europeans were not willing to assume any larger share of the economic burden, especially as long as the United States refused to relinquish its military primacy within the alliance.

Risse-Kappen (1995) examines the relationship between the United States and its European allies by focusing on the Korean War, Suez Crisis, and the Test-Ban Treaty. Risse-Kappen demonstrates how European concerns influenced the US decisions regarding the Cuban missile crisis as well, particularly in its decision to enforce a blockade and agree to the Turkish missile deal. He argues that Berlin was a central issue throughout the missile crisis.

Trachtenberg (1999) posits the centrality of Germany in the East–West struggle. Both Kennedy and Khrushchev wanted to keep nuclear weapons out of Germany. The 1948 Berlin blockade had made Berlin a symbol of US resolve, however; thus Kennedy could not back out of Berlin, particularly if such a move appeared designed to appease Khrushchev. A showdown seemed inevitable. According to Trachtenberg, it came, not in Europe, but in Cuba. In turn, after Khrushchev blinked at US resolve in Cuba, he became more amenable to a modus vivendi in Germany. As Trachtenberg's work indicates, scholars have speculated that Kennedy's failure in the Bay of Pigs incident made him more bellicose in dealing with Khrushchev and the Soviets than he otherwise would have been. Whether or not this was true, Soviet–American relations deteriorated sharply during the summer of 1961, as the two nations faced off once again over the Berlin issue. The first week in June, Kennedy and Khrushchev held a summit meeting in Vienna where the Soviet leader attempted to browbeat and intimidate his much younger counterpart. The main topic was the divided city.

Smith (1963) argues that the Kennedy administration was less aggressive on the issue than Truman and Eisenhower mainly because of the influence of "softline" advisers Adlai Stevenson, Charles Bohlen, and Arthur Schlesinger, Jr. The Kennedy administration saw Berlin as a burden, a costly symbol with little substance, and in the winter of 1961–3 desperately tried to negotiate a deal with the Soviets that would extricate the United States from a seemingly untenable position. Schick (1971) criticizes Kennedy for failing to establish clear objectives in Berlin and for trying to bully the Soviets; the administration's policy, he argues, was really a mirror image of the Kremlin's. Kelleher (1975) chronicles the development of German nuclear weapons policy from German rearmament to 1966. Kelleher argues that the German position was shaped and constrained by its unequal status in NATO, its dependence on the United States, its internal division, and the Soviet threat. Based on interviews and German political writings during the period, Kelleher's work constitutes a clear analysis of Germany's interests and how Bonn attempted to defend them, at times independent of their Western allies. Political scientist Roger Morgan (1974) also discusses the relations between the two nations and attempts to construct a theory as to how alliances operate.

Soviet historian Robert M. Slusser (1973) argues that the Soviet Union's nuclear testing program was more a result of a domestic political tug-of-war inside the Kremlin than anything said or done by Washington. According to Slusser, those who blame Kennedy for the Berlin crisis are totally misguided. Historian Michael Beschloss (1991) agrees with Slusser on the importance of understanding the politics of the Kremlin, but criticizes Kennedy for failing to take that dynamic into account. He faults Khrushchev for bullying Kennedy, but ultimately places the responsibility for the crisis on the American president. According to Beschloss, Kennedy confused the Soviets by appearing inexperienced and vulnerable to intimidation and at the same time more aggressive than Eisenhower. Beschloss argues that if Kennedy had made it clear to the Soviets that offensive weapons in Cuba would not be tolerated, the crisis would never have taken place. The president was also guilty of political double-dealing. Even though Kennedy planned to accept a public plea by the United Nations to remove US missiles in Turkey, he only reluctantly made the same offer to the Soviets and insisted that the deal remain secret. Political scientist Honoré Marc Catudal (1980) looks at the development of the Kennedy administration's Berlin policy from January 1961 through August 1961. Catudal focuses on the domestic political challenges that Kennedy faced at the time. Kennedy's actions on Berlin were more a political compromise designed to simultaneously appease hawks and doves than a reaction to great power diplomacy or theories of strategy. Trachtenberg (1991) calls for a more interdisciplinary approach to strategic studies and war/peace studies. In an essay on the Berlin Crisis of 1958–62, Trachtenberg argues that political stability in Western Europe was not simply a consequence of the presence of nuclear weapons in the region. Stability was achieved for more compli- cated political and economic reasons. Ultimately, the Soviet Union and the United States were unwilling to risk nuclear war over Berlin; thus the crisis precipitated an agreement between the two powers and "cleared the air."

Gearson (1998) provides insight into London's view of the Cold War and its alliances with the Western world. Macmillan's attempts to act as an intermediary between the United States and the USSR ultimately failed, according to Gearson. He criticizes Macmillan's initial indecisiveness during the Berlin crisis and argues that this is what caused members of the Western alliance to discount Britain as a serious player in the game. William R. Smyser's *From Yalta to Berlin* (1999) is a recent synthesis of German history geared toward a general readership. Smyser, who lived in Hitler's Germany and worked both for the State and Defense Departments in German affairs, echoes Trachtenberg in placing Germany at the center of the Cold War struggle between the United States and the Soviet Union. Smyser depicts Kennedy as inexperienced and unaware of Germany's strategic importance and views Khrushchev's deployment of missiles in Cuba as leverage against a future planned crisis in Berlin. Historian Frank Mayer (1996) focuses on the tense interaction between Washington and Bonn during the Berlin crisis. The Kennedy administration was distrustful of West Germany and frustrated with its chancellor, Konrad Adenauer. While Adenauer was committed to German unification, the Kennedy administration was content with the status quo and did not want to push the Soviets. Mayer demonstrates that, despite its public protests, the Kennedy administration was privately relieved.

John C. Ausland's *Kennedy, Khrushchev and the Berlin–Cuba Crisis* (1996) is a memoir that was originally written in 1966 by a member of the Berlin Task Force. Ausland argues that Washington underestimated the Soviets and their threats to close down East Berlin. He discusses the difficulties associated with getting things done through the alliance system and explains the legal complexities of the US presence in Berlin. Ausland fails to give much Cold War context, however, which is a profound weakness. British writer Ann Tusa (1996) details the diplomatic maneuverings between the Soviets and the Americans during the crisis. The general information Tusa gives as a background is frequently inaccurate, but her discussion of the political personalities of the late 1950s and early 1960s is noteworthy. She argues that Eisenhower refused to budge for fear of losing prestige; Kennedy was authentically committed to a sweeping reappraisal of policy on Berlin but was thwarted by domestic politics, overt Soviet bullying, and the ineptness of his allies. She considers Macmillan a pest for his attempted mediation and accuses Adenauer of following a course based on narrow German nationalism.

For Kennedy and advisers Robert McNamara and Dean Rusk, the nuclear arms race was just one of many contests with the communist powers. During the 1960 presidential campaign, Kennedy had been sharply critical of the Eisenhower policy of massive retaliation. His impression that conventional forces had been woefully neglected was reinforced by reading retired General Maxwell Taylor's *Uncertain Trumpet* (1960) and by McNamara's alarmist report that the US army consisted of a mere fourteen divisions, only eleven of which were combat ready. During his first year, the president increased the regular military budget by 15 percent, doubled the number of army divisions in ready reserve, and increased the number of combat units in both the navy and the marines. In response to the counterinsurgency theories then being espoused by Taylor and others, Kennedy instructed the Special Warfare Center at Ft. Bragg, North Carolina, to train a new type of soldier capable of meeting communist guerrillas on their own terms. In the 1950s, anti-communist forces in Malaya, the Philippines, and Greece had successfully employed guerrilla tactics to defeat insurgents, and the administration was convinced that these techniques were suitable for dealing with Khrushchev's wars of national liberation. Special Forces units at Ft. Bragg – the green berets – increased from fewer than 1,000 to 12,000 and the White House created a special group (counterinsurgency) chaired by General Taylor and including Attorney General Robert Kennedy. The Taylor group saw the Special Forces not only as a paramilitary unit capable of sabotage and counterterrorism, but also as a progressive political and social force that would assist local governments in winning the hearts and minds of indigenous peoples. Coupled with a hyperactive CIA that had moved under the Eisenhower administration from purely information gathering to covert operations, the Special Forces were to be the answer to international communism's efforts to conquer the Third World.

Allen Dulles' *The Craft of Intelligence* (1963) is a defense of the CIA from one of its most influential former-chiefs. The author attempts to debunk the myth of the CIA and allay fears of a clandestine organization running amok overseas by arguing that it is overseen by the president and congressional subcommittees and checked by other national security organizations. Former CIA employee Douglas Blaufarb (1977) discusses the Kennedy Doctrine and focuses on six insurgencies in the Philippines, Malaya, Vietnam, Laos, Thailand, and Latin America. Blaufarb sometimes gives the Kennedy administration poor marks for execution, but sees counterinsurgency as an antidote to Sino-Soviet imperialism as entirely justified. Thomas (1995) examines the careers of Frank Wisner, Desmond Fitzgerald, Tracy Barnes, and Richard Bissell. Thomas characterizes these men as products of World War II who continued the ideological battle against communism in the early years of the Cold War. Powers (1979) argues that the actions of the CIA were in direct response to the Cold War environment and that the agency acted with the approval of the executive branch. Powers believes that the CIA was not, as Sen. Frank Church (D. – Idaho) and his committee found, a "rogue elephant."

FitzSimons (1972) argues in her critical assessment that Kennedy was the ultimate Cold Warrior. She defines the Kennedy Doctrine as the right to intervene, both politically and militarily, in the affairs of lesser powers to prevent the growth of communist influence. The chief manifestations of this policy were the confrontations in Cuba and Berlin and the introduction of counterinsurgency forces into Vietnam and Laos. In his comprehensive look at JFK's foreign policy, Freedman (2000) sees the president as less tunnel-visioned than FitzSimons portrays him. Freedman depicts a president whose foremost aim was to avoid nuclear war while at the same time not losing the battles over hearts and minds to the Soviets. Thus, a character emerges that was adept at crisis management and one, according to Freedman, who left the Cold War world less dangerous than he found it. Jeffreys-Jones (1989) argues that the CIA has been relatively successful in achieving its goals without abusing its power, especially in its efforts toward intelligence gathering. However, Jeffreys-Jones does criticize the agency for its covert activities in Third World nations. The author details the successes in Iran (1953) and Guatemala (1954) and the abject failure in Cuba (1961), a blunder that did almost irreparable damage to the agency's reputation. Charges by the Church committee further damaged the prestige of the CIA, but also forced the agency to reorient itself from cloak-and-dagger operations to its central function of intelligence gathering. Johnson (1989) attempts to explain the history of the CIA from its inception in 1947 through the Iran–Contra affair of 1987. Johnson suggests a course to resolve the conflict posed by the competing demands of an agency that utilizes covert means to ensure the security of an open, democratic society. He admits that abuses take place; zealots like Oliver North, for example, have compromised democratic values to obtain their objectives. However, Johnson concludes that through congressional oversight the public trust can be safeguarded. Johnson's survey adds nothing new that hasn't already been covered by Powers or Jeffreys-Jones.

Former Foreign Service officer Lucien S. Vandenbroucke (1993) outlines four cases in which special operations were conducted and failed, including the mission to liberate the American hostages in Iran under the Carter administration and the Bay of Pigs fiasco under Kennedy. Vandenbroucke argues that faulty intelligence and poor interagency cooperation and coordination were at least partly to blame.

Chapter 18 of this volume, on Vietnam, covers the most important literature on Special Forces. The Special Forces were the military aspect of a larger effort to identify the United States with the themes of anti-colonialism and nationalism. Another Kennedy initiative designed to demonstrate America's commitment to economic progress and social change was the Peace Corps. The stated objectives of the program were to provide a skill to an interested country, to teach other cultures about America, and to increase young America's understanding of other peoples. For Kennedy, the Peace Corps was more than an exercise in altruism, however. He spoke of halting communist expansion by helping to develop the resources of the Third World. This New Frontier foreign policy experiment has, to say the least, received mixed reviews from scholars and from participants.

A number of books relate personal experiences in the Peace Corps, both by bureaucratic leaders as well as volunteers, and attempt to resolve the stated mission with practical result. Sargent Shriver's *Point of the Lance* (1964) is a first-hand account from the Corps' founding director. The book contains a selection of Shriver's speeches and writings as well as a history of the origins and first years of the Corps. Hoopes' (1968) edited volume includes popular and personal stories of the volunteers. Lowther and Lucas (1978) is one of several accounts written by former Peace Corps participants that charges that the Corps did not live up to expectations, but still has the potential to do so. Lowther and Lucas describe the Corps as a Cold War invention to spread US influence and make a case for retooling the organization to meet present-day demands for global service. Another former-volunteer, Zane Reeves, discusses the bureaucratic struggles that have characterized the Corps throughout its lifetime. Reeves (1988) argues that the rigid anti-communism of various Cold War administrations has repeatedly brought them into conflict with agency personnel, who had for the most part embraced antiwar activism and the ideal of social justice both at home and abroad. Amin (1992) focuses on the Corps' programs in secondary education and community development in West Cameroon from 1962 to 1966. Amin describes the personal strides made by volunteers, whom the author believes ultimately failed at the bureaucratic objective of community development. Schwarz (1991) is a more recent survey of the volunteers' experiences and provides a general history of the Corps from Kennedy to George Bush, Sr. The essays within Schwarz's work are often cynical and reflect the author's belief that early on the Corps represented an idealized portrait of American character. According to Schwarz, the personal friendships forged between the volunteers and natives come across as the Corps' most significant accomplishment, while bureaucratic bungling seems to have been its most glaring failure.

Rice (1986) provides a history of the organization and emphasizes the popularity of the program among young college graduates. Rice draws on Peace Corps records, interviews, and personal manuscript collections to provide a thorough study. The program had a positive impact on both the host countries and the volunteers, he concludes. Overwhelmingly, the participants volunteered to help humanity, rather than to fight communism. Thus, the Peace Corps volunteers fulfilled a noble and positive role in the global community, while at the same time their government was frequently using the organization to pursue narrowly anti-communist goals in the Third Word. Fischer (1998) examines the dilemma volunteers found themselves in when they were confronted with the realities of the Third World, realities that frequently did not match the cultural preconceptions that had been instilled in them by the Peace Corps leadership in Washington. The volunteers, according to Fischer, began to recraft their own mission philosophy; the new goal was to refrain from imposing American values on other cultures. Hoffman (1998) takes a more institutional approach by focusing on the Corps under the Kennedy, Johnson, and Nixon administrations. According to Hoffman, Kennedy created it, and then ignored it; Johnson embraced it; Nixon tried unsuccessfully to get rid of it. Hoffman also focuses on the experience of the volunteer and praises the Peace Corps as having kept alive the best traditions of the nation, especially the belief in the right of self-determination for all peoples. (See also Searles (1997), which claims that the Peace Corps became more professionalized and useful under President Nixon, who appointed an able Joseph Blatchford as the Corps' new director.)

Outside of Southeast Asia, the New Frontier's dual penchant for social uplift and anti-communism is best seen in Latin America. And nowhere were the contradictions inherent in the Kennedy Doctrine more apparent. According to Schlesinger (1965), Kennedy fully understood that in Latin America "the militantly anti-revolutionary line" of the past was the policy most likely to strengthen the communists and lose the hemisphere. He and his advisers planned openings to the Left to facilitate "democratic development." Specifically, the administration projected an ambitious foreign aid program that would promote social justice and economic progress in the developing nations and in the process funnel nationalist energy into pro-democracy, anti-communist channels. Modernization through American aid would ensure that the newly emerging nations would achieve prosperity and political stability through evolution rather than revolution.

At the same time, the administration saw any significant change in the balance of world power as a threat to American security. Kennedy, McGeorge Bundy, Dean Rusk, and Robert McNamara took Soviet Premier Nikita Khrushchev's January 1961 speech very seriously. The problem was, of course, that anti-communist regimes in the Third World were as likely as not to be undemocratic. And, like so many of his predecessors, Kennedy was to learn that intervention, no matter how lofty the justification, was generally counterproductive, rallying popular support within and without the country intervened for the very regime that was alleged to be embracing communism. This was true in the cultural and political sphere no less than in the military.

Not surprisingly, the literature on Latin America and the Kennedy administration focuses on Cuba. It is both voluminous and conflicted. Smith (1962) is a firsthand account of Castro's rise and first years in power by a former ambassador to the island nation. US ambassador to Cuba in 1959 and 1960, Philip W. Bonsal (1971) focuses on the economic ties between the United States and Cuba. He argues that Castro's desire to rid his nation of American interests and corporate dominance was and is his most important objective. Bonsal comes to the conclusion that US policies made it virtually inevitable that Castro would fall into the arms of the Soviets. *The Hovering Giant* (1976) by political scientist Cole Blasier is a study of the US response to revolution in Mexico, Bolivia, Guatemala, and Cuba. Blasier concludes that strategic considerations dictated US policies, despite influences from business interests. He agrees with Bonsal that US policies served to radicalize the revolutionary movement in Cuba. Smith (1987) offers a critical look at US foreign policy toward the island by a former-State Department official and ambassador to Cuba. As a junior research analyst with the State Department during Fidel Castro's rise to power, Smith found no evidence that Castro was a communist and concludes that US policy toward Cuba has been an abject failure. Benjamin (1990) chronicles US influence in Cuba from the Spanish–American War through the end of the Cold War. The United States used threats of military intervention to influence the young republic and after the abrogation of the Platt Amendment in 1934 wielded its economic dominance to shape Cuban policies. He agrees with Bonsal and Smith that US policies have been primarily responsible for the rise of a nationalist Fidel Castro who was driven to seek support from the Soviets. Political scientist Morris H. Morley (1987), who emphasizes the economic origins of conflict between the United States and Cuba, also falls into this critical school. Paterson (1994) provides one of the most recent and sophisticated critiques of US policy. He concludes that the Eisenhower administration's obsession with communism blinded it to the realization of just how unpopular the Batista regime had become with its own people. Paterson argues that Castro was not a communist early on in the revolution and criticizes US policies toward Cuba before 1959 for facilitating post-'59 Cuban hostility toward the US government.

More balanced is Richard E. Welch, Jr.'s *Response to Revolution* (1985), which describes the response to Castro of the different governmental organizations as well as the press, and conservative and liberal camps within the United States during the two years following his seizure of power. Welch tends to blame historical circumstance, the structure of American capitalism, and ideology, rather than Castro or the presidents who dealt with him for the poor condition of Cuban–American relations. In a similar vein, Pérez (1988) places the Cuban Revolution in the context of Cuban history and nationalism. In Cuba and the United States Pérez explores the social, cultural, political, and economic forces that have shaped US–Cuban relations. Pérez-Stable (1993) describes the economic, social, and political impoverishment of pre-Castro Cuba and argues that one of the reasons for Castro's initial success was his appeal to the masses through promises of social justice. Pérez-Stable argues that partly because of Soviet monies flowing to the government, Castro was able to pioneer a system of state welfare that ultimately paved the way for a degree of social mobility in Cuba. Sweig (2002) utilizes Cuban documents and argues that during the early years of the revolution the *llano*, or the urban, middle-class militia had more influence over the revolution than Fidel Castro or his comrades in the Sierra Maestre. Sweig, a deputy director of the Latin American Program at the Council on Foreign Relations, argues that from February 1957 to January 1959 Castro and the *llano* functioned as rivals. Sweig's study and the opening up of Cuban archives to US scholars will no doubt provide evidence for future revision of the revolutionary period. (See also Gosse (1993), which details the Fair Play For Cuba Committee and its link to the New Left.)

By 1960, Castro had nationalized approximately $1 billion of American-owned property, announced that he was a Marxist-Leninist, and publicly embraced Nikita Khrushchev. Almost as soon as Kennedy took up residence in the White House he was briefed on the American-sponsored scheme in which a band of Cuban exiles would land at the Bay of Pigs, stimulate a popular uprising, and rescue the island from the Castroites. Despite the objections of Galbraith, adviser Arthur Schlesinger, Jr., and Sen. J. William Fulbright (D. – AR), Kennedy approved the CIA-authored plot with the stipulation that there be no overt participation by US armed forces.

The Bay of Pigs invasion on April 17, 1961 was a dismal failure. Cuba was prepared for the attack and held the numerical and weapons advantage. Kennedy rejected a request by members of the Joint Chiefs of Staff and the CIA for US intervention to rescue the exiles and topple Castro. Such blatant aggression, Kennedy declared, would only weaken the nation's hand in the global struggle against communism. The president accepted full responsibility for the fiasco. Most scholars have concluded that the blame was well placed.

Johnson (1964) provides an early, journalistic account of events from the perspective of the exile leaders, and details the activities of the brief, but storied career of the CIA's Richard Bissell. The memoir provides a detailed account behind the planning for the Bay of Pigs invasion. Wyden (1979) is another well-written account of the invasion by a journalist. Wyden uses interviews from participants and planners and concludes that Kennedy was weak and indecisive; his failure to provide air cover doomed the operation. *Operation Zapata* edited by Luis Aguilar (1981) consists of transcripts from meetings of top leaders from the White House, Pentagon, and CIA on why the Bay of Pigs operation failed. Much of the record is still classified, so the testimony is uneven. However, the report does identify Operation Zapata, the Bay of Pigs landing site, as a hurried replacement for Operation Trinidad. Also, the report shows that many agency planners were not aware of the final operation's specific details and that different agencies had different notions of the operation's objectives. Higgins (1987) views the invasion in the context of events in Guatemala in 1954 and compares it to subsequent failures in Laos and Vietnam. According to Higgins, Kennedy relied too heavily on the advice of Robert McNamara and the acquiescence of the joint chiefs, neither of whom were particularly well informed about the invasion plans. Thus, the invasion was more a consequence of CIA influence and inertia left over from the Eisenhower administration, than well thought out planning by the Kennedy administration. Dominguez (1989) examines the triangular relationship between Washington, Moscow, and Havana. Written before the breakup of the Soviet Union, Dominguez's work pays particular attention to Cuba's economic dependency on the USSR. Grayston L. Lynch's *Decision for Disaster* (1998) is a recent indictment of the Kennedy administration for the failure of the Bay of Pigs invasion. Lynch, who was a member of the CIA and accompanied the brigade of Cubans during the landing, gives his version of events in riveting detail. He has no qualms about showing his anti-Camelot bias. For example, the first chapter is entitled, "Into the Bay of Death." According to Lynch, Kennedy's weakness betrayed the Cuban freedom-fighters, doomed Cuba to rule by a communist dictator, and allowed the Soviets to become a real threat to the Western hemisphere. Castro and Fernandez (2001) is an equally biased look at events, but from the opposite point of view. Castro points out that the invasion was not a "fiasco," but rather a defeat for a well-trained and well-equipped American invasion force. Not surprisingly, he sees the event as a victory over US imperialism and justification for his revolution. (See also Rodriquez and Weisman (1989), which details Rodriquez's life as a CIA operative during the Bay of Pigs, the CIA's hunt for revolutionary Che Guevara, and Rodriquez's later involvement in Vietnam and with the Iran–Contra Affair.)

The declassification of materials on US–Cuban relations during this period and the opening up of Soviet archives within the past decade has resulted in a flood of new scholarship on US–Cuban relations. In 1997 the State Department released *Foreign Relations of the United States*, Vol. 10, Cuba 1961–1962, which presents a comprehensive look at events during the Kennedy administration. The FRUS volume includes documents from the White House and the CIA as well as the State Department and provides extremely useful editorial comment throughout. Any new researcher on the subject will find the volumes a treasure-trove of information. However, for those who have watched the painfully slow declassification of documents relating to Cuba, the volumes will be disappointing because they include little material that hasn't already been released through FOIA requests.

In addition to the FRUS volume, a rich, multi-archival literature is emerging on the subject of US–Cuban relations, partly because of a series of conferences held by the principal participants. In April 2001 a handful of Cold Warriors from the United States and as many from Cuba gathered in Havana for a conference commemorating the 40th anniversary of the failed invasion. Media reports from the event described the debate as intense but respectful and even friendly. Even *el líder* Fidel Castro engaged former CIA official Bob Reynolds in a friendly discussion, even though forty years before Reynolds had served as the CIA station chief in Miami and been in charge of recruiting *brigadistas* for the invasion. Prior to the Bay of Pigs reunion, Peter Kornbluh of the National Security Archive and James Blight of Brown University's Watson Institute for International Studies put together an oral history of the event. Blight and Kornbluh (1998) includes relevant documents and edited transcripts from meetings with former CIA officials and anti-Castro Cuban operatives. Though the participants in the meetings tended to defer to the version of events as interpreted by Kennedy-defender Arthur Schlesinger, Jr. and former ambassador Wayne Smith, what comes out in the end is a consensus that the invasion was ill-conceived and poorly executed. The planners seem more embarrassed than guilt-ridden. Bay of Pigs veteran Rafael Quintero charges that the CIA took advantage of naive émigrés and accused the operation's planners of being caught up in the John Wayne syndrome: America is always right and never loses. A supplement to Blight and Kornbluh's *Politics of Illusion* (1998) is *Bay of Pigs Declassified: The Top Secret Report of the CIA Inspector General on the Invasion of Cuba* (Kornbluh 1998). This volume consists of documents that were not released when *Politics of*

Illusion went to press. As the title suggests, the dominant document is a biting critique written by then CIA Inspector Gen. Lyman Kirkpatrick in 1961 of the mishandling and miscommunication of the operation by all government agencies involved in its planning.

When Fidel Castro began complaining to Nikita Khrushchev in 1961 that the United States was trying to overthrow his government by assassination or invasion, the Soviet Union began sending weapons and military personnel to protect its Cuban ally. Such a move had the added benefit in Khrushchev's eyes of placating hardliners within the Politburo who were worried about the massive imbalance in nuclear delivery systems that then existed. The buildup included medium-range ballistic missiles (MRBMs) capable of raining down nuclear warheads on American cities, ILB-28 bombers, and Soviet troops.

Because no offensive weapons had been sighted in Cuba and because Soviet Ambassador Anatoly Dobrynin had guaranteed that there were none, the Kennedy administration responded to rumors of an arms buildup by publicly announcing that there were no offensive weapons in Cuba and that none would be tolerated. Dobrynin was in fact deceiving the Kennedy administration. U-2 photographs analyzed on October 15, 1962 revealed that Soviet technicians were building sites from which both 1,000-mile MRBMs and 2,200-mile IRBMs could be launched against the United States. The president was frightened and angry. It seemed to him that Khrushchev was deliberately and deceitfully upsetting the balance of power. To monitor the situation and suggest options, Kennedy created the Executive Committee of the National Security Council (ExComm).

On October 22 Kennedy went on national television to announce the presence of the missiles and the imposition of a naval quarantine. Khrushchev immediately denounced the move as American piracy and declared that he was ordering ships on the high seas to ignore the blockade and proceed to Cuba. Two days later, as the world held its breath, the Soviet flotilla stopped just short of the naval picket line set up some 500 miles east of Cuba. Nevertheless, aerial photographs of the island showed that Soviet technicians were continuing work on the sites.

As tensions continued to mount, Khrushchev sent the president two remarkable and contradictory letters. The first, an absolutely confidential communication, offered to dismantle the Soviet missile sites in return for an American promise not to invade Cuba. A second letter, apparently written under pressure from hardliners in the Kremlin, offered to remove the Soviet MRBMs and IRBMs in return for withdrawal of American Jupiter missiles in Turkey as well as a promise not to invade Cuba. After much discussion, several members of ExComm suggested that the president ignore the second letter and respond to the first. He did just that. In a telegram, the White House proposed that in return for removal of the offensive missiles in Cuba under United Nations supervision, the United States would lift its quarantine and give assurances against an invasion. Determined to allow Khrushchev as much maneuvering room as possible, Kennedy, referring to the missiles in Turkey, indicated that the United States would be willing to discuss other weapons installations at a later date. On October 28, Moscow Radio broadcast Khrushchev's reply. He agreed fully with the president's proposal, thus ignoring the second letter. Horrified that Castro had urged him to launch strategic nuclear missiles against the United States at the height of the crisis, Khrushchev subsequently ordered all nuclear warheads, tactical and strategic, out of Cuba by December 1962. Not surprisingly, the Cuban missile crisis has produced a wealth of scholarship which has focused for the most part on the skill or lack of it with which the Kennedy administration handled the situation, on Soviet motives, and on the Cuban–Soviet dynamic.

Mary S. McAuliffe's *CIA Documents on the Cuban Missile Crisis* (1962) is an early compilation of intelligence data and evaluations – policy deliberations are not covered. McAuliffe highlights the role played by Director John McCone in uncovering Soviet duplicity in placing offensive missiles in Cuba. Chang and Kornbluh's *Cuban Missile Crisis* (1992) is a compilation of documents that provide insight into the ExComm meetings during the crisis. Documents are taken from 18,000 pages that the Archive forced the government to release through an FOI lawsuit.

Any scholar who first begins to dig through historical analysis of the crisis must consult Graham T. Allison's *Essence of Decision* (1971). First published less than a decade after the event, the work includes an engaging narrative of events and provides three models for understanding the crisis, models which are of use to historians and political scientists alike. An expanded second edition by Allison and Zelikow appeared in 1999. Robert Kennedy's *Thirteen Days* (1969) is an insider's account and apologia for the administration. Khrushchev (1974) presents an ideologically biased interpretation of events from the Soviet point of view. However, the work includes useful insights into Khrushchev the man and his personality. Khrushchev (1990) is a more unvarnished and more complete look at the leader and his positions. Relying primarily on Soviet and Cuban press reports for his research, Dinerstein (1976) rejects any single explanation as to why Khrushchev placed missiles in Cuba. Rather, he argues that the political elites within each nation were pursuing different objectives, all of which added up to nuclear confrontation. Uppermost in Khrushchev's mind, according to the author, was to restore the strategic balance of power created by the Kennedy–McNamara nuclear buildup. By placing the missile crisis in the context of the Guatemalan intervention of 1954, the Cuban Revolution, and the Cuban–Soviet alliance, Dinerstein adds valuable insight. A staff-level adviser in the State Department during the crisis, Raymond L. Garthoff (1989) emphasizes the strategic factor, arguing that Khrushchev deliberately upset the balance of power and Kennedy acted justifiably to remove an unacceptable threat to American security. Hilsman's *Cuban Missile Crisis* (1996) is a rehashing of his earlier book, *To Move A Nation* (1967). Hilsman fails to take into account new findings, especially from Soviet archives.

Former State Department legal adviser Abram Chayes (1987) examines the crisis from an institutional and legal perspective. He concludes that international law influenced decision-making during the crisis, especially in ExComm's decision to employ a "quarantine," and that the Kennedy administration desperately wanted to be able to justify its actions in the court of world opinion.

Beschloss (1991) depicts Kennedy as an inexperienced, yet increasingly adept diplomat and Khrushchev as ideological and mistrustful to the point of paranoia. According to Beschloss, Khrushchev concluded in the wake of the Bay of Pigs fiasco that Kennedy was weak, and despite the president's demonstration of spine at Vienna, the impression never left him. By exposing Soviet nuclear supremacy as a myth, Kennedy backed Khrushchev into a corner. The Soviet leader's decision to send missiles to Cuba had much more to do with restoring the strategic balance than with defending Castro's Cuba. Beschloss criticizes both leaders for bringing on the ensuing missile crisis, but gives Kennedy credit for being an effective crisis manager. Brugioni (1991) emphasizes the importance of the photographic evidence of missiles in Cuba to the ultimate showdown. That Brugioni was a photographic interpreter working for the CIA at the National Photographic Interpretation Center during the crisis helps explain the narrowness of his interpretation. Thompson (1992) portrays Kennedy as a man bent on proving himself to his father by demonstrating his toughness in diplomatic crises. He consistently underestimated his enemies: Castro and Khrushchev. Thompson argues that Kennedy knew about the missiles and attempted to set Khrushchev up for a confrontation – a confrontation which, based on US missile superiority, Kennedy was sure to win.

A collection of essays compiled by James A. Nathan (1992) is generally unsympathetic to Kennedy. In that volume, an essay by Laurence Chang accuses the president of misreading Khrushchev's intentions. Rather than signaling a new Soviet initiative in the Cold War, the decision to place the missiles in Cuba was primarily defensive in nature. James Hershberg echoes Chang's arguments and emphasizes that Operation Mongoose could have easily been construed by the Soviets as a precursor to another invasion attempt. Barton Bernstein and Ned Lebow point out that Kennedy's motivations were based in part on the fear of a political loss. Scott (1999) provides a full analysis of the British role during the crisis.

Recently declassified documents relating to the crisis have produced a wealth of new material. Released with *FRUS*, vol. 10 in 1997, the eleventh volume, *FRUS 1961–63, Cuban Missile Crisis and Aftermath*, provides a comprehensive look at the event. The recently declassified transcripts from the ExComm meetings in the White House are not included in the volume, but can be found in May and Zelikow (1997), a compilation that provides a more accurate and comprehensive record of the ExComm debate than any previous account. Based not on telephone records, but on actual meetings, it reveals that Attorney General Robert Kennedy was more hawkish on Cuba than has previously been known. Conversely, Kennedy advisers Robert McNamara and Dean Rusk come off as much less aggressive than they had previously been portrayed. The volume also highlights the importance of Berlin in the minds of ExComm officials as they dealt with the crisis in Cuba. May and Zelikow also provide a glimpse into the administration's pre-crisis invasion plans for Cuba, a topic that is worthy of further research. The editors later published *The Presidential Recordings* (Zelikow et al. 2001) which includes in its third volume a more accurately transcribed version of the missile crisis meetings.

Blight, Allyn, and Welch's *Cuba on the Brink* (1993) is a transcription from a 1992 meeting in Havana of participants in the crisis, including Fidel Castro. The exchange served to confirm that Khrushchev's concern with a US invasion of Cuba, coupled with the desire for a rough strategic balance in nuclear weapons, served as the primary justifications for placing missiles in Cuba. Another revelation coming out of *Cuba on the Brink* was just how close Washington and Moscow came to waging nuclear war. Nuclear warheads had been delivered to Cuba to be deployed on intermediate and short-range missiles in the event of an American invasion; it was clear that Castro would have launched if an invasion had taken place. Blight and Welch's earlier work, *On the Brink* (1989), had downplayed the threat of nuclear war. At a 1989 meeting between Soviet and US participants at Harvard University,

McGeorge Bundy revealed that Kennedy would have accepted a public request by the United Nations to remove missiles in Turkey in exchange for Soviet withdrawal of missiles in Cuba if the Soviets had not unilaterally agreed to their removal within six months. Blight, a psychologist, wrote *The Shattered Crystal Ball* (1992) as an analysis of the findings of the 1989 conference. Blight argues that the crisis perpetuated an adaptive response from the participants, allowing them to act cautiously and prevent a nuclear war.

Mark J. White's *Cuban Missile Crisis* (1996) constitutes a valiant attempt at a balanced approach to the topic. White zeros in on political personalities, including the roles of Sen. Kenneth Keating, Adlai Stevenson, and Dean Acheson, whom White portrays as three of Kennedy's most influential advisers, and through them discusses the various political, strategic, and historical factors acting on the president. White subsequently published a shortened version entitled *Missiles in Cuba* (1997) and also edited *The Kennedys and Cuba* (1999). Nash (1997) focuses on the part played in the crisis by the intermediate-range Jupiter missiles. Nash stresses the issue of credibility in the foreign policymaking decisions of both the Eisenhower and Kennedy administrations and how throughout the missile crisis with Cuba Kennedy and his advisers were cognizant of the merits of a trade involving the Jupiters in Turkey. Kennedy comes off in Nash's account as a leader better suited to deal with short-term crises than with long-term policies.

Fursenko and Naftali (1997), an analysis based on Soviet archives, presents the Soviet and to a degree the Cuban version of events. This study sheds new light on the Soviet–Cuban relationship in the months before the crisis and reveals that the Soviets were well aware of assassination plots on Castro's life by the CIA and the Kennedy administration's updating of a contingency plan for an invasion of the island. Thus, Fursenko and Naftali argue, Khrushchev's decision to defend the island by sending in nuclear missiles is both more credible and understandable than previous scholars have portrayed it. The authors do not, however, simply dismiss the other motivations that historians have attributed to Khrushchev: namely, that he wanted to remind the United States of Soviet power. Fursenko and Naftali also provide insight into Khrushchev's decision to withdraw the missiles. According to the authors, the Soviet leader had already decided to remove them before he was informed of Kennedy's pledge to pull the Jupiters out of Turkey. Thus, it seems, Kennedy's no-invasion pledge had already convinced Khrushchev to back down.

The Kennedy administration responded to the perceived threat of communist infiltration in Latin America in two very different ways. Professing fears that Castro would make good on his promise to spread his revolution throughout Latin America, the administration worked to alleviate poverty and promote social justice throughout the Americas. In the spring of 1961 the president announced an "alliance for progress," a vast aid program designed to speed the modernization process in Latin America. Economic and finance ministers from all American republics except Cuba signed the charter of the Alliance for Progress, which promised $20 billion for economic development from the United States and international lending institutions. Some scholars give the Kennedy administration high marks for vision but fault it in the area of implementation. Others portray the Alliance as a transparent mechanism to perpetuate United States dominance of the hemisphere.

LaFeber (1993) impugns not only the administration of the Alliance, but also the motives that underlay it. For him, the initiative was nothing less than counterrevolutionary. LaFeber criticizes Kennedy, among other US presidents, for ignoring the socioeconomic realities of Central America and choosing to funnel money to the corrupt oligarchies of the region. Thus, Kennedy's "revolution" in Central America served to bolster the status quo and resulted in inevitable discontent among the masses. Similarly, Hanson (1970) sees the Alliance as another form of dollar diplomacy and Blasier (1976) accuses the Kennedy administration of adopting a carrot and stick approach to social change in Latin America. Smith (1994) views the Alliance in a much more positive light. He portrays Kennedy's Alliance as simply another chapter in the ongoing story of United States humanitarianism toward the region. Historian Stephen G. Rabe (1999) analyzes Kennedy's Alliance for Progress and finds that like Eisenhower, Kennedy allowed the communist bogey-man to distort if not undermine his noble quest for social and economic justice in the hemisphere. Rabe also looks at the Kennedy administration's interventions in Haiti and the Dominican Republic and efforts to undermine administrations in Argentina, Brazil, and Guatemala. Rabe examines the role of the Kennedy administration's brainchild, counterinsurgency, which ultimately put anti-communist guns before butter in Latin America.

In the wake of the Cuban missile crisis, Kennedy and his advisers sensed a slight thaw in Soviet–American relations. The Russians had made good on their promise to allow the US navy to inspect ships carrying dismantled missiles out of Cuba. In 1963, as a result of the Cuban confrontation, Kennedy and Khrushchev agreed to an emergency phone and teletype, or "hotline," connection between Washington, DC, and Moscow. In March Kennedy authorized his arms control representatives in Geneva to begin discussions in earnest on a nuclear test-ban treaty. In June he announced that the United States would no longer test nuclear arms in the atmosphere "so long as other states do not do so." Khrushchev was interested. He wanted to relieve the pressure the military budget was exerting on the Soviet Union's slumping economy. On June 10, 1963, Kennedy announced that representatives from Russia, Britain, and the United States would meet in Moscow to discuss a nuclear test-ban treaty. The three delegations reached an agreement within three days and signed a pact that outlawed all nuclear tests in the atmosphere, in outer space, on land, and under water, but allowed them to continue underground.

Seaborg (1981) is a candid account by insider Seaborg, who was chairman of the Atomic Energy Commission from 1961 to 1971. Using mostly British and US archival sources, Oliver (1998) looks at US–British relations on the issue of the nuclear arms limitations. Oliver argues that Macmillan played a key role in US–Soviet negotiations and was instrumental in working out a compromise between the two powers.

Lyndon B. Johnson was in basic agreement with the foreign policies of the Kennedy administration: military preparedness and realistic diplomacy, he believed, would contain communism within its existing bounds. To keep up morale among America's allies and satisfy hardline anti-communists at home, the United States would have to continue to hold fast in Berlin, oppose the admission of communist China to the United Nations, and continue to confront and blockade Cuba. LBJ was aware of the growing split between the Soviet Union and communist China, and the possibilities inherent in it for dividing the communist world. He also took a flexible, even hopeful view of the Soviet Union and Nikita Khrushchev. It was just possible, he believed, that Russia was becoming a status quo power and as such would be a force for stability rather than chaos in the world. The United States must continue its "flexible response" of military aid, economic assistance, and technical/political advice in response to the threat of communism in the developing world. However, there was nothing wrong with negotiating with the Soviets at the same time in an effort to reduce tensions. Insofar as Latin America was concerned, Johnson was an enthusiastic supporter of the Alliance for Progress. As a progressive Democrat, he was drawn to the Schlesinger–Goodwin philosophy of seeking openings to the democratic Left. At the outset of his administration, it appeared that the new president did not buy into the myth of a monolithic communist threat. He was a staunch supporter of trade with Yugoslavia and Poland. To all appearances then, Johnson was a Cold Warrior, but a flexible, pragmatic one.

The Texan felt compelled, for practical as well as political reasons, to carry out the policies of his predecessor. After all, he had not been elected in his own right, and he was acutely sensitive to the dangers of appearing disloyal to Kennedy. Moreover, Johnson felt constrained to demonstrate to the world, allies and antagonists alike, that America's period of grief and self-searching would not diminish its strength or weaken its commitment to its allies. Thus, in his first message to Congress and the nation on November 27, 1963, Johnson assured his audience that he would uphold American commitments "from South Vietnam to West Berlin." And thus did he set himself up to pursue the same contradictory Cold War policies as John F. Kennedy.

A number of works compare the policies of Kennedy and Johnson. One of the main tasks *The Diplomacy of a Crucial Decade* (Kunz 1994) sets for itself is to measure the continuity between the Kennedy and Johnson administrations. An essay in that collection by Robert Schulzinger on Vietnam policy is the strongest in arguing for continuity. Other authors, David Kaiser and William O. Walker among them, stress the shifts in policy under Johnson from Latin America to East Asia. Schertz (1992) looks at the approaches by the Kennedy and Johnson administrations toward Germany and emphasizes the differing perspectives of the two presidents' advisers. Schertz says that Kennedy used global-minded academics including McGeorge Bundy and Arthur Schlesinger, while Johnson listened to State Department Europeanists, among them George Ball and George McGhee, whose main concern was to keep West Germany satisfied and within the fold of the Western alliance.

Led by Vietnam scholars, most members of the academy have been critical of Lyndon Johnson's handling of American foreign policy – but that is changing, particularly among historians who deal with areas other than Southeast Asia. Some have criticized Johnson for his lack of knowledge regarding foreign affairs; he was, they argue, a provincial and a legislative politician. Logevall (1999) depicts Johnson as completely unaware of the subtleties of diplomacy, while Brands (1995) accuses LBJ of at times overreacting and of showing a lack of imagination, especially in regard to Vietnam. Bruce Kuklick (in Winterstein 2000) surmises that Johnson felt culturally inadequate compared to the Kennedys; thus did he rely too heavily on his predecessor's advisers in foreign policy decision-making. Gardner (1995) sees Vietnam and the Johnson foreign policies in general as merely an extension of the president's social philosophy and domestic priorities. Gardner focuses on the interconnectedness of Johnson's war on poverty at home, the military conflict in Vietnam, and the struggle to bring political and economic development to East Asia. All of which, according to Gardner, unraveled simultaneously.

Thomas A. Schwartz and noted Johnson biographer Robert Dallek have called for historians to go beyond Vietnam in their scholarship and focus more on Johnson's other forays into foreign policy. In so doing, they argue, students of the Johnson presidency will find a different, more complex chief executive. Schwartz (2001) looks at LBJ and US relations with Europe and concludes that Johnson was a quick learner and ultimately an astute practitioner of alliance politics in Europe. Schwartz argues that Johnson was not the "ugly American" as he has so often been depicted. Dallek (1999) contends that apart from Vietnam, Johnson's foreign policy contributions were positive, especially given the volatile international environment he faced. Brands (1995) depicts LBJ, outside of Vietnam and the Dominican Republic, as a pragmatic, accomplished practitioner of the diplomatist's art. Cohen and Tucker (1994) is a compilation of essays examining Johnson's policies toward the Dominican Republic, the Western European allies, Vietnam, and the Middle East, using a traditional diplomatic history approach. The contributors remain unconvinced about the man, if not his policies. As a whole the essays depict Johnson as uninterested in foreign affairs and content to form policy based on his advisers' recommendations. As a result the essays focus more on the president's advisers, their philosophies, the bureaucratic conflicts over policymaking, and the histories of America's relationship with the regions in question than they do on the person of Johnson.

As Dallek, Brands, and Schwartz have pointed out, at the same time Johnson was struggling with the complex issues of Southeast Asia, he had to deal with a whole host of other areas and problems: rioting in Panama, chaos in the Dominican Republic, a major outbreak of fighting in the Middle East, the ongoing campaign to achieve détente with the Soviet Union, and the dual effort to either oust or co-opt Fidel Castro. None of these topics was more complex or troublesome than Latin America.

The conditions in Latin America that had prompted the Kennedy administration to launch the Alliance for Progress and search for "openings on the Left" continued to persist. Although some republics had taken tentative steps down the road to democracy, most were still ruled by military strong men, who represented the army, the large landowners, and foreign capitalists, particularly US capitalists. Huge economic gaps separated tiny elites from an impoverished peasantry and proletariat.

Lyndon Johnson was sensitive to the plight of the Latin masses, but he was more sensitive to the continuing threat Fidel Castro posed to his administration – in a political if not a strategic sense. Johnson could not forget how much public support the GOP had attracted by accusing Kennedy and the Democrats of failing to liberate Cuba. The direction that his Latin American policy would take became apparent when he appointed Thomas Mann, a Texas lawyer and former ambassador to Mexico, as assistant secretary of state for Latin American affairs. A strident anti-communist, Mann was committed to maintaining political stability in the republics to the south, ensuring that they would continue to be lucrative investment fields for US capitalists. When revolution erupted in the Dominican Republic, toppling the existing government and producing chaos in the capital city, it was Mann's philosophy that prevailed.

The causes of the Dominican Republic's many troubles were varied, but most were rooted in the thirty-year dictatorship of Rafael Leonidas Trujillo Molina. Trujillo had brutally suppressed all opposition, turned the army into his personal palace guard, and ravaged his country's fragile economy. Then, in the summer of 1961, assassins shot him in the head. His family tried to perpetuate his tyranny without him, but failed and then fled into exile. In December 1962, the Dominicans elected the liberal intellectual, Juan Bosch, to the presidency. Seven months later, a military coup overthrew him, its leaders charging that he was too tolerant of communists and Marxism. Despite support from the Johnson administration for the new government of Donald Reid Cabral and the presence of some 2,500 Americans on the island, stability eluded the Dominicans. Drought, widespread unemployment, strikes, sabotage, and the continuing opposition from dissidents kept the country in constant turmoil. From exile in Puerto Rico, where he was employed as a college professor, Juan Bosch directed the disruptive activities of the Dominican Revolutionary Party (PRD).

The spring of 1965 found the Dominican military deeply divided. A minority was devoted to Bosch's return, but the majority regarded him as a dangerous revolutionary who would "open the door to the communists" and, more to the point, do away with the military's privileges. After a general uprising led by the PRD in Santo Domingo, the military attacked Bosch strongholds that were, in the minds of the military, seedbeds of communist agitation. The attacks inflamed the population, which flooded into the streets in response to calls from the PRD. Santo Domingo teetered on the edge of chaos. Panicked, Ambassador W. Tapley Bennett urgently requested the dispatch of a contingent of marines to protect American lives and to thwart a possible Castroite takeover of the island. Johnson and his advisers quickly concurred and soon 20,000 troops were occupying Santo Domingo. The president went on television and informed the American people that another Cuba seemed likely in the Dominican Republic. "We don't intend to sit here in our rocking chair with our hands folded and let the communists set up any governments in the Western hemisphere," he declared.

Much of the earliest writing on the Dominican crisis was by participants who seek to defend Washington's policies and by reporters, many of whom were veterans of the Latin American beat, who were extremely dubious concerning administration claims about the potential for a Castroite takeover in the republic. More recently, scholars have attempted a more detached stance. While faulting Johnson for acting unilaterally and for exaggerating the extent of communist influence, they see his actions in the context of the Cold War, early reports from Santo Domingo, and the heritage of the Bay of Pigs, as not unreasonable.

Two works examine the state of the Cuban Revolution during the Johnson administration. Halperin (1981) is essentially an examination of the speeches of Fidel Castro in the mid-1960s. Halperin concludes that by the time Johnson was elected in his own right in 1964, Castro had become a stooge of the Soviet Union and had wrecked the Cuban economy. Halperin does not see Castro as a product of Cuban history, but rather as an opportunist who seized upon Marxism-Leninism as a device to serve his own personal ambition. Like many liberals within the Cuban exile community, Halperin resents Castro and the revolution for not living up to their promise. Bunck (1994) argues that Fidel Castro and his political cohorts have failed to promote a viable culture of the revolution. Only attempts to incorporate an already existent sports culture have succeeded, according to Bunck, and that is precisely because such a culture already existed. When Cuban leaders have attempted to create and mold cultural attitudes toward youth, women, and labor, Bunck says, they have failed.

Wiarda and Kryzanek's *Dominican Republic* (1982) is a general history of the island nation. The authors discuss the nation's geography, culture, economy, and political institutions and argue that based on development-related issues, the Dominican Republic represented a microcosm of change in lesser developed nations around the world. The Dominicans' history of foreign intervention, dictatorship, economic exploitation, civil war, class tension, and relative stability symbolizes the Third World experience. Bosch (1965) presents a version of events during the Dominican crisis from the perspective of the left-leaning, ousted president. Bosch offers a critical analysis of Dominican society and politics and the role the military has played in Dominican history. Martin's *Overtaken by Events* (1966) is a look at events from the perspective of a former US ambassador to the country. The work is highly readable – Martin had worked as a speechwriter for Adlai Stevenson and John F. Kennedy. Martin details day-to-day events but leaves out any controversial or heretofore secret information about US involvement in the fall of Trujillo. Thus, the work is a sanitized version of the Dominican crisis from the perspective of a high-ranking State Department official. General Bruce Palmer, Jr. commanded the military forces in the Dominican Republic and provides a relatively balanced account of the operation. Palmer (1989) ultimately defends the US government's use of the military to ensure that a second communist regime would not take hold in the hemisphere. Draper's *Dominican Revolt* (1968) is an account based on magazine articles the author published in 1965 and 1966 during and after the crisis. Draper criticizes the US intervention and the tendency of Washington to raise the specter of communism wherever in the hemisphere instability occurs. Similarly, Slater (1970) argues that the communist threat was minimal. He also criticizes the US policymakers for leaving the Dominican military intact. José A. Moreno was a Jesuit priest in the Dominican Republic working on his doctoral dissertation when the civil war broke out. Much of his brief work (Moreno 1970) details what it was like to live in the midst of events. Abraham Lowenthal (1970) was also a witness to events on the island and attempts to retell what he saw. Reflecting Graham Allison's work, Lowenthal discounts the rational-actor policy model as a conceptual framework for understanding the Dominican intervention. Instead, he argues, officials on many levels, acting upon their fears, ambitions, and inaccurate assumptions, were responsible for events. Uruguayan journalist Carlos María Gutiérrez's *Dominican Republic* (1972) consists of a series of vignettes of Dominican life. The work's chief value lies in its interviews with prominent Dominican leftists, including Juan Bosch.

Historian William O. Walker III (1999) emphasizes Johnson's obsession with Fidel Castro in explaining his Dominican policy. So does Peter Felton (1999), who argues that this preoccupation shaped Johnson's policy toward Latin America as a whole. Felton notes Johnson's reliance on advisers and contacts throughout the crisis, including Supreme Court Justice Abe Fortas, who regularly communicated with Juan Bosch. In so doing Johnson partially insulated himself from liberal criticism within and without, enabling him to weather the crisis and make American policy stick. Gleijeses (1979) utilizes Dominican sources in discussing the various political factions that emerged in Dominican politics after 1961. His book is an expanded and revised version of the author's doctoral dissertation at the University of Geneva, which was written in French. Gleijeses is meticulous in his detail and provides a useful chronological survey of events. He is generally critical of the Kennedy and Johnson administrations' involvement in affairs and concludes that the opportunists won the day.

Gleijeses (2002) analyzes the US and Cuban foreign policies toward Africa. Gleijeses identifies Cuban policy as separate from Soviet objectives on the continent and that the Cubans were not acting as a Soviet pawn as US policymakers believed. Gleijeses' access to Cuban documents and oral histories makes this work a significant addition to the literature of US–Cuban relations.

There are still nationalist historians willing to defend Johnson's Dominican policy and intervention in general. Smith (1994) downplays the United States' imperialistic designs on the Caribbean and argues that US policy toward the region has been based, in keeping with the Monroe Doctrine, on excluding European imperialism from the hemisphere. Blechman and Kaplan (1978) argue that the use of military forces to achieve political objectives historically has been successful.

Much recent scholarship has argued that Johnson's anti-communism was political rather than philosophical and emotional. The Dominican intervention stemmed from his fear that the GOP would accuse him of presiding over the creation of another Cuba. Similarly, he remembered Joe McCarthy's vicious and profitable attacks on Truman and Acheson for "losing" China to the communists. In support of their interpretation, these historians cite the fact that while pursuing bellicose policies in Southeast Asia and Central America, Johnson worked quietly to further the policy of détente that had begun during the last days of the Kennedy administration. Nikita Khrushchev was suddenly deposed in October 1964, but his successors, Leonid Brezhnev and Alexei N. Kosygin, indicated their willingness to work on improved relations with the West. In 1964 Russian and American diplomats hammered out an agreement providing for the exchange of scholars, artists, and scientists. They inaugurated a direct air service between Washington, DC, and Moscow. President Johnson took up the cause of nuclear non-proliferation. Following three years of difficult negotiations, the Soviet Union, the United States, Great Britain, and 58 other nations signed the historic document. It constrained the nuclear powers from transferring atomic weapons technology to third parties and committed the non-nuclear powers to refrain from manufacturing or receiving nuclear weapons.

America's North Atlantic allies generally welcomed the Johnson administration's efforts to achieve détente, but a number of allies believed that they did not go far enough. At the time NATO was losing its cohesiveness due in no small part to the nationalism of France's Charles de Gaulle. The French leader advocated an independent course for Europe, made overtures toward various communist governments, and announced that his country no longer wanted to be tied to an alliance dominated by the United States and Great Britain, which he called non-European powers.

Thus, de Gaulle withdrew France from NATO in 1966 and continued to block Britain's entry into the Common Market. Trade relations between the United States and the Common Market remained strong, however, as a round of trade negotiations cut tariffs on goods traded between the United States and the Common Market countries by an average of 35 percent.

The body of historical literature on NATO is massive. Cleveland (1966), Beaufre (1966), and Fox and Fox (1967) were all written during the Johnson administration and reflect the collective desire among government officials for a period of détente between the United States and Soviet Union. They all focus on US leadership within NATO and the other members' ambivalence concerning that situation. The authors emphasize that given NATO was a military alliance and that the threat posed by the Soviet Union was lessening, the fractures that were developing within the alliance system were inevitable and not unhealthy. Cleveland and Beaufre both believe that détente depended upon the continuation of a stable strategic balance. Fox and Fox discuss the problems inherent in NATO to the United States, its dominant member, and focus on the decision-making process within the United States and how it affected NATO. Beer (1969) examines the process of integration within the organizational structure of the alliance system. Beer sees NATO as more of a traditional alliance than something radically new. Kaplan (1988) is a general history of NATO, covering its origins to 1986. Because the United States played the leading role in the founding of NATO and because it alone possessed the military might to protect the region from Soviet encroachment, its dominance has been inevitable and indeed necessary to the existence of the alliance. Kaplan traces the evolution of NATO and demonstrates how each crisis shaped its organizational structure and objectives. A not inconsiderable side benefit is that NATO has served as an umbrella under which nations like Germany and France could develop supranational relations. Kaplan admits, however, that the dominating role of the United States has to a degree retarded European integration. Kugler (1994) is a detailed history of NATO from its founding in 1949 to the early 1990s. Almost three times the length of Kaplan's general history, Kugler chronicles the political battles of the alliance and includes more quantitative data, including details on military and defense budgets. A former NATO planner at the Pentagon, Kugler calls for an expansion of NATO in both membership and mission in the future.

Richard Barnet's *The Alliance – America, Europe and Japan* (1983) tackles an immense subject and provides both fact and analysis. He argues that the United States became the dominant power in Europe to prevent the continent from being dominated by the Soviet Union or Germany rather than to co-opt European prosperity and enrich itself. Barnet attempts to weave personalities, such as Adenauer and MacArthur, into a narrative of the major events of the post-World War II era. Grosser (1980) turns standard interpretations on their head. He describes a NATO that features France and Germany as its primary members, although his work focuses on their relations with the United States. To Grosser, Britain's role was frequently peripheral.

Lundestad (1998) argues that the United States took the lead in European integration because France and Great Britain were too weak to do so. The United States supported European integration and cooperative ventures such as the Common Market and the European Coal and Steel Community, but then during the

1960s and early 1970s shifted its focus to increased European defense spending. In keeping with his anti-New Left, corporatist position, Lundestad attributes de Gaulle's aggressiveness to his desire for French glory, not commercial imperatives. The economic argument is advanced by Moravcsik (1998). Burk and Stokes (1999) analyze the strengths and weaknesses of the transatlantic alliance. The essays in their collection deal with the language of power, key personalities, financial and trade ties among members, and the concept of a special relationship.

During the 1960s much of the debate within NATO dealt with the issue of massive retaliation vs. flexible response. That is, should the allies continue to rely on the threat of a massive nuclear strike to defend the West, or should it include conventional warfare or even limited nuclear conflict in their list of viable options? Stromseth (1988) is a comprehensive study developed from the author's doctoral dissertation on the origins of and arguments over flexible response. Haftendorn (1996) describes the diplomatic wrangling among Alliance members that led to the new strategy of flexible response, which according to the author, held the European alliance together through the 1970s. Along with flexible response, the Nuclear Planning Group gave the non-nuclear members of NATO a greater say in decision-making and resulted in a less US-dominated organization.

Historian Thomas Schwartz (1999) considers Johnson's efforts in Europe as one of his most important foreign policy achievements. Schwartz maintains that Johnson learned on the job and grew more diplomatically astute with time. Johnson balanced domestic forces, both political and economic, with international pressures from the European allies. According to Schwartz, LBJ "recognized how to assemble cross-national coalitions and work towards his goals and objectives." In contrast to his handling of Vietnam, Johnson's diplomacy in Europe was ultimately successful.

Dobson (1995) traces the Anglo-American relationship from the late nineteenth century through the majority of the twentieth century. Dobson sees the 1960s and 1970s as a time of transition in the connection as each nation concentrated on different goals – for Britain, joining the EEC was most important, while the Americans were consumed with Vietnam and fighting communists. However, the 1980s witnessed a return to the "special relationship" between the two nations similar to that which existed during World War II. Sean Greenwood's *Britain and the Cold War* (2000) is one of the few accounts of Britain's role in the East–West conflict dominated by the United States and Soviet Union. The majority of this slim volume chronicles British concerns from 1945 to 1956, when Britain's contribution to the East–West dynamic was much greater than it was to be later.

Lacouture (1990, 1991) provides an objective biography of one of France's most influential leaders. Lacouture argues that de Gaulle's popularity and mythologized life were very much products of his own creation. His two-volume work begins with a diary entry by the teenage de Gaulle forecasting his leading a French army to greatness. Lacouture takes the reader through de Gaulle's first departure from power in 1946, his "years in the desert," his return to power in 1958, and his departure ten years later. Grosser (1967) is a sound analysis of Gaullist aims and methods in foreign policy. Grosser argues that the Fifth Republic's foreign policy was a continuation of the Fourth's. While de Gaulle's tactics may have differed from one to the other, his objective – equality for France within the Atlantic system – did not. Newhouse (1970) is a study of Gaullist foreign policy toward Great Britain and the

United States. Newhouse explicates de Gaulle's concept of nationality and deter-
mines that it was impossible for the United States and Great Britain to negotiate
with de Gaulle in terms of alliance politics. To de Gaulle, geography and history
were more important than ideology or strategic theory as factors in determining
foreign policy. De Carmoy (1970) accepts Grosser and Newhouse's explanation of
de Gaulle's motives, but criticizes him for not being more successful in his efforts to
increase France's global, political presence.

Political scientist Edward L. Morse's *Foreign Policy and Interdependence in
Gaullist France* (1973) comprises another early examination of de Gaulle's foreign
policy. Because of the global trend toward interdependence, Morse opines, the
General's policy was doomed to failure. A number of conditions allowed France to
assert its independence in the early 1960s: the East–West détente that followed the
Berlin crisis, America's ongoing commitment to protect France, and de Gaulle's
leadership in the EEC. Eventually, however, conditions changed, and the fragility of
the French policy of grandeur became glaringly apparent. Finally, Morse argues, US
disillusionment in Vietnam and the Soviet incursion into Czechoslovakia finished off
de Gaulle's dream of a new France. America's commitment to French defense was
uncertain at the very time when the threat of Soviet incursion into Western Europe
appeared more likely. French strategic vulnerability stood fully revealed. Kohl (1971)
argues that the goals of de Gaulle's foreign policy were basically contradictory. He
wanted to lead the European community in arbitrating between East and West,
while at the same time rejecting the American leadership that in many ways served
as the glue for that community. He spends much time describing efforts by French
leaders to wield the issue of control over nuclear weapons as a political weapon
against both the Soviet Union and the other members of NATO. Vaïsse (1998)
chronicles French foreign, colonial, and European policies during de Gaulle's second
stint as president. Based on newly released documents, Vaïsse's work focuses on the
president's policies toward Algeria. The author praises de Gaulle for his efforts in
behalf of decolonization, but criticizes de Gaulle's failed overtures toward the Soviet
Union and Germany. The French leader's attempts to create a "European Europe"
by blocking Britain's entrance into the EEC only served to prevent European
integration.

Though a minority, several scholars view Gaullist foreign policies in a positive
light. Harrison (1981) focuses on de Gaulle's response to the NATO alliance.
Harrison argues that de Gaulle's policies were appropriate and reasonable and that
they were successful in no small part because they were so popular with the French
populace. To Harrison, the aims of the Fourth Republic concerning security, the
desire for international prestige, and military superiority over Germany were consistent with de Gaulle's goals. Gordon (1993) assesses the Gaullist legacy on French
military policies and strategies from 1958 to 1992 and finds a remarkable continuity
despite changing world politics. Gaullist foreign policy helped maintain a healthy
distance between the United States and Western Europe and paved the way for a
truly independent European Union.

The most recent and in many ways the most balanced chronicle of the Franco-
American dialogue is Costigliola (1992). In this survey of the political and cultural
relationship between the United States and France from World War II to 1991,
Costigliola concludes that the United States wanted a French ally that would toe the

line, while the French were determined to pursue an independent course. With the return of de Gaulle to power in 1958, the French became increasingly assertive in foreign policy matters and presented a series of challenges to US policy. Costigliola explains how and why the unilateralist policy of de Gaulle was frequently ineffective in securing de Gaulle's objectives, but was nonetheless wildly popular with the French populace. Interestingly, in times of crisis Gaullist policies assumed a much more multilateral and dependent tone. The alliance between the two nations, the author demonstrates, has been complicated by their divergent and often competing cultures. French scholar Frédéric Bozo (2001) examines the second presidency of de Gaulle (1958–69), adding important detail but little new insight.

A number of scholars have described the Johnson administration's policy toward Europe as one of double containment – of the Soviet Union and Germany. They point out that many Europeans – and Americans for that matter – were as worried about a rebirth of German imperialism as they were about Soviet expansionism. The key for the US was to keep a democratized and healthy West Germany within the NATO fold without arming it to the point that it threatened its other allies and the Soviet Union. More often than not, the issue boiled down to the degree Germany would have control over its own nuclear force.

For a forthright defense of American policy toward the Federal Republic, see Bark and Gress (1989), the second part of a two-volume work on West Germany by the authors. Bark and Gress argue that the Soviet threat to the republic was real; they see the integration of West Germany into the Western world as crucial to the preservation of democracy and prosperity in Europe, and view West German democracy as one of the great achievements of the Cold War era. McGhee (1989), a memoir of McGhee's life in Bonn from 1963 to 1968, also renders a positive verdict, but with qualifications. He doesn't hesitate to provide details on West Germany's growing pains and the problems they caused in the republic's relations with the United States. McGhee views past policy failures as a result of individual incompetence and sees a strong future bond between Germans and Americans.

For the double containment policy, see Hanrieder (1989). In this survey of the German–American relationship in the post-World War II period, Hanrieder concludes that American policy preserved the Federal Republic from Soviet domination but at the same time kept it from plotting an independent foreign policy. Schwartz (1991) is a thoroughly researched account of US–German relations from 1949 to 1955 with the mission of John J. McCloy as US member of the Allied high commission to the Federal Republic of Germany as its organizing principle. Schwartz commends McCloy and his colleagues for successfully pursuing the double containment strategy, while managing at the same time to hold the Western alliance together. Bird (1992) offers a more skeptical, critical view of McCloy. Lest one be tempted to portray the proconsul as the personification of American ideals, it should be noted that he supported the Japanese–American internment camps and argued against the bombing of railroad lines leading to German concentration camps. Bird describes McCloy as a man who believed that almost any act could be justified in the name of national security.

For German–American cultural relations and their impact on the strategic relationship, see Ninkovich (1995). Hans-Peter Schwarz (1991) and Prittie (1979) provide valuable insights into the personalities and goals of the men who ruled in

Bonn during the 1960s. In his later years as a statesman, Schwarz argues, Adenauer pursued two sometimes-conflicting goals: the preservation of German security and the removal of Germany from the center of Cold War intrigue in Europe. Prittie compares the five "velvet chancellors" who have held sway in postwar Germany favorably to forerunner Otto von Bismarck. He argues that the Germans have learned the lessons of history and are capable and ready to reenter the Western fold, which for the most part already embraces them.

Though Johnson's dual commitment to guns and butter posed a threat to the economic health of the nation by the end of the decade, America prospered during the 1960s. Some historians of international economics argue that that prosperity was due in no small part to the administration's efforts to control the outward flow of gold, maintain a reasonable balance of payments, and shore up the international trading system. Others maintain that Johnson and his aides were merely fiddling while Rome smoldered, and then after the administration's departure, burst into flames with massive payments deficits and runaway inflation.

Coombs (1976) is a memoir of Coombs' fifteen years (1961–75) as Senior Vice President responsible for all US Treasury and Federal Reserve operations in the international gold and foreign exchange markets. Coombs provides a colorful and generally uncritical account (an exception being the Nixon administration) of members of the international finance community and the crises that they handled. He also makes clear that one should not ignore or underestimate the forces of the market, nor the political character of monetary policy. Weil and Davidson (1970) trace international finance from Bretton Woods to the late 1960s. Weil and Davidson's non-technical treatise criticizes de Gaulle for attempting to build up French gold reserves and blame US military ventures for the US payment deficits and the resulting inflation. Anderson and Hazelton (1986) is an analysis of fiscal, monetary, wage-price, and foreign economic policy of the Johnson administration. Anderson, a political scientist, and Hazelton, an economist, have put together this work as part of the Administrative History of the Johnson Presidency series. The authors discuss the personalities and the institutions that aided the president in the development and implementation of economic policy, a policy they portray in a generally favorable light. Barry Eichengreen's *Globalizing Capital* (1996) details the evolution of the system from the bimetallic to the gold standard, to the Bretton Woods system, to the mechanism of floating exchange rates among major currencies, to the European efforts to create a monetary union. James (1996) analyzes international monetary issues from the creation of the International Monetary Fund (IMF) and the World Bank at Bretton Woods in 1944 through the 1990s. James was selected by the IMF to write its history; his conclusions about various multilateral efforts, if not Washington's role in them, are generally positive. He points out that international trade has evolved toward a rules-based system, which is epitomized by the World Trade Organization, while the international monetary system moved in the opposite direction toward flexible cooperation. The special treatment that the United States received under Bretton Woods because of the preeminence of its currency distorted the system and was partially responsible for its demise.

Ilgen (1985) argues that autonomy and interdependence in the economic sphere are incompatible but that both have been objectives of US policy. When conflict has inevitably arisen out of the dual policy, the desire for autonomy in domestic economic management has generally won out over the desire for economic interdependence. Thus, Ilgen contends, the United States' economic nationalism in the face of increasing global interdependence has worked to the nation's economic disadvantage. Kunz (1997) traces the economic diplomacy of the United States from the Marshall Plan to the disintegration of the Soviet Union. She argues that the United States had its cake and ate it too. That is, the United States built a permanent military establishment that ultimately triumphed over communism, while experiencing unprecedented prosperity at home. According to Kunz, foreign and domestic economic policy went hand in hand with containment strategy as military spending primed the pump of the American economy. Zeiler (1992) argues that the Kennedy–Johnson administrations demonstrated a solid grasp of tariff and protectionist issues as well as an appreciation of the economic interests of America's allies. Zeiler argues that Kennedy and subsequently Johnson embraced the Wilsonian vision of a liberalized world economy and viewed GATT as a mechanism to realize that vision. Ultimately, however, strategic interests – the desire to create a strong and economically dynamic Atlantic alliance as a bastion against communism – was the driving force behind Washington's approach to the Trade Expansion Act and the Kennedy Round of the General Agreement on Tariffs and Trade (GATT).

Funigiello (1988) examines why and how the United States imposed trade sanctions on the Soviet Union, communist China, and Eastern Europe throughout the Cold War. Funigiello concludes that the sanctions were an unqualified failure. Not only was the policy wrong headed, it was never truly enforced. As a result, Soviet and satellite economic power grew apace in the 1960s and 1970s. Those federal bureaucrats whose task it was to promote international trade supported loose restrictions on commerce with the enemy nations; so too did those politicians and diplomats who believed that increased trade promoted peace. Those whose primary concern was security and strategic advantage, along with anti-communist ideologues, were the chief advocates of trade restrictions. The latter lost out to the former. Funigiello praises Eisenhower for his "bridge-building" approach to Eastern Europe. Eisenhower did not want to isolate communist nations by refusing to trade with them; closer trade ties would in the end loosen the ties binding Eastern Europe to the Soviet Union. (See also Mastanduno 1992.)

Treverton (1978) discusses the conflict between the United States and Germany over the Troop Offset issue in 1966–7. The arrangement called for the West German government to buy an agreed amount of US military equipment to help offset the cost of stationing US troops inside West Germany. The Federal Republic dragged its feet, resisting the linkage of troops to America's deteriorating balance of payments position. Either it was in the United States' strategic interests to defend Western Europe or it was not, Bonn argued. Frustrated, the Johnson administration linked the two, blaming the threat to withdraw on isolationists and fiscal conservatives in Congress. At the same time, the Germans, who wanted US troops on German soil, were becoming frustrated with US threats to withdraw their forces in the absence of Germany's reluctance to pay for them.

As noted previously, the bedrock of Johnson's European policy was détente with the Soviet Union. One of the keys to better relations, policymakers recognized, was a cooling off of the dangerous arms race that Sputnik and the McNamara arms buildup had touched off. Scholars are now recognizing that the serious negotiations concerning limits on the construction and deployment of new weapons systems and eventually the destruction of existing stockpiles that culminated in the late 1980s and 1990s began during Johnson's administration. They differ as to how effective those negotiations were and how truly committed the avowedly anti-communist administration was to their success.

Seaborg (1987) chronicles the progress made toward arms control under the Johnson administration. As former chairman of the Atomic Energy Commission, Seaborg is able to provide an insider's look into bureaucratic and inter-agency struggles and the conflicts during the early 1960s between the United States and its allies over the Multilateral Force, the negotiation with the Soviets that produced the Non-Proliferation Treaty of 1968, and the origins of the Strategic Arms Limitation Talks. Seaborg provides a useful if uncritical survey of Johnson's arms control policy and the whole arms control process. Richelson (1990) describes the origins of the US reconnaissance satellite program in the early 1950s to the present day. Richelson blends technical details with bureaucratic politics and a history of various intelligence estimates.

Ikenberry (2001) argues that victors can win the peace by showing strategic restraint. His work constitutes a sweeping justification for the policy of détente, including that practiced by the Johnson administration. Conventional wisdom holds that victors have the opportunity to reshape the structure of the international system in ways that benefit their own strategic interests. A true Wilsonian, Ikenberry argues that liberal internationalism, which manifested itself at Vienna in 1815 and after World War II, has not weakened the United States, but rather strengthened it as well as helping less powerful nations.

Lyndon Johnson hoped to end his administration with a Soviet–American summit conference that would give substance to the policy of détente. That hope was shattered by the Soviet invasion of Czechoslovakia in late 1968. Valenta (1979) examines the Soviet decision to intervene in Czechoslovakia. Valenta employs a bureaucratic-politics paradigm, which proves as useful in examining Soviet diplomatic decision-making as American. He shows that sharp differences existed within the Kremlin, and that different personalities and power centers favored intervention or non-intervention based on self-interest, political perception, and ideology. From the outset, the Johnson administration made it clear to Prague and Moscow that the American response would be limited to official protests.

Kovrig (1991) surveys US policy toward the Soviet satellites from World War II to their demise in 1989. Kovrig, who apparently failed to take advantage of recently released documentary sources, argues that US policy as a whole was flexible and well carried out. He does criticize Washington for not trying to bluff the Soviets into abandoning their plans to invade Czechoslovakia in 1968, though the author's criticism is a bit understated. Kovrig argues that when dealing with the Soviet satellite states, the US government inevitably placed security interests ahead of economic and human rights issues.

At a time when alliances with the Western world were strained, events in the Middle East would present an even more formidable task to US policymakers. In the aftermath of World War II the United States had defined its role as protector of the non-communist world from Soviet and subsequently Chinese imperialism and from the scourge of Marxism-Leninism. With the growing importance of such non-

Cold War issues as anti-colonialism and the socioeconomic gap between the northern and southern hemispheres, America's ability to act as arbiter of world affairs diminished sharply. The United States would have to pick and choose, George Kennan and others argued, intervening in those areas that bore directly on its national interest strategically and economically defined. Vietnam, some scholars have argued, made pursuit of such a rational course impossible. Indeed, America's inability to prevent the outbreak of the Six Day War in the Middle East in 1967 and the polarization that followed indicated just how out of balance United States foreign policy was in the 1960s. Given America's increasing dependence on the Middle East for oil and its special relationship with the new state of Israel, critics argued, its interests were far more compelling in that area of the world than in Southeast Asia.

Like its predecessors, the Johnson administration had to maneuver between the Scylla of American dependency on Middle Eastern oil and the Charybdis of US sympathy for Israel, a sympathy made all the stronger by Israel's assumption of the role as the region's principal bastion against communist imperialism. A number of important works explore this conundrum generally and specifically as it related to the Johnson administration.

Spiegel (1985) discusses decision-making in regard to the Arab–Israeli conflict within the US bureaucracy. He concludes that the pro-Israeli lobby and the petroleum interests have held less sway on US policymaking than it appears. Kelly (1980) provides a masterful account of the modern history of the Middle East, its connection with the West, and the development of the oil market. Kelly delves into the conflict of cultures between the Islamic Middle East and the Christian West, as well as the differences that exist among the region's diverse peoples. Kelly emphasizes the importance of history to the peoples and institutions of the region, thereby challenging the validity of constructs such as the bureaucratic decision-making model and international relations theories. Peter Grose's *Israel in the Mind of America* (1983) is a general history of America's role in the creation of the state of Israel.

In May 1967 Nasser persuaded the United Nations to withdraw the peacekeeping force that had been inserted between Egyptian and Israeli forces following the Suez imbroglio. As a result, the two adversaries faced each other directly across a huge demilitarized zone for the first time since 1956. Nasser moved quickly to fill the void. He ordered his army and air force to occupy the Sinai Peninsula, which it did, in the process seizing the strategically crucial town of Sharm el-Sheikh, which overlooked the Gulf of Aqaba. This waterway, separating Egypt from the Arabian Peninsula, was Israel's only outlet to the Indian Ocean. At the same time, PLO fedayeen guerrillas launched attacks against Jewish settlements from their bases in the Sinai as well as from Jordan and Syria.

Convinced that the front-line states and the PLO intended to attack, the Israelis decided to stage a preemptive strike. On June 6 the Israeli air force flew across the Mediterranean to avoid Egyptian radar and then attacked from the north. Catching Egypt's planes on the ground, the Israelis virtually destroyed Nasser's air force. This scene was repeated in Jordan and Syria. For the next six days, the Israeli army followed up on this initial success, invading and occupying the Sinai, the old city of Jerusalem, the West Bank of the Jordan, and the strategic Golan Heights just inside Syria's border. With the capture of Sharm el-Sheikh, the Israelis once again controlled an outlet to the Arabian Gulf and through it to the Indian Ocean.

Moscow and Washington stayed in close contact throughout the crisis using the "hotline" telephone, lessening the chance that the Six Day War would escalate into a great power confrontation. Indeed, it was the Soviet Union that on June 11 introduced and ushered through a ceasefire resolution through the UN Security Council. When that measure passed and the combatants signed off on it, the fighting came to an end. In November the Security Council approved Resolution 242, which was designed to bring about a negotiated settlement to the ongoing Middle East crisis. It called for a multilateral guarantee of Israel's borders in exchange for a return of the territory seized in the Six Day War. In addition, Israel would enjoy free access to "regional waterways" (Nasser had ordered the Suez Canal blocked with sunken ships shortly after Israel attacked) in the area, whereas the Palestinians could look forward to "a just settlement of the refugee problem," a provision they interpreted to mean the conversion of what used to be called Palestine (Israel and parts of the current state of Jordan) into a multinational state, including both Jews and Palestinians.

The United States supported Resolution 242 but was at the same time extremely sympathetic to Israel's fears concerning its security. The Jewish state insisted that the Arab nations would have to extend formal recognition and give guarantees before the land seized in the Six Day War was returned. As the United States continued to replace Israeli military equipment and to subsidize the Israeli economy, an angry Nasser severed diplomatic ties with Washington. When Israel refused to evacuate the Sinai and return the Gaza Strip, the West Bank, and the Golan Heights, Moscow severed relations with Tel Aviv. The US government and various third parties attempted mediation but with no success

Predictably, the debate over the wisdom of American policy toward Israel and the Arabs during the 1960s has been sharp and at times rancorous. Johnson and his advisers have their defenders. Pro-Zionists defend the administration's acquiescence in Israeli gains, although some argue that US aid was too little, too late. Apologists emphasize Nasser's mindless nationalism and Soviet meddling. Others criticize the administration for not anticipating the Egyptian seizure and the subsequent Israeli response, and for unwittingly abetting the crisis. There are of course scholars who argue that American support for Israel against the Palestinians flew in the face of traditional US ideals, especially respect for human rights and the right of national self-determination. They tend to blame failed American policy on the Johnson administration's blind anti-communism and/or its subservience to the Jewish lobby in the United States.

Safran (1969) discusses the origins of the conflict and stresses the role played by clashing nationalisms and the massive arms buildup in the region. Almost half of the work deals with the Six Day War and its causes and consequences. It is particularly strong on the motives of the Great Powers. Safran's survey leaves many questions still unanswered, but provides an informative and comprehensive narrative of events. O'Neill (1978) discusses the Palestinian effort to defeat Israel by military means and the impact of Israel's policy of retaliation on the Palestinian Liberation Organization and the Arab world in general. Schulze (1999) is a brief (148-page) chronology of events. The author begins with a look at Arab and Jewish nationalism and deals with the major issues affecting war and peace in the Middle East from Israel's creation to the late 1990s.

Churba (1977) emphasizes Israel's strategic importance to the United States and criticizes the United States for having appeased the Arab nations. The author argues that it was in the United States' interest to support Israel in its campaign to keep its Arab neighbors weak and off balance lest, among other things, Soviet influence in the area become overwhelming. Churba opposes a Palestinian state because he believes that its creation would lead to a war between the Israelis and the Palestinians allied with the Soviets. Safran (1978) discusses the recent history of the Jewish nation, including its founding, its demographic, social, and economic problems, and its relationship with the United States. Safran maintains that the Six Day War marked a turning point in the Israeli–American relationship, converting the latter into a full-fledged ally of the former. Schoenbaum (1993) chronicles the US–Israeli special relationship, but argues that close ties were not always the norm. Before and after what Schoenbaum terms the "golden age" of US–Israeli relations from 1961 to 1973, American officials frequently evinced disapproval of Israeli policies. The author goes beyond politics and analyzes popular culture and interaction between the Jewish communities of the two nations. Klinghoffer (1999) blames US involvement in Southeast Asia for the occurrence of the Six Day War. With US attention focused on Vietnam, the Soviet Union managed to insert itself into Arab counsels and convince Nasser and his minions to attack Israel. In turn, because of the war, Israel was forced to rely more heavily on the United States and in the process lost all of its standing in the Third World. Brands (1995) devotes a chapter to the Six Day War. He sees Johnson as a man trapped by policies of his predecessors. The Arab–Israeli conflict was fifteen years old when Johnson took power. The US decision to send tanks to Israel angered Nasser, but Johnson did his best to preserve the delicate balance that had maintained a hostile peace since 1956. He failed. To Johnson's credit, he was able to keep the war brief and somewhat limited.

Palestinian professor of English Edward Said's *The Question of Palestine* (1979) is a cry for justice for the Palestinian people. The text waxes and wanes from polemic to reasoned arguments on both sides of the Palestinian–Israeli issue. The effects of Zionism on the Palestinian people is Said's greatest concern. He accuses the Israelis of participating in state-sponsored terrorism and international lawlessness. At the same time, Said laments the disastrous impact the Holocaust has had on the Jews and depicts both the Israelis and Palestinians as victims. Aronson (1978) is a discussion of Israeli foreign policy by a political scientist at Hebrew University. Aronson criticizes Israeli foreign policymaking as a simple exercise in reaction to Arab hostility. He criticizes post-1967 Israeli officials for complacency regarding the territorial status quo, their insistence on absolute security, and their refusal to admit the legitimacy of a Palestinian national movement. Shadid (1981) describes the relationship between the United States and the Palestinian people. He criticizes the United States for its unwavering commitment to the security of Israel, but credits it with a sincere effort to work out a resolution of the Palestinian refugee problem. Shadid notes as well how over time Washington has progressed from viewing the Palestinians as a non-people to accepting them as a distinct cultural and political entity. One of the principal reasons that no progress has been made toward recognition of a Palestinian state, Shadid contends, is the lack of a cohesive and monied Arab lobby in the United States in contrast to the existence of a powerful Jewish lobby.

Tillman (1982) focuses on the Camp David peace process and the Arab–Palestinian–Israeli conflict. He argues that the US commitment to Israeli security has complicated the achievement of its other objectives, namely access to oil, détente with the Soviets, and promotion of the principle of the right of national self-determination. The only way to restore balance, to achieve lasting peace in the Middle East, and to make US resources and attention available to other regions and crises, he contends, is for Washington to support the creation of a Palestinian state. Ball and Ball (1992) detail America's relationship with the Jewish state from its creation to the Gulf War. The authors criticize those presidents who have displayed "passionate attachments" to Israel by providing aid and support at all costs. They portray Israeli leaders as bullies and blame the American Israel Public Affairs Committee and anti-Arab sentiments of members of the national security bureaucracy for America's slanted policy. According to historian Douglas Little (1994, 1999), Johnson and his national security adviser Walt Rostow were obsessed with Nasser and his increasing involvement with the Soviet Union. Indeed, it was fear of Arab nationalism and its possible co-option by the Kremlin, rather than a pro-Israeli bias, which was the chief explanatory factor in Johnson's policy decisions in the region. Ben-Zvi (1998) points out that an important by-product of the Six Day War was an intensification of the Israeli drive to develop the capacity to manufacture nuclear weapons. Ben-Zvi credits Kennedy with being deeply concerned about nuclear proliferation and with providing the Israelis with incentives to slow down. In his blind support for Israel security, Lyndon Johnson gave only lip service to non-proliferation in the Middle East. (See also Little 1994; Cohen 1994.)

The consensus among critics of US foreign policy during the 1960s is fairly clear. Both the Kennedy and Johnson administrations were committed to peaceful coexistence with the communist superpowers and desirous of promoting social justice and democracy in the developing world. Indeed, the presidents and their foreign policy advisers recognized that the United States would have to disassociate itself from the vestiges of Western imperialism if it and the free world were to win the battle for hearts and minds. Unfortunately, the American people and many of their political representatives were unwilling or unable to distinguish between Marxism-Leninism as a social and economic theory and Sino-Soviet imperialism. Thus, it was when revolutions in Cuba and Vietnam – revolutions that were primarily indigenous and aimed at overthrowing entrenched oligarchies and their foreign sponsors – endorsed Marxism-Leninism and accepted aid from the communist superpowers, the US government threw caution to the winds, going to war with North Vietnam and seeking the overthrow of Castro.

America's obsession with Cuba and Vietnam distorted its relationship with the rest of the world. Its opposition to revolutions in those countries destroyed its credibility with revolutionary nationalists from all nations and of every ideological persuasion. It stretched the nation's military and economic resources to the breaking point and polarized American society. The United States was not able to overthrow Castro, but it made allegiance to the anti-Castro crusade a litmus test for every government in the hemisphere. Neither was it able to defeat revolutionary nationalism in Vietnam. The ongoing war strained the North Atlantic alliance, creating fears among America's allies that the United States had lost both the will and the ability to help defend Western Europe. In its determination to combat communism on every front, it seemed America had rendered itself incapable of defeating it on every front. Many policymakers and sophisticated observers in the United States understood the imbalance and distortion Vietnam and Cuba had introduced into American foreign policy, but the strength of domestic anti-communism barred them from pursuing a more pragmatic course.

Defenders of Kennedy and Johnson agree that both presidents were pragmatic Cold War warriors who were under constant pressure from ideologues, political opportunists, and the military–industrial complex to take a hardline against Sino-Soviet communism. They conclude, however, that in the face of the very real threat of communist imperialism and domestic extremism, the presidents in question successfully steered a middle course, containing the red menace abroad and the anti-communist threat at home. In the dangerous world of the 1960s, Washington succeeded in holding NATO together, preventing the fall of Thailand, Indonesia, Burma, and the Philippines to the communists, and defeating Castroism in the Western hemisphere.

REFERENCES

Aguilar, Luis (ed.): *Operation Zapata: The "Ultrasensitive" Report and Testimony of the Board of Inquiry on the Bay of Pigs* (Frederick, MD: Aletheia Books, 1981).

Allison, Graham T.: *Essence of Decision: Explaining the Cuban Missile Crisis* (Boston, MA: Little, Brown, 1971); 2nd edn. with Philip Zelikow (New York: Longman, 1999).

Amin, Julius A.: *The Peace Corps in Cameroon* (Kent, OH: Kent State University Press, 1992).

Anderson, James E. and Jared E. Hazelton: *Managing Macroeconomic Policy: The Johnson Presidency* (Austin: University of Texas Press, 1986).

Aronson, Shlomo: *Conflict and Bargaining in the Middle East: An Israeli Perspective* (Baltimore, MD: Johns Hopkins University Press, 1978).

Ausland, John C.: *Kennedy, Khrushchev and the Berlin–Cuba Crisis, 1961–1964* (Oslo: Scandinavian University Press, 1996).

Ball, Desmond: *Politics and Force Levels: The Strategic Missile Program of the Kennedy Administration* (Berkeley: University of California Press, 1981).

Ball, George and Douglas Ball: *The Passionate Attachment: America's Involvement with Israel, 1947 to Present* (New York: W. W. Norton, 1992).

Bange, Oliver: *The EEC Crisis of 1963: Kennedy, Macmillan, de Gaulle and Adenauer in Conflict* (Basingstoke: Macmillan, 2000).

Bark, Dennis L. and David R. Gress: *A History of West Germany, Vol. 2: Democracy and its Discontents 1963–1988* (Oxford: Blackwell, 1989).

Barnet, Richard: *The Alliance – America, Europe and Japan: Makers of the Postwar World* (New York: Simon and Schuster, 1983).

Beaufre, André: *NATO and Europe* (New York: Alfred A. Knopf, 1966).

Beer, Francis: *Integration and Disintegration in NATO: Processes of Alliance Cohesion and Prospects for Atlantic Community* (Columbus: Ohio State University Press, 1969).

Ben-Zvi, Abraham: *Decade of Transition: Eisenhower, Kennedy, and the Origins of the American–Israeli Alliance* (New York: Columbia University Press, 1998).

Benjamin, Jules R.: *The United States and the Origins of the Cuban Revolution: An Empire of Liberty in an Age of National Liberation* (Princeton, NJ: Princeton University Press, 1990).

Beschloss, Michael: *Mayday: Eisenhower, Khrushchev and the U-2 Affair* (New York: Harper, 1986).

Beschloss, Michael: *The Crisis Years: Kennedy and Khrushchev 1960–1963* (New York: Harper Collins, 1991).

Bird, Kai: *The Chairman: John J. McCloy: The Making of the American Establishment* (New York: Simon and Schuster, 1992).

Bissell, Richard M. with Johnathan Lewis and Frances Pudlo: *Reflections of a Cold Warrior: From Yalta to the Bay of Pigs* (New Haven, CT: Yale University Press, 1996).

Blasier, Cole: *The Hovering Giant: US Responses to Revolutionary Change in Latin America* (Pittsburgh, PA: University of Pittsburgh Press, 1976).

Blaufarb, Douglas: *The Counter-Insurgency Era: US Doctrine and Performance* (New York: Free Press, 1977).

Blechman, Barry M. and Stephen S. Kaplan (eds.): *Force without War: US Armed Forces as a Political Instrument* (Washington, DC: Brookings Institution, 1978).

Blight, James G.: *The Shattered Crystal Ball: Fear and Learning in the Cuban Missile Crisis* (Lanham, MD: Rowman and Littlefield, 1992).

Blight, James and Peter Kornbluh: *Politics of Illusion: The Bay of Pigs Invasion Reexamined* (Boulder, CO: Lynne Rienner, 1998).

Blight, James G. and David A. Welch: *On the Brink: Americans and Soviets Reexamine the Cuban Missile Crisis* (New York: Hill and Wang, 1989).

Blight, James G., Bruce J. Allyn, and David A. Welch with David Lewis: *Cuba on the Brink: Castro, the Missile Crisis, and the Soviet Collapse* (New York: Pantheon, 1993).

Bonsal, Philip W.: *Cuba, Castro and the United States* (Pittsburgh, PA: University of Pittsburgh Press, 1971).

Bosch, Juan: *The Unfinished Experiment: Democracy in the Dominican Republic* (New York: Praeger, 1965).

Bose, Meena: *Shaping and Signaling Presidential Policy: The National Security Decision Making of Eisenhower and Kennedy* (College Station: Texas A&M University Press, 1998).

Bozo, Frédéric: *Two Strategies for Europe: De Gaulle, the United States and the Atlantic Alliance*, trans. Susan Emanuel (Lanham, MD: Rowman and Littlefield, 2001).

Brands, H. W.: *The Wages of Globalism* (New York: Oxford University Press, 1995).

Brands, H. W. (ed.): *Beyond Vietnam: The Foreign Policies of Lyndon Johnson* (College Station: Texas A&M University Press, 1999).

Brinkley, Douglas: *Dean Acheson: The Cold War Years, 1953–1971* (New Haven, CT: Yale University Press, 1992).

Brinkley, Douglas and Richard T. Griffiths: *John F. Kennedy and Europe* (Baton Rouge: Louisiana State University Press, 1999).

Brugioni, Dino: *Eyeball to Eyeball: The Inside Story of the Cuban Missile Crisis* (New York: Random House, 1991).

Bunck, Julie Marie: *Fidel Castro and the Quest for a Revolutionary Culture in Cuba* (University Park: Pennsylvania State University Press, 1994).

Bundy, McGeorge: *Danger and Survival: Choices About the Bomb in the First Fifty Years* (New York: Random House, 1988).

Burk, Kathleen and Melvyn Stokes (eds.): *The United States and the European Alliance since 1945* (New York: Oxford University Press, 1999).

Burner, David: *John F. Kennedy and a New Generation* (Boston, MA: Little, Brown, 1988).

Castro, Fidel and José Ramon Fernandez: *Playa Girón: Bay of Pigs: Washington's First Military Defeat in the Americas* (New York: Pathfinder, 2001).

Catudal, Honoré Marc: *Kennedy and the Berlin Wall Crisis: A Case Study in US Decision Making* (Berlin: Verlag, 1980).

Chang, Laurence and Peter Kornbluh (eds.): *The Cuban Missile Crisis, 1962: A National Security Archive Documents Reader* (New York: New Press, 1992).

Chayes, Abram: *The Cuban Missile Crisis: International Crisis and the Role of Law* (Lanham, MD: University Press of America, 1987).

Churba, Joseph: *The Politics of Defeat: America's Decline in the Middle East* (New York: Cyrco Press, 1977).

Cleveland, Harold Van B.: *The Atlantic Idea and Its European Rivals* (New York: McGraw-Hill, 1966).

Cohen, Warren I.: *Dean Rusk* (Totowa, NJ: Cooper Square, 1980).

Cohen, Warren I.: "Balancing American Interests in the Middle East: Lyndon Baines Johnson vs. Gamal Abdul Nasser." In Warren I. Cohen and Nancy Bernkopf Tucker (eds.) *Lyndon Johnson Confronts the World: American Foreign Policy, 1963–1968* (New York: Cambridge University Press, 1994).

Cohen, Warren I. and Nancy Berkopf Tucker (eds.): *Lyndon Johnson Confronts the World: American Foreign Policy, 1963–1968* (New York: Cambridge University Press, 1994).

Coombs, Charles: *The Arena of International Finance* (New York: Wiley, 1976).

Costigliola, Frank: *France and the United States: The Cold Alliance Since World War II* (New York: Twayne, 1992).

Craig, Campbell: *Destroying the Village: Eisenhower and Thermonuclear War* (New York: Columbia University Press, 1998).

Dallek, Robert: "Lyndon Johnson as a World Leader." In H. W. Brands (ed.) *The Foreign Policies of Lyndon Johnson: Beyond Vietnam* (College Station: Texas A&M University Press, 1999).

de Carmoy, Guy: *The Foreign Policies of France: 1944–1968*, trans. Elaine Halperin (Chicago, IL: University of Chicago Press, 1970).

Dinerstein, Herbert: *The Making of a Missile Crisis: October 1962* (Baltimore, MD: Johns Hopkins University Press, 1976).

Dobson, Alan P.: *Anglo American Relations in the Twentieth Century: Of Friendship, Conflict, and the Rise and Decline of Superpowers* (London: Routledge, 1995).

Dominguez, Jorge: *To Make a World Safe for Revolution: Cuba's Foreign Policy* (Cambridge, MA: Harvard University Press, 1989).

Draper, Theodore: *The Dominican Revolt: A Case Study in American Policy* (New York: Commentary, 1968).

Dulles, Allen: *The Craft of Intelligence* (London: Weidenfeld and Nicolson, 1963).

Eichengreen, Barry: *Globalizing Capital: A History of the International Monetary System* (Princeton, NJ: Princeton University Press, 1996).

Felton, Peter: "Yankee, Go Home and Take Me with You: Lyndon Johnson and the Dominican Republic." In H. W. Brands (ed.) *Beyond Vietnam: The Foreign Policies of Lyndon Johnson* (College Station: Texas A&M University Press, 1999).

Fischer, Fritz: *Making Them Like Us: Peace Corps Volunteers in the 1960s* (Washington, DC: Smithsonian Institution Press, 1998).

FitzSimons, Louise: *The Kennedy Doctrine* (New York: Random House, 1972).

Foreign Relations of the United States, Vol. 10, Cuba, 1961–1962 (Washington, DC: Government Printing Office, 1997).

Fox, William T. R. and Annette Baker Fox: *NATO and the Range of American Choice* (New York: Columbia University Press, 1967).

Freedman, Lawrence: *US Intelligence and the Soviet Strategic Threat* (Boulder, CO: Westview Press, 1977).

Freedman, Lawrence: *Kennedy's Wars: Berlin, Cuba, Laos and Vietnam* (Oxford: Oxford University Press, 2000).

FRUS: Vol. 11, Cuban Missile Crisis and Aftermath, October 1962–December 1963 (Washington, DC: Government Printing Office, 1997).

Funigiello, Philip J.: *American–Soviet Trade in the Cold War* (Chapel Hill: University of North Carolina Press, 1988).

Fursenko, Aleksandr and Timothy Naftali: *"One Hell of a Gamble": Khrushchev, Castro, and Kennedy, 1958–1964* (New York: Norton, 1997).

Gardner, Lloyd: *Pay Any Price: Lyndon Johnson and the Wars for Vietnam* (Chicago, IL: Dee, 1995).

Garthoff, Raymond L.: *Reflections on the Cuban Missile Crisis*, 2nd edn. (Washington, DC: Brookings Institution, 1989).

Gearson, John: *Harold Macmillan and the Berlin Wall Crisis, 1958–1962: The Limits of Interest and Force* (London: Macmillan, 1998).

Giglio, James: *The Presidency of John F. Kennedy* (Lawrence: University of Kansas Press, 1991).

Gleijeses, Piero: *The Dominican Crisis: The 1965 Constitutional Revolt and American Intervention*, trans. Lawrence Lipson (Baltimore, MD: Johns Hopkins University Press, 1979).

Gleijeses, Piero: *Conflicting Missions: Havana, Washington, and Africa, 1959–1976* (Chapel Hill: University of North Carolina Press, 2002).

Gordon, Philip H.: *A Certain Idea of France: French Security Policy and the Gaullist Legacy*. Princeton Studies in International History and Politics (Princeton, NJ: Princeton University Press, 1993).

Gosse, Van: *Where the Boys Are: Cuba, Cold War America and the Making of the New Left* (New York: Verso, 1993).

Greenwood, Sean: *Britain and the Cold War, 1945–1991* (New York: St. Martin's Press, 2000).

Grose, Peter: *Israel in the Mind of America* (New York: Knopf, 1983).

Grosser, Alfred: *French Foreign Policy Under de Gaulle*, trans. Lois Ames Pattison (Boston, MA: Little, Brown, 1967).

Grosser, Alfred: *The Western Alliance: European–American Relations since 1945*, trans. Michael Shaw (New York: Seabury Press, 1980).

Gutiérrez, Carlos María: *The Dominican Republic: Rebellion and Repression* (New York: Monthly Review Press, 1972).

Haftendorn, Helga: *NATO and the Nuclear Revolution: A Crisis of Credibility, 1966–1967* (Oxford: Clarendon Press, 1996).

Halperin, Maurice: *The Taming of Fidel Castro* (Berkeley: University of California Press, 1981).

Hamilton, Nigel: *JFK: Reckless Youth* (London: Arrow, 1992).

Hanrieder, Wolfram F.: *Germany, America, Europe: Forty Years of German Foreign Policy* (New Haven, CT: Yale University Press, 1989).

Hanson, Simon: *Dollar Diplomacy Modern Style: Chapters in the Failure of the Alliance for Progress* (Washington, DC: Inter-American Affairs Press, 1970).

Harrison, Michael: *The Reluctant Ally: France and Atlantic Security* (Baltimore, MD: Johns Hopkins University Press, 1981).

Henggeler, Paul: *The Kennedy Persuasion: The Politics of Style Since JFK* (Chicago, IL: University of Chicago Press, 1995).

Herken, Greg: *Counsels of War* (New York: Alfred A. Knopf, 1985).

Hersh, Seymour: *The Dark Side of Camelot* (New York: Little, Brown, 1997).

Higgins, Trumbell: *The Perfect Failure: Kennedy, Eisenhower and the CIA at the Bay of Pigs* (New York: W. W. Norton, 1987).

Hilsman, Roger: *To Move a Nation: The Politics of Foreign Policy in the Administration of John F. Kennedy* (Garden City, NY: Doubleday, 1967).

Hilsman, Roger: *The Cuban Missile Crisis: The Struggle Over Policy* (Westport, CT: Praeger, 1996).

Hoffman, Elizabeth Cobbs: *All You Need Is Love: The Peace Corps and the Spirit of the 1960s* (Cambridge, MA: Harvard University Press, 1998).

Hoopes, Roy (ed.): *The Peace Corps Experience* (New York: Clarkson N. Potter, 1968).

Horelick, Arnold and Myron Rush: *Strategic Power and Soviet Foreign Policy* (Chicago, IL: University of Chicago Press, 1966).

Ikenberry, John G.: *After Victory: Institutions, Strategic Restraint, and the Rebuilding of Order After Major Wars* (Princeton, NJ: Princeton University Press, 2001).

Ilgen, Thomas: *Autonomy and Interdependence: US–Western European Monetary and Trade Relations, 1958–1984* (Totowa, NJ: Rowman and Allanheld, 1985).

Isaacson, Walter and Evan Thomas: *The Wise Men: Six Friends and the World They Made* (New York: Simon and Schuster, 1986).

James, Harold: *International Monetary Cooperation Since Bretton Woods* (New York: Oxford University Press, 1996).

Jeffreys-Jones, Rhodri: *The CIA and American Diplomacy* (New Haven, CT: Yale University Press, 1989).

Johnson, Haynes B.: *The Bay of Pigs: The Leaders' Story of Brigade 2506* (New York: W. W. Norton, 1964).

Johnson, Loch K.: *America's Secret Power: The CIA in a Democratic Society* (New York: Oxford University Press, 1989).

Kaplan, Lawrence: *NATO and the United States: The Enduring Alliance* (Boston, MA: Twayne, 1988).

Kelleher, Catherine McArdle: *Germany and the Politics of Nuclear Weapons* (New York: Columbia University Press, 1975).

Kelly, J. B.: *Arabia, the Gulf and the West* (New York: Basic Books, 1980).

Kennedy, Robert: *Thirteen Days: A Memoir of the Cuban Missile Crisis* (New York: Norton, 1969).

Kern, Montague, Patricia Levering, and Ralph B. Levering: *The Kennedy Crisis: The Press, the Presidency and Foreign Policy* (Chapel Hill: University of North Carolina Press, 1983).

Khrushchev, Nikita Sergeevich: *Khrushchev Remembers: The Last Testament*, trans. Strobe Talbott (Boston, MA: Little, Brown, 1974).

Khrushchev, Nikita Sergeevich: *Khrushchev Remembers: The Glasnost Tapes*, trans. Jerrold Schechter and Vyacheslav Luchkov (Boston, MA: Little, Brown, 1990).

Klinghoffer, Judith: *Vietnam, Jews, and the Middle East: Unintended Consequences* (New York: St. Martin's Press, 1999).

Kohl, Wilfried L.: *French Nuclear Diplomacy* (Princeton, NJ: Princeton University Press, 1971).

Kornbluh, Peter: *Bay of Pigs Declassified: The Secret CIA Report on the Invasion of Cuba* (New York: New Press, 1998).

Kovrig, Bennet: *Of Walls and Bridges: The United States and Eastern Europe* (New York: New York University Press, 1991).

Kugler, Richard: *Commitment to Purpose: How Alliance Partnership Won the Cold War* (Santa Monica, CA: Rand Corporation Study, 1994).

Kunz, Diane B.: *Butter and Guns: America's Cold War Economic Diplomacy* (New York: Free Press, 1997).

Kunz, Diane B. (ed.): *The Diplomacy of a Crucial Decade: American Foreign Relations During the 1960s* (New York: Columbia University Press, 1994).

Lacouture, Jean: *De Gaulle: The Rebel, 1890–1944*, trans. Patrick O'Brian (New York: W. W. Norton, 1990).

Lacouture, Jean: *De Gaulle: The Ruler 1945–70* (New York: W. W. Norton, 1991).

LaFeber, Walter: *Inevitable Revolutions: The United States in Central America*, 2nd edn. (New York: W. W. Norton, 1993).

Latham, Michael E.: *Modernization as Ideology: American Social Science and "Nation-Building" in the Kennedy Era* (Chapel Hill: University of North Carolina Press, 2000).

Little, Douglas: "Choosing Sides: Lyndon Johnson and the Middle East." In Robert A. Divine (ed.) *The Johnson Years, Vol. 3: LBJ at Home and Abroad* (Lawrence: University of Kansas Press, 1994).

Little, Douglas: "Nasser Delenda Est: Lyndon Johnson, the Arabs, and the 1967 Six-Day War." In H. W. Brands (ed.) *Beyond Vietnam: The Foreign Policies of Lyndon Johnson* (College Station: Texas A&M University Press, 1999).

Logevall, Fredrik: *Choosing War: The Lost Chance for Peace and the Escalation of War in Vietnam* (Berkeley: University of California Press, 1999).

Lowenthal, Abraham: *Dominican Intervention* (Cambridge, MA: Harvard University Press, 1970).

Lowther, Kevin and C. Payne Lucas: *Keeping Kennedy's Promise: The Peace Corps: Unmet Hope of the New Frontier* (Boulder, CO: Westview Press, 1978).

Lundestad, Geir: *"Empire" by Integration: The United States and European Integration, 1945–1997* (New York: Oxford University Press, 1998).

Lynch, Grayston L.: *Decision for Disaster: Betrayal at the Bay of Pigs* (Washington, DC: Brassey's, 1998).

McAuliffe, Mary S. (ed.): *CIA Documents on the Cuban Missile Crisis, 1962* (Washington, DC: CIA, 1962).

McGhee, George: *At the Creation of a New Germany: From Adenauer to Brandt, An Ambassador's Account* (New Haven, CT: Yale University Press, 1989).

Maga, Timothy P.: *John F. Kennedy and the New Frontier Diplomacy, 1961–1963* (Malabar, FL: Krieger Publishing, 1994).

Martin, John Barlow: *Overtaken by Events: The Dominican Crisis from the Fall of Trujillo to the Civil War* (New York: Doubleday, 1966).

Mastanduno, Michael: *Economic Containment: CoCom and the Politics of East–West Trade* (Ithaca, NY: Cornell University Press, 1992).

May, Ernest R. and Philip D. Zelikow (eds.): *The Kennedy Tapes: Inside the White House during the Cuban Missile Crisis* (Cambridge, MA: Belknap Press of Harvard University Press, 1997).

Mayer, Frank A.: *Adenauer and Kennedy: A Study in German–American Relations, 1961–1963* (New York: St. Martin's Press, 1996).

Moravcsik, Andrew: *The Choice for Europe: Social Purpose and State Power from Messina to Maastricht* (Ithaca, NY: Cornell University Press, 1998).

Moravcsik, Andrew: "De Gaulle Between Grain and Grandeur: The Political Economy of French EC Policy, 1958–1970 (Parts 1 and 2)." *Journal of Cold War Studies* 2, 2 (spring 2000), 3–43; and 2, 3 (fall 2000), 4–68.

Moreno, José A.: *Barrios in Arms* (Pittsburgh, PA: University of Pittsburgh Press, 1970).

Morgan, Roger: *The United States and West Germany, 1945–1973* (Oxford: Oxford University Press, 1974).

Morley, Morris H.: *Imperial State and Revolution: The United States and Cuba, 1952–1986* (New York: Cambridge University Press, 1987).

Morse, Edward L.: *Foreign Policy and Interdependence in Gaullist France* (Princeton, NJ: Princeton University Press, 1973).

Murray, Donette: *Kennedy, Macmillan and Nuclear Weapons* (New York: St. Martin's Press, 2000).

Nash, Philip: *The Other Missiles of October: Eisenhower, Kennedy and the Jupiters, 1957–1963* (Chapel Hill: University of North Carolina Press, 1997).

Nathan, James A. (ed.): *The Cuban Missile Crisis Revisited* (New York: St. Martin's Press, 1992).

Neustadt, Richard E.: *Report to JFK: The Skybolt Crisis in Perspective* (Ithaca, NY: Cornell University Press, 1999).

Newhouse, John: *De Gaulle and the Anglo-Saxons* (New York: Viking Press, 1970).

Ninkovich, Frank: *Germany and the United States: The Transformation of the German Question since 1945*, 2nd edn. (New York: Twayne, 1995).

O'Neill, Bard E.: *Armed Struggle in Palestine: A Political–Military Analysis* (Boulder, CO: Westview Press, 1978).

Oliver, Kendrick: *Kennedy, Macmillan and the Nuclear Test-Ban Debate, 1961–1963* (London: Macmillan, 1998).

Palmer, General Bruce, Jr.: *Intervention in the Caribbean: The Dominican Crisis of 1965* (Lexington: University of Kentucky Press, 1989).

Parmet, Herbert S.: *JFK: The Presidency of John F. Kennedy* (New York: Dial Press, 1983).

Paterson, Thomas G.: *Kennedy's Quest for Victory: American Foreign Policy, 1961–1963* (New York: Oxford University Press, 1989).

Paterson, Thomas G.: *Contesting Castro: The United States and the Triumph of the Cuban Revolution* (New York: Oxford University Press, 1994).

Pérez, Louis A., Jr.: *Cuba: Between Reform and Revolution* (New York: Oxford University Press, 1988).

Pérez, Louis A., Jr.: *Cuba and the United States: Ties of Singular Intimacy* (Athens, GA: University of Georgia Press, 1990).

Pérez-Stable, Marifeli: *The Cuban Revolution: Origins, Course and Legacy* (New York: Oxford University Press, 1993).

Powers, Thomas: *The Man Who Kept Secrets: Richard Helms and the CIA* (New York: Knopf, 1979).

Prados, John: *The Soviet Estimate* (New York: Dial, 1982).

Prados, John: *Keepers of the Keys: A History of the National Security Council from Truman to Bush* (New York: William Morrow Publishers, 1991).

Prittie, Terence: *The Velvet Chancellors: A History of Postwar Germany* (London: Muller, 1979).

Rabe, Stephen G.: *The Most Dangerous Area in the World: John F. Kennedy Confronts Communist Revolution in Latin America* (Chapel Hill: University of North Carolina Press, 1999).

Reeves, Thomas C.: *A Question of Character: A Life of John F. Kennedy* (New York: Free Press, 1991).

Reeves, Zane: *The Politics of the Peace Corps and VISTA* (Tuscaloosa: University of Alabama Press, 1988).

Rice, Gerard T.: *The Bold Experiment: JFK's Peace Corps* (Notre Dame, IN: University of Notre Dame Press, 1986).

Richelson, Jeffrey T.: *America's Secret Eyes in Space: The US Keyhole Spy Satellite Program* (New York: Harper and Row, 1990).

Risse-Kappen, Thomas: *Cooperation Among Democracies: The European Influence on US Foreign Policy*. Princeton Studies in International History and Politics (Princeton, NJ: Princeton University Press, 1995).

Rodriquez, Felix and John Weisman: *Shadow Warrior: The CIA Hero of a Hundred Unknown Battles* (New York: Simon and Schuster, 1989).

Rusk, Dean with Richard Rusk and Daniel S. Papp: *As I Saw It* (New York: W. W. Norton, 1990).

Safran, Nadav: *From War to War: The Arab–Israeli Confrontation, 1948–1967* (New York: Pegasus, 1969).

Safran, Nadav: *Israel: The Embattled Ally* (Cambridge, MA: Belknap Press of Harvard University Press, 1978).

Said, Edward: *The Question of Palestine* (New York: Times Books, 1979).

Schertz, Arian W.: *Die Deutschlandpolitik Kennedys and Johnsons: Unterschiedliche Ansatze innerhalb der Amerikanishen Regierung (Kennedy and Johnson's Policies Toward Germany: Different Approaches within the American Government)* (Cologne: Bohlau, 1992).

Schick, Jack M.: *The Berlin Crisis, 1958–1962* (Philadelphia: University of Pennsylvania Press, 1971).

Schlesinger, Arthur M., Jr.: *A Thousand Days: John F. Kennedy in the White House* (Boston, MA: Houghton Mifflin, 1965).

Schoenbaum, David: *The United States and the State of Israel* (New York: Oxford University Press, 1993).

Schoenbaum, Thomas J.: *Waging Peace and War: Dean Rusk in the Truman, Kennedy and Johnson Years* (New York: Simon and Schuster, 1988).

Schulze, Kirsten E.: *The Arab–Israeli Conflict: Seminar Studies in History Series* (London: Addison Wesley Longman, 1999).

Schwartz, Thomas A.: *America's Germany: John J. McCloy and the Federal Republic of Germany* (Cambridge, MA: Harvard University Press, 1991).

Schwartz, Thomas A.: "Lyndon Johnson and Europe: Alliance Politics, Political Economy, and 'Growing Out of the Cold War'." In H. W. Brands (ed.) *Beyond Vietnam: The Foreign Policies of Lyndon Johnson* (College Station: Texas A&M University Press, 1999).

Schwartz, Thomas A.: *In the Shadow of Vietnam: Lyndon Johnson and Europe* (unpublished manuscript, 2001).

Schwarz, Hans-Peter: *Adenauer, vol. 2: Der Staatsmann: 1952–1967* (Stuttgart: Deutsche-Verlags Anstalt, 1991).

Schwarz, Karen: *What You Can Do for Your Country: An Oral History of the Peace Corps* (New York: William Morrow, 1991).

Scott, Len: *Macmillan, Kennedy and the Cuban Missile Crisis: Political, Military and Intelligence Aspects* (London: Macmillan, 1999).

Seaborg, Glenn T.: *Stemming the Tide: Arms Control in the Johnson Years* (Lexington, MA: D. C. Heath, 1987).

Seaborg, Glenn T. with Benjamin S. Loeb: *Kennedy, Khrushchev and the Test Ban* (Berkeley: University of California Press, 1981).

Searles, David: *The Peace Corps Experience: Challenge and Change, 1969–1976* (Lexington: University of Kentucky Press, 1997).

Shadid, Mohammed K.: *The United States and the Palestinians* (New York: St. Martin's Press, 1981).

Shriver, Sargent: *Point of the Lance* (New York: Harper and Row, 1964).

Slater, Jerome: *Intervention and Negotiation: The United States and the Dominican Revolution* (New York: Harper and Row, 1970).

Slusser, Robert M.: *The Berlin Crisis of 1961: Soviet–American Relations and the Struggle for Power in the Kremlin* (Baltimore, MD: Johns Hopkins University Press, 1973).

Smith, Earl E. T.: *The Fourth Floor: An Account of the Castro Communist Revolution* (New York: Random House, 1962).

Smith, Jean Edward: *The Defense of Berlin* (Baltimore, MD: Johns Hopkins University Press, 1963).

Smith, Robert Freeman: *The Caribbean World and the United States: Mixing Rum and Coca-Cola* (New York: Twayne, 1994).

Smith, Wayne S.: *The Closest of Enemies: A Personal and Diplomatic Account of US–Cuban Relations since 1957* (New York: W. W. Norton, 1987).

Smyser, William R.: *From Yalta to Berlin: The Cold War Struggle Over Germany* (New York: St. Martin's Press, 1999).

Sorensen, Theodore C.: *Kennedy* (New York: Harper and Row, 1965).

Spiegel, Steven L.: *The Other Arab–Israeli Conflict: Making America's Middle East Policy from Truman to Reagan* (Chicago, IL: University of Chicago Press, 1985).

Stromseth, Jane E.: *The Origins of Flexible Response: NATO's Debate over Strategy in the 1960s* (Basingstoke: Macmillan, 1988).

Sweig, Julia E.: *Inside the Cuban Revolution: Fidel Castro and the Urban Underground* (Cambridge, MA: Harvard University Press, 2002).

Taylor, Maxwell: *The Uncertain Trumpet* (New York: Harper, 1960).

Thomas, Evan: *The Very Best Men: Four Who Dared; The Early Years of the CIA* (New York: Simon and Schuster, 1995).

Thompson, Robert Smith: *The Missiles of October: The Declassified Story of John F. Kennedy and the Cuban Missile Crisis* (New York: Simon and Schuster, 1992).

Tillman, Seth P.: *The United States in the Middle East* (Bloomington: Indiana University Press, 1982).

Trachtenberg, Marc: *History and Strategy* (Princeton, NJ: Princeton University Press, 1991).

Trachtenberg, Marc: *A Constructed Peace: The Making of the European Settlement, 1945–1963.* Princeton Studies in International History and Politics (Princeton, NJ: Princeton University Press, 1999).

Treverton, Gregory F.: *The Dollar Drain and American Forces in Germany: Managing the Political Economics of Alliance* (Athens, OH: University of Ohio Press, 1978).

Tusa, Ann: *The Last Division: Berlin and the Wall* (London: Hodder and Stoughton, 1996).

Vaïsse, Maurice: *Le Gandeur: politique étrangère du general de Gaulle 1958–1969* (Paris: Librairie Arthème Fayard, 1998).

Valenta, Jiri: *Soviet Intervention in Czechoslovakia, 1968: Anatomy of a Decision* (Baltimore, MD: Johns Hopkins University Press, 1979).

Vandenbroucke, Lucien S.: *Perilous Options: Special Operations as an Instrument of US Foreign Policy* (New York: Oxford University Press, 1993).

Walker, William O., III: "The Struggle for the Americas: The Johnson Administration and Cuba." In H. W. Brands (ed.) *Beyond Vietnam: The Foreign Policies of Lyndon Johnson* (College Station: Texas A&M University Press, 1999).

Weil, Gordon L. and Ian Davidson: *The Gold War: The Story of the World's Monetary Crisis* (New York: Holt, Rinehart, and Winston, 1970).

Welch, Richard E., Jr.: *Response to Revolution: The United States and the Cuban Revolution, 1959–1961* (Chapel Hill: University of North Carolina Press, 1985).

White, Mark J.: *The Cuban Missile Crisis* (New York: New York University Press, 1996).

White, Mark J.: *Missiles in Cuba: Kennedy, Khrushchev, Castro and the 1962 Crisis* (Chicago, IL: Ivan R. Dee, 1997).

White, Mark J. (ed.): *Kennedy: The New Frontier Revisited* (New York: New York University Press, 1998).

White, Mark J. (ed.): *The Kennedys and Cuba: The Declassified Documentary History* (Chicago, IL: Ivan R. Dee, 1999).

Wiarda, Howard J. and Michael J. Kryzanek: *Dominican Republic: A Caribbean Crucible* (Boulder, CO: Westview Press, 1982).

Wills, Garry: *The Kennedy Imprisonment: A Meditation on Power* (New York: Little, Brown, 1985).

Winand, Pascaline: *Eisenhower, Kennedy and the United States of Europe* (London: Macmillan, 1993).

Winterstein, Stephen: "Teaching the Vietnam War: A Conference Report." Foreign Policy Research Institute *Newsletter* 6, 4 (July 2000).

Wyden, Peter: *Bay of Pigs: The Untold Story* (New York: Simon and Schuster, 1979).

Zeiler, Thomas W.: *American Trade and Power in the 1960s* (New York: Columbia University Press, 1992).

Zelikow, Philip D. et al. (eds.): *The Presidential Recordings: John F. Kennedy; The Great Crises*, 3 vols. (New York: Norton, 2001).

Zubok, Vladislav and Constantine Pleshakov: *Inside the Kremlin's Cold War: From Stalin to Khrushchev* (Cambridge, MA: Harvard University Press, 1996).

CHAPTER TWENTY

The United States and the Middle East since 1967

PETER L. HAHN

Since 1967, the Middle East has posed a series of great challenges to the United States. The region's Cold War dynamics, intra-regional rivalries, anti-American nationalism, and wars and revolutions have tested the resolve of US diplomats. Americans have found it difficult clearly to understand the region's multiplicity of cultures, religions, ethnic groups, and political systems. Historians, political scientists, journalists, and others have recorded and analyzed the legacy of US involvement with the region. This essay seeks to identify and analyze the most significant works of scholarship dealing with US diplomacy in the Middle East since 1967.

General US policy in the Middle East since 1967 is included in a number of overview, synthetic, and interpretive works that range over the post-1945 period. Tillman (1982), Fraser (1989), and Lenczowski (1990) evaluate the relative importance of such objectives as access to oil, containment of Soviet influence, preservation of Israel, and domestic political interests in the making of US policy in the region since World War II. During the Cold War, Sayigh and Shlaim (1997) conclude, the local powers of the Middle East resisted US pressures in their international, regional, and domestic politics. Brands (1994), a text suitable for undergraduate instruction, covers the broad parameters of US policy.

Several works adopt specific interpretive frameworks toward US policy in the Middle East. Stivers (1986) critically analyzes the US tendency to side with conservative political forces in the region against radical and nationalist alternatives, noting that Nixon's "Twin Pillars" strategy of relying on Saudi Arabia and Iran as bastions of stability merely blinded the United States to the imminent Iranian revolution. Kolko (1988) stresses economic objectives – specifically a quest to capture markets and trade routes – as the defining motives behind US policy in the Middle East and elsewhere in the Third World. Cooley (1991) faults US officials for stumbling aimlessly in the 1970s–1990s into the power vacuum left by collapsed European empires in Iran, Lebanon, Saudi Arabia, and Iraq, and thereby provoking consequences such as terrorism against US civilians. A perceptive overview of great power dynamics in the Middle East during the twentieth century, Shlaim (1994) suggests that the Persian Gulf War of 1990–1 signaled the triumph of US hegemony over the Middle East but also revealed that the United States had failed to mitigate the disorder that characterized the region since the collapse of the Ottoman Empire. Rossi (1998) emphasizes that the US anti-Soviet containment doctrine culminated in the Persian Gulf War, which established US dominance but failed to avoid anti-US backlash in the region.

Scholars have reached different conclusions about the importance of public opinion on the making of US foreign policy. Bard (1991), for example, examines in detail lobbying by pro-Israel US citizens and concludes that such activity, while not uncontested, exerted disproportional and measurable influence on US decision-making, to Israel's advantage over the Arab states. Smith (2000) concludes that pro-Israel Jews developed more political strength than any other ethnic group inside the United States and used it effectively (and in his judgment excessively) to shape national policy. Alexander DeConde (1992), by contrast, concludes that pro-Israel US citizens exercised no more influence over the policymaking process than other ethnic groups within the United States.

The literature on US oil interests in the Middle East since 1967 has not reached the maturity or range of such scholarship on the mid-twentieth century, but several noteworthy studies exist. A structured and theoretical study of oil corporations in the earlier era, Sampson (1975) addresses the impact of OPEC price controls in the early 1970s. Yergin (1991), with an engaging, popular style, and Bromley (1991), with a more scholarly apparatus, study the growing importance of oil in world power calculations during the twentieth century and deal with adjustments the United States made in the 1970s and 1980s as Saudi Arabia and Iran gained control over oil production. Han (1994) surveys the business, trade, and local political contexts of Persian Gulf oil production since the 1970s, while Hollis (1998) studies the economic and political dynamics of the Middle East oil industry in the 1990s.

Several scholars examine the background and origins of the Iranian Revolution of 1979, in which forces loyal to the Ayatollah Ruhollah Khomeini overthrew the US-supported Shah Mohammed Reza Pahlavi. The first major analysis published after the revolution, Rubin (1980) surveys US–Iran relations after World War II and argues that the traditional US quest to bolster the Shah as an anti-communist bulwark reflected ignorance and poor judgment among officials in Washington. On the basis of more extensive research, including examination of sources in Persian, Bill (1988) adds that bureaucratic infighting within the US government and domestic political pressures exerted by the pro-Shah lobby contributed to the unwise reliance on the Shah. Goode (1997), also based on bilingual research, faults US officials for only vaguely understanding Iran during their long relationship with the Shah. Implicitly exonerating US officials, Dorman and Farhang (1987) note that ethnocentrism also prevented US media experts from foreseeing the anti-Shah revolution, while Sick (1985) notes that other Western states were also unprepared to deal with a revolutionary movement with powerful, religious undertones.

The literature on the Iranian Revolution addresses in particular the hostage crisis of 1979–81, in which Iranian authorities incarcerated more than fifty US government personnel as hostages against counter-revolutionary activity by the United States. Bill (1988) suggests that the hostage ordeal resulted from revolutionary Iran's passionate anti-US fervor, which had been aggravated by President Jimmy Carter's inept policy toward Iran and failure to control his own policymaking bureaucracy before the revolution. In a detailed analysis of Carter's efforts to liberate the hostages, Moses (1996) concludes that their release resulted from changing political dynamics within Iran rather than US diplomacy. More sympathetic to

Carter, Sick (1985) applauds Carter's determination to settle the crisis peacefully. David, Carrol, and Selden (1993) use theories from psychology and bureaucratic politics to explain Carter's missteps toward Iran, while Hemmer (2000) cites Carter's handling of the hostage crisis to illustrate his thesis that US leaders used historical analogies not merely to justify predetermined policies, but to evaluate prospective options before reaching decisions.

Passionate debate also centers on the "October Surprise" controversy. Honegger (1989) and Sick (1991) allege that during the US presidential election campaign of 1980, members of the Ronald Reagan campaign staff secretly negotiated with Iranian officials to keep the hostages in captivity until after the election, in order to deny Carter a last-minute hostage settlement that might secure his reelection, in exchange for weapons to be delivered by the new Republican government. Such activity by the Reagan team, the accusers note, would have constituted criminal (as well as immoral) behavior. Despite intriguing circumstantial evidence amassed by the accusers, however, Moses (1996) observes that the charges remained unproven, if still tantalizing, after extensive investigations by Congress and the media.

Scholars also examine the Iran–Contra affair of the mid-1980s, in which officials of the Ronald Reagan administration covertly sold weapons to Iran and diverted some of the financial proceeds to the Contra rebels in Nicaragua. Reagan approved such arms supply apparently to win release of hostages held in Lebanon by political groups affiliated with Tehran. But revelations about the arms deal embarrassed him because it contradicted his public refusals to negotiate with hostage-takers and violated an international embargo against arms supply to Iran. (The diversion of funds to the Contras also circumvented US laws.) Bill (1988, 1990) clarifies the complex affair, assesses Reagan's motives, details the domestic political backlash that tarnished the president's image, and censures Reagan for undermining US credibility and demonizing Iran at a cost to future relations. Insider accounts of the scandal by North (1991) and Teicher and Teicher (1993) detail operations inside the Reagan administration while deflecting blame for the scandal toward other officials.

On a more general plane, the US role in the Persian Gulf since the 1970s has attracted academic attention. Palmer (1992) examines how the United States assumed the duty of protecting Western interests in the Gulf after Britain withdrew from it in the 1970s, clarifying its position in the Carter Doctrine of 1980 and in Reagan's decision to protect Kuwaiti tankers from Iran in the 1980s. Applying a paradigm regarding third party diplomacy, Yetiv (1995) concludes that the United States unexpectedly gained strategic strength in the Persian Gulf by responding to the Soviet invasion of Afghanistan, the Iran–Iraq War, and the Iraqi invasion of Kuwait. Hiro (1991) probes the diplomatic and intelligence support the United States provided Iraq during its war against Iran in the 1980s. According to Sick (1999), the Bill Clinton administration abandoned an earlier assumption of bolstering either Iran or Iraq as a check against the other and enunciated a strategy of containing both states. A prescriptive analysis, Kemp (1994) approves a firm but accommodating US approach to Iran.

Scholars address US–Arab relations in several different dimensions. A major debate has ensued on the US approach to Arab nationalism. Stookey (1975), for instance, argues that US officials through the early 1970s misunderstood Arab nationalism, equated it with Soviet-inspired communism, and squandered opportunities to build healthy relationships with nationalist leaders. Stivers (1986), by contrast, recognizes that US officials understood the vitality of Arab nationalism and distinguished it from communism, but nonetheless considered accommodation with nationalists less important than preserving conflicting security interests.

Scholars have also explored the importance of culture and perception in determining US relations with Arab peoples. Said (1988) suggests that Western culture enhanced imperialism by lacing an anti-Oriental bias and a sense of exceptionalism into Western perceptions of Arab peoples. Said (1993) adds that anti-Arab tendencies in US popular culture aggravated the violence and exceptionalism in the US war against Iraq and blinded US observers to Iraq's anti-colonial legacy. Gerges (1999a, b) critiques US officials in the 1970s to 1990s for failing to comprehend the nature of modern Islam or to understand its importance in international diplomacy, which strained political relations with Iran and Arab states. Terry (1987), Suleiman (1988), and Christison (1999) argue that US popular perceptions of Arab peoples – abetted by press reporting and a traditional affinity for Jews over Muslims – created in the mindset of US leaders an anti-Arab frame of reference. Suleiman (1995) notes that the American people inherited such biases from European culture but added to them their own peculiarly American ideas about race and culture. Ranging beyond the Arab world, McAlister (2001) illustrates how popular cultural representations of the Middle East shaped the identities of various groups of Americans.

Several scholars probe the bilateral relationships between the United States and specific Arab countries. In a survey of US relations with Arab states from 1945 through the 1990s, Kaufman (1996) emphasizes the importance of containment and oil in US policy calculations, the impact of Arab–Israeli and Arab–Arab conflicts on US diplomacy, and the US response to nationalism in various Arab states. Others explore US policy with specific Arab states. Al Madfai (1993) examines US–Jordanian relations from Amman's perspective in 1974–91; Vitalis (1997) examines US imperialism in Saudi Arabia in the 1990s; Joyce (1998) and Ghabra (1999) study US policy toward Kuwait after Britain's departure in the 1960s; and Gause (1994) analyzes the delicate US balance between maintaining friendly regimes and promoting democratic reform in six Arab states in the Persian Gulf. Shadid (1981), Rabie (1995), and DeGeorgio-Lutz (1999) examine US relations with the stateless Palestinians, including a Palestinian perspective.

US relations with Iraq are heavily examined in the literature on the Persian Gulf War of 1990–1. Initial accounts such as Palmer (1992) celebrate US military exploits, reflecting the popular euphoria that swept the United States immediately after the war. Revisionists criticize US military policy and diplomacy. Smith (1992) and Hilsman (1992) suggest that President George H. W. Bush provoked an unnecessary war that he was sure to win, in order to serve his domestic political purposes and to revive US military might. Situating Iraq's invasion of Kuwait in a 75-year-old border and oil controversy, Khadduri and Ghareeb (1997) suggest that Bush should have settled the dispute with diplomacy rather than force. Amirahmadi (1993) notes that Bush waged war to reverse aggression, protect friends in Saudi Arabia and Kuwait, and defend oil, but suspects that a desire to establish US hegemony in the Middle East and bolster US global power in the post-Cold War era formed greater motives. An extreme revisionist, Clark (1992) tendentiously accuses Bush of committing war crimes against the people of Iraq.

A post-revisionist, moderate interpretation of the Persian Gulf War also exists. Hiro (1992), Brune (1993), Atkinson (1993), and Freedman and Karsh (1993) offer both defenses and criticisms of military and political moves by the Bush administration. Baram (1999) retraces the evolution of US–Iraqi relations from the indirect US support of Iraq during the Iran–Iraq War of the 1980s to the hostile US reaction to Iraq's attack on Kuwait in 1990, stressing that both powers miscalculated the consequences of their actions.

Israel is a subject of sustained attention in the literature on US policy in the Middle East. Many scholars believe that in the late 1900s the United States and Israel were linked by a "special relationship" that featured unusual levels of mutual friendliness, interaction, dependency, and support. Schoenbaum (1993) and Sheffer (1997) examine various aspects of US–Israeli relations from the 1940s to the 1990s and conclude that the two states experienced conflicts and controversies but nonetheless developed a special relationship on a fundamental level. Mansour (1994) emphasizes the evolution of US reliance on Israel as a defense partner.

Numerous scholars argue that Israel occupied a special place in the realm of US domestic culture and politics. According to Gilboa (1987), measurements of US public opinion consistently revealed a pro-Israel disposition through the 1980s, while Tivnan (1987) and Spiegel (1985) describe the influential network of pro-Israel political pressure groups that participated in public debates on US policy in the Middle East. Boyer (1992) demonstrates that many US Christians supported the establishment of Israel because they considered it a fulfillment of biblical prophecy. Kaufman (1994) highlights the emergence of collaboration between US Jewish groups and Israel after the Six Day War.

Several scholars who emphasize the special relationship thesis affirm the propriety of US friendship and support for Israel. Reich (1977, 1984, 1995) consistently and approvingly argues that close friendship linked the two states in various chronological periods. Raviv and Melman (1994) emphasize the secret connections, both official and unofficial, that bound the two states in a close and intimate partnership. Druks (1991) and Arens (1995) indirectly endorse the special relationship idea by faulting the United States for showing inadequate support of Israel.

Conversely, several scholars affirm that a special relationship linked the United States and Israel but criticize it. According to Rubenberg (1986), US leaders shaped their policy through 1980 to benefit Israel in deference to the political and financial clout of pro-Israel citizens, even when US national interests were imperiled. Ball and Ball (1992) regret that a popular attachment to Israel prevented US officials from formulating a balanced policy in the Middle East, while Chomsky (1999) blames the United States for tolerating Israeli misdeeds in Lebanon and elsewhere. Cockburn and Cockburn (1991) and Hersh (1991) argue with a tone of censure that US and Israeli officials covertly coordinated intelligence operations and Israel's development of nuclear weaponry. At the extreme, Green (1984, 1988) and Hussain (1991) criticize the United States for supplying Israel with military and economic aid while it aggressively expanded against its neighbors, and Findley (1985) posits that the pro-Israel lobby inside the United States influenced US policy by nefarious means such as suppressing books, restricting free speech, and unduly pressuring government officials.

By contrast, other scholars of US–Israeli relations have disputed the special relationship thesis. Bar-Siman-Tov (1987) and Ben-Zvi (1993) find that the United States, during major security episodes of the 1950s–1990s, frequently disagreed with Israel's policy and restrained Israel from assertive diplomacy even though US public opinion supported such action. Klieman (1990) and Quandt (1993) consider Israel's relationship with the United States normal and unexceptional, featuring both amity and conflict.

Scholars examine at length US policy toward the Arab–Israeli conflict since 1967. Substantial inquiry and debate has focused on the Six Day War of June 1967, in which Israel reacted to threats from Egypt by striking preemptively against it, provoking a war that also involved Jordan and Syria. In his "yellow-light thesis" Quandt (1993) posits that the Johnson administration subtly signaled Israel that it would not oppose its preemptive strike, thereby creating political conditions conducive to the eruption of war. Little (1999) affirms the yellow-light thesis by stressing Johnson's inclination to see Egypt bloodied by Israeli firepower; Brands (1995) withholds judgment while analyzing Johnson's decision-making during the war. Oren (2002) cogently analyzes the complex multinational diplomacy surrounding the war that, in his reckoning, fundamentally reshaped the Middle East political balance. US ability to prevent the war or alter its outcome, according to Oren, paled in comparison to the forces of chance, circumstance, and miscalculation by other powers that triggered the war and shaped its unintended yet profound consequences.

Scholarship on the Six Day War includes other interpretations. Klinghoffer (1999) hypothesizes that international dynamics stemming from the Vietnam War influenced the unfolding of US and Israeli policies toward the Six Day War. According to Gerges (1999), Arab states detected US support of Israel during the Six Day War and therefore mistrusted the United States in the peace process that followed. In a concise and dramatic account of the war, Neff (1984) displays a tone of sympathy for the Arab powers. Ennes (1979) criticizes Johnson's passivity during the *Liberty* episode, in which Israeli warplanes attacked a US navy intelligence ship and killed US sailors at the height of the war.

Scholars also probe the position of the United States during the Egyptian–Israeli War of Attrition (1967–70), the Arab–Israeli War of October 1973, the civil war in Lebanon, and the peace process of the middle and late 1970s. In an expert scholarly analysis, Quandt (1977) evaluates the relative importance of national security concerns, domestic political interests, and bureaucratic dynamics in US policymaking, concluding that presidential leadership – more than a rational application of national security goals – determined policy. Parker (1993) details US miscalculations that exacerbated the Six Day War and the war of attrition, while Bar-Siman-Tov (1980) and Korn (1992) stress that US officials learned, from their failures to end the war of attrition, the means to build a framework for the peacemaking that followed the 1973 war.

Much scholarship focuses on the role of Henry Kissinger in negotiating the disengagement accords of the mid-1970s and nurturing the peace process that led to the Israel–Egypt peace treaty of 1979. While not uncritical of Kissinger, Sheehan (1976) gives the diplomat enormous credit for stabilizing the Arab–Israeli situation and repairing the strain in US relations with Arab states. Examining US diplomacy in an intricate multinational dimension, K. Stein (1999) thematically emphasizes that Kissinger and other US, Israeli, and Egyptian leaders made peace creatively and heroically. By contrast, Golan (1976) – rumored to have been inspired by the Israeli government – censures Kissinger for producing agreements that undermined Israeli interests and for using deception and duplicity in the process. J. Stein (1999) faults Kissinger for undermining détente by excluding the Soviet Union from the peace-making of the mid-1970s. AlRoy (1975) censures Kissinger's peacemaking from a decidedly pro-Israel perspective.

Several scholars explain and analyze US peacemaking from the late 1970s to the present day. A wide-ranging and episodic survey of US policy toward various facets of the Arab–Israeli controversy from 1945 to 1995, Neff (1995) focuses sympathet-ically on the Palestinian perspective. Quandt (1993) expertly summarizes and evaluates the initiatives shown by US diplomats from the late 1960s to the early 1990s. Focusing more on the process of policy formulation from Truman to Reagan rather than policy per se, Spiegel (1985) concludes that presidential leadership, as a determinant of US policy, outweighed other factors such as congressional and public opinion, bureaucratic forces, and episodes in the Middle East. Safty (1992) analyzes the impact of US diplomacy on Palestinian interests from the Camp David meeting through the Persian Gulf War, and suggests that the United States unjustly backed Israel's expansive ambitions and denied Palestinian statehood. Spiegel (1992), Eisenberg and Caplan (1998), and Rabinovich (1998) chart the US role in the peace process of the 1990s.

Situated geographically, politically, and ideologically on the Middle East–Euro-pean border, Turkey has attracted modest scholarly attention. While the United States successfully applied containment in Greece and Turkey in the early Cold War era, Stearns (1992) observes, after the 1950s it mismanaged Greek–Turkish confron-tations over Cyprus, the Aegean, and other issues. Bolukbasi (1988) concludes that US–Turkish relations declined during confrontations over Cyprus in 1964, 1967, and 1974. Watanabe (1984) and Halley (1985) attribute the US arms embargo on Turkey during the Cyprus dispute of the 1970s to the skilled lobbying of Greek-Americans on behalf of the country of their ancestral origins. Abramowitz (2000) presents a range of contemporary reflections on US–Turkish relations since the 1990s.

This brief survey of the literature on US policy in the Middle East since 1967 leads to several broad conclusions. First, understanding US policy in the post-1967 era sometimes demands an exploration of trends that date to the dawn of official US involvement in the region and the collapse of European empires there in the 1940s–1950s. Second, understanding US policy might necessitate blending various interpre-tive models employed by individual scholars. In other words, there is no strong consensus that any single model offers a superior mode of inquiry.

Scholars who deal with US policy in the Middle East since 1967 fall readily into categories based on geographic borders (Iran, Turkey, Israel, individual Arab states) or another, topical consideration (oil, the Arab–Israeli conflict, Islam). Aside from a few general textbooks, no one has yet attempted a grand synthesis that covers US policy toward the region as a whole on the basis of exhaustive research and a comprehensive paradigm. To contribute to the prospect of such a grand narrative, scholarship must focus on certain neglected areas, especially Turkey and the Arab states. Moreover, scholarship should move beyond, without abandoning, the traditional concerns of high policy and national security and probe the concerns of the so-called new diplomatic history, such as culture, ethnicity and race, and perceptions of the "Other."

REFERENCES

Abramowitz, Morton (ed.): *Turkey's Transformation and American Policy* (New York: Century Foundation Press, 2000).

Al Madfai, Madiha Rashid: *Jordan, the United States, and the Middle East Peace Process, 1974–1991* (New York: Cambridge University Press, 1993).

AlRoy, Gil C.: *The Kissinger Experience: American Policy in the Middle East* (New York: Horizon, 1975).

Amirahmadi, Hooshang: "Global Restructuring, the Persian Gulf War, and the US Quest for World Leadership." In Hooshang Amirahmadi (ed.) *The United States and the Middle East: A Search for New Perspectives* (Albany: State University of New York Press, 1993).

Arens, Moshe: *Broken Covenant: American Foreign Policy and the Crisis Between the US and Israel* (New York: Simon and Schuster, 1995).

Atkinson, Rick: *Crusade: The Untold Story of the Persian Gulf War* (Boston, MA: Houghton Mifflin, 1993).

Ball, George W. and Douglas B. Ball: *The Passionate Attachment: America's Involvement with Israel, 1947 to the Present* (New York: Norton, 1992).

Bar-Siman-Tov, Yaacov: *The Israeli–Egyptian War of Attrition, 1969–1970: A Case Study of Limited Local War* (New York: Columbia University Press, 1980).

Bar-Siman-Tov, Yaacov: *Israel, the Superpowers, and the War in the Middle East* (New York: Praeger, 1987).

Baram, Amatzia: "US Input into Iraqi Decisionmaking, 1988–1990." In David W. Lesch (ed.) *The Middle East and the United States: A Historical and Political Reassessment* (Boulder, CO: Westview Press, 1999).

Bard, Mitchell Geoffrey: *The Water's Edge and Beyond: Defining the Limits to Domestic Influence on United States Middle East Policy* (New Brunswick, NJ: Transaction Books, 1991).

Ben-Zvi, Abraham: *The United States and Israel: The Limits of the Special Relationship* (New York: Columbia University Press, 1993).

Bill, James A.: *The Eagle and the Lion: The Tragedy of American–Iranian Relations* (New Haven, CT: Yale University Press, 1988).

Bill, James A.: The US Overture to Iran, 1985–1986: An Analysis." In Nikki R. Keddie and Mark J. Gasiorowski (eds.) *Neither East Nor West: Iran, the Soviet Union, and the United States* (New Haven, CT: Yale University Press, 1990).

Bolukbasi, Suha: *The Superpowers and the Third World: Turkish–American Relations and Cyprus* (Lanham, MD: University Press of America, 1988).

Boyer, Paul: *When Time Shall Be No More: Prophecy Belief in Modern American Culture* (Cambridge, MA: Belknap Press, 1992).

Brands, H. W: *Into the Labyrinth: The United States and the Middle East, 1945–1993* (New York: McGraw-Hill, 1994).

Brands, H. W: *The Wages of Globalism: Lyndon Johnson and the Limits of American Power* (New York: Oxford University Press, 1995).

Bromley, Simon: *American Hegemony and World Oil: The Industry, the State System, and the World Economy* (University Park: Pennsylvania State University Press, 1991).

Brune, Lester H.: *America and the Iraq Crisis, 1990–1992: Origins and Aftermath* (Claremont, CA: Regina Books, 1993).

Chomsky, Noam: *The Fateful Triangle: The United States, Israel, and the Palestinians* (Cambridge, MA: South End Press, 1999).

Christison, Kathleen: *Perceptions of Palestine: Their Influence on US Middle East Policy* (Berkeley: University of California Press, 1999).

Clark, Ramsey: *The Fire This Time: US War Crimes in the Gulf* (New York: Thunder's Mouth Press, 1992).

Cockburn, Andrew and Leslie Cockburn: *Dangerous Liaison: The Inside Story of the US–Israeli Covert Relationship* (New York: Harper Collins, 1991).

Cooley, John K.: *Payback: America's Long War in the Middle East* (Washington, DC: Brassey's, 1991).

David, Charles-Philippe, Nancy Ann Carrol, and Zachary A. Selden: *Foreign Policy Failure in the White House: Reappraising the Fall of the Shah and the Iran–Contra Affair* (Lanham, MD: University Press of America, 1993).

DeConde, Alexander: *Ethnicity, Race, and American Foreign Policy: A History* (Boston, MA: Northeastern University Press, 1992).

DeGeorgio-Lutz, JoAnn A.: "The US–PLO Relationship: From Dialogue to the White House Lawn." In David W. Lesch (ed.) *The Middle East and the United States: A Historical and Political Reassessment* (Boulder, CO: Westview Press, 1999).

Dorman, William A. and Maneur Farhang: *The US Press and Iran: Foreign Policy and the Journalism of Deference* (Berkeley: University of California Press, 1987).

Druks, Herbert J.: *The US and Israel, 1945–1990* (New York: Speller, 1991).

Eisenberg, Laura Zittrain, and Neil Caplan: *Negotiating Arab–Israeli Peace: Patterns, Problems, Possibilities* (Bloomington: Indiana University Press, 1998).

Ennes, James M.: *Assault on the Liberty: The True Story of the Israeli Attack on an American Intelligence Ship* (New York: Random House, 1979).

Findley, Paul: *They Dare to Speak Out: People and Institutions Confront Israel's Lobby* (Chicago, IL: Lawrence Hill Books, 1985).

Fraser, T. G.: *The USA and the Middle East Since World War II* (New York: St. Martin's Press, 1989).

Freedman, Lawrence and Efraim Karsh: *The Gulf Conflict, 1990–1991: Diplomacy and War in the New World Order* (Princeton, NJ: Princeton University Press, 1993).

Gause, F. Gregory: *Oil Monarchies: Domestic and Security Challenges in the Arab Gulf States* (New York: Council on Foreign Relations Press, 1994).

Gerges, Fawaz A.: *America and Political Islam: Clash of Cultures or Clash of Interests?* (Cambridge: Cambridge University Press, 1999a).

Gerges, Fawaz A.: "The 1967 Arab–Israeli War: US Actions and Arab Perceptions." In David W. Lesch (ed.) *The Middle East and the United States: A Historical and Political Reassessment* (Boulder, CO: Westview Press, 1999b).

Ghabra, Shafeeq: "Kuwait and the United States: The Reluctant Ally and US Policy Toward the Gulf." In David W. Lesch (ed.) *The Middle East and the United States: A Historical and Political Reassessment* (Boulder, CO: Westview Press, 1999).

Gilboa, Eytan: *American Public Opinion toward Israel and the Arab–Israeli Conflict* (Lexington, MA: Heath, 1987).

Golan, Matti: *The Secret Conversations of Henry Kissinger: Step-by-step Diplomacy in the Middle East*, trans. Ruth Geyra Stern and Sol Stern (New York: Quadrangle, 1976).

Goode, James F.: *The United States and Iran: In the Shadow of Musaddiq* (New York: St. Martin's Press, 1997).

Green, Stephen F.: *Taking Sides: America's Secret Relations with a Militant Israel* (New York: Morrow, 1984).

Green, Stephen F.: *Living by the Sword: America and Israel in the Middle East, 1968–87* (Brattleboro, VT: Amana Books, 1988).

Halley, Laurence: *Ancient Affections: Ethnic Groups and Foreign Policy* (New York: Praeger, 1985).

Han, Vo Xuan: *Oil, the Persian Gulf, and the United States* (Westport, CT: Praeger, 1994).

Hemmer, Christopher M.: *Which Lessons Matter? American Foreign Policy Decision Making in the Middle East, 1979–1987* (Albany: State University of New York Press, 2000).

Hersh, Seymour M.: *The Samson Option: Israel's Nuclear Arsenal and American Foreign Policy* (New York: Random House, 1991).

Hilsman, Roger: *George Bush vs. Saddam Hussein: Military Success! Political Failure?* (Novato, CA: Lyford Books, 1992).

Hiro, Dilip: *The Longest War: The Iran–Iraq Military Conflict* (New York: Routledge, 1991).

Hiro, Dilip: *Desert Shield to Desert Storm: The Second Gulf War* (New York: Routledge, 1992).

Hollis, Rosemary (ed.): *Oil and Regional Developments in the Gulf* (London: RIIA, 1998).

Honegger, Barbara: *October Surprise* (New York: Tudor, 1989).

Hussain, Asaf: *The United States and Israel: Politics of a Special Relationship* (Islamabad: Quaid-i-Azam University Press, 1991).

Joyce, Miriam: *Kuwait, 1945–1996: An Anglo-American Perspective* (London: Cass, 1998).

Kaufman, Burton I.: *The Arab Middle East and the United States: Inter-Arab Rivalry and Superpower Diplomacy* (New York: Twayne, 1996).

Kaufman, Menahem: "From Philanthropy to Commitment: The Six Day War and the United Jewish Appeal." *Journal of Israeli History* 15, 2 (1994), 161–91.

Kemp, Geoffrey: *Forever Enemies? American Policy and the Islamic Republic of Iran* (New York: Carnegie Endowment, 1994).

Khadduri, Majid and Edmund Ghareeb: *War in the Gulf, 1990–91: The Iraq–Kuwait Conflict and its Implications* (New York: Oxford University Press, 1997).

Klieman, Aaron S.: *Israel and the World After 40 Years* (Washington, DC: Pergamon–Brassey's, 1990).

Klinghoffer, Judith A.: *Vietnam, Jews, and the Middle East: Unintended Consequences* (New York: St. Martin's Press, 1999).

Kolko, Gabriel: *Confronting the Third World: United States Foreign Policy, 1945–1980* (New York: Pantheon, 1988).

Korn, David A.: *Stalemate: The War of Attrition and Great Power Diplomacy in the Middle East, 1967–1970* (Boulder, CO: Westview Press, 1992).

Lenczowski, George: *American Presidents and the Middle East* (Durham: Duke University Press, 1990).

Little, Douglas: "Nasser Delenda Est: Lyndon Johnson, the Arabs, and the 1967 Six Day War." In H. W. Brands (ed.) *Beyond Vietnam: The Foreign Policies of Lyndon Johnson* (College Station: Texas A&M University Press, 1999).

McAlister, Melani: *Epic Encounters: Culture, Media, and US Interests in the Middle East, 1945–2000* (Berkeley: University of California Press, 2001).

Mansour, Camille: *Beyond Alliance: Israel and US Foreign Policy*, trans. James A. Cohen (New York: Columbia University Press, 1994).

Moses, Russell Leigh: *Freeing the Hostages: Reexamining US–Iranian Negotiations and Soviet Policy, 1979–1981* (Pittsburgh, PA: University of Pittsburgh Press, 1996).

Neff, Donald: *Warriors for Jerusalem: The Six Days that Changed the Middle East* (New York: Linden Press, 1984).

Neff, Donald: *Fallen Pillars: US Policy Towards Palestine and Israel, 1947–1994* (Washington, DC: Institute for Palestine Studies, 1995).

North, Oliver L., with William Novak: *Under Fire: An American Story* (New York: Harper Collins, 1991).

Oren, Michael B.: *Six Days of War: June 1967 and the Making of the Modern Middle East* (New York: Oxford University Press, 2002).

Palmer, Michael A.: *Guardians of the Gulf: A History of America's Expanding Role in the Persian Gulf, 1833–1992* (New York: Free Press, 1992).

Parker, Richard B.: *The Politics of Miscalculation in the Middle East* (Bloomington: Indiana University Press, 1993).

Quandt, William B.: *Decade of Decisions: American Policy Toward the Arab–Israeli Conflict, 1967–1976* (Berkeley: University of California Press, 1977).

Quandt, William B.: *Peace Process: American Diplomacy and the Arab–Israeli Conflict since 1967* (Washington, DC: Brookings Institution, 1993).

Rabie, Muhammed: *US–PLO Dialogue: Secret Diplomacy and Conflict Resolution* (Gainesville: University of Florida Press, 1995).

Rabinovich, Itamar: *The Brink of Peace: The Israeli–Syrian Negotiations* (Princeton, NJ: Princeton University Press, 1998).

Raviv, Dan and Yossi Melman: *Friends in Deed: Inside the US–Israeli Alliance* (New York: Hyperion, 1994).

Reagan, Ronald: *An American Life* (New York: Simon and Schuster, 1990).

Reich, Bernard: *Quest for Peace: United States–Israel Relations and the Arab–Israeli Conflict* (New Brunswick, NJ: Transaction Books, 1977).

Reich, Bernard: *The United States and Israel: Influence in the Special Relationship* (New York: Praeger, 1984).

Reich, Bernard: *Securing the Covenant: United States–Israeli Relations After the Cold War* (Westport, CT: Greenwood Press, 1995).

Rossi, Lorenza: *Who Shall Guard the Guardians Themselves? An Analysis of US Strategy in the Middle East since 1945* (New York: Lang, 1998).

Rubenberg, Cheryl A.: *Israel and the American National Interest: A Critical Examination* (Urbana: University of Illinois Press, 1986).

Rubin, Barry: *Paved with Good Intentions: The American Experience in Iran* (Oxford: Oxford University Press, 1980).

Safty, Adel: *From Camp David to the Gulf: Negotiations, Language and Propaganda, and War* (New York: Black Rose, 1992).

Said, Edward W.: *Orientalism* (New York: Vintage, 1988).

Said, Edward W.: *Culture and Imperialism* (New York: Knopf, 1993).

Sampson, Anthony: *The Seven Sisters: The Great Oil Companies and the World They Shaped* (New York: Viking, 1975).

Sayigh, Yezid and Avi Shlaim (eds).: *The Cold War and the Middle East* (Oxford: Clarendon Press, 1997).

Schoenbaum, David: *The United States and the State of Israel* (New York: Oxford University Press, 1993).

Shadid, Mohammed K.: *The United States and the Palestinians* (London: Croom Helm, 1981).

Sheehan, Edward R. F.: *The Arabs, Israelis, and Kissinger: A Secret History of American Diplomacy in the Middle East* (New York: Reader's Digest Press, 1976).

Sheffer, Gabriel: *US–Israeli Relations at the Crossroads* (London: Cass, 1997).

Shlaim, Avi: *War and Peace in the Middle East: A Critique of American Policy* (New York: Whittle, 1994).

Sick, Gary: *All Fall Down: America's Tragic Encounter with Iran* (New York: Random House, 1985).

Sick, Gary: *October Surprise: America's Hostages in Iran and the Election of Ronald Reagan* (New York: Random House, 1991).

Sick, Gary: "The United States in the Persian Gulf: From Twin Pillars to Dual Containment." In David W. Lesch (ed.) *The Middle East and the United States: A Historical and Political Reassessment* (Boulder, CO: Westview Press, 1999).

Smith, Jean Edward: *George Bush's War* (New York: Holt, 1992).

Smith, Tony: *Foreign Attachments: The Power of Ethnic Groups in the Making of American Foreign Policy* (Cambridge, MA: Harvard University Press, 2000).

Spiegel, Steven L.: *The Other Arab–Israeli Conflict: Making America's Middle East Policy, from Truman to Reagan* (Chicago, IL: University of Chicago Press, 1985).

Spiegel, Steven L. (ed.): *The Arab–Israeli Search for Peace* (Boulder, CO: Rienner, 1992).

Stearns, Monteagle: *Entangled Allies: US Policy Toward Greece, Turkey, and Cyprus* (New York: Council on Foreign Relations Press, 1992).

Stein, Janice Gross: "Flawed Strategies and Missed Signals: Crisis Bargaining Between the Superpowers, October 1973." In David W. Lesch (ed.) *The Middle East and the United States: A Historical and Political Reassessment* (Boulder, CO: Westview Press, 1999).

Stein, Kenneth: *Heroic Diplomacy: Sadat, Kissinger, Carter, Begin, and the Quest for Arab–Israeli Peace* (New York: Routledge, 1999).

Stivers, William: *America's Confrontation with Revolutionary Change in the Middle East, 1948–1983* (New York: St. Martin's Press, 1986).

Stookey, Robert: *America and the Arab States: An Uneasy Encounter* (New York: Wiley, 1975).

Suleiman, Michael W.: *The Arabs in the Mind of America* (Brattleboro, VT: Amana Books, 1988).

Suleiman, Michael: "Palestine and the Palestinians in the Mind of America." In Michael W. Suleiman (ed.) *US Policy in Palestine from Wilson to Clinton* (Normal, IL: Association of Arab–American University Graduates, 1995).

Teicher, Howard and Gayle Radley Teicher: *Twin Pillars to Desert Storm: America's Flawed Vision in the Middle East from Nixon to Bush* (New York: Morrow, 1993).

Terry, Janice J.: *Mistaken Identity: Arab Stereotypes in Popular Writing* (Washington, DC: Arab–American Affairs Council, 1987).

Tillman, Seth P.: *The United States in the Middle East: Interests and Obstacles* (Bloomington: Indiana University Press, 1982).

Tivnan, Edward: *The Lobby: Jewish Political Power and American Foreign Policy* (New York: Simon and Schuster, 1987).

Vitalis, Robert: "The Closing of the Arabian Oil Frontier and the Future of Saudi–American Relations." *Middle East Report* 27, 3 (July–September 1997), 15–25.

Watanabe, Paul Y.: *Ethnic Groups, Congress, and American Foreign Policy: The Politics of the Turkish Arms Embargo* (Westport, CT: Greenwood Press, 1984).

Weinberger, Caspar: *Fighting For Peace: Seven Critical Years in the Pentagon* (New York: Warner, 1990).

Yergin, Daniel: *The Prize: The Epic Quest for Oil, Money, and Power* (New York: Simon and Schuster, 1991).

Yetiv, Steve A.: *America and the Persian Gulf: The Third Party Dimension in World Politics* (Westport, CT: Praeger, 1995).

CHAPTER TWENTY-ONE

US Relations with Latin America, 1961 to the Present: A Historiographic Review

STEPHEN G. RABE

The voluminous literature on US relations with Latin America since 1961 could be characterized in several distinct ways. Most scholars took a critical stance in analyzing inter-American relations. They criticized the United States for its repeated overt and covert interventions in Latin America and held the United States partially responsible for violence, poverty, and despair within the region. Scholars differed, however, on whether the United States was capable of reforming its approach and uplifting Latin Americans. Many questioned whether, given the vast differences in wealth and power, US interests could ever be made compatible with those of Latin American nations. Beyond being critical, the literature on inter-American relations can also be dubbed, in scholarly terms, "traditional." Authors offered a "view from Washington" perspective, focusing on the development of US policies and asking how those policies affected Latin Americans. They compared and contrasted the policies of the individual presidential administrations from John F. Kennedy to George W. Bush. They further emphasized the momentous Cold War confrontations that marked the era, from the invasion at the Bay of Pigs in 1961 to the destabilization campaign in Chile in the 1970s, to the mercenary wars in Central America in the 1980s. This emphasis on the "crisis-event" also reflected the four-decade-long US obsession with Fidel Castro and the Cuban Revolution. But in the aftermath of the Cold War, scholars have broadened their definition of inter-American relations, writing about topics like trade, narcotics trafficking, and immigration and exploring the activities of non-governmental groups such as religious organizations and human rights activists. In view of the new issues and the growing power of the new groups, these authors have speculated that the United States might encounter restraints on its awesome power in the post-Cold War era.

Richard Immerman's award-winning study, *The CIA in Guatemala* (1982), is a good place to start to highlight the basic historiographic approaches toward inter-American relations for the Cold War period after 1961. Although Immerman recounted an event of the 1950s – the US destruction of the popularly elected Guatemalan government of Jacobo Arbenz Guzmán (1950–4) – his study set the tone for analyses of subsequent US policies. Since 1954 it had been widely assumed that the United States bore some responsibility for the overthrow of President

Arbenz, but scholars could not verify the degree of US involvement. Using newly declassified documents, Immerman detailed how the Truman and Eisenhower administrations came to suspect the Guatemalan Revolution (1944–54) and then moved, by covert means, to overturn it. US officials interpreted policies and events through a Cold War prism, placing regional developments in a global context. Guatemala's agrarian reform law, which called for the redistribution of fallow land including the holdings of the United Fruit Company of Boston, came to be seen as part of a deliberate process designed to lead Guatemala down the path of communism. Beyond openly consorting with members of the Guatemalan Communist Party, Arbenz advocated policies that reminded US leaders of actions taken in the Soviet bloc and communist China rather than the nationalistic reforms of the Mexican Revolution. Immerman argued that Arbenz eschewed radical policies and that US officials had no hard evidence linking him or his close advisers to the international communist movement. Nonetheless, President Eisenhower authorized the CIA to destabilize the Arbenz regime, which it successfully did with a sophisticated program, code-named PBSUCCESS, of military pressures and propaganda. Immerman lamented the CIA intervention, suggesting that Arbenz's land reforms could have helped produce the stable, prosperous, anti-communist society that the United States professed it favored. He further noted that the 1954 intervention set off a ghastly cycle of violence in Guatemala that led to the slaughter by the mid-1990s of 150,000–200,000 people, most at the hands of the Guatemalan military and anti-communist "death squads." The United States frequently armed these conservative groups. Indeed, in March 1999, President Bill Clinton publicly apologized for the US role in the Guatemalan terror.

Other authors, such as Schlesinger and Kinzer (1982), who have studied the Guatemalan intervention, have suggested that economic concerns primarily motivated the Eisenhower administration. Practicing traditional "dollar diplomacy," the administration presumably wanted to rescue the holdings of United Fruit. But no scholar has effectively undermined Immerman's national security or anti-communism theme. Piero Gleijeses (1991), who interviewed Arbenz's wife and friends, pointed out that Arbenz had more radical political beliefs than Immerman realized. Gleijeses dismissed notions, however, that Arbenz was a secret agent of the Soviet Union. He characterized the CIA action as "wanton, criminal negligence" and compared it to the ugly Soviet intervention in Hungary in 1956. Gleijeses' denunciation appeared in an afterword he wrote for Nick Cullather's *Secret History* (1999). Cullather, who worked in the CIA's historical office, wrote a history of PBSUCCESS that was to serve as a training manual for covert operators. The study sustained Immerman's thesis that the Eisenhower administration feared a Soviet beachhead in the Western hemisphere. The techniques and deceptions that CIA agents used in Guatemala would also become apparent during subsequent interventions in the 1960s in Cuba, British Guiana, and Brazil. In my own survey of inter-American relations in the 1950s (Rabe 1988), I agreed with Immerman that the administration pursued a foreign policy of anti-communism.

My other study (Rabe 1999) continued the anti-communist theme. In private conversations with US and foreign officials, President Kennedy insisted that communism in the Western hemisphere imperiled the United States, impeded the ability of the United States to act elsewhere, and threatened to become a divisive domestic political issue. As Secretary of State Dean Rusk put it to Latin Americans, the Soviet Union would question US resolve in West Berlin, if the United States appeared weak "in our own backyard" (p. 60). In part, the president intended to vanquish the specter of communist revolution with his Alliance for Progress, a $20 billion economic aid program designed to create socially progressive, democratic Latin American societies. But the Kennedy administration also responded to its fears with increased military aid to the region, a counterinsurgency program, a police assistance initiative, and destabilization campaigns in Argentina, Brazil, Guatemala, and British Guiana. Such policies tended to strengthen conservative, anti-democratic forces in the hemisphere. The administration also covertly intervened in Chile's democratic political process. In his last speech on inter-American affairs, the president pronounced his "Kennedy Doctrine," suggesting a restoration of Theodore Roosevelt's famous corollary to the Monroe Doctrine. Kennedy implied that, as part of its "international responsibility," the United States was prepared to send the US marines to prevent another Cuba in the hemisphere. Tulchin (1988, 1994) and Walker (1994), who have also surveyed inter-American relations in the 1960s, have agreed that the Kennedy administration's fears of communist expansion overwhelmed its commitment to democracy and social change. As Walker concluded, "it would be a mistake to underestimate the effect of the Cold War in the Americas" (p. 42). This was a remarkable statement from an innovative scholar who has been in the forefront of efforts to expand the field of diplomatic history beyond its traditional political and military boundaries.

The Kennedy administration launched the campaign to undermine the constitutional government of João Goulart (1961–4) of Brazil. The Lyndon Johnson administration finished the job. US officials decided that President Goulart was either a communist, sympathetic to communists, or blind to the international communist conspiracy. In specific, they disliked Goulart's rhetoric, his willingness to accept political support from Brazilian radicals, and his refusal to break diplomatic relations with Castro's Cuba. Like the 1954 intervention in Guatemala, the analysis of the US move to oust Goulart is based on substantial archival evidence. Parker (1979) found documents in the Kennedy and Johnson libraries that revealed that the United States encouraged Brazilian generals to strike and prepared to support them militarily if they encountered resistance from Goulart's supporters. Black (1977) astutely demonstrated how agencies like the US Information Service and the American Institute for Free Labor Development formed alliances with anti-Goulart factions. Leacock (1990) argued that the United States undermined the Alliance for Progress with its attack on Goulart. Multi-archival research particularly distinguished Michael Weis' *Cold Warriors and Coups d'Etat* (1993). Weis placed Goulart's overthrow within the larger context of the growing Brazilian–American estrangement over Brazil's place in the international economy. Although the four above-named authors took contrasting approaches to their subject, they agreed that the United States had badly exaggerated the appeal of communism in Brazil. They judged Goulart a political opportunist, not a communist. The overthrow of Goulart ushered in more than two decades of harsh military rule in Brazil accompanied by gross violations of basic human rights. An analysis of US support for military authoritarianism in Brazil can be found in Huggins (1998). Huggins interviewed Brazilian police who were supported by the US Office of Public Safety from 1962 to

1974. The Brazilian officers confessed to torturing and murdering political dissidents.

When, in 1965, over 20,000 US marines landed in the Dominican Republic, it represented the first US invasion of Latin America since the Franklin D. Roosevelt administration pronounced the Good Neighbor policy. Johnson had ordered what Kennedy had vowed to do in his Kennedy Doctrine speech. Although the Dominican invasion differed in form from the "quiet intervention" in Brazil, journalists and scholars have offered similar interpretations about both interventions. Offering eyewitness accounts, journalists Dan Kurzman (1965) and Tad Szulc (1965) alleged that US officials both in Washington and Santo Domingo misunderstood the politics of the island and badly exaggerated the threat of communist expansion. Slater (1970), Lowenthal (1972), and Gleijeses (1979) agreed in their scholarly studies that the Johnson administration mistakenly labeled the constitutionalist revolt as Castro-oriented rather than as a legitimate movement to end political repression and restore the deposed Juan Bosch to the presidency. Although Gleijeses conducted interviews both in the Dominican Republic and the United States and Lowenthal had privileged access to some US documents, research on the Dominican invasion and subsequent US actions has remained inadequate. Agencies like the Central Intelligence Agency and the National Security Council have resisted the declassification of vital records. As of 2002, scholars could count on reasonably complete access to documents only through the Kennedy presidency.

The US war against President Salvador Allende (1970–3), the Marxist leader of Chile, is a crisis-event that has ignited passionate scholarly debate. In their respective memoirs, President Nixon (1978) and Henry A. Kissinger (1982) disparaged Allende for his socialism, but they denied that the United States had incited or assisted the Chilean coup or *golpe de estado*. Nixon and Kissinger were responding to two post-Watergate studies by the US Congress (1975) on covert activities in Chile and the alleged US involvement in the assassination in 1970 of General Rene Schneider, a Chilean military leader who respected constitutional processes. The studies suggested that the United States conducted a massive destabilization campaign against Allende's Chile. Scholarly studies have focused on the issue of US responsibility. Alexander (1976) and Falcoff (1989) absolved the United States for Allende's overthrow, arguing that Allende caused his own political problems with his radical schemes that alienated middle-class Chileans. The US ambassador to Chile, Nathaniel Davis, offered a similar interpretation in his 1985 memoir. Sigmund (1977) staked out a middle ground. In his view, the extensive US intervention contributed to political and social polarization in Chile but was not entirely responsible for the breakdown in constitutional processes. Harsher indictments of the Nixon–Kissinger years can be found in Jensen's (1988) two-volume study and journalist Seymour Hersh's (1983) relentless critique. Further debate awaited declassification of critical documents in Chile and the United States. Some declassification, in fact, took place after the indictment, both at home and abroad, of the Chilean dictator, General Augusto Pinochet (1973–89), for human rights violations. The Jimmy Carter administration's response to Pinochet's bloody dictatorship can be found in Schoultz (1981).

Although it happened on a tiny, English-speaking island in the Caribbean, the

1983 invasion of Grenada by US troops had implications for inter-American relations. The invasion presumably served as a warning to Cuba, the Soviet Union, and to leftists and radicals in El Salvador and Nicaragua that the United States had recovered from the "political malaise" and defeatism or "Vietnam syndrome" of the Carter years. The assertive Ronald Reagan administration would defend US global interests and would not hesitate to respond decisively to the expansion of communism in the Western hemisphere. Among journalists and scholars, however, the familiar debate broke out over the nature of political leftists in the hemisphere – in this case the New Jewel Movement in Grenada. In their separate, extensive essays, Schoenhals and Melanson (1985) reasoned that Maurice Bishop, the leader of the New Jewel Movement, intended to transform Grenada into a Marxist-Leninist state and that President Reagan acted responsibly in ordering the invasion. Armed with documents seized from Grenada, Valenta and Elison (1986) edited a series of essays by political conservatives that alleged a strong Soviet and Cuban influence on minuscule Grenada. The 200 pages of documents offered in the volume did not, however, sustain the charge of international communism. Taking the middle ground, Burrowes (1988) noted that the US invasion probably prevented a Grenadian civil war, because the New Jewel Movement had broken into warring factions. But Burrowes cast doubt on the external threat to Grenada and the Reagan administration's claim that US citizens were endangered on the island. British journalist Hugh O'Shaughnessey (1985), who was on the island in 1983, labeled the invasion as illegal and unnecessary. Bell (1986) averred that President Reagan engaged in "Orwellian fiction" in trying to justify the US invasion, for the threats to the United States from Grenada were potential, not real (pp. 564–86).

Contemporary arguments about Grenada echoed the angry debate that erupted in the United States in the 1980s over the Reagan administration's military campaigns in Central America. As in the other regional Cold War crises, the arguments focused on the character and nature of the left-wing groups that vied for power in Nicaragua and El Salvador. Were the Nicaraguan Sandinistas led by President Daniel Ortega (1985–90) and the Salvadorean guerrillas, the Farubundo Martí National Liberation Front, surrogates for communist Cuba and the Soviet Union or home-grown revolutionaries committed to attacking poverty and injustice in their respective homelands? The Reagan administration unequivocally answered that question by propping up conservative governments in El Salvador, Guatemala, and Honduras with massive amounts of economic and military assistance and by openly aiding the counterrevolutionary exile army or "Contras" in Nicaragua. The administration justified its anti-communist intervention by pointing to the conclusions of *The Report of the National Bipartisan Commission on Central America* (1984), chaired by Henry Kissinger. The report actually presented a nuanced analysis, suggesting that the sources of turmoil were both foreign and indigenous. The US Congress ultimately wearied of the mercenary wars and restricted funding. The administration defied legislators and creatively and illegally found funds for the Contras. Within its own terms, the Reagan administration proved successful in Central America, successfully harassing guerrilla groups and containing the Sandinistas. The Central American civil wars left, however, an appalling record of death and destruction. Perhaps 75,000 died in tiny El Salvador – most at the hands of right-wing terrorist groups.

A chilling narrative of the horror can be found in Mark Danner (1994). In late 1981 the US-trained Alcatel battalion murdered 500 civilians in a Salvadorean village. The Reagan administration tried to explain away the massacre.

Mastering the literature of the Central American crisis of the 1980s would prove a daunting assignment. In a historiographic review, Leonard (1993) reported that between 1979 and 1992 over 900 books appeared that purported to explain the Central American upheavals. Perhaps the best place to start is with incisive surveys of the region, such as Woodward's (1999) standard account and Booth and Walker (1999). Booth and Walker discounted the Kissinger Commission's contention that external forces played a major role in inciting revolution. They pointed to rapid socioeconomic change in the region, such as the development of export agriculture, as underlying the discontent. In their latest edition, the authors also analyzed how Central America had fared in the 1990s in the aftermath of the civil wars. Economic explanations also informed Coatsworth (1994) and LaFeber (1993). These distinguished historians both used a form of dependency analysis to explain that the US domination of Central America's economy and its reflexive support for socioeconomic elites who ignored Central America's poverty and injustice made revolution "inevitable." In his survey, Leonard (1991) criticized historians who focused solely on US economic and geopolitical drives. Leonard emphasized that Central American elites, like the wealthy landowners of El Salvador, were perfectly capable of directing US policy for their own purposes to maintain the domestic status quo. Latin Americans' ability to make their own history was evident in Armony (1997). In his well-investigated study, Armony demonstrated that the Argentine military did not merely respond to US requests in aiding anti-Sandinista forces in Nicaragua. Of their own volition and for their own purposes, the Argentines taught the Contras the tactics of counterterror and "dirty war."

LeoGrande (1998) composed the most comprehensive account of the rancorous debates over Central America that rocked Washington in the 1980s. LeoGrande highlighted the showdown between the executive and legislative branches as well as the internal squabbles between ideologues and pragmatists within the Reagan administration. The fight to control policy can also be followed in Arnson (1993). Although she disapproved of the policy, Arnson fully conceded that Reagan and his followers kept control of Central American policy, because they effectively played the anti-communist tune. Kagan (1996) provided a supportive account of Reagan's war against the Contras that was not excessively polemical. Kagan, who worked for Reagan, reasoned that his president's policy proved successful, because it led to a democratic transition with the election in 1990 of Violetta Chamorro as president of Nicaragua. Thomas Carothers (1991), who served in the State Department during the Reagan years, found another victory emerging from the war against the Sandinistas. In order to demonstrate to US allies that its anti-communism was rooted in a respect for democracy, the administration began to spurn authoritarian, anti-communist allies like Chile's General Pinochet. Carothers attributed the collapse of dictatorial regimes in the 1980s in key countries like Argentina, Brazil, and Chile to the new US emphasis on representative government.

Disputes among policymakers and scholars alike over the repeated Cold War interventions by the United States ultimately centered on the essential issue of the designs of the Soviet Union in Latin America. Scholars such as Blasier (1987), Miller

(1989), and Prizel (1990), who have conducted research in Moscow, interviewed the Soviet Union's Latin American experts, and read Russian-language sources, do not support allegations that agents of the Soviet Union penetrated the region. They found that Moscow favored national liberation movements, the expansion of Soviet influence, and the triumph of socialism in Latin America. But the Soviet Union faced a variety of restraints in achieving those ideological and strategic goals. The power of the United States, the lack of economic complementarity with Latin America, the daunting barriers to physical communication, and the deep hostility of Latin America's elites to communism forced Soviet authorities to take a cautious approach. These scholars pointed out, for example, that the Soviet Union provided only limited support to Salvador Allende's Chile, because it did not need copper, lacked the technology to assist Chile's mining development, and simply could not afford a massive economic aid program. In the 1980s, the Soviet Union traded extensively with Argentina and Brazil, but the balance of trade overwhelmingly favored the Latin Americans. Hungry Russians desperately needed Argentine wheat, whereas Argentines found Soviet consumer goods to be of shoddy quality, especially when compared to items manufactured in the West. To be sure, the Soviets provided military assistance to the Sandinistas. The Sandinistas came to power, however, without the aid of the Soviet Union or Nicaragua's Communist Party, and Moscow carefully calibrated what it would provide to Managua. It sent only defensive arms and let the Reagan administration define what was unacceptable military aid, such as advanced jet fighter aircraft. The Soviet Union had no desire to risk a confrontation with the United States, albeit it saw Nicaragua as a target of opportunity to counter US support for anti-communist fighters in Afghanistan. Perhaps the opening of Soviet archives will reveal that the Soviet Union secretly and effectively sponsored revolution in Latin America. But short of such evidence, scholars generally agreed that the political and economic needs of the Soviet state mattered more than the ideological imperatives of the international communist movement.

Cuba was the Soviet Union's only real diplomatic success story in Latin America. As in Nicaragua, however, a radically nationalist movement came to power without the active assistance of Moscow or local communists. Properly assessing the scholarly literature on the perpetual US confrontation with Fidel Castro's Cuba would easily require a book-length study. Normal diplomatic relations will resume presumably only after Castro dies. In May 2001, President George W. Bush rejected normalization and smugly predicted that time was not on Castro's side. The Cuban strongman could have responded by observing that he had already outlasted nine US presidents. During those presidencies, critical events – the Bay of Pigs invasion, Operation Mongoose, the Cuban missile crisis, Cuba's intervention in Africa, the Mariel boatlift – shaped inter-American relations and the history of the Cold War. Since 1989, the issues of immigration, narcotics trafficking, and trade have become the key items on the US–Cuban agenda, as well as for inter-American relations in general.

Students of the forty-year war between the United States and Cuba might begin with Paterson (1994). Although the author focused on the pre-1959 period, this study proved essential to understanding subsequent conflicts. What Paterson documented was that the FBI and CIA spied on and harassed the young Cuban and that the Eisenhower administration repeatedly tried to block the 26th of July Movement's rise to power. Whereas Castro's anti-Americanism was rooted in his personal experiences and the widespread Cuban disdain for the US political, economic, and cultural domination of the island, his intellectual journey toward Marxism-Leninism and an alliance with the Soviet Union was not preordained. Most Castro biographers, like Quirk (1993), reasoned that Castro gradually and willingly moved politically leftward, because he concluded that communism provided solutions to Cuba's problems and because a dictatorship of the proletariat would enhance his own power. On the other hand, Szulc (1986) opined, based on personal interviews with Castro, that the Cuban hid his radical views during the 1950s. In any case, two years before Castro announced his conversion to Marxism-Leninism, the United States decided to eliminate him. Trumbull Higgins prepared a standard account of the Bay of Pigs invasion in *The Perfect Failure* (1987). As indicated in Higgins' title, scholars have probed why the Eisenhower and Kennedy administrations incorrectly and perhaps foolishly believed that they could overthrow Castro with a 1,400-man exile army. Blight and Kornbluh (1989), Gleijeses (1995), and Kornbluh (1998) have published new studies based on recently declassified documents and interviews with and conferences among US policymakers, Cuban officials, and Cuban exiles. Most participants agreed that the United States badly underestimated the depth and intensity of support among the Cuban people that Castro enjoyed in the early 1960s.

More crisis-events followed the Bay of Pigs debacle. US efforts to destabilize the Castro regime and murder its leader can be found in the previously cited study by the US Congress (1975a) on the assassination of foreign leaders. Fursenko and Naftali (1997) skillfully survey the course and conduct of the missile crisis. The authors gained some access to Soviet archives and demonstrated that both the Cubans and Soviets believed that the Kennedy administration contemplated a military invasion of the island. The missile crisis ended with the United States pledging not to invade Cuba. But in a new article (Rabe 2000), I found that Kennedy and his advisers continued to plot Castro's overthrow right through November 1963. Inside the White House, the president, dubbed "Higher Authority" in CIA parlance, personally approved terrorist and sabotage activities aimed at Cuba.

After October 1962 neither the United States nor the Soviet Union risked further confrontation over Cuba. Nonetheless, over the next twenty-five years, US officials objected to the revolutionary machinations of Cuba, assuming that Cuba acted as a surrogate for the Soviet Union. The Soviets provided Cuba with $2–3 billion a year in assistance. But the aid apparently did not guarantee Cuba's subservience. Domín-guez (1989) and especially Gleijeses in his brilliant study, *Conflicting Missions* (2002), challenged prevailing Cold War wisdom about a vast global conspiracy. Based on their interviews with Cuban political and military authorities and access to Cuban archives, they argued that in its desire "to make the world safe for revolution" Cuba pursued its own foreign policy. At times, Cuban goals may have coincided with Soviet objectives. The authors insisted, however, that whereas Cuba aided socialist movements, it hardly created them. Gleijeses found that fewer than forty Cubans actually fought in Latin America in the 1960s (p. 377). Cuba's inability to foment revolution was particularly apparent in Bolivia, where Ernesto "Che" Gue-vara lost his life in 1967. In his pathetic effort to rally Bolivian *campesinos*, Guevara lacked the steadfast support of Castro. Anderson (1997) interviewed Guevara's friends and family and conducted extensive research in Cuba. Henry Butterfield

Ryan, a retired foreign service officer, celebrated the CIA's capture of Guevara and recounted the events leading to the revolutionary's execution in *The Fall of Che Guevara* (1998).

As exemplified by the Helms–Burton law (1996), which threatened other countries with sanctions if they traded with Cuba, US relations with the island may have actually deteriorated in the aftermath of the Cold War. Conventional wisdom assigns responsibility for the unending confrontation with Castro to the political clout of the Cuban exile community. More than 10 percent of Cuba's population resided in the United States, especially in south Florida. In *Havana USA* (1996), María Cristina García, who studied the 600,000 Cubans and Cuban Americans in Dade County, observed that Cubans rejected complete assimilation into US society, defining themselves instead as exiles. Masud-Piloto (1996) confirmed that the Cuban community remained committed opponents of Castro, because since 1959 the United States had used immigration as a way to destabilize the Castro regime. Evidence that cute, little Elián Gonzalez, who became the object of an international custody battle in 2000, was not the first child to become a pawn in the war against Castro could be found in Victor Andrés Triay's *Fleeing Castro* (1998). Other scholars have tried to move beyond the politics of south Florida to explain the "Colder War." Domínguez (1997) reminded that domestic groups in Cuba also opposed a *rapprochement*. Bernell (1994) theorized that, beyond national security considerations, the United States could not abide challenges to its presumption of hegemony in the hemisphere. In an earlier imaginative essay, Edward Cuddy (1986) suggested the use of psychology to explain the US fear and loathing of Castro. US policy was geared toward meeting its psychic needs, presumably a craving for power and domination, rather than fulfilling strategic demands.

Emotionalism and irrationality often characterized US–Panamanian relations. The ratification of the Panama Canal Treaties and the US invasion of Panama in 1989 were unique crisis-events for the Cold War period, for neither directly involved fear of the international communist conspiracy. Coniff (1992) and LaFeber (1989) surveyed the "forced and unequal relationship" that fueled Panamanian nationalism, leading to Panamanian demands for sovereignty over the canal. Others have analyzed the histrionics that surrounded the 1977–8 debates over the treaties. Hogan (1986) happily concluded that political conservatives gained in defeat, assembling a mass political base that rallied behind Ronald Reagan, an ardent opponent of the treaties. George D. Moffett, III, who worked on President Carter's White House staff, sadly agreed that Carter's international victory had significant domestic costs. Moffett (1985) conceded that a political backlash followed the US Senate's vote to transfer the canal to Panama in 2000. Carter had done an excellent job of convincing elite opinion to support the treaties but failed to persuade the public.

The US public reacted enthusiastically, however, to the December 1989 invasion of Panama and the ousting of General Manuel Antonio Noriega (1981–9). "Operation Just Cause" seemed a fitting title for the seizure, trial, and imprisonment in the United States of a dictator, drug trafficker, and sexual pervert. Donnelly, Roth, and Baker (1991) and Bob Woodward (1991), the famous *Washington Post* journalist, wrote celebratory accounts of the invasion. Coming just a month after the collapse of the Berlin Wall, the overthrow of Noriega seemed to signal that the United States had a new post-Cold War agenda for Latin America. Although agreeing that Washington now assigned importance to democracy and the control of the international flow of illegal narcotics, other scholars and journalists remembered that Noriega was a Cold War relic. The CIA had put the Panamanian strongman on its payroll, and the Reagan administration had ignored his corruption and drug trafficking, because Noriega allowed the United States to use Panama as a base for Reagan's war against the Sandinistas of Nicaragua. As Buckley (1991), Dinges (1991), Kempe (1990), and Scranton (1991) colorfully noted, the "whole story" was that "our man in Panama" was a "monster" that the United States helped to create. The Bush administration "divorced the dictator," not because Noriega had been unfaithful, but because the United States had discovered new, alluring interests.

Indeed, since 1989, with the Soviet Union/Russia in retreat, Cuba in a hapless state, and the US economy dominating a globalized market, the United States has enjoyed unchallenged supremacy in the Western hemisphere. Drugs, migration, and trade have become preeminent inter-American issues. Skidmore and Smith (2001: 391) have dubbed them "intermesic issues – that is, international questions with substantial domestic implications." The scholarly literature has tracked these new concerns. With a declaration of a "war on drugs" during the Bush and Clinton administrations, the United States has defined narcotics trafficking as the major national security threat in the Americas. In 2000, the US Congress provided Colombia with $1.3 billion mostly to arm its military for war against cocaine producers and traffickers, and US personnel and the CIA cooperated with Peruvians in shooting suspicious airplanes out of the sky. Washington spent nearly $20 billion annually fighting the illicit drug trade, with about two-thirds of the money being devoted to reducing supply both at home and abroad through coercive measures. Only about one-third of US resources were devoted to reducing demand within the United States through education and drug-treatment programs.

As they did in analyzing US interventions during the Cold War, scholars take a critical view of Washington's approach to the hemispheric drug trade. Walker (1981) and in his imaginative (1988) article set the tone for the debate. Reviewing the twentieth-century history of US efforts to stem the flow of narcotics from Latin America, Walker found that US authorities invariably defined the drug trade as a criminal enterprise. US efforts to eliminate the trade through crime-fighting strategies inevitably failed, because officials ignored the cultural significance of narcotics in Latin America, especially among Amerindian communities in the Andean countries of Bolivia and Peru. Riley (1996) validated Walker's insights. Riley analyzed the US campaign in the 1980s and early 1990s to eradicate cocaine production in the Andean countries. The use of defoliants and herbicides disrupted peasant communities and posed alarming health and environmental risks for the population. Edited collections of essays by Smith (1992) and Bagley and Walker (1996) reported that the hemispheric drug trade had become a huge multinational enterprise that, by the mid-1990s, had surpassed $100 billion in annual value. The drug trade was creating political and social havoc throughout the hemisphere. The essayists largely concluded that narcotics trafficking was a demand-driven business and that American nations, including the United States, had to develop strategies to reduce the demand for drugs among their urban and suburban populations. Latin American "narco-traffickers" were apparently more resistant to US power than had been the political leftists and radicals that the United States had contained and eliminated during the Cold War.

People also increasingly crossed the US border in the post-1961 period. The US census of 2000 classified approximately 35 million people or 12 percent of the population as "Hispanic," a loose and imprecise definition of people who had different national, ethnic, and racial backgrounds. Approximately 60 percent of the Hispanic population claimed Mexican ancestry. Others came from Cuba, the Dominican Republic, and Puerto Rico. Many others fled the civil wars in Central America in the 1980s. In the 1990s, increasing numbers of Colombians arrived in the United States, seeking safety from the violence and terrorism perpetrated by the narco-traffickers. Mitchell (1992) and Pastor (1984) provided fine overviews of the shifting US attitudes and policies toward immigration from Latin America. Frank Bean and colleagues (1997) emphasized in their essays that changes in working and living patterns in Mexico, as much as the attractions of the US labor market, explained the migration of Mexicans to "El Norte." The massive influx of immigrants from Mexico has especially transformed the 2,000-mile border region. In his survey of US–Mexican relations, Raat (1997) devoted a chapter to what he called "Mexamerica." Ruiz (1998) studied the daily contacts among border dwellers and the vast differences in their wealth and power. Ruiz agreed with Raat that a distinct culture had evolved along the border. Dunn (1997) worried about the growing militarization of the border. In their efforts to apprehend drug runners and illegal migrants, US authorities increasingly deployed police and paramilitary outfits along the border. By 2001, almost 10,000 agents served in the US Border Patrol. Dunn doubted whether military-based strategies could address problems that had deep economic and cultural roots.

The evolution of Mexamerica pointed to growing economic interdependence between the United States and Mexico and the expansion of trade throughout the hemisphere. In 1993 the US Congress ratified the North American Free Trade Agreement or NAFTA, establishing a free-trade zone between the United States, Canada, and Mexico. The new president of Mexico, Vicente Fox (2000–) envisioned the day when the US–Mexican border would be a Western European-like "open" border, and Mexican citizens could freely cross the border to work in the United States. President Fox actually created a new cabinet-level position, the Ministry of Migrant Affairs, to represent the millions of Mexicans and Mexican Americans living and working in the United States. Latin Americans also saw advantages to free trade. In 1991, Argentina, Brazil, Uruguay, and Paraguay formed an economic association, MERCOSUR, that envisioned a "Common Market of the South," based on the model of the European Union. In the 1990s the volume of trade and investment grew rapidly within MERCOSUR. The success of NAFTA and MERCOSUR prompted calls for a hemispheric-wide free-trade association. Preliminary discussions among the region's heads of state took place in Miami in 1994 and in Quebec in 2001.

These Latin American desires for economic interdependence and their renewed faith in free trade and investment, dubbed "neoliberalism," caught many scholars by surprise. The dominant mode of interpretation had been the dependency theory or *dependencia*. Dependency theorists held that Latin America's underdevelopment and poverty could be explained by their participation in the international capitalist system. Argentine economist Raúl Prebisch attacked the theory of trading from comparative advantage, offering his theory of "unequal exchange" that held that trade between the industrialized "center" (the United States) and the non-industrial "periphery" (Latin America) inevitably accrued to the benefit of the industrialized nation. Other theorists took a more doctrinaire approach, arguing that center nations manipulated the international financial machinery to maintain their economic dominance over the periphery. The privileged few in the periphery, such as owners of vast plantations and *haciendas*, collaborated with the international capitalists, leaving Latin America in an impoverished and unjust state. Chilcote (1984) and Kláren and Bossert (1986) provided excellent surveys on Latin American thinking on development and change. Pérez (1991) concisely presented dependency thinking. Packenham (1992), however, dissected the dependency movement, suggesting that political agendas rather than economic analyses informed the approach of those who employed the dependency model. The economic decisions of Brazilian President Fernando Henrique Cardoso (1995–) seemingly sustained Packenham's critique. As a leftist intellectual, Cardoso, with Enzo Faletto, had stimulated dependency thinking in the 1960s with his *Dependencia y desarrollo en America Latina* (1967). But once in office, this founding father of the dependency movement advocated neoliberal policies, privatizing, for example, many of Brazil's national industries.

Whereas dependency theory now suffered from credibility problems, it remained uncertain whether scholars had concluded that a harmony of interests could exist between the United States and Latin America in the post-Cold War, globalized era. Generally upbeat assessments of the future of inter-American relations could be read in the collections edited by Bulmer-Thomas and Dunkerley (1999) and Domínguez (2000). The essayists predicted growing economic interdependence, suggesting perhaps some concomitant restraints on US power. They also wrote about the new influence of non-governmental actors like businessmen, environmental groups, and human rights activists. But vast differences persisted in wealth and power between the United States and its Latin American neighbors at the beginning of the twenty-first century. For example, the hourly minimum wage in the United States was higher than the daily minimum wage in Mexico. Would the United States continue to accept Latin America's products and its ambitious but poor people, when a lengthy economic recession gripped the US economy? How would the United States react when desperately poor Haiti suffered another political and social breakdown? Would pressure build in the US Congress for decisive action if the Colombian government could not subdue its narco-terrorists? Most important, what would ensue if neoliberal doctrines and the brave, new world of the Internet did not produce the economic growth and social justice that Latin Americans yearned for? International investors, led by US financiers, were purchasing high-profile businesses, like Latin American banks. Latin American citizens might grant extreme nationalists a hearing if the surrender of their economic sovereignty did not produce real benefits within a reasonable period.

What could be predicted with certainty was that the study of US relations with Latin America would continue as a vibrant endeavor. Historians Coerver and Hall (1999), Gilderhus (1999), Longley (2002), Schoultz (1999), and Smith (1999) recently published textbooks on inter-American relations for the higher education market. The authors were probably responding to the growing public interest in

Latin America relating to issues like immigration, narcotics trafficking, preservation of the Brazilian rainforests, and NAFTA. The increasing numbers of college and university students of Hispanic heritage were also naturally interested in enrolling in courses with Latin American themes. Faithful to the dominant themes in recent scholarship, these authors asked students to think critically about the costs and consequences of the twentieth-century domination of Latin America by the United States.

REFERENCES

Alexander, Robert: *The Tragedy of Chile* (Westport, CT: Greenwood Press, 1976).

Anderson, Jon: *Che Guevara: A Revolutionary Life* (New York: Grove Press, 1997).

Armony, Ariel C.: *Argentina, the United States, and the Anti-Communist Crusade in Central America, 1977–1984* (Athens, OH: Ohio University Press, 1997).

Arnson, Cynthia: *Crossroads: The Congress, the President, and Central America, 1976–1993*, 2nd edn. (University Park: Pennsylvania State University Press, 1993).

Bagley, Wesley and William O. Walker, III (eds.): *Drug Trafficking in the Americas* (Coral Gables: University of Miami North–South Center Press, 1996).

Bean, Frank et al. (eds.) *At the Crossroads: Mexico and US Immigration Policy* (Lanham, MD: Rowman and Littlefield, 1997).

Bell, Wendell: "The Invasion at Grenada: A Note on False Prophecy." *Yale Review* 75 (summer 1986), 564–86.

Bernell, David: "The Curious Case of Cuba in American Foreign Policy." *Journal of Inter-American Studies and World Affairs* 36 (summer 1994), 65–103.

Black, Jan Knippers: *United States Penetration of Brazil* (Philadelphia: University of Pennsylvania Press, 1977).

Blasier, Cole: *The Giant's Rival: The USSR and Latin America*, revd. edn. (Pittsburgh, PA: University of Pittsburgh Press, 1987).

Blight, James G. and Peter Kornbluh: *Politics of Illusion: The Bay of Pigs Invasion Re-examined* (Boulder, CO: Lynne Reinner Publishers, 1989).

Booth, John A. and Thomas W. Walker: *Understanding Central America*, 3rd edn. (Boulder, CO: Westview Press, 1999).

Buckley, Kevin: *Panama: The Whole Story* (New York: Simon and Schuster, 1991).

Bulmer-Thomas, Victor and James Dunkerley (eds.) *The United States and Latin America: The New Agenda* (London and Cambridge, MA: Institute of Latin American Studies, University of London and David Rockefeller Center for Latin American Studies, Harvard University, 1999).

Burrowes, Reynold A.: *Revolution and Rescue in Grenada: An Account of the US–Caribbean Invasion* (Westport, CT: Greenwood Press, 1988).

Cardoso, Fernando Henrique and Enzo Faletto: *Dependencia y desarrollo en America Latina* (Lima: Instituto de Estudios Peruanos, 1967).

Carothers, Thomas: *In the Name of Democracy: US Policy toward Latin America in the Reagan Years* (Berkeley: University of California Press, 1991).

Chilcote, Ronald H.: *Theories of Development and Underdevelopment* (Boulder, CO: Westview Press, 1984).

Coatsworth, John: *Central America and the United States: The Clients and the Colossus* (New York: Twayne, 1994).

Coerver, Don and Linda B. Hall: *Tangled Destinies: Latin America and the United States* (Albuquerque: University of New Mexico Press, 1999).

Coniff, Michael: *Panama and the United States: The Forced Alliance* (Athens, GA: University of Georgia Press, 1992).

Cuddy, Edward: "America's Cuban Obsessions: A Case Study in Diplomacy and Psycho-History." *The Americas* 43 (October 1986), 183–96.

Cullather, Nick: *Secret History: The CIA's Classified Account of Its Operations in Guatemala, 1952–1954.* Afterword by Piero Gleijeses (Stanford, CA: Stanford University Press, 1999).

Danner, Mark: *The Massacre at El Mozote: A Parable of the Cold War* (New York: Vintage, 1994).

Davis, Nathaniel: *The Last Two Years of Salvador Allende* (Ithaca, NY: Cornell University Press, 1985).

Dinges, John: *Our Man in Panama: The Shrewd Rise and Brutal Fall of Manuel Noriega* (New York: Times Books/Random House, 1991).

Domínguez, Jorge I.: *To Make a World Safe for Revolution: Cuba's Foreign Policy* (Cambridge, MA: Harvard University Press, 1989).

Domínguez, Jorge I.: "US–Cuban Relations: From the Cold War to the Colder War." *Journal of Inter-American Studies and World Affairs* 39 (fall 1997), 49–75.

Domínguez, Jorge I. (ed.): *The Future of Inter-American Relations* (New York: Routledge, 2000).

Donnelly, Thomas, Margaret Roth, and Caleb Baker: *Operation Just Cause: The Storming of Panama* (New York: Lexington Books, 1991).

Dunn, Timothy J.: *The Militarization of the US–Mexico Border, 1978–1992: Low-Intensity Conflict Doctrine Comes Home* (Austin: Center for Mexican American Studies, University of Texas, 1997).

Falcoff, Mark: *Modern Chile, 1970–1989: A Critical History* (New Brunswick, NJ: Transaction Books, 1989).

Fursenko, Alexsandr and Timothy Naftali: *"One Hell of a Gamble": Khrushchev, Castro, and Kennedy, 1958–1964* (New York: W. W. Norton, 1997).

García, María Cristina: *Havana USA: Cuban Exiles and Cuban Americans in South Florida, 1959–1994* (Berkeley: University of California Press, 1996).

Gilderhus, Mark T.: *The Second Century: US–Latin American Relations since 1889* (Wilmington, DE: Scholarly Resources, 1999).

Gleijeses, Piero: *The Dominican Crisis: The 1965 Constitutionalist Revolt and American Intervention* (Baltimore, MD: Johns Hopkins University Press, 1979).

Gleijeses, Piero: *Shattered Hope: The Guatemalan Revolution and the United States* (Princeton, NJ: Princeton University Press, 1991).

Gleijeses, Piero: "Ships in the Night: The CIA, the White House, and the Bay of Pigs." *Journal of Latin American Studies* 27 (February 1995), 1–42.

Gleijeses, Piero: *Conflicting Missions: Havana, Washington, and Africa, 1959–1976* (Chapel Hill: University of North Carolina Press, 2002).

Hersh, Seymour: *The Price of Power: Kissinger in the Nixon White House* (New York: Summit Books, 1983).

Higgins, Trumbull: *The Perfect Failure: Kennedy, Eisenhower, and the CIA at the Bay of Pigs* (New York: W. W. Norton, 1987).

Hogan, Michael J.: *The Panama Canal in American Politics: Domestic Advocacy and the Evolution of Policy* (Carbondale: Southern Illinois University Press, 1986).

Huggins, Martha K.: *Political Policing: The United States and Latin America* (Durham, NC: Duke University Press, 1998).

Immerman, Richard H.: *The CIA in Guatemala: The Foreign Policy of Intervention* (Austin: University of Texas Press, 1982).

Jensen, Poul: *The Garrote: The United States and Chile, 1970–1973*, 2 vols. (Aarhus, Denmark: Aarhus University Press, 1988).

Kagan, Robert: *A Twilight Struggle: American Power and Nicaragua, 1977–1990* (New York: Free Press, 1996).

Kempe, Frederick: *Divorcing the Dictator: America's Bungled Affair with Noriega* (New York: G. P. Putnam's Sons, 1990).

Kissinger, Henry A.: *Years of Upheaval* (Boston, MA: Little, Brown, 1982).

Kláren, Peter F. and Thomas J. Bossert (eds.): *Promise of Development: Theories of Change in Latin America* (Boulder, CO: Westview Press, 1986).

Kornbluh, Peter: *Bay of Pigs Declassified: The Secret CIA Report* (New York: New Press, 1998).

Kurzman, Dan: *Santo Domingo: Revolt of the Damned* (New York: Putnam, 1965).

LaFeber, Walter: *The Panama Canal: The Crisis in Historical Perspective*, updated edn. (New York: Oxford University Press, 1989).

LaFeber, Walter: *Inevitable Revolutions: The United States in Central America*, 2nd edn. (New York: W. W. Norton, 1993).

Leacock, Ruth: *Requiem for Revolution: The United States and Brazil, 1961–1969* (Kent, OH: Kent State University Press, 1990).

LeoGrande, William M.: *Our Own Backyard: The United States in Central America, 1977–1992* (Chapel Hill: University of North Carolina Press, 1998).

Leonard, Thomas M.: *Central America and the United States: The Search for Stability* (Athens, GA: University of Georgia Press, 1991).

Leonard, Thomas M.: "Central America and the United States: Overlooked Foreign Policy Objectives." *The Americas* 50 (July 1993), 1–30.

Longley, Kyle: *In the Eagle's Shadow: The United States and Latin America* (Wheeling, IL: Harlan Davidson, 2002).

Lowenthal, Abraham: *The Dominican Intervention* (Cambridge, MA: Harvard University Press, 1972).

Masud-Piloto, Félix Roberto: *From Welcomed Exiles to Illegal Immigrants: Cuban Migration to the United States, 1959–1995* (Lanham, MD: Rowman and Littlefield, 1996).

Miller, Nicola: *Soviet Relations with Latin America, 1959–1987* (New York: Cambridge University Press, 1989).

Mitchell, Christopher (ed.): *Western Hemisphere Immigration and United States Foreign Policy* (University Park: Pennsylvania State University Press, 1992).

Moffett, George D., III: *The Limits of Victory: The Ratification of the Panama Canal Treaties* (Ithaca, NY: Cornell University Press, 1985).

Nixon, Richard M.: *RN: The Memoirs of Richard Nixon* (New York: Grosset and Dunlap, 1978).

O'Shaughnessey, Hugh: *Grenada: An Eyewitness Account of the US Invasion and the Caribbean History That Provoked It* (New York: Dodd, Mead, 1985).

Packenham, Robert A.: *The Dependency Movement: Scholarship and Politics in Development Studies* (Cambridge, MA: Harvard University Press, 1992).

Parker, Phyllis R.: *Brazil and the Quiet Intervention, 1964* (Austin: University of Texas Press, 1979).

Pastor, Robert A.: "US Immigration Policy and Latin America: In Search of the 'Special Relationship'." *Latin American Research Review* 19, 3 (1984), 35–56.

Paterson, Thomas G.: *Contesting Castro: The United States and the Triumph of the Cuban Revolution* (New York: Oxford University Press, 1994).

Pérez, Louis A.: "Dependency." In Michael J. Hogan and Thomas G. Paterson (eds.) *Explaining the History of American Foreign Relations* (New York: Cambridge University Press, 1991).

Prizel, Illya: *Latin America through Soviet Eyes: The Evaluation of Soviet Perceptions during the Brezhnev Era, 1964–1982* (New York: Cambridge University Press, 1990).

Quirk, Robert: *Fidel Castro* (New York: W. W. Norton, 1993).

Raat, Dirk: *Mexico and the United States: Ambivalent Vistas* (Athens, GA: University of Georgia Press, 1997).

Rabe, Stephen G.: *Eisenhower and Latin America: The Foreign Policy of Anticommunism* (Chapel Hill: University of North Carolina Press, 1988).

Rabe, Stephen G.: *The Most Dangerous Area in the World: John F. Kennedy Confronts Communist Revolution in Latin America, 1961–1963* (Chapel Hill: University of North Carolina Press, 1999).

Rabe, Stephen G.: "After the Missiles of October: John F. Kennedy and Cuba, November 1962 to November 1963." *Presidential Studies Quarterly* 30 (December 2000), 714–26.

Report of the National Bipartisan Commission on Central America. Foreword by Henry A. Kissinger (New York: Macmillan, 1984).

Riley, Kevin Jack: *Snow Job? The War Against International Cocaine Trafficking* (New Brunswick, NJ: Transaction Books, 1996).

Ruiz, Ramón Eduardo: *On the Rim of Mexico: Encounters of the Rich and Poor* (Boulder, CO: Westview Press, 1998).

Ryan, Henry Butterfield: *The Fall of Che Guevara: A Story of Soldiers, Spies, and Diplomats* (New York: Oxford University Press, 1998).

Schlesinger, Stephen and Stephen Kinzer: *Bitter Fruit: The Untold Story of the American Coup in Guatemala* (Garden City, NY: Anchor Press, 1982).

Schoenhals, Kai P. and Richard A. Melanson: *Revolution and Intervention in Grenada: The New Jewel Movement, the United States, and the Caribbean* (Boulder, CO: Westview Press, 1985).

Schoultz, Lars: *Human Rights and United States Policy toward Latin America* (Princeton, NJ: Princeton University Press, 1981).

Schoultz, Lars: *Beneath the United States: A History of US Policy toward Latin America* (Cambridge, MA: Harvard University Press, 1999).

Scranton, Margaret E.: *The Noriega Years: US–Panamanian Relations, 1981–1990* (Boulder, CO: Lynne Reinner, 1991).

Sigmund, Paul: *The Overthrow of Allende and the Politics of Chile, 1964–1976* (Pittsburgh, PA: University of Pittsburgh Press, 1977).

Skidmore, Thomas E. and Peter H. Smith: *Modern Latin America*, 5th edn. (New York: Oxford University Press, 2001).

Slater, Jerome: *Intervention and Negotiation: The United States and the Dominican Revolution* (New York: Harper and Row, 1970).

Smith, Peter H. (ed.): *Drug Policy in the Americas* (Boulder, CO: Westview Press, 1992).

Smith, Peter H.: *Talons of the Eagle: Dynamics of US–Latin American Relations*, 2nd edn. (New York: Oxford University Press, 1999).

Szulc, Tad: *Dominican Diary* (New York: Delacorte, 1965).

Szulc, Tad: *Fidel: A Critical Portrait* (New York: William Morrow, 1986).

Triay, Victor Andrés: *Fleeing Castro: Operation Pedro Pan and the Cuban Children's Program* (Gainesville: University of Florida Press, 1998).

Tulchin, Joseph S.: "The United States and Latin America in the 1960s." *Journal of Inter-American Studies and World Affairs* 30 (spring 1988), 1–36.

Tulchin, Joseph S.: "The Promise of Progress: US Relations with Latin America during the Administration of Lyndon B. Johnson." In Warren I. Cohen and Nancy Bernkopf Tucker (eds.) *Lyndon Johnson Confronts the World: American Foreign Policy, 1963–1968* (New York: Cambridge University Press, 1994).

US Congress. Senate. Select Committee to Study Governmental Operations with Respect to Intelligence Activities. *Alleged Assassination Plots Involving Foreign Leaders*. Senate Report No. 465 (Washington, DC: Government Printing Office, 1975a).

US Congress. Senate. Select Committee to Study Governmental Operations with Respect to

Intelligence Activities. *Covert Action in Chile, 1963–1973: Staff Report.* (Washington, DC: Government Printing Office, 1975b).

Valenta, Jiri and Herbert J. Elison (eds.): *Grenada and Soviet/Cuban Policy: Internal Crisis and US/OECS Intervention* (Boulder, CO: Westview Press, 1986).

Walker, William O., III: *Drug Control in the Americas* (Albuquerque: University of New Mexico Press, 1981).

Walker, William O., III: "Mixing the Sweet with the Sour: Kennedy, Johnson, and Latin America." In Diane B. Kunz (ed.) *The Diplomacy of the Crucial Decade: American Foreign Relations during the 1960s* (New York: Columbia University Press, 1994).

Walker, William O., III: "Drug Control and the Issue of Culture in American Foreign Relations." *Diplomatic History* 12 (fall 1998), 365–82.

Weis, Michael: *Cold Warriors and Coups d'Etat: Brazilian–American Relations, 1945–* (Albuquerque: University of New Mexico Press, 1993).

Woodward, Bob: *The Commanders* (New York: Simon and Schuster, 1991).

Woodward, Ralph Lee, Jr.: *Central America: A Nation Divided*, 3rd edn. (New York: Oxford University Press, 1999).

CHAPTER TWENTY-TWO

Presidential Elections and the Cold War

MELVIN SMALL

Near the end of a three-day conference at the Lyndon Baines Johnson Library on making peace in Vietnam someone from the audience asked: "It is all well and good to examine the many initiatives from all over the world that could have helped the United States to extricate itself from Vietnam, but how can one evaluate their significance unless we take into consideration the importance of the 1964 and 1968 presidential elections in *all* of Johnson's diplomatic and military interventions?" At that point, another member of the audience chimed in: "And the same goes for the Vietnam policies of Kennedy and Nixon." Why did it take until the eleventh hour for a room full of experienced diplomatic historians to move to that subject?

In the first place, despite a good deal of circumstantial evidence to the contrary, almost all presidents have maintained that they never considered their reelections when determining national security policy. It would be unseemly of them, they assert self-righteously, to consider such a selfish issue when confronting decisions concerning war and peace. Indeed, the minutes of presidential meetings concerning responses to foreign crises rarely reveal evidence that those in attendance discussed the domestic implications of their policy choices. But like the pink elephant in the room that nobody talks about, those unstated implications are almost always of concern to the decision-makers. Does anyone seriously believe that because John F. Kennedy did not mention the upcoming congressional elections during the Cuban missile crisis that they had little to do with his responses to the Russians? Why was he unwilling to safely escape from the most serious crisis of the Cold War by simply trading missiles in Cuba for poorly designed and soon-to-be-removed missiles in Turkey?

In addition, foreign policy has rarely been the central or even a major issue in a presidential election. Only in the elections of 1800, 1812, 1846, 1900, 1920, 1952, and 1980 did foreign affairs figure prominently, and even in most of those elections, other issues were more salient. But merely evaluating election issues in a vacuum does not tell the entire story about the impact of foreign policy on presidential elections or, especially, the impact of presidential elections on foreign policy.

In fact, the most interesting connection between elections and foreign policy has to do with the way domestic political considerations have altered and limited the options available to America's chief executives. During the Cold War years in particular, the need for the president or his party's chosen successor to stand for reelection or election every four years limited those in the Oval Office who contemplated taking unusual or potentially unpopular foreign policy initiatives that might have been in the nation's best national security interests. There is a good deal of evidence to suggest that, since presidents were more responsive to public opinion during election years than at other times (Foyle 1999: 272), they were nervous about rocking the boat. Moreover, by adopting politically popular campaign rhetoric, the winners in presidential campaigns found themselves bound by promises they never really meant to keep. According to one scholar, new presidents inherit "issues typically . . . central to the rhetoric and debate of the campaign," and they become, whether they like it or not, their agenda (Jones 1994: 180–1).

Further, as elections approached, presidents and their opponents had to worry about "October Surprises" when candidates might make major foreign policy moves or declarations primarily to affect the electorate. Finally, we cannot ignore the importance of US presidential elections for the nation's friends and foes, who sometimes adjusted their foreign policies in ways that supported their necessarily unstated preferences among the presidential candidates and who also had to deal with the impact of the campaign on their relations with the United States during the following four years.

It is interesting to note that one of the events that ushered in the Cold War, Josef Stalin's February 1946 speech, was directed not to the United States but to his own electorate, which was preparing to go through the motions of a Supreme Soviet election. Most Kremlinologists viewed the speech as a call to arms against the West. Harry Truman ultimately accepted that erroneous interpretation, even though his first response was "Well, you know we always have to demagogue a little, before elections" (Costigliola 2000: 46).

In this chapter, I will examine the relationship between the Cold War and US presidential elections. I will narrow my focus to the Soviet Union and its allies, ignoring such key issues as Israel, the Panama Canal, and the Iranian Revolution. For the period from 1940 to 1972, historian Robert A. Divine (1976) provides a comprehensive history of the role of foreign policy issues in presidential elections.

Throughout American history it has been difficult for political leaders to adopt positions that made them seem less patriotic, nationalistic, and muscular than their opponents (DeConde 2000). During the Cold War in particular, the Democratic Party, with its relativist, liberal, internationalist, even at times anti-military bent, found itself under continual Republican attack for not being tough enough with the Russians and their allies – and also with communists and radicals at home. Consequently, the party often had to adopt hardline positions that made many of its more liberal followers quite uncomfortable. Of course, when the Cold War ended after the presidency of Ronald Reagan, some observers noted that the Republicans had been correct all along: tough talk and tough actions were far more effective than liberal attempts to conciliate the communists.

As early as the 1946 congressional elections, anti-communism as a campaign issue began to assume prominence. On the East Coast, running for political office for the first time, a young navy veteran, Democrat John F. Kennedy, talked about getting tough with Russia, while on the West Coast, another young navy veteran running for Congress, Richard M. Nixon, launched his political career by accusing his Democratic opponent of being soft on communism.

By the time of the 1948 presidential election, few could accuse Democratic president Harry S. Truman of being soft on communism. In 1947, in order to sell his unprecedented Truman Doctrine, which provided aid to Greece and Turkey because of perceived external communist threats to their survival, the president painted the emerging conflict with the Soviet Union in apocalyptic terms. By the fall of that year, as he prepared for the election campaign, his advisers told him that "the battle with the Kremlin" could help him politically in 1948. "The worse matters get . . . the more is there a sense of crisis. In times of crisis, the American citizen tends to back up his president" (Divine 1976: 172). Confronted by a Republican Congress that failed to enact much of his social and economic legislation, Truman realized, as did all of his successors, that he enjoyed a far freer hand in foreign affairs than domestic affairs. A failing presidency at home could be rescued by a vigorous presidency abroad.

This is not to say that the blunt-speaking Truman did not sincerely believe in assertive rhetoric and muscular actions in the Cold War. But he did recognize how such a posture could aid him in the 1948 election. After Czechoslovakia fell in a coup to communism in March of that year, the administration, and the aircraft industry in particular, helped to create a crisis atmosphere that not only convinced Congress to increase defense-related appropriations but also made the president appear to be more of a leader to the electorate (Kofsky 1993). At home, assailed by the Right for not doing enough about American communists, he had earlier introduced a government employee loyalty program.

The war scare and crackdown on domestic communists, combined with sensational revelations about Soviet spying, contributed to tensions in East–West relations. When the left-wing Progressive Party formed in response to Truman's Cold War at home and abroad, Republicans had a difficult time pinning the soft-on-communism label on the president. The Progressive's candidate, former Vice President Henry Wallace, ran against "the bipartisan reactionary war policy which is dividing the world into two armed camps." Truman aide Clark Clifford advised the president "to identify him and isolate him in the public mind with the communists" (Divine 1976: 171, 172). The Progressives were supported by the American Communist Party, some of whose members took leadership roles in the campaign, while Wallace had eagerly accepted Stalin's call for bilateral peace negotiations that Truman had rejected.

Stalin unwittingly helped Truman in the summer of 1948 when, on the same day that the Republicans nominated Thomas E. Dewey for the presidency, he launched a blockade of Berlin in response to US German policy. Truman's vigorous response, through a daring airlift, further contributed to his anti-Soviet reputation. But one wonders how important his need to seem tough, maybe even recklessly so, affected his strategies, even though he felt "we are very close to war" (DeConde 2000: 143). This concern, as well as his perception that the public favored a peaceful resolution of the dispute, led him to contemplate the first "October Surprise," the dispatch of Chief Justice Fred Vinson to Moscow to talk directly with Stalin just before the election.

The hardline Republicans made it easier for Truman by nominating the moderate Dewey, who while generally critical of his failures in Eastern Europe and China, supported the airlift. (This was to some degree a repeat of the 1940 election when

Franklin Roosevelt ran against Wendell Willkie, a moderate Republican who did not support the isolationism of many of his colleagues.) In 1948, some Republicans had begun railing about the 1945 Yalta conference, where they claimed, a sick or pro-communist Democratic president, Franklin Delano Roosevelt, had surrendered Eastern Europe to Stalin.

Dewey, himself, stressed bipartisanship with another moderate, Republican senator Arthur Vandenberg, warning the Russians that even during an election year, "America is united" on foreign policy (Divine 1976: 233). Along with virtually all the pollsters and pundits, Dewey was so confident that he would win the election that he took the high road on Cold War issues. It was not just the high road. He did not want any strident attack on the Russians to come back to haunt him once he became the relatively moderate president that he planned to be.

After Truman was reelected, international events took a turn for the worse for the Democrats, beginning with the Russian explosion of an atomic bomb in August 1949. According to the Republican litany, the Democrats were responsible for turning a blind eye to communist spying that gave Moscow the secret of the bomb. On top of that sensation, the communists won the Chinese Civil War in October 1949. The Republicans were quick to blame the Democrats for not doing enough to aid the Chinese nationalists, with some even claiming that communists and fellow travelers in the State Department were responsible for the "loss of China." Joseph McCarthy, then a relatively obscure Republican senator from Wisconsin, began making such charges in February 1950, which were believed by more than 50 percent of those polled. This soon became a hot-button issue for many Americans, which would not be forgotten by Democratic presidents John F. Kennedy and Lyndon Johnson as they contemplated policies that might have resulted in a communist takeover of South Vietnam.

More immediately, the Democrats under Truman were not going to be blamed for losing Korea, after losing much of Eastern Europe and China. Despite earlier writing off Korea as not a prime national security interest, Truman felt compelled to intervene in June 1950 when communist North Korea invaded pro-Western South Korea. After American forces pushed the invaders back across the 38th parallel later that summer, Truman sanctioned the conquest of North Korea, despite the opposition of his European allies, who, after all, did not have to worry about the Republicans breathing down their necks as the 1950 congressional elections neared.

Despite Truman's resolute actions in Korea and unassailable anti-communist credentials marked by the success of the containment policy in Europe, his party suffered from another Republican assault against its Cold War policies in 1952. The Korean War had become bogged down in a war of attrition after the Chinese and North Koreans pushed the Americans back down the peninsula and across the 38th parallel at the end of 1950. It was a "no-win" war that the president seemed incapable of ending. The main hangup revolved around the nature of the armistice agreement, particularly the disposition of the North Korean and Chinese prisoners of war. Truman felt he could not afford appearing to appease communists by meeting them halfway in the peace talks that had begun in 1951. In the meantime, the Republican candidate, celebrated war hero General Dwight David Eisenhower, scored politically by promising that "in the cause of peace" he would "go to Korea" to try to end the "tragic war" (DeConde 2000: 155). The seemingly interminable

Korean War had become the Democrats' major political weakness (Pierpaoli 1999). The formula for Republican success in 1952 was two-thirds Cold War related – "K1C2," or Korea, Communism, and Corruption.

It was during this election that many Republicans, but not their Olympian candidate, talked about "Twenty Years of Treason" in the Democratic White Houses, especially Franklin Roosevelt's sell-out to the Russians at Yalta (Theoharis 1970). Much of the dirty work was left to the vice-presidential candidate, Senator Richard Nixon, who had risen quickly to national prominence after he took the lead in investigating Alger Hiss, a high government official who was accused of being a communist agent and who ultimately was sentenced to jail for perjury. Nixon called Adlai Stevenson, the Democratic presidential candidate, "a graduate of [Secretary of State] Dean Acheson's Cowardly College of Communist Containment" (Small 1999: 14). Containment was cowardly because it promised only to keep the Russians from expanding further. For his part, Senator McCarthy referred to "Alger – I mean Adlai" during the campaign (White 1997: 96).

The Republican policy would be "Rollback," an offensive policy aimed at ejecting the communists from Eastern Europe. It is difficult to say with precision how important this line was for Eisenhower's victory. Polish Americans, for example, who usually voted overwhelmingly for Democrats, gave 50 percent of their votes to the Republicans, who promised to liberate their homeland. But Eisenhower would have won without such a promise. He was a very popular, almost apolitical hero, the Democrats had been in power for twenty years, and their recent domestic policies had not been especially successful. Nonetheless, the emphasis on new directions in foreign policy, overseen by a man experienced in foreign and military affairs, certainly contributed to the confidence Americans expressed in Eisenhower during a time when there were far more nominal Democrats than Republicans in the country.

Needless to say, the talk of a literal rollback, which was not taken seriously by Eisenhower or even his strongly anti-communist secretary of state, John Foster Dulles, made it less likely that the Russians would try to reach a peaceful resolution of their disputes with the pugnacious Americans who took over the White House. Although Stalin died in March 1953, the time was not propitious for the new Russian leaders to try to affect a limited détente with the new American leaders, even had they wanted to do so. Indeed, there are indications that in 1951 and 1952, even Stalin was serious about proposals for the neutralization of Germany and the relaxation of East–West tensions, initiatives that were rejected by the Democrats facing the soft-on-communism charges.

Once in office, the Eisenhower administration continued the containment policy of its predecessor, while giving just a little bit more than lip service to rollback. Its intelligence and propaganda agencies did encourage Eastern Europeans to believe that if they took up arms against their oppressors, the United States would assist them. Under a CIA program codenamed RED SOX/RED CAP, the agency trained Hungarian and other Eastern European émigrés for paramilitary missions behind the Iron Curtain. Some of those operatives took the lead in the revolution in Budapest. Thus it was in 1956, when the Hungarians did rebel against the Russians, they expected some sort of support from Washington. Sadly for them, none was forthcoming, as they confused the exaggerated rhetoric of conservative Republicans with the far more sober policies of President Eisenhower, who was not about to start World War III over the disposition of a nation thousands of miles away from US shores.

Adlai Stevenson tried again for the presidency in 1956 against a still popular Republican administration. In a departure from Eisenhower's policy, Stevenson called for a ban on the testing of hydrogen bombs. The test ban was something that the administration was contemplating, but only as part of a larger more complex agreement with the Russians. Eisenhower strongly resented Stevenson's undercutting of his position for apparent partisan gain. In the end, Stevenson was wounded on this issue when the Soviet premier publicly endorsed the Democratic candidate's position, demonstrating to many Americans that it was unsound, even treasonous. In later elections the Russians learned to keep their mouths shut in such situations.

Desperate for issues, Stevenson criticized Eisenhower from the right for "losing" North Vietnam in a sort of payback for the Republican refrain, "Who lost China?" At the Geneva conference in 1954 the administration did nothing when the French ended their war in Indochina by giving up the northern part of Vietnam to the communists. The refrain "Who lost Vietnam?" did not resonate with many Americans.

Although Eisenhower was not responsible for his October surprises, during the month before the 1956 election, the British, French, and Israelis attacked Egypt and the Russians put down the revolution in Hungary. The Suez War became an international crisis when the Soviet premier threatened to bombard London and Paris with rockets if they did not withdraw from Egypt. The president feared that these setbacks to American policy could hurt at the polls. The electorate, however, felt it was better to have an experienced leader at the helm than Stevenson, a former governor of Illinois, during a crisis.

In 1956, Eisenhower had been a popular president whose domestic and foreign policies enjoyed widespread support. He was still personally popular in 1960, but by the end of his second term, his foreign policies were in disarray. In 1957, the Russians had beaten the United States into space when they launched the first satellite, Sputnik. On top of that blow to American prestige and potentially to national security, by late 1959, Fidel Castro's revolutionary regime in Cuba had begun moving into the Soviet orbit. Finally, Eisenhower's attempt to lower tensions in Soviet–American relations boomeranged in the spring of 1960 after the Russians shot down an American spy plane and then, after failing to receive an apology from the president, scuttled a summit conference in Paris.

The Democrats launched a furious attack against the Eisenhower administration's foreign policy failures and against the Republican presidential nominee, Vice President Richard Nixon. It was the soft-on-communism's party's turn to use the Cold War in an election by accusing their opponents of losing ground to the Russians. Their problem was demonstrating the gravitas and foreign policy experience of their young nominee, Senator John F. Kennedy. In the first of a series of four televised debates, Kennedy handled that problem easily by appearing confident and knowledgeable. During those debates and elsewhere, he hammered Nixon for being part of an administration that had permitted the Soviets to take the lead in missile production and for permitting Cuba to go communist: "Today the Iron Curtain is

90 miles off the coast of the United States" (DeConde 2000: 174). He also referred to a recent poll that revealed that US allies had lost confidence in the nation's military superiority.

On the first charge, the dangerous "missile gap," Kennedy contended that the administration had left the United States vulnerable to Khrushchev's rocket-rattling. After all, the fact that the Soviets could launch a satellite apparently meant that they could easily launch missiles across the ocean. There was no missile gap, which Kennedy may have suspected and soon discovered when he became president. If there was a gap, it was the Soviets who were in the inferior position, despite Sputnik. Khrushchev had convinced much of the world, but not American intelligence, that he was far mightier than he really was. Indeed, during the 1962 Cuban missile crisis, Castro behaved recklessly because he believed the Russians' bluster that they were at the least a match for the United States in extra continental ballistic missiles.

As for the charge that Eisenhower had done nothing to get rid of Castro, when Kennedy broached that issue in one of the debates, Nixon could not respond that the administration had secretly been training a Cuban émigré force to invade the island. Kennedy had received intelligence briefings about Cuba, although his advisers later claimed that they were never told specifics about the plan. Nixon was furious with Kennedy for scoring debating points on a secret national security matter, which Republicans could not reveal. Kennedy knew what he was up to. He asked one of his aides rhetorically, "How would we have saved Cuba if we had the power?" He answered his own question: "What the hell, they never told us how they would have saved China" (Beschloss 1991: 28).

Despite the Democrats' campaign rhetoric, the Russians preferred them to Nixon, whom they perceived to be an inveterate anti-communist hardliner. Soviet leader Nikita S. Khrushchev later told Kennedy that he "participated" in the election of 1960 by delaying the release of two American RB-47 spy-plane pilots who had been shot down earlier in the year until the Democrat eked out a victory.

Even though the Democrats won, Soviet–American relations did not improve dramatically. In part, this was a legacy of campaign rhetoric. The Democrats had run as virile anti-communists who could fight the Cold War better than the Republicans. In his inaugural address, Kennedy announced, "Let every nation know that we shall pay any price, bear any burden, support any friend, oppose any foe to assure the survival and success of liberty." To turn around and begin talking about a *rapprochement* with communist China, for example, would have been impossible for this new Democratic Party that did not want to go through the 1952 election all over again.

Almost upon assuming office, first-term presidents begin thinking about their reelection. Kennedy was no different. He could not be seen as the man who gave away more territory to the communists. After failing to overthrow Castro with his Bay of Pigs invasion in April 1961 and agreeing to the neutralization of Laos in August 1962, which some interpreted as losing another round in the Cold War, he decided that he could not afford to even neutralize the American-backed government in South Vietnam that had been engaged in a civil war with the communist National Liberation Front (Viet Cong) since 1958.

By the time of his assassination in November 1963, he had become concerned about the drift of the war, in which the United States kept sending in more military advisers (from 800 in 1961 to 16,000 at the end of 1963) without affecting the steady progress of the communists against a corrupt, unpopular, and inept government in Saigon. But those who think that Kennedy was so discouraged that he planned to disengage from Vietnam point out that he could not do so until after the 1964 election. He could not run as the president who bugged out of Vietnam.

The domestic political context was even more important during the very dangerous Cuban missile crisis in 1962. It occurred in October, just before the congressional elections. Many observers considered Kennedy's administration a failure, with major foreign policy losses and virtually no significant New Frontier domestic legislation enacted. If many more Republicans were elected in the fall, his liberal programs would be dead in the water, leaving him with a meager record on which to run in 1964. On top of this, with turnabout being fair play, the Republicans had been attacking him for doing nothing about Cuba after the horribly botched Bay of Pigs invasion.

Thus, when he finally was convinced that the Russians had been secretly implanting missiles in Cuba capable of carrying nuclear warheads, he took a tough line in tense negotiations during the thirteen days that constituted the crisis. When he ordered them to remove the missiles, they proposed as a quid pro quo that he remove NATO missiles in Turkey. Those missiles were of an old and rather ineffective generation that was destined for replacement in the very near future. Kennedy refused the deal and established an illegal blockade (he called it a "quarantine") and the world watched as the Russians came closer and closer to the blockade line and Americans stood poised to fire on their vessels. More important, when it appeared that the Russians would not back down, Kennedy was on the verge of ordering a full-scale attack on the missile emplacements in Cuba, not suspecting that some of them were already operative. His air attack on the missile sites would have led to a direct Soviet–American military confrontation and, perhaps, an apocalyptic World War III.

When Kennedy agreed to the final settlement, he assured Khrushchev through intermediaries that he would soon remove the missiles from Turkey but they could not be part of any public deal; if the Russians revealed it, all bets would be off. He could not be seen as "losing" the Cuban missile crisis to the Soviet Union. His defenders claim that US international prestige was at stake – had Khrushchev won the crisis, he would have been emboldened to attempt even more dangerous probes in the American sphere.

Others who are less generous see domestic political considerations playing an unseemly large role in a crisis that easily could have led to Armageddon. Kennedy received kudos for his handling of the missile crisis, his party did better than expected in the November elections (Richard Nixon blamed his loss in the California gubernatorial race on Kennedy's celebrated triumph over Khrushchev), and his reputation as a wise and cool statesman was insured. Yet considering that some of his colleagues reported that at the time, they thought the chances for nuclear war were 50–50, one wonders about the chances Kennedy took to protect his political reputation. When Khrushchev was deposed by his colleagues in 1964, one of the charges against *him* was starting and then "losing" the Cuban missile crisis.

When Vice President Lyndon Johnson assumed the presidency after Kennedy's assassination, he immediately became concerned about the presidential election that was less than one year away. Like Kennedy, even had he wanted to do so, he could not consider pulling out of Vietnam. Most Americans supported the commitment to Saigon but were leery about any significant escalation. Here Johnson was helped by the Republican candidate, Arizona senator Barry Goldwater, who appeared to many Americans to be too hawkish for their tastes.

Goldwater owed his rise in the party to the growth of the Sunbelt or "Gunbelt" states (Hogan 1999: 359), where Republican leaders did not share the moderate views on the Cold War of many in the primarily eastern Republican establishment. Because of cheap labor, good weather, and clever congressional politics, those states in the south and west received a disproportionate share of defense expenditures, with, for example, California raking in 20 percent of all the domestic defense expenditures between 1951 and 1965. The Gunbelt thrived on the Cold War.

But 1964 was not the Gunbelt's year. Most Americans approved the peaceful resolution of the missile crisis, the achievement of a limited Test Ban Treaty in 1963, and the easing of tensions in the Cold War. Johnson worried about his opponent: "He's a man who had two nervous breakdowns. He's not a stable fellow at all." Goldwater was alleged to have said that he wanted "to lob one [Atomic bomb] into the men's room of the Kremlin" (Roper 2000: 69, 70). In one of the first negative television ads, the Democrats featured a little girl counting the petals from a daisy she plucked, a scene that morphed into the countdown for a nuclear explosion. The message was clear: a vote for Goldwater was a vote for nuclear war. The Republican complaints of foul play compelled the Democrats to drop the ad after one day, but when it was repeated many times over on newscasts, Johnson received free advertising. Americans wanted their presidents to be resolute with the communists, but not reckless.

As for the Vietnam War, despite the fact that many of his advisers were advocating a dramatic increase in American military involvement in order to save Saigon, Johnson assumed the dovish position to Goldwater's hawkish one – as he maintained, "We don't want our boys to do the fighting for Asian boys." Walt Rostow, his hawkish future national security adviser, warned him that he should be careful with his language so as not to close out his options "in a future tough situation" (Gardner 1995: 144, 142). This was the beginning of Johnson's politically crippling credibility gap. When he decided to start bombing North Vietnam in a major escalation in February 1965, a wag noted ironically, "They told me if I voted for Goldwater we would bomb North Vietnam. I voted for Goldwater and we bombed North Vietnam."

The election also figured significantly in the debate over the Gulf of Tonkin Resolution in early August. That resolution, which the president interpreted as his declaration of war against North Vietnam ("like granny's nightshirt it covers just about everything"), was supported by virtually every Democrat, including a somewhat skeptical Senator J. William Fulbright, the chair of the Foreign Relations Committee. Fulbright was so concerned about the election of Goldwater, whom he considered a "Neanderthal" on foreign policy, that he energetically pushed the resolution through the Senate in what he soon labeled "a source of neither pleasure nor pride to me" (Fulbright 1967: 52). Within a year, he emerged as one of the most important and outspoken critics of the president's Vietnam policy. After the Gulf of Tonkin incident, Johnson's approval ratings on his handling of the war issue rose from 48 percent to 72 percent. He won the election in a landslide.

Despite the size of his victory, Johnson was convinced that like Kennedy before him, he could not lose Vietnam to the communists and win reelection. Had he pulled out early in 1965, before he adopted policies that made the war an American war, the North Vietnamese and Viet Cong would have taken over South Vietnam well before the 1968 election. It would be like losing China all over again. And within the party, Johnson feared "Robert Kennedy out in front leading the fight against me, telling everyone that I had betrayed John Kennedy's commitment to Vietnam" (Kearns 1976: 264).

Thus it was that Johnson hung on in Vietnam, adopting a military policy between that of the doves who wanted to pull out and that of the hawks who wanted to blow North Vietnam to smithereens. Most of the doves were in his party, which self-destructed over the war. Confronted by the candidacies of senators Eugene McCarthy and Robert F. Kennedy for the Democratic presidential nomination in 1968, no immediate end to the war in sight, and the probability that although he could win the nomination he would lose the general election, Johnson decided at the end of March 1968 not to seek reelection. He told the nation that he wanted to devote all of his attention to trying to end the war in Vietnam during the little more than eight months of his tenure.

The Republican nominee, Richard Nixon, as had Willkie and Dewey before him, rallied around the president during a time of national crisis, and refrained from directly criticizing his military and political policies in Vietnam. However, when asked, he did tell a journalist, "Yes I have a plan to end the war" (Small 1999: 28). The media turned that response into Nixon's "secret plan" to end the war, which made many Republican and independent doves more comfortable with him. Not having to reveal his plan because he did not want to undercut the president was fine with Nixon, since he had no specific plan to end the war.

His opponent, Vice President Hubert H. Humphrey, supported the president's policies as well but these did not go far enough to please the millions of those who wanted a speedy end to the war. When he genuflected a bit toward the doves' position at the end of September, his poll numbers began to rise. More important to his chances for victory was the change in October in Hanoi's negotiating position concerning the ground rules for establishing peace talks. Here the Russians played a role. Fearing the "profoundly anti-communist" Nixon (Dobrynin 1995: 189), they pressured their North Vietnamese allies to be more conciliatory. (They were so concerned about a Nixon victory that Ambassador Anatoly Dobrynin even clumsily offered the cash-starved Humphrey camp financial support, which, of course, Humphrey refused; ibid: 190.) Pressure was also exerted by the chief American negotiator, Democratic loyalist W. Averell Harriman, who so disliked the idea of a Nixon presidency that he went beyond his instructions to try to sweeten a deal for the North Vietnamese.

So it came to be, in the most famous October surprise in history, one week before the election, Johnson announced a breakthrough in the talks about peace negotiations, which led to another rise in Humphrey's poll numbers to a point where the race became too close to call. Suspecting that the Democrats were playing politics with national security and fearing that the breakthrough would lead to Humphrey's victory, on the weekend before the election, Nixon campaign officials instructed an operative to urge the South Vietnamese government not to accept the deal Johnson had arranged. She told her contacts that they would get a better deal under a Republican administration. The South Vietnamese did not need much urging to nix the deal in a public announcement, which resulted in Humphrey falling back in the polls.

Because the FBI was illegally listening to the messages going back and forth between the Republicans and the South Vietnamese embassy in Washington, Johnson knew about Nixon's actions and came close to going public with what he labeled "treason" (Small 1999: 29). But he was missing an explicit smoking gun and, moreover, would have had to reveal that he was illegally wiretapping the Republicans and his South Vietnamese allies.

The formal peace talks did begin after President-Elect Nixon quickly informed the South Vietnamese to accept the deal he had earlier urged them to reject. Yet despite formal talks in Paris and later, more important secret negotiations between his national security adviser Henry Kissinger and North Vietnamese diplomat Le Duc Tho, the new president was not able to end US involvement in the war until January 1973. Like his predecessors, he feared that were American forces to leave South Vietnam early in his term, the communists would take it over before his reelection campaign. Consequently, he announced that he would only accept a "peace with honor," which at the start of four years of negotiations meant the American-backed government in place in Saigon at war's end and all North Vietnamese troops out of the south.

An honorable peace in Vietnam was one of the issues he discussed with the Russians and Chinese as he carefully constructed his triangulated diplomacy that would end with his unprecedented and triumphal visits to China in February 1972 and to the Soviet Union in May. As US relations with Hanoi's two communist allies improved, he hoped that they would help him extricate American forces from Vietnam in a way that maintained American – and his – political credibility and prestige. Chinese leader Mao Zedong understood enough about US politics as early as the fall of 1970 to tell a visiting American that Nixon would be welcome in his country in 1972, which, he noted with a smile, was an election year. The opening to China, which was popular with almost all Americans, did occur early in 1972, but only after Nixon had extracted a promise from the Chinese that "No Democrat is to go to China before the President" (Small 1999: 121).

The Russians and to a lesser degree the Chinese did pressure the North Vietnamese to be more forthcoming at the peace table in the fall of 1972, when they finally agreed that President Nguyen Van Thieu could remain as leader of South Vietnam until new elections were held. In May, the Russians had conveyed a message from Nixon to the communists: "The United States would not tolerate drawn-out negotiations in an election year" (Berman 2001: 126). The United States the previous year had already given up its demand that all North Vietnamese troops had to leave South Vietnam at war's end. Hanoi believed that it could get better terms from candidate Nixon in 1972 than from a second-term president in 1973. They knew that American polls were predicting close to a landslide win for the president over his Democratic opponent, Senator George McGovern, whose program to end the war was assailed by Republicans and even by his rival for the nomination, Hubert Humphrey, as appeasement. McGovern, Nixon's favorite candidate because of his perceived weakness, owed his nomination in part to Cold War politics. After antiwar demonstrators and the Chicago police clashed violently during the 1968 convention, the Democratic Party reformed its convention rules so as to allow significantly increased representation at the 1972 convention from the most liberal wing of the party. As in 1952, the Republicans introduced a formula into the campaign, as McGovern became the "AAA" candidate, a presumed supporter of appeasement, amnesty for draft dodgers, and abortion. They did not know that in private negotiations with Senator McGovern in Paris in October 1971, a North Vietnamese diplomat promised not to do "anything during negotiations" that might help Nixon (Berman 2001: 95).

Kissinger finally achieved a breakthrough with Le Duc Tho in the middle of October. Fearing that the United States might renege, on October 25, the North Vietnamese announced that they had reached agreement with the United States. The next day, Kissinger confirmed the October surprise stressing "peace is at hand." Kissinger later told McGovern that he made that statement not to hurt him in the upcoming election but to convince President Thieu and hawks in the Nixon administration that there could be no turning back from the peace table (Berman 2001: 174).

But peace was not at hand. After the national security adviser outlined the terms to South Vietnamese president Thieu, the South Vietnamese leader became so angry that he "wanted to punch Kissinger in the mouth" and rejected the draft treaty (Small 1999: 90). Unlike 1968's October surprise, American voters were not told that the South Vietnamese had squelched the deal. Indeed, after the election, when negotiations fell apart, Americans believed Nixon, who maintained that the North Vietnamese were the renegers.

Nixon's attempt to run for reelection as the master of the international system also had a significant impact on Soviet–American relations. He was so concerned about leaving the Moscow summit in May 1972 with major accomplishments that he and Kissinger blundered in two key areas. Although they concluded a generally salutary Strategic Arms Limitation Treaty (SALT I), their haste to proclaim success, coupled with their personal lack of detailed knowledge about missile systems, left the Soviets with an advantage in several key areas. More important, as part of the détente process, the two Americans promoted a trade agreement involving the Soviet purchase of American grain that helped Moscow to corner the world market and push up prices for American consumers in what Democratic senator Henry Jackson labeled "one of the most notorious foulups in American history" (Small 1999: 114). Jackson, a hawkish Democrat, had his eye on Jewish-American support for the Democratic nomination in 1976, when in 1974 he scuttled Nixon's Soviet trade deal by leading Congress to attach an amendment to the authorization bill relating to Jewish emigration.

To be fair to Nixon, he had more on his mind than the election when he journeyed to Moscow. He demonstrated his willingness to jettison the summit conference and all the good publicity it would engender, when just days before he was to leave the country, he ordered a major escalation of the war in Vietnam, and the mining of the harbors of Hanoi and Haiphong in response to the North Vietnamese spring offensive. Although he was confident that the Russians would not cancel the meeting, in part because he had already made his telegenic visit to their arch enemy, the Chinese, many Kremlinologists were not as certain.

With the end of the Vietnam War and the end to the turbulent 1960s, as one journalist noted during the 1976 presidential election, "issues were no more important than the price of hoopskirts" to most American voters, since the philosophic distance between moderate-conservative Republican Gerald Ford and moderate Democrat Jimmy Carter was not very large (Carroll 1982: 201). And if any specific issues interested voters, they were the domestic issues which they cited as more important than foreign policy by a 12 to 1 margin (Sobel 2000: 22).

But this was an important election for the way it shaped diplomacy in the years to come. The Republican Party was coming apart on Soviet policy in the same way that the Democrats had come apart over the Vietnam War ten years earlier. Leading the conservative assault against the détente policy of Nixon and Ford was Ronald Reagan who charged, "Under Messrs. Kissinger and Ford, the nation has become Number Two in military power in a world where it is dangerous – if not fatal – to be second best" (Carroll 1982: 198). Desperately trying to save his nomination from the charismatic "Great Communicator," Ford accepted a platform that criticized his own détente policy, SALT, and the recently initialed Helsinki Agreement, as it appeared, at least for the majority of Republicans, that the darkest days of the Cold War were upon them.

As in 1960, the foreign policy issue in the presidential debates was pivotal for some voters. Ford had been a long-time congressional leader, vice president, and president; Carter had been a governor of Georgia whose main claim to foreign policy expertise was allegedly a nefarious one: his membership in the elitist Trilateral Commission, an internationalist global organization sponsored by Rockefeller interests. However, during one of the televised debates, Ford blurted out, "There is no Soviet domination of Eastern Europe" (Cannon 1994: 408). He later claimed that he meant to say that the United States did not accept Soviet domination and that by making such a comment he wanted to hold out hope to independence-minded Eastern Europeans. But his gaffe made it difficult for Republicans to contend that it was dangerous to leave foreign policy in the hands of a diplomatic novice like Carter.

For his part, Carter opposed the cold-blooded, amoral realism of the Nixon–Ford–Kissinger team, some of which was revealed during the Watergate hearings in 1973 and 1974 as well as during the 1975 investigations of the illegal activities of the CIA and FBI. He promised that under his presidency, the United States would be "a beacon light for human rights throughout the world," and he would not interfere in the internal affairs of other nations because of perceived Cold War exigencies (DeConde 2000: 223). Many citizens thrilled to his idealistic rhetoric during the campaign. But like his campaign promise never to lie to the American people, he encountered difficulties trying to implement his policy with any degree of consistency when confronted by new threats to national security. In addition, he paid severely in 1980 when Republicans attributed Soviet gains around the world on his watch in part to the restraints he placed on the CIA's covert activities in keeping with the recommendations of the intelligence investigatory commissions.

It is interesting to note that the fall of South Vietnam, Cambodia, and Laos in 1975 to communism was not a campaign issue. In 1973, the prime minister of Singapore had hoped South Vietnam would last until 1976 "so that you will have a strong President" (Berman 2001: 261). But most Americans were happy to be out of the region in 1973 and realized that there was little that President Ford could have done to have saved those countries. Of course, it was more difficult for Democrats to criticize Republicans for being soft on communism than vice versa, especially since the party and its leaders, except for Jackson and his followers, supported détente.

As in 1976, the key issue in the 1980 election was the feeble US economy, which was wallowing in stagflation. Because of that and also because of his perceived foreign policy failures, many Americans considered Carter to be a weak president. It did not help that he also talked realistically about the limits of America's global reach. Ronald Reagan appeared to be anything but weak and inspired his listeners with talk about America's greatness through increased defense expenditures and taking a tough line towards its enemies.

In the last year of his presidency, Carter had to deal with two serious diplomatic problems: the Iranian hostage crisis, which was not directly related to the Cold War except insofar as the Shah of Iran had been a loyal anti-communist ally, and the Soviet invasion of Afghanistan. In December 1979, when the Kremlin announced that it had been invited into Afghanistan to assist its allies against revolutionaries, Carter proclaimed hyperbolically that we confronted "the most serious threat to world peace since the Second World War." One of his critics from the pro-détente Democratic Left charged, "Afghanistan has given Carter a useful excuse . . . to reveal publicly [a] much earlier decision. He has sacrificed the hope for peace on the altar of his own political ambition" (Carroll 1982: 341).

After several years during which time Republicans had accused him of coddling the Russians, he overreacted, perhaps trying to demonstrate that he was a tough-minded leader. Among other punitive actions against the Soviet Union, he reinstituted draft registration, compelled the US Olympic team to boycott the 1980 Olympics, cut off American wheat sales, and even, in Presidential Directive 59 in July 1980, retargeted American missiles from Russian cities to missile sites, signaling a readiness to use nuclear weapons against the foe in a limited war.

The Olympic boycott fell flat when he was unable to convince most of his allies to join him. Reagan claimed that this demonstrated that "Our allies are losing confidence in us" while "our adversaries no longer respect us" (Carroll 1982: 343). The Russians were upset about losing the revenue from American television coverage as well as the prestige of beating the United States in their capital. They returned the favor when, for trumped-up reasons, they boycotted the 1984 Los Angeles Olympics. As for the wheat ban, the Russians easily found alternate sources, while American farmers howled about their losses. The fiercely anti-communist President Reagan answered their pleas early in his administration by ending the ban.

Like Kennedy in 1960 and Carter in 1976, Reagan appeared to many to be inexperienced in handling foreign affairs compared to his opponent. And like Kennedy and Carter, Reagan was helped by the debates, particularly when President Carter implied that he took advice about nuclear weapons policy from his pre-pubescent young daughter Amy during breakfast table chats (Carter did not know at the time that Reagan made some decisions about his own policies based upon his wife Nancy's astrologer's readings). Although Reagan scored points during the campaign by ticking off the countries in Africa and Central America that had gone "communist" since a Republican left the White House, the Iran hostage issue overshadowed all foreign policy issues, and it was overshadowed by the general issue of Reagan's perceived strength and Carter's perceived weaknesses.

The Russians took note of the dramatic change in tone in the White House when Reagan continued his campaign rhetoric about a more assertive United States in his presidency, culminating in 1983 with his description of them as "evil." They were so worried about the words and policies of the wild man in the White House that they seriously feared he was contemplating launching a preemptive war and took special intelligence measures to deal with that problem. Not just the Russians were scared. With the intensity of the Cold War reaching 1950s levels, many Americans became concerned again about the dangers of nuclear war. In response, the peace movement came alive as a nuclear freeze campaign enjoyed widespread popularity. It did not help that as he approached the 1984 election, Reagan had become the first president not to hold a summit conference with a Russian leader since Herbert Hoover.

During the campaign, owing in good measure to the prodding of his most important adviser, Nancy Reagan (and perhaps her astrologer), he began to adopt a noticeably softer tone to meet the public's concerns about the trajectory of Soviet–American relations. Whether or not he came to that decision for political reasons, he did follow through during his second term with a dramatically improved relationship with Moscow. During the 1984 campaign, the Soviet intelligence service, the KGB, launched an extensive if discrete anti-Reagan propaganda blitz in order to influence Americans to vote for the Democratic candidate, Walter Mondale. Mondale tried to play upon voters' fears of nuclear confrontation produced by Reagan's hardline policies, but the president sounded more moderate in 1984 than he had sounded earlier in the year. Of all Mondale's issues, Reagan's controversial Central American policy was the highest-ranked foreign policy issue with his supporters. But it ranked only fifth in importance and added, at most, 2.4 percent to his meager vote totals in Reagan's landslide victory (Sobel 2000: 22).

The last American election to be held during the Cold War was in 1988 when Reagan's vice president, George Bush, ran against Massachusetts governor Michael Dukakis. Many conservative Republicans worried about Bush policies and especially about his less-than-muscular persona, compared to Reagan. One year before the election, *Newsweek* headlined a cover story on Bush, "Fighting the Wimp Factor." To demonstrate his toughness during the campaign, Bush moved away from the developing love feast between the president and Soviet leader Mikhail Gorbachev to appeal to skeptics on the Right. Though privately supporting the drift of Russian–American relations, he told Gorbachev in 1987 not to pay attention to his anti-communist rhetoric during the campaign.

Dukakis, whose lack of foreign policy and military experience worried many voters, also tried to look like a tough guy by taking a ride in a tank at a Michigan factory. Unfortunately, someone gave him a goofy-looking helmet to wear during his ride that produced a ludicrous photo opportunity for the Democratic candidate. In a tough negative campaign, Bush was not above red-baiting by using a phrase from the Red Scare of the fifties, describing his opponent as "card-carrying member" of the American Civil Liberties Union (White 1997: 151).

Vietnam became a minor issue when it was discovered that Bush's vice presidential choice, Indiana senator Dan Quayle, had used influence after graduating from college in 1969 to obtain admission to the National Guard, most likely, like thousands of other young men, to escape having to serve in Vietnam. Bush's opponent in the 1992 campaign, Bill Clinton, had an even more difficult time explaining what he did in the Cold War. For one thing, Clinton did not tell the entire truth about the way he tried to use the ROTC to stay out of the draft and the Vietnam War. In addition, while he was on a Rhodes Scholarship in London, he helped lead several protests in the fall of 1969 against America's Vietnam policy. Fortunately for Clinton, the Bush campaign's operative who was sent to England to try to find photographs of the long-haired student doing something unpatriotic in front of the American embassy came up empty handed.

Almost as damning for Republicans and their supporters was the fact that Clinton visited the Soviet Union while he was at Oxford, which led one Republican congressman to suggest that he was a "Manchurian Candidate" selected by the KGB to take over the United States. When Larry King asked Bush about Clinton's trip on his television show, the Republican candidate responded, "I don't want to tell you what I *really* think" (Goldman 1994: 531). When the issue came up during a presidential debate, Clinton wondered what Bush's father, Senator Prescott Bush, a noted anti-McCarthyite, would have thought about his son's position.

Bush did take credit for the fact that he was president in 1991 when the United States "won the Cold War." Gorbachev, with whom he enjoyed cordial relations, thought it was "our common victory" (DeConde 2000: 257). Whoever won the Cold War, foreign policy was a relatively minor issue in 1992, even though Clinton's chief experience in that area was commanding the Arkansas National Guard. Only 6 percent of those polled in the first year after the Cold War ended thought that foreign policy was the most important issue in the election.

Aside from questions relation to candidates' experiences during the Vietnam War, including George W. Bush's somewhat mysterious tour of duty in the Texas National Guard, by the turn of the new century, it appeared that the Cold War had finally disappeared as a factor in presidential politics.

American diplomacy, politics, culture, religion, science and technology, and the institution of the family were all dramatically affected by the nation's longest "war," the Cold War. As we have seen in the nation's most important political activity, the quadrennial election of a president, it played a prominent role for over forty years, if not always as a central issue for voters, at least always as a central issue for the way presidents selected their diplomatic strategies. In the late 1830s, Alexander de Tocqueville had expressed concern about the negative role politics might play in American foreign policy once the young nation became an active member of the international system. The prescient French observer of the American scene was right to have been concerned.

REFERENCES

Berman, L.: *No Peace, No Honor: Nixon, Kissinger, and Betrayal in Vietnam* (New York: Free Press, 2001).

Beschloss, M. R.: *The Crisis Years: Kennedy and Khrushchev, 1960–1963* (New York: Harper Collins, 1991).

Cannon, J.: *Time and Change: Gerald Ford's Appointment with History* (New York: Harper Collins, 1994).

Carroll, P. N.: *It Seemed Like Nothing Happened: America in the Seventies* (New Brunswick, NJ: Rutgers University Press, 1982).

Costigliola, F.: "The Creation of Memory and Myth: Stalin's 1946 Election Speech and the Soviet Threat." In Martin J. Medhurst and H. W. Brands (eds.) *Critical Reflections on the Cold War: Linking Rhetoric and History* (College Station: Texas A&M University Press, 2000).

DeConde, A.: *Presidential Machismo: Executive Authority, Military Intervention, and Foreign Relations* (Boston, MA: Northeastern University Press, 2000).

Divine, R. A.: *Foreign Policy and US Presidential Elections, 1940–1972*, 2 vols. (New York: New Viewpoints, 1976).

Dobrynin, A.: *In Confidence: Moscow's Ambassador to America's Six Cold War Presidents* (New York: Times Books, 1995).

Foyle, D. C.: *Counting the Public In: Presidents, Public Opinion, and Foreign Policy* (New York: Columbia University Press, 1999).

Fulbright, J. W.: *The Arrogance of Power* (New York: Vintage, 1967).

Gardner, L. C.: *Pay Any Price: Lyndon Johnson and the Wars for Vietnam* (Chicago, IL: Ivan Dee, 1995).

Goldman, P. et al.: *Quest for the Presidency: 1992* (College Station: Texas A&M Press, 1994).

Greene, J. R.: *The Presidency of George Bush* (Lawrence: University of Kansas Press, 2000).

Hogan, M. J.: "Partisan Politics and Foreign Policy in the American Century." In M. Hogan (ed.) *The Ambiguous Legacy: US Foreign Relations in the "American Century"* (Cambridge: Cambridge University Press, 1999).

Jones, C. O.: *The Presidency in a Separated System* (Washington, DC: Brookings Institution, 1994).

Kearns, D.: *Lyndon Johnson and the American Dream* (New York: Signet, 1976).

Kofsky, F.: *Harry S. Truman and the War Scare of 1948: A Successful Campaign to Deceive a Nation* (New York: St. Martin's Press, 1993).

Pierpaoli, P. G.: *Truman and Korea: The Political Culture of the Early Cold War* (Columbia: University of Missouri Press, 1999).

Roper, J.: *The American Presidents: Heroic Leadership from Kennedy to Clinton* (Edinburgh: Edinburgh University Press, 2000).

Small, M.: *The Presidency of Richard Nixon* (Lawrence: University of Kansas Press, 1999).

Sobel, R.: *The Impact of Public Opinion on US Foreign Policy since Vietnam: Constraining the Colossus* (New York: Oxford University Press, 2000).

Theoharis, A.: *The Yalta Myths: An Issue in US Politics, 1945–1955* (Columbia: University of Missouri Press, 1970).

White, J. K.: *Still Seeing Red: How the Cold War Shapes the New American Politics* (Boulder, CO: Westview Press, 1997).

FURTHER READING

Anderson, D. (ed.): *Shadow on the White House: Presidents and the Vietnam War* (Lawrence: University of Kansas Press, 1993).

Appy, C. G. (ed.): *Cold War Constructions: The Political Culture of United States Imperialism: 1945–1966* (Amherst: University of Massachusetts Press, 2000).

Barnet, R. J.: *The Rockets Red Glare: When America Goes to War: The Presidents and the People* (New York: Simon and Schuster, 1990).

Berman, W. C.: *America's Right Turn: From Nixon to Bush* (Baltimore, MD: Johns Hopkins University Press, 1994).

Beschloss M. R. and S. Talbott: *At the Highest Levels: The Inside Story of the End of the Cold War* (Boston, MA: Little, Brown, 1993).

Brace, P. and B. Hinckley: *Follow the Leader: Opinion Polls and the Modern Presidency* (New York: Basic Books, 1993).

Briggs, P.: *Making American Foreign Policy: President–Congress Relations from the Second World War to Vietnam* (Lanham, MD: University Press of America, 1991).

Caldwell, D.: *American Soviet Relations: From 1947 to the Nixon–Kissinger Grand Design* (Westport, CT: Greenwood Press, 1981).

Caridi, R. J.: *The Korean War and American Politics: The Republican Party as a Case Study* (Philadelphia: University of Pennsylvania Press, 1968).

Chester, L. et al.: *An American Melodrama: The Presidential Campaign of 1968* (New York: Viking, 1969).

Cramer, R. B.: *What it Takes: Promise and the Presidency* (New York: Random House, 1992).

Dietz, T.: *Republicans and Vietnam, 1961–1968* (Westport, CT: Greenwood Press, 1986).

Dionne, E. J.: *Why Americans Hate Politics* (New York: Simon and Schuster, 1991).

Farber, D. R.: *Chicago '68* (Chicago, IL: University of Chicago Press, 1988).

Freeland, R. M.: *The Truman Doctrine and the Origins of McCarthyism: Foreign Policy, Domestic Politics, and Internal Security, 1946–1948* (New York: Knopf, 1972).

Garthoff, R.: *Détente and Confrontation* (Washington, DC: Brookings Institution, 1985).

Haldeman, H. R. *The Haldeman Diaries: Inside the Nixon White House* (New York: Putnam's, 1994).

Johnson, H.: *Sleepwalking Through History: America in the Reagan Years* (New York: Norton, 1992).

Johnson, R. H.. *Improbable Dangers: US Conceptions of Threat in the Cold War and After* (New York: St. Martin's Press, 1994).

Kernell, S.: *Going Public: New Strategies of Presidential Leadership* (Washington, DC: CQ Press, 1993).

Logevall, F.: *Choosing War: The Lost Chance for Peace and the Escalation of the War in Vietnam* (Berkeley: University of California Press, 1999).

Mueller, J. E.: *War, Presidents, and Public Opinion* (New York: Wiley, 1973).

Nelson, K.: *The Making of Détente: Soviet–American Relations in the Shadow of Vietnam* (Baltimore, MD: Johns Hopkins University Press, 1995).

Small, M.: *Democracy and Diplomacy: The Impact of Domestic Politics on US Foreign Policy, 1789–1994* (Baltimore, MD: Johns Hopkins University Press, 1996).

Walker M.: *The Cold War: A History* (New York: Henry Holt, 1994).

White, T. A.: *The Making of the President, 1960* (New York: Atheneum, 1961).

White, T. A.: *The Making of the President, 1964* (New York: Atheneum, 1965).

CHAPTER TWENTY-THREE

Détente Over Thirty Years

KEITH L. NELSON

It should come as no surprise that the passage of three astounding decades and the release of much classified and even previously unknown documentation have combined to render the widely hailed "achievements" of the Nixon–Kissinger era somewhat more problematic. We have lived to witness not only the unexpected collapse of the Soviet Union but also the rise and fall of Cold War II in the 1980s and the globalization, terrorism, and hegemonic militarism of more recent years. On the evidential front we have experienced not just a substantial increase in data relevant to the subject, but a dramatic series of major revelations as presidential papers came to be opened (after 1987), Soviet and Chinese materials appeared (after 1991), and unique diaries and tapes were released (after 1994 and 1999). Such developments, each in its own way, have forced us to reconceptualize the era of détente and to reassess the roles and contributions of its major authors. The decade of the 1970s is still seen as a crucial one, even a turning point, but its meaning is less clear now and the reputations of the statesmen are far less brilliant.

To be sure, the claims of Nixon, Kissinger, Brezhnev, and others at the time almost cried out to be deflated. Nixon had come to the presidency very much aware that the United States now faced strategic parity with the Soviet Union and hoping that, by accepting this, he could usher in a new "era of negotiation." He also hoped that, by taking a less obviously competitive approach, he could gain Soviet and even Chinese assistance in ending the exhausting war in Vietnam. What he had not expected, of course, was the extent to which his failure to end the conflict in Southeast Asia would impel him to offer the "opening to China" and détente with Russia to the American electorate in 1972 as the primary evidence of his statesmanship. Still, having made this choice, he had not been loath to emphasize just how realistic and creative he had been or how much had been achieved in building a "structure of peace" and transforming the American–Soviet relationship.[1] Secretary of State Kissinger had presented détente to the American Congress and people as a powerful means to "manage the emergence of Soviet power," suggesting that, by enmeshing Moscow in a network of relationships, Washington had given it more to lose and more reason to avoid a confrontation.[2]

Such perspectives regarding East–West relations were echoed in several contemporary discussions by journalists who, though not uncritical, were clearly appreciative of the Nixon administration's efforts. Brandon (1972), the earliest of these, described the president and his "impresario" Kissinger as cleverly arranging the disengagement of an over-extended United States, employing balance of power diplomacy in order better to cope with the increasing strength of allies and communist adversaries. Newhouse (1973), with information provided by Kissinger's staff, gave the first authentic account of administration debates on SALT, though its slant on these almost always reflected the views of the White House. Kalb and Kalb (1974) benefited in its foreign policy discussions from many hours of interviews with Kissinger, but it also suffered from being overly dependent on what Kissinger chose to disclose about his intentions.

In any event, as the 1970s wore on, bringing a new Arab–Israeli war, an oil embargo, Watergate, the collapse of South Vietnam, and Soviet–American friction over Angola and the Horn of Africa, the mood of the American people shifted perceptibly in the direction of more suspicion and less passivity. The most obvious indication of this change came in 1974 with Senator Henry Jackson's success in undercutting the new trade agreements with Russia and in 1976 with the formation of the Committee on the Present Danger to oppose the SALT II arms control negotiations. Yet, interestingly, despite the energetic and ultimately successful nature of those endeavors, most of their written attack upon détente was spelled out in magazine articles and not in books (e.g., Wohlstetter 1974; Podhoretz 1975). The most extensive criticism of the Nixon–Kissinger foreign policies during this period came from independent journalists. Schell (1975), for example, produced a biting and frightening analysis of the way in which détente preserved world peace in a nuclear age by allowing innumerable issues to be "linked" to American "credibility" and to the swollen powers of the presidency. Three years later, Szulc (1978) was an impressively detailed and damning exposé (unfortunately, without footnotes) of Nixon's entire diplomatic stewardship. Conceding that the broad conceptual strokes of the president's policies (détente with the Soviet Union and an opening to China) had been "undoubtedly correct," Szulc proceeded to anticipate many later critics by faulting Nixon for his secrecy, overselling of détente, prolonging of the Vietnam War, and intensification of the arms race. In addition, he argued, over-centralization of control had led to serious tactical errors, as at the Moscow summit of 1972, where Nixon and Kissinger were "beaten diplomatically and technically" on the vital ICBM issue.

By this time scholars as well as journalists had begun to venture into these subjects. Bell (1977) summarized American strategy incisively and concluded that what truly made it new was the opportunity Nixon and Kissinger saw to gain diplomatic leverage from a triangular relationship among the United States, Russia, and China. Hoffman (1978) was more critical, focusing on Kissinger's actual behavior and accusing him, despite rhetoric to the contrary, of striving to preserve the international primacy that the United States had previously possessed. Hoffman noted Kissinger's promises to achieve savings by means of disengagement and more maneuverability, but he insisted that American dominance was clearly still the object, though, to be sure, Kissinger could guarantee neither linkage of issues nor consistent moderation on the part of other major powers. A third professor, Seyom Brown (1979), was less negative, willing to explore and admire the "diplomatic virtuosity and rhetorical artistry" of Dr. Kissinger.[3] Kissinger's contribution, he believed, was "to help the country adapt to the enlarging strategic power of the Soviet Union" and to translate the tactical requirements of a post-containment strategy into a "world order vision." Nevertheless, Brown argued, Kissinger's vision was too geopolitical to sit comfortably with influential segments of the American public, something even he began to realize after his failure in Angola in 1976.

The debate was now in full swing, but at the beginning of the 1980s two new factors were to transform the historiography of the subject: the publication of the memoirs of the principal participants, especially two massive and rich volumes by Henry Kissinger, and simultaneously, the political eclipse of the détente idea in the United States under the impact of the Soviet invasion of Afghanistan and the election of Ronald Reagan. From this time on, students of the subject found themselves asking more explicitly than before, "how did détente come about in the first place?" and "what went wrong?"

Nixon and Kissinger were anxious to defend and justify themselves. As a result, not surprisingly, they had recourse to many of the same explanations, presenting themselves as daring but realistic, omitting deception and illegality from the story, and blaming others (especially Congress and the Watergate crisis) for the ultimate failure of their "grand design." Each sought implicitly to show that he was the principal architect of their administration's foreign policy, but Kissinger got the better of the argument at this stage. Nixon's (1978) account was disappointing, predictable, even flat.[4] Kissinger (1979) was more thorough, analytical, and revealing. With volume 2, published in 1982, he brought the story down to Nixon's resignation, offering the reader 2,400 pages of proof that these years had witnessed a positive turning point in the Cold War.[5]

Spurred by the new evidence, new challenge, and Reagan's new confrontationism, scholars and observers now swarmed to re-examine détente. Among the most original and provocative was the neo-realist John Lewis Gaddis, whose *Strategies of Containment* (1982) soon became a standard text for courses in American diplomatic history. Standing back to take a long view, Gaddis suggested that in fact the Nixon–Kissinger foreign policy fitted into a recurrent thirty-year pattern in which the United States had oscillated between, on the one hand, attempting to "contain" the Soviet Union on all fronts and all levels of power (symmetrically) and, on the other, pursuing containment on only those fronts that were considered to be of vital importance (asymmetrically). To Gaddis' eye, the Nixon détente strategy was clearly in the asymmetric tradition of George Kennan (and Dwight Eisenhower), deriving its importance, as did Kennan's original doctrine, from the recognition that the economic means available for waging cold war were severely limited. Gaddis found such a policy to be eminently realistic, but at the same time acknowledged not only that asymmetries in weaponry often set off public "insecurities," but also that Nixon and Kissinger had undercut their own effectiveness by being excessively secretive, expecting too much of "linkage," failing to rebuild US military capabilities, and focusing exclusively on superpower relations.

Other students of détente extended Gaddis' effort to place the phenomenon in a comparative and theoretical perspective. The political scientist Robert Litwak (1984) pointed out that to compensate for the prospective decline in American activism following Vietnam, Nixon had turned to the nascent strength of regionalism as an alternative. Thus the Nixon Doctrine emerged as one of the two central elements of his strategy of retrenchment without disengagement. Indeed, the establishment of a "limited adversary" relationship with communist great power rivals had been intended to create a political atmosphere favorable to the orderly devolution of

American power to incipient regional powers. As it turned out, however, Nixon's reappraisal of Soviet intentions beginning with the Arab–Israeli War of October 1973 resulted in a shift in administration policy from the new "pluralism" to a reworked "containment" of the USSR.

Richard W. Stevenson (1985), a British scholar, attempted to understand his topic better by examining the occasions on which a relaxation of tension had occurred during the Cold War (i.e., the periods following the Geneva conference (1955), the Camp David summit (1959), the October missile crisis (1962), and the Moscow summit (1972)) and by identifying those factors working for or against the specific détente. Among the elements he found generally contributing to an easing of tension, Stevenson emphasized four: (1) fear of nuclear war, (2) feelings of strength and security *vis-à-vis* the opponent, (3) leaders with qualifications and commitments to pursue détente, and (4) convergence of such special concerns as the need for crisis management or the need to control allies. More specifically, he saw the Soviet–American détente of 1972 as having benefited especially from (1) the emergence of a Sino-American relationship, (2) the US withdrawal from Vietnam, (3) the achievement of strategic parity, (4) mutual interest in increased trade, and (5) Nixon's and Brezhnev's personal creativity. He saw it weakened subsequently by (1) the collapse of the trade treaty, (2) the failure of the superpowers to agree on a code of behavior, (3) the tendency of détente to promote polycentrism, and (4) Nixon's attempt to survive Watergate by exaggerating its accomplishments.[6]

Meanwhile, just before Stevenson published his volume, a book had appeared that astounded many and would leave a major imprint on future détente studies. This was *The Price of Power* (1983), a scathing attack on Henry Kissinger's diplomacy during the Nixon years (one reviewer called it the "Kissinger anti-memoirs"), authored by Seymour M. Hersh, a Pulitzer Prize-winning reporter for the *New York Times*. Rich in detail and personal recollection (the author claims to have interviewed over 1,000 American and foreign officials), *The Price of Power* ripped off the veil to show just how deceitful, manipulative, self-serving, arrogant, and fearful Kissinger really was. Hersh was widely accused of "overkill," but his work was extremely valuable in alerting readers to the mistakes, tensions, and hidden agendas of the individuals involved – those parts of the story that Nixon and Kissinger often simply left out. Hersh's discussions of SALT, MIRV, the backchannel, the "crisis" of fall 1970, the grain deal, China visit, and Moscow summit were amazing and revealing.

Important as Hersh's volume was, however, it was soon surpassed in significance by a study that has come to be recognized as one of the great books of the genre: Raymond Garthoff's *Détente and Confrontation* (1985). In one sense a memoir (since Garthoff was second in command of the first American SALT delegation), *Détente and Confrontation* transcended the author's personal experience to become an exemplary piece of serious scholarship. Massive in size (over 1,100 pages) and scope (it chronicled every significant episode in American Soviet relations between 1969 and 1984), it was also unusual in its careful analysis and attention to detail.

An advocate of détente, Garthoff found more than enough blame to go around in explaining its ultimate failure during the 1970s. Though he credited Nixon and Kissinger for adopting it, he charged them with viewing it primarily as a strategy, not an objective, and with having no real sense of its possibilities. Their willingness to treat SALT as a bargaining chip, to pass up a MIRV ban and a comprehensive weapons freeze, to ignore their own experts and negotiate secretly, and, finally, to pursue unilateral American advantage in the Third World, he condemned with understandable harshness. Nor did the Russians escape his judgment. One of Garthoff's special strengths was his ability to look at the same event, first, through American, and then through Soviet eyes, demonstrating how ideology and experience affect perceptions and how differing perceptions often lead to unintended conflict. In this case he showed that a simple code of conduct was insufficient in the face of what each side perceived as "natural" about the course of historical change.

Another of Garthoff's contributions lay in the fact that his study was the first to examine the diplomatic record of the Ford years with any thoroughness. In four lengthy chapters Garthoff described the ups and downs of Soviet–American ties during this period, from the successes at the Vladivostok summit and the Helsinki conference to the "shocks" of Jackson–Vanik, the fall of South Vietnam, and the Angola crisis. Though he had no simple explanation of the weakening of American support for détente, he offered telling criticisms of congressional interference in diplomacy, obstinacy at the Pentagon, and Kissinger's inability to think beyond waging covert war in Africa.[7]

Garthoff's views tended to become the new orthodoxy among scholars, but not everyone fell into line. Kissinger's one-time assistant and later the editor of *Foreign Affairs*, William Hyland, for one, quickly defended his old boss in a new survey of Soviet–American relations (Hyland 1987). In Hyland's view, Nixon and Kissinger succeeded under the most adverse circumstances in revolutionizing American foreign policy, effecting a classical reversal of alliances, and achieving a new "global structure." By keeping control in the hands of a tiny group, Kissinger and his colleagues were able to play upon subtle shifts in the balance of power to end the Vietnam War, introduce arms control, and in general pursue America's advantage. They continued to be largely successful in doing this, argued Hyland, until Watergate, the intervention of the public and Congress, and the perfidy of the Defense Department under Ford severely weakened their hand.

Two other interesting if idiosyncratic interpretations of détente appeared in the late 1980s. Franz Schurmann (1987), a Berkeley sociologist, argued vehemently that Nixon had seized the opportunity provided by America's Vietnam crisis and the Chinese–Soviet split to devise a "grand design" (*à la* Charles de Gaulle), which guided all his subsequent actions. The president's intention was to put the United States in a position of global economic "centrality" and to "liberate the presidency" to maintain this advantage. The necessary steps were three: (1) to extricate the United States from its involvement in Asia and other mainland areas; (2) to achieve détente with Russia after turning China into a friend (according to Schurmann, Nixon had launched détente in December 1970, probably with an offer of economic aid to Brezhnev); and (3) to stabilize the Middle East and restructure the political economy of oil (Schurmann argued that Nixon was using the Shah of Iran to encourage OPEC to raise oil prices, thus making America's allies dependent on it while Russia was being forced out of the area).

Two years later, in the first volume of a trilogy on "American Foreign Policy during 1968–1988," Richard Thornton (1989) described the strategies and counter-strategies of the major powers with surprising certainty. Noting that Nixon took office at a time when the American position was gravely weakened, Thornton contended that the new president had embarked on a gradual reshaping of the country's international relationships in order to permit, even require, that Germany and Japan play greater security roles. To this end, Nixon had not only made clear his intention to withdraw from Vietnam, but also as early as 1969 (!) had achieved a working relationship with China that prompted, first, a Soviet counter-thrust in the Middle East and Caribbean (1970) and, following that, a decision by Moscow to accept Nixon's offer of "détente" (1972). Still later, after Watergate had incapacitated Nixon, Kissinger had adopted a strategy involving a "tripolar" set, whose object was to establish a new equilibrium with the two communist giants, and a "trilateral" set designed to reinforce America's partnership with Western Europe and Japan. According to Thornton, trilateralism failed in the aftermath of the 1973 war and Arab oil embargo. Meanwhile, the USSR was moving aggressively in Angola under the rubric of détente to demonstrate its strength and America's weakness.

An important new factor was added to the historiographic equation in 1988 when the National Archives began to grant scholars access to a substantial part of the 42 million pages in the Nixon presidential papers. Though the files of the National Security Council and much additional foreign policy material (not to speak of the Nixon tapes and the Kissinger papers) remained closed, enough holdings were released so that the study of Nixon–Kissinger diplomacy would never be quite the same. This is not to say, of course, that the grounds for disagreement were about to fade away.

The first scholarship to profit from the new documentation was the second volume of Stephen Ambrose's biography, *Nixon* (1989), a study focused on the years from 1962 to 1972. The expanded sources allowed Ambrose to offer the reader a more detailed and more human Nixon than we had seen before, though the author's final verdict on the statesman remained mixed. Ambrose credited him with courage (and with wisdom) in accepting the idea of strategic parity and also in initiating the opening to China, but at the same time he found the president obsessive, secretive, and over-reliant on Kissinger during crucial arms control negotiations. Following Raymond Garthoff, he accused both Nixon and Kissinger of, among other things, mistakenly converting the Indo-Pakistani War of 1991 into a superpower crisis. In general, Ambrose showed little appreciation of Kissinger, whom he saw not as a "generator of ideas" but as an "agent, tool, and sometimes adviser."

An almost simultaneous study, equally if not more enriched by the Nixon (and Gerald Ford) papers, came to a rather different conclusion. Schulzinger (1989) presented a nuanced if still critical picture of Kissinger. Not really addressing the question of Kissinger's responsibility for policy, Schulzinger often simply assumed it with statements like, "Henry Kissinger's greatest achievement was the opening of relations between the United States and the People's Republic of China." In the author's view, when the North Vietnamese had proved recalcitrant about granting "peace with honor," Kissinger in particular had had the sense to realize that "fruitful areas for possible foreign policy success" lay in relations with Russia and with China. Convinced that a realistic strategic objective was to bring the communist giants into a balance of power requiring moderation and restraint, Kissinger was less interested in the details of arms treaties and specific bargains than in the very fact that they were made. All of this Schulzinger deftly explained and even praised, yet he was not blind to Kissinger's role in undermining his own creation. Kissinger's secrecy, his

promising too much to others, his doing too much himself, his disdain for colleagues, and his lack of interest in morality, human rights, and the fate of poorer
nations all contributed to the fact that many of his apparent achievements collapsed
even before the end of Ford's term in office.[8]

A second biographer of Henry Kissinger would not have seriously disagreed.
Isaacson (1992), relying more than Schulzinger on secondary sources but supple-
menting these with widespread interviewing (even of Nixon and Kissinger), offered
a lengthy and complex portrait. Describing his subject as "the foremost American
negotiator of this century" and, aside from George Kennan, our "most influential
foreign policy intellectual," Isaacson pointed out that the main lines of his policy
(containment and cooperation with Moscow; a realistic attitude toward China)
continued to be followed throughout the next two decades. Nevertheless, the author
said, Kissinger's tendency to see every crisis in East–West terms (as in September
1970), his terrible mistakes in the "back channel" (as in May 1971), his off-the-cuff
diplomacy at the Moscow summit (May 1972), and his constant dismissal of the
ethical dimension combined to alienate potential supporters and ultimately to
prompt the backlash against détente.

Not all the relevant publications of these years made use of the new presidential
documentation. Tom Wicker's (1991) biography of Nixon was largely dependent on
memoirs – Kissinger and Garthoff particularly – but it presented a well-written and
provocative summary of the president's arms control efforts in which the author
challenged the rationale for Nixon's decision on MIRV and questioned the very
need for a Kissinger back channel. Analytical volumes by Froman (1991) and
Melanson (1991) harkened back to the work of John Lewis Gaddis and Richard
Stevenson in deriving lessons from a comparison of Nixon's diplomacy with the
foreign policies of other American presidents.[9] Froman used the term "détente" to
refer to all efforts, from Eisenhower to Reagan, to improve United States–Soviet
relations. He suggested that, whereas the Kennedy, Johnson, and Reagan administrations had valued détente primarily as an expression of coexistence, the Eisenhower,
Nixon, and Ford administrations had valued it as a means of transforming fundamental elements of Soviet foreign policy (in Nixon's case, through "linkage") or the
Soviet system itself. The balance struck by each administration, Froman concluded,
"may have as much to do with evolving perceptions of American resources . . . as
with interpretations of the Soviet challenge."

Melanson's study proceeded from the insight that, following the breakdown of
America's original Cold War consensus in the Vietnam decade, each succeeding
presidential administration had tried and failed to reconstruct that consensus along
the lines of its own beliefs about the nature of the conflict. In the case of the Nixon
presidency, Melanson argued, because both Nixon and Kissinger assumed that the
structure of international relations was changing significantly, the foreign policy
design envisioned "the emergence of a stable multipolar balance managed by the
United States and animated by a shared sense of international legitimacy." However,
in Melanson's opinion, Nixon's decision to describe his objectives to the public as a
"full generation of peace" shrouded his realpolitik in largely Wilsonian ideology and
created a situation in which the concrete results were subjected to "simultaneous
liberal and conservative critiques." Attempts under Ford to emphasize the competi-

tive side of détente only provoked liberals all the more and catalyzed public demands for greater morality in foreign policy.

No sooner were arguments like these mounted, however, than again the context began to shift, as the realization that the Cold War had ended raised unprecedented questions and brought increasing commentary from the former Soviet side. Perhaps no writing was more symbolic of this new world than that of Joan Hoff (1994), who turned the field of Nixon scholarship on its head.[10] Having carefully examined the existing evidence (and interviewed Nixon himself extensively), Hoff had come to a number of surprising conclusions: that scholars had praised Nixon's foreign policy much too much, that they had attributed too much of its relative success to Kissinger, and that they had almost entirely ignored the president's considerable domestic achievements by focusing on Watergate. Calling Kissinger's appointment as national security adviser "one of the most unfortunate decisions the president-elect [had] made," she described the former as a "geopolitical follower," not a leader, the Tonto, not the Lone Ranger, of United States foreign policy. As for Nixon, Hoff (like so many others) conceded that his new relationship with China was a lasting achievement, but she insisted that his Third World policy was a disaster and that his general diplomatic legacy was weaker than he and many others had maintained. In her opinion, "the steps that Nixon and Kissinger took away from traditional containment seem less impressive than they did . . . twenty years ago." "Now that the Cold War is over, his imaginative ways for fighting it . . . have lost their importance, in part because they were not followed by his successors . . . and in part because they were never designed to end the Cold War."

A very different but equally provocative perspective was offered in the same year that Hoff wrote by Lebow and Stein (1994). They presented detailed case studies of the perceptions of decision-makers during two of the tensest moments of Soviet–American relations: the Cuban missile crisis of 1962 and the confrontations during the Arab–Israeli War of 1973. In both instances the authors profited from the new opportunity to interview participants from both sides and to encounter them in situations where they were unconstrained. The authors found both crisis situations enlightening, but the Arab–Israeli conflict, they believed, had direct implications for the meaning and effectiveness of détente. On that occasion the crisis became a crisis because the responsible leaders (1) possessed very self-serving definitions of what détente allowed them, (2) failed to face up to difficult choices and painful tradeoffs, (3) overestimated the extent to which, and the speed with which, they could influence their allies, and (4) suffered the effects of anger, stress, and psychological denial during the event. Ironically, it seems, détente had made the responsible parties over-confident by masking profound if unanticipated disagreements among them. In ordering a DEFCON III alert Kissinger had compounded the problem with an "ineffective, potentially dangerous, and ill-considered" action. "Both the Soviet Union and the US miscalculated badly and did serious damage to their relationship."

The comparison of perceptions employed by Lebow and Stein was in some ways reminiscent of their use by Raymond Garthoff, and it is not surprising, considering the changed international circumstances, that Garthoff thought it timely to publish a revised edition of *Détente and Confrontation* in 1994. The essential interpretation, of course, remained unchanged, but the author chose now to conclude the story of détente at the end of the 1970s and to deal with the period that followed in a sequel entitled *The Great Transition* (1994b; see also Garthoff 2001). This time he cited his earlier sources more explicitly, while pointing out that the chapters on the "road to détente" and the "1972 summit" also included new material and acknowledging a special debt to Lebow and Stein for their work on the 1973 Arab–Israeli War. Perhaps the most interesting change from the first edition was a final chapter devoted to placing Nixon's détente in the broadest context. Here he began by asserting that, though "real alleviation of an adversarial relationship would only have been possible after a change in the basic underlying [ideological] framework," detente *could* have been more successful. What mistakes were made? Garthoff suggested at least three: (1) allowing excessively permissive limits in arms control agreements; (2) overlooking the need for frequent consultation and strategic dialogue between the rivals; and (3) not developing a common conception of détente or specific agreements on geopolitical conduct. He concluded with a two-pronged contention: (1) that "such external influences as détente – and confrontation – affected the internal causes of the collapse of . . . the Soviet bloc only marginally," and (2) that "the most significant of these influences was the contribution of détente to the gradual development . . . of what came to be called 'the new political thinking' in the Gorbachev years."

By the mid-1990s the flood of new documentation and foreign memoirs with relevance to our subject had reached truly impressive proportions. Granted, not all, or even most, of this material was integrated quickly into the secondary literature, but as time went on it began to have an impact on discourse and analysis. Perhaps the most unexpected windfall turned out to be the appearance of the diary that Nixon's chief of staff and confidante, H. R. Haldeman, wrote or dictated each night after interacting with the president during the day. This commentary began with Nixon's inauguration and continued through April 30, 1973, when Haldeman was fired by the president. It totaled about 750,000 words, although the published version (Haldeman 1994) represents only about 40 percent of the text available on CD-Rom. The diary included, of course, an enormous amount of repetition and trivia, and the book version was heavily focused on Watergate, but together they were a marvelously rewarding source, since Haldeman was always present, even in China and in Russia. Nowhere else can one witness so clearly the mental health of the president, his hatred of the media and bureaucracy, his interactions (and at times, dismay) with Kissinger, and the emotional ups and downs of Kissinger (with whom Haldeman talked a great deal).

Another useful contribution to our understanding of the Nixon diplomacy was the publication of the memoirs of the former Soviet ambassador to the United States, Anatoly Dobrynin (1995).[11] Envoy to six presidents from Kennedy to Reagan, Dobrynin was not only experienced and perceptive but also refreshingly non-ideological. He well comprehended that "Nixon and Kissinger sought to create a more stable and predictable strategic situation without reducing the high level of armaments." His recollections were a mine of significant information, ranging from reports of previously unknown meetings (e.g., the January 1971 Politburo session at which Gromyko and Andropov pushed for more active involvement with Nixon) to assessments of diplomatic bargaining (e.g., Gromyko's requiring an agreement on Berlin before agreeing to a summit only helped to insure Nixon's visiting Beijing before Moscow) and asides about personalities (e.g., Gromyko simply couldn't stand "the smart Henry").

Meanwhile, scholars continued to investigate and ponder the development and the meaning of détente. Among the more speculative at this point were the authors of two essays included in a book edited by Westad (1997). One of these was the editor himself, the other a scholar we have encountered before, John Lewis Gaddis.[12] The volume was actually a by-product of the "Carter–Brezhnev Project" (an international collaboration) and was focused primarily on the period 1977–81, but the Westad and Gaddis contributions were more general in scope and relevance. Westad's essay began by emphasizing the extent to which American failure in Vietnam and the acceptance of the USSR as a military equal generated an overly optimistic scenario in the minds of the Brezhnev Politburo about the future of their country. In light of this, Westad argued, détente may be seen to have furthered the ultimate collapse of the Soviet Union in a most ironic way: by causing its leaders to expend precious resources (resources that could have given their regime another lease on life) in an effort to maintain the nuclear parity and global role they believed were necessary to preserve peaceful coexistence, or détente.

Gaddis, in his essay, attempted to answer the question of why the Cold War lasted as long as it did. Of relevance here is that, among the factors he thought may have played a role (e.g., nuclear weapons, bipolarity, fear of another world war), Gaddis identified the Vietnam War as important in several ways: because it distracted Lyndon Johnson's attention from efforts to resolve Soviet–American differences that had begun under Kennedy and Khrushchev; because it made it more difficult for the new Brezhnev–Kosygin regime to pursue these initiatives; and because it led the normally cautious Brezhnev to conclude that the Third World's "correlation of forces" had shifted permanently in Moscow's favor, thus enticing him ultimately to advance along his own path of "adolescent imperial overextension."

Not every historian would have agreed with Gaddis in seeing the Vietnam conflict as an unmitigated setback to peace. Nelson (1995), for example, argued that the trauma America experienced as a result of the prolonged Asian struggle was a major factor in (1) breaking down the public consensus that had made the Cold War possible and (2) forcing postwar political leadership to consider other options. Basing my interpretation on extensive archival work as well as interviews with participants, I went on to propose a more general thesis, that in both the Soviet and American cases a general shortage of resources (e.g., public support, economic means, alliance loyalty) had been at the root of the simultaneous and fortunate willingness to become more cooperative. Alternating my explorations of the two countries' situations, I offered evidence to demonstrate the validity of this thesis while at the same time examining the diplomacy that was employed. Both Nixon and Kissinger played an important role in this story, though I was highly critical of their (and Brezhnev's) unwillingness to exploit more fully the opportunity for change. Among the themes I emphasized were (1) Brezhnev's use of détente as a vehicle to establish his personal political authority; (2) Nixon's use of it to assuage public disappointment at the failure to end the war in Vietnam; (3) the significance of grain, trade, and capital in Moscow's calculations and in Soviet–American negotiations; and (4) the importance of the pending ratification of Soviet–West

German treaties in Brezhnev's decision to proceed with the Moscow summit despite Nixon's bombing of North Vietnam.

Some of these same themes were largely reaffirmed three years later with the publication of a lengthy and careful assessment of the entire Nixon foreign policy by William Bundy (1998), an assistant secretary of state in the Johnson administration and editor of *Foreign Affairs* magazine from 1972 to 1984. His study, though largely derived from secondary sources, attested to both his impressive personal connections and his command of the essential literature. Addressing what he calls "the most crucial historical issue" (i.e., why Nixon's "great successes" collapsed or became inactive in just two to three years), Bundy found himself drawn to largely negative conclusions about Nixon's thought and behavior. Nixon had gone further than any of his predecessors in pursuit of serious negotiations with Moscow, Bundy said, yet *vis-à-vis* the Russians he remained essentially a Cold Warrior, and what he had accomplished he undermined with short-sighted political calculations and his "unshakable bent to deceive." Watergate was only part of the reason his foreign policy fell apart. The key factor was that Congress and the people were rebelling against his persistent record of misrepresenting his policies and pursuing strategies at odds with what he disclosed. The opening to China, in Bundy's view, was important, but not so important as the structural changes that resulted from Brandt's Ostpolitik. Nixon's treatment of Cambodia was a disgrace and so was his policy toward Chile. His record was much better in the Middle East, where Bundy believed it made sense for him to try to keep the Soviets out. In fact, Bundy lauded Kissinger, who otherwise was not given much credit, for being particularly effective in the Middle East, both in 1973 and during the Ford era.

A much more specific and highly relevant book which appeared the same year as Bundy's was also written by a former governmental official, this time from the Carter administration. Cahn (1998) constituted a fascinating investigation of the way in which the CIA was besieged and used by conservative intellectuals in the 1970s to cast doubt upon the adequacy of Nixon and Ford's defense policies. Though not without its own bias, the study offered the reader considerable evidence from both sides of the debate, evidence gleaned from interviewing, archival research, and use of the Freedom of Information Act. Cahn told the story well, from its beginnings in Nixon and Kissinger's animosity toward the CIA, through the agency's reorganization and involvement in Watergate, to the attacks from the Right on its National Intelligence Estimates and the disastrous decision (by Ford's last CIA director, George Bush) to appoint a small group of "outside experts" to perform an alternative threat assessment (Team B). Why was the CIA so vulnerable? Cahn pointed not only to the lack of support from Nixon, Kissinger, and Ford, but also to such factors as the antagonism generated by the CIA's "realism" about Vietnam, public anger at discovering a host of illegal CIA activities, congressional reassertion of its oversight prerogatives, and rapid turnover in CIA directors from 1973 to 1977. What was the net effect of the Team B "experiment" and the pessimistic estimates of Soviet military strength it generated (and leaked)? Détente was weakened, she asserted, the country driven to the Right, and billions of dollars wasted on unnecessary armaments.

At this point, we should stop to note once again the progress of the National Archives in opening its Nixon collections to scholars. Until very recently those studies of Nixon's foreign policy that utilized original government sources were forced to rely almost entirely on the so-called "Special File," an often rich but hardly central trove of documentation, opened in 1987 and comprising approximately a sixth of the 40 million pages in the archival holdings. This has now changed. In March 1998 the National Archives announced a major release of Nixon National Security Council (NSC) documents and it followed this up with substantial NSC openings in 2000 and 2001. Simultaneously, the archive committed itself to releasing all remaining Nixon tapes (approximately 3,700 hours) in five equal installments from 1999 to 2004.[13]

The sheer volume of these declassifications is astonishing and virtually guarantees that it will be a number of years before historians can penetrate the material effectively. For the time being, the most the public is likely to see is an occasional newspaper article reporting that discoveries in the presidential papers have contradicted an account in Kissinger's or someone else's memoirs. Such was the case, for example, in March 2002, when the press disclosed that newly declassified documents showed that what Kissinger had written about Taiwan being "barely discussed" in his July 1971 meetings with Zhou Enlai was "breathtakingly not true" (Mann 2002; see Sciolino 2002). A similar article in April 2002 reported that documents had been uncovered indicating that United States' covert intervention in Angola in 1975 actually occurred weeks before Kissinger claimed it had (French 2002).

Since Kissinger's own papers remain under lock and key in the Library of Congress until five years after his death, one of the more significant recent publications for the study of Nixon–Ford diplomacy has been an unauthorized collection of many of Kissinger's conversations during the 1970s with the leaders of Beijing and Moscow. Edited by William Burr, *The Kissinger Transcripts* (1999) was put together by the National Security Archive (a research library at George Washington University) from State Department files and papers of Kissinger's assistant, Winston Lord, which had been deposited in the National Archives. Though the "mem-cons" of the meetings with the Soviets, with one exception, were entirely from 1974–6, the negotiations with Zhou, Mao, Deng Xiaoping, and Huang Hua (Chinese Ambassador to Canada and Representative to the United Nations) were themselves revealing of the state of Soviet–American relations. Among the more startling revelations was that Kissinger practiced triangular diplomacy in a manner very favorable to China. He gave Chinese leaders briefings about his meetings in Moscow but did not tell the Soviets much about his talks in Beijing. He repeatedly offered classified military intelligence to the Chinese as a way of demonstrating how the United States could be of help to China. Meanwhile, though he and Brezhnev got along well personally, their discussions showed that détente was coming under severe strain as the two of them wrangled over MIRV, the Middle East, and Angola. It was also noteworthy that both he and Brezhnev badly underestimated the importance of the Helsinki agreements in 1975.[14]

As if to challenge historians to get on with their work of evaluation, Henry Kissinger finally completed his own memoirs with the publication of its third volume, *Years of Renewal* (1999). Sensitive to the criticisms he had endured and profiting from twenty-five years of hindsight, Kissinger, in introducing his comments on the Ford era, fashioned a very elegant reinterpretation of what he and Nixon did together and what later happened to it. The two of them (who had a "nearly identical perspective") had tried to take the middle road, he said. They had seen the need not only to extricate the United States from Vietnam in a way that "preserved American leadership," but also to define a role for the United States in the post-Vietnam world that avoided "the extremes of abdication and heroic posturing." Détente with Russia had been but one aspect of the strategy, designed as it was to control a crucial adversarial relationship. Moreover, by the end of Nixon's first term, it had been shown to work. "The Soviet Union was being constrained from geopolitical adventures by the stick of our opening to China and the carrot of . . . increased trade." We had helped to channel Willy Brandt's Ostpolitik "into a direction compatible with Allied cohesion" by linking recognition of East Germany to a guarantee of free access to Berlin. We had negotiated "a strategic arms agreement freezing the Soviet numerical missile build-up without modifying any established American program" (note the absence of second thoughts about MIRV). Then, in 1972, Kissinger contended, the national consensus "broke down," and for the remainder of Nixon's term the administration found itself increasingly whipsawed between the Wilsonianism of the Left and the Wilsonianism of the Right. This was not so much the result of Watergate (which seemed now a less central matter to Kissinger) but of other factors, the most important of which was that "Nixon and I underestimated the impact on the public psyche of the sharp difference between our approach to foreign policy and . . . [that of American] Wilsonianism."

With Ford, Kissinger maintained, Providence smiled on America. To Kissinger, the new president was a person who embodied our nation's deepest and simplest values, a genuine healer. Yet even Ford could not overcome the burgeoning split between the conservatives/neo-cons, on the one hand, and the liberals on the other, and both sides harassed him unmercifully, even from within his own administration. Despite this, according to Kissinger, Ford could take pride in a long list of foreign policy accomplishments. In East–West relations he had conducted a policy of strength, resisted the Kremlin's attempt to enlarge the Soviet sphere, and, in spite of strong opposition, signed the Helsinki Treaty (now acclaimed by Kissinger as a landmark). In the long run, the author asserted, détente would survive, since Reagan's policy was in fact a "canny reassertion of the geopolitical strategies of the Nixon and Ford administrations clothed in the rhetoric of Wilsonianism."

Though only indirectly a response to Kissinger, the most recent commentary by professional historians on détente appeared in three balanced and well-written books – one a study of his administration, one a biography of Nixon, and one a survey of the Cold War. Small (1999) drew a sharp line between Nixon's great power diplomacy, to which the author gave high marks, and his record with the rest of the world, whose nations suffered painfully from being viewed entirely through the prism of Soviet–American relations. With the Soviets and Chinese, Small suggested, Nixon's policy of triangulation succeeded brilliantly. Though the grain deal backfired through carelessness, the SALT treaty was less than perfect, and détente itself was puffed up to the American public, Nixon's openings to China and Russia marked the "beginning of the end" of the Cold War.

Morgan (2002) also conceded a great deal to the president before concluding that historians must resist the "overselling" of Nixon's wisdom in the handling of international affairs. Attributing to Nixon "more sophisticated geopolitical vision than any other US president," and giving him, not Kissinger, the credit for the insight, Morgan praised him for envisioning "a new global equilibrium based on the recognition that both Soviet and American power was limited, that a multipolar world was emerging and that different ideologies could have similar interests." However, Morgan noted, Nixon's road to détente was far from smooth and exacted a fearful price in terms of deceitfulness, the exclusion of both experts and public, bad crisis management, and a very limited SALT agreement. Furthermore, the endurance of his Cold War mentality, his failure to appreciate the Third World, and his brutality in Vietnam were very costly. Détente may have shown that America and the communist world could coexist, but Nixon did not get clear enough that it might mean different things to each of them.[15]

Loth (2002) placed us in a rather different framework, examining how the East–West Cold War evolved and was eventually "defeated" through continued efforts to produce "détente" (a relaxation of tension). This was a refreshing approach because, though the Nixon years and policy remained important, Loth shined his spotlight on other periods and other countries, especially on Europe and Germany.[16] There had been chances to reduce the East–West confrontation ever since there had been a Cold War, he contended. What it took to succeed was imaginative, confident leaders and perseverance against the coalition of forces that was profiting from the confrontation. Though Loth's account of the 1970s was relatively straightforward, it was clear that he had a very high regard for the contribution to détente of Willy Brandt, whose resignation as West Germany's chancellor on May 6, 1974, he viewed as almost as severe a blow to improved international ties as Nixon's Watergate problems. Two general developments, he argued, threatened the "precarious network of cooperative relations woven first by the Brandt government and then somewhat later and with another accent by the Nixon administration." One threat came from the criticism of groups in the American public who were either mistrustful or who idealistically misunderstood the actual possibilities. The second arose from the rapid technological change within the field of nuclear arms. In Loth's view, largely because Nixon had so inadequately explained his détente policy "to a public which had always equated balance of power with American superiority," Ford did not at all understand how to cope with either development. Brezhnev was confused as well. The important point, Loth concluded, was not to accept the thesis, advanced after 1989, that Western détente policy unnecessarily prolonged the Cold War. On the contrary, he asserted, the insights that were needed for the leaders of the Soviet system to give up on Leninist ideology were actually derived from the repeated attempts on the part of the West to communicate as much as possible about the realities of life here and to exhibit cooperative behavior toward them – the essence of détente policy.

So the debate on our subject continues, reflecting, as it always does, the assumptions of the viewer as well as the reality of the past. Relative consensus does seem to have emerged about certain things; for example, about the unusually malleable nature of the era, about the value of Nixon's "opening" to China, about Nixon's failure to understand the Third World, about the destructive impact of excessive secrecy and centralization. But on other matters there is still wide-ranging disagreement; on questions such as the contributions of Kissinger to détente, whether Nixon and Kissinger pushed arms control as hard as they could or should have, to what extent they themselves contributed to détente's demise, and what the real meaning of détente was for each side and for the Cold War. We can be sure of only one thing. The unusual quality of the personalities involved, the significance of these questions to a country still struggling to define its role in the world, and the known existence of vast, untapped historical sources mean that we shall hear much more about détente in the not too distant future.[17]

NOTES

1   The phrase is from Nixon's inaugural address. See also Nixon (1972: xii).
2   See "Secretary Kissinger's News Conference of December 23 [1975]," *State Bulletin* 74 (January 19, 1976), 70.
3   It was also in 1979 that Paula Stern produced a volume entitled *To The Water's Edge*, an examination of the interaction of domestic and foreign affairs surrounding the Jackson–Vanik amendment that has remained a minor classic in the field.
4   Of the eight books Nixon wrote after his memoirs, the most relevant to our subject is *The Real War* (1980). It is there that he speaks of the need for "hard-headed détente."
5   Other revealing memoirs of close Nixon associates include Safire (1975), Price (1977), Haldeman (1978), and Erlichman (1982). President Ford's (1979) memoirs also date from this period.
6   This comparative approach was also taken by Wallensteen (1989).
7   See also the revealing memoirs of the chairmen of the SALT delegations: Smith (1980) and Johnson (1984). A third useful memoir (and history) is Maresca (1985).
8   Gerald Ford's presidential papers are housed in the Gerald R. Ford Library in Ann Arbor, Michigan, and were made available to the public after 1981.
9   Another insightful British interpretation of this period is Bowker and Williams (1988).
10   It is ironic, considering the position she takes on Kissinger's creative role, that it was Hoff who coined the word "Nixinger" to describe the foreign policy of the administration.
11   Other relevant Soviet memoirs include Gromyko (1989), Arbatov (1992), Keworkow (1995), Aleksandrov-Argentov (1994, in Russian), Kornienko (1995, in Russian), and Israelyan (1995). Helpful secondary works on Soviet policy include Edmonds (1983), Ulam (1983), Gelman (1984), Breslauer (1982), and Anderson (1993).
12   Gaddis' chapter is a revised and briefer version of an essay he published in *The Long Peace* (1987).
13   See the bibliographical essay by Jonathan Cassidy in Reeves (2001), pp. 663–9.
14   Rewarding discussions of China's indirect contributions to détente can be found in Garver (1982), Chang (1990), Harding (1992), and Foot (1995).
15   Two other recent biographies of Nixon, Summers (2000) and Reeves (2001), do not address the subject of détente directly. Nor do the otherwise admirable and well researched studies by Kimball (1998) and Berman (2001).
16   Germany's important role in the development of détente can be traced in two important memoirs: Brandt (1976) and Bahr (1996). See also the valuable studies by Haftendorn (1985), Sodaro (1990), and Sarotte (2001). On Europe and détente, see Dyson (1986) and White (1992).
17   In addition to the evidence already mentioned, there are alleged to be 10,000 handwritten pages in Nixon's personal diaries.

REFERENCES

Aleksandrov-Agentov, Andrei M.: *Ot Kollontai do Gorbacheva [From Kollontai to Gorbachev]* (Moscow: Mezhdunar otnosheniia, 1994).

Ambrose, Stephen E.: *Nixon, Vol. 2: The Triumph of a Politician 1962–1972* (New York: Simon and Schuster, 1989).

Anderson, Richard D., Jr.: *Public Politics in an Authoritarian State: Making Foreign Policy During the Brezhnev Years* (Ithaca, NY: Cornell University Press, 1993).

Arbatov, Georgi: *The System: An Insider's Life in Soviet Politics* (New York: Times Books, 1992).

Bahr, Egon: *Zu Meiner Zeit* (Munich: Karl Blessing, 1996).

Bell, Coral: *The Diplomacy of Détente: The Kissinger Era* (London: Martin Robertson, 1977).

Berman, Larry: *No Peace, No Honor: Nixon, Kissinger, and Betrayal in Vietnam* (New York: Free Press, 2001).

Bowker, Mike and Phil Williams: *Superpower Détente: A Reappraisal* (London: Royal Institute of International Affairs, 1988).

Brandon, Henry: *The Retreat of American Power* (New York: Norton, 1972).

Brandt, Willy: *People and Politics: The Years 1960–1975* (Boston, MA: Little, Brown, 1976).

Breslauer, George: *Khrushchev and Brezhnev as Leaders: Building Authority in Soviet Politics* (London: Allen and Unwin, 1982).

Brown, Seyom: *The Crisis of Power: An Interpretation of United States Foreign Policy During the Kissinger Years* (New York: Columbia University Press, 1979).

Bundy, William: *A Tangled Web: The Making of Foreign Policy in the Nixon Presidency* (New York: Hill and Wang, 1998).

Burr, William: *The Kissinger Transcripts: Top Secret Talks with Beijing and Moscow* (New York: New Press, 1999).

Cahn, Anne H.: *Killing Détente: The Right Attacks the CIA* (University Park: Pennsylvania State University Press, 1998).

Chang, Gordon H.: *Friends and Enemies: The United States, China, and the Soviet Union, 1948–1972* (Stanford, CA: Stanford University Press, 1990).

Dobrynin, Anatoly: *In Confidence: Moscow's Ambassador to America's Six Cold War Presidents* (New York: Times Books, 1995).

Dyson, Kenneth (ed.): *European Détente: Case Studies of the Politics of East–West Relations* (London: Frances Pinter, 1986).

Edmonds, Robin: *Soviet Foreign Policy: The Brezhnev Years* (Oxford: Oxford University Press, 1983).

Erlichman, John: *Witness to Power* (New York: Simon and Schuster, 1982).

Foot, Rosemary: *The Practice of Power: US Relations with China since 1949* (Oxford: Oxford University Press, 1995).

Ford, Gerald R.: *A Time to Heal: The Autobiography of Gerald R. Ford* (New York: Harper and Row, 1979).

French, Howard W. "Old Files Contradict US Account of War." *International Herald Tribune* (April 2, 2002).

Froman, Michael B.: *The Development of the Idea of Détente: Coming to Terms* (New York: St. Martin's Press, 1991).

Gaddis, John Lewis: *Strategies of Containment: A Critical Appraisal of Postwar American National Security Policy* (New York: Oxford University Press, 1982).

Gaddis, John Lewis: *The Long Peace: Inquiries Into the History of the Cold War* (Oxford: Oxford University Press, 1987).

Garthoff, Raymond L.: *Détente and Confrontation: American–Soviet Relations from Nixon to Reagan* (Washington, DC: Brookings Institution, 1985).

Garthoff, Raymond L.: *Détente and Confrontation: American–Soviet Relations from Nixon to Reagan*, 2nd edn. (Washington, DC: Brookings Institution, 1994a).

Garthoff, Raymond L.: *The Great Transition: American–Soviet Relations and the End of the Cold War* (Washington, DC: Brookings Institution, 1994b).

Garthoff, Raymond L.: *A Journey Through the Cold War: A Memoir of Containment and Coexistence* (Washington, DC: Brookings Institution, 2001).

Garver, James W.: *China's Decision for Rapprochement With the United States, 1968–1971* (Boulder, CO: Westview Press, 1982).

Gelman, Harry: *The Brezhnev Politburo and the Decline of Détente* (Ithaca, NY: Cornell University Press, 1984).

Gromyko, Andrei: *Memories* (London: Hutchinson, 1989).

Haftendorn, Helga: *Security and Détente: Conflicting Priorities in German Foreign Policy* (New York: Praeger, 1985).

Haldeman, H. R. with Joseph Dimona: *The Ends of Power* (New York: Times Books, 1978).

Haldeman, H. R.: *The Haldeman Diaries: Inside the Nixon White House* (New York: Putnam's, 1994).

Harding, Harry: *A Fragile Relationship: The United States and China since 1972* (Washington, DC: Brookings Institution, 1992).

Hersh, Seymour M.: *The Price of Power: Kissinger in the Nixon White House* (New York: Summit Books, 1983).

Hoff, Joan: *Nixon Reconsidered* (New York: Basic Books, 1994).

Hoffman, Stanley: *Primacy or World Order: American Foreign Policy since the Cold War* (New York: McGraw-Hill, 1978).

Hyland, William G.: *Mortal Rivals: Superpower Relations from Nixon to Reagan* (New York: Random House, 1987).

Isaacson, Walter: *Kissinger: A Biography* (New York: Simon and Schuster, 1992).

Israelyan, Victor: *Inside the Kremlin During the Yom Kippur War* (University Park: Pennsylvania State University Press, 1995).

Johnson, U. Alexis: *The Right Hand of Power* (Englewood Cliffs, NJ: Prentice-Hall, 1984).

Kalb, Marvin and Bernard Kalb: *Kissinger* (Boston, MA: Little, Brown, 1974).

Keworkow, Wjatscheslav: *Der Geheime Kanal: Moskau, Der KGB And Die Bonner Ostpolitik* (Berlin: Rowohlt, 1995).

Kimball, Jeffrey: *Nixon's Vietnam War* (Lawrence: University of Kansas Press, 1998).

Kissinger, Henry: *White House Years* (Boston, MA: Little, Brown, 1979).

Kissinger, Henry: *Years of Renewal* (New York: Simon and Schuster, 1999).

Kornienko, G. M.: *Kholodnaia Voina [The Cold War]* (Moscow: Mezhdunar Otnosheniia, 1995).

Lebow, Richard Ned and Janice Gross Stein: *We All Lost the Cold War* (Princeton, NJ: Princeton University Press, 1994).

Litwak, Robert S.: *Détente and the Nixon Doctrine: American Foreign Policy and the Pursuit of Stability, 1969–1976* (Cambridge: Cambridge University Press, 1984).

Loth, Wilfried: *Overcoming the Cold War: A History of Détente, 1950–1991* (Basingstoke: Palgrave, 2002).

Maresca, John J.: *To Helsinki: The Conference on Security and Cooperation in Europe 1973–1975* (Durham, NC: Duke University Press, 1985).

Melanson, Richard A.: *Reconstructing Consensus: American Foreign Policy since the Vietnam War* (New York: St. Martin's Press, 1991).

Morgan, Iwan: *Nixon* (London: Arnold, 2002).

Nelson, Keith L.: *The Making of Détente: Soviet–American Relations in the Shadow of Vietnam* (Baltimore, MD: Johns Hopkins University Press, 1995).

Newhouse, John: *Cold Dawn: The Story of SALT* (New York: Holt, Rinehart, and Winston, 1973).

Nixon, Richard M.: *US Foreign Policy for the 1970s: The Emerging Structure of Peace* (Washington, DC: Government Printing Office, 1972).

Nixon, Richard M.: *RN: The Memoirs of Richard Nixon* (New York: Grosset and Dunlap, 1978).

Nixon, Richard M.: *The Real War* (New York: Warner Books, 1980).

Podhoretz, Norman: "Making the World Safe for Communism." *Commentary* (April 1975), 31–41.

Price, Raymond: *With Nixon* (New York: Viking, 1977).

Reeves, Richard: *President Nixon: Alone in the White House* (New York: Simon and Schuster, 2001).

Safire, William: *Before the Fall: An Inside Look at the Pre-Watergate Nixon White House* (Garden City, NY: Doubleday, 1975).

Sarotte, M. E.: *Dealing with the Devil: East Germany, Détente, and Ostpolitik, 1969–1973* (Chapel Hill: University of North Carolina Press, 2001).

Schell, Jonathan: *The Time of Illusion* (New York: Knopf, 1975).

Schulzinger, Robert D.: *Henry Kissinger: Doctor of Diplomacy* (New York: Columbia University Press, 1989).

Schurmann, Franz: *The Foreign Politics of Richard Nixon: The Grand Design* (Berkeley: Institute of International Studies, 1987).

Sciolino, Elaine: "Kissinger in China: 2 Versions of Secret '71 Talks." *International Herald Tribune* (March 1, 2002).

Small, Melvin: *The Presidency of Richard Nixon* (Lawrence: University of Kansas Press, 1999).

Smith, Gerard: *Doubletalk: The Story of SALT I* (New York: Doubleday, 1980).

Sodaro, Michael J.: *Moscow, Germany, and the West from Khrushchev to Gorbachev* (Ithaca, NY: Cornell University Press, 1990).

Stern, Paula: *To The Water's Edge: Domestic Politics and the Making of American Foreign Policy* (Westport, CT: Greenwood Press, 1979).

Stevenson, Richard W.: *The Rise and Fall of Détente: Relaxations of Tension in US–Soviet Relations 1953–84* (Basingstoke: Macmillan, 1985).

Summers, Anthony: *The Arrogance of Power: The Secret World of Richard Nixon* (New York: Viking, 2000).

Szulc, Tad: *The Illusion of Peace: Foreign Policy in the Nixon Years* (New York: Viking, 1978).

Thornton, Richard C.: *The Nixon–Kissinger Years: Reshaping America's Foreign Policy* (New York: Paragon House, 1989).

Ulam, Adam B.: *Dangerous Relations: The Soviet Union in World Politics, 1970–1982* (New York: Oxford University Press, 1983).

Wallensteen, Peter: "Recurrent Detentes." *Journal of Peace Research* 26 (1989), 225–31.

Westad, Odd Arne: *The Fall of Détente: Soviet–American Relations During the Carter Years* (Oslo: Scandinavian University Press, 1997).

White, Brian: *Britain, Détente and Changing East–West Relations* (London: Routledge, 1992).

Wicker, Tom: *One of Us: Richard Nixon and the American Dream* (New York: Random House, 1991).

Wohlstetter, Albert: "Is There a Strategic Arms Race?" *Foreign Policy* 15 (summer 1974).

CHAPTER TWENTY-FOUR

Nationalism and Regionalism in an Era of Globalization: US Relations with South and Southeast Asia, 1975–2000

ROBERT J. MCMAHON

The final quarter of the twentieth century proved a substantially less tumultuous chapter in US–Asian relations than the quarter-century that preceded it. Between the end of World War II in 1945 and the conclusion of the Second Indochina War in 1975, much of South and Southeast Asia suffered from persistent warfare, wrenching, often bloody independence struggles, bitter ideological conflicts, debilitating economic dislocation, and incessant political turmoil. The United States, for its part, tended to filter all those developments through a Cold War lens. American strategists believed that the eventual pro-Western orientation of South and Southeast Asian nations could be instrumental to the achievement of overall Cold War goals and hence sought to calibrate US regional policies accordingly. Global priorities, in the event, invariably trumped more focused regional and bilateral perspectives in US policymaking.

The post-1975 period, while hardly placid, brought much greater stability and a significant reduction in violence and outside intervention, especially to Southeast Asia. The regional cooperation and cohesion that has so markedly shaped Southeast Asia over the past twenty-five years has been paralleled by striking economic progress and political stability as well. Despite those achievements, and despite the strengthening commercial ties between the United States and Southeast Asia in an era of burgeoning globalization, America's interest in and engagement with the region has declined precipitously since the mid-1970s. The global interests of the United States have once again conditioned its attitudes and policies toward Southeast Asia – but since the end of the Vietnam War, those have with only a few exceptions pushed the region to the outer edges of American consciousness.

The post-1975 history of the South Asian region has evolved in starkly different directions. Parts of the region, from Pakistan to Afghanistan to Sri Lanka, have remained a cauldron of seething political discontent, destabilizing religious fundamentalism, terrorism, and economic retardation. India, on the other hand, the region's dominant power, has exhibited robust economic growth and, despite the assassination of two prime ministers and a series of ugly separatist insurgencies, has displayed an impressive degree of political stability and an abiding commitment to democratic governance. Despite these significant regional variations, US policymakers have tended to view post-1975 South Asia in much the same terms as they have viewed post-1975 Southeast Asia: as an area of peripheral interest and concern; occasionally important, as shifting global priorities might dictate, but almost never vital.

The pages that follow sketch key trends in Southeast and South Asia, since the end of the Vietnam War, beginning with the former region. Each section also offers an assessment of the preliminary secondary literature that has thus far appeared on US relations with these two distinctive regions, emphasizing the more significant and useful books and articles. I close with some brief concluding remarks.

Southeast Asia

The triumph of North Vietnam over longtime US ally South Vietnam in April 1975, along with the near-simultaneous victories of communist insurgencies in Cambodia and Laos over the US-backed regimes there, brought the most conflict-ridden chapter in US–Southeast Asian relations to a dramatic – and rather ignominious – close. Despite the loss of over 58,000 American lives and 2–3 million Vietnamese, Cambodian, and Laotian lives, the expenditure of billions of dollars, and humankind's most extensive bombing campaign, Americans had failed in their principal purpose. They could not preserve the independent South Vietnamese government that so much US blood, treasure, and prestige had been tied to; nor could they prevent the emergence of hostile, communist regimes in neighboring Cambodia and Laos. In the wake of those embarrassing, prestige-sapping defeats, the United States sought to forge new relationships with the nations of Southeast Asia while adopting a lowered profile in a region that now seemed far less central to the overall goals of US foreign policy than it had from the late 1940s to the early 1970s.

Newly elected President Richard M. Nixon had, back in 1969, first set in motion the process of gradual US disengagement from Southeast Asia with his three-cornered policy of phased troop withdrawals from South Vietnam, peace negotiations with North Vietnam, and "Vietnamization" of the still-raging conflict on the ground. That policy aimed at a compromise peace settlement that would leave intact US credibility and prestige, in Southeast Asia and worldwide, while permitting the gradual reduction of the US presence in the region. Nixon's approach stemmed from his conviction that the United States had become grievously overcommitted in an area of secondary importance to the overall balance of global power. His opening to China of the early 1970s confirmed the profound shift taking place in US strategic thinking. The power long identified as so menacing a threat to regional order that its containment necessitated a powerful US military presence in vulnerable Southeast Asia had overnight metamorphosed into America's newest strategic partner. The fundamental shift in threat perception underlying that transformation justified a lowered US profile in Southeast Asia just as Nixon's realization of the limits of US power made such a lowered profile imperative.

Under Nixon's immediate successors, Presidents Gerald R. Ford and Jimmy Carter, US diplomats sought to lessen the negative political and psychological fallout of defeat in Indochina by demonstrating a continuing, if decidedly more modest and circumscribed, commitment to the region. Key to that strategy was the need to reassure Thailand and the Philippines, two formal allies, that the United States was not abandoning them while, at the same time, persuading friendly, non-aligned states such as Indonesia, Malaysia, and Singapore that it was not withdrawing entirely from Southeast Asia. Ford and Carter, despite initial skepticism from indigenous elites, managed at least partially to accomplish that goal. They did so through quiet face-to-face diplomacy, through public professions of America's intent to remain a Pacific power, through generous economic and developmental assistance, and through vigorous expressions of support for the Association of Southeast Asian Nations (ASEAN).

The latter organization assumed greatly enhanced importance to US–Southeast Asian relations in the aftermath of the Vietnam War. Founded in 1967, at the height of the war, ASEAN represented a nascent effort by the region's non-communist nations – Thailand, Malaysia, Singapore, the Philippines, and Indonesia – to cooperate on a range of common economic, political, and security matters. Support for ASEAN, still tepid under Ford, became the hallmark of America's Southeast Asian policy by the advent of the Carter administration. As Cyrus R. Vance, Carter's first secretary of state, noted in his memoirs: "One of the building blocks of our post-Vietnam policy, not only in East Asia but throughout the world, was support of regional economic or political organizations that could bear an increasing role in maintaining stability in the world." ASEAN, in his words, ranked as "perhaps the outstanding example of such an organization" (Vance 1983: 125). Beginning in 1977, US representatives met annually with ASEAN foreign ministers to discuss matters of mutual concern, a pattern that continued during the administration of Ronald Reagan and thereafter. Indeed, in September 1982, Reagan remarked publicly that "ASEAN now stands as a model for regional cooperation" and "regional resilience" and that US support for ASEAN "has been and will continue to be the keystone of American policy in Southeast Asia" (McMahon 1999: 197).

Yet the fallout from the Vietnam War and the detritus of a still-virulent Cold War also continued to influence US policy toward Southeast Asia throughout the Ford, Carter, and Reagan presidencies. Preliminary talk about normalizing relations with unified, communist Vietnam in the immediate postwar period foundered, largely on the rock of US domestic politics. Vietnam's invasion of Cambodia in December 1978, its subsequent occupation of that war-ravaged country, the brief Sino-Vietnamese conflict of 1979, and the deepening ties between Hanoi and Moscow, all served both to harden Cold War tensions in the region and to render moribund any prospect for the early normalization of US–Vietnamese relations.

The return of Cold War patterns of thought and diplomacy, first evident during the last two years of the Carter presidency, became even more pronounced during Reagan's tenure in the White House. By the 1980s, global geopolitical priorities were once again conditioning most US actions in the region. The Reagan administration identified Vietnam as a stalking horse for the Soviet Union and insisted upon the need to contain the regional power and influence of each. Toward that end, US–ASEAN security cooperation strengthened, particularly with regard to the construction of a common front against Vietnam's continued occupation of Cambodia. Reagan's de-emphasis on the human rights campaign launched by Carter also derived in large measure from his determination to hold together a strong anti-Soviet coalition. Doing so, he was convinced, in Southeast Asia as elsewhere, demanded the cultivation of close working relationships with friendly, anti-communist regimes – regardless of their human rights records at home.

It also bears emphasizing, however, that American policymakers, despite their genuine concern about Vietnamese expansionism and apprehension about the Soviet–Vietnamese alliance, have not since the end of the Vietnam War regarded Southeast Asia as an area of vital interest. That was amply evident during the Carter and Reagan years, as the Cold War entered its final phase; it has certainly been the case ever since. Indeed, as Asian expert John Bresnan correctly observes: "Since the fall of Saigon in 1975, Washington's attention has been drawn back to the region only briefly, at moments of high drama" (Bresnan 1994: 13). Northeast Asia, the Middle East, Central America, Eastern Europe – all grabbed far more headlines during the post-1975 period, and all absorbed far more of the limited attention span of senior American diplomats.

The abrupt end of the Cold War at the close of the 1980s further consigned the region to peripheral status in American eyes. The Cold War's demise hastened the withdrawal of Vietnamese troops from Cambodia, thereby eliminating the only regional security issue still of cardinal concern to the United States. In October 1991 a peace treaty was signed under United Nations auspices that brought at least a partial halt to the bloody, destabilizing civil war in Cambodia. With the movement toward peace in that fractured country and with Vietnam's tentative embrace of economic reforms and opening toward ASEAN (it was accepted as a member in 1995), the security fears that had for so long dominated US policy in Southeast Asia faded from view. When, in November 1992, the United States closed down its sprawling air and naval bases in the Philippines, in response to a combination of Philippine opposition and a devastating volcanic eruption, defense analysts in Washington betrayed little anxiety. Bases deemed critical to the US defense posture in the Pacific ever since the end of World War II now seemed superfluous in the new security environment of the post-Cold War era. As the twenty-first century opened, a small logistics base in Singapore housing a mere 200 US troops was all that was left of America's once-formidable military presence in Southeast Asia.

The precipitous decline in America's military–security stake in Southeast Asia has been paralleled by an equivalent surge in its economic–commercial stake. As the Southeast Asian nations increased their gross domestic product fourteen-fold between 1965 and 1990, US trade with the region soared. John Bresnan's slim but suggestive book, *From Dominoes to Dynamos* (1994), took the new policy challenges posed by that economic revitalization as its central focus. "In 1990," Bresnan noted, "US two-way trade with the ASEAN economies, totaling $49.5 billion, was larger than US trade with South America, with the Middle East, with Africa, or with the former Soviet Union and eastern Europe. US exports of $20.6 billion were larger, as well." Despite the serious economic downturn that afflicted Southeast Asia in 1997–8, Bresnan's central point retains its validity: "US investment in the ASEAN economies and US trade with them have given the United States a substantial economic stake in Southeast Asia" (pp. 27–8).

The secondary literature touching on these major events and trends in post-1975 US–Southeast Asian relations is still in its infancy. Compared to the voluminous and richly documented corpus of scholarship examining US–Southeast Asian relations from World War II through the end of the Vietnam War, serious work on this more recent period is spare, episodic, and based on exceedingly thin documentary evidence. On the one hand, this relative inattention simply mimics the normal evolution of historical scholarship: historians ordinarily await both the opening of essential archival records and the perspective afforded by the lapse of sufficient time before seeking to write full-blown accounts of recent events. This is a pattern amply attested to by many of the essays in the present volume. Journalists, memoirists, and contemporary policy analysts and advocates invariably produce the first cut of diplomatic history, a pattern that has held for early studies of post-1975 US–Southeast Asian relations, as discussed below. Yet the thinness of even this kind of work is striking in the case of the United States and Southeast Asia. It doubtless reflects the relative inattention paid to the region by American policymakers and the public at large in the aftermath of the Vietnam War, and stems, to put it baldly, from the relegation of Southeast Asia once more to the peripheral status it occupied prior to the Cold War.

While the divergent memories of and lessons thought to be derived from the Vietnam War have proved absolutely critical to the overall shape and direction of recent US foreign policy, the Southeast Asian region itself has largely dropped off the radar screen since the war. It is telling that in lengthy memoirs devoted to their respective tenures as secretary of state, neither George P. Shultz (1993), James A. Baker, III (1995), nor Warren Christopher (2001) offer much more than a passing glance in the direction of an area that so thoroughly absorbed the energies of several of their predecessors at Foggy Bottom. Likewise, general works covering US foreign policy since the Vietnam War pay but cursory attention, if that, to Southeast Asian developments. Former government official Raymond L. Garthoff's seminal *Détente and Confrontation* (1985) largely ignores the region. That is the case as well with historian H. W. Brands' useful survey, *Since Vietnam* (1996), journalist David Halberstam's sweeping account of the foreign policy debates of the 1990s, *War in a Time of Peace* (2001), and most of the books devoted to individual post-Vietnam War presidencies as well.

There are exceptions, of course. The final chapter of my own book (McMahon 1999) sketches a preliminary narrative of the 1975–98 period, pieced together largely from the public record, contemporary journalism, memoirs, statements of top officials, trade statistics, and the like. I argue that economic interests supplanted geopolitical imperatives after 1975 as the key force driving US policy, a trend that became even more pronounced in the 1990s. I also contend that powerful nationalist and regionalist currents within Southeast Asia have dominated the region's recent history. ASEAN, a product of those forces, has become instrumental in the forging of a new, indigenous order and sense of regional identity. Southeast Asian governments and societies have, as a consequence, become arbiters of their own destiny to a far greater extent than at any previous point in the modern era, even as the phenomenon of globalization challenges their economic, political, and cultural autonomy in new ways.

John Bresnan's *From Dominoes to Dynamos*, a Council on Foreign Relations-sponsored publication, is one of the few books to focus centrally on contemporary Southeast Asia's significance to US foreign policy. In addition to the valuable compendium of economic data that it provides, Bresnan's study serves as a work of vigorous policy advocacy. Noting that US policy toward Asia has tended to focus principally on China, Japan, and to a lesser extent Korea, he argues that the ASEAN states – whose "economies are already a major market for US exports among world regions" – demand far greater attention than they have received of late from American policymakers (Bresnan 1994: 103–4).

US–Philippine relations, especially during the Ferdinand Marcos era, stand as an important exception to the general pattern of scholarly neglect of Southeast Asian topics. Solid overviews by Karnow (1989) and Brands (1992), the former a Pulitzer Prize-winner, ably trace the story of the Filipino–American encounter from the pre-colonial period to the overthrow of the Marcos dictatorship in 1986 and the immediate post-Marcos years. Raymond Bonner's ironically titled *Waltzing with a Dictator* (1987) is an outstanding journalistic account of US policy toward the Marcos regime, based on a range of interviews with leading figures from both countries.

US policy *vis-à-vis* Vietnam and Cambodia has proven the most significant exception to the general slighting of Southeast Asian developments. A varied and rich literature has developed on US relations with Vietnam and Cambodia since 1975. Much of this work has, perforce, represented a continuation of the scholarly fascination with the Vietnam War and its consequences. Several scholars have, for example, carefully scrutinized the Carter administration's decision to abandon its original pursuit of normalized relations with Vietnam. Some see that policy reversal as a product of the marked tilt toward China that characterized Carter's shifting global priorities from 1979 onward. Smith (1986), Jespersen (1995), and Hurst (1997), among others, have more convincingly traced the decision to US domestic politics and to America's solicitous attitude toward ASEAN, which resolutely opposed Vietnam's aggression. A handful of valuable books and articles have also appeared on US policy toward Cambodia. As the title of one – *Cambodia, Pol Pot, and the United States: The Faustian Pact* (Haas 1991) – quite plainly suggests, a spirited debate has swirled around the morality, or immorality, of US policy. Various authors have sought to explicate – in some cases to condemn – the gap separating Washington's professed commitment to human rights and its expedient decision to support the remnants of the murderous Khmer Rouge regime as a way of exerting pressure on Hanoi and its Moscow patron. Brown and Zasloff (1998) stands as perhaps the strongest and most balanced of these works, offering an admirably detailed and thorough analysis of the diplomatic activity surrounding the vexing Cambodian problem. Former Assistant Secretary of State Richard H. Solomon (2000) has produced a noteworthy insider account.

Much work remains to be done on post-1975 US–Southeast Asian relations, however. Surprisingly few bilateral studies extend into the more recent period. In addition to the Karnow and Brands books on the Philippines, noted above, there are Pamela Sodhy's *US–Malaysian Nexus* (1991) and Paul F. Gardner's *Shared Hopes, Separate Fears: Fifty Years of US–Indonesian Relations* (1997), each usefully broad if also thin. Region-wide subjects, including ASEAN, certainly demand more careful scrutiny than they have thus far received. Although important studies exist on the association and its evolution, including solid monographs by Leifer (1989), Antolik (1990), and Acharya (2001), they generally give short shrift to the US–ASEAN diplomatic relationship. Washington's support for Southeast Asian regionalism has, arguably, loomed as the most important single theme in America's Southeast Asian policy over the past quarter-century, yet the phenomenon has yet to find its chronicler. Rostow's slim monograph (1986), part history and part memoir, is helpful on the early years, though hardly definitive.

The US response to and role in the economic upsurge of the 1970s, 1980s, and 1990s have, similarly, attracted far less scholarly attraction than they warrant. Relatedly, globalization's impact on the region, especially its role in the solidification, and the simultaneous disruption, of economic, cultural, and political ties between the United States and Southeast Asia demands sustained analysis. So, too, do the region's political flashpoints, from the US response to human rights abuses and political repression in Burma, Indonesia, Malaysia, and elsewhere, to the East Timor crisis, separatist challenges in Indonesia, and the rise of Islamic fundamentalism. The role of Congress, organized interest groups, and the public at large in the making of America's Southeast Asia policy also requires scholarly assessment, along with the more diffuse impact of culture and ideology in US perceptions and actions *vis-à-vis* this part of the world.

South Asia

The year 1975 forms a less meaningful break point for US–South Asian relations than it does for US–Southeast Asian relations. American disengagement from South Asia was underway a full decade before the collapse of the Saigon regime, precipitated by the Indo-Pakistani War of 1965 and President Lyndon B. Johnson's decision, in the war's wake, to curtail sharply all US aid programs to India and Pakistan. The Pakistani–American alliance became moribund from that point forward, and Pakistani accusations of American betrayal continued to resound well into the 1970s and after. The year 1971 serves as another critical date in the US–South Asian relationship, since that year brought the third Indo-Pakistani War, this one leaving Pakistan dismembered as the former province of East Pakistan became the independent state of Bangladesh. The support of the Nixon administration for Pakistan in that conflict, a decision stemming especially from Pakistan's role in the high-priority opening toward China, wound up infuriating and alienating India without fully repairing the breach between Washington and Islamabad.

The year 1974 marks another key date in the subcontinent's recent history. India detonated its first atomic bomb in that year, raising the specter of a nuclearized South Asia and setting in motion events destined to reshape the subcontinent's diplomatic landscape over the next two-and-a-half decades. Indeed, Pakistan's determination to match India's nuclear capability became the driving force behind its foreign policy for the remainder of the twentieth century – and put it on a collision course with the United States. In February 1975 the United States lifted its decade-old embargo against lethal arms transfers to Pakistan, adding military sales to its substantial economic aid program and seeming to herald a new cordiality in relations between the two former allies. But late in 1977, Washington suddenly suspended its aid programs on account of Pakistan's importation of nuclear fuel preprocessing technology, action judged to be in violation of the Glenn Amendment. The aid suspension severely strained relations between the Jimmy Carter administration and the newly installed regime of General Mohammed Zia ul-Haq.

On July 5, 1977, Zia and the military had ousted Prime Minister Zulfikar Ali Bhutto in a bloodless coup. Under Zia's leadership, the Pakistani government declared martial law, which remained in effect until December 31, 1985. It arrested former Prime Minister Bhutto, on questionable charges, and, despite American protestations, hanged the former leader on April 4, 1979. An angry mob sacked the US Embassy in Islamabad later that year, which "brought the bilateral relationship to its lowest point ever" (Kux 2001: 244). In the aftermath of the attack on the embassy, according to National Security Council staff member Thomas Thornton, US relations with Pakistan were "about as bad as with any country in the world, except perhaps Albania or North Korea" (ibid: 245).

The Soviet invasion of Afghanistan on December 27, 1979, overnight changed American attitudes and policies toward Pakistan. Viewing the South Asian nation once again as a front line state in the Cold War, President Carter swallowed his misgivings about its checkered human rights record and ongoing nuclear program. In a nationally televised speech of January 4, 1980, in which he spelled out his administration's concerns about the Soviet thrust into Afghanistan, Carter stated: "We will provide military equipment, food and other assistance to help Pakistan defend its independence and national security against the seriously increased threat from the north" (ibid: 247). Yet, much to the American leader's dismay, Zia contemptuously dismissed a $400 million US aid offer as "peanuts," characterizing it as "terribly disappointing." Dennis Kux, who has written the fullest and most incisive account of US–Pakistani relations during the post-1975 period, observes that "the turndown marked an embarrassing diplomatic setback" for the Carter administration (ibid: 251).

The advent, in January 1981, of the Ronald Reagan administration, which was determined to prosecute the Cold War with renewed vigor, brought a significant upping of the ante for Pakistani cooperation. Reagan proposed a $3.2 billion, five-year aid package, much more to Zia's liking; the Pakistani general, as it turned out, had shrewdly gauged his country's rising strategic stock. Pakistan thereafter figured centrally in the so-called Reagan Doctrine, an extensive program of covert support for anti-communist guerrillas across the Third World, becoming the principal conduit for US aid to the Afghan mujahideen who were battling the Soviet occupiers. By the mid-1980s the United States and Saudi Arabia were together pumping more than $1 billion per year into Pakistan to help supply the anti-Soviet fighters in Afghanistan. As a reward, the United States granted Pakistan, in May 1981, a six-year waiver protecting it against the anti-nuclear sanctions that had previously barred American aid. In effect, the United States was signaling its willingness to live with the Pakistani nuclear program, provided that Islamabad did not actually explode a bomb. The new partnership between Washington and Islamabad was based on the temporary convergence of interest between countries determined, for their own reasons, to force Soviet troops from Afghanistan. Almost inevitably, the very success of those efforts – and by the late 1980s Soviet forces found themselves increasingly on the defensive – would remove the partnership's *raison d'être*, propelling the nuclear issue once again to the fore.

Indo-American relations followed a very different path between the mid-1970s and the late 1980s. Emulating a pattern that had prevailed throughout the 1950s and 1960s, the strengthening of US–Pakistani ties led directly to a weakening of

US–Indian ties – and vice versa. When the Ford administration, in early 1975, resumed arms sales to Pakistan, India complained vociferously and Indo-American relations suffered yet another body blow. The Indian defense minister charged that the decision would "retard the process of normalization of relations in the subcontinent," while Prime Minister Indira Gandhi likened the renewed arms shipments to a "reopening of old wounds" (Brands 1990: 153). US relations with India at that time were already strained as a result of several factors: bitter Indian memories of the US "tilt" toward Pakistan during the 1971 war; India's close ties to the Soviet Union; the widespread perception in the United States that the haughty Gandhi was reflexively anti-American; and deep-seated unease about India's nuclear program. The latter factor proved especially touchy. India's 1974 atomic test not only generated outrage in the United States, but also, in the apt assessment of Thomas Thornton, "marked the most severe setback to the global nonproliferation regime since the Chinese test a decade earlier" (Thornton 1992: 111).

Relations deteriorated further when, on June 24, 1975, Indira Gandhi proclaimed a national emergency, imposing *de facto* martial law and arresting prominent political opponents and thousands of their followers. "Seig heil, Indira!" mocked William F. Buckley's conservative *National Review* (Brands 1990: 154). In a much-repeated quip, Daniel Patrick Moynihan, a former ambassador to India, bluntly told an interviewer: "When India ceased to be a democracy, our actual interest there just plummeted. I mean, what does it export but communicable disease?" (Kux 1993: 337).

The surprise victory of the Janata Front in India's national elections of 1977, which elevated Morarji Desai to the prime ministership, brought a temporary improvement to Indo-American relations. The Carter administration hailed the return of democracy to India. Desai, for his part, sought to move India's international posture closer to true non-alignment and hence less open hostility to the United States, and President Carter was greeted warmly during a 1978 visit to India (he pointedly did not visit Pakistan on that trip). But the collapse of the Janata coalition, the return of Indira Gandhi to power following Indian elections in January 1980, and, most significantly, the Soviet invasion of Afghanistan, led to an abrupt reversal in the short-lived warming trend.

India's refusal to condemn unequivocally the aggression of its Soviet ally, together with Prime Minister Gandhi's denunciation of US military aid to Pakistan, produced a predictable anti-Indian backlash in the United States. Throughout the Reagan presidency, relations between Washington and New Delhi remained chilly. Massive US support for Pakistan, India's principal rival, proved a near-insuperable obstacle to closer ties between what pundits on both sides liked to call the world's two largest democracies. "The Reagan administration initially wrote off India as politically opposed and economically irrelevant to US interests," notes Dennis Kux (ibid: 417), a view that never fundamentally changed. Although the diplomatic and political atmospherics improved following the replacement of Indira Gandhi by her son Rajiv, following the former's assassination in October 1984, core differences in interest and perspective continued to plague the bilateral relationship.

Stephen P. Cohen, an influential South Asian policy analyst who served on the State Department's Policy Planning Staff from 1985 to 1987, insists that Reagan's India policy actually achieved a modicum of success – at least if judged by the exceedingly low expectations that obtained in both Washington and New Delhi. "A new, limited strategic relationship was forged with Pakistan, a relationship that did not commit the United States against India but did stiffen Pakistani resistance against the Soviets," emphasizes Cohen (1992: 149). The Reagan administration managed not only to gain India's reluctant acceptance of the Pakistani aid program, but also to engineer a modest "opening" to the Rajiv Gandhi government in the mid-1980s. Yet, as Sumit Ganguly rightly observes: "India's close ties to Moscow and lack of strategic or economic importance to the United States limited the prospects of any sharp upswing in relations" (Ganguly 1999: 164).

The withdrawal of Soviet troops from Afghanistan, the last of whom departed in February 1989, and the simultaneous winding down of the Cold War fundamentally altered the strategic–diplomatic equation in South Asia, with profound implications for Pakistan, for India, and for Afghanistan. As America's strategic fears about Soviet expansion receded, the US–Pakistani partnership collapsed. For the first George Bush administration and for the Bill Clinton administration that followed, Pakistan increasingly loomed not as a strategic asset but as a diplomatic and political problem. Not only did Islamabad continue to flout non-proliferation norms with its ongoing nuclear program, but also by 1989–90 it provocatively began stoking the embers of the long-smoldering Kashmir dispute with India. "Although Pakistan did not start the uprising in Kashmir," states Kux (2001), "the temptation to fan the flames was too great for Islamabad to resist. Using guerrilla-warfare expertise gained during the Afghan war, Pakistan's ISI [Inter-Services Intelligence Network] began to provide active backing for Kashmiri Muslim insurgents" (p. 305). The growing violence in the Indian-controlled portion of Kashmir, where New Delhi assumed direct rule in early 1990, pushed the two nations to the very brink of military confrontation later that year.

Then, on October 1, 1990, the Bush administration dropped the hammer on Pakistan. No longer able, or willing, to certify that Pakistan did not possess a nuclear device, it permitted the automatic suspension of all military and economic aid to its former ally under terms mandated by the Pressler Amendment. That decision, which abruptly terminated the intimate security partnership that had flourished throughout the 1980s, was met with shock and fury throughout Pakistan. Pakistanis quite understandably complained that "You Americans have discarded us like a piece of used Kleenex" (ibid: 310), a charge that continued to echo throughout the 1990s.

Persistent political instability within Pakistan further tarnished that nation's international image as well as its reputation with the American policymaking elite and with Congress. Between 1988, when Zia was killed in a suspicious plane crash, and 1999, when General Pervez Musharraf assumed power in a coup, Benazir Bhutto and Nawaz Sharif alternated as heads of unstable, fractious, and highly corrupt governments. Knowledgeable American observers wondered, openly at times, if Pakistan was not fast approaching the status of a failed state, with problems too enormous to overcome. Support for terrorism, drug trafficking, chronic instability, endemic societal violence, the rise of Islamic extremism – all proved deeply disquieting to America's Pakistan-watchers. But, at least until the terrorist attacks on New York and Washington on September 11, 2001, US experts were agreed that the biggest single issue of concern was Pakistan's nuclear capability. On May 28, 1998, Pakistan unmistakably demonstrated that capability, to the dismay of the

United States and the wider world community, by exploding five underground nuclear devices in Baluchistan. The Pakistani tests followed close on the heels of India's series of underground nuclear tests seventeen days earlier. In response, the United States immediately invoked a new set of sanctions on both countries.

Throughout the 1990s, and especially after the nuclear tests of May 1998, the non-proliferation imperative dominated US relations with South Asia. Indeed, as Cohen (1999) contends: "The balance of American policy in South Asia was dramatically tilted in the early 1990s toward a single issue: nuclear nonproliferation" (p. 198). The early post-Cold War years initially offered numerous hopeful indications that a corner had been turned in Indo-American relations; the collapse of both the Cold War and the Soviet Union had, after all, removed the core policy difference that had clouded the bilateral relationship in the past. Talk of a new strategic dialogue soon emanated from policy circles in Washington and New Delhi, and senior US officials began to tout India as an emerging world power buoyed by an increasingly vibrant, market-oriented economy. During the 1990s the United States became India's largest trading partner, its major source of overseas investment, and its principal supplier of advanced technology. At the same time, Indian immigration to the United States increased substantially, with the Indo-American community becoming a significant advocate within the United States of closer diplomatic ties. Yet the more salient factor shaping Indo-American relations remained the relative indifference on the part of the United States toward a country, and a region, that offered few critical strategic or economic assets, and that posed nettlesome obstacles – in terms of regional instability, nuclear proliferation, drug trafficking, terrorism, and more – to the post-Cold War order Washington sought. The major US concern at the beginning of the new century was that unresolved regional tensions, especially over Kashmir and the Pakistani-supported Taliban regime in Afghanistan, would lead not just to conflict but to a nuclear holocaust. All other issues paled to significance.

The secondary literature on US relations with South Asia since 1975 has been richer and more extensive than that dealing with US–Southeast Asian relations during the same period. Particularly notable have been the two invaluable bilateral studies written by former State Department South Asian expert Dennis Kux (1993, 2001), which should long prove indispensable to scholars. I have drawn heavily upon each for the above summary of key trends in the post-1975 period. Kux's insider perspective, his careful, balanced judgments, and the scores of interviews that he conducted with top US, Indian, and Pakistani officials and that inform his narratives at every stage, make these books the essential starting point for any serious historical analysis of the post-1975 period. A handful of other surveys of Indo-American relations exist that treat at least part of the post-1975 period, including H. W. Brands' informative if breezy *India and the United States* (1990) and M. Srinivas Chary's less satisfying *The Eagle and the Peacock* (1995). Shirin R. Tahir-Kheli's Council on Foreign Relations-sponsored book, *India, Pakistan, and the United States* (1997), a work of explicit policy advocacy, is also worthy of mention. Additionally, several volumes of collected essays have been published that focus on the international politics of South Asia, with particular emphasis on security issues.

Policy analysts have thus far dominated the literature on post-1975 US–South

Asian relations. The work of Kux, the foreign service officer turned historian, stands as the major exception to that rule. It bears emphasizing in this regard that, despite important areas of overlap, the work of policy analysts and that of foreign relations historians differ substantially in terms of purpose, audience, and sources. Those who write about contemporary issues typically seek to influence the direction of current and future policy, with decision-makers serving as a key target audience. The immediacy of their purpose precludes the wait for the declassification of essential sources that the writing of authoritative history necessitates. Yet, in lieu of the obvious limitations of a genre based on public sources and interviews, even historians cannot fail to be impressed by the manifest contributions offered by this type of scholarly work. Two unusually incisive South Asia scholars, Stephen P. Cohen and Sumit Ganguly, have made especially noteworthy contributions to the literature on recent US–South Asian relations. Their work has concentrated, naturally enough, on the contemporary issues of greatest concern to US officials; namely, the problems of Kashmir and nuclear proliferation. Ganguly's *Crisis in Kashmir* (1997) ranks as perhaps the most essential study of that dispute's latest and most violent phase. The prolific Cohen's contributions can be found in numerous journal articles, book chapters, op-ed pieces, and monographs, the most recent of which is the broadly focused *India: Emerging Power* (2001). In addition to the numerous essays and articles addressing the contemporary nuclear proliferation tangle by Ganguly, Cohen, and other policy analysts, one work of historical breadth deserves to be singled out. George Perkovich's impressively researched *India's Nuclear Bomb* (1999) provides both needed historical context and astute analysis of India's nuclear dilemma.

As with the United States and Southeast Asia, much work remains to be done before a fuller picture of US–South Asian relations during the 1975–2000 period can emerge. The literature to date, and hence this essay, has concentrated on India and Pakistan to the exclusion of South Asia's other states. Those two nations, which together constitute fully one-fifth of the world's population, dominate the region, of course. Yet we certainly need some studies of US relations with Bangladesh, Nepal, Sri Lanka, and Afghanistan. The latter country has factored in the broader literature on the Cold War's final phase – unavoidably so in view of the importance of the Soviet–Afghan war – but the evolving nature of US–Afghan relations before, during, and after the Soviet occupation remains woefully understudied. That observation leads to a related one: the scholarship on US–South Asian relations since 1975 has mostly been written by regional specialists with regional concerns. These authors have not shown much interest in integrating the story of US–South Asian relations into the broader narrative of post-Vietnam War US foreign relations. Yet that task is crucial.

Concluding Remarks

As the release of essential governmental documentation pertaining to these years transpires in, one hopes, the not-too-distant future, the policy analysts, memoirists, and journalists who have produced the initial wave of studies of the post-1975 period will gradually give way to the historians. The latter will bring to the examination of this fascinating transitional period in international relations different scholarly agendas, higher standards of evidence, and, with luck, fresh vistas and new sets of questions. As they enter the scholarly fray and seek to make sense out of the post-1975 era, a time in which the world moved from détente, to renewed Cold War, to the promise and uncertainties of the post-Cold War era, they should find the corners of the globe that this essay has been concerned with to be especially fruitful terrain.

During these years the United States lurched suddenly and unexpectedly from a security-obsessed Cold War system to a new era of globalization, in which the dictates of the marketplace seemed to overshadow all else. Yet, in South and Southeast Asia, as in so many other parts of the world, nationalism and regionalism persisted, ofttimes uneasily, with a globalized, Americanized world order led by the planet's sole remaining superpower. Future foreign relations historians must examine the manifold intricacies and complexities of this transitional era in international affairs – and not just for the United States and other core, industrialized nations, but for the states and societies along the Third World periphery as well. South and Southeast Asia, where so substantial a portion of the world's people reside, must be integrated fully into that larger story if it is to have the breadth and scope that an international history of the final quarter of the twentieth century demands.

REFERENCES

Acharya, Amitav: *Constructing a Security Community in Southeast Asia: ASEAN and the Problem of Regional Order* (New York: Routledge, 2001).

Antolik, Michael: *ASEAN and the Diplomacy of Accommodation* (Armonk, NY: Sharpe, 1990).

Baker, James A., III: *The Politics of Diplomacy: Revolution, War, and Peace, 1989–1992* (New York: Putnam's, 1995).

Bonner, Raymond: *Waltzing with a Dictator: The Marcoses and the Making of American Policy* (New York: Times Books, 1987).

Brands, H. W.: *India and the United States: The Cold Peace* (Boston, MA: Twayne, 1990).

Brands, H. W.: *Bound to Empire: The United States and the Philippines* (New York: Oxford University Press, 1992).

Brands, H. W.: *Since Vietnam: The United States in World Affairs, 1973–1995* (New York: McGraw Hill, 1996).

Bresnan, John: *From Dominoes to Dynamos: The Transformation of Southeast Asia* (New York: Council on Foreign Relations Press, 1994).

Brown, MacAlister and Joseph J. Zasloff: *Cambodia Confounds the Peacemakers, 1979–1998* (Ithaca, NY: Cornell University Press, 1998).

Chary, M. Srinivas: *The Eagle and the Peacock: US Foreign Policy towards India since Independence* (Westport, CT: Greenwood Press, 1995).

Christopher, Warren: *Chances of a Lifetime* (New York: Scribner, 2001).

Cohen, Stephen P.: "The Reagan Administration and India." In Harold A. Gould and Sumit Ganguly (eds.) *The Hope and the Reality: US–Indian Relations from Roosevelt to Reagan* (Boulder, CO: Westview Press, 1992).

Cohen, Stephen P.: "The United States, India, and Pakistan: Retrospect and Prospect." In Selig S. Harrison, Paul H. Kreisberg, and Dennis Kux (eds.) *India and Pakistan: The First Fifty Years* (New York: Cambridge University Press, 1999).

Cohen, Stephen P.: *India: Emerging Power* (Urbana: University of Illinois Press, 2001).

Ganguly, Sumit: *The Crisis in Kashmir: Portents of War, Hopes of Peace* (New York: Cambridge University Press, 1997).

Ganguly, Sumit: "India: Policies, Past and Future." In Selig S. Harrison, Paul H. Kreisberg, and Dennis Kux (eds.) *India and Pakistan: The First Fifty Years* (New York: Cambridge University Press, 1999).

Gardner, Paul F.: *Shared Hopes, Separate Fears: Fifty Years of US–Indonesian Relations* (Boulder, CO: Westview Press, 1997).

Garthoff, Raymond L.: *Détente and Confrontation: American–Soviet Relations from Nixon to Reagan* (Washington: Brookings Institution, 1985).

Haas, Michael: *Cambodia, Pol Pot, and the United States: The Faustian Pact* (New York: Praeger, 1991).

Halberstam, David: *War in a Time of Peace* (New York: Scribner, 2001).

Hurst, Steven: "Regionalism or Globalism? The Carter Administration and Vietnam." *Journal of Contemporary History* 32 (January 1997), 81–95.

Jespersen, T. Christopher: "The Politics and Culture of Nonrecognition: The Carter Administration and Vietnam." *Journal of American–East Asian Relations* 4 (winter 1995), 397–412.

Karnow, Stanley: *In Our Image: America's Empire in the Philippines* (New York: Ballantine, 1989).

Kux, Dennis: *India and the United States: Estranged Democracies, 1941–1991* (Washington, DC: National Defense University Press, 1993).

Kux, Dennis: *The United States and Pakistan, 1947–2000: Disenchanted Allies* (New York: Cambridge University Press, 2001).

Leifer, Michael: *ASEAN and the Security of South-East Asia* (London: Routledge, 1989).

McMahon, Robert J.: *The Limits of Empire: The United States and Southeast Asia since World War II* (New York: Columbia University Press, 1999).

Perkovich, George: *India's Nuclear Bomb: The Impact on Global Proliferation* (Berkeley: University of California Press, 1999).

Rostow, W. W.: *The United States and the Regional Organization of Asia and the Pacific, 1965–1985* (Austin: University of Texas Press, 1986).

Shultz, George P.: *Turmoil and Triumph* (New York: Scribners, 1993).

Smith, Gaddis: *Morality, Reason, and Power: American Diplomacy in the Carter Years* (New York: Hill and Wang, 1986).

Sodhy, Pamela: *The US–Malaysian Nexus: Themes in Superpower–Small State Relations* (Kuala Lumpur: Institute of Strategic and International Studies, 1991).

Solomon, Richard H.: *Exiting Indochina: US Leadership of the Cambodia Settlement and Normalization of Relations with Vietnam* (Washington, DC: United States Institute of Peace Press, 2000).

Tahir-Kheli, Shirin R.: *India, Pakistan, and the United States: Breaking with the Past* (New York: Council on Foreign Relations Press, 1997).

Thornton, Thomas P.: "US–Indian Relations in the Nixon and Ford Years." In Harold A. Gould and Sumit Ganguly (eds.) *The Hope and the Reality: US–Indian Relations from Roosevelt to Reagan* (Boulder, CO: Westview Press, 1992).

Vance, Cyrus: *Hard Choices: Critical Years in America's Foreign Policy* (New York: Simon and Schuster, 1983).

FURTHER READING

Ayoob, Mohammed: "Nuclear India and Indian–American Relations." *Orbis* 43 (winter 1999), 59–74.

Bajpai, Kanti P. and Stephen P. Cohen (eds.) *South Asia after the Cold War: International Perspectives* (Boulder, CO: Westview Press, 1993).

Bertsch, Gary K., Seema Gahlaut, and Anupam Srivastava (eds.): *Engaging India: US Strategic Relations with the World's Largest Democracy* (New York: Routledge, 1999).

Chandler, David P.: *The Tragedy of Cambodian History: Politics, War, and Revolution* (New Haven, CT: Yale University Press, 1991).

Cohen, Stephen P. (ed.): *The Security of South Asia: American and Asian Perspectives* (Urbana: University of Illinois Press, 1987).

Ganguly, Sumit: *The Origins of War in South Asia: The Indo-Pakistani Conflicts since 1947*, 2nd revd. edn. (Boulder, CO: Westview Press, 1994).

Grasselli, Gabriella: *British and American Responses to the Soviet Invasion of Afghanistan* (Aldershot: Dartmouth, 1996).

Hegerty, Devin T.: "Nuclear Deterrence in South Asia: The 1990 India–Pakistani Crisis." *International Security* 20 (winter 1995–6), 79–114.

Palmer, Norman: *The United States and India: The Dimensions of Influence* (New York: Praeger, 1985).

Palmer, Ronald D. and Thomas J. Reckford: *Building ASEAN: Twenty Years of Southeast Asia Cooperation* (New York: Praeger, 1987).

Thornton, Thomas P.: "Between Two Stools?: US Policy Towards Pakistan in the Carter Administration." *Asian Survey* 22 (October 1982), 959–77.

Wirsing, Robert G.: *Pakistan's Security under Zia, 1977–1988: The Policy Imperatives of a Peripheral Asian State* (New York: St. Martin's Press, 1991).

Wirsing, Robert G.: *India, Pakistan, and the Kashmir Dispute: On Regional Conflict and Its Resolution* (New York: St. Martin's Press, 1994).

Zasloff, Joseph J. (ed.): *Postwar Indochina: Old Enemies and New Allies* (Washington, DC: Foreign Service Institute, 1988).

Conclusion

From the End of the Cold War to the Beginning of the Twenty-First Century

Robert D. Schulzinger

The next assignment for historians of American foreign relations will be to explain the remarkable end to the Cold War. Few predicted it. Nearly everyone was astonished by it. Successive American administrations from 1977 until 1991 wrestled first with the intensification of the Cold War and then with its dramatic end. The immediate aftermath of the Cold War was nearly as tumultuous. The administrations of George H. W. Bush and Bill Clinton both tried to fashion policies for a world in which the United States stood alone as a superpower.

How did these changes occur? Who most successfully grasped the nettle of profound changes in the international environment? Who relied for too long on outmoded ways of thinking? What role did fortune play in the end of the Cold War? Who was able to fashion lasting, effective structures of foreign relations? What were the alternatives? Could the Cold War have ended sooner? Could the tumult of the post-Cold War world have been better managed? These are some of the most important questions likely to animate scholars of diplomatic history in the coming decades.

A large literature already has appeared. For the most part, however, it is fragmentary, journalistic, and personal. The vast documentary record of the last years of the twentieth century will emerge gradually over the next decades. The United States government operates under a twenty-five year rule for the supposedly automatic declassification of its government records. In actuality, twenty-five years is only a rough starting point. Some government files dealing with foreign affairs appear sooner than that, and many are released many years after twenty-five years. Anyone can request records less than twenty-five years old under the terms of the Freedom of Information Act, but it is nearly impossible under the terms of FOIA to obtain a systematic range of documents. Most serious historical work involving records of the US government begins about twenty-five to thirty years after the events in question. Once that documentary record becomes available, most of the works discussed below will become obsolete. But the arguments they set forth will set the parameters of future discussions.

While the documentary evidence is far from complete, the contours of the discussion of great power relations have emerged. The Carter administration initially sought to expand détente with the Soviet Union. Kaufman (1993) and Smith (1986) demonstrate that officials in the Carter administration, deeply affected by the debacle of Vietnam, initially sought to turn American attention away from the confrontation with the Soviet Union. Hyland (1987) ridicules Carter for *naïveté* in his application of détente. Garthoff (1992) employs an impressive array of published documents, memoirs, and journals in both Russian and English. Garthoff argues convincingly that détente was not doomed by the supposed *naïveté* of Carter and his principal advisers. Instead, Garthoff shows how many articulate Americans undermined the basis for détente.

The memoirs of the principal foreign policy actors of the Carter administration show the range of opinion of how the high hopes of 1977 were dashed after the Soviet invasion of Afghanistan in 1979. The books by President Carter (1982), Secretary of State Cyrus Vance (1983), and National Security Adviser Zbigniew Brzezinski (1983) all were based on documents that the authors had access to, but which, for the most part, are still not available to other researchers. Carter laments the constant squabbling among his advisers. He wishes Vance and Brzezinski could have worked out their differences. The president eventually came to rely more on his national security adviser than on Vance. Still, Carter personally found Vance's hopefulness more appealing than Brzezinski's sour pessimism toward the Soviet Union. For his part, Vance writes that infighting within the administration did more to undermine support for détente than did growing fears or militancy on the part of the Soviet Union. Brzezinski presents precisely the opposite point of view. He argues that Carter's initial softer line toward the Soviet Union made sense as a test of Soviet intentions. But the great rival of the United States clearly failed by 1978. Brzezinski relished precisely the sort of bureaucratic infighting Vance deplored. Brzezinski's memoirs argue that he successfully educated Carter into taking a more confrontational position toward the Soviet Union.

The Reagan administration's stance toward the Soviet Union has produced some of the starkest opposing views. Veterans of the Reagan administration express triumphal jubilation over the end of the Cold War and the demise of the Soviet Union. Secretary of State Alexander Haig (1984), National Security Council staff member Constantine Menges (1988), and Secretary of Defense Caspar Weinberger (1991) argue the Reagan administrational position toward the Soviet Union forced Moscow to spend itself into destruction. Secretary of State George Shultz presents a more nuanced view (1993). Shultz and Weinberger engaged in bureaucratic battles almost as fierce as those that dominated the earlier Nixon, Ford, and Carter administrations. Shultz's memoirs argue both that the defense buildup of the early Reagan years *and* the president's nimble appreciation of the novelty of Mikhail Gorbachev's approach led to the end of the Cold War.

Garthoff (1994), which is also based upon a wide range of published documentary sources, sustains Shultz's view. Garthoff is no supporter of the confrontational stance of the early Reagan administration. Yet he is struck by the paradox of Reagan, a visceral anti-communist, forming a friendship with President Gorbachev. Garthoff attributes Reagan's change to his political boldness. Gaddis (1992) also notes the paradox of Reagan grasping at Gorbachev's new thinking and ending the Cold War.

Fitzgerald (2000) is having none of the argument that Reagan's political astuteness led to the end of the Cold War. Fitzgerald argues that Reagan and his principal foreign policy lieutenants had an almost theological commitment to the development of a missile defense system. The development of Star Wars, as it was called, cost more to the United States than it did the Soviet Union. According to Fitzgerald, the end of the Cold War came far more through Gorbachev's vision than Reagan's response.

The four-year administration of George H. W. Bush, sandwiched between those of two far more popular presidents, seems almost forgotten. Yet when the Cold War actually ended, Bush, his Secretary of State James A. Baker, and his national security adviser Brent Scowcroft were lauded as masters of foreign policy. Together they won praise for navigating the peaceful transition from communism to capitalism in Eastern Europe and the Soviet Union and they presided over the creation of a Europe whole and free. Bush himself originally proclaimed the dawn of a new world order. But the phrase fell into disfavor when war erupted in the Persian Gulf in 1990–1. The economic difficulties of the United States in 1991 and 1992 also undermined the appeal of new world orders. When Bush lost the 1992 election to Bill Clinton, most Americans thought that foreign affairs mattered less than at any time since the 1920s.

Bush and Scowcroft (1998) and Baker (1995) outline the view that their administration reached the highest level of calm, professional diplomacy in its relations with the Soviet Union and the states of Eastern Europe. Zelikow and Rice (1995) based their massive work on the largest Freedom of Information Act request ever filed for national security documents. Both served as staff members on the National Security Council. They concluded that there was nothing inevitable about the peaceful reunification of Germany. They give themselves and their colleagues high marks for managing the end of Soviet control over Eastern Europe. Beschloss and Talbott (1993) made use of interviews and personal contacts to describe an administration far angrier and more divided than the outward appearance of tight discipline would suggest.

Garthoff (1994) is not convinced of the virtuosity of the Bush administration's conduct of relations with the collapsing communist world. He makes the intriguing point that the very depth of experience of Bush and his principal advisers made them slow to grasp the great changes underway in the communist world. American leaders had grown comfortable with the categories of the Cold War, Garthoff argues. They could hardly imagine any alternative future. When one came crashing down with the Berlin Wall, American officials were slow to understand the implications.

It fell to the Clinton administration to shape the post-Cold War world. The literature on those eight years is only beginning to emerge, and the works that have already appeared are likely to be the ones that disappear most quickly. Still, the outline of a debate has appeared. Hyland (1999) is scathing in his indictment of the Clinton administration. He taunts them as rank amateurs. They thought that the end of the Cold War meant that the United States could fritter its resources in costly humanitarian interventions. Brune (1998) is more nuanced, but still critical of humanitarian interventions in Somalia, Haiti, and Bosnia. Cohen (2001) argues that the Clinton administration mishandled relations with post-Soviet Russia. Litwak (2000) argues that the Clinton administration played the hand it was dealt in containing "rogue states."

Talbott (2002) strongly defends the Clinton administration's policies toward the former Soviet Union. The "Russia hand" of Talbott's title is not the author, Clinton's deputy secretary of state, himself a legitimate Russia expert. Instead, it is the president himself who takes center stage as the man who defined and implemented a sophisticated policy toward post-Soviet Russia. Talbott's well-written account, based on a significant amount of documents, argues that Clinton's quick mind, openness to new ideas, and keen political sense ideally suited him to form a personal bond with Boris Yeltsin and understand the fluidity of Russia in the 1990s.

The breakup of Yugoslavia led to the human catastrophes of Bosnia and Kosovo. The Clinton administration's handling of war in the Balkans provoked controversy at the time and in retrospect. Richard Holbrooke was the Clinton administration's negotiator in the Balkans. His book (Holbrooke 1998) lays down the case that the administration skillfully negotiated the end of the Bosnian conflict. Daalder (2000) is more critical, although he believes the final result had much merit. Daalder and O'Hanlon (2000) and Ignatieff (2000) describe how the United States came almost too late to recognize the depth of the human catastrophe unfolding in Kosovo. Constrained by a recalcitrant Congress, an uncertain public, and a military reluctant to undertake another humanitarian intervention, they argue that the Clinton administration made the best of a nearly impossible situation.

As the archives open in the next generation, historians will revisit all of these issues. Few of the works mentioned above will probably stand up against the volumes based on more complete documentation and the perspective of time. Some will seem thin or ephemeral. Some will appear tendentious or wrong. But they have all addressed enduring questions.

REFERENCES

Baker, James A., III with Thomas M. DeFrank: *The Politics of Diplomacy: Revolution, War and Peace, 1989–1992* (New York: G. P. Putnam's, 1995).

Beschloss, Michael and Strobe Talbott: *At the Highest Levels: The Inside Story of the End of the Cold War* (Boston, MA: Little, Brown, 1993).

Brune, Lester: *The United States and Post-Cold War Interventions: Bush and Clinton in Somalia, Haiti and Bosnia, 1992–1998* (Claremont, CA: Regina Books, 1998).

Brzezinski, Zbigniew: *Power and Principle: Memoirs of the National Security Adviser, 1977–1981* (New York: Farrar, Straus, and Giroux, 1983).

Bush, George H. W. and Brent Scowcroft: *A World Transformed* (New York: Knopf, 1998).

Carter, Jimmy: *Keeping Faith: The Memoirs of a President* (New York: Bantam, 1982).

Cohen, Stephen: *Failed Crusade: America and the Tragedy of Post Communist Russia* (New York: W. W. Norton, 2001).

Daalder, Ivo: *Getting to Dayton: The Making of America's Bosnia Policy* (Washington, DC: Brookings Institution, 2000)

Daalder, Ivo and Michael O'Hanlon: *Winning Ugly: NATO's War to Save Kosovo* (Washington, DC: Brookings Institution, 2000).

Fitzgerald, Frances: *Way Out There in the Blue: Reagan, Star Wars, and the End of the Cold War* (New York: Simon and Schuster, 2000).

Gaddis, John Lewis: *The United States and the End of the Cold War* (New York: Oxford University Press, 1992).

Garthoff, Raymond: *Détente and Confrontation: American–Soviet Relations from Nixon to Reagan* (Washington, DC: Brookings Institution, 1992).

Garthoff, Raymond: *The Great Transition: American–Russian Relations and the End of the Cold War* (Washington, DC: Brookings Institution, 1994).

Haig, Alexander: *Caveat: Reagan, Realism, and Foreign Policy* (New York: Macmillan, 1984).

Holbrooke, Richard: *To End a War* (New York: Random House, 1998).

Hyland, William: *Mortal Rivals: Superpower Relations from Nixon to Reagan* (New York: Random House, 1987).

Hyland, William: *Clinton's World: Remaking American Foreign Policy* (Westport, CT: Praeger, 1999).

Ignatieff, Michael: *Virtual War: Kosovo and Beyond* (New York: Henry Holt, 2000).

Kaufman, Burton I.: *The Presidency of James E. Carter, Jr.* (Lawrence: University of Kansas Press, 1993).

Litwak, Robert: *Rogue States and US Foreign Policy: Containment After the Cold War* (Washington, DC: Woodrow Wilson Center Press, 2000).

Menges, Constantine: *Inside the National Security Council: The True Story of the Making and Unmaking of Reagan's Foreign Policy* (New York: Simon and Schuster, 1988).

Shultz, George P.: *Turmoil and Triumph: My Years as Secretary of State* (New York: Charles Scribner's, 1993).

Smith, Gaddis: *Morality, Reason, and Power: American Diplomacy in the Carter Years* (New York: Hill and Wang, 1986).

Talbott, Strobe: *The Russia Hand: A Memoir of Presidential Leadership* (New York: Random House, 2002).

Vance, Cyrus: *Hard Choices: Critical Years in America's Foreign Policy* (New York: Simon and Schuster, 1983).

Weinberger, Caspar: *Fighting for Peace: Seven Critical Years at the Pentagon* (New York: Warner Books, 1991).

Zelikow, Philip and Condoleezza Rice: *Germany Unified and Europe Transformed: A Study in Statecraft* (Cambridge, MA: Harvard University Press, 1995).

Bibliography

Abramowitz, Morton (ed.): *Turkey's Transformation and American Policy* (New York: Century Foundation Press, 2000).

Accinelli, Robert: *Crisis and Commitment: United States Policy Toward Taiwan, 1950–1955* (Chapel Hill: University of North Carolina Press, 1996).

Accinelli, Robert: "A Thorn in the Side of Peace: The Eisenhower Administration and the 1958 Offshore Islands Crisis." In Robert S. Ross and Jiang Changbin (eds.) *Re-examining the Cold War: US–China Diplomacy, 1954–1973* (Cambridge, MA: Harvard University Press, 2001).

Acharya, Amitav: *Constructing a Security Community in Southeast Asia: ASEAN and the Problem of Regional Order* (New York: Routledge, 2001).

Acheson, Dean G.: *Present at the Creation: My Years in the State Department* (New York: Norton, 1969).

Adams, Henry: *History of the United States under the Administrations of Jefferson and Madison*, 9 vols. (New York: Scribner and Sons, 1889–91).

Adams, Michael C. C.: *The Best War Ever: America and World War II* (Baltimore, MD: Johns Hopkins University Press, 1994).

Adler, Les K. and Thomas G. Paterson: "Red Fascism: The Merger of Nazi Germany and Soviet Russia in the American Image of Totalitarianism, 1930s–1950s." *American Historical Review* 75 (April 1970), 1046–64.

Aga-Rossi, Elena: "Roosevelt's European Policy and the Origins of the Cold War: A Reevaluation." *Telos* 96 (summer 1993), 65–85.

Aguilar, Luis (ed.): *Operation Zapata: The "Ultrasensitive" Report and Testimony of the Board of Inquiry on the Bay of Pigs* (Frederick, MD: Aletheia Books, 1981).

Al Madfai, Madiha Rashid: *Jordan, the United States, and the Middle East Peace Process, 1974–1991* (New York: Cambridge University Press, 1993).

Albert, Bill: *South America and the First World War: The Impact of the War on Brazil, Argentina, Peru, and Chile* (New York: Cambridge University Press, 1988).

Aldrich, Richard J.: *Intelligence and the War Against Japan: Britain, America, and the Politics of Secret Service* (New York: Columbia University Press, 2000).

Aleksandrov-Agentov, Andrei M.: *Ot Kollontai do Gorbacheva [From Kollontai to Gorbachev]* (Moscow: Mezhdunar otnosheniia, 1994).

Alexander, Bevin: *Korea: The First War We Lost* (New York: Hippocrene, 1986).

Alexander, Robert: *The Tragedy of Chile* (Westport, CT: Greenwood Press, 1976).

Alin, Erika: *The United States and the 1958 Lebanon Crisis* (Lanham, MD: University Press of America, 1994).

Allgor, Catherine: "'A Republican in a Monarchy': Louisa Catherine Adams in Russia." *Diplomatic History* 21 (winter 1997), 15–43.

Allison, Graham T.: *Essence of Decision: Explaining the Cuban Missile Crisis* (Boston, MA: Little, Brown, 1971); 2nd edn. with Philip Zelikow (New York: Longman, 1999).

Alperovitz, Gar: *Atomic Diplomacy, Hiroshima and Potsdam: The Use of the Atomic Bomb and* the American Confrontation with Soviet Power (New York: Vintage, 1965; revd. edn. London: Penguin Books, 1985).

Alperovitz, Gar: *The Decision to Use the Atomic Bomb and the Architecture of an American Myth* (New York: Alfred A. Knopf, 1995).

AlRoy, Gil C.: *The Kissinger Experience: American Policy in the Middle East* (New York: Horizon, 1975).

Alteras, Isaac: *Eisenhower and Israel: US–Israeli Relations, 1953–1960* (Gainesville: University of Florida Press, 1993).

Ambrose, Stephen E.: *Eisenhower and Berlin: The Decision to Halt at the Elbe* (New York: W. W. Norton, 1967).

Ambrose, Stephen E.: *Eisenhower*, 2 vols. (New York: Simon and Schuster, 1983–4).

Ambrose, Stephen E.: *Nixon, Vol. 2: The Triumph of a Politician 1962–1972* (New York: Simon and Schuster, 1989).

Ambrose, Stephen E.: " 'Just Dumb Luck': American Entry into World War II." In Robert W. Love, Jr. (ed.) *Pearl Harbor Revisited* (New York: St. Martin's Press, 1995).

Ambrose, Stephen E. and Richard H. Immerman: *Ike's Spies: Eisenhower and the Espionage Establishment* (Garden City, NY: Doubleday, 1981).

Ambrosius, Lloyd E.: *Woodrow Wilson and the American Diplomatic Tradition: The Treaty Fight in Perspective* (Cambridge: Cambridge University Press, 1987).

Ambrosius, Lloyd E.: *Wilsonian Statecraft: Theory and Practice of Liberal Internationalism during World War I* (Wilmington, DE: Scholarly Resources, 1991).

Ambrosius, Lloyd E.: *Wilsonianism: Woodrow Wilson and His Legacy in American Foreign Relations* (New York: Palgrave/Macmillan, 2002).

Ameringer, Charles D.: *The Democratic Left in Exile: The Anti-Dictatorial Struggle in the Caribbean, 1945–1975* (Coral Gables, FL: University of Miami Press, 1974).

Ameringer, Charles D.: *The Caribbean Legion: Patriots, Politicians, Soldiers of Fortune, 1946–1950* (University Park: Pennsylvania State University Press, 1996).

Amin, Julius A.: *The Peace Corps in Cameroon* (Kent, OH: Kent State University Press, 1992).

Amirahmadi, Hooshang: "Global Restructuring, the Persian Gulf War, and the US Quest for World Leadership." In Hooshang Amirahmadi (ed.) *The United States and the Middle East: A Search for New Perspectives* (Albany: State University of New York Press, 1993).

Ammon, Harry: *The Genet Mission* (New York: W. W. Norton, 1971).

Anders, Roger M.: "The Atomic Bomb and the Korean War: Gordon Dean and the Issue of Civilian Military Control." *Military Affairs* 52, no. 1 (January 1988), 1–6.

Anderson, Carol: "From Hope to Disillusion: African Americans, the United Nations, and the Struggle for Human Rights, 1944–1947." *Diplomatic History* 20 (1996), 531–63.

Anderson, David L.: *Imperialism and Idealism: American Diplomats in China, 1861–1898* (Bloomington: Indiana University Press, 1985).

Anderson, David L.: *Trapped by Success: The Eisenhower Administration and Vietnam* (New York: Columbia University Press, 1991).

Anderson, David L. (ed.): *Shadow on the White House: Presidents and the Vietnam War, 1945–1975* (Lawrence: University of Kansas Press, 1993).

Anderson, David L.: *The Columbia Guide to the Vietnam War* (New York: Columbia University Press, 2002).

Anderson, Irvine H.: *Aramco, the United States, and Saudi Arabia: A Study in the Dynamics of Foreign Oil Policy, 1933–1950* (Princeton, NJ: Princeton University Press, 1981).

Anderson, James E. and Jared E. Hazelton: *Managing Macroeconomic Policy: The Johnson Presidency* (Austin: University of Texas Press, 1986).

Anderson, Jon: *Che Guevara: A Revolutionary Life* (New York: Grove Press, 1997).

Anderson, Richard D., Jr.: *Public Politics in an Authoritarian State: Making Foreign Policy During the Brezhnev Years* (Ithaca, NY: Cornell University Press, 1993).

Anderson, Terry H.: *The United States, Great Britain, and the Cold War, 1944–1947* (Columbia: University of Missouri Press, 1981).

Andrew, Christopher: *The Missing Dimension: Governments and Intelligence Communities in the Twentieth Century* (Urbana: University of Illinois Press, 1984).

Antelyes, Peter: *Tales of Adventurous Enterprise: Washington Irving and the Poetics of Western Expansion* (New York: Columbia University Press, 1990).

Antolik, Michael: *ASEAN and the Diplomacy of Accommodation* (Armonk, NY: Sharpe, 1990).

Appadurai, Arjun: *Modernity at Large: Cultural Dimensions of Globalization* (Minneapolis: University of Minnesota Press, 1996).

Appadurai, Arjun (ed.): *Globalization* (Durham, NC: Duke University Press, 2001).

Appiah, K. Anthony: "The Multiculturalist Misunderstanding." *The New York Review of Books* (October 9, 1997), 30–6.

Appleman, Roy E.: *South to the Naktong, North to the Yalu* (Washington, DC: US Government Printing Office, 1961).

Appy, Christian G. (ed.): *Cold War Constructions: The Political Culture of United States Imperialism, 1945–1966* (Amherst: University of Massachusetts Press, 2000).

Arbatov, Georgi: *The System: An Insider's Life in Soviet Politics* (New York: Times Books, 1992).

Arens, Moshe: *Broken Covenant: American Foreign Policy and the Crisis Between the US and Israel* (New York: Simon and Schuster, 1995).

Armony, Ariel C.: *Argentina, the United States, and the Anti-Communist Crusade in Central America, 1977–1984* (Athens, OH: Ohio University Press, 1997).

Arnson, Cynthia: *Crossroads: The Congress, the President, and Central America, 1976–1993*, 2nd edn. (University Park: Pennsylvania State University Press, 1993).

Aronson, Shlomo: *Conflict and Bargaining in the Middle East: An Israeli Perspective* (Baltimore, MD: Johns Hopkins University Press, 1978).

Ashcroft, Bill et al.: *The Empire Writes Back* (London: Routledge, 1989).

Ashcroft, Bill, Gareth Griffiths, and Helen Tiffin (eds.) *The Post-colonial Studies Reader* (New York: Routledge, 1995).

Asher, Harvey: "Hitler's Decision to Declare War on the United States Revisited: A Synthesis of the Secondary Literature." *Newsletter of the Society for Historians of American Foreign Relations* 31 (September 2000), 2–20.

Ashton, John N.: *Eisenhower, Macmillan and the Problem of Nasser: Anglo-American Relations and Arab Nationalism, 1955–1959* (New York: St. Martin's Press, 1997).

Atkins, G. Pope.: *Latin America in the International Political System* (Boulder, CO: Westview Press, 1989).

Atkins, G. Pope and Larman C. Wilson: *The United States and the Trujillo Regime* (New Brunswick, NJ: Rutgers University Press, 1972).

Atkins, G. Pope and Larman C. Wilson: *The Dominican Republic and the United States: From Imperialism to Transnationalism* (Athens, GA: University of Georgia Press, 1998).

Atkinson, Rick: *Crusade: The Untold Story of the Persian Gulf War* (Boston, MA: Houghton Mifflin, 1993).

Ausland, John C.: *Kennedy, Khrushchev and the Berlin–Cuba Crisis, 1961–1964* (Oslo: Scandinavian University Press, 1996).

Axson, S.: *"Brother Woodrow": A Memoir of Woodrow Wilson* (Princeton, NJ: Princeton University Press, 1993).

Ayoob, Mohammed: "Nuclear India and Indian–American Relations." *Orbis* 43 (winter 1999), 59–74.

Bacino, L. J.: *Reconstructing Russia: US Policy in Revolutionary Russia, 1917–1922* (Kent, OH: Kent State University Press, 1999).

Bacon, Margaret H.: *One Woman's Passion for Peace and Freedom: The Life of Mildred Scott Olmsted* (Syracuse, NY: Syracuse University Press, 1993).

Bagby, Wesley M.: *The Eagle–Dragon Alliance: America's Relations with China in World War II* (Newark: University of Delaware Press, 1992).

Bagley, Wesley and William O. Walker, III (eds.): *Drug Trafficking in the Americas* (Coral Gables: University of Miami North–South Center Press, 1996).

Bahr, Egon: *Zu Meiner Zeit* (Munich: Karl Blessing, 1996).

Bailey, Fred A.: "A Virginia Scholar in Chancellor Hitler's Court: The Tragic Ambassadorship of William Edward Dodd." *Virginia Magazine of History and Biography* 100 (July 1992), 323–42.

Bailey, Sydney D.: *The Korean Armistice* (New York: St. Martin's Press, 1992).

Bailey, Thomas: "The North Pacific Sealing Convention of 1911." *Pacific Historical Review* 4 (1935), 1–14.

Bailey, Thomas A.: *A Diplomatic History of the American People*, 9th edn. (Englewood Cliffs, NJ: Prentice-Hall, 1974).

Baily, Samuel L.: *The United States and the Development of South America, 1945–1975* (New York: New Viewpoints, 1976).

Bajanov, Evgueni: "Assessing the Politics of the Korean War, 1949–1951." *Cold War International History Project Bulletin*, Issues 6–7 (winter 1995/1996), 54, 87–91.

Bajpai, Kanti P. and Stephen P. Cohen (eds.) *South Asia after the Cold War: International Perspectives* (Boulder, CO: Westview Press, 1993).

Baker, James A., III with Thomas M. DeFrank: *The Politics of Diplomacy: Revolution, War and Peace, 1989–1992* (New York: G. P. Putnam's, 1995).

Baldwin, David A.: *Economic Development and American Foreign Policy, 1943–1962* (Chicago, IL: University of Chicago Press, 1966).

Baldwin, Frank (ed.): *Without Parallel: The American–Korean Relationship since 1945* (New York: Pantheon Books, 1975).

Baldwin, Hanson W.: *Great Mistakes of the War* (New York: Harper and Brothers, 1949).

Ball, Desmond: *Politics and Force Levels: The Strategic Missile Program of the Kennedy Administration* (Berkeley: University of California Press, 1981).

Ball, George W. and Douglas B. Ball: *The Passionate Attachment: America's Involvement with Israel, 1947 to the Present* (New York: Norton, 1992).

Bange, Oliver: *The EEC Crisis of 1963: Kennedy, Macmillan, de Gaulle and Adenauer in Conflict* (Basingstoke: Macmillan, 2000).

Bannister, Robert C.: *Social Darwinism: Science and Myth in Anglo-American Social Thought* (Philadelphia, PA: Temple University Press, 1979).

Baptiste, Fitzroy A.: *War, Cooperation, and Conflict: The European Possessions in the Caribbean, 1939–1945* (New York: Greenwood Press, 1988).

Baram, Amatzia: "US Input into Iraqi Decisionmaking, 1988–1990." In David W. Lesch (ed.) *The Middle East and the United States: A Historical and Political Reassessment* (Boulder, CO: Westview Press, 1999).

Baram, Philip J.: *The Department of State in the Middle East, 1919–1945* (Philadelphia: University of Pennsylvania Press, 1978).

Barber, Benjamin R.: *Jihad vs. McWorld* (New York: Times Books, 1995).

Bard, Mitchell G.: *The Water's Edge and Beyond: Defining the Limits to Domestic Influence on United States Middle East Policy* (New Brunswick, NJ: Transaction Books, 1991).

Baritz, Loren: *Backfire: A History of How American Culture Led Us into Vietnam and Made Us Fight the Way We Did* (New York: Ballantine Books, 1985).

Bark, Dennis L. and David R. Gress: *A History of West Germany, Vol. 2: Democracy and its Discontents 1963–1988* (Oxford: Blackwell, 1989).

Barker, Elisabeth: *Churchill and Eden at War* (London: St. Martin's Press, 1978).

Barnet, R. J.: *The Rockets Red Glare: When America Goes to War: The Presidents and the People* (New York: Simon and Schuster, 1990).

Barnet, Richard: *The Alliance – America, Europe and Japan: Makers of the Postwar World* (New York: Simon and Schuster, 1983).

Barnhart, Michael A.: "Hornbeck Was Right: The Realist Approach to American Policy Toward Japan." In Hilary Conroy and Harry Wray (eds.) *Pearl Harbor Reexamined: Prologue to the Pacific War* (Honolulu: University of Hawaii Press, 1990).

Barnhart, Michael A. "The Origins of the Second World War in Asia and the Pacific: Synthesis Impossible?" In Michael J. Hogan (ed.) *Paths to Power: The Historiography of American Foreign Relations to 1941* (New York: Cambridge University Press, 2000).

Barrett, D. M.: *Uncertain Warriors: Lyndon Johnson and his Vietnam Advisers* (Lawrence: University of Kansas Press, 1993).

Bar-Siman-Tov, Yaacov: *The Israeli–Egyptian War of Attrition, 1969–1970: A Case Study of Limited Local War* (New York: Columbia University Press, 1980).

Bar-Siman-Tov, Yaacov: *Israel, the Superpowers, and the War in the Middle East* (New York: Praeger, 1987).

Bassett, L. J. and S. E. Pelz: "The Failed Search for Victory: Vietnam and the Politics of War." In T. G. Paterson (ed.) *Kennedy's Quest for Victory: American Foreign Policy, 1961–1963* (New York: Oxford University Press, 1989).

Beach, Edward L.: *Scapegoats: A Defense of Kimmel and Short at Pearl Harbor* (Annapolis, MD: Naval Institute Press, 1995).

Beale, Howard K.: *Theodore Roosevelt and the Rise of the United States to World Power* (Baltimore, MD: Johns Hopkins University Press, 1956).

Bean, Frank et al. (eds.) *At the Crossroads: Mexico and US Immigration Policy* (Lanham, MD: Rowman and Littlefield, 1997).

Beard, Charles A. (with G. H. E. Smith): *The Idea of the National Interest: An Analytical Study of American Foreign Policy* (New York: Macmillan, 1934).

Beaufre, André: *NATO and Europe* (New York: Alfred A. Knopf, 1966).

Becker, William H. and Samuel F. Wells, Jr. (eds.): *Economics and World Power: An Assessment of American Diplomacy since 1789* (New York: Columbia University Press, 1984).

Beer, Francis: *Integration and Disintegration in NATO: Processes of Alliance Cohesion and Prospects for Atlantic Community* (Columbus: Ohio State University Press, 1969).

Beisner, Robert L.: *Twelve Against Empire: The Anti-Imperialists, 1898–1900* (New York: McGraw-Hill, 1968).

Beisner, Robert L.: *From the Old Diplomacy to the New, 1865–1900*, 2nd edn. (Arlington Heights, IL: Harlan Davidson, 1986).

Beitzell, Robert: *The Uneasy Alliance: America, Britain and Russia, 1941–1943* (New York: Knopf, 1972).

Bell, Christopher M.: "Thinking the Unthinkable: British and American Strategies for an Anglo-American War, 1918–1931." *International History Review* 19 (November 1997), 789–808.

Bell, Coral: *The Diplomacy of Détente: The Kissinger Era* (London: Martin Robertson, 1977).

Bell, P. M. H.: *John Bull and the Bear: British Public Opinion, Foreign Policy and the Soviet Union, 1941–1945* (London: Edward Arnold, 1990).

Bell, Philip and Roger Bell (eds.): *Americanization and Australia* (Sydney: University of New South Wales Press, 1998).

Bell, Roger J.: *Unequal Allies: Australian–American Relations and the Pacific War* (Melbourne: Melbourne University Press, 1977).

Bell, Wendell: "The Invasion at Grenada: A Note on False Prophecy." *Yale Review* 75 (summer 1986), 564–86.

Belohlavek, John: *"Let The Eagle Soar!" The Foreign Policy of Andrew Jackson* (Lincoln: University of Nebraska Press, 1985).

Bemis, Samuel Flagg: *Pinckney's Treaty: A Study of America's Advantage from Europe's Distress, 1783–1800* (Baltimore, MD: Johns Hopkins University Press, 1926).

Bemis, Samuel Flagg: *John Quincy Adams and the Foundations of American Foreign Policy* (New York: A. A. Knopf, 1949).

Bemis, Samuel Flagg: *The Latin American Policy of the United States: A Historical Interpretation* (New York: W. W. Norton, 1967 [1943]).

Ben-Atar, Doron S.: *The Origins of Jeffersonian Commercial Policy and Diplomacy* (London: Macmillan, 1993).

Ben-Atar, Doron S.: "Nationalism, Neo-Mercantilism, and Diplomacy: Rethinking the Franklin Mission." *Diplomatic History* 22 (winter 1998), 103–14.

Benedick, Richard: *Ozone Diplomacy: New Directions in Safeguarding the Planet* (Cambridge, MA: Harvard University Press, 1991).

Benjamin, Jules R.: *The United States and Cuba: Hegemony and Dependent Development, 1880–1934* (Pittsburgh, PA: University of Pittsburgh Press, 1977).

Benjamin, Jules R.: *The United States and the Origins of the Cuban Revolution: An Empire of Liberty in an Age of National Liberation* (Princeton, NJ: Princeton University Press, 1990).

Bennett, Edward M.: *Franklin D. Roosevelt and the Search for Victory: American–Soviet Relations, 1939–1945* (Wilmington, DE: Scholarly Resources, 1990).

Bennett, Todd: "Culture, Power, and *Mission to Moscow*: Film and Soviet–American Relations during World War II." *Journal of American History* 88 (September 2001), 489–518.

Ben-Zvi, Abraham: *The United States and Israel: The Limits of the Special Relationship* (New York: Columbia University Press, 1993).

Ben-Zvi, Abraham: *Decade of Transition: Eisenhower, Kennedy, and the Origins of the American–Israeli Alliance* (New York: Columbia University Press, 1998).

Berg, A. Scott: *Lindbergh* (New York: G. P. Putnam, 1998).

Bergamini, David: *Japan's Imperial Conspiracy* (New York: William Morrow, 1971).

Berger, Carl: *The Korean Knot: A Military–Political History* (Philadelphia: University of Pennsylvania Press, 1964).

Berger, Henry W.: *A William Appleman Williams Reader: Selections from his Major Historical Writings* (Chicago, IL: Ivan R. Dee, 1992).

Berger, Mark T.: *Under Northern Eyes: Latin American Studies and United States Hegemony in the Americas, 1898–1990* (Bloomington: Indiana University Press, 1995).

Bergerud, E. M.: *The Dynamics of Defeat: The Vietnam War in Hau Nghia Province* (Boulder, CO: Westview Press, 1990).

Bergerud, E. M.: *Red Thunder, Tropic Lightning: The World of a Combat Division in Vietnam* (Boulder, CO: Westview Press, 1993).

Berghahn, Volker: "Philanthropy and Diplomacy in the 'American Century'." *Diplomatic History* 23 (summer, 1999), 393–419.

Berman, Larry: *Planning a Tragedy: The Americanization of the War in Vietnam* (New York: Norton, 1982).

Berman, Larry: *Lyndon Johnson's War* (New York: Norton, 1989).

Berman, Larry: "NSAM 263 and NSAM 273: Manipulating History." In L. C. Gardner and T. Gittinger (eds.) *Vietnam: The Early Decisions* (Austin: University of Texas Press, 1997).

Berman, Larry: *No Peace, No Honor: Nixon, Kissinger, and Betrayal in Vietnam* (New York: Free Press, 2001).

Berman, W. C.: *America's Right Turn: From Nixon to Bush* (Baltimore, MD: Johns Hopkins University Press, 1994).

Bernell, David: "The Curious Case of Cuba in American Foreign Policy." *Journal of Inter-American Studies and World Affairs* 36 (summer 1994), 65–103.

Bernstein, Barton J.: "Foreign Policy in the Eisenhower Administration." *Foreign Service Journal* 50 (1973), 17–20, 29–30, 38.

Bernstein, Barton J.: "Roosevelt, Truman and the Atomic Bomb, 1941–1945: A Reinterpretation." *Political Science Quarterly* 90 (spring 1975), 23–69.

Bernstein, Barton J.: "The Uneasy Alliance: Roosevelt, Churchill, and the Atomic Bomb, 1940–1945." *Western Political Science Quarterly* 29 (June 1976), 202–30.

Bernstein, Barton J.: "A Postwar Myth: 500,000 Lives Saved." *Bulletin of the Atomic Scientists* 42 (June/July 1986), 38–40.

Bernstein, Barton J.: "Understanding the Atomic Bomb and the Japanese Surrender: Missed Opportunities, Little-Known Near Disasters, and Modern Memory." In Michael J. Hogan (ed.) *Hiroshima in History and Memory* (Cambridge: Cambridge University Press, 1996).

Bertsch, Gary K., Seema Gahlaut, and Anupam Srivastava (eds.): *Engaging India: US Strategic Relations with the World's Largest Democracy* (New York: Routledge, 1999).

Beschloss, Michael: *Mayday: Eisenhower, Khrushchev and the U-2 Affair* (New York: Harper, 1986).

Beschloss, Michael: *The Crisis Years: Kennedy and Khrushchev 1960–1963* (New York: Harper Collins, 1991).

Beschloss, Michael and Strobe Talbott: *At the Highest Levels: The Inside Story of the End of the Cold War* (Boston, MA: Little, Brown, 1993).

Bethell, Leslie and Ian Roxborough (eds.): *Latin America Between the Second World War and the Cold War, 1944–1948* (Cambridge: Cambridge University Press, 1992).

Bhabha, Homi (ed.): *Nation and Narration* (London: Routledge, 1990).

Bill, James A.: *The Eagle and the Lion: The Tragedy of American–Iranian Relations* (New Haven, CT: Yale University Press, 1988).

Bill, James A.: The US Overture to Iran, 1985–1986: An Analysis." In Nikki R. Keddie and Mark J. Gasiorowski (eds.) *Neither East Nor West: Iran, the Soviet Union, and the United States* (New Haven, CT: Yale University Press, 1990).

Billings-Yun, Melanie: *Decision Against War: Eisenhower and Dien Bien Phu, 1954* (New York: Columbia University Press, 1988).

Billington, Ray A. and Martin Ridge: *Westward Expansion*, 5th edn. (New York, 1982).

Bills, Scott: *Empire and Cold War: The Roots of US–Third World Antagonism, 1945–1947* (New York: St. Martin's Press, 1990).

Bird, Kai: *The Chairman: John J. McCloy: The Making of the American Establishment* (New York: Simon and Schuster, 1992).

Bischof, Guenter and Saki Dockrill (eds.): *Cold War Respite: The Geneva Summit of 1955* (Baton Rouge: Louisiana State University Press, 2000).

Bissell, Richard M. with Johnathan Lewis and Frances Pudlo: *Reflections of a Cold Warrior: From Yalta to the Bay of Pigs* (New Haven, CT: Yale University Press, 1996).

Bix, Herbert P.: "Japan's Delayed Surrender: A Reinterpretation." In Michael J. Hogan (ed.) *Hiroshima in History and Memory* (Cambridge: Cambridge University Press, 1996).

Bix, Herbert P.: *Hirohito and the Making of Modern Japan* (New York: HarperCollins, 2000).

Black, Jan K.: *United States Penetration of Brazil* (Philadelphia: University of Pennsylvania Press, 1977).

Blair, Clay: *The Forgotten War: America in Korea, 1950–1953* (New York: Times Books, 1987).

Bland, Larry I. (ed.) *George C. Marshall Interviews and Reminiscences for Forrest C. Pogue* (Lexington, VA: George C. Marshall Research Foundation, 1991).

Blasier, Cole: *The Hovering Giant: US Responses to Revolutionary Change in Latin America* (Pittsburgh, PA: University of Pittsburgh Press, 1976).

Blasier, Cole: *The Giant's Rival: The USSR and Latin America* (Pittsburgh, PA: University of Pittsburgh Press, 1983, revd. edn. 1987).

Blasier, Cole: *The Hovering Giant: US Responses to Revolutionary Change in Latin America, 1910–1985*, revd. edn. (Pittsburgh, PA: University of Pittsburgh Press, 1985).

Blaufarb, Douglas: *The Counter-Insurgency Era: US Doctrine and Performance* (New York: Free Press, 1977).

Blechman, Barry M. and Stephen S. Kaplan (eds.): *Force without War: US Armed Forces as a Political Instrument* (Washington, DC: Brookings Institution, 1978).

Blight, James G.: *The Shattered Crystal Ball: Fear and Learning in the Cuban Missile Crisis* (Lanham, MD: Rowman and Littlefield, 1992).

Blight, James G. and Peter Kornbluh: *Politics of Illusion: The Bay of Pigs Invasion Re-examined* (Boulder, CO: Lynne Reinner Publishers, 1989).

Blight, James G. and David A. Welch: *On the Brink: Americans and Soviets Reexamine the Cuban Missile Crisis* (New York: Hill and Wang, 1989).

Blight, James G., Bruce J. Allyn, and David A. Welch with David Lewis: *Cuba on the Brink: Castro, the Missile Crisis, and the Soviet Collapse* (New York: Pantheon, 1993).

Blondheim, Menahem: *News Over the Wires: The Telegraph and the Flow of Information in America, 1844–1897* (Cambridge, MA: Harvard University Press, 1994).

Blum, R. M.: *Drawing the Line: The Origins of the American Containment Policy in East Asia* (New York: Norton, 1982).

Boemeke, M. F., G. D. Feldman, and E. Glaser, E. (eds.): *The Treaty of Versailles: A Reassessment after 75 Years* (Cambridge: Cambridge University Press, 1998).

Bolukbasi, Suha: *The Superpowers and the Third World: Turkish–American Relations and Cyprus* (Lanham, MD: University Press of America, 1988).

Bonner, Raymond: *Waltzing with a Dictator: The Marcoses and the Making of American Policy* (New York: Times Books, 1987).

Bonsal, Philip W.: *Cuba, Castro and the United States* (Pittsburgh, PA: University of Pittsburgh Press, 1971).

Booth, John A. and Thomas W. Walker: *Understanding Central America*, 3rd edn. (Boulder, CO: Westview Press, 1999).

Borden, W. S.: *The Pacific Alliance: United States Foreign Economic Policy and Japanese Trade Recovery, 1947–1955* (Madison: University of Wisconsin Press, 1984).

Borg, Dorothy: *American Policy and the Chinese Revolution, 1925–1928* (New York: Macmillan, 1947).

Borg, Dorothy: *The United States and the Far Eastern Crisis of 1933–1938* (Cambridge, MA: Harvard University Press, 1964).

Borg, Dorothy and Waldo Heinrichs (eds.): *Uncertain Years: Chinese–American Relations, 1947–1950* (New York: Columbia University Press, 1980).

Borstelmann, Thomas: *Apartheid's Reluctant Uncle: The United States and South Africa in the Early Cold War* (New York: Oxford University Press, 1993).

Borstelmann, Thomas: " 'Hedging Our Bets and Buying Time': John Kennedy and Racial Revolutions in the American South and Southern Africa." *Diplomatic History* 24 (2000), 435–63.

Borstelmann, Thomas: *The Cold War and the Color Line: American Race Relations in the Global Arena* (Cambridge, MA: Harvard University Press, 2001).

Bosch, Juan: *The Unfinished Experiment: Democracy in the Dominican Republic* (New York: Praeger, 1965).

Bose, Meena: *Shaping and Signaling Presidential Policy: The National Security Decision Making of Eisenhower and Kennedy* (College Station: Texas A&M University Press, 1998).

Bouvier, Virginia (ed.): *Whose America? The War of 1898 and the Battles to Define the Nation* (Baltimore, MD: Johns Hopkins University Press, 2001).

Bowie, Robert R. and Richard H. Immerman: *Waging Peace: How Eisenhower Shaped an Enduring Cold War Strategy* (New York: Oxford University Press, 1998).

Bowker, Mike and Phil Williams: *Superpower Détente: A Reappraisal* (London: Royal Institute of International Affairs, 1988).

Bowler, Peter J.: *The Eclipse of Darwinism: Anti-Darwinian Evolution Theories in the Decade Around 1900* (Baltimore, MD, 1983).

Bowler, Peter J.: *The Non-Darwinian Revolution: Reinterpreting a Historical Myth* (Baltimore, MD: Johns Hopkins University Press, 1988).

Boyer, Paul: *When Time Shall Be No More: Prophecy Belief in Modern American Culture* (Cambridge, MA: Belknap Press, 1992).

Bozo, Frédéric: *Two Strategies for Europe: De Gaulle, the United States and the Atlantic Alliance*, trans. Susan Emanuel (Lanham, MD: Rowman and Littlefield, 2001).

Brace, P. and B. Hinckley: *Follow the Leader: Opinion Polls and the Modern Presidency* (New York: Basic Books, 1993).

Bradley, Mark P.: *Imagining Vietnam and America: The Making of Postcolonial Vietnam, 1919–1950* (Chapel Hill: University of North Carolina Press, 2000).

Bradley, Mark P. and R. K. Brigham: "Vietnamese Archives and Scholarship of the Cold War Period: Two Reports." Cold War International History Project, Working Paper No. 7 (1993).

Braeman, John: *Albert Beveridge: American Nationalist* (Chicago, IL: University of Chicago Press, 1971).

Braestrup, P.: *Big Story: How the American Press and Television Reported and Interpreted the Crisis of Tet 1968 in Vietnam and Washington* (Boulder, CO: Westview Press, 1977).

Brandon, Henry: *The Retreat of American Power* (New York: Norton, 1972).

Brands, H. W.: *Cold Warriors: Eisenhower's Generation and American Foreign Policy* (New York: Columbia University Press, 1988).

Brands, H. W.: "Milton Eisenhower and the Coming Revolution in Latin America." In *Cold Warriors: Eisenhower's Generation and American Foreign Policy* (New York: Columbia University Press, 1988).

Brands, H. W.: "Testing Massive Retaliation: Credibility and Crisis Management in the Taiwan Strait." *International Security* 12 (1988), 124–51.

Brands, H. W.: "The Age of Vulnerability: Eisenhower and the National Insecurity State." *American Historical Review* 94 (1989), 963–89.

Brands, H. W.: *The Specter of Neutralism: The United States and the Emergence of the Third World, 1947–1960* (New York: Columbia University Press, 1989).

Brands, H. W.: *India and the United States: The Cold Peace* (Boston, MA: Twayne, 1990).

Brands, H. W.: *Inside the Cold War: Loy Henderson and the Rise of the American Empire, 1918–1961* (New York: Oxford University Press, 1991).

Brands, H. W.: *Bound to Empire: The United States and the Philippines* (New York: Oxford University Press, 1992).

Brands, H. W: *Into the Labyrinth: The United States and the Middle East, 1945–1993* (New York: McGraw-Hill, 1994).

Brands, H. W.: *The Reckless Decade* (New York: St. Martin's Press, 1995).

Brands, H. W: *The Wages of Globalism: Lyndon Johnson and the Limits of American Power* (New York: Oxford University Press, 1995).

Brands, H. W.: *Since Vietnam: The United States in World Affairs, 1973–1995* (New York: McGraw Hill, 1996).

Brands, H. W.: *TR: The Last Romantic* (New York: Basic Books, 1997).

Brands, H. W.: *What America Owes the World: The Struggle for the Soul of Foreign Policy* (New York: Cambridge University Press, 1998).

Brands, H. W. (ed.): *Beyond Vietnam: The Foreign Policies of Lyndon Johnson* (College Station: Texas A&M University Press, 1999).

Brands, H. W.: "The Idea of the National Interest." In Michael J. Hogan (ed.), *The Ambiguous Legacy: US Foreign Relations in the "American Century"* (New York: Cambridge University Press, 1999).

Brands, H. W. (ed.): *The Use of Force after the Cold War* (College Station, TX: Texas A&M University Press, 2000).

Brandt, Willy: *People and Politics: The Years 1960–1975* (Boston, MA: Little, Brown, 1976).

Breitman, Richard: *Official Secrets: What the Nazis Planned, What the British and Americans Knew* (New York: Hill and Wang, 1998).

Breitman, Richard and Alan M. Kraut: *American Refugee Policy and European Jewry, 1933–1945* (Bloomington: Indiana University Press, 1987).

Breslauer, George: *Khrushchev and Brezhnev as Leaders: Building Authority in Soviet Politics* (London: Allen and Unwin, 1982).

Bresnan, John: *From Dominoes to Dynamos: The Transformation of Southeast Asia* (New York: Council on Foreign Relations Press, 1994).

Brewer, Susan: *To Win the Peace: British Propaganda in the United States during World War II* (Ithaca, NY: Cornell University Press, 1997).

Briggs, P.: *Making American Foreign Policy: President–Congress Relations from the Second World War to Vietnam* (Lanham, MD: University Press of America, 1991).

Brigham, R. K.: *Guerrilla Diplomacy: The NLF's Foreign Relations and the Viet Nam War* (Ithaca, NY: Cornell University Press, 1999).

Brinkley, Douglas: *Dean Acheson: The Cold War Years, 1953–1971* (New Haven, CT: Yale University Press, 1992).

Brinkley, Douglas and Richard T. Griffiths: *John F. Kennedy and Europe* (Baton Rouge: Louisiana State University Press, 1999).

Britton, John A.: *Revolution and Ideology: The Image of the Mexican Revolution in the United States, 1910–1960* (Lexington: University of Kentucky Press, 1995).

Brodie, Bernard: *The Absolute Weapon: Atomic Power and World Order* (New York: Harcourt Brace, 1946).

Brodie, Bernard: *Strategy in the Missile Age* (Princeton, NJ: Princeton University Press, 1959).

Bromley, Simon: *American Hegemony and World Oil: The Industry, the State System, and the World Economy* (University Park: Pennsylvania State University Press, 1991).

Brookhiser, Richard: *Alexander Hamilton, American* (New York: Free Press, 1999).

Brower, Charles F., IV: "Sophisticated Strategist: General George A. Lincoln and the Defeat of Japan, 1944–1945." *Diplomatic History* 15 (summer 1991), 317–37.

Brown, Anthony C. and Thomas F. Troy: *Wild Bill and Intrepid: Bill Donovan, Bill Stephenson, and the Origins of the CIA* (New Haven, CT: Yale University Press, 1996).

Brown, Charles H.: *The Correspondents' War: Journalists in the Spanish–American War* (New York: Scribner, 1967).

Brown, Jonathan C.: *Oil and Revolution in Mexico* (Berkeley: University of California Press, 1992).

Brown, MacAlister and Joseph J. Zasloff: *Cambodia Confounds the Peacemakers, 1979–1998* (Ithaca, NY: Cornell University Press, 1998).

Brown, Michael E., Owen R. Cote, Jr., Sean M. Lynn-Jones, and Steven E. Miller (eds.) *The Rise of China* (Cambridge, MA: MIT Press, 2000)

Brown, Roger H.: *The Republic in Peril: 1812* (New York: Columbia University Press, 1964).

Brown, Seyom: *The Crisis of Power: An Interpretation of United States Foreign Policy During the Kissinger Years* (New York: Columbia University Press, 1979).

Bruckheimer, Jerry et al. (ed.): *Pearl Harbor: The Movie and the Moment* (New York: Hyperion, 2001).

Brügger, Mads: "Six Days that Shocked the World." *Virus* 5 (May 2000).

Brugioni, Dino: *Eyeball to Eyeball: The Inside Story of the Cuban Missile Crisis* (New York: Random House, 1991).

Brune, Lester H.: *America and the Iraq Crisis, 1990–1992: Origins and Aftermath* (Claremont, CA: Regina Books, 1993).

Brune, Lester H.: *The United States and Post-Cold War Interventions: Bush and Clinton in Somalia, Haiti and Bosnia, 1992–1998* (Claremont, CA: Regina Books, 1998).

Brzezinski, Zbigniew: *The Grand Failure* (New York: Scribner, 1979).

Brzezinski, Zbigniew: *Power and Principle: Memoirs of the National Security Adviser, 1977–1981* (New York: Farrar, Straus, and Giroux, 1983).

Buckley, Kevin: *Panama: The Whole Story* (New York: Simon and Schuster, 1991).

Buckley, Thomas H.: "The Icarus Factor: The American Pursuit of Myth in Naval Arms Control, 1921–36." In Eric Goldstein and John H. Maurer (eds.) *The Washington Conference, 1921–22: Naval Rivalry, East Asian Stability and the Road to Pearl Harbor* (Portland, OR: Frank Cass, 1994).

Buckley, Thomas H. and E. B. Strong, Jr.: *American Foreign and National Security Policies, 1914–1945* (Knoxville: University of Tennessee Press, 1987).

Buhite, Russell D.: "'Major Interests': American Policy Toward China, Taiwan, and Korea, 1945–1950." *Pacific Historical Review* 47, 3 (August 1978), 425–51.

Buhite, Russell D.: *Decisions at Yalta: An Appraisal of Summit Diplomacy* (Wilmington, DE: Scholarly Resources, 1986).

Buhle, Paul M. and Edward Rice-Maxim: *William Appleman Williams and the Tragedy of Empire* (New York: Routledge, 1995).

Bui, D. and D. Chanoff: *In the Jaws of History* (Boston, MA: Houghton Mifflin, 1987).

Bullitt, William C.: "How We Won the War and Lost the Peace." *Life* 25 (August 30, 1948), 82–97.

Bullock, Mary Brown: *An American Transplant: The Rockefeller Foundation and Peking Union Medical College* (Berkeley: University of California Press, 1980).

Bulmer-Thomas, Victor and James Dunkerley (eds.) *The United States and Latin America: The New Agenda* (London and Cambridge, MA: Institute of Latin American Studies, University of London and David Rockefeller Center for Latin American Studies, Harvard University, 1999).

Bunck, Julie M.: *Fidel Castro and the Quest for a Revolutionary Culture in Cuba* (University Park: Pennsylvania State University Press, 1994).

Bundy, McGeorge: *Danger and Survival: Choices About the Bomb in the First Fifty Years* (New York: Random House, 1988).

Bundy, William: *A Tangled Web: The Making of Foreign Policy in the Nixon Presidency* (New York: Hill and Wang, 1998).

Burk, Kathleen: "The Lineaments of Foreign Policy: The United States and a 'New World Order,' 1919–1939." *Journal of American Studies* 26 (1992), 377–91.

Burk, Kathleen and Melvyn Stokes (eds.): *The United States and the European Alliance since 1945* (New York: Oxford University Press, 1999).

Burke, Bernard V.: *Ambassador Frederic Sackett and the Collapse of the Weimar Republic, 1930–1933: The United States and Hitler's Rise to Power* (New York: Cambridge University Press, 1994).

Burke, John P. and Fred I. Greenstein: *How Presidents Test Reality: Decisions on Vietnam, 1954 and 1965* (New York: Russell Sage, 1989).

Burner, David: *John F. Kennedy and a New Generation* (Boston, MA: Little, Brown, 1988).

Burns, James M.: *Roosevelt: The Soldier of Freedom, 1940–1945* (New York: Harcourt, Brace, Jovanovich, 1970).

Burr, William (ed.): *The Kissinger Transcripts: The Top Secret Talks with Beijing and Moscow* (New York: New Press, 1998).

Burr, William: *The Kissinger Transcripts: Top Secret Talks with Beijing and Moscow* (New York: New Press, 1999).

Burr, William: "Sino-American Relations, 1969: The Sino-Soviet Border War and Steps Towards Rapprochement." *Cold War History* 1, 3 (April 2001), 73–112.

Burr, William and Jeffrey T. Richelson: "Whether to 'Strangle the Baby in the Cradle': The United States and the Chinese Nuclear Program, 1960–64." *International Security* 25, 3 (winter 2000/1), 54–99.

Burrow, J. W.: *Evolution and Society: A Study in Victorian Social Theory* (Cambridge: Cambridge University Press, 1966).

Burrowes, Reynold A.: *Revolution and Rescue in Grenada: An Account of the US–Caribbean Invasion* (Westport, CT: Greenwood Press, 1988).

Burton, David H.: *Theodore Roosevelt: Confident Imperialist* (Philadelphia, PA, 1968).

Busch, Briton C.: *"Whaling Will Never Do For Me": The American Whalemen in the Nineteenth Century* (Lexington: University of Kentucky Press, 1994).

Bush, George H. W. and Brent Scowcroft: *A World Transformed* (New York: Knopf, 1998).

Butler, J. R. M. (ed.): *Grand Strategy*, 6 vols. (London: Her Majesty's Stationery Office, 1956–76).

Butler, Michael A.: *Cautious Visionary: Cordell Hull and Trade Reform* (Kent, OH: Kent State University Press, 1998).

Butow, Robert J. C.: *The John Doe Associates: Backdoor Diplomacy for Peace, 1941* (Stanford, CA: Stanford University Press, 1974).

Buzzanco, R.: *Masters of War: Military Dissent and Politics in the Vietnam Era* (Cambridge: Cambridge University Press, 1996).

Buzzanco, R.: *Vietnam and the Transformation of American Life* (Cambridge, MA: Blackwell, 1999).

Cable, L.: *Unholy Grail: The US and the Wars in Vietnam, 1965–8* (New York: Routledge, 1991).

Cahn, Anne H.: *Killing Détente: The Right Attacks the CIA* (University Park: Pennsylvania State University Press, 1998).

Calder, Bruce J.: *The Impact of Intervention: The Dominican Republic During the US Occupation of 1916–1924* (Austin: University of Texas Press, 1984).

Caldwell, D.: *American Soviet Relations: From 1947 to the Nixon–Kissinger Grand Design* (Westport, CT: Greenwood Press, 1981).

Calhoun, Frederick S.: *Power and Principle: Armed Intervention in Wilsonian Foreign Policy* (Kent, OH: Kent State University Press, 1986).

Calhoun, Frederick S.: *Uses of Force and Wilsonian Foreign Policy* (Kent, OH: Kent State University Press, 1993).

Calingaert, Daniel: "Nuclear Weapons and the Korean War." *Journal of Strategic Studies* 11 (June 1988), 177–202.

Callahan, Raymond A.: *Churchill: Retreat from Empire* (Wilmington, DE: Scholarly Resources, 1984).

Calloway, Colin G.: *Our Hearts Fell to the Ground: Plains Indians Views of How The West Was Lost* (Boston, MA: Bedford Books, 1996).

Campbell, Charles, Jr.: *Special Business Interests and the Open Door Policy* (New Haven, CT: Yale University Press, 1951).

Campbell, Charles, Jr.: "The Anglo-American Crisis in the Bering Sea, 1890–1891." *Mississippi Valley Historical Review* 66 (1961), 395–410.

Campbell, Charles, Jr.: "The Bering Sea Settlements of 1892." *Pacific Historical Review* 32 (1963), 347–68.

Campbell, Thomas M.: *Masquerade Peace: America's UN Policy, 1944–1945* (Tallahassee: Florida State University Press, 1973).

Cannon, J.: *Time and Change: Gerald Ford's Appointment with History* (New York: Harper Collins, 1994).

Cardoso, Fernando Henrique and Enzo Faletto: *Dependencia y desarrollo en America Latina* (Lima: Instituto de Estudios Peruanos, 1967).

Caridi, Ronald J.: *The Korean War and American Politics: The Republican Party as a Case Study* (Philadelphia: University of Pennsylvania Press, 1968).

Carothers, Thomas: *In the Name of Democracy: US Policy toward Latin America in the Reagan Years* (Berkeley: University of California Press, 1991).

Carr, P. J. and A. G. Hopkins: *British Imperialism*, 2 vols. (London, 1993).

Carr, Raymond: *Puerto Rico: A Colonial Experiment* (New York: Vintage Books, 1984).

Carroll, John: *Environmental Diplomacy: An Examination and Prospective of Canadian–US Transboundary Environmental Relations* (Ann Arbor: University of Michigan Press, 1983).

Carroll, Peter N.: *It Seemed Like Nothing Happened: America in the Seventies* (New Brunswick, NJ: Rutgers University Press, 1982).

Carson, James T.: *Searching for the Bright Path: The Mississippi Choctaws from Prehistory to Removal* (Lincoln: University of Nebraska Press, 1999).

Carter, Jimmy: *Keeping Faith: The Memoirs of a President* (New York: Bantam, 1982).

Cashman, Richard and Anthony Hughes: "Sport." In Philip Bell and Roger Bell (eds.) *Americanization and Australia* (Sydney: University of New South Wales Press, 1998).

Castle, Alfred A.: *Diplomatic Realism: William R. Castle Jr. and American Foreign Policy, 1919–1953* (Honolulu: Samuel L. and Mary Castle Foundation, 1998).

Castro, Fidel and José Ramon Fernandez: *Playa Girón: Bay of Pigs: Washington's First Military Defeat in the Americas* (New York: Pathfinder, 2001).

Catchpole, Brian: *The Korean War 1950–53* (London: Constable and Robinson, 2000).

Catudal, Honoré M.: *Kennedy and the Berlin Wall Crisis: A Case Study in US Decision Making* (Berlin: Verlag, 1980).

Chandler, David P.: *The Tragedy of Cambodian History: Politics, War, and Revolution* (New Haven, CT: Yale University Press, 1991).

Chang, Gordon H.: "JFK, China, and the Bomb." *Journal of American History* 74, 4 (March 1988), 1289–310.

Chang, Gordon H.: "To the Nuclear Brink: Eisenhower, Dulles, and the Quemoy–Matsu Crisis." *International Security* 12 (1988), 96–123.

Chang, Gordon H.: *Friends and Enemies: The United States, China, and the Soviet Union, 1948–1972* (Stanford, CA: Stanford University Press, 1990).

Chang, Gordon: *Friends and Enemies: The United States, China, and the Soviet Union, 1948–1972* (Stanford, CA: Stanford University Press, 1990).

Chang, Iris: *The Rape of Nanking: The Forgotten Holocaust of World War II* (New York: Basic Books, 1997).

Chang, Laurence and Peter Kornbluh (eds.): *The Cuban Missile Crisis, 1962: A National Security Archive Documents Reader* (New York: New Press, 1992).

Charles, Douglas M. and John P. Rossi: "FBI Political Surveillance and the Charles Lindbergh Investigation, 1939–1944." *Historian* 59 (summer 1997), 831–47.

Charmley, John: *Churchill: The End of Glory; A Political Biography* (New York: Harcourt Brace, 1993).

Charmley, John: *Churchill's Grand Alliance. The Anglo-American Special Relationship, 1940–1957* (New York: Harcourt Brace, 1995).

Chary, M. Srinivas: *The Eagle and the Peacock: US Foreign Policy towards India since Independence* (Westport, CT: Greenwood Press, 1995).

Chavezmontes, J.: *Heridas Que No Cierran* [Wound That Will Not Heal] (Mexico City: Grijalbo, 1988).

Chayes, Abram: *The Cuban Missile Crisis: International Crisis and the Role of Law* (Lanham, MD: University Press of America, 1987).

Chen, Jian: *China's Road to the Korean War: The Making of the Sino-American Confrontation* (New York: Columbia University Press, 1994).

Chen, Jian: "The Myth of America's 'Lost Chance' in China: A Chinese Perspective in Light of New Evidence." *Diplomatic History* 21, 1 (winter 1997), 77–86.

Chen, Jian: *Mao's China and the Cold War* (Chapel Hill: University of North Carolina Press, 2001).

Chen, Jian and James Hershberg: "Informing the Enemy: Sino-American 'Signalling' and the Vietnam War, 1965." Paper presented at CWIHP workshop on "New Evidence on China, Southeast Asia, and the Vietnam War," January 2000, Hong Kong University, Hong Kong.

Chen, Jian and David L. Wilson: "'All Under Heaven is Great Chaos': Beijing, the Sino-Soviet Border Clashes, and the Turn Toward Sino-American Rapprochement, 1968–69." *Cold War International History Project Bulletin* 11 (winter 1998), 155–75.

Chester, L. et al.: *An American Melodrama: The Presidential Campaign of 1968* (New York: Viking, 1969).

Chickering, R. and S. Forster (eds.): *Great War, Total War: Combat and Mobilization on the Western Front* (Cambridge: Cambridge University Press, 2000).

Chilcote, Ronald H.: *Theories of Development and Underdevelopment* (Boulder, CO: Westview Press, 1984).

Childs, Marquis: *Eisenhower: Captive Hero: A Critical Study of the General and the President* (New York: Harcourt, Brace, 1958).

Chi-Pao Cheng (ed.): *Chinese American Cultural Relations* (New York: China Institute in America, 1965).

Cho Soon-sung: *Korea in World Politics, 1940–1950: An Evaluation of American Responsibility* (Berkeley: University of California Press, 1967).

Chomsky, Noam: *The Fateful Triangle: The United States, Israel, and the Palestinians* (Cambridge, MA: South End Press, 1999).

Christensen, Thomas J.: *Useful Adversaries: Grand Strategy, Domestic Mobilization, and Sino-American Conflict, 1947–1958* (Princeton, NJ: Princeton University Press, 1996).

Christensen, Thomas J.: "Posing Problems without Catching Up: China's Rise and Challenges for US Security Policy." *International Security* 25, 4 (spring 2001), 5–40.

Christison, Kathleen: *Perceptions of Palestine: Their Influence on US Middle East Policy* (Berkeley: University of California Press, 1999).

Christman, Calvin L.: "Franklin D. Roosevelt and the Craft of Strategic Assessment." In Williamson Murray and Allan R. Millett (eds.) *Calculations: Net Assessment and the Coming of World War II* (New York: Free Press, 1992).

Christopher, Warren: *Chances of a Lifetime* (New York: Scribner, 2001).

Churba, Joseph: *The Politics of Defeat: America's Decline in the Middle East* (New York: Cyrco Press, 1977).

Churchill, Winston S.: *The Second World War*, 6 vols. (Boston, MA: Houghton Mifflin, 1948–53).

CIA Clandestine Service History: "Overthrow of Premier Mossadeq of Iran, November 1952– August 1953," March 1954, by Dr. Donald Wilber, available on the National Security Archive web page at: http://www.gwu.edu/'nsarchiv/NSAEBB/NSAEBB28/index.html#documents

Clark, Mark W.: *From the Danube to the Yalu* (New York: Harper, 1954).

Clark, Paul C., Jr.: *The United States and Somoza, 1933–1956: A Revisionist Look* (Westport, CT: Praeger, 1992).

Clark, Ramsey: *The Fire This Time: US War Crimes in the Gulf* (New York: Thunder's Mouth Press, 1992).

Clausen, Henry C. and Bruce Lee: *Pearl Harbor: Final Judgment* (New York: Crown, 1992).

Clavin, Patricia M.: *The Failure of Economic Diplomacy: Britain, Germany, France, and the USA, 1931–36* (New York: St. Martin's Press, 1996).

Clayton, Lawerence A.: *Peru and the United States: The Condor and the Eagle* (Athens, GA: University of Georgia Press, 1999).

Clemens, Diane S.: *Yalta* (New York: Oxford University Press, 1970).

Clements, K. A.: *William Jennings Bryan: Missionary Isolationist* (Knoxville: University of Tennessee Press, 1982).

Clements, K. A.: *Woodrow Wilson: World Statesman* (Boston, MA: Twayne Publishers, 1987).

Clements, K. A.: *The Presidency of Woodrow Wilson* (Lawrence: University of Kansas Press, 1992).

Cleveland, Harold Van B.: *The Atlantic Idea and Its European Rivals* (New York: McGraw-Hill, 1966).

Clodfelter, Mark: *The Limits of Air Power: The American Bombing of North Vietnam* (New York: Free Press, 1989).

Clodfelder, Mark: "Pinpointing Devastation: American Air Campaign Planning before Pearl Harbor." *Journal of Military History* 58 (January 1994), 75–101.

Clymer, Kenton J.: *Protestant Missionaries in the Philippines 1898–1916* (Urbana, IL, 1986).

Coatsworth, John H.: *Central America and the United States: The Clients and the Colossus* (New York: Twayne, 1994).

Cobbs, Elizabeth A.: *The Rich Neighbor Policy: Rockefeller and Kaiser in Brazil* (New Haven, CT: Yale University Press, 1992).

Cockburn, Andrew and Leslie Cockburn: *Dangerous Liaison: The Inside Story of the US–Israeli Covert Relationship* (New York: Harper Collins, 1991).

Coerver, Don and Linda B. Hall: *Tangled Destinies: Latin America and the United States* (Albuquerque: University of New Mexico Press, 1999).

Cohen, Stephen P. (ed.): *The Security of South Asia: American and Asian Perspectives* (Urbana: University of Illinois Press, 1987).

Cohen, Stephen P.: "The Reagan Administration and India." In Harold A. Gould and Sumit Ganguly (eds.) *The Hope and the Reality: US–Indian Relations from Roosevelt to Reagan* (Boulder, CO: Westview Press, 1992).

Cohen, Stephen P.: "The United States, India, and Pakistan: Retrospect and Prospect." In Selig S. Harrison, Paul H. Kreisberg, and Dennis Kux (eds.) *India and Pakistan: The First Fifty Years* (New York: Cambridge University Press, 1999).

Cohen, Stephen P.: *Failed Crusade: America and the Tragedy of Post Communist Russia* (New York: W. W. Norton, 2001).

Cohen, Stephen P.: *India: Emerging Power* (Urbana: University of Illinois Press, 2001).

Cohen, Warren I.: *Dean Rusk* (Totowa, NJ: Cooper Square, 1980).

Cohen, Warren I.: "Acheson, His Advisers, and China, 1949–1950." In Dorothy Borg and Waldo Heinrichs (eds.) *Uncertain Years: Chinese–American Relations, 1947–1950* (New York: Columbia University Press, 1980), 15–52.

Cohen, Warren I.: *Empire Without Tears: American Foreign Relations, 1921–1933* (New York: Knopf, 1987).

Cohen, Warren I.: "American Leaders and East Asia, 1931–1938." In Akira Iriye and Warren

I. Cohen (eds.) *American, Chinese, and Japanese Perspectives on Wartime Asia, 1931–1949* (Wilmington, DE: Scholarly Resources, 1990).

Cohen, Warren I.: *The United States and China* (New York: Columbia University Press, 1990).

Cohen, Warren I.: *East Asian Art and American Culture* (New York: Columbia University Press, 1992).

Cohen, Warren I.: "Balancing American Interests in the Middle East: Lyndon Baines Johnson vs. Gamal Abdul Nasser." In Warren I. Cohen and Nancy Bernkopf Tucker (eds.) *Lyndon Johnson Confronts the World: American Foreign Policy, 1963–1968* (New York: Cambridge University Press, 1994).

Cohen, Warren I. (ed.): *Pacific Passages: The Study of American–East Asian Relations on the Eve of the Twenty-First Century* (New York: Columbia University Press, 1996).

Cohen, Warren I.: *Empire Without Tears: American Foreign Relations, 1921–1933*, 2nd edn. (New York: McGraw Hill, 1998).

Cohen, Warren I.: *America's Response to China: A History of Sino-American Relations*, 4th edn. (New York: Columbia University Press, 2000).

Cohen, Warren I. and Nancy Berkopf Tucker (eds.): *Lyndon Johnson Confronts the World: American Foreign Policy, 1963–1968* (New York: Cambridge University Press, 1994).

Colby, W. and J. McCargar: *Lost Victory: A Firsthand Account of America's Sixteen-Year Involvement in Vietnam* (Chicago, IL: Contemporary Books, 1989).

Cole, Wayne S.: *Roosevelt and the Isolationists, 1932–45* (Lincoln: University of Nebraska Press, 1983).

Cole, Wayne S.: "American Appeasement." In David F. Schmitz and Richard D. Challener (eds.) *Appeasement in Europe: A Reassessment of US Policies* (Westport, CT: Greenwood Press, 1990).

Cole, Wayne S.: "The America First Committee – A Half-Century Later." In Wayne S. Cole, *Determinism and American Foreign Relations During the Franklin D. Roosevelt Era* (Lanham, MD: University Press of America, 1995).

Cole, Wayne S.: "Franklin D. Roosevelt: Great Man or Man for His Times?" In Wayne S. Cole, *Determinism and American Foreign Relations During the Franklin D. Roosevelt Era* (Lanham, MD: University Press of America, 1995).

Coletta, Paolo A.: "Prelude to War: Japan, the United States, and the Aircraft Carrier, 1919–1945." *Prologue* 23 (winter 1991), 342–59.

Collin, Richard H.: *Theodore Roosevelt, Culture, Diplomacy, and Expansion: A New View of American Imperialism* (Baton Rouge: Louisiana State University Press, 1985).

Collin, Richard H.: *Theodore Roosevelt's Caribbean: The Panama Canal, the Monroe Doctrine, and the Latin American Context* (Baton Rouge: Louisiana State University Press, 1990).

Collins, J. Lawton: *War in Peacetime: The History and Lessons of Korea* (Boston, MA: Houghton Mifflin, 1969).

Colville, John: *The Fringes of Power: 10 Downing Street Diaries, 1939–1955* (New York: W. W. Norton, 1985).

Colville, John: "How the West Lost the Peace in 1945." *Commentary* 80 (September 1985), 41–7.

Combs, Jerald A.: *American Diplomatic History: Two Centuries of Changing Interpretations* (Berkeley: University of California Press, 1983).

Condit, Doris M.: *History of the Office of the Secretary of Defense, Vol. 2: The Test of War, 1950–1953* (Washington, DC: US Government Printing Office, 1988).

Coniff, Michael: *Panama and the United States: The Forced Alliance* (Athens, GA: University of Georgia Press, 1992).

Connell-Smith, Gordon: *The Inter-American System* (Oxford: Oxford University Press, 1966).

Connell-Smith, Gordon: *The United States and Latin America: An Historical Analysis of Inter-American Relations* (New York: John Wiley and Sons, 1974).

Conniff, Michael L.: *Panama and the United States: The Forced Alliance* (Athens, GA: University of Georgia Press, 1992).

Conyne, G. R.: *Woodrow Wilson: British Perspectives, 1912–21* (London: Macmillan, 1992).

Coogan, J. W.: *The End of Neutrality: The United States, Britain, and Maritime Rights, 1899–1915* (Ithaca, NY: Cornell University Press, 1981).

Cook, Blanche W.: *The Declassified Eisenhower* (Garden City, NY: Doubleday, 1981).

Cook, Haruko Taya: "The Myth of the Saipan Suicides." In Robert Cowley (ed.) *No End Save Victory: Perspectives on World War II* (New York: G. P. Putnam's Sons, 2001).

Cooley, John K.: *Payback: America's Long War in the Middle East* (Washington, DC: Brassey's, 1991).

Coombs, Charles: *The Arena of International Finance* (New York: Wiley, 1976).

Cooper, C. L.: *The Lost Crusade: America in Vietnam* (New York: Dodd, Mead, 1970).

Cooper, J. M., Jr.: *Walter Hines Page: The Southerner as American, 1855–1918* (Chapel Hill: University of North Carolina Press, 1977).

Cooper, J. M., Jr.: *The Warrior and the Priest: Theodore Roosevelt and Woodrow Wilson* (Cambridge, MA: Harvard University Press, 1983).

Cooper, J. M., Jr.: *Breaking the Heart of the World: Woodrow Wilson and the Fight for the League of Nations* (Cambridge: Cambridge University Press, 2001).

Cooper, J. M., Jr. and C. E. Neu: *The Wilson Era: Essays in Honor of Arthur S. Link* (Arlington Heights, IL: Harlan Davidson, 1991).

Costigliola, Frank: *Awkward Dominion: American Political, Economic, and Cultural Expansion, 1919–1933* (Ithaca, NY: Cornell University Press, 1984).

Costigliola, Frank: *France and the United States: The Cold Alliance Since World War II* (New York: Twayne, 1992).

Costigliola, Frank: "'Unceasing Pressure for Penetration': Gender, Pathology, and Emotion in George Kennan's Formation of the Cold War." *Journal of American History* 83 (March 1997), 1309–39.

Costigliola, Frank: "The Creation of Memory and Myth: Stalin's 1946 Election Speech and the Soviet Threat." In Martin J. Medhurst and H. W. Brands (eds.) *Critical Reflections on the Cold War: Linking Rhetoric and History* (College Station: Texas A&M University Press, 2000).

Cottam, Martha L.: *Images and Intervention: US Policies in Latin America* (Pittsburgh, PA: University of Pittsburgh Press, 1994).

Coulter, Matthew W.: *The Senate Munitions Inquiry of the 1930s: Beyond the Merchants of Death* (Westport, CT: Greenwood Press, 1997).

Craig, Campbell: *Destroying the Village: Eisenhower and Thermonuclear War* (New York: Columbia University Press, 1998).

Cramer, R. B.: *What it Takes: Promise and the Presidency* (New York: Random House, 1992).

Crapol, Edward D.: "Coming to Terms With Empire: The Historiography of Late Nineteenth Century American Foreign Relations." In Michael J. Hogan (ed.) *Paths to Power: The Historiography of American Foreign Relations to 1941* (New York, 2000).

Craven, Wesley F. and James L. Cate (eds.): *The Army Air Forces in World War II*, 7 vols. (Chicago, IL: University of Chicago Press, 1948–58).

Creighton, Margaret S.: *Rites and Passages: The Experience of American Whaling, 1830–1870* (Cambridge: Cambridge University Press, 1995).

Crocker, Chester: *High Noon in Southern Africa: Making Peace in a Rough Neighborhood* (New York: Norton, 1992).

Croog, Charles E.: "FBI Political Surveillance and the Isolationist–Interventionist Debate, 1931–1941." *Historian* 54 (spring 1992), 441–58.

Crook, Paul: *Darwinism, War and History: The Debate Over the Biology of War from the 'Origin of Species' to the First World War* (Cambridge: Cambridge University Press, 1994).

Crowley, James: *Japan's Quest for Autonomy* (Princeton, NJ: Princeton University Press, 1966).

Cuddy, Edward: "America's Cuban Obsessions: A Case Study in Diplomacy and Psycho-History." *The Americas* 43 (October 1986), 183–96.

Cueto, Marcos (ed.): *Missionaries of Science: The Rockefeller Foundation and Latin America* (Bloomington: Indiana University Press, 1994).

Cull, Nicholas J.: "Radio Propaganda and the Art of Understatement: British Broadcasting and American Neutrality, 1939–1941." *Historical Journal of Film, Radio and Television* 13 (1993), 403–31.

Cull, Nicholas J.: *Selling War: The British Propaganda Campaign Against American "Neutrality" in World War II* (New York: Oxford University Press, 1995).

Cullather, Nick: *Illusions of Influence: The Political Economy of United States–Philippine Relations, 1942–1960* (Stanford, CA: Stanford University Press, 1994).

Cullather, Nick: *Secret History: The CIA's Classified Account of Its Operations in Guatemala, 1952–1954.* Afterword by Piero Gleijeses (Stanford, CA: Stanford University Press, 1999).

Cumings, Bruce: *The Origins of the Korean War*, 2 vols (Princeton, NJ: Princeton University Press, 1981, 1990).

Cumings, Bruce (ed.): *Child of Conflict: The Korean–American Relationship, 1945–1953* (Seattle: University of Washington Press, 1983).

Cumings, Bruce: "Korean–American Relations: A Century of Contact and Thirty-Five Years of Intimacy." In Warren I. Cohen (ed.) *New Frontiers in American–East Asian Relations: Essays Presented to Dorothy Borg* (New York: Columbia University Press, 1983).

Cumings, Bruce: "The Wicked Witch of the West is Dead. Long Live the Wicked Witch of the East." In M. J. Hogan (ed.) *The End of the Cold War: Its Meanings and Implications* (Cambridge: Cambridge University Press, 1992).

Curti, Merle: *American Philanthropy Abroad: A History* (New Brunswick, NJ: Rutgers University Press, 1963).

Daalder, Ivo: *Getting to Dayton: The Making of America's Bosnia Policy* (Washington, DC: Brookings Institution, 2000)

Daalder, Ivo and Michael O'Hanlon: *Winning Ugly: NATO's War to Save Kosovo* (Washington, DC: Brookings Institution, 2000).

Dallek, Robert: *Franklin D. Roosevelt and American Foreign Policy, 1932–1945* (New York: Oxford University Press, 1979).

Dallek, Robert: *The American Style of Foreign Policy: Cultural Politics and Foreign Affairs* (New York: Oxford University Press, 1983).

Dallek, Robert: *Flawed Giant: Lyndon Johnson and His Times, 1961–1973* (New York: Oxford University Press, 1998).

Dallek, Robert: "Lyndon Johnson as a World Leader." In H. W. Brands (ed.) *The Foreign Policies of Lyndon Johnson: Beyond Vietnam* (College Station: Texas A&M University Press, 1999).

Dalton, Kathleen: *Theodore Roosevelt: A Strenuous Life* (New York: Knopf, 2001).

Danchev, Alex: *Very Special Relationship: Field-Marshal Sir John Dill and the Anglo-American Alliance, 1941–1944* (London: Brassey's, 1986).

Danchev, Alex: *On Specialness: Essays in Anglo-American Relations* (New York: St. Martin's Press, 1998).

Dangerfield, George: *Chancellor Robert R. Livingston of New York* (New York: Harcourt Press, 1960).

Danner, Mark: *The Massacre at El Mozote: A Parable of the Cold War* (New York: Vintage, 1994).

Darby, Philip: *The Faces of Imperialism: British and American Approaches to Asia and Africa, 1870–1970* (New Haven, CT: Yale University Press, 1987).

David, Charles-Philippe, Nancy Ann Carrol, and Zachary A. Selden: *Foreign Policy Failure in the White House: Reappraising the Fall of the Shah and the Iran–Contra Affair* (Lanham, MD: University Press of America, 1993).

Davidann, Jon T.: *A World of Crisis and Progress: The American YMCA in Japan, 1890–1930* (Bethlehem: Lehigh University Press. 1998).

Davidson, P. B.: *Vietnam at War: The History, 1946–1975* (Novato, CA: Presidio, 1988).

Davis, Lance E., Robert E. Gallman, and Karen Gleiter: *In Pursuit of Leviathan: Technology, Institutions, Productivity, and Profits in American Whaling, 1816–1906* (Chicago, IL: University of Chicago Press, 1997).

Davis, Lynn E.: *The Cold War Begins: Soviet–American Conflict Over Eastern Europe, 1943–1947* (Princeton, NJ: Princeton University Press, 1974).

Davis, Nathaniel: *The Last Two Years of Salvador Allende* (Ithaca, NY: Cornell University Press, 1985).

De Bevoise, Ken: *Agents of Apocalypse: Epidemic Disease in the Philippines* (Princeton, NJ, 1995).

de Carmoy, Guy: *The Foreign Policies of France: 1944–1968*, trans. Elaine Halperin (Chicago, IL: University of Chicago Press, 1970).

De Santis, Hugh: "The Imperialist Impulse and American Innocence, 1865–1900." In Gerald K. Haines and Samuel K. Walker (eds.) *American Foreign Relations: A Historiographical Review* (Westport, CT, 1981).

de Tocqueville, Alexis: *L'Ancien régime et la révolution* (Paris: 1856); trans. Alan S. Kahan, *The Old Regime and the Revolution* (Chicago, IL: University of Chicago Press, 1998).

Dean, Robert D.: "Masculinity as Ideology: John F. Kennedy and the Domestic Politics of Foreign Policy." *Diplomatic History* 22 (winter 1998), 29–62.

Deane, John R.: *The Strange Alliance: The Story of Our Wartime Co-operation with Russia* (New York: Viking, 1947).

DeBenedetti, C. and C. Chatfield: *An American Ordeal: The Antiwar Movement of the Vietnam Era* (Syracuse, NY: Syracuse University Press, 1990).

DeConde, Alexander: *The Quasi War: The Politics and Diplomacy of the Undeclared War with France, 1797–1801* (New York: Scribner, 1966).

DeConde, Alexander: *This Affair of Louisiana* (New York: Scribner, 1976).

DeConde, Alexander (ed.) *Encyclopedia of American Foreign Policy: Studies of the Principal Movements and Ideas* (New York: Scribner, 1978).

DeConde, Alexander: *Ethnicity, Race, and American Foreign Policy: A History* (Boston, MA: Northeastern University Press, 1992).

DeConde, Alexander: *Presidential Machismo: Executive Authority, Military Intervention, and Foreign Relations* (Boston, MA: Northeastern University Press, 2000).

DeGeorgio-Lutz, JoAnn A.: "The US–PLO Relationship: From Dialogue to the White House Lawn." In David W. Lesch (ed.) *The Middle East and the United States: A Historical and Political Reassessment* (Boulder, CO: Westview Press, 1999).

DeGroot, G. J.: *A Noble Cause? America and the Vietnam War* (Harlow: Longman, 2000).

Delpar, Helen: *The Enormous Vogue of Things Mexican: Cultural Relations between the United States and Mexico, 1920–1935* (Tuscaloosa: University of Alabama Press, 1992).

DeNovo, John: "The Culbertson Economic Mission and Anglo-American Tensions in the Middle East, 1944–1945." *Journal of American History* 63 (March 1977), 913–36.

DeRoche, Andrew: "Standing Firm for Principles: Jimmy Carter and Zimbabwe." *Diplomatic History* 23 (1999), 657–85.

DeRoche, Andrew: *Black, White, and Chrome: The United States and Zimbabwe, 1953–1998* (Trenton, NJ: Africa World Press, 2001).

Dickinson, Frederick R.: *War and National Reinvention: Japan in the Great War, 1914–1919* (Cambridge, MA: Harvard University Press, 1999).

Dietz, T.: *Republicans and Vietnam, 1961–1968* (Westport, CT: Greenwood Press, 1986).

DiLeo, D. L.: *George Ball, Vietnam, and the Rethinking of Containment* (Chapel Hill: University of North Carolina Press, 1991).

Dilks, David (ed.): *The Diaries of Sir Alexander Cadogan, 1938–1945* (New York: G. P. Putnam's Sons, 1972).

Dinerstein, Herbert: *The Making of a Missile Crisis: October 1962* (Baltimore, MD: Johns Hopkins University Press, 1976).

Dinges, John: *Our Man in Panama: The Shrewd Rise and Brutal Fall of Manuel Noriega* (New York: Times Books/Random House, 1991).

Dingman, Roger: "Atomic Diplomacy during the Korean War." *International Security* 13, 3 (winter 1988/1989), 61–89.

Dionne, E. J.: *Why Americans Hate Politics* (New York: Simon and Schuster, 1991).

Divine, Robert A.: *Second Chance: The Triumph of Internationalism during World War II* (New York: Atheneum, 1967).

Divine, Robert A.: *Roosevelt and World War II* (Baltimore, MD: Johns Hopkins University Press, 1969).

Divine, Robert: *Second Chance: The Triumph of Internationalism in America during World War II* (New York: Atheneum, 1971).

Divine, Robert A.: *Foreign Policy and US Presidential Elections, 1940–1972*, 2 vols. (New York: New Viewpoints, 1976).

Divine, Robert: *Eisenhower and the Cold War* (New York: Oxford University Press, 1981).

Divine, Robert A.: "Vietnam Reconsidered." *Diplomatic History* 12 (1988), 79–93.

Divine, Robert: *The Sputnik Challenge: Eisenhower's Response to the Soviet Satellite* (New York: Oxford University Press, 1993).

Dobbs, Charles M.: *The Unwanted Symbol: American Foreign Policy, the Cold War, and Korea, 1945–1950* (Kent, OH: Kent State University Press, 1981).

Dobrynin, A.: *In Confidence: Moscow's Ambassador to America's Six Cold War Presidents* (New York: Times Books, 1995).

Dobson, Alan P.: *US Wartime Aid to Britain, 1940–1946* (London: Croom Helm, 1986).

Dobson, Alan P.: *Anglo-American Relations in the Twentieth Century: Of Friendship, Conflict, and the Rise and Decline of Superpowers* (London: Routledge, 1995).

Dockrill, Saki: *Eisenhower's New-Look National Security Policy, 1953–61* (New York: St. Martin's Press, 1996).

Doenecke, Justus D. (ed.): *In Danger Undaunted: The Anti-Interventionist Movement of 1940–1941 as Revealed in the Papers of the America First Committee* (Stanford, CA: Hoover Institution Press, 1990).

Doenecke, Justus D.: "Reinhold Niebuhr and His Critics: The Interventionist Controversy in World War II." *Anglican and Episcopal History* 64 (December 1995), 459–81.

Doenecke, Justus D.: "Scribner's Commentator, 1939–1942." In Ronald Lora and William Henry Longton (eds.) *The Conservative Press in Twentieth-Century America* (Westport, CT: Greenwood Press, 1999).

Doenecke, Justus D.: "Weekly Foreign Letter, 1938–1942." In Ronald Lora and William Henry Longton (eds.) *The Conservative Press in Twentieth-Century America* (Westport, CT: Greenwood Press, 1999).

Doenecke, Justus D.: *Storm on the Horizon: The Challenge to American Intervention, 1939–1941* (Lanham, MD: Rowman and Littlefield, 2000).

Doenecke, Justus D.: "The United States and the European War, 1939–1941: A Historiographical Review." In Michael J. Hogan (ed.) *Paths to Power: The Historiography of American Foreign Relations to 1941* (New York: Cambridge University Press, 2000).

Doerries, R. R.: *Imperial Challenge: Ambassador Count Bernstorff and German–American Relations, 1908–1917* (Chapel Hill: University of North Carolina Press, 1989).

Dominguez, Jorge I,: *To Make a World Safe for Revolution: Cuba's Foreign Policy* (Cambridge, MA: Harvard University Press, 1989).

Domínguez, Jorge I.: "US–Cuban Relations: From the Cold War to the Colder War." *Journal of Inter-American Studies and World Affairs* 39 (fall 1997), 49–75.

Domínguez, Jorge I. (ed.): *The Future of Inter-American Relations* (New York: Routledge, 2000).

Domínguez, Jorge I., Robert A. Pastor, and R. DeLisle Worrell (eds.) *Democracy in the Caribbean: Political, Economic, and Social Perspectives* (Baltimore, MD: Johns Hopkins University Press, 1993).

Dommen, A. J.: *The Indochinese Experience of the French and the Americans: Nationalism and Communism in Cambodia, Laos, and Vietnam* (Bloomington: Indiana University Press, 2001).

Donnelly, Thomas, Margaret Roth, and Caleb Baker: *Operation Just Cause: The Storming of Panama* (New York: Lexington Books, 1991).

Dorman, William A. and Maneur Farhang: *The US Press and Iran: Foreign Policy and the Journalism of Deference* (Berkeley: University of California Press, 1987).

Dorsey, Kurk: "Scientists, Citizens, and Statesmen: US–Canadian Wildlife Protection Treaties in the Progressive Era." *Diplomatic History* 19 (1995), 407–30.

Dorsey, Kurk: *The Dawn of Conservation Diplomacy: US–Canadian Wildlife Protection Treaties in the Progressive Era* (Seattle: University of Washington Press, 1998).

Dosal, Paul J.: *Doing Business With the Dictators: A Political History of the United Fruit Company in Guatemala, 1899–1944* (Wilmington, DE: Scholarly Resources, 1993).

Douglas, Roy: *From War to Cold War, 1942–1948* (New York: St. Martin's Press, 1981).

Dower, John W.: *War Without Mercy: Race and Power in the Pacific War* (New York: Pantheon Books, 1986).

Dower, John W.: "Three Narratives of Our Humanity." In Edward T. Linenthal and Tom Engelhardt (eds.) *History Wars: The Enola Gay and Other Battles for the American Past* (New York: Henry Holt, 1996).

Dower, John W.: *Embracing Defeat: Japan in the Wake of World War II* (New York: W. W. Norton, 1999).

Downs, Jacques M.: *The Golden Ghetto: The American Commercial Community at Canton and the Shaping of American China Policy, 1784–1844* (Bethlehem: Lehigh University Press, 1997).

Doyle, M. W.: *Ways of War and Peace: Realism, Liberalism, and Socialism* (New York: W. W. Norton, 1997).

Doyle, Michael: *Empires* (Ithaca, NY: Cornell University Press, 1986).

Dozer, Donald M.: *Are We Good Neighbors? Three Decades of Inter-American Relations, 1930–1960* (Pittsburgh, PA: University of Pittsburgh Press, 1961).

Drachman, Edward R.: *United States Policy toward Vietnam, 1940–1945* (Rutherford, NJ: Fairleigh Dickinson University Press, 1970).

Drake, Paul W.: *The Money Doctor in the Andes: The Kemmerer Missions, 1923–1933* (Durham, NC: Duke University Press, 1989).

Draper, Theodore: *The Dominican Revolt: A Case Study in American Policy* (New York: Commentary, 1968).

Draper, Theodore: "Neoconservative History." *New York Review of Books* (January 16 and 24; and April 24, 1986).

Draper, Theodore: *A Present of Things Past: Selected Essays* (New York: Hill and Wang, 1990).

Druks, Herbert J.: *The US and Israel, 1945–1990* (New York: Speller, 1991).

Dudziak, Mary L.: *Cold War Civil Rights: Race and the Image of American Democracy* (Princeton, NJ: Princeton University Press, 2000).

Duiker, W. J.: *US Containment Policy and the Conflict in Indochina* (Stanford, CA: Stanford University Press, 1994).

Duiker, W. J.: *Sacred War: Nationalism and Revolution in a Divided Vietnam* (New York: McGraw-Hill, 1995).

Duiker, W. J.: *The Communist Road to Power in Vietnam*, 2nd edn. (Boulder, CO: Westview Press, 1996).

Duiker, W. J.: *Ho Chi Minh* (New York: Hyperion, 2000).

Dulles, Allen: *The Craft of Intelligence* (London: Weidenfeld and Nicolson, 1963).

Dunlay, Tom: *Kit Carson and the Indians* (Lincoln: University of Nebraska Press, 2000).

Dunn, Dennis J.: *Caught Between Roosevelt and Stalin: America's Ambassadors to Moscow* (Lexington: University of Kentucky Press, 1998).

Dunn, Timothy J.: *The Militarization of the US–Mexico Border, 1978–1992: Low-Intensity Conflict Doctrine Comes Home* (Austin: Center for Mexican American Studies, University of Texas, 1997).

Dunn, Walter S.: *Second Front Now 1943* (University Park: University of Alabama Press, 1980).

Dyer, Thomas G.: *Theodore Roosevelt and the Idea of Race* (Baton Rouge: Louisiana State University Press, 1980).

Dyson, Kenneth (ed.): *European Détente: Case Studies of the Politics of East–West Relations* (London: Frances Pinter, 1986).

Ealy, L. O.: *Yanquí Politics and the Isthmian Canal* (University Park: Pennsylvania State University Press, 1971).

Economy, Elizabeth and Michel Oksenberg: *China Joins the World: Progress and Prospects* (New York: Council on Foreign Relations, 1999).

Edmonds, Robin: *Soviet Foreign Policy: The Brezhnev Years* (Oxford: Oxford University Press, 1983).

Edmonds, Robin: *The Big Three: Churchill, Roosevelt, and Stalin in Peace and War* (New York: W. W. Norton, 1991).

Ehrman, John: *The Rise of Neoconservatism: Intellectuals and Foreign Affairs, 1945–1994* (New Haven, CT: Yale University Press, 1995).

Eichengreen, Barry: *Globalizing Capital: A History of the International Monetary System* (Princeton, NJ: Princeton University Press, 1996).

Eisenberg, Carolyn Woods: *Drawing the Line: The American Decision to Divide Germany, 1944–1949* (New York: Cambridge University Press, 1996).

Eisenberg, Laura Zittrain and Neil Caplan: *Negotiating Arab–Israeli Peace: Patterns, Problems, Possibilities* (Bloomington: Indiana University Press, 1998).

Eisenhower, David: *Eisenhower: At War, 1943–1945* (New York: Random House, 1986).

Eisenhower, Dwight D.: *The White House Years, Vol. 2: Mandate for Change, 1953–1956* (Garden City, NY: Doubleday, 1963).

Ellis, L. Ethan: *Republican Foreign Policy, 1921–1933* (New Brunswick, NJ: Rutgers University Press, 1968).

Ellsberg, D.: *Papers on the War* (New York: Simon and Schuster, 1972).

Emerson, William: "Franklin Roosevelt as Commander-in-Chief in World War II." *Military Affairs* 22 (winter 1958–9), 181–207.

"Empires and Intimacies: Lessons From (Post) Colonial Studies: A Round Table." *Journal of American History* 88 (December 2001), 829–93.

Endicott, Stephen L. and Edward Hagerman: *The United States and Biological Warfare: Secrets from the Early Cold War and Korea* (Bloomington: Indiana University Press, 1997).

Engstrand, Iris W.: Poniatowska, Elena: *Culture y Cultura: Consequences of the US–Mexican War, 1846–1848* (Los Angeles: Autry Museum of Western Heritage, 1998).

Ennes, James M.: *Assault on the Liberty: The True Story of the Israeli Attack on an American Intelligence Ship* (New York: Random House, 1979).

Epstein, Mark: "The Coolidge Conference of 1927: Disarmament in Disarray." In Brian J. C. McKercher (ed.) *Arms Limitation and Disarmament: Restraints on War, 1899–1939* (Westport, CT: Praeger, 1992).

Erb, Claude C.: "Prelude to Point Four: The Institute of Inter-American Affairs." *Diplomatic History* 9 (summer 1985), 249–69.

Erlichman, John: *Witness to Power* (New York: Simon and Schuster, 1982).

Espinoza, J. Manuel: *Inter-American Beginnings of US Cultural Diplomacy, 1936–1948* (Washington, DC: Bureau of Educational and Cultural Affairs, US Department of State, 1976).

Esposito, D. M.: *The Legacy of Woodrow Wilson: American War Aims in World War I* (Westport, CT: Praeger, 1996).

Esthus, Raymond: *Theodore Roosevelt and the International Rivalries* (Claremont, CA: Regina Books, 1970).

Eubank, Keith: *Summit at Teheran* (New York: William Morrow, 1985).

Everest, Allan S.: *The War of 1812 in the Champlain Valley* (Syracuse, NY: Syracuse University Press, 1981).

Everett, Dianna: *The Texas Cherokees: A People Between Two Fires, 1819–1840* (Norman: University of Oklahoma Press, 1990).

Ewell, Judith: *Venezuela and the United States: From Monroe's Hemisphere to Petroleum's Empire* (Athens, GA: University of Georgia Press, 1996).

Eykholt, Mark: "Aggression, Victimization, and Chinese Historiography of the Nanjing Massacre." In Joshua A. Fogel (ed.) *The Nanjing Massacre in History and Historiography* (Berkeley: University of California Press, 2000).

Fairbank, John K.: *Chinese–American Interactions: A Historical Summary* (Rahway, NJ: Rutgers University Press, 1975).

Fairbank, John K.: *Chinabound: A Fifty Year Memoir* (New York: Harper and Row, 1982).

Fairbank, John K.: *The United States and China*, 4th edn., enlarged (Cambridge, MA: Harvard University Press, 1983).

Falcoff, Mark: *Modern Chile, 1970–1989: A Critical History* (New Brunswick, NJ: Transaction Books, 1989).

Fanning, Richard W.: *Peace and Disarmament: Naval Rivalry and Arms Control, 1922–1933* (Lexington: University of Kentucky Press, 1995).

Faragher, John M. (ed.): *Rereading Frederick Jackson Turner: The Significance of the Frontier and Other Essays* (New York: Henry Holt, 1994).

Farber, D. R.: *Chicago '68* (Chicago, IL: University of Chicago Press, 1988).

Farnham, Barbara Rearden: *Roosevelt and the Munich Crisis: A Study of Political Decision-Making* (Princeton, NJ: Princeton University Press, 1997).

Farrar-Hockley, Anthony: *The British Part in the Korean War, Vol. 1: A Distant Obligation* (London: Her Majesty's Stationery Office, 1987).

Fehrenbach, T. R.: *This Kind of War: A Study in Unpreparedness* (New York: Macmillan, 1963).

Fein, Seth: "Everyday Forms of Transnational Collaboration: US Film Propaganda in Cold War Mexico." In Gilbert M. Joseph, Catherine C. LeGrand, and Ricardo D. Salvatore (eds.) *Close Encounters of Empire: Writing the Cultural History of US–Latin American Relations* (Durham, NC: Duke University Press, 1998).

Feis, Herbert: *Churchill, Roosevelt and Stalin: The War They Waged and the Peace They Sought* (Princeton, NJ: Princeton University Press, 1957).

Feis, Herbert: *Japan Subdued: The Atomic Bomb and the End of the War in the Far East* (Princeton, NJ: Princeton University Press, 1961).

Felton, Peter: "Yankee, Go Home and Take Me with You: Lyndon Johnson and the Dominican Republic." In H. W. Brands (ed.) *Beyond Vietnam: The Foreign Policies of Lyndon Johnson* (College Station: Texas A&M University Press, 1999).

Fernandez, Ronald: *The Disenchanted Island: Puerto Rico and the United States in the Twentieth Century* (Westport, CT: Praeger, 1992).

Ferrell, R. H.: *Woodrow Wilson and World War I, 1917–1921* (New York: Harper and Row, 1985).

Field, James A., Jr.: "American Imperialism: The Worst Chapter in Almost Any Book." *American Historical Review* 83 (1978), 665.

Field, James A., Jr.: "Novus Ordo Seclorum" [Feature review on Michael Hunt's *Ideology and US Foreign Policy*]. *Diplomatic History* 13 (winter 1989), 113–22.

Fieldhouse, D. K.: *The Colonial Empires: A Comparative Survey From the Eighteenth Century* (New York: Delacorte Press, 1965).

Fifer, J. Valerie: *United States Perceptions of Latin America, 1850–1930: A "New West" South of Capricorn?* (Manchester: Manchester University Press, 1991).

Figueroa, E. R.: *La Guerra De Corso De Mexico Durante La Invasion Norteamericana, 1845–1848* [The War In Mexico During the North American Invasion, 1845–1848] (Mexico City: Instituto Tecnologico Autonomo De Mexico, 1996).

Findlay, Eileen Suarez: *Imposing Decency: The Politics of Sexuality and Race in Puerto Rico 1870–1920* (Durham, NC, 1999).

Findley, Paul: *They Dare to Speak Out: People and Institutions Confront Israel's Lobby* (Chicago, IL: Lawrence Hill Books, 1985).

Findling, John E.: *Close Neighbors, Distant Friends: United States–Central American Relations* (New York: Greenwood Press, 1987).

Findling, John E.: *Dictionary of American Diplomatic History*, 2nd edn. New York: Greenwood Press, 1989).

Finer, Herman: *Dulles Over Suez: The Theory and Practice of His Diplomacy* (Chicago, IL: Quadrangle, 1964).

Fischer, Fritz: *Making Them Like Us: Peace Corps Volunteers in the 1960s* (Washington, DC: Smithsonian Institution Press, 1998).

Fitzgerald, F.: *Fire in the Lake: The Vietnamese and the Americans in Vietnam* (Boston, MA: Little, Brown, 1972).

Fitzgerald, Frances: *Way Out There in the Blue: Reagan, Star Wars, and the End of the Cold War* (New York: Simon and Schuster, 2000).

Fitzsimons, David M.: "Idealistic Internationalism in the Ideology of Early American Foreign Relations." *Diplomatic History* 19 (fall 1995), 569–82.

FitzSimons, Louise: *The Kennedy Doctrine* (New York: Random House, 1972).

Flanders, Stephen E.: *Dictionary of American Foreign Affairs* (New York: Macmillan, 1993).

Fleming, Denna F.: *The Cold War and Its Origins, 1917–1960*, 2 vols. (New York: Doubleday, 1961).

Floto, I.: *Colonel House in Paris: A Study of American Policy at the Paris Peace Conference 1919* (Princeton, NJ: Princeton University Press, 1980).

Flynt, Wayne and Gerald W. Berkley: *Taking Christianity to China: Alabama Missionaries in the Middle Kingdom, 1850–1950* (Tuscaloosa: University of Alabama Press, 1997).

Fogel, Joshua A. (ed.): *The Nanjing Massacre in History and Historiography* (Berkeley: University of California Press, 2000).

Fogelsong, David S.: *America's Secret War Against Bolshevism: US Intervention in the Russian Civil War, 1917–1920* (Chapel Hill: University of North Carolina Press, 1995).

Foglesong, David S.: "'Roots of Liberation': American Images of the Future of Russia in the Early Cold War, 1948–1953." *International History Review* 21 (March 1999), 57–79.

Foot, Rosemary: *The Wrong War: American Policy and the Dimensions of the Korean Conflict, 1950–1953* (Ithaca, NY: Cornell University Press, 1985).

Foot, Rosemary: "Nuclear Coercion and the Ending of the Korean Conflict." *International Security* 13, 3 (winter 1988/1989), 92–112.

Foot, Rosemary: *A Substitute for Victory: The Politics of Peacemaking at the Korean Armistice Talks* (Ithaca, NY: Cornell University Press, 1990).

Foot, Rosemary: "Making Known the Unknown War: Policy Analysis of the Korean Conflict Since the 1980s." In Michael J. Hogan (ed.) *America in the World: The Historiography of American Foreign Relations since 1941* (New York: Cambridge University Press, 1995).

Foot, Rosemary: *The Practice of Power: US Relations with China since 1949* (Oxford: Oxford University Press, 1995).

Foot, Rosemary: "Redefinitions: The Domestic Context and America's China Policy in the 1960s." In Robert S. Ross and Jiang Changbin (eds.) *Re-examining the Cold War: US–China Diplomacy, 1954–1973* (Cambridge, MA: Harvard University Press, 2001).

Forcey, Charles: *The Crossroads of Liberalism: Croly, Weyl, Lippmann, and the Progressive Era, 1900–1925* (New York: Oxford University Press, 1961).

Ford, Gerald R.: *A Time to Heal: The Autobiography of Gerald R. Ford* (New York: Harper and Row, 1979).

Foreign Relations of the United States, 1946, Vol. 6 (Washington, DC: US Government Printing Office, 1969).

Foreign Relations of the United States, Vol. 10: Cuba, 1961–1962 (Washington, DC: Government Printing Office, 1997).

Foreign Relations of the United States, Vol. 11, Cuban Missile Crisis and Aftermath, October 1962–December 1963 (Washington, DC: Government Printing Office, 1997).

Foreign Relations of the United States 1964–8, Vol. 30 (Washington, DC: US Government Printing Office, 1998).

Foster, Carrie A.: *The Women and the Warriors: The US Section of the Women's International League for Peace and Freedom, 1915–1946* (Syracuse, NY: Syracuse University Press, 1995).

Fox, Frank W.: *J. Reuben Clark: The Public Years* (Provo, UT: Brigham Young University Press, 1980).

Fox, William T. R. and Annette Baker Fox: *NATO and the Range of American Choice* (New York: Columbia University Press, 1967).

Foyle, D. C.: *Counting the Public In: Presidents, Public Opinion, and Foreign Policy* (New York: Columbia University Press, 1999).

Francis, Michael L.: *The Limits of Hegemony: United States Relations with Argentina and Chile during World War II* (Notre Dame, IN: University of Notre Dame Press, 1977).

Frank, Andre G.: *Capitalism and Underdevelopment in Latin America: Historical Studies of Chile and Brazil* (New York: Monthly Review Press, 1967).

Frank, Gary: *Struggle for Hegemony in South America: Argentina, Brazil, and the United States during the Second World War* (Miami, FL: University of Miami, 1979).

Frank, Gary: *Juan Perón v. Spruille Braden: The Story Behind the Blue Book* (Lanham, MD: University Press of America, 1980).

Fraser, Cary: "Crossing the Color Line in Little Rock: The Eisenhower Administration and the Dilemma of Race in US Foreign Policy." *Diplomatic History* 24 (2000), 233–64.

Fraser, David: *Alanbrooke* (New York: Atheneum, 1982).

Fraser, T. G.: *The USA and the Middle East Since World War II* (New York: St. Martin's Press, 1989).

Fredrickson, George: *Black Liberation: A Comparative History of Black Ideologies in the United States and South Africa* (New York: Oxford University Press, 1995).

Freedman, Lawrence: *US Intelligence and the Soviet Strategic Threat* (Boulder, CO: Westview Press, 1977).

Freedman, Lawrence: *Kennedy's Wars: Berlin, Cuba, Laos and Vietnam* (Oxford: Oxford University Press, 2000).

Freedman, Lawrence and Efraim Karsh: *The Gulf Conflict, 1990–1991: Diplomacy and War in the New World Order* (Princeton, NJ: Princeton University Press, 1993).

Freeland, R. M.: *The Truman Doctrine and the Origins of McCarthyism: Foreign Policy, Domestic Politics, and Internal Security, 1946–1948* (New York: Knopf, 1972).

Freiberger, Steven Z.: *Dawn Over Suez: The Rise of American Power in the Middle East, 1953–1957* (Chicago, IL: University of Chicago Press, 1992).

French, Hilary: *Partnership for the Planet: An Environmental Agenda for the United Nations* (Washington, DC: Worldwatch, 1995).

French, Howard W. "Old Files Contradict US Account of War." *International Herald Tribune* (April 2, 2002).

Friedberg, Aaron L.: *In the Shadow of the Garrison State: America's Anti-Statism and its Cold War Grand Strategy* (Princeton, NJ: Princeton University Press, 2000).

Friedberg, Aaron L.: "11 September and the Future of Sino-American Relations." *Survival* 44, 1 (spring 2002), 33–50.

Friedman, Edward: "Nuclear Blackmail and the End of the Korean War." *Modern China* 1, 1 (January 1975), 75–91.

Friedman, Thomas L.: *The Lexus and the Olive Tree* (New York: Farrar Straus Giroux, 2000).

Friend, Theodore: *Between Two Empires: The Ordeal of the Philippines, 1929–1946* (New Haven, CT: Yale University Press, 1965).

Froman, Michael B.: *The Development of the Idea of Détente: Coming to Terms* (New York: St. Martin's Press, 1991).

Fry, Joseph A.: "William McKinley and the Coming of the Spanish–American War: A Study of the Besmirching and Redemption of an Historical Image." *Diplomatic History* 3 (winter 1979), 77–98.

Fryd, Vivien Green: *Art and Empire: The Politics of Ethnicity in the United States Capitol, 1815–1860* (New Haven, CT: Yale University Press, 1992).

Fujiwara Ikira: "The Road to Pearl Harbor." In Hilary Conroy and Harry Wray (eds.) *Pearl Harbor Reexamined: Prologue to the Pacific War* (Honolulu: University of Hawaii Press, 1990).

Fukuyama, Francis: "The End of History?" *National Interest* (summer 1989).

Fukuyama, Francis: *The End of History and the Last Man* (New York: Free Press, 1992).

Fulbright, J. W.: *The Arrogance of Power* (New York: Vintage, 1967).

Funigiello, Philip J.: *American–Soviet Trade in the Cold War* (Chapel Hill: University of North Carolina Press, 1988).

Funk, Arthur L.: *The Politics of TORCH: The Allied Landings and the Algiers Putsch, 1942* (Lawrence: University of Kansas Press, 1974).

Fursenko, Alexsandr and Timothy Naftali: *"One Hell of a Gamble": Khrushchev, Castro, and Kennedy, 1958–1964* (New York: W. W. Norton, 1997).

Gaddis, John L.: *The United States and the Origins of the Cold War, 1941–1947* (New York: Columbia University Press, 1972).

Gaddis, John L.: *Strategies of Containment: A Critical Appraisal of Postwar American National Security Policy* (New York: Oxford University Press, 1982).

Gaddis, John L.: *The Long Peace: Inquiries Into the History of the Cold War* (Oxford: Oxford University Press, 1987).

Gaddis, John L.: "The American 'Wedge Strategy,' 1949–1958." In Harry Harding and Yuan Ming (eds.) *Sino-American Relations 1945–1955: A Joint Assessment of a Critical Decade* (Wilmington, DE: Scholarly Resources, 1989).

Gaddis, John L.: *The United States and the End of the Cold War* (New York: Oxford University Press, 1992).

Gaddis, John L.: *We Now Know: Rethinking Cold War History* (New York: Oxford University Press, 1997).

Gallicchio, Marc S.: *The Cold War Begins in Asia: American East Asian Policy and the Fall of the Japanese Empire* (New York: Columbia University Press, 1988).

Gallicchio, Marc S.: "Coloring the Nationalists: The African-American Construction of China in the Second World War." *International History Review* 20 (September 1998), 571–96.

Gallicchio, Marc S.: *The African American Encounter with Japan and China: Black Internationalism in Asia, 1895–1945* (Chapel Hill: University of North Carolina Press, 2000).

Gambone, Michael: *Eisenhower, Somoza and the Cold War in Nicaragua, 1953–1961* (Westport, CT: Praeger, 1997).

Ganguly, Sumit: *The Origins of War in South Asia: The Indo-Pakistani Conflicts since 1947*, 2nd revd. edn. (Boulder, CO: Westview Press, 1994).

Ganguly, Sumit: *The Crisis in Kashmir: Portents of War, Hopes of Peace* (New York: Cambridge University Press, 1997).

Ganguly, Sumit: "India: Policies, Past and Future." In Selig S. Harrison, Paul H. Kreisberg, and Dennis Kux (eds.) *India and Pakistan: The First Fifty Years* (New York: Cambridge University Press, 1999).

García, María C.: *Havana USA: Cuban Exiles and Cuban Americans in South Florida, 1959–1994* (Berkeley: University of California Press, 1996).

Gardner, Lloyd C.: *Economic Aspects of New Deal Diplomacy* (Madison: University of Wisconsin Press, 1964).

Gardner, Lloyd C.: *Architects of Illusion: Men and Idea in American Foreign Policy, 1941–1949* (Chicago, IL: Quadrangle, 1970).

Gardner, Lloyd C.: *Safe for Democracy: The Anglo-American Response to Revolution, 1913–1923* (New York: Oxford University Press, 1984).

Gardner, Lloyd C.: *Approaching Vietnam: From World War II Through Dienbienphu, 1941–1954* (New York: Norton, 1988).

Gardner, Lloyd: *Spheres of Influence: The Great Powers Partition Europe, from Munich to Yalta* (Chicago, IL: Ivan R. Dee, 1993).

Gardner, Lloyd C.: *Pay Any Price: Lyndon Johnson and the Wars for Vietnam* (Chicago, IL: Ivan R. Dee, 1995).

Gardner, Paul F.: *Shared Hopes, Separate Fears: Fifty Years of US–Indonesian Relations* (Boulder, CO: Westview Press, 1997).

Garfinkle, A. M.: *Telltale Hearts: The Origins and Impact of the Vietnam Antiwar Movement* (New York: St. Martin's Press, 1995).

Garrett, Banning N.: "The Strategic Basis of Learning in US Policy Toward China, 1948–1988." In George W. Breslauer and Philip Tetlock (eds.) *Learning in US and Soviet Foreign Policy* (Boulder, CO: Westview Press, 1991).

Garthoff, Raymond L.: *Détente and Confrontation: American–Soviet Relations from Nixon to Reagan* (Washington, DC: Brookings Institution, 1985).

Garthoff, Raymond L.: *Reflections on the Cuban Missile Crisis*, 2nd edn. (Washington, DC: Brookings Institution, 1989).

Garthoff, Raymond: *Détente and Confrontation: American–Soviet Relations from Nixon to Reagan* (Washington, DC: Brookings Institution, 1992).

Garthoff, Raymond L.: *Détente and Confrontation: American–Soviet Relations from Nixon to Reagan*, 2nd edn. (Washington, DC: Brookings Institution, 1994).

Garthoff, Raymond L.: *The Great Transition: American–Soviet Relations and the End of the Cold War* (Washington, DC: Brookings Institution, 1994).

Garthoff, Raymond L.: *A Journey Through the Cold War: A Memoir of Containment and Coexistence* (Washington, DC: Brookings Institution, 2001).

Garver, James W.: *China's Decision for Rapprochement With the United States, 1968–1971* (Boulder, CO: Westview Press, 1982).

Garver, John: "Little Chance." *Diplomatic History* 21, 1 (winter 1997), 87–94.

Garver, John: *The Sino-American Alliance: Nationalist China and American Cold War Strategy in Asia* (New York: M. E. Sharpe, 1997).

Garver, John: "Food for Thought: Reflections on Food Aid and the Idea of Another Lost Chance in Sino-American Relations." *Journal of American–East Asian Relations* 7, 1–2 (spring/summer 1998), 101–6.

Gasiorowski, Marc J.: "The 1953 Coup D'État." *International Journal of Middle East Studies* 19 (1987), 261–86.

Gatewood, William B., Jr.: *Black Americans and the White Man's Burden 1898–1903* (Urbana: University of Illinois Press, 1975).

Gause, F. Gregory: *Oil Monarchies: Domestic and Security Challenges in the Arab Gulf States* (New York: Council on Foreign Relations Press, 1994).

Gearson, John: *Harold Macmillan and the Berlin Wall Crisis, 1958–1962: The Limits of Interest and Force* (London: Macmillan, 1998).

Gelb, L. and R. K. Betts: *The Irony of Vietnam: The System Worked* (Washington, DC: Brookings Institution Press, 1979).

Gellman, Irwin F.: *Roosevelt and Batista: Good Neighbor Diplomacy in Cuba* (Albuquerque: University of New Mexico Press, 1973).

Gellman, Irwin F.: *Good Neighbor Diplomacy: United States Policies in Latin America, 1933–1945* (Baltimore, MD: Johns Hopkins University Press, 1979).

Gellman, Irwin F.: *Secret Affairs: Franklin Roosevelt, Cordell Hull, and Sumner Welles* (Baltimore, MD: Johns Hopkins University Press, 1995).

Gelman, Harry: *The Brezhnev Politburo and the Decline of Détente* (Ithaca, NY: Cornell University Press, 1984).

Gendzier, Irene E.: *Notes from the Minefield: United States Intervention, Lebanon and the Middle East, 1945–1958* (New York: Columbia University Press, 1996).

George, Alexander L.: *The Chinese Communist Army in Action: The Korean War and Its Aftermath* (New York: Columbia University Press, 1967).

Georgi-Findlay, Brigitte: *The Frontiers of Women's Writing: Women's Narratives and the Rhetoric of Westward Expansionism* (Tucson: University of Arizona Press, 1996).

Gerges, Fawaz A.: *America and Political Islam: Clash of Cultures or Clash of Interests?* (Cambridge: Cambridge University Press, 1999).

Gerges, Fawaz A.: "The 1967 Arab–Israeli War: US Actions and Arab Perceptions." In David W. Lesch (ed.) *The Middle East and the United States: A Historical and Political Reassessment* (Boulder, CO: Westview Press, 1999).

Ghabra, Shafeeq: "Kuwait and the United States: The Reluctant Ally and US Policy Toward the Gulf." In David W. Lesch (ed.) *The Middle East and the United States: A Historical and Political Reassessment* (Boulder, CO: Westview Press, 1999).

Giangreco, D. M.: "Casualty Projections for the US Invasion of Japan, 1945–1946: Planning and Policy Implications." *Journal of Military History* 61 (July 1997), 521–81.

Giauque, Jeffrey Glen: *Grand Designs and Visions of Unity: The Atlanatic Powers and the Reorganization of Western Europe, 1955–1963* (Chapel Hill: University of North Carolina Press, 2002).

Gibbons, W. C.: *The US Government and the Vietnam War: Executive and Legislative Roles and Relationships*, 4 vols. (Princeton, NJ: Princeton University Press, 1986–95).

Gibbs, David: *The Political Economy of Third World Intervention: Mines, Money, and US Policy in the Congo Crisis* (Chicago, IL: University of Chicago Press, 1991).

Gibson, J. W.: *The Perfect War: The War We Couldn't Lose and How We Did* (New York: Vintage, 1986).

Gienow-Hecht, Jessica: *Transmission Impossible: American Journalism as Cultural Diplomacy in Postwar Germany 1945–1955* (Baton Rouge: Louisiana State University Press, 1999).

Giglio, James: *The Presidency of John F. Kennedy* (Lawrence: University of Kansas Press, 1991).

Gilbert, Felix: *To the Farewell Address: Ideas of Early American Foreign Policy* (Princeton, NJ: Princeton University Press, 1961).

Gilbert, M. J. and W. Head (eds.): *The Tet Offensive* (Westport, CT: Praeger, 1996).

Gilbert, Martin: *Auschwitz and the Allies* (New York: Holt, Rinehart and Winston, 1981).

Gilbert, Martin: *Winston S. Churchill, 7: Road to Victory, 1941–1945* (Boston, MA: Houghton Mifflin, 1986).

Gilboa, Eytan: *American Public Opinion toward Israel and the Arab–Israeli Conflict* (Lexington, MA: Heath, 1987).

Gilderhus, Mark T.: *Diplomacy and Revolution: US–Mexican Relations under Wilson and Carranza, 1913–1921* (Tucson: University of Arizona Press, 1977).

Gilderhus, Mark T.: *Pan American Visions: Woodrow Wilson in Latin America, 1913–1921* (Tucson: University of Arizona Press, 1986).

Gilderhus, Mark T.: "Founding Father: Samuel Flagg Bemis and the Study of US–Latin American Relations." *Diplomatic History* 21 (winter 1997), 1–13.

Gilderhus, Mark T.: *The Second Century: US–Latin American Relations Since 1889* (Wilmington, DE: Scholarly Resources, 2000).

Gitlin, Jay: "Private Diplomacy to Private Property: States, Tribes and Nations in the Early National Period." *Diplomatic History* 22 (winter 1998), 85–99.

Gittings, John: "Talks, Bombs and Germs – Another Look at the Korean War." *Journal of Contemporary Asia*, 5, 2 (1975), 205–17.

Giunta, Mary A. (ed.): *The Emerging Nation: A Documentary History of the Foreign Relations of the United States under the Articles of Confederation, 1780–1789*, 3 vols. (Washington, DC: Scholarly Resources, 1996).

Gleijeses, Piero: *The Dominican Crisis: The 1965 Constitutional Revolt and American Intervention*, trans. Lawrence Lipson (Baltimore, MD: Johns Hopkins University Press, 1979).

Gleijeses, Piero: *Shattered Hope: The Guatemalan Revolution and the United States, 1944–1954* (Princeton, NJ: Princeton University Press, 1991).

Gleijeses, Piero: "'Flee! The White Giants Are Coming!': The United States, the Mercenaries, and the Congo, 1964–65." *Diplomatic History* 18 (1994), 207–37.

Gleijeses, Piero: "Ships in the Night: The CIA, the White House, and the Bay of Pigs." *Journal of Latin American Studies* 27 (February 1995), 1–42.

Gleijeses, Piero: *Conflicting Missions: Havana, Washington, and Africa, 1959–1976* (Chapel Hill: University of North Carolina Press, 2002).

Goetzmann, William H.: *Exploration and Empire: The Explorer and the Scientist in the Winning of the American West* (New York: Knopf, 1966).

Goetzmann, William H.: *New Lands, New Men: America and the Second Great Age Of Discovery* (New York: Viking, 1986).

Golan, Matti: *The Secret Conversations of Henry Kissinger: Step-by-step Diplomacy in the Middle East*, trans. Ruth Geyra Stern and Sol Stern (New York: Quadrangle, 1976).

Goldman, P. et al.: *Quest for the Presidency: 1992* (College Station: Texas A&M Press, 1994).

Goldstein, Jonathan, Jerry Israel, and Hilary Conroy (eds.) *America Views China: American Images of China Then and Now* (Bethlehem, PA: Lehigh University Press, 1991).

Goncharov, Sergei N., John W. Lewis, and Litai Xue: *Uncertain Partners: Stalin, Mao and the Korean War* (Stanford, CA: Stanford University Press, 1993).

Goode, James F.: *The United States and Iran: In the Shadow of Musaddiq* (New York: St. Martin's Press, 1997).

Goodman, Allan E.: *The Lost Peace: America's Search for a Negotiated Settlement of the Vietnam War* (Stanford, CA: Hoover Institution Press, 1978).

Goodman, Allan E. (ed.): *Negotiating While Fighting: The Diary of Admiral C. Turner Joy at the Korean Armistice Conference* (Stanford, CA: Hoover Institution Press, 1978).

Goodman, David S. G. and Gerald Segal (eds.) *China Rising: Nationalism and Interdependence* (London: Routledge, 1997).

Gordon, David: *The United States and Africa: A Post-Cold War Perspective* (New York: Norton, 1998).

Gordon, Philip H.: *A Certain Idea of France: French Security Policy and the Gaullist Legacy.* Princeton Studies in International History and Politics (Princeton, NJ: Princeton University Press, 1993).

Gorodetsky, Gabriel: *Stafford Cripps' Mission to Moscow, 1940–1942* (Cambridge: Cambridge University Press, 1984).

Gosse, Van: *Where the Boys Are: Cuba, Cold War America and the Making of the New Left* (New York: Verso, 1993).

Gough, Terrence J.: "Soldiers, Businessmen, and US Industrial Mobilization Planning Between the Two Wars." *War and Society* 9 (May 1991), 68–98.

Gould, Lewis L.: *The Presidency of William McKinley* (Lawrence: Regents Press of Kansas, 1980).

Gould, Lewis L.: *The Presidency of Theodore Roosevelt* (Lawrence: University of Kansas Press, 1991).

Goulden, Joseph C.: *Korea: The Untold Story of the War* (New York: Times Books, 1982).

Graebner, Norman A.: *Empire on the Pacific: A Study in American Continental Expansion* (New York, 1955).

Graebner, Norman A.: *Ideas and Diplomacy: Readings in the Intellectual Tradition of American Foreign Policy* (New York: Oxford University Press, 1964).

Graebner, Norman A. (ed.): *Manifest Destiny* (Indianapolis, IN, 1968).

Graebner, Norman A.: "Isolationism and Antifederalism: The Ratification Debates." *Diplomatic History* 11 (fall 1987), 337–70.

Graebner, Norman A.: "Nomura in Washington: Conversations in Lieu of Diplomacy." In Hilary Conroy and Harry Wray (eds.) *Pearl Harbor Reexamined: Prologue to the Pacific War* (Honolulu: University of Hawaii Press, 1990).

Graff, Henry F.: (ed.): *American Imperialism and the Philippine Insurrection* (Boston, MA: Little, Brown, 1969).

Grasselli, Gabriella: *British and American Responses to the Soviet Invasion of Afghanistan* (Aldershot: Dartmouth, 1996).

Gray, John: *False Dawn: The Delusions of Global Capitalism* (New York: New Press, 1998).

Green, David: *The Containment of Latin America: A History of the Myths and Realities of the Good Neighbor Policy* (Chicago, IL: Quadrangle Books, 1971).

Green, Stephen F.: *Taking Sides: America's Secret Relations with a Militant Israel* (New York: Morrow, 1984).

Green, Stephen F.: *Living by the Sword: America and Israel in the Middle East, 1968–87* (Brattleboro, VT: Amana Books, 1988).

Greene, J. R.: *The Presidency of George Bush* (Lawrence: University of Kansas Press, 2000).

Greenfield, Kent Roberts: *The Historian and the Army* (New Brunswick, NJ: Rutgers University Press, 1954).

Greenfield, Kent Roberts (ed.): *Command Decisions* (Washington, DC: US Government Printing Office, 1960).

Greenfield, Kent Roberts: *American Strategy in World War II: A Reconsideration* (Baltimore, MD: Johns Hopkins University Press, 1963).

Greenstein, Fred I.: *The Hidden-Hand Presidency: Eisenhower as Leader* (New York: Basic Books, 1982).

Greenwood, Sean: *Britain and the Cold War, 1945–1991* (New York: St. Martin's Press, 2000).

Greider, William: *One World Ready or Not: The Manic Logic of Global Capitalism* (New York: Simon and Schuster, 1997).

Grimshaw, Patricia: *Paths Of Duty: American Missionary Wives in Nineteenth Century Hawaii* (Honolulu: University of Hawaii Press, 1989).

Griswold del Castillo, Richard: *The Treaty of Guadelupe-Hidalgo: A Legacy of Conflict* (Norman: University of Oklahoma Press, 1990).

Gromyko, Andrei: *Memories* (London: Hutchinson, 1989).

Grose, Peter: *Israel in the Mind of America* (New York: Knopf, 1983).

Grosser, Alfred: *French Foreign Policy Under de Gaulle*, trans. Lois Ames Pattison (Boston, MA: Little, Brown, 1967).

Grosser, Alfred: *The Western Alliance: European–American Relations since 1945*, trans. Michael Shaw (New York: Seabury Press, 1980).

Grosz, George: *Ein kleines Ja und ein grosses Nein* [1946], trans. Nora Hodges, *George Grosz: An Autobiography* (Berkeley: University of California Press, 1998).

Grow, Michael: *The Good Neighbor Policy and Authoritarianism in Paraguay: United States Economic Expansion and Great-Power Rivalry in Latin America during World War II* (Lawrence: University of Kansas Press, 1981).

Gupta, Karunakar: "How Did the Korean War Begin?" *China Quarterly* 52 (October–December 1972), 699–716.

Gutiérrez, Carlos M.: *The Dominican Republic: Rebellion and Repression* (New York: Monthly Review Press, 1972).

Haas, Michael: *Cambodia, Pol Pot, and the United States: The Faustian Pact* (New York: Praeger, 1991).

Hackworth, D. H. and J. Sherman: *About Face: The Odyssey of an American Soldier* (New York: Simon and Schuster, 1989).

Haddow, Robert H.: *Pavilions of Plenty: Exhibiting American Culture Abroad in the 1950s* (Washington, DC: Smithsonian Institution Press, 1997).

Haftendorn, Helga: *Security and Détente: Conflicting Priorities in German Foreign Policy* (New York: Praeger, 1985).

Haftendorn, Helga: *NATO and the Nuclear Revolution: A Crisis of Credibility, 1966–1967* (Oxford: Clarendon Press, 1996).

Hagan, Kenneth J.: *This People's Navy: The Making of American Sea Power* (New York: Free Press, 1991).

Hagedorn, Hermann: *Leonard Wood: A Biography* (New York: Kraus, 1969).

Hague, Harlan: *Thomas O. Larkin: A Life Of Patriotism and Profit in Old California* (Norman: University of Oklahoma Press, 1990).

Hahn, Peter L.: *The United States, Great Britain, and Egypt, 1945–1946: Strategy and Diplomacy in the Early Cold War* (Chapel Hill: University of North Carolina Press, 1991).

Haig, Alexander, Jr.: *Caveat: Realism, Reagan, and Foreign Policy* (New York: Macmillan, 1984).

Haines, Gerald K.: "Under the Eagle's Wing: The Franklin Roosevelt Administration Forges an American Hemisphere." *Diplomatic History* 1 (fall 1977), 373–88.

Haines, Gerald K.: *The Americanization of Brazil: A Study of US Cold War Diplomacy in the Third World, 1945–1954* (Wilmington, DE: Scholarly Resources, 1989).

Halberstam, David: *The Making of a Quagmire* (New York: Random House, 1964).

Halberstam, David: *The Best and the Brightest* (New York: Random House, 1972).

Halberstam, David: *War in a Time of Peace* (New York: Scribner, 2001).

Haldeman, H. R.: *The Haldeman Diaries: Inside the Nixon White House* (New York: Putnam's, 1994).

Haldeman, H. R. with Joseph Dimona: *The Ends of Power* (New York: Times Books, 1978).

Hall, Linda B.: *Oil, Banks, and Politics: The United States and Postrevolutionary Mexico, 1917–1924* (Austin: University of Texas Press, 1995).

Hall, Linda B. and Don M. Coerver: *Texas and the Mexican Revolution: A Study in State and National Border Policy, 1910–1920* (San Antonio, TX: Trinity University Press, 1984).

Hall, Linda B. and Don M. Coerver: *Revolution on the Border: The United States and Mexico, 1910–1920* (Albuquerque: University of New Mexico Press, 1988).

Hall, Michael R.: *Sugar and Power in the Dominican Republic: Eisenhower, Kennedy, and the Trujillos* (Westport, CT: Greenwood Press, 2000).

Halley, Laurence: *Ancient Affections: Ethnic Groups and Foreign Policy* (New York: Praeger, 1985).

Halliday, Jon and Bruce Cumings: *Korea: The Unknown War* (New York: Pantheon, 1988).

Hallin, D. C: *The "Uncensored War": The Media and Vietnam* (New York: Oxford University Press, 1986).

Halperin, Maurice: *The Taming of Fidel Castro* (Berkeley: University of California Press, 1981).

Halperin, Morton H.: *Limited War in the Nuclear Age* (New York: Wiley, 1963).

Hamby, Alonzo L.: *Man of the People: A Life of Harry S. Truman* (New York: Oxford University Press, 1995).

Hamilton, Nigel: *JFK: Reckless Youth* (London: Arrow, 1992).

Hammack, James W., Jr.: *Kentucky and the Second American Revolution* (Lexington: University of Kentucky Press, 1976).

Hammer, E. J.: *A Death in November: America in Vietnam, 1963* (New York: Dutton, 1987).

Hammond, W. M.: *Reporting Vietnam: Media and Military at War* (Lawrence: University of Kansas Press, 1998).

Han, Vo Xuan: *Oil, the Persian Gulf, and the United States* (Westport, CT: Praeger, 1994).

Hanrieder, Wolfram F.: *Germany, America, Europe: Forty Years of German Foreign Policy* (New Haven, CT: Yale University Press, 1989).

Hanson, Simon: *Dollar Diplomacy Modern Style: Chapters in the Failure of the Alliance for Progress* (Washington, DC: Inter-American Affairs Press, 1970).

Hao Yufan and Zhai Zhihai: "China's Decision to Enter the Korean War: History Revisited." *China Quarterly* 121 (March 1990), 94–115.

Harbutt, Fraser J.: *The Iron Curtain: Churchill, America, and the Origins of the Cold War* (New York: Oxford University Press, 1986).

Harding, Harry: "From China with Disdain: New Trends in the Study of China." *Asian Survey* 22, 10 (October 1982).

Harding, Harry: *A Fragile Relationship: The United States and China since 1972* (Washington, DC: Brookings Institution, 1992).

Hardt, Michael and Antonio Negri: *Empire* (Cambridge, MA: Harvard University Press, 2000).

Hargreaves, Mary W. M.: *The Presidency of John Quincy Adams* (Lawrence: University of Kansas Press, 1985).

Harlow, Neal: *California Conquered: War and Peace on the Pacific, 1846–1850* (Berkeley: University of California Press, 1982).

Harper, John L.: *American Visions: Franklin D. Roosevelt, George F. Kennan, and Dean G. Acheson* (New York: Cambridge University Press, 1994).

Harris, Joseph: *African-American Reactions to War in Ethiopia, 1936–1941* (Baton Rouge: Louisiana State University Press, 1994).

Harris, Stuart and Gary Klintworth (eds.): *China as a Great Power: Myths, Realities and Challenges in the Asia–Pacific Region* (Sydney: Longman, 1995).

Harrison, J. P.: *The Endless War: Vietnam's Struggle for Independence* (New York: Columbia University Press, 1989).

Harrison, Michael: *The Reluctant Ally: France and Atlantic Security* (Baltimore, MD: Johns Hopkins University Press, 1981).

Harrison, Richard A.: "The United States and Great Britain: Presidential Diplomacy and Alternatives to Appeasement in the 1930s." In David F. Schmitz and Richard D. Challener (eds.) *Appeasement in Europe: A Reassessment of US Policies* (Westport, CT: Greenwood Press, 1990).

Hastings, Max: *The Korean War* (New York: Simon and Schuster, 1987).

Hatcher, P. L.: *The Suicide of an Elite: American Internationalists and Vietnam* (Stanford, CA: Stanford University Press, 1990).

Hathaway, Robert M.: *Ambiguous Partnership: Britain and America, 1944–1947* (New York: Columbia University Press, 1981).

Hatzenbueler, Ronald L. and Robert L. Ivie: *Congress Declares War: Rhetoric, Leadership, and Partisanship in the Early Republic* (Kent, OH: Kent State University Press, 1983).

He, Di and Gordon H. Chang: "The Absence of War in the US–China Confrontation over Quemoy-Matsu in 1954–1955: Contingency, Luck, Deterrence?" *American Historical Review* 98 (December 1993), 1500–24.

Heald, Morrell and Lawrence S. Kaplan: *Culture and Diplomacy: The American Experience* (Westport, CT: Greenwood Press, 1977).

Healy, David F.: *The United States in Cuba, 1898–1902: Generals, Politicians, and the Search for Policy* (Madison: University of Wisconsin Press, 1963).

Healy, David F.: *US Expansionism: The Imperialist Urge in the 1890s* (Madison, 1970).

Healy, David F.: *Drive to Hegemony: The United States in the Caribbean, 1898–1917* (Madison: University of Wisconsin Press, 1988).

Hearden, Patrick J.: "John Cudahy and the Pursuit of Peace." *Mid-America* (April–June 1986), 99–114.

Hearden, Patrick J.: *Roosevelt Confronts Hitler: America's Entry into World War II* (DeKalb: Northern Illinois University Press, 1987).

Hearden, Patrick J.: *The Tragedy of Vietnam* (New York: Harper Collins, 1991).

Heater, D.: *National Self-Determination: Woodrow Wilson and His Legacy* (New York: St. Martin's Press, 1994).

Heckscher, A.: *Woodrow Wilson: A Biography* (New York: Charles Scribner's Sons, 1991).

Hegerty, Devin T.: "Nuclear Deterrence in South Asia: The 1990 India–Pakistani Crisis." *International Security* 20 (winter 1995–6), 79–114.

Heinrichs, Waldo: *Threshold of War: Franklin D. Roosevelt and American Entry into World War II* (New York: Oxford University Press, 1988).

Heinrichs, Waldo: "Franklin D. Roosevelt and the Risks of War, 1939–1941." In Akira Iriye and Warren I. Cohen (eds.) *American, Chinese, and Japanese Perspectives on Wartime Asia, 1931–1949* (Wilmington, DE: Scholarly Resources, 1990).

Heinrichs, Waldo: "The United States Prepares for War." In George C. Chalou (ed.) *The Secrets War: The Office of Strategic Services in World War II* (Washington, DC: National Archives and Records Administration, 1992).

Heinrichs, Waldo: "Pearl Harbor in a Global Context." In Robert W. Love, Jr. (ed.) *Pearl Harbor Revisited* (New York: St. Martin's Press, 1995).

Heiss, Mary A.: *Empire and Nationhood: The United States, Great Britain, and Iranian Oil, 1950–1954* (New York: Columbia University Press, 1997).

Held, David and Anthony McGrew (eds.): *The Global Transformations Reader: An Introduction to the Globalization Debate* (Cambridge, MA: Blackwell, 2000).

Heller, Frances H. (ed.): *The Korean War: A 25-Year Perspective* (Lawrence: University of Kansas Press, 1977).

Hemmer, Christopher M.: *Which Lessons Matter? American Foreign Policy Decision Making in the Middle East, 1979–1987* (Albany: State University of New York Press, 2000).

Henggeler, Paul: *The Kennedy Persuasion: The Politics of Style Since JFK* (Chicago, IL: University of Chicago Press, 1995).

Henrikson, Alan: "The Map as an 'Idea': The Role of Cartographic Imagery During the Second World War." *The American Cartographer* 2 (April 1975), 19–53.

Herken, Greg: *Counsels of War* (New York: Alfred A. Knopf, 1985).

Herman, Sondra: *Eleven against War: Studies in American Internationalist Thought, 1898–1921* (Stanford, CA: Stanford University Press, 1969).

Hermes, Walter G.: *Truce Tent and Fighting Front* (Washington, DC: US Government Printing Office, 1966).

Hernández, José M.: *Cuba and the United States: Intervention and Militarism, 1868–1933* (Austin: University of Texas Press, 1993).

Herring, George C.: *Aid to Russia, 1941–1946: Strategy, Diplomacy, and the Origins of the Cold War* (New York: Columbia University Press, 1973).

Herring, George C.: *America's Longest War: The United States and Vietnam, 1950–1975* (New York: McGraw Hill, 1979, 1986, 1996).

Herring, George C.: "America and Vietnam: The Debate Continues." *American Historical Review* 92 (1987), 350–62.

Herring, George C.: *LBJ and Vietnam: A Different Kind of War* (Austin: University of Texas Press, 1994).

Hersh, Seymour M.: *The Price of Power: Kissinger in the Nixon White House* (New York: Summit Books, 1983).

Hersh, Seymour M.: *The Samson Option: Israel's Nuclear Arsenal and American Foreign Policy* (New York: Random House, 1991).

Hersh, Seymour M.: *The Dark Side of Camelot* (New York: Little, Brown, 1997).

Herwig, Holger H.: *Germany's Vision of Empire in Venezuela: 1871–1914* (Princeton, NJ: Princeton University Press, 1986).

Herzstein, Robert E.: *Roosevelt and Hitler: Prelude to War* (New York: Scribner's, 1989).

Herzstein, Robert E.: *Henry R. Luce: A Political Portrait of the Man Who Created the American Century* (New York: Scribner's, 1993).

Hess, Gary R.: *America Encounters India, 1941–1947* (Baltimore, MD: Johns Hopkins University Press, 1971).

Hess, Gary R.: "Franklin Roosevelt and Indochina." *Journal of American History* 59 (September 1972), 353–68.

Hess, Gary R.: "The Military Perspective on Strategy in Vietnam: Harry G. Summers's *On Strategy* and Bruce Palmer's *The 25 Year War.*" *Diplomatic History* 10 (1986), 91–106.

Hess, Gary R.: *The United States' Emergence as a Southeast Asian Power, 1940–1950* (New York: Columbia University Press, 1987).

Hess, Gary R.: "Historians and the Vietnam War." *Diplomatic History* 18 (1994), 239–64.

Hess, Gary R.: *Vietnam and the United States: Origins and Legacy of War*, revd. edn. (New York: Macmillan Library Reference, 1998).

Hickey, Donald R.: *The War of 1812: A Forgotten Conflict* (Urbana: University of Illinois Press, 1989).

Hickey, Michael: *The Korean War: The West Confronts Communism, 1950–1953* (London: John Murray, 1999).

Higgins, H.: *Vietnam*, 2nd revd. edn. (London: Heineman, 1982).

Higgins, Trumbull: *Truman and the Fall of MacArthur: A Precis on Limited War* (New York: Oxford University Press, 1960).

Higgins, Trumbull: *Soft Underbelly: The Anglo-American Controversy over the Italian Campaign* (New York: Macmillan, 1968).

Higgins, Trumbull: *The Perfect Failure: Kennedy, Eisenhower, and the CIA at the Bay of Pigs* (New York: W. W. Norton, 1987).

Hilderbrand, Robert C.: *Dumbarton Oaks: The Origins of the United Nations and the Search for Postwar Security* (Chapel Hill: University of North Carolina Press, 1990).

Hill, Peter P.: *French Perceptions of the Early American Republic, 1783–1793* (Philadelphia, PA: American Philosophical Society, 1988).

Hilsman, Roger: *To Move a Nation: The Politics of Foreign Policy in the Administration of John F. Kennedy* (Garden City, NY: Doubleday, 1967).

Hilsman, Roger: *George Bush vs. Saddam Hussein: Military Success! Political Failure?* (Novato, CA: Lyford Books, 1992).

Hilsman, Roger: *The Cuban Missile Crisis: The Struggle Over Policy* (Westport, CT: Praeger, 1996).

Hilton, Stanley E.: *Brazil and the Great Powers, 1930–1939: The Politics of Trade Rivalry* (Austin: University of Texas Press 1975).

Hilton, Stanley E.: *Hitler's Secret War in South America, 1939–1945: German Military Espionage and Allied Counterespionage in Brazil* (Baton Rouge: Louisiana State University Press, 1981).

Hilton, Stanley E.: "The United States, Brazil, and the Cold War, 1945–1969: End of the Special Relationship." *Journal of American History* 68 (December 1981), 599–624.

Hiro, Dilip: *The Longest War: The Iran–Iraq Military Conflict* (New York: Routledge, 1991).

Hiro, Dilip: *Desert Shield to Desert Storm: The Second Gulf War* (New York: Routledge, 1992).

Hirobe, Izumi: *Japanese Pride, American Prejudice: Modifying the Exclusion Clause of the 1924 Immigration Act* (Stanford, CA: Stanford University Press, 2001).

Hitchcock, Wilbur W.: "North Korea Jumps the Gun." *Current History* 20, 115 (March 20, 1951), 136–44.

Hixson, Walter L.: *Parting the Curtain: Propaganda, Culture, and the Cold War, 1945–1961* (New York: St. Martin's Press, 1997).

Hobson, John: *Imperialism* (London, 1902).

Hoff, Joan: *Nixon Reconsidered* (New York: Basic Books, 1994).

Hoffman, Elizabeth Cobbs: *All You Need Is Love: The Peace Corps and the Spirit of the 1960s* (Cambridge, MA: Harvard University Press, 1998).

Hoffman, Stanley: *Primacy or World Order: American Foreign Policy since the Cold War* (New York: McGraw-Hill, 1978).

Hofstadter, Richard: *Social Darwinism in American Thought* (Boston, MA: Beacon Press, 1955).

Hofstadter, Richard: "Cuba, the Philippines, and Manifest Destiny." In *The Paranoid Style in American Politics and Other Essays* (New York: Vintage Books, 1997).

Hogan, Michael J.: *The Panama Canal in American Politics: Domestic Advocacy and the Evolution of Policy* (Carbondale: Southern Illinois University Press, 1986).

Hogan, Michael J.: *The Marshall Plan: America, Britain, and the Reconstruction of Western Europe, 1947–1952* (New York: Cambridge University Press, 1987).

Hogan, Michael J. (ed.): *Hiroshima in History and Memory* (Cambridge: Cambridge University Press, 1996).

Hogan, Michael J.: *A Cross of Iron: Harry S. Truman and the Origins of the National Security State, 1945–1954* (New York: Cambridge University Press, 1998).

Hogan, Michael J.: "Partisan Politics and Foreign Policy in the American Century." In M. Hogan (ed.) *The Ambiguous Legacy: US Foreign Relations in the "American Century"* (Cambridge: Cambridge University Press, 1999).

Hogan, Michael J. (ed.): *The Ambiguous Legacy: US Foreign Relations in the "American Century"* (New York: Cambridge University Press, 2000).

Hogan, Michael J. and Thomas G. Paterson (eds.): *Explaining the History of American Foreign Relations* (New York: Cambridge University Press, 1991).

Hoganson, Kristin L.: *Fighting for American Manhood: How Gender Politics Provoked the Spanish–American and Philippine–American War* (New Haven, CT: Yale University Press, 1998).

Hoganson, Kristin: "Cosmopolitan Domesticity: Importing the American Dream, 1865–1920." *American Historical Review* 107 (February 2002), 55–83.

Holbrooke, Richard: *To End a War* (New York: Random House, 1998).

Hollis, Rosemary (ed.): *Oil and Regional Developments in the Gulf* (London: RIIA, 1998).

Holloway, David: *Stalin and the Bomb: The Soviet Union and Atomic Energy, 1939–1956* (New Haven, CT: Yale University Press, 1994).

Honegger, Barbara: *October Surprise* (New York: Tudor, 1989).

Hoopes, Roy (ed.): *The Peace Corps Experience* (New York: Clarkson N. Potter, 1968).

Hoopes, Townsend: *The Devil and John Foster Dulles* (Boston, MA: Little Brown, 1973).

Hopkins, A. G. (ed.): *Globalization in World History* (London: Pimlico, 2002).

Horelick, Arnold and Myron Rush: *Strategic Power and Soviet Foreign Policy* (Chicago, IL: University of Chicago Press, 1966).

Horsman, Reginald: *Race and Manifest Destiny: The Origins of American Racial Anglo-Saxonism* (Cambridge, MA: Harvard University Press, 1981).

Horsman, Reginald: "Feature Review; The War of 1812 Revisited." *Diplomatic History* 15 (winter 1991), 115–24.

"How has the United States Met its Major Challenges since 1945: A Symposium." *Commentary* 80 (November 1985), 25–8, 50–2, 56–60, 73–6.

Howard, Michael: *The Mediterranean Strategy in the Second World War* (New York: Praeger, 1968).

Howland, Nina Davis: "Ambassador John Gilbert Winant: Friend of an Embattled Britain, 1941–1946." PhD dissertation, University of Maryland, 1983).

Huggins, Martha K.: *Political Policing: The United States and Latin America* (Durham, NC: Duke University Press, 1998).

Humphreys, R. A.: *Latin America and the Second World War, 1938–1945*, 2 vols. (London: University of London, 1981–2).

Hunt, Michael H.: "The American Remission of the Boxer Indemnity: A Reappraisal." *Journal of Asian Studies* 31 (May 1972).

Hunt, Michael H.: *Frontier Defense and the Open Door: Manchuria in Chinese–American Relations, 1885–1911* (New Haven, CT: Yale University Press, 1973).

Hunt, Michael H.: *The Making of a Special Relationship: The United States and China to 1914* (New York: Columbia University Press, 1983).

Hunt, Michael H.: *Ideology and US Foreign Policy* (New Haven, CT: Yale University Press, 1987).

Hunt, Michael H.: "Beijing and the Korean Crisis, June 1950–June 1951." *Political Science Quarterly* 107, 3 (fall 1992), 453–78.

Hunt, Michael H.: *Ideology and US Foreign Policy* (New Haven, CT: Yale University Press, 1997).

Hunt, R. A.: *Pacification: The American Struggle for Vietnam's Hearts and Minds* (Boulder, CO: Westview Press, 1995).

Hunter, Jane: *The Gospel of Gentility: American Women Missionaries in Turn-of-the-Century China* (New Haven, CT: Yale University Press, 1984).

Huntington, Samuel: "The Clash of Civilizations?" *Foreign Affairs* (summer 1993).

Huntington, Samuel: *The Clash of Civilizations and the Remaking of World Order* (New York: Simon and Schuster, 1996).

Hurst, Steven: "Regionalism or Globalism? The Carter Administration and Vietnam." *Journal of Contemporary History* 32 (January 1997), 81–95.

Hurstfield, Julian G.: *America and the French Nation, 1939–1945* (Chapel Hill: University of North Carolina Press, 1986).

Hussain, Asaf: *The United States and Israel: Politics of a Special Relationship* (Islamabad: Quaid-i-Azam University Press, 1991).

Hutchison, William R.: *Errand to the World: American Protestant Thought and Foreign Missions* (Chicago, IL: University of Chicago Press, 1987).

Hutson, James H.: "Intellectual Foundations of Early American Diplomacy." *Diplomatic History* 1 (winter 1977), 1–19.

Hyam, Ronald: Empire and Sexuality: The British Experience (New York: St. Martin's Press, 1992).

Hyland, William: *Mortal Rivals: Superpower Relations from Nixon to Reagan* (New York: Random House, 1987).

Hyland, William: *Clinton's World: Remaking American Foreign Policy* (Westport, CT: Praeger, 1999).

Ignatieff, Michael: *Virtual War: Kosovo and Beyond* (New York: Henry Holt, 2000).

Ikenberry, John G.: *After Victory: Institutions, Strategic Restraint, and the Rebuilding of Order After Major Wars* (Princeton, NJ: Princeton University Press, 2001).

Ilgen, Thomas: *Autonomy and Interdependence: US–Western European Monetary and Trade Relations, 1958–1984* (Totowa, NJ: Rowman and Allanheld, 1985).

Immerman, Richard H.: *The CIA in Guatemala: The Foreign Policy of Intervention* (Austin: University of Texas Press, 1982).

Immerman, Richard H.: "Prologue: Perceptions by the United States of its Interests in Indochina." In L. S. Kaplan, D. Artaud, and M. R. Rubin (eds.) *Dien Bien Phu and the Crisis of Franco-American Relations, 1945–1955* (Wilmington, DE: Scholarly Resources, 1990).

Immerman, Richard H.: *John Foster Dulles: Piety, Pragmatism, and Power in US Foreign Policy* (Wilmington, DE: Scholarly Resources, 1999).

Inis, Claude L., Jr.: "The OAS, the UN, and the United States." In Richard A. Falk and Saul H. Mendlovitz (eds.) *Regional Politics and World Order* (San Francisco: W. H. Freeman, 1973).

Innis, Harold: *The Cod Fisheries: The History of an International Economy* (New Haven, CT: Yale University Press, 1940).

Iriye, Akira: *Across the Pacific: An Inner History of American–East Asian Relations* (New York: Harcourt, Brace, 1967).

Iriye, Akira: *Power and Culture: The Japanese–American War, 1941–1945* (Cambridge, MA: Harvard University Press, 1981).

Iriye, Akira: *After Imperialism: The Search for a New Order in the Far East, 1921–1931* (Chicago, IL: Imprint Publications, 1990).

Iriye, Akira: "Culture and International History." In Michael J. Hogan and Thomas G. Paterson (eds.) *Explaining the History of American Foreign Relations* (New York: Cambridge University Press, 1991).

Iriye, Akira: *The Globalizing of America, 1913–1945* (Cambridge: Cambridge University Press, 1993).

Iriye, Akira: "Cultural Diplomacy." In Bruce W. Jentleson and Thomas G. Paterson (eds.) *Encyclopedia of US Foreign Relations* (New York: Oxford University Press, 1997).

Iriye, Akira: *Cultural Internationalism and World Order* (Baltimore, MD: Johns Hopkins University Press, 1997).

Iriye, Akira: "A Century of NGOs." *Diplomatic History* 23 (summer 1999), 421–35.

Iriye, Akira: "Americanization of East Asia: Writings on Cultural Affairs Since 1900." In Warren Cohen (ed.) *New Frontiers in American–East Asian Relations.*

Iriye, Akira and Yonosuke Nagai (eds.): *The Origins of the Cold War in Asia* (New York: Columbia University Press, 1977).

Irvine, Reed J.: "American Trade with the Philippines." In Robert J. Barr (ed.) *American Trade With Asia and the Far East* (Milwaukee, WI: Marquette University Press, 1959).

Isaacs, A. R.: *Without Honor: Defeat in Vietnam and Cambodia* (Baltimore, MD: Johns Hopkins University Press, 1983).

Isaacs, A. R.: *Vietnam Shadows: The War, Its Ghosts, and Its Legacy* (Baltimore, MD: Johns Hopkins University Press, 1997).

Isaacs, Harold: *Scratches on Our Minds: American Views of China and India* (Armonk, NY: M. E. Sharpe, 1980).

Isaacson, Walter: *Kissinger: A Biography* (New York: Simon and Schuster, 1992).

Isaacson, Walter and Evan Thomas: *The Wise Men: Six Friends and the World They Made* (New York: Simon and Schuster, 1986).

Israel, Jerry: *Progressivism and the Open Door: America and China, 1905–1921* (Pittsburgh, PA: University of Pittsburgh Press, 1971).

Israelyan, Victor: *Inside the Kremlin During the Yom Kippur War* (University Park: Pennsylvania State University Press, 1995).

Jacobs, S.: "'Our System Demands the Supreme Being': The US Religious Revival and the 'Diem Experiment,' 1954–55." *Diplomatic History* 25 (2001), 589–624.

Jakub, Jay: *Spies and Saboteurs: Anglo-American Collaboration and Rivalry in Human Intelligence Collection and Special Operations, 1940–45* (New York: St. Martin's Press, 1999).

James, D. Clayton: *The Years of MacArthur*, 3 vols. (Boston, MA: Houghton Mifflin, 1970–85).

James, D. Clayton: *A Time for Giants: The Politics of the American High Command in World War II* (New York: Franklin Watts, 1987).

James, Harold: *International Monetary Cooperation Since Bretton Woods* (New York: Oxford University Press, 1996).

James, Robert R. (ed.): *Churchill Speaks: Winston S. Churchill in Peace and War, Collected Speeches, 1897–1963* (New York: Chelsea House, 1980).

Jařab, Josef: "The Story of the Jazz Section in Czechoslovakia." In Rob Kroes, Robert W. Rydell, and Doeko F. J. Bosscher (eds.) *Cultural Transmissions and Receptions: American Mass Culture in Europe* (Amsterdam: Vu University Press, 1993).

Jarvie, Ian: *Hollywood's Overseas Campaign: The North Atlantic Movie Trade, 1920–1950* (New York: Cambridge University Press, 1992).

Jeffreys-Jones, Rhodri: *Eagle Against Empire: American Opposition to European Imperialism* (Aix-en-Provence: Université de Provence, 1983).

Jeffreys-Jones, Rhodri: *The CIA and American Diplomacy* (New Haven, CT: Yale University Press, 1989).

Jeffreys-Jones, Rhodri: *Peace Now! American Society and the Ending of the Vietnam War* (New Haven, CT: Yale University Press, 1999).

Jenkins, Shirley: *American Economic Policy Toward the Philippines* (Stanford, CA: Stanford University Press, 1954).

Jensen, Poul: *The Garrote: The United States and Chile, 1970–1973*, 2 vols. (Aarhus, Denmark: Aarhus University Press, 1988).

Jentleson, Bruce W. and Thomas G. Peterson (eds.): *Encyclopedia of US Foreign Relations* (New York: Oxford University Press, 1997).

Jervis, Robert: "The Impact of the Korean War on the Cold War." *Journal of Conflict Resolution* 24, 4 (December 1980), 563–92.

Jervis, Robert: "Was the Cold War a Security Dilemma?" *Journal of Cold War Studies* 3 (2001), 36–60.

Jespersen, T. Christopher: "The Politics and Culture of Nonrecognition: The Carter Administration and Vietnam." *Journal of American–East Asian Relations* 4 (winter 1995), 397–412.

Jesperson, T. Christopher: *American Images of China 1931–1949* (Stanford, CA: Stanford University Press, 1996).

Johannsen, Robert H.: *To the Halls of the Montezumas: The Mexican War in the American Imagination* (New York: Oxford University Press, 1985).

Johnson, H.: *Sleepwalking Through History: America in the Reagan Years* (New York: Norton, 1992).

Johnson, Haynes B.: *The Bay of Pigs: The Leaders' Story of Brigade 2506* (New York: W. W. Norton, 1964).

Johnson, John H.: *Latin America in Caricature* (Austin: University of Texas Press, 1980).

Johnson, John J.: *A Hemisphere Apart: The Foundations of US Policy toward Latin America* (Baltimore, MD: Johns Hopkins University Press, 1990).

Johnson, Loch K.: *America's Secret Power: The CIA in a Democratic Society* (New York: Oxford University Press, 1989).

Johnson, R. H.: *Improbable Dangers: US Conceptions of Threat in the Cold War and After* (New York: St. Martin's Press, 1994).

Johnson, Robert D.: *Ernest Gruening and the American Dissenting Tradition* (Cambridge, MA: Harvard University Press, 1988).

Johnson, Robert D.: "The Transformation of Pan-Americanism." In Robert David Johnson (ed.) *On Cultural Ground: Essays in International History* (Chicago, IL: Imprint Publications, 1994).

Johnson, Robert D.: *The Peace Progressives and American Foreign Relations* (Cambridge, MA: Harvard University Press, 1995).

Johnson, Robert D.: *Ernest Gruening and the American Dissenting Tradition* (Cambridge, MA: Harvard University Press, 1998).

Johnson, U. Alexis: *The Right Hand of Power* (Englewood Cliffs, NJ: Prentice-Hall, 1984).

Johnston, Alastair, and Robert S. Ross (eds.): *Engaging China: The Management of an Emerging Power* (London: Routledge, 1999).

Jones, Bartlett: *Flawed Triumphs: Andy Young at the United Nations* (New York: University Press of America, 1996).

Jones, C. O.: *The Presidency in a Separated System* (Washington, DC: Brookings Institution, 1994).

Jones, Matthew: *Britain, the United States and the Mediterranean War, 1942–44* (New York: St. Martin's Press, 1996).

Joseph, Gilbert M.: *Revolution from Without: Yucatán, Mexico, and the United States, 1880–1924* (New York: Cambridge University Press, 1982).

Joseph, Gilbert M., Catherine C. Legrand, and Ricardo D. Salvatore (eds.) *Close Encounters of Empire: Writing the Cultural History of US–Latin American Relations* (Durham, NC: Duke University Press, 1998).

Joy, C. Turner: *How Communists Negotiate* (New York: Macmillan, 1955).

Joyce, Miriam: *Kuwait, 1945–1996: An Anglo-American Perspective* (London: Cass, 1998).

Kagan, Robert: *A Twilight Struggle: American Power and Nicaragua, 1977–1990* (New York: Free Press, 1996).

Kahin, G. M.: *Intervention: How America Became Involved in Vietnam* (New York: Knopf, 1986).

Kahin, G. M. and J. W. Lewis: *The United States in Vietnam* (New York: Delta, 1969).

Kahn, Herman: *On Thermonuclear War* (Princeton, NJ: Princeton University Press, 1960).

Kalb, Madeleine G.: *The Congo Cables: The Cold War in Africa – From Eisenhower to Kennedy* (New York: Macmillan, 1982).

Kalb, Marvin and Bernard Kalb: *Kissinger* (Boston, MA: Little, Brown, 1974).

Kaplan, Amy and Donald Pease (eds.) *Cultures of Imperialism* (Durham, NC: Duke University Press, 1993).

Kaplan, Lawrence S.: *Jefferson and France* (New Haven, CT: Yale University Press, 1967).

Kaplan, Lawrence S.: "Reflections on Jefferson as a Francophile." *South Atlantic Quarterly* 79 (winter 1980), 38–50.

Kaplan, Lawrence S.: *Entangling Alliances with None: American Foreign Policy in the Age of Jefferson* (Kent, OH: Kent State University Press, 1987).

Kaplan, Lawrence S.: "Jefferson and the Constitution: The View from Paris, 1786–89." *Diplomatic History* 11 (fall 1987), 321–35.

Kaplan, Lawrence S.: *NATO and the United States: The Enduring Alliance* (Boston, MA: Twayne, 1988).

Kaplan, Lawrence S., Denise Artaud, and Mark R. Rubin (eds.): *Dien Bien Phu and the Crisis of Franco-American Relations, 1954–1955* (Wilmington, DE: Scholarly Resources, 1989).

Kaplan, Robert D.: *The Coming Anarchy: Shattering the Dreams of the Post Cold War* (New York: Yale University Press, 2000).

Karnow, Stanley: *In Our Image: America's Empire in the Philippines* (New York: Random House, 1989).

Karnow, Stanley: *Vietnam: A History* (New York: Viking Press, 1992).

Karsten, Peter: *The Naval Aristocracy: The Golden Age of Annapolis and the Emergence of Modern American Navalism* (New York, 1972).

Kattenburg, P. M.: *The Vietnam Trauma in American Foreign Policy, 1945–75* (New Brunswick, NJ: Rutgers University Press, 1980).

Katz, Friedrich: *The Secret War in Mexico: Europe, the United States, and the Mexican Revolution* (Chicago, IL: University of Chicago Press, 1981).

Katz, Friedrich: *The Life and Times of Pancho Villa* (Stanford, CA: Stanford University Press, 1998).

Kaufman, Burton I.: *Trade and Aid: Eisenhower's Foreign Economic Policy, 1953–1961* (Baltimore, MD: Johns Hopkins University Press, 1982).

Kaufman, Burton I.: *The Korean War: Challenges in Crises, Credibility, and Command* (Philadelphia, PA: Temple University Press, 1986).

Kaufman, Burton I.: *The Presidency of James E. Carter, Jr.* (Lawrence: University of Kansas Press, 1993).

Kaufman, Burton I.: *The Arab Middle East and the United States: Inter-Arab Rivalry and Superpower Diplomacy* (New York: Twayne, 1996).

Kaufman, Menahem: "From Philanthropy to Commitment: The Six Day War and the United Jewish Appeal." *Journal of Israeli History* 15, 2 (1994), 161–91.

Kaufman, Robert G.: *Arms Control in the Pre-Nuclear Era: The United States and Naval Limitation Between the World Wars* (New York: Columbia University Press, 1990).

Kawamura, Noriko: *Turbulence in the Pacific: Japanese–US Relations during World War I* (New York: Praeger, 2000).

Kearns, D.: *Lyndon Johnson and the American Dream* (New York: Harper and Row, 1976).

Keefer, Edward C.: "President Dwight D. Eisenhower and the End of the Korean War." *Diplomatic History* 10, 3 (summer 1986), 267–89.

Keefer, Edward C.: "The Truman Administration and the South Korean Political Crisis of 1952: Democracy's Failure?" *Pacific Historical Review* 60, 2 (May 1991), 145–68.

Keiichiro Komatsu: *Origins of the Pacific War and the Importance of Magic* (New York: St. Martin's Press, 1999).

Kelleher, Catherine McArdle: *Germany and the Politics of Nuclear Weapons* (New York: Columbia University Press, 1975).

Kelly, J. B.: *Arabia, the Gulf and the West* (New York: Basic Books, 1980).

Kemp, Geoffrey: *Forever Enemies? American Policy and the Islamic Republic of Iran* (New York: Carnegie Endowment, 1994).

Kempe, Frederick: *Divorcing the Dictator: America's Bungled Affair with Noriega* (New York: G. P. Putnam's Sons, 1990).

Kennan, George F.: *American Diplomacy 1900–1950* (Chicago, IL: University of Chicago Press, 1950).

Kennan, George F.: *Memoirs 1925–1950* (Boston, MA: Little, Brown, 1967).

Kennedy, David M.: *Over Here: The First World War and American Society* (New York: Oxford University Press, 1980).

Kennedy, George C.: "The 1930 London Naval Conference and Anglo-American Maritime Strength, 1927–1930." In Brian J. C. McKercher (ed.) *Arms Limitation and Disarmament: Restraints on War, 1899–1939* (Westport, CT: Praeger, 1992).

Kennedy, Greg: "Depression and Security: Aspects Influencing the United States Navy During the Hoover Administration." *Diplomacy and Statecraft* 6 (July 1995), 342–72.

Kennedy, John F. and Richard M. Nixon: Transcript of First Joint Radio–Television Broadcast, September 26, 1960, available on John F. Kennedy Library web page at: http://www.jfklibrary.org/60–1st.htm

Kennedy, Paul: *The Rise and Fall of the Great Powers: Economic Change and Military Conflict from 1500 to 2000* (New York: Random House, 1987).

Kennedy, Robert: *Thirteen Days: A Memoir of the Cuban Missile Crisis* (New York: Norton, 1969).

Kern, Montague, Patricia Levering, and Ralph B. Levering: *The Kennedy Crisis: The Press, the Presidency and Foreign Policy* (Chapel Hill: University of North Carolina Press, 1983).

Kernell, S.: *Going Public: New Strategies of Presidential Leadership* (Washington, DC: CQ Press, 1993).

Keworkow, Wjatscheslav: *Der Geheime Kanal: Moskau, Der KGB And Die Bonner Ostpolitik* (Berlin: Rowohlt, 1995).

Khadduri, Majid and Edmund Ghareeb: *War in the Gulf, 1990–91: The Iraq–Kuwait Conflict and its Implications* (New York: Oxford University Press, 1997).

Khong, Yen Foon: *Analogies at War: Korea, Munich, Dien Bien Phu, and the Vietnam Decision of 1965* (Princeton, NJ: Princeton University Press, 1992).

Khrushchev, Nikita S.: *Khrushchev Remembers* (Boston, MA: Little, Brown, 1970).

Khrushchev, Nikita S.: *Khrushchev Remembers: The Last Testament*, trans. Strobe Talbott (Boston, MA: Little, Brown, 1974).

Khrushchev, Nikita S.: *Khrushchev Remembers: The Glasnost Tapes*, trans. Jerrold Schechter and Vyacheslav Luchkov (Boston, MA: Little, Brown, 1990).

Kidwell, Clara S.: *Choctaws and Missionaries in Mississippi, 1818–1918* (Norman: University of Oklahoma Press, 1995).

Kiernan, V. G.: *America: The New Imperialism* (London: Zed Books, 1978).

Killen, L.: *The Russian Bureau: A Case Study in Wilsonian Diplomacy* (Lexington: University of Kentucky Press, 1983).

Kim Chull Baum: *The Truth About the Korean War: Testimony 40 Years Later* (Seoul: Eulyoo, 1991).

Kim Chull Baum and James I. Matray (eds.): *Korea and the Cold War: Division, Destruction, and Disarmament* (Claremont, CA: Regina, 1993).

Kim Chum-gon: *The Korean War* (Seoul: Kwongmyong, 1973).

Kimball, Jeffrey P.: "The Stab-in-the-back Legend and the Vietnam War." *Armed Forces and Society* 14 (1988), 433–58.

Kimball, Jeffrey P.: "How Wars End: The Vietnam War." *Peace and Change* 20 (1995), 183–202.

Kimball, Jeffrey P.: *Nixon's Vietnam War* (Lawrence: University of Kansas Press, 1998).

Kimball, Warren F.: *The Most Unsordid Act: Lend-Lease, 1939–1941* (Baltimore, MD: Johns Hopkins University Press, 1969).

Kimball, Warren F.: *Swords or Plowshares?: The Morgenthau Plan for Defeated Nazi Germany, 1943–1946* (Philadelphia, PA: Lippincott, 1976).

Kimball, Warren F. (ed.): *Churchill and Roosevelt: The Complete Correspondence* (Princeton, NJ: Princeton University Press, 1984).

Kimball, Warren F.: *The Juggler: Franklin Roosevelt as Wartime Statesman* (Princeton, NJ: Princeton University Press, 1991).

Kimball, Warren F. (ed.): *America Unbound: World War II and the Making of a Superpower* (New York: St. Martin's Press, 1992).

Kimball, Warren F.: "Wheel Within a Wheel: Churchill, Roosevelt and the Special Relationship." In Robert Blake and William Roger Louis (eds.) *Churchill* (New York: W. W. Norton, 1993).

Kimball, Warren F.: *Forged in War: Roosevelt, Churchill and the Second World War* (New York: William Morrow, 1997).

Kimball, Warren F.: *Times Literary Supplement*, February 20, 1998, 24.

Kimball, Warren F.: "The Incredible Shrinking War: The Second World War, Not (just) the Origins of the Cold War." *Diplomatic History* 25 (summer 2001), 347–65.

Kingseed, Cole C.: *Eisenhower and the Suez Crisis of 1956* (Baton Rouge: Louisiana State University Press, 1995).

Kinnard, D.: *The War Managers* (Hanover, NH: University Press of New England, 1976).

Kinnard, D.: *The Certain Trumpet: Maxwell Taylor and the American Experience in Vietnam* (Washington, DC: Government Printing Office, 1991).

Kirkpatrick, Charles E.: *An Unknown Future and a Doubtful Present: Writing the Victory Plan in 1941* (Washington, DC: Center of Military History, United States Army, 1990).

Kirkpatrick, Jeane: "Dictatorships and Double Standards." *Commentary* (November 1979).

Kissinger, Henry A.: *Nuclear Weapons and Foreign Policy* (New York: Council on Foreign Relations/Harper, 1957).

Kissinger, Henry A.: *White House Years* (Boston, MA: Little, Brown, 1979).

Kissinger, Henry A.: *Years of Upheaval* (Boston, MA: Little, Brown, 1982).

Kissinger, Henry A.: *Diplomacy* (New York: Simon and Schuster, 1994).

Kissinger, Henry A.: *Years of Renewal* (New York: Simon and Schuster, 1999).

Kitchen, Martin: *British Policy Towards the Soviet Union During the Second World War* (New York: St. Martin's Press, 1986).

Kláren, Peter F. and Thomas J. Bossert (eds.): *Promise of Development: Theories of Change in Latin America* (Boulder, CO: Westview Press, 1986).

Klieman, Aaron S.: *Israel and the World After 40 Years* (Washington, DC: Pergamon–Brassey's, 1990).

Klinghoffer, Judith A.: *Vietnam, Jews, and the Middle East: Unintended Consequences* (New York: St. Martin's Press, 1999).

Knock, Thomas J.: *To End All Wars: Woodrow Wilson and the Quest for a New World Order* (New York: Oxford University Press, 1992).

Knox, Donald: *The Korean War: Pusan to Chosin* (New York: Harcourt, Brace, Jovanovich, 1985).

Knox, Donald: *The Korean War: Uncertain Victory* (New York: Harcourt, Brace, Jovanovich, 1988).

Kochavi, Arieh J.: *Prelude to Nuremberg: Allied War Crimes Policy and the Question of Punishment* (Chapel Hill: University of North Carolina Press, 1998).

Kochavi, Noam: "Kennedy, China, and the Tragedy of No Chance." *Journal of American–East Asian Relations* 7, 1–2 (spring/summer 1998), 107–16.

Kochavi, Noam: *A Conflict Perpetuated: China Policy During the Kennedy Years* (Westport, CT: Praeger, 2002).

Koebner, Richard and Helmut Dan Schmidt: *Imperialism: The Story and Significance of a Political Word, 1840–1960* (Cambridge: Cambridge University Press, 1965).

Kofas, Jon V.: *The Struggle for Legitimacy: Latin American Labor and the United States, 1930–1960* (Tempe: Arizona State University Press, 1992).

Kofsky, F.: *Harry S. Truman and the War Scare of 1948: A Successful Campaign to Deceive a Nation* (New York: St. Martin's Press, 1993).

Kohl, Wilfried L.: *French Nuclear Diplomacy* (Princeton, NJ: Princeton University Press, 1971).

Kohn, Richard H.: "History at Risk: The Case of the *Enola Gay.*" In Edward T. Linenthal and Tom Engelhardt (eds.) *History Wars: The Enola Gay and Other Battles for the American Past* (New York: Henry Holt, 1996).

Koistinen, Paul A. C.: *Planning War, Pursuing Peace: The Political Economy of American Warfare, 1920–1939* (Lawrence: University of Kansas Press, 1998).

Kolko, Gabriel: *The Politics of War: The World and United States Foreign Policy, 1943–1945* (New York: Random House, 1968).

Kolko, Gabriel: *The Roots of American Foreign Policy* (Boston, MA: Beacon Press, 1969).

Kolko, Gabriel: *Anatomy of a War* (New York: Pantheon Books, 1985).

Kolko, Gabriel: *Confronting the Third World: United States Foreign Policy, 1945–1980* (New York: Pantheon Books, 1988).

Kolko, Joyce and Gabriel Kolko: *The Limits of Power: The World and United States Foreign Policy, 1945–1954* (New York: Harper and Row, 1972).

Kolodney, Annette: *The Land Before Her: Fantasy and Experience of the American Frontiers, 1630–1860* (Chapel Hill: University of North Carolina Press, 1984).

Komer, R. W.: *Bureaucracy at War: US Performance in the Vietnam Conflict* (Boulder, CO: Westview Press, 1986).

Korn, David A.: *Stalemate: The War of Attrition and Great Power Diplomacy in the Middle East, 1967–1970* (Boulder, CO: Westview Press, 1992).

Kornbluh, Peter: *Bay of Pigs Declassified: The Secret CIA Report on the Invasion of Cuba* (New York: New Press, 1998).

Kornienko, G. M.: *Kholodnaia Voina [The Cold War]* (Moscow: Mezhdunar Otnosheniia, 1995).

Kovrig, Bennet: *Of Walls and Bridges: The United States and Eastern Europe* (New York: New York University Press, 1991).

Krebs, Ronald R.: *Dueling Visions: US Strategy Toward Eastern Europe under Eisenhower* (College Station: Texas A&M University Press, 2001).

Krenn, Michael L.: *United States Policy toward Economic Nationalism in Latin America, 1917–1929* (Wilmington, DE: Scholarly Resources, 1990).

Krenn, Michael L.: *The Chains of Interdependence: US Policy Toward Central America, 1945–1954* (Armonk, NY: Sharpe, 1996).

Krenn, Michael L.: *Black Diplomacy: African Americans and the State Department, 1945–1969* (Armonk, NY: M. E. Sharpe, 1999).

Krepinevich, A. F., Jr.: *The Army and Vietnam* (Baltimore, MD: Johns Hopkins University Press, 1986).

Kroes, Rob: *If You've Seen One, You've Seen the Mall: Europeans and American Mass Culture* (Urbana: University of Illinois Press, 1996).

Kroes, Rob, Robert W. Rydell, and Doeko F. J. Bosscher (eds.): *Cultural Transmissions and Receptions: American Mass Culture in Europe* (Amsterdam: Vu University Press, 1993).

Kuehl, Warren F. and Lynne K. Dunn: *Keeping the Covenant: American Internationalists and the League of Nations, 1920–1939* (Kent, OH: Kent State University Press, 1997).

Kugler, Richard: *Commitment to Purpose: How Alliance Partnership Won the Cold War* (Santa Monica, CA: Rand Corporation Study, 1994).

Kuisel, Richard: *Seducing the French: The Dilemma of Americanization* (Berkeley: University of California Press, 1993).

Kuisel, Richard: "Americanization for Historians." *Diplomatic History* 24 (summer 2000), 509–15.

Kunz, Diane B.: *The Economic Diplomacy of the Suez Crisis* (Chapel Hill: University of North Carolina Press, 1991).

Kunz, Diane B. (ed.): *The Diplomacy of a Crucial Decade: American Foreign Relations During the 1960s* (New York: Columbia University Press, 1994).

Kunz, Diane B.: *Butter and Guns: America's Cold War Economic Diplomacy* (New York: Free Press, 1997).

Kurzman, Dan: *Santo Domingo: Revolt of the Damned* (New York: Putnam, 1965).

Kusnitz, Leonard: *Public Opinion and Foreign Policy: America's China Policy, 1949–1979* (Westport, CT: Greenwood Press, 1984).

Kux, Dennis: *India and the United States: Estranged Democracies, 1941–1991* (Washington, DC: National Defense University Press, 1993).

Kux, Dennis: *The United States and Pakistan, 1947–2000: Disenchanted Allies* (New York: Cambridge University Press, 2001).

Lacouture, Jean: *De Gaulle: The Rebel, 1890–1944*, trans. Patrick O'Brian (New York: W. W. Norton, 1990).

Lacouture, Jean: *De Gaulle: The Ruler 1945–70* (New York: W. W. Norton, 1991).

LaFeber, Walter: *The New Empire: An Interpretation of American Expansion 1860–1898* (Ithaca, NY: Cornell University Press, 1963).

LaFeber, Walter: "Roosevelt, Churchill, and Indochina, 1942–1945." *American Historical Review* 80 (December 1975), 1277–95.

LaFeber, Walter: *Inevitable Revolutions: The United States in Central America* (New York: W. W. Norton, 1983).

LaFeber, Walter: *The Panama Canal: The Crisis in Historical Perspective*, updated edn. (New York: Oxford University Press, 1989).

LaFeber, Walter: *The American Search for Opportunity, 1865–1913*. Vol. 2 in *The Cambridge History of American Foreign Relations* (New York: Cambridge University Press, 1993).

LaFeber, Walter: *America, Russia, and the Cold War, 1945–92*, 7th edn. (New York: McGraw-Hill, 1993).

LaFeber, Walter: *Inevitable Revolutions: The United States in Central America*, 2nd edn. (New York: W. W. Norton, 1993).

LaFeber, Walter: "The World and the United States." *American Historical Review* 100 (October 1995), 1015–33.

LaFeber, Walter: *The Clash: US–Japanese Relations Throughout History* (New York: Norton, 1997).

LaFeber, Walter: *Michael Jordan and the New Global Capitalism* (New York: W.W. Norton, 1999).

Lampton, David M.: "America's China Policy in the Age of the Finance Minister: Clinton ends Linkage." *China Quarterly* 139 (September 1994).

Lampton, David M.: *Same Bed, Different Dreams: Managing US–China Relations, 1989–2000* (Berkeley: University of California Press, 2001).

Landes, David S.: "The Nature of Economic Imperialism." In Kenneth E. Boulding and Tapan Muskerjee (eds.) *Economic Imperialism: A Book of Readings* (Ann Arbor: University of Michigan Press, 1972).

Landry, Donna and Gerald MacLean (eds.) *The Spivak Reader* (New York: Routledge, 1996).

Lane, Ann and Howard Temperly (eds.): *The Rise and Fall of the Grand Alliance, 1941–1945* (New York: St. Martin's Press, 1995).

Lane, Jack C.: *Armed Progressive: General Leonard Wood.*

Langer, William L.: *The Diplomacy of Imperialism*, 2nd edn. (New York: Knopf, 1972).

Langguth, A. J.: *Our Vietnam: The War, 1954–1975* (New York: Simon and Schuster, 2000).

Langley, Lester D.: *The Banana Wars: An Inner History of American Empire, 1900–1934* (Lexington: University of Kentucky Press, 1983).

Langley, Lester D.: *America and the Americas: The United States in the Western Hemisphere* (Athens, GA: University of Georgia Press, 1989).

Langley, Lester D.: *The United States and the Caribbean in the Twentieth Century* (Athens: University of Georgia Press, 1992).

Langley, Lester D. and Thomas Schoonover: *The Banana Men: American Mercenaries and Entrepreneurs in Central America, 1880–1930* (Lexington: University of Kentucky Press, 1995).

Laqueur, Walter: *The Terrible Secret: Suppression of the Truth About Hitler's "Final Solution"* (Boston, MA: Little, Brown, 1980).

Larrabee, Eric: *Commander in Chief: Franklin D. Roosevelt, His Lieutenants, and Their War* (New York: Harper and Row, 1987).

Lasch, Christopher: *The American Liberals and the Russian Revolution* (New York: McGraw-Hill, 1972).

Latham, Michael E.: "Ideology, Social Science, and Destiny: Modernization and the Kennedy-Era Alliance for Progress." *Diplomatic History* 22 (spring 1998).

Latham, Michael E.: *Modernization as Ideology: American Social Science and "Nation-Building" in the Kennedy Era* (Chapel Hill: University of North Carolina Press, 2000).

Lawrence, Mark A.: *Constructing Vietnam: The United States, European Colonialism, and the Making of the Cold War in Indochina* (Berkeley: University of California Press, forthcoming.)

Layton, Thomas N.: *The Voyage of the Frolic: New England Merchants and the Opium Trade* (Palo Alto, CA: Stanford University Press, 1997).

Leacock, Ruth: *Requiem for Revolution: The United States and Brazil, 1961–1969* (Kent, OH: Kent State University Press, 1990).

Lebow, Richard N. and Janice Gross Stein: *We All Lost the Cold War* (Princeton, NJ: Princeton University Press, 1994).

Leckie, Robert: *Conflict: The History of the Korean War, 1950–1953* (New York: Putnam's, 1962).

Lee, Loyd E.: "We Have Just Begun to Write." *Diplomatic History* 25 (summer 2001), 367–81.

Lee, Steven H.: *Outposts of Empire: Korea, Vietnam and the Origins of the Cold War, 1949–1954* (Montreal: McGill-Queen's University Press, 1995).

Lee, Steven H.: *The Korean War* (New York: Longman, 2001).

Leech, Margaret: *In the Days of McKinley* (New York: Harper, 1959).

Leffler, Melvyn P.: "Expansionist Impulses and Domestic Constraints, 1921–32." In William H. Becker and Samuel F. Wells, Jr. (eds.) *Economics and World Power: An Assessment of American Diplomacy since 1789* (New York: Columbia University Press, 1984).

Leffler, Melvyn P.: "Adherents to Agreements: Yalta and the Experiences of the Early Cold War." *International Security* 11 (summer 1986), 88–123.

Leffler, Melvyn P.: *A Preponderance of Power: National Security, the Truman Administration, and the Cold War* (Stanford, CA: Stanford University Press, 1992).

Leffler, Melvyn P.: "New Approaches, Old Interpretations, and Prospective Reconfigurations." *Diplomatic History* 19 (1995), 173–96.

Leffler, Melvyn P.: "The Cold War: What Do 'We Now Know.'" *American Historical Review* 104 (1999), 501–24.

Lehman, Kenneth D.: *Bolivia and the United States: A Limited Partnership* (Athens, GA: University of Georgia Press, 1999).

Leifer, Michael: *ASEAN and the Security of South-East Asia* (London: Routledge, 1989).

Leigh, Michael: *Mobilizing Consent: Public Opinion and American Foreign Policy, 1937–1947* (Westport, CT: Greenwood Press, 1976).

Lemmon, Sarah M.: *Frustrated Patriots: North Carolina and the War of 1812* (Chapel Hill: University of North Carolina Press, 1973).

Lenczowski, George: *American Presidents and the Middle East* (Durham: Duke University Press, 1990).

LeoGrande, William M.: *Our Own Backyard: The United States in Central America, 1977–1992* (Chapel Hill: University of North Carolina Press, 1998).

Leonard, Thomas M.: *The United States and Central America, 1944–1949: Perceptions of Political Dynamics* (University Park: University of Alabama Press, 1984).

Leonard, Thomas M.: *Central America and the United States: The Search for Stability* (Athens, GA: University of Georgia Press, 1991).

Leonard, Thomas M.: "Central America and the United States: Overlooked Foreign Policy Objectives." *The Americas* 50 (July 1993), 1–30.

Lesch, David: *Syria and the United States: Eisenhower's Cold War in the Middle East* (Boulder, CO: Westview Press, 1993).

Leuchtenberg, William E.: "Progressivism and Imperialism: The Progressive Movement and American Foreign Policy, 1898–1916." *Mississippi Valley Historical Review* 39 (June 1952).

Levering, Ralph B.: *American Opinion and the Russian Alliance, 1939–1945* (Chapel Hill: University of North Carolina Press, 1976).

Levering, Ralph B. and Miriam Levering: *Citizen Action for Global Change: The Neptune Group and Law of the Sea* (Syracuse, NY: Syracuse University Press, 1999).

Levin, N. Gordon, Jr.: *Woodrow Wilson and World Politics: America's Response to War and Revolution* (New York: Oxford University Press, 1968).

Levine, Steven I.: "Sino-American Relations: Testing the Limits." In Samuel S. Kim (ed.) *China and the World: Chinese Foreign Relations in the Post-Cold War Era* (Boulder, CO: Westview Press, 1994).

Levy, D. W.: *The Debate over Vietnam* (Baltimore, MD: Johns Hopkins University Press, 1995).

Lewis, James E., Jr.: *John Quincy Adams: Policymaker for the Union* (Wilmington, DE: Scholarly Resources, 2001).

Lewy, G.: *America in Vietnam* (New York: Oxford University Press, 1978).

Limerick, Patricia N.: *The Legacy of Conquest: The Unbroken Past of the American West* (New York: W. W. Norton, 1987).

Limerick, Patricia N.: *Something in the Soil: Legacies and Reckonings in the New West* (New York: W. W. Norton, 2000).

Limerick, Patricia N.: "Dilemmas in Forgiveness: William Appleman Williams and Western American History." *Diplomatic History* 25 (2001), 293–300.

Limerick, Patricia N. and Clyde A. Milner: *Trails: Toward a New Western History* (Lawrence: University of Kansas Press, 1991).

Lind, M.: *Vietnam: The Necessary War* (New York: Free Press, 1999).

Linenthal, Edward T. and Tom Engelhardt (eds.): *History Wars: The Enola Gay and Other Battles for the American Past* (New York: Henry Holt, 1996).

Link, A. S.: *The Higher Realism of Woodrow Wilson and Other Essays* (Nashville, TN: Vanderbilt University Press, 1971).

Link, A. S.: *Woodrow Wilson: Revolution, War, and Peace* (Arlington Heights, IL: AHM Publishing, 1979).

Linn, Brian M.: *Guardian of Empire: The US Army and the Pacific, 1902–1940* (Chapel Hill: University of North Carolina Press, 1997).

Lipstadt, Deborah: *Beyond Belief: The American Press and the Coming of the Holocaust, 1933–1945* (New York: Free Press, 1985).

Liss, Sheldon B.: *The Canal: Aspects of United States Panamanian Relations* (Notre Dame, IN: University of Notre Dame Press, 1967).

Litoff, Judy B. and David C. Smith (eds.): *What Kind of World Do We Want? American Women Plan for Peace* (Wilmington, DE: Scholarly Resources, 2000).

Little, Douglas: "Antibolshevism and Appeasement: Great Britain, the United States, and the Spanish Civil War." In David F. Schmitz and Richard D. Challener (eds.) *Appeasement in Europe: A Reassessment of US Policies* (Westport, CT: Greenwood Press, 1990).

Little, Douglas: "Cold War and Covert Action: The United States and Syria, 1945–1958." *Middle East Journal* 44 (1990), 51–75.

Little, Douglas: "Influence Without Responsibility: American Statecraft and the Munich Conference." In Melvin Small and O. Feinstein (eds.) *Appeasing Fascism: Articles from the Wayne State University Conference on Munich After Fifty Years* (Lanham, MD: University Press of America, 1991).

Little, Douglas: "Choosing Sides: Lyndon Johnson and the Middle East." In Robert A. Divine (ed.) *The Johnson Years, Vol. 3: LBJ at Home and Abroad* (Lawrence: University of Kansas Press, 1994).

Little, Douglas: "A Puppet in Search of a Puppeteer? The United States, King Hussein, and Jordan, 1951–1970." *International History Review* 17 (1995), 512–44.

Little, Douglas: "His Finest Hour? Eisenhower, Lebanon, and the 1958 Middle East Crisis." *Diplomatic History* 20 (1996), 27–54.

Little, Douglas: "Nasser Delenda Est: Lyndon Johnson, the Arabs, and the 1967 Six-Day War." In H. W. Brands (ed.) *Beyond Vietnam: The Foreign Policies of Lyndon Johnson* (College Station: Texas A&M University Press, 1999).

Litwak, Robert S.: *Détente and the Nixon Doctrine: American Foreign Policy and the Pursuit of Stability, 1969–1976* (Cambridge: Cambridge University Press, 1984).

Litwak, Robert S.: *Rogue States and US Foreign Policy: Containment After the Cold War* (Washington, DC: Woodrow Wilson Center Press, 2000).

Liu Xiaoyuan: "Sino-American Diplomacy over Korea during World War II." *Journal of American–East Asian Relations* 1, 2 (summer 1992), 223–64.

Lockmiller, David: *Magoon in Cuba: A History of the Second Intervention, 1906–1909* (Chapel Hill: University of North Carolina Press, 1938).

Loewenheim, Francis L., Harold L. Langley, and Manfred Jonas (eds.) *Roosevelt and Churchill: The Secret Wartime Correspondence* (New York: Saturday Review Press/Dutton, 1975).

Logevall, Fredrik: *Choosing War: The Lost Chance for Peace and the Escalation of War in Vietnam* (Berkeley: University of California Press, 1999).

Lomperis, T. J.: *From People's War to People's Rule: Insurgency, Intervention, and the Lessons of Vietnam* (Chapel Hill: University of North Carolina Press, 1996).

Long, David F.: *Gold Braid and Foreign Relations: Diplomatic Activities of US Naval Officers, 1798–1883* (Annapolis, MD: Naval Institute Press, 1988).

Longley, Kyle: *The Sparrow and the Hawk: Costa Rica and the United States during the Rise of José Figueres* (Tuscaloosa: University of Alabama Press, 1997).

Longley, Kyle: *In the Eagle's Shadow: The United States and Latin America* (Wheeling, IL: Harlan Davidson, 2002).

Loth, Wilfried: *Overcoming the Cold War: A History of Détente, 1950–1991* (Basingstoke: Palgrave, 2002).

Louis, William R. (ed.): *Imperialism: The Robinson and Gallagher Controversy* (New York: New Viewpoints, 1976).

Louis, William R.: *Imperialism at Bay: The United States and the Decolonization of the British Empire, 1941–1945* (New York: Oxford University Press, 1978).

Louis, William R.: "Dulles, Suez, and the British." In Richard H. Immerman (ed.) *John Foster Dulles and the Diplomacy of the Cold War* (Princeton, NJ: Princeton University Press, 1990).

Louria, Margot: *Triumph and Downfall: America's Pursuit of Peace and Prosperity, 1921–1933* (Westport, CT: Greenwood Press, 2001).

Love, Jr., Robert W.: "FDR as Commander in Chief." In Robert W. Love, Jr. (ed.) *Pearl Harbor Revisited* (New York: St. Martin's Press, 1995).

Lowe, Peter: *Origins of the Korean War* (New York: Longman, 1986).

Lowenheim, Francis L., Harold Langley, and Manfred Jonas (eds.): *Roosevelt and Churchill: Their Secret Wartime Correspondence* (New York: Saturday Review Press/E. P. Dutton, 1975).

Lowenthal, Abraham: *Dominican Intervention* (Cambridge, MA: Harvard University Press, 1970).

Lowenthal, Abraham: *The Dominican Intervention* (Cambridge, MA: Harvard University Press, 1972).

Lowenthal, Abraham (ed.): *Exporting Democracy: The United States and Latin America* (Baltimore, MD: Johns Hopkins University Press, 1991).

Lowenthal, Mark M.: "INTREPID and the History of World War II." *Military Affairs* 41 (April 1977), 88–90.

Lower, Richard C.: *A Bloc of One: The Politics and Career of Hiram W. Johnson* (Stanford, CA: Stanford University Press, 1993).

Lowther, Kevin and C. Payne Lucas: *Keeping Kennedy's Promise: The Peace Corps: Unmet Hope of the New Frontier* (Boulder, CO: Westview Press, 1978).

Lucas, W. Scott: *Divided We Stand: Britain, the US and the Suez Crisis* (London: Hodder and Stoughton, 1991).

Lukas, Richard C.: *Eagles East: The Army Air Forces and the Soviet Union, 1941–1945* (Tallahassee: Florida State University Press, 1970).

Lukas, Richard C.: *The Strange Allies: The United States and Poland, 1941–1945* (Knoxville: University of Tennessee Press, 1978).

Lundestad, Geir: *The American Non-Policy towards Eastern Europe, 1943–1947: Universalism in an Area Not of Essential Interest to the United States* (New York: Humanities Press, 1975).

Lundestad, Geir: *The United States and the World, 1945–1989* (Washington, DC, 1989).

Lundestad, Geir: *The American "Empire" and Other Studies of US Foreign Policy in Contemporary Perspective* (New York: Oxford University Press, 1990).

Lundestad, Geir: *"Empire" by Integration: The United States and European Integration, 1945–1997* (New York: Oxford University Press, 1998).

Lynch, Cecelia: *Beyond Appeasement: Interpreting Interwar Peace Movements in World Politics* (Ithaca, NY: Cornell University Press, 1999).

Lynch, Grayston L.: *Decision for Disaster: Betrayal at the Bay of Pigs* (Washington, DC: Brassey's, 1998).

Lyon, Judson: "Informal Imperialism: The United States in Liberia, 1897–1912." *Diplomatic History* 5 (1981), 221–43.

Lyon, Peter: *Eisenhower: Portrait of a Hero* (Boston, MA: Little, Brown, 1974).

Lytle, Mark H.: *The Origins of the Iranian–American Alliance, 1941–1953* (New York: Holmes and Meier, 1987).

Lytle, Mark H.: "An Environmental Approach to American Diplomatic History." *Diplomatic History* 20 (1996), 279–300.

Lytle, Mark H.: "NGOs and the New Transnational Politics." *Diplomatic History* 25 (winter 2001), 121–8.

McAlister, Melani: *Epic Encounters: Culture, Media, and US Interests in the Middle East, 1945–2000* (Berkeley: University of California Press, 2001).

MacArthur, Douglas: *Reminiscences* (New York: McGraw Hill, 1964).

McAuliffe, Mary S. (ed.): *CIA Documents on the Cuban Missile Crisis, 1962* (Washington, DC: CIA, 1962).

McBeth, B. S.: *Juan Vicente Gómez and the Oil Companies in Venezuela, 1908–1935* (New York: Cambridge University Press, 1983).

McCagg, William O.: *Stalin Embattled, 1943–1948* (Detroit, MI: Wayne State University Press, 1978).

McCann, Frank D.: *The Brazilian–American Alliance, 1937–1945* (Princeton, NJ: Princeton University Press, 1973).

McClintock, Anne: *Imperial Leather: Race, Gender, and Sexuality in the Colonial Conquest* (New York: Routledge, 1994).

McCormack, Gavan: *Cold War/Hot War* (Sydney: Hale and Iremonger, 1983).

McCormick, T. J.: *America's Half-Century: United States Foreign Policy in the Cold War* (Baltimore, MD: Johns Hopkins University Press, 1989).

McCormick, Thomas: *The China Market: America's Quest for Informal Empire, 1893–1901* (Chicago, IL, 1967).

McCullough, David: *The Path Between the Seas: The Creation of the Panama Canal 1870–1914* (New York: Simon and Schuster, 1977).

McCullough, David: *Truman* (New York: Simon and Schuster, 1992).

McCune, George M. and Arthur L. Grey, Jr.: *Korea Today* (Cambridge, MA: Harvard University Press, 1950).

MacDonald, Callum A.: *Korea: The War Before Vietnam* (New York: Free Press, 1986).

MacDonald, Callum A.: *Britain and the Korean War* (Oxford: Blackwell, 1990).

MacDonald, Robert H.: *The Language of Empire: Myths and Metaphors of Popular Imperialism, 1880–1918* (Manchester: Manchester University Press, 1994).

MacDonnell, Francis: *Insidious Foes: The Axis Fifth Column and the American Home Front* (New York: Oxford University Press, 1995).

MacDougall, Walter A.: *Let the Sea Make a Noise: A History of the North Pacific from Magellan to MacArthur* (New York: Basic Books, 1993).

McDougall, W. A.: *Promised Land, Crusader State: The American Encounter with the World Since 1776* (Boston, MA: Houghton Mifflin, 1997).

McDougall, Walter: *The Heavens Can Wait: A Political History of the Space Age* (New York: Basic Books, 1985).

McFadden, D. W.: *Alternative Paths: Soviets and Americans, 1917–1920* (New York: Oxford University Press, 1993).

McGhee, George: *At the Creation of a New Germany: From Adenauer to Brandt, An Ambassador's Account* (New Haven, CT: Yale University Press, 1989).

McGibbon, Ian: *New Zealand and the Korean War* (New York: Oxford University Press, 1992).

McGlothen, Ronald L.: *Controlling the Waves: Dean Acheson and US Policy in East Asia* (New York: Norton, 1993).

McJimsey, George T.: *Harry Hopkins: Ally of the Poor and Defender of Democracy* (Cambridge, MA: Harvard University Press, 1987).

McKee, Delber L.: *Chinese Exclusion Versus the Open Door Policy 1900–1906* (Detroit, MI: Wayne State University Press, 1977).

McKercher, Brian J. C.: " 'Our Most Dangerous Enemy': Great Britain Pre-eminent in the 1930s." *International History Review* (November 1991), 565–98.

McKercher, Brian J. C.: "No Eternal Friends or Enemies: British Defence and the Problem of the United States, 1919–1939." *Canadian Journal of History/Annales Canadiennes d'Histoire* 28 (April 1993), 258–93.

McKercher, Brian J. C.: *Transition of Power: Britain's Loss of Global Pre-eminence to the United States, 1930–1945* (New York: Columbia University Press, 1999).

McKercher, Brian J. C.: "Reaching for the Brass Ring: The Recent Historiography of Interwar American Foreign Relations." In Michael J. Hogan (ed.) *Paths to Power: The Historiography of American Foreign Relations to 1941* (New York: Cambridge University Press, 2000).

McLean, David: "American Nationalism, the China Myth, and the Truman Doctrine: The Question of Accommodation with Peking, 1949–50." *Diplomatic History* 10 (winter 1986), 25–42.

MacLean, Elizabeth Kimball: *Joseph E. Davies: Envoy to the Soviets* (Westport, CT: Praeger, 1992).

McLoughlin, William G.: *Cherokees and Missionaries: 1789–1839* (New Haven, CT: Yale University Press, 1984).

McLoughlin, William G.: *Cherokee Renascence in the New Republic* (Princeton, NJ: Princeton University Press, 1986).

McLoughlin, William G.: *After the Trail of Tears: The Cherokees Struggle For Survival, 1839–1880* (Chapel Hill: University of North Carolina Press, 1993).

McMahon, Robert J.: *Colonialism and Cold War: The United States and the Struggle for Indonesian Independence, 1945–1949* (Ithaca, NY: Cornell University Press, 1981).

McMahon, Robert J.: "Eisenhower and Third World Nationalism: A Critique of the Revisionists." *Political Science Quarterly* 101 (Centennial Year 1986), 453–73.

McMahon, Robert J.: *The Cold War on the Periphery: The United States, India, and Pakistan* (New York: Columbia University Press, 1994).

McMahon, Robert J.: "The Cold War in Asia: The Elusive Synthesis." In Michael J. Hogan (ed.) *America in the World: The Historiography of American Foreign Relations since 1941* (New York: Cambridge University Press, 1995).

McMahon, Robert J.: "US–Vietnamese Relations: A Historigraphical Survey." In W. I. Cohen (ed.) *Pacific Passage: The Study of American–East Asian Relations on the Eve of the Twenty-First Century* (New York: Columbia University Press, 1996).

McMahon, Robert J.: *The Limits of Empire: The United States and Southeast Asia since World War II* (New York: Columbia University Press, 1999).

McMahon, Robert J.: "Contested Memory: The Vietnam War and American Society, 1975–2001." *Diplomatic History* 26 (2002), 159–84.

McMaster, H. R.: *Dereliction of Duty: Johnson, McNamara, the Joint Chiefs of Staff, and the Lies that Led to Vietnam* (New York: Harper Collins, 1997).

McNamara, R. S.: *In Retrospect: The Tragedy and Lessons of Vietnam* (New York: Times Books, 1995).

McNamara, R. S., Blight, J. G., and Brigham, R. K.: *Argument without End: In Search of Answers to the Vietnam Tragedy* (New York: Public Affairs, 1999).

McNeill, John: *Something New Under the Sun: An Environmental History of the Twentieth-Century World* (New York: W. W. Norton, 2000).

McNeill, William H.: *America, Britain and Russia: Their Cooperation and Conflict, 1941–1946* (New York: Oxford University Press, 1953).

McPoil, William D.: "The Development and Defense of Wake Island, 1934–1942." *Prologue* 23 (winter 1991), 360–6.

Madsen, Richard: *China and the American Dream: A Moral Inquiry* (Berkeley: University of California Press, 1995).

Maga, Timothy P.: *John F. Kennedy and the New Frontier Diplomacy, 1961–1963* (Malabar, FL: Krieger Publishing, 1994).

Mahl, Thomas E.: *Desperate Deception: British Covert Operations in the United States, 1939–44* (Washington, DC: Brassey's, 1998).

Maier, Charles: "Foreword." In Joshua A. Fogel (ed.) *The Nanjing Massacre in History and Historiography* (Berkeley: University of California Press, 2000).

Major, John: *Prize Possession: The United States and the Panama Canal 1903–1979* (New York: Cambridge University Press, 1993).

Malone, Dumas: *Jefferson the President: Second Term, 1805–1809*, vol. 5 in *Jefferson and His Time* (Boston, MA: Little, Brown, 1974).

Mann, James: *About Face: A History of America's Curious Relationship with China, From Nixon to Clinton* (New York: Knopf, 1998).

Mann, R.: *A Grand Delusion: America's Descent into Vietnam* (New York: Basic Books, 2001).

Mansour, Camille: *Beyond Alliance: Israel and US Foreign Policy*, trans. James A. Cohen (New York: Columbia University Press, 1994).

Mansourov, Alexandre Y.: "Stalin, Mao, Kim, and China's Decision to Enter the Korean War, September 16–October 15, 1950: New Evidence from the Russian Archives." *Cold War International History Project Bulletin*, Issues 6–7 (winter 1995/1996), 100–5.

Marcus, Harold: *The Politics of Empire: Ethiopia, Great Britain and the United States, 1941–1974* (Trenton, NJ: Red Sea Press, 1995).

Maresca, John J.: *To Helsinki: The Conference on Security and Cooperation in Europe 1973–1975* (Durham, NC: Duke University Press, 1985).

Mark, Edward: "American Policy toward Eastern Europe and the Origins of the Cold War, 1941–1946: An Alternative Interpretation." *Journal of American History* 68 (September 1981), 313–36.

Mark, Edward: "October or Thermidor? Interpretations of Stalinism and the Perception of Soviet Foreign Policy in the United States, 1927–1947." *American Historical Review* 94 (October 1989), 937–62.

Marks, Frederick W., III: *Velvet on Iron: The Diplomacy of Theodore Roosevelt* (Lincoln: University of Nebraska Press, 1979).

Marks, Frederick W., III: *Independence on Trial* (Wilmington, DE: Scholarly Resources, 1986).

Marks, Frederick W., III: *Wind over Sand: The Diplomacy of Franklin Roosevelt* (Athens, GA: University of Georgia Press, 1988).

Marks, Frederick W., III: "The CIA and Castillo Armas in Guatemala, 1954: New Clues to an Old Puzzle." *Diplomatic History* 14 (winter 1990), 67–86.

Marks, Frederick W., III: "Prelude to Pearl Harbor: The Diplomatic Dress Rehearsal." In Robert W. Love, Jr. (ed.) *Pearl Harbor Revisited* (New York: St. Martin's Press, 1995).

Marshall, Jonathan: *To Have and Have Not: Southeast Asian Raw Materials and the Origins of the Pacific War* (Berkeley: University of California Press, 1995).

Mart, Michelle: "Tough Guys and American Cold War Policy: Images of Israel, 1948–1960." *Diplomatic History* 20 (summer 1996), 357–80.

Martel, Leon: *Lend-Lease, Loans, and the Coming of the Cold War: A Study of the Implementation of Foreign Policy* (Boulder, CO: Westview Press, 1979).

Martin, John Barlow: *Overtaken by Events: The Dominican Crisis from the Fall of Trujillo to the Civil War* (New York: Doubleday, 1966).

Masaaki, Tanaka: *What Really Happened in Nanking: The Refutation of a Common Myth* (Tokyo: Sekai Shuppan, 2000).

Massie, Robert: *Loosing the Bonds: The United States and South Africa in the Apartheid Years* (New York: Doubleday, 1997).

Mastanduno, Michael: *Economic Containment: CoCom and the Politics of East–West Trade* (Ithaca, NY: Cornell University Press, 1992).

Mastny, Vojtech: *Russia's Road to the Cold War: Diplomacy, Wafare, and the Politics of Communism, 1941–1945* (New York: Columbia University Press, 1979).

Mastny, Vojtech: *The Cold War and Soviet Insecurity: The Stalin Years* (New York: Oxford University Press, 1996).

Masud-Piloto, Félix Roberto: *From Welcomed Exiles to Illegal Immigrants: Cuban Migration to the United States, 1959–1995* (Lanham, MD: Rowman and Littlefield, 1996).

Matloff, Maurice: "Franklin Delano Roosevelt as War Leader." In Harry L. Coles (ed.) *Total War and Cold War: Problems in Civilian Control of the Military* (Columbus: Ohio State University Press, 1962).

Matray, James I.: "Truman's Plan for Victory: National Self-Determination and the Thirty-Eighth Parallel Decision in Korea." *Journal of American History* 66, 2 (September 1979), 314–33.

Matray, James I.: *The Reluctant Crusade: American Foreign Policy in Korea, 1941–1950* (Honolulu: University of Hawaii Press, 1985).

Matray, James I.: "Dean Acheson's National Press Club Speech Reexamined." *Journal of Conflict Studies* 22, 1 (spring 2002).

Maurer, John H. Maurer: "Arms Control and the Washington Conference." In Eric Goldstein and John H. Maurer (eds.) *The Washington Conference, 1921–22: Naval Rivalry, East Asian Stability and the Road to Pearl Harbor* (Portland, OR: Frank Cass, 1994).

May, Elaine Tyler: *Homeward Bound: American Families in the Cold War Era* (New York: Basic Books, 1988).

May, Ernest: *American Imperialism: A Speculative Essay* (New York: Atheneum, 1968).

May, Ernest: *Imperial Democracy: The Emergence of the United States as Great Power* (New York: Harper Torchbooks, 1973).

May, Ernest R.: *"Lessons of the Past": The Use and Misuse of History in American Foreign Policy* (New York: Oxford University Press, 1973).

May, Ernest R.: "'The Bureaucratic Politics' Approach: US–Argentine Relations, 1942–1947." In Julio Cotler and Richard R. Fagan (eds.) *Latin America and the United States: The Changing Political Realities* (Stanford, CA: Stanford University Press, 1974).

May, Ernest: "The Alliance for Progress in Historical Perspective." In Akira Iriye (ed.) *Rethinking International Relations: Ernest R. May and the Study of Foreign Affairs* (Chicago, IL: Imprint Publications, 1998).

May, Ernest R. and Philip D. Zelikow (eds.): *The Kennedy Tapes: Inside the White House during the Cuban Missile Crisis* (Cambridge, MA: Belknap Press of Harvard University Press, 1997).

May, Glenn A.: *Social Engineering in the Philippines: The Aims, Execution, and Impact of American Colonial Policy, 1900–1913* (Westport, CT: Greenwood Press, 1980).

May, Glenn A.: "Why the United States Won the Philippine–American War, 1899–1902." *Pacific Historical Review* 52 (1983), 353–77.

May, Glenn A.: *Battle for Batangas: A Philippine Province at War* (New Haven, CT: Yale University Press, 1991).

May, Glenn A.: "The Unfathomable Other: Historical Studies of US–Philippine Relations." In Warren I. Cohen (ed.) *Pacific Passages: The Study of American–East Asian Relations on the Eve of the Twenty-First Century* (New York: Columbia University Press, 1996).

Mayer, Frank A.: *Adenauer and Kennedy: A Study in German–American Relations, 1961–1963* (New York: St. Martin's Press, 1996).

Mayers, David: *Cracking the Monolith: US Policy Against the Sino-Soviet Alliance, 1949–1955* (Baton Rouge: Louisiana State University Press, 1986).

Mayers, David: *George Kennan and the Dilemmas of US Foreign Policy* (New York: Oxford University Press, 1988).

Mayers, David: "Ambassador Joseph Davies Reconsidered." *Society for Historians of American Foreign Relations Newsletter* 23 (September 1992), 1–16.

Mayers, David: *The Ambassadors and America's Soviet Policy* (New York: Oxford University Press, 1995).

Meade, E. Grant: *American Military Government in Korea* (New York: King's Crown Press, 1951).

Mecham, J. Lloyd: *The United States and Inter-American Security, 1889–1960* (Austin: University of Texas Press, 1961).

Meinig, D. W.: *The Shaping of America: A Geographical Perspective on 500 Years of History, Vol. 2: Continental America, 1800–1867* (New Haven, CT: Yale University Press, 1993).

Meinig, D. W.: *The Shaping Of America: A Geographical Perspective on 500 Years of History, Vol. 3: Transcontinental America, 1850–1915* (New Haven, CT: Yale University Press, 1998).

Melanson, Richard A.: *Reconstructing Consensus: American Foreign Policy since the Vietnam War* (New York: St. Martin's Press, 1991).

Menges, Constantine: *Inside the National Security Council: The True Story of the Making and Unmaking of Reagan's Foreign Policy* (New York: Simon and Schuster, 1988).

Merk, Frederick: *Manifest Destiny and Mission in American History: A Reinterpretation* (New York: Knopf, 1963).

Merk, Frederick: *The Oregon Question: Essays in Anglo-American Diplomacy and Politics* (Cambridge, MA: Harvard University Press, 1967).

Merrill, Dennis: *Bread and the Ballot: The United States and India's Economic Development, 1947–1963* (Chapel Hill: University of North Carolina Press, 1990).

Merrill, Dennis: "Negotiating Cold War Paradise: US Tourism, Economic Planning, and Cultural Modernity in Twentieth-Century Puerto Rico." *Diplomatic History* 25 (spring 2001), 179–214.

Merrill, John: *Korea: The Peninsular Origins of the War* (Newark: University of Delaware Press, 1985).

Merry, Sally Engle: *Colonizing Hawaii: The Cultural Power of Law* (Princeton, NJ: Princeton University Press, 2000).

Meyer, Gail E.: *Egypt and the United States: The Formative Years* (Rutherford, NJ: Fairleigh Dickinson University Press, 1980).

Meyer, Lorenzo: *Mexico and the United States in the Oil Controversy, 1917–1942*, trans. Muriel Vasconcellos (Austin: University of Texas Press, 1972).

Middleton, Harry: *The Compact History of the Korean War* (New York: Hawthorne, 1965).

Miles, Rufus E., Jr.: "Hiroshima: The Strange Myth of Half a Million Lives Saved." *International Security* 10 (fall 1985), 121–40.

Military History Institute of Vietnam: *Victory in Vietnam: The Official History of the People's Army of Vietnam, 1954–1975*, trans. M. L. Pribbenow, foreword by W. J. Duiker (Lawrence: University of Kansas Press, 2002).

Miller, Aaron D.: *Search for Security: Saudi Arabian Oil and American Foreign Policy, 1939–1949* (Chapel Hill: University of North Carolina Press, 1980).

Miller, Angela: *The Empire of the Eye: Landscape Representation and American Cultural Politics, 1825–1875* (Ithaca, NY: Cornell University Press, 1993).

Miller, Edward S.: *War Plan Orange: The US Strategy to Defeat Japan, 1897–1945* (Annapolis, MD: Naval Institute Press, 1991).

Miller, John C.: *Crisis in Freedom: The Alien and Sedition Acts* (Boston, MA: Little, Brown, 1951).

Miller, John E.: *The United States and Italy, 1940–1950* (Chapel Hill: University of North Carolina Press, 1986).

Miller, Nicola: *Soviet Relations with Latin America, 1959–1987* (New York: Cambridge University Press, 1989).

Miller, Richard H. (ed.): *American Imperialism in 1898: The Quest for National Fulfillment* (New York: John Wiley and Sons, 1970).

Miller, Stuart C.: *"Benevolent Assimilation": The American Conquest of the Philippines, 1899–1903* (New Haven, CT: Yale University Press, 1982).

Millett, Allan R.: *The Politics of Intervention: The Military Occupation of Cuba 1906–1909* (Columbus: Ohio State University Press, 1968).

Miner, Steven M.: *Between Churchill and Stalin: The Soviet Union, Great Britain, and the Origins of the Grand Alliance* (Chapel Hill: University of North Carolina Press, 1988).

Minger, Ralph E.: *William Howard Taft and United States Foreign Policy: The Apprenticeship Years, 1900–1908* (Urbana: University of Illinois Press, 1975).

Ministry of Foreign Affairs, USSR: *Russia: Correspondence between the Chairman of the Council of Ministers of the USSR and the Presidents of the USA and the Prime Ministers of Great Britain during the Great Patriotic War of 1941–1945*, 2 vols. (Moscow: Foreign Languages Publishing House, 1957).

Minter, William: *King Solomon's Mines Revisited: Western Interests and the Burdened History of Southern Africa* (New York: Basic Books, 1986).

Miscamble, Wilson D.: *George Kennan and the Making of American Foreign Policy, 1947–1950* (Princeton, NJ: Princeton University Press, 1992).

Mitchell, Christopher (ed.): *Western Hemisphere Immigration and United States Foreign Policy* (University Park: Pennsylvania State University Press, 1992).

Mitchell, Nancy: *The Danger of Dreams: German and American Imperialism in Latin America* (Chapel Hill: University of North Carolina Press, 1999).

Mitrovich, Gregory: *Undermining the Kremlin: America's Strategy to Subvert the Soviet Bloc, 1947–1956* (Ithaca, NY: Cornell University Press, 2000).

Moffett, George D., III: *The Limits of Victory: The Ratification of the Panama Canal Treaties* (Ithaca, NY: Cornell University Press, 1985).

Moïse, E. E.: *Tonkin Gulf and the Escalation of the Vietnam War* (Chapel Hill: University of North Carolina Press, 1996).

Mommsen, Wolfgang J.: *Theories of Imperialism*, trans. P. S. Falla (New York: Random House, 1980).

Moravcsik, Andrew: *The Choice for Europe: Social Purpose and State Power from Messina to Maastricht* (Ithaca, NY: Cornell University Press, 1998).

Moravcsik, Andrew: "De Gaulle Between Grain and Grandeur: The Political Economy of French EC Policy, 1958–1970 (Parts 1 and 2)." *Journal of Cold War Studies* 2, 2 (spring 2000), 3–43; and 2, 3 (fall 2000), 4–68.

Moreno, José A.: *Barrios in Arms* (Pittsburgh, PA: University of Pittsburgh Press, 1970).

Morgan, H. Wayne: *America's Road to Empire: The War with Spain and Overseas Expansion* (New York: Wiley, 1965).

Morgan, Iwan: *Nixon* (London: Arnold, 2002).

Morgan, Roger: *The United States and West Germany, 1945–1973* (Oxford: Oxford University Press, 1974).

Morgenthau, Hans J.: *Politics Among Nations: The Struggle for Power and Peace* (New York: Knopf, 1948).

Morison, Samuel E.: *History of United States Naval Operations in World War II*, 15 vols. (Boston, MA: Little, Brown, 1947–62).

Morley, Morris H.: *Imperial State and Revolution: The United States and Cuba, 1952–1986* (New York: Cambridge University Press, 1987).

Morris, Edward: *Theodore Rex* (New York: Random House, 2001).

Morris, M. Wayne: *Stalin's Famine and Roosevelt's Recognition of Russia* (Lanham, MD: University Press of America, 1994).

Morse, Edward L.: *Foreign Policy and Interdependence in Gaullist France* (Princeton, NJ: Princeton University Press, 1973).

Moser, John E.: *Twisting the Lion's Tail: American Anglophobia Between the World Wars* (New York: New York University Press, 1999).

Moses, Russell L.: *Freeing the Hostages: Reexamining US–Iranian Negotiations and Soviet Policy, 1979–1981* (Pittsburgh, PA: University of Pittsburgh Press, 1996).

Moss, G. D.: *Vietnam: An American Ordeal*, 4th edn. (Upper Saddle River, NJ: Prentice-Hall, 2002).

Moynihan, D. P.: *Pandaemonium: Ethnicity in International Politics* (New York: Oxford University Press, 1993).

Mueller, J. E.: *War, Presidents, and Public Opinion* (New York: Wiley, 1973).

Mugridge, Ian: *The View from Xanadu: William Randolph Hearst and United States Foreign Policy* (Montreal: McGill–Queen's University Press, 1995).

Munro, Dana G.: *Intervention and Dollar Diplomacy in the Caribbean, 1900–1921* (Princeton, NJ: Princeton University Press, 1964).

Munro, Dana G.: *The United States and the Caribbean Republics, 1921–1933* (Princeton, NJ: Princeton University Press, 1974).

Murfett, Malcolm H.: "Look Back in Anger: The Western Powers and the Washington Conference of 1921–22." In Brian J. C. McKercher (ed.) *Arms Limitation and Disarmament: Restraints on War, 1899–1939* (Westport, CT: Praeger, 1992).

Murray, Donette: *Kennedy, Macmillan and Nuclear Weapons* (New York: St. Martin's Press, 2000).

Musicant, Ivan: The Banana Wars: A History of United States Military Intervention in Latin America from the SpanishAmerican War to the Invasion of Grenada (New York: Macmillan, 1990).

Musicant, Ivan: *Empire By Default* (New York: Henry Holt, 1998).

Nadeau, Remi: *Stalin, Churchill, and Roosevelt Divide Europe* (New York: Praeger, 1990).

Naftali, Timothy J.: "Intrepid's Last Deception: Documenting the Career of William Stephenson." *Intelligence and National Security* 8 (July 1993), 72–92.

Naimark, Norman M.: *The Russians in Germany: A History of the Soviet Zone of Occupation, 1945–1949* (Cambridge, MA: Harvard University Press, 1995).

Nash, Philip: *The Other Missiles of October: Eisenhower, Kennedy and the Jupiters, 1957–1963* (Chapel Hill: University of North Carolina Press, 1997).

Nathan, James A. (ed.): *The Cuban Missile Crisis Revisited* (New York: St. Martin's Press, 1992).

Nearing, Scott and Joseph Freeman: *Dollar Diplomacy: A Study in American Imperialism* (New York: Modern Reader Paperbacks, 1969).

Neary, Ian and James Cotton (eds.): *The Korean War in History* (Atlantic Highlands, NJ: Humanities Press International, 1989).

Neff, Donald: *Warriors at Suez: Eisenhower Takes America into the Middle East* (New York: Linden Press/Simon and Schuster, 1981).

Neff, Donald: *Warriors for Jerusalem: The Six Days that Changed the Middle East* (New York: Linden Press, 1984).

Neff, Donald: *Fallen Pillars: US Policy Towards Palestine and Israel, 1947–1994* (Washington, DC: Institute for Palestine Studies, 1995).

Nehru, Jawaharlal: *Visit to America* (New York: John Day, 1950).

Nelson, Anna Kasten: "The 'Top of Policy Hill': President Eisenhower and the National Security Council." *Diplomatic History* 7 (1983), 307–26.

Nelson, Keith L.: *The Making of Détente: Soviet–American Relations in the Shadow of Vietnam* (Baltimore, MD: Johns Hopkins University Press, 1995).

Neu, Charles: *An Uncertain Friendship: Theodore Roosevelt and Japan, 1906–1909* (Cambridge, MA: Harvard University Press, 1967).

Neustadt, Richard E.: *Report to JFK: The Skybolt Crisis in Perspective* (Ithaca, NY: Cornell University Press, 1999).

Newhouse, John: *De Gaulle and the Anglo-Saxons* (New York: Viking Press, 1970).

Newhouse, John: *Cold Dawn: The Story of SALT* (New York: Holt, Rinehart, and Winston, 1973).

Newman, J. M.: *JFK and Vietnam: Deception, Intrigue, and the Struggle for Power* (New York: Warner Books, 1992).

Newman, Robert P.: *Truman and the Hiroshima Cult* (East Lansing: Michigan State University Press, 1995).

Newton, Verne W. (ed.): *FDR and the Holocaust* (New York: St. Martin's Press, 1996).

Niblo, Stephen R.: *War, Diplomacy, and Development: The United States and Mexico, 1938–1954* (Wilmington, DE: Scholarly Resources, 1995).

Niebuhr, Reinhold: *The Irony of American History* (New York: Scribner, 1952).

Niebuhr, Reinhold: *Christian Realism and Political Problems* (New York: Scribner, 1953).

Ninkovich, Frank A.: "Cultural Relations and American China Policy, 1942–1945." *Pacific Historical Review* 49 (August 1980), 471–98.

Ninkovich, Frank A.: *The Diplomacy of Ideas: US Foreign Policy and Cultural Relations, 1938–1950* (New York: Cambridge University Press, 1981).

Ninkovich, Frank A.: "The Rockefeller Foundation, China, and Cultural Change." *Journal of American History* 70 (March 1984), 799–820.

Ninkovich, Frank A.: "Theodore Roosevelt: Civilization as Ideology." *Diplomatic History* 10 (summer 1986), 221–45.

Ninkovich, Frank A.: *Modernity and Power: A History of the Domino Theory in the Twentieth Century* (Chicago, IL: University of Chicago Press, 1994).

Ninkovich, Frank A.: *Germany and the United States: The Transformation of the German Question since 1945*, 2nd edn. (New York: Twayne, 1995).

Ninkovich, Frank A.: *The Wilsonian Century: US Foreign Policy since 1900* (Chicago, IL: University of Chicago Press, 1999).

Ninkovich, Frank A.: *The United States and Imperialism* (Oxford, 2000).

Nisbet, Robert: *Roosevelt and Stalin: The Failed Courtship* (Washington, DC: Regnery Gateway, 1988).

Nixon, Richard M.: *US Foreign Policy for the 1970s: The Emerging Structure of Peace* (Washington, DC: Government Printing Office, 1972).

Nixon, Richard M.: *RN: The Memoirs of Richard Nixon* (New York: Grosset and Dunlap, 1978).

Nixon, Richard M.: *The Real War* (New York: Warner Books, 1980).

Nixon, Richard M.: *No More Vietnams* (New York: Arbor House, 1985).

Noble, Harold J.: *Embassy at War* (Seattle: University of Washington Press, 1975).

Noer, Thomas J.: "The New Frontier and African Neutralism: Kennedy, Nkrumah, and the Volta River Project." *Diplomatic History* 8 (1984), 61–79.

Noer, Thomas J.: *Cold War and Black Liberation: The United States and White Rule in Africa, 1948–1968* (Colombia: University of Missouri Press, 1985).

Nordholt, J. W. S.: *Woodrow Wilson: A Life for World Peace* (Berkeley: University of California Press, 1991).

North, Oliver L., with William Novak: *Under Fire: An American Story* (New York: Harper Collins, 1991).

Notoji, Masako: "Cultural Transformation of John Philip Sousa and Disneyland in Japan." In

Reinhold Wagnleitner and Elaine Tyler May (eds.) *"Here, There, and Everywhere": The Foreign Politics of American Popular Culture* (Hanover, NH: University Press of New England, 2000).

Nwaubani, Ebere: *The United States and Decolonization in West Africa, 1950–1960* (Rochester, NY: University of Rochester Press, 2001).

Nye, Joseph S.: *Bound to Lead: The Changing Nature of American Power* (New York: Basic Books, 1990).

O'Brien, Conor Cruise: *The Long Affair: Thomas Jefferson and the French Revolution, 1785–1800* (Chicago, IL: University of Chicago Press, 1996).

O'Brien, Thomas F.: *The Revolutionary Mission: American Enterprise in Latin America, 1900–1945* (New York: Cambridge University Press, 1996).

O'Connor, Raymond G.: *Perilous Equilibrium: The United States and the London Naval Conference of 1930* (New York: Greenwood Press, 1962).

O'Connor, Raymond G.: *Diplomacy for Victory: FDR and Unconditional Surrender* (New York: W. W. Norton, 1971).

O'Neill, Bard E.: *Armed Struggle in Palestine: A Political–Military Analysis* (Boulder, CO: Westview Press, 1978).

O'Neill, Robert: *Australia in the Korean War, 1950–1953, Vol. 1: Strategy and Diplomacy* (Canberra: Australian Government Publishing Service, 1981).

O'Shaughnessey, Hugh: *Grenada: An Eyewitness Account of the US Invasion and the Caribbean History That Provoked It* (New York: Dodd, Mead, 1985).

Oberdorfer, D.: *Tet!* (Garden City, NY: Doubleday, 1971).

Offner, Arnold A.: *American Appeasement: United States Foreign Policy and Germany, 1933–1938* (Cambridge, MA: Harvard University Press, 1969), 268.

Offner, Arnold A.: "Influence Without Responsibility: American Statecraft and the Munich Conference." In Melvin Small and O. Feinstein (eds.) *Appeasing Fascism: Articles from the Wayne State University Conference on Munich After Fifty Years* (Lanham, MD: University Press of America, 1991).

Offner, Arnold A.: *Another Such Victory: President Truman and the Cold War, 1945–1953* (Stanford, CA: Stanford University Press, 2002).

Offner, John L.: *An Unwanted War: The Diplomacy of the United States and Spain over Cuba, 1895–1898* (Chapel Hill: University of North Carolina Press, 1992).

Oliver, Kendrick: *Kennedy, Macmillan and the Nuclear Test-Ban Debate, 1961–1963* (London: Macmillan, 1998).

Oliver, Robert T.: *Syngman Rhee: The Man Behind the Myth* (Tokyo: Tuttle, 1955).

Olson, J. S. and R. Roberts: *Where the Domino Fell: America and Vietnam, 1945 to 1995* (St. James, NY: Brandywine Press, 1999).

Onuf, Peter S.: "A Declaration of Independence for Diplomatic Historians." *Diplomatic History* 22 (winter 1998), 71–83.

Orde, Anne: *The Eclipse of Great Britain: The United States and British Imperial Decline, 1895–1956* (New York: St. Martin's Press, 1996).

Oren, Michael B.: *Six Days of War: June 1967 and the Making of the Modern Middle East* (New York: Oxford University Press, 2002).

Osborne, Thomas J.: *"Empire Can Wait": American Opposition to Hawaiian Annexation, 1893–1898* (Kent, OH, 1981).

Osgood, Robert E.: *Limited War: The Challenge to American Strategy* (Chicago, IL: University of Chicago Press, 1957).

Osterhammel, Jürgen: *Colonialism: A Theoretical Overview*, trans. Shelley L. Frisch (Princeton, NJ: M. Wiener, 1996).

Osterhammel, Jürgen and Wolfgang J. Mommsen (eds.) *Imperialism and After: Continuities and Discontinuities* (London: Allen and Unwin, 1986).

Pach, Chester J., Jr.: "The Containment of US Military Aid to Latin America, 1944–1949." *Diplomatic History* 6 (summer 1982), 225–44.

Pach, Chester J., Jr.: *Arming the Free World: The Origins of the United States Military Assistance Program, 1945–1950* (Chapel Hill: University of North Carolina Press, 1991).

Pach, Chester J., Jr. and Elmo Richardson: *The Presidency of Dwight D. Eisenhower* (Lawrence: University of Kansas Press, 1991).

Packenham, Robert A.: *Liberal America and the Third World: Political Development Ideas in Foreign Aid and Social Science* (Princeton, NJ: Princeton University Press, 1989).

Packenham, Robert A.: *The Dependency Movement: Scholarship and Politics in Development Studies* (Cambridge, MA: Harvard University Press, 1992).

Paige, Glenn D.: *The Korean Decision: June 24–30, 1950* (New York: Free Press, 1968).

Paik Sun Yup: *From Pusan to Panmunjom* (New York: Brassey's, 1992).

Painter, David S.: *Oil and the American Century: The Political Economy of US Foreign Oil Policy, 1941–1954* (Baltimore, MD: Johns Hopkins University Press, 1986).

Palmer, B., Jr.: *The 25-Year War: America's Military Role in Vietnam* (Lexington: University of Kentucky Press, 1984).

Palmer, D. R.: *Summons of the Trumpet: US–Vietnam in Perspective* (San Rafael, CA: Novato, 1978).

Palmer, General Bruce, Jr.: *Intervention in the Caribbean: The Dominican Crisis of 1965* (Lexington: University of Kentucky Press, 1989).

Palmer, Michael A.: *Guardians of the Gulf: A History of America's Expanding Role in the Persian Gulf, 1833–1992* (New York: Free Press, 1992).

Palmer, Norman: *The United States and India: The Dimensions of Influence* (New York: Praeger, 1985).

Palmer, Ronald D. and Thomas J. Reckford: *Building ASEAN: Twenty Years of Southeast Asia Cooperation* (New York: Praeger, 1987).

Park Hong-kyu: "From Pearl Harbor to Cairo: America's Korean Diplomacy, 1941–1943." *Diplomatic History* 13, 3 (summer 1989), 343–58.

Park, James W.: *Latin American Underdevelopment: A History of Perspectives in the United States, 1870–1965* (Baton Rouge: Louisiana State University Press, 1995).

Parker, Phyllis R.: *Brazil and the Quiet Intervention, 1964* (Austin: University of Texas Press, 1979).

Parker, Richard B.: *The Politics of Miscalculation in the Middle East* (Bloomington: Indiana University Press, 1993).

Parkinson, F.: *Latin America, the Cold War, and the World Powers, 1945–1973.* Sage Library of Social Research, no. 9 (Beverly Hills, CA: Sage Publishers, 1974).

Parmet, Herbert S.: *Eisenhower and the American Crusades* (New York: Macmillan, 1972).

Parmet, Herbert S.: *JFK: The Presidency of John F. Kennedy* (New York: Dial Press, 1983).

Parrish, Michael E.: "Soviet Espionage and the Cold War." *Diplomatic History* 25 (winter 2001), 105–20.

Pastor, Robert A.: "US Immigration Policy and Latin America: In Search of the 'Special Relationship'." *Latin American Research Review* 19, 3 (1984), 35–56.

Paterson, Thomas G.: "Foreign Aid Under Wraps: The Point Four Program." *Wisconsin Magazine of History* 56, 2 (winter 1972–3), 119–26.

Paterson, Thomas G.: *Soviet–American Confrontation: Postwar Reconstruction and the Origins of the Cold War* (Baltimore, MD: Johns Hopkins University Press, 1973).

Paterson, Thomas G.: *Kennedy's Quest for Victory: American Foreign Policy, 1961–1963* (New York: Oxford University Press, 1989).

Paterson, Thomas: "Defining and Doing the History of American Foreign Relations: A Primer." *Diplomatic History* 14 (1990), 584–601.

Paterson, Thomas G.: "Defining and Doing the History of American Foreign Relations: A Primer." In Michael J. Hogan and Thomas G. Paterson (eds.) *Explaining the History of American Foreign Relations* (New York: Cambridge University Press, 1991).

Paterson, Thomas G.: *Contesting Castro: The United States and the Triumph of the Cuban Revolution* (New York: Oxford University Press, 1994).

Paz, María E.: *Strategy, Security, and Spies: Mexico and the US as Allies in World War II* (University Park: Pennsylvania State University Press, 1997).

Peattie, Mark: *Ishiwara Kanji and Japan's Confrontation with the West* (Princeton, NJ: Princeton University Press, 1976).

Pells, Richard: *Not Like Us: How Europeans Have Loved, Hated, and Transformed American Culture Since World War II* (New York: Basic Books, 1997).

Penkower, Monty N.: *The Jews Were Expendable: Free World Diplomacy and the Holocaust, 1933–1945* (Urbana: University of Illinois Press, 1983).

Pérez, Louis A., Jr.: "International Dimensions of Inter-American Relations, 1944–1960." *Inter-American Economic Affairs* 27, 1 (summer 1973), 47–68.

Pérez, Louis A., Jr.: "Intervention, Hegemony, and Dependency: The United States in the Circum-Caribbean, 1898–1980." *Journal of American History* 51 (May 1982), 165–94.

Pérez, Louis A., Jr.: *Cuba Under the Platt Amendment, 1902–1934* (Pittsburgh, PA: University of Pittsburgh Press, 1986).

Pérez, Louis A., Jr.: *Cuba: Between Reform and Revolution* (New York: Oxford University Press, 1988).

Pérez, Louis A., Jr.: *Cuba and the United States: Ties of Singular Intimacy* (Athens, GA: University of Georgia Press, 1990).

Pérez, Louis A., Jr.: "Dependency." In Michael J. Hogan and Thomas G. Paterson (eds.) *Explaining the History of American Foreign Relations* (New York: Cambridge University Press, 1991).

Pérez, Louis A., Jr.: *Cuba and the United States: Ties of Singular Intimacy* (Athens, GA: University of Georgia Press, 1997).

Pérez, Louis A., Jr.: *The War of 1898: The United States and Cuba in History and Historiography* (Chapel Hill: University of North Carolina Press, 1998).

Pérez, Louis A., Jr.: *On Becoming Cuban: Identity, Nationality, and Culture* (New York: Ecco Press, 1999).

Pérez-Stable, Marifeli: *The Cuban Revolution: Origins, Course and Legacy* (New York: Oxford University Press, 1993).

Perkins, Bradford: *Prologue to War: England and the United States, 1805–1812* (Berkeley: University of California Press, 1961).

Perkins, Bradford: *The Causes of the War of 1812: National Honor or National Interest?* (Malabar, FL: Krieger Publishing, 1983).

Perkins, Bradford: *The Creation of a Republican Empire, 1776–1865, vol. 1: The Cambridge History of American Foreign Relations*, ed. Warren I. Cohen (New York: Cambridge University Press, 1993).

Perkins, Bradford: "Early American Foreign Relations: Opportunities and Challenges." *Diplomatic History* 22 (winter 1998), 115–20.

Perkins, Whitney T.: *Constraint of Empire: The United States and Caribbean Interventions* (Westport, CT: Greenwood Press, 1981).

Perkovich, George: *India's Nuclear Bomb: The Impact on Global Proliferation* (Berkeley: University of California Press, 1999).

Perlmutter, Amos: *FDR and Stalin: A Not So Grand Alliance, 1943–1945* (Columbia: University of Missouri Press, 1993).

Perlmutter, Amos: *Making the World Safe for Democracy: A Century of Wilsonianism and Its Totalitarian Challengers* (Chapel Hill: University of North Carolina Press, 1997).

Perret, Geoffrey: *Old Soldiers Never Die: The Life of Douglas MacArthur* (New York: Random House, 1996).

Perry, John C.: *Facing West: Americans and the Opening of the Pacific* (Westport, CT: Praeger, 1994).

Peskin, Lawrence A.: "Caught in the Web: Algerian Pirates and the Early National Public Sphere." Paper presented at the Washington Area Early American Seminar, College Park, MD, September 20, 2001.

Phillips, George H.: *Indians and Intruders in Central California, 1769–1849* (Norman: University of Oklahoma Press, 1993).

Phillips, George H.: *Indians and Indian Agents: The Origins of the Reservation System in California, 1849–1852* (Norman: University of Oklahoma Press, 1997).

Pickett, William: *Dwight D. Eisenhower and American Power* (Wheeling, IL: Harlan Davidson, 1995).

Pierpaoli, Paul G., Jr.: *Truman and Korea: The Political Culture of the Early Cold War* (Columbia: University of Missouri Press, 1999).

Pike, D.: *Viet Cong: The Organization and Techniques of the National Liberation Front of South Vietnam* (Cambridge, MA: MIT Press, 1966).

Pike, D.: *History of Vietnamese Communism* (Stanford, CA: Stanford University Press, 1978).

Pike, D.: *PAVN: People's Army of Vietnam* (Novato, CA: Presidio, 1986).

Pike, Frederick B.: *The United States and Latin America: Myths and Stereotypes of Civilization and Nature* (Austin: University of Texas Press, 1992).

Pike, Fredrick B.: *FDR's Good Neighbor Policy: Sixty Years of Generally Gentle Chaos* (Austin: University of Texas Press, 1995).

Platt, Rorin M.: *Virginia in Foreign Affairs, 1933–1941* (Lanham, MD: University Press of America, 1991).

Platt, Rorin M.: "The Triumph of Interventionism: Virginia's Political Elite and Aid to Britain, 1933–1941." *Virginia Magazine of History and Biography* 100 (July 1992), 343–64.

Pletcher, David M.: *The Awkward Years: American Foreign Relations under Garfield and Arthur* (Columbia: University of Missouri Press, 1962).

Pletcher, David M.: *The Diplomacy of Trade and Investment: American Economic Expansion in the Hemisphere, 1865–1900* (Columbia: University of Missouri Press, 1998).

Plummer, Brenda G.: *Haiti and the Great Powers, 1902–1915* (Baton Rouge: Louisiana State University Press, 1988).

Plummer, Brenda G.: *Haiti and the United States: The Psychological Moment* (Athens, GA: University of Georgia Press, 1992).

Plummer, Brenda G.: *Rising Wind: Black Americans and US Foreign Affairs, 1935–1960* (Chapel Hill: University of North Carolina Press, 1996).

Poats, Rutherford B.: *Decision in Korea* (New York: McBride, 1954).

Podhoretz, Norman: "Making the World Safe for Communism." *Commentary* (April 1975), 31–41.

Podhoretz, Norman: *The Present Danger: Do We Have the Will to Reverse the Decline of American Power?* (New York: Simon and Schuster, 1980).

Podhoretz, Norman: *Why We Were in Vietnam* (New York: Simon and Schuster, 1983).

Pogue, Forrest C.: *George C. Marshall*, 4 vols. (New York: Viking, 1963–87).

Poiger, Uta G.: *Jazz, Rock, and Rebels: Cold War Politics and American Culture in a Divided Germany* (Berkeley: University of California Press, 2000).

Pomeroy, William J.: *American Neo-Colonialism: Its Emergence in the Philippines and Asia* (New York: International Publishers, 1970).

Porter, G.: *A Peace Denied: The United States, Vietnam and the Paris Agreement* (Bloomington: Indiana University Press, 1975).

Powers, Thomas: *The Man Who Kept Secrets: Richard Helms and the CIA* (New York: Knopf,
1979).

Prados, John: *The Soviet Estimate* (New York: Dial, 1982).

Prados, John: *Keepers of the Keys: A History of the National Security Council from Truman to
Bush* (New York: William Morrow Publishers, 1991).

Pratt, Julius: *Expansionists of 1898: The Acquisition of Hawaii and the Spanish Islands* (New
York: Quadrangle Books, 1936).

Pratt, Julius: *America's Colonial Experiment: How the United States Gained, Governed, and in
Part Gave Away Its Colonial Empire* (New York: Prentice-Hall, 1950).

Prevots, Naima: *Dance for Export: Cultural Diplomacy and the Cold War* (Hanover, NH:
University Press of New England, 1998).

Price, Raymond: *With Nixon* (New York: Viking, 1977).

Pringle, Robert: *Indonesia and the Philippines: American Interests in Island Southeast Asia*
(New York: Columbia University Press, 1980).

Prittie, Terence: *The Velvet Chancellors: A History of Postwar Germany* (London: Muller,
1979).

Prizel, Illya: *Latin America through Soviet Eyes: The Evaluation of Soviet Perceptions during the
Brezhnev Era, 1964–1982* (New York: Cambridge University Press, 1990).

Prucha, Francis P.: *American Indian Treaties: The History of a Political Anomaly* (Berkeley:
University of California Press, 1994).

Quandt, William B.: *Decade of Decisions: American Policy Toward the Arab–Israeli Conflict,
1967–1976* (Berkeley: University of California Press, 1977).

Quandt, William B.: *Peace Process: American Diplomacy and the Arab–Israeli Conflict since
1967* (Washington, DC: Brookings Institution, 1993).

Quirk, Robert: *Fidel Castro* (New York: W. W. Norton, 1993).

Raat, W. Dirk: *Revoltosos: Mexico's Rebels in the United States, 1903–1923* (College Station:
Texas A&M University Press, 1981).

Raat, W. Dirk: *Mexico and the United States: Ambivalent Vistas* (Athens, GA: University of
Georgia Press, 1997).

Rabe, Stephen G.: "The Elusive Conference: United States Economic Relations with Latin
America, 1945–1952." *Diplomatic History* 2 (summer 1978), 79–294.

Rabe, Stephen G.: *The Road to OPEC: United States Relations with Venezuela, 1919–1976*
(Austin: University of Texas Press, 1982).

Rabe, Stephen G.: *Eisenhower and Latin America: The Foreign Policy of Anti-Communism*
(Chapel Hill: University of North Carolina Press, 1988).

Rabe, Stephen G.: *The Most Dangerous Area in the World: John F. Kennedy Confronts
Communist Revolution in Latin America* (Chapel Hill: University of North Carolina Press,
1999).

Rabe, Stephen G.: "After the Missiles of October: John F. Kennedy and Cuba, November
1962 to November 1963." *Presidential Studies Quarterly* 30 (December 2000),
714–26.

Rabie, Muhammed: *US–PLO Dialogue: Secret Diplomacy and Conflict Resolution* (Gainesville:
University of Florida Press, 1995).

Rabinovich, Itamar: *The Brink of Peace: The Israeli–Syrian Negotiations* (Princeton, NJ:
Princeton University Press, 1998).

Race, J.: *War Comes to Long An: Revolutionary Conflict in a Vietnamese Province* (Berkeley:
University of California Press, 1972).

Randall, Stephen J.: *Colombia and the United States: Hegemony and Interdependence* (Athens,
GA: University of Georgia Press, 1992).

Raviv, Dan and Yossi Melman: *Friends in Deed: Inside the US–Israeli Alliance* (New York: Hyperion, 1994).

Reagan, Ronald: *An American Life* (New York: Simon and Schuster, 1990).

Reed, James: *The Missionary Mind and American East Asia Policy 1911–1915* (Cambridge, MA: Harvard University Press, 1983).

Rees, David: *Korea: The Limited War* (New York: St. Martin's Press, 1964).

Reeves, Richard: *President Nixon: Alone in the White House* (New York: Simon and Schuster, 2001).

Reeves, Thomas C.: *A Question of Character: A Life of John F. Kennedy* (New York: Free Press, 1991).

Reeves, Zane: *The Politics of the Peace Corps and VISTA* (Tuscaloosa: University of Alabama Press, 1988).

Reich, Bernard: *Quest for Peace: United States–Israel Relations and the Arab–Israeli Conflict* (New Brunswick, NJ: Transaction Books, 1977).

Reich, Bernard: *The United States and Israel: Influence in the Special Relationship* (New York: Praeger, 1984).

Reich, Bernard: *Securing the Covenant: United States–Israeli Relations After the Cold War* (Westport, CT: Greenwood Press, 1995).

Remini, Robert V.: *Andrew Jackson and his Indian Wars* (New York: Viking Press, 2001).

Renda, Mary A.: *Taking Haiti: Military Occupation and the Culture of US Imperialism, 1915–1940* (Chapel Hill: University of North Carolina Press, 2001).

Report of the National Bipartisan Commission on Central America. Foreword by Henry A. Kissinger (New York: Macmillan, 1984).

Resis, Albert: "The Churchill–Stalin 'Percentages' Agreement on the Balkans, Moscow, October 1944." *American Historical Review* 83 (April 1978), 368–87.

Resis, Albert: "Spheres of Influence in Soviet Wartime Diplomacy." *Journal of Modern History* 53 (September 1981), 417–39.

Reynolds, David: *The Creation of the Anglo-American Alliance 1937–41* (Chapel Hill: University of North Carolina Press, 1982).

Reynolds, David: "Roosevelt, the British Left, and the Appointment of John G. Winant as United States Ambassador to Britain in 1941." *International History Review* 4 (August 1982), 393–413.

Reynolds, David: "Roosevelt, Churchill, and the Wartime Anglo-American Alliance: Towards a New Synthesis." In William Roger Louis and Hedley Bull (eds.) *The "Special Relationship": Anglo-American Relations since 1945* (Oxford: Oxford University Press, 1986).

Reynolds, David: "The 'Big Three' and the Division of Europe, 1945–1948: An Overview." *Diplomacy and Statecraft* 1 (July 1990), 111–36.

Reynolds, David: "The Atlantic 'Flop': British Foreign Policy and the Churchill–Roosevelt Meeting of August 1941." In Douglas Brinkley and David R. Facey-Crowther (eds.) *The Atlantic Charter* (New York: St. Martin's Press, 1994).

Reynolds, David: *Rich Relations: The American Occupation of Britain, 1942–1945* (New York: Random House, 1995).

Reynolds, David: "World War II and Modern Meanings." *Diplomatic History* 25 (summer 2001), 457–72.

Reynolds, David, Warren F. Kimball, and A. O. Chubarian (eds.) *Allies at War: The Soviet, American, and British Experience, 1939–1945* (New York: St. Martin's Press, 1994).

Rhonda, James P.: *Astoria and Empire* (Lincoln: University of Nebraska Press, 1990).

Rice, Gerard T.: *The Bold Experiment: JFK's Peace Corps* (Notre Dame, IN: University of Notre Dame Press, 1986).

Richelson, Jeffrey T.: *America's Secret Eyes in Space: The US Keyhole Spy Satellite Program* (New York: Harper and Row, 1990).

Ridgway, Matthew B.: *The Korean War* (Garden City, NY: Doubleday, 1967).

Riley, Kevin J.: *Snow Job? The War Against International Cocaine Trafficking* (New Brunswick, NJ: Transaction Books, 1996).

Rippy, J. Fred: *Globe and Hemisphere: Latin America's Place in the Postwar Foreign Relations of the United States* (Chicago, IL: H. Regnery, 1958).

Risse-Kappen, Thomas: *Cooperation Among Democracies: The European Influence on US Foreign Policy*. Princeton Studies in International History and Politics (Princeton, NJ: Princeton University Press, 1995).

Rivas, Darlene: *Missionary Capitalist: Nelson Rockefeller in Venezuela* (Chapel Hill: University of North Carolina Press, 2002).

Roberts, Geoffrey: "Litvinov's Lost Peace, 1941–1946." *Journal of Cold War Studies* 4 (2002), 23–54.

Roberts, John W.: *Putting Foreign Policy to Work: The Organized Labor in American Foreign Relations, 1932–1941* (New York: Garland, 1995).

Roberts, Walter R.: *Tito, Mihailovic and the Allies, 1941–1945* (New Brunswick, NJ: Rutgers University Press, 1973).

Robin, Ron: *The Making of the Cold War Enemy: Culture and Politics in the Military–Industrial Complex* (Princeton, NJ: Princeton University Press, 2001).

Robinson, Ronald and John Gallagher, with Alice Denny: *Africa and the Victorians: The Official Mind of Imperialism* (London: Macmillan, 1961).

Rodriquez, Felix and John Weisman: *Shadow Warrior: The CIA Hero of a Hundred Unknown Battles* (New York: Simon and Schuster, 1989).

Rohrs, Richard C.: "The Federalist Party and the Convention of 1800." *Diplomatic History* 12 (summer 1998), 237–60.

Roman, Peter: *Eisenhower and the Missile Gap* (Ithaca, NY: Cornell University Press, 1995).

Roorda, Eric P.: *The Dictator Next Door: The Good Neighbor Policy and the Trumillo Regime in the Dominican Republic, 1930–1945* (Durham, NC: Duke University Press, 1998).

Roper, J.: *The American Presidents: Heroic Leadership from Kennedy to Clinton* (Edinburgh: Edinburgh University Press, 2000).

Rosen, Stephen P.: "Alexander Hamilton and the Domestic Uses of International Law." *Diplomatic History* 5 (summer 1981), 183–202.

Rosenberg, David A.: "The Origins of Overkill: Nuclear Weapons and American Strategy, 1945–1960." *International Security* 7 (1983), 3–71.

Rosenberg, Emily S.: *Spreading the American Dream: American Economic and Cultural Expansion, 1890–1945* (New York: Hill and Wang, 1982).

Rosenberg, Emily: "The Invisible Protectorate: The United States, Liberia, and the Evolution of Neocolonialism, 1909–1940." *Diplomatic History* 9 (1985), 191–214.

Rosenberg, Emily S.: "Walking the Borders." *Diplomatic History* 14 (fall 1990), 565–73. Also ch. 3 in Michael J. Hogan and Thomas G. Paterson (eds.) *Explaining the History of American Foreign Relations* (Cambridge: Cambridge University Press, 1991).

Rosenberg, Emily S.: "Cultural Interactions." In Stanley Kutler (ed.) *Encyclopedia of the United States in the Twentieth Century* (New York: Scribners, 1996).

Rosenberg, Emily S.: "A Call to Revolution: A Roundtable on Early US Foreign Relations." *Diplomatic History* 22 (winter 1998), 63–70.

Rosenberg, Emily S.: "Turning to Culture." In Gilbert M. Joseph, Catherine C. LeGrand, and Ricardo Salvatore (eds.) *Close Encounters of Empire: Writing the Cultural History of US–Latin American Relations* (Durham, NC: Duke University Press, 1998).

Rosenberg, Emily S.: *Financial Missionaries to the World: The Politics and Culture of Dollar Diplomacy, 1900–1930* (Cambridge, MA: Harvard University Press, 1999).

Ross, Robert S.: "National Security, Human Rights, and Domestic Politics: The Bush Administration and China." In Kenneth Oye, Robert J. Lieber, and D. Rothchild (eds.)

Eagle in a New World: American Grand Strategy in the Post-Cold War Era (New York: Harper Collins, 1992).

Ross, Robert S. (ed.): *China, the United States, and the Soviet Union: Tripolarity and Policy Making in the Cold War* (Armonk, NY: M. E. Sharpe, 1993).

Ross, Robert S.: *Negotiating Cooperation: The United States and China, 1969–1989* (Stanford, CA: Stanford University Press, 1995).

Ross, Robert S.: *After the Cold War: Domestic Factors and US–China Relations* (Armonk, NY: M. E. Sharpe, 1998).

Rossi, Lorenza: *Who Shall Guard the Guardians Themselves? An Analysis of US Strategy in the Middle East since 1945* (New York: Lang, 1998).

Rossi, Mario: *Roosevelt and the French* (Westport, CT: Praeger, 1993).

Rossignol, Marie-Jeanne: *Le Ferment nationale: aux origines de la politique extérieures des Etats-Unis, 1789–1812* (Paris: Editions Belin, 1994).

Rostow, W. W.: *The United States and the Regional Organization of Asia and the Pacific, 1965–1985* (Austin: University of Texas Press, 1986).

Rothwell, Victor: *Britain and the Cold War, 1941–1947* (London: Jonathan Cape, 1982).

Rotter, Andrew J.: *The Path to Vietnam: Origins of the American Commitment to Southeast Asia* (Ithaca, NY: Cornell University Press, 1987).

Rotter, Andrew J.: "Gender Relations, Foreign Relations: The United States and South Asia, 1947–1964." *Journal of American History* 81 (September 1994), 518–42.

Rotter, Andrew J.: *Comrades at Odds: The United States and India, 1947–1964* (Ithaca, NY: Cornell University Press, 2000).

Rotter, Andrew J.: "Feeding Beggars: Class, Caste, and Status in Indo–US Relations, 1947–1964." In Christian G. Appy (ed.) *Cold War Constructions: The Political Culture of United States Imperialism, 1945–1966* (Amherst: University of Massachusetts Press, 2000).

Rotter, Andrew J.: "Saidism without Said: *Orientalism* and US Diplomatic History." *American Historical Review* 105 (October 2000), 1205–17.

Rout, Leslie B., Jr., and John F. Bratzel: *The Shadow War: German Espionage and United States Counterespionage in Latin America during World War II* (Frederick, MD: University Publications of America, 1986).

Rovere, Richard and Arthur M. Schlesinger, Jr.: *The General and the President and the Future of American Foreign Policy* (New York: Farrar, Straus, and Giroux, 1951).

Rowe, John C.: *Literary Culture and US Imperialism: From the Revolution to World War II* (New York: Oxford University Press, 2000).

Rubenberg, Cheryl A.: *Israel and the American National Interest: A Critical Examination* (Urbana: University of Illinois Press, 1986).

Rubin, Barry: *The Great Powers in the Middle East, 1941–1947: The Road to the Cold War* (New York: Oxford University Press, 1980).

Rubin, Barry: *Paved with Good Intentions: The American Experience in Iran* (Oxford: Oxford University Press, 1980).

Rubinstein, William: *The Myth of Rescue: Why the Democracies Could Not Have Saved More Jews from the Holocaust* (New York: Routledge, 1997).

Ruiz, Ramón E.: *On the Rim of Mexico: Encounters of the Rich and Poor* (Boulder, CO: Westview Press, 1998).

Rusbridger, James and Eric Nave: *Betrayal at Pearl Harbor: How Churchill Lured Roosevelt into World War II* (New York: Summit, 1991).

Rusk, Dean with Richard Rusk and Daniel S. Papp: *As I Saw It* (New York: W. W. Norton, 1990).

Russell, Greg: *John Quincy Adams and the Public Virtues of Diplomacy* (Columbia: University of Missouri Press, 1995).

Rust, W. J.: *Kennedy in Vietnam* (New York: Scribners, 1985).

Ryan, Henry B.: *The Fall of Che Guevara: A Story of Soldiers, Spies, and Diplomats* (New York: Oxford University Press, 1998).

Ryan, Mark A.: *Chinese Attitudes toward Nuclear Weapons: China and the United States During the Korean War* (Armonk, NY: M. E. Sharpe, 1989).

Rydell, Robert W.: *All the World's a Fair: Visions of Empire at American International Expositions, 1876–1916* (Chicago, IL: University of Chicago Press, 1984).

Rystad, Goran: *Ambiguous Imperialism: American Foreign Policy and Domestic Politics at the Turn-of-the-Century* (Lund, Sweden, 1975).

Safire, William: *Before the Fall: An Inside Look at the Pre-Watergate Nixon White House* (Garden City, NY: Doubleday, 1975).

Safran, Nadav: *From War to War: The Arab–Israeli Confrontation, 1948–1967* (New York: Pegasus, 1969).

Safran, Nadav: *Israel: The Embattled Ally* (Cambridge, MA: Belknap Press of Harvard University Press, 1978).

Safty, Adel: *From Camp David to the Gulf: Negotiations, Language and Propaganda, and War* (New York: Black Rose, 1992).

Said, Edward W.: *The Question of Palestine* (New York: Times Books, 1979).

Said, Edward W.: *Orientalism* (New York: Vintage, 1988).

Said, Edward W.: *Culture and Imperialism* (New York: Knopf, 1993).

Sainsbury, Keith: *The Turning Point: Roosevelt, Stalin, Churchill, and Chiang Kai-shek, 1943: The Moscow, Cairo and Teheran Conferences* (New York: Oxford University Press, 1985).

Salamanca, Bonifacio S.: *The Filipino Reaction to American Rule, 1901–1913* (Shoe String Press, 1968).

Salisbury, Richard V.: *Anti-Imperialism and International Competition in Central America, 1920–1929* (Wilmington, DE: Scholarly Resources, 1989).

Sampson, Anthony: *The Seven Sisters: The Great Oil Companies and the World They Shaped* (New York: Viking, 1975).

Sandler, Stanley: *The Korean War: No Victors, No Vanquished* (Lexington: University of Kentucky Press, 1999).

Sandos, James A.: *Rebellion in the Borderlands: Anarchism and the Plan of San Diego, 1904–1923* (Norman: University of Oklahoma Press, 1992).

Sandusky, Michael C.: *America's Parallel* (Alexandria, VA: Old Dominion Press, 1983).

Sapio, Victor A.: *Pennsylvania and the War of 1812* (Lexington: University of Kentucky Press, 1970).

Sarotte, M. E.: *Dealing with the Devil: East Germany, Détente, and Ostpolitik, 1969–1973* (Chapel Hill: University of North Carolina Press, 2001).

Sater, William F.: *Chile and the United States: Empires in Conflict* (Athens, GA: University of Georgia Press, 1990).

Sawyer, Robert K. and Walter G. Hermes: *Military Advisors in Korea: KMAG in Peace and War* (Washington, DC: US Government Printing Office, 1979).

Sayigh, Yezid and Avi Shlaim (eds).: *The Cold War and the Middle East* (Oxford: Clarendon Press, 1997).

Sbrega, John J.: *Anglo-American Relations and Colonialism in East Asia* (New York: Garland, 1983).

Schaller, Michael: *The United States and China in the Twentieth Century* (New York: Oxford University Press, 1979).

Schaller, Michael: *The US Crusade in China, 1937–1945* (New York: Columbia University Press, 1979).

Schaller, Michael: *The American Occupation of Japan: The Origins of the Cold War in Asia* (New York: Oxford University Press, 1985).

Schaller, Michael: *Douglas MacArthur: The Far Eastern General* (New York: Oxford University Press, 1989).

Scheer, Arthur: "Louis Ludlow's War Referendum of 1938: A Reappraisal." *Mid-America* 76 (spring–summer 1994), 133–55.

Schell, Jonathan: *The Time of Illusion* (New York: Knopf, 1975).

Schelling, Thomas: *The Strategy of Conflict* (Cambridge, MA: Harvard University Press, 1960).

Schertz, Arian W.: *Die Deutschlandpolitik Kennedys and Johnsons: Unterschiedliche Ansatze innerhalb der Amerikanishen Regierung (Kennedy and Johnson's Policies Toward Germany: Different Approaches within the American Government)* (Cologne: Bohlau, 1992).

Schick, Jack M.: *The Berlin Crisis, 1958–1962* (Philadelphia: University of Pennsylvania Press, 1971).

Schirmer, Daniel B.: *Republic or Empire: American Resistance to the Philippine War* (Morristown, NJ: Schenkman Books, 1972).

Schirmer, Daniel B. and Stephen Rosskamm Shalom (eds.) *The Philippines Reader: A History of Colonialism, Neocolonialism, Dictatorship, and Resistance* (Boston, MA: South End Press, 1987).

Schlesinger, Arthur M., Jr.: *A Thousand Days: John F. Kennedy in the White House* (Boston, MA: Houghton Mifflin, 1965).

Schlesinger, Arthur M., Jr.: *The Bitter Heritage: Vietnam and American Democracy, 1941–1966* (Boston, MA: Houghton Mifflin, 1966).

Schlesinger, Arthur M., Jr.: *Reviews in American History* 11 (1983), 1–11.

Schlesinger, Arthur M., Jr.: "Effective National Security Advising: A Most Dubious Precedent." *Political Science Quarterly* 115 (2000), 347–51.

Schlesinger, Stephen and Stephen Kinzer: *Bitter Fruit: The Untold Story of the American Coup in Guatemala* (Garden City, NY: Doubleday, 1982).

Schmidt, Hans: *The United States Occupation of Haiti, 1915–1934* (New Brunswick, NJ: Rutgers University Press, 1971).

Schmitz, David F.: " 'Speaking the Same Language': The US Response to the Italo-Ethiopian War and the Origins of American Appeasement." In David F. Schmitz and Richard D. Challener (eds.) *Appeasement in Europe: A Reassessment of US Policies* (Westport, CT: Greenwood Press, 1990).

Schmitz, David F.: *Thank God They're on Our Side: The United States and Right-Wing Dictatorships, 1921–1965* (Chapel Hill: University of North Carolina Press, 1999).

Schnabel, James F.: *Policy and Direction: The First Year* (Washington, DC: US Government Printing Office, 1972).

Schnabel, James F. and Robert J. Watson: *History of the Joint Chiefs of Staff, Vol. 3: The Korean War* (Washington, DC: US Government Printing Office, 1988).

Schoenbaum, David: *The United States and the State of Israel* (New York: Oxford University Press, 1993).

Schoenbaum, Thomas J.: *Waging Peace and War: Dean Rusk in the Truman, Kennedy and Johnson Years* (New York: Simon and Schuster, 1988).

Schoenhals, Kai P. and Richard A. Melanson: *Revolution and Intervention in Grenada: The New Jewel Movement, the United States, and the Caribbean* (Boulder, CO: Westview Press, 1985).

Scholes, Walter V. and Marie V. Scholes: *The Foreign Policies of the Taft Administration* (Columbia: University of Missouri Press, 1970).

Schonberger, H. B.: "The Cold War and the American Empire in Asia." *Radical History Review* 33 (1985), 140–8.

Schoonover, Thomas: *The United States in Central America, 1860–1911: Episodes of Social Imperialism and Imperial Rivalry in the World System* (Durham, NC: Duke University Press, 1991).

Schoultz, Lars: *Human Rights and United States Policy toward Latin America* (Princeton, NJ: Princeton University Press, 1981).

Schoultz, Lars: *National Security and United States Policy toward Latin America* (Princeton, NJ: Princeton University Press, 1987).

Schoultz, Lars: *Beneath the United States: A History of US Policy Toward Latin America* (Cambridge, MA: Harvard University Press, 1998).

Schraeder, Peter: *United States Foreign Policy Toward Africa: Incrementalism, Crisis and Change* (Cambridge: Cambridge University Press, 1994).

Schrijvers, Peter: *The Crash of Ruin: American Combat Soldiers in Europe during World War II* (Washington Square, NY: New York University Press, 1998).

Schroeder, John H.: *Shaping a Maritime Empire: The Commercial and Diplomatic Role of the American Navy, 1829–1861* (Westport, CT: Greenwood Press, 1985).

Schuler, Friedrich E.: *Mexico between Hitler and Roosevelt: Mexican Foreign Relations in the Age of Lázaro Cárdenas, 1934–1940* (Albuquerque: University of New Mexico Press, 1998).

Schulze, Kirsten E.: *The Arab–Israeli Conflict: Seminar Studies in History Series* (London: Addison Wesley Longman, 1999).

Schulzinger, Robert D.: *Henry Kissinger: Doctor of Diplomacy* (New York: Columbia University Press, 1989).

Schulzinger, Robert D.: *A Time of War: The United States and Vietnam, 1941–1975* (New York: Oxford University Press, 1997).

Schurmann, Franz: *The Foreign Politics of Richard Nixon: The Grand Design* (Berkeley: Institute of International Studies, 1987).

Schwabe, K.: *Woodrow Wilson, Revolutionary Germany, and Peacemaking, 1918–1919: Missionary Diplomacy and the Realities of Power* (Chapel Hill: University of North Carolina Press, 1985).

Schwartz, Thomas A.: *America's Germany: John J. McCloy and the Federal Republic of Germany* (Cambridge, MA: Harvard University Press, 1991).

Schwartz, Thomas A.: "Lyndon Johnson and Europe: Alliance Politics, Political Economy, and 'Growing Out of the Cold War'." In H. W. Brands (ed.) *Beyond Vietnam: The Foreign Policies of Lyndon Johnson* (College Station: Texas A&M University Press, 1999).

Schwartz, Thomas A.: *In the Shadow of Vietnam: Lyndon Johnson and Europe* (unpublished manuscript, 2001).

Schwarz, Hans-Peter: *Die Ära Adenauer* [The Adenauer Era] (Stuttgart: Deutsche Verlags-Anstalt, 1981–3).

Schwarz, Hans-Peter: *Adenauer, vol. 2: Der Staatsmann: 1952–1967* (Stuttgart: Deutsche-Verlags Anstalt, 1991).

Schwarz, Karen: *What You Can Do for Your Country: An Oral History of the Peace Corps* (New York: William Morrow, 1991).

Sciolino, Elaine: "Kissinger in China: 2 Versions of Secret '71 Talks." *International Herald Tribune* (March 1, 2002).

Scott, Len: *Macmillan, Kennedy and the Cuban Missile Crisis: Political, Military and Intelligence Aspects* (London: Macmillan, 1999).

Scott, William: *The Sons of Sheba's Race: African Americans and the Italo–Ethiopian War, 1935–1941* (Bloomington: Indiana University Press, 1993).

Scranton, Margaret E.: *The Noriega Years: US–Panamanian Relations, 1981–1990* (Boulder, CO: Lynne Reinner, 1991).

Scully, Eileen: *Bargaining with the State from Afar: American Citizenship in Treaty Port China, 1844–1942* (New York: Columbia University Press, 2001).

Seaborg, Glenn T.: *Stemming the Tide: Arms Control in the Johnson Years* (Lexington, MA: D. C. Heath, 1987).

Seaborg, Glenn T. with Benjamin S. Loeb: *Kennedy, Khrushchev and the Test Ban* (Berkeley: University of California Press, 1981).

Searles, David: *The Peace Corps Experience: Challenge and Change, 1969–1976* (Lexington: University of Kentucky Press, 1997).

Sears, John F.: "Bierstadt, Buffalo Bill, and the Wild West in Europe." In Rob Kroes, Robert W. Rydell, and Doeko F. J. Bosscher (eds.) *Cultural Transmissions and Receptions: American Mass Culture in Europe* (Amsterdam: Vu University Press, 1993).

Semmel, Bernard: *Imperialism and Social Reform: English Social-imperial Thought, 1895–1914* (Cambridge, MA: Harvard University Press, 1960).

Semmel, Bernard: *The Rise of Free Trade Imperialism: Classical Political Economy, the Empire of Free Trade and Imperialism 1750–1850* (Cambridge: Cambridge University Press, 1970).

Sestanovich, Stephen: "US Policy Toward the Soviet Union, 1970–90: The Impact of China." In Robert S. Ross (ed.) *China, the United States, and the Soviet Union: Tripolarity and Policy Making in the Cold War* (Armonk, NY: M. E. Sharpe, 1993).

Sevostianov, G. N. and W. F. Kimball (eds.): *Soviet–US Relations, 1933–1942* (Moscow: Progress Publishers, 1989).

Sexton, Donal J., Jr. (compiler): *Signals Intelligence in World War II: A Research Guide* (Westport, CT: Greenwood Press, 1996).

Shadid, Mohammed K.: *The United States and the Palestinians* (New York: St. Martin's Press, 1981).

Shalom, Stephen R.: *The United States and the Philippines: A Study of Neocolonialism* (Philadelphia, PA: Institute for the Study of Human Issues, 1981).

Shannon, Thomas: *An Introduction to the World-System Perspective* (Boulder, CO: Westview Press, 1989).

Shaplen, R.: *The Lost Revolution: The US in Vietnam, 1946–1966* (New York: Harper and Row, 1966).

Sharp, U. S. G.: *Strategy for Defeat* (San Rafael, CA: Presidio, 1978).

Sheehan, Edward R. F.: *The Arabs, Israelis, and Kissinger: A Secret History of American Diplomacy in the Middle East* (New York: Reader's Digest Press, 1976).

Sheehan, N.: *A Bright Shining Lie: John Paul Vann and America in Vietnam* (New York: Random House, 1988).

Sheffer, Gabriel: *US–Israeli Relations at the Crossroads* (London: Cass, 1997).

Sheinen, David: *Searching for Authority: Pan Americanism, Diplomacy and Politics in United States–Argentine Relations, 1910–1930* (New Orleans, LA: University Press of the South, 1998).

Sheng, Michael M.: *Battling Western Imperialism: Mao, Stalin, and the United States* (Princeton, NJ: Princeton University Press, 1997).

Sheng, Michael M.: "The Triumph of Internationalism: CCP–Moscow Relations before 1949." *Diplomatic History* 21, 1 (winter 1997), 95–104.

Shepard, Robert: *Nigeria, Africa, and the United States: From Kennedy to Reagan* (Bloomington: Indiana University Press, 1991).

Sheridan, Eugene R.: "The Recall of Edmond Charles Genet: A Study in Transatlantic Politics and Diplomacy." *Diplomatic History* 18 (fall 1994), 463–88.

Sherry, Michael S.: *Preparing for the Next War: American Plans for Postwar Defense, 1941–1945* (New Haven, CT: Yale University Press, 1977).

Sherry, Michael S.: *The Rise of American Air Power: The Creation of Armageddon* (New Haven, CT: Yale University Press, 1987).

Sherry, Michael S.: *In the Shadow of War: The United States Since the 1930s* (New Haven, CT: Yale University Press, 1995).

Sherry, Michael S.: "Projections of Hegemony and Consent in Film." *Diplomatic History* 19 (fall 1995), 713–18.

Sherwin, Martin J.: *A World Destroyed: The Atomic Bomb and the Grand Alliance* (New York: Vintage, 1975).

Shizhang Hu: *Stanley K. Hornbeck and the Open Door Policy, 1919–1937* (Westport, CT: Greenwood Press, 1995).

Shlaim, Avi: *War and Peace in the Middle East: A Critique of American Policy* (New York: Whittle, 1994).

Shogan, Robert: *Hard Bargain: How FDR Twisted Churchill's Arm, Evaded the Law, and Changed the Role of the American Presidency* (New York: Scribner, 1995).

Short, A.: *The Origins of the Vietnam War* (London: Longman, 1989).

Shriver, Sargent: *Point of the Lance* (New York: Harper and Row, 1964).

Shulman, Holly C.: *The Voice of America: Propaganda and Democracy, 1941–1945* (Madison: University of Wisconsin Press, 1990).

Shultz, George P.: *Turmoil and Triumph: My Years as Secretary of State* (New York: Charles Scribner's, 1993).

Sick, Gary: *All Fall Down: America's Tragic Encounter with Iran* (New York: Random House, 1985).

Sick, Gary: *October Surprise: America's Hostages in Iran and the Election of Ronald Reagan* (New York: Random House, 1991).

Sick, Gary: "The United States in the Persian Gulf: From Twin Pillars to Dual Containment." In David W. Lesch (ed.) *The Middle East and the United States: A Historical and Political Reassessment* (Boulder, CO: Westview Press, 1999).

Siekmeier, James F.: *Aid, Nationalism, and Inter-American Relations: Guatemala, Bolivia, and the United States, 1945–1961* (Lewiston, NY: Mellen Press, 1999).

Sigal, Leon V.: *Fighting to a Finish: The Politics of War Termination in the United States and Japan, 1945* (Ithaca, NY: Cornell University Press, 1988).

Sigmund, Paul: *The Overthrow of Allende and the Politics of Chile, 1964–1976* (Pittsburgh, PA: University of Pittsburgh Press, 1977).

Simmons, Robert R.: *The Strained Alliance: Peking, Pyongyang, Moscow and the Politics of the Korean Civil War* (New York: Free Press, 1975).

Sittser, Gerald L.: *A Cautious Patriotism: The American Churches and the Second World War* (Chapel Hill: University of North Carolina Press, 1997).

Skates, John Ray: *The Invasion of Japan: Alternative to the Bomb* (Columbia: University of South Carolina Press, 1994).

Skidmore, Thomas E.: *Politics in Brazil, 1930–1964: An Experiment in Democracy* (New York: Oxford University Press, 1967).

Skidmore, Thomas E. and Peter H. Smith: *Modern Latin America*, 5th edn. (New York: Oxford University Press, 2001).

Skinner, Elliott: *African Americans and US Policy Toward Africa, 1850–1924* (Washington, DC: Howard University Press, 1992).

Slater, Jerome: *Intervention and Negotiation: The United States and the Dominican Revolution* (New York: Harper and Row, 1970).

Slusser, Robert M.: *The Berlin Crisis of 1961: Soviet–American Relations and the Struggle for Power in the Kremlin* (Baltimore, MD: Johns Hopkins University Press, 1973).

Small, Melvin: *Johnson, Nixon, and the Doves* (New Brunswick, NJ: Rutgers University Press, 1988).

Small, Melvin: *Democracy and Diplomacy: The Impact of Domestic Politics on US Foreign Policy, 1789–1994* (Baltimore, MD: Johns Hopkins University Press, 1996).

Small, Melvin: *The Presidency of Richard Nixon* (Lawrence: University of Kansas Press, 1999).

Smelser, Marshall: *The Democratic Republic, 1801–1815* (New York: Harper and Row, 1968).

Smith, Amanda (ed.): *Hostage to Fortune: The Letters of Joseph P. Kennedy* (New York: Viking, 2001).

Smith, Bradley F.: *The Ultra-Magic Deals and the Most Secret Special Relationship, 1940–1946* (Novato, CA: Presidio, 1993).

Smith, Bradley F.: *Sharing Secrets with Stalin: How the Allies Traded Intelligence, 1941–1945* (Lawrence: University of Kansas Press, 1996).

Smith, Earl E. T.: *The Fourth Floor: An Account of the Castro Communist Revolution* (New York: Random House, 1962).

Smith, Gaddis: *American Diplomacy During the Second World War, 1941–1945*, 2nd edn. (New York: Alfred A. Knopf, 1985).

Smith, Gaddis: *Morality, Reason, and Power: American Diplomacy in the Carter Years* (New York: Hill and Wang, 1986).

Smith, Gaddis: *The Last Years of the Monroe Doctrine, 1945–1993* (New York: Hill and Wang, 1994).

Smith, Geoffrey S.: "National Security and Personal Isolation: Sex, Gender, and Disease in the Cold-War United States." *International History Review* 14 (May 1992), 307–37.

Smith, Gerard: *Doubletalk: The Story of SALT I* (New York: Doubleday, 1980).

Smith, James M.: *Freedom's Fetters: The Alien Sedition Laws and American Civil Liberties* (Ithaca, NY: Cornell University Press, 1956).

Smith, Jean E.: *The Defense of Berlin* (Baltimore, MD: Johns Hopkins University Press, 1963).

Smith, Jean E.: *George Bush's War* (New York: Holt, 1992).

Smith, Joseph: *Unequal Giants: Diplomatic Relations between the United States and Brazil, 1889–1930* (Pittsburgh, PA: University of Pittsburgh Press, 1991).

Smith, Page: *John Adams* (Garden City, NY: Doubleday, 1962).

Smith, Peter H. (ed.): *Drug Policy in the Americas* (Boulder, CO: Westview Press, 1992).

Smith, Peter H.: *Talons of the Eagle: Dynamics of US–Latin American Relations* (New York: Oxford University Press, 1996).

Smith, Peter H.: *Talons of the Eagle: Dynamics of US–Latin American Relations*, 2nd edn. (New York: Oxford University Press, 1999).

Smith, R. B.: *An International History of the Vietnam War*, 3 vols. (New York: St. Martin's Press, 1984–90).

Smith, Robert F.: *The United States and Revolutionary Nationalism in Mexico, 1916–1932* (Chicago, IL: University of Chicago Press, 1972).

Smith, Robert F.: "The Good Neighbor Policy: The Liberal Paradox in United States Relations with Latin America." In Leonard P. Liggio and James Martin (eds.) *Watershed of Empire: Essays on New Deal Foreign Policy* (Colorado Springs, CO: Ralph Myles, 1976).

Smith, Robert F.: *The Caribbean World and the United States: Mixing Rum and Coca-Cola* (New York: Twayne, 1994).

Smith, Shannon: "From Relief to Revolution: American Women and the Russian–American Relationship, 1890–1917." *Diplomatic History* 19 (fall 1995), 601–16.

Smith, Tony: *The Pattern of Imperialism: The United States, Great Britain, and the Late-industrializing World since 1815* (New York: Cambridge University Press, 1981).

Smith, Tony: *America's Mission: The United States and the Worldwide Struggle for Democracy in the Twentieth Century* (Princeton, NJ: Princeton University Press, 1994).

Smith, Tony: *Foreign Attachments: The Power of Ethnic Groups in the Making of American Foreign Policy* (Cambridge, MA: Harvard University Press, 2000).

Smith, Wayne S.: *The Closest of Enemies: A Personal and Diplomatic Account of US–Cuban Relations since 1957* (New York: W. W. Norton, 1987).

Smyser, William R.: *From Yalta to Berlin: The Cold War Struggle Over Germany* (New York: St. Martin's Press, 1999).

Snead, David: *The Gaither Committee, Eisenhower, and the Cold War* (Columbus: Ohio State University Press, 1999).

Snell, John L. (ed.): *The Meaning of Yalta: Big Three Diplomacy and the New World Balance of Power* (Baton Rouge: Louisiana State University Press, 1956).

Snell, John L.: *Illusion and Necessity: The Diplomacy of Global War, 1939–1945* (Boston, MA: Houghton Mifflin, 1963).

Sobel, R.: *The Impact of Public Opinion on US Foreign Policy since Vietnam: Constraining the Colossus* (New York: Oxford University Press, 2000).

Sodaro, Michael J.: *Moscow, Germany, and the West from Khrushchev to Gorbachev* (Ithaca, NY: Cornell University Press, 1990).

Sodhy, Pamela: *The US–Malaysian Nexus: Themes in Superpower–Small State Relations* (Kuala Lumpur: Institute of Strategic and International Studies, 1991).

Sofka, James R.: "The Jeffersonian Idea of Security: Commerce, the Atlantic Balance of Power, and the Barbary War, 1786–1805." *Diplomatic History* 21 (fall 1997), 519–44.

Solomon, Richard H.: *Chinese Negotiating Behaviour: Pursuing Interests through "Old Friends"* (Washington, DC: USIP, 1999).

Solomon, Richard H.: *Exiting Indochina: US Leadership of the Cambodia Settlement and Normalization of Relations with Vietnam* (Washington, DC: United States Institute of Peace Press, 2000).

Sorensen, Theodore C.: *Kennedy* (New York: Harper and Row, 1965).

Spanier, John W.: *The Truman–MacArthur Controversy and the Korean War* (New York: Norton, 1959).

Spector, R. H.: *The United States Army in Vietnam: Advice and Support: The Early Years, 1941–1960* (Washington, DC: Government Printing Office, 1983).

Spence, Jonathan: *To Change China: Western Advisers in China 1620–1960* (Boston, MA: Little, Brown, 1969).

Spiegel, Steven L.: *The Other Arab–Israeli Conflict: Making America's Middle East Policy, from Truman to Reagan* (Chicago, IL: University of Chicago Press, 1985).

Spiegel, Steven L. (ed.): *The Arab–Israeli Search for Peace* (Boulder, CO: Rienner, 1992).

Spivak, Burton: *Jefferson's English Crisis* (Charlottesville: University Press of Virginia, 1979).

Spurr, David: *The Rhetoric of Empire: Colonial Discourse in Journalism, Travel Writing, and Imperial Administration* (Durham, NC: Duke University Press, 1993).

Spurr, Russell: *Enter the Dragon: China's Undeclared War Against the US In Korea, 1950–1951* (New York: Newmarket Press, 1988).

Stagg, J. C. A.: *Mr. Madison's War: Politics, Diplomacy and Warfare in the Early American Republic, 1783–1830* (Princeton, NJ: Princeton University Press, 1983).

Stairs, Denis: *The Diplomacy of Constraint: Canada, the Korean War, and the United Nations* (Toronto: University of Toronto Press, 1974).

Staniland, Martin: *American Intellectuals and African Nationalists, 1955–1970* (New Haven, CT: Yale University Press, 1991).

Stanley, Peter W.: *A Nation in the Making: The Philippines and the United States, 1899–1921* (Cambridge, MA: Harvard University Press, 1974).

Stanley, Peter W. (ed.): *Reappraising an Empire: New Perspectives on Philippine–American History* (Cambridge, MA: Harvard University Press, 1984).

Stanton, S. L.: *The Rise and Fall of an American Army: US Ground Forces in Vietnam, 1965–1973* (San Rafael, CA: Presidio, 1985).

Stead, William.T.: *The Americanization of the World or the Trend of the Twentieth Century* [1902] (New York: Garland Publishing, 1972).

Stearns, Monteagle: *Entangled Allies: US Policy Toward Greece, Turkey, and Cyprus* (New York: Council on Foreign Relations Press, 1992).

Steel, Ronald: *Walter Lippmann and the American Century* (Boston, MA: Houghton Mifflin, 1980).

Steel, Ronald: *Temptations of a Superpower* (Cambridge, MA: Harvard University Press, 1995).

Steel, Ronald: "Mr. Fix-It." *New York Review of Books* 47 (October 5, 2000), 19–21.

Steele, Richard W.: *The First Offensive, 1942: Roosevelt, Marshall and the Making of American Strategy* (Bloomington: Indiana University Press, 1973).

Steigerwald, D.: *Wilsonian Idealism in America* (Ithaca, NY: Cornell University Press, 1994).

Steigerwald, D.: "Reclamation of Woodrow Wilson." *Diplomatic History* 23 (1999), 79–99.

Stein, Janice Gross: "Flawed Strategies and Missed Signals: Crisis Bargaining Between the Superpowers, October 1973." In David W. Lesch (ed.) *The Middle East and the United States: A Historical and Political Reassessment* (Boulder, CO: Westview Press, 1999).

Stein, Kenneth: *Heroic Diplomacy: Sadat, Kissinger, Carter, Begin, and the Quest for Arab–Israeli Peace* (New York: Routledge, 1999).

Stephanson, Anders: *Kennan and the Art of Foreign Policy* (Cambridge, MA: Harvard University Press, 1989).

Stephanson, Anders: "Commentary: Ideology and Neorealist Mirrors." *Diplomatic History* 17 (spring 1993), 285–95.

Stephanson, Anders: *Manifest Destiny: American Expansion and the Empire of Right* (New York: Hill and Wang, 1995).

Stern, Paula: *To The Water's Edge: Domestic Politics and the Making of American Foreign Policy* (Westport, CT: Greenwood Press, 1979).

Stevens, Kenneth R.: "Thomas Jefferson, John Quincy Adams, and Foreign Policy in the Early Republic" [feature review]. *Diplomatic History* 19 (fall 1995), 705–11.

Stevenson, Richard W.: *The Rise and Fall of Détente: Relaxations of Tension in US–Soviet Relations 1953–84* (Basingstoke: Macmillan, 1985).

Steward, Dick: *Trade and Hemisphere: The Good Neighbor Policy and Reciprocal Trade* (Columbia: University of Missouri Press, 1975).

Stinnett, Robert B.: *Day of Deceit: The Truth About FDR and Pearl Harbor* (New York: Touchstone, 2000).

Stivers, William: *America's Confrontation with Revolutionary Change in the Middle East, 1948–1983* (New York: St. Martin's Press, 1986).

Stocking, George W., Jr.: *Race, Culture, and Evolution: Essays in the History of Anthropology* (New York, 1968).

Stocking, George W., Jr.: *Race, Culture, and Victorian Anthropology* (New York: Free Press, 1987).

Stoff, Michael: *Oil, War and American Security: The Search for a National Policy on Foreign Oil, 1941–1947* (New Haven, CT: Yale University Press, 1980).

Stokesbury, James L.: *A Short History of the Korean War* (New York: William Morrow, 1988).

Stoler, Mark A.: *The Politics of the Second Front: American Military Planning and Diplomacy in Coalition Warfare, 1941–1943* (Westport, CT: Greenwood Press, 1977).

Stoler, Mark A.: *George C. Marshall: Soldier–Statesman of the American Century* (Boston, MA: Twayne, 1989).

Stoler, Mark A.: "A Half Century of Conflict: Interpretations of US World War II Diplomacy." *Diplomatic History* 18 (summer 1994), 375–403.

Stoler, Mark A.: *Allies and Adversaries: The Joint Chiefs of Staff, the Grand Alliance, and US Strategy in World War II* (Chapel Hill: University of North Carolina Press, 2000).

Stoler, Mark A.: "The Second World War in US History and Memory." *Diplomatic History* 25 (summer 2001), 383–92.

Stone, I. F.: *The Hidden History of the Korean War* (New York: Monthly Review Press, 1952).

Stookey, Robert: *America and the Arab States: An Uneasy Encounter* (New York: Wiley, 1975).

Stout, Joseph A., Jr.: *Border Conflict: Villistas, Carrancistas and the Punitive Expeditions, 1915–1920* (Fort Worth: Texas Christian University Press, 1999).

Streeter, Stephen M.: *Managing the Counterrevolution: The United States and Guatemala, 1954–1961* (Athens, GA: University of Ohio Press, 2000).

Stromseth, Jane E.: *The Origins of Flexible Response: NATO's Debate over Strategy in the 1960s* (Basingstoke: Macmillan, 1988).

Stuart, Reginald C.: "Confederation Diplomacy" [feature review]. *Diplomatic History* 22 (spring 1999), 371–8.

Stueck, William W., Jr.: *Road to Confrontation: American Policy Toward China and Korea, 1947–1950* (Chapel Hill: University of North Carolina Press, 1981).

Stueck, William W., Jr.: *The Korean War: An International History* (Princeton, NJ: Princeton University Press, 1995).

Suleiman, Michael W.: *The Arabs in the Mind of America* (Brattleboro, VT: Amana Books, 1988).

Suleiman, Michael W.: "Palestine and the Palestinians in the Mind of America." In Michael W. Suleiman (ed.) *US Policy in Palestine from Wilson to Clinton* (Normal, IL: Association of Arab–American University Graduates, 1995).

Summers, Anthony: *The Arrogance of Power: The Secret World of Richard Nixon* (New York: Viking, 2000).

Summers, H. G., Jr.: *On Strategy: A Critical Analysis of the Vietnam War* (Novato, CA: Presidio, 1982).

Susskind, Lawrence: *Environmental Diplomacy: Negotiating More Effective Global Agreements* (New York: Oxford University Press, 1994).

Sutter, Robert G.: *US Policy Toward China: An Introduction to the Role of Interest Groups* (Lanham, MD: Rowman and Littlefield, 1998).

Sweig, Julia E.: *Inside the Cuban Revolution: Fidel Castro and the Urban Underground* (Cambridge, MA: Harvard University Press, 2002).

Szulc, Tad: *Dominican Diary* (New York: Delacorte, 1965).

Szulc, Tad: *The Illusion of Peace: Foreign Policy in the Nixon Years* (New York: Viking, 1978).

Szulc, Tad: *Fidel: A Critical Portrait* (New York: William Morrow, 1986).

Tahir-Kheli, Shirin R.: *India, Pakistan, and the United States: Breaking with the Past* (New York: Council on Foreign Relations Press, 1997).

Takemoto, Tadao and Yasuo Ohara: *The Alleged "Nanking Massacre": Japan's Rebuttal to China's Forged Claims* (Tokyo: Meisei-sha, 2000).

Talbott, Strobe: *The Russia Hand: A Memoir of Presidential Leadership* (New York: Random House, 2002).

Tang Tsou, *America's Failure in China*.

Taubman, William: *Stalin's American Policy: From Entente to Détente to Cold War* (New York: W. W. Norton, 1982).

Taylor, Graham D.: "The Axis Replacement Program: Economic Warfare and the Chemical Industry in Latin America, 1942–1944." *Diplomatic History* 8 (spring 1984), 145–64.

Taylor, Maxwell: *The Uncertain Trumpet* (New York: Harper, 1960).

Tebbel, John: *America's Great Patriotic War With Spain* (Manchester, VT: Marshall Jones, 1996).

Teicher, Howard and Gayle Radley Teicher: *Twin Pillars to Desert Storm: America's Flawed Vision in the Middle East from Nixon to Bush* (New York: Morrow, 1993).

Teles, Steven M.: "Public Opinion and Interest Groups in the Making of US–China Policy." In Robert S. Ross (ed.) *After the Cold War: Domestic Factors and US–China Relations* (Armonk, NY: M. E. Sharpe, 1998).

Terry, Janice J.: *Mistaken Identity: Arab Stereotypes in Popular Writing* (Washington, DC: Arab–American Affairs Council, 1987).

Thelen, David et. al.: "History and the Public: What Can We Handle? A Round Table about History after the *Enola Gay* Controversy." *Journal of American History* 82 (December 1995), 1029–135.

Theoharis, Athan: *The Yalta Myths: An Issue in US Politics, 1945–1955* (Columbia: University of Missouri Press, 1970).

Thies, W. J.: *When Governments Collide: Coercion and Diplomacy in the Vietnam Conflict, 1964–1968* (Berkeley: University of California Press, 1980).

Thomas, Evan: *The Very Best Men: Four Who Dared; The Early Years of the CIA* (New York: Simon and Schuster, 1995).

Thomas, Leonard: *The United States and Central America, 1944–1949: Perceptions of Political Change* (1984).

Thompson, J. A.: *Woodrow Wilson: Profiles in Power* (London: Longman, 2002).

Thompson, J. C.: *Rolling Thunder: Understanding Policy and Program Failure* (Chapel Hill: University of North Carolina Press, 1980).

Thompson, Robert S.: *The Missiles of October: The Declassified Story of John F. Kennedy and the Cuban Missile Crisis* (New York: Simon and Schuster, 1992).

Thomson, James C., Jr.: *While China Faced West: American Reformers in Nationalist China, 1928–1937* (Cambridge, MA: Harvard University Press 1969).

Thomson, James C., Jr.: "On the Making of China Policy, 1961–9: A Study in Bureaucratic Politics." *China Quarterly* 50 (1972), 220–43.

Thomson, James C., Jr., Peter W. Stanley, and John Curtis Perry: *Sentimental Imperialists: The American Experience in East Asia* (New York: Harper and Row, 1982).

Thorne, Christopher: "Indochina and Anglo-American Relations, 1942–1945." *Pacific Historical Review* 45 (February 1976), 73–96.

Thorne, Christopher: *Allies of a Kind: The United States, Britain and the War against Japan, 1941–1945* (New York: Oxford University Press, 1978).

Thorne, Christopher: *The Issue of War: States, Societies, and the Far Eastern Conflict of 1941–1945* (New York: Oxford University Press, 1985).

Thornton, A. P.: *Doctrines of Imperialism* (New York, 1965).

Thornton, Richard C.: *The Nixon–Kissinger Years: Reshaping America's Foreign Policy* (New York: Paragon House, 1989).

Thornton, Thomas P.: "Between Two Stools?: US Policy Towards Pakistan in the Carter Administration." *Asian Survey* 22 (October 1982), 959–77.

Thornton, Thomas P.: "US–Indian Relations in the Nixon and Ford Years." In Harold A. Gould and Sumit Ganguly (eds.) *The Hope and the Reality: US–Indian Relations from Roosevelt to Reagan* (Boulder, CO: Westview Press, 1992).

Thorp, Rosemary: "Latin America and the International Economy from the First World War to the World Depression." In Leslie Bethell (ed.) *The Cambridge History of Latin America*, Vol. 4: c. 1870–1930 (New York: Cambridge University Press, 1986).

Tillapaugh, J.: "Closed Hemisphere and Open World? The Dispute over Regional Security at the UN Conference, 1945." *Diplomatic History* 2 (winter 1978), 25–42.

Tillman, Seth P.: *The United States in the Middle East: Interests and Obstacles* (Bloomington: Indiana University Press, 1982).

Tivnan, Edward: *The Lobby: Jewish Political Power and American Foreign Policy* (New York: Simon and Schuster, 1987).

Toland, John: *In Mortal Combat: Korea, 1950–1953* (New York: William Morrow, 1991).

Tolba, Mostafa: *Global Environmental Diplomacy: Negotiating Environmental Agreements for the World, 1973–1992* (Cambridge, MA: MIT Press, 1998).

Tomedi, Rudy: *No Bugles, No Drums: An Oral History of the Korean War* (New York: Wiley, 1993).

Tomlinson, John: *Cultural Imperialism: A Critical Introduction* (Baltimore, MD: Johns Hopkins University Press, 1991).

Tomlinson, John: *Globalization and Culture* (Chicago, IL: University of Chicago Press, 1999).

Tompkins, E. Berkely: *Anti-Imperialism in the United States: The Great Debate 1890–1920* (Philadelphia, PA).

Trachtenberg, Marc: "A 'Wasting Asset': American Strategy and the Shifting Nuclear Balance." *International Security* 13 (1988/1989), 5–49.

Trachtenberg, Marc: *History and Strategy* (Princeton, NJ: Princeton University Press, 1991).

Trachtenberg, Marc: *A Constructed Peace: The Making of the European Settlement, 1945–1963*. Princeton Studies in International History and Politics (Princeton, NJ: Princeton University Press, 1999).

Trask, David F.: *The War with Spain in 1898* (New York: Macmillan, 1981).

Trask, David F.: *The AEF and Coalition Warmaking, 1917–1918* (Lawrence: University of Kansas Press, 1993).

Trask, Roger R.: "The Impact of the Cold War on United States–Latin American Relations, 1945–1949." *Diplomatic History* 1 (summer 1977), 271–84.

Trask, Roger R.: "George F. Kennan's Report on Latin America (1950)." *Diplomatic History* 2 (summer 1978), 307–11.

Trask, Roger R.: "Spruille Brade versus George Messersmith: World War II, the Cold War, and Argentine Policy, 1945–1947." *Journal of Inter-American Studies and World Affairs* 26 (February 1984), 69–95.

Traxel, David: *1898: The Birth of the American Century* (New York: Knopf, 1998).

Treverton, Gregory F.: *The Dollar Drain and American Forces in Germany: Managing the Political Economics of Alliance* (Athens, OH: University of Ohio Press, 1978).

Triay, Victor A.: *Fleeing Castro: Operation Pedro Pan and the Cuban Children's Program* (Gainesville: University of Florida Press, 1998).

Truett, Samuel: "Neighbors by Nature: Rethinking Region, Nation, and Environmental History in the US–Mexican Borderlands." *Environmental History* 2 (1997), 160–78.

Trullinger, J. W.: *Village at War. An Account of Revolution in Vietnam* (New York: Longman, 1980).

Truman, Harry S.: *Memoirs, Vol. 2: Years of Trial and Hope* (Garden City, NY: Doubleday, 1956).

Tsunoda Jun: "On the So-called Hull–Nomura Negotiations." In Hilary Conroy and Harry Wray (eds.) *Pearl Harbor Reexamined: Prologue to the Pacific War* (Honolulu: University of Hawaii Press, 1990).

Tuchman, Barbara W.: *Stilwell and the American Experience in China, 1911–1945* (New York: Macmillan, 1970).

Tucker, Nancy Bernkopf: "Nationalist China's Decline and Its Impact on Sino-American Relations, 1949–1950." In Dorothy Borg and Waldo Heinrichs (eds.) *Uncertain Years: Chinese–American Relations, 1947–1950* (New York: Columbia University Press, 1980).

Tucker, Nancy Bernkopf: *Patterns in the Dust: Chinese–American Relations and the Recognition Controversy, 1949–1950* (New York: Columbia University Press, 1983).

Tucker, Nancy Bernkopf: "John Foster Dulles and the Taiwan Roots of the "two Chinas" Policy." In Richard H. Immerman (ed.) *John Foster Dulles and the Diplomacy of the Cold War* (Princeton, NJ: Princeton University Press, 1990).

Tucker, Nancy Bernkopf: *Taiwan, Hong Kong and the United States 1945–1992: Uncertain Friendships* (New York: Twayne, 1994).

Tucker, Nancy Bernkopf: "Continuing Controversies in the Literature on US–China Relations Since 1945." In Warren I. Cohen (ed.) *Pacific Passage: The Study of American–East Asian Relations on the Eve of the Twenty-first Century* (New York: Columbia University Press, 1996).

Tucker, Nancy Bernkopf: *China Confidential: American Diplomats and Sino-American Relations, 1945–1996* (New York: Columbia University Press, 2001).

Tucker, Richard: *Insatiable Appetite: The United States and the Degradation of the Tropical World* (Berkeley: University of California Press, 2000).

Tucker, Robert W. and David C. Hendrickson: *Empire of Liberty: The Statecraft of Thomas Jefferson* (New York: Oxford University Press, 1990).

Tucker, S. C.: *Vietnam* (Lexington: University of Kentucky Press, 1999).

Tulchin, Joseph S.: "The United States and Latin America in the 1960s." *Journal of Inter-American Studies and World Affairs* 30 (spring 1988), 1–36.

Tulchin, Joseph S.: "The Promise of Progress: US Relations with Latin America during the Administration of Lyndon B. Johnson." In Warren I. Cohen and Nancy Bernkopf Tucker (eds.) *Lyndon Johnson Confronts the World: American Foreign Policy, 1963–1968* (New York: Cambridge University Press, 1994).

Turley, W. S.: *The Second Indochina War: A Short Political and Military History, 1954–1975* (Boulder, CO: Westview Press, 1986).

Turner, Frederick J. and Martin Ridge: *History, Frontier, and Section: Three Essays* (Albuquerque: University of New Mexico Press, 1993).

Tusa, Ann: *The Last Division: Berlin and the Wall* (London: Hodder and Stoughton, 1996).

Tuttle, Dwight W.: *Harry L. Hopkins and Anglo-American–Soviet Relations, 1941–1945* (New York: Garland, 1983).

Tyler, Patrick: *A Great Wall: Six Presidents and China, An Investigative History* (New York: Century Foundation, 1999).

Ulam, Adam B.: *Dangerous Relations: The Soviet Union in World Politics, 1970–1982* (New York: Oxford University Press, 1983).

Underwood, Jeffrey S.: *The Wings of Democracy: The Influence of Air Power on the Roosevelt Administration, 1931–1941* (College Station: Texas A&M University Press, 1991).

United States Army, Center for Military History: *United States Army in World War II*, 79 vols. (Washington, DC: US Government Printing Office).

Unrau, William E.: *The White Man's Wicked Water: The Alcohol Trade and Prohibition in Indian Country, 1802–1892* (Lawrence: University of Kansas Press, 1996).

Unterberger, B. M.: *The United States, Revolutionary Russia, and the Rise of Czechoslovakia* (Chapel Hill: University of North Carolina Press, 1989).

US Congress. Senate. Select Committee to Study Governmental Operations with Respect to Intelligence Activities. *Alleged Assassination Plots Involving Foreign Leaders*. Senate Report No. 465 (Washington, DC: Government Printing Office, 1975).

US Congress. Senate. Select Committee to Study Governmental Operations with Respect to Intelligence Activities. *Covert Action in Chile, 1963–1973: Staff Report*. (Washington, DC: Government Printing Office, 1975).

Utley, Jonathan G.: *Going to War with Japan, 1937–1941* (Knoxville: University of Tennessee Press, 1985).

Vaïsse, Maurice: *Le Gandeur: politique étrangère du general de Gaulle 1958–1969* (Paris: Librairie Arthème Fayard, 1998).

Valenta, Jiri: *Soviet Intervention in Czechoslovakia, 1968: Anatomy of a Decision* (Baltimore, MD: Johns Hopkins University Press, 1979).

Valenta, Jiri and Herbert J. Elison (eds.): *Grenada and Soviet/Cuban Policy: Internal Crisis and US/OECS Intervention* (Boulder, CO: Westview Press, 1986).

Van Ree, Erik: *Socialism in One Zone: Stalin's Policy in Korea, 1945–1947* (Oxford: Berg, 1989).

Vance, Cyrus: *Hard Choices: Critical Years in America's Foreign Policy* (New York: Simon and Schuster, 1983).

VanDeMark, B.: *Into the Quagmire: Lyndon Johnson and the Escalation of the Vietnam War* (New York: Oxford University Press, 1991).

Vandenbroucke, Lucien S.: *Perilous Options: Special Operations as an Instrument of US Foreign Policy* (New York: Oxford University Press, 1993).

Varg, Paul: *Missionaries, Chinese, and Diplomats.*

Vatcher, William H.: *Panmunjom: The Story of the Korean Military Armistice Negotiations* (New York: Praeger, 1958).

Villa, Brian J.: "The US Army, Unconditional Surrender, and the Potsdam Declaration." *Journal of American History* 63 (June 1976), 66–92.

Villa, Brian J.: "The Atomic Bomb and the Normandy Invasion." *Perspectives in American History* 11 (1977–8), 463–502.

Viorst, Milton: *Hostile Allies: FDR and Charles de Gaulle* (New York: Macmillan, 1965).

Vitalis, Robert: "The Closing of the Arabian Oil Frontier and the Future of Saudi–American Relations." *Middle East Report* 27, 3 (July–September 1997), 15–25.

Vogel, Ezra F. (ed.): *Living With China: US–China Relations in the Twenty-First Century* (New York: Norton, 1997).

Von Eschen, Penny M.: *Race Against Empire: Black Americans and Anticolonialism, 1937–1957* (Ithaca, NY: Cornell University Press, 1997).

Von Eschen, Penny M.: " 'Satchmo Blows Up the World': Jazz, Race and Empire during the Cold War." In Reinhold Wagnleitner and Elaine Tyler May (eds.) *"Here, There and Everywhere": The Foreign Politics of American Popular Culture* (Hanover, NH: University Press of New England, 2000).

Wagnleitner, Reinhold: *Coca-Colonization and the Cold War: The Cultural Mission of the United States in Austria after the Second World War* (Chapel Hill: University of North Carolina Press, 1994).

Wagnleitner, Reinhold and Elaine Tyler May (eds.): *"Here, There and Everywhere": The Foreign Politics of American Popular Culture* (Hanover, NH: University Press of New England, 2000).

Wainstock, Dennis D.: *Truman, MacArthur, and the Korean War* (Westport, CT: Greenwood Press, 1999).

Waldron, Arthur: *How the Peace Was Lost: The 1935 Memorandum – Developments Affecting American Policy in the Far East* (Stanford, CA: Hoover Institution Press, 1992).

Walker, J. Samuel: "The Decision to Use the Bomb: A Historiographical Update." *Diplomatic History* 14 (winter 1990), 97–114.

Walker, J. Samuel: "The Decision to Use the Bomb: A Historiographical Update." In Michael J. Hogan (ed.) *Hiroshima in History and Memory* (Cambridge: Cambridge University Press, 1996).

Walker, J. Samuel: *Prompt and Utter Destruction: Truman and the Use of the Atomic Bombs Against Japan* (Chapel Hill: University of North Carolina Pres, 1997).

Walker, M.: *The Cold War: A History* (New York: Henry Holt, 1994).

Walker, William O., III: *Drug Control in the Americas* (Albuquerque: University of New Mexico Press, 1981).

Walker, William O., III: "Mixing the Sweet with the Sour: Kennedy, Johnson, and Latin America." In Diane B. Kunz (ed.) *The Diplomacy of the Crucial Decade: American Foreign Relations during the 1960s* (New York: Columbia University Press, 1994).

Walker, William O., III (ed.): *Drugs in the Western Hemisphere: An Odyssey of Cultures in Conflict* (Wilmington, DE: Scholarly Resources, 1996).

Walker, William O., III: "Drug Control and the Issue of Culture in American Foreign Relations." *Diplomatic History* 12 (fall 1998), 365–82.

Walker, William O., III: "The Struggle for the Americas: The Johnson Administration and Cuba." In H. W. Brands (ed.) *Beyond Vietnam: The Foreign Policies of Lyndon Johnson* (College Station: Texas A&M University Press, 1999).

Wall, Irwin: "The United States, Algeria, and the Fall of the Fourth French Republic." *Diplomatic History* 18 (1994), 489–511.

Wallensteen, Peter: "Recurrent Detentes." *Journal of Peace Research* 26 (1989), 225–31.

Wallerstein, Immanuel: *The Modern World System I: Capitalist Agriculture and the Origins of the European World Economy in the Sixteenth Century* (New York: Academic Press, 1974).

Wang Xi: "A Test of the Open Door Policy: America's Silver Policy and Its Effects on East Asia, 1934–1937." In Akira Iriye and Warren I. Cohen (eds.) *American, Chinese, and Japanese Perspectives on Wartime Asia, 1931–1949* (Wilmington, DE: Scholarly Resources, 1990).

Ward, Geoffrey: "On Writing about FDR." *American Heritage* 23 (summer 1991).

Wasserman, Mark: *Capitalists, Caciques, and Revolution: The Native Elite and Foreign Enterprise in Chihuahua, Mexico, 1854–1911* (Chapel Hill: University of North Carolina Press, 1984).

Watanabe, Paul Y.: *Ethnic Groups, Congress, and American Foreign Policy: The Politics of the Turkish Arms Embargo* (Westport, CT: Greenwood Press, 1984).

Watt, Donald C.: "Britain and the Historiography of the Yalta Conference and the Cold War." *Diplomatic History* 13 (winter 1989), 67–98.

Weathersby, Kathryn: "New Findings on the Korean War." *Cold War International History Project Bulletin*, Issue 3 (fall 1993), 1, 14–18.

Weathersby, Kathryn: "The Soviet Role in the Early Phase of the Korean War: New Documentary Evidence." *Journal of American–East Asian Relations* 2, 4 (winter 1993), 425–58.

Weathersby, Kathryn: "The Soviet Role in the Early Phase of the Korean War: New Documentary Evidence." *Journal of American–East Asian Relations* 3, 4 (winter 1994), 446–7.

Weeks, William E.: *John Quincy Adams and American Global Empire* (Lexington: University of Kentucky Press, 1992).

Weeks, William E.: "New Directions in the Study of Early American Foreign Relations." *Diplomatic History* 17 (winter 1994), 73–96.

Weeks, William E.: *Building the Continental Empire: American Expansion from the Revolution to the Civil War* (Chicago, IL: American Way Series, 1996).

Weil, Gordon L. and Ian Davidson: *The Gold War: The Story of the World's Monetary Crisis* (New York: Holt, Rinehart, and Winston, 1970).

Weinberg, Albert K.: *Manifest Destiny: A Study of National Expansion in American History* (Baltimore, MD: Johns Hopkins University Press, 1935).

Weinberg, Gerhard: "Pearl Harbor: The German Perspective." In Gerhard Weinberg (ed.) *Germany, Hitler, and World War II: Essays in Modern German and World History* (New York: Cambridge University Press, 1992).

Weinberg, Gerhard: "Why Hitler Declared War on the United States." *MHQ: The Quarterly Journal of Military History* 4 (spring 1992), 18–23.

Weinberg, Gerhard: *A World at Arms: A Global History of World War II* (Cambridge: Cambridge University Press, 1995).

Weinberger, Caspar: *Fighting for Peace: Seven Critical Years at the Pentagon* (New York: Warner Books, 1991).

Weintraub, Stanley: *MacArthur's War: Korea and the Undoing of an American Hero* (New York: Free Press, 2000).

Weis, Michael: *Cold Warriors and Coups d'Etat: Brazilian–American Relations, 1945–* (Albuquerque: University of New Mexico Press, 1993).

Weiss, Steve: *Allies in Conflict: Anglo-American Strategic Negotiations, 1938–1944* (New York: St. Martin's Press, 1996).

Welch, Richard E., Jr.: *Response to Imperialism: The United States and the Philippine War, 1899–1902* (Chapel Hill: University of North Carolina Press, 1965).

Welch, Richard E., Jr.: "American Atrocities in the Philippines: The Indictment and the Response." *Pacific Historical Review* 43 (1974), 233–53.

Welch, Richard E., Jr.: *Response to Revolution: The United States and the Cuban Revolution, 1959–1961* (Chapel Hill: University of North Carolina Press, 1985).

Wells, Henry: *The Modernization of Puerto Rico: A Political Study of Changing Values and Institutions* (Cambridge, MA: Harvard University Press, 1969).

Wells, T.: *The War Within: America's Battle over Vietnam* (Berkeley: University of California Press, 1994).

Wells, T.: *Wild Man: The Life and Times of Daniel Ellsberg* (New York: Palgrave, 2001).

Wenger, Andreas: *Living with Peril: Eisenhower, Kennedy, and Nuclear Weapons* (Lanham, MD: Rowman and Littlefield, 1997).

Werrell, Kenneth P.: *Blankets of Fire: US Bombers over Japan during World War II* (Washington, DC: Smithsonian Institution Press, 1996).

Westad, Odd A.: *The Fall of Détente: Soviet–American Relations During the Carter Years* (Oslo: Scandinavian University Press, 1997).

Westad, Odd A.: "Losses, Chances, and Myths: The United States and the Creation of the Sino-Soviet Alliance, 1945–1950." *Diplomatic History* 21, 1 (winter 1997), 105–15.

Westad, Odd A. (ed.): *Brothers in Arms: The Rise and Fall of the Sino-Soviet Alliance 1945–1963* (Stanford, CA: Stanford University Press; Washington, DC: Woodrow Wilson Center Press, 1998).

Westmoreland, W. C.: *A Soldier Reports* (Garden City, NY: Doubleday, 1976).

Whelan, Richard L.: *Drawing the Line: The Korean War, 1950–1953* (Boston, MA: Little, Brown, 1990).

Whitaker, Arthur Preston: *The Western Hemisphere Idea: Its Rise and Decline* (Ithaca, NY: Cornell University Press, 1954).

White, Brian: *Britain, Détente and Changing East–West Relations* (London: Routledge, 1992).

White, Dorothy S.: *Seeds of Discord: De Gaulle, Free France and the Allies* (Syracuse, NY: Syracuse University Press, 1964).

White, George: "Holding the Line: Race, Racism, and American Foreign Policy, 1953–1961." PhD dissertation, Temple University, 2000.

White, J. K.: *Still Seeing Red: How the Cold War Shapes the New American Politics* (Boulder, CO: Westview Press, 1997).

White, Mark J.: *The Cuban Missile Crisis* (New York: New York University Press, 1996).

White, Mark J.: *Missiles in Cuba: Kennedy, Khrushchev, Castro and the 1962 Crisis* (Chicago, IL: Ivan R. Dee, 1997).

White, Mark J. (ed.): *Kennedy: The New Frontier Revisited* (New York: New York University Press, 1998).

White, Mark J. (ed.): *The Kennedys and Cuba: The Declassified Documentary History* (Chicago, IL: Ivan R. Dee, 1999).

White, Richard: *The Middle Ground: Indians, Empires, and Republics in the Great Lakes Region, 1650–1815* (New York: Cambridge University Press, 1991).

White, T. A.: *The Making of the President, 1960* (New York: Atheneum, 1961).

White, T. A.: *The Making of the President, 1964* (New York: Atheneum, 1965).

Whitham, Charlie: "On Dealing with Gangsters: The Limits of British 'Generosity' in the Leasing of Bases to the United States, 1940–41." *Diplomacy and Statecraft* 7 (November 1996), 589–630.

Whiting, Allen S.: *China Crosses the Yalu: The Decision to Enter the Korean War* (Stanford, CA: Stanford University Press, 1960).

Whiting, Allen S.: *China Crosses the Yalu: The Decision to Enter the Korean War* (Stanford, CA: Stanford University Press, 1970).

Wiarda, Howard J. and Michael J. Kryzanek: *Dominican Republic: A Caribbean Crucible* (Boulder, CO: Westview Press, 1982).

Wicker, Tom: *One of Us: Richard Nixon and the American Dream* (New York: Random House, 1991).

Widenor, William C.: *Henry Cabot Lodge and the Search for an American Foreign Policy* (Berkeley: University of California Press, 1980).

Widenor, William C.: "American Planning for the United Nations: Have We Been Asking the Right Question?" *Diplomatic History* 6 (summer 1982), 245–65.

Wiley, Peter B.: *Yankees in the Land of the Gods: Commodore Perry and the Opening of Japan* (New York: Viking Penguin, 1991).

Wilkins, Mira: *Maturing of Multinational Enterprise, 1941–1970* (Cambridge, MA: Harvard University Press, 1974).

Williams, G. Mennen: *Africa For The Africans* (Grand Rapids, MI: William Eerdmans, 1969).

Williams, Raymond: *Keywords: A Vocabulary of Culture and Society* (London: Croom Helm, 1976).

Williams, W. A., C. McCormick, L. Gardner, and W. LaFeber (eds.) *America in Vietnam: A Documentary History* (New York: Norton, 1989).

Williams, Walter: "The United States Indian Policy and the Debate Over Philippine Annexation: The Implications for the Origins of American Imperialism." *Journal of American History* 66 (March 1980), 810–31.

Williams, William A.: *The Tragedy of American Diplomacy* (1959; expanded edn., New York: Dell, 1962).

Williams, William A.: *The Contours of American History* (Chicago, IL: Quadrangle Books, 1966).

Williams, William A.: *The Tragedy of American Diplomacy and the Roots of the American Empire: A Study of the Growth and Shaping of Social Consciousness in a Mass-Market Society* (New York, 1969).

Willmott, H. P. with Tohmatsu Haruo and W. Spencer Johnson: *Pearl Harbor* (London: Cassell, 2001).

Wills, Garry: *The Kennedy Imprisonment: A Meditation on Power* (New York: Little, Brown, 1985).

Wilmot, Chester: *The Struggle for Europe* (New York: Harper and Brothers, 1952).

Wilson, Joan Hoff: *American Business and Foreign Policy, 1920–1933* (Lexington: University of Kentucky Press, 1971).

Wilson, Theodore A.: *The First Summit: Roosevelt and Churchill at Placentia Bay, 1941* (Boston, MA: Houghton Mifflin, 1969; revd. edn. Lawrence: University of Kansas Press, 1991), 230, 235.

Wilson, Theodore A.: "The First Summit and the Riddle of Personal Diplomacy." In Douglas Brinkley and David R. Facey-Crowther (eds.) *The Atlantic Charter* (New York: St. Martin's Press, 1994).

Wiltz, John E.: *In Search of Peace: The Senate Munitions Inquiry, 1934–36* (Baton Rouge: Louisiana State University Press, 1963).

Wilz, John E.: "The MacArthur Hearings of 1951: The Secret Testimony." *Military Affairs* 39, 4 (December 1975), 167–73.

Winand, Pascaline: *Eisenhower, Kennedy, and the United States of Europe* (New York: St. Martin's Press, 1993).

Windchy, E. C.: *Tonkin Gulf* (Garden City, NY: Doubleday, 1971).

Winkler, Allan M.: *The Politics of Propaganda: The Office of War Information, 1942–1945* (New Haven, CT: Yale University Press, 1978).

Winter, J., G. Parker, and M. R. Habeck (eds.): *The Great War and the Twentieth Century* (New Haven, CT: Yale University Press, 2000).

Winterbotham, F. W.: *The Ultra Secret* (London: Weidenfeld, 1974).

Winterstein, Stephen: "Teaching the Vietnam War: A Conference Report." Foreign Policy Research Institute *Newsletter* 6, 4 (July 2000).

Wirsing, Robert G.: *Pakistan's Security under Zia, 1977–1988: The Policy Imperatives of a Peripheral Asian State* (New York: St. Martin's Press, 1991).

Wirsing, Robert G.: *India, Pakistan, and the Kashmir Dispute: On Regional Conflict and Its Resolution* (New York: St. Martin's Press, 1994).

Wirth, John: *Smelter Smoke in North America: The Politics of Transborder Pollution* (Lawrence: University Press of Kansas, 2000).

Wisan, Joseph E.: *The Cuban Crisis as Reflected in the New York Press (1895–1898)* (New York: Columbia University Press, 1934).

Wohlstetter, Albert: "Is There a Strategic Arms Race?" *Foreign Policy* 15 (summer 1974).

Wolff, Leon: *Little Brown Brother: How the United States Purchased and Pacified the Philippines* (New York: Oxford University Press, 1991).

Wood, Bryce: *The Making of the Good Neighbor Policy* (New York: Columbia University Press, 1961).

Wood, Bryce: *The Dismantling of the Good Neighbor Policy* (Austin: University of Texas Press, 1985).

Woods, Randall B.: *The Roosevelt Foreign Policy Establishment and the Good Neighbor: The United States and Argentina, 1941–1945* (Lawrence: University of Kansas Press, 1979).

Woods, Randall B.: *A Changing of the Guard: Anglo-American Relations, 1941–1946* (Chapel Hill: University of North Carolina Press, 1990).

Woodward, Bob: *The Commanders* (New York: Simon and Schuster, 1991).

Woodward, D. R.: *Trial by Friendship: Anglo-American Relations, 1917–1918* (Lexington: University of Kentucky Press, 1993).

Woodward, Ralph Lee, Jr.: *Central America: A Nation Divided*, 3rd edn. (New York: Oxford University Press, 1999).

Woodward, Sir Llewellyn: *British Foreign Policy in the Second World War*, 1 vol. abridged and 5 vols. (London: Her Majesty's Stationery Office, 1962, 1970–6).

Worster, Donald: "World Without Borders: The Internationalizing of Environmental History." In Kendall Bailes (ed.) *Environmental History: Critical Issues in Comparative Perspective* (Lanham, MD: University Press of America, 1985).

Wyden, Peter: *Bay of Pigs: The Untold Story* (New York: Simon and Schuster, 1979).

Wyman, David S.: *The Abandonment of the Jews: America and the Holocaust, 1941–1945* (New York: Pantheon, 1984).

Yang, Daqing: "The Challenges of the Nanjing Massacre: Reflections on Historical Inquiry." In Joshua A. Fogel (ed.) *The Nanjing Massacre in History and Historiography* (Berkeley: University of California Press, 2000).

Yang, Kuisong: "The Sino-Soviet Border Clash of 1969: From Zhenbao Island to Sino-American Rapprochement." *Cold War History* 1, 1 (winter 2000/1), 21–52.

Yergin, Daniel: *Shattered Peace: The Origins of the Cold War and the National Security State* (Boston, MA: Houghton Mifflin, 1977; revd. edn., New York: 1990).

Yergin, Daniel: *The Prize: The Epic Quest for Oil, Money, and Power* (New York: Simon and Schuster, 1991).

Yetiv, Steve A.: *America and the Persian Gulf: The Third Party Dimension in World Politics* (Westport, CT: Praeger, 1995).

Yoshida, Takashi: "A Battle over History: The Nanjing Massacre in Japan." In Joshua A. Fogel (ed.) *The Nanjing Massacre in History and Historiography* (Berkeley: University of California Press, 2000).

Young, Marilyn B.: *The Rhetoric of Empire: American China Policy 1895–1901* (Cambridge, MA, 1968).

Young, Marilyn B.: *The Vietnam Wars, 1945–1990* (New York: Harper Collins, 1991).

Young, Marilyn B.: "The Age of Global Power." In Thomas Bender (ed.) *Rethinking American History in a Global Age* (Berkeley: University of California Press, 2002).

Young, Oran, George Demko, and Kilaparti Ramakrishna (eds.): *Global Environmental Change and International Governance* (Hanover, NH: University Press of New England, 1996).

Zahnheiser, Marvin R. and W. Michael Weiss: "A Diplomatic Pearl Harbor: Richard Nixon's Goodwill Mission to Latin America in 1958." *Diplomatic History* 13 (1989), 163–90.

Zaroulis, N. and G. Sullivan: *Who Spoke Up? American Protest against the War in Vietnam, 1963–1975* (New York: Doubleday, 1984).

Zasloff, Joseph J. (ed.): *Postwar Indochina: Old Enemies and New Allies* (Washington, DC: Foreign Service Institute, 1988).

Zeiler, Thomas W.: *American Trade and Power in the 1960s* (New York: Columbia University Press, 1992).

Zelikow, Philip and Condoleezza Rice: *Germany Unified and Europe Transformed: A Study in Statecraft* (Cambridge, MA: Harvard University Press, 1995).

Zelikow, Philip D. et al. (eds.): *The Presidential Recordings: John F. Kennedy; The Great Crises*, 3 vols. (New York: Norton, 2001).

Zhai, Qiang: *China and the Vietnam Wars, 1950–1975* (Chapel Hill: University of North Carolina Press, 2000).

Zhang, Shu Guang: *Deterrence and Strategic Culture: Chinese–American Confrontations, 1949–1958* (Ithaca, NY: Cornell University Press, 1992).

Zhang, Shu Guang: *Mao's Military Romanticism: China and the Korean War, 1950–53* (Lawrence: University of Kansas Press, 1995).

Zhang, Shu Guang: *Economic Cold War: America's Embargo Against China and the Sino-Soviet Alliance, 1943–1963* (Washington, DC: Woodrow Wilson Center Press, 2000).

Zoumaras, Thomas: "Containing Castro: Promoting Homeownership in Peru, 1956–1961." *Diplomatic History* 10 (spring 1986), 161–81.

Zoumaras, Thomas: "Eisenhower's Economic Policy, The Case of Latin America." In Richard A. Melanson and David Mayers (eds.) *Reevaluating Eisenhower: American Foreign Policy in the 1950s* (Urbana: University of Illinois Press, 1987).

Zubok, Vladislav and Constantine Pleshakov: *Inside the Kremlin's Cold War: From Stalin to Khrushchev* (Cambridge, MA: Harvard University Press, 1996).

Zweig, David: "Sino-American Relations and Human Rights: June 4 and the Changing Nature of a Bilateral Relationship." In William T. Tow (ed.) *Building Sino-American Relations: An Analysis for the 1990s* (New York: Paragon House, 1991).

Zwick, Jim (ed.): *Mark Twain's Weapons of Satire: Anti-Imperialist Writings on the Philippine–American War*.

Index